Ethnologue®

Languages of Asia

Ethnologue®

Languages of Asia

Seventeenth Edition

M. Paul Lewis, Gary F. Simons, and Charles D. Fennig
Editors

SIL International

Dallas

Library of Congress Control Number: 2014938714
ISBN: 978-1-55671-370-5
ISSN: 0364-9288

Previous Editions
First edition 1951. Second edition 1952. Third edition 1953. Fourth edition 1953. Fifth edition 1958. Sixth edition 1965. Seventh edition 1969. Eighth edition 1974. Ninth edition 1978. Tenth edition 1984. Eleventh edition 1988. Twelfth edition 1992. Thirteenth edition 1996. Fourteenth edition 2000. Fifteenth edition 2005. Sixteenth edition 2009.

SIL International Publications
7500 West Camp Wisdom Road
Dallas, Texas 75236-5629 USA

Voice: +1 972 708 7404
FAX: +1 972 708 7363
Email: publications_intl@sil.org
www.sil.org/resources/publications, www.ethnologue.com

Editorial and Production Staff

Executive Editor	Gary F. Simons
General Editor	M. Paul Lewis
Managing Editor	Charles D. Fennig
Editor Emerita	Barbara F. Grimes†
Research Editors	Colleen Ahland, Michael Ahland, Stan Anonby, Ted G. Bergman, J. Albert Bickford, Kendall D. Decker, William C. Hall, Mark E. Karan, Lorna Priest Evans, Stuart D. Showalter, Jürg Stalder
Research Assistants	Robert Johnson, Linda Simons
Editorial Assistants	Denise Hovland, Louise Hunt
Senior Copy Editor	Bonnie Brown
Lead Cartographer	Irene Tucker
Cartographers	Matt Benjamin, Eva Horton, Michael McMillan, Stephen Tucker
Production Manager	Gayle Sheehan
Graphic Design	Barbara Alber, Patrick Gourley
Technical Support	Lars Huttar
Database Support	Joseph McCarthy, Roger Hanggi, Ray Uehara
Webmaster	Chad White
Web Site Design	LevelTen Interactive

Contents

Abbreviations

ACFLC	Act Creating the Filipino Language Commission, No. 07104
alt.	alternate name for
alt. dial.	alternate dialect name for
BI	Bibles International
Class	Language classification
dial.	primary dialect name for
FTT	Finishing the Task
GXLOUS	Guangxi Language and Orthography Use Situation
IICCC	India Institute for Cross Cultural Communication
IMA	India Missions Association
IMB	International Mission Board
ISO	International Organization for Standardization
JHEOA	Jabatan Hal Ehwal Orang Asli
km	kilometer(s)
L1 / L2	first language / second (or other additional) language
Lg Dev	Language development
Lg Use	Language use
LWC	language of wider communication
m	meter(s)
NLCI	New Life Computer Institute
NP	noun phrase
NT	New Testament
NTM	New Tribes Mission
NWFP	Northwest Frontier Province
OMF	Overseas Missionary Fellowship
OT	Old Testament
pej.	pejorative
pl.	plural
sg.	singular
SIL	SIL International
SOV	Subject-Object-Verb
SVO	Subject-Verb-Object
Type	Typological information
UBS	United Bible Societies
UKAW	Artha Wacana Christian University
UN	United Nations
UNESCO	United Nations Educational, Scientific, and Cultural Organization
UNSD	United Nations Statistics Division
USCWM	US Center for World Missions
USDS	US Department of State
VDC	Village Development Committee
VOS	Verb-Object-Subject
VP	verb phrase
VSO	Verb -Subject-Object
WT	World Team

Introduction

The purpose of the *Ethnologue* is to provide a comprehensive listing of the known living languages of the world. The *Ethnologue* is intended more as a catalog than as an encyclopedia and so provides summary data rather than more extensive descriptions of identified languages. Information comes from numerous sources and is confirmed by consulting both reliable published sources and a large network of field correspondents.

Much of the focus of *Ethnologue* is on the less commonly known languages. Even the most basic information is not available for every language, so the scope of *Ethnologue's* descriptions varies. The information is organized within specific categories as described in "Language information" (page 24). With each new edition of *Ethnologue* the range and focus of the categories we use is refined and adapted to better serve those who use the *Ethnologue* as a reference and research tool. However, we can report little data beyond those categories. Greater detail and depth of description of many of the languages, especially the larger, more commonly studied languages, can best be found in other works.

Because languages are dynamic, variable, and constantly changing, the total number of living languages in the world cannot be known precisely. As knowledge of the world's languages increases, so does the number of identified languages. This edition reflects the net addition of 69 living languages that have been identified by the ISO 639-3 standard since the previous edition of *Ethnologue* was published (2009). This is the result of adding 156 languages previously unidentified (59 through splitting off what were previously considered dialects of another language and 97 as new varieties not previously associated with another language) and the subtraction of 87 languages (69 being merged with other languages and 18 removed because they were duplicates or could not be substantiated as ever having been a language).

In this edition, we tally 7,106 languages worldwide which are known to be in use. This is actually an increase of 195 over the previous edition, which is considerably more than the 69 explained above. The larger increase is due to the fact that in this edition we have changed the way we count "living" languages. Previously we counted only languages that have living speakers who learned them, for the most part, by transmission from parent to child as the primary language of day-to-day communication. These languages are commonly referred to as a person's "first language" or "mother tongue". With this edition, we institute the use of a greatly expanded system for classifying the vitality of every known language of the world. That system, known as EGIDS, is described below in "Language status" (page 13). Next to the bottom end of the scale is the Dormant category (EGIDS 9). These languages were counted as extinct in the previous edition, but are now being distinguished from Extinct (EGIDS 10) and counted as living. In many cases there are revitalization efforts underway to preserve and even revive these languages as part of the heritage of living ethnic communities. While there may be no fully proficient speakers, some symbolic uses of these languages remain and they cannot be accurately identified as extinct. We believe this change aligns with the general consensus of language communities themselves and with the understanding of language preservation and documentation activists.

In addition to living languages as defined above, *Ethnologue* also contains data on languages which have gone out of use since the first appearance of the publication over 60 years ago. This edition lists 373 such recently extinct languages. Ancient, classical, and long-extinct languages are not listed (even though the ISO 639-3 standard assigns codes to them), unless they are in current use, such as in the scriptures or liturgy of a faith community. Such languages are classed as Dormant.

Another innovation in this edition is the reporting in much greater detail in each country of the functions of those languages which serve as officially recognized languages at the national and provincial levels. A description of the categories *Ethnologue* uses to describe these functions is given in "Official recognition" (page 15).

The information included in this volume on the demography, geography, typology, vitality, and development of the known living languages of the world can be useful to linguists, translators, anthropologists, bilingual educators, language planners, government officials, aid workers, potential field investigators, missionaries, students, and others with language interests.

History of the *Ethnologue*

The *Ethnologue* was founded by Richard S. Pittman, who was motivated by the desire to share information on language development needs around the world with his colleagues in SIL International as well as with other language researchers.

The first edition in 1951 was 10 mimeographed pages and included information on 46 languages or groups of languages. Hand-drawn maps were included for the first time in the fourth edition (1953). The publication transitioned from mimeographed pages to a book in the fifth edition (1958).

Dr. Pittman continued to expand his research through the seventh edition (1969), which listed 4,493 languages.

In 1971 Barbara F. Grimes became editor. She had assisted with the *Ethnologue* since the fourth edition (1953) and took on the role of research editor in 1967 for the seventh edition (1969). She continued as editor through the fourteenth edition (2000). In 1971 information was expanded from primarily minority languages to encompass all known languages of the world. Between 1967 and 1973 she completed an in-depth revision of the information on Africa, the Americas, the Pacific, and a few countries of Asia. During her years as editor, the number of identified languages grew from 4,493 to 6,809 and the information about each language expanded so that the published work more than tripled in size. In 2000, Raymond G. Gordon, Jr. became the third editor of the *Ethnologue* and produced the fifteenth edition (2005). Shortly after the publication of the fifteenth edition, M. Paul Lewis became the general editor. Under his direction, the editorial staff of the *Ethnologue* has expanded to include a managing editor and a distributed team of research editors in response to the growing scope and importance of the *Ethnologue* as a global research project.

The seventeenth edition marks a major milestone in the history of the *Ethnologue*. In the previous editions, the primary product was a book. Beginning in 1997 with the thirteenth edition, the complete contents of the book were also shared on the web. However, with the seventeenth edition, *Ethnologue* has shifted to a web-centric paradigm in which the website is the primary product standing at the center of a whole family of more-focused derivative products. The seventeenth edition was released to the web in 2013, with a revision of that edition appearing both on the web and in other formats (including print) in 2014.

The published data are generated from a computerized database on languages of the world first created in 1971 by then consulting editor, Joseph Grimes, from the typesetting tapes for the seventh edition (1969). The work was done at the University of Oklahoma under a grant from the National Science Foundation. In 1974 the database was moved to a computer at Cornell University where Dr. Grimes was professor of linguistics, and it was then moved to a personal computer in 1979. Since 2000 it has been housed and maintained at the headquarters of SIL International in Dallas, Texas. The structure of the database continues developing over time to meet the ongoing research needs of the *Ethnologue*. The fact that the entries are partially constructed by computer accounts for a certain stiffness or redundancy in the phrasing.

One feature of the database since its inception has been a system of three-letter language identifiers. The codes were first published with the following explanation in a monograph reporting the results of the grant to create the database:

> Each language is given a three-letter code on the order of international airport codes. This aids in equating languages across national boundaries, where the same language may be called by different names, and in distinguishing different languages called by the same name. (Grimes 1974:i)

While the codes were used behind the scenes in the database that generated the eighth and ninth editions, it was not until the tenth edition (1984) that they appeared in the publication itself.

In 1998, the International Organization for Standardization (ISO) adopted ISO 639-2, a standard for three-letter language identifiers. It is based on a convergence of ISO 639-1 (an earlier standard for two-letter language identifiers originally adopted in 1967) and of ANSI Z39.53 (also known as the MARC language codes, a set of three-letter identifiers developed within the library community and adopted as an American National Standard in 1987). The ISO 639-2 standard was insufficient for many purposes since it has identifiers for fewer than 400 individual languages. Thus in 2002, ISO TC37/SC2 formally invited SIL International to prepare a new standard that would reconcile the complete set of codes used in the *Ethnologue* with the codes already in use in the earlier ISO standard. In addition, codes developed by Linguist List to handle ancient and constructed languages were incorporated. The result, which was officially approved by the subscribing national standards bodies in 2006 and published in 2007, is a standard named ISO 639-3 that provides unique three-letter codes for over 7,500 languages (ISO 2007). SIL International was named as the registration authority for the standard and administers the annual cycle for changes and updates as a function separate from the *Ethnologue*. It is the editorial policy of *Ethnologue* to follow ISO 639-3 in determining what should be listed as languages.

This edition of *Ethnologue* is the third to use the ISO 639-3 language identifiers. In the fifteenth edition (2005) the codes had the status of Draft International Standard. In this edition they are based on the standard as originally adopted plus all the adopted change requests through January 2014. Information about the ISO 639-3 standard and procedures for requesting additions, deletions, and other modifications to the ISO 639-3 inventory of identified languages can be found at the ISO 639-3 website: http://www.sil.org/iso639-3.

The problem of language identification

How one chooses to define a language depends on the purposes one has in identifying one language as being distinct from another. Some base their definition on purely linguistic grounds, focusing on lexical and grammatical differences. Others may see social, cultural, or political factors as being primary. In addition, speakers themselves often have their own perspectives on what makes a particular language uniquely theirs. Those are frequently related to issues of heritage and identity much more than to the actual linguistic features. In addition, it is important to recognize that not all languages are oral. Sign languages constitute an important class of linguistic varieties that merit consideration.

Due to the nature of language and the various perspectives brought to its study, it is not surprising that a number of issues prove controversial. Of preeminence in this regard is the definition of the basic unit which the *Ethnologue* reports on: what constitutes *a* language?

Language as particle, wave, and field. Scholars recognize that languages are not always easily nor best treated as discrete, identifiable, and countable units with clearly defined boundaries between them (Makoni and Pennycook 2006). Rather, a language is more often comprised of continua of features that extend across time, geography, and social space. There is growing attention being given to the roles or functions that language varieties play within the linguistic ecology of a region or a speech community. The *Ethnologue* approach to listing and counting languages as though they were discrete units does not preclude a more dynamic understanding of the linguistic makeup of the countries and regions we report on.

While discrete linguistic varieties can be distinguished, we also recognize that those varieties exist in a complex set of relationships to each other. Languages can be viewed simultaneously as discrete units (particles) amenable to being listed and counted, as continua of features across time and space (waves) that are best studied in terms of variational tendencies as examples of "change in progress" (Weinreich, Labov and Herzog 1968), and as parts of a larger ecological matrix (field), where functional roles and usage of the linguistic codes for a wide range of purposes are more in focus. All three of these, language as particle, wave, and field (Lewis 1999; Pike 1959), are useful and important perspectives. *Ethnologue* focuses primarily on the unitary nature of languages without prejudice against the other perspectives.

Language and dialect. As part of the wave-like nature of language in general, every language is characterized by variation within the speech communities that use it. Innovations of new features and retentions of long-standing lexical, phonological or grammatical features spread like waves across geographic and social space and come and go over time. Varieties which share similar features diverge from one another to different degrees. Divergent varieties are often referred to as dialects. In some cases, they may be distinct enough that some would consider them to be separate languages. In other cases, the varieties may be sufficiently similar to be considered merely characteristic of a particular geographic region, social grouping, or historical era. Sometimes speakers may be very aware of dialect variation and be able to label a particular dialect with a name. In other cases, the variation may go largely unnoticed or overlooked. For many, the term dialect is a pejorative term that identifies a variety as being in some way deficient or inadequate.

Not all scholars share the same set of criteria for distinguishing what level of divergence distinguishes a "language" from a "dialect" and therefore the terms are not always consistently applied. Since the fifteenth edition (2005), *Ethnologue* has followed the ISO 639-3 inventory of identified languages (http://www.sil.org/iso639-3) as the basis for our listing of languages.

ISO 639-3 criteria for language identification. The ISO 639-3 standard applies the following basic criteria for defining a language in relation to varieties which may be considered dialects:

- Two related varieties are normally considered varieties of the same language if speakers of each variety have inherent understanding of the other variety at a functional level (that is, can understand based on knowledge of their own variety without needing to learn the other variety).
- Where spoken intelligibility between varieties is marginal, the existence of a common literature or of a common ethnolinguistic identity with a central variety that both understand can be a strong indicator that they should nevertheless be considered varieties of the same language.
- Where there is enough intelligibility between varieties to enable communication, the existence of well-established distinct ethnolinguistic identities can be a strong indicator that they should nevertheless be considered to be different languages.

These criteria make it clear that the identification of "a language" is not based on linguistic criteria alone.

The language entries in *Ethnologue* include a listing of dialect names. In most cases, those listings are not based on rigorous dialectology. Rather, these lists include all names reported to us which may, at one time or another, have been used in reference to a local variety of a language. Names listed may be alternate names for the same linguistic variety.

Macrolanguages. In addition to defining three-letter codes for individual languages, the ISO 639-3 standard also defines codes for macrolanguages. The latter are defined in the standard as "multiple, closely related individual languages that are deemed in some usage contexts to be a single language." Macrolanguages were introduced into the standard in order to handle cases in which varieties would be considered distinct languages by the criterion of non-intellgibility, but had already been given a code as a single language by the previously existing ISO 639-2 standard. For instance, Arabic [ara] and Chinese [zho] were already defined in ISO 639-2 on the basis of a writing system and literature shared across many spoken varieties.

Languages like these (with their existing three-letter codes) entered into ISO 639-3 as macrolanguages, and the varieties that were so distinct as not to be intelligible to each other received new three-letter codes as individual languages. The standard then enumerates the set of individual languages that are the members of each macrolanguage. It is important to note that macrolanguages are more than just groups of related languages. The individual languages that comprise a macrolanguage must be closely related, and there must be some domain in which they are commonly viewed as comprising a single language.

This volume includes entries for 26 macrolanguages as identified in the ISO 639-3 standard. The addition of this conceptualization of language provides us with a way to represent the fact that linguistic varieties function simultaneously as both individual units and within a larger functional matrix. Macrolanguage entries are brief, consisting largely of a listing of the individual languages that comprise them.

Sign languages. There are hundreds of sign languages in the world, created and used by deaf people. This volume lists 34 living sign languages. As the primary language of daily face-to-face communication for their respective communities of users, these languages fall within the scope of the *Ethnologue.* The deaf sign languages listed in language entries are those used exclusively within deaf communities. The listings include only natural sign languages, not signed versions of spoken languages (manual codes), which typically have names like "Signed English" or "Signed French." Manual codes are, however, sometimes mentioned in the entries for individual sign languages. Generally, we do not include manual systems invented primarily for use by hearing people that are not full languages (e.g., hand signals in sports), though some manual systems that have been assigned ISO 639-3 codes and are used as second languages only are included in our listings.

Language development

While the news seems to highlight the mounting external and internal pressures that are driving language endangerment, not all languages are endangered. Many languages have well-established literary traditions and are being used for a wide variety of functions in society. Many other communities, which have not yet achieved that status for their languages, are nevertheless taking steps to preserve the vitality of their languages and to find new ways of using them. *Ethnologue* records and reports data about these aspects of language use under the rubric of language development.

Defining language development. The term *language development* is commonly used among psychologists and educators with reference to individuals to refer to the phenomenon of child language acquisition (that is, how infants acquire language). The term is also used at the societal level. *Ethnologue* uses the term in the sense given to it by Charles Ferguson (1968) who defined language development as primarily dealing with three areas of concern:

- *graphization*—the development of a system of writing,
- *standardization*—the development of a norm that overrides regional and social dialects, and
- *modernization*—the development of the ability to translate and carry on discourse about a broad range of topics in ways characteristic of "industrialized, secularized, structurally differentiated, 'modernized' societies".

These development activities are now generally known as language planning activities, subsumed specifically within what is called "corpus planning" (Cooper 1989). More broadly, *Ethnologue* defines language development as follows:

> Language development is the result of the series of on-going planned actions that language communities take to ensure that they can effectively use their languages to achieve their social, cultural, political, economic, and spiritual goals.

As Ferguson proposed, those planned actions most often consist of the development of writing systems, the standardization of norms, and the elaboration of terminology designed to expand the "reach" of a language. They may also go well beyond that and cover a broad range of activities including advocacy on behalf of minority languages and other actions outside of the realm of linguistics proper. This broader definition of language development encompasses not only the acquisition of the means of reading and writing the language, but also the uses of the language in a variety of media and for as many functions as the speech community finds useful.

Evaluating language development. *Ethnologue* provides data not only on the factors which are indicators of endangerment but also on numerous indicators of development. Notable among the data that we report are:

- Identification of the writing systems in use both currently and historically
- Literacy rates in the language as well as in the dominant languages in the region

- The existence of various kinds of literature including poetry, stories, translated materials (including health and development literature and the Bible), and other print media such as newspapers and magazines
- The use of the language in the broadcast media (radio, television, recorded materials on compact disc, tape, digital video discs, etc.), or in films and videos
- The use of the language in so-called "new media" such as on web pages, in chat rooms, podcasts and MP3 downloads, and for SMS texting on mobile phones or other electronic devices
- The use of the language in the "official" functions of government
- Comments on the use of the language by others as their second language

These indicators of the state of development of a language are presented within the language entries according to their nature and focus; see "Language development" (page 10). In those cases where most of these development types are amply present, rather than listing them all separately, we simply categorize a language as "fully developed".

Language development and the EGIDS. With this edition of the *Ethnologue* we are able to dramatically increase our reporting of vitality of the languages of the world by using the Expanded Graded Intergenerational Disruption Scale or EGIDS (Lewis and Simons 2010), an adaptation and expansion of Fishman's (1991) Graded Intergenerational Disruption Scale (GIDS). For the first time, we report in each language entry (under the label *Status*) an estimate of the development versus endangerment of every identified language in each country where that language is spoken. This is done by reporting its estimated EGIDS level; see "Language status" (page 13) for the definitions of the levels.

In the middle of the scale is level 6a (Vigorous). These languages are represented by the green bars in the summary graphs for each country; these are not developing, but neither are they endangered since they enjoy vigorous face-to-face use in daily life by all generations. We report this to be the condition of 2,544 (or 36%) of the 7,105 known living languages in the world. With respect to the area covered in this volume, we report this to be the case for 857 (or 37%) of the 2,303 known living languages of Asia.

The first step up the development side of the EGIDS scale is level 5 (Developing). These languages are represented by the blue bars in the summary graphs for each country; they are in the initial stages of development (graphization, standardization, modernization). Literature in a standardized form is being used by some though this is not yet widespread or sustainable. We report this to be the condition of 1,563 (or 22%) of the 7,105 known living languages in the world. With respect to the area covered in this volume, we report this to be the case for 363 (or 16%) of the 2,303 known living languages of Asia.

All of the remaining levels on the development side of the EGIDS scale (4 and higher) have in common that the language has been developed to the point that it is used and sustained by institutions beyond the home and community. These languages are represented by the violet bars in the summary graphs for each country; as a class they are referred to as "Institutional" languages. We report this to be the condition of 561 (or 8%) of the 7,105 known living languages in the world. With respect to the area covered in this volume, we report this to be the case for 203 (or 9%) of the 2,303 known living languages of Asia. EGIDS levels 4 and higher are referred to individually as Educational, Wider Communication, Provincial, National, and International. These successively stronger levels on the scale take into account the growing number of both uses and users of the language, including its native community as well as those who have learned it as a second language.

Language development and language endangerment are not mutually exclusive. Indeed, many languages that had once risen above level 6a (due to language development efforts when they were in vigorous use by all generations) are now losing users. The endangerment indicators are given precedence in EGIDS; therefore, such languages are classed at 6b or lower. There are also many communities whose languages are endangered (at EGIDS levels weaker than 6a) who are engaging in planned actions designed to improve the vitality of their languages. Even if such activities result in widely adopted standardization and literature, the EGIDS level will not rise above level 6a until the community also achieves sustainable face-to-face use by all generations. The threshold of stable oral use identified by EGIDS 6a serves as a categorical boundary line for overall classification as developed versus endangered, though each specific case may be characterized by a complex configuration of indicators of both endangerment and development.

Endangered languages

Language endangerment is a serious concern to which linguists and language planners have turned their attention in the last several decades. For a variety of reasons, speakers of many smaller, less dominant languages stop using their heritage language and begin using another. Parents may begin to use only that second language with their children and gradually the intergenerational transmission of the heritage language is reduced and may even cease. As a consequence there may be no speakers who use the language as their first or primary language and eventually the language may no longer be used at all. A language may become dormant or extinct, existing perhaps only in recordings or written records and transcriptions. Languages which have not been adequately documented disappear altogether.

Defining language endangerment. Language endangerment is a matter of degree. At one end of the scale are languages that are vigorous, and perhaps are even expanding in numbers of speakers or functional areas of use, but nevertheless exist under the shadow of a more dominant language. At the other end are languages that are on the verge of extinction (that is, loss of all individuals who continue to identify the language as being related to their identity). In between are many degrees of greater or lesser vitality.

There are two dimensions to the characterization of endangerment: the number of *users* who identify with a particular language and the number and nature of the *functions* for which the language is used. A language may be endangered because there are fewer and fewer people who claim that language as their own and therefore neither use it nor pass it on to their children. It may also, or alternatively, be endangered because it is being used for fewer and fewer daily activities and so loses the characteristically close association of the language with particular social or communicative functions. Since form follows function, languages which are being used for fewer and fewer domains of life also tend to lose structural complexity, which in turn may affect the perceptions of users regarding the suitability of the language for use in a broader set of functions. This can lead to a downward spiral which eventually results in the complete loss of the language.

The concern about language endangerment is centered, first and foremost, around the factors which motivate speakers to abandon their language and the social and psychological consequences of language death for the community of (former) speakers of that language. Since language is closely linked to culture, loss of language almost always is accompanied by social and cultural disruptions. More broadly, the intangible heritage of all of human society is diminished when a language disappears. Secondarily, those concerned about language endangerment recognize the implications of the loss of linguistic diversity both for the linguistic and social environment generally and for the academic community which is devoted to the study of language as a human phenomenon.

Evaluating language endangerment. The best way to identify the level of vitality of a language has not always been clear. However, a scholarly consensus that can be applied worldwide is developing, and a global evaluation of the state of language vitality is becoming increasingly possible. Sociolinguists and linguistic anthropologists seek to identify trends in language use through the description of some direct measures of language vitality such as changes in the number of speakers or in the use of the language in certain domains or functions. Less directly, an increase in bilingualism, both in the number of bilinguals and in their proficiency levels, is often associated with these trends, though a high level of bilingualism is not, in itself, a sufficient condition for language shift or death. In addition there are numerous economic, political and social factors that affect a community's self perception and motivations.

Ethnologue reports data that are indicators of the two major dimensions of language use (users and functions). When data are available, we report the following factors which may contribute to the assessment of language endangerment:

- The speaker population
- The number of those who connect their ethnic identity with the language (whether or not they speak the language)
- The stability of and trends in that population size
- Residency and migration patterns of speakers
- The use of second languages
- The use of the language by others as a second language
- Language attitudes within the community
- The age range of the speakers
- The domains of use of the language
- Official recognition of languages within the nation or region
- Means of transmission (whether children are learning the language at home or being taught the language in schools)
- Non-linguistic factors such as economic opportunity or the lack thereof

Such factors interact within a society in dynamic ways that are not entirely predictable but which do follow recognizable patterns and trends. The general scholarly consensus, however, is that the key factor in gauging the relative safety of an endangered language is the degree to which intergenerational transmission of the language remains intact.

Language endangerment and the EGIDS. Because of the complexity of the interrelated factors, it is helpful to categorize the vitality of a language using a summary label. Various schemas have been proposed, each with a particular focus. For various reasons, none of these have proved adequate for a comprehensive global assessment of the state of the world's languages. The Expanded Graded Intergenerational Disruption Scale or EGIDS (Lewis and Simons 2010) was developed specifically to fill this gap.

For the first time, with this edition of the *Ethnologue*, we report a vitality estimate for every identified language in each country where that language is spoken. This is done by reporting the estimated EGIDS level in each language entry (under the label *Status*); see "Language status" (page 13) for the definitions of the levels.

The summary of the world language situation in terms of Institutional, Developing, and Vigorous languages is described in the preceding section. On the endangerment side of the EGIDS scale we distinguish three additional summary categories.

The first two steps down the endangerment side of the EGIDS scale are levels 6b (Threatened) and 7 (Shifting). These two levels have in common that intergenerational transmission is in the process of being broken, but the child-bearing generation can still use the language. These languages are represented by the yellow bars in the summary graphs for each country; as a class they are referred to as "In Trouble" languages. Since parents can still use the language, it is not too late to restore natural intergenerational transmission in the home. It is possible that revitalization efforts could achieve this by focusing on the motivations of parents. We report this to be the condition of 1,518 (or 21%) of the 7,105 known living languages in the world. With respect to the area covered in this volume, we report this to be the case for 691 (or 30%) of the 2,303 known living languages of Asia.

The next summary category includes levels 8a through 9 which are classed as "Dying" languages. These languages are represented by the red bars in the summary graphs for each country. At these levels, the child-bearing generation is no longer able to transmit the language to the next generation, since the only fluent users (if any remain) are above that age. Revitalization efforts would need to develop mechanisms outside the home in order to transmit the language. We report this to be the condition of 919 (or 13%) of the 7,105 known living languages in the world. With respect to the area covered in this volume, we report this to be the case for 189 (or 8%) of the 2,303 known living languages of Asia.

Finally, there are the "Extinct" languages at level 10. These languages have fallen completely out of (even symbolic) use, since no one retains a sense of ethnic identity associated with the language. With extinct languages, the *Ethnologue* lists only those that have become extinct since 1950 (which is when the *Ethnologue* began publication). We report 373 such languages in the current edition. This is a rate of loss amounting to 6 languages per year. With respect to the area covered in this volume, we report 48 extinct languages for Asia.

Language status

In this edition of *Ethnologue* we introduce a new category of information to summarize the status of each language in each country where it is used. The *Status* element of a language entry includes two types of information. The first is an estimate of the overall development versus endangerment of the language using the EGIDS scale (Lewis and Simons 2010). The second is a categorization of the "Official recognition" (page 15) given to a language within the country.

The EGIDS consists of 13 levels with each higher number on the scale representing a greater level of disruption to the intergenerational transmission of the language. Table 1 provides summary definitions of the 13 levels of the EGIDS.

Table 1. Expanded Graded Intergenerational Disruption Scale

Level	Label	Description
0	International	The language is widely used between nations in trade, knowledge exchange, and international policy.
1	National	The language is used in education, work, mass media, and government at the national level.
2	Provincial	The language is used in education, work, mass media, and government within major administrative subdivisions of a nation.
3	Wider Communication	The language is used in work and mass media without official status to transcend language differences across a region.
4	Educational	The language is in vigorous use, with standardization and literature being sustained through a widespread system of institutionally supported education.
5	Developing	The language is in vigorous use, with literature in a standardized form being used by some though this is not yet widespread or sustainable.
6a	Vigorous	The language is used for face-to-face communication by all generations and the situation is sustainable.
6b	Threatened	The language is used for face-to-face communication within all generations, but it is losing users.
7	Shifting	The child-bearing generation can use the language among themselves, but it is not being transmitted to children.
8a	Moribund	The only remaining active users of the language are members of the grandparent generation and older.

Table 1. Expanded Graded Intergenerational Disruption Scale (cont.)

Level	Label	Description
8b	Nearly Extinct	The only remaining users of the language are members of the grandparent generation or older who have little opportunity to use the language.
9	Dormant	The language serves as a reminder of heritage identity for an ethnic community, but no one has more than symbolic proficiency.
10	Extinct	The language is no longer used and no one retains a sense of ethnic identity associated with the language.

The EGIDS levels are designed to largely coincide with Fishman's Graded Intergenerational Disruption Scale, or GIDS (Fishman 1991). We refer users to Fishman's work for an orientation to this approach to evaluating endangerment and to the original work on EGIDS (Lewis and Simons 2010) for the rationale behind the development of the expanded framework. The descriptions of the levels used in this edtion of the Ethnologue have been adjusted to take into account significant feedback on the scale that has been received since its initial development. Most notably, the EGIDS level descriptions have been reworded to take into account signed languages. Like the GIDS, the EGIDS at its core measures the level of disruption of intergenerational transmission. Therefore, stronger, more vital languages have lower numbers on the scale and weaker, more endangered languages have higher numbers.

In comparison to GIDS, the EGIDS includes some additional factors at both the stronger and weaker levels of the scale and thus adds some levels not included in the original scale. As a result, the EGIDS can be applied to all of the languages of the world. In addition, two of the levels in the GIDS (6 and 8) have been split (6a, 6b, 8a, 8b) in the EGIDS in order to allow for a finer-grained description of the state of intergenerational transmission in the presence of language shift (or revitalization). We have used letters to distinguish these divided levels in order to maintain numbering alignment with Fishman's better-known GIDS. Each number on the EGIDS has also been assigned a one or two word label that summarizes the state of development or vitality of the language. The labels are intended to provide mnemonics for those who prefer to use words rather than numbers. In a few cases, alternative labels are assigned to a level in order to distinguish significantly different situations that are associated with the same level on the scale. Table 2 lists the alternative labels that are used.

Table 2. Alternative labels for other special situations

Level	Label	Description
5	Dispersed	The language is fully developed in its home country, so that the community of language users in a different country has access to a standardized form and literature, but these are not promoted in the country in focus via institutionally supported education.
9	Reawakening	The ethnic community associated with a dormant language is working to establish more uses and more users for the language with the results that new L2 speakers are emerging.
9	Second language only	The language was originally vehicular, but it is not the heritage language of an ethnic community and it no longer has enough users to have significant vehicular function.

How the EGIDS Works. The EGIDS is a multi-dimensional scale which focuses on different aspects of vitality at different levels. Like Fishman's GIDS, the EGIDS, at its core, measures disruption in use. At the weakest levels of vitality, EGIDS 9 (Dormant) and EGIDS 10 (Extinct) the primary factor in focus is the function of the language as a marker of identity. If no one still associates the language with their identity, the language can be considered to be Extinct. If there is an ethnic group that associates its identity with the language but uses the language only for symbolic purposes to remind themselves of that identity, the language can be categorized as Dormant (EGIDS 9).

At EGIDS levels 6a (Vigorous), 6b (Threatened), 7 (Shifting), 8a (Moribund), and 8b (Nearly extinct) the primary factor in focus is the state of daily face-to-face use and intergenerational transmission of the language. Each successively weaker level on the scale represents the loss of use, generation by generation.

EGIDS 4 (Educational) and EGIDS 5 (Developing) bring into focus the degree to which the ongoing use of the language is supported and reinforced by the use of the language in education. This largely focuses around issues of standardization and literacy acquisition and the degree to which those are institutionally supported and have been adopted by the community of language users.

EGIDS 3 (Wider Communication) focuses primarily on the notion of vehicularity. If a language (whether written or not) is widely used by others as a second language and as a means of intergroup communication, it has greater vitality than a language with a smaller number of users and which is seen as being less useful by outsiders. Where we have data, we report the use of each language by speakers of other languages.

EGIDS 2 (Provincial) and EGIDS 1 (National) focus on the level of recognition and use given to the language by government. Beyond purely official use, however, the focus includes the widespread use of the language in media and the workplace at either the provincial (sub-national) or national levels. EGIDS 0 (International) is a category reserved for those few languages that are used as the means of communication in many countries for the purposes of diplomacy and international commerce. Because the Ethnologue organizes the language entries by country, EGIDS 1 (National) is the strongest vitality level that we report.

The EGIDS levels are hierarchical in nature. With only one exception, the scale assumes that each stronger level of vitality entails the characteristics of the levels below it. Thus, for example, a language cannot be characterized as EGIDS 5 (Developing) if it cannot also be characterized as being at EGIDS 6a (Vigorous). A language with written materials which is not used for day-to-day communication by all generations and which is not being passed on to all children cannot be categorized as EGIDS 5 (Developing). The one exception to this principle is EGIDS 3 (Wider Communication) where the vehicularity of languages of wider communication is counted as being weightier than the existence of an orthography and the use of the language in education. Some languages that are widely used for intergroup communication are not used in formal education and have no written materials. Were these languages to lose that vehicularity, they would drop directly to EGIDS 6a (Vigorous).

Methodology. The EGIDS levels reported in this edition of the *Ethnologue* were initially arrived at by inspecting our database and analyzing the factors that we categorized as indicators of vitality. In many cases, we had sufficient data to allow an initial EGIDS evaluation. Where the data were not sufficient, we set the EGIDS default value at EGIDS 6a. The initial estimates were then distributed to a large number of correspondents who were asked to review the data and make corrections based on their knowledge of specific countries, regions, language families and individual languages. This review process resulted in a large number of corrections and revisions. Any remaining unreviewed or uncertain estimates were more closely scrutinized by the editors and, after soliciting additional commentary from knowledgeable sources, decisions made as to how best to evaluate the EGIDS level in each case. The EGIDS estimates, though based on the best information available to us, are preliminary and the review process is ongoing. We encourage users of the *Ethnologue* to provide us with comments and corrections that will lead to a more accurate assessment for inclusion in future editions.

In a few cases, there is real doubt as to whether the language actually exists as a distinct variety. Although an ISO 639-3 code has been assigned, data on the existence of the language is not convincing. In such cases, we do not report an EGIDS level but identify the language status as "Unattested".

The existence of an EGIDS estimate for every known language in every country provides a useful new resource for the assessment of language vitality globally, regionally, and country-by-country. For instance, this volume provides a visualization of the language situation in each country by means of a histogram that plots the distribution of the languages in that country according to their EGIDS levels. The existence of such data opens up the possibility for other kinds of analysis, such as the evaluation of the vitality of language families (see, for example, Whalen and Simons 2012).

Official recognition

If a language has an official function within a country or is specifically recognized in legislation, the entry for the language includes a description of the nature of its recognition. When that recognition is by statute, the specific law is also cited. Table 3 lists and defines (with examples) the fourteen language recognition categories that are used.

In developing these recognition categories, we have adapted the general framework described by Cooper (1989:99-103). Following Stewart's (1968) identification of the official function of languages in a country, Cooper further distinguishes between statutory, working, and symbolic official languages. To that we have added a further distinction between those same functions at either the national or the provincial level. This descriptive framework identifies the legal foundation (if any) for the recognition, the nature of the official use of the language, and the geopolitical scope of that use and recognition. The combination of these three parameters (legal status, nature of use, and scope of application) results in the first twelve function categories that are listed in table 3. The final two categories represent any other kind of statutory recognition for a language.

The distinction between statutory and de facto functions is relatively straightforward. When a language function is described as statutory, it means that there is a legal document such as the constitution of the country, language or diversity policy legislation, or the like, that specifies the functions for which the language will be used. Whenever a language is assigned a function that is statutory, we provide the name of the relevant statute. We are unable at this time to distinguish in all cases between legislation that is in force and legislation which may not be enforced though it is still legally viable. As for de facto status, in many countries languages are commonly used for governance functions but there is no formal legislative mandate for that use. In those cases, we identify the function as de facto.

Table 3. Official recognition categories and definitions

Function	Definition	Example
Statutory national language	This is the language in which the business of the national government is conducted and this is mandated by law. It is also the language of national identity for the citizens of the country.	Bengali [ben] in Bangladesh Indonesian [ind] in Indonesia Spanish [spa] in Spain
Statutory national working language	This is a language in which the business of the national government is conducted and this is mandated by law. However it is not the language of national identity for the citizens of the country.	Amharic [amh] in Ethiopia Bislama [bis] in Vanuatu English [eng] in India
Statutory language of national identity	This is the language of national identity and this is mandated by law. However, it is not developed enough to function as the language of government business.	Kituba [mkw] in Congo Maori [mri] in New Zealand Rarotongan [rar] in Cook Islands
De facto national language	This is the language in which the business of the national government is conducted but this is not mandated by law. It is also the language of national identity for the citizens of the country.	Standard German [deu] in Germany Japanese [jpn] in Japan Tswana [tsn] in Botswana
De facto national working language	This is a language in which the business of the national government is conducted, but this is not mandated by law. Neither is it the language of national identity for the citizens of the country.	Brunei [kxd] in Brunei Tagalog [tgl] in Philippines Shona [sna] in Zimbabwe
De facto language of national identity	This is the language of national identity but this is not mandated by law. Neither is it developed enough or known enough to function as the language of government business.	Algerian Arabic [arq] in Algeria Jamaican Creole English [jam] in Jamaica Tokelauan [tkl] in Tokelau
Statutory provincial language	This is the language in which the business of provincial government is conducted and this is mandated by law. It is also the language of identity for the citizens of the province.	Assamese [asm] in India Slovene [slv] in Italy Uyghur [uig] in China
Statutory provincial working language	This is a language in which the business of the provincial government is conducted and this is mandated by law. However, it is not the language of identity for the citizens of the province.	Afar [aar] in Ethiopia Corsican [cos] in France Lü [khb] in China
Statutory language of provincial identity	This is the language of identity for the citizens of the province and this is mandated by law. However, it is not developed enough or known enough to function as the language of government business.	Maithili [mai] in India Rotokas [roo] in Papua New Guinea Walloon [wln] in Belgium
De facto provincial language	This is the language in which the business of the provincial government is conducted, but this is not mandated by law. It is also the language of identity for the citizens of the province.	Chinese, Yue [yue] in China Faroese [fao] in Denmark Hausa [hau] in Nigeria

Table 3. Official recognition categories and definitions (cont.)

Function	Definition	Example
De facto provincial working language	This is a language in which the business of provincial government is conducted, but this is not mandated by law. Neither is it the language of identity for the citizens of the province.	Greek [ell] in Albania Kurdish, Central [ckb] in Iran
De facto language of provincial identity	This is the language of identity for citizens of the province, but this is not mandated by law. Neither is it developed enough or known enough to function as the language of government business.	Fulfulde, Adamawa [fub] in Nigeria Khinalugh [kjj] in Azerbaijan Thai, Northeastern [tts] in Thailand
Recognized language	There is a law that names this language and recognizes its right to be used and developed for some purposes.	New Zealand Sign Language [nzs] in New Zealand Sénoufo, Mamara [myk] in Mali Candoshi-Shapra [cbu] in Peru
Language of recognized nationality	There is a law that names the ethnic group that uses this language and recognizes their right to use and develop their identity.	Lisu [lis] in China Puma [pum] in Nepal

The nature of the use of a language in government operations is specified using the term "working" or "identity" or the absence of these terms. When a language is identified as a working language, it means that the operations of the government (debate in parliament, the language of the laws, the language used in government offices, on official forms,) may be carried out in the language, but the language is not the language of identity of the majority of the citizens. There are many countries where, for very practical reasons, an international language or the language of a colonial power is used for day-to-day operations of the government, but national (or provincial) identity is linked to a different language. On the other hand, when a language is identified as a language of identity, the reverse is true. The majority of citizens identify that language as being closely associated with their identity but for practical reasons the language is not generally used for governmental operations. In these cases, the language often has a very strong symbolic use to reinforce a common identity and to build national or provincial unity. In the final case, in which the language functions both as the working language of the government and as the language of identity for the majority of the citizens, the label for the category is simply "national language" or "provincial language", implying both the working function and the identify function.

In terms of geopolitical scope, we distinguish between the national and provincial levels of recognition and use. When a language is identified as performing a particular function at the provincial level, we describe the geopolitical regions involved. If there are many, that description may be reduced to a summary statement.

Some languages are not used or recognized for all of the functions of governance as described above, but may instead be granted only partial or limited recognitions by law. Those languages have been identified more generically as a "recognized language". Though our data is admittedly incomplete, we attempt to describe the nature of the recognition and its geopolitical scope in as many cases as possible. In addition, in some countries, ethnic groups or nationalities are given official recognition rather than their languages. In some cases these recognized nationalities speak multiple languages. We attempt to identify the languages of such officially recognized nationalities using the label "language of recognized nationality".

The recognition category for each language is based on the best research available to us. As with all *Ethnologue* information, we welcome corrections and updates from informed users.

Language maps

Maps showing the locations of language homelands are available for most countries of the world. Most of the maps make use of polygons to show the approximate boundaries of the language groups. No claim is made for precision in the placement of these boundaries, which in many instances overlap with those of other languages. Reference numbers are used on some maps where space does not allow the placement of language names. For some maps where the language boundaries are not known, the names or numbers alone appear.

The earliest maps in *Ethnologue* were developed as part of the Language Mapping Project carried out jointly with Global Mapping International (GMI). For the 16th edition, all of the maps were redrawn with a new and clearer design. We took advantage of the capabilities afforded to us by a new generation of software to improve the way that we show the family association of each language and the overlap of languages. A greater level of geographic detail is now included in the maps to aid in the location of languages within countries. All of the maps in this edition were created using ArcGIS® software by Environmental Systems Research Institute, Inc. (Esri®). ArcGIS® and ArcMap™ are the intellectual property of Esri® and are used herein under license. For more information about Esri® software, please visit www.esri.com.

The maps are drawn using the Digital Chart of the World as the underlying geographic database which has a finer level of resolution than the base map used in editions prior to the 16th. In that edition, all the language polygons were repositioned to fit the greater detail of geographic features offered by that new database. This is an ongoing process and we continue to improve the accuracy and precision with which the language areas are plotted particularly with the increased use of location data collected by GPS units which enables locations to be plotted directly into the existing databases. The complete geographic database used to produce these maps (including the language polygons) is available in a product jointly published with GMI named the World Language Mapping System; see http://www.gmi.org/wlms/.

For the 17th edition we have continued to expand the list of countries for which maps are provided. Most notably, in the 17th edition, maps of India and Myanmar have been included for the first time.

African equatorial countries use the Sinusoidal projection. Other equatorial countries use the Mercator (cylindrical) projection. Maps of countries in higher latitudes use the Lambert Conformal Conic projection.

As with all of the content of the *Ethnologue,* no political statement is intended by the identification of any territory separately in a map or in the language listings nor by the placement of any boundary lines for any languages or countries on any map.

Acknowledgments

The compilation of a body of information as large as the *Ethnologue* requires the cooperation and participation of hundreds of contributors. The data in this edition are the contributions of researchers, language fieldworkers, and native speakers of the languages who have freely given their time and expertise to improve the accuracy and quality of the *Ethnologue*. Lamentably, space does not permit a listing of every correspondent who has communicated with us since the sixteenth edition was released in 2009. Moreover, the list of contributors over the nearly six decades of *Ethnologue* publication defies documentation.

Gary Simons, as Executive Editor, has provided vision, guidance, and most importantly, coordination and technical assistance for the task of bringing this edition into existence. Paul Lewis, as General Editor, provides overall direction for the research and data gathering activities of the Ethnologue. Charles Fennig, Managing Editor, has supervised the data entry process, tracked changes, dealt with thousands of electronic and hard copy communications, and has been a thoughtful and patient collaborator in the production of this edition. The Research Editors, Colleen Ahland, Michael Ahland, Stan Anonby, Ted Bergman, Albert Bickford, Ken Decker, William Hall, Mark Karan, Lorna Priest, Stuart Showalter, and Jürg Stalder, have provided valuable advice and assistance. Denise Hovland has patiently and diligently entered volumes of data. We have also benefited from the research and editorial assistance provided by Robert Johnson. Louise Hunt served as a summer intern and made an invaluable contribution in a number of ways. Linda Simons has assisted us as the Ethnologue Bibliographer. The Editor Emerita, Barbara F. Grimes, provided timely assistance whenever asked.

Significant reviews of portions of the language family classifications have taken place since the last edition under the general supervision of Colleen and Michael Ahland. Research on the classifications of the languages of the Americas was carried out by Chris Fiorello. John Duerksen provided advice and guidance in updating the Bantu classifications. The entire genetic classification for Tibeto-Burman languages (representing roughly 450 languages) was also thoroughly reviewed and updated. The current classification is a modification of Bradley (1997; 2002). The work on the classification was done by Ken Manson, Christopher P. Wilde, and Erik Andvik. Feedback on various aspects of the reclassification was provided by the Senior Management Committee of the Linguistic Survey of Nepal (LINSUN), made up of Chura Mani Bhandu, Madhav Pokharel, Dan Raj Regmi, Yogendra P. Yadava, with additional contributions and comments from David Bradley, Andrea Csépe, George van Driem, John W. Eppele, Jana Fortier, Warren Glover, Austin Hale, Ken Hugoniot, Karen Grunow-Hårsta, Tej R. Kansakar, Mari-Sisko Khadgi, Brian Migliazza, Novel Kishore Rai, Lal-Shyãkarelu Rapacha, Anju Saxena, Sueyoshi Toba, and Claus Peter Zoller. Karl Anderbeck, David Mead, and Charles E. Grimes have assisted us in reviewing and updating the Austronesian language classifications. We regret that additional revisions and updates were not processed in time for inclusion in this edition.

Intensive data reviews were carried out in Nepal and the Philippines in an effort to improve the quality and timeliness of the data. We are grateful for the enthusiastic participation of both local and expatriate scholars and representatives of many of the speech communities in these events.

The Nepal review involved a large number of linguists from the Central Department of Linguistics at Tribhuvan University and from the Linguistic Society of Nepal, with technical and logistical assistance from the staff of the Nepali National Languages Preservation Institute (NNLPI), along with many others met multiple times to engage in the largest and most comprehensive data review carried out by the *Ethnologue* to date. The effort was coordinated by John Eppele, Prof. Dan Raj Regmi, and Prof. Yogendra Yadava. Participants both on site and via correspondence included: Brataraj Acharya, Bikram Angdembe, Tej Man Angdembe, Chura Mani Bandhu, Cathy Bartram, Nirajan Rai Batas, Bhabendra Bhandari, Chura Mani Bandhu, Tapasi Bhattacharya, Toya Nath Bhattarai, Shangbu Bhote, Balthasar Bickel, Edward Boehm, Dörte Borchers, Ross Caughley, Krishna Prasad Chalise, Gobinda Chantyal, Balman Chhantyal, Indrajit Chhantyal, Kwang-Ju Cho, R. D. Chataut, Prem Chaulagain, Andrea Csépe, Dankaji, Rabinddra Prasad Das, Dubi Nanda Dhakal, Marius Doornenbal, Karen Ebert, Stephanie Eichentopf, John Eppele, Jana Fortier, Martin Gaenszle, Tej P. Gauchan, Bhim Lal Gautam, Narayan Prasad Gautam, Narayan Sharma Gautam, Carol Genetti, Warren Glover, D. Gnanasekaran, Kent Gordon, David Greninger, Christy Grimes, Karen Grunow Harsta, Anna Maria Hari, Matthew Hedlin, Kristine Hildebrandt, Benamin Hilty, Holly Hilty, Hope Hurlbut, René Baptist Huysmans, Hyung-Joon Jung, Tej R. Kansakar, Mari-Sisko Khadgi, Karnakhar Khatiwala, Ramesh Khatri, Bhim Kissan, Kevin Kopp, Bhim Lal, Bipi Lawati, Maureen Lee, Ching Chippa Lhomi, Shobha K. Mahato, Anita Malbaum, Jessi Mitchell, Kedar Bilash Nagila, Til Bikram Nembang, Jean Robert Opgenort, Laxmi Raj Pandit, Krishna Paudel, Krishna Prasad Parajuli, Lekhnath S. Pathak, Vishna Nath Pathak, Krishna Prasad Paudyal, Madhav P. Pokharel, Margaret Potter, Kamal Poudel, Kedar Prasad Poudel, Krishna Poudel, Jyoti Pradhan, Balaram Prasain, Netra Mani Dumi Rai, Jeewan Khaling Rai, Yona Khaling Rai, Novel Kishore Rai, Ichchha Puma Rai, S. K. Rai, Purna Bahadur Rana, Lal-Shyakarelu Rapacha, Kavita Rastogi, Ambika Regmi, Danraj Regmi, Johan Reinhard, Roland Rutgers, Missy Ryan, Dankaji Sampang, Sulochana Sapkota, Suren Sapkota, Diana Schackow, Narayan Sharma, Sekhar Sheeba, Reema Shresta, Dwarika Shrestha, Vishwambhar Nath Shukla, Esther Strahm, K. Subba, Ajitman Tamang, Gopal Thakur, Indresh Thakur, Sueyoshi Toba, G. J. Tolsma, Vikram Mani Tripathi, Dipak Tuladhar, Nirmal Man Tuladhar, Govinda Bahadur Tumbahang, Mark Turin, Ram Kishun Uranw, Bryan Varenkamp, Olavi Vesalainen, Daniel Watters, Stephen Watters, Jeff Webster, Christopher Wilde, Curtis Wong, Kerry Woods, Dev Narayan Yadav, Yogendra Yadava, and Amrit Yonjan-Tamang.

The Philippines review was coordinated by William Hall and Sue McQuay. Participants included: Erica Arcenas, Mel Awid, Emy Ballenas, Dietlinde Behrens, Keith Benn, Loren Billings, Ruth Biral-Schroeder, Scott Burton, Marie Caluza, Bel Caress, Tim Castagna, Albert Castelijn, Richard Elkins, Ross Errington, Doug Fraiser, JoAnn Gault, Ryn Jean Fe Gonzales, Jacqueline Huggins, Marc Jacobson, Daniel Kaufman, Vera Khor, Lani Leano-Mallorca, Jason Lobel, Helen Madrid, Curtis McFarland, Alfred Mijares, Raquel Mijares, Ricardo Nolasco, Kemp Pallesen, Carol Pebley, Andy Peña, Laurie Reid, Mary Rhea, Carl Rubino, Brenda Scheller, Don Scheller, Donna Schumacher, Ron Schumacher, Craig Soderberg, Glenn Stallsmith, Roger Stone, Kermit Titrud, Torine Tolentino, Ena Vander Molen, Chari S. Viloria, Chuck Walton, Sally Winter, Hazel Wrigglesworth, Ritsuko Yamami, Catherine Young, and others.

In addition to these more focused and intensive reviews, the updated data reported in this edition reflect the cooperation and communications over the last five years from hundreds of researchers in the field in SIL and other organizations, but especially the following who participated by reviewing, correcting, and updating data: Joshua Ahn, Sang-Hyuk Ahn, Silvia Allen, Sean Allison, Daniel Anade, Karl Anderbeck, Mike Anderson, Lisa Andrews, Erik Anonby, Stan Anonby, Erika Arcenas, Hilkka Arminen, Gift Asaku, Michael Ayotte, Joan Baart, Denise Bailey, Jonathan Barnhoorn, Aireen Barrios, Keith Beavon, Simone Beck, Ted Bergman, John Berthelette, Albert Bickford, Laura Blackburn, Leonard Bolioki, Douglas Boone, Katrina Boutwell, Richard Boutwell, Leoni Bouwer, Ginger Boyd, David Bradley, Ginny Bradley, Robert Bradshaw, Sherri Brainard, Arjan Branger, Amanda Brotchie, Alan Brown, Bob Brown, John Brownie, Erika Browning, Mike Bryant, Dana Buell, Bob Bugenhagen, Philip Burgess, Larry Burke, Cate Burnett, Scott Burton, Bruce Cain, Bill Callister, Stuart Cameron, Carl Campbell, Alan Canavan, Evelyn Carress, Andy Castro, Sune Ceder, Brad Chamberlain, Nate Cheeseman, Richard Chen, Debbie Chi, Monie Chiong, Katia Chirkova, Nicky Chong, Scott Clark, Stephen Clark, Diana Cohen, Arnie Coleman, Karen Coleman, Kim Colich, Millard Collins, Jeanice Conner, Matt Connor, Bruce Cox, Tom Crabtree, Davy Crockett, Nico Daams, Henriette Daudey, Ken Decker, Marc Deneufchâtel, Lynn Dennis, Christine Derungs, Roselle Dobbs, Keith Doust, Rebekah Drew, Daniel Duke, Robert Early, Helen Eaton, Stephen M. Echerd, William Eckermann, Jim Elliot, Thomas Elvis Guenekean Stephen Emerton, Leif Engkvist, John Eppele, Urs Ernst, Jonathan Evans, Jim Farr, Tim Farrell, Craig Farrow, Ian Flaws, Sebastian Floor, Carl Follingstad, Dorothy Forsberg, Suzie Foster, Mick Foster, Joanna Frampton, Mike Frecette, Robb Fried, Cameron Fruit, Mark Gaddis, Ryan Galorport, O. J. Gamache, Jesse Gates, JoAnn Gault, Maggie Gaved, John Gibbens, Ruth Gisileng, Sep Gisileng, Víctor Gómez, Jan Gossner, Syd Gould, Steve Graham, Richard Gravina, Jeff Green, Jason Griffiths, Charles E. Grimes, Barbara D. Grimes, John Grummitt, Brad Guderian, Bob Gunn, William Hall, Calinda Hallberg, Dan Hallberg, Joshua Ham,

Jongseok Han, Newton Hamlin, Cameron Hamm, Bruce Hansen, Marcus Hansley, Sue Hasselbring, David Healey, Dan Heath, David Heath, Ria Hedinger, Robert Hedinger, Gail Hendrickson, Dusty Hill, Tod Hoatson, Lee Hochstetler, Barbara Hodder, Stephen Hoff, Bruce Hooley, Joan Hooley, Jacqueline Huggins, Jock Hughes, Ken Hugoniot, Robert Hunt, Daniel Hunziker, Elisabeth Hunziker, Greg Huteson, Saleh Mahmud Idris, Kendall Isaac, Eric Jackson, Marc Jacobson, Jeremiah James, Taeho Jang, Juha Janhunen, Dorothy Jauncey, Linda Jekel, Michael Jemphrey, Lucie Jeong, Eric Johnson, Ross Jones, Linda Jordan, Andreas Joswig, André Kamphuis, Andrew Kellogg, Jason Kerr, Paulus-Jan Kieviet, Heather Jean Kilgour, Stephen Kim, Annuka Kinnaird, Arne Kirchner, Geerhard Kloppenburg, Brad Koenig, Dongwan Koo, Issifou Korogo, Tinindjotobe Samuel Kpagheri, Susanne Krüger, Emma Kuipers, Birgitta Kurzan, Daisy Lai, Edwin Lam, Peter Langeveld, Randy LaPolla, Julia Larsen, Ginny Larson, Rence Law, Yong-Seop Lee, Ritva Lehonkoski, Christine Léonard, Yves Leonard, Henrik Liljegren, Katri Linnasalo, Pauline Linton, John Livingstone, Arjen Lock, Larry Lovell, Joseph Lovestrand, Margie Lumawan, Wayne Lunsford, Pirrko Luoma, Antje Maass, James MacDonell, Julie MacKay, Bonnie MacKenzie, Loren Maggard, John Shukurani Magundo, Rundell Maree, Jeremiah Markley, Craig Marshall, Sarah Marshall, Mila Mata, Kina Isaac Matchoudo, Rich Mattocks, Steve McEvoy, Stuart McGill, Ed McGuckin, Greg McLean, David Mead, Paul Nyanduru Meja, Christine Meme, Johannes Merz, Sharon Merz, Jens Meyer, Miriam Meyerhoff, Joseph Mfonyam, David Miller, Rao Min, Bernadette Mitterhofer, Gideon M'mbetsa, Ena Vander Molen, Lee Montgomery, Fiona Morgan, Gareth Mort, Anna Mrisi, Peter Sigak Mudogo, Katja Mueller, Bea Myers, Takashi Nakamura, Prossy Nannyombi, Ken Nehrbass, Elvire Ngnoulaye, Michael Nicholls, Jacques Nicole, Elizabeth Nicoleti, Kelvin Nicolle, Rick Nivens, Prosper Nongnide, Russell Norton, Tatchum Noussi, Misheck Nyirenda, Richard Nzogi, Rainer Oetzel, Clif Olson, Richard Olson, Sam Oluka, Mark Osborne, Linus Otronyi, Jim Owen, Brian Paris, Hannah Paris, Joseph Park, Wilma Parker, David Pate, Eric Pawley, Elizabeth Pearce, Jamin Pelkey, Gary Persons, Andrew Persson, Shiloh Peterson, Tom Phinnemore, Tom Pinson, Justin Power, Ken Prettol, Angela Prinz, Greg Pruett, Ruth Raharimanantsoa, Wes Reed, Neil Rees, David Riggs, Jim Roberts, Ali Robinson, Louis Rose, Patrick Rosendall, Heidi Rosendall, David Ross, Tim Roth, Ed Ruch, Mike Rueck, Mary Salisbury, Andrew Sandeen, Misha Sandeen, Mridul Sangma, Zenith Sarker, Ken Sawka, Donald Scheller, Terrill Schrock, Larry Seguin, Satoko Shirai, Stuart Showalter, Aaron Shryock, Rindu Simanjuntak, Yulanti Sisca, Bruce Skoropinski, Scott Smith, Tony Smith, Jacques Sossoukpe, Juerg Stalder, Erik Stapleton, Carey Statezni, Nathan Statezni, Oliver Stegen, Tim Stirtz, Scot Stober, Roger Stone, Bernard Talah, Gerhard Tauberschmidt, Charles Tessaro, Keno Tesoro, Nick Thieberger, David Thormoset, Jonathan Thurley, Kermit Titrud, Edward Tong, Doug Trick, Steven Ttopoqogo, Aaron Uche, Krijn van der Jagt, Melanie Viljoen, Michael Viljoen, Kathy Vanaria, Rosario Viloria, Kilu von Prince, Andy Warren-Rothlin, Karla Watt, Albinus Waynse, Ross Webb, Joan Weber, Martin Weber, Manasseh Wekunda, Rachelle Wenger, Brigitte Werner, Sandra Whang, Patricia Wilkendorf, Carl Williams, Angi Williams-Ngumbu, Paul Williamson, Jim Winters, Cathryn Yang, Zach Yoder, Juhong Yun, Stefanie Zaske, and Carsten Ziegart.

In addition, the following have made significant contributions to the data and its accuracy through personal communications to the editors: Julia Ciupek-Reed, Matt Connor, Colin M. Davis, Daniel Eberle, Jeff German, Amy Kim, Jason Lobel, John E. McLaughlin, Kirk Miller, Bill Morrison, Liahey Ngwazah, Elizabeth Parks, Lawrence Reid, P. R. Shinu, Glenna Sollenberger, Ian Tupper, Sara van Cott, Angela Williams, among many others.

The proofreading of the text of the 17th edition was organized by Cyndi Conner who coordinated the thorough and careful efforts of: Elinor Abbot, Heidi Aboutaj, Judy Benjamin, Raymond Bergthold, Bonnie Brown, Mickey Brussow, Mike Cahill, Vurnell Cobbey, Cindy Crosbie, Paul Crosbie, Dennis Felkner, Lynn Frank, Joyce Franklin, Karl Franklin, Sharon Hallisy, Randy Hasty, Denise Hovland, Ken Hubel, Louise Hunt, George Huttar, Mary Huttar, Robert Johnson, Rhonda Hartell Jones, Dirk Kievit, Eric Kindeberg, Marj Liedtke, Lucy Lindholm, Melinda Lyons, Lana Martens, Martha Martens, Julia Anne McCord, Georgetta MacDonald, Jason Naylor, Janell Nordmoe, Joyce Park, Becky Quick, Ron Radke, Paul Schmidt, Linda Simons, Glenna Sollenberger, Martie Tracy, Paul Vollrath, Barb Waugh, Bev Woodward, Tom Woodward, Diane Wroge, and Mae Zook.

Technical support for the *Ethnologue* database and the systems that allow us to edit the information and produce publications from it has been provided by Roger Hanggi, Lars Huttar, Joe McCarthy, Ray Uehara, and Chad White. Joan Spanne and Melinda Lyons, ISO 639-3 Registrars, along with Anthony Aristar at LinguistList, have assisted us in keeping our database aligned with the ISO 639-3 inventory of identified languages.

The language maps have been produced under the direction of SIL's Lead Cartographer, Irene Tucker, by Matt Benjamin, Michael McMillan and Eva Horton with quality assurance and technical assistance from Stephen Tucker and additional research by Colin Davis.

Production of this edition was implemented by the staff of SIL International's Global Publishing Services Department under the leadership of Alan Conner and with particular assistance from Gayle Sheehan. Chad White did extensive work on website development and implementation.

Though there are many names listed above, we have almost certainly omitted others who have made significant contributions. To them we offer both apologies and gratitude.

Updates and corrections

New and updated editions of the *Ethnologue* are published on a regular basis. Although this edition contains nearly 60,000 updates and corrections from the previous one, we make no claims for completeness. While we aim for accuracy, advancing knowledge from ongoing research and the continuously changing situations of the 7,106 known living languages of the world inevitably lead to inaccuracies and discrepancies. We welcome corrections and new information that will improve both the accuracy and the completeness of the data.

Language additions or deletions. Requests for the addition of a previously unidentified language or for other modifications to the inventory of identified languages should be made directly to the ISO 639-3 Registrar since it is the editorial policy of *Ethnologue* to follow the ISO 639-3 standard when determining the inventory of languages to be listed. Go to the ISO 639-3 website at http://www.sil.org/iso639-3/ and click on "Submitting change requests" to find the change request form and the filing instructions.

Corrections. If you believe any of the information about a language is in error, send your proposed change to the editor using one of the addresses given below. Please provide details about the sources of your information, including full bibliographic citations of published sources when applicable.

The submitter of any correction can expect to receive an initial acknowledgment from the Managing Editor of the *Ethnologue*. Our staff will then seek to verify the proposed change before it is accepted. This process may take months as it generally involves making enquiries of individuals who are resident in the country or region where the language is spoken. These persons may in turn make enquiries of others or consult published materials in order to perform the verification. While we make every effort to inform the submitter of the results of our research and verification, we cannot guarantee that a report of the outcome will be sent in every case. Corrections, even after they are accepted and entered in our database, will only appear online or in print when the next edition of the Ethnologue is released.

Submit corrections and additions by e-mail to:

Ethnologue_Editor@sil.org

Or by post to:

Editor, Ethnologue
SIL International
7500 West Camp Wisdom Road
Dallas, TX 75236, U.S.A.

How to Use This Book

This *Ethnologue* volume is organized into four parts as follows:

Part I, "Statistical Summaries", gives a summary view of the language situation both globally and in Asia. Specifically, it offers numerical tabulations of languages and number of speakers by world area, by language size, by language status, by language family, and by country.

Part II, "Language Listings", provides detailed information on the 2,351 languages listed in the *Ethnologue* as originating in Asia. Language entries are organized by country; a total of 52 countries are included in this volume. Each country is introduced by an overview paragraph containing the information elements described below in "Country information". The overview is followed by an entry for each language of the country that is not a language of recent immigrants or of temporary residents. Language entries within each country are in alphabetical order by primary language name and provide a summary description structured by a set of categories described below in "Language information". The section for "Other Languages" (page 319) includes the primary entries for languages used in Asia that originate outside of that area. A bibliography listing all (and only) the published references cited within the country and language descriptions is included at the end of Part II beginning on page 325. See "How references are cited" (page 29) for a description of how source citations are formatted.

Part III, "Language Maps", locates the languages described in Part II on a series of 68 maps. Language maps have been produced for 32 of the countries of Asia. Continent maps are given to help orient the user to the location of specific countries. The maps are ordered by continent, then by country name. However, there are occasional deviations from strict alphabetical order of country names in order to maintain the integrity of maps on facing pages. No political statement is intended by the placement of any boundary lines for any languages or countries on any map. See "Language maps" (page 17) for more details on the maps and how they were produced.

Part IV, "Indexes", offers three ways of finding information in this volume:

- "Language Name Index" (page 419) is an index of the 16,433 unique names that are associated with the 2,351 languages described in this volume. It is an alphabetical list of all the language names, alternate names, dialect names, and alternate dialect names that appear in the language entries. Each index entry has page references back to the language entries in which the given name appears. Instructions for using the index are given on its first page.
- "Language Code Index" (page 543) is an alphabetical list of the three-letter codes from ISO 639-3 that are used to uniquely identify the languages in this volume. Each index entry has a page reference back to the main entry for the language. Instructions for using the index are given on its first page.
- "Country Index" (page 557) is an alphabetical list of country names with a page reference back to the page on which the section for that country begins. If there are maps for the country, their first page is also indicated.

Country information

Languages are listed in Part II by country within the major geographic areas of Asia. The country names used as headings are not official names, but are the commonly known names of the countries in English. *Ethnologue* follows the ISO 3166 standard in determining what geopolitical entities to list as countries. As a consequence, some political dependencies are listed in a country section of their own while others are included within the larger country with which they are associated. The *Ethnologue* takes no position on issues of national sovereignty by this arrangement which is intended solely to facilitate the navigation of the published information.

The entry for a country begins with a pair of header paragraphs giving summary information about the country. This header is followed by an entry for each language of the country that is not a recent immigrant. The country header has the following form:

> Official name. Sovereignty status. Population. General remarks. Principal languages. Literacy rate. Immigrant languages. General references. Deaf population. Recognized nationalities.
>
> Language counts (with profile graphic). Map information.

Official name. If the name used by the country in its official documents differs from the popular English name as given in the heading, the official name of the country is listed here. There may be more than one official name listed in more than one language. In a few cases, additional or former names used to identify a country are also included.

Sovereignty status. If the country is not a

fully sovereign nation, a comment is given here to describe its status in relation to the sovereign state with which it is associated.

Population. These figures are taken from the most recent national census data where available or are the current estimated population from the United Nations or another reliable source, which is identified.

General remarks. The country information may also contain general remarks about the political status, the geography, or the population.

Principal languages. Languages that have been identified as having a function at the nation-wide level are listed here. This includes all the languages that function at the national level as a working language or a language of identity or both, whether this is by statute or is the de facto situation. For a fuller discussion, see "Official recognition" (page 15).

Literacy rate. This is an estimate of the percentage of the population in the country that is literate in any language of the country. Data are primarily from UNESCO but may also come from various other sources if more recent estimates are available.

Immigrant languages. Immigrant languages are categorized as such if they are spoken by relatively recently arrived or transient populations which do not have a well-established, multi-generational community of language users in the country. Population estimates, if known, are shown in parentheses immediately following the language name. These languages do not have a separate language entry in the language listings for the country and are not included in the language counts for the country. Given the transitory nature of these populations and the difficulty in obtaining up-to-date information, this listing may be inaccurate or incomplete.

General references. This lists author-year citations for published sources of general information about the country and its languages. See "Bibliography" (page 325) for the full bibliographic references for the cited works. This list includes only suggestions for those who wish to begin to explore the language situation of the country in greater depth. It is not intended to be an exhaustive list and more current works may be missing. Suggestions for additional or more up-to-date general works on the languages of the country are solicited. See "Updates and corrections" (page 21) for submission instructions.

Deaf population. There are millions of deaf and hearing-impaired people in the world. The country overview gives information on the number of audiologically deaf people (which is generally larger than the number of deaf people who use a sign language) and an approximate count of the deaf institutions (schools, clubs, associations). The deaf sign languages listed in language entries are those used exclusively within deaf communities. They do not include those, like Signed English, that spell out spoken languages used in the country. See the fuller discussion under "Sign languages" (page 10). Additional information on deafness and deaf sign languages is welcomed. See "Updates and corrections" (page 21) for submission instructions.

Recognized nationalities. If the country has a system for officially recognizing nationalities within its borders, it is described here. The language entries for the country then use the *Status* section to identify the officially recognized nationality with which the individual languages are associated.

Language counts (with profile graphic). The number of individual languages indigenous to the country is given with a breakdown of the number of living languages versus extinct languages. The counts of living languages are further broken down into the summary categories of Institutional (EGIDS 0-4), Developing (EGIDS 5), Vigorous (EGIDS 6a), In trouble (EGIDS 6b-7), and Dying (EGIDS 8a-9). These counts are then represented visually in a country profile histogram that shows the relative number of languages in each of these five summary categories. These categories are represented by bars of purple, blue, green, yellow, and red, respectively. See "Language status" (page 13) for a detailed discussion of the EGIDS levels that make up these summary categories. Macrolanguages are not included in these counts since they are not distinct from, but overlap, the individual languages that are already counted.

Map information. If the location of languages within the country in focus is shown on one or more maps in Part III, a reference is given to the exact page number on which the set of maps begins.

Language information

Many languages are spoken in more than one country, and so are listed under several countries. One of the countries is considered primary, usually the country of origin or country where most of the speakers are located. More information about a language is given in its entry in the primary country than in the others. An entry for a language in a non-primary country ends with the words "See more information under..." giving a cross-reference to the primary country. This system results in 2,999 entries for the 2,351 languages listed in this volume.

A complete entry for the primary country has the following form and content:

Primary language name [ISO 639-3 code] (Alternate names). Country speaker population. Population stability comment. Population in all countries. Monolingual population. Population remarks. Ethnic population. Location. *Status:* EGIDS level. Language function in country. *Class:* Linguistic classification. Macrolanguage membership. *Dialects:* Dialect names. Intelligibility and dialect relations. Lexical similarity. *Type:* Linguistic typology information. *Lg Use:* Viability remarks. Domains of use. User age groups. Language attitudes. Bilingualism remarks. Use as second language. *Lg Dev:* Literacy rates. Literacy remarks. Use in elementary or secondary schools. Publications and use in media. *Writing:* Scripts used. *Other:* General remarks. Religion. Macrolanguage member languages. *Map:* Map location.

Each language entry begins with language identification information, population information, and location information. Beyond these initial parts of the entry, italicized labels are used to organize the entry into topical sections. A label appears in a given entry only if the entry contains one or more of the pieces of information associated with that topic. Nine such labels are used:

- *Status* for the EGIDS level and recognized functions of the language in the country;
- *Class* for the language classification, including macrolanguage membership if applicable;
- *Dialects* for information about the names of dialects of the language, including information on lexical similarity and intelligibility with other varieties if available;
- *Type* for typological information, including brief descriptions of basic word order, significant phonological, morphological, and syntactic features, and other matters of interest to linguists;
- *Lg Use* for information about the use and viability of the language, as well as the use of other languages by the community;
- *Lg Dev* for information about language development, including literacy rates, written materials, and use in education;
- *Writing* for information about writing systems and scripts used for the language;
- *Other* for all additional information; and
- *Map* for cross-references to the language maps

Information in all of these categories is not available for every language.

Language identification

This part of the entry lists names that have been used to identify the language, as well as the international three-letter code that is used to identify it uniquely.

Primary language name. Each entry begins with the name used to refer in English to that language in that country. In most cases the name is the one that the speakers prefer if such a preference is known. However, speakers within a language community may have different opinions about which name they prefer. Known preferred names are recorded using English spellings, though diacritical marks may be included. Among Khoisan languages and a few other languages in southern Africa special symbols are used in language names to represent the "click" sounds produced with ingressive mouth air.

ISO 639-3 code The code assigned to the language by the ISO 639-3 standard (ISO 2007) is given in lower-case letters within square brackets. When a given language is spoken in multiple countries, all of the entries for that language use the same three-letter code. The code distinguishes the language from other languages with the same or similar names and identifies those cases in which the name differs across country borders. These codes ensure that each language is counted only once in world or area statistics.

Alternate names Many languages are known by or have been referenced in the literature by more than one name. The entries in this volume list 7,945 alternate names to assist the reader in identifying a language. These are enclosed in parentheses and listed in alphabetical order separated from each other by commas. Alternate names come from many diverse sources: speakers may have more than one name for their language, or neighboring groups may use different names. Other names may have been assigned by outsiders and used in ethnographic or linguistic publications before the name used by the speakers themselves was known. Another source of alternate names is variant spellings of what is essentially the same name. In many cases, spellings used in languages of wider communication or in regional languages are also included in the list. Names for the ethnic group and place names that have been used in the literature as names for the language are listed in the *Other comments* part of the entry.

Some names in use by others are offensive to the speakers of the language. Those are identified, wherever they are listed, by enclosing the name in double quotation marks and appending the label *pej.* (pejorative) following the name. We include these names as a means of helping users find languages they may have only heard of or seen referred to by such names. By so doing, *Ethnologue* in no way implies any endorsement of the pejorative names.

Population

This part of the entry gives the number of L1 speakers in the country, plus the total number of L1 speakers worldwide if it is used in multiple countries. Also included may be an indication of population stability, number of monolingual speakers, population of ethnic community, and other comments about population.

Country speaker population. The first population figure given is the estimated number of first-language (L1) speakers in the country in focus. Population data have been provided from many different sources over a number of years. This diversity among sources and dates frequently causes the totals of the populations for all of the languages in any given country to differ markedly from the total current population of the country.

We do not extrapolate population estimates to bring them up-to-date, since populations of language communities do not increase at the same rate within a country and since some initial estimates themselves turn out to have been incorrect to start with. However, some population data submitted to the *Ethnologue* may be the result of extrapolation.

The *Ethnologue* provides the number of first-language speakers wherever possible. It is often difficult to get an accurate figure for the speakers of a language. All figures are only estimates; this is true even for census figures. Some sources do not include all dialects in their figures or may count as a single language two languages identified separately in the ISO 639-3 inventory. Some sources count members of ethnic groups, who, in some cases, may not be speakers of the language. Some sources do not make clear whether they refer to the total number of speakers in all countries, or only to those in one of the countries. Some do not distinguish first-language (L1) speakers from second-language (L2) speakers.

Languages that are no longer in use, but still have ethnic group members who identify with the language, are listed as having "No known speakers" in place of a population figure. Languages that have neither societal use nor remaining ethnic group members are described as "Extinct". Languages which have no L1 speakers but which are used for specific purposes by a community are identified as "Second Language Only".

Dates and sources for population data are given where available using the conventions described in "How references are cited" (page 29). Where the word "census" appears as the source, it is generally the national census of the country and is not included in the list of references. In some cases the source is a government agency (but not the official census) or another organization. Only when the citation has the form "Author Year" will the source appear in the bibliography; see "How references are cited" (page 29).

Population stability comment. For some languages, we are able to indicate whether the L1 speaker population is increasing or decreasing. This information also contributes to an overall evaluation of ethnolinguistic vitality. There may be a few cases where the actual speaker population count is not known or is unreported, but the stability and general trend of the population is evident and has been commented on.

Population in all countries. When a language has first-language speakers in more than one country, the entry for the primary country lists the calculated total speaker population for all countries. Since information may come from multiple sources, the sum of the individual country populations may not equal the figure given for all countries in other sources. In some cases, the L1 speaker population of one or more countries may not be available and is not included in this calculation.

Monolingual population. Where the data are available, the number of those who are monolingual is reported. In some cases it is reported as a percentage of the L1 speaker population. This figure can be compared with the total speaker population as an indicator of the vitality of the language.

L2 speaker population. Where the data are available, the number of those who speak this language as a second language is reported. Two numbers may be reported: the number of L2 speakers within the country, and the number of L2 speakers worldwide.

Population remarks. Additional information concerning populations may include population breakdowns (by dialect, gender, ethnic groups, or specific villages or communities), the population of the deaf community, or other comments on demographics.

Ethnic population. Where it is known, the population of those who identify themselves as part of the ethnic group, whether or not they speak the language, is given. A language with no first-language speakers will be reported as extinct when the ethnic population figure is zero, absent, or unknown. When the reported speaker population is zero but there is an ethnic population figure, the language will be reported as having "No known speakers".

Location

A description of the location where the language is spoken is included in each entry where a specific area can be defined. Those languages that are scattered through a country or wide region may not have this information in the entry or may be reported as "Widespread". These languages may not appear on the country maps. A list of all countries where the language is spoken is provided in the primary entry for a language that is spoken in multiple countries. Generally, regional locations are listed in descending order from largest geopolitical unit to the smallest. The list of locations may not be exhaustive. When the language is used in multiple countries, this part of the entry for the primary country also includes a listing of all the other countries in which it is used.

Language status

This part of the entry reports the estimate of the status of the language in the country on the Expanded Graded Intergeneratonal Disruption Scale (EGIDS); see the complete section on "Language status" (page 13) for a listing of the levels. If the language has been officially recognized in legislation or serves official functions at the national or provincial levels, there is an additional note naming the nature of the recognition and function. If the recognition is statutory, the statute is identified. The categories for recognition and function are described in the section on "Official recognition" (page 15).

If the reported language status is EGIDS 3 (Wider Communication) and the data are available, L1 speakers of other languages who use this language as a language of wider communication are identified.

Classification

This part of the entry names the linguistic affiliation of the language, including macrolanguage membership if applicable.

All languages are slowly changing, and linguistically related varieties may be diverging or merging. Most languages are related to other languages–to some more closely and to others more distantly. Linguists have used terms such as phylum, stock, family, branch, group, language, and dialect to refer to these relationships in increasing order of linguistic similarity.

Linguistic classification. The classification information for each language follows the general order from largest grouping to smallest. More inclusive group names are given first, followed by the names for less inclusive subgroups, separated by commas.

Language classification information comes from a variety of sources. The *Ethnologue* attempts to report the generally accepted consensus of scholars working in the language family based on published works and scholarly review. For this edition, the language classifications for several major families have undergone thorough review and revision. The sources on which the classifications are based are not overtly cited in the language entry but may be included in the list of general references listed at the country level. The sources used for classifications are available on request by contacting the Editor; see "Updates and corrections" (page 21) for contact information.

Macrolanguage membership. If an individual language is a member of a macrolanguage , that fact is reported following the language classification information. See "Macrolanguages" (page 9) for a discussion of this concept. The listing gives the name of the macrolanguage of which the individual language is a member, the name of the primary country under which its entry is found (if different from the current country), and the ISO code for the macrolanguage. By looking up that entry, it is possible to find a list of all the members of the macrolanguage.

Dialects

This part of the entry gives information about the names of dialects of the language. It may also describe the relationships among dialects or to other languages in terms of dialect intelligibility and lexical similarity.

Dialect names. Speech varieties which are functionally intelligible to each others' speakers because of linguistic similarity are generally considered dialects of the same language and the names of all such dialects are listed under that language. In addition, alternate names for individual dialects are listed in parentheses following the primary name for the dialect. When one of these names is known to be offensive to its speakers, it is placed in double quotes (and tagged as pejorative with the abbreviation "*pej.*" as is also done for alternate language names).

The listing of dialect names does not represent the results of rigorous dialectological investigations. As with the alternate names, the list of dialect names includes all names reported to us which may, at one time or another, have been used in reference to a local variety of a language. Some of these names are village or regional names and may not actually represent significant linguistic variants. In a few cases, the ISO 639-3 standard has assigned individual language identification codes to varieties which we, on the advice of our contributors and consultants, have included in our list of dialects. In those very few cases, we depart from the ISO 639-3 standard and do not list these varieties separately as individual languages.

Intelligibility and dialect relations. A measure of inherent intelligibility with other varieties is given by percent. Values of less than 85% are likely to signal difficulty in comprehension of the indicated language.

The ability of the users of one variety to understand another variety, based only on the similarity of those two varieties, is called *inherent* intelligibility. Intelligibility may not be reciprocal or mutual, thus the wording of the intelligibility description may indicate the direction of the intelligibility (e.g., 85% intelligibility *of* another variety, or 85% intelligibility *by* speakers of another variety). If the direction of intelligibility is not indicated (e.g., 85% intelligibility *with* another variety) or is identified as being mutual, it should be understood as being reciprocal with speakers of each of the varieties mentioned understanding each other equally well.

The ability of speakers to understand another variety because of previous exposure to it or learning is called *acquired* intelligibility and may be commented on in some language entries.

Lexical similarity. The percentage of lexical similarity between two linguistic varieties is determined by comparing a set of standardized wordlists and counting those forms that show similarity in both form and meaning. Percentages higher than 85% usually indicate a speech variant that is likely a dialect of the language with which it is being compared. Unlike intelligibility, lexical similarity is bidirectional or reciprocal.

Typology

For some languages, brief lists of linguistic phenomena found in the language are given. Constituent order (e.g. Subject, Object, Verb = SOV) is the most commonly reported feature. Other basic features that are of particular interest to linguists are also reported when the data is available. In a growing number of cases these listings are more extensive and cover a range of linguistic features, including information about the existence of prepositions versus postpositions, constituent order in noun phrases, gender, case, transitivity and ergativity, canonical syllable patterns, the number of consonants and vowels, the existence of tone, and in some cases whether users of the language also use "whistle speech". These descriptions are no more than brief mentions, however, and do not constitute adequate descriptions of the language. A list of the typological features that we wish to collect data on is available upon request.

Language use

This part of the entry gives information about the use and viability of the language, as well as the use of other languages by members of the community.

Viability remarks. A number of viability indicators are given. As a general summary, where the language is being passed on to children as their first language, or where it is used frequently and widely within the community, the term "Vigorous" is most often used.

Other indicators are the number of people who use the language as their second language, and the degree of language shift of speakers of this language to a another language (in some cases indicated by the percentage of speakers within the ethnic community). General estimates of viability may be given. These indicators and general comments are taken into account in assigning the EGIDS status.

Domains of use. When more than one language is used in a community, speakers often establish patterns of language use for specific configurations of speakers, topics, and locations. These domains of language use can be described by answering the well-known question, "Who is speaking to whom, about what, and where?" In some language entries, we are able to specify a set of identified domains of use and we also report whether the domain is associated exclusively with the language or is one where mixed language use is prevalent.

The *Ethnologue* does not have sufficient data about each language to permit a full description of the domains of use in this technical sense, but uses the term to refer most often to a general set of categories most often associated with a particular location (e.g., home, school, community) and thus only indirectly related to the topics and speakers most generally associated with those settings. Knowledge of these patterns of language use can help in evaluating ethnolinguistic vitality and in developing strategies for language revitalization or language development.

User age groups. Data reported in this category is most often reported in terms of generations (children, adolescents, young adults, adults, older adults) but occasionally specific age ranges may be identified.

As language use shifts from a traditional language to one of wider communication, differences in use appear between age groups. As language change takes place, older adults tend to be the final speakers of the traditional language. The use of a language by children is thus a significant indicator of the patterns of intergenerational language transmission which is key to language maintenance.

Language attitudes. We report only summary attitude evaluations as positive attitudes, neutral attitudes, or negative attitudes. In some cases these general categories may include an additional modifier, such as, "somewhat positive attitudes."

What people think and how they feel about their own language is important to those promoting literacy or other development activities as more positive attitudes generally correspond to stronger ethnolinguistic vitality. Attitudes are difficult to assess directly and equally difficult to describe adequately.

Bilingualism remarks. Brief comments about the use and users of second languages are included. Unless specific information is provided to us, we generally do not characterize levels of proficiency or domains of use of second languages. Generally the remark consists of the phrase "Also use" followed by the name(s) of the additional languages.

Because second languages are usually learned later than first languages and access to the means of acquiring proficiency in a second language is not always equally available, bilingualism is usually not uniform across a community. When communities use a second language, different speakers usually have varying degrees of bilingual proficiency, ranging from the ability to use only greetings, to engage in trade, or proficiency adequate for freely expressing anything in the second language. Leaders, educated, men, traders, those who travel, those in population centers, and people in certain age groups may be more bilingual than other members of their community. Where information is available, these factors about bilingualism are described.

Use as second language. When the language in focus is used by others as a second language (as reported in the bilingualism remarks of other language entries), this is indicated with the phrase "Used as L2 by ...". Following this introductory phrase is a list of the other languages that are reported to use this one as a second language.

Language development

This part of the entry gives information about literacy rates, written materials, and use in education.

Literacy rates. Where available, percentages of the speaker population who are literate are given for the first (L1) and second (L2) languages. Where the L2 is not specifically identified, it is assumed to be the dominant language of the country in focus or another major language in the vicinity.

Literacy remarks. Information concerning motivation for literacy and existence of government (and other) literacy programs are given where available. Additional information concerning literacy that does not appear in related categories may also be reported here.

Use in elementary or secondary schools. The language may be used either as a language of instruction or taught as a subject within one or more schools in the language area. Generally, we only include a statement in this category if the language is used in the schools. Occasionally some additional information about the nature of that use is also available and is reported.

Publications and use in media. The existence of materials that have been produced in the language such as linguistic documentation (dictionaries, grammars), printed materials, broadcast media, and new media (SMS, email, websites, etc.) is indicated when known. We report the existence of such materials but do not list titles individually. Where extensive literature and media exist, we identify the language as "Fully developed". For many languages this information is very incomplete at this time. More information is welcomed though it is unlikely that the *Ethnologue* will ever be able to document existing literature in a comprehensive way.

The most widely published book in the world is the Bible with at least portions having been translated and published in 2,865 or 40% of the living languages listed in the *Ethnologue*. This figure is based on the thorough archival efforts of the United Bible Societies and the American Bible Society. Information about Bible publication for each language is given with the dates of the earliest and most recent published Bible, New Testament (NT), Old Testament (OT), or complete books (portions).

Writing

For each language, the script used for written materials is given if known. Where multiple scripts are in use they are reported in alphabetical order. Where possible we also report any specific style of a script that is used, the years when a script began to be used or ceased to be used, and other comments regarding writing and orthography. Languages which are known to be unwritten are so identified. Since many languages use the Latin script, that fact is not always reported if its use is obvious. Scripts other than transcription systems also exist for some Sign Languages but are not in wide use and so are not currently reported.

Other Comments

This part of the entry gives additional information that does not fit under the above categories.

General remarks. These are general statements about the language or its context that do not fall into other specific categories. Alternate identifications of the language community or ethnic group may be identified here. These may include government recognized or official nationalities, ethnic names (usually identified by the label "Ethnonym:"), or the identification of the meanings or derivations of certain names. Other historical or ethnographic information may be included here as well.

Religion. The religious affiliations of the speakers of the language are given where known. These are generally listed in descending order of number of adherents.

Macrolanguage member languages. If the entry is describing a macrolanguage , then a complete list is given of the individual languages that fall within the scope of the macrolanguage. See "Macrolanguages" (page 9) for a discussion of this concept.

Second Language Only status. While there are many languages that are used as second languages by large populations of speakers, the phrase "Second language only" is used to identify a specific category made up of those languages which are used as second languages but have no mother-tongue speakers and generally weak or secondary ethnic or identity associations.

These may include languages of special use, such as languages of initiation, languages of interethnic communication such as American Plains Indian Sign Language, liturgical languages, as well as cants and jargons. Most often these languages are given a status of EGIDS 3 (Wider Communication) but are identified here as well because of the absence of L1 speakers.

Crossreference to primary entry. When this entry is not the primary entry for the language being described, there is a crossreference to the specific page on which the primary entry may be found. Information like the total population, all the countries where spoken, linguistic relationships, linguistic typology, products of language development, and writing systems are included only in the primary entry.

Map information

If the location of the language within the country in focus is shown on one or more maps, page number references to those maps are given. If the language is identified on a map by name, but that name differs from the primary name in the language entry, the name on the map is also given here in parentheses. If the language is represented on a map by an index number, rather than by its name, the index number is given following the page number (with a colon as separator).

How references are cited

Because the *Ethnologue* is produced by extracting data from a database, there is a great deal of uniformity, and some stiffness in the wording and phrases used. Frequently the data is maintained using a set of predetermined categories and labels. Because of this, the *Ethnologue* rarely quotes any source verbatim. Sources are acknowledged wherever specific statements or facts can be directly attributed to them.

Three kinds of source citations are used:

- **Published works** are identified using standard in-text citations enclosed in parentheses. These consist of the author's or editor's surname followed by the year of publication. Up to three authors are listed in the citation. Published works authored or edited by more than three persons are cited using the first author's surname followed by "et al." and the year of publication. Citations do not distinguish between multiple works by the same person published in the same year. Neither are persons with the same surname distinguished in the citations. Generally, the corresponding references identified by such ambiguous citations can be identified clearly based on the language entry in which the citation is made and the title of the work in the bibliography (page 325) where the bibliographic details of all cited published works are included.
- **Unpublished sources** are also acknowledged when specific statements or facts are attributed to them. Unpublished works may include personal communications, manuscripts, unpublished reports, and other materials submitted to us. They are identified using in-text citations enclosed in parentheses in which the year of the communication is given first, followed by the source's first initial and surname. Unpublished sources with multiple authors are handled in the same way as published source citations, except for the inversion of the order of the citation elements as just described. Unpublished sources are not further described in the bibliography.
- **Census data** are cited like unpublished sources with the year first followed only by the word "census". Though there may be electronic or print publications where such data can be accessed, we treat them this way in order to avoid swelling the bibliography beyond a manageable size.

We have made strenuous efforts to track and identify all the sources cited in the text and we are happy to supply additional details upon request.

Part I
Statistical Summaries

Global Summary

Part II, "Language Listings" (page 45), provides a detailed listing of all the languages of Asia. This section steps back from that detail to offer a summary view of the language situation in that area of the world. First, however, we set the global context by offering numerical tabulations of languages and number of speakers in the world at large by geographic area, by language size, and by language status.

Summary by area

The language listings in the three volumes of *Ethnologue* are organized under five world areas: Africa, the Americas, Asia, Europe, and the Pacific. Table 4 summarizes the distribution of languages and their populations by these areas. Note that the areas differ widely with respect to typical language size (Grimes 1986, 1995).

The first *Count* column in table 4 gives the number of living languages that originate in the specified area. A living language is defined as one that has at least one speaker for whom it is their first language; extinct languages and languages that are used only as a second language are excluded from these counts. In this tabulation, each language is counted only once so that the total at the bottom of the column represents the total number of living languages in the world. A language that is spoken in more than one country is counted under the area of its primary country. This has the effect of counting the languages by their area of origin.

The second *Count* column gives the total number of people who use those languages as their first language, regardless of where in the world they may live. Note, for instance, that the population given in the row for Europe is nearly twice the actual population of Europe. This is because it is a count of speakers of European languages, some of which are now used as a first language in other parts of the world due to the colonial expansion of the last few centuries. Since it is a count of first-language speakers, any given person should be counted only once. As a result the total at the bottom of the column approximates the total world population. Note, however, that the total is somewhat less than the actual world population at present. This is because the *Ethnologue* lacks population estimates for about 4% of the languages and because it does not automatically extrapolate population estimates to the current year, but waits for reports from reliable sources.

The *Percent* columns give the share of the count for that area as a percentage of the total number listed at the bottom of the Count column. The *Mean* column gives the average number of speakers per language, while the *Median* column gives the middle value in the distribution of language populations (that is, half of the languages have more speakers than that number and half have that number or fewer).

Table 4. Distribution of world languages by area of origin

Area	Living languages		Number of speakers			
	Count	*Percent*	*Total*	*Percent*	*Mean*	*Median*
Africa	2,146	30.2	810,209,997	12.9	377,544	27,000
Americas	1,060	14.9	51,456,819	0.8	48,544	1,150
Asia	2,303	32.4	3,745,496,032	59.7	1,626,355	12,000
Europe	285	4.0	1,656,808,477	26.4	5,813,363	50,000
Pacific	1,312	18.5	6,740,866	0.1	5,138	950
Totals	7,106	100.0	6,270,712,191	100.0	882,453	7,000

Summary by language status

Table 5 summarizes the distribution of languages in the world by their status in terms of language development or language endangerment. The *EGIDS* column categorizes the languages by their level on the EGIDS scale. Consult "Language status" (page 13) for a description of the levels in the scale.

The next six columns are as in Table 6. In addition, the *Mean* column gives the average population of all the languages with the given EGIDS level and the *Median* column gives the median population for the languages at that level, that is, half of the languages at that level have a higher population and half have a lower population. If there are any languages with an unknown population, these are ignored in the calculation of the mean and the median.

Table 5. Distribution of world languages by vitality status

EGIDS	Living languages			Number of speakers				
	Count	*Percent*	*Cumulative*	*Total*	*Percent*	*Cumulative*	*Mean*	*Median*
0	6	0.1	0.1%	1,839,439,858	29.3338	29.3338%	306,573,310	335,148,868
1	95	1.3	1.4%	1,925,647,667	30.7086	60.0424%	20,269,975	6,408,985
2	69	1.0	2.4%	703,103,562	11.2125	71.2549%	10,189,907	1,300,000
3	175	2.5	4.9%	553,839,750	8.8322	80.0871%	3,164,799	684,000
4	215	3.0	7.9%	159,717,369	2.5470	82.6341%	742,871	123,000
5	1,563	22.0	29.9%	616,297,678	9.8282	92.4623%	394,304	27,000
6a	2,549	35.9	65.7%	403,200,700	6.4299	98.8922%	158,180	10,000
6b	1,055	14.8	80.6%	55,965,859	0.8925	99.7847%	53,048	3,000
7	464	6.5	87.1%	12,705,302	0.2026	99.9873%	27,382	1,080
8a	288	4.1	91.2%	721,897	0.0115	99.9988%	2,507	270
8b	424	6.0	97.1%	72,549	0.0012	100.0000%	171	15
9	203	2.9	100.0%	0	0.0000	100.0000%	0	0
Totals	7,106	100.0		6,270,712,191	100.0000			

Summary by language size

Table 6 summarizes the distribution of languages in the world by number of L1 speakers. The *Population range* column categorizes the languages by the number of digits in their population of first-language speakers.

The *Count* column gives the number of living languages within the specified population range. The *Percent* column gives the share of the count for that population range as a percentage of the total number of languages given at the bottom of the Count column. The *Cumulative* column gives the cumulative sum of the percentage of languages going from top to bottom in the column.

The *Total* column gives the total population of all the languages in the given range category. The second *Percent* column gives the percentage of the total country population as estimated at the bottom of the Total column. Note that if the table has a row for Unknown, representing languages for which the *Ethnologue* does not have a population estimate; the calculation of population percentage is not able to take those languages into account. The final *Cumulative* column gives the cumulative sums of the population percentages going from top to bottom in the column.

Table 6. Distribution of world languages by number of first-language speakers

Population range	Living languages			Number of speakers		
	Count	*Percent*	*Cumulative*	*Total*	*Percent*	*Cumulative*
100,000,000 to 999,999,999	8	0.1	0.1%	2,543,460,358	40.56095	40.56095%
10,000,000 to 99,999,999	79	1.1	1.2%	2,433,383,987	38.80554	79.36649%
1,000,000 to 9,999,999	305	4.3	5.5%	929,591,638	14.82434	94.19083%
100,000 to 999,999	937	13.2	18.7%	294,626,823	4.69846	98.88929%
10,000 to 99,999	1,811	25.5	44.2%	61,556,414	0.98165	99.87094%
1,000 to 9,999	1,978	27.8	72.0%	7,613,358	0.12141	99.99235%
100 to 999	1,062	14.9	87.0%	466,128	0.00743	99.99978%
10 to 99	338	4.8	91.7%	12,944	0.00021	99.99999%
1 to 9	137	1.9	93.7%	541	0.00001	100.00000%
0	204	2.9	96.5%	0	0.00000	100.00000%
Unknown	247	3.5	100.0%			
Totals	7,106	100.0		6,270,712,191	100.00000	

Table 7 lists the largest languages of the world in descending order of population of first-language speakers. The *Primary Country* column names the country in which the primary entry for the language is found. The *Total Countries* column gives the number of countries in the world in which the language is listed either with a full entry or as an immigrant language in the country header. The *Speakers* column gives the number of first-language speakers in millions. The table rows in italic type represent macrolanguages (see *Introduction*, page 9); in these cases the *Total Countries* and *Speakers* columns are totals for all the individual languages listed in the macrolanguage entry as members of the macrolanguage. Individual languages that are members of a macrolanguage are not counted in the ranking, but are listed as indented entries below the macrolanguage. Note that the indented listing of individual languages does not include all member languages; it includes only those that have at least one million speakers.

Table 7. Languages with at least 50 million first-language speakers

Rank	Language	Primary Country	Total Countries	Speakers (millions)
1	*Chinese [zho]*	*China*	*33*	*1,197*
	Chinese, Gan [gan]	China	1	20.6
	Chinese, Hakka [hak]	China	13	30.1
	Chinese, Huizhou [czh]	China	1	4.60
	Chinese, Jinyu [cjy]	China	1	45.0
	Chinese, Mandarin [cmn]	China	13	848
	Chinese, Min Bei [mnp]	China	2	10.3
	Chinese, Min Dong [cdo]	China	6	9.12
	Chinese, Min Nan [nan]	China	10	46.6
	Chinese, Min Zhong [czo]	China	1	3.10
	Chinese, Pu-Xian [cpx]	China	3	2.56
	Chinese, Wu [wuu]	China	1	77.2
	Chinese, Xiang [hsn]	China	1	36.0
	Chinese, Yue [yue]	China	10	62.2
2	Spanish [spa]	Spain	31	414
3	English [eng]	United Kingdom	99	335
4	Hindi [hin]	India	4	260
5	*Arabic [ara]*	*Saudi Arabia*	*60*	*237*
	Arabic, Algerian Spoken [arq]	Algeria	1	28.0
	Arabic, Chadian Spoken [shu]	Chad	4	1.14
	Arabic, Eastern Egyptian Bedawi Spoken [avl]	Egypt	4	1.69
	Arabic, Egyptian Spoken [arz]	Egypt	1	54.0
	Arabic, Gulf Spoken [afb]	Kuwait	9	2.34
	Arabic, Hijazi Spoken [acw]	Saudi Arabia	2	6.02
	Arabic, Libyan Spoken [ayl]	Libya	3	4.32
	Arabic, Mesopotamian Spoken [acm]	Iraq	4	15.1
	Arabic, Moroccan Spoken [ary]	Morocco	2	21.0
	Arabic, Najdi Spoken [ars]	Saudi Arabia	4	9.67
	Arabic, North Levantine Spoken [apc]	Syria	2	14.4
	Arabic, North Mesopotamian Spoken [ayp]	Iraq	3	6.30
	Arabic, Sa'idi Spoken [aec]	Egypt	1	19.0
	Arabic, Sanaani Spoken [ayn]	Yemen	1	7.60
	Arabic, South Levantine Spoken [ajp]	Jordan	3	6.20
	Arabic, Sudanese Spoken [apd]	Sudan	3	16.8
	Arabic, Ta'izzi-Adeni Spoken [acq]	Yemen	2	7.08
	Arabic, Tunisian Spoken [aeb]	Tunisia	1	9.41
6	Portuguese [por]	Portugal	12	203
7	Bengali [ben]	Bangladesh	4	193
8	Russian [rus]	Russian Federation	16	167
9	Japanese [jpn]	Japan	3	122
10	Javanese [jav]	Indonesia	3	84.3
11	*Lahnda [lah]*	*Pakistan*	*6*	*82.6*
	Hindko, Northern [hno]	Pakistan	1	1.88
	Pahari-Potwari [phr]	Pakistan	1	2.50

Table 7. Languages with at least 50 million first-language speakers (cont.)

Rank	Language	Primary Country	Total Countries	Speakers (millions)
	Panjabi, Mirpur [pmu]	India	1	1.04
	Panjabi, Western [pnb]	Pakistan	2	62.6
	Seraiki [skr]	Pakistan	2	14.0
12	German, Standard [deu]	Germany	18	78.2
13	Korean [kor]	South Korea	5	77.2
14	French [fra]	France	51	75.0
15	Telugu [tel]	India	2	74.0
16	Marathi [mar]	India	1	71.8
17	Turkish [tur]	Turkey	8	70.8
18	Tamil [tam]	India	6	68.8
19	Vietnamese [vie]	Viet Nam	3	67.8
20	Urdu [urd]	Pakistan	6	63.9
21	Italian [ita]	Italy	10	63.7
22	*Malay [msa]*	*Malaysia*	*13*	*59.5*
	Banjar [bjn]	Indonesia	2	3.50
	Indonesian [ind]	Indonesia	1	23.2
	Malay [zlm]	Malaysia	3	15.8
	Malay, Jambi [jax]	Indonesia	1	1.00
	Malay, Kedah [meo]	Malaysia	2	2.60
	Malay, Pattani [mfa]	Thailand	1	1.00
	Minangkabau [min]	Indonesia	1	5.53
	Musi [mui]	Indonesia	1	3.10
23	*Persian [fas]*	*Iran*	*29*	*56.6*
	Dari [prs]	Afghanistan	2	9.60
	Persian, Iranian [pes]	Iran	6	47.0

Asia

This section provides a summary view of the language situation in Asia. Specifically, it offers numerical tabulations of languages and numbers of speakers by language size, by language status, by language family, and by country.

Summary by language status

Table 8 summarizes the 2,303 languages that originate in Asia (see table 5) in terms of language status. It gives the distribution of languages by their status in terms of language development or language endangerment. The *EGIDS* column categorizes the languages by their level on the Expanded Graded Intergenerational Disruption Scale.

The *Count* column gives the number of living languages within the specified population range. The *Percent* column gives the share of the count for that population range as a percentage of the total number of languages given at the bottom of the Count column. The *Cumulative* column gives the cumulative sum of the percentage of languages going from top to bottom in the column.

The *Total* column gives the total population of all the languages in the given range category. The second *Percent* column gives the percentage of the total population as estimated at the bottom of the Total column. Note that if the table has a row for Unknown, representing languages for which the *Ethnologue* does not have a population estimate; the calculation of population percentage is not able to take those languages into account. The final *Cumulative* column gives the cumulative sums of the population percentages going from top to bottom in the column.. The *Mean* column gives the average population of all the languages with the given EGIDS level and the *Median* column gives the median population for the languages at that level, that is, half of the languages at that level have a higher population and half have a lower population. If any languages have an unknown population, they are ignored in the calculation of mean and median.

Table 8. Distribution of Asian languages by vitality status

EGIDS	Living languages			Number of speakers				
	Count	*Percent*	*Cumulative*	*Total*	*Percent*	*Cumulative*	*Mean*	*Median*
0	2	0.1	0.1%	847,808,270	22.6354	22.6354%	423,904,135	847,808,270
1	34	1.5	1.6%	1,199,557,120	32.0267	54.6621%	35,281,092	14,792,300
2	25	1.1	2.6%	589,425,130	15.7369	70.3990%	23,577,005	12,828,220
3	70	3.0	5.7%	295,975,240	7.9022	78.3011%	4,228,218	940,000
4	72	3.1	8.8%	104,281,450	2.7842	81.0853%	1,448,353	106,000
5	364	15.8	24.6%	374,284,894	9.9929	91.0782%	1,028,255	57,700
6a	857	37.2	61.8%	287,985,326	7.6888	98.7671%	336,039	13,000
6b	500	21.7	83.5%	38,100,442	1.0172	99.7843%	76,201	4,640
7	192	8.3	91.9%	7,703,060	0.2057	99.9900%	40,120	2,950
8a	80	3.5	95.4%	359,705	0.0096	99.9996%	4,496	745
8b	77	3.3	98.7%	15,395	0.0004	100.0000%	200	37
9	30	1.3	100.0%	0	0.0000	100.0000%	0	0
Totals	2,303	100.0		3,745,496,032	100.0000			

Summary by language size

Table 9 summarizes the 2,303 languages that originate in Asia (see table 5) in terms of population. It gives the distribution by their number of first-language speakers. The *Population range* column categorizes the languages by the number of digits in their population of first-language speakers. This is not limited to the population within Asia; rather, the populations reported in this table are the number of L1 speakers worldwide of languages that have their origin in Asia. The next six columns are as in table 9.

Table 10 lists the 20 largest individual languages that originate in Asia. They are listed in descending order of population of first-language speakers. The *Primary Country* column names the country in which the primary entry for the language is found in part II, "Language Listings" (page 45). The *Total Countries* column gives the number of countries of the world in which the language is listed either with a full entry or as an immigrant language in the country header. The *Speakers* column gives the total number of L1 speakers worldwide in millions.

Table 9. Distribution of Asian languages by number of first-language speakers

Population range	Living languages			Number of speakers		
	Count	*Percent*	*Cumulative*	*Total*	*Percent*	*Cumulative*
100,000,000 to 999,999,999	4	0.2	0.2%	1,423,460,030	38.00458	38.00458%
10,000,000 to 99,999,999	52	2.3	2.4%	1,737,646,950	46.39297	84.39755%
1,000,000 to 9,999,999	142	6.2	8.6%	451,803,342	12.06258	96.46013%
100,000 to 999,999	329	14.3	22.9%	107,327,804	2.86552	99.32565%
10,000 to 99,999	663	28.8	51.7%	22,717,620	0.60653	99.93218%
1,000 to 9,999	627	27.2	78.9%	2,413,575	0.06444	99.99662%
100 to 999	284	12.3	91.2%	124,388	0.00332	99.99994%
10 to 99	54	2.3	93.6%	2,261	0.00006	100.00000%
1 to 9	13	0.6	94.1%	62	0.00000	100.00000%
0	30	1.3	95.4%	0	0.00000	100.00000%
Unknown	105	4.6	100.0%			
Totals	2,303	100.0		3,745,496,032	100.00000	

Table 10. Twenty largest languages of Asia

Rank	Language	Primary Country	Total Countries	Speakers (millions)
1	Chinese, Mandarin [cmn]	China	13	848
2	Hindi [hin]	India	4	260
3	Bengali [ben]	Bangladesh	4	193
4	Japanese [jpn]	Japan	3	122
5	Javanese [jav]	Indonesia	3	84.3
6	Chinese, Wu [wuu]	China	1	77.2
7	Korean [kor]	South Korea	5	77.2
8	Telugu [tel]	India	2	74.0
9	Marathi [mar]	India	1	71.8
10	Turkish [tur]	Turkey	8	70.8
11	Tamil [tam]	India	6	68.8
12	Vietnamese [vie]	Viet Nam	3	67.8
13	Urdu [urd]	Pakistan	6	63.9
14	Panjabi, Western [pnb]	Pakistan	2	62.6
15	Chinese, Yue [yue]	China	10	62.2
16	Persian, Iranian [pes]	Iran	6	47.0
17	Gujarati [guj]	India	6	46.6
18	Chinese, Min Nan [nan]	China	10	46.6
19	Chinese, Jinyu [cjy]	China	1	45.0
20	Bhojpuri [bho]	India	3	39.7

Summary by language family

The genetic classifications given in the language entries of part II, "Language Listings" (page 45), name 37 different top-level genetic groups for the 2,303 languages that originate in Asia (see table 5). Table 11 summarizes the distribution of languages and their populations within these families. The columns are as for table 8, with two differences: (1) the *Cumulative* column is excluded since there is no inherent ordering of the families, and (2) a final *Countries* column is added listing the countries of Asia under which the main entries for the languages of that family are found in Part II.

Table 11. Distribution of Asian languages by language family

Language family	Living languages		Number of speakers				Countries
	Count	Percent	Total	Percent	Mean	Median	
Afro-Asiatic	51	2.2	83,017,540	2.2	1,627,795	26,000	Bahrain, Cyprus, Georgia, Iran, Iraq, Israel, Jordan, Kuwait, Oman, Palestine, Saudi Arabia, Syria, Tajikistan, Turkey, United Arab Emirates, Uzbekistan, Yemen
Altaic	34	1.5	153,677,010	4.1	4,519,912	172,350	Afghanistan, Azerbaijan, China, Georgia, Iran, Kazakhstan, Kyrgyzstan, Mongolia, Turkey, Turkmenistan, Uzbekistan
Andamanese	4	0.2	501	0.0	125	122	India
Austro-Asiatic	170	7.4	102,502,739	2.7	602,957	9,000	Bangladesh, Cambodia, China, India, Laos, Malaysia, Myanmar, Thailand, Viet Nam
Austronesian	722	31.4	301,544,721	8.1	417,652	10,000	Brunei, Cambodia, China, East Timor, Indonesia, Malaysia, Myanmar, Philippines, Taiwan, Thailand, Viet Nam
Bayono-Awbono	2	0.1	200	0.0	100	100	Indonesia
Border	3	0.1	1,100	0.0	367	350	Indonesia
Creole	24	1.0	9,255,630	0.2	385,651	22,500	East Timor, India, Indonesia, Macao, Malaysia, Philippines, Singapore, Sri Lanka
Deaf sign language	34	1.5	3,080,449	0.1	90,601	3,000	Afghanistan, Armenia, China, Hong Kong, India, Indonesia, Iran, Israel, Japan, Jordan, Laos, Malaysia, Mongolia, Nepal, Pakistan, Philippines, Saudi Arabia, Singapore, South Korea, Sri Lanka, Taiwan, Thailand, Turkey, Viet Nam
Dravidian	84	3.6	229,294,360	6.1	2,729,695	26,000	India, Nepal, Pakistan
East Bird's Head-Sentani	8	0.3	71,730	0.0	8,966	5,875	Indonesia
East Geelvink Bay	12	0.5	8,005	0.0	667	300	Indonesia
Hmong-Mien	38	1.7	9,334,840	0.2	245,654	65,500	China, Laos, Viet Nam
Indo-European	302	13.1	1,297,584,890	34.6	4,296,639	107,500	Afghanistan, Armenia, Azerbaijan, Bangladesh, China, India, Iran, Iraq, Israel, Maldives, Myanmar, Nepal, Oman, Pakistan, Sri Lanka, Tajikistan, Turkey
Japonic	12	0.5	123,067,790	3.3	10,255,649	5,000	Japan
Kartvelian	5	0.2	4,854,510	0.1	970,902	79,800	Georgia, Israel, Turkey
Kaure	3	0.1	900	0.0	300	250	Indonesia
Lakes Plain	19	0.8	8,455	0.0	445	300	Indonesia
Language isolate	11	0.5	77,281,868	2.1	7,025,624	2,000	India, Indonesia, Japan, Nepal, Pakistan, South Korea
Lower Mamberamo	2	0.1	800	0.0	400	400	Indonesia

Table 11. Distribution of Asian languages by language family (cont.)

Language family	Living languages		Number of speakers				Countries
	Count	*Percent*	*Total*	*Percent*	*Mean*	*Median*	
Mairasi	3	0.1	4,385	0.0	1,462	1,000	Indonesia
Maybrat	2	0.1	25,000	0.0	12,500	12,500	Indonesia
Mixed language	3	0.1	32,050	0.0	10,683	2,000	Armenia, China
Nimboran	5	0.2	8,500	0.0	1,700	2,000	Indonesia
North Caucasian	7	0.3	152,623	0.0	21,803	5,000	Azerbaijan, Georgia
Pauwasi	4	0.2	2,570	0.0	642	225	Indonesia
Pidgin	3	0.1	0	0.0	0	0	India, Indonesia
Senagi	1	0.0	1,690	0.0	1,690	1,690	Indonesia
Sino-Tibetan	455	19.8	1,268,218,984	33.9	2,787,294	15,000	Bangladesh, Bhutan, China, India, Kyrgyzstan, Laos, Myanmar, Nepal, Pakistan, Thailand, Viet Nam
Skou	1	0.0	700	0.0	700	700	Indonesia
Somahai	2	0.1	2,200	0.0	1,100	1,100	Indonesia
South-Central Papuan	7	0.3	3,250	0.0	464	120	Indonesia
Tai-Kadai	94	4.1	80,772,252	2.2	859,279	52,300	China, India, Laos, Myanmar, Thailand, Viet Nam
Tor-Kwerba	24	1.0	16,195	0.0	675	400	Indonesia
Trans-New Guinea	114	5.0	1,048,160	0.0	9,194	3,000	East Timor, Indonesia
Unclassified	15	0.7	350,010	0.0	23,334	530	Afghanistan, China, India, Indonesia, Viet Nam
West Papuan	23	1.0	269,425	0.0	11,714	3,310	Indonesia
Totals	2,303	100.0	3,745,496,032	100.0			

Summary by country

Table 12 summarizes the distribution of languages and their populations within the countries of Asia. The *Count* column gives the total count of living languages used as a first language in that country, and *Percent* translates that to a percentage of all living languages in the world. Unlike the preceding tables, this table counts all languages regardless of their area of origin. Therefore, no grand totals are given for these columns since the same language can be counted as being used in multiple countries. The next two columns break the language count into *Indigenous* languages versus *Immigrant* languages. The next three columns summarize populations: *Total* gives the total number of first-language speakers in that country for all languages for which population figures are known, *Mean* gives the average size of those language groups for which population figures are known, and *Median* gives the middle size of a language group (that is, half are larger and half are smaller). The last two columns are explained in the next paragraph.

Table 13 repeats the information in table 12 but presents the countries of Asia in order of their linguistic diversity, from most diverse to least diverse. The *Index* column reports Greenberg's diversity index. This is the probability that any two people of the country selected at random would have different mother tongues (Lieberson 1981). The highest possible value, 1, indicates total diversity (that is, no two people have the same mother tongue) while the lowest possible value, 0, indicates no diversity at all (that is, everyone has the same mother tongue). The computation of the diversity index is based on the population of each language as a proportion of the total population. The *Coverage* column indicates the completeness of the computation by reporting the percentage of languages in the country for which population estimates are available.

Table 12. Distribution of living languages in Asia by country

Country	Living languages				Number of speakers			Diversity	
	Count	*Per-cent*	*Indige-nous*	*Immi-grant*	*Total*	*Mean*	*Median*	*Index*	*Cover-age*
Afghanistan	41	0.58	40	1	22,964,800	574,120	8,000	0.790	98%
Armenia	11	0.15	7	4	3,361,230	336,123	45,000	0.125	91%
Azerbaijan	37	0.52	17	20	8,400,700	247,079	20,000	0.457	92%
Bahrain	12	0.17	4	8	557,600	61,956	300,000	0.663	75%
Bangladesh	45	0.63	41	4	142,218,220	3,307,400	15,000	0.386	96%
Bhutan	34	0.48	24	10	712,100	25,432	5,000	0.851	82%
British Indian Ocean Territory	1	0.01	1	0	3,500	3,500	3,500	0.000	100%
Brunei	17	0.24	15	2	345,195	24,657	10,000	0.590	82%
Cambodia	27	0.38	22	5	13,728,360	572,015	6,540	0.116	89%
China	301	4.24	298	3	1,212,660,788	4,124,697	27,700	0.511	98%
Cyprus	6	0.08	4	2	1,281,040	320,260	177,000	0.244	67%
East Timor	19	0.27	19	0	1,033,506	54,395	18,400	0.817	100%
Georgia	28	0.39	19	9	6,185,700	237,912	40,000	0.582	93%
Hong Kong	8	0.11	7	1	6,454,600	922,086	77,600	0.126	88%
India	454	6.39	447	7	1,074,901,321	2,493,971	34,300	0.913	95%
Indonesia	707	9.95	706	1	220,398,286	313,958	3,500	0.815	99%
Iran	80	1.13	76	4	88,785,020	1,432,016	60,000	0.705	78%
Iraq	26	0.37	22	4	25,917,820	1,178,083	60,000	0.728	85%
Israel	52	0.73	35	17	8,672,175	192,715	45,000	0.665	87%
Japan	16	0.23	15	1	123,232,863	9,479,451	5,100	0.036	81%
Jordan	16	0.23	10	6	5,084,210	391,093	50,000	0.496	81%
Kazakhstan	44	0.62	14	30	15,140,140	420,559	332,000	0.699	82%
Kuwait	7	0.10	3	4	819,400	163,880	500,000	0.556	71%
Kyrgyzstan	32	0.45	5	27	5,062,800	187,511	657,000	0.670	84%
Laos	92	1.29	86	6	5,693,284	66,201	5,000	0.692	93%
Lebanon	9	0.13	6	3	4,266,900	533,362	75,000	0.161	89%
Macao	5	0.07	5	0	401,420	80,284	6,660	0.134	100%
Malaysia	146	2.05	138	8	24,355,505	261,887	3,500	0.761	64%
Maldives	2	0.03	2	0	331,000	331,000	331,000	?	50%
Mongolia	14	0.20	12	2	2,613,100	326,638	35,000	0.187	57%
Myanmar	117	1.65	117	0	46,528,905	404,599	15,000	0.519	98%
Nepal	125	1.76	120	5	26,686,940	222,391	7,780	0.756	96%
North Korea	1	0.01	1	0	23,300,000	23,300,000	23,300,000	0.000	100%
Oman	19	0.27	16	3	1,578,400	98,650	25,000	0.702	84%
Pakistan	77	1.08	72	5	152,371,460	2,208,282	80,000	0.795	90%
Palestine	8	0.11	6	2	1,812,000	302,000	2,000	0.208	75%
Philippines	193	2.72	181	12	72,208,122	392,435	21,300	0.843	95%
Qatar	6	0.08	3	3	205,700	41,140	104,000	0.608	83%
Saudi Arabia	20	0.28	5	15	16,440,720	913,373	6,000,000	0.626	90%
Singapore	32	0.45	24	8	3,502,170	129,710	10,000	0.756	84%
South Korea	3	0.04	2	1	48,581,000	24,290,500	48,400,000	0.007	67%
Sri Lanka	7	0.10	7	0	19,326,030	3,865,206	46,000	0.319	71%
Syria	22	0.31	16	6	13,170,000	731,667	70,000	0.527	82%
Taiwan	27	0.38	22	5	22,093,698	960,596	8,490	0.489	85%
Tajikistan	32	0.45	13	19	4,825,660	178,728	15,000	0.485	84%
Thailand	85	1.20	73	12	51,693,913	749,187	15,000	0.740	81%
Turkey	46	0.65	35	11	87,612,140	2,367,896	25,000	0.394	80%
Turkmenistan	27	0.38	4	23	4,417,220	169,893	317,000	0.385	96%

Table 12. Distribution of living languages in Asia by country (cont.)

Country	Living languages				Number of speakers			Diversity	
	Count	*Per-cent*	*Indige-nous*	*Immi-grant*	*Total*	*Mean*	*Median*	*Index*	*Cover-age*
United Arab Emirates	35	0.49	7	28	1,773,560	68,214	100,000	0.777	74%
Uzbekistan	39	0.55	9	30	21,977,893	646,409	808,000	0.426	87%
Viet Nam	110	1.55	108	2	76,935,370	769,354	13,800	0.267	91%
Yemen	14	0.20	10	4	15,700,000	1,570,000	57,000	0.578	71%

Table 13. Linguistic diversity of countries in Asia (highest to lowest)

Country	Diversity		Living languages				Number of speakers		
	Index	*Cover-age*	*Total*	*Per-cent*	*Indige-nous*	*Immi-grant*	*Count*	*Mean*	*Median*
India	0.913	95%	454	6.39	447	7	1,074,901,321	2,493,971	34,300
Bhutan	0.851	82%	34	0.48	24	10	712,100	25,432	5,000
Philippines	0.843	95%	193	2.72	181	12	72,208,122	392,435	21,300
East Timor	0.817	100%	19	0.27	19	0	1,033,506	54,395	18,400
Indonesia	0.815	99%	707	9.95	706	1	220,398,286	313,958	3,500
Pakistan	0.795	90%	77	1.08	72	5	152,371,460	2,208,282	80,000
Afghanistan	0.790	98%	41	0.58	40	1	22,964,800	574,120	8,000
United Arab Emirates	0.777	74%	35	0.49	7	28	1,773,560	68,214	100,000
Malaysia	0.761	64%	146	2.05	138	8	24,355,505	261,887	3,500
Nepal	0.756	96%	125	1.76	120	5	26,686,940	222,391	7,780
Singapore	0.756	84%	32	0.45	24	8	3,502,170	129,710	10,000
Thailand	0.740	81%	85	1.20	73	12	51,693,913	749,187	15,000
Iraq	0.728	85%	26	0.37	22	4	25,917,820	1,178,083	60,000
Iran	0.705	78%	80	1.13	76	4	88,785,020	1,432,016	60,000
Oman	0.702	84%	19	0.27	16	3	1,578,400	98,650	25,000
Kazakhstan	0.699	82%	44	0.62	14	30	15,140,140	420,559	332,000
Laos	0.692	93%	92	1.29	86	6	5,693,284	66,201	5,000
Kyrgyzstan	0.670	84%	32	0.45	5	27	5,062,800	187,511	657,000
Israel	0.665	87%	52	0.73	35	17	8,672,175	192,715	45,000
Bahrain	0.663	75%	12	0.17	4	8	557,600	61,956	300,000
Saudi Arabia	0.626	90%	20	0.28	5	15	16,440,720	913,373	6,000,000
Qatar	0.608	83%	6	0.08	3	3	205,700	41,140	104,000
Brunei	0.590	82%	17	0.24	15	2	345,195	24,657	10,000
Georgia	0.582	93%	28	0.39	19	9	6,185,700	237,912	40,000
Yemen	0.578	71%	14	0.20	10	4	15,700,000	1,570,000	57,000
Kuwait	0.556	71%	7	0.10	3	4	819,400	163,880	500,000
Syria	0.527	82%	22	0.31	16	6	13,170,000	731,667	70,000
Myanmar	0.519	98%	117	1.65	117	0	46,528,905	404,599	15,000
China	0.511	98%	301	4.24	298	3	1,212,660,788	4,124,697	27,700
Jordan	0.496	81%	16	0.23	10	6	5,084,210	391,093	50,000
Taiwan	0.489	85%	27	0.38	22	5	22,093,698	960,596	8,490
Tajikistan	0.485	84%	32	0.45	13	19	4,825,660	178,728	15,000
Azerbaijan	0.457	92%	37	0.52	17	20	8,400,700	247,079	20,000
Uzbekistan	0.426	87%	39	0.55	9	30	21,977,893	646,409	808,000
Turkey	0.394	80%	46	0.65	35	11	87,612,140	2,367,896	25,000
Bangladesh	0.386	96%	45	0.63	41	4	142,218,220	3,307,400	15,000
Turkmenistan	0.385	96%	27	0.38	4	23	4,417,220	169,893	317,000
Sri Lanka	0.319	71%	7	0.10	7	0	19,326,030	3,865,206	46,000
Viet Nam	0.267	91%	110	1.55	108	2	76,935,370	769,354	13,800

Table 13. Linguistic diversity of countries in Asia (highest to lowest, cont.)

Country	Diversity		Living languages				Number of speakers		
	Index	*Coverage*	*Total*	*Percent*	*Indigenous*	*Immigrant*	*Count*	*Mean*	*Median*
Cyprus	0.244	67%	6	0.08	4	2	1,281,040	320,260	177,000
Palestine	0.208	75%	8	0.11	6	2	1,812,000	302,000	2,000
Mongolia	0.187	57%	14	0.20	12	2	2,613,100	326,638	35,000
Lebanon	0.161	89%	9	0.13	6	3	4,266,900	533,362	75,000
Macao	0.134	100%	5	0.07	5	0	401,420	80,284	6,660
Hong Kong	0.126	88%	8	0.11	7	1	6,454,600	922,086	77,600
Armenia	0.125	91%	11	0.15	7	4	3,361,230	336,123	45,000
Cambodia	0.116	89%	27	0.38	22	5	13,728,360	572,015	6,540
Japan	0.036	81%	16	0.23	15	1	123,232,863	9,479,451	5,100
South Korea	0.007	67%	3	0.04	2	1	48,581,000	24,290,500	48,400,000
British Indian Ocean Territory	0.000	100%	1	0.01	1	0	3,500	3,500	3,500
North Korea	0.000	100%	1	0.01	1	0	23,300,000	23,300,000	23,300,000

Part II
Language Listings

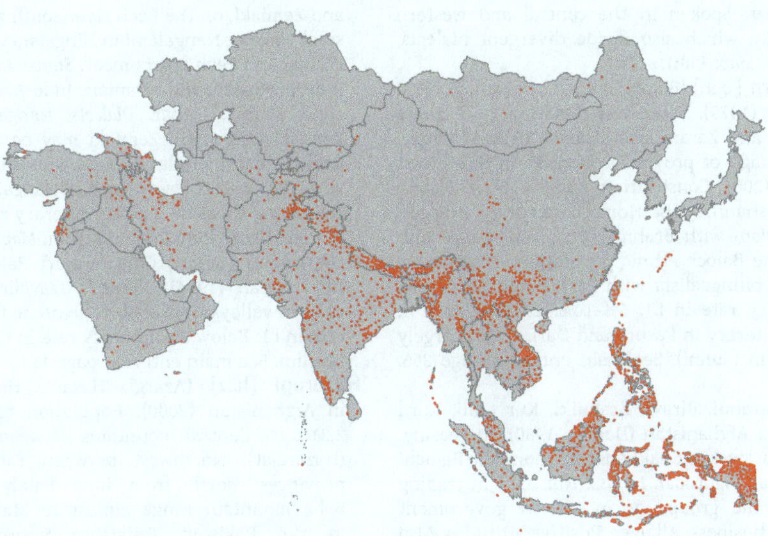

Asia

Afghanistan

Islamic Republic of Afghanistan. 26,000,000 (2010 UNSD). Principal languages: Dari, Northeast Pashayi, Southern Pashto. Literacy rate: 28% (2008 USDS). Immigrant language: Uyghur (3,000). General references: Bashir 2003; Dupree 1980; Farhadi and Raven 1967; Grjunberg 1968; Morgenstierne 1974; Payne 1987; Sebeok 1970; Strand 1973, 2001.

The number of individual languages listed for Afghanistan is 40. Of these, 39 are living and 1 is extinct. Of the living languages, 4 are institutional, 5 are developing, 20 are vigorous, 5 are in trouble, and 5 are dying. See map on page 338.

Afghan Sign Language [afg] (Afghan Sign, AFSL). 1,000 (2012). Kabul Province, Kabul city; Parwan Province; Nangarhar Province, Jalalabad city and many surrounding districts; Laghman Province; Kandahar Province, Kandahar city; Herat Province, Herat city; Balkh Province, Mazar-e Sharif; Takhar Province, Faizabad; Bamiyan Province, Bamiyan city. The vast majority live in Kabul and Jalalabad. *Status:* 5 (Developing). *Class:* Deaf sign language. *Dialects:* None known. Influenced by American Sign Language [ase] used by foreign workers in some of the deaf schools in Afghanistan. *Lg Use:* Home, university, work. Children through adults 50 years old. *Lg Dev:* Taught in at least 3 schools for the deaf in Afghanistan. Taught in primary and secondary schools. New media. Videos. Dictionary. *Other:* Muslim.

Aimaq [aiq] (Barbari, Berberi, Chahar-Aimaq, Char Aimaq). 480,000 in Afghanistan (1993). Population total all countries: 650,000. Central northwest Afghanistan, west of Hazara, eastern Iran, and Tajikistan (Jamshidi and Khazara). Centers in Ghor, Badghis, and Herat provinces. Also in Iran, Tajikistan. *Status:* 6a (Vigorous). *Class:* Indo-European, Indo-Iranian, Iranian, Western, Southwestern, Persian. *Dialects:* Chinghizi, Firozkohi, Jamshidi (Djamchidi, Dzhemshid, Jamshedi, Yemchidi), Maliki, Mizmast, Taimani, Taimuri (Taimouri, Teimuri, Timuri), Zainal, Zohri (Zuri). Dialect names could well be ethnic names, probably dialect of Dari [prs], at least Jamshidi is not much different from the Herati dialect of Dari. *Lg Dev:* Literacy rate in L2: 5%–15%. *Writing:* Unwritten. *Other:* Muslim (Hanafi Sunni). *Map:* 338.

Arabic, Tajiki Spoken [abh]. 5,000 in Afghanistan (Farhadi and Raven 1967), decreasing. Balkh Province, Dawlatabad district, Yakhdan, Khushalabad; Jawzjan Province, Mingajik district, Sultan Arigh; Sheberghan district, Hasanabad. *Status:* 6b (Threatened). *Dialect:* Balkh Arabic. *Lg Use:* Home, community. Positive attitudes. Also use Dari [prs], Tajiki [tgk]. *Lg Dev:* Some can read traditional Arabic, but unlikely any literature exists in this dialect. *Other:* While no others speak this dialect of Arabic, it is highly possible that some other people use a mixture of Arabic and Dari [prs] when communicating with mother tongue speakers of Tajiki Spoken Arabic. Muslim (Sunni). See main entry on page 298. *Map:* 338.

Ashkun [ask] (Ashkund, Ashkuni, Wamais, Wamayi). 40,000 (2011), increasing. 4,000 monolinguals. Ethnic population: 40,000. Nuristan Province, Pech Valley in Wama District, eastern side of the Lower Alingar Valley in Nurgaram and Duab districts, Malil wa Mushfa, Titin, Kolatan and Bajagal valleys. *Status:* 6a (Vigorous). *Class:* Indo-European, Indo-Iranian, Indo-Aryan, Nuristani. *Dialects:* Ashuruviri (Kolata, Titin Bajaygul), Gramsukraviri, Suruviri (Wamai). Not intelligible with the other Nuristani languages. *Lg Use:* All domains. All ages. Positive attitudes. 36,000 also use Northern Pashto [pbu]. *Lg Dev:* Literacy rate in L1: 0%. Literacy rate in L2: 5%–15%. Poetry. *Writing:*

Unwritten. *Other:* Spoken in the central and western Nuristan valleys, which also divide divergent dialects. Muslim (Sunni). *Map:* 338:1.

Balochi, Western [bgn] (Baloci, Baluchi, Baluci). 200,000 in Afghanistan (1979). Southwest Desert region, along Helmand river and Zaranj area. *Status:* 5 (Developing). Statutory language of provincial identity in Southwest Desert Region (2004, Constitution, Article 16(2)). *Dialect:* Rakhshani (Raxshani). *Lg Use:* Home, community. All ages. Much bilingualism with Brahui [brh], a language also belonging to the Baloch ethnic population. Otherwise a high degree of bilingualism with Pashto and Dari [prs]. *Lg Dev:* Literacy rate in L1: 5%–10%. Literacy rate in L2: 15%–25%. Literacy in Pashto and Dari. *Other:* Largely nomadic. Muslim (Sunni). See main entry on page 266. *Map:* 338.

Brahui [brh] (Birahui, Biravi, Brahuiki, Kur Galli, Kurd Gali). 200,000 in Afghanistan (Dupree 1980), increasing. South, from Shorawak to Chakhansoor among the Baluchi [bgn]. *Status:* 6a (Vigorous). *Lg Use:* Not used in trading with other ethnic groups or in official government domain. Home, business. All ages. Positive attitudes. Also use Southern Pashto [pbt] for trading and government relations. Used as L2 by Western Balochi [bgn]. *Lg Dev:* Literacy rate in L1: Below 1%. Literacy rate in L2: 20% (men only). *Other:* Muslim (Sunni). See main entry on page 266. *Map:* 338.

Dari [prs] (Afghan Persian, East Farsi, Farsi, Parsi, Persian, Tajik, Tajiki). 7,600,000 in Afghanistan (2011 census), increasing. Population total all countries: 9,600,000. Ethnic population: 7,600,000. L2 users: All other language groups have Dari speakers, especially those who live in the city of Kabul. Western, Central, Northern, and Northeastern Afghanistan; Kabul Province. Also in Iran, Pakistan. *Status:* 1 (National). Statutory national language (2004, Constitution, Article 16 (1)). *Class:* Indo-European, Indo-Iranian, Iranian, Western, Southwestern, Persian. A member of macrolanguage Persian [fas] (Iran). *Dialects:* Darwazi, Tangshew (Tangshuri). Radio Afghanistan broadcasts promote a standardized pronunciation of the literary language based on the old dictional tradition of the country, with archaic phonetic characteristics. Phonological and lexical differences between Iran and Afghanistan cause little difficulty in comprehension. Most Afghan dialects are reportedly more similar to literary Persian than Iranian dialects are. Lexical similarity: 86%–90% among Dari dialects. *Lg Use:* All domains. All ages. Positive attitudes. *Lg Dev:* Literacy rate in L1: 28%. Taught in primary and secondary schools. Poetry. Magazines. Newspapers. New media. Radio programs. Films. TV. Videos. Dictionary. Grammar. Bible: 2008. *Writing:* Arabic script. *Other:* Muslim (Sunni), Muslim (Shi'a). *Maps:* 338, 338:2.

Domari [rmt] (Ghorbati). L2 users: 0 in Afghanistan. Scattered. *Status:* 6a (Vigorous). *Dialect:* Churi-Wali. *Lg Use:* Home and in communication with other speakers. *Lg Dev:* Literacy rate in L2: Below 5%. *Other:* Muslim. See main entry on page 202.

Gawar-Bati [gwt] (Arandui, Gowari, Narisati, Narsati, Satre). 8,000 in Afghanistan. Population total all countries: 9,500. Kunar valley. 8 or 9 villages. Also in Pakistan. *Status:* 6b (Threatened). *Class:* Indo-European, Indo-Iranian, Indo-Aryan, Northwestern zone, Dardic, Kunar. *Dialects:* None known. Lexical similarity: 47% with Shumashti [sts], 44% with Dameli [dml], 42% with Savi [sdg] and Grangali [nli]. *Lg Use:* Also use Southern Pashto [pbt]. *Lg Dev:* Literacy rate in L2: 5%–15%. *Writing:* Unwritten. *Other:* Muslim (Sunni). *Map:* 338:3.

Grangali [nli] (Gelangali, Jumiaki). 5,000 (1994). Grangali and Zemiaki, on the Pech river south side at Kandai, in 2 small valleys; Nangalami in Ningalam village is where the Waigal and Pech rivers meet. *Status:* 6a (Vigorous). *Class:* Indo-European, Indo-Iranian, Indo-Aryan, Northwestern zone, Dardic, Kunar. *Dialects:* Nangalami (Ningalami), Zemiaki (Zamyaki). Zemiaki may be related to Waigali [wbk]. Lexical similarity: 63% with Shumashti [sts], 42% with Gawar-Bati [gwt]. *Lg Use:* Nangalami may have no remaining speakers. *Lg Dev:* Literacy rate in L2: 5%–15%. *Writing:* Unwritten. *Other:* Muslim. *Map:* 338:4.

Gujari [gju] (Gojari, Gojri, Gujuri Rajasthani). 2,000 in Afghanistan (1994). Nomads traveling in summer in eastern valleys. *Status:* 6b (Threatened). *Lg Dev:* Literacy rate in L1: Below 1%. Literacy rate in L2: Below 5%. *Other:* Muslim. See main entry on page 113.

Hazaragi [haz] (Azargi, Hazara, Hezareh). 1,770,000 in Afghanistan (2000). Population total all countries: 2,210,000. Central mountains between Kabul and Herat (Hazarajat); Northwest between Faryab and Saripul provinces; north from immediately south of Koh-i Baba mountain range almost to Mazar-e Sharif. Also in Iran, Pakistan, Tajikistan. *Status:* 5 (Developing). *Class:* Indo-European, Indo-Iranian, Iranian, Western, Southwestern, Persian. *Dialects:* None known. Related to Dari [prs]; possibly distinct. *Lg Use:* Vigorous. All ages. Also use Dari [prs]. *Lg Dev:* Literacy rate in L1: Below 1%. Literacy rate in L2: Possibly 10%–20%. Radio programs. Bible portions. *Writing:* Arabic script. *Other:* Ethnic group names are Dai Kundi, Dai Zangi, Behsud, Yekaulang, Polada, Urusgani, Jaguri, Ghazni Hazaras, Dai Miradad. Muslim (Shi'a). *Map:* 338.

Ishkashimi [isk] (Eshkashimi, Ishkashim, Ishkashmi). 2,500 in Afghanistan (2009 S. Beck), decreasing. Population total all countries: 3,000. 0 monolinguals. North of the town of Ishkashim, Xermani, Bahar Bazar, Zargaran, Darwan, Zayad, Qaz Deh villages. Also in Tajikistan. *Status:* 6b (Threatened). *Class:* Indo-European, Indo-Iranian, Iranian, Eastern, Southeastern, Pamir. *Dialects:* None known. Ishkashimi intelligible to Sanglechi [sgy] speakers, but Sanglechi not intelligible to Ishkashimi speakers. Lexical similarity: 70% with Sanglechi [sgy]. *Lg Use:* Some parents used Dari [prs] with their children to provide them with better chances in school. Only now do the people realize that this might cause the language to become endangered. About half the households use Ishkashimi with the younger generation. Home, village. Older and middle generations; some younger people only speak Dari [prs]. Positive attitudes. 100% also use Dari [prs]. *Lg Dev:* Literacy rate in L2: 15%–25%. Most children now become literate in Dari [prs] because they attend school. *Writing:* Unwritten. *Other:* Most Sanglechi [sgy] have a positive attitude toward Ishkashimi and consider it closely related, whereas the Ishkashimi do not have a good attitude toward Sanglechi. Muslim (Ismaili). *Map:* 338.

Kamviri [xvi] (Kamdeshi, Kamik, Lamertiviri, Shekhani). 18,000 in Afghanistan (2011), increasing. Population total all countries: 20,000. 3,600 monolinguals. Ethnic population: 18,000. Lower Bashgal valley, Kamdesh and Kishtoz villages. Also in Pakistan. *Status:* 6a (Vigorous). *Class:* Indo-European, Indo-Iranian, Indo-Aryan, Nuristani. *Dialect:* Shekhani. Related to Kati [bsh]. *Lg Use:* Outside of language area, shifting towards majority language. All domains. All ages. Positive attitudes. 14,400 also use Northern Pashto [pbu]. *Lg Dev:* Literacy rate in L2: 10%. Dictionary. Grammar. *Writing:* Unwritten. *Other:* Muslim (Sunni). *Map:* 338:5.

Kati [bsh] (Bashgali, Kativiri, Nuristani). 15,000 in Afghanistan (1994), increasing. Population total all countries: 18,700. Ethnic population: 114,000. 110,000 in Nuristan and 4,000 in diaspora. L2 users: Some Nuristani people from other language groups can also speak Kati. Western Kativiri dialect: Mondul and Duab districts, Ramgal, Kulam, Ktivi (Kantiwo), and Paruk (Papruk) valleys; Mumviri dialect: Mangul, Sasku, Gabalgrom villages in the Bashgal valley; Eastern Kativiri dialect: upper Bashgal valley (Barg-e-Matal). Also in Pakistan. *Status:* 6a (Vigorous). Statutory language of provincial identity in Nuristan Province (2004, Constitution, Article 16(2)). *Class:* Indo-European, Indo-Iranian, Indo-Aryan, Nuristani. *Dialects:* Eastern Kativiri, Mumviri, Western Kativiri (Jadidi, Ramgulviri). Mumviri may be a separate language. Eastern and Western Kataviri are very similar dialects and almost completely mutually intelligible. *Type:* Agglutinative suffixes; CVC, CCVC, CV, CCCVC, CCVCC, CCCVCC. *Lg Use:* Outside of language area, shifting towards Dari [prs]. All domains. All ages. Positive attitudes. Also use Dari [prs] in the west. Also use Pashto [pbt] in the east. *Lg Dev:* Literacy rate in L1: 0%. Literacy rate in L2: 1%–3%. Textbooks for teaching Kati as a subject in school not widely used and are unacceptable to those from other Kati dialects. The Afghanistan Ministry of Education plans to produce Eastern Kati language textbooks for 1st through 12th grades; the 1st grade textbook is in progress (2010). Poetry. TV. Dictionary. *Writing:* Arabic script, limited usage, in development. *Other:* Kati is different from Kamviri [xvi], but the two are significantly mutually intelligible and speakers may refer to them as the same language. Muslim (Sunni). *Map:* 338:6.

Kyrgyz [kir] (Kirghiz, Kirghizi, Kirgiz). 750 in Afghanistan (2000). 450 in the Great Pamir; a few in Badakhshan. Extreme northeast, Great Pamir and Little Pamir valleys. *Status:* 5 (Dispersed). *Lg Dev:* Literacy rate in L1: Below 1%. Afghan Kyrgyz do not read Cyrillic script. *Other:* Muslim (Sunni). See main entry on page 213. *Map:* 338.

Mogholi [mhj] (Moghol, Mogol, Mogul, Mongul). No known L1 speakers. Ethnic population: 2,000. Near Herat, Kundur and Karez-i-Mulla. 2 villages. *Status:* 9 (Dormant). *Class:* Altaic, Mongolic, Western. *Dialects:* Karez-I-Mulla, Kundur. Unintelligible to other Mongol speakers; linguistically relatively well explored. *Writing:* Unwritten. *Other:* Muslim (Sunni).

Munji [mnj] (Munjani, Munjigi, Munjiwar). 5,300 (2008 D. Beyer and S. Beck). Very few monolinguals. Ethnic population: 5,300. Northeastern Afghanistan, Badakhshan Province, Kuran wa Munjan district, in the Munjan and Mamalgha valleys. *Status:* 6a (Vigorous). Statutory language of provincial identity in Badakhshan Province (2004, Constitution, Article 16(2)). *Class:* Indo-European, Indo-Iranian, Iranian, Eastern, Southeastern, Pamir. *Dialects:* Northern Munji, Southern Munji. Northern Munji and Southern Munji are mutually intelligible. The differences are found mostly in regular sound changes and some lexical items. Lexical similarity: 68% among dialects, 56%–80% with Yidgha [ydg] in Pakistan. *Lg Use:* Speakers view it as their secret language, and they perceive it as an advantage to have a language that is not commonly understood by outsiders. Home, community, at school. All ages. Positive attitudes. Nearly all adults also speak Dari [prs]. *Lg Dev:* Literacy rate in L1: Below 1%. Literacy rate in L2: 15%–25%. Poetry. Dictionary. *Writing:* Arabic script, in development. *Other:* Little contact with Yidgha [ydg]. Muslim (Ismaili). *Maps:* 338, 338:7.

Ormuri [oru] (Baraks, Bargista, Oormuri, Ormui). 50 in Afghanistan (2011 SIL), decreasing. Ethnic population: 2,000. L2 users: 0 in Afghanistan. Logar, Baraki-Barak. *Status:* 8b (Nearly extinct). *Dialects:* Kanigurami, Logar. *Lg Use:* Elderly only. *Other:* Muslim. See main entry on page 270. *Map:* 338.

Pahlavani [phv]. No known L1 speakers. Nimroz Province, Chakhansur district. *Status:* 9 (Dormant). *Class:* Indo-European, Indo-Iranian, Iranian, Western, Southwestern, Persian. *Dialects:* None known. Reportedly similar to Dari [prs]. *Other:* Muslim.

Parachi [prc]. 3,500 (Kiefer 2009). Hindu Kush valley near Kabul, Nijrau and Tagau villages, Pachaghan, Shutul, Ghujulan. *Status:* 7 (Shifting). *Class:* Indo-European, Indo-Iranian, Iranian, Western, Northwestern, Ormuri-Parachi. *Dialects:* Ghujulan, Pachaghan, Shutul. Dialect diversity seems slight. *Lg Dev:* Literacy rate in L2: 5%–15%. Dictionary. *Writing:* Unwritten. *Other:* Muslim. *Map:* 338:10.

Parya [paq] (Afghana-Yi Nasfurush, Afghana-Yi Siyarui, Laghmani). No known L1 speakers in Afghanistan. Ethnic population: 240. Kunduz Province. *Status:* 9 (Dormant). See main entry on page 299.

Pashayi, Northeast [aee] (Pashai). 54,400 (2000). Kunar Province west of Asadabad, side valleys between Kunar and Pech rivers. *Status:* 6a (Vigorous). Statutory language of national identity (2004, Constitution, Article 16(2)). *Class:* Indo-European, Indo-Iranian, Indo-Aryan, Northwestern zone, Dardic, Pashayi. *Dialects:* Aret, Chalas (Chilas), Kandak, Kurangal, Kurdar. Unintelligible of other Pashayi speakers. Lexical similarity: approximately 30% with Southeast Pashayi [psi] and Southwest Pashayi [psh]. *Type:* SOV. *Lg Dev:* Literacy rate in L2: 5%–15%. Poetry. *Writing:* Unwritten. *Other:* Kandak, Shemul, Aret, Shumasht, and Kordar villages belong to the Chugani people; Chalas and Kurangal are separate. Muslim (Sunni). *Map:* 338:8.

Pashayi, Northwest [glh] (Pashai). 70,000 (2011 SIL). Kapisa and Laghman provinces, Gulbahar to Nuristan on Alingar river, Alisheng valley, valleys north of Sarobi. *Status:* 6a (Vigorous). *Class:* Indo-European, Indo-Iranian, Indo-Aryan, Northwestern zone, Dardic, Pashayi. *Dialects:* Alasai, Bolaghain, Gulbahar, Kohnadeh, Laurowan, Najil, Nangarach, Pachagan, Pandau, Parazhghan, Pashagar, Sanjan, Shamakot, Shutul, Uzbin, Wadau. Unintelligible of other Pashayi speakers. Lexical similarity: approximately 30% with Southeast Pashayi [psi]. *Type:* SOV. *Lg Dev:* Literacy rate in L2: 5%–15%. *Writing:* Unwritten. *Other:* Muslim (Sunni). *Map:* 338:9.

Pashayi, Southeast [psi] (Pashai). 180,000 (2011 Pashai Language Development Project), increasing. 100,000 monolinguals. Ethnic population: 400,000. Upper and Lower Darrai Nur valley, Damench, Shale (Shari); Nangarhar Province, north of Shewa; south Laghman Province, Alingar valley area. *Status:* 6a (Vigorous). Statutory language of provincial identity in Nangahar, Laghman provinces (2004, Constitution, Article 16(2)). *Class:* Indo-European, Indo-Iranian, Indo-Aryan, Northwestern zone, Dardic, Pashayi. *Dialects:* None known. Somewhat intelligible of Southwest Pashayi [psh]; hardly intelligible of Northeast Pashayi [aee] and Northwest Pashayi [glh]. Lexical similarity: about 30% with Southwest Pashayi [psh], Northeast Pashayi [aee], and Northwest Pashayi [psh]. *Type:* SOV. *Lg Use:* Vigorous. Home, market, all informal settings. All ages. Positive attitudes. Also use Northern Pashto [pbu], Southern Pashto [pbt]. *Lg Dev:* Literacy rate in L1: Below 1%. Literacy rate in L2: Less than 20%. Many books for early readers have been produced by the Pashayi people as part of their literacy program. The Afghanistan Ministry of Education plans to produce Pashayi Language textbooks for 1st through 12th grades. The 1st grade textbook is in progress. Poetry. Radio programs. Dictionary. *Writing:* Arabic script. *Other:* Muslim (Sunni). *Map:* 338:14.

Pashayi, Southwest [psh] (Pashai). 100,000 (2011 SIL). Northeast of Kabul, north of Sarobi, Tagau (Tagab) valley. *Status:* 6a (Vigorous). *Class:* Indo-European, Indo-Iranian, Indo-Aryan, Northwestern zone, Dardic, Pashayi. *Dialects:* Ishpi, Isken, Tagau. Not intelligible of other Pashayi languages. Lexical similarity: Less than 30% with other Pashayi languages. *Type:* SOV. *Lg Dev:* Literacy rate in L2: 5%–15%. *Writing:* Unwritten. *Other:* Pashayi peoples have rich folklore and songs preserved by oral tradition. Muslim (Sunni). *Map:* 338:16.

Pashto, Northern [pbu] (Afghan, Eastern Afghan Pashto, Northwestern Pakhto, Pakhtoo, Pakhtu, Paktu, Sharqi). 1,700,000 in Afghanistan (2008), increasing. Nangarhar Province and surrounding regions. *Status:* 3 (Wider communication). *Dialects:* Ghilzai, Khogyani. *Lg Use:* Pashto is 1 of 2 national languages taught in schools. Ghilzai are nomadic, 24% of the Pashto population. All domains. All ages. Positive attitudes. Educated people and speakers in Dari-speaking majority areas also use Dari [prs]. Monolingualism high in Pashto majority areas. Used as L2 by Ashkun [ask], Kamviri [xvi], Southeast Pashayi [psi], Tregami [trm], Waigali [wbk], Wotapuri-Katarqalai [wsv]. *Lg Dev:* Literacy rate in L1: 5%–10%. Literacy rate in L2: 15%–25%. Taught in primary and secondary schools. *Other:* Called Pakhtoon in the north, Pashtoon in the south, and Pakhtun in the central regions. Pashto clans include: Mohmandi, Ghilzai, Durani, Yusufzai, Afridi, Kandahari (Qandahari), Waziri, Chinwari (Shinwari), Mangal, and Wenetsi. Muslim (Sunni). See main entry on page 271.

Pashto, Southern [pbt] (Kandahar Pashto, Qandahar Pashto, Southwestern Pashto). 6,000,000 in Afghanistan (2008). Population total all countries: 10,810,100. Kandahar area; Zabul, Kandahar, Uruzgan, Helmand, Nimroz, Farah, Herat, and Badghis provinces. Also in Iran, Pakistan, Tajikistan, United Arab Emirates, United Kingdom. *Status:* 1 (National). Statutory national language (2004, Constitution, Article 16(1)). *Class:* Indo-European, Indo-Iranian, Iranian, Eastern, Southeastern, Pashto. A member of macrolanguage Pushto [pus] (Pakistan). *Dialect:* Durani. Lexical similarity: 80% between northern and southern varieties of Pashto. *Lg Use:* Afghan government has worked since 1930s to standardize and publicize it. All domains. All ages. Positive attitudes. Only those who are educated or have business in Dari-speaking provinces are bilingual in Dari [prs]. Some have spent time in Pakistan and are bilingual in Urdu [urd]; otherwise, speakers are monolingual. *Lg Dev:* Pashto is one of two national languages taught in schools. Low literacy rate, especially in non-urban locations and among women. Taught in primary and secondary schools. Poetry. Magazines. Newspapers. New media. Radio programs. Films. TV. Videos. Dictionary. Grammar. Bible portions: 2011. *Writing:* Arabic script. *Other:* Muslim (Sunni). *Maps:* 338, 338:15.

Prasuni [prn] (Parun, Paruni, Prasun, Veron, Verou, Veruni, Wasi-Veri). 8,000 (2011), increasing. 1,600 monolinguals. Ethnic population: 8,000. Nuristan Province, Prasun (Parun) valley on upper reaches of Pech river, Shupu (Ishtivi, Shtevgrom), Sech, Ucu, Ushut, Zumu villages. *Status:* 6a (Vigorous). *Class:* Indo-European, Indo-Iranian, Indo-Aryan, Nuristani. *Dialects:* Central Prasun, Lower Prasun (Pashki, Ushut), Upper Wasi-Weri (Ishtivi). Related to Kati [bsh] but more archaic. The most aberrant Nuristani language. No mutual intelligibility of other Nuristani languages. *Lg Use:* All domains. All ages. Positive attitudes. Traditionally bilingual in Dari. Now increasingly bilingual in Pashto. *Lg Dev:* Literacy rate in L2: 15%. Poetry. *Writing:* Unwritten. *Other:* Muslim (Sunni). *Map:* 338:11.

Sanglechi [sgy] (Dargi). 2,200 (2009 S. Beck). Ethnic population: 2,200. Badakhshan Province, Zebok district, Sanglechi valley, Sar-Sanglech, Esketul, Takya, Faruq, Flaxmadek, Dashte Rubat villages. *Status:* 6a (Vigorous). *Class:* Indo-European, Indo-Iranian, Iranian, Eastern, Southeastern, Pamir. *Dialects:* None known. Ishkashimi [isk] is moderately intelligible to Sanglechi speakers. Lexical similarity: 70% with Ishkashimi [isk]. *Lg Use:* Home, village. All ages. Positive attitudes. Dari [prs] is partly or exclusively used in the education, administration, media, travel and trade domain, but only men have access to these domains. *Lg Dev:* Literacy rate in L2: 15%–25%. *Writing:* Unwritten. *Other:* Muslim (Ismaili). *Map:* 338.

Savi [sdg] (Sau, Sauji, Sawi). 3,000 in Afghanistan (1983). Kunar river, Sau village. Also in Pakistan. *Status:* 6a (Vigorous). *Class:* Indo-European, Indo-Iranian, Indo-Aryan, Northwestern zone, Dardic, Shina. *Dialects:* None known. Savi, Palula [phl], and Kalkoti [xka] form a cluster of closely related varieties within the Shina group. Lexical similarity: 56%–58% with Palula [phl]. *Lg Use:* Home, community. All ages. Positive attitudes. 100% also use Southern Pashto [pbt]. *Lg Dev:* Literacy rate in L2: 5%–15%. Pashto is the medium of instruction in the school, which goes up to class 12. Dari, Arabic, and English are taught as subjects. *Writing:* Unwritten. *Other:* Muslim (Sunni). *Map:* 338:12.

Shughni [sgh] (Khughnani, Khughni, Khughnoni, Khugnone, Shighnani, Shighni, Shughnani, Shughnoni, Shugni). 40,000 in Afghanistan (2009). Most are monolingual. Both sides of the Afghanistan-Tajikistan border, 50 km north of Ishkashim, Pamir mountains. *Status:* 6a (Vigorous). *Dialect:* Rushani (Oroshani, Roshan, Roshani, Rushan). *Lg Use:* All domains; in Faizabad City, home only. All ages. Very positive attitudes. *Lg Dev:* Literacy rate in L1: Below 1%. Literacy rate in L2: Over 60%. Shughni are highly interested in literature in their own language. Taught in primary schools unofficially. *Other:* Muslim (Ismaili). See main entry on page 299. *Map:* 338.

Shumashti [sts] (Shumasht). 1,000 (1994). West side of Kunar valley between Pech valley and Jalalabad city. *Status:* 6a (Vigorous). *Class:* Indo-European, Indo-Iranian, Indo-Aryan, Northwestern zone, Dardic, Kunar. *Dialects:* None known. Lexical similarity: 63% with Grangali [nli], 47% with Gawar-Bati [gwt]. Heavily influenced by Northeast Pashayi [aee]. *Lg Dev:* Literacy rate in L2: 5%–15%. *Writing:* Unwritten. *Other:* Muslim. *Map:* 338:13.

Tirahi [tra]. 100. Ethnic population: 5,000. Southeast of Jalalabad, west of Khyber Pass, Nangarhar village. *Status:* 8b (Nearly extinct). *Class:* Indo-European, Indo-Iranian, Indo-Aryan, Northwestern zone, Dardic, Kohistani. *Dialects:* None known. Most closely related to Kohistani languages of Pakistan. *Lg Use:* Most shifted to Southern Pashto [pbt]. Older adults. *Writing:* Unwritten. *Other:* It is very likely that this language is extinct. The Tirahi are "a group of unclear origin, almost completely assimilated by Pashtun" (Pstrusinska and Gray 1990). Muslim.

Tregami [trm] (Katar Gambir, Trigami). 3,500 (2011), increasing. 700 monolinguals. Ethnic population: 3,500. Nuristan Province, Want (Waygal) district, Tregam valley, Katar and Gambir villages. *Status:* 6a (Vigorous). *Class:* Indo-European, Indo-Iranian, Indo-Aryan, Nuristani. *Dialects:* None known. Lexical similarity: 76%–80% with Waigali [wbk]. *Lg Use:* 2,800 also use Northern Pashto [pbu]. Men and some women. *Lg Dev:* Literacy rate in L2: 15%. Poetry. *Writing:* Unwritten. *Other:* It is not clear whether Tregami is a separate language or a dialect of

Waigali [wbk]. Muslim (Sunni). *Map:* 338:17.

Turkmen [tuk] (Turkman, Turkmencha, Turkmeni). 1,500,000 in Afghanistan (2009). Herat, Faryab, Jawzjan, Balkh, Baghlan, Samangan, Badghis, Helmand, Kunduz, and Kabul. A majority live outside cities. *Status:* 5 (Dispersed). Statutory language of provincial identity in Turkmenistan border areas (2004, Constitution, Article 16(2)). *Dialects:* Ärsare (Arsariy), Bayat, Shirik, Teke (Taka), Xatap, Yomut. *Lg Use:* Vigorous. In villages, all domains; in larger cities, home and among other Turkmen. All ages. Positive attitudes. Very few of the Turkmen speak Dari [prs]; only those living in big cities speak it. About 70%–80% of the Turkmen can reasonably understand Uzbek [uzs]. *Lg Dev:* Literacy rate in L1: Below 1%. Literacy rate in L2: Very low. Girls and women especially low. In remote areas, few children, especially girls, are able to attend school. Near cities, a sharp increase in the next generation attending school. Textbooks up to grade 12. Turkmen teachers are few and use of primers not widespread. *Other:* Most Turkmen in Afghanistan use Ärsare. Muslim (Sunni). See main entry on page 307. *Map:* 338.

Uzbek, Southern [uzs] (Usbeki, Uzbak, Uzbeki). 2,910,000 in Afghanistan (2011 UNSD), increasing. Population total all countries: 2,961,980. 1,000,000 monolinguals. Ethnic population: 2,910,000. Faryab, Saripul, Jawzjan, Balkh, Samangan, Baghlan, Kunduz, Takhar, and Badakhshan provinces, in Maimana, Sheberghan, Aqcha, and Saripul towns. Also in Pakistan, Turkey. *Status:* 2 (Provincial). Statutory language of provincial identity in Fariab, Jawzjan, Saripul, other northern provinces (2004, Constitution, Article 16(2)). *Class:* Altaic, Turkic, Eastern. A member of macrolanguage Uzbek [uzb] (Uzbekistan). *Dialects:* None known. Somewhat intelligible of, but differences in grammar from, Northern Uzbek [uzn]. Many loan words from Dari [prs]. *Type:* SOV; postpositions; noun head final; content q-word final; one prefix in words borrowed from Dari [prs], many suffixes (agglutinative); verbal affixation marks of person and number for subject and object; verb tense and aspect marked by suffixes; nontonal; no vowel harmony (unlike some other, closely-related Turkic languages). *Lg Use:* Vigorous. All domains. All ages. Mostly positive attitudes. 1,700,000 also use Dari [prs]. Used primarily by city dwellers; village dwellers have limited ability in Dari. Also use Southern Pashto [pbt]. Used as L2 by Turkmen [tuk]. *Lg Dev:* Literacy rate in L1: 1%. Literacy rate in L2: 20% in Dari [prs]. L1 Literacy in larger towns increasing among younger population. The Afghanistan Ministry of Education has produced Southern Uzbek textbooks for grades 1–3; planned through 12th grade. Taught in secondary schools. Poetry. Magazines. Newspapers. New media. TV. Videos. Dictionary. Bible portions: 2004–2006. *Writing:* Arabic script. *Other:* Muslim (Sunni). *Map:* 338.

Waigali [wbk] (Suki, Wai, Wai-Ala, Waigala, Waigalii, Waigeli, Zhonjigali). 11,500 (2011), increasing. 2,300 monolinguals. Ethnic population: 11,500. Southeast Nuristan Province, Central Kunar Province north of Pech. Varjan in north Waigal valley, Waigal, Zonchigal, Jamach, Ameshdesh villages, and east in Veligal valley villages; Chima-Nishey in lower valley villages. *Status:* 6a (Vigorous). *Class:* Indo-European, Indo-Iranian, Indo-Aryan, Nuristani. *Dialects:* Chima-Nishey, Varjan. Lexical similarity: 76%–80% with Tregami [trm]. *Lg Use:* All domains. All ages. Positive attitudes. 9,200 also use Northern Pashto [pbu]. *Lg Dev:* Literacy rate in L2: 15%. Poetry. *Writing:* Unwritten. *Other:* Muslim (Sunni). *Map:* 338:18.

Wakhi [wbl] (Khik, Khikwar, Vakhan, Wakhani, Wakhigi). 17,000 in Afghanistan (2011 S. Beck), increasing. Population total all countries: 58,000. Ethnic population: 17,000. Badakhshan Province, Wakhan district, along the Panj river as far as Sarhad village. 42 villages. The center of the Wakhi-speaking area is Khandud village. Also in China, Pakistan, Tajikistan. *Status:* 6a (Vigorous). *Class:* Indo-European, Indo-Iranian, Iranian, Eastern, Southeastern, Pamir. *Dialects:* Dialect intelligibility reportedly not a serious problem even with those in other countries, although intelligibility may not be complete on initial contact between speakers from different countries. Lexical similarity: 84% with Ishkoman and Gojal dialects, 89% with Yasin and Gojal, 91% with Ishkoman and Yasin. *Type:* SOV. *Lg Use:* Vigorous. Home, community, work. All ages. Positive attitudes. 5,000 also use Dari [prs]. Men are bilingual in Dari in order to function in every-day situations. Very few women are bilingual. *Lg Dev:* Literacy rate in L1: Below 1%. Literacy rate in L2: 3%–15%. Pilot L1 literacy project ongoing (2012). Poetry. New media. Radio programs. Dictionary. Grammar. Bible portions: 2001. *Writing:* Arabic script, used in Afghanistan. Cyrillic script, used in Tajikistan. Latin script, used in Tajikistan, preferred script, not firmly established. *Other:* Muslim (Ismaili). *Map:* 338.

Warduji [wrd]. 5,000 (1994). Northeast, Werdoge river area west of Ishkashim. *Status:* 6a (Vigorous). *Class:* Unclassified. *Dialects:* Probably a Dari [prs] dialect. *Lg Dev:* Literacy rate in L1: Below 1%. Literacy rate in L2: 5%–15%. *Other:* Muslim. *Map:* 338.

Wotapuri-Katarqalai [wsv]. No known L1 speakers. Nuristan, south of Waigali area, Wotapuri and Katarqalai towns. *Status:* 10 (Extinct). *Class:* Indo-European, Indo-Iranian, Indo-Aryan, Northwestern zone, Dardic, Kohistani. *Lg Use:* Shifted to Pashto [pbu] or [pbt]. Also use Northern Pashto [pbu], Southern Pashto [pbt]. *Lg Dev:* Literacy rate in L2: 15%–25%. *Writing:* Unwritten.

Armenia

Republic of Armenia. 3,019,000 (2011 UNSD). Principal language: Armenian. Literacy rate: 99% (2010 UNESCO). Immigrant languages: Georgian (1,560), Greek (1,300), Karachay-Balkar (320), Russian (14,800), Ukrainian (8,000). Deaf population: 3,500.

The number of individual languages listed for Armenia is 7. All are living languages. Of these, 2 are institutional, 2 are developing, 1 is vigorous, and 2 are in trouble.

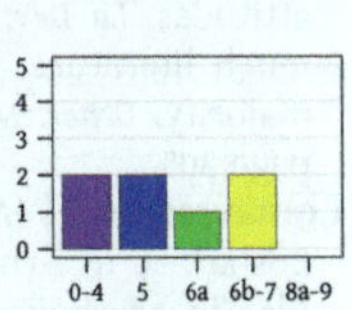

Armenian [hye] (Armjanski Yazyk, Ena, Ermeni Dili, Ermenice, Somkhuri). 3,140,000 in Armenia (2001 census). Population total all countries: 5,902,970. Widespread. Also in Azerbaijan, Bulgaria, Canada, Cyprus, Egypt, Estonia, France, Georgia, Greece, Honduras, Hungary, India, Iran, Iraq, Israel, Jordan, Kazakhstan, Kyrgyzstan, Lebanon, Palestine, Romania, Russian Federation, Syria, Tajikistan, Turkey, Turkmenistan, Ukraine, United States, Uzbekistan. *Status:* 1 (National). Statutory national language (1995, Constitution, Article 12). *Class:* Indo-European, Armenian. *Dialects:* Agulis, Akn, Arabkir, Ararat, Artvin (Artwin), Ashkharik, Astrakhan (Astrachan), Constantinople (Istanbul, Konstantinopel), Crimea (Krim), Dzhulfa (Dschugha, Dschulfa), Eastern Armenian, Erevan (Eriwan), Ewdokia (Tokat), Hamshen (Hamschen), Karabagh, Karin (Erzerum, Erzurum), Kharberd (Charberd, Erzenka, Erzincan), Khvoy-Salmst (Choi-Salmst), Kilikien, Malatya (Malatia), Mus (Musch), North Komedia, Rodosto, Sebaste, Shabin-Karahissar (Schabin-Karahissar), Shamakhi (Schamachi), Smyrna (Izmir), Syria (Syrien), Tbilisi (Tiflis), Tigranakert (Diarbekir, Diyarbakir), Trabzon (Trapezunt), Urmia-Maragheh (Urmia-Maragha), Van (Wan). Eastern Armenian (4,341,000) in Armenia and its Turkish and Iranian borderlands; Western Armenian (879,612) used elsewhere and only understood by some in Iran. In Syria, people in Kessaberen (northeastern mountain village of Kessab) and Musa Dagh village (now relocated to Lebanon) speak related varieties which other Western Armenian speakers do not understand. Most Kessaberen users now learn Western Armenian. Western Armenian (Turkey) and Ararat (Russian Federation) are easily intelligible. *Type:* SVO. *Lg Use:* 91% of the ethnic group in Russia spoke it as L1 (1979 census). All ages. Also use Russian [rus]. *Lg Dev:* Fully developed. Bible: 1883–1994. *Writing:* Armenian script, primary usage. Braille script. *Other:* Ethnic autonym: Haieren. Christian (Miaphysite).

Armenian Sign Language [aen]. *Status:* 6a (Vigorous). *Class:* Deaf sign language.

Assyrian Neo-Aramaic [aii] (Aisorski, Sooreth). 3,500 in Armenia (2001 census). Ethnic population: 15,000. Transcaucasia, Erevan and scattered. *Status:* 7 (Shifting). *Lg Use:* Mainly older adults. Many use Russian [rus] as L1. *Other:* 'Aisor' is the Russian name for the people. The Assyrian and Chaldean separated denominationally during the 16th century. Christian (Nestorian). See main entry on page 206.

Azerbaijani, North [azj] (Azerbaydzhani, Azeri Turk, Turkler). 161,000 in Armenia (Johnstone 1993). *Status:* 5 (Dispersed). *Dialects:* Airym, Baku, Borcala, Derbent, Erevan, Karapapak, Kazakh, Kirovabad, Kuba, Kutkasen, Kyzylbash, Lenkoran, Nakhichevan, Nukha, Ordubad, Saliany, Semakha, Susa (Karabakh), Terekeme, Zakataly (Mugaly). *Lg Use:* Also use Armenian [hye]. *Lg Dev:* Literacy rate in L2: High. *Other:* Muslim (Shi'a). See main entry on page 52.

Erzya [myv]. 500 in Armenia. *Status:* 5 (Developing). See main entry on page 320.

Kurdish, Northern [kmr] (Êzdîkî, Kurmancî, Kurmanji). 45,000 in Armenia (2002). Aragats, Armavir, Talin, Artashat, Abovian, Echmiadzin, Masis, and other main towns and cities. *Status:* 4 (Educational). *Lg Use:* Positive attitudes. *Lg Dev:* Well-developed literary standard and much literature. Some schools where speakers are the majority. *Other:* Majority are Yezidi. See main entry on page 305.

Lomavren [rmi] (Armenian Bosa, Armenian Bosha, Bosa, Bosha). 50 in Armenia (2004). Armenia, south Caucasus. Also in Azerbaijan, Russian Federation, Syria. *Status:* 6b (Threatened). *Class:* Mixed language, Armenian-Romani. *Dialects:* None known. Grammatically restructured like Armenian [hye] with phonology and lexicon also influenced by Armenian.

Azerbaijan

Republic of Azerbaijan, Azerbaycan Respublikasi. 8,922,000 (2009 census). Principal languages: North Azerbaijani, Russian. Literacy rate: 100% (2010 UNESCO). Immigrant languages: Assyrian Neo-Aramaic (1,230), Belarusian (5,210), Dargwa (860), Erzya (1,150), Georgian (16,300), Iranian Persian (1,200), Karachay-Balkar (180), Korean (1,000), Lak (1,210), Lishán Didán (100), Ossetic (2,520), Polish (1,260), Romanian (1,400), South Azerbaijani (248,000), Tabassaran (280), Tatar (31,800), Turkish (18,000), Ukrainian (32,000). General references: Kibrik 1991; Salminen 2007; Sebeok 1963.

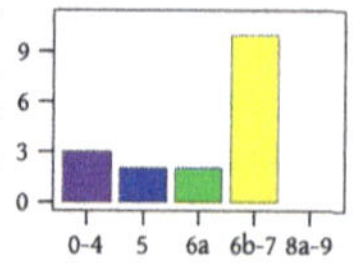

The number of individual languages listed for Azerbaijan is 17. All are living languages. Of these, 3 are institutional, 2 are developing, 2 are vigorous, and 10 are in trouble. See map on page 339.

Akhvakh [akv]. Expatriate community of Akhvakh-dere in Kuba county. *Status:* 6b (Threatened). See main entry on page 319.

Armenian [hye] (Armjanski, Ermenice, Haieren, Somkhuri). 152,000 in Azerbaijan. Nagorno-Karabakh region. *Status:* 7 (Shifting). *Dialect:* Western Armenian. *Lg Use:* Used as L2 by Udi [udi]. *Other:* Christian. See main entry on page 51. *Map:* 339.

Avar [ava] (Avaro, Dagestani). 44,000 in Azerbaijan (1989 census). Northwest, Zaqatala and Balakan regions. *Status:* 6b (Threatened). De facto language of provincial identity in Balakan and Zaqatala. *Dialect:* Zaqatala (Char, Zakataly). *Other:* Muslim (Sunni). See main entry on page 319. *Map:* 339.

Azerbaijani, North [azj] (Azerbaijan, Azerbaydzhani, Azeri Turk). 6,100,000 in Azerbaijan (2007 census). Population total all countries: 7,324,060. 4,000,000 monolinguals. Ethnic population: 6,230,000. L2 users: 8,000,000 in Azerbaijan. Also in Armenia, Estonia, Georgia, Kazakhstan, Kyrgyzstan, Russian Federation, Turkmenistan, Ukraine, Uzbekistan. *Status:* 1 (National). Statutory national language (1995, Constitution, Article 21(1)). *Class:* Altaic, Turkic, Southern, Azerbaijani. A member of macrolanguage Azerbaijani [aze] (Iran). *Dialects:* Airym, Baku, Borcala, Derbend, Ganja, Karapapak, Lenkaran, Nakhchivan, Nukha, Ordubad, Qabala, Qazakh, Quba, Qyzylbash, Salyan, Shamakhi, Shusha (Karabakh), Terekeme, Yerevan, Zaqatala (Mugaly). Slight dialect differences. Qazakh dialect is not related to Kazakh [kaz]. Significant differences from South Azerbaijani [azb] in phonology, lexicon, morphology, syntax, and loanwords. *Lg Dev:* Literacy rate in L2: High. Taught as L2 in Russian language schools. Radio programs. TV. Dictionary. Grammar. Bible: 1891–2004. *Writing:* Arabic script, used until 1920s. Braille script. Cyrillic script, widely used in Armenia. Latin script, official script in Azerbaijan since 1992. *Other:* North and South Azerbaijani are spoken by 1 ethnic group. Each language group is reluctant to accept the written form of the other. Muslim (Shi'a), Muslim (Sunni). *Map:* 339.

Budukh [bdk] (Budug, Budugi, Budux, Bukukhi). 200 (Bril 2010). Ethnic population: 1,000 (1990 A. Kibrik). Quba county, Budukh village; in expatriate communities of Deli-Kaya, Pirusti. *Status:* 7 (Shifting). *Class:* North Caucasian, East Caucasian, Lezgic, Nuclear Lezgic, South Lezgic. *Dialects:* Budukh, Yergyuch. *Lg Use:* All domains. Used by 30%–50% of children. Positive attitudes. Azerbaijani [azj] is literary language. *Writing:* Unwritten. *Other:* Muslim (Sunni). *Map:* 339.

Judeo-Tat [jdt] (Bik, Dzhuhuric, Jewish Tat, Judeo-Tatic, Juhur, Juhuri, Juwri). 24,000 in Azerbaijan (1989 census). Northeast, Quba region, Baku and Krasnaya Sloboda village; Vartashen region, Vartashen village. *Status:* 6a (Vigorous). De facto language of provincial identity in Quba, Baku districts. *Lg Use:* Tats attending the Gregorian (Armenian) church lived in Madrasa village until the late 1980s, and spoke a variety of Tat similar to Judeo-Tat. May have migrated to Armenia or the Russian Federation. *Other:* Jewish. See main entry on page 321. *Map:* 339.

Khalaj [kjf]. Also in Iran. *Status:* 6a (Vigorous). *Class:* Indo-European, Indo-Iranian, Iranian, Western,

Northwestern. *Lg Dev:* NT: 2011. *Other:* Different from Turkic Khalaj [klj] in Iran. *Map:* 339.

Khinalugh [kjj] (Khinalug, Khinalugi, Xinalug). 1,000 (Salminen 2007). Quba county, Khinalug village. *Status:* 6b (Threatened). De facto language of provincial identity in Quba District. *Class:* North Caucasian, East Caucasian, Khinalugh. *Lg Use:* All domains. Some child speakers. Positive attitudes. Azerbaijani [azj] is literary language. *Writing:* Unwritten. *Other:* Muslim. *Map:* 339.

Kryts [kry] (Dzek, Dzhek, Dzheki, Katsy, Kryc, Kryz, Kryzy). 5,000 (Salminen 2007). Quba county, Kryz, Jek, Khaput, Yergyuj, and Alyk villages. *Status:* 6b (Threatened). *Class:* North Caucasian, East Caucasian, Lezgic, Nuclear Lezgic, South Lezgic. *Dialects:* Alyk, Dzhek, Kryts, Xaput (Khaput), Yergyudzh. Dialects quite distinct; perhaps separate languages. *Lg Use:* All domains. Used by 30%–50% of children, but number of child speakers decreasing (Salminen 2007). Positive attitudes. Azerbaijani [azj] is literary language. *Writing:* Unwritten. *Other:* Muslim (Sunni). *Map:* 339.

Kurdish, Northern [kmr] (Kurdî, Kurmancî, Kurmanji). 20,000 in Azerbaijan (1989 census). Basargechar, Minkend, Kubatly, Zangelan, especially Kelbajar and Lachin. Many displaced. *Status:* 5 (Developing). Statutory language of provincial identity in Jabrayil, Kelbajar, Lachan, Qubadly, Zangilan districts (1995, Constitution, Articles 25(3) and 45). *Other:* Muslim (Sunni). See main entry on page 305. *Map:* 339.

Lezgi [lez] (Kiurinty, Lezghi, Lezgian, Lezgin). 364,000 in Azerbaijan (2007). Qusar and Zachmaz provinces, near Russian Federation border on the northeast; southern slopes of main Caucasus chain. *Status:* 6b (Threatened). De facto language of provincial identity in Qusar and Zachmaz. *Dialect:* Quba. *Lg Use:* Also use North Azerbaijani [azj]. *Other:* Muslim. See main entry on page 321. *Map:* 339.

Russian [rus]. 475,000 in Azerbaijan. *Status:* 3 (Wider communication). De facto national working language. *Lg Use:* Used as L2 by Udi [udi]. See main entry on page 322.

Rutul [rut]. 17,000 in Azerbaijan. Sheik and Kax counties. *Status:* 6b (Threatened). *Lg Use:* Home, community. Majority of children do not speak LWC before entering school. See main entry on page 322. *Map:* 339.

Talysh [tly] (Talesh, Talish, Talyshi). 800,000 in Azerbaijan (1996). Population total all countries: 915,400. Caspian coast south of Viliazh-Chai River. May be in Central Asia and Siberia. Also in Iran, Russian Federation. *Status:* 4 (Educational). De facto language of provincial identity in Astara, Lankaran, Lerik, Masally districts. *Class:* Indo-European, Indo-Iranian, Iranian, Western, Northwestern, Talysh. *Dialects:* Astara, Lenkoran, Lerik, Massali. Northern Talyshi in Azerbaijan and Iran. Dialects in Azerbaijan are similar. Dialects in Iran may be separate languages. Reportedly similar to Harzani [hrz]. *Lg Use:* Also use North Azerbaijani [azj]. *Lg Dev:* Taught in primary schools. Newspapers. Dictionary. Grammar. *Writing:* Arabic script. Cyrillic script. *Other:* Muslim (Sunni), Muslim (Shi'a). *Map:* 339.

Tat, Muslim [ttt] (Muslim Tat, Mussulman Tati, Tati). 18,000 in Azerbaijan (1989 census). Population total all countries: 28,010. Ethnic population: 22,000 (1990 A. Kibrik). Widespread in mountains near Qonaqkend; Kuba, Davichi, Sizan, Vartashen, Baku cities; Apsheron peninsula: Balakhan, Surakhan; Lakhij, Matrasa, Konakhkend, Afruja, Chichi, Dagkushu, and Genvab villages. Also in Iran, Russian Federation. *Status:* 7 (Shifting). De facto language of provincial identity in Quba, Shabran, Siazan. *Class:* Indo-European, Indo-Iranian, Iranian, Western, Southwestern, Tat. *Dialects:* Absheron, Aruskush-Daqqushchu (Khyzy), Balakhani, Devechi, Lahyj, Malham, Qonaqkend, Quba, Qyzyl Qazma, Surakhani. Difficult intelligibility of Judeo-Tat [jdt]. Reportedly similar to Farsi [pes]. Balakhani are recent exiles from Iran. Lahyj dialect may be a separate language. *Lg Use:* Rapidly shifting to Azerbaijani (Salminen 2007). Community. Few children. Positive attitudes. Lahyj use Northern Azerbaijani [azj] as literary language. *Lg Dev:* Taught in primary schools. Poetry. Radio programs. Dictionary. Grammar. *Writing:* Cyrillic script, not used in Iran. Latin script, official usage in Azerbaijan, not used in Iran. *Other:* Different from Takestani [tks] of Iran. Muslim (Shi'a). *Map:* 339.

Tsakhur [tkr] (Caxur, Sakhur, Tsakhury, Tsaxur, Yikbi). 13,000 in Azerbaijan (1989 census). Population total all countries: 23,673. Ethnic population: 13,300 (1989 census). Northwest, Zakatal and Kakh counties, 16 villages. Also in Russian Federation, Uzbekistan. *Status:* 6b (Threatened). De facto language of provincial identity in Tovuz District. *Class:* North Caucasian, East Caucasian, Lezgic, Nuclear Lezgic, West Lezgic. *Lg Use:* Most families still transmit it to children. *Lg Dev:* Studied as a subject in local schools (Salminen 2007). Newspapers. Grammar. Bible portions: 2003–2012. *Writing:* Cyrillic script. Latin script, used in Azerbaijan. *Other:* Muslim. *Map:* 339.

Udi [udi] (Udin, Uti). 3,800 in Azerbaijan (2009 census). Population total all countries: 6,590. Oghuz town, Qabala, Niç (about 4,000 speakers), and Mirzabeyli villages. Also in Georgia, Russian Federation, Turkmenistan. *Status:* 5 (Developing). De facto language of provincial identity in Qabala District. *Class:* North Caucasian, East Caucasian, Lezgic, Udi. *Dialects:* Nidzh (Nic, Nij, Nizh), Oghuz (Vartashen), Oktomberi. Oktomberi dialect more divergent from Nic Udi than from Oghuz Udi. One of the most divergent Lezgian (Lezgic) languages. *Lg Use:* Home, community. Used by 30%–50% of children. Neutral attitudes. Udi not seen as prestigious as Russian [rus]. Also use Armenian [hye], Georgian [kat], Russian [rus]. *Lg Dev:* Discussing how their language can be saved. Taught in primary schools, through 4th grade. Dictionary. Grammar. Bible portions: 1902. *Writing:* Cyrillic script. *Other:* Nic dialect is vigorous (6a). Oghuz dialect is moribund (8a), as only about 100 persons remain in Oghuz. Christian. *Map:* 339.

Bahrain

Kingdom of Bahrain. 1,195,000 (2011 UNSD). Principal languages: Baharna Spoken Arabic, English, Standard Arabic. Literacy rate: 90% (2010 UNESCO). Immigrant languages: Iranian Persian (48,000), Kerinci (25,000), Korean (1,200), Malayalam (23,600), Tamil (18,000), Telugu (13,000), Urdu (28,800). General references: Al-Tajir 1982; Fischer and Jastrow 1980; Holes 1990; Johnstone 1967. Deaf population: 600.

The number of individual languages listed for Bahrain is 4. All are living languages. Of these, 3 are institutional and 1 is vigorous.

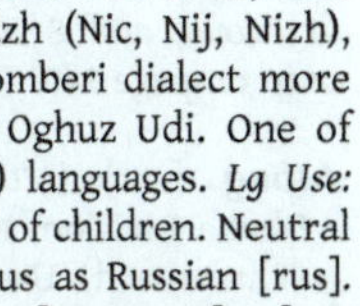

Arabic, Baharna Spoken [abv] (Baharna, Baharnah, Bahraini Shi'ite Arabic). 300,000 in Bahrain (1995). Population total all countries: 310,000. Also in Oman. *Status:* 3 (Wider communication). De facto national working language. *Class:* Afro-Asiatic, Semitic, Central, South, Arabic. A member of macrolanguage Arabic [ara] (Saudi Arabia). *Lg Use:* Negative attitudes. Also use Gulf

Spoken Arabic [afb]. *Writing:* Arabic script. *Other:* Muslim (Shi'a).

Arabic, Gulf Spoken [afb] (Gulf Arabic, Khaliji). 100,000 in Bahrain (1995). *Status:* 6a (Vigorous). *Dialect:* Bahraini Gulf Arabic. *Lg Use:* Used as L2 by Baharna Spoken Arabic [abv]. *Other:* Muslim (Sunni). See main entry on page 213.

Arabic, Standard [arb]. Widespread. *Status:* 1 (National). Statutory national language (2002, Constitution, Article 2). *Lg Use:* Education, official purposes. See main entry on page 293.

English [eng]. *Status:* 3 (Wider communication). De facto national working language. *Lg Use:* Used for most business communication. Many Bahraini children learn English before Arabic [arb] because it is easier to learn (2004). See main entry on page 319.

Bangladesh

People's Republic of Bangladesh. 149,772,000 (2011 UNSD). Principal language: Bengali. Literacy rate: 52% (2010 UNESCO). Immigrant languages: Eastern Panjabi (23,700), Gujarati (250), Hindi (346,000), Oriya (32,500). General references: Comrie 1987; Hale 1982; Matisoff, Baron, and Lowe 1996; Voegelin and Voegelin 1977. Deaf population: 7,596,500. Deaf institutions: 14.

The number of individual languages listed for Bangladesh is 41. All are living languages. Of these, 4 are institutional, 12 are developing, 17 are vigorous, and 8 are in trouble. See map on page 340.

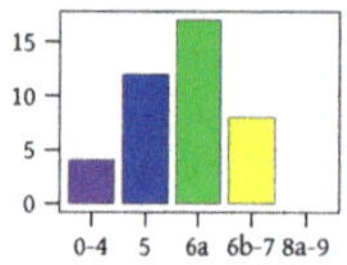

Atong [aot] (A'tong, Attong). 5,400 in Bangladesh. Dhaka Division, Northern Netrokona district. *Status:* 6b (Threatened). Used as LWC among all Mandi. *Lg Use:* Will possibly become more mixed with the Abeng dialect of Garo [grt] and Bengali [ben]. Home, village. All ages, but many children can speak Abeng before starting school. Good proficiency in Bengali [ben]. Also use Garo [grt]. Used as L2 by Megam [mef]. *Other:* Seen by themselves and other Garos to be Garos, but the languages are not mutually intelligible. Christian. See main entry on page 102. *Map:* 340 (as A'tong).

Bengali [ben] (Bangala, Bangla, Bangla-Bhasa). 110,000,000 in Bangladesh (2001 census). Population total all countries: 193,261,200. L2 users: 140,000,000 in Bangladesh. West. Also in Canada, India, Malawi, Nepal, Saudi Arabia, Singapore, United Arab Emirates, United Kingdom, United States. *Status:* 1 (National). Statutory national language (1972, Constitution, Article 3). *Class:* Indo-European, Indo-Iranian, Indo-Aryan, Eastern zone, Bengali-Assamese. *Dialects:* Barisal, Khulna, Mymensingh, Noakhali. Reportedly similar to Assamese [asm]. Lexical similarity: 40% with Nepali [npi]. *Type:* SOV; postpositions; noun head both initial and final; 3 genders: male, female, neuter; content q-word initial and final; clause constituents indicated by case-marking and word order; tense; passives and voice; tonal; 35 consonant and 5 vowel phonemes. *Lg Use:* All ages. Also use Chak [ckh] in Khagrachari and Rangamati districts. Also use Chittagonian [ctg], War-Jaintia [aml]. *Lg Dev:* Taught in primary and secondary schools. Fully developed. Bible: 1809–2000. *Writing:* Bengali script, primary usage. Braille script. Newar (Prachalit Nepal) script, no longer in use. *Other:* Muslim. *Maps:* 340, 341.

Bihari [urd] (Urdu). 250,000 in Bangladesh (2003 SIL). Mainly refugee camps in 13 districts. *Status:* 5 (Dispersed). *Lg Use:* Home, village, religion, market. All ages. Positive attitudes. Also use Bengali [ben], English [eng], Standard Arabic [arb]. *Lg Dev:* Literacy rate in L1: Below 50%, probably 25%. Literacy rate in L2: 50%. Many more literate in Bengali than Urdu. See main entry on page 272 (as Urdu). *Maps:* 340, 341.

Bishnupriya [bpy] (Bishnupria, Bishnupuriya, Bisna Puriya). 40,000 in Bangladesh (2003). 400 monolinguals. Sylhet Division, Moulvibazar district; southern Habiganj district, Sylhet city, 1 village; Sunamganj district, 2 villages. *Status:* 6a (Vigorous). *Dialects:* Madai Gang, Rajar Gang. *Lg Use:* Vigorous. Home, village. All ages. Positive attitudes. Also use Bengali [ben], Meitei [mni]. Used as L2 by Meitei [mni]. *Lg Dev:* Literacy rate in L2: 75% in Bengali. Those who are literate in Bengali are also able to read Bishnupriya though they have little practice at doing so. *Other:* Dialects are not attached to localities but exist side by side: Madai Gang (of the village of the queen) and Rajar Gang (of the village of the king). Intelligibility between the 2 caste dialects sufficient to understand complex and abstract discourse. Hindu. See main entry on page 105. *Map:* 340.

Chak [ckh] (Sak, Tsak). 3,000 in Bangladesh (Bradley 2007). Southeastern Chittagong district, Arakan Blue mountains, Baishari, Bandarban, south Naikhongchari area, Bishar Chokpra, 14 villages. *Status:* 6a (Vigorous). *Lg Use:* All ages. 80% also use Marma [rmz]. Including most Chak living near Bandarban. Also use Bengali [ben]. Used as L2 by Bengali [ben], Marma [rmz], Tangchangya [tnv], Tippera [tpe]. *Lg Dev:* Literacy rate in L2: 25% Bengali [ben]. *Other:* Distinct from Chakma [ccp]. Traditional religion. See main entry on page 230. *Map:* 341.

Chakma [ccp] (Sakma, Sangma, Takam). 150,000 in Bangladesh (2007). Population total all countries: 326,000. Southeast, Chittagong Hills area, and Chittagong city. Also in India, Myanmar. *Status:* 5 (Developing). *Class:* Indo-European, Indo-Iranian, Indo-Aryan, Eastern zone, Bengali-Assamese. *Dialects:* Chakma of India [ccp] understand Bangladesh Chakma with difficulty. Some dialect variation within Myanmar. Lexical similarity: 58%–67% with Tanchangya [tnv]. *Lg Use:* All domains. All ages. Positive attitudes. Educated and most men also use Bengali [ben]. Also use Chittagonian [ctg]. Used as L2 by Riang [ria]. *Lg Dev:* Literacy rate in L1: 70%. Literacy rate in L2: 70%. NT: 1926–1991. *Writing:* Bengali script. Chakma script, no longer in use. Latin script. *Other:* Buddhist, Christian. *Maps:* 340, 341.

Chin, Asho [csh] (Khyang, Khyeng, Qin, Sho, Shoa). 4,000 in Bangladesh (2011). Chittagong Division, Bandarban, Chittagong, and Rangamati districts. Laitu dialect in the plain area; Kongtu in the hill area. *Status:* 6a (Vigorous). *Dialects:* Khyang, Kongtu, Laitu. *Lg Use:* All ages. 80% also use Marma [rmz]. See main entry on page 230. *Map:* 341.

Chin, Bawm [bgr] (Bawm, Bawn, Bawng, Bom). 10,000 in Bangladesh (2011). Chittagong hills. *Status:* 5 (Developing). *Lg Use:* All ages. 50% also use Marma [rmz]. See main entry on page 108. *Map:* 341.

Chin, Khumi [cnk] (Khami, Khuni, Khweymi). 2,090 in Bangladesh (2005). Chittagong Division, Bandarban district, Thanchi, Ruma, and Rowanchari subdistricts. *Status:* 6a (Vigorous). *Dialects:* Khami, Khimi, Yindi (Yindu). *Lg Use:* All ages. 80% also use Marma [rmz]. See main entry on page 231. *Map:* 341.

Chittagonian [ctg] (Chatgaiyan Buli, Chatgaya, Chittagonian Bengali). 13,000,000 (2006 SIL). Chittagong region. *Status:* 3 (Wider communication). Used as an L2 in Rangamati, Bandarban, Cox' s Bazar, and Chittagong districts primarily for business and market. *Class:* Indo-European, Indo-Iranian, Indo-Aryan, Eastern zone, Bengali-Assamese. *Dialects:* Not inherently intelligible with Bengali [ben], although considered a nonstandard Bengali dialect. Dialects form a continuum from north to south, with a larger religious distinction between Muslim and others. Rohingya [rhg] in Myanmar is reportedly similar to the southern dialect of Chittagonian. Lexical similarity: 43%–64% with Bangla [ben]. *Lg Use:* Home, family, religion. 60% also use Bengali [ben]. Village women without access to TV do not understand Bengali. Educated people understand some Bengali, but are not comfortable using it. Education is in standard Bengali. Used as L2 by Bengali [ben], Chakma [ccp], Marma [rmz], Mru [mro], Rakhine [rki], Rohingya [rhg], Tippera [tpe]. *Lg Dev:* Lower literacy rate than most of the country. TV. *Writing:* Arabic script. Latin script. *Other:* Muslim, Christian, Hindu. *Map:* 341.

Garo [grt] (Garrow, Mande, Mandi). 120,000 in Bangladesh (2005). Mymensingh plains, Tangail Sherpur, Madhupur, Jamalpur, Netrokona, Sylhet, Dhaka. *Status:* 5 (Developing). *Dialects:* Abeng, Achik, Brak, Chibok, Dual. *Lg Use:* All ages. Also use Bengali [ben], Hajong [haj]. Used as L2 by Atong [aot], Hajong [haj], Koch [kdq], Megam [mef]. *Lg Dev:* Literacy rate in L1: 25%. Literacy rate in L2: 80% in Bengali [ben]. Parents want their children to read and write Garo. *Other:* Abeng dialect is spoken but writing is in Achik. Christian, Hindu, traditional religion. See main entry on page 112. *Map:* 340.

Hajong [haj] (Hajang). 8,000 in Bangladesh. Dhaka Division, Rangpur district east to Sunamganj district. *Status:* 5 (Developing). *Lg Use:* Home, village, religion. All ages. Positive attitudes. In India, Hajong has more prestige than in Bangladesh due to more population and language development. Nearly all use some Bengali [ben], young speak it better. Educated use standard Bengali. Nearly all can buy and sell in Bengali. An increasing number (young and educated) can use Bengali for abstract concepts. Also use Garo [grt]. Used as L2 by Garo [grt]. *Lg Dev:* Literacy rate in L1: 20% can read Hajong in Bengali script. Literacy rate in L2: 20% in Bengali. *Other:* Hindu. See main entry on page 114. *Map:* 340.

Indian Sign Language [ins]. *Status:* 6a (Vigorous). *Other:* The Indian manual English system is barely understandable to American Signed English. See main entry on page 115.

Khasi [kha] (Cossyah, Kahasi, Khasie, Khasiyas, Khassee, Khuchia, Kyi). Very few speakers. *Status:* 6b (Threatened). *Lg Use:* Also use Bengali [ben]. Used as L2 by War-Jaintia [aml]. *Other:* The Lyngngam [lyg], Pnar [pbv], and War-Jaintia [aml] of Bangladesh identify ethnically with the Khasi. See main entry on page 119. *Map:* 340.

Koch [kdq] (Koc, Kocch, Koce, Kochboli, Konch). 6,000 in Bangladesh (2006 SIL). Dhaka Division, northern Sherpur district. *Status:* 6a (Vigorous). *Dialects:* Chapra, Margan, Tintekiya. *Lg Use:* Home, community. All ages. Positive attitudes. Also use Garo [grt]. See main entry on page 120. *Map:* 340.

Koda [cdz]. 1,300 in Bangladesh (2005). Rajshahi Division, Puthia, Mohonpur and Mundumala areas. *Status:* 6a (Vigorous). *Lg Use:* May be in slow transition to colloquial Bengali [ben]. Education rate low. 60% say Bengali is their best language. Home, community. All ages. Negative attitudes. Considered inferior to Bengali [ben] which is favored for education and economic advancement. Those who travel often speak some Santhali [sat]. Also use Bengali [ben]. *Lg Dev:* Literacy rate in L1: 0%. Literacy rate in L2: Below 10% in Bengali. *Other:* Hindu, traditional religion. See main entry on page 120. *Map:* 340.

Kok Borok [trp] (Debbarma, Tipura, Tripura, Tripuri). 5,000 in Bangladesh. *Status:* 6a (Vigorous). *Lg Use:* All ages. See main entry on page 120. *Maps:* 340, 341.

Kol [ekl] (Hor). 1,660 (2012 SIL). Godagari subdistrict of Rajshahi district in northwest Bangladesh. *Status:* 6a (Vigorous). *Class:* Austro-Asiatic, Munda, North Munda, Kherwari, Mundari. *Dialects:* None known. Lexical similarity: 62%–64% with Santhali [sat], 58% with Mundari [unr], 57%–60% with Koda [cdz], 37% with Ho (Lanka Kol) [hoc]. *Lg Use:* All ages. *Writing:* Latin script. *Other:* Hindu, Christian, traditional religion. *Map:* 340.

Kurux [kru] (Kurukh, Oraoan, Uraon). 50,000 in Bangladesh (2011), decreasing. Ethnic population: 50,000. *Status:* 6b (Threatened). *Lg Use:* Not as vital as other indigenous languages. All ages, but more adults. Neutral attitudes. Positive attitude toward Bangla [ben], which is used in most settings outside the home or village. *Other:* Different from Sadri, Oraon [sdr]. See main entry on page 124. *Map:* 340.

Lyngngam [lyg] (Megam). 1,000 in Bangladesh. Dhaka Division, Netrokona district. *Status:* 7 (Shifting). *Other:* Previously listed as dialect of Khasi. Culturally intermediate between the Khasi and the Garo. Resemble Garos in appearance and customs. (Singh 1994) Lyngngam is a former Garo clan, but do not mix with the Garo, and consider themselves to be Khasi (Breton 1997). Megam [mef] and Lyngngam are sometimes used interchangeably for the same language in Netrokona district. Christian. See main entry on page 126. *Map:* 340.

Mahali [mjx] (Mahle). 3,000 in Bangladesh (2010 SIL). Ethnic population: 3,000 (2004 SIL). Rajshahi Division, Abirpara, Matindor, and Mundumala-Pachondor villages. *Status:* 6a (Vigorous). *Lg Use:* Home, village. All ages. 100% also use Bengali [ben]. 15% also use English [eng]. 12% also use Sadri [sck]. 91% also use Santhali [sat]. *Lg Dev:* Literacy rate in L1: 37%. Literacy rate in L2: 50%. Multilingual education projects within the Mahali community since 2006. See main entry on page 126.

Marma [rmz] ("Mogh" *pej.*). 150,000 in Bangladesh (2007). Population total all countries: 180,600. Chittagong Division, Rangamati, Bandarban, and Khagrachari districts. Also in India. *Status:* 3 (Wider communication). Largest and earliest language group to settle in the area. Used in Cox's Bazar and Bandarban districts in religious ceremonies, market, stores, and churches. *Class:* Sino-Tibetan, Tibeto-Burman, Ngwi-Burmese, Burmish, Southern. *Lg Use:* Home, village. Also use Chak [ckh] in Khagrachari and Rangamati districts. Also use Chittagonian [ctg]. Used as L2 by Asho Chin [csh], Bawm Chin [bgr], Chak [ckh], Khumi Chin [cnk], Mru [mro], Tippera [tpe]. *Writing:* Myanmar (Burmese) script, used in India. *Other:* Buddhist, Christian, Muslim. *Map:* 341.

Megam [mef] (Migam, Negam). 6,870 (2000). Dhaka Division, Netrokona district, Kalmakanda subdistrict. *Status:* 6a (Vigorous). *Class:* Sino-Tibetan, Tibeto-Burman, Sal, Bodo-Garo-Northern Naga, Bodo-Koch, Bodo-Garo. *Dialects:* Lexical similarity: 7%–9% with the Abeng dialect of Garo [grt], 60% with Lyngngam [lyg]. *Lg Use:* Home, village. All ages. Positive attitudes. Also use the Abeng dialect of Garo [grt] with most other Mandi speakers. Also use Atong [aot]. *Writing:* Unwritten. *Other:* Identify ethnically with the Garo [grt]. Christian. *Map:* 340.

Meitei [mni] (Manipuri, Meetei, Meithei). 15,000 in Bangladesh (2003). 300 monolinguals. Sylhet district, Moulvi Bazar district (Kamalganj subdistrict) and Sylhet dity. *Status:* 5 (Developing). *Dialects:* Hindu Meitei, Pangan (Pangal). *Lg Use:* Vigorous. Home, village. All ages. Positive attitudes. Youth also use Bengali [ben]. Also use Bishnupriya [bpy], Sylheti [syl]. Used as L2 by Bishnupriya [bpy]. *Lg Dev:* Literacy rate in L1: Low. Literacy rate in L2: 70% in Bengali. Those literate in Bengali are able to read Meitei but have little practice doing so. *Other:* Preferred name is Meitei Manipuri. Outsiders don't distinguish between Meitei and Bishnupriya, calling both of them Manipuri. Meitei is a well-developed language with much literature in India, but little is available in Bangladesh. Hindu, Muslim. See main entry on page 129. *Map:* 340.

Mizo [lus] (Hualngo, Lei, Lusai, Lushai, Lushei, Sailau, Whelngo). 250 in Bangladesh (2007 census). Chittagong Division, Rangamati, Sajek. *Status:* 6b (Threatened). *Lg Use:* Vigorous. *Other:* Most moved from Bangladesh to India. Christian. See main entry on page 131. *Map:* 341.

Mru [mro] (Maru, Mrung, Murung). 30,000 in Bangladesh (2007). Population total all countries: 50,000. Chittagong, Division, Bandarban district. Also in India, Myanmar. *Status:* 5 (Developing). *Class:* Sino-Tibetan, Tibeto-Burman, Ngwi-Burmese, Mru. *Dialects:* Anok, Dowpreng, Sungma. Lexical similarity: 13% with Mro-Khimi Chin [cmr], 72%–76% with Anu-Hkongso Chin [anl]; lexical similarity with Anok, Dowpreng, and Sungma dialects in Bangladesh is high: 91%-98%. *Type:* SOV. *Lg Use:* All ages. 80% also use Marma [rmz]. Also use Bengali [ben], Chittagonian [ctg]. *Lg Dev:* Literacy rate in L2: 10%. Literacy materials are being developed using the Krama script. NT: 1994. *Writing:* Latin script. Mro script, invented in 1980s. *Other:* Ethnically related to the Khumi. 5 linguistically distinct groups: Anok (largest and central) and Tshungma in the north, Domrong in the lowlands north of the Matamuri, Dopreng and Rumma in far south and into Arakan (Brauns and Loffler 1990). Traditional religion. *Map:* 341.

Mundari [unr] (Colh, Horo, Mandari, Mondari, Munari, Munda). 2,500 in Bangladesh (2005 Caritas Bangladesh). Ethnic population: 5,000. Rajshahi Division, Dinajpur and Naogaon districts; Sylhet Division, various tea estates. *Status:* 6a (Vigorous). *Dialects:* Hasada', Kera', Latar, Naguri. *Lg Use:* Primarily in Rajshahi Division. Among the Mundaris living on Sylhet tea estates, Mundari language use is much lower. Home, village. All ages. Positive attitudes. *Lg Dev:* Literacy rate in L1: Below 1%. See main entry on page 131. *Map:* 340.

Pangkhua [pkh] (Pangkhu, Pankho, Pankhu, Panko). 3,200 in Bangladesh (2012 SIL). Chittagong Division, Rangamati district. Also in India (Pankhu). *Status:* 6a (Vigorous). *Class:* Sino-Tibetan, Tibeto-Burman, Sal, Kuki-Chin-Naga, Kuki-Chin, Central. *Lg Use:* All ages. Education is in Bengali [ben]. *Writing:* Devanagari script. Latin script. *Other:* Christian. *Maps:* 340, 341.

Pnar [pbv]. 4,000 in Bangladesh (2002). Northeast along India border; Sylhet Division, Sylhet district, near Jaflong, Tamabil, Jaintiapur, and north of Raipur; Moulvi Bazar district, near Fenchuganj, Madhabkunda, Barlekha, Goalbari, Fultala, Alinagar, Islampur, Khajori, Rashidpur, Satgoan, and Kamalganj. *Status:* 6a (Vigorous). *Lg Use:* Also use War-Jaintia [aml]. *Other:* Identify ethnically with the Khasi [kha]. See main entry on page 139. *Map:* 340.

Rakhine [rki] (Mogh, Rakhain, Rakkhaine). 200,000 in Bangladesh (2011 SIL). Southeast, Chittagong district. *Status:* 5 (Developing). *Dialects:* Rakhine, Sitwe. *Lg Use:* All ages. Positive attitudes. Many men also use Bengali [ben]. Also use Burmese [mya], Chittagonian [ctg]. *Lg Dev:* Literacy rate in L1: 80%. Literacy rate in L2: 60% Rakhine [rhg]; 30% Marma [rmz]. *Other:* Buddhist, Hindu, Muslim. See main entry on page 240. *Map:* 341.

Rangpuri [rkt] (Anchalit Bangla, Bahe Bangla, Kamta, Polia). 10,000,000 in Bangladesh (2007). Population total all countries: 15,000,000. Rangpur Division north from Bogra, also known as the greater Dinajpur and Rangpur areas, now subdivided into Rangpur, Lalmonihat, Nilphamari, Gaibanda, Panchagar, Thakurgaon, and Dinajpur districts. Also in India (Kamta). *Status:* 5 (Developing). *Class:* Indo-European, Indo-Iranian, Indo-Aryan, Eastern zone, Bengali-Assamese. *Lg Dev:* Dictionary. Grammar. Bible portions: 2008–2011. *Writing:* Bengali script. *Map:* 340.

Riang [ria] (Kau Bru, Reang). 500 in Bangladesh (2007). Chittagong Division, Rangamati district. *Status:* 7 (Shifting). *Lg Use:* Most Riang in Bangladesh now speak Chakma [ccp] as L1. *Other:* Different from Riang [ril] of Myanmar, a Mon-Khmer language. See main entry on page 141. *Maps:* 340, 341.

Rohingya [rhg] (Rohinga). 200,000 in Bangladesh (2006). Chittagong Division, Cox's Bazaar district. *Status:* 6b (Threatened). *Lg Use:* Also use Chittagonian [ctg]. *Other:* Muslim. See main entry on page 241. *Map:* 341.

Sadri, Oraon [sdr]. 166,000 (2000). Throughout Rajshahi Division; Sylhet Division, Moulvibazar and Habiganj districts; Khulna Division, Jhenaidah district (Jhenaidah, Moheshpur subdistricts), Kushtia district (Mirpur subdistrict), Magura district (Magura subdistrict). *Status:* 5 (Developing). *Class:* Indo-European, Indo-Iranian, Indo-Aryan, Eastern zone, Bihari. *Dialects:* Borail Sadri, Mokkan Tila Sadri, Nurpur Sadri, Uchai Sadri. Dialects may need separate literature. Inherent intelligibility of 7 Sadri varieties on Borail ranges from 70%–93%; of 8 varieties on Nurpur from 78%–94%. Lexical similarity: 88%–97% with 14 Sadri varieties with the Borail Sadri dialect. *Lg Use:* Vigorous but some educated people do not use Oraon with their children. All ages. Low proficiency in Bengali [ben]. *Lg Dev:* Literacy rate in L2: 30%. Bangladesh Oraon Foundation has committed to language maintenance. NT: 2003. *Writing:* Bengali script. Latin script. *Other:* The Oraon people came from India over 100 years ago. Sometime in the past some Oraon shifted from Kurux [kru], a Dravidian language, to Sadri, which is Indo-Aryan. Some Oraon people still speak Kurux. Traditional religion, Hindu. *Map:* 340.

Santhali [sat] (Har, Hor, Sandal, Sangtal, Santal, Santali, Satar, Sonthal). 225,000 in Bangladesh (2011). Rajshahi Division. *Status:* 5 (Developing). *Lg Use:* Home, village, church, market. All ages. Positive attitudes. Used as L2 by Koda [cdz], Mahali [mjx]. *Lg Dev:* Literacy rate in L1: 50%. See main entry on page 142. *Map:* 340.

Sauria Paharia [mjt] (Malto, Paharia). 7,000 in Bangladesh (2007). *Status:* 7 (Shifting). See main entry on page 143. *Map:* 340.

Sylheti [syl] (Sileti, Siloti, Srihattia, Sylhetti, Sylhetti Bangla, Syloti, Syloty). 7,000,000 in Bangladesh. Population total all countries: 10,300,000. L2 users: 1,500,000 in Bangladesh. Sylhet Division, Sylhet, Sunamganj, Habiganj, and Moulvibazar districts. Also in Canada, India, Malaysia, Singapore, United Kingdom, United States. *Status:* 3 (Wider communication). *Class:* Indo-European, Indo-Iranian, Indo-Aryan, Eastern zone, Bengali-Assamese. *Dialects:* None known. Reportedly similar to Assamese [asm]. Lexical similarity: 70% with Bengali [ben]. *Lg Use:* All ages. Also use Bengali [ben], primarily men. Bengali used in education and media. Used as L2 by Meitei [mni], War-Jaintia [aml]. *Lg Dev:* Literacy rate in L2: 35%. Educated can read Bengali. Few women are educated. Bible portions: 1993. *Writing:* Bengali script. Latin script. Syloti Nagri script, no longer in use. *Other:* Muslim, Hindu. *Map:* 340.

Tangchangya [tnv] (Tanchangya). 21,600 (1991 census). Chittagong hills. *Status:* 6a (Vigorous). *Class:* Indo-European, Indo-Iranian, Indo-Aryan, Eastern zone, Bengali-Assamese. *Dialects:* None known. 90% intelligibility of Chakma [ccp]. Lexical similarity: 58%–67% with Chakma [ccp]. *Lg Use:* All ages. Also use Chak [ckh] in

Khagrachari and Rangamati districts. *Writing:* Chakma script. *Map:* 341.

Tippera [tpe] (Kok Borok, Tipperah, Tippurah, Tipra, Tipura, Triperah, Tripura). 85,000. Chittagong Division, Khagrachari district, Chittagong district, Fatikchari subdistrict. *Status:* 6a (Vigorous). *Class:* Sino-Tibetan, Tibeto-Burman, Sal, Bodo-Garo-Northern Naga, Bodo-Koch, Bodo-Garo, Bodo. *Dialects:* Anok, Aslong, Dendak, Gabing, Kema, Kewa, Khali, Naitong, Phatung, Tongpai. Lexical similarity: 56%–85% among dialects, 61%–74% with Kok Borok [trp], 53%–65% with Riang [ria], 37%–59% with Usoi Tripura [usi]. *Lg Use:* All ages. Many men also use some Bengali [ben]. Also use Chak [ckh] in Khagrachari and Rangamati districts. 50% also use Marma [rmz]. Also use Chittagonian [ctg]. *Writing:* Bengali script. Latin script. *Other:* Traditional religion, Hindu. *Maps:* 340, 341.

Usoi [usi] (Kau Brung, Unshoi, Unsuiy, Ushoi). 22,400. Chittagong Division, Bandarban district. *Status:* 5 (Developing). *Class:* Sino-Tibetan, Tibeto-Burman, Sal, Bodo-Garo-Northern Naga, Bodo-Koch, Bodo-Garo, Bodo. *Dialects:* Joloi, Panji. Lexical similarity: 88% with Panji and Joloi dialects, 59%–67% with Riang [ria], 47%–58% with Kok Borok [trp], 37%–59% with Tippera [tpe]. *Lg Use:* All ages. *Lg Dev:* NT: 1995. *Writing:* Bengali script. Latin script. *Other:* Hindu, Christian, traditional religion. *Map:* 341.

War-Jaintia [aml]. 16,000 in Bangladesh (2003 SIL). Population total all countries: 41,900. 4,000 monolinguals. Northeast along India border; Sylhet Division, Sylhet district, near Jaflong, Tamabil, Jaintiapur, and north of Raipur; Moulvi Bazar district, near Fenchuganj, Madhabkunda, Barlekha, Goalbari, Fultala, Alinagar, Islampur, Khajori, Rashidpur, Satgoan and Kamalganj. Also in India. *Status:* 6a (Vigorous). *Class:* Austro-Asiatic, Mon-Khmer, Northern Mon-Khmer, Khasian. *Dialects:* War-Jaintia, War-Khasi. Lexical similarity: 86%–92% with dialects in Bangladesh; 83%–89% with War-Jaintia in India and Bangladesh; India variety 41%–45% with Pnar [pbv] (from scant data); 27%–35% with standard Khasi [kha]; 24%–28% with War dialect of Khasi. *Type:* SVO; prepositions; articles before noun heads; CV, CVC, CVV, V, VCV, CCV, CCVC; nontonal. *Lg Use:* Vigorous. Home, village. All ages. Also use Bengali [ben], English [eng], Khasi [kha], Sylheti [syl]. Used as L2 by Bengali [ben], Pnar [pbv]. *Lg Dev:* Literacy rate in L2: 40% Bengali; many are literate in standard Khasi [kha]. Using Latin script for War-Jaintia produces some pronunciation problems but eases transition into Khasi. Taught in primary schools. Grammar. *Writing:* Unwritten. *Other:* Learning standard Khasi [kha] is important due to affinity with the larger Khasi ethnic group. Standard Khasi has high prestige. Christian, traditional religion. *Map:* 340.

Bhutan

Kingdom of Bhutan. 681,000 (2012 census). Principal languages: Dzongkha, English. Literacy rate: 39% (2005 UNESCO). Immigrant languages: Adi (2,100), Assamese (27,000), Bantawa (19,200), Hindi (11,000), Santhali (13,600), Sherpa (4,200). General references: Coelho 1967; Matisoff 1991; Matisoff, Baron, and Lowe 1996; Singh 1972; Van Driem 1997, 2007; White 1971. Deaf population: 6,170.

The number of individual languages listed for Bhutan is 24. All are living languages. Of these, 3 are institutional, 1 is developing, 14 are vigorous, and 6 are in trouble. See map on page 342.

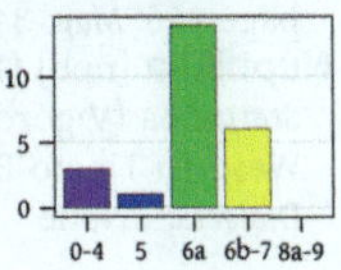

Adap [adp]. South central, Wangdue Phodrang District, from Damphu to Shemgang, Ada villages. *Status:* 6a (Vigorous). *Class:* Sino-Tibetan, Tibeto-Burman, Western Tibeto-Burman, Bodish, Central Bodish, Central, Southern. *Dialects:* None known. Lexical similarity: 77% with Dzongkha [dzo], 62%–65% with Bumthangkha [kjz], 41% with Tshangla [tsj]. *Writing:* Unwritten.

Brokkat [bro] (Brokskad, Jokay). 300 (Van Driem 1993). Central Bumthang District, Dur. *Status:* 6a (Vigorous). *Class:* Sino-Tibetan, Tibeto-Burman, Western Tibeto-Burman, Bodish, Central Bodish, Central, Southern. *Writing:* Unwritten. *Other:* Different from Brokpake [sgt] (Van Driem 1993). *Map:* 342.

Brokpake [sgt] (Brokpa, Dakpa, Damilo, Dap, Drokpakay, Jobikha, Mera Sagtengpa, Meragsagstengkha, Mira Sagtengpa, Sagtengpa). 5,000 (2006 census). Trashigang District, Sakteng valley east, mainly in Merak and Sakteng villages. *Status:* 6a (Vigorous). *Class:* Sino-Tibetan, Tibeto-Burman, Western Tibeto-Burman, Bodish, Central Bodish, Central, Southern. *Writing:* Unwritten. *Other:* Buddhist. *Map:* 342.

Bumthangkha [kjz] (Bhumtam, Bumtang, Bumtangkha, Bumtanp, Bumthang, Bumthapkha, Kebumtamp). 20,000 (2011 SIL). Central Bhutan, Bumthang, Mangdi District around Tongsa in Mangdikha; northeast border of Kurto in Tsamangkha on the east; Yangtse District in Salabekha; Tawang; southeast Tibet. *Status:* 6a (Vigorous). *Class:* Sino-Tibetan, Tibeto-Burman, Western Tibeto-Burman, Bodish, East Bodish, Bumthang. *Dialects:* Chogor, Chunmat, Tang, Ura. Some northern varieties of Khengkha [xkf] and some southern varieties of Bumthangkha are reported by one source to likely be mutually intelligible. Tawang Monpa [twm] in India (Tawan Monba in China) is the same as, or closely related to, Bumthangkha. Lexical similarity: 92% with Khengkha [xkf], 47%–52% with Dzongkha [dzo], 62%–65% with Adap [adp], 40%–50% with Tshangla [tsj], 75%–77% with Nyenkha [neh], 70%–73% with Kurtokha [xkz]. *Lg Use:* Used as L2 by Khengkha [xkf]. *Lg Dev:* Bible portions: 1938. *Writing:* Tibetan script, Uchen style. *Other:* Buddhist. *Map:* 342.

Chalikha [tgf] (Chali, Chalipkha, Tshali, Tshalingpa). 1,500 (2011 SIL). East Bhutan Mongar District, Chali area, east bank of Kurichhu river; central and eastern Bhutan in Wangmakhar, Gorsum and Tormazhong villages. *Status:* 6a (Vigorous). *Class:* Sino-Tibetan, Tibeto-Burman, Western Tibeto-Burman, Bodish, East Bodish, Bumthang. *Dialects:* None known. Related to Bumthangkha [kjz] and Kurtokha [xkz]. *Writing:* Unwritten. *Map:* 342.

Chocangacakha [cgk] (Kursmadkha, Maphekha, Rtsamangpa'ikha, Tsagkaglingpa'ikha). 30,000 (2011 SIL). Mongar District, lower areas east of Dzongkha, Tsamang and Tsakaling; Lhuntsi District, Kurmet; Kurmey, Jarey, Tamochhu, Lingmithang, Thridangbi, Minje, Tormazhog, Autsho, Karmashangshang, Gorgen, Budur, Kupinyelsa. *Status:* 6a (Vigorous). *Class:* Sino-Tibetan, Tibeto-Burman, Western Tibeto-Burman, Bodish, Central Bodish, Central, Southern. *Dialects:* None known. Related to Dzongkha [dzo]. *Writing:* Unwritten. *Map:* 342.

Dakpakha [dka]. 2,000 (2011 SIL). North Trashigang District, near Brokpake, in Chaleng, Phongmey, Yobinang, Dangpholeng and Lengkhar near Radhi. *Status:* 6a (Vigorous). *Class:* Sino-Tibetan, Tibeto-Burman, Western Tibeto-Burman, Bodish, East Bodish. *Dialects:* May be dialect of Brokpake [sgt]. Has been influenced by Dzalakha [dzl], and Brokpake has not. *Writing:* Unwritten. *Map:* 342.

Dzalakha [dzl] (Dzala, Dzalamat, Yangtsebikha). 22,000

(2011 SIL). East Lhuntse and Yangtse districts. *Status:* 6a (Vigorous). *Class:* Sino-Tibetan, Tibeto-Burman, Western Tibeto-Burman, Bodish, East Bodish, Bumthang. *Dialect:* Khomakha. *Writing:* Unwritten. *Map:* 342.

Dzongkha [dzo] (Bhotia of Bhutan, Bhotia of Dukpa, Bhutanese, Drukha, Drukke, Dukpa, Jonkha, Rdzongkha, Zongkhar). 160,000 in Bhutan (2006). Population total all countries: 171,080. Ha, Paru, Punakha districts. Also in India, Nepal. *Status:* 1 (National). Statutory national language (2008, Constitution, Article 1(8)). *Class:* Sino-Tibetan, Tibeto-Burman, Western Tibeto-Burman, Bodish, Central Bodish, Central, Southern. *Dialects:* Ha, Northern Thimphu, Wang-The (Thimphu-Punakha). As different from Central Tibetan [bod] as Nepali [npi] is from Hindi [hin]. Partially intelligible with Sikkimese [sip] (Denjoke). Dialects may be separate languages. Lexical similarity: 48% with Tshangla [tsj], 47%–52% with Bumthangkha [kjz], 77% with Adap [adp]. *Lg Use:* Also use Dzongkha [dzo]. *Lg Dev:* Literacy rate in L1: 54%. Literacy rate in L2: Below 5%. Common school language. Radio programs. Grammar. NT: 2000. *Writing:* Tibetan script, official usage. *Other:* Buddhist. *Map:* 342.

English [eng]. *Status:* 3 (Wider communication). De facto national working language. *Lg Use:* Education, government, commerce, media. Used as L2 by Khengkha [xkf]. *Lg Dev:* Taught in primary and secondary schools. See main entry on page 319.

Gongduk [goe] (Gongdubikha). 2,000 (2006). East Bhutan, Mongar District, Gongdu Gewog; Dagsa, Damkhar, Pangthang, Pam, Yangbari, Bala. *Status:* 6b (Threatened). *Class:* Sino-Tibetan, Tibeto-Burman, Western Tibeto-Burman, Bodish. *Writing:* Unwritten. *Other:* Retains the complex verbal agreement system of Proto-Tibeto-Burman. Said to belong to an ancient population of Bhutan. *Map:* 342.

Khengkha [xkf] (Ken, Keng, Kenkha, Khen, Khenkha, Kyengkha). 50,000 (2003 SIL). 30,000 monolinguals. L2 users: 15,000. Zhemgang, Mongar districts; near Bumthangkha. Middle Kheng in Northwest Zhemgang; Upper Khen northeast of Zhemgang; also Mongar District; Lower Kheng in southern Zhemgang. *Status:* 6a (Vigorous). *Class:* Sino-Tibetan, Tibeto-Burman, Western Tibeto-Burman, Bodish, East Bodish, Bumthang. *Dialects:* Lower Kheng, Middle Kheng, Upper Kheng. Bumthangkha [kjz] reportedly most similar related language, but comprehension not sufficient for complex discourse. Comprehend Kurtokha [xkz] with difficulty. Lexical similarity: 75%–85% with Bumthangkha [kjz], 70% with Kurtokha [xkz] and Nyengkha [neh], 65% with Adap [adp], 34% with Dzongkha [dzo], 40% with Tshangla [tsj], and 75%–100% between dialects. *Type:* SOV; postpositions; genitives, relatives before noun heads, articles, adjective after noun heads; maximum prefixes 1; maximum suffixes 4; affixes indicate case; ergative; passives; causatives; some comparatives; CCVC; tonal. *Lg Use:* Vigorous. Home, commerce, local politics, traditional religion, but not allowed in school. All ages. Negative attitudes toward Gonphu village speaking style. Lower Kheng considered most backward; Middle Kheng most prestigious. Bumthangkha [kjz] spoken by those who travel or have intermarried. Dzongkha [dzo] spoken well only by educated and some older males. English [eng] used by educated young people (10%). Kurtokha [xkz] spoken by those who travel or have intermarried. Nepali [npi] spoken by those who live near the road (20%). Nyengkha [neh] spoken by those who travel or have intermarried. Tshangla [tsj] spoken by those who travel east of Kheng area. *Lg Dev:* Literacy rate in L2: 20% in Dzongkha [dzo]. Bible portions: 2008. *Writing:* Tibetan script, Uchen style, unofficial usage. *Other:* Middle Kheng region strongest and most developed economically; Lower Kheng least developed. Buddhist. *Map:* 342.

Kurtokha [xkz] (Gurtü, Kurteopkha, Kürthöpka, Kurthopkha, Kurtobikha, Kurtopakha). 15,000 (2011 SIL). Northwest Lhuntsi District, especially Kurto. Bounded by Kurichhu river east and north, Tangmachhu village south and Rodula Pass west. *Status:* 6a (Vigorous). *Class:* Sino-Tibetan, Tibeto-Burman, Western Tibeto-Burman, Bodish, East Bodish, Bumthang. *Dialects:* The dialect around Tangmachhu is more divergent. Lexical similarity: 69% with Nyengkha [neh], 70%–73% with Bumthangkha, 66%–74% with Khengkha. *Lg Use:* Used as L2 by Khengkha [xkf]. *Writing:* Unwritten. *Map:* 342.

Kurux [kru] (Kurukh, Oraoan, Uraon). 4,200 in Bhutan (2002). *Status:* 6b (Threatened). See main entry on page 124.

Lakha [lkh] (Tshangkha). 8,000 (Van Driem 1993). *Status:* 6b (Threatened). *Class:* Sino-Tibetan, Tibeto-Burman, Western Tibeto-Burman, Bodish, Central Bodish, Central, Southern. *Writing:* Unwritten. *Map:* 342.

Layakha [lya]. 1,100 (2003). North Punakha District, around Laya; Gasa District; Thimphu District, Lingzhi Gewog. *Status:* 6a (Vigorous). *Class:* Sino-Tibetan, Tibeto-Burman, Western Tibeto-Burman, Bodish, Central Bodish, Central, Southern. *Dialects:* None known. Reportedly similar to Dzongkha [dzo], but many divergent grammatical features significantly limit mutual intelligibility. Spoken by Layabs, alpine yakherds in northern Bhutan, and Lingzhibs in Western Bhutan. *Writing:* Unwritten. *Map:* 342.

Lepcha [lep] (Lapcha, Nünpa, Rong, Rongke, Rongpa). 2,000 in Bhutan (2006). West and south lower valleys. *Status:* 6b (Threatened). *Dialects:* Ilammu, Rengjongmu, Tamsangmu. *Other:* Traditional religion, Buddhist (Lamaist). See main entry on page 125. *Map:* 342.

Lhokpu [lhp] (Lhobikha, Taba-Damey-Bikha). 2,500 (Van Driem 1993). Southwest Bhutan, Samtsi District between Samtsi and Phuntsoling; Taba Damtey, Loto Kuchu, Sanglong, Sataka, and Lotu villages. *Status:* 6b (Threatened). *Class:* Sino-Tibetan, Tibeto-Burman, Western Tibeto-Burman, Bodish. *Writing:* Unwritten. *Other:* An ancient population of Bhutan. *Map:* 342.

Lunanakha [luk]. 700 (1998). Punakha District, north, northeast quadrant, Lunana, on Pho Chhu river north from Punakha, right fork halfway up the valley. *Status:* 6a (Vigorous). *Class:* Sino-Tibetan, Tibeto-Burman, Western Tibeto-Burman, Bodish, Central Bodish, Central, Southern. *Dialects:* None known. Reportedly similar to Dzongkha [dzo], but many divergent grammatical features limit intelligibility between them. *Writing:* Unwritten. *Other:* Take herds over to Gasa District, north from Punakha up the Mo Chhu River. *Map:* 342.

Nepali [npi] (Eastern Pahari, Gorkhali, Gurkhali, Khaskura, Lhotshammikha, Nepalese, Parbatiya). 156,000 in Bhutan (2006). Foothills the entire length of Bhutan, especially south central. *Status:* 5 (Dispersed). De facto language of provincial identity in entire length of foothills, especially south central region. *Lg Use:* Used as L2 by Khengkha [xkf]. *Other:* May be majority language of the south. Many are Bhutanese citizens. Hindu. See main entry on page 256. *Map:* 342.

Nupbikha [npb] (Trongsakha). 2,200 (2006). Trongsa area. *Status:* 6a (Vigorous). *Class:* Sino-Tibetan, Tibeto-Burman, Western Tibeto-Burman, Bodish, East Bodish, Bumthang. *Dialects:* None known. Phonological similarities to

Khengkha [xkf]. *Writing:* Unwritten. *Other:* View their language as different from Bumthangkha [kjz]. *Map:* 342.

Nyenkha [neh] (Henkha, Lap, Mangdhika, Mangsdekha). 10,000 (2006 Royal Gov't of Bhutan). Mangdi (Trongsa) District, Tongsa town, Sephu Geo area; Black river passes below their villages: Taktse, Usar and Tashidingkha, Phobjikha, Ridha, Dangchhu; surrounding hamlets southeast of Wangdue-Phodrang District. *Status:* 6a (Vigorous). *Class:* Sino-Tibetan, Tibeto-Burman, Western Tibeto-Burman, Bodish, East Bodish, Bumthang. *Dialects:* Chutobikha, Phobjikha. Lexical similarity: 69% with Kurtokha [xkz], 75%-77% with Bumthangkha [kjz], 65%-78% with Khengkha [xkf]. *Lg Use:* Used as L2 by Khengkha [xkf]. *Writing:* Unwritten. *Map:* 342.

Olekha [ole] (Black Mountain Language, Monkha, Monpa, Ole Mönpa). 500 (Van Driem 2007). 5 villages: Adha, Rukha, Wangling, Jangji, Thrumzur. The 2 dialects are separated by the Black mountains. *Status:* 6b (Threatened). *Class:* Sino-Tibetan, Tibeto-Burman, Western Tibeto-Burman, Bodish. *Dialects:* None known. Retained complex verbal system of Proto-Tibeto-Burman. *Writing:* Unwritten. *Other:* Reportedly an ancient population of Bhutan. *Map:* 342.

Tshangla [tsj] (Menba, Monpa, Sangla, Sarchapkkha, Shachobiikha, Shachopkha, Sharchagpakha, Sharchhop-kha, Tsangla, Tshalingpa). 140,000 in Bhutan (1999 SIL). Population total all countries: 158,200. East and southeast Bhutan, especially Trashigang and Dungsam. Also in China, India. *Status:* 4 (Educational). De facto language of provincial identity in eastern and southeastern Bhutan. *Class:* Sino-Tibetan, Tibeto-Burman, Western Tibeto-Burman, Bodish. *Dialects:* None known. Standard variety in Tashigang. Tshangla is nearly identical to that of eastern Bhutan, except for the loss of initial voicing and tonogenesis in Tibet. Differs from Tawan Monba [twm] in phonology, vocabulary, and grammar, and Tawan Monba and Tshangla are not mutually intelligible. Lexical similarity: 40%-50% with Bumthangkha [kjz], 48% with Dzongkha [dzo], 41% with Adap [adp]. *Type:* SOV; numbers and adjectives follow noun head; singular-dual-plural personal pronouns; nontonal. *Lg Use:* Also use Dzongkha [dzo]. Used as L2 by Khengkha [xkf]. *Lg Dev:* Literacy rate in L1: 47% (2003 SIL). Literacy rate in L2: Below 1%. Radio programs. Grammar. Bible portions: 2000. *Writing:* Tibetan script, Uchen style, used in India. *Other:* Ethnonym: Schachop (sg.), Sharchhokpa (pl.) in Dzongkha. Not the same as Tsanglo (Angami Naga) of Assam, India. May also be classified as North Assam, Monpa. Buddhist. *Map:* 342.

British Indian Ocean Territory

British Overseas Territory. 4,000 (2004 census). Principal language: English. Indigenous population removed. Military personnel only.

Only 1 language is listed for British Indian Ocean Territory. It is living and institutional.

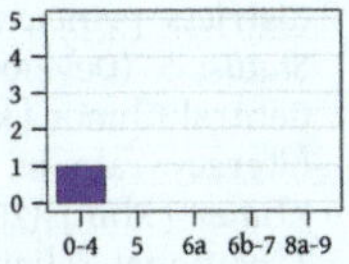

English [eng]. 3,500 in British Indian Ocean Territory (2004). *Status:* 1 (National). De facto national language. *Other:* The indigenous population no longer resides in the islands. Current residents include members of the United States military, a small detachment of British officials, and support staff, mainly of Mauritian and Philippine origin. See main entry on page 319.

Brunei

State of Brunei Darussalam, Negara Brunei Darussalam. 393,000 (2011 census). Principal languages: Brunei, Brunei Bisaya, English, Standard Malay. Literacy rate: 94% (2011 USDS). General references: Martin 1995; Martin, Oxog, and Poedjosoedarmo 1996; Purnama 1991; Wurm and Hattori 1981.

The number of individual languages listed for Brunei is 14. All are living languages. Of these, 7 are institutional, 3 are developing, 1 is vigorous, and 3 are in trouble. See map on page 387.

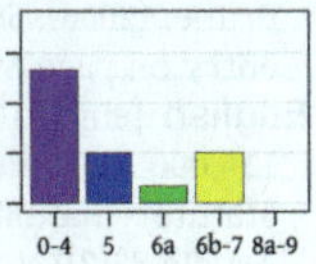

Belait [beg] (Balait Jati, Lemeting, Meting). 1,000 in Brunei. Scattered in Belait District; Tutong District in Kampung Kiudang. Also in Malaysia. *Status:* 7 (Shifting). *Class:* Austronesian, Malayo-Polynesian, North Borneo, North Sarawakan, Berawan-Lower Baram, Lower Baram, Central, A. *Dialects:* None known. Lexical similarity: 54% with Tutong [ttg]. *Lg Use:* Shifting to Brunei Malay [kxd]. Mainly adults. *Writing:* Unwritten. *Other:* Recognized indigenous group. Muslim Belait are Malay in orientation. Non-Muslims retain their Belait identity more. Heavy intermarriage with Bisaya and Chinese. Muslim. *Map:* 387:64.

Bisaya, Brunei [bsb] (Basaya, Bekiau, Besaya, Bisaia, Bisaya Bukit, Bisayah, Dusun, Jilama Bawang, Jilama Sungai, Lorang Bukit, Southern Bisaya, Tutong 1, Visayak). 37,600 in Brunei (2007 SIL). Population total all countries: 57,600. Central and interior Belait and Tutong districts, south of Tutong [ttg] language area; Brunei dialect around Seria town and a few villages near Sarawak border. Also in Malaysia. *Status:* 5 (Developing). De facto language of national identity. *Class:* Austronesian, Malayo-Polynesian, North Borneo, Sabahan, Dusunic, Bisaya, Southern. *Dialects:* Brunei Bisaya, Sarawak Bisaya, Tutong 1. Lexical similarity: 78% with dialects spoken in Brunei and Sarawak, lower with other Dusunic languages. *Lg Use:* Also use Brunei [kxd]. *Lg Dev:* Radio programs. Bible portions: 1938. *Writing:* Latin script. *Other:* Recognized indigenous group. *Map:* 387:66.

Brunei [kxd] (Brunei-Kadaian, Orang Bukit). 215,000 in Brunei (1984 SIL), increasing. Population total all countries: 266,000. Bandar Seri Bagawan; Mara District, Kedayan; the coastal strip; Tutong District. Also in Malaysia. *Status:* 3 (Wider communication). De facto national working language. *Class:* Austronesian, Malayo-Polynesian, Malayo-Chamic, Malayic, Malay. A member of macrolanguage Malay [msa] (Malaysia). *Dialects:* Brunei Malay, Kampong Ayer, Kedayan (Kadaian, Kadayan, Kadian, Kadien, Kadyan, Karayan, Kedien, Kedyan, Kerayan). Lexical similarity: 94%-95% between Brunei and the Kampong Ayer dialects, 80%-82% with Standard Malay [zsm]. *Lg Use:* Vigorous. Used in Bandar Seri Begawan and surrounding areas, and by young people and educated older people from different language or dialect backgrounds. All ages. Positive attitudes. Also use Standard Malay [zsm]. Used as L2 by Brunei Bisaya [bsb], Central Melanau [mel]. *Other:* Brunei and Kadayan are recognized indigenous groups. Ethnic autonym: Orang Bukit. Muslim. *Map:* 387:63.

Chinese, Hakka [hak] (Hakka). 5,650 in Brunei (2006). *Status:* 3 (Wider communication). See main entry on page 67.

Chinese, Mandarin [cmn]. 10,600 in Brunei (2006). *Status:* 3 (Wider communication). See main entry on page 67.

Chinese, Min Dong [cdo]. 7,060 in Brunei (2006). *Status:* 3 (Wider communication). *Dialect:* Foochow. *Other:* Buddhist, Christian, Daoist. See main entry on page 68.

Chinese, Min Nan [nan] (Min Nan, Minnan). 13,100 in Brunei (2006). *Status:* 3 (Wider communication). *Dialects:* Hainan, Hokkien (Fujian), Teochew (Chaochow, Tiuchiu). See main entry on page 68.

Chinese, Yue [yue] (Cantonese, Yue, Yueh). 6,350 in Brunei (2006). *Status:* 3 (Wider communication). See main entry on page 69.

English [eng]. 10,000 in Brunei (Crystal 2003). L2 users: 134,000 in Brunei (Crystal 2003). *Status:* 1 (National). Statutory national working language (1984, Constitution, Article 82(2)). *Lg Use:* Government, education, and by the educated as L1 or L2. See main entry on page 319.

Iban [iba] (Sea Dayak). 21,400 in Brunei. Rural areas of Belait and Tutong districts; Temburong District. *Status:* 5 (Developing). *Dialects:* Batang Lupar, Bugau. See main entry on page 221. *Map:* 387:42.

Lun Bawang [lnd] (Lun Daya, Lun Dayah, Lun Daye, Lun Dayoh, Lundaya, Southern Murut). 500 in Brunei (2006 SIL). Interior, from Brunei Bay to Padas, then to Baram river headwaters, Temburong District. 7 villages. *Status:* 5 (Developing). *Dialects:* Long Iluk, Lun Ba, Trusan. *Other:* Not Murutic, although sometimes called Southern Murut. Murut is a recognized indigenous group. Christian, traditional religion. See main entry on page 175. *Map:* 387:74.

Malay, Standard [zsm] (Formal Malay, Malay, Malayu, Melayu, Melayu Baku). L2 users: L2 only. *Status:* 1 (National). Statutory national language (1984, Constitution, Article 82(1)). *Lg Use:* Formal domains, religion, government. *Lg Dev:* Taught through third grade; used in the classroom through the final year. *Other:* L2 only. See main entry on page 224.

Melanau, Central [mel] (Belana'u, Melanau, Milanau, Milano). 280 in Brunei (2006 SIL). Around Kuala Belait town. *Status:* 6a (Vigorous). *Dialect:* Mukah-Oya (Muka, Mukah, Oga, Oya, Oya'). *Lg Use:* Also use Brunei [kxd]. *Other:* Mukah dialect is spoken in Brunei. Muslim. See main entry on page 224. *Map:* 387:38.

Penan, Eastern [pez]. 55 in Brunei (2003 P. Sercombe). West of the Baram river. *Status:* 6b (Threatened). *Dialects:* Bok Penan (Bok), Jelalong Penan, Nibong (Nibon, Penan Nibong), Penan Gang (Gang), Penan Lanying, Penan Lusong (Lusong), Penan Silat, Sipeng (Speng). See main entry on page 225. *Map:* 387:70.

Tutong [ttg] (Tutong 2, Tutung). 16,600 (2006 SIL). Around Tutong town on the coast and central Tutong District. *Status:* 6b (Threatened). *Class:* Austronesian, Malayo-Polynesian, North Borneo, North Sarawakan, Berawan-Lower Baram, Lower Baram, Central, B. *Dialects:* None known. Lexical similarity: 54% with Belait [beg] in Malaysia. *Lg Use:* Used with other ethnic groups. Parents in mixed marriages tend to use Brunei Malay [kxd] with their children. Positive attitudes. *Lg Dev:* Grammar. *Other:* Different from Brunei Bisaya [bsb] in Dusunic, Bisaya Group. Recognized indigenous group. Muslim. *Map:* 387:65.

Cambodia

Kingdom of Cambodia. 15,200,000 (2013 World Factbook). Principal languages: Central Khmer, English. Literacy rate: 66% (2007 UNESCO). Immigrant languages: Min Nan Chinese (350,000), Yue Chinese (20,000). General references: Bradley 2007; Diffloth and Zide 1992; Lebar, Hickey, and Musgrave 1964; Thomas and Headley 1970; Voegelin and Voegelin 1977; Wurm and Hattori 1981. Deaf population: 85,000.

The number of individual languages listed for Cambodia is 22. All are living languages. Of these, 1 is institutional, 5 are developing, 2 are vigorous, 10 are in trouble, and 4 are dying. See map on page 343.

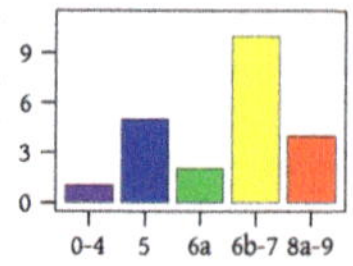

Brao [brb] (Braou, Brou, Lave, Laveh, Love, Proue). 9,030 in Cambodia (2008 census). About 2,000 of the Brao counted in the census are Brao Tanap, which is actually more similar to Krung [krr]. 4,520 monolinguals. Ethnic population: 9,030. Northeast Cambodia, north Ratanakiri Province, especially Ta Veaeng district, north of Sesan river. *Status:* 5 (Developing). *Dialects:* Hamong, Jrii, Ka-nying, Lun, Ombaa. *Lg Use:* All ages. Positive attitudes. 50% also use Central Khmer [khm]. *Lg Dev:* Literacy rate in L2: 34% can read Khmer [khm]. Government-run classes. *Other:* Krung [krr], Brao [brb], Kavet [krv], and Lun dialect [brb] form a mutually-intelligible cluster. At times, Brao may be used as a cover term for all groups. Traditional religion, Christian. See main entry on page 215 (as Lave). *Map:* 343.

Cham, Western [cja] (Cambodian Cham, Cham, New Cham, Tjam). 204,000 in Cambodia (2008 census). Population total all countries: 246,990. 0 monolinguals. Ethnic population: 400,000. Near major cities; Kampong Cham and Kampong Chnang along Mekong and Tonle Sap rivers. Also in France, Libya, Malaysia, Saudi Arabia, Thailand, United States, Viet Nam, Yemen. *Status:* 6a (Vigorous). *Class:* Austronesian, Malayo-Polynesian, Malayo-Chamic, Chamic, Coastal, Cham. *Dialects:* None known. Cannot communicate with Eastern Cham [cjm] of central Viet Nam. Lexical similarity: 84% with Eastern Cham [cjm] of Vietnam (Pawley 2010), 69% with Jarai [jra] of northeast Cambodia. *Lg Use:* All domains. All ages. Positive attitudes. 100% also use Central Khmer [khm]. *Lg Dev:* Literacy rate in L1: 30%. Literacy rate in L2: 50% in Khmer [khm]. Many children learn to read Cham using Arabic-based script in madrassah schools. In one sect, most people over age 50 can read using the ancient Cham script called Kakha. Radio programs. Dictionary. *Writing:* Arabic script. Cham script. Latin script. *Other:* Small ethnic groups from Cambodia settled in Thailand but no longer speak Cham (Bradley 2007). Muslim (Sunni). *Map:* 343.

Chinese, Hakka [hak]. 500 in Cambodia (2011 SIL). Stung Treng, Ratanakiri. *Status:* 6a (Vigorous). See main entry on page 67. *Map:* 343.

Jarai [jra] (Chor, Cho-Rai, Chrai, Djarai, Gia-Rai, Gio-Rai, Jorai, Mthur). 20,800 in Cambodia (2008 census). Ratanakiri Province, Bar Kaev, Andoung Meas, Ou Ya Dav districts principally, northeast border near Viet Nam. *Status:* 5 (Developing). *Lg Use:* All ages. 50% also use Central Khmer [khm]. Used as L2 by Kaco' [xkk]. *Lg Dev:* Literacy rate in L1: 20%. Literacy rate in L2: 20% in Khmer [khm] (2010 E. Pawley and M-S. Pawley). *Other:* Traditional religion, Christian. See main entry on page 311. *Map:* 343.

Kaco' [xkk] (Kachah'). 3,370 (2007). Ratanakiri Province, Andoung Meas and Veun Sai districts. *Status:* 6b (Threatened). *Class:* Austro-Asiatic, Mon-Khmer, Eastern Mon-Khmer, Bahnaric, North Bahnaric. *Lg Use:* Also use Central Khmer [khm], Jarai [jra], Lao [lao], Vietnamese [vie]. *Map:* 343.

Kavet [krv] (Khvek, Kowet, Kravet). 6,220 (2008 census).

Stung Treng and Ratanakiri provinces, Laos-Cambodia border area. *Status:* 6b (Threatened). *Class:* Austro-Asiatic, Mon-Khmer, Eastern Mon-Khmer, Bahnaric, West Bahnaric, Brao-Kravet. *Writing:* Khmer script. *Map:* 343.

Khmer, Central [khm] (Cambodian, Khmer). 12,900,000 in Cambodia (2008 census). Population total all countries: 14,224,500. L2 users: 1,000,000 in Cambodia. Widespread. Also in Canada, China, France, Laos, United States, Viet Nam. *Status:* 1 (National). Statutory national language (1993, Constitution, Article 5). *Class:* Austro-Asiatic, Mon-Khmer, Eastern Mon-Khmer, Khmer. *Dialects:* Battambang Khmer, Cardamom Khmer, Khmer Kandal (Central), Khmer Keh (Stung Treng), Khmer Krom (Southern). Distinct from Northern Khmer [kxm] of Thailand. *Type:* SVO. *Lg Dev:* 35% of the population over 15 cannot read or write Khmer. Radio programs. Grammar. Bible: 1954–1998. *Writing:* Khmer script.

Kraol [rka]. 4,200 (2008 census). 4,200 monolinguals. Kratie Province. *Status:* 6b (Threatened). *Class:* Austro-Asiatic, Mon-Khmer, Eastern Mon-Khmer, Bahnaric, South Bahnaric, Sre-Mnong, Mnong, Southern-Central Mnong. *Dialects:* None known. Not intelligible to speakers of Central Mnong [cmo]. *Other:* Different from Kraol dialect of Kuy [kdt]. *Map:* 343.

Kru'ng 2 [krr] (Brao Krung, Kreung). 20,700 (2008 census). Stung Treng and Ratanakiri provinces, Laos-Cambodia border area. *Status:* 6b (Threatened). *Class:* Austro-Asiatic, Mon-Khmer, Eastern Mon-Khmer, Bahnaric, West Bahnaric, Brao-Kravet. *Dialects:* Brao Tanap, Lun. Brao [brb] and Kavet [krv] are reportedly inherently intelligible with Kru'ng 2. *Lg Use:* Also use Central Khmer [khm], Lao [lao]. *Lg Dev:* Bible portions: 2012. *Writing:* Khmer script. *Other:* Different from Krung 1 dialect of Rade [rad] in Viet Nam. *Map:* 343.

Kuy [kdt] (Kuay). 10,000 in Cambodia. Ethnic population: 37,700. Northeast Cambodia, Preah Vihear Province, most districts; east Siem Reap, north Kampong Thom, west Stung Traeng, and Kratie provinces. *Status:* 7 (Shifting). *Dialects:* Kuy Ak, Kuy Anthua, Kuy Antra, Kuy May (Kuy Ma'ay), Kuy Mlor. *Lg Use:* Also use Central Khmer [khm]. *Lg Dev:* Literacy rate in L2: 50%. *Other:* Central Khmer used in schools. Dialects are based on the use of their word for 'what': Kuy Antra (northern Kompong Thom, southern Preah Vihear), Kuy Anthua (central Preah Vihear), Kuy May or Ma'ay (in Kratie), Kuy Mlor (1 village in northern Preah Vihear); only the older people still speak the last 2 dialects. See main entry on page 301. *Map:* 343.

Lao [lao]. 21,600 in Cambodia. *Status:* 6b (Threatened). *Lg Use:* Used as L2 by Kaco' [xkk], Kru'ng 2 [krr], Tampuan [tpu]. See main entry on page 215. *Map:* 343.

Lao Phuon [phu]. 1,000 in Cambodia (2013). Ethnic population: 2,000 (2013 SIL). Banteay Meanchey Province, Mongkol Borei district, Pong Ror, Rohat Teak, Ta Sal, Sranal, Prey To Teang, Pouy Ta Sek, Boung Preang, Sdey Leu, Sdey Kraom, and Kok Thnong villages. *Status:* 6b (Threatened). See main entry on page 303 (as Phuan).

Mnong, Central [cmo] (Budong, Bunong, Phanong, Phnong, Phong). 37,500 in Cambodia (2008 census). Northeast, 80% of Mondolkiri Province, all districts. *Status:* 5 (Developing). *Dialects:* Biat, Bu Dang, Bu Nar, Bu Rung, Dih Bri, Preh. *Lg Use:* All ages. Most have low proficiency in Central Khmer [khm]. Used as L2 by Bulo Stieng [sti]. *Lg Dev:* Literacy rate in L2: Low. *Other:* Biat is main dialect. See main entry on page 313. *Map:* 343.

Pear [pcb] (Por). 1,670 (2011). Ethnic population: 1,830 (2008 census). Preah Vihear Province, Rovieng district, 3 to 4 villages. *Status:* 8a (Moribund). *Class:* Austro-Asiatic, Mon-Khmer, Eastern Mon-Khmer, Pearic, Eastern. *Map:* 343.

Samre [sxm]. No known L1 speakers. Ethnic population: 200 (2000 D. Bradley). *Status:* 9 (Dormant). *Class:* Austro-Asiatic, Mon-Khmer, Eastern Mon-Khmer, Pearic, Western, Samre. *Lg Use:* Shifting to Khmer [khm].

Sa'och [scq] (Saotch, Sauch). 10 (2009 Filipi), decreasing. Ethnic population: 450. Southwest near Kompong Som on the coast. *Status:* 8b (Nearly extinct). *Class:* Austro-Asiatic, Mon-Khmer, Eastern Mon-Khmer, Pearic, Western, Chong. *Lg Use:* Even elders rarely speak the language and are forgetting it. Negative attitudes. *Map:* 343.

Somray [smu]. 4,100 (2005 J. Ironside). Pursat Province, north, east, and west of Phum Tasanh, and Tanyong river around Phum Pra Moi; 2 areas. *Status:* 8a (Moribund). *Class:* Austro-Asiatic, Mon-Khmer, Eastern Mon-Khmer, Pearic, Western, Samre. *Map:* 343.

Stieng, Bulo [sti] (Kajiang). 6,540 in Cambodia (2008 census). East, Kratie Province, Snuol district, and southern Mondolkiri. *Status:* 6b (Threatened). *Dialects:* Budip, Bulo. *Lg Use:* Also use Central Khmer [khm], Central Mnong [cmo]. *Lg Dev:* Literacy rate in L2: Low. See main entry on page 315. *Map:* 343.

Suoy [syo] (Su'ung). 860 (Bradley 2007), decreasing. Kompong Speu Province. *Status:* 7 (Shifting). *Class:* Austro-Asiatic, Mon-Khmer, Eastern Mon-Khmer, Pearic, Western, Suoy. *Lg Use:* Religion. Mainly older adults. 100% also use Central Khmer [khm]. *Map:* 343.

Tampuan [tpu] (Campuon, Kha Tampuon, Proon, Proons, Tamphuan, Tampuen, Tampuon). 31,000 in Cambodia (2008 census). Northeast border area, Central Ratanakiri Province, south of Brao, west of Jarai. Also in Laos. *Status:* 6b (Threatened). *Class:* Austro-Asiatic, Mon-Khmer, Eastern Mon-Khmer, Bahnaric, Central Bahnaric. *Lg Use:* Vigorous. All domains. All ages. Also use Central Khmer [khm], Lao [lao]. *Lg Dev:* Literacy rate in L1: 5%. Literacy rate in L2: 10%. Taught in primary schools. Pilot formal education programme begun in 3 elementary schools in 2003. *Writing:* Khmer script. *Other:* Exogamous clans, together with Kaco' and Jarai, override ethnic and linguistic boundaries. *Map:* 343.

Thai [tha]. 2,460 in Cambodia (2008 census). Thai Koh Kong in Koh Kong Province; Thai Norkor Raja in Banteay Meanchey Province. *Status:* 5 (Dispersed). *Dialects:* Thai Koh Kong, Thai Norkor Raja (Siam Nokor, Siam Trang). See main entry on page 304. *Map:* 343.

Vietnamese [vie]. 72,800 in Cambodia (2008 census). *Status:* 5 (Dispersed). *Lg Use:* All ages. Used as L2 by Kaco' [xkk]. See main entry on page 316.

China

People's Republic of China. 1,282,780,000 (2010 census). Principal language: Mandarin Chinese. Literacy rate: 91% (2010 USDS). Immigrant languages: Central Khmer (1,000), Parsi (5,000). General references: Bradley 1997, 2005, 2007; Dreyer 1976; Janhunen 1989, 2003; Li Fang-gui 1973; Matisoff, Baron, and Lowe 1996; Pelkey 2008, 2011; Ramsey 1987; Salminen 2007; Wurm et al. 1987; Xiong and Yang 1991. Deaf population: 20,040,000 (2006 China Disabled Persons' Federation). Deaf institutions: There are 550 schools for the deaf in addition to 683 special education schools in mainland China, some of which have classes for the deaf. Recognized nationalities: Minority languages in China are associated with one or more officially recognized nationalities by the State Ethnic Affairs Commission.

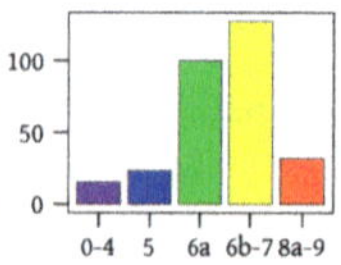

The number of individual languages listed for China is 298. All are living languages. Of these, 15 are institutional, 23 are developing, 100 are vigorous, 128 are in trouble, and 32 are dying. See maps beginning on page 344.

Achang [acn] (Acang, Ach'ang, Achung, Ahchan, Atsang, Maingtha, Mönghsa, Ngacang, Ngac'ang, Ngachang, Ngatsang, Ngo Chang, Ngochang, Xiandao). 27,700 in China (1990 census). Population total all countries: 62,700. Ethnic population: 34,000 (2000 census). Western Yunnan Province, Dehong Dai-Jingpo autonomous prefecture and Baoshan district, along the Myanmar border, Longchuan, Liangge, Yingjiang, and Luxi counties; Baoshan prefecture, Tengchong and Longling counties; Dali Bai autonomous prefecture, Yunlong county. Also in Myanmar. *Status:* 7 (Shifting). Language of recognized nationality: Achang. *Class:* Sino-Tibetan, Tibeto-Burman, Ngwi-Burmese, Burmish, Northern. *Dialects:* Husa (Chintaw, Xiandao), Lianghe, Longchuan, Luxi. Each of the 3 main counties has a distinctive dialect (Statistical Bureau of Yunnan Province 2004). No reported intelligibility between dialects. Longchuan differs more from the others, with more Dai loanwords. Lianghe and Luxi use many Chinese loanwords. There are also Burmese [mya] loanwords. Related to Hpon [hpo], Maru [mhx], Lashi [lsi], Zaiwa [atb]. *Type:* SOV; tonal, 4 tones. *Lg Use:* Longchuan dialect is stable, but other dialect speakers are shifting to Chinese. Many Han people in Longchuan County use Achang in informal situations. All domains. Mainly adults. Also use Chinese [zho], Jingpho [kac], Tai Nüa [tdd]. *Lg Dev:* Literacy rate in L2: 86% (2000 census). Bible: 2011. *Writing:* Latin script. *Other:* Mingled with Lashi [lsi]. Buddhist (Hinayana). *Map:* 345.

Ache [yif]. 35,000 (2003). Yunnan Province, Shuangbai, Yimen, Eshan, and Lufeng counties. *Status:* 6b (Threatened). Language of recognized nationality: Yi. *Class:* Sino-Tibetan, Tibeto-Burman, Ngwi-Burmese, Ngwi, Southeastern. *Other:* Traditional religion. *Map:* 345.

Ai-Cham [aih] (Atsam, Jiamuhua, Jin, Jinhua). 2,700 (2000). Southern Guizhou Province, Qiannan Buyi-Miao autonomous prefecture, Libo county, Di'e and Boyao townships. 13 villages. *Status:* 6b (Threatened). Language of recognized nationality: Bouyei. *Class:* Tai-Kadai, Kam-Tai, Kam-Sui. *Dialects:* Boyao, Di'e. Dialects have phonological differences, but are largely intelligible. Reportedly similar to Mak [mkg]. *Type:* SVO; tonal, 6 tones. *Other:* Traditional religion. *Maps:* 345, 346:38.

Ainu [aib] (Abdal, Aini, Aynu). 6,570 (2000). Southwest Xinjiang Autonomous Region, Hetian, Luopu, Moyu, Shache, Yingjisha, and Shulekuche counties; Kashgar area, Yengixar (Shule) town, Hanalik and Paynap villages, and Gewoz village near Hoban. *Status:* 6b (Threatened). Language of recognized nationality: Uygur. *Class:* Altaic, Turkic, Eastern. *Dialects:* Has the same grammar as Uyghur [uig] but much Persian [pes] vocabulary. Some consider it a dialect of Uyghur, others an Iranian language heavily influenced by Uyghur. *Lg Use:* Home. Also use Uyghur [uig] with outsiders. *Other:* Do not intermarry with ethnic Uyghur. Muslim (Sunni). *Map:* 344.

Akeu [aeu] (Aki, Akui). 10,000 in China (2007). Population total all countries: 12,400. South Yunnan Province, Xishuangbanna prefecture, most villages in Jinhong county, some in Mengla county. Also in Laos, Myanmar, Thailand. *Status:* 7 (Shifting). Language of recognized nationality: Hani. *Class:* Sino-Tibetan, Tibeto-Burman, Ngwi-Burmese, Ngwi, Southern. *Dialects:* None known. Reportedly similar to Akha [ahk]. *Lg Use:* Also use Akha [ahk]. *Lg Dev:* Bible portions. *Writing:* Latin script, developed in 2005, used mainly in Thailand and Myanmar. *Map:* 345.

Akha [ahk] (Ahka, Aini, Aka, Ak'a, Ekaw, Ikaw, Ikor, Kaw, Kha Ko, Khako, Khao Kha Ko, Ko, Yani). 240,000 in China (Bradley 2007), increasing. Ethnic population: 240,000 (Bradley 2007). Southwest Yunnan Province, Xishuangbanna and Simao prefectures. *Status:* 5 (Developing). Language of recognized nationality: Hani. *Lg Use:* All domains. All ages. Positive attitudes. Also use Mandarin Chinese [cmn]. Used as L2 by Akeu [aeu]. *Lg Dev:* Literacy rate in L1: 5%. Literacy rate in L2: 70% in any language (2000 census, Hani nationality); but functional literacy is low in Mandarin [cmn]. Orthographies in fairly wide use, but not in public schools (Bradley 2007). Taught in primary schools. *Other:* Traditional religion, Christian. See main entry on page 230. *Map:* 345.

Alugu [aub] (Muji, Phula, Phupha). 3,500 (Pelkey 2011), increasing. Ethnic population: 3,500. Yunnan Province, Yuanyang county, Fengchunling township across Honghe river; Gejiu county, Manhao township. *Status:* 6a (Vigorous). Language of recognized nationality: Yi. *Class:* Sino-Tibetan, Tibeto-Burman, Ngwi-Burmese, Ngwi, Southeastern. *Dialects:* None known. Reportedly similar to, but not intelligible with, Phupha [yph]. *Lg Use:* Home, village, market. All ages. *Lg Dev:* Taught in primary schools. *Writing:* Unwritten. *Map:* 345.

Aluo [yna] (Gan Yi, Laka, Lila, Niluo, Yala). 25,000 (2007). Ethnic population: 40,000 (Bradley 2007). Yunnan Province, north Wuding, Luquan, and Yuanmou counties; Sichuan Province, Huili and Miyi counties. *Status:* 7 (Shifting). Language of recognized nationality: Yi. *Class:* Sino-Tibetan, Tibeto-Burman, Ngwi-Burmese, Ngwi, Northern. *Lg Use:* Being replaced by Chinese or varieties of closely related Nasu or both. Severely endangered in all 3 villages in Miyi County, endangered in most other places (Bradley 2007). *Map:* 345.

Anong [nun] (Anoong, Anu, Anung, Fuch'ye, Khanung, Khupang, Kwingsang, Kwinp'ang, Lu, Lutze, Lutzu, Nu, Nung). 50 in China (Bradley 2007). One-third are speakers and another one-third have passive knowledge (Bradley 2007). 0 monolinguals. Ethnic population: 7,300 (Bradley 2007). Thanlwin (Salween) (Nu) river area: northwest Yunnan Province, Nujian Lisu autonomous prefecture, central Fugong county, Shangpa town, Mugujia village cluster. *Status:* 8a (Moribund). Language of recognized nationality: Nu. *Dialects:* Cholo, Gwaza, Miko. *Lg Use:* Most ethnic Nung have shifted to Lisu [lis] (Bradley 2007). Only adults, mainly elderly. Neutral attitudes. A few leaders are concerned about its loss. The ethnic Anong who have not shifted to Lisu [lis] are bilingual in it. Also use Mandarin Chinese [cmn]. Used as L2 by Central Bai [bca]. *Lg Dev:* Literacy rate in L2: 68% literate in any language (2000 census, Nu nationality). *Other:* Different from Nung [nut] (Tai family) of Viet Nam, Laos, and China, Nong Zhuang (Tai family) of China, and from Chinese Nung (Yue [yue]) of Viet Nam. Due to intense linguistic contact with the Lisu, Anong is being radically restructured (Sun Hong Kai and Liu Guangkun 2009). Traditional religion, Buddhist (Lamaist), Christian. See main entry on page 230. *Map:* 345.

A'ou [aou] (|Auo, Ayo). 50 (2011 SIL). West central Guizhou Province, Qianxi county, Xintian, Shawo, and Lannigou villages; Zhijin county, Longjia village; Dafang county, Jindi village. *Status:* 8b (Nearly extinct). Language of recognized nationality: Gelao. *Class:* Tai-Kadai, Kra, Western Kra. *Lg Use:* All elderly. *Writing:* Unwritten. *Map:* 345.

Awa [vwa] (Ava, Awa Wa, Va). 98,000 (Zhou Zhizhi, Qixiang Yan, and Guoqing Chen 2004). Masan Dialect: 33,000 in Ximeng County; Xiyun Dialect: 2,200 in Lancang and Menglian counties; Dawangnuo Dialect: 30,000 in Menglian and Ximeng counties; Awalei Dialect: 2,200 in Ximeng County; Awa proper: 30,600 In Lancan County. Southwest Yunnan Province, Simao prefecture: Ximeng Va, Menglian Dai, Lahu and Va, and Lancang Lahu autonomous counties. *Status:* 6b (Threatened). Language of recognized nationality: Wa. *Class:* Austro-Asiatic, Mon-Khmer, Northern Mon-Khmer, Palaungic, Eastern Palaungic, Waic, Wa. *Dialects:* Awalei ('A vo' loi, Awalai), Dawangnuo (Damangnuo, Mangnuo, Vo', Wangnuo), Masan ('A Vo', La via', Ro via', Vo'), Xiyun (Shixi, Va'). Closely related languages: Vo [wbm], Parauk [prk], and Blang [blr]. *Lg Use:* Also use Mandarin Chinese [cmn]. *Lg Dev:* Literacy rate in L2: 76% (2000 census). *Other:* Possibly also spoken in Myanmar. *Map:* 345.

Awu [yiu] (Luowu, Luwu). 20,000 (2002). Yunnan Province, primarily north Honghe prefecture, Mile and Luxi counties; south Qujing prefecture, Shizong and Luoping counties. *Status:* 6b (Threatened). Language of recognized nationality: Yi. *Class:* Sino-Tibetan, Tibeto-Burman, Ngwi-Burmese, Ngwi, Northern. *Dialects:* Northern Awu, Southern Awu. *Other:* Traditional religion. *Map:* 345.

Axi [yix] (Ahi, Axibo, Axipo). 100,000 (Bradley 2007), decreasing. Elderly and women over 35 are monolingual. L2 users: L2 users are only those who have married into Axi families. Southeast Yunnan Province, Mile and Luxi counties. Shilin county, 1 village. *Status:* 6b (Threatened). Language of recognized nationality: Yi. *Class:* Sino-Tibetan, Tibeto-Burman, Ngwi-Burmese, Ngwi, Southeastern. *Type:* SOV. *Lg Use:* Many Axi aged 30 or less are unfamiliar with botanical or zoological terms, and tend to be unfamiliar with traditional stories and legends. All domains. All ages. Positive attitudes. Those early 30's and under are highly proficient in the local Chinese dialect and Mandarin. *Lg Dev:* Literacy rate in L1: 0%. Literacy rate in L2: Low. Taught in primary schools. Poetry. Dictionary. Grammar. *Writing:* Unwritten. *Other:* Traditional religion. *Map:* 345.

Ayizi [yyz]. 50 (2007), decreasing. Ethnic population: 2,000 (Bradley 2007). Yunnan Province, Shilin county, Beidacun district, mainly in Aimalong village; also other villages of Beidacun and Banqiao districts. *Status:* 8b (Nearly extinct). Language of recognized nationality: Yi. *Class:* Sino-Tibetan, Tibeto-Burman, Ngwi-Burmese, Ngwi, Northern. *Lg Use:* Extinct in most places; moribund at best in Aimalong (Bradley 2007). *Map:* 345.

Azha [aza] (Aji, Ajiwa, A'ndze, A'ntsaozo, Azan, Black Phula, Cowtail Phula, Golden Phula, Han Phula, Hei Phula, Hua Phula, Hua Yi, Jin Phula, Nimitso, Niuweiba Phula, Phula, Phuphje, Shaoji Phula, Sifter Basket Phula). 53,000 (2007). Yunnan Province, primarily along the border between Wenshan and Yanshan counties. *Status:* 6a (Vigorous). Language of recognized nationality: Yi. *Class:* Sino-Tibetan, Tibeto-Burman, Ngwi-Burmese, Ngwi, Southeastern. *Lg Use:* All ages. *Map:* 345.

Azhe [yiz]. 54,000 (Bradley 2007). Ethnic population: 60,000. Yunnan Province, Mile county: Xun Jian, Wushan, and Jiangbian districts; Huaning county, Panxi district; north Kaiyuan county, Xiaolongtan district, Xiaolongtan community; Lebaidao district, Jiedian community; Mazheshao district, Chongzi community; northeast Jianshui county, 1 village. *Status:* 6a (Vigorous). Language of recognized nationality: Yi. *Class:* Sino-Tibetan, Tibeto-Burman, Ngwi-Burmese, Ngwi, Southeastern. *Lg Use:* Also use Mandarin Chinese [cmn]. *Other:* Traditional religion. *Map:* 345.

Bai, Central [bca] (Labbu, Minchia, Minjia, Minkia, Nama, Pai). 800,000 (2003 census). Ethnic population: 800,000. Northwest Yunnan Province, Jianchuan, Heqing, Lanping, Eryuan, and Yunlong; small enclave in Guizhou Province. *Status:* 6a (Vigorous). Language of recognized nationality: Bai. *Class:* Sino-Tibetan, Tibeto-Burman, Northeastern Tibeto-Burman, Bai. *Dialects:* Eryuan, Heqing, Jianchuan, Lanping, Yunlong. *Type:* SVO; attributives precede noun heads; number classifier constructions follow noun heads; tense-lax vowel distinction; tonal, 5 to 8 tones. *Lg Use:* Vigorous. All domains. All ages. Positive attitudes. A few also speak Naxi [nxq]. Also use Anong [nun], Lisu [lis], Mandarin Chinese [cmn]. Used as L2 by Lisu [lis], Naxi [nxq], Northern Pumi [pmi], Southern Pumi [pmj], Zaiwa [atb], Zauzou [zal]. *Lg Dev:* Literacy rate in L1: 0%. Literacy rate in L2: 70%. 1 experimental program. Poetry. Radio programs. Dictionary. *Writing:* Han (Hanzi, Kanji, Hanja) script, dating from 9th century, limited use in folk songs and ritual texts, favoured by older people. Latin script, pinyin-based, used since 1982, experimental, small-scale use in education, administration, and literature. *Other:* Classification difficult due to heavy borrowing (60%–70%) from Chinese. Considered genetically related to Chinese, or a mixed language with Chinese, or an independent branch of Tibeto-Burman. Traditional religion, Buddhist, Daoist. *Map:* 345.

Bai, Lama [lay] (Lama, Lan-Bi Bai, Nama, Northern Bai). 60,000 (1995). Yunnan Province, Nujiang Lisu autonomous prefecture, Lanping Bai Pumi autonomous county, Hexi district, Lajing township, in the mountains on both banks of the Lancang river. Also in Diqing Tibetan autonomous prefecture. *Status:* 6a (Vigorous). Language of recognized nationality: Bai. *Class:* Sino-Tibetan, Tibeto-Burman, Northeastern Tibeto-Burman, Bai. *Type:* SVO. *Other:* Classification difficult due to heavy borrowing (60%–70%) from Chinese. Northern Bai comprises two separate languages, Panyi [bfc] and Lama. Traditional religion, Buddhist, Daoist. *Map:* 345 (as Lama).

Bai, Panyi [bfc] (Bijiang Bai, Lan-Bi Bai, Leme, Lemo, Northern Bai, Panyi). 12,000 (2005). Yunnan Province, Nujiang prefecture, Lushui county, Luobenzhuo Bai autonomous district, Gudeng, Chenggan, and Shangjiang districts, Liuku and Pianma townships; Baoshan Municipality, Mangkuan township; Pu'er Municipality. *Status:* 6a (Vigorous). Language of recognized nationality: Bai. *Class:* Sino-Tibetan, Tibeto-Burman, Northeastern Tibeto-Burman, Bai. *Dialects:* Da-E, Yu-Teu. *Type:* SOV. *Other:* Classification difficult due to heavy borrowing (60%–70%) from Chinese and influence from Lisu [lis]. Northern Bai comprises two separate languages, Panyi and Lama [lay]. Traditional religion, Buddhist, Christian, Daoist. *Map:* 345 (as Bai, Northern).

Bai, Southern [bfs]. 400,000 (2003). Northwest Yunnan Province, Dali Bai autonomous prefecture, Xiangyun. *Status:* 6a (Vigorous). Language of recognized nationality: Bai. *Class:* Sino-Tibetan, Tibeto-Burman, Northeastern Tibeto-Burman, Bai. *Dialects:* Dali, Xiangyun. *Type:* SVO; attributives precede noun heads; number classifier constructions follow noun heads; tense-lax vowel distinction; tonal, 5 to 8 tones. *Lg Use:* All ages. *Writing:* Han (Hanzi, Kanji, Hanja) script, dating from 9th century, limited use in folk songs and ritual texts, favoured by older people. Latin script, pinyin-based, used since 1993, experimental, small-scale use in education, administration, and literature. *Other:* Classification difficult due to heavy borrowing (60%–70%) from

Chinese. Considered genetically related to Chinese, or a mixed language with Chinese, or related to Yi, or an independent branch of Tibeto-Burman. Traditional religion, Buddhist, Daoist. *Map:* 345.

Baima [bqh] (Bai Ma, Pe). 10,000 (Bradley 2007). Older adults and a few middle aged are monolingual. Ethnic population: 14,000 (Bradley 2007). North central Sichuan Province, Pingwu, Jiuzhaigou, and Songpan counties; Gansu Province, Wenxian county. *Status:* 6b (Threatened). Language of recognized nationality: Tibetan. *Class:* Sino-Tibetan, Tibeto-Burman, Northeastern Tibeto-Burman, Baima. *Dialects:* Northern Baima (Wenxian Baima), Southern Baima (Pingwu Baima), Western Baima (Jiuzhaigou Baima, Songpan Baima). *Type:* SOV; initial consonant clusters; no consonantal codas; mostly monosyllabic morphemes; loans from Chinese and Tibetan; tonal, 4 tones. *Lg Use:* Vigorous among adults in Pingwu and Jiuzhaigou counties. All domains. Neutral attitudes. Also use Amdo Tibetan [adx], Mandarin Chinese [cmn]. *Lg Dev:* Schools use Chinese. Poetry. Dictionary. *Other:* The Baima clan has a distinct ethnic identity from other Tibetans. Classified Tibetan, though some scholars consider it in the Tibeto-Burman language family, Qiangic subgroup. Traditional religion. *Map:* 344.

Biao [byk] (Gang Bau, Kang Bau, Kang Beu, Kang Pau). 80,000 (Liang Min and Zhang Junru 2002). 10,000 monolinguals. Women and small children are monolingual. Ethnic population: 120,000. Guangdong Province, southwest corner of Huaiji county, Shidong, Yonggu, Dagang, Liangcun, and Qiaotou districts; Fengkai county, Chang'an, Jinzhuang, and Qixing districts, several villages. *Status:* 6a (Vigorous). Language of recognized nationality: Han. *Class:* Tai-Kadai, Kam-Tai, Kam-Sui. *Dialects:* Minor dialect differences, but all mutually intelligible. *Lg Use:* Vigorous. All domains. All ages. Positive attitudes. With Biao people, Biao usually used. Most Biao have frequent contact with Chinese-speaking Han and Zhuang people, and then use a local Yue Chinese [yue] dialect, often Bai hua. *Lg Dev:* There is an effort to use more standard Mandarin in schools in the Biao area. Grammar. *Writing:* Unwritten. *Other:* Consider themselves a distinct ethnic group from Chinese-speaking Han people around them. Traditional religion, Buddhist, Daoist. *Map:* 346.

Biao Mon [bmt] (Biao Mien, Biaoman, Biao-Mian, Changping, Min Yao, Sida Min Yao). 20,000 (Wang Fushi and Mao Zhongwu 1995). Guangxi Zhuang Autonomous Region, Mengshan, Zhaoping, Pingle, Lipu, and Gongcheng counties. *Status:* 6a (Vigorous). Language of recognized nationality: Yao. *Class:* Hmong-Mien, Mienic, Mian-Jin. *Dialects:* Biao Mon (Min Yao), Shi Mun (Sida Min Yao). May be intelligible with some dialects of Iu Mien [ium]. Quite different from and unintelligible with Biao Jiao Mien [bje] or its dialect Biaomin, also called Biao Mien. *Other:* Daoist. *Map:* 346.

Biao-Jiao Mien [bje] (Biao Chao, Byau Min, Dongshan Biao Min). 43,000 (Wang Fushi and Mao Zhongwu 1995). Biaomin (Dongshan) has a much larger speaker population (approximately 35,700) than Jiaogong (Shikou; approximately 10,900). Northeast Guangxi Zhuang Autonomous Region, Quanzhou, Guanyang, and Gongcheng Yao autonomous counties; south Hunan Province, Shuangpai, and Daoxian counties. *Status:* 6a (Vigorous). Language of recognized nationality: Yao. *Class:* Hmong-Mien, Mienic, Biao-Jiao. *Dialects:* Biao Min (Ao Yao, Biao Mien, Biaomin, Byaumin, Dongshan Yao), Jiaogong Mian (Chao Kong Meng, Shikou, Tsaukongmeng). Dialects Biaomin (Dongshan) and Jiaogong (Shikou) reportedly mutually unintelligible. Quite different from and unintelligible with Biao Mon [bmt] (Biaoman). Lexical similarity: 70% with Iu Mien [ium], 67% with Kim Mun [mji], 58% with Dzao Min [bpn]. *Lg Dev:* Grammar. *Other:* Daoist. *Map:* 346.

Bisu [bzi] (Lawa, Lua, Mbi, Mibisu, Misu, Pin). 240 in China (Xu Shixuan 2005). 0 monolinguals. Ethnic population: 240. Southwest Yunnan Province, Xishuangbanna Dai autonomous prefecture, Menghai county, Mengzhe township, Manghong village cluster, one village: Laopinzhai. Also in Thailand. *Status:* 6b (Threatened). Language of recognized nationality: Hani. *Class:* Sino-Tibetan, Tibeto-Burman, Ngwi-Burmese, Ngwi, Southern, Bisoid. *Dialects:* Dakao, Huaipa, Lanmeng. Reportedly similar to Mpi [mpz] and Pyen [pyy]. Lexical similarity: 36% with Hani [hni], 32% with Lahu [lhu], 31% with Lisu [lis]. *Type:* SVO; simple syllable structure; certain obstruent onsets may be prenasalized, aspirated, or palatalized, but otherwise no consonant clusters; syllables may be closed by stop or nasal; 3 tones, tone sandhi; words have 1 or 2 syllables; modifiers follow heads; loanwords from Dai and Chinese. *Lg Use:* Home, village. Positive attitudes. Also use Hani [hni], Lahu [lhu], Lü [khb], Mandarin Chinese [cmn]. *Lg Dev:* Literacy rate in L2: 70%. Grammar. Bible portions: 2009–2011. *Writing:* Latin script, used since 2002, used in Myanmar. Thai script, used since 1998, used in Thailand. *Other:* Others officially classified as Undetermined Nationality. Some view Bisu as an important link to their culture and hope to preserve it. Traditional religion. *Map:* 345.

Biyo [byo] (Bio, Biyue, Piyo). 120,000 (Bradley 1997). Yunnan Province, southeast Simao prefecture, Mojiang, Jiangcheng, Zhenyuan, and Jingdong counties. *Status:* 6a (Vigorous). Language of recognized nationality: Hani. *Class:* Sino-Tibetan, Tibeto-Burman, Ngwi-Burmese, Ngwi, Southern. *Lg Use:* Also use Mandarin Chinese [cmn]. *Lg Dev:* Literacy rate in L2: 70%. Observed functional literacy in Chinese is low. Official literacy rate for the Hani Nationality is registered much higher. *Other:* A distinct language from Akha [ahk] and Kaduo [ktp]. Traditional religion, Christian. *Map:* 345.

Blang [blr] (Bulang, K'ala, Kawa, Kontoi, Plang, Pula, Pulang). 42,000 in China (2000 census). Population total all countries: 55,200. Southwest Yunnan Province, Xishuangbanna Dai autonomous prefecture, Menghai county, Bulangshan, Bada, Xiding, and Daluo districts; Jinghong county, Damengnong district. Also in Myanmar, Thailand. *Status:* 6a (Vigorous). Language of recognized nationality: Blang. *Class:* Austro-Asiatic, Mon-Khmer, Northern Mon-Khmer, Palaungic, Eastern Palaungic, Waic, Bulang. *Dialects:* Kem Degne, Phang. In Thailand, the group from Mae Sai came from Sipsongpanna, Yunnan, China, stayed in Myanmar for a while, and have been in Thailand since 1974. 6 to 10 dialects represented in one refugee village in Thailand. Samtao [stu] of Myanmar and China is not intelligible with Plang, but is closely related to Plang and Wa [wbm]. *Type:* SVO; modifiers follow noun heads; voiceless nasal initials; singular-dual-plural pronoun distinction; rich in morphophonemic processes; tonal, 4 tones. *Lg Use:* Vigorous. All domains. All ages. Positive attitudes. Also use Lü [khb], Mandarin Chinese [cmn], Vo Wa [wbm]. Used as L2 by Lahu [lhu]. *Lg Dev:* Literacy rate in L2: 77% (2000 census). Grammar. Bible portions. *Writing:* Latin script. Tai Le script, used in Dehong and Lincang, Yunnan, China. Tai Tham (Lanna) script, used in Xishuangbanna, Yunnan, China. Thai script. *Other:* Buddhist (Hinayana), Christian. *Map:* 345.

Bokha [ybk] (Akapa, Aphu, Black Muji, Bokho, Flowery Phula, Hei Muji, Hua Phula, Lao Phula, Pao Tle).

10,000 (Pelkey 2011), decreasing. Ethnic population: 12,000. Yunnan Province, central Pingbian county, Dishuiceng township; east Jinping county, Mengqiao and Ma'andi townships; west Hekou county, Lianhuatan township. *Status:* 6b (Threatened). Language of recognized nationality: Yi. *Class:* Sino-Tibetan, Tibeto-Burman, Ngwi-Burmese, Ngwi, Southeastern. *Dialects:* None known. Reportedly similar to Phuma [ypm]. *Lg Use:* Some young people, all adults. *Map:* 345.

Bolyu [ply] (Baliu, Lai, Lailai, Paliu, Palju, Palyu, Polyu). 500 (Bradley 2007). Ethnic population: 1,770 (Bradley 2007). Far west Guangxi on the Guizhou and Yunnan borders, Xilin and Longlin counties, in 2 groups. Possibly in Yunnan. *Status:* 8a (Moribund). Language of recognized nationality: Gelao. *Class:* Austro-Asiatic, Mon-Khmer, Palyu. *Dialects:* None known. May be similar to Bugan [bbh], which is the nearest Mon-Khmer language geographically. *Type:* SVO; modifiers follow heads; grammatical relations marked mainly by word order and particles; reported to have long and half long versus short vowel distinction; uvular stops; 6 tone categories in unchecked syllables plus 5 in checked syllables. Shows similarities to Kadai languages. *Other:* Ethnonym: Lai in Chinese. Traditional religion. *Map:* 345.

Bonan [peh] (Bao'an, Baonan, Boan, Paoan, Paongan). 6,000. Very few monolinguals. Ethnic population: 24,500. Includes 16,500 Jishishan and 8000 Tongren. Southwest Gansu Province, Linxia Hui autonomous prefecture, Jishishan Bao'an-Dongxiang-Sala Autonomous county; east Qinghai Province, Tongren county. *Status:* 7 (Shifting). Language of recognized nationality: Blang. Speakers of the Jishishan dialect moved from Qinghai Province to Gansu, 1858–1863; officially classified within Bonan nationality. *Class:* Altaic, Mongolic, Eastern, Mongour. *Dialects:* Jishishan (Dahejia, Dajiahe, Dakheczjha), Tongren (Tungyen). Jishishan subdialects are Ganhetan and Dadun; Tongren subdialects are Nianduhu, Guomari, Gajiuri, and Lower Bao'an. Jishishan dialect has been influenced by Mandarin Chinese [cmn], Tongren by Tibetan [bod]. There are phonological and grammatical differences between them, and inherent intelligibility may be low. *Type:* SOV; stress on final syllable; modifiers precede noun heads; Tongren dialect allows onset consonant clusters which resemble Tibetan; Jishishan dialect has Chinese-type syllable structure. *Lg Use:* Religion, local administration, home; for Tongren, not used for religion. Tongren: all ages. Positive attitudes, except in Tongren. Also use Amdo Tibetan [adx], Mandarin Chinese [cmn]. *Lg Dev:* Literacy rate in L2: 44% (2000 census, Baoan nationality). No written language; no desire for one. Amdo Tibetan is local LWC. Chinese required to excel in school and find a good job. Dictionary. Grammar. *Other:* Muslim (Sunni), Buddhist (Lamaist), traditional religion. *Map:* 344.

Bouyei [pcc] (Bo-I, Bui, Buyei, Buyi, Buyui, Chung-Chia, Dioi, Giay, Pui, Pu-I, Pujai, Pu-Jui, Puyi, Puyoi, Shuihu, Tujia, Zhongjia). 2,600,000 in China (2000 census). Population total all countries: 2,649,200. Ethnic population: 2,950,000 (2000 census). South and southwest Guizhou Province, Guizhou-Yunnan plateau, mainly Buyi-Miao and Miao-Dong autonomous prefectures, Zhenning and Guanling counties; Yunnan Province, Luoping county; Sichuan Province, Ningnan and Huidong counties. Also in France (Giáy), Viet Nam (Giáy). *Status:* 6a (Vigorous). Language of recognized nationality: Bouyei. *Class:* Tai-Kadai, Kam-Tai, Tai, Northern. *Dialects:* Qiannan (Bouyei 1, Southern Guizhou), Qianxi (Bouyei 3, Western Guizhou), Qianzhong (Bouyei 2, Central Guizhou). *Type:* SVO; modifiers follow heads; highly monosyllabic; tonal, 6 tone categories in open syllables and 4 in closed syllables. *Lg Use:* Vigorous. Rare oral use in local administration, commerce, education. All ages. Also use Mandarin Chinese [cmn], Sui [swi]. Used as L2 by Bu-Nao Bunu [bwx], Mak [mkg], T'en [tct]. *Lg Dev:* Literacy rate in L1: Very low. Literacy rate in L2: 76% (2000 census). Poetry. Films. Dictionary. *Writing:* Han (Hanzi, Kanji, Hanja) script, dating from late Ming/early Qing dynasty, limited use in ritual texts and folk literature. Latin script, used since 1982, experimental, small-scale use in education and literature in China. *Other:* Ethnonym: Giay in Viet Nam. Quinnan hua (Quinnan speech) also refers to a dialect of southwestern Mandarin spoken in Guizhou, and should not be confused with the Qiannan Bouyei dialect. Traditional religion, Buddhist, Daoist. *Map:* 345.

Bugan [bbh] (Bengan, Bogan, Bugeng, Hualo, Huazu, Pukan, Puqeng). 2,700 (Yunbin 2005). Southeast Yunnan Province, Wenshan Zhuang and Miao autonomous prefecture, Guangnan and Xichou counties, South Guangnan Nasa township, 4 Bugan villages: Laowalong, Xinwalong, Xinpingzhai, and Nala; Guangnan county, Zhuanjiao district, 2 Bugan villages: Jiuping, Shibeipo; Northern Yanshan county, Jijie district, Manlong and 6 other villages. *Status:* 6a (Vigorous). Language of recognized nationality: Yi. *Class:* Austro-Asiatic, Mon-Khmer, Palyu. *Dialects:* None known. Very minor accent differences between villages. *Type:* Prenasalized and plain stop and affricate initials; tense and lax vowel contrast; nasal and stop variation word final; tone sandhi, 6 tones. *Lg Use:* Vigorous. All ethnic Bugan speak Bugan. All ages. Some middle aged and older people and children who have not attended school do not understand local Chinese or Mandarin [cmn] but many adults speak some local Chinese. Also use Chuanqiandian Cluster Miao [cqd], Nong Zhuang [zhn]. *Other:* Language and culture are very different from the surrounding Yi nationality groups. They maintain their own festivals and are endogamous. Ethnonyms: Hualuo and Huazu, multi-colored tribe, are used by surrounding Han, Zhuang and other groups and are due to traditional costumes worn by women. Traditional religion. *Map:* 345.

Bumang [bvp] (Manzhang Dai). 200 (Jie 2007). Yunnan Province, Honghe and Yi autonomous prefectures, Jinping Miao-Yao-Dai autonomous county, Mengla district, Manzhang-Shangzhai and Mangzhang-Xiazhai villages. *Status:* 6a (Vigorous). Language of recognized nationality: Dai. *Class:* Austro-Asiatic, Mon-Khmer, Northern Mon-Khmer, Palaungic, Eastern Palaungic, Waic, Bulang. *Lg Use:* Also use Tai Dam [blt], Tai Dón [twh]. *Other:* Language is unlike the other 3 Dai language groups in their home county. Traditional religion. *Map:* 345.

Bunu, Bu-Nao [bwx] (Bunao, Po-Nau, Punu). 258,000 (McConnell 1995). 97,000 monolinguals. Ethnic population: 439,000 (1982 census). 100,000 ethnic Bunu speak Central Hongshuihe Zhuang [zch] as L1. Western Guangxi Zhuang Autonomous Region, 22 counties: Du'an, Bama, Dahua, Lingyun, Nandan, Tiandong, Tianyang, Pingguo, Fengshan, Donglan, Hechi, Mashan, Bose, Tianlin, Leye, Tiandeng, Xincheng, Shanglin, Long'an, Debao, Laibin, and Luocheng; Guizhou Province, Libo county; Yunnan Province, Funing county. Southwest Hunan Province, near Guangxi border. *Status:* 6b (Threatened). Language of recognized nationality: Yao. *Class:* Hmong-Mien, Hmongic, Bunu. *Dialects:* Bunuo (Pu No), Cingsui Longlin, Dongnu (Bunu, Punu, Tung Nu), Hontou Longlin, Naogelao (Baonuo, Nao Khalo, Nao Klao, Nau Klau, Pounou), Numao (Hong Yao, Nu Mhou), Nunu. The dialects listed may be at least 5 languages (Strecker 1987), communication is difficult (McConnell 1995). *Type:* SVO; modifiers follow heads; up to 11 affixes; complex set of initials including prenasalized stops; relatively simple rhymes; tonal, most dialects have 8 tones. *Lg Use:* Vigorous. All domains. All ages. Positive attitudes. Also use Chinese [cmn]. Mandarin Chinese used in schools. Also use Bouyei [pcc]. *Lg Dev:* Dictionary. *Writing:* Latin script, used at least since 1988. *Other:* Daoist, traditional religion. *Maps:* 345, 346:47.

Bunu, Jiongnai [pnu] (Hualan Yao, Jiongnai, Jiongnaihua, Kiong Nai, Punu, Qiungnai). 1,080 (1999 Mao Zongwu). 270 monolinguals. Ethnic population: 1,500 (Bradley 2007). East Guangxi Zhuang Autonomous Region, Jinxiu Yao autonomous county. *Status:* 6b (Threatened). Language of recognized nationality: Yao. *Class:* Hmong-Mien, Hmongic, Bunu. *Dialects:* None known. Very different from and unintelligible to surrounding Yao and other Bunu speakers. Lexical similarity: 52% with Bu-Nao Bunu [bwx]. *Lg Use:* Vigorous in most families. All domains. All ages. Neutral attitudes. Also use Hmong Njua [hnj], Iu Mien [ium], Lakkia [lbc], Mandarin Chinese [cmn]. *Lg Dev:* Grammar. *Other:* Ethnonym: Hualan Yao by Han Chinese, Patterned Blue Yao (from womens' traditional dress). Bunu is a cover term for separate languages. Daoist, traditional religion. *Map:* 346.

Bunu, Wunai [bwn] (Hm Nai, Ngnai, Punu, Wunai). 5,800 (Shearer and Sun Hong Kai 2002), decreasing. Ethnic population: 8,000 (Bradley 2007). West Hunan Province, Longhui, Xupu, Tongdao, Chenxi, Dongkou, Chengbu, and Xinning counties; small area, northern Guangxi Province. *Status:* 7 (Shifting). Language of recognized nationality: Yao. *Class:* Hmong-Mien, Hmongic, Bunu. *Type:* SVO; has uvular onsets; only final nasal is velar. *Lg Use:* Also use Mandarin Chinese [cmn]. *Other:* Bunu is a cover term for separate languages. Daoist. *Map:* 346.

Bunu, Younuo [buh] (Pu No, Punu, Younuo, Yuno, Yunuo). 9,720 (McConnell 1995). Northeast Guangxi Zhuang Autonomous Region, Xing'an and Longsheng counties. *Status:* 7 (Shifting). Language of recognized nationality: Yao. *Class:* Hmong-Mien, Hmongic, Bunu. *Type:* SVO; relatively simple set of initials; many Chinese loans; tonal, 6 tones. *Lg Use:* Also use Mandarin Chinese [cmn]. *Writing:* Latin script. *Other:* Bunu is a cover term for several separate languages (Strecker 1989). Daoist. *Map:* 346:42.

Buriat, China [bxu] (Ba'erhu-Buliyate, Bargu Buriat, Buriat-Mongolian, Buryat, Northeastern Mongolian, Northern Mongolian). 65,000 (1982 census). 47,000 New Bargu, 14,000 Old Bargu, 4,500 Buriat. Nei Mongol Province, Inner Mongolia Autonomous Region, Hulun-Buyr district, near Russia (Siberia) and Mongolia borders. *Status:* 7 (Shifting). Language of recognized nationality: Mongolian. *Class:* Altaic, Mongolic, Eastern, Oirat-Khalkha, Khalkha-Buriat, Buriat. A member of macrolanguage Buriat [bua] (Russian Federation). *Dialects:* Aga, Buriat (Buliyate, Buryat), Khori, New Bargu (Xin Ba'erhu), Old Bargu (Chen Ba'erhu). Differs from Buriat of Mongolia [bxm] and the Russian Federation [bxr] due to influences of other languages. *Lg Use:* Shifting to Mongolian. *Lg Dev:* Written Mongolian is the literary language. *Other:* Buddhist (Lamaist), traditional religion. *Map:* 344.

Buxinhua [bgk] (Boxing, Buxing, Buxing Khmu, Khabit, Pasing, Phsin, Phsing). 200 in China (1994). Ethnic population: 500 (Bradley 2007). Southwest Yunnan Province, Xishuangbanna Dai autonomous prefecture, Mengla county. *Status:* 6b (Threatened). *Other:* Traditional religion. See main entry on page 214 (as Bit). *Map:* 345.

Buyang, Baha [yha] (Buyang, Buyang Zhuang, Guangnan Buyang, Western Buyang). 600 (Li Jinfang 1997), decreasing. Yunnan Province, Wenshan Zhuang-Miao autonomous prefecture, northern Guangnan county, Dixu district, Yanglian village; Bada district, Anshe village. *Status:* 6b (Threatened). Language of recognized nationality: Zhuang. *Class:* Tai-Kadai, Kra, Central Kra. *Dialects:* Ecun, Langjia, Yalang. Lexical similarity: 50% with Langnian Buyang [yln], 48% with E'ma Buyang [yzg], 46% with Yerong (Yalang Buyang) [yrn], 45% with Pubiao [laq], 41% with Laji (Lachi) [lbt], 40% with Lao [lao], 35% with Mulao [mlm], 32% with Lingao [onb], 28% with Northern Zhuang, 27% with Dong, 22% with Cun [cuq]. *Type:* SVO; adjectives follow nouns; tonal, 6 tones (combining categories in checked and unchecked syllables). *Lg Use:* As of 1995, still used by all ages in Dixu district's Yanglian village, but only older people can speak it in Bada district's Anshe village. In Anshe, younger people shifted to Guibian Zhuang [zgn]. All adults also use local Guibian Northern Zhuang [zgn]. Some also use local Southwest Mandarin Chinese [cmn]. *Other:* Traditional religion. *Map:* 345.

Buyang, E'ma [yzg] (Buozaang, Buyang Zhuang, Eastern Buyang, Funing Buyang, Langjia Buyang). 600 (Li Jinfang 1997). Yunnan Province, Wenshan Zhuang-Miao autonomous prefecture, Funing county, Gula township, 6 villages: E'cun, Maguan, Dugan, Zhelong, Nada, and Longna. *Status:* 8a (Moribund). Language of recognized nationality: Zhuang. *Class:* Tai-Kadai, Kra, Eastern Kra. *Dialects:* None known. Lexical similarity: 78% with Langnian Buyang [yln], yet not intelligible despite frequent contact, 63% with Yerong (Yalang Buyang) [yrn], 48% with Baha Buyang [yha]. Also reportedly quite similar to En [enc] (200 speakers) of Northern Vietnam. (Li Jinfang 2006). *Lg Use:* Those 15–50 speak local Guibian Zhuang language [zgn]. Some, especially men, can speak the local southwestern Mandarin [cmn] dialect. *Other:* Traditional religion. *Map:* 345:18.

Buyang, Langnian [yln] (Buozaang, Buyang Zhuang, Eastern Buyang, E'cun Buyang). 300 (Li Jinfang 1997), decreasing. Yunnan Province, Wenshan Zhuang-Miao autonomous prefecture, Funing county, Gula district, Longse community, Langjia village; Gutao community, Nianlang village. *Status:* 8a (Moribund). Language of recognized nationality: Zhuang. *Class:* Tai-Kadai, Kra, Eastern Kra. *Dialects:* None known. 78% with E'ma Buyang [yzg], yet not intelligible despite frequent contact, 67% with Yerong (Yalang Buyang) [yrn], 50% with Baha Buyang [yha], 45% with Pubiao [laq], 42% with Laji (Lachi) [lbt]. Also reportedly quite similar to En [enc] (200 speakers) of Northern Vietnam. (Li Jinfang 2006). *Lg Use:* Those 15–50 years of age also use local Guibian Zhuang [zgn]. Some, especially men, use local Southwest Mandarin [cmn]. *Other:* Traditional religion. *Map:* 345:19.

Cao Miao [cov] (Grass Miao, Mjiuniang, Sanjiang Miao). 63,600 (2000). Southeast Guizhou Province, Liping county; southwest Hunan Province, Tongdao Dong autonomous county; northeast Guangxi Zhuang Autonomous Region, Sanjiang Dong autonomous county, near South Dong, small villages. *Status:* 6a (Vigorous). Language of recognized nationality: Miao. *Class:* Tai-Kadai, Kam-Tai, Kam-Sui. *Dialects:* Lexical similarity: with Northern Dong [doc] and sometimes referred to as a special dialect of Dong. *Type:* Tonal, 6 tones. *Lg Use:* Daily communication. All ages. Also use Mandarin Chinese [cmn], including in singing. *Other:* Traditional religion. *Map:* 346.

Chadong [cdy] (Cha Dong, Chadonghua, Chadongyu). 20,000 (Li Jinfang 2006). Northeast Guangxi Zhuang Autonomous Region, Lingui county, Guilin muncipality; Chadong district (most villages), Liangjiang township; Yongfu county, Longjiang district. *Status:* 6a (Vigorous).

Language of recognized nationality: Hani. *Class:* Tai-Kadai, Kam-Tai, Kam-Sui. *Lg Use:* Home. Also use Guiliu dialect of southwest Mandarin Chinese [cmn]. Also use Iu Mien [ium], Yue Chinese [yue], Zhuang [zha]. *Other:* Traditional religion, Daoist. *Map:* 346.

Chesu [ych]. 3,300 (2007), decreasing. Ethnic population: 6,600 (Bradley 2007). Yunnan Province, northwest Xinping, southeast Shuangbai, and southwest Eshan counties. *Status:* 7 (Shifting). Language of recognized nationality: Yi. *Class:* Sino-Tibetan, Tibeto-Burman, Ngwi-Burmese, Ngwi, Northern. *Dialects:* None known. Related to Samtao [stu]. *Lg Use:* Shifting to Chinese, endangered in many areas (Bradley 2007). Used as L2 by Hlersu [hle]. *Map:* 345.

Chinese [zho]. A macrolanguage (see page 9). *Lg Use:* Used as L2 by Achang [acn], Iu Mien [ium], Sui [swi]. *Other:* Includes: Gan Chinese [gan], Hakka Chinese [hak], Huizhou Chinese [czh], Jinyu Chinese [cjy], Mandarin Chinese [cmn], Min Bei Chinese [mnp], Min Dong Chinese [cdo], Min Nan Chinese [nan], Min Zhong Chinese [czo], Pu-Xian Chinese [cpx], Wu Chinese [wuu], Xiang Chinese [hsn], Yue Chinese [yue].

Chinese Sign Language [csl] (China Coast Pidgin, Zhongguo Shouyu). *Status:* 5 (Developing). *Class:* Deaf sign language. *Dialect:* Southern Chinese Sign Language (Shanghai Sign Language). Survey needed. Few signs of foreign origin. Negative clauses reportedly share similarity with British Sign Language. *Lg Use:* Classmates and factory coworkers are channels of dissemination. Now specialized deaf colleges use CSL. All domains. All ages. *Lg Dev:* Literacy rate in L1: 0%. In 2006, school age deaf children enrollment rate was approximately 82% (China Disabled Persons' Federation). TV. Videos. Dictionary. Grammar. *Other:* Developed late 1980s. There are also Chinese character signs. Others use home sign languages. 550 schools for the deaf, 77 schools for the deaf and the blind. In addition to signs, Chinese Sign Language also uses an alphabetic spelling system (analogous to pinyin in Mandarin [cmn]) and can signify tones with facial gestures. Shanghai Sign Language is the prestige dialect.

Chinese, Gan [gan] (Gan, Jiangxi hua, Jiangxinese, Kan). 20,600,000 (1984). Jiangxi Province and southeast corner of Hubei Province, including Dachi, Xianning, Jiayu, Chongyang, and parts of Anhui; east Hunan and Fujian provinces. Chang-Jing in Nanchang city, Xiuhui, and Jing'an; Yi-Liu in Yichun (Ichun) in Jiangxi, Liuyang in Hunan. *Status:* 6a (Vigorous). Language of recognized nationality: Han. *Class:* Sino-Tibetan, Chinese. A member of macrolanguage Chinese [zho]. *Dialects:* Chang-Jing, Datong, Dongsui, Fu-Guang, Hauiyue, Ji-Cha, Leizi, Nanchang, Yilu (Yi-Liu), Ying-Yi. Marginally intelligible with Mandarin [cmn] and Wu [wuu] Chinese. Lexical similarity: with Hakka Chinese [hak]. *Type:* Tonal. *Lg Use:* All ages. Also use Mandarin Chinese [cmn]. *Lg Dev:* 91% (2000 census, Han nationality). *Writing:* Han script, Simplified variant. Han script, Traditional variant. Latin script, from 1891 to some time after last publication in 1922. *Other:* Nanchang is representative dialect. *Map:* 346.

Chinese, Hakka [hak] (Hakka, Hokka, Ke, Kechia, Kejia, Majiahua, Tu Guangdonghua, Xinminhua). 25,700,000 in China (1984). Population total all countries: 30,082,810. Widespread with other dialects. Greatest concentration in east and northeast Guangdong Province; also in west and southwest Fujian, south Jiangxi, Guangxi, Hunan, Sichuan, and Hainan provinces. Also in Brunei, Cambodia, Canada, Hong Kong, Taiwan, French Guiana, French Polynesia, Indonesia, Malaysia, Mauritius, Panama, Singapore, South Africa, Suriname, Thailand, United Kingdom, United States. *Status:* 5 (Developing). Language of recognized nationality: Han. *Class:* Sino-Tibetan, Chinese. A member of macrolanguage Chinese [zho]. *Dialects:* Changting, Hailu, Huayang, Huizhou, Ning-Long (Longnan), Pingdong, Tingzhou (Min-Ke), Tonggu, Yuebei, Yue-Tai (Meixian, Raoping, Taiwan Kejia), Yuezhong, Yugui. Yue-Tai (Meixian) is standard dialect. Lexical similarity: with Gan Chinese [gan]. *Type:* SVO; tonal. *Lg Use:* All ages. Also use Mandarin Chinese [cmn]. Used as L2 by She [shx]. *Lg Dev:* Literacy rate in L2: 91% (2000 census, Han nationality). Highly literate in Chinese and they use that literature. Radio programs. Bible: 1916. *Writing:* Han script, Traditional variant. Latin script, used since early 19th century. *Map:* 346.

Chinese, Huizhou [czh] (Hui, Huizhou). 4,600,000 (2000 census). Jixi dialect: 988,000; Xiuyi dialect: 861,000; Qide dialect: 798,000; Yanzhou dialect: 638,000; Jingzhan dialect: 134,000. South or southeast Anhui Province, Huizhou region, Jixi, She (Xi), Ningguo, Jingde, Tunxi, Xiuning, Yi, Qimen, and Dongzhi counties; north and west Zhejiang Province, Chun'an county, Jiande municipality; northeast Jiangxi Province, Wuyuan, Dexing, and Fuliang counties. *Status:* 6a (Vigorous). Language of recognized nationality: Han. *Class:* Sino-Tibetan, Chinese. A member of macrolanguage Chinese [zho]. *Dialects:* Jingzhan, Jixi, Qide, Tunxi, Xiuyi, Yanzhou. Formerly considered part of Jianghuai dialect of Mandarin Chinese [cmn], but now considered by many a major dialect of Chinese. Dialects reportedly differ greatly from each other. Different from Huizhou dialect of Hakka Chinese [hak]. *Lg Use:* All ages. Also use Mandarin Chinese [cmn]. *Lg Dev:* Literacy rate in L2: 91% (2000 census, Han nationality). Highly literate in Chinese and they use that literature. *Writing:* Han script, Simplified variant. Han script, Traditional variant. *Map:* 344.

Chinese, Jinyu [cjy] (Jin, Jinyu). 45,000,000 (1995). Mainly Shanxi, Nei Mongol, and Shaanxi provinces; some in west Hebei, Henan, Beijing and Gansu provinces. *Status:* 6a (Vigorous). Language of recognized nationality: Han. *Class:* Sino-Tibetan, Chinese. A member of macrolanguage Chinese [zho]. *Dialects:* Changzhi, Pingyao. Formerly considered part of Xibei Guanhua dialect of Mandarin Chinese [cmn], but now considered by many a separate major dialect of Chinese. Unlike Mandarin, it has contrastive glottal-checked syllables and other distinctive features. *Type:* SVO; tonal. *Lg Use:* All ages. Also use Mandarin Chinese [cmn]. *Lg Dev:* Literacy rate in L2: 91% (2000 census, Han nationality). Highly literate in Chinese and they use that literature. *Writing:* Han script, Simplified variant. Han script, Traditional variant. *Map:* 344.

Chinese, Mandarin [cmn] (Beifang Fangyan, Guanhua, Guoyu, Hanyu, Huayu, Mandarin, Northern Chinese, Putonghua, Standard Chinese, Zhongguohua, Zhongwen). 840,000,000 in China (2000 census), increasing. 70% of Chinese language users speak a Mandarin dialect as L1. Population total all countries: 847,808,270. L2 users: 178,000,000 in China. Widespread north of Changjiang river, a belt south of the Changjiang from Qiujiang (Jiangxi) to Zhenjiang (Jiangsu), Hubei Province, except southeast corner, Sichuan, Yunnan, Guizhou provinces, northwest Guangxi Zhuang Autonomous Region, and northwest corner of Hunan Province. Also in Australia, Brunei, Cambodia, Canada, Hong Kong, Macao, Taiwan, Equatorial Guinea, Indonesia, South Korea, Laos, Libya, Malaysia, Mauritius, Mongolia, Mozambique, Myanmar, New Zealand, Philippines, Russian Federation, Singapore, Thailand, United Kingdom, United States, Viet Nam, Zambia. *Status:* 1 (National). De facto national language.

Class: Sino-Tibetan, Chinese. A member of macrolanguage Chinese [zho]. *Dialects:* Huabei Guanhua (Northern Mandarin), Jinghuai Guanhua (Eastern Mandarin, Jiangxia Guanhua, Lower Yangze Mandarin), Xibei Guanhua (Northwestern Mandarin), Xinan Guanhua (Southwestern Mandarin). Speakers of Kokang variety in Myanmar are reportedly most similar to the dialect spoken in Yunnan Province, China. *Type:* SVO; analytic; aspect; 6 full (concrete meaning) word classes; tonal. *Lg Use:* Vigorous. All domains. All ages. Also use Korean in predominantly Korean-speaking provinces of China. Also use English [eng], French [fra], Japanese [jpn], Russian [rus], Vietnamese [vie]. *Lg Dev:* Literacy rate in L2: 91% (2000 census, Han nationality). Official language taught in all schools in mainland China and Taiwan. Taught in secondary schools. Fully developed. Bible: 1874–1983. *Writing:* Bopomofo script, used since 1913, mainly used in Taiwan. Braille script. Han script, Simplified variant, used since 1956, official in Mainland China (1956) and Singapore (1969), also used elsewhere. Han script, Traditional variant, used since mid-19th century, official in Taiwan, also used elsewhere. Latin script. *Other:* There are Mandarin speakers in all 56 official nationalities of China, but the majority in China are classified under Han, Manchu and Hui nationalities. Traditional religion, Buddhist, Christian, Confucianist, Daoist, Jewish, Muslim (Hui). *Map:* 344.

Chinese, Min Bei [mnp] (Min Pei, Northern Min). 10,300,000 in China (1984). Population total all countries: 10,304,000. North Fujian Province, 7 counties around Jian'ou. Some in Jiangxi and Zhejiang provinces. Also in Singapore. *Status:* 5 (Developing). Language of recognized nationality: Han. *Class:* Sino-Tibetan, Chinese. A member of macrolanguage Chinese [zho]. *Dialects:* None known. The Chinese now divide Chinese Min into 5 major varieties: Min Nan [nan], Min Bei [mnp], Min Dong [cdo], Min Zhong [czo], and Pu-Xian [cpx]. Others say there are at least 9 varieties which are inherently mutually unintelligible. *Type:* Tonal. *Lg Use:* All ages. Also use Mandarin Chinese [cmn]. *Lg Dev:* Literacy rate in L2: 91% (2000 census, Han nationality). Highly literate in Chinese and they use that literature. NT: 1934. *Writing:* Latin script, from 1896 to some time after last publication in 1922. *Other:* Buddhist, Christian, Daoist. *Map:* 346.

Chinese, Min Dong [cdo] (Eastern Min). 8,820,000 in China (2000). Population total all countries: 9,115,930. Fujian Province, Fu'an in northeast to Fuzhou in east central; southern border, Zhejiang Province, near Luoyang. Also in Brunei, Indonesia, Malaysia, Singapore, Thailand, United States. *Status:* 5 (Developing). Language of recognized nationality: Han. *Class:* Sino-Tibetan, Chinese. A member of macrolanguage Chinese [zho]. *Dialect:* Fuzhou (Foochow, Fuchow, Guxhou). The prestige dialect is spoken in Fujian. *Lg Use:* All ages. *Lg Dev:* Literacy rate in L1: 91% (2000 census, Han nationality). Highly literate in Chinese, and they use that literature. Bible: 1884–1905. *Writing:* Han script, Simplified variant, used since 1987. Han script, Traditional variant. Latin script, devised and revised to final form during late 19th century. *Map:* 346.

Chinese, Min Nan [nan] (Minnan, Southern Min). 25,700,000 in China (Johnstone and Mandryk 2001). Population total all countries: 46,619,500. South Fujian, Guangdong, south Hainan, south Zhejiang, and south Jiangxi provinces. Xiamen in south Fujian and Jiangxi provinces; Hainan in Hainan; Leizhou on Leizhou peninsula of southwest Guangdong Province; Chao-Shan in far east corner of Guangdong Province in Chaozhou-Shantou area; Longdu is a dialect island around Zhongshan city and Shaxi in Guangdong Province, south of Guangzhou; Zhenan Min in southeast Zhejiang Province around Pingyang and Cangnan and on Zhoushan archipelago of northeast Zhejiang Province. Also in Brunei, Cambodia, Canada, Hong Kong, Macao, Taiwan, Indonesia, Malaysia, Philippines, Singapore, Thailand, United States. *Status:* 6a (Vigorous). Language of recognized nationality: Han. *Class:* Sino-Tibetan, Chinese. A member of macrolanguage Chinese [zho]. *Dialects:* Chao-Shan (Chaozhou, Choushan, Teochew), Hainan (Hainanese, Qiongwen Hua, Wenchang), Leizhou (Lei Hua, Li Hua), Longdu, Quanzhou (Chinchew), Xiamen (Amoy), Zhangzhou (Changchew), Zhenan Min. Amoy is the prestige dialect. Amoy and Taiwanese are easily mutually intelligible. Chao-Shan has difficult intelligibility with Amoy; Hainan quite different from other dialects. Most speakers in Thailand use Chaoshou dialect. Min Nan most widely distributed and influential Min variety. *Type:* SVO; tone sandhi, tonal. *Lg Use:* Other speakers use it for commerce. Most domains. All ages. Positive attitudes. Also use English [eng], Mandarin Chinese [cmn], Yue Chinese [yue]. Used as L2 by Lingao [onb], She [shx], Tsat [huq]. *Lg Dev:* Literacy rate in L2: 91% (2000 census, Han nationality). Highly literate in Chinese and they use that literature. Poetry. Dictionary. Grammar. Bible: 1884–1933. *Writing:* Bopomofo script, used since 1998, used in Taiwan. Katakana script, 1895–1945, once used in Taiwan. Latin script, used since 1850. *Other:* Traditional religion, Buddhist, Christian, Daoist. *Map:* 346.

Chinese, Min Zhong [czo] (Central Min). 3,100,000 (2000 census). Central Fujian Province, Sha county, Yong'an and Sanming municipalities. *Status:* 6a (Vigorous). Language of recognized nationality: Han. *Class:* Sino-Tibetan, Chinese. A member of macrolanguage Chinese [zho]. *Type:* Tonal. *Lg Use:* All ages. *Lg Dev:* 91% (2000 census, Han nationality). *Map:* 346.

Chinese, Pu-Xian [cpx] (Henghua, Hinghua, Hsienyu, Hsinghua, Putian, Putten, Xianyou, Xinghua). 2,520,000 in China (2000). Population total all countries: 2,558,800. East central Fujian Province, Putian and Xianyou counties. Also in Malaysia, Singapore. *Status:* 5 (Developing). Language of recognized nationality: Han. *Class:* Sino-Tibetan, Chinese. A member of macrolanguage Chinese [zho]. *Lg Use:* All ages. Also use Mandarin Chinese [cmn]. *Lg Dev:* Literacy rate in L2: 91% (2000 census, Han nationality). Highly literate in Chinese, and they use that literature. Poetry. Bible: 1912. *Writing:* Latin script, 1890–1950, once used in a newspaper. *Map:* 346.

Chinese, Wu [wuu] (Jiangnan hua, Jiangsu-Zhujiang hua, Jiangzhe hua, Wu, Wuyue). 77,200,000 in China (1984). Population total all countries: 77,202,480. Jiangsu Province south of Changjiang river, east of Zhenjiang, on Chongming Island, mouth of and north of the Changjiang in Nantong area, Haimen, Qidong, and Qingjiang; Zhejiang Province south to Quzhou, Jinhua, and Wenzhou; southeast Anhui Province; Shanghai municipality; northeast Jiangxi Province; northern Fujian Province, Shangrao area. Also in United States. *Status:* 5 (Developing). Language of recognized nationality: Han. *Class:* Sino-Tibetan, Chinese. A member of macrolanguage Chinese [zho]. *Dialects:* Chongming, Chuqu, Danyang, Hangzhou, Jinhua, Jinhua (Kinhwa), Oujiang, Quzhou, Shanghai, Shaoxing, Suzhou, Taihu, Taizhou, Tangxi, Wenling, Wenzhou, Wuzhou, Xuanzhou, Youngkang, Zhenhai. Varieties of Taihu dialect are Piling, Su-Hu-Jia, Tiaoxi, Hangzhou, Lin-Shao, and Yongjiang; Chuqu subdialects are Chuzhou and Longqu; Xuanzhou varieties are Tongjing, Taigao, and Shiling. *Type:* SVO; tone sandhi, tonal. *Lg Use:* All ages. Also use Mandarin Chinese

[cmn]. *Lg Dev:* Literacy rate in L2: 91% (2000 census, Han nationality). Fully developed. Bible: 1908–1914. *Writing:* Han script, Simplified variant, used since 1981. Han script, Traditional variant. Latin script, used since mid/late 19th century. *Map:* 344.

Chinese, Xiang [hsn] (Hsiang, Hunan, Hunanese, Xiang). 36,000,000 in China (1984). Population total all countries: 36,000,290. Hunan Province, over 20 counties; parts of Guangxi Zhuang Autonomous Region, Guizhou and Hubei provinces. Also in United States. *Status:* 6a (Vigorous). Language of recognized nationality: Han. *Class:* Sino-Tibetan, Chinese. A member of macrolanguage Chinese [zho]. *Dialects:* Changsha, Changyi, Jishou, Jishu, Jixu, Loudi, Luoshao, Shaoyang, Xupu, Yiyang. Linguistically between Mandarin [cmn] and Wu [wuu] Chinese and marginally intelligible with them. Reportedly becoming more similar to (southwestern) Mandarin [cmn] and is losing non-northern features. 3 main dialect groups: Changyi (includes Changsha and Yiyang), Luoshao (includes Loudi and Shaoyang), and Jixu (Jishu) (includes Xupu and Jishou). *Lg Use:* All ages. Also use Mandarin Chinese [cmn]. *Lg Dev:* Literacy rate in L2: 91% (2000 census, Han nationality). Highly literate in Chinese, and they use that literature. *Writing:* Han script, Simplified variant. Han script, Traditional variant. Nüshu script, used at least since mid-19th century, mainly used by women. *Map:* 346.

Chinese, Yue [yue] (Cantonese, Gwong Dung Waa, Yue, Yueh, Yuet Yue, Yueyu). 52,000,000 in China (1984). Population total all countries: 62,221,560. Mainly Guangdong, except Hakka-speaking areas northeast, and Min Nan-speaking areas east. and in east Guangxi provinces. Other areas: Hainan and Hunan provinces. Also in Australia, Brunei, Cambodia, Canada, Hong Kong, Macao, Costa Rica, Honduras, Indonesia, Laos, Malaysia, Mauritius, Nauru, Netherlands, New Zealand, Panama, Philippines, Singapore, South Africa, Sweden, Thailand, United Kingdom, United States, Viet Nam. *Status:* 2 (Provincial). De facto provincial language in Guangdong Province. Language of recognized nationality: Han. *Class:* Sino-Tibetan, Chinese. A member of macrolanguage Chinese [zho]. *Dialects:* Bobai, Cangwu, Gaolei (Gaoyang), Guangzhou, Guinan, Ping, Qinlian, Siyi (Hoisan, Schleiyip, Seiyap, Taishan, Toisan), Tengxian, Yangjiang, Zhongshan. The Guangzhou variety considered the standard. *Type:* SVO; prepositions; genitives, relatives, articles, adjectives, numerals before noun heads; tonal. *Lg Use:* Second only to Mandarin [cmn] in use. All domains. All ages. Positive attitudes. Though many Yue speakers can understand Mandarin [cmn], many have difficulty speaking it. Used as L2 by Biao [byk], Chadong [cdy], E [eee], Min Nan Chinese [nan], Tsat [huq], Vietnamese [vie], Yang Zhuang [zyg], Yongnan Zhuang [zyn], Zuojiang Zhuang [zzj]. *Lg Dev:* Literacy rate in L1: 91% (2000 census, Han nationality). Speakers are highly literate in Chinese. Taught in primary and secondary schools. Fully developed. Bible: 1894–1981. *Writing:* Braille script, used in Hong Kong. Han script, Simplified variant. Han script, Traditional variant, official usage in Hong Kong and Macau, also used elsewhere. Latin script, used since mid-19th century. *Other:* Many members of other nationalities in Guangxi, Guangdong and Hainan also speak Yue dialects. *Map:* 346.

Choni [cda] (Chona, Chone, Cone, Jone, Zhuoni). 154,000 (2004). South Gansu Province, east Gannan prefecture, Lintan, Zhuoni, Diebu, and Zhouqu counties; northern Sichuan Province. *Status:* 7 (Shifting). Language of recognized nationality: Tibetan. *Class:* Sino-Tibetan, Tibeto-Burman, Western Tibeto-Burman, Bodish, Central Bodish. *Dialects:* Hbrugchu (Zhouqu), Thewo (Diebu). *Lg Dev:* Tibetan vernaculars are not written, but education in written Tibetan is available where Choni speakers live. Teachers probably speak either Choni or Amdo [adx]. *Map:* 344.

Cun [cuq] (Cunhua, Cun-Hua, Ngao Fon). 80,000 (1999 O. Jueya). 47,200 monolinguals. Mainly children, elders, and some women. Hainan Province, north Dongfang county, south bank of Changhua river, north bank in Changjiang county. *Status:* 6a (Vigorous). Language of recognized nationality: Han. *Class:* Tai-Kadai, Kra, Eastern Kra. *Dialects:* None known. Lexical similarity: 40% with Hlai [lic]. Many loanwords from Chinese. *Type:* SVO; tonal, 10 tones (5 in checked syllables and 5 in unchecked syllables). *Lg Use:* Vigorous. All domains. All ages. Positive attitudes. Very few also use Hlai [lic]. 41% can use Mandarin Chinese [cmn]. *Lg Dev:* Grammar. *Other:* Traditional religion. *Map:* 346.

Darang Deng [mhu] (Darang, Darang Dengyu, Digaro, Digaro-Mishmi). 850 in China (1999 Sun Hong Kai). 750 monolinguals. Southeast Xizang Tibet Autonomous Region, Chayu (Zayü) county along Dulai river valley, Xiazayu, Qu'antong, and Gayao townships, Nyingchi prefecture. *Status:* 6b (Threatened). *Lg Use:* Vigorous. A few Geman Deng speak it as second language. All domains. All ages. Positive attitudes. Also use Central Tibetan [bod], Mandarin Chinese [cmn], Miju-Mishmi [mxj]. Used as L2 by Geman Deng [mxj]. *Other:* Some Chinese scholars believe them to be in the Jingpo branch. Officially classified as Undetermined Nationality. Traditional religion. See main entry on page 110 (as Digaro-Mishmi). *Map:* 345.

Daur [dta] (Daguor, Dagur, Dawar, Dawo'er, Tahuerh, Tahur). 96,100 in China (1999 D. Ying), decreasing. 35,000 Buteha dialect, 35,000 Qiqiha'er dialect, 15,500 Haila'er dialect, 4500 Ili dialect. 24,300 monolinguals. Ethnic population: 132,000 (2000 census). Nei Mongol Province, Inner Mongolia Autonomous Region, Hulun Buir league, Hailar prefecture, Morin Dawa (Molidawa) Daur autonomous banner, Oroqen autonomous banner and Ewenki autonomous banner; Heilongjiang Province, Nenjiang prefecture, Fuyu and Nehe counties; Qiqihar prefecture, Qiqihar city; northwest Xinjiang Uyghur Autonomous Region, Tacheng prefecture (Ili dialect). Also in Mongolia. *Status:* 7 (Shifting). Statutory language of provincial identity in Inner Mongolia Autonomous Region, Hulun Buir League (1984, Ethnic Regional Autonomy Act, Articles 10 and 21). Language of recognized nationality: Daur. *Class:* Altaic, Mongolic, Eastern, Dagur. *Dialects:* Buteha (Aihui, Bataxan, Butah, Darbin, Mergen, Nawen, Nemor), Haila'er (Hailar, Mokertu, Nantun), Ili, Qiqiha'er (Fularji, Jiangdong, Jingxi, Qiqihar, Tsitsikhar). Definitely distinct from other Mongolian languages (Voegelin and Voegelin 1977). Some identify Haila'er dialect as a dialect of Evenki [evn]. *Type:* SOV; grammatical function marked mainly by suffixes; some vowel harmony; many consonant clusters; palatalized and labialized consonants; loans from Chinese, Manchu, Evenki. *Lg Use:* In Hulun Buir the language is being retained well; in Heilongjiang not transmitted to children among most groups (Bradley 2007). All domains. Mainly adults. Neutral attitudes. Also use Evenki [evn], Kazakh [kaz], Manchu [mnc], Mandarin Chinese [cmn], Oroqen [orh], Peripheral Mongolian [mvf]. Used as L2 by Evenki [evn], Oroqen [orh]. *Lg Dev:* Literacy rate in L2: 97% (2000 census, Daur nationality). Some literacy in Mongolian among those 30 to 50 years of age in Hala'er. Poetry. Radio programs. Films. Dictionary. Grammar. *Writing:* Cyrillic script, 1916–?, 1957–1958. Han script, Simplified variant. Latin script, used from 1920 to some time after 1928, then from 1981. Mongolian script, Manchu style, used since the Qing dynasty. *Other:* Traditional religion. *Map:* 344.

Dong, Northern [doc] (Gam, Kam, Tong, Tung, Tung-Chia). 463,000 in China (2003). Area where west Hunan Province and north Guangxi Zhuang Autonomous Region meet, southeast Guizhou (Yuping autonomous county); Guangxi Zhuang Autonomous Region, 20 contiguous counties. Also in Viet Nam. *Status:* 6b (Threatened). Language of recognized nationality: Dong. *Class:* Tai-Kadai, Kam-Tai, Kam-Sui. *Dialects:* None known. Zhanglu speech in Rongjiang County, Guizhou Province is standard variety. Reportedly similar to Mulam [mlm]. Lexical similarity: 80% with Northern Dong varieties, 71% with Southern Dong [kmc], 46% with Lakkia [lbc], 29% with Qabiao [laq], 26% with Hlai [lic], 24% with Gelao, 22% with Lachi [lbt], 6% with Hmong Njua [hnj], 4% with Iu Mien [ium]. *Type:* Tonal, 9 tones. *Lg Use:* Vigorous. All domains. All ages. Also use Mandarin Chinese [cmn]. Used as L2 by Pa-Hng [pha], Southern Dong [kmc]. *Lg Dev:* Literacy rate in L2: 55%. Dictionary. Grammar. *Writing:* Latin script, pinyin-based, used since 1981, experimental, small-scale use in education and literature. *Other:* Ethnic autonym: Kam; Dong is the Chinese name. Traditional way of life relatively undisturbed. Traditional religion. *Map:* 346:35.

Dong, Southern [kmc] (Gam, Kam, Tong, Tung, Tung-Chia). 1,000,000. Area where west Hunan Province and north Guangxi Zhuang Autonomous Region meet, southeast Guizhou (Yuping autonomous county); Guangxi Zhuang Autonomous Region, 20 contiguous counties. *Status:* 6a (Vigorous). Language of recognized nationality: Dong. *Class:* Tai-Kadai, Kam-Tai, Kam-Sui. *Dialects:* Reportedly similar to Mulam [mlm]. Lexical similarity: 93% with Southern Dong dialects, 71% with Northern Dong [doc], 46% with Lakkia [lbc], 29% with Qabiao [laq], 26% with Hlai [lic], 24% with Gelao, 22% with Lachi [lbt], 6% with Hmong Njua [hnj], 4% with Iu Mien [ium]. *Type:* Tonal, 9 tones. *Lg Use:* All domains. All ages. Neutral attitudes. Use Mandarin [cmn] for literature. Northern Dong [doc] users are more bilingual than Southern Dong. *Lg Dev:* Poetry. Magazines. New media. Films. TV. Videos. Dictionary. Grammar. NT: 2006. *Writing:* Han (Hanzi, Kanji, Hanja) script, dating from late-Ming dynasty, used in ritual texts and folk domains. Latin script, pinyin-based, 1958–1966 and from 1981, experimental, small-scale use in education, administration, and literature. *Other:* Ethnic autonym: Kam; Dong is Chinese name. Traditional way of life relatively undisturbed. Traditional religion. *Map:* 346:40.

Dongxiang [sce] (Santa, Tung, Tunghsiang). 200,000 (Bradley 2007). Half in Suonanba dialect. 80,000 monolinguals. Ethnic population: 514,000 (Bradley 2007). Southwest Gansu Province, Linxia Hui autonomous prefecture, 7 counties and a city; Xinjiang Uyghur Autonomous Region, Ili Kazak autonomous prefecture, Yining and Huocheng counties. *Status:* 6b (Threatened). Language of recognized nationality: Dongxiang. *Class:* Altaic, Mongolic, Eastern, Mongour. *Dialects:* Sijiaji, Suonanba (Xiaonan), Wangjiaji. Some intelligibility with Bonan [peh]. Minor dialect differences in pronunciation and borrowed words. Suonanba considered the standard. *Type:* SOV; no vowel harmony or vowel length distinction; rich in consonants including uvulars; case marking. *Lg Use:* Shifting to Chinese. Home, religion, local commerce, oral tradition. Positive attitudes. Written Chinese in common use. *Lg Dev:* Literacy rate in L2: 12%. Radio programs. Dictionary. Grammar. *Other:* 30% of vocabulary borrowed from Chinese. Muslim (Sunni). *Map:* 344.

Drung [duu]. 14,000 in China (2000 census). 8,500 in Nu River dialect, 5,500 in Dulong River dialect. Total population all countries: 14,000. Population total all countries: 14,225. 13,300 monolinguals. L2 users: Other speakers living among them use Drung as L2. Dulong River dialect (5,500): Far northwest Yunnan Province, Gongshan Dulong-Nu autonomous county, both sides of Dulong river. Nu River dialect (8,500): From Gongshan Dulong-Nu autonomous county west to Chayu (Zayü) county in Xizang Tibet Autonomous Region; Bingzhongluo of Gongshang county and the Chawalong district of Chayu county in Tibet. Also in Myanmar. *Status:* 6a (Vigorous). Language of recognized nationality: Dulong. *Class:* Sino-Tibetan, Tibeto-Burman, Central Tibeto-Burman, Nungish. *Dialects:* Dulong River (Central Dulongjiang, Derung River, Northern Dulongjiang, Southern Dulongjiang), Nu River (Nujiang Dulong). Dialects reportedly inherently intelligible (Thurgood and LaPolla 2003). Nu River Drung is not the same as Tibeto-Burman Anong [nun], which is also in Myanmar. Different from Rawang [raw] in Myanmar. Other possible dialect names are Melam, Metu, Tamalu, and Tukiumu. Lexical similarity: 74% with Matwang dialect of Rawang [raw]. *Type:* SOV; 2 tones. *Lg Use:* Vigorous. All domains. All ages. Positive attitudes. Also use Burmese [mya], Lisu [lis], Mandarin Chinese [cmn]. *Lg Dev:* Literacy rate in L2: 68%–73% (2000 census, Nu nationality). 68%–73%. *Writing:* Latin script, pinyin-based, used between 1984 and 1990s. *Other:* Ethnonym: Qiuzu is an old term for the people. Traditional religion. *Map:* 345.

Duoluo [giw] (Bai Gelo, White Gelao). 1,200 in China (1987 Z. Guo-qiao). Population total all countries: 1,220. North central Guizhou Province, Zunyi county, Jianshan village; Zhijin county, Agong village; Langdai county, Zhuijiao and Ruojiao villages; Guanling county, Dingyinxiao village. Also in Guangxi Province, Longlin county, Muji village. Tu'lu is spoken in Yunnan Province, Malipo. Also in Viet Nam (White Gelao). *Status:* 8b (Nearly extinct). Language of recognized nationality: Gelao. *Class:* Tai-Kadai, Kra, Western Kra. *Dialect:* Tu'lu. *Lg Use:* Elderly only. *Map:* 345.

Dzao Min [bpn] (Ba Pai Yao, Yao Min, Yau Min, Zaomin). 60,000 (Wang Fushi and Mao Zhongwu 1995). Northern Guangdong Province, Liannan and Yangshan counties; south Hunan Province, Yizhang county. *Status:* 6a (Vigorous). Language of recognized nationality: Yao. *Class:* Hmong-Mien, Mienic, Zaomin. *Dialects:* None known. Not intelligible with other Mienic languages. Lexical similarity: 61% with Iu Mien [ium], 59% with Kim Mun [mji], 58% with Biao-Jiao Mien [bje]. *Other:* Daoist. *Map:* 346.

E [eee] (Eahua, Kjang E, "Wuse Hua" *pej.*, "Wusehua" *pej.*). 30,000 (Edmondson 1992). North Guangxi Zhuang Autonomous Region, Rongshui Hmong autonomous county, Yongle district, Xiatan, Simo, Xinglong (Xingyou) and other villages; Luocheng Mulam autonomous county border areas. *Status:* 6b (Threatened). Language of recognized nationality: Zhuang. *Class:* Mixed language. *Dialects:* A mixed language, with large amounts of Tuguai Hua (also called Pinghua, a Yue Chinese [yue] dialect) and Guiliu Hua (a southwest Mandarin [cmn] dialect) vocabulary, tone category, voice quality, and some word structure. The grammar has been more resistant to Chinese influence. Chinese scholars consider E a mixture of Northern Zhuang languages, Mulam [mlm], Dong [doc] and Chinese. *Type:* Tonal. *Lg Use:* Also use the Guiliu dialect of southwestern Mandarin Chinese [cmn]. Also use Yue Chinese [yue]. *Other:* Ethnic autonym: E. Northern Zhuang languages are not used. Traditional religion. *Map:* 346.

Enu [enu] (Ximoluo). 30,000 (Dai Qingxia and Duan Kuangle 1995). South Yunnan Province, Simao municipality, Mojiang county, Yayi, Baliu, and Sinanjiang townships; Jiangcheng county, Jiahe and Qushui townships; Honghe prefecture, Luchun county. *Status:* 6b (Threatened). Language of recognized nationality: Hani. *Class:* Sino-Tibetan, Tibeto-Burman, Ngwi-Burmese, Ngwi, Southern. *Dialects:* None known. Lexical similarity: 76% with Biyo [byo] (17 % of similarities are Han loanwords that both have borrowed), 74% with Kaduo [ktp]. *Type:* Tonal, 3 tones. *Lg Use:* Some young people, all adults. *Other:* Ximoluo is an exonym given to Enu by other Hani peoples. Not known if it is pejorative. *Map:* 345.

Ersu [ers] (Bu'erci, Bu'erzi, Bu'erzi Ersu, Doxu, Duoxu, Erhsu, Lizu, Lusu, T'osu). 20,000 (Shearer and Sun Hong Kai 2002), decreasing. Eastern Ersu (Ersu) 13,000, Central Ersu (Duoxu) 10 or less, Western Ersu (Lizu) 4,000. South central Sichuan Province, lower reaches of the Dadu river; Liangshan Yi autonomous prefecture, Ganluo, Yuexi, Mianning, and Muli counties; Ya'an prefecture, Shimian and Hanyuan counties; Ganzi Tibetan autonomous prefecture, Jiulong county; dispersed among Yi, Chinese, and Tibetan peoples. *Status:* 7 (Shifting). Language of recognized nationality: Tibetan. *Class:* Sino-Tibetan, Tibeto-Burman, Northeastern Tibeto-Burman, Ersuish. *Dialects:* Duoxu (Central Ersu), Ersu (Eastern Ersu), Lisu (Liru, Lüzü, Western Ersu). *Type:* SOV; adjectives and number-classifier constructions follow noun heads; consonant cluster onsets; most morphemes monosyllabic; 2 tones, word-template zone. *Lg Use:* Decreasing from language attrition. Mainly older adults. Neutral attitudes. 400 also use Lipo [lpo]. 8,000 also use Mandarin Chinese [cmn]. Used as L2 by Namuyi [nmy]. *Lg Dev:* About 10 people can read the Shaba script. Poetry. Videos. Dictionary. *Writing:* Ersu Shaba Picture Writing, used until some time before 2003, limited usage, used in religious ceremonies. *Other:* Traditional religion. *Map:* 345.

Evenki [evn] (Ewenk, Ewenke, Ewenki, Khamnigan, Owenke, Solon, Solong, Sulong, Suolun). 11,000 in China (Salminen 2007). Population total all countries: 17,130. Ethnic population: 30,500 (2000 census). Nei Mongol Province, Inner Mongolia Autonomous Region, Hulunbuir banners; Ewenki, Moriadawa, Oronchon, Chen Bargu, Arong, Ergune East, and Huisuomu; Heilongjiang Province, Nale prefecture; a few in Xinjiang Uyghur Autonomous Region. Also in Mongolia, Russian Federation, United States. *Status:* 7 (Shifting). Language of recognized nationality: Ewenki. *Class:* Altaic, Tungusic, Northern, Evenki. *Dialects:* Aoluguya (Olguya), Chenba'erhu (Old Bargu), Haila'er, Huihe (Hoy), Morigele (Mergel). Standard dialect is Huihe. Dialectal differences within Evenki are small and the case for regarding Evenki and Orochen as separate languages is weak (Salminen 2007). *Lg Use:* Other speakers in the area also use Evenki. All domains. Very few children except among the Khamnigan. Positive attitudes. Bilinguals use Mandarin Chinese [cmn] as L2. Written Chinese used as literary languages. Farmers use Chinese. Also use Mongolian [mvf]. Written Mongolian used as literary language. Herdsmen use Mongolian as L2. Also use Daur [dta], Oroqen [orh]. Used as L2 by Daur [dta], Oroqen [orh]. *Lg Dev:* Literacy rate in L2: 96%, literacy in any language (2000 census, Ewenki nationality). Radio programs. TV. Dictionary. Grammar. Bible portions: 1995. *Writing:* Cyrillic script, used since 1937, small-scale use in Russia. Latin script, used in Russia in 1931–1937, limited use in a few publications in China and on internet from 1983. *Other:* Ethnic autonym: Solon in China, but also now use the official name Ewenke. Traditional religion, Buddhist (Lamaist). *Map:* 344.

Ge [hmj] (Chonganjiang Miao, Ge Jia, Gedang, Gedong, Gedou, Gedou Miao, Gedoudiu, Gedu, Gejia, Ge-Mong, Gho-mhon, Keh Deo). 60,000 (Wang Fushi and Mao Zhongwu 1995). East central Guizhou Province, Huangping county, Chong'an township; Kaili municipality, Longchang township. *Status:* 6b (Threatened). Language of recognized nationality: Miao. *Class:* Hmong-Mien, Hmongic, Chuanqiandian. A member of macrolanguage Hmong [hmn]. *Dialects:* None known. Not inherently intelligible with other varieties of Miao. *Lg Use:* All domains. *Lg Dev:* Bible portions: 1937. *Other:* Given special status as Gejia in Guizhou Province. Traditional religion. *Maps:* 345, 346.

Gelao, Red [gir]. A few speakers. Yunnan Province, Wenshan prefecture, Malipo county. *Status:* 8b (Nearly extinct). Language of recognized nationality: Gelao. See main entry on page 310. *Map:* 345.

Geman Deng [mxj] (Kaman, Keman, Miji, Miju, Mishmi). 200 in China (1999 Sun Hong Kai), decreasing. Xizang Province, southeast corner of Tibet Autonomous Region, Chayu (Zayü) county, Nyingchi prefecture, several townships, on tablelands either side of lower reaches of Chayu (Zayü) river in their own small villages. *Status:* 6b (Threatened). *Lg Use:* Facing extinction. Intermarriage with Darang Deng leads to switch to Darang [mhu]. Limited to home domain in which both parents are Geman. All ages. Some young people also use Chinese or Tibetan [bod] or both. Also use Digaro-Mishmi [mhu]. Used as L2 by Darang Deng [mhu]. *Other:* Officially classified as Undetermined nationality. Some Chinese linguists believe the language to be similar to Jingpo [kac]. Traditional religion. See main entry on page 130 (as Miju-Mishmi). *Map:* 345.

Gepo [ygp] (Baiyi, Gepu, Guo, Gupu, Guzu, Jiantouyi, Köpu, Nasu, Pingtouyi). 100,000 (2007), decreasing. Northeast Yunnan Province, Luquan, Fumin, Xundian, Luxi, Shizong, Luoping, Malong, Songming, Huize, Mile, Shilin, and Dongchuan counties. *Status:* 6a (Vigorous). Language of recognized nationality: Yi. *Class:* Sino-Tibetan, Tibeto-Burman, Ngwi-Burmese, Ngwi, Northern. *Dialects:* Luquan Naso, Wuding Naisu. Related to Nasu [ywq]. *Lg Use:* All ages. *Map:* 345.

Groma [gro] (Tromowa). 12,800 in China (1993). Population total all countries: 26,800. Xizang Tibet Autonomous Region, Chambi Valley, between Sikkim and Bhutan. Also in India. *Status:* 6a (Vigorous). Language of recognized nationality: Tibetan. *Class:* Sino-Tibetan, Tibeto-Burman, Western Tibeto-Burman, Bodish, Central Bodish, Central, Southern. *Dialects:* Lower Groma, Upper Groma. Possible dialects or related languages: Spiti, Tomo (Chumbi). *Other:* Traditional religion, Buddhist (Lamaist). *Map:* 344.

Guiqiong [gqi] (Guichong, Guiqiang, Yutong). 6,000 (2000 Sun Hong Kai). 1,000 monolinguals. Ethnic population: 7,000 (2000 D. Bradley). About 1,000 ethnic Guiqiong reportedly understand Guiqiong, but do not speak it. West central Sichuan Province, Ganzi (Garzê) Tibetan autonomous prefecture, 4 townships: Shiji, Maibeng, Qianqi, Shelian West; also Guza town; plateaus on both sides of north Dadu river. *Status:* 6b (Threatened). Language of recognized nationality: Tibetan. *Class:* Sino-Tibetan, Tibeto-Burman, Northeastern Tibeto-Burman, Qiangic. *Dialects:* Phonological dialect differences, but communication is possible. 2 or 3 varieties have difficult mutual intelligibility. Loanwords from Tibetan and Chinese. *Type:* SOV; adjectives and number-classifier constructions follow noun heads; tonal, 4 tones. *Lg Use:* Vigorous. Only in the village with their own people. Children rarely use it. Negative attitudes. 100% also use Mandarin Chinese [cmn]. *Lg Dev:* Poetry. Dictionary. *Other:* Buddhist (Lamaist). *Map:* 344.

Hagei [giq] (Hakei). North central Guizhou Province, Renhuai county, Anliang and Taiyang villages; Zunyi county, Qinglong village; Qingzhen county, Maixiang village; Zhenning county, Huajiangzhen and Ma'ao villages; Qinglong county, Liangshuiyang; Guanling county, Dingying village. Also in Guangxi Province, Longlin county, Sanchong village. *Status:* 8a (Moribund). Language of recognized nationality: Gelao. *Lg Use:* Older adults and elderly. See main entry on page 310 (as Gelao, Green). *Map:* 345.

Hani [hni] (Hanhi, Hani Proper, Haw). 740,000 in China (Bradley 2007). Population total all countries: 758,620. 444,000 monolinguals. South Yunnan Province, Jingdong and Jinggu counties, Yuanjiang and Lancang (Mekong) river basins, Ailao mountains. Also in Laos, Viet Nam. *Status:* 6a (Vigorous). Language of recognized nationality: Hani. *Class:* Sino-Tibetan, Tibeto-Burman, Ngwi-Burmese, Ngwi, Southern. *Dialects:* Hani has numerous dialects and is reportedly fairly similar to Akha [ahk]. *Type:* SOV; tonal, 3 tones. *Lg Use:* Vigorous. Some users of nearby languages also speak Hani. Taught at Kunming Institute. All domains. All ages. Positive attitudes. 40% also use Mandarin Chinese [cmn]. Written Chinese is in common use. Also use Lipo [lpo], Lü [khb]. Used as L2 by Bisu [bzi], Kucong [lkc], Lahu [lhu], Sangkong [sgk]. *Lg Dev:* 40,000 can read and write Hani. Newspapers. Radio programs. Films. TV. Dictionary. Grammar. *Writing:* Latin script, pinyin-based, used in 1958–1964 and from 1982, experimental, used in education, literature, and media. *Other:* Includes Hani, Akha, Biyo, Kaduo, Honi, and other groups, all speaking Southern Ngwi languages. The Hanhi ethnic group in Viet Nam and Laos speak Hani. Traditional religion. *Map:* 345.

Hlai [lic] (Bli, Dai, Day, Dli, Klai, La, Lai, Le, Li, Loi, Slai). 667,000 (1999 O. Jueya). 160,000 monolinguals. Ethnic population: 1,248,000 (2000 census). Includes about 52,300 Jiamao [jio] speakers. Central and southern Hainan Province, Wanning, Tunchang, Danxiang, Chengmai, Baisha. *Status:* 6a (Vigorous). Language of recognized nationality: Li. *Class:* Tai-Kadai, Hlai. *Dialects:* Bendi (Baisha-Yuanmen, Local Li, Zwn), Ha (Luohua-Hayan-Baoxian), Meifu (Moifau), Qi (Gei, Tongshi-Qiandui-Baocheng). Some dialects may be separate languages. Matisoff (1988) lists 8 varieties: Baoding, Xifang, Tongshi, Baisha, Qiandiu, Heitu, Yuanmen, and Baocheng. Luowo subdialect of Ha dialect is considered the standard. Lexical similarity: 27% with Gelao, 26% with Dong [doc] and Qabiao [laq], 25% with Lachi [lbt]. *Lg Use:* Vigorous. Some local Han can also speak Hlai. All domains. All ages. Positive attitudes. Also use Iu Mien [ium], Mandarin Chinese [cmn]. Used as L2 by Cun [cuq]. *Lg Dev:* Literacy rate in L2: 88% (2000 census, Li nationality). Dictionary. *Writing:* Latin script, pinyin-based, used from 1958 to early 1960s and from 1985, small-scale use in literacy. *Other:* Together with speakers of Jiamao [jio]. Traditional culture. Traditional religion. *Map:* 346.

Hlersu [hle] (Lesu, Sansu, Shansu). 15,000 (2007), decreasing. Central Yunnan Province, Zhenyuan and Shuangbai counties, scattered mountaintop locations; Yuanjiang county, 38 villages; Xinping county, 40 villages; Eshan county, 6 villages; Shiping county, 5 villages. *Status:* 6b (Threatened). Language of recognized nationality: Yi. *Class:* Sino-Tibetan, Tibeto-Burman, Ngwi-Burmese, Ngwi, Central. *Dialects:* None known. Related to Lolopo [ycl]. *Lg Use:* Being replaced by Nisu and Chinese (Bradley 2007). Home, village. Also use Chesu [ych] (Bradley 2007). Also use Nisu [nos] (Bradley 2007). *Map:* 345.

Hmong [hmn]. A macrolanguage (see page 9). *Other:* Includes: Central Huishui Miao [hmc], Central Mashan Miao [hmm], Chuanqiandian Cluster Miao [cqd], Eastern Huishui Miao [hme], Eastern Qiandong Miao [hmq], Eastern Xiangxi Miao [muq], Ge [hmj], Hmong Daw [mww], Hmong Njua [hnj] (Laos), Horned Miao [hrm], Large Flowery Miao [hmd], Luopohe Miao [hml], Northern Guiyang Miao [huj], Northern Huishui Miao [hmi], Northern Mashan Miao [hmp], Northern Qiandong Miao [hea], Sinicized Miao [hmz], Small Flowery Miao [sfm], Southern Guiyang Miao [hmy], Southern Mashan Miao [hma], Southern Qiandong Miao [hms], Southwestern Guiyang Miao [hmg], Southwestern Huishui Miao [hmh], Western Mashan Miao [hmw], Western Xiangxi Miao [mmr].

Hmong Daw [mww] (Bai Miao, Banded Arm Hmong, Hmong Dleu, Hmong Qua Mpa, Meo Do, Meo Kao, Mong Do, Mong Trang, Pe Miao, Peh Miao, Striped Arm Hmong, Striped Hmong, White Hmong, White Lum, White Meo, White Miao). 233,000 in China (2004). Population total all countries: 1,698,400. Ethnic population: All Hmong in China: 8,950,000 (2000 census). South and southwest Guizhou Province, northwest Guangxi, southeast and southwest Yunnan provinces. Also in France, Laos, Thailand, United States, Viet Nam. *Status:* 5 (Developing). Language of recognized nationality: Miao. *Class:* Hmong-Mien, Hmongic, Chuanqiandian. A member of macrolanguage Hmong [hmn]. *Dialects:* None known. Largely intelligible with Hmong Njua [hnj], but sociolinguistic factors require separate literature for Hmong Daw. *Type:* Tonal, 7 tones. *Lg Use:* All ages. Also use Mandarin Chinese [cmn]. *Lg Dev:* Literacy rate in L2: 42% in Mandarin Chinese [cmn]. Radio programs. Dictionary. Bible: 2000. *Writing:* Lao script. Latin script, used since 1953, primary usage. Miao (Pollard) script, used in China. Pahawh Hmong script, used since 1959. Thai script, used in Thailand. *Other:* Traditional religion, Christian. *Map:* 345.

Hmong Njua [hnj] (Blue Hmong, Blue Meo, Ching Miao, Green Hmong, Green Meo, Hmong Leng, Hmong Nzhua, Hmoob Leeg, Lu Miao, Meo Dam, Meo Lai, Mong Leng, Mong Ntsua, Qing Miao, Tak Miao). 40,000 in China (Hattaway 2000). Southeast Yunnan Province, Maguan and Malipo counties, scattered areas to west; far west Guangxi, southwest Guizhou and south Sichuan provinces. *Status:* 6a (Vigorous). Language of recognized nationality: Miao. *Lg Use:* Vigorous. Home, community, market. All ages. Also use Mandarin Chinese [cmn]. Used as L2 by Jiongnai Bunu [pnu], Northern Tujia [tji], Pa-Hng [pha], Qabiao [laq]. *Lg Dev:* Taught in primary schools. *Other:* Unique in culture and language from other Miao groups. See main entry on page 214. *Map:* 345.

Honi [how] (Baihong, Hao-Bai, Haoni, Ho, Ouni, Uni, Woni). 140,000 (Bradley 2007). South Yunnan Province, east Simao prefecture, Mojiang Hani, Pu'er Hani, Yi, and Dai autonomous counties; Yuxi municipal prefecture, Yuanjiang Hani, Yi, and Dai autonomous counties. *Status:* 6a (Vigorous). Language of recognized nationality: Hani. *Class:* Sino-Tibetan, Tibeto-Burman, Ngwi-Burmese, Ngwi, Southern. *Dialects:* Baihong, Haoni. Dialects may be separate languages. *Lg Use:* Also use Mandarin Chinese [cmn]. *Lg Dev:* Literacy rate in L2: 70%. Observed functional literacy in Chinese is low. Official literacy rate for the Hani nationality is registered much higher. *Writing:* Han (Hanzi, Kanji, Hanja) script, no longer in use, used in ritual texts and folk literature. *Other:* Language is distinct from Hani proper. Traditional religion, Christian. *Map:* 345.

Horpa [ero] (Bawang, Bopa, Danba, Daofu, Daofuhua, Dawu, Ergong, Geshitsa, Geshiza, Geshizahua, Hor, Hórsók, Huo'er, Nyagrong-Minyag, Pawang, Rgu, rTau, sTau, Western Gyarong, Western Jiarong, Xinlong-Muya). 45,000 (Shearer and Sun Hong Kai 2002). sTau: 23,000, Geshitsa: 21,000, Nyagrong-Minyak: 1,000. 15,000 monolinguals. Sichuan Province, Ganzi (Garzê) Tibetan autonomous prefecture, Daofu (rTau, sTau, Dawu), Luhuo, Xinlong (Brag-'go), Danba (Rong-brag), and Xinlong (Nyagrong) counties. *Status:* 6a (Vigorous). Language of recognized nationality: Tibetan. *Class:* Sino-Tibetan, Tibeto-Burman, Northeastern Tibeto-Burman, rGyalrongic. *Dialects:* Geshitsa (Geshiza), Nyagrong-Minyag (Xinlong-Muya), sTau (Daofu, Dawu, rTau). The dialects of Horpa reportedly are not mutually intelligible. *Type:* SOV; adjectives and number-classifier constructions follow noun heads; affixation; compounding; reduplication; complex consonant cluster onsets; nontonal. *Lg Use:* All domains. Mainly adults but also a large percentage of children speak Horpa vigorously. Neutral attitudes. 1,000 also use Central Tibetan [bod]. 20,000 also use Mandarin Chinese [cmn]. *Lg Dev:* Dictionary. *Other:* Buddhist (Lamaist). *Map:* 344.

Hu [huo]. 1,000 (Li Jinfang 2006). Southwest Yunnan Province, Xishuangbanna Dai autonomous prefecture, Mengla and Jinghong counties, 5 villages, including Nahuopa village in Jinghong, Mengyang township. *Status:* 6b (Threatened). *Class:* Austro-Asiatic, Mon-Khmer, Northern Mon-Khmer, Palaungic, Eastern Palaungic, Angkuic. *Dialects:* Possibly a dialect of U [uuu]. 76% similar lexically with U of Shuangjiang County. *Type:* Affixes; tonal. *Other:* Officially classified as Undetermined Nationality. Traditional religion. *Map:* 345:30.

Ili Turki [ili] (Ili Turk, Tuerke, Tu'erke, T'urk). 120 in China (1980 R. Hahn), decreasing. The language of about 30 families (Salminen 2007). Xinjiang Uyghur Autonomous Region, Ili Kazak autonomous prefecture, Tekes, Nilka, Xinyuan, Gongliu, Zhaosu, and other counties, Ili valley near Kuldja. Also in Kazakhstan. *Status:* 8a (Moribund). Language of recognized nationality: Uzbek. *Class:* Altaic, Turkic, Eastern. *Type:* SOV; vowel harmony; influenced greatly by Kazakh and Uyghur; has Arabic, Persian, Chinese, and Russian loans. *Lg Use:* Younger generations are shifting to Kazakh [kaz] or Uygur [uig] (Salminen 2007). Older adults. Also use Kazakh [kaz], Uyghur [uig]. *Other:* Ethnically and linguistically distinct, discovered in 1956. Their oral history says they came from the Ferghana Valley (Uzbekistan and Kyrgyzstan) about 200 years ago. Muslim (Sunni). *Map:* 344.

Iu Mien [ium] (Ban Yao, Highland Yao, Mian, Mien, Myen, Pan Yao, Yao, Yiu Mien, Youmian). 383,000 in China (Wang Fushi and Mao Zhongwu 1995). Population total all countries: 819,800. Guangxi Zhuang Autonomous Region, Dayao mountains; Guangdong Province, Ruyuan county, Yunnan and Hunan provinces; Guizhou Province, Rongjiang, Congjiang, and Libo counties. some in Jiangxi Province. Also in Belgium, Denmark, France, Laos, Switzerland, Thailand, United States, Viet Nam. *Status:* 5 (Developing). Language of recognized nationality: Yao. *Class:* Hmong-Mien, Mienic, Mian-Jin. *Dialect:* Guoshan Yao. Dialects may not be intelligible. Biao Mon [bmt] may be a dialect of Iu Mien. Differences from other Mienic languages are in the tone system, consonants, vowel quality, vowel length. Chinese linguists consider the Iu Mien spoken in Changdong, Jinxiu Yao Autonomous County, Guangxi to be the standard. May be most similar to Mandarin Chinese [cmn]. Lexical similarity: 78% with Kim Mun [mji], 70% with Biao-Jiao Mien [bje], 61% with Dzao Min [bpn]. *Type:* Tonal, 7 tones. *Lg Use:* Vigorous. All domains. All ages. Positive attitudes. Adults also use Chinese [zho]. Used as L2 by Chadong [cdy], Hlai [lic], Jiongnai Bunu [pnu], Lakkia [lbc]. *Lg Dev:* Radio programs. Dictionary. Grammar. Bible: 2008. *Writing:* Han (Hanzi, Kanji, Hanja) script, dating from before Yuan dynasty, used in folk domains and text messaging. Lao script, used in Laos. Latin script, used at least since 1930s, used in China, Thailand, United States, France, Canada. Thai script, used in Thailand. *Other:* Ethnic groups: Hua Lan, Hua, Hung, Cao Long, Coc, Khoc, Quan Coc, Quan Trang, Son Trang, Sung, Tien (Tiao Tchaine), Yaya. The Lakkia, Mun, Bunu languages, plus speakers of other Mienic and Hmongic languages, and ethnic Yao who speak Chinese, are officially classified within Yao nationality in China. Pingdi Yao (Piongtuojo, Piongtoajeu) is a variety of Chinese with 1,000,000 speakers, half of whom are members of Yao nationality, Guangdong Province, Hunan-Guangxi border. Daoist, traditional religion. *Map:* 346:41.

Jiamao [jio] (Gevou, Kamau, Ku vou, Tai). 52,300 (Wurm et al. 1987). South Hainan Province, Baoting, Lingshui, and Qiongzhong counties, near Wuzhi mountain. *Status:* 6a (Vigorous). Language of recognized nationality: Li. *Class:* Tai-Kadai, Hlai. *Dialects:* Considered by Chinese linguists a dialect of Hlai [lic], but very different from Hlai dialects in phonology, grammar, and vocabulary. *Lg Use:* Also use Mandarin Chinese [cmn]. *Lg Dev:* Literacy rate in L2: 88% (2000 census, Li nationality). *Other:* Together with Hlai [lic] speakers. Traditional religion. *Map:* 346.

Jiarong [jya] (Chiarong, Gyarong, Gyarung, Jarong, Jyarung, Keru, Rgyarong). 83,000 (1999 Sun Hong Kai). 25,000 monolinguals. Ethnic population: 151,000 (Lin Xiangrong 1993). Includes 139,000 in Situ Jiarong, 12,200 in Chabao and Sidaba. North central Sichuan Province. Situ is in the traditional territory of 4 chieftaincies: Zhuokeji, Suomo, Songgang, Dangba. Chabao is in northeast corner of Maerkang county, Chabao district, Longerjia, Dazang, and Shaerzong townships. Sidaba is in Maerkang county, Sidaba district, Caodeng, Kangshan, and Ribu townships; north in southwest corner of Aba county, Kehe and Rongan townships; west along middle Duke river, Rangtang county, between Wuyi and Shili townships; and Seda county at the confluence of Seda and Duke rivers, a small town. *Status:* 6a (Vigorous). Language of recognized nationality: Tibetan. *Class:* Sino-Tibetan, Tibeto-Burman, Northeastern Tibeto-Burman, rGyalrongic. *Dialects:* Chabao (Central Jiarong, Dazang, Northeastern Jiarong, Northern Jiarong), Sidaba (Caodeng, Northwestern Jiarong, Western Jiarong), Situ (Eastern Jiarong). Varieties of Situ are: Ma'erkang, Lixian, Jinchuan (Dajin), and Xiaojin. Varieties of Sidaba are Caodeng and Ribu. Western and Northern phonology are fairly similar but differ greatly from Eastern. Dialects are likely three separate mutually unintelligible languages. Lexical similarity: 75% between Eastern and Northern Jiarong (with significant phonological differences), 60% between Western and Northern, 13% between the Situ dialect and Horpa [ero]. *Type:* SOV; phonologically and lexically similar to Tibetan, grammatically more similar to Pumi and Qiang; complex consonant clusters; limited pitch contrast. *Lg Use:* Vigorous. All domains. All ages. Positive attitudes, but intellectuals worry about diminishing use. 950 also use Central Tibetan [bod]. 56,000 also use Mandarin Chinese [cmn]. 50 also use Northern Qiang

[cng]. *Lg Dev:* Radio programs. Dictionary. *Writing:* Tibetan script. *Other:* Traditional religion, Buddhist (Lamaist). *Map:* 344.

Jingpho [kac] (Chingpaw, Chingp'o, Dashanhua, Jinghpaw, Jingpo, Kachin, Marip). 40,000 in China (1999 X. Xijian). 20,000 monolinguals. Ethnic population: 132,000 (2000 census). Includes Atsi [atb], Maru [mhx] and Lashi [lsi] speakers (2000 census). West Yunnan Province, Dehong Dai-Jingpo autonomous prefecture, Yingjiang, Longchuan, and Ruili counties; Baoshan prefecture,Tengchong county. *Status:* 6a (Vigorous). Language of recognized nationality: Jingpo. *Dialects:* Dulong, Dzili (Jili), Enkun (Nkhum, Nkhumka), Hkaku (Hka-Hku), Kauri (Gauri, Hkauri, Kauri, Kauzhika, Khauri), Mengzhi, Shidan (Satanka, Xidan). *Lg Use:* Vigorous. All domains. Positive attitudes. Also use Chinese [cmn]. Chinese used in some secondary schools. Also use Lashi [lsi], Lhao Vo [mhx], Zaiwa [atb]. Used as L2 by Achang [acn], Lhaovo [mhx], Lisu [lis], Lü [khb], Ruching Palaung [pce], Zaiwa [atb]. *Lg Dev:* Literacy rate in L2: 84% (2000 census, Jingpho nationality). Chinese used in some secondary schools. *Other:* Also includes Zaiwa [atb], Maru [mhx], and Lashi [lsi] speakers. Kachin refers to the cultural rather than the linguistic group. Traditional religion, Buddhist, Christian. See main entry on page 234. *Map:* 345.

Jinuo, Buyuan [jiy] (Buyuan, Jino). 1,000 (1994). Most monolingual. Ethnic population: All Jinuo: 20,900 (Bradley 2007). South Yunnan Province, Xishuangbanna Dai autonomous prefecture, near Laos and Myanmar borders, east of Jinghong. Youle mountains. 40 villages. *Status:* 6b (Threatened). Language of recognized nationality: Jinuo. *Class:* Sino-Tibetan, Tibeto-Burman, Ngwi-Burmese, Ngwi, Central. *Dialects:* Buyuan and Youle dialects not inherently intelligible. Chinese used for communication. *Type:* SOV; initial consonant clusters (stop or nasal plus, r); no syllable-final consonants; mostly monosyllabic words; tonal, 6 tones. *Lg Use:* Vigorous. All domains. All ages. Also use Lü [khb], Mandarin Chinese [cmn]. *Lg Dev:* Literacy rate in L2: 83% in any language (2000 census, Jinuo nationality). Grammar. *Writing:* Latin script. *Other:* Traditional religion. *Map:* 345:26.

Jinuo, Youle [jiu] (Jino, Youle). 10,000 (Bradley 2007). Ethnic population: All Jinuo: 20,900 (Bradley 2007). South Yunnan Province, Xishuangbanna Dai autonomous prefecture, near Laos and Myanmar borders, east of Jinghong. Youle mountains. 40 villages. *Status:* 6b (Threatened). Language of recognized nationality: Jinuo. *Class:* Sino-Tibetan, Tibeto-Burman, Ngwi-Burmese, Ngwi, Central. *Dialects:* Youle and Buyuan dialects not mutually inherently intelligible. Chinese used to communicate. *Type:* SOV; initial consonant clusters (stop or nasal plus, r); no syllable-final consonants; mostly monosyllabic words; tonal, 6 tones. *Lg Use:* Vigorous. All domains. All ages. Positive attitudes. Some also use Chinese [cmn]. Chinese used in education. Also use Lü [khb]. *Lg Dev:* Literacy rate in L2: 83%. Films. *Writing:* Latin script. *Other:* Traditional religion. *Map:* 345:25.

Kaduo [ktp] (Khatu). 180,000 in China (Bradley 2007), increasing. Population total all countries: 185,000. Many monolinguals. Yunnan Province, primarily southeast Simao prefecture, Pu'er, Mojiang, and Jiangcheng counties. Also in Laos. *Status:* 6a (Vigorous). Language of recognized nationality: Hani. *Class:* Sino-Tibetan, Tibeto-Burman, Ngwi-Burmese, Ngwi, Southern. *Type:* SOV; CV(V); a voiced-voiceless distinction only for fricatives; no tense or nasalized vowels; nouns mostly polysyllabic, other words mostly monosyllabic; many loanwords from Chinese; tonal, 8 tones. *Lg Use:* Home, village. All ages. *Lg Dev:* Literacy rate in L2: Some in Chinese. *Writing:* Miao (Pollard) script, no longer in use. *Other:* Different from Kadu [zkd] in Myanmar. *Map:* 345.

Kalmyk-Oirat [xal] (Oirat, Weilate, Western Mongol, Xinjiang Mongolian). 130,000 in China (Salminen 2007). Xinjiang Uyghur Autonomous Region, Jungaria region; Qinghai Province, Kukunor region, Lake Qinghai northwest; Nei Mongol, western Inner Mongolia Autonomous Region, Alashan league; Gansu Province northern border area. *Status:* 7 (Shifting). Statutory language of provincial identity in Inner Mongolia Autonomous Region (1984, Ethnic Regional Autonomy Act, Articles 10 and 21). Language of recognized nationality: Mongolian. *Dialects:* Bayit, Dorbot, Jakhachin, Khoshut (Khoshuud), Kök Nur (Qinghai), Mingat, Olot (Eleuth, Elyut, Ööld), Torgut (Torghut, Tu'erhute). *Lg Use:* Continues to be used as a community language in most areas (Salminen 2007). Schooling in Chahar Mongolian [mvf]. High bilingualism in Chahar Mongolian. Used as L2 by Tuva [tyv]. See main entry on page 321. *Map:* 344.

Kang [kyp] (Tai Khang). 34,100 in China (1993). Southwest Yunnan Province. *Status:* 6a (Vigorous). Language of recognized nationality: Dai. *Other:* Related ethnic groups, dialects, or languages in the area: Chang Teo Fah, Kentse, Mengka (Mengkah). See main entry on page 214. *Map:* 345.

Kangjia [kxs] (Kangyang Hui). 1,000 (Bradley 2007). Ethnic population: 2,000 (Bradley 2007). Qinghai Province, Tongren county. *Status:* 8a (Moribund). Language of recognized nationality: Hui. *Class:* Altaic, Mongolic, Eastern, Mongour. *Lg Use:* Local commerce. Mainly older adults. Neutral attitudes. Also use Central Tibetan [bod], Mandarin Chinese [cmn]. *Lg Dev:* Dictionary. Grammar. *Writing:* Unwritten. *Other:* Muslim (Jahaliyah). *Map:* 344.

Kathu [ykt] (Gasu). 5,000 (2007), decreasing. Yunnan Province, Guangnan county, Balong district. Possibly in Guangxi Province. *Status:* 6b (Threatened). Language of recognized nationality: Yi. *Class:* Sino-Tibetan, Tibeto-Burman, Ngwi-Burmese, Ngwi, Southeastern. *Map:* 345.

Katso [kaf] (Gazhuo, Gezhuo, Kazhuo). 4,000 (Bradley 1997), decreasing. Most young people are semi-speakers, speaking Chinese instead (Bradley 2007). Ethnic population: 6,340 (Bradley 2007). Yunnan Province, Yuxi prefecture, Tonghai county, Xingmeng Mongolian autonomous township. *Status:* 7 (Shifting). Language of recognized nationality: Mongolian. *Class:* Sino-Tibetan, Tibeto-Burman, Ngwi-Burmese, Ngwi, Northern. *Dialects:* None known. All are proficient in Southwest Mandarin [cmn]. *Lg Use:* Home, village. All ages, but a decreasing number of children. *Lg Dev:* High literacy in Chinese. Grammar. *Other:* Remnants of an outpost dating back to the Yuan Dynasty. *Map:* 345.

Kazakh [kaz] (Hazake, Kazak, Kazax). 1,250,000 in China (2000 census). 830,000 Northeastern Kazakh, 70,000 Southwestern Kazakh (1982). 1,060,000 monolinguals. Northern Xinjiang Uygur Autonomous Region, Yili Kazakh autonomous prefecture; eastern Xinjiang Uyghur Autonomous Region, Mulei Kazakh autonomous county, Balikun Kazakh autonomous county; northwest Gansu Province, Akesai Kazakh autonomous county; northwest Qinghai Province. *Status:* 3 (Wider communication). Language of recognized nationality: Kazakh. *Dialects:* Northeastern Kazakh, Southwestern Kazakh. *Lg Use:* Vigorous. All domains. All ages. Positive attitudes. 15% also use Mandarin Chinese [cmn]. Used as L2 by Daur [dta], Ili Turki [ili], Northern Uzbek [uzn], Peripheral Mongolian [mvf], Tatar [tat], Tuva [tyv], Xibe [sjo]. *Lg Dev:* Literacy rate in L2: 97% (2000 census, Kazak nationality). *Other:* Muslim (Sunni), traditional religion. See main entry on page 212. *Map:* 344.

Kemiehua [kfj]. 1,000 (1991). Southwest Yunnan Province, Xishuangbanna Dai autonomous prefecture, Jinghong county. *Status:* 6a (Vigorous). *Class:* Austro-Asiatic, Mon-Khmer, Unclassified. *Type:* SVO; most modifiers follow heads, although adverbial phrases precede heads; simple syllable structure; tonal. *Other:* Officially classified as Undetermined Nationality. Traditional religion. *Map:* 345:28.

Khakas [kjh] (Abakan Tatar, Fuyü Gïrgïs, Fuyu Ka'erkezi, Hakasi, Khakhas, Khakhass, Manchurian Kirghiz, Yenisei Tatar). 10 in China (Salminen 2007). Ethnic population: 880. Heilongjiang Province, Fuyu county, north of Qiqihar. *Status:* 8b (Nearly extinct). Language of recognized nationality: Kyrghyz. *Dialects:* Beltir, Kacha, Kamassian, Kyzyl, Sagai, Shor. *Lg Use:* In 1980s, only about 10 very old people were fluent, others used some words, but mainly spoke Mongolian or Chinese. Young people are monolingual in Chinese. *Other:* Buddhist (Lamaist), traditional religion. See main entry on page 321. *Map:* 344.

Khlula [ykl] (Alapha, Black Phula, Black Zokhuo, Hei Phula, Mo, Namupha, Pao, Phulapha, Shaoji Phula, Sifter Basket Phula, Tula, Zokhuo Na). 21,000 (Pelkey 2011), decreasing. Ethnic population: 34,000. Yunnan Province, southeast Wenshan county, Liujin township; north and central Maguan county, Renhe, Dalishu, Muchang, and Miechang townships. *Status:* 6b (Threatened). Language of recognized nationality: Yi. *Class:* Sino-Tibetan, Tibeto-Burman, Ngwi-Burmese, Ngwi, Southeastern. *Dialects:* Dalishu, Liujing, Muchang. Closely related to Zokhuo [yzk]; some marriage networks maintained with Hlepho Phula [yhl], but not mutually intelligible with either language. *Map:* 345.

Khmu [kjg] (Chaman, Damai, Damailao, Damaile, Kamhmu, Kammu, Kamu, Kemu, Khamu, Khamuk, Khmu', Khomu, Lao Terng, Mou, Pouteng, Theng). 1,600 in China (1990). Southwest Yunnan Province, Xishuangbanna Dai autonomous prefecture, Jinghong county, 9 villages, some in Mengla county. *Status:* 6b (Threatened). *Other:* Officially classified as Undetermined Nationality. See main entry on page 215. *Map:* 345.

Khuen [khf] (Khouen, Khween, Kween). 1,000 in China (1993). *Status:* 6a (Vigorous). See main entry on page 215.

Kim Mun [mji] (Chasan Yao, Gem Mun, Hainan Miao, Jim Mun, Jinmen, Kem Mun, Kimmun, Lan Tin, Lanten, Lowland Yao, Man Lantien, Men, Mun, Shanzi Yao). 200,000 in China (Wang Fushi and Mao Zhongwu 1995). 61,000 in Hainan Province (2000 census). Population total all countries: 374,500. Guizhou Province, Quiandongnan Miao and Dong autonomous prefecture, Congjiang county. Also in Laos, Viet Nam. *Status:* 6a (Vigorous). Language of recognized nationality: Yao. The majority officially classified within Yao nationality. *Class:* Hmong-Mien, Mienic, Mian-Jin. *Dialects:* Dao Ho, Dao Quan Trang. Not intelligible with Iu Mien [ium]. Lexical similarity: 78% with Iu Mien [ium], 67% with Biao-Jiao Mien [bje], 59% with Dzao Min [bpn]. *Lg Dev:* Dictionary. *Writing:* Latin script, used since 1983, experimental, used in China. *Other:* The largest Yao group after Iu Mien. Daoist. *Maps:* 345, 346.

Kon Keu [kkn] (Kongge). 6,300 (2000). Southwest Yunnan Province, Xishuangbanna autonomous prefecture; Dai Lincang, Baoshan or Simao prefectures. Possibly also in Myanmar or Laos. *Status:* 6a (Vigorous). Language of recognized nationality: Blang. *Class:* Austro-Asiatic, Mon-Khmer, Northern Mon-Khmer, Palaungic, Eastern Palaungic, Angkuic. *Lg Use:* Also use Mandarin Chinese [cmn]. *Lg Dev:* Literacy rate in L2: 77%. *Other:* Traditional religion. *Map:* 345.

Korean [kor] (Chaoxian, Hanguohua). 2,710,000 in China (2012 census). 1,200,000 monolinguals. 60% of Korean speakers live in Jilin (Kirin) Province, in Yanbian (Hyanbian) Korean autonomous prefecture; 20% live in Heilongjiang Province; 13% in Liaoning Province; some in Beijing Municipality, Hebei and Shandong provinces, and Inner Mongolia Autonomous Region. *Status:* 4 (Educational). Language of recognized nationality: Chaoxian (Korean). *Lg Use:* All domains. All ages. Positive attitudes. 70,000 also use Mandarin Chinese [cmn]. Also use Japanese [jpn], Russian [rus]. Used as L2 by Mandarin Chinese [cmn]. *Lg Dev:* Literacy rate in L1: 97% (2000 census). *Other:* Buddhist, Christian. See main entry on page 294. *Map:* 344.

Kuamasi [yku]. 1,000 (2011 SIL). Yunnan Province, Heqing county, Liuhe township. *Status:* 6a (Vigorous). Language of recognized nationality: Yi. *Class:* Sino-Tibetan, Tibeto-Burman, Ngwi-Burmese, Ngwi, Southeastern. *Dialects:* None known. Reportedly similar to Sonaga [ysg] and Kua-nsi [ykn]. *Lg Use:* All ages. *Writing:* Unwritten. *Map:* 345.

Kuanhua [xnh] (Damai). 1,000 (1991). Southwest Yunnan Province, Xishuangbanna Dai autonomous prefecture, Jinghong county. *Status:* 6a (Vigorous). *Class:* Austro-Asiatic, Mon-Khmer, Unclassified. *Type:* SVO. *Other:* Officially classified as Undetermined Nationality, but are locally considered part of Khmu peoples. Traditional religion. *Map:* 345:29.

Kua-nsi [ykn] (Baiyi ren, Kua'ensi, Kua'eshi). 5,000 (2009 SIL). Yunnan Province, Heqing county, Liuhe township. *Status:* 6a (Vigorous). Language of recognized nationality: Yi. *Class:* Sino-Tibetan, Tibeto-Burman, Ngwi-Burmese, Ngwi, Southeastern. *Dialects:* None known. Reportedly similar to Kuamasi [yku] and Sonaga [ysg]. *Lg Use:* All ages. *Writing:* Unwritten. *Map:* 345.

Kucong [lkc] (Cosung, Lahlu). 40,000 in China (Bradley 2007), decreasing. Central Yunnan Province, Jinping, Luchun, Jiangcheng, Mengla, Yuanjiang, Xinping, Jinggu, and other counties. *Status:* 6b (Threatened). Language of recognized nationality: Lahu. *Lg Use:* Starting to be replaced by Hani [hni] and Mandarin [cmn] (Bradley 2007). All ages. Neutral attitudes. Also use Hani [hni], Mandarin Chinese [cmn]. See main entry on page 312. *Map:* 345.

Kyerung [kgy] (Kyerong, Kyirong). 100 in China (2002). Population total all countries: 600. Xizang Tibet Autonomous Region, Western Central Tibet, Shigatse prefecture, Kyirong district, lower Kyirong (26 villages) and Lende valley (16 villages). Also in Nepal (Kyirong). *Status:* 6a (Vigorous). Language of recognized nationality: Tibetan. *Class:* Sino-Tibetan, Tibeto-Burman, Western Tibeto-Burman, Bodish, Central Bodish, Central, gTsang. *Dialects:* None known. Reportedly most similar with Kagate [syw]. Lexical similarity: 89% with Helambu Sherpa [scp], 83% with Tibetan [bod]. *Type:* SOV; postpositions; content q-word placed directly before copula and main verb; clause constituents indicated by case-marking; ergativity: Split S system; 26 consonant and 24 vowel phonemes; tonal. *Lg Dev:* Dictionary. Grammar. *Writing:* Unwritten. *Other:* Buddhist (Lamaist). *Map:* 344.

Kyrgyz [kir] (Kara, Ke'erkez, Kirgiz). 160,000 in China (2000 census). 60,000 Northern Kirghiz, 40,000 Southern Kirghiz (Shearer and Sun Hong Kai 2002). Older adults monolingual. Ethnic population: 161,000 (2000 census). West and southwest Xinjiang Uyghur Autonomous Region, Wuqia, Akqi, Akto, Tekes, Zhaosu, Baicheng, and Wushi counties. *Status:* 2 (Provincial). Statutory provincial language in Xinjiang Uyghur Autonomous Region (1984, Ethnic Regional Autonomy Act, Articles 10 and 21). Language of recognized nationality: Kyrgyz. *Dialects:* Northern Kyrgyz, Southern Kyrgyz. *Lg Use:* Vigorous. All domains. All ages. Positive attitudes. Also use Dari [prs], Mandarin Chinese [cmn], Uyghur [uig]. Used as L2 by Sarikoli [srh]. *Lg Dev:* Literacy rate in L1: 80%–85%. Literacy rate in L2: 59%. Taught in primary and secondary schools. *Other:* Muslim (Sunni), traditional religion. See main entry on page 213. *Map:* 344.

Lachi [lbt] (I To, Ku Te, La Chi, Laji, Lati, Lipuljo, Tai Lati, Y Mia, Y Poong, Y To). 200 in China (Bradley 2007), decreasing. 0 monolinguals. Ethnic population: 2,600. Yunnan Province, Wenshan Zhuang and Miao autonomous prefectures, southern Maguan county, several villages. *Status:* 8b (Nearly extinct). Language of recognized nationality: Zhuang. *Dialects:* Lipuke (Red Lachi), Lipuliongtco (Flowery Lachi), Lipupi (Long-Haired Lachi), Liputcio (Han Lachi), Lipute (Bag Lachi), Liputiõ (Black Lachi). *Lg Use:* Most ethnic Lachi in China have shifted to either Nong Southern Zhuang [zhn] or local Southwestern Mandarin [cmn] as L1, though some still understand Lachi. Elderly. Positive attitudes. Language preservation important to them. All ethnic Lachi speak 2, 3, or 4 languages. The few who only speak one other, use local Chinese (Southwest Mandarin) [cmn]. Used as L2 by Zaiwa [atb]. *Other:* Ethnic Lachi in Nanlao (Bag Lachi), Renhe (Han or Sinocized Lachi), Jiahanqing (Han or Sinocized Lachi) and Xiaobazi (Red Lachi) no longer speak Lachi fluently, but understand some. See main entry on page 312. *Map:* 345.

Ladakhi [lbj] (Ladak, Ladaphi, Ladhakhi, Ladwags). 12,000 in China (1995). Western Xizang Tibet Autonomous Region. *Status:* 6b (Threatened). Language of recognized nationality: Tibetan. *Dialects:* Leh (Central Ladakhi), Nubra Ladakhi, Shamma (Lower Ladakhi, Sham, Shamskat). *Other:* Buddhist (Lamaist). See main entry on page 125.

Lahu [lhu] (Kaixien, Kucong, Kutsong, Lahuna, Laku, Lohei, Moso, Muhso, Mussar, Musso, Mussuh, Namen). 280,000 in China (Bradley 2007). Population total all countries: 530,350. L2 users: Some speakers of other languages use Lahu as L2 for commerce. Southwest Yunnan Province, Simao prefecture, Lancang Lahu, Menglian Dai, Lahu, and Va autonomous counties; Lincang prefecture, Gengma Dai, and Va autonomous counties. Also in Laos, Myanmar, Thailand, Viet Nam. *Status:* 4 (Educational). Language of recognized nationality: Lahu. *Class:* Sino-Tibetan, Tibeto-Burman, Ngwi-Burmese, Ngwi, Central. *Dialects:* Na (Black Lahu, Lohei, Musser Dam, Northern Lahu), Nyi (Musse Daeng, Red Lahu, Southern Lahu), Shehleh. Standard dialect: Na. Black Lahu dialect and Lahu Shi [lhi] have difficult intelligibility. Lahu Shi and Kucong Lahupu (White Lahu dialect, in Zhenyuan County, China) are distinct. *Type:* SOV; Lü [khb] and Hani [hni] loanwords. *Lg Use:* Vigorous. All domains. All ages. Positive attitudes. Also use Blang [blr], Hani [hni], Lü [khb], Mandarin Chinese [cmn], Vo Wa [wbm]. Used as L2 by Bisu [bzi], Lahu Shi [lhi], Laomian [lwm], Sangkong [sgk], Shixing [sxg], Vo Wa [wbm]. *Lg Dev:* Literacy rate in L1: 63%. Literacy rate in L2: Low in Chinese. Taught in primary schools. Newspapers. Radio programs. Dictionary. Grammar. Bible: 1989. *Writing:* Latin script. *Other:* Traditional religion, Buddhist, Christian. *Map:* 345.

Lahu Shi [lhi] (Kur, Kwi, Lahu Xi, Shi, Yellow Lahu). 117,000 in China (Bradley 2007), increasing. Population total all countries: 196,200. Few monolinguals. Ethnic population: 120,000. South Yunnan Province, Xishuangbanna Dai autonomous prefecture, Menghai district, Menghai county, Menghai township; Simao prefecture, Lancang Lahu autonomous county, Nuofu district, other areas. Also in Laos, Myanmar, Thailand, United States. *Status:* 5 (Developing). Language of recognized nationality: Lahu. *Class:* Sino-Tibetan, Tibeto-Burman, Ngwi-Burmese, Ngwi, Central. *Dialects:* Bakeo, Banlan. Reportedly most similar to Lahu [lhu]. *Type:* SOV. *Lg Use:* Vigorous. All domains. All ages. Neutral attitudes. 50% also use Lahu [lhu]. 70% also use Mandarin Chinese [cmn]. *Lg Dev:* Literacy rate in L1: Fairly high among Christians. Bible portions: 2009. *Writing:* Latin script. *Map:* 345.

Lakkia [lbc] (Chashan Yao, Lajia, Laka, Lakia, Lakja, Lakkja, Tai Laka, Tea Mountain Yao). 9,000 (Bradley 2007). 4,000 monolinguals. Ethnic population: 12,000 (Bradley 2007). Eastern Guangxi Zhuang Autonomous Region, Jinxiu Yao autonomous county. *Status:* 6a (Vigorous). Language of recognized nationality: Yao. *Class:* Tai-Kadai, Kam-Tai, Lakkja. *Dialects:* Phonetically similar to Iu Mien [ium], word order to Bunu [bwx]. Not intelligible with Hmong Djua [hnj] or Bunu. Minimal variation within Lakkia. Lexical similarity: 45% with Dong [doc], 23% with Lachi [lbt] and Qabiao [laq], 22% with Gelao. *Type:* SVO; modifiers follow heads; consonant clusters and palatalized and labialized onsets; voiced and voiceless nasal onsets; long-short vowel distinction; 6 basic tone categories in unchecked syllables and 2 in checked with further split in checked syllables according to vowel length. *Lg Use:* Vigorous. Some speakers of other languages use Lakkia for trade. All domains. All ages. Positive attitudes. Also use Iu Mien [ium], Liuqian Zhuang [zlq], Mandarin Chinese [cmn]. Used as L2 by Jiongnai Bunu [pnu]. *Lg Dev:* Dictionary. Grammar. *Other:* The language is nonetheless Tai-Kadai (1990 J-O. Svantesson). Daoist, traditional religion. *Map:* 346.

Lalo, Central [ywt] (Lalo, Lalopa, Laluo, Misapa, Xishanba Lalo). 213,000 (2010 SIL). Over 500,000 in subgroup; many living further west, south or east do not speak the language; less than half are speakers, not all fluent and not many children (Bradley 2007). West Yunnan Province, Weishan, Fengqing, Midu, Changning, Jingdong, Nanjian, Yangbi, and Yunlong counties. *Status:* 6b (Threatened). Language of recognized nationality: Yi. *Class:* Sino-Tibetan, Tibeto-Burman, Ngwi-Burmese, Ngwi, Central. *Dialects:* None known. Not intelligible with other Lalo languages. *Type:* SOV; 5 tones. *Lg Use:* In many areas it is extinct or severely endangered; vital in some areas where parents teach their children and use it in most domains. High bilingualism in Chinese [cmn], especially among young people. *Lg Dev:* Poetry. Dictionary. Grammar. *Other:* Western Yi dialect. Traditional religion. *Map:* 345.

Lalo, Dongshanba [yik] (Lalu, Lalupa, Lalupu). 30,000 (2002). Over 500,000 in the ethnic group. West Yunnan Province, Weishan, Yangbi, Midu, Xiaguan, Yongping, Baoshan, and Lancang counties. *Status:* 6b (Threatened). Language of recognized nationality: Yi. *Class:* Sino-Tibetan, Tibeto-Burman, Ngwi-Burmese, Ngwi, Central. *Lg Use:* Extinct, moribund or severely endangered in many areas, and not many children using it; in some areas less so (Bradley 2007). *Other:* Daoist, traditional religion. *Map:* 345.

Lalu, Eastern [yit]. 38,000 (2002). Yunnan Province, Xinping, Zhenyuan, Mojiang, and Yuanjiang counties. *Status:* 7 (Shifting). Language of recognized nationality: Yi. *Class:* Sino-Tibetan, Tibeto-Burman, Ngwi-Burmese, Ngwi, Central. *Map:* 345.

Lalu, Western [ywl]. 38,000 (2002). West Yunnan Province, in Baoshan, Shidian, Zhenkang, Longling, and Luxi counties. *Status:* 6b (Threatened). Language of recognized nationality: Yi. *Class:* Sino-Tibetan, Tibeto-Burman, Ngwi-Burmese, Ngwi, Central. *Other:* Traditional religion. *Map:* 345.

Lamu [llh]. 120 (2007), decreasing. Ethnic population: 300. Yunnan Province, Dali prefecture, northeast Binchuan county. *Status:* 8b (Nearly extinct). Language of recognized nationality: Lahu. *Class:* Sino-Tibetan, Tibeto-Burman, Ngwi-Burmese, Ngwi, Central. *Lg Use:* Intermarried with Lipo [lpo] (Bradley 2007). Home, village. 100% also use Lipo [lpo]. Also use Lolopo [ycl]. *Map:* 345.

Lang'e [yne] (La'u). 2,000 (2007). Yunnan Province, southwest Yongsheng county. *Status:* 6a (Vigorous). Language of recognized nationality: Yi. *Class:* Sino-Tibetan, Tibeto-Burman, Ngwi-Burmese, Ngwi, Central. *Lg Use:* All ages. *Map:* 345.

Laomian [lwm] (Bisu, Guba, Lawmeh). 1,600 (2007), decreasing. 240 Laopin (Bradley 2007). Ethnic population: 5,000 (Bradley 2007). Ethnic population does not include Laopin. Yunnan Province, Lancang, Menglian, and Ximeng counties. Laopin dialect: Menghai county, Mengzhe township, Van Phin (Laopinzhai) village. *Status:* 6b (Threatened). Language of recognized nationality: Lahu. *Class:* Sino-Tibetan, Tibeto-Burman, Ngwi-Burmese, Ngwi, Southern, Bisoid. *Dialect:* Laopin. Reportedly similar to Pyen [pyy] and Bisu [bzi]. Lexical similarity: 93%–95% between Laopin and Laomian, 88% with Bisu [bzi] in Thailand. *Lg Use:* Use of Chinese [cmn] is increasing and leading to language shift. Home. Neutral attitudes. High levels of bilingualism in Lahu [lhu]. High levels of bilingualism in Chinese [cmn]. *Other:* The name 'Laomian' is the Chinese derivation of the Lahu name 'Lawmeh'. *Map:* 345.

Lashi [lsi] (Acye, Chashanhua, Lachikwaw, Laji, Laqi, Lasi, Leqi, Leshi, Letsi). 1,800 in China (1997). Yunnan Province, Dehong Dai-Jingpo autonomous prefecture, Luxi, Longchuan, Yingjiang, and Ruili counties. *Status:* 6b (Threatened). Language of recognized nationality: Jingpo. *Lg Use:* Used as L2 by Jingpho [kac]. *Other:* Intermixed with others of Jingpo nationality who use other languages, but call themselves Le Chi (Tshi). See main entry on page 237. *Map:* 345.

Lavrung [jiq] (Guanyingqiao, Western Jiarong, Zhongzhai). 50,000 (1993 Lin). North central Sichuan Province, southwest tip of Maerkang county, Jinchuan river tributaries; northwest Jinchuan county; southeast Rangtang county. *Status:* 6a (Vigorous). Language of recognized nationality: Tibetan. *Class:* Sino-Tibetan, Tibeto-Burman, Northeastern Tibeto-Burman, rGyalrongic. *Dialects:* Ere, Ergali, Guanyingqiao, Muerzong, Siyaowu, Taiyanghe, Xiaoyili, Yelong. Phonologically Western and Northern are fairly similar and differ greatly from Eastern. Lexical similarity: 60% between Western and Northern Jiarong dialects. *Type:* SOV; phonologically and lexically similar to Tibetan, grammatically more similar to Pumi and Qiang; complex consonant clusters; limited pitch contrast. *Lg Dev:* Grammar. *Other:* Buddhist (Lamaist), traditional religion. *Map:* 344.

Lawu [lwu]. 50 (2012 C. Yang). Yunnan Province, Yuxi prefecture, Xinping county, Shuitang district, Jiuha village. Possibly some speakers in Yunnan Province, Pu'er prefecture, Zhenyuan county, Jijujia district. *Status:* 8b (Nearly extinct). Language of recognized nationality: Lahu. *Class:* Sino-Tibetan, Tibeto-Burman, Ngwi-Burmese, Ngwi, Central. *Dialects:* None known. Related to Central Lalo [ywt], Kucong [lkc], Lahu [lhu], and Lisu [lis]. *Lg Use:* Only elderly speakers. *Map:* 345.

Lhaovo [mhx] (Diso, Lang'e, Langwa, Laungaw, Laungwaw, Lawng, Liangsu, Malu, Maru, Matu, Nyky, Zi). 3,500 in China (2000). West Yunnan Province, Dehong Dai-Jingpo autonomous prefecture, Luxi, Longchuan, Yingjiang, Ruili, and Lianghe counties. *Status:* 6b (Threatened). Language of recognized nationality: Jingpo. *Lg Use:* Also use Jingpho [kac], Mandarin Chinese [cmn], Zaiwa [atb]. Used as L2 by Jingpho [kac], Zaiwa [atb]. *Lg Dev:* Literacy rate in L2: 84% (2000 census, Jingpho nationality). *Other:* Different from the Matu variety of Khumi Chin [cnk]. Ethnic autonym: Lovo. Ethnonym: Langsu for Chinese; Maru for Jingpho. Maru speakers reportedly preserve ancient cultural characteristics more than other ethnic groups. See main entry on page 237 (as Lhao Vo). *Map:* 345.

Lhomi [lhm] (Lhoket, Shing Saapa). 1,000 in China. Xizang Tibet Autonomous Region. *Status:* 6b (Threatened). Language of recognized nationality: Tibetan. *Other:* Traditional religion, Buddhist (Lamaist). See main entry on page 252. *Map:* 344.

Limi [ylm] (Liumi). 29,000 (2002). Yunnan Province, Yongde, Fengqing, and Yunxian counties. *Status:* 6a (Vigorous). Language of recognized nationality: Yi. *Class:* Sino-Tibetan, Tibeto-Burman, Ngwi-Burmese, Ngwi, Central. *Lg Use:* All ages. *Other:* Traditional religion. *Map:* 345.

Lingao [onb] (Bê, Limkow, Linkow, Ongbe, Ong-Be, Vo Limkou). 600,000 (2000 Liang Min). 350,000 Lincheng, 170,000 Qiongshan. 100,000 monolinguals. Hainan Province, north central coast, Lingao county, parts of Danxian, Chengmai, and Qiongshan counties, Haikou city suburbs. *Status:* 6a (Vigorous). Language of recognized nationality: Han. *Class:* Tai-Kadai, Kam-Tai, Lakkja. *Dialects:* Lincheng (Lingao Proper-Dengmai), Qiongshan. *Type:* SVO; Lincheng reportedly has 7 tone categories, Qiongshan 13. Loans from Cantonese [yue] and Hainan variety of Min Nan Chinese [nan]. *Lg Use:* Vigorous. Other speakers in the area use it. All domains. All ages. Positive attitudes. Urban residents also use Hainan dialect of Min Nan Chinese [nan]. 300,000 also speak Chinese, 200,000 use the Hainan dialect, 100,000 speaking Jun or Danzhou dialects. Chinese used in secondary schools. *Lg Dev:* Chinese characters read with Lingao pronounciation. Taught in primary schools. Radio programs. Dictionary. Grammar. *Other:* Traditional religion, Buddhist, Daoist. *Map:* 346.

Lipo [lpo] (Central Lisu, Dayao, Eastern Lisu, Lolongo). 250,000 (Bradley 2007). Few monolinguals. North central Yunnan Province, Luquan, Wuding, Lufeng, Yuanmo, Yongsheng, Dayao, Binchuan, Yuanmo, Yongren, and Yao'an counties; south Sichuan Province, Renhe county. *Status:* 6b (Threatened). Language of recognized nationality: Lisu. Language of recognized nationality: Yi. Only those in Dayao and Yongren counties of Western Chuxing Prefecture. *Class:* Sino-Tibetan, Tibeto-Burman, Ngwi-Burmese, Ngwi, Central. *Dialects:* Eastern Lipo, Western Lipo. Both dialects are reportedly similar to Lisu [lis], but neither is intelligible with Lisu. *Lg Use:* Home, village. All ages. Neutral attitudes. Chinese [cmn] widely used, even between speakers of different dialects of Lipo. Used as L2 by Ersu [ers], Hani [hni], Lamu [llh], Namuyi [nmy], Northern Pumi [pmi], Southern Pumi [pmj]. *Lg Dev:* Literacy rate in L1: Very low. Literacy rate in L2: High in Chinese. NT: 1951. *Writing:* Lisu (Fraser) script, no longer in use. Miao (Pollard) script, used from about 1910, primary usage among Christians. *Other:* Ethnonym: Lolopo or Lolongo prefered, especially in Yongren County. Christian, traditional religion. *Map:* 345.

Lisu [lis] (Chedi, Cheli, Chung, Khae, Leisu, Leshuoopa, Lesuo, Li, Li-Hsaw, Lip'a, Lisaw, Li-Shaw, Lishu, Liso,

Lissu, Loisu, Lusu, Lu-Tzu, Yao Yen, Yaw Yin, Yaw-Yen, Yeh-Jen). 600,000 in China (2000 census), increasing. Population total all countries: 942,700. West Yunnan Province, 11 prefectures, 63 counties, upper reaches of Salween and Mekong rivers; Sichuan Province, southwest Liangshan prefecture. Also in India, Myanmar, Thailand. *Status:* 3 (Wider communication). Language of recognized nationality: Lisu. Some 7,000 members of the Nu nationality in China, and more in Myanmar, speak only Lisu. *Class:* Sino-Tibetan, Tibeto-Burman, Ngwi-Burmese, Ngwi, Central. *Dialects:* Bai Lisu (White Lisu), Dechang Lisu, Hei Lisu (Black Lisu), Hua Lisu (Flowery Lisu), Lu Shi Lisu, Ninglang Lisu, Northern Lisu, Nujiang Lisu, Shibacha Lisu, Western Lisu. Much dialectal variation; some do not understand each other. *Type:* SOV; tonal, 6 tones. *Lg Use:* Vigorous. Speakers of other languages in the area use Lisu for administration, religion, and bilingual education in schools. In Drung and Nu areas, oral and written Lisu are used for Christian activities. All domains. All ages. Positive attitudes. Also use Chinese [cmn]. Chinese is used in secondary schools. Also use Central Bai [bca], Central Tibetan [bod], Jingpho [kac], Lü [khb], Naxi [nxq]. Used as L2 by Anong [nun], Central Bai [bca], Drung [duu], Northern Pumi [pmi], Nusu [nuf], Southern Pumi [pmj], Zaiwa [atb], Zauzou [zal]. *Lg Dev:* Literacy rate in L1: High. Literacy rate in L2: Medium. Chinese. Literacy taught through churches, rather than schools. Taught in primary schools. Newspapers. Radio programs. Dictionary. Grammar. Bible: 1968–1986. *Writing:* Latin script, used in 1915–1918, 1958–1966, and from 1981. Lisu (Fraser) script, used since 1918, primary usage. *Other:* Traditional religion, Christian. *Map:* 345.

Lolopo [ycl] (Bai Yi, Central Yi, Gaoshanzu, Hei Yi, Lolopho, Lulupu, Luolu). 380,000 (2007). Central Yunnan Province, Nanhua, Chuxiong, Yao'an, Jingdong, Shuangbai, Mouding, and Lufeng counties primarily. *Status:* 6a (Vigorous). Language of recognized nationality: Yi. *Class:* Sino-Tibetan, Tibeto-Burman, Ngwi-Burmese, Ngwi, Central. *Dialects:* Nanhua Lolopo, Shuangbai Lolopo, Yao'an Lolopo. *Type:* SOV. *Lg Use:* Vigorous. All ages. Positive attitudes. Used as L2 by Lamu [llh]. *Other:* Traditional religion, Christian. *Map:* 345.

Lolopo, Southern [ysp]. 190,000 (2002). Yunnan Province, Jingdong, Jinggu, Lancang, Zhenyuan, Simao, and Pu'er counties. *Status:* 6b (Threatened). Language of recognized nationality: Yi. *Class:* Sino-Tibetan, Tibeto-Burman, Ngwi-Burmese, Ngwi, Central. *Lg Use:* Some young people, all adults. *Other:* Traditional religion. *Map:* 345.

Lopi [lov]. Yunnan Province, Yuanyang, Yuanjiang, and Mojiang counties. *Status:* 6a (Vigorous). Language of recognized nationality: Hani. *Class:* Sino-Tibetan, Tibeto-Burman, Ngwi-Burmese, Ngwi, Southern. *Type:* SOV.

Lü [khb] (Dai, Dai Le, Lu, Lue, Ly, Pai'i', Pai-I, Shui-Pai-I, Sipsongpanna Dai, Tai Lu, Xishuangbanna Dai). 280,000 in China (2000 census). Population total all countries: 550,960. 140,000 monolinguals. Southern Yunnan Province, Xishuangbanna Dai autonomous prefecture, 3 counties: Jinghong (Chiang Hung, Chien Rung), Menghai, and Mengla; also a few in Simao municipal prefecture, Jiangcheng Hani and Yi Autonomous counties. Also in Laos, Myanmar, Thailand, Viet Nam. *Status:* 2 (Provincial). Statutory provincial working language in South Yunnan and other places (1984, Ethnic Regional Autonomy Act, Articles 10 and 21). Language of recognized nationality: Dai. Some speakers of other languages use Lü as L2 for trade. *Class:* Tai-Kadai, Kam-Tai, Tai, Southwestern. *Dialect:* Jinghong. Muang Yong and dialects in northern Thailand may converge phonologically with Northern Thai [nod] (Diller and Juntanamalaga 1990). Low intelligibility with Shan [shn] and Tai Nüa [tdd]. Different from Tai Nüa [tdd], each having their own literary tradition. Lexical similarity: 95% with Northern Thai [nod], 86% with Central Thai [tha], 92%–93% with Shan [shn], 92%–95% with Khün [kkh]. *Type:* SVO; modifiers follow noun heads. *Lg Use:* Vigorous. All domains. All ages. Positive attitudes. Also use Chinese [cmn]. Some schools only teach in Chinese. Also use Jingpho [kac]. Used as L2 by Bisu [bzi], Blang [blr], Buyuan Jinuo [jiy], Hani [hni], Lahu [lhu], Lisu [lis], Ruching Palaung [pce], Samtao [stu], Sangkong [sgk], Vo Wa [wbm], Youle Jinuo [jiu]. *Lg Dev:* Literacy rate in L1: 84% literate in any language (2000 census, Dai nationality). Given that Tai Lü has a traditional script and tradition of literacy, the literacy figure probably includes significant percentages literate in Lü Scripts, as well as percentages educated in Chinese, as well as some literate in both languages. Taught in primary and secondary schools. Magazines. Newspapers. Radio programs. TV. Dictionary. Grammar. NT: 1933. *Writing:* New Tai Lue script, used in Yunnan Province, China. Tai Tham (Lanna) script, still used by some, particularly in Buddhist monasteries in Yunnan Province, China. *Other:* Traditional Lü script is used in monastaries and reformed version used in some government functions. Traditional religion, Buddhist. *Map:* 345.

Luoba, Boga'er [adi] (Abor, Adi, Adi-Bokar, Bengni-Boga'er, Boga'er, Bokar, Lhoba, Lho-Pa). 1,090 in China (1999 O. Jueya). 400 monolinguals. Southeast Xizang Tibet Autonomous Region, Lhunze and Mainling counties, south of Yaluzangjiang river, Luoyu area. *Status:* 6b (Threatened). Language of recognized nationality: Lhoba (Luoba). *Lg Use:* Vigorous. All domains. All ages. Also use Central Tibetan [bod], Mandarin Chinese [cmn], Tawang Monpa [twm]. *Lg Dev:* 27% attended school, 31% have some degree of literacy, less than 1% have a university degree. *Other:* Different from Loke [loy] (Loba) in Nepal. Traditional religion, Buddhist (Lamaist). See main entry on page 100 (as Adi). *Map:* 344.

Luoba, Yidu [clk] (Chulikata, Idu Lhoba, Idu Mishmi, Lhoba, Lho-Pa, Yidu). 80 in China (1999 Sun Hong Kai). 50 monolinguals. Southeast Xizang Tibet Autonomous Region, Nyingchi prefecture, Chayu county, Xia Chayu (Zayu) zone, Xia Chayu (Zayu) and Ba'antong townships, in Danba river valley and adjoining mountain slopes, near Bhutan border. *Status:* 6b (Threatened). Language of recognized nationality: Lhoba (Luoba). *Lg Use:* Vigorous. All domains. All ages. Neutral attitudes. Also use Central Tibetan [bod], Mandarin Chinese [cmn]. *Other:* Different from Loke (Loba) [loy] in Nepal. 27% attended primary school, 31% have some degree of literacy. Traditional religion, Buddhist (Lamaist). See main entry on page 115 (as Idu-Mishmi). *Map:* 345.

Mak [mkg] (Ching, Mo, Mochiahua, Mohua, Mo-Hua, Mojiahua). 5,000 (Bradley 2007). Ethnic population: 10,000 (2000 D. Bradley). Guizhou Province, northwest Libo county, Yangfeng, Fangcun, Jialiang, and Di'e villages; some in neighboring Dushan county. *Status:* 7 (Shifting). Language of recognized nationality: Bouyei. *Class:* Tai-Kadai, Kam-Tai, Kam-Sui. *Dialects:* Chi, Ching (Cham), Hwa, Lyo, Mak. Dialect differences are minor. Reportedly similar to Ai-Cham [aih]. *Lg Use:* Also use local Chinese or Bouyei [pcc]. *Other:* Traditional religion. *Maps:* 345, 346:37.

Man Met [mml] (Manmi, Manmit). 900 (1990 J-O. Svantesson). Southwest Yunnan Province, 5 communities in Xishuangbanna Dai autonomous prefecture near the Hu. *Status:* 6a (Vigorous). *Class:* Austro-Asiatic,

Mon-Khmer, Northern Mon-Khmer, Palaungic, Eastern Palaungic, Angkuic. *Type:* Affixes; tonal. *Other:* Reportedly similar to Hu [huo]. Officially classified as Undetermined Nationality. Buddhist, traditional religion. *Map:* 345:27.

Manchu [mnc] (Man). 20 (Bradley 2007). Some additional semi-speakers in 3 remote villages (Bradley 2007). Ethnic population: 10,700,000 (2000 census). Liaoning, Jilin, Hebei, and Beijing provinces; Heilongjiang Province, a few Manchu-speaking villages in Aihui and Fuyu counties; small enclave in northeast Nei Mongol Province, Inner Mongolia Autonomous Region. *Status:* 8b (Nearly extinct). Language of recognized nationality: Manchu (Man). *Class:* Altaic, Tungusic, Southern, Southwest. *Dialects:* Alechuxa, Bala, Jing, Lalin. *Lg Use:* Long extinct among the mainly urbanized Manchu, but still studied in an ongoing scholarly tradition (Bradley 2007). Older adults, 50 and older. Positive attitudes. All bilingual. Nonspeakers of Manchu in the ethnic group speak Mandarin [cmn]. Written Chinese in common use. Used as L2 by Daur [dta]. *Lg Dev:* Literacy rate in L1: About 50 read and write. Literacy rate in L2: 82%. Dictionary. NT: 1835. *Writing:* Mongolian script, Manchu style, used since 1599. Mongolian script, Old Manchu style, no longer in use. *Other:* Traditional religion, Buddhist. *Map:* 344.

Mang [zng] (Ba'e, Chaman, Manbu, Mang U, Nieng Ó, Xá Lá Vàng, Xá Mang, Xá Ó, Xamang). 500 in China. Ethnic population: 1,220 (Bradley 2007). Southeastern Yunnan Province, Honghe Hani and Yi autonomous prefectures, Jinping county, Mengla district; 4 villages: Nanguo Xin Zhai, Heping Zhong Zhai, Heping Xia Zhai, Dadui Leigongdaniu Zhai. *Status:* 6b (Threatened). *Other:* Officially classified as Undetermined Nationality. Traditional religion. See main entry on page 313. *Map:* 345.

Maonan [mmd] (Ai Nan). 30,000 (GXLOUS 2005), decreasing. A few thousand women and children are monolingual. Ethnic population: 107,000 (2000 census). North central Guangxi, Huanjiang Maonan autonomous county, Xianan area: Yishan, Nandan, Yizhou; a few in Hechi and Du'an counties; small border area, south central Guizhou Province. *Status:* 6b (Threatened). Language of recognized nationality: Maonan. *Class:* Tai-Kadai, Kam-Tai, Kam-Sui. *Type:* SVO; numbers and adjectives follow nouns; reduplication; glottalized, prenasalized, palatalized, and labialized onsets; nasal and stop finals; many Chinese loans; tonal, 6 tone categories in unchecked syllables, 2 in checked (split into 4 according to vowel length). *Lg Use:* 75% use it at home; 62% use it outside the home; 72% speak it to their children (GXLOUS 2005). Positive attitudes. Also use Chinese [cmn] or other local languages. More than 90% are bilingual or trilingual (GXLOUS 2005). *Lg Dev:* Literacy rate in L2: 93% (2000 census, Manon nationality). Taught in primary schools. Radio programs. Grammar. *Writing:* Han script, Simplified variant. Han script, Traditional variant. *Other:* Daoist, Christian. *Maps:* 345, 346.

Miao, Central Huishui [hmc] (Central Huishui Hmong). 40,000 (Wang Fushi and Mao Zhongwu 1995). Central Guizhou Province, Huishui and Changshun counties, suburbs of south Guiyang municipality. *Status:* 6a (Vigorous). Language of recognized nationality: Miao. *Class:* Hmong-Mien, Hmongic, Chuanqiandian. A member of macrolanguage Hmong [hmn]. *Dialects:* None known. Inherently unintelligible of other Miao varieties. 30 to 40 different Hmong (Miao) languages in China. Great linguistic differences. *Lg Use:* All domains. *Other:* Traditional religion. *Map:* 345:12.

Miao, Central Mashan [hmm] (Central Mashan Hmong). 70,000 (Wang Fushi and Mao Zhongwu 1995). South central Guizhou Province, Ziyun, Wangmo, and Luodian counties. *Status:* 6a (Vigorous). Language of recognized nationality: Miao. *Class:* Hmong-Mien, Hmongic, Chuanqiandian. A member of macrolanguage Hmong [hmn]. *Dialects:* None known. Not inherently intelligible of other varieties of Miao. *Type:* Tonal, 11 tones. *Lg Use:* All domains. *Lg Dev:* Dictionary. *Other:* Traditional religion. *Map:* 345:15.

Miao, Chuanqiandian Cluster [cqd] (Chuanchientien Miao, Chuanqiandian Miao, Core Farwestern Hmongic, Hua Miao, Sichuan-Guizhou-Yunnan Miao, Western Miao). 1,400,000 (Wang Fushi and Mao Zhongwu 1995). West Guizhou Province, west Guangxi Zhuang Autonomous Region, south Sichuan and southeast and northeast Yunnan provinces. *Status:* 5 (Developing). Language of recognized nationality: Miao. *Class:* Hmong-Mien, Hmongic, Chuanqiandian. A member of macrolanguage Hmong [hmn]. *Dialects:* Bai Miao, Black Hmong, Black Meo, Black Mong, Blue Hmong, Blue Meo, Ching Miao, Chuan Miao, Clear Water Hmong, Dananshan Miao, Dianxi Miao, Downhill Hmong, Flowery Meo, Green Hmong, Green Meo, Hei Miao, Hmong Be, Hmong Bua, Hmong Den, Hmong Dle Ncha, Hmong Dlo, Hmong Dou, Hmong Drout Raol, Hmong La, Hmong Len, Hmong Shi, Hmong Shua Bua, Hmong Sou, Hongxian Miao, Hua Miao, Hwa Miao, Light Hmong, Liuzhai Miao, Lu Miao, Luzhai Miao, Magpie Miao, Meo Dam, Meo Den, Meo Lai, Mong Hoa, Mong La Hou, Mong Leng, Mong Lenh, Mong Shi, Mong Si, Mountain Hmong, Paddyfield Miao, Qing Miao, Qingshui Miao, Red Mong, Red Thread Miao, Red-headed Hmong, River Miao, Sa Pa Hmong, Sichuan Miao, Six Village Miao, Striped Hmong, Tak Miao, Variegated Mong, Western Yunnan Miao, White Miao, Yaque Miao. *Type:* SVO; 7–9 tones. *Lg Use:* Vigorous. Home, community, market. All ages. Positive attitudes. Younger generation and urban residents also use Mandarin Chinese [cmn]. Used as L2 by Bugan [bbh]. *Lg Dev:* Literacy rate in L1: 10% or less. Literacy rate in L2: 42% in Mandarin Chinese [cmn]. Taught in primary schools. Radio programs. *Writing:* Latin script, pinyin-based, 1958–1960 and from 1981, experimental. *Other:* Consider themselves Miao nationality. *Map:* 345:1.

Miao, Eastern Huishui [hme] (Eastern Huishui Hmong). 14,000 (Wang Fushi and Mao Zhongwu 1995). Central and south Guizhou Province, Huishui, Pingba, and Luodian counties. *Status:* 6a (Vigorous). Language of recognized nationality: Miao. *Class:* Hmong-Mien, Hmongic, Chuanqiandian. A member of macrolanguage Hmong [hmn]. *Dialects:* None known. Inherently unintelligible of other Miao varieties. *Lg Use:* Home, community, market. *Other:* Traditional religion. *Map:* 345:13.

Miao, Eastern Qiandong [hmq] (Black Miao, Central Miao, Chientung Miao, Eastern East-Guizhou Miao, Eastern Hmu, Hei Miao, Hmu). 350,000 (Wang Fushi and Mao Zhongwu 1995). East Guizhou Province, Jianhe, Jinping, and Liping counties; west Hunan Province, Huitong, Jingzhou, and Tongdao counties. *Status:* 6a (Vigorous). Language of recognized nationality: Miao. *Class:* Hmong-Mien, Hmongic, Qiandong. A member of macrolanguage Hmong [hmn]. *Dialects:* None known. Not intelligible of other Miao varieties. Corresponds more or less to Ma's Central Miao and Purnell's Eastern Miao. *Lg Dev:* Dictionary. Bible portions: 1928. *Other:* Traditional religion. *Map:* 346:36.

Miao, Eastern Xiangxi [muq] (Eastern Ghao-Xong, Eastern Miao, Eastern West-Hunan Miao, Ghao-Xong, Hsianghsi Miao, Meo Do, Northern Miao, Red Meo, Red Miao). 80,000 (Wang Fushi and Mao Zhongwu 1995). West Hunan Province, Luxi, Guzhang, Jishou, and Longshan counties; some in Guizhou, Hubei, and Chongqing provinces, and in Guangxi Zhuang autonomous region. *Status:* 6a (Vigorous). Language of recognized nationality: Miao. *Class:* Hmong-Mien, Hmongic, Xiangxi. A member of macrolanguage Hmong [hmn]. *Dialects:* None known. Not inherently intelligible of other varieties of Miao. *Other:* Traditional religion. *Map:* 346:32.

Miao, Horned [hrm] (A-Hmo, Bai Miao, Changjiao Miao, Forest Miao, Hmong Khua Shua Ndrang, Hmong Ndong, Hmong Ndou, Hmong Sou, Jiao Miao, Jiaojiao Miao, Kha-Nzi, Longhorn Miao, Qing Miao, White Miao). 50,000 (Hattaway 2000). Northeast Yunnan Province, Zhenxiong county; northwest and central Guizhou Province, Dafang, Nayong, and Zhijin counties, Anshun, Guiyang, Bijie, and Qingzhen municipalities. *Status:* 6a (Vigorous). Language of recognized nationality: Miao. *Class:* Hmong-Mien, Hmongic, Chuanqiandian. A member of macrolanguage Hmong [hmn]. *Dialects:* None known. May have inherent intelligibility of Small Flowery Miao [sfm] (1998 M. Johnson); not inherently intelligible with other Miao varieties. *Lg Use:* Vigorous. Home, community, market. Also use Mandarin Chinese [cmn]. *Other:* Consider themselves Miao nationality but unique in culture and language from other Miao groups. *Map:* 345.

Miao, Large Flowery [hmd] (A-Hmao, Big Flowery Miao, Da Hua Bei Miao, Da Hua Miao, Diandongbei Miao, Flowery Miao, Great Flowery Tribe, Hua Miao, Hwa Miao, Northeastern Dian Miao, Northeastern Yunnan Miao, Ta Hwa Miao). 300,000 (Wang Fushi and Mao Zhongwu 1995). Northwest Guizhou Province, Weining, Hezhang, Shuicheng, Pu'an, Zhenning, and Ziyun counties, Liupanshui municipality; northeast and central Yunnan Province, Zhaotong area, Yongshan, Yiliang, Daguan, Suijiang, Qiaojia, Xundian, Fumin, Luquan, Lufeng, and Wuding counties, Xuanwei, Qujing, Kunming, Anning, and Chuxiong municipalities; south Sichuan Province, Panzhihua municipality. *Status:* 5 (Developing). Language of recognized nationality: Miao. *Class:* Hmong-Mien, Hmongic, Chuanqiandian. A member of macrolanguage Hmong [hmn]. *Dialects:* None known. Inherently unintelligible of other Miao varieties. *Type:* Tonal, 5–7 tones. *Lg Use:* Vigorous. Home, community, market. *Lg Dev:* High level of literacy among the older generation in original Pollard script. Dictionary. Bible: 2009. *Writing:* Latin script, 1909–1917, 1951–1956, 1958–1966, and from 1982. Miao (Pollard) script, used since 1905, primary usage. Pahawh Hmong script. *Other:* Traditional religion, Christian. *Map:* 345:2.

Miao, Luopohe [hml] (Lobohe Miao, Luobo River Miao, Luobohe Hmong, Luopohe Hmong, Xi, Xijia Miao, Ximahe Miao). 61,000 (Wang Fushi and Mao Zhongwu 1995). Central Guizhou Province east of Guiyang, Weng'an, Guiding, Longli, and Kaiyang counties, Fuquan and Kaili municipalities. *Status:* 6a (Vigorous). Language of recognized nationality: Miao. Most officially classified within Miao nationality, except for Xijia group. *Class:* Hmong-Mien, Hmongic, Chuanqiandian. A member of macrolanguage Hmong [hmn]. *Dialects:* 2 dialects. Not inherently intelligible of other Miao varieties. *Lg Use:* Home, community, market. All ages. *Other:* Traditional religion. *Map:* 345.

Miao, Northern Guiyang [huj] (Northern Guiyang Hmong). 84,000 (Wang Fushi and Mao Zhongwu 1995). Central Guizhou Province, Jinsha, Qianxi, Xifeng, Kaiyang, Xiuwen, and Pingba Guiding counties, west Guiyang municipality suburbs. *Status:* 6a (Vigorous). Language of recognized nationality: Miao. *Class:* Hmong-Mien, Hmongic, Chuanqiandian. A member of macrolanguage Hmong [hmn]. *Dialects:* None known. Inherently unintelligible of other Miao varieties. *Lg Use:* Home, community, market. *Other:* Traditional religion. *Map:* 345:6.

Miao, Northern Huishui [hmi] (Northern Huishui Hmong). 70,000 (Wang Fushi and Mao Zhongwu 1995). Central Guizhou Province, Guiyang municipality, Gaopo district; Huishui, Longli and Guiding counties. *Status:* 6a (Vigorous). Language of recognized nationality: Miao. *Class:* Hmong-Mien, Hmongic, Chuanqiandian. A member of macrolanguage Hmong [hmn]. *Dialects:* None known. Inherently unintelligible of other Miao varieties. *Lg Use:* Home, community, market. *Other:* Traditional religion. *Map:* 345:8.

Miao, Northern Mashan [hmp] (Northern Mashan Hmong). 35,000 (Wang Fushi and Mao Zhongwu 1995). South central Guizhou Province, Changshun, Luodian, and Huishui counties. *Status:* 6a (Vigorous). Language of recognized nationality: Miao. *Class:* Hmong-Mien, Hmongic, Chuanqiandian. A member of macrolanguage Hmong [hmn]. *Dialects:* None known. Inherently unintelligible of other Miao varieties. *Type:* Tonal, 13 tones. *Lg Use:* Home, community, market. *Other:* Traditional religion. *Map:* 345:14.

Miao, Northern Qiandong [hea] (Black Miao, Central Miao, Chientung Miao, East Guizhou Miao, Gha Ne, Gha Ne Dlai, Heh Miao, Hei Miao, Hmu, Northern East Guizhou Miao, Northern Hmu). 1,250,000 (Wang Fushi and Mao Zhongwu 1995), decreasing. East and south Guizhou Province, Majiang, Danzhai, Leishan, Taijiang, Huangping, Shibing, Jianhe, Zhenyuan, Sansui, Fuquan, Pingba, Zhenning, Xingren, Anlong, Guanling, Zhenfeng, and Ziyun counties, Kaili and Qingzhen municipalities; northwest Guangxi Zhuang Autonomous Region, Longlin county. *Status:* 5 (Developing). Language of recognized nationality: Miao. *Class:* Hmong-Mien, Hmongic, Qiandong. A member of macrolanguage Hmong [hmn]. *Dialects:* Inherently unintelligible of other Miao varieties. Corresponds more or less to Ma's Central Miao and Purnell's Eastern Miao. At least 4 dialects (vernaculars). The official standard variety of Qiandong Miao is based on Yanghao, but with some similarities to other varieties. *Lg Use:* Most domains. All ages. Youth move to the city and abandon more of their culture and language. Positive attitudes in countryside; neutral to negative attitudes in city. Children often learn standard Mandarin [cmn] in school, but speak Miao at home. *Lg Dev:* Literacy rate in L1: Low. Literacy rate in L2: Many literate in Chinese [cmn], but many older women are illiterate. Large-scale literacy programs stopped but supportive attitude toward literacy promoters. Taught in primary schools. A few village schools still use Miao to teach Mandarin. 1 or 2 offer Miao classes. Dictionary. Grammar. NT: 1934. *Other:* Traditional religion. *Maps:* 345:7, 346:7.

Miao, Small Flowery [sfm] (Atse, Ghab-Mvb Ghab-Svd, Ghuab-Hmongb Ghuab-Soud, Hsiao Hwa Miao, Xiao Hua Miao). 84,000 (Wang Fushi and Mao Zhongwu 1995). West Guizhou Province, Hezhang, Guanling, Nayong, Shuicheng, and Zhenning counties. *Status:* 6a (Vigorous). Language of recognized nationality: Miao. *Class:* Hmong-Mien, Hmongic, Chuanqiandian. A member of macrolanguage Hmong [hmn]. *Dialects:* None known. Inherently unintelligible of other Miao varieties (Hattaway 2000). *Lg Use:* Vigorous. Home, community, market. All ages. Also use Mandarin Chinese [cmn]. *Other:* Traditional religion, Christian. *Map:* 345:5.

Miao, Southern Guiyang [hmy] (Southern Guiyang Hmong). 28,000 (Wang Fushi and Mao Zhongwu 1995). South central Guizhou Province, Changshun, Ziyun, and Zhenning counties, Anshun municipality. *Status:* 6a

(Vigorous). Language of recognized nationality: Miao. *Class:* Hmong-Mien, Hmongic, Chuanqiandian. A member of macrolanguage Hmong [hmn]. *Dialects:* None known. Inherently unintelligible of other Miao varieties. *Lg Use:* Home, community, market. *Other:* Traditional religion. *Map:* 345:9.

Miao, Southern Mashan [hma] (Southern Mashan Hmong). 10,000 (Wang Fushi and Mao Zhongwu 1995). South Guizhou Province, Wangmo county. *Status:* 6a (Vigorous). Language of recognized nationality: Miao. *Class:* Hmong-Mien, Hmongic, Chuanqiandian. A member of macrolanguage Hmong [hmn]. *Dialects:* None known. Inherently unintelligible of other Miao varieties. *Type:* Tonal, 13 tones. *Lg Use:* Home, community, market. *Other:* Traditional religion. *Map:* 345:17.

Miao, Southern Qiandong [hms] (Black Miao, Central Miao, Chientung Miao, Hei Miao, Hmu, Southern East-Guizhou Miao, Southern Hmu). 500,000 (Wang Fushi and Mao Zhongwu 1995). All Miao in China: 8,950,000 (2000 census). Southeast Guizhou Province, Sandu, Danzhai, Libo, and Rongjiang Congjiang counties; north Guangxi Province, Rongshui and Sanjiang counties. *Status:* 6a (Vigorous). Language of recognized nationality: Miao. *Class:* Hmong-Mien, Hmongic, Qiandong. A member of macrolanguage Hmong [hmn]. *Dialects:* None known. Inherently unintelligible of other Miao varieties. Corresponds more or less to Ma's Central Miao and Purnell's Eastern Miao. *Lg Dev:* Dictionary. *Other:* Traditional religion, Christian. *Map:* 346:39.

Miao, Southwestern Guiyang [hmg] (Southwestern Guiyang Hmong). 70,000 (Wang Fushi and Mao Zhongwu 1995). Central Guizhou Province, Pingba and Changshun counties, suburbs of Guiyang, Qingzhen and Anshun municipalities. *Status:* 6a (Vigorous). Language of recognized nationality: Miao. *Class:* Hmong-Mien, Hmongic, Chuanqiandian. A member of macrolanguage Hmong [hmn]. *Dialects:* None known. Inherently unintelligible of other Miao varieties. *Lg Use:* Home, community, market. *Other:* Traditional religion. *Map:* 345:10.

Miao, Southwestern Huishui [hmh] (Miao, Southwestern Huishui Hmong). 56,000 (Wang Fushi and Mao Zhongwu 1995). Central Guizhou Province, Huishui, Sandu, and Changshun counties. *Status:* 6a (Vigorous). Language of recognized nationality: Miao. *Class:* Hmong-Mien, Hmongic, Chuanqiandian. A member of macrolanguage Hmong [hmn]. *Dialects:* None known. Inherently unintelligible of other Miao varieties. *Lg Use:* Home, community, market. *Other:* Traditional religion. *Map:* 345:11.

Miao, Western Mashan [hmw] (Western Mashan Hmong). 14,000 (Wang Fushi and Mao Zhongwu 1995). South Guizhou Province, Wangmo and Ziyun counties. *Status:* 6a (Vigorous). Language of recognized nationality: Miao. *Class:* Hmong-Mien, Hmongic, Chuanqiandian. A member of macrolanguage Hmong [hmn]. *Dialects:* None known. Inherently unintelligible of other Miao varieties. *Type:* Tonal, 13 tones. *Lg Use:* Home, community, market. *Other:* Traditional religion. *Map:* 345:16.

Miao, Western Xiangxi [mmr] (Eastern Miao, Ghao-Xong, Hsianghsi Miao, Huayuan Miao, Meo Do, Northern Miao, Red Meo, Red Miao, West Hunan Miao, Western Ghao-Xong, Western West-Hunan Miao). 820,000 (Wang Fushi and Mao Zhongwu 1995), decreasing. Northwest Hunan Province, Huadan, Fenghuang, Baojing, Jishou, Guzhang, Longshan, and Xinhuang Mayang counties; northeast Guizhou Province, Songtao county, Tongren and southeast Chongqing municipalities; Xiushan and Youyang counties; southwest Hubei Province, Xuan'en county; north Guangxi Zhuang Autonomous Region, Hechi municipality; Nandan county. *Status:* 6a (Vigorous). Language of recognized nationality: Miao. *Class:* Hmong-Mien, Hmongic, Xiangxi. A member of macrolanguage Hmong [hmn]. *Dialects:* None known. Inherently unintelligible of other Miao varieties. *Lg Use:* Vigorous, strong sense of ethnic identity. Most domains except education. Positive attitudes. Also use Mandarin Chinese [cmn]. *Lg Dev:* Literacy rate in L2: 40% or more. Dictionary. *Writing:* Latin script, pinyin-based, 1951–1956, 1958–1969, and from 1978, experimental. *Other:* Traditional religion. *Map:* 345:22.

Mili [ymh]. 23,000 (2002). Yunnan Province, Jingdong, Yunxian, Zhenyuan, and Xinping counties. *Status:* 6b (Threatened). Language of recognized nationality: Yi. *Class:* Sino-Tibetan, Tibeto-Burman, Ngwi-Burmese, Ngwi, Central. *Other:* Traditional religion. *Map:* 345.

Miqie [yiq] (Micha, Mielang, Minqi). 30,000 (Bradley 2007), decreasing. Ethnic population: 50,000. Yunnan Province, Wuding (Jincheng, Jiuchang, and Chadian districts), north Fumin, north Lufeng, south Luquan counties, parts of Yongren, Dayao, Yao'an, Nanhua, Jingdong, Zhenyuan, Jinggu, and Yimen counties. *Status:* 7 (Shifting). Language of recognized nationality: Yi. *Class:* Sino-Tibetan, Tibeto-Burman, Ngwi-Burmese, Ngwi, Central. *Lg Use:* No remaining speakers in Jinning and Anning counties; declining elsewhere. Home. Neutral attitudes. Also use Mandarin Chinese [cmn]. *Map:* 345.

Moji [ymi] (Flathead Phulai, Muji, Phula, Phulawa, Pingtou Phula). 2,000 (Pelkey 2011), decreasing. Ethnic population: 7,000. Yunnan Province, south and southwest Wenshan county; west Xichou county, Luchaichong village; possibly east Fumin county. *Status:* 7 (Shifting). Language of recognized nationality: Yi. *Class:* Sino-Tibetan, Tibeto-Burman, Ngwi-Burmese, Ngwi, Southeastern. *Dialect:* Luchaichong. Moji patterns with the Proto-Muji subgroup phylogenetically, but Luchaichong dialect (the most vital dialect) heavily influenced by contact with Khlula [ykl] and Zokhuo [yzk]. *Other:* Traditional religion. *Map:* 345.

Monba, Cuona [twm] (Buruomiba, Cona Monba, Cuona Menba, Cuona Monpa, Dakpa, Dwags, Menba, Menpa, Moinba, Momba, Mompa, Monba, Monpa, Pramipa, Takpa, Tawan Monba). 1,300 in China (2000 census). 600 Southern Cuona, 700 Northern Cuona. Less than half monolingual: Young children, older people, some young adults. Southeast Xizang Tibetan Autonomous Region; Southern Cuona, Shannan prefecture, Cuona county, Lebu district, Northern Cuona, Linzhi prefecture, Motuo county, Dexing district, Wenlang village. *Status:* 6b (Threatened). Language of recognized nationality: Menba. *Dialects:* Northern Cuona, Southern Cuona. *Lg Use:* Vigorous. All domains. All ages. Positive attitudes. Over half also use Central (Lhasa) Tibetan [bod]; about one-third are literate in Tibetan script. Classical Tibetan used for recitation of Buddhist Scriptures. Used as L2 by Boga'er Luoba [adi]. *Lg Dev:* Literacy rate in L2: 44% (2000 census, Monba nationality). Most are literate in Tibetan [bod]. *Other:* Cuona Monba [twm] differs from Tshangla in phonology, vocabulary, and grammar, and is not mutually intelligible. Shares many Tibetan language characteristics. Is the same as, or closely related to, Bumthangkha of Bhutan. May also be classified as North Assam, Monpa. Buddhist (Lamaist). See main entry on page 131 (as Monpa, Tawang). *Map:* 344.

Mongolian, Peripheral [mvf] (Inner Mongolian, Menggu, Monggol, Mongol, Southern-Eastern Mongolian). 3,380,000 in China (1982). Population includes 299,000 Chakhar, 317,000 Bairin, 1,347,000 Khorain, 593,00 Karachin, 123,000 Ordos, 34,000 Ejine. 2,500,000 monolinguals. Nei Mongol Province,Inner Mongolia Autonomous Region; Liaoning, Jilin, Hebei, Gansu, Ningxia, and Heilongjiang provinces, Urumchi to Hailar. Also in Mongolia. *Status:* 2 (Provincial). Statutory provincial working language in Inner Mongolia Autonomous Region and other places (1984, Ethnic Regional Autonomy Act, Articles 10 and 21). Language of recognized nationality: Mongolian. *Class:* Altaic, Mongolic, Eastern, Oirat-Khalkha, Khalkha-Buriat, Mongolian Proper. A member of macrolanguage Mongolian [mon] (Mongolia). *Dialects:* Chahar (Chaha'er, Chakhar, Qahar), Ejine, Jirim (Gorlos, Jalait, Kalaqin, Khorchin), Jostu (Eastern Tumut, Ke'erqin, Kharachin, Kharchin, Kharchin-Tumut), Jo-Uda (Bairin, Balin, Keshikten, Naiman), Ordos (E'erduosite), Shilingol (Ujumchin), Tumut (Tumet), Ulanchab (Mingan, Urat). Largely intelligible of Halh Mongolian [khk], but there are phonological and important loanword differences. *Type:* SOV. *Lg Use:* Vigorous. Chinese living in the area can also speak it. All domains. All ages. Positive attitudes. Also use Kazakh [kaz], Mandarin Chinese [cmn], Uyghur [uig]. Used as L2 by Daur [dta], Evenki [evn], Kalmyk-Oirat [xal], Oroqen [orh], Tuva [tyv]. *Lg Dev:* Literacy rate in L2: 71%. Taught in primary and secondary schools. Magazines. Newspapers. Radio programs. TV. Grammar. Bible: 2003. *Writing:* Mongolian script. Phags-pa script, no longer in use. *Other:* Includes China Buriat [bxu], Tuva [tyv], Kalmyk-Oirat [xal], and speakers of other varieties. In Xinjiang, Torgut, Oold, Korbet, and Hoshut peoples are known as the Four tribes of Oirat. Buddhist (Lamaist), traditional religion. *Map:* 344.

Muda [ymd]. 2,000 (2007), decreasing. Yunnan Province, Jinghong county, Nanpianshan district. *Status:* 6b (Threatened). Language of recognized nationality: Hani. *Class:* Sino-Tibetan, Tibeto-Burman, Ngwi-Burmese, Ngwi, Southern. *Map:* 345.

Muji, Northern [ymx] (Bokha, Hlaka Mujima, Phula). 9,000 (Pelkey 2011). Ethnic population: 15,000. Yunnan Province, south Mengzi county, Shuitian, Lengquan, and Qilubai townships; west Pingbian county, Xinxian township. *Status:* 7 (Shifting). Language of recognized nationality: Yi. *Class:* Sino-Tibetan, Tibeto-Burman, Ngwi-Burmese, Ngwi, Southeastern. *Dialects:* None known. Reportedly similar to Southern Muji [ymc]. *Other:* Traditional religion. *Map:* 345.

Muji, Qila [ymq] (Doka, Mujitsu, Phutsu). 1,500 (2008), decreasing. Ethnic population: 1,500. Yunnan Province, south Jinping county. 2 isolated villages. *Status:* 7 (Shifting). Language of recognized nationality: Yi. *Class:* Sino-Tibetan, Tibeto-Burman, Ngwi-Burmese, Ngwi, Southeastern. *Other:* Traditional religion. *Map:* 345.

Muji, Southern [ymc] (Aga, Khlaka, Lahi, Muzi, Phula, Tjeki, Tshebu, Tshibu). 26,000 (Pelkey 2011), increasing. Ethnic population: 28,000. Yunnan Province, north Jinping county; some in southwest and east Jinping county, south Mengzi county, southeast Gejiu county. *Status:* 6a (Vigorous). Language of recognized nationality: Yi. *Class:* Sino-Tibetan, Tibeto-Burman, Ngwi-Burmese, Ngwi, Southeastern. *Dialects:* Dazhai, Gamadi, Jinhe, Ma'andi, Tongchang, Yingpan. *Lg Use:* Vigorous. Home, village, business. All ages. Positive attitudes. *Lg Dev:* Taught in primary schools. *Other:* Traditional religion. *Map:* 345.

Mulam [mlm] (Abo, Kyam, Molao, Mulao, Mulao Miao, Muliao, Mulou). 86,000 (2005 GXLOUS). Fewer than 10,000 monolinguals (including women and preschool children). Ethnic population: 210,000 (2000 census). North central Guangxi Zhuang Autonomous Region, Hechi prefecture, Luocheng Mulao autonomous county (90% in Dongmen and Siba communes), also Yizhou county. *Status:* 6b (Threatened). Language of recognized nationality: Mulam. *Class:* Tai-Kadai, Kam-Tai, Kam-Sui. *Dialects:* None known. Lexical similarity: 65% with Dong (probably Southern Dong [kmc]). *Type:* SVO; reduplication; aspirated, palatalized, labialized, voiceless nasal, lateral onsets; nasal and stop finals; many Chinese loans; 6 tone categories in unchecked syllables, 2 in checked (split into 4 according to vowel length). *Lg Use:* Vigorous. Most domains, Daoist and Buddhist services. 87% speak Mulam at home; 57% speak it outside the home. 82% speak Mulam to their children. (2005 GXLOUS). Mainly older adults. Positive attitudes. Written Chinese [cmn] in common use. Also use various Chinese varieties or a Northern Zhuang language. *Lg Dev:* Literacy rate in L2: 94% (2000 census, Mulao nationality). Taught in primary schools. Radio programs. *Other:* They live near the Han, Dong [doc], Hmong Njua [hnj], and Iu Mien [ium]. They call themselves Mulam. Some around Luocheng call themselves Kyam. Different from the nearly extinct Western Kra Tai-Kadai language also called Mulao [giu], previously spoken by Gelao nationality people in Guizhou. Traditional religion, Buddhist, Daoist. *Map:* 346:45.

Mulao [giu] (Ayo). A few elderly speakers. Guizhou Province, Majiang county, Longli. *Status:* 8b (Nearly extinct). Language of recognized nationality: Gelao. *Class:* Tai-Kadai, Kra, Western Kra. *Lg Use:* Only elderly. *Writing:* Unwritten. *Other:* Mulao do not understand other Gelao languages. Not to be confused with Mulam [mlm].

Muya [mvm] (Boba, Manyak, Menya, Minyag, Minyak, Miyao, Munya). 10,000 (Bradley 2007), decreasing. 2,000 monolinguals. Ethnic population: 15,000 (Bradley 2007). West central Sichuan Province, Kangbo (Kangding) and Jiulong (Gyaisi), Ganzi (Garzê) Tibetan autonomous prefecture, Simian (Shimian) county, Ya'an district. *Status:* 6b (Threatened). Language of recognized nationality: Tibetan. *Class:* Sino-Tibetan, Tibeto-Burman, Northeastern Tibeto-Burman, Qiangic. *Dialects:* Eastern Muya, Western Muya. Dialects reportedly not mutually inherently intelligible. Loanwords from Tibetan and Chinese. *Type:* SOV; adjectives and number-classifier constructions follow noun heads; compounding; affixation; reduplication; consonant cluster onsets; tense-lax vowel distinction; nasalized vowels; tonal, 4 tones. *Lg Use:* All village domains. All ages. Neutral attitudes. 3,000 also use Khams Tibetan [khg]. In the west, they tend to be more fluent in Tibetan. 7,000 also use Mandarin Chinese [cmn]. In the east, they tend to be more fluent in Chinese. *Lg Dev:* Videos. Dictionary. OT. *Other:* Consider themselves Tibetan. Proper Tibetan Wylie spelling: Minyag. Buddhist (Lamaist). *Map:* 344.

Muzi [ymz] (Mogeha, Muji). 10,000 (2008). Yunnan Province, south and east Gejiu county; west Mengzi county, scattered villages. *Status:* 7 (Shifting). Language of recognized nationality: Yi. *Class:* Sino-Tibetan, Tibeto-Burman, Ngwi-Burmese, Ngwi, Southeastern. *Dialects:* None known. Reportedly similar to Notthern Muji [ymx]. *Other:* Traditional religion. *Map:* 345.

Naluo [ylo] (Gan Yi, Laluo, Naruo, Shui Yi, Shuitian). 15,000 (Bradley 2007). Mostly in Yunnan, with about 2,000 in Pingjiang and Futian townships of Panzhihua (Bradley 2007). Yunnan Province, southern Huaping and eastern Yongsheng counties; Sichuan, western Panzhihua city. *Status:* 6b (Threatened). Language of recognized nationality: Yi. *Class:* Sino-Tibetan, Tibeto-Burman, Ngwi-Burmese, Ngwi, Northern. *Lg Use:* Moribund to extinct in Sichuan, potentially endangered to endangered in Yunnan (Bradley 2007). *Other:* Traditional religion, Christian. *Map:* 345.

Namuyi [nmy] (Naimuci, Naimuzi). 5,000 (Bradley 2007).

200 monolinguals. Mainly older adults. Ethnic population: 5,000 (Bradley 2007). Sichuan Province, Liangshan Yi autonomous prefecture, Mianning, Muli, Xichang, and Yanyuan counties; southwest Sichuan, Ganzi (Garzê) Tibetan autonomous prefecture, Jiulong (Gyaisi) county. *Status:* 6b (Threatened). Language of recognized nationality: Tibetan. *Class:* Sino-Tibetan, Tibeto-Burman, Northeastern Tibeto-Burman, Naic. *Dialects:* Eastern Namuyi, Western Namuyi. Low intelligibility between dialects, with lexical and phonological differences. *Type:* SOV; adjectives and number-classifier constructions follow noun heads; compounding; affixation; consonant cluster onsets but no consonantal codas; tense-lax vowel distinction; nasalized and retroflexed vowels; tonal, 4 tones. *Lg Use:* Vigorous. All domains. All ages. Positive attitudes. 500 also use Lipo [lpo]. 2,000 also use Mandarin Chinese [cmn]. 500 also use Northern Pumi [pmi]. Also use Central Tibetan [bod], Ersu [ers]. *Lg Dev:* Generally better educated than Yi or Tibetan peoples. Dictionary. Grammar. *Other:* Traditional religion, Buddhist, Daoist. *Map:* 345.

Nanai [gld] (Gold, Goldi, Hezhe, Hezhen, Juchen, Nanay, Sushen). 40 in China (Salminen 2007). About half speak Sungari dialect, half speak Nanai proper (Salminen 2007). Ethnic population: 4,640 (2000 census). Northeast corner of Heilongjiang Province, near merge of Heilong, Songhua, and Wusuli rivers, Tongjiang county, Bacha and Jiejinkou villages; Raohe county, Sipai village. *Status:* 8b (Nearly extinct). Language of recognized nationality: Hezhe. *Dialects:* Qileng (Kilen, Kili, Kirin, Qile'en), Sungari. *Lg Use:* 47 understand Nanai. Religion. Older adults, 60 and older. Negative attitudes. People have lost hope that it will survive. All are L1 or L2 speakers of Chinese. Written Chinese in common use. *Lg Dev:* Literacy rate in L2: 97% (2000 census, Hezhe nationality). *Other:* Formerly called Sushen. Traditional religion, Buddhist. See main entry on page 321. *Map:* 344.

Narua [nru] (Eastern Naxi, Moso, Mosso, Mosuo, Na, Naru, Nazu). 47,000 (2010 SIL). Ethnic population: 47,000. Sichuan and Yunnan provinces border area near Lugu lake, Ninglang Yi autonomous county, Muli Tibetan autonomous county and Yanuyuan county. *Status:* 6b (Threatened). Language of recognized nationality: Mongolian. Sichuan Province speakers assigned to the Mongolian nationality. Language of recognized nationality: Naxi. Yunnan Province speakers officially classified within Naxi nationality. *Class:* Sino-Tibetan, Tibeto-Burman, Northeastern Tibeto-Burman, Naic. *Dialects:* None known. Lexical similarity: 40%–60% with Naxi [nxq]. *Type:* SOV; prolific compounding; some prefixing; noun classes; noun heads NP; some vowel harmony; approx 38 Cs, 14 Vs, including some nasalised vowels; tonal. *Lg Use:* Frequent. Home, village, friends. All ages. Also use local Chinese dialect [cmn]; written Chinese in common use. Also use Northern Pumi [pmi], Nuosu [iii]. Used as L2 by Central Tibetan [bod], Northern Pumi [pmi], Nuosu [iii]. *Lg Dev:* Literacy rate in L1: 0%. Literacy rate in L2: Most under age 40 literate in Mandarin Chinese [cmn]. Grammar. *Writing:* Unwritten. *Other:* Buddhist, traditional religion. *Map:* 345.

Nasu, Wumeng [ywu] (Wumeng Yi, Wusa Yi, Yuan-Mo Yi). 150,000 (2007). Ethnic population: 200,000. West Guizhou and east Yunnan provinces, Weining, Shuicheng, Hezhang, Nayong, Xuanwei, Huize, and Yiliang counties; Northwest Yunnan Province, Zhaotong, Yongshan, Daguan, and Ludian counties. *Status:* 6b (Threatened). Language of recognized nationality: Yi. *Class:* Sino-Tibetan, Tibeto-Burman, Ngwi-Burmese, Ngwi, Northern. *Dialects:* Hen-Ke Yi, Hezhang Yi, Weining Yi. *Other:* Traditional religion, Christian. *Map:* 345:3.

Nasu, Wusa [yig] (Eastern Yi). 500,000 (2007), decreasing. Ethnic population: 700,000. Yunnan Province, Chuxiong autonomous prefecture and Kumming city, and scattered areas to east; Guizhou Province, Weining Yi-Hui-Miao and Dafang autonomous counties, Hezhang and Pan counties; west Guangxi Zhuang Autonomous Region. *Status:* 5 (Developing). Language of recognized nationality: Yi. *Class:* Sino-Tibetan, Tibeto-Burman, Ngwi-Burmese, Ngwi, Northern. *Dialects:* Bijie, Dafang, Qian Xi. Reported low intelligibility between dialects. *Type:* SOV. *Lg Use:* Home, village, market. All ages. Neutral attitudes. Also use Mandarin Chinese [cmn]. *Lg Dev:* Literacy rate in L1: Low. Literacy rate in L2: Moderate in Chinese. Taught at Guizhou Institute of Nationalities. Taught in primary schools. Dictionary. *Writing:* Yi script, traditional. *Map:* 345:4.

Naxi [nxq] (Lomi, "Moso" *pej.*, "Mosso" *pej.*, "Mo-Su" *pej.*, Mu, Nahsi, Nakhi, Naqxi, Nasi). 300,000 (2000 census). 100,000 monolinguals. Ethnic population: 300,000. Northwest Yunnan Province, a majority (over 200,000) in Yulong (formerly Lijiang) Naxi autonomous county. Some scattered through Weixi, Zhongdian, Ninglang, Deqing, Yongsheng, Heqing, Jianchuan, and Lanping counties. Some in Sichuan Province, Yanyuan, Yanbian, and Muli counties. A few in Tibet Autonomous Region, Mangkang county. *Status:* 5 (Developing). Language of recognized nationality: Naxi. Official ethnic language of the Narua nationality. *Class:* Sino-Tibetan, Tibeto-Burman, Northeastern Tibeto-Burman, Naic. *Dialects:* Lapao, Lijiang, Ludian. Reportedly similar to Narua [nru]. *Type:* SOV; no checked syllables; tonal, 4 tones (some sub-dialects have only 3 tones). *Lg Use:* Lijiang Old Town attitudes somewhat negative, decreasing number of young speakers. All domains. All ages. Positive attitudes. Also use Mandarin Chinese [cmn]; written Chinese in common use. Also use Central Bai [bca], Central Tibetan [bod], English [eng]. Used as L2 by Central Bai [bca], Central Tibetan [bod], Lisu [lis], Northern Pumi [pmi], Nuosu [iii], Shixing [sxg], Southern Pumi [pmj]. *Lg Dev:* Literacy rate in L1: 5%. Literacy rate in L2: 40% in Mandarin Chinese. Used as the medium of communication in several Naxi area primary schools. Taught in some schools as a subject for 1 or 2 years. Poetry. Radio programs. TV. Videos. Dictionary. Grammar. Bible portions: 1932. *Writing:* Latin script, developed in the 1950s and revised in 1984. Nakhi Geba script, no longer in use. Naxi Dongba script. *Other:* Official ethnic language of the Narua nationality. Buddhist (Lamaist), Buddhist, Confucianist, Daoist. *Map:* 345.

Nisi [yso]. 36,000 (2002), decreasing. Southeast Yunnan Province, Wenshan, Yanshan, Maguan, Funing, Xichou, Malipo, and Honghe counties. *Status:* 6a (Vigorous). Language of recognized nationality: Yi. *Class:* Sino-Tibetan, Tibeto-Burman, Ngwi-Burmese, Ngwi, Southeastern. *Other:* Probably similar to the language spoken by Lolo nationality in Viet Nam. *Map:* 345.

Nisu, Eastern [nos] (Nisu, Shiping-Jianshui Nisu, Shiping-Jianshui Yi). 75,000 (2004), decreasing. Yunnan Province, Jianshui, Tonghai, Gejiu, Kaiyuan, Mengzi, Pingbian, and Hekou counties. *Status:* 6b (Threatened). Language of recognized nationality: Yi. *Class:* Sino-Tibetan, Tibeto-Burman, Ngwi-Burmese, Ngwi, Southeastern. *Lg Use:* Language is active in areas with high concentrations of Nisu. Language use higher for older people, women, uneducated men, or villages further removed from main roads. Nisu living in cities or counties are generally Sinicized. Many parents teach their children the Chinese local dialect as L1 so they can do well in school. There is increasing borrowing of lexical items from Chinese. Code switching between Nisu and Chinese is common. Many men and women spend part of the year working in predominantly Chinese towns or cities. Home, in the fields, with village friends and relatives. Active use by people middle-aged and older. Neutral attitudes. Also use local Chinese [cmn] dialect. Chinese is the L2, spoken with outsiders, non-Nisu government officials, non-Nisu markets, or elementary school teachers. Also use Northern Nisu [yiv]. Village children eventually learn Nisu (with many loan words from Chinese). Used as L2 by Hlersu [hle], Northern Nisu [yiv]. *Lg Dev:* Literacy rate in L1: 0%. *Writing:* Yi script, traditional, limited usage. *Other:* Traditional religion. *Map:* 345.

Nisu, Northern [yiv] (E-Xin Yi). 160,000, decreasing. Yunnan Province, Eshan, Xinping, Shiping (North), Yimen, Yuxi, Jiangchuan, Shuangbai, Jinning, Chengjiang, and northern Yuanjiang counties. *Status:* 6b (Threatened). Language of recognized nationality: Yi. *Class:* Sino-Tibetan, Tibeto-Burman, Ngwi-Burmese, Ngwi, Southeastern. *Dialects:* Nasu, Nisu. Nasu dialect is distinct from the Nasu language continuum located further north. *Lg Use:* The language is active in areas with high concentrations of Nisu. However, there is increasing borrowing of lexical items from Chinese. Code switching between Nisu and Chinese is common. Many men and women spend part of the year working in predominantly Chinese towns or cities. Home, village, work. Mainly adults. Neutral attitudes. Also use Eastern Nisu [nos], Mandarin Chinese [cmn]. Used as L2 by Eastern Nisu [nos]. *Map:* 345.

Nisu, Northwestern [nsf]. 24,000 (2004 SIL). 7,000 in Yunlong, 7,000 in Yangbi, 8,000 in Yongping districts (2004). Northwest Yunnan Province, Dali Bai autonomous prefecture, Yangbi county, Fuheng district; Yunlong county, Tuanjie Yi district; Yongping county, Beidou Yi district. *Status:* 6a (Vigorous). Language of recognized nationality: Yi. *Class:* Sino-Tibetan, Tibeto-Burman, Ngwi-Burmese, Ngwi, Southeastern. *Lg Use:* All ages. *Writing:* Unwritten.

Nisu, Southern [nsd] (Yuan-Mo Yi). 210,000 (2007), decreasing. Yunnan Province, Honghe, Yuanyang, Lüchun (Eastern), Jinping, Shiping (Southern), and Yuanjiang (Southeastern) counties. *Status:* 6b (Threatened). Language of recognized nationality: Yi. *Class:* Sino-Tibetan, Tibeto-Burman, Ngwi-Burmese, Ngwi, Southeastern. *Dialects:* Mojiang Nisu, Yuanyang Nisu. *Lg Use:* Use active in areas with high concentrations of Nisu. However, increasing lexical borrowing from Chinese. Code switching common between Nisu and Chinese. Many men and women spend part of the year working in predominantly Chinese towns or cities. Home, village. Actively used by people middle-aged and above. Neutral attitudes. Many parents teach their children the Chinese [cmn] local dialect as L1 so they can do well in school. Village children eventually learn Nisu (with many loan words from Chinese). Chinese is the L2, spoken with outsiders, government officials who are not Nisu, non-Nisu people in township markets, elementary school teachers. *Lg Dev:* Literacy rate in L1: 0%. *Writing:* Yi script, traditional, limited usage. *Other:* Traditional religion. *Map:* 345.

Nisu, Southwestern [nsv]. 15,000 (2007), decreasing. Yunnan Province, Jiangcheng, Simao, Mojiang, Lüchun (western), Pu'er counties. *Status:* 6b (Threatened). Language of recognized nationality: Yi. *Class:* Sino-Tibetan, Tibeto-Burman, Ngwi-Burmese, Ngwi, Southeastern. *Dialects:* Mojiang Nisu, Yuanyang Nisu. *Lg Use:* Use higher for older people, women, uneducated men, or villages further removed from main roads. Nisu living in cities or counties are generally Sinicized. Mainly adults. Also use Mandarin Chinese [cmn]. *Writing:* Yi script, traditional, limited usage. *Map:* 345:24.

Nuosu [iii] (Black Yi, Liangshan Yi, Northern Yi, Nosu Yi, Sichuan Yi). 2,000,000 (2000 census), increasing. 1,200,000 monolinguals (Jiafa 1994). North Yunnan and south Sichuan provinces, mainly in Greater and Lesser Liangshan mountains. Spoken in over 40 counties. *Status:* 4 (Educational). Language of recognized nationality: Yi. *Class:* Sino-Tibetan, Tibeto-Burman, Ngwi-Burmese, Ngwi, Northern. *Dialects:* Northern Shypnra, Southern Shypnra, Suondi (Adu), Yynuo. Chinese linguists recognize 3 primary dialects: Shengzha (standard), Northern (Lindimu-Yinuo), and Southern (Adur-Suondi) (Bradley 2007). Some dialects, such as Lindimu, are likely distinct languages. *Lg Use:* Many Chinese loan words are appearing. All domains. All ages. Positive attitudes. 40% also use Mandarin Chinese [cmn]. Also use Narua [nru], Naxi [nxq]. Used as L2 by Narua [nru]. *Lg Dev:* Literacy rate in L1: Moderate in central Liangshan. Low elsewhere. Literacy rate in L2: Moderate. Nearly all literate Nuosu are literate in Chinese; some are also literate in Nuosu. Written Nuosu is used in rituals by shamans in every community. Some educated Nuosu use standardized syllabary in academic contexts. The culture is orally oriented so most would not think of writing a letter or a set of procedures in Nuosu, nor would they think of reading written instructions. The educated prefer to write in Chinese for these tasks. Taught in primary and secondary schools. Poetry. Magazines. Newspapers. Dictionary. Grammar. NT: 2005. *Writing:* Latin script, 1951–1957, 1958–1960, and from 1975. Yi script, standardized, used since 1975, official (1980), primary usage. *Other:* When applied to the Nuosu, terms Black Yi (Hei Yi) and White Yi (Bai Yi) refer to caste distinctions rather than to ethnic or linguistic distinctions. However, the same terms often do refer to ethnic and linguistic distinctions when applied to Yi groups in Yunnan. Also, some outsiders refer to Nuosu as Black Yi. Traditional religion, Christian. *Map:* 345.

Nusu [nuf]. 12,000 in China (Bradley 2007). 2,000 Northern Nusu; 4,000 Southern; 6,000 Central. Population total all countries: 12,670. 1,000 monolinguals. Northwestern Yunnan Province, Nujiang Lisu autonomous prefecture, southern Fugong (formerly Bijiang) county, Pihe town area. Northern Nusu: Wawa, Kongtong, and Youduoluo villages; Southern Nusu: Guoke, Puluo, Tuoping (Tongping), and Jiajiu (Jiajia) villages; Central Nusu: Zhiziluo, Laomudeng, Miangu, Shawa, and Zileng villages. Also in Myanmar. *Status:* 6a (Vigorous). Language of recognized nationality: Nu. *Class:* Sino-Tibetan, Tibeto-Burman, Ngwi-Burmese, Ngwi, Central. *Dialects:* Other dialect speakers comprehend the prestige dialect Miangu (Central Nusu, Miangu, Laomudeng) fairly well. *Type:* SOV; grammatical relations indicated mainly by word order and particles; tonal, 4 tones with relatively complex sandhi; loans from Lisu, Chinese, and a few from Burmese. *Lg Use:* Vigorous. All domains. All ages. Mixed attitudes. Intellectuals want to preserve it. 9,000 also use Lisu [lis]. *Lg Dev:* Literacy rate in L2: 68% literate in any language (2000 census, Nu nationality). Bible portions: 2010. *Writing:* Latin script. *Other:* With Ayi, Anong, 1,500 Zauzou, and 5,500 Drung. Traditional religion. *Map:* 345.

Oroqen [orh] (Elunchun, Olunchun, Orochen, Orochon, Oronchon, Ulunchun). 1,200 (Li Fengxiang and Whaley 2009). 30% of ethnic group (Salminen 2007). Only 12 fluent speakers in 1990, all over 65 yrs (Li Fengxiang and Whaley 2009). 800 monolinguals. Ethnic population: 8,200 (2000 census). Heilongjiang Province, Da Hinggan Ling prefecture, Tahe and Huma counties; Heihe prefecture, Xunke county; Yichun prefecture, Jiayin county, Heihe city; Nei Mongol, Inner Mongolia Autonomous Region, Hulun Buir league, Oroqen and Butha banners. *Status:* 8b (Nearly extinct). Language of recognized nationality: Oroqen. *Class:* Altaic, Tungusic, Northern, Evenki. *Dialects:* Birarchen, Kumarchen, Orochen, Selpechen. Gankui in Inner Mongolia is the standard dialect. *Lg Use:* Kumarchen dialect has some child speakers; Birarchen is moribund (Salminen 2007). All domains. Mostly middle-aged or elderly (Salminen 2007). Positive attitudes. Also use Daur [dta], Evenki [evn], Mandarin Chinese [cmn], Peripheral Mongolian [mvf], Russian [rus]. Used as L2 by Daur [dta], Evenki [evn]. *Lg Dev:* Literacy rate in L2: 97% in any language (2000 census, Oroqen nationality). Radio programs. *Other:* Maintain native language and customs. Came to China from the Russian Federation. Traditional religion. *Map:* 344.

Pa Di [pdi] (Padi). 1,000 in China. Population total all countries: 1,300. Yunnan Province, Honghe Hani and Yi prefectures, Hekou and Jinping counties. Also in Viet Nam. *Status:* 6b (Threatened). Language of recognized nationality: Dai. *Class:* Tai-Kadai, Kam-Tai, Tai, Southwestern. *Type:* Tonal. *Other:* In China probably Dai nationality. Traditional religion. *Map:* 345.

Pa-Hng [pha] (Baheng, Bahengmai, Man Pa Seng, Meo Lai, Pa Hng, Pa Ngng, Pa Then, Paheng, Tóng). 26,800 in China (McConnell 1995). 45,000 total ethnic population in China and Vietnam (Bradley 2007). Population total all countries: 33,610. 10,000 monolinguals. Ethnic population: 26,800. Yunnan Province, Wenshan Zhuang and Miao autonomous prefecture. Also in Viet Nam. *Status:* 6b (Threatened). Language of recognized nationality: Yao. *Class:* Hmong-Mien, Hmongic, Pa-hng. *Dialects:* Northern Pa-Hng, Southern Pa-Hng. *Type:* SVO; uvular onsets; no nasal-final syllables but has nasalized vowels. *Lg Use:* Vigorous. All domains. Positive attitudes. Also use Hmong Njua [hnj] (Bradley 2007). Also use Mandarin Chinese [cmn] (Bradley 2007). Also use Dong [doc] (Bradley 2007). *Lg Dev:* Grammar. *Other:* Official ethnic community in Viet Nam, although the variety spoken there may be a distinct language. Daoist. *Map:* 346.

Palaung, Ruching [pce] (Bulai, Bulei, Da'ang, Dlang, Ngwe Palaung, Palay, Pale, Pale Palaung, Pulei, Silver Palaung, Southern Ta'ang). 9,000 in China (2000). West Yunnan Province, Dehong prefecture, Luxi county, east of Rumai. *Status:* 6b (Threatened). Language of recognized nationality: De'ang. *Dialects:* Bulei, Da'ang, Raojin. *Lg Use:* Vigorous. 50% of the De'ang nationality speak Palaung. All domains. All ages. Also use Jingpho [kac], Lü [khb], Mandarin Chinese [cmn]. *Lg Dev:* Literacy rate in L2: 79% in any language for Deang nationality (to which Palaung speakers belong) (2000 census). *Other:* Total De'ang nationality in China (17,935, 2000 census). Buddhist (Hinayana). See main entry on page 239. *Map:* 345.

Palaung, Rumai [rbb] (Humai, Rumai, Ta'ang). 3,600 in China (2000 census). Far western Yunnan Province, Dehong prefecture, Longchuan and Ruili counties, on Myanmar border. *Status:* 6b (Threatened). Language of recognized nationality: De'ang. *Lg Use:* 20% of the De'ang speak Rumai. Also use Mandarin Chinese [cmn]. *Lg Dev:* Literacy rate in L2: 79% in any language for Deang nationality (to which Palaung speakers belong) (2000 census). *Other:* Total De'ang nationality in China (17,935, 2000 census). See main entry on page 239. *Map:* 345.

Palaung, Shwe [pll] (Golden Palaung, Liang Palaung, Shwe). 2,000 in China (1995 SIL). Southwest Yunnan Province, Lincang prefecture, Zhenkang county; Baoshan prefecture, Longyang county. *Status:* 6b (Threatened). Language of recognized nationality: De'ang. *Lg Use:* Also use Mandarin Chinese [cmn]. *Lg Dev:* Literacy rate in L2: 79% in any language for Deang nationality (to which Palaung speakers belong) (2000 census). *Other:* Buddhist (Hinayana). See main entry on page 240. *Map:* 345.

Pela [bxd] (Bela, Bola, Bula, Pala, Polo). 400 (2000 D. Bradley). Ethnic population: 1,000 (2001 J. Edmondson). Yunnan Province, Dehong prefecture, Luxi county, Santaishan township; Yingjiang and Lianghe counties. Maybe also Myanmar. *Status:* 7 (Shifting). Language of recognized nationality: Jingpo. *Class:* Sino-Tibetan, Tibeto-Burman, Ngwi-Burmese, Burmish, Northern. *Dialects:* Reportedly similar to Zaiwa [atb]. Considered by some a Zaiwa dialect. *Type:* SOV; only voiceless affricates and stops; no consonant clusters; palatalized and nonpalatalized series of labials and velars; nasal and stop codas; tense-lax and nasal unnasalized vowels; Chinese, Jingpo, Dai, and Burmese loans; tonal, 4 tones, tone sandhi. *Lg Use:* Home. Used by half the children. Neutral attitudes. All are multilingual, speaking other languages from within the cluster natively, as well as some Chinese and a local Tai language (Bradley 2007). *Other:* Live among the Jingpo majority and wear Jingpo clothing. They regard themselves as different from Zaiwa and Jingpo and have different traditions. Traditional religion. *Map:* 345.

Phala [ypa] (Black Phula, Bola, Hei Phula, Khapho, Phula, Phulepho). 12,000 (Pelkey 2011). Ethnic population: 13,000. Yunnan Province, Shiping and Honghe counties, north and south banks of Yuanjiang (Honghe) river; Yuanyang and Jianshui counties, a few isolated villages downriver. *Status:* 6b (Threatened). Language of recognized nationality: Yi. *Class:* Sino-Tibetan, Tibeto-Burman, Ngwi-Burmese, Ngwi, Southeastern. *Dialects:* None known. Most similar to Phola [ypg]. *Lg Use:* Home, village. *Other:* Traditional religion. *Map:* 345.

Phola [ypg] (Bola, Flowery Phula, Hua Phula, Phula, Phulepho, Tsha Phula). 13,000 (Pelkey 2011). Ethnic population: 13,000. Yunnan Province, Yuanjiang, Shiping, and Honghe counties, along confluence of Yuanjiang (Honghe) and Xiaohedi rivers. *Status:* 6b (Threatened). Language of recognized nationality: Yi. *Class:* Sino-Tibetan, Tibeto-Burman, Ngwi-Burmese, Ngwi, Southeastern. *Dialects:* None known. Reportedly most similar to Phala [ypa]. *Other:* Traditional religion. *Map:* 345.

Phola, Alo [ypo] (Bola, Pula). 500 (Pelkey 2011). Ethnic population: 500. Yunnan Province, Yuanjiang county, Tuguozhai village. *Status:* 6b (Threatened). Language of recognized nationality: Yi. *Class:* Sino-Tibetan, Tibeto-Burman, Ngwi-Burmese, Ngwi, Southeastern. *Dialects:* None known. Reportedly similar to Phola [ypg], but reportedly unintelligible due to contact with a Tai-Kadai variety. *Other:* Traditional religion. *Map:* 345.

Pholo [yip] (Black Phula, Flowery Phula, Phu, Phula). 30,000 (Pelkey 2011), decreasing. Ethnic population: 34,000. Yunnan Province, northeast Yanshan county, southeast Qiubei county; east Yanshan, west Guangnan, and northeast Malipo counties, scattered. *Status:* 6b (Threatened). Language of recognized nationality: Yi. *Class:* Sino-Tibetan, Tibeto-Burman, Ngwi-Burmese, Ngwi, Southeastern. *Lg Use:* All ages. *Other:* Affiliated with the Phula ethnic group historically but not phylogenetically; Ngwi isolate. Traditional religion. *Map:* 345.

Phowa, Ani [ypn] (Anipho, Flowery Phu, Hua Phu, Laotshipu, Pho, Phula). 10,000 (Pelkey 2011). Ethnic population: 10,000. Yunnan Province, north central Mengzi county, Xibeile district; south Kaiyuan county, Yangjie district. *Status:* 6b (Threatened). Language of recognized nationality: Yi. *Class:* Sino-Tibetan, Tibeto-Burman, Ngwi-Burmese, Ngwi, Southeastern. *Dialects:* Daheineng, Dayongsheng, Xibeile. *Lg Use:* Home, village, market. All ages. *Other:* Traditional religion. *Map:* 345.

Phowa, Hlepho [yhl] (Abo, Boren, Bozi, Conehead Phula, Cowtail Phula, Daizhanpho, Digaopho, Flowery Phula, Hua Phula, Jiantou Phula, Minjia, Niuweiba Phula, Paola, Pho, Phula, Sandaohong Phula, Shaoji Phula, Sifter Basket Phula, Thrice Striped Red Phula, Xiuba). 36,000 (Pelkey 2011), decreasing. Ethnic population: 50,000. Yunnan Province, Kaiyuan county, eastern Beige township; Yanshan county, southeastern Ashe township; also northern Mengzi, western Weshan, and northern Pingbian counties. *Status:* 6b (Threatened). Language of recognized nationality: Yi. *Class:* Sino-Tibetan, Tibeto-Burman, Ngwi-Burmese, Ngwi, Southeastern. *Lg Use:* Dialects spoken in Wenshan County are most endangered. Home, village, market. All ages. *Other:* Traditional religion. *Map:* 345.

Phowa, Labo [ypb] (Asaheipho, Asahopho, Ekhepho, Labopho, Pho, Phula, White Phu, Zemapho). 17,000 (Pelkey 2011), decreasing. Ethnic population: 21,000. Yunnan Province, central, north-central and southeast Kaiyuan county, primarily in western Beige township; also in Mazheshao, Laozhai, Zhongheying, Yanggai, Mazheshao, and Lebaidao townships. *Status:* 6b (Threatened). Language of recognized nationality: Yi. *Class:* Sino-Tibetan, Tibeto-Burman, Ngwi-Burmese, Ngwi, Southeastern. *Dialects:* None known. Transitional with Hlepho Phowa [yhl]. *Lg Use:* Dialects spoken in Kaiyuan County are most endangered. Home, village, market. All ages. *Other:* Traditional religion. *Map:* 345.

Phukha [phh] (Fu Khla, Phu Khla, Phù Lá, Phù Lá Hán). 5,000 in China (Pelkey 2011). Ethnic population: 7,000. Yunnan Province, southeast Maguan and southwest Malipo counties. *Status:* 6b (Threatened). Language of recognized nationality: Yi. *Other:* Also classified as Phula nationality in Viet Nam. See main entry on page 314 (as Phula).

Phuma [ypm] (Black Muji, Hei Muji, Muji, Paotlo, Phula, Phuli, Shaoji Phula, Sifter Basket Phula). 8,000 (Pelkey 2011), increasing. Ethnic population: 8,000. Yunnan Province, east central Pingbian county, Baihe township; also Wantang and Baiyun townships. *Status:* 6b (Threatened). Language of recognized nationality: Yi. *Class:* Sino-Tibetan, Tibeto-Burman, Ngwi-Burmese, Ngwi, Southeastern. *Lg Use:* Vigorous. *Map:* 345.

Phupa [ypp] (Hlagho, Laghï, Lala, Lamu, La'ou, Lapa, Larhwo, Muzi, Phula, Phupha, Tshebu). 3,000 (Pelkey 2011), decreasing. Ethnic population: 4,000. Yunnan Province, southwest Mengzi county; southeast corner of Gejiu panhandle: southeast Shuitian and southeast Lengquan townships. *Status:* 6b (Threatened). Language of recognized nationality: Yi. *Class:* Sino-Tibetan, Tibeto-Burman, Ngwi-Burmese, Ngwi, Southeastern. *Dialects:* Baiwushan, Da Fengkou, Gamadi, Jiangnanbo, Nuogumi, Xiao Fengkou. *Map:* 345.

Phupha [yph] (Phula, Phupho, Tsapho). 1,300 (2007), decreasing. Ethnic population: 1,500. Yunnan Province, southwest Gejiu county, 4 villages; Yuangyang county, across Honghe river, 1 village. *Status:* 6b (Threatened). Language of recognized nationality: Yi. *Class:* Sino-Tibetan, Tibeto-Burman, Ngwi-Burmese, Ngwi, Southeastern. *Dialects:* None known. Closely related to, but not intelligible of, Alugu [aub]. *Lg Use:* 4 villages linguistically vital, 1 is shifting to Nisu [nsd]. *Map:* 345.

Phuza [ypz] (Hei Phu, Phu'a, Phujitsu, Phula). 6,000 (2007), decreasing. Ethnic population: 8,000. Yunnan Province, southwest Mengzi county, west Lengquan township; and southeast Gejiu county, southeast Kafang township. *Status:* 6b (Threatened). Language of recognized nationality: Yi. *Class:* Sino-Tibetan, Tibeto-Burman, Ngwi-Burmese, Ngwi, Southeastern. *Dialects:* Bujibai, Dabaqi. Not intelligible of Phupa [ypp]. *Lg Use:* Also use Mandarin Chinese [cmn]. *Map:* 345.

Pumi, Northern [pmi] (Ch'rame, Pimi, P'ömi, Primmi, P'rome, Pruumi, P'umi). 35,000 (1999). 5,000 in Pumi nationality, 30,000 in Tibetan nationality (1994). 10,000 monolinguals. Southwest Sichuan Province, Muli, Yanyuan, and Jiulong counties; northwest Yunnan Province, Ninglang county, Yongning district. *Status:* 6a (Vigorous). Language of recognized nationality: Tibetan. *Class:* Sino-Tibetan, Tibeto-Burman, Northeastern Tibeto-Burman, Qiangic. *Dialect:* Taoba. 4 other dialects. Intelligibility of Southern Pumi [pmj] is low. Lexical similarity: between Northern Pumi and Southern Pumi [pmj] is 60%, grammatical differences minor. *Lg Use:* Vigorous. All domains. All ages. Positive attitudes. Also use Central Bai [bca], Central Tibetan [bod], Lipo [lpo], Lisu [lis], Mandarin Chinese [cmn], Narua [nru], Naxi [nxq]. Used as L2 by Namuyi [nmy], Narua [nru], Shixing [sxg]. *Lg Dev:* Literacy rate in L1: 0%. Literacy rate in L2: 70% for Pumi nationality (2000 census). Trial use in 1 school. Poetry. Grammar. *Other:* Traditional religion, Buddhist (Lamaist). *Map:* 345.

Pumi, Southern [pmj] (Pimi, P'ömi, Primmi, P'rome, Pruumi, P'umi). 19,000 (1999). 6,000 monolinguals. Ethnic population: 28,000 (2000 census). Northwest Yunnan Province, Lanping, Weixi, Yongsheng, and Lijiang counties; Ninglang county, Xinyingpan district; western Sichuan Province, Garze Tibetan autonomous prefecture. *Status:* 6a (Vigorous). Language of recognized nationality: Pumi. *Class:* Sino-Tibetan, Tibeto-Burman, Northeastern Tibeto-Burman, Qiangic. *Dialect:* Qinghua. 4 other dialects. Intelligibility of Northern Pumi [pmi] is difficult. Lexical similarity: 60% between Northern Pumi [pmi] and Southern Pumi. *Type:* SOV; adjectives and numbers follow noun heads; uvular obstruents; initial s + consonant clusters; different vowels from N. Pumi; tonal, 2 tones. *Lg Use:* Vigorous. All domains. Positive attitudes. Also use Central Bai [bca], Central Tibetan [bod], Lipo [lpo], Lisu [lis], Mandarin Chinese [cmn], Naxi [nxq]. Used as L2 by Shixing [sxg]. *Lg Dev:* Literacy rate in L2: 70% for Pumi nationality (2000 census). *Writing:* Unwritten. *Other:* Buddhist (Lamaist). *Map:* 345.

Qabiao [laq] (Bendi Lolo, Ka Bao, Ka Biao, Kabeo, Laqua, Man La Qua, Phubyau, Pu Beo, Pu Péo, Pubiao, Pupeo, Qabiau, Qaqiau). 18 in China (2002 Li Yunbing), decreasing. A few fluent elderly speakers in 2001 (Li Jinfang 2006). Ethnic population: 400 (Li Jinfang 2006). Southeast Yunnan Province, Malipo county, Wenshan Zhuang and Miao autonomous prefectures, Donggan township, villages on Vietnam border: Matong, Punong, Pucha, and Makun; Tiechang district, Pufeng village; Babu district, Longlong village; Liuhe district, Xinfa and Meitang villages; Longlin village. (Ethnic Pubiao live in these villages, but the language is no longer spoken in all villages). *Status:* 8b (Nearly extinct). Language of recognized nationality: Yi. *Lg Use:* All located speakers were over 55 years old in 2000. Neutral attitudes. Also use Hmong Njua [hnj] in Matong village. Everyone also uses southwestern Mandarin [cmn]. Qabiao at Longlong (Babu district) switched to southwestern Mandarin. Qabiao at Longlong (Babu district) switched to Nong Zhuang [zhn]. *Other:* Ethnic autonym: Qa Biau (Ka Biao) or Qa Qiau; Ethnonym: Pubiao in Chinese. Intermarriage with Han, Zhuang, Miao and Dai nationality peoples is common.

See main entry on page 314. *Map:* 345.

Qau [gqu] (Aqao, Gao). 2,000 (2011 SIL). Central Guizhou Province, Shuicheng county, Dongkou village; Zhijin county, Niudong village; Pingba county, Dagoufang; Anshun county, Mosu and Wanzi villages; Puding county, Wozi village; Langdai county, Longxia village. *Status:* 8b (Nearly extinct). Language of recognized nationality: Gelao. *Class:* Tai-Kadai, Kra, Western Kra. *Lg Use:* Elderly only. *Writing:* Unwritten. *Map:* 345.

Qiang, Northern [cng] (Ch'iang). 57,800 (1999), decreasing. 14,000 Mawo, 14,000 Weigu, 11,000 Luhua, 8,000 Cimulin, and 9,000 Yadu. 130,000 total for Northern and Southern Qiang languages, including 80,000 as Qiang nationality and 50,000 as Tibetan nationality (1990 J-O. Svantesson). 0 monolinguals. Ethnic population: 306,000 (2000 census). North central Sichuan Province, Mao, Songpan, Heishui, and Beichuan counties. *Status:* 7 (Shifting). Language of recognized nationality: Qiang. *Class:* Sino-Tibetan, Tibeto-Burman, Northeastern Tibeto-Burman, Qiangic. *Dialects:* Cimulin, Luhua, Mawo, Weigu, Yadu. *Type:* SOV; more consonants than Southern Qiang; heavy phonemic inventory; consonant clusters in syllable onsets; nontonal. *Lg Use:* Parents encourage children to excel in school, which means learning Mandarin Chinese [cmn] well. Some use Qiang at home. Home. Mainly adults. Negative attitudes. Also use Mandarin Chinese [cmn]. Written Chinese used. Also use Central Tibetan [bod]. Used as L2 by Jiarong [jya]. *Lg Dev:* Literacy rate in L1: 0%. Literacy rate in L2: 100%. Men are more literate than women. Those under 30 are fairly literate in Chinese. Taught in primary schools, only for 1st and maybe 2nd grades. Dictionary. Grammar. *Writing:* Latin script, used since 1990, experimental (1993). *Other:* Buddhist (Lamaist), Daoist, traditional religion. *Map:* 344.

Qiang, Southern [qxs] (Ch'iang). 81,300 (1999 J. Evans), decreasing. 8,300 Daqishan, 4,100 Taoping, 3,100 Longxi, 14,500 Mianchi, 31,000 Hehu. Around 130,000 total for Northern and Southern Qiang. 80,000 officially classified within Qiang nationality and speakers 50,000 within Tibetan nationality (1990 J-O. Svantesson). 0 monolinguals. Ethnic population: 306,000 (2000 census). North central Sichuan Province, Wenchuan and Li counties; South Mao county, which transitions into Northern Qiang [cng]. *Status:* 7 (Shifting). Language of recognized nationality: Qiang. *Class:* Sino-Tibetan, Tibeto-Burman, Northeastern Tibeto-Burman, Qiangic. *Dialects:* Dajishan (Daqishan), Heihu, Jiaochang, Longxi, Mianchi, Sanlong, Taoping. *Type:* SOV; heavy phonemic inventory; few consonant clusters in syllable onsets; tonal, 2–6 tones. *Lg Use:* Parents encourage children's excellence at school which means learning Mandarin Chinese [cmn]. Some families still use Qiang at home. Home. Older adults. Negative attitudes. Also use Mandarin Chinese [cmn]. *Lg Dev:* Those under 35 are functionally literate in Chinese. Dictionary. OT. *Other:* Buddhist (Lamaist), Daoist, traditional religion. *Map:* 344.

Queyu [qvy] (Choyo, Zhaba). 7,000 (1995). West Sichuan Province, Ganzi (Garzê) Tibetan autonomous prefecture, Xinlong (Nyagrong) and Yajiang (Nyagquka) Litang counties. *Status:* 6b (Threatened). Language of recognized nationality: Tibetan. *Class:* Sino-Tibetan, Tibeto-Burman, Northeastern Tibeto-Burman, Qiangic. *Dialects:* None known. Reportedly similar to Zhaba [zhb]. *Type:* SOV; adjectives and number-classifier constructions follow noun heads; consonant cluster initials; tonal, 4 tones. *Lg Use:* Use Tibetan [bod] as a liturgical language (Bradley 2007). *Other:* Glossonym: Zhaba is used in Tuanjie Township of Yajiang County. Different from Zhaba language in Zhamai District. Buddhist (Lamaist), traditional religion. *Map:* 344.

Riang [ril]. 3,000 in China (1995). Ethnic population: 17,900 (2000 census). Southwest Yunnan Province, Lincang prefecture, Zhenkang county; Baoshan prefecture, Longyang county. *Status:* 8b (Nearly extinct). Language of recognized nationality: De'ang. *Dialects:* De'ang, Liang, Liang Palaung, Na'ang, Riang-Lang, Xiaoan'gou, Xiaochanggou, Yang Sek, Yang Wan Kun, Yanglam, Yin. *Other:* Along with Palaung speakers. Traditional religion. See main entry on page 241. *Map:* 345.

Russian [rus] (Eluosi, Olossu, Russ, Russki). 2,940 in China (Shearer and Sun Hong Kai 2002). Ethnic population: 15,600 (2000 census). North Xinjiang Uyghur Autonomous Region, Urumqi, Karamay (Kelamayi), Changji, and Tacheng cities; Yili prefecture (especially Yi'ning city); Inner Mongolia Autonomous Region, E'erguna Enhe Russian autonomous district (Hulunbeier banner); Heilongjiang Province, Heihe city. *Status:* 5 (Dispersed). Language of recognized nationality: Russian. *Lg Use:* Mostly neutral attitudes. Also use Mandarin Chinese [cmn], Uyghur [uig]. Used as L2 by Korean [kor], Mandarin Chinese [cmn], Oroqen [orh], Uyghur [uig], Xibe [sjo]. *Lg Dev:* Literacy rate in L2: 96% in any language for Russian nationality (2000 census). *Other:* Christian. See main entry on page 322. *Map:* 344.

Salar [slr] (Sala). 70,000 (2002), increasing. 10,000 monolinguals. Ethnic population: 105,000 (2000 census). L2 users: Some, especially men of other area languages, use Salar. Qinghai Province, Xunhua Salar and Hualong Hui autonomous counties; Gansu Province, Jishishan autonomous county; Xinjiang Uyghur Autonomous Region, Yilli. Kazakh autonomous prefecture. *Status:* 6b (Threatened). Language of recognized nationality: Salar. *Class:* Altaic, Turkic, Southern. *Dialects:* Ili, Jiezi, Mengda. Salar is spoken by descendants of an Oghuz-Turkic-speaking subtribe. Has an Oghuz Turkic base, and took on a medieval Chaghatay Turkic stratum through Central Asian contacts and finally acquired a stratum of features from local languages (1989 R. Hahn). Jiezi often seen as standard dialect. *Type:* SOV; postpositional; verbs take up to 3 or 4 suffixes, no prefixes; no person or gender marking; 27 consonant and 8 vowel phonemes; nontonal. *Lg Use:* Some speakers of other languages in the area use Salar, especially men. Domestic, informal domains. All ages, but children less. Positive attitudes. Also use Central Tibetan [bod], Mandarin Chinese [cmn], Uyghur [uig]. *Lg Dev:* Literacy rate in L1: 0%. Literacy rate in L2: 60%. Dictionary. Grammar. *Writing:* Unwritten. *Other:* Muslim (Sufi), Muslim (Ikhwan), Muslim (Sunni). *Map:* 344.

Samatao [ysd] (Samadu, Samaduo, Samou). 400 (2007), decreasing. Ethnic population: 2,810 (Bradley 2007). Yunnan Province, Guandu district, Kunming municipality, Zijun village. A few elderly speakers in Zhenkang and Yongde. *Status:* 8a (Moribund). Language of recognized nationality: Yi. *Class:* Sino-Tibetan, Tibeto-Burman, Ngwi-Burmese, Ngwi, Northern. *Dialects:* None known. Similar to Samei [smh] and Sanie [ysy], but not mutually intelligible (Bradley 2007). *Lg Use:* Some language heritage activities underway in the village school (Bradley 2007). No fluent speakers under 50. Also use Mandarin Chinese [cmn]. *Map:* 345.

Samei [smh]. 20,000 (Bradley 2007). Very few monolinguals. Ethnic population: 28,000 (Bradley 2007). Yunnan Province, Guandu district, Kunming city, Ala and surrounding communities, 47 villages; west Yiliang County, 7 villages. *Status:* 8a (Moribund). Language of recognized nationality: Yi. *Class:* Sino-Tibetan, Tibeto-Burman, Ngwi-Burmese, Ngwi, Northern. *Lg Use:* Extinct in some villages close to Kunming, severely endangered to the east in northeast Guandu and Yiliang, endangered in Ala Township, which is the center of the Samei distribution and where most villages are entirely or largely Samei (Bradley 2007). Few fluent young speakers, though many children have a passive understanding (Bradley 2007). Nearly all also use Chinese [cmn]. *Lg Dev:* Literacy rate in L2: High in Chinese. *Writing:* Yi script, traditional, no longer in use. *Other:* Traditional religion.

Samtao [stu] (Samtau, Samtuan). 100 in China (1993). Southwest Yunnan Province, Xishuangbanna prefecture. *Status:* 8a (Moribund). Language of recognized nationality: Blang. *Lg Use:* Also use Burmese [mya], Khün [kkh], Lü [khb], Mandarin Chinese [cmn], Shan [shn], Thai [tha]. Women are less bilingual than men. *Other:* No recent evidence that this language is still spoken in China. May be officially classified within Blang nationality or Undetermined nationality. Buddhist (Theravada), traditional religion. See main entry on page 241.

Sangkong [sgk] (Buxia). 1,500 (1995 D. Bradley), decreasing. Ethnic population: 2,000. South Yunnan Province, Xishuangbanna Dai autonomous prefecture, Jinghong county, Xiaojie (3 villages) and Menglong (1 village) districts. *Status:* 6b (Threatened). Language of recognized nationality: Hani. *Class:* Sino-Tibetan, Tibeto-Burman, Ngwi-Burmese, Ngwi, Southern. *Dialects:* None known. Reportedly similar to Bisu [bzi] and Phunoi [pho]. *Type:* Prenasalized initial consonants. Both -p -t -k endings and open syllables with tense vowels. Verbal particles which agree in number with the subject of the sentence. *Lg Use:* Negative attitudes. Most also use Hani [hni] (particularly the Yani variety of Haya dialect). Also use Lahu [lhu], Lü [khb], Mandarin Chinese [cmn]. *Map:* 345.

Sani [ysn]. 100,000 (2007). Southeast Yunnan Province, Shilin, Yilang, Mile, Luxi, and Qiubei counties. *Status:* 6a (Vigorous). Language of recognized nationality: Yi. *Class:* Sino-Tibetan, Tibeto-Burman, Ngwi-Burmese, Ngwi, Central. *Dialects:* Northern Sani, Southern Sani. *Type:* SOV. *Lg Use:* All ages. Also use Mandarin Chinese [cmn]. *Lg Dev:* Dictionary. *Writing:* Yi script, traditional, limited usage. *Other:* Population 7,762,300 (2000 census). The Samei, an Eastern Yi group east of Kunming in the Guandu region, call themselves Sani, but are not part of the Sani in Shilin. Tones differ on the 2 names, sa21 ni53 versus sa21 ni21. An Eastern Yi group with a similar name call themselves Sanie, immediately west of Kunming in Xishan region and in Anning and Fumin counties. For the Samei, Sani is their autonym. For the Sani in Shilin, Sani is an exonym. The Sani of Shilin call themselves ni21, but outsiders know them by the Chinese name Sani. Traditional religion. *Map:* 345.

Sanie [ysy] (Bai Lolo, Bai Yi, Sa'nguie, Sanyie, Shanie, Shaniepu, White Yi). 8,000 (2007), decreasing. Ethnic population: 17,200 (Bradley 2007). Yunnan Province, north Anning county, Kunming municipality, Xishan district; southwest Fumin county. *Status:* 8a (Moribund). Language of recognized nationality: Yi. *Class:* Sino-Tibetan, Tibeto-Burman, Ngwi-Burmese, Ngwi, Northern. *Dialects:* None known. Reportedly similar to Samatao [ysd]. *Lg Use:* Closer to Kunming spoken only by elderly; further away only by adults; furthest away a few children speak L1, which is being replaced by Chinese and Nasu (Bradley 2007). Few older adults. Also use Mandarin Chinese [cmn]. *Writing:* Miao (Pollard) script. *Map:* 345.

Sarikoli [srh] (Saliku'er, Salikur, Sarikuli, Sariqul, Sarykoly, Tadzik, Tajik, Tajiki). 16,000 (2000 G. Erqing). Ethnic population: 20,400 (2000 G. Erqing). Southwest Xinjiang Uyghur Autonomous Region, Taxkorgan (Tashkurghan) area, Sarikol valley. *Status:* 6b (Threatened). Language of recognized nationality: Tajik. *Class:* Indo-European, Indo-Iranian, Iranian, Eastern, Southeastern, Pamir, Shugni-Yazgulami. *Dialects:* None known. Not intelligible with Shughni [sgh] of Tajikistan and Afghanistan. *Type:* SOV. *Lg Use:* Vigorous. All ages. Positive attitudes. Also use Dari [prs], Kyrgyz [kir], Mandarin Chinese [cmn], Uyghur [uig]. *Lg Dev:* Literacy rate in L2: 87% in any language for Tajik nationality (2000 census). Taught in primary schools. Dictionary. Grammar. *Other:* Different from Tajiki [tgk] of Tajikistan, Afghanistan, and Iran. The label Tajik is used in different ways in different countries. Muslim (Ismaili). *Map:* 344.

Shan [shn] (Dehong). Yunnan Province, Myanmar border area, 1 village. *Status:* 5 (Developing). Language of recognized nationality: Dai. *Lg Use:* Used as L2 by Samtao [stu]. See main entry on page 241.

She [shx] (Huo Nte). 910 (1999 Mao Zongwu). 580 Luofu, 390 Lianhua (McConnell 1995). 200 monolinguals. Ethnic population: 710,000 (2000 census). 375,000 (Fujian Province), 171,000 (Zhejiang Province), 78,000 (Jiangxi Province), 45,000 (Guizhou Province), 28,000 (Guangdong). Southeast Guangdong Province. Luofu: Boluo and Zengcheng counties; Lianhua: Haifeng and Huidong counties. More than 10 villages. *Status:* 8b (Nearly extinct). Language of recognized nationality: She. *Class:* Hmong-Mien, Ho Nte. *Dialects:* Lianhua (Western She), Luofu (Eastern She). Major linguistic differences with Iu Mien [ium]. Reportedly most similar to Jiongnai Bunu [pnu]. Dialects inherently intelligible. Classification within Hmong-Mien is in dispute (McConnell 1995:1320). *Type:* SVO; modifiers precede noun heads; mainly monosyllabic roots, but mainly compound words; loans from Hakka and Cantonese Chinese; tonal, 8 tones. *Lg Use:* Most ethnic She use Hakka Chinese [hak] as L1 and other Chinese as well (Bradley 2007). All domains. Mainly adults. Neutral attitudes. Also use Hakka Chinese [hak], Mandarin Chinese [cmn], Min Nan Chinese [nan]. *Lg Dev:* Literacy rate in L2: 88% in any language for She nationality (2000 census). Grammar. *Other:* Shehua refers to Hakka [hak] variety spoken by the She. Daoist. *Map:* 346.

Sherpa [xsr] (Serwa, Sharpa, Sharpa Bhotia, Xiaerba). 800 in China (1994). Xizang Tibet Autonomous Region. *Status:* 6b (Threatened). Language of recognized nationality: Tibetan. *Other:* Buddhist (Lamaist). See main entry on page 258. *Map:* 344.

Shixing [sxg] (Xumi). 1,800 (2000 D. Bradley). 1,000 monolinguals. Ethnic population: 2,000 (2000 D. Bradley). Southwest Sichuan Province, Liangshan Yi autonomous prefecture, Muli Tibetan autonomous county, Shuiluo township. Two dialects: upper reaches of the Shuiluo river, lower reaches of the Shuiluo river. *Status:* 6b (Threatened). Language of recognized nationality: Tibetan. *Class:* Sino-Tibetan, Tibeto-Burman, Northeastern Tibeto-Burman, Naic. *Dialects:* Restricted mutual intelligibility between the Upper and the Lower Reaches dialects; salient phonological, lexical and grammatical differences between the two varieties. *Type:* SOV; adjectives and number-classifier constructions follow noun heads; consonant cluster initials; tonal, 2 tones, word-template tone. *Lg Use:* Vigorous. All domains. All ages. Tibetan [bod] is used in temples. 500 also use Mandarin Chinese [cmn]. Also use Khams Tibetan [khg], Lahu [lhu], Naxi [nxq], Northern Pumi [pmi], Southern Pumi [pmj]. *Lg Dev:* Poetry. Dictionary. *Other:* Buddhist (Lamaist), traditional religion. *Map:* 345.

Sinicized Miao [hmz] (Biantou Miao, Changshu Miao, Curved Comb Miao, Flat Head Miao, Han Miao, Hmong

Nzi, Hmong Sa, Hmong Shua, Hmong Sua, Long Comb Miao, Lopsided Comb Miao, Mushu Maio, Shuixi Miao, Waishu Miao, Water Miao, West of the Water Miao, Wooden Comb Miao). 250,000 in China (Hattaway 2000). Population total all countries: 252,000. West Guizhou Province, Dafang, Guanling, Nayong, Pu'an, Puding, Qianxi, Qinglong, Shuicheng, Xingren, Zhenning, Zhijin, and Ziyun counties, Anshun municipality; southeast Yunnan Province, Guangnan, Funing, and Jinping counties, Gejiu municipality; northwest Guangxi Zhuang Autonomous Region, Longlin county. Also in Viet Nam. *Status:* 6a (Vigorous). Language of recognized nationality: Miao. *Class:* Hmong-Mien, Hmongic, Chuanqiandian. A member of macrolanguage Hmong [hmn]. *Dialects:* None known. Not inherently intelligible with other Miao varieties. *Type:* SOV; 7 or 8 tones. *Lg Use:* Vigorous. Home, community, market. *Writing:* Latin script, pinyin-based, favoured by the educated. Miao (Pollard) script, favoured by peasants. *Other:* Traditional religion, Christian. *Map:* 345.

Sonaga [ysg] (Suoneiga). 2,000 (2009 SIL). Yunnan Province, Heqing county, Liuhe township. *Status:* 6a (Vigorous). Language of recognized nationality: Yi. *Class:* Sino-Tibetan, Tibeto-Burman, Ngwi-Burmese, Ngwi, Southeastern. *Dialects:* None known. Reportedly similar to Kuamasi [yku] and Kua-nsi [ykn]. *Lg Use:* All ages. *Writing:* Unwritten. *Map:* 345.

sTodsde [jih] (Shangzhai, Western Jiarong). 4,100 (2004). North central Sichuan Province, south Rangthang county, Shangzhai district, Shili, Zongke, and Puxi townships, near confluence of Duke river and its tributary, Zhongke river. *Status:* 6a (Vigorous). Language of recognized nationality: Tibetan. *Class:* Sino-Tibetan, Tibeto-Burman, Northeastern Tibeto-Burman, rGyalrongic. *Dialects:* Dayili, Puxi, Zongke. Phonologically Western and Northern are fairly similar and differ greatly from Eastern. Lexical similarity: 75% between Eastern and Northern Jiarong, 60% between Western and Northern Jiarong. *Type:* SOV; phonologically and lexically similar to Tibetan, grammatically more similar to Pumi and Qiang; complex consonant clusters; limited pitch contrast. *Other:* Buddhist (Lamaist), traditional religion. *Map:* 344.

Sui [swi] (Ai Sui, Shui, Sui Li, Suipo). 300,000 in China (Bradley 2007). Population total all countries: 300,120. Ethnic population: 407,000 (2000 census). Guizhou Province, centered in Sandu; Duyun, Dushan, Libo, Rongjiang, Danzhai, Leishan, and Congjiang counties; Guangxi Zhuang Autonomous Region, Nandan, and Rongshui counties; Yunnan Province, Fuyuan county. Also in Viet Nam. *Status:* 6a (Vigorous). Language of recognized nationality: Shui. *Class:* Tai-Kadai, Kam-Tai, Kam-Sui. *Dialects:* Pandong, Sandong (Central Sui, Southern Sui), Yang'an. Some communication difficulty between dialects. Sandong (Central) is the standard and most intelligible in the area (Castro 2011). *Type:* SVO; noun head initial; 70 onsets, 50 rhymes; 8 tones (Wei and Edmondson 2008). *Lg Use:* Vigorous. All domains. All ages. Positive attitudes. 100,000 also use Chinese [zho]. Bilingualism is low in the main areas. Written Chinese is in use. Used as L2 by Bouyei [pcc]. *Lg Dev:* Literacy rate in L1: 0%. Literacy rate in L2: 78% in any language for Shui nationality (2000 census). Not formally taught. Poetry. Dictionary. *Writing:* Han (Hanzi, Kanji, Hanja) script, used by folk singers aged 40–60. *Other:* Traditional religion. *Maps:* 345, 346.

Tai Dam [blt] (Black Tai, Hei Dai, Jinping Dai, Tailam, Tailon). 10,000 in China (1995). Southeast Yunnan Province, Honghe Hani and Yi autonomous prefectures, Jinping Miao, Yao, and Dai autonomous counties. *Status:* 5 (Developing). Language of recognized nationality: Dai. *Lg Use:* Used as L2 by Bumang [bvp]. See main entry on page 315. *Map:* 345.

Tai Dón [twh] (Bai Dai, Tai Jinping, White Tai). 15,000 in China (2000 census). Population figure 90% of Dai nationality in Jinping County in 2000. Southeast Yunnan Province, Honghe Hani and Yi autonomous prefectures, Jinping Miao, Yao and Dai autonomous counties. *Status:* 6a (Vigorous). Language of recognized nationality: Dai. *Lg Use:* Used as L2 by Bumang [bvp]. See main entry on page 315. *Map:* 345.

Tai Hongjin [tiz]. 85,000 (2000 census). Southeast and north Yunnan Province. Yongwu dialect: Chuxiong Yi autonomous prefecture, Yongren, Wuding and Dayao counties, and Kunming prefecture, Luquan Yi and Miao autonomous counties; Maguan dialect: Wenshan Zhuang and Miao autonomous prefectures, Maguan county; Yuanjiang dialect: Honghe Hani and Yi autonomous prefectures, Honghe and Yuanyang counties, as well as Yuxi prefecture, Yuanjiang Hani, Yi, and Dai autonomous counties; Lüshi dialect: Honghe Hani and Yi autonomous prefectures, Lüchun, Shiping, and Jianshui counties. *Status:* 7 (Shifting). Language of recognized nationality: Dai. *Class:* Tai-Kadai, Kam-Tai, Tai, Southwestern. *Dialects:* Lüshi, Maguan, Yongwu, Yuanjiang (Shui Dai). Dialects are significantly different and probably not all mutually intelligible. Tai Hongjin is a subgroup of scattered non-Buddhist Southwestern Tai language groups, who have some common phonological traits, but many differences as well. Tai Hongjin dialects have undergone more influence from Chinese and surrounding Ngwi languages (Yi and Hani) than other Yunnan Tai languages, and are only 50%–60% lexically similar to other Tai languages. *Lg Use:* All adults. *Lg Dev:* Literacy rate in L1: 0%. *Other:* Traditional religion. *Map:* 345.

Tai Nüa [tdd] (Chinese Shan, Chinese Tai, Dai Kong, Dai Na, Dai Nuea, Daide, Dehong, Dehong Dai, Tai Dehong, Tai Le, Tai Mao, Tai Neua, Tai nö, Tai Nü, Tai Nue, Tai taü, Tai-Kong, Tai-Le, Yunannese Shan, Yunnan Shant'ou). 540,000 in China (Zhou Yaowen and Luo Meizhen 2001). Population total all countries: 717,400. Ethnic population: 610,000 (Zhou Yaowen and Luo Meizhen 2001). Includes Tai Lü, Tai Hongjin, Tai Ya, Tai Dam and Tai Dón. Southwest Yunnan Province, Dehong Dai and Jingpo autonomous prefectures, Baoshan, Simao, and Lincang municipal prefectures. Mangshi dialect: Dehong Dai and Jingpo autonomous prefectures, Luxi, Yingjiang, Lianghe, Longchuan, and Wanding counties, Baoshan municipal prefecture, Baoshan, Tengchong, Longling, and Shidian counties. Menggeng dialect: Simao municipal prefecture, Menglian Dai-Lahu-Va, Jinggu Dai-Yi, Lancang Hani, Zhenyuan Yi-Hani-Lahu, Ximeng Va, Jingdong Yi, Pu'er Hani-Yi, and Mojiang Hani autonomous counties, as well as Simao county, Baoshan municipal prefecture, Changning county, Lincang municipal prefecture, Lincang, Yongde, Zhenkang, Yun, and Fengqing counties, and Shuangjiang Lahu-Va-Blang-Dai, and Cangyuan Va autonomous counties; southern Sichuan Province, Liangshan autonomous prefecture. Also in Laos, Myanmar, Viet Nam. *Status:* 4 (Educational). Language of recognized nationality: Dai. *Class:* Tai-Kadai, Kam-Tai, Tai, Southwestern. *Dialects:* Mangshi (Debao, Dehong, Taile), Menggeng (Taita), Tai Pong (Ka, La, Sai, Tai Ka, Ya, You), Yongren. *Type:* SVO; modifiers follow heads. *Lg Use:* Also use Mandarin Chinese [cmn]. Used as L2 by Achang [acn]. *Lg Dev:* Literacy rate in L2: 84% literate in any language (2000 census, Dai nationality). Tai Nüa has traditional script and tradition of literacy, so percentages probably include literacy in Liek or Chinese script or both. Taught in primary and secondary schools. Dictionary. Bible portions: 1931–1948. *Writing:* Tai Le script, used in the Dehong Dai and Jingpho Autonomous Prefecture, Yunnan Province, China. *Other:* Northern Shan-like varieties in China are referred to collectively as Tai Na, or Dehong Dai in Chinese. Buddhist (Theravada), traditional religion. *Map:* 345.

Tai Ya [cuu] (Cung, Daiya, Huayao Dai, Multi-colored Waistband Tai, Tai Cung, Tai-Chung, Tai-Cung, Ya, Yuanxin Hongjin Dai). 50,000 in China (2000 census). Population total all countries: 50,400. Ethnic population: 50,000 (2000 census). Based on county level Dai populations. Central and south Yunnan Province, Yuxi prefecture, Xinping Yi-Dai autonomous county, Mosha district; Yuanjiang Hani, Yi, and Dai autonomous counties; Honghe Hani and Yi autonomous prefectures, Yuanyang and Honghe counties. Also in Thailand. *Status:* 6a (Vigorous). Language of recognized nationality: Dai. *Class:* Tai-Kadai, Kam-Tai, Tai, Southwestern. *Dialects:* Tai Chung (Cung, Dai Zhong), Tai Kha (Dai Ka), Tai Sai (Dai Sai), Tai Ya. Dialects mutually intelligible, though speakers of the latter 3 may understand Tai Ya dialect (the largest) more easily than speakers of Tai Ya understand the other 3 dialects. Some linguists have analyzed Tai Ya as most similar to Tai Nüa [tdd], others have grouped Tai Ya with other non-Buddhist Southwestern Tai groups. Tai Ya is probably not easily intelligible with other varieties of Tai. *Type:* SVO; tonal, 6 tone categories in unchecked syllables, 2 (split into 4 according to vowel length) in checked syllables; nasal and stop finals. *Lg Use:* Most domains. All ages. Positive attitudes. *Lg Dev:* Dictionary. Grammar. Bible portions: 1922. *Other:* Called Daiya or Huayao Dai (Multi-colored Waistband Dai) in China. Traditional religion, Christian. *Map:* 345.

Talu [yta] (Tagu, Taliu, Tazhi). 13,600 (2007), decreasing. Yunnan Province, Yongsheng county, mainly in 4 villages of Liude township; Ninglang county, Ninglangping townhip; Huaping county, Tongda township. *Status:* 6b (Threatened). Language of recognized nationality: Yi. *Class:* Sino-Tibetan, Tibeto-Burman, Ngwi-Burmese, Ngwi, Central. *Dialects:* None known. Similar to Lolopo [ycl] (Bradley 2007). *Lg Use:* Also use Mandarin Chinese [cmn]. *Map:* 345.

Tanglang [ytl] (Tholo). 950 (Bradley 2007), decreasing. Northwest Yunnan Province, south Lijiang county, Tai'an district, Hongmai community. Locals call this area Tanglangba or Tanglang basin. *Status:* 6b (Threatened). Language of recognized nationality: Yi. *Class:* Sino-Tibetan, Tibeto-Burman, Ngwi-Burmese, Ngwi, Central. *Dialects:* None known. Reportedly similar to Lisu [lis]. *Lg Use:* Most, including children, can speak the language (Bradley 2007). Home, village, market. Also use Mandarin Chinese [cmn]. *Lg Dev:* Taught in primary schools. *Map:* 345.

Tatar [tat] (Tartar, Tata'er). 800 in China (1999 C. Zongzhen), decreasing. Ethnic population: 4,890 (2000 census). North Xinjiang Uyghur Autonomous Region, Yining (Ghulja, Kulja), Qvqek, and Ürümqi. *Status:* 7 (Shifting). Language of recognized nationality: Tatar. *Lg Use:* Oral tradition, songs. Older adults. Written Kazakh [kaz] is used as literary language; nearly all use it. Written Uyghur [uig] is used as literary language; nearly all use it. *Lg Dev:* Literacy rate in L2: 98% literate in any language (2000 census, Tatar nationality). *Other:* Some speak only Kazakh. Speech in different areas is influenced by Uyghur and Kazakh. Muslim (Sunni). See main entry on page 322. *Map:* 344.

T'en [tct] (Rao, Rau, Then, Yang Hwang, Yanghuang). 20,000 (Bradley 2007). Ethnic population: 25,000 (2000 D. Bradley). Guizhou Province, east Pingtang county; Dushan county; Huishui, just south of Guiyang; some in Guangxi Zhuang Autonomous Region. *Status:* 6b (Threatened). Language of recognized nationality: Bouyei. *Class:* Tai-Kadai, Kam-Tai, Kam-Sui. *Dialects:* Hedong, Hexi, Huishui. Reportedly similar to Sui [swi], some scholars consider T'en to be a dialect of Sui (Shearer and Sun 2002). *Lg Use:* Moderately vigorous. Chinese and Bouyei [pcc] in the area also speak T'en. Religion. All ages. Not used by children and young people as often as adults. Also use local Chinese or Bouyei [pcc]. *Lg Dev:* Dictionary. Grammar. *Other:* Traditional religion. *Map:* 345.

Thangmi [thf] (Dolakha, Thami). 300 in China (2002). Xizang Tibetan Autonomous Region. *Status:* 7 (Shifting). See main entry on page 261.

Thopho [ytp] (Black Hat Folk, Black Phula, Hei Mao Ren, Phula). 200 (Pelkey 2011), decreasing. Ethnic population: 500. Yunnan Province, Guangnan county, South central Zhetu district; northeast Zhulin district, 2 villages. *Status:* 6b (Threatened). Language of recognized nationality: Yi. *Class:* Sino-Tibetan, Tibeto-Burman, Ngwi-Burmese, Ngwi, Southeastern. *Lg Use:* Also use Mandarin Chinese [cmn], Nong Zhuang [zhn]. *Other:* Substantial subsequent contact with Pholo [yip] and Tai-Kadai varieties. *Map:* 345.

Tibetan, Amdo [adx] (Amdo, Anduo, Ngambo, Panang). 1,800,000 (2005 C. Lhungrub). Tibet Autonomous Region, Huangnan, Hainan, Haibei, and Guoluo (Golog) autonomous prefectures; Qinghai Province, Haixi Mongolian-Tibetan-Kazakh autonomous prefecture and Gannan Tibetan autonomous prefecture; southwest Gansu Province, Tianzhu autonomous county; west and north Sichuan Province, Ganzi and Aba (Ngaba) Tibetan autonomous prefectures. *Status:* 6a (Vigorous). Language of recognized nationality: Tibetan. *Class:* Sino-Tibetan, Tibeto-Burman, Western Tibeto-Burman, Bodish, Central Bodish, Amdo. *Dialects:* Hbrogpa, Panang (Banag, Banang, Panags, Panakha, Pananag, Sbanag, Sbranag), Rongba, Rongmahbrogpa, Rtahu. Central Tibetan [bod] or Khams Tibetan [khg] varieties not intelligible. Lexical similarity: 70% with Central Tibetan [bod] and Khams Tibetan [khg]. *Type:* SOV; many onset clusters. *Lg Use:* All ages. Used as L2 by Baima [bqh], Bonan [peh]. *Lg Dev:* Classroom teachers use it it, but Modern Literary Tibetan is the language of literature. Films. TV. Videos. Dictionary. Grammar. *Writing:* Tibetan script. *Other:* Those in Golog are called Golog, Ngolok, Mgolog, Ggolo, or Gugoluo. Buddhist (Lamaist). *Map:* 344.

Tibetan, Central [bod] (Bhotia, Dbus, Dbusgtsang, Phoke, Tibetan, U, Wei, Weizang, Zang). 1,070,000 in China (1990 census). 570,000 Dbus, 460,000 Gtsang, 40,000 Mngahris out of 4,593,000 in the official nationality. Population total all countries: 1,172,940. 920,000 monolinguals. Xizang Province,Tibet Autonomous Region; some in Xinjiang Province. Also in Taiwan (Tibetan), India (Tibetan), Nepal (Tibetan), Norway (Tibetan), Switzerland (Tibetan), United States (Tibetan). *Status:* 2 (Provincial). Statutory provincial language in Xizang Autonomous Region (Tibet) (1984, Ethnic Regional Autonomy Act, Articles 10 and 21). Language of recognized nationality: Tibetan. *Class:* Sino-Tibetan, Tibeto-Burman, Western Tibeto-Burman, Bodish, Central Bodish, Central. *Dialects:* Dbus, Deqing Zang, Gtsang (Lhasa, Tsang), Mngahris (Ngari). In the exile community a so-called diaspora Tibetan has developed. *Type:* SOV; tonal, 4 tones. *Lg Use:* Vigorous. Speakers of other languages in the area can also speak Tibetan. All domains. All ages. Positive attitudes. Also use Mandarin Chinese [cmn], Narua [nru], Naxi [nxq]. Used as L2 by Boga'er Luoba [adi], Cuona Monba [twm], Darang Deng [mhu], Geman Deng [mxj], Horpa [ero], Jiarong [jya], Kangjia [kxs], Lisu [lis], Namuyi [nmy], Naxi [nxq], Northern Pumi [pmi], Northern Qiang [cng], Salar [slr], Shixing [sxg], Southern Pumi [pmj], Tshangla [tsj], Tu [mjg], Yidu Luoba [clk]. *Lg Dev:* Literacy rate in L2: 30%. Motivation for literacy is high. Taught in primary and secondary schools. Magazines. Newspapers. Radio programs. Dictionary. Grammar. Bible: 1948. *Writing:* Phags-pa script. Tibetan script, Uchen, Umed and a less-widely known and more priestly style. *Other:* Xifan (Hsifan) and Bhotia are general terms for Tibetan. Probably includes many languages: Groma, Niarong, Lhomi, Panang, Sherpa, Tseku, Tinan Lahul. Nomads in central and northern Tibet in Phala on the 4,500-meter Chang Tang plateau are known as Drokba. They number around 500,000. Written Tibetan is reportedly based on a southern dialect. Buddhist (Lamaist), Muslim. *Map:* 344.

Tibetan, Khams [khg] (Kam, Kang, Khamba, Khampa, Khams, Khams Bhotia, Khams-Yal). 1,380,000 in China (1994). 996,000 Eastern, 135,000 Southern, 158,000 Western, 91,000 Northern. Population total all countries: 1,380,300. West, northeast Xizang Tibet Autonomous Region, Changdu (Qamdo) and Naqu (Nagqu) districts; west Sichuan Province, Ganzi (Garzê) Tibetan autonomous prefecture; northwest Yunnan Province, Diqing (Dechen) Tibetan autonomous prefecture; southwest Qinghai Province, Yushu Tibetan autonomous prefecture. Also in Myanmar. *Status:* 6a (Vigorous). Language of recognized nationality: Tibetan. *Class:* Sino-Tibetan, Tibeto-Burman, Western Tibeto-Burman, Bodish, Central Bodish, Khams. *Dialects:* Eastern Khams, Northern Khams, Southern Khams, Western Khams. Dialects may be distinct languages; large differences reported. Lexical similarity: 80% with Central Tibetan [bod]. *Type:* SOV; tonal, 4 tones. *Lg Use:* All ages. Used as L2 by Muya [mvm], Shixing [sxg]. *Lg Dev:* Grammar. *Writing:* Tibetan script. *Other:* Different from Western Parbate [kjl], Eastern Parbate [kif], Sheshi Kham [kip], and Gamale Kham [kgj] of Nepal. Buddhist (Lamaist). *Map:* 344.

Tinani [lbf] (Bhotia of Lahul, Gondla, Lahauli, Lahouli, Lahuli Tinan, Rangloi). 450 in China (Voegelin and Voegelin 1977). Western border of Xizang Tibet Autonomous Region. *Status:* 7 (Shifting). Language of recognized nationality: Tibetan. See main entry on page 146. *Map:* 344.

Tsat [huq] (Hainan Cham, Hui, Huihui, Sanya Hui, Utsat, Utset). 4,000 (Bradley 2007). Ethnic population: 5,000 (2000 D. Bradley). South Hainan Prefecture; Yaxian (Sanya) County, Yanglan District, Huixin and Huihui villages. *Status:* 6b (Threatened). Language of recognized nationality: Hui. *Class:* Austronesian, Malayo-Polynesian, Malayo-Chamic, Chamic, Highlands, Chru-Northern, Northern Cham. *Dialects:* None known. Reportedly most similar to Northern Roglai [rog], but very different. Tsat is structurally changed to be like Chinese. *Type:* Tonal. *Lg Use:* Vigorous. All domains. All ages. Positive attitudes. Also use Mandarin Chinese [cmn] for school. Also use the Fukienese dialect of Min Nan Chinese [nan] for commerce. Also use Yue Chinese [yue] for commerce. *Other:* The phonology suggests a history of some independence from other Chamic languages (Maddieson 1991). Their name for themselves is Utsat, for their language Tsat. Huihui or Hui is the Chinese name. Muslim. *Map:* 346.

Tseku [tsk] (Tsuku, Tzuku). 12,600 (2000). Population total all countries: 19,000. Xizang Tibetan Autonomous Region. *Status:* 6a (Vigorous). Language of recognized nationality: Tibetan. *Class:* Sino-Tibetan, Tibeto-Burman, Western Tibeto-Burman, Bodish, Central Bodish. *Writing:* Unwritten.

Tshangla [tsj] (Canglo Monba, Cangluo Menba, Cangluo Monba, Central Monpa, Menba, Monba, Monpa, Motuo Menba, Sangla, Tsangla Monba, Tsanglo). 7,000 in China (2000 census). Majority are monolingual. Ethnic population: 8,920 (2000 census). Includes Moinba (Cuona Monba) [twm] speakers. Southeast Xizang Tibet Autonomous Region, Linzhi prefecture, Motuo (Medoz, Medog) county, Beibeng, Motuo, Bangxing, and Dexing districts; Dongjiu district, Linzhi (Ngingchi) county. *Status:* 6b (Threatened). Language of recognized nationality: Menba. *Lg Use:* Vigorous. All domains, except for Buddhist scriptures which are recited in Classical Tibetan. Positive attitudes. Also use Central Tibetan [bod], Mandarin Chinese [cmn]. *Lg Dev:* Literacy rate in L2: A minority are literate in either Tibetan script or Chinese script. *Other:* Different from Angami Naga [njm] of India. Buddhist (Lamaist). See main entry on page 59. *Map:* 344.

Tu [mjg] (Mongor, Mongour, Monguor). 152,000 (2000 census). Very few monolinguals. Ethnic population: 190,000. East Qinghai Province, Huzhu Tu, Minhe Tu, and Hui autonomous counties; Gansu Province. *Status:* 7 (Shifting). Language of recognized nationality: Tu. *Class:* Altaic, Mongolic, Eastern, Mongour. *Dialects:* Huzhu (Halchighol, Mongghul, Naringhol), Minhe (Mangghuer). Reportedly most divergent of all Mongolian languages. Dialects reported not inherently mutually intelligible. Huzhu: 150,000 people, 50,000 speakers; Minhe: 25,000. Dongren Huzhu considered standard. Dialects of Huzhu: Halchi, Karlong (18,000), and Naringhol. *Type:* SOV; postpositions; genitives, adjectives, numerals, and relative clauses precede head noun; question word appears in the position of the thing being questioned; verbs may bear up to 3 or 4 suffixes; word order distinguishes subject and direct object; topicalized noun phrases are often fronted; case is marked by enclitic postpositions; verbs are marked for the pragmatic category of perspective (a binary distinction between the perspective of the speaker and that of anyone else); causatives are extremely common; syllables (C)(C)V(C) (clusters must involve a glide in Mangghuer, while Mongghul allows a wider range of onset clusters); stress falls on the final syllable of a phonological word; no vowel harmony (in Mangghuer). *Lg Use:* Varies with location. Positive attitudes. Also use Central Tibetan [bod], Mandarin Chinese [cmn]. *Lg Dev:* Literacy rate in L1: About 2,000 can read, 200 can write. Literacy rate in L2: 77% literate in any language (2000 census, Tu nationality). Poetry. Magazines. Films. Dictionary. Grammar. *Writing:* Latin script, pinyin-based. *Other:* Buddhist (Lamaist), traditional religion. *Map:* 344.

Tujia, Northern [tji] (Tuchia, Tudja). 70,000 (Brassett and Brassett 2005). Regularly used but increasingly the young prefer to speak Chinese and are encouraged by their parents. In most areas children acquire a passive knowledge only. No longer used in southeastern Sichuan, northeastern Guizhou, and southwestern Hubei provinces. No longer used or moribund in northwestern Hunan and severely endangered in the remaining areas (Bradley 2007). 100 monolinguals. Ethnic population: 8,030,000 (2000 census). Ethnic population includes 1,500 speakers of Southern Tujia [tjs]. Northwest Hunan Province, Yingjiang and Yanhe counties; southwest Hubei and southeast Chongqing provinces, Wuling mountain range; some in Guizhou Province. *Status:* 8a (Moribund). Language of recognized nationality: Tujia. *Class:*

Sino-Tibetan, Tibeto-Burman, Northeastern Tibeto-Burman, Tujia. *Dialects:* Baojing, Longshan. Northern and Southern Tujia [tjs] are not mutually intelligible. Lexical similarity: 40% with Southern Tujia [tjs]. *Type:* SOV; tonal, 4 tones; no voiced stops or affricates. *Lg Use:* Regularly used but increasingly the young prefer to speak Chinese and are encouraged by their parents. In most areas children acquire a passive knowledge only. No longer used in southeastern Sichuan, northeastern Guizhou and southwestern Hubei provinces. No longer used or moribund in northwestern Hunan and severely endangered in the remaining areas (Bradley 2007). All domains. 60% older than 50 years, 30% between 20 and 50, 10% under 25. Most also use Mandarin Chinese [cmn]. Written Chinese in use and used in schools. Also use Hmong Njua [hnj]. *Lg Dev:* Literacy rate in L2: 88% in Chinese (2000 census, Tujia nationality). Grammar. *Other:* Traditional religion, Buddhist. *Map:* 346:31.

Tujia, Southern [tjs] (Tuchia). 1,500 (Brassett and Brassett 2005), decreasing. Monolinguals are mainly women, children, and older adults. Ethnic population: 8,030,000 (2000 census). Includes 70,000 in Northern Tujia. Northwest Hunan Province, Luxi county, 3 villages. *Status:* 8a (Moribund). Language of recognized nationality: Tujia. *Class:* Sino-Tibetan, Tibeto-Burman, Northeastern Tibeto-Burman, Tujia. *Dialects:* None known. Northern [tji] and Southern Tujia are not mutually intelligible. Lexical similarity: 40% with Northern Tujia [tji], but with phonological and grammatical differences. *Type:* SOV; voiced stops and affricates; tonal, 5 tones. *Lg Use:* In Boluozhai, all speak the language; in Puzhu, some children can speak it; in Xiaqieji, only adults speak it (Bradley 2007). Home, village. Mainly older people. Positive attitudes. Also use Mandarin Chinese [cmn]. Chinese used in schools. *Lg Dev:* Literacy rate in L1: 0%. Literacy rate in L2: 88% in Chinese (2000 census, Tujia nationality). *Other:* Traditional religion, Buddhist. *Map:* 346:34.

Tuva [tyv] (Diba, Kök Mungak, Tuvin, Tuwa). 2,400 in China (1999 W. Hongwei). 0 monolinguals. Xinjiang Uyghur Autonomous Region, Altay prefecture, Burjin, Habahe, Fuyun, and Altay counties. *Status:* 6b (Threatened). Language of recognized nationality: Mongolian. *Lg Use:* Vigorous. Religious services. All ages. Positive attitudes. 30% also use Kalmyk-Oirat [xal]. More than 90% also use Kazakh [kaz]. Peripheral Mongolian [mvf] used in education. Also use Mandarin Chinese [cmn]. *Other:* Buddhist (Lamaist), traditional religion. See main entry on page 323. *Map:* 344.

U [uuu] (A'erwa, Awa Blang, Puman, P'uman, Wa, Wu, Wu Blang). 40,000 (2000). Southwest Yunnan Province, Baoshan municipal prefecture, Shidian and Changning counties. May be in Myanmar. *Status:* 7 (Shifting). Language of recognized nationality: Blang. *Class:* Austro-Asiatic, Mon-Khmer, Northern Mon-Khmer, Palaungic, Eastern Palaungic, Angkuic. *Dialects:* Not closely related to Plang [blr] (1990 J-O. Svantesson). May be same as Wu dialect of Wa [wbm] in Myanmar and Hu [huo] of China. *Lg Use:* Also use Mandarin Chinese [cmn]. *Lg Dev:* Literacy rate in L2: 77%. *Other:* Buddhist (Theravada), traditional religion. *Map:* 345.

Uyghur [uig] (Uighuir, Uighur, Uiguir, Uigur, Uygur, Weiwu'er, Wiga). 8,400,000 in China (2000 census). 4,700,000 Central Uyghur, 1,150,000 Hotan, 25,000 Lop. Population total all countries: 8,791,610. Most are monolingual. Mainly in Xinjiang Province, Uyghur Autonomous Region. Small areas in Gansu and Xizang provinces. Also in Afghanistan, Australia, Taiwan, Germany, India, Kazakhstan, Kyrgyzstan, Mongolia, Pakistan, Russian Federation, Saudi Arabia, Tajikistan, Turkey, United States, Uzbekistan. *Status:* 2 (Provincial). Statutory provincial language in Xinjiang Uyghur Autonomous Region (1984, Ethnic Regional Autonomy Act, Articles 10 and 21). Language of recognized nationality: Uygur. *Class:* Altaic, Turkic, Eastern. *Dialects:* Central Uyghur, Hotan (Hetian), Lop (Luobu). The Akto Türkmen speak a dialect of Uyghur with 500 different seldom-used words. There are 2,000 in 2 villages, Kösarap and Oytak in Akto County, south of Kashgar, Xinjiang. Dolan is a dialect spoken around the fringes of the Taklimakan Desert in Xinjiang. Chinese linguists recognize 3 dialects. Others have used the following dialect names: Kashgar-Yarkand (Kashi-Shache), Yengi Hissar (Yengisar), Khotan-Kerya (Hotan-Yutian), Charchan (Qarqan, Qiemo), Aksu (Aqsu), Qarashahr (Karaxahar), Kucha (Kuqa), Turfan (Turpan), Kumul (Hami), Ili (Kulja, Yining, Taranchi), Urumqi (Urumchi), Lopnor (Lopnur), and Dolan, Akto Türkmen. There are significant dialect differences between China, Kazakhstan, Kyrgyzstan, and Uzbekistan. *Type:* SOV; postpositions; genitives, adjectives, numerals, relatives before noun heads; question words initial; a few prefixes; 3 suffixes on nouns; 6 suffixes on verbs; word order distinguishes subjects and indirect objects, topic and comment; 8 noun cases shown by suffixes; verb suffixes mark subject person, number, 2nd person marks plural and 3 levels of respect; passive, reflexive, reciprocal and causative; comparatives; CV, CVC, CVCC syllables; nontonal. *Lg Use:* Widely used in print media in Kashgar. Vigorous. All domains. All ages. Positive attitudes. Young people and intellectuals also use Chinese [cmn]. Also use English [eng], Russian [rus]. Used as L2 by Ainu [aib], Ili Turki [ili], Kyrgyz [kir], Northern Uzbek [uzn], Peripheral Mongolian [mvf], Russian [rus], Salar [slr], Sarikoli [srh], Tatar [tat], Xibe [sjo]. *Lg Dev:* Literacy rate in L2: 91% in any language (2000 census, Uyghur nationality). Literacy based on Central Uyghur as spoken in the area between Yili (Ili) and Urumqi, and includes literates in Uyghur or Chinese or both. Newspapers. Radio programs. TV. Grammar. Bible: 1950. *Writing:* Arabic script, official and primary usage in China, also used in Afghanistan. Cyrillic script, used in Kazakhstan, past usage in China. Latin script, used in China and Turkey. *Other:* Some speakers classified within other official nationalities, such as Kyrghyz. Those in the north are more influenced by modern Chinese culture. Muslim (Sunni). *Map:* 344.

Uzbek, Northern [uzn] (Ouzbek, Ozbek, Usbaki, Usbeki). 5,000 in China (2000 A. Chentgshiliang). Ethnic population: 12,400 (2000 census). North and west Xinjiang Uyghur Autonomous Region; Urumqi, Kashgar, and Yining (Ghulja) cities, especially Ili. *Status:* 5 (Dispersed). Language of recognized nationality: Uzbek. *Dialects:* Andizhan, Fergana, Samarkand, Tashkent. *Lg Use:* Vigorous. Some speakers of other languages in the area can also speak Uzbek. All domains. All ages. Positive attitudes. Also use Kazakh [kaz], Mandarin Chinese [cmn], Uyghur [uig]. *Lg Dev:* Literacy rate in L2: 98% (2000 census, Uzbek nationality). *Other:* Muslim (Sunni). See main entry on page 308. *Map:* 344.

Vietnamese [vie] (Annamese, Ching, Gin, Jing, Kinh). 7,200 in China (1999 O. Jueya). South coast of Guangxi Zhuang Autonomous Region, on Shanxin, Wanwei, and Wutou peninsulas (the '3 peninsulas'), Fangcheng Pan-Nationality autonomous county; Jiangping region. *Status:* 6b (Threatened). Language of recognized nationality: Jing. *Lg Use:* Moderately vigorous. In parts of Fangcheng County most shifting to Yue Chinese [yue]. Due to increased commerce and contact with Viet Nam since mid 1990s, the language could revive in China. Most domains in the"3 peninsulas', although interchangeably with Yue Chinese [yue]; only restricted domains elsewhere. All ages in the '3 peninsulas'; elsewhere older people. Most also use Yue Chinese [yue] of Guangxi. A few also use Yue. Bilinguals use Chinese as a written language. A few also use Mandarin Chinese [cmn]. Bilinguals use Chinese as a written language. Used as L2 by Mandarin Chinese [cmn]. *Lg Dev:* Literacy rate in L2: 92% in Chinese (2000 census, Jing nationality). *Other:* Christian, Daoist. See main entry on page 316. *Map:* 346:52.

Wa, Parauk [prk] (Baraog, Baroke, Buliu, Bulu, Burao, Phalok, Praok, Wa). 399,000 in China (2008 P. Hopple). Speaker population based on 2000 census. Southwest Yunnan Province, Lincang prefecture, Cangyuan Va autonomous, Shuangjiang Lahu, Blang, Dai autonomous, Gengma Dai, and Yongde counties; Simao prefecture, Lancang Lahu autonomous county; Xishuangbanna Dai autonomous prefecture, Menghai county, Mengman district. *Status:* 5 (Developing). Language of recognized nationality: Blang. Around 10,000 Parauk speakers are classified as being within Blang nationality. Language of recognized nationality: Wa. The vast majority of speakers are assigned to the Wa nationality. *Dialects:* Aishuai, Alwa, Banhong, Dazhai. *Lg Use:* All ages. Also use Mandarin Chinese [cmn]. *Lg Dev:* Literacy rate in L2: 76% in any language for Va nationality (to which some Parauk speakers belong) (2000 census). *Other:* According to Chinese sources. Buddhist (Hinayana), Christian. See main entry on page 242. *Map:* 345.

Wa, Vo [wbm] (Ban, Kawa, K'awa, La, Pan, Pinyin, Va, Vo, Wa Pwi, Wakut). 40,000 in China (Zhou Zhizhi, Qixiang Yan, and Guoqing Chen 2004). Population total all countries: 40,700. Many monolinguals. Southwest Yunnan Province, Lincang prefecture, Yongde and Zhenkang counties; Simao prefecture, Lancang Lahu autonomous county. Also in Myanmar. *Status:* 5 (Developing). Language of recognized nationality: Wa. *Class:* Austro-Asiatic, Mon-Khmer, Northern Mon-Khmer, Palaungic, Eastern Palaungic, Waic, Wa. *Lg Use:* Vigorous. All domains. All ages. Positive attitudes. Also use Lahu [lhu], Lü [khb], Mandarin Chinese [cmn]. Used as L2 by Blang [blr], Lahu [lhu]. *Lg Dev:* Literacy rate in L1: 1%. Literacy rate in L2: 76% in any language (2000 census, Va nationality). NT: 1938. *Writing:* Latin script. *Other:* Traditional religion, Buddhist, Christian. *Map:* 345.

Wakhi [wbl] (Khik, Vakhan, Wakhani, Wakhigi). 6,000 in China. Ethnic population: 41,000 (2000 census). Includes Sarikoli [srh] speakers. Xinjiang Uyghur Autonomous Region, Taxkorgan Tajik autonomous county (especially Daftar); mountains south of Pishan. *Status:* 7 (Shifting). Language of recognized nationality: Tajik. *Dialect:* Eastern Wakhi. *Lg Use:* Also use Mandarin Chinese [cmn]. *Lg Dev:* Literacy rate in L2: 87% in any language (2000 census, Tajik nationality). *Other:* Muslim (Ismaili). See main entry on page 51. *Map:* 344.

Waxianghua [wxa] (Wogang, Xianghua). 300,000 (1995). West Hunan Province, a 6,000 square km area, Wuling mountains, including Yuanling, Chunxi, Jishou, Guzhang, and Dayong. *Status:* 6b (Threatened). Language of recognized nationality: Han. *Class:* Unclassified. *Dialects:* None known. Classified as Han nationality. It differs greatly from both Southwestern Mandarin (Xinan Guanhua) [cmn] and Xiang Chinese (Hunanese) [hsn], but is relatively uniform within itself. Neighboring Han Chinese, Miao, and Tujia people do not understand it. Some view it as a special variety of Chinese, others as a minority language, perhaps related to Miao. *Map:* 346:33.

Wutunhua [wuh] (Wutong, Wutun). 2,000 (1995). East Qinghai Province, Huangnan Tibetan autonomous prefecture, Tongren county, Longwu township, Upper and Lower Wutun and Jiangchama villages. *Status:* 7 (Shifting). Language of recognized nationality: Tu. *Class:* Mixed language, Chinese-Tibetan-Bonan Mongour. *Type:* SOV; adjectives follow nouns; adverbials precede predicate; case and number marked on nouns; prenasalized consonants; 11 different syllable-final consonants; tone and stress have low functional load; most words polysyllabic; 60% Chinese, 20% Tibetan vocabulary with the rest having mixed Chinese and Tibetan elements. *Other:* A variety of Chinese heavily influenced by Tibetan or perhaps a Tibetan language undergoing relexification with Chinese forms. Also described as Chinese which converged to an agglutinative language, Tibetan or Mongolian, using only Chinese material. Neighboring Tibetans refer to the Wutun people use ethnonym: Sanggaixiong, center of the lion. Known for their paintings of Buddha. Buddhist (Lamaist). *Map:* 344.

Xibe [sjo] (Sibe, Sibin, Sibo, Xibo). 30,000 (2000 A. Jun). Few monolinguals. Ethnic population: 189,000 (2000 census). L2 users: Chinese, Uyghur, or Kazakh speakers in the area can also speak Xibe. Xinjiang Uyghur Autonomous Region, Qapqal, Huocheng, Gongliu, Xinyuan, Nilka, Tekes, and Zhaosu counties; Ili prefecture, Yining city; Tacheng prefecture, Tacheng county; Bortala prefecture, Bole county, Ürümqi city. *Status:* 6b (Threatened). Statutory language of provincial identity in Xinjiang Uyghur Autonomous Region (1984, Ethnic Regional Autonomy Act, Articles 10 and 21). Language of recognized nationality: Xibe. *Class:* Altaic, Tungusic, Southern, Southwest. *Dialects:* None known. Inherently intelligible of Manchu [mnc]. *Type:* SOV; genitives, articles, adjectives, numerals precede noun heads; question word initial; complex vowel harmony. *Lg Use:* Vigorous. All domains. All ages in rural areas. Positive attitudes. Also use English [eng], Kazakh [kaz], Mandarin Chinese [cmn], Russian [rus], Uyghur [uig]. *Lg Dev:* Literacy rate in L1: 50%. Literacy rate in L2: 52%. Taught in primary schools. Newspapers. Radio programs. Dictionary. Grammar. *Writing:* Cyrillic script, 1957–1958, experimental, limited use in education. Latin script, used in 1939–1941 and since internet became popular, mainly used on internet and text messaging, favoured by younger people. Mongolian script, Sibe style, used in 1947–1966 and from 1974, official, primary usage, all domains, favoured by older generations. Mongolian script, Manchu style, used from Qing dynasty to 1947. *Other:* Descendants of an 18th century Qing dynasty military garrison. Loans from Uyghur, Kazakh, and Chinese. Traditional religion. *Map:* 344.

Yerong [yrn] (Ban Yao, Da Ia, Daban Yao, Eastern Buyang, Guangxi Buyang, Ia Hrong, Iron Yao, Khyung Buyang, Liu Yao, Napo Buyang, Six Yao, Tie Yao, Tu Yao Indigenous Yao, Yalang, Yang Khyung, Yerong Buyang). 380 (2000). West Guangxi Zhuang Autonomous Region, Baise prefecture, Napo county, on the Yunnan Province and Viet Nam border; Longhe district, Rongtun and Gonghe villages; Pohe district, Shanhe, Yong'an and Guoba. *Status:* 6b (Threatened). Language of recognized nationality: Yao. *Class:* Tai-Kadai, Kra, Eastern Kra. *Dialects:* None known. Not mutually intelligible of the 3 Buyang languages. May be most similar to En [enc] of Northern Viet Nam. Lexical similarity: 67% with Langnian Buyang [yln], 63% with E'ma Buyang [yzg], and 46% with Baha Buyang [yha]. *Lg Use:* Vigorous. Home. All ages. Most men also use local southwest Mandarin Chinese [cmn] (Li Jinfang 2006). Also use Guibian Zhuang [zgn], Yang Zhuang [zyg]. Children still learn Yerong first, but begin learning Zhuang at a young age, and are fluent by adulthood. (Li Jinfang 2006). *Other:* Traditional religion. *Map:* 345.

Yi, Wuding-Luquan [ywq] (Black Yi, Dian Dongbei Yi, Hei Yi, Nasu, Wu-Lu Yi). 250,000 (2007). Yunnan Province, Luquan, Wuding, Yongren, Lufeng, Yuanmou, Qujing, Xundian, and Huize counties; south Sichuan Province, Huili county. *Status:* 5 (Developing). Language of recognized nationality: Yi. *Class:* Sino-Tibetan, Tibeto-Burman, Ngwi-Burmese, Ngwi, Northern. *Dialects:* Luquan Naso, Wuding Naisu. The Naisu dialect is also called Hong Yi (Red Yi). Degrees of similarity between dialects, and also with Naluo [ylo], needs further investigation. *Lg Use:* All ages. *Lg Dev:* NT: 1948. *Writing:* Miao (Pollard) script, used at least since 1923, primary usage among Christians. Yi script, traditional, dating from Han dynasty, limited usage. *Other:* Hei Yi means Black Yi. Christian, traditional religion. *Map:* 345.

Yugur, East [yuy] (Eastern Yogor, Enge'er, Enger, Shera Yogur, Shira Yugur, Yogor, Yögur, Yugar, Yugu). 4,000 (Bradley 2007). Ethnic population: 6,000 (2000 D. Bradley). Northwest Gansu Province, east Sunan Yugur autonomous county, Kangle, Mati, and Dahe districts; some in Qinghai Province. *Status:* 8a (Moribund). Language of recognized nationality: Yugur. *Class:* Altaic, Mongolic, Eastern, Mongour. *Lg Use:* Also use Mandarin Chinese [cmn]. *Lg Dev:* Literacy rate in L2: 85% (2000 census, Yugur nationality). Written Chinese is in use. Dictionary. Grammar. *Other:* Traditional religion, Buddhist (Lamaist). *Map:* 344.

Yugur, West [ybe] (Sari Yogur, Sarig, Sarygh Uygur, Sary-Uighur, Ya Lu, Yellow Uighur, Yugu, Yuku). 4,600 (Bradley 2007). Ethnic population: 7,000 (Bradley 2007). Northwest Gansu Province, Sunan Yugur autonomous county near Zhangye (Kanchow). *Status:* 8a (Moribund). Language of recognized nationality: Yugur. *Class:* Altaic, Turkic, Eastern. *Type:* SOV. *Lg Use:* Decreasing use. Religion, some commerce, oral literature. Positive attitudes. Also use Mandarin Chinese [cmn]. *Lg Dev:* Literacy rate in L2: 85% (2000 census, Yugur nationality). Written Chinese is in use. *Other:* Buddhist (Lamaist), traditional religion. *Map:* 344.

Zaiwa [atb] (Aci, Aji, Atshi, Atsi, Atsi-Maru, Atzi, Azi, Szi, Tsaiwa, Xiaoshanhua). 80,000 in China (1999 X. Xijian). Population total all countries: 110,000. 20,000 monolinguals. Yunnan Province, Dehong Dai-Jingpo autonomous prefecture, Luxi, Ruili, Longchuan, Yingjiang, and Bangwa counties. Also in Myanmar. *Status:* 5 (Developing). Language of recognized nationality: Jingpo. *Class:* Sino-Tibetan, Tibeto-Burman, Ngwi-Burmese, Burmish, Northern. *Dialects:* Bengwa, Longzhun, Tingzhu. Some consider Pela [bxd] (Bola, Polo, Pala), Lashi [lsi] (Leqi), and Maru [mhx] (Langsu, Langwa) to be dialects of Zaiwa. Dialects have only minor phonological differences. *Type:* SOV; 3 tone categories in unchecked syllables and 2 in checked; tense-lax vowel contrast. *Lg Use:* Vigorous. Speakers of other languages in the area also speak Zaiwa. All domains. All ages. Used less by young people and children. Positive attitudes. Intellectuals are concerned about preservation of Zaiwa. Also use Central Bai [bca], Jingpho [kac], Lachi [lbt], Lhao Vo [mhx], Lisu [lis], Mandarin Chinese [cmn]. Used as L2 by Jingpho [kac], Lhaovo [mhx]. *Lg Dev:* Literacy rate in L1: 50,000 can read and write. Taught in primary schools. Newspapers. Radio programs. TV. Dictionary. NT: 2009. *Writing:* Latin script, developed in 1957, modified in 1997. Lisu (Fraser) script, no longer in use. *Other:* Traditional religion, Christian, Daoist. *Map:* 345.

Zakhring [zkr] (Zaiwa, Zha). 600 in China (Bradley 2007). Population total all countries: 900. Southeast Xizang Tibet Autonomous Region, Zayul county, Lower Zayul township, 3 villages: Songgu, Lading, and Tama. Also in India. *Status:* 7 (Shifting). *Class:* Sino-Tibetan, Tibeto-Burman, Central Tibeto-Burman, Keman. *Dialects:* None known. Similar to Tibetan [bod] (Singh 1994), Miju-Mishmi [mxj] (Bradley 2007). Not related to Zaiwa [atb] in Yunnan. *Lg Use:* All are multilingual (Bradley 2007).

Zauzou [zal] (Jaojo, Raorou, Rourou). 2,100 (Bradley 2007). 210 monolinguals. Mainly older adults. Ethnic population: 2,500 (1999 Sun Hong Kai). Northwest Yunnan Province, Nujiang Lisu autonomous prefecture, Lanping county, Tu'e, Biji, Wupijiang, Guoli, Xiaocun, and Jiangmo districts; Lushui county, Luzhang, Shuilizhai and Liukuzhen districts and townships. *Status:* 6b (Threatened). Language of recognized nationality: Nu. *Class:* Sino-Tibetan, Tibeto-Burman, Ngwi-Burmese, Ngwi, Central. *Dialects:* Bijilan, Wupijiang. *Type:* SOV; no consonant clusters; no checked syllables; tense-lax and nasalized-unnasalized vowel distinctions; tonal, 6 tones. *Lg Use:* Vigorous. All domains. All ages. Used less by young people and children. Positive attitudes. 40% also use Lisu [lis]. Also use Central Bai [bca], Mandarin Chinese [cmn]. *Lg Dev:* Literacy rate in L2: 68% in any language (2000 census, Nu nationality). Grammar. *Other:* Also Nusu [nuf], and 5,500 ethnic Nung who speak Drung [duu]. Traditional religion, Daoist. *Map:* 345.

Zhaba [zhb] (Bazi, Bozi, Draba, nDrapa, Zaba, Zha). 7,800 (Genxia Wengmu and Hu Shujin 2008), decreasing. Many young monolingual speakers in Zhaba and Zhamai districts. Ethnic population: 9,000 (Gong 2007). Sichuan Province, Ganzi (Garzê) Tibetan autonomous prefecture, Yajiang (Nyagquka) county, Zhamai district; Daofu (Dawu) county, Zhaba district. *Status:* 6b (Threatened). Language of recognized nationality: Tibetan. *Class:* Sino-Tibetan, Tibeto-Burman, Northeastern Tibeto-Burman, Qiangic. *Dialects:* Drame (Southern nDrapa, Zhami), Drate (Northern nDrapa). Reportedly similar to Stau (Horpa [ero]) and Queyu [qvy], but no mutual intelligibility. Many loanwords from Tibetan and Chinese varieties. *Type:* Verb-final; agglutinating; suffixes and prefixes, case-marking employs postpositions, case system nominative-accusative; tonal. *Lg Use:* Most use Chinese or Tibetan varieties even when they speak with other Zhaba people. Personal communication among themselves. All ages. Negative attitudes. Regarded as useless. Users strongly desire to learn/improve Chinese varieties. *Lg Dev:* Literacy rate in L2: Low. Many in elder generation illiterate. No written tradition. Poetry. Dictionary. *Other:* Different from Queyu [qvy]. Buddhist (Lamaist). *Map:* 344.

Zhuang [zha]. A macrolanguage (see page 9). *Lg Use:* Used as L2 by Chadong [cdy]. *Other:* Includes: Central Hongshuihe Zhuang [zch], Dai Zhuang [zhd], Eastern Hongshuihe Zhuang [zeh], Guibei Zhuang [zgb], Guibian Zhuang [zgn], Lianshan Zhuang [zln], Liujiang Zhuang [zlj], Liuqian Zhuang [zlq], Minz Zhuang [zgm], Nong Zhuang [zhn], Qiubei Zhuang [zqe], Yang Zhuang [zyg], Yongbei Zhuang [zyb], Yongnan Zhuang [zyn], Youjiang Zhuang [zyj], Zuojiang Zhuang [zzj].

Zhuang, Central Hongshuihe [zch]. 1,080,000 (2007). Guangxi Zhuang Autonomous Region, either side of central stretch of Hongshuihe river, including Du'an, Dahua, Mashan, north Shanglin and possibly other border areas such as east Pingguo. *Status:* 6a (Vigorous). Language of recognized nationality: Zhuang. *Class:* Tai-Kadai, Kam-Tai, Tai, Northern. A member of macrolanguage Zhuang [zha]. *Lg Use:* All domains. All ages. Positive attitudes. *Writing:* Han (Hanzi, Kanji,

Hanja) script, dating from Han dynasty, mainly used in non-official domains, gaining popularity. *Map:* 346:48.

Zhuang, Dai [zhd] (Bu Dai, Kau Ndae, Khaau Daai, Thu Lao, Tu, Tuliao, Tuzu, Wen-Ma Southern Zhuang, Zhuangyu Nanbu fangyan Dejing tuyu, Zhuangyu Nanbu Fangyan Wen-Ma Tuyu). 100,000 in China (Wang Mingfu and Johnson 2008). Population total all countries: 100,200. Very few monolinguals, though it is L1 learned by children in most Dai Zhuang villages. Ethnic population: 120,000. Southeast Yunnan Province, Wenshan Zhuang and Miao autonomous prefectures, Wenshan county, Matang, Dehou, Laohuilong, Panzhihua, and Kaihua townships; Yanshan county, Pingyuan township; Guangnan county, Zhulin township; Maguan and Malipo (western edge) counties. Also in Viet Nam. *Status:* 6b (Threatened). Language of recognized nationality: Zhuang. *Class:* Tai-Kadai, Kam-Tai, Tai, Central. A member of macrolanguage Zhuang [zha]. *Dialects:* Central Wenshan (Ping Tou Tu), Guangnan (Pian Tou Tu), Maguan-Malipo (Jian Tou Tu), Western Yanshan-Northern Wenshan (Da Tou Tu). Most similar language is Nong Zhuang [zhn], but not mutually intelligible of Nong Zhuang, Min Zhuang [zgm] or Yang Zhuang [zyg] (2010 E. Johnson). Lexical similarity: 63%–70% among Nong, Yang [zhn], Yongnan [zyn], Zuojiang [zzj], and Dai [zhd]; 54% with Yongbei Zhuang [zyb] (2011 E. Johnson). *Type:* SVO; voiced oral stop onsets, all final oral stops have been lost except for glottal stops in some locations; 5–6 tones, depending on dialect. *Lg Use:* Vigorous in most areas except Wenshan Municipality. Home, village, religious and traditional ceremonies. All ages in rural areas where L1 is dominant, but only the elders in other areas. Positive attitudes. Preserving traditional artforms through video, books, etc.. Almost all bilingual in local southwestern Mandarin [cmn]. Also use Nong Zhuang [zhn]. *Lg Dev:* No orthography for L1 by government. Speakers use like-sounding Chinese characters to record folk songs, linguists use International Phonetic Alphabet to record pronunciation, so literacy is not possible at present. Poetry. Videos. *Writing:* Han (Hanzi, Kanji, Hanja) script, dating from Han dynasty, mainly used in non-official domains (e.g., speakers use like-sounding Chinese characters to record folk-songs). Latin script, used between 1984 and 1990s, experimental use in education in Wenshan, Yunnan, China. *Other:* Buddhist, Daoist. *Map:* 345.

Zhuang, Eastern Hongshuihe [zeh]. 1,200,000 (2007). Guangxi Zhuang Autonomous Region, south of eastern Hongshuihe river and south of Qianjiang river, includes south Shanglin, south Xincheng, south Xingbin, north Guigang, west Guiping, and south Wuxuan; some in Guangdong Province. *Status:* 6a (Vigorous). Language of recognized nationality: Zhuang. *Class:* Tai-Kadai, Kam-Tai, Tai, Northern. A member of macrolanguage Zhuang [zha]. *Lg Use:* All domains. All ages. Positive attitudes. *Writing:* Han (Hanzi, Kanji, Hanja) script, dating from Han dynasty, mainly used in non-official domains, gaining popularity. *Map:* 346:49.

Zhuang, Guibei [zgb]. 1,500,000 (2007). Guangxi Zhuang Autonomous Region, Longsheng, Sanjiang, Yongfu, Rongan, Rongshui, Luocheng, Huanjiang, Hechi, Nandan, Tian'e, Donglan, and Bama. Also in Hunan and Guizhou provinces. *Status:* 6a (Vigorous). Language of recognized nationality: Zhuang. *Class:* Tai-Kadai, Kam-Tai, Tai, Northern. A member of macrolanguage Zhuang [zha]. *Lg Use:* All domains. Positive attitudes. *Writing:* Han (Hanzi, Kanji, Hanja) script, dating from Han dynasty, mainly used in non-official domains, gaining popularity. *Map:* 346:46.

Zhuang, Guibian [zgn] (Buyei, Buyoi, Kang Yei, Northern Zhuang). 1,000,000 (2007). 420,000 monolinguals. Guangxi Zhuang Autonomous Region, Fengshan, Tianlin, Longlin, Xilin, Lingyun, Leyun; Yunnan, Funing, and north Guangnan. *Status:* 3 (Wider communication). Language of recognized nationality: Zhuang. In concentrated Guibian areas, the main trade language on market days. *Class:* Tai-Kadai, Kam-Tai, Tai, Northern. A member of macrolanguage Zhuang [zha]. *Dialects:* None known. Some intelligibility of standard Bouyei [pcc]; none of Qiubei Zhuang [zqe], Yongbei Zhuang [zyb], or Nong Zhuang [zhn] (2011 E. Johnson). Lexical similarity: 71% with Yongbei Zhuang [zyb], 83% with Qiubei Zhuang [zqe] (northern Taic), 64%–66% with Nong Zhuang [zhn] (central Taic). *Type:* SVO. *Lg Use:* All domains. All ages. Positive attitudes. Some also use Nong Zhuang [zhn] in northern Guangnan County (Yunnan) due to intensive contact. Used as L2 by Baha Buyang [yha], E'ma Buyang [yzg], Langnian Buyang [yln], Minz Zhuang [zgm], Yerong [yrn]. *Lg Dev:* Poetry. TV. Videos. *Writing:* Han (Hanzi, Kanji, Hanja) script, dating from Han dynasty, mainly used in non-official domains, gaining popularity. *Other:* Traditional religion. *Map:* 345.

Zhuang, Lianshan [zln]. 48,000 (2007 census). West Guangdong Province, Lianshan Zhuang Yao autonomous county, Huaji county, Xiashuai and Zhongzhou districts; some in Guangxi Zhuang Autonomous Region. *Status:* 8a (Moribund). Language of recognized nationality: Zhuang. *Class:* Tai-Kadai, Kam-Tai, Tai, Northern. A member of macrolanguage Zhuang [zha]. *Lg Use:* Older adults and elderly. Positive attitudes. *Writing:* Han (Hanzi, Kanji, Hanja) script, dating from Han dynasty, mainly used in non-official domains, gaining popularity. *Map:* 346.

Zhuang, Liujiang [zlj]. 1,560,000 (2007). Guangxi Zhuang Autonomous Region, Liujiang, North Laibin, Yishan, Liucheng, and north Xincheng. *Status:* 6a (Vigorous). Language of recognized nationality: Zhuang. *Class:* Tai-Kadai, Kam-Tai, Tai, Northern. A member of macrolanguage Zhuang [zha]. *Lg Use:* All domains. Positive attitudes. *Writing:* Han (Hanzi, Kanji, Hanja) script, dating from Han dynasty, mainly used in non-official domains, gaining popularity. Latin script, 1952–1955, experimental use in education. *Map:* 346:44.

Zhuang, Liuqian [zlq]. 370,000 (2007). Guangxi Zhuang Autonomous Region, east of Liujiang and north of Qianjiang rivers; includes north Wuxuan, Xiangzhou, and Luzhai; possibly Pingle, Yangshuo, and Hezhou. *Status:* 6b (Threatened). Language of recognized nationality: Zhuang. *Class:* Tai-Kadai, Kam-Tai, Tai, Northern. A member of macrolanguage Zhuang [zha]. *Lg Use:* All domains. Some young people, all adults. Positive attitudes. Used as L2 by Lakkia [lbc]. *Writing:* Han (Hanzi, Kanji, Hanja) script, dating from Han dynasty, mainly used in non-official domains, gaining popularity. *Map:* 346:43.

Zhuang, Minz [zgm] (Black Zhuang, Bu Xiong, Heiyi Zhuang, Kon Min, Sung, Zong Zhuang). 173,000 (2004). Southwest Guangxi Zhuang Autonomous Region, Dejing area, Napo, Jingxi, and Debao counties; southeast Yunnan Province, Wenshan Zhuang and Miao autonomous prefectures, Funing county, Langheng district (now in Tianbeng township), Sankeshu, Xionggu, Shangmabu, Tianfang, Getao, Gezao, Gecai, Bagan, Na'en, Longnong, and Anha villages. *Status:* 6a (Vigorous). Language of recognized nationality: Zhuang. *Class:* Tai-Kadai, Kam-Tai, Tai, Central. A member of macrolanguage Zhuang [zha]. *Dialects:* Cuengh (Zong), Minz (Min). Nong Zhuang [zhn] is reportedly most similar. *Type:* SVO; phonemic distinction between aspirated, unaspirated voiceless, and preglottalized voiced plosives; 6 tones on unchecked, 3–4 on checked syllables, depending on dialect. *Lg Use:* Home, village, traditional ceremonies. All ages. Also use Guibian Zhuang [zgn], Mandarin Chinese [cmn], Yang Zhuang [zyg]. *Writing:* Han (Hanzi, Kanji, Hanja) script, dating from Han dynasty, mainly used in non-official domains, gaining popularity. *Other:* Traditional religion. *Map:* 345:23.

Zhuang, Nong [zhn] (Daez, Kau Nong, Khaau Nong, Noangx, Nong hua, Phu Nong, Phu Tei, Yan-Guang Southern Zhuang, Zhuangyu Nanbu fanyan Yan-Guang tuyu). 500,000 (Wang Mingfu and Johnson 2008). 125,000 monolinguals. Ethnic population: 600,000 (2007). Southeast Yunnan Province, Wenshan Zhuang and Miao autonomous prefectures, central and west Guangnan, east Yanshan, north Wenshan, Maguan, Xichou, and Malipo counties. A few in Funing and Qiubei counties. *Status:* 3 (Wider communication). Language of recognized nationality: Zhuang. *Class:* Tai-Kadai, Kam-Tai, Tai, Central. A member of macrolanguage Zhuang [zha]. *Dialects:* Central Zhuang, Liancheng, Southern Zhuang, Western Guangnan. Reportedly most similar Tày [tyz], and Min Zhuang [zgm]. Some Tày dialects near Viet Nam-Yunnan border reportedly mutually intelligible. Nong Dialects mutually intelligible for simple topics. Not intelligible of Dai Zhuang [zhd], Min Zhuang [zgm], Yang Zhuang [zyg], Guibian Zhuang [zgn], or Qiubei Zhuang [zqe]. Lexical similarity: over 70% with Nong, Yang [zyg], Yongnan [zyn], and Zuojiang [zzj]; about 67% with Dai [zhd]; 54% with Yongbei Zhuang [zyb]. *Type:* SVO; modifiers follow nouns, directional verbs precede objects; phonemic distinction between aspirated, unaspirated voiceless, and preglottalized voiced plosives; 6 tones on unchecked, 3–4 on checked syllables. *Lg Use:* Vigorous. All domains. All ages. Positive attitudes. 75% also use Mandarin Chinese [cmn]. Used as L2 by Bugan [bbh], Dai Zhuang [zhd], Guibian Zhuang [zgn], Qabiao [laq], Thopho [ytp], Zokhuo [yzk]. *Lg Dev:* Literacy rate in L1: A few teachers and linguists can read the recent Yunnan government approved experimental orthography. Literacy rate in L2: Rapidly increasing due to free education begun in 2008, including women and girls. In 2011, 300 Nong 7th graders received a few hours of Nong instruction. Taught in primary schools, pilot projects. Poetry. Magazines. Radio programs. Films. Dictionary. *Writing:* Han (Hanzi, Kanji, Hanja) script, dating from Han dynasty, mainly used in non-official domains, gaining popularity. Latin script, used in 1984–1990s and from 2006, experimental use in education and official publications. *Other:* 'Phu Nong', Nong People; 'Khau Nong', Nong Language. Over half the Nong live in Guangnan and Yanshan counties. Nong represent a majority of Zhuang in all their counties except for Funing and Qiubei, where mostly northern Taic Zhuang languages are spoken. Traditional religion. *Map:* 345.

Zhuang, Qiubei [zqe] (Bau i, Bui, Buyi, Northern Zhuang, Qiubei Sha). 140,000 (2007 census). 28,000 monolinguals. Ethnic population: 150,000. Southeast Yunnan Province, Qiubei county (and west edge Guangnan county), Wenshan Zhuang Miao autonomous prefecture; Qujing municipal prefecture, Shizong county, Longqing Yi-Zhuang and Wulong Zhuang autonomous districts. *Status:* 6a (Vigorous). Language of recognized nationality: Zhuang. *Class:* Tai-Kadai, Kam-Tai, Tai, Northern. A member of macrolanguage Zhuang [zha]. *Dialects:* None known. Not mutually intelligible with Guibian Zhuang [zgn], Nong Zhuang [zhn], or Dai Zhuang [zhd]. Lexical similarity: 83% with Guibian Zhuang [zgn], 69% with Yongbei (standard) Zhuang [zyb], 64%–66% with Nong Zhuang [zhn] and Yang Zhuang [zyg], 55% with Dai Zhuang [zhd]. (2011 E. Johnson). *Type:* SVO. *Lg Use:* All village domains. All ages. Positive attitudes. *Writing:* Han (Hanzi, Kanji, Hanja) script, dating from Han dynasty, mainly used in non-official domains, gaining popularity. Latin script, 1985–early 1990s, experimental use in education. *Other:* Traditional religion. *Map:* 345.

Zhuang, Yang [zyg] (Dejing Zhuang, Gen Yang, Jingxi Zhuang, Lang, Nong, Nung Giang, Tianbao, Tuhua, Yangyu, Yangzhou, Zhuangyu Nanbu fangyan Dejing tuyu). 765,000 in China (2004). 745,000 in the Dejing area (Jingxi, Napo, and Debao Counties, Guangxi). Guangxi Zhuang Autonomous Region, most Zhuang populations of Jingxi, Debao, and Napo counties; Yunnan Province, Funing county, scattered in Bo'ai, Xinhua, Zhesang, Dongbo, Guichao, and Banlun townships and districts. Also in Viet Nam. *Status:* 6a (Vigorous). Language of recognized nationality: Zhuang. *Class:* Tai-Kadai, Kam-Tai, Tai, Central. A member of macrolanguage Zhuang [zha]. *Dialects:* Caj coux (Jiazhou, Zouzhou), Fouh (Fu), Sengh (Sheng), Tianbao (Dianbao, Tianpao), Yang (Tuhua, Yangyu). Most similar languages are Zuojiang Zhuang [zzj] and other Nung languages of Viet Nam. Lexical similarity: 70% with Nong Zhuang [zhn], Yang [zyg], Yongnan [zyn], Zuojiang, and Dai [zhd], 65% with Yongbei Zhuang [zyb]. *Lg Use:* Vigorous. All domains. All ages. Also use southwestern dialect of Mandarin [cmn]. Also use Ping dialect of Yue Chinese (Cantonese) [yue]. Used as L2 by Minz Zhuang [zgm], Yerong [yrn]. *Writing:* Han (Hanzi, Kanji, Hanja) script, dating from Han dynasty, mainly used in non-official domains, gaining popularity. Nüshu script, used by women only. *Other:* Traditional religion, Buddhist (Mahayana), Daoist. *Map:* 345:21.

Zhuang, Yongbei [zyb]. 1,980,000 (2007). Guangxi Zhuang Autonomous Region, north Yongning, Hengxian, Bingyang, Wuming, and Pingguo. *Status:* 6a (Vigorous). Language of recognized nationality: Zhuang. *Class:* Tai-Kadai, Kam-Tai, Tai, Northern. A member of macrolanguage Zhuang [zha]. *Lg Use:* All domains. All ages. Positive attitudes. *Lg Dev:* Newspapers. Radio programs. Dictionary. Grammar. Bible portions: 1904. *Writing:* Han (Hanzi, Kanji, Hanja) script, dating from Han dynasty, mainly used in non-official domains, gaining popularity. Latin script, pinyin-based, used since 1982, official, mainly used in official domains. *Map:* 346:50.

Zhuang, Yongnan [zyn] (Bou Rau, Long An, Long'an, Nung An, Southern Zhuang, Yongnan Vernacular of the Southern Dialect of the Zhuang Language, Zhuangyu nanbu fangyan Yongnan tuyu). 1,800,000 in China (2000 J. Edmondson). Population total all countries: 1,810,000. South Guangxi Zhuang Autonomous Region, south Yongning, Longan, Fusui, Shangsi, Qinzhou, and Fangcheng counties; some in Jingxi county; Yunnan Province, Funing county. Also in Viet Nam. *Status:* 6a (Vigorous). Language of recognized nationality: Zhuang. *Class:* Tai-Kadai, Kam-Tai, Tai, Central. A member of macrolanguage Zhuang [zha]. *Dialects:* None known. Most similar languages are Zuojiang Zhuang [zzj] (Nung Chao), Yongbei Zhuang [zyb], Yang Zhuang [zyg] (Nung Giang), and other Nung languages of Viet Nam. Lexical similarity: 70% with Nong [zhn], Yang [zyg], Yongnan [zyn], Zuojiang [zzj], and Dai [zhd], 65% with Yongbei Zhuang [zyb]. *Type:* Voiced oral onsets have merged into nasal onsets. *Lg Use:* Vigorous. All domains, especially in rural homes when no outsiders are present. All ages. Also use southwestern dialect of Mandarin [cmn]. Also use Yue Chinese dialects [yue]. Many are partially or fully bilingual in one or more dialects and often use them in business, education, government, market and other domains. *Writing:* Han (Hanzi, Kanji, Hanja) script, dating from Han dynasty, mainly used in non-official domains, gaining popularity. *Other:* Traditional religion, Buddhist (Mahayana), Daoist. *Maps:* 345, 346:51.

Zhuang, Youjiang [zyj]. 870,000 (2007). Guangxi Zhuang Autonomous Region, Tiandong, Tianyang, and Baise; some in Yunnan Province. *Status:* 6a (Vigorous). Language of recognized nationality: Zhuang. *Class:* Tai-Kadai, Kam-Tai, Tai, Northern. A member of macrolanguage Zhuang [zha]. *Lg Use:* All domains. Positive attitudes. *Writing:* Han (Hanzi, Kanji, Hanja) script, dating from Han dynasty, mainly used in non-official domains, gaining popularity. Latin script, pinyin-based, used since 1982, official, mainly used in official domains. *Map:* 345:20.

Zhuang, Zuojiang [zzj] (Ken Tho, Longyin, Longzhou, Pho Thai, Pu Tho, Southern Zhuang, Zhuangyu nanbu fangyan Zuojiang tuyu). 1,500,000 in China (2000 census). 35,000 in Jingxi and Napo counties. Population total all countries: 1,840,000. Southwest Guangxi Zhuang Autonomous Region, Tiandeng, Daxin, Chongzuo, Ningming, Longzhou, Pingxiang, and Jingxi counties; Yunnan Province, Funing county, a few villages. Also in Viet Nam. *Status:* 6a (Vigorous). Language of recognized nationality: Zhuang. *Class:* Tai-Kadai, Kam-Tai, Tai, Central. A member of macrolanguage Zhuang [zha]. *Dialects:* None known. Most similar languages are Yang Zhuang [zyg], Yongnan Zhuang [zyn], Nong Zhuang [zhn], and other Nung languages of Viet Nam. Lexical similarity: 70% between Nong [zhn], Yang [zyg], Yongnan, and Dai [zhd], 65% with Yongbei Zhuang [zyb]. *Lg Use:* Vigorous. All domains. All ages. Also use southwestern dialect of Mandarin [cmn]. Also use Yue Chinese [yue]. *Writing:* Han (Hanzi, Kanji, Hanja) script, dating from Han dynasty, mainly used in non-official domains, gaining popularity. *Other:* The language is named for Zuojiang river that runs through this area, from northern Viet Nam into Longzhou, Chongzuo, and Fusui counties. Traditional religion, Buddhist (Mahayana), Daoist. *Map:* 345.

Zokhuo [yzk] (Cowtail Phula, Nimitso, Niuweiba Phula, Phula, Ruoke, Tshokha, Zekhe, Zuoke). 13,000 (Pelkey 2011), decreasing. Ethnic population: 17,000. Yunnan Province, southeast Wenshan county, north Zhuiligai and south Dongshan townships; south Yanshan county. *Status:* 6b (Threatened). Language of recognized nationality: Yi. *Class:* Sino-Tibetan, Tibeto-Burman, Ngwi-Burmese, Ngwi, Southeastern. *Dialects:* Daxingzhai, Longle. Most closely related to, but not mutually intelligible with, Khlula [ykl]. *Lg Use:* Also use Mandarin Chinese [cmn], Nong Zhuang [zhn]. *Map:* 345.

Cyprus

Republic of Cyprus. 1,143,000 (2011 census). Principal language: Greek. Literacy rate: 97% (2010 UNESCO). General references: Borg 1985. Deaf population: 49,300. Deaf institutions: 2.

The number of individual languages listed for Cyprus is 4. All are living languages. Of these, 2 are institutional, 1 is in trouble, and 1 is dying. See map on page 348.

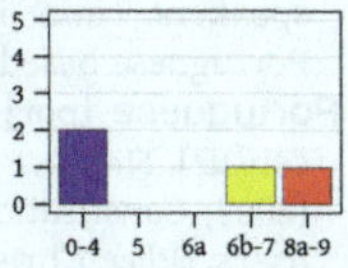

Arabic, Cypriot Spoken [acy] (Cypriot Maronite Arabic, Maronite, Sanna). 1,300 (1995). Ethnic population: 6,000. 140 Maronites in Kormatiki, 80 to 100 in Limassol, the rest in the Maronite community in Nicosia. Northern Cyprus, Kormakiti, one of 4 Maronite villages in the mountains. *Status:* 8a (Moribund). *Class:* Afro-Asiatic, Semitic, Central, South, Arabic. A member of macrolanguage Arabic [ara] (Saudi Arabia). *Lg Use:* Revitalization effort producing written materials. All older than 30 years. 140 mainly older adults in Kormatiki. No diglossia with Standard Arabic [arb]. Also use Greek [ell], Turkish [tur]. *Writing:* Arabic script, no longer in use. Greek script, no longer in use. Latin script, revitalization efforts in one town. *Other:* A hybrid language with roots in the Arabic of both Anatolia and Levant. Many borrowings from Syriac [syc] and Greek [ell]. Ethnonym: Maronites. Christian (Maronite). *Map:* 348.

Armenian [hye] (Armjanski, Ermenice, Haieren, Somkhuri). 2,740 in Cyprus (1987). *Status:* 7 (Shifting). *Dialect:* Western Armenian. *Lg Use:* Elderly also use Turkish [tur]. Also use Greek [ell]. *Other:* Urban population. Christian. See main entry on page 51.

Greek [ell]. 1,100,000 in Cyprus (ELDIA 2012). L2 users: 57,000 in Cyprus (ELDIA 2012). Nearly all in south Cyprus. *Status:* 1 (National). Statutory national language (1960, Constitution, Article 3(1)). *Dialect:* Cypriot Greek. *Lg Use:* 514,000 also use English [eng]. 81,000 also use French [fra]. 33,800 also use Standard German [deu]. *Other:* Christian. See main entry on page 320. *Map:* 348.

Turkish [tur] (Osmanli). 177,000 in Cyprus (1995). Nearly all in north Cyprus. *Status:* 2 (Provincial). De facto provincial language in north Cyprus. *Lg Use:* Used as L2 by Armenian [hye], Cypriot Spoken Arabic [acy]. *Other:* Muslim. See main entry on page 306. *Map:* 348.

East Timor

Democratic Republic of East Timor, República Democrática de Timor-Leste, Repúblika Demokrátika Timor Lorosa'e. 1,067,000 (2010 census). Principal languages: Portuguese, Tetun, Tetun Dili. Literacy rate: 53% (2010 UNESCO). General references: Fox 1991; Gray, Drummond, and Greenhill 2009; Grimes et al. 1997; Ross 2005; Wurm 2007; Wurm and Hattori 1981.

The number of individual languages listed for East Timor is 20. Of these, 19 are living and 1 is extinct. Of the living languages, 2 are institutional, 1 is developing, 10 are vigorous, 5 are in trouble, and 1 is dying. See map on page 349.

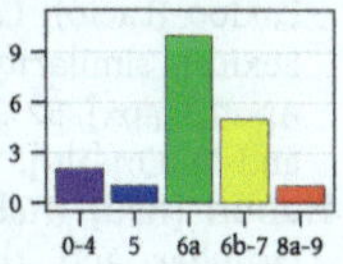

Adabe [adb] (Ataura, Atauran, Atauro, Atauru, Raklu Un, Raklu-Un). 5,000 (2010 census). Atauro island, Timor island north of Dili. *Status:* 6a (Vigorous). *Class:* Trans-New Guinea, West, Timor-Alor-Pantar, Timor. *Dialects:* Munaseli Pandai, Rahesuk, Raklungu, Resuk. Different from Galolen [gal] dialects on Atauro. *Type:* SOV. *Writing:* Latin script. *Map:* 349.

Baikeno [bkx] (Ambeno, Ambenu, Baikenu, Biqueno, "Dawan" *pej.*, Lais Meto, Molok Meto, Oe Cusi, Oecusse, Oecussi, Oekusi, Uab Meto, Uab Pah Meto, Vaikenu, Vaikino). 72,000 (2011 Baikeno Language Council). Several thousand speakers in Dili and Indonesian west Timor. 15 clans of Nu'af (mountains); 3 clans of Amnesat (plains). 15 clans of Nu'af (mountains); 3 clans of Amnesat (plains). Many monolinguals. Oekusi enclave. *Status:* 6a (Vigorous). *Class:* Austronesian, Malayo-Polynesian, Central-Eastern Malayo-Polynesian, Timor-Babar, Nuclear Timor, Uab Meto. *Dialects:* Amnesat, Nu'af. Part of Uab Meto dialect chain, which includes several languages. Partial intelligibility of the Uab Meto of Amfo'an, northern Mollo, and Insana. Significant differences with Amarasi

[aaz] block intelligibility. *Lg Use:* Vigorous. All domains. All ages. Many have difficulty with Indonesian [ind]. Less than 1% can perform job-related functions in Portuguese [por]. Only those who have studied or worked in Dili can function in Tetun Dili [tdt]. *Lg Dev:* Bible portions: 2004. *Writing:* Latin script. *Other:* Speakers see themselves as part of the wider Atoni cultural, linguistic, and historical network, in contrast to Tetun, Helong, or Rote. Ethnic autonym: atoni, person, speaking uab meto, the language of the dry. Uab Meto refers to the language chain of which Baikeno is a part. Ambeno refers to traditional kingship. Oekusi is the main town in Ambeno, but people in other parts of East Timor use it to refer to the whole enclave. Locals object to this usage. Dawan is considered derogatory by many (the language does not have a, d, and dawan is said to mean enemy). Traditional religion, Christian. *Map:* 349.

Bunak [bfn] (Buna, Bunake, Bunaq, Gae', Marae). 55,000 in East Timor (2010 census). Population total all countries: 76,000. Timor island central interior, south coast. Also in Indonesia. *Status:* 6a (Vigorous). *Class:* Trans-New Guinea, West, Timor-Alor-Pantar, Timor. *Dialects:* None known. Not closely related to other languages. *Lg Use:* Also use Tetun [tet]. *Lg Dev:* Grammar. NT. *Writing:* Latin script. *Other:* Small groups scattered among other languages. Traditional religion, Christian. *Map:* 349.

Fataluku [ddg] (Dagada, Dagaga, Dagoda'). 37,000 (2010 census). Timor island east tip, Los Palos area. *Status:* 6a (Vigorous). *Class:* Trans-New Guinea, West, Timor-Alor-Pantar, Timor. *Dialects:* May be related to Oirata [oia] on nearby Kisar Island. Significant dialect variation. May be several languages. *Type:* Verb final. *Lg Dev:* Bible portions. *Writing:* Latin script. *Other:* Christian, traditional religion. *Map:* 349.

Galolen [gal] (Galole, Galolem, Galoli, Galolin). 13,000 in East Timor (2010 census). Population total all countries: 13,680. North coast between Mambae, Makasae, and Lakloo. Also in Indonesia. *Status:* 6a (Vigorous). *Class:* Austronesian, Malayo-Polynesian, Central-Eastern Malayo-Polynesian, Timor-Babar, Nuclear Timor. *Dialects:* Lakloo (Lacló), Laleia, Manatutu (Vila), Wetar (Iliwaki). Lexical similarity: 94%-98% with dialects, 57% with Aputai [apx], 52% with Tugun [tzn], 51% with Perai [wet] and Ili'uun [ilu]. *Writing:* Latin script. *Map:* 349.

Habun [hbu] (Habu). 2,700 (2010 census). Northeast of Laclubar and the Idate [idt] language area. *Status:* 6b (Threatened). *Class:* Austronesian, Malayo-Polynesian, Central-Eastern Malayo-Polynesian, Timor-Babar, Nuclear Timor. *Dialects:* None known. Reportedly many loanwords from Trans-New Guinea languages similar to Makasae [mkz], but with Austronesian structure. Classification needs further investigation. *Lg Use:* Potentially endangered because of size and location. *Writing:* Latin script. *Map:* 349.

Idaté [idt]. 13,500 (2010 census). Central East Timor, Laclubar mountains, surrounded by Mambae [mgm], Galolen [gal], Kairui [krd], and Tetun [tet] language areas. *Status:* 6b (Threatened). *Class:* Austronesian, Malayo-Polynesian, Central-Eastern Malayo-Polynesian, Timor-Babar, Nuclear Timor. *Dialects:* None known. Reportedly most similar to Lakalei [lka] and Galolen [gal]. *Writing:* Latin script. *Map:* 349.

Kairui-Midiki [krd] (Cairui, Midiki). 15,000 (2010 census). Central small mountainous area surrounded by Makasae [mkz], Waima'a [wmh], Tetun [tet], Galolen [gal] language areas. *Status:* 6b (Threatened). *Class:* Austronesian, Malayo-Polynesian, Central-Eastern Malayo-Polynesian, Timor-Babar, Nuclear Timor. *Dialects:* Kairui, Midiki (Midik). Vocabulary predominantly Trans-New Guinea, structure is Austronesian. Classification needs further investigation. May be co-dialect with Waima'a. *Writing:* Latin script. *Map:* 349.

Kemak [kem] (Ema). 62,000 in East Timor (2010 census). Population total all countries: 72,000. North central Timor island border between East Timor and West Timor, mostly east. Also in Indonesia. *Status:* 6a (Vigorous). *Class:* Austronesian, Malayo-Polynesian, Central-Eastern Malayo-Polynesian, Timor-Babar, Nuclear Timor. *Dialects:* Kemak, Nogo (Nogo-Nogo). Most closely related to Mambae [mgm] and Tukudede [tkd]. *Type:* SVO. *Writing:* Latin script. *Other:* Traditional religion, Christian. *Map:* 349.

Lakalei [lka]. 3,250 (2010 census). Central Timor island, north of Same, northeast of Ainaro. *Status:* 6b (Threatened). *Class:* Austronesian, Malayo-Polynesian, Central-Eastern Malayo-Polynesian, Timor-Babar, Nuclear Timor. *Dialects:* None known. Reportedly similar to Idate [idt], Tetun [tet], and Galolen [gal]. *Writing:* Latin script. *Other:* Loanwords from Tetun [tet], Mambae [mgm], and Idate [idt]. *Map:* 349.

Makasae [mkz] (Ma'asae, Macassai, Makasai, Makassai, Maksae). 102,000 (2010 census). Timor island, east Baucau area and inland, west of Fataluku, from north to south coast in a dialect chain. *Status:* 6a (Vigorous). *Class:* Trans-New Guinea, West, Timor-Alor-Pantar, Timor. *Dialects:* Makasae, Maklere. Not closely related to other languages. *Writing:* Latin script. *Other:* Traditional religion, Christian. *Map:* 349.

Makuva [lva] (Lovaea, Lovaia, Lóvaia, Maku'a, Makua, Makuwa). 56 (2010 census). Timor island northeast, Tutuala area. *Status:* 8b (Nearly extinct). *Class:* Austronesian, Malayo-Polynesian, Central-Eastern Malayo-Polynesian, Timor-Babar, Nuclear Timor. *Lg Use:* Almost all shifted to Fataluku [ddg] (Wurm 2007). *Writing:* Latin script. *Map:* 349.

Mambae [mgm] (Mambai, Manbae). 131,000 (2010 census). Central Timor mountains, Ermera, Aileu, and Ainaro areas. *Status:* 6a (Vigorous). *Class:* Austronesian, Malayo-Polynesian, Central-Eastern Malayo-Polynesian, Timor-Babar, Nuclear Timor. *Dialects:* Damata, Lolei, Mambae, Manua. North Mambae and South Mambae show significant differences. *Lg Use:* Second most widely spoken language of East Timor. *Writing:* Latin script. *Other:* Very little productive morphology compared to Tetun [tet], Uab Meto [aoz], or Galolen [gal]. Traditional religion, Christian. *Map:* 349.

Nauete [nxa] (Naóti, Naueti, Nauhete, Nauote, Nauoti). 15,000 (2010 census). South coast, Timor island east tip, west of Tiomar, Uato Lari is main town. *Status:* 6a (Vigorous). *Class:* Austronesian, Malayo-Polynesian, Central-Eastern Malayo-Polynesian, Timor-Babar, Nuclear Timor. *Dialects:* Naumik, Oso Moko. Not closely related to any other language. Loanwords from Trans-New Guinea languages like Makasae [mkz]. *Lg Use:* Vigorous. *Writing:* Latin script. *Map:* 349.

Pidgin, Timor [tvy] (Bidau Creole Portuguese, Português de Bidau, Timor Creole Portuguese). No known L1 speakers. Timor island. *Status:* 10 (Extinct). *Class:* Creole, Portuguese based.

Portuguese [por] (Português). 600 in East Timor (2010 census). *Status:* 1 (National). Statutory national language (2002, Constitution, Article 13). *Lg Use:* Very few fluent users. *Other:* Christian. See main entry on page 321.

Tetun [tet] (Belo, Belu, Fehan, Teto, Tettum, Tetu, Tetum, Tetun Belu, Tetun Loos, Tetun Terik, Tetung). 63,500 in East Timor (2010 census). Western East Timor, south coast from Suai to Soibada and Viqueque, east of Atoni. *Status:* 5 (Developing). De facto language of national identity. *Dialects:* Eastern Tetun (Lakluta, Natarbora, Soibada, Tetun Loos, Tetun Los), Northern Tetun (Belu Utara, Hill Tetun, Lia Foho, North Belu, Tasi Feto, Tetun Terik, Tetun Therik), Southern Tetun (Belu Selatan, Lia Fehan, Plain Tetun, South Belu, South Tetun, Tasi Mane). *Lg Use:* Used as L2 by Bunak [bfn], Tetun Dili [tdt]. *Other:* Christian, traditional religion. See main entry on page 194. *Map:* 349.

Tetun Dili [tdt] (Dili Tetum, Tetum, Tetum Dili, Tetum Praça, Tetum Prasa, Tetun). 385,000 (2009). East Timor north coast, L1 in Dili area; L2 scattered in western part of East Timor. *Status:* 1 (National). Statutory national language (2002, Constitution, Article 13). *Class:* Creole, Tetun based. *Dialects:* None known. Heavy Portuguese [por] and Mambae [mgm] influence; some Indonesian [ind] or Malay influence. *Type:* Compared to Tetun [tet]: many more Portuguese [por] loanwords; does not inflect V-initial verb roots for person or number; uses more periphrastic constructions than morphological constructions (e.g., causatives); differences in possessive constructions and negatives. *Lg Use:* Increasing in use in urban areas. All domains. All ages. North and South Tetun speakers have significant difficulty understanding it in many speech domains, and vice versa. Some L1 speakers of Tetun Dili consider themselves bilingual in Tetun [tet] due to contact, but when pressed, admit there are domains in which communication is completely blocked. *Lg Dev:* Dictionary. Grammar. NT. *Writing:* Latin script. *Other:* Cultural rituals and themes in Tetun [tet] are not as deeply rooted in Tetun Dili. Christian. *Map:* 349.

Tukudede [tkd] (Tocod, Tokodé, Tokodede, Tukude). 39,500 (2010 census). Timor island, north coast, Maubara and Liquisa regions from Lois river banks to Dili. *Status:* 6a (Vigorous). *Class:* Austronesian, Malayo-Polynesian, Central-Eastern Malayo-Polynesian, Timor-Babar, Nuclear Timor. *Dialects:* Keha (Keia), Tukudede. *Writing:* Latin script. *Other:* Christian. *Map:* 349.

Waima'a [wmh] (Uai Ma'a, Uaimo'a, Waimaha, Waimoa). 18,400 (2012 census). Northeast coast Timor island, enclave within Makasae [mkz] language area. *Status:* 6b (Threatened). *Class:* Austronesian, Malayo-Polynesian, Central-Eastern Malayo-Polynesian, Timor-Babar, Nuclear Timor. *Dialects:* Many Trans-New Guinea loanwords reportedly similar to Makasae. Classification needs further investigation. May be a co-dialect with Kairui-Midiki. *Writing:* Latin script. *Map:* 349.

Georgia

Georgia. 4,793,000 (2012 census). Principal languages: Georgian, Russian. Census does not include results from Abkhazia. Literacy rate: 100% (2010 UNESCO). Immigrant languages: Greek (38,000), Lezgi (3,650), Lishán Didán (120), Pontic (120,000), Tatar (3,100), Turkish (3,100), Udi (500), Ukrainian (52,000). General references: Naby 1975; Kibrik 1991; Sebeok 1963.

The number of individual languages listed for Georgia is 19. All are living languages. Of these, 3 are institutional, 5 are developing, 2 are vigorous, and 9 are in trouble.

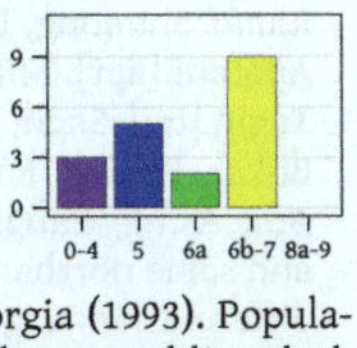

Abkhaz [abk] (Abxazo). 101,000 in Georgia (1993). Population total all countries: 112,740. Abkhaz Republic, Black Sea coast. Also in Russian Federation, Turkey, Ukraine. *Status:* 2 (Provincial). Statutory provincial language in Abkhazia, co-official with Georgian (1995, Constitution, Article 8). *Class:* North Caucasian, West Caucasian, Abkhaz-Abazin. *Dialects:* Abzhui, Bzyb, Samurzakan. *Lg Use:* 94% speak it as L1. *Lg Dev:* NT: 1912–2004. *Writing:* Cyrillic script, used since 1860s. Georgian (Mkhedruli) script, no longer in use. *Other:* Christian, Muslim.

Armenian [hye] (Somkhuri). 448,000 in Georgia. *Status:* 5 (Dispersed). See main entry on page 51.

Assyrian Neo-Aramaic [aii] (Aisorski). 3,000 in Georgia (1999). Ethnic population: 14,000. Erevan and scattered in Transcaucasia. *Status:* 7 (Shifting). *Lg Use:* Mostly older adults. Also use Russian [rus]. *Other:* 'Aisor' is the Russian name for the people. Christian (Nestorian). See main entry on page 206.

Avar [ava]. 2,000 in Georgia (2002 census). Kakheti Region, Qvareli district, Tivi village. *Status:* 6b (Threatened). *Dialect:* Antsukh. See main entry on page 319.

Azerbaijani, North [azj]. 360,000 in Georgia (2007). *Status:* 5 (Dispersed). See main entry on page 52.

Bats [bbl] (Bac, Batsaw, Batsba, Batsbi, Batsbiitsy, Batsi, Tsova-Tush, Tush). 3,420 (2000). Active users may be far fewer than 3,000 (Salminen 2007). Kakheti Region, Talavei district, Zemo-Alvani (Upper Alvani). *Status:* 7 (Shifting). *Class:* North Caucasian, East Caucasian, Nakh, Batsi. *Lg Use:* Modern Bats heavily influenced by Georgian [kat]. Traditional Bats perhaps known by a few elders (Salminen 2007). Few domains. Used by few children. Neutral attitudes. Georgian [kat] used in school and for wider group communication (Salminen 2007). *Lg Dev:* Georgian [kat] is literary language. Dictionary. Grammar. *Writing:* Unwritten. *Other:* Traditional territory and way of life. Christian.

Bezhta [kap]. 700 in Georgia (2006). Kakheti Region, Qvareli district, Chatliskure and Saruso villages. *Status:* 5 (Developing). See main entry on page 319.

Bohtan Neo-Aramaic [bhn]. 1,000 in Georgia (1999 S. Fox). Mainly Garbadani village. Also in Russian Federation. *Status:* 7 (Shifting). *Class:* Afro-Asiatic, Semitic, Central, Aramaic, Eastern, Central, Northeastern. *Lg Use:* Mainly older adults. *Other:* Christian.

Dido [ddo]. Kakheti Region, Qvareli district, Ibtsokhi village. *Status:* 6b (Threatened). See main entry on page 319.

Georgian [kat] (Common Kartvelian, Gruzinski, Kartuli). 3,900,000 in Georgia (1993 UBS). Population total all countries: 4,237,710. Ethnic population: 3,980,000 (1993 UBS). Also in Armenia, Azerbaijan, Iran, Kazakhstan, Kyrgyzstan, Russian Federation, Tajikistan, Turkey, Turkmenistan, Ukraine, Uzbekistan. *Status:* 1 (National). Statutory national language (1995, Constitution, Article 8). *Class:* Kartvelian, Georgian. *Dialects:* Adzhar (Acharian), Ferejdan, Gurian, Imeretian, Imerxev Kartlian, Ingilo, Kaxetian (Kakhetian), Meskhur-Javakhuri, Moxev (Mokhev), Mtiul, Pshav, Racha-Lexchxum (Lechkhum), Tush, Xevsur (Kheysur). Imerxev is in Turkey, Ferejdan may no longer be spoken in Iran. *Type:* SVO. *Lg Use:* Meskhi are ethnically Georgian, speak Georgian, are Eastern Orthodox, and live in southwest Georgia. *Lg Dev:* Fully developed. Bible: 1743–2002. *Writing:* Braille script. Georgian (Mkhedruli) script, primary usage. Khutsuri (Asomtavruli and Nuskhuri) script, no longer in use. *Other:* Adzhai Muslims are in Armenia. South Caucasian also called Kartvelian; Gruzinski is the Russian name. Christian, Muslim (Shi'a), Muslim (Sunni).

Hunzib [huz]. 410 in Georgia (Koryakov 2006). Tkhilistsqaro, Qvareli district, Chatliskure village. *Status:* 6b (Threatened). See main entry on page 320.

Judeo-Georgian [jge]. 20,000 in Georgia (1995). *Status:* 6a (Vigorous). *Other:* Oriental and Ashkenazic Jews in Georgia live separately. Judeo-Georgians live separately from non-Jewish Georgians. Jewish. See main entry on page 209.

Kurdish, Northern [kmr] (Kurdî, Kurmancî, Kurmanji). 40,000 in Georgia (1991). Tblisi area. *Status:* 5 (Developing). *Other:* Yezidi. See main entry on page 305.

Laz [lzz] (Chan, Chanuri, Chanzan, Laze, Zan). 1,000 in Georgia (Salminen 2007). Adjara Republic, a few villages. *Status:* 7 (Shifting). *Dialects:* Atina, Chxala (Ckhala), Samurzakan-Zugdidi, Senaki, Vice-Arxava (Vital-Arkhava), Xopa (Hopa). *Lg Use:* Rapid language shift to Georgian [kat] (Salminen 2007). Georgian [kat] is literary language. *Other:* Ethnic autonym: Lazuri. Muslim. See main entry on page 306.

Mingrelian [xmf] (Margaluri, Megrel, Megruli). 500,000 (1989 B. Hewitt). West lowland. *Status:* 6a (Vigorous). *Class:* Kartvelian, Zan. *Dialects:* None known. Officially considered a single language with Laz [lzz] called Zan, but linguists recognize they are not inherently mutually intelligible. *Lg Use:* Younger generation uses the language less (Salminen 2007). Also use Georgian [kat]. *Writing:* Georgian (Mkhedruli) script. *Other:* Ethnic autonym: Margaluri. Christian.

Ossetic [oss] (Osetin, Ossete, Ossetian). 100,000 in Georgia (Johnstone and Mandryk 2001). South Ossetia. *Status:* 5 (Developing). *Dialects:* Digor (Digorian, Digoron, Dogor), Iron, Kudar (South Osetin). *Other:* Christian (Orthodox). See main entry on page 321.

Russian [rus]. 372,000 in Georgia. *Status:* 3 (Wider communication). De facto national working language. *Lg Use:* Used as L2 by Assyrian Neo-Aramaic [aii], Svan [sva]. See main entry on page 322.

Svan [sva] (Svanuri). 15,000 (2000 A. Kibrik). Ethnic population: 15,000 (2000 A. Kibrik). Svanetia Region, Mestiya and Lentekhi districts. *Status:* 7 (Shifting). *Class:* Kartvelian, Svan. *Dialects:* Lashx, Lentex, Lower Bal, Upper Bal. *Lg Use:* All domains. Mainly adults. Positive attitudes. Also use Georgian [kat], Russian [rus]. *Writing:* Cyrillic script. Georgian (Mkhedruli) script. Latin script. *Other:* Many Georgian [kat] speakers still claim Svan ethnicity (Salminen 2007). Christian (Lakhamul).

Urum [uum]. 97,700 in Georgia (2000). Population total all countries: 192,700. Trialeti. Also in Greece, Ukraine. *Status:* 6b (Threatened). *Class:* Altaic, Turkic. *Dialects:* A number of inherently intelligible dialects. *Lg Use:* Few child speakers (Salminen 2007). *Lg Dev:* Grammar. *Writing:* Cyrillic script. Greek script, occasional usage. *Other:* Ethnic autonym: Greeks.

Hong Kong

Hong Kong Special Administrative Region of the People's Republic of China, Zhonghua Renmin Gongheguo, Xianggang Tibie Xingzheng Qu. As a Special Administrative Region, Hong Kong has a significant amount of autonomy in all areas except defence and foreign affairs. 6,864,000 (2006 census). Principal language: Chinese. Literacy rate: 97% (2011 USDS). Immigrant language: Japanese (10,800). Deaf population: 5,500–224,000. Deaf institutions: 4.

The number of individual languages listed for Hong Kong is 7. All are living languages. Of these, 3 are institutional, 1 is developing, 1 is vigorous, 1 is in trouble, and 1 is dying.

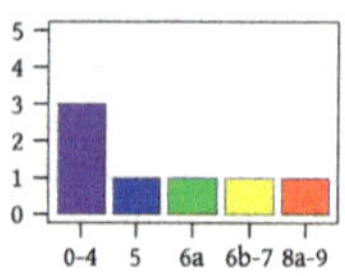

Chinese, Hakka [hak]. 68,300 in Hong Kong (2006 census). *Status:* 6b (Threatened). *Lg Use:* Some young people, all adults. See main entry on page 67.

Chinese, Mandarin [cmn]. 60,900 in Hong Kong (2006 census). *Status:* 1 (National). See main entry on page 67.

Chinese, Min Nan [nan]. 77,600 in Hong Kong (2006 census). *Status:* 5 (Developing). See main entry on page 68.

Chinese, Yue [yue] (Cantonese, Guangfu, Hong Kong Cantonese, Shatou, Shiqi, Wancheng, Yuehai). 6,030,000 in Hong Kong (2006 census). *Status:* 2 (Provincial). De facto provincial language in Hong Kong. See main entry on page 69.

English [eng]. 187,000 in Hong Kong (2006 census), increasing. L2 users: 2,200,000 in Hong Kong (Crystal 2003). *Status:* 1 (National). Statutory provincial working language in Hong Kong (1997, Basic Law, Article 9). *Lg Use:* Positive attitudes. *Lg Dev:* Taught in primary and secondary schools. See main entry on page 319.

Hong Kong Sign Language [hks] (Heung Kong Sau Yue, HKSL). 20,000 (2007). *Status:* 6a (Vigorous). *Class:* Deaf sign language. *Dialects:* None known. 40% similarity with Chinese Sign Language [csl], 42%–52% similarity with Taiwan Sign Language [tss]. *Lg Use:* All domains. All ages. Positive attitudes. Also use Mandarin Chinese [cmn]. *Lg Dev:* Literacy rate in L2: 70%–80% in written Chinese. Dictionary.

Macanese [mzs]. *Status:* 8b (Nearly extinct). See main entry on page 218.

India

Republic of India. 1,210,727,000 (2011 census). Principal languages: English, Hindi, Sanskrit. Literacy rate: 51% (2006 UNESCO). Immigrant languages: Armenian (500), Burushaski, Iranian Persian (18,000), Judeo-Iraqi Arabic (51,700), Northern Pashto (11,100). General references: Bradley 1997, 2005; Breton 1997; Hugoniot 1970; Marrison 1967; Masica 1991; Matisoff, Baron, and Lowe 1996; Singh, 1994, 1995; van Bik 2006; Van Driem 2001, 2007. Deaf population: 9,400,000–14,000,000 (2001). Deaf institutions: 850.

The number of individual languages listed for India is 456. Of these, 442 are living and 14 are extinct. Of the living languages, 63 are institutional, 129 are developing, 186 are vigorous, 53 are in trouble, and 11 are dying. See maps beginning on page 351.

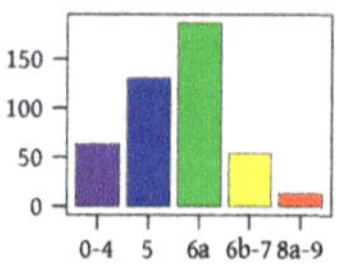

Adi [adi] (Abhor, Abor, Boga'er Luoba, Lhoba, Luoba). 97,000 in India (2001 census). Population total all countries: 100,190. Arunachal Pradesh, East, West, and Upper Siang districts, Upper Subansiri and Dibang Valley districts; Assam, north hills of Assam Valley, between Bhutan and Buruli rivers. Also in Bhutan, China (Boga'er Luoba). *Status:* 5 (Developing). *Class:* Sino-Tibetan, Tibeto-Burman, Central Tibeto-Burman, Tani. *Dialects:* Ashing, Bokar (Boga'er Luoba), Bori, Karko, Komkar, Milang, Minyong, Padam, Pailibo, Pangi, Pasi, Ramo, Shimong, Tangam. Sun (1993) lists Tani varieties as Apatani [apt], Milang, Damu, Mising [mrg], Bangni [njz], Tagin [tgj], Sagli, south Aya, Leli, and perhaps the Padam, Bokar, Pailibo, Ramo, Bori, Minyong and Pasi dialects of Adi; Asing, Panggi, Simong, Karok, Hill, Mising [mrg], and some northern and western dialects of Nyishi [njz]. A different language from Yidu Lhoba [clk]. Bokar, Milang, Pailibo, and Ramo are very divergent—possibly separate languages. *Type:* SOV; particles indicate grammatical relations; long-short vowel distinction; most words polysyllabic; loans mainly from Tibetan. *Lg Use:* Also use

Assamese [asm], Hindi [hin], Nepali [npi]. Used as L2 by Tshangla [tsj]. *Lg Dev:* Literacy rate in L2: 59% (2001 census). Radio programs. Grammar. Bible: 2005–2009. *Writing:* Latin script. Tibetan script, used in China. *Other:* A Scheduled Tribe with several subgroups. 'Adi', hillman, is a cover term for eastern Tani languages. Traditional religion. *Map:* 356:186.

Adi, Galo [adl] (Adi, Adi-Gallong, Adi-Galo, Gallong, Galo, Galong). 30,000. 62,000 (2001 census). A few older adult monolinguals. L2 users: Used as L2 by some commerce people from Bihar and Nepal who have settled in Adi areas. Arunachal Pradesh, West Siang, East Siang, Dibang Valley (south), Lohit (east), Changlang (northeast), and some in Upper Subansiri (west) districts; Assam. *Status:* 5 (Developing). *Class:* Sino-Tibetan, Tibeto-Burman, Central Tibeto-Burman, Tani. *Dialects:* Karka, Lare, Pugo. Lare is the main dialect and is accepted by all Galo. *Type:* SOV; postpositions; genitives after noun heads; articles, adjectives, numerals before and after noun heads; relatives after noun heads or without; question word initial; maximum prefixes 2, maximum suffixes 4–5; affixes indicate case of noun phrase; causatives and comparatives; CV, CVC, CVV patterns; nontonal. *Lg Use:* Village, home. All ages. Nearly all also use Assamese [asm]. English [eng] is spoken by the educated and the young. Nearly all speak some Hindi [hin]. Also Hindi [hin] is used with the military. *Lg Dev:* Literacy rate in L2: 60%. More men can read than women but more girls and women are learning. Radio programs. Grammar. NT: 2008. *Writing:* Latin script. *Other:* A Scheduled Tribe. Traditional religion, Buddhist, Christian. *Map:* 356:185.

Agariya [agi] (Agaria, Agharia, Agoria). 72,000 (2007). Madhya Pradesh, Mandla and Rewa districts, Maikal hills; Chhattisgarh, Bilaspur District; Uttar Pradesh, Agra, Mathura, and Mirzapur districts. *Status:* 6a (Vigorous). *Class:* Austro-Asiatic, Munda, North Munda, Kherwari. *Lg Use:* Also use Hindi [hin]. *Lg Dev:* Literacy rate in L2: 5%. *Other:* A Scheduled Caste in Uttar Pradesh. Chhattisgarhi [hne] L1 of tribe (Singh 1995). Traditional religion, Hindu. *Map:* 354:102.

Ahirani [ahr] (Ahiri). 1,870,000 (2001 census). Gujarat and Maharashtra states. In Maharashtra: Dhulia, Jalgaon, Nandurbar, Nasik, and Aurangabad districts. *Status:* 6a (Vigorous). *Class:* Indo-European, Indo-Iranian, Indo-Aryan, Central zone, Khandesi. *Dialects:* None known. Ahirani may be distinct from Khandesi [khn]. *Lg Use:* Also use Hindi [hin], Marathi [mar]. Used as L2 by Palya Bareli [bpx], Pauri Bareli [bfb], Rathwi Bareli [bgd]. *Lg Dev:* Dictionary. Grammar. *Other:* Hindu. *Map:* 358:303.

Ahom [aho] (Tai Ahom). No known L1 speakers. Assam. *Status:* 9 (Second language only). *Class:* Tai-Kadai, Kam-Tai, Tai, Southwestern. *Lg Use:* Not spoken in daily life; used in religious chants and literary materials. Attempts to revive the spoken language are underway, with assistance of scholars from the Aiton [aio] and Phake [phk] communities (2007). *Writing:* Ahom script. *Other:* Former language of the Tai-Ahom king. Possibly 8,000,000 Assamese [asm] speakers claim to be of Ahom descent (1990 A. Diller).

Aimol [aim]. 2,640 (2001 census). Manipur State, Chandel district, Unapal, Satu, Kumbirei, Chingunghut, Aimol Tampak, Khodamphai, Ngairong Aimol, Chandonpokpi, Soibong (Khudengthabi), and Khomayai (Khunjai); Senapati district, Tuikhong; Churachandpur district, Luichungbum (Louchulbung); Bishnupur district, Kha-Aimol; Assam State. *Status:* 5 (Developing). *Class:* Sino-Tibetan, Tibeto-Burman, Sal, Kuki-Chin-Naga, Kuki-Chin, Northern. *Dialect:* Langrong. Langrong may be a distinct language. Reportedly intelligible to Koireng [nkd]. *Lg Use:* Home, church. Most also use Meitei [mni]. *Lg Dev:* Literacy rate in L2: 60%–70%. *Writing:* Latin script. *Other:* A Scheduled Tribe. Christian. *Map:* 357:268.

Aiton [aio] (Aitonia). 1,500 (Morey 2006). Assam, Jorhat and Karbi Anglong districts, Doboroni, Banlung, Ahomoni, Balipathar, Kaliyani, Chakihula, Tengani, and Barhula villages. *Status:* 6b (Threatened). *Class:* Tai-Kadai, Kam-Tai, Tai, Southwestern. *Dialects:* None known. Reportedly similar to Phake [phk]. *Lg Use:* Vigorous. Also use Assamese [asm], English [eng], Hindi [hin]. *Lg Dev:* Literacy rate in L1: Below 1%. *Writing:* Myanmar (Burmese) script. *Other:* Buddhist. *Map:* 356:221.

Aka-Bea [abj] (Aka-Beada, Bea, Beada, Biada, Bogijiab, Bojigniji, Bojigyab). No known L1 speakers. Andaman Islands, South Andaman island except northeast coast, and north and east interiors; Rutland island except south coast; small islands southeast of Rutland; Labyrinth Islands. *Status:* 10 (Extinct). *Class:* Andamanese, Great Andamanese, Central.

Aka-Bo [akm] (Ba, Bo). No known L1 speakers. Andaman Islands, east central coast of North Andaman island, North Reef island. *Status:* 10 (Extinct). *Class:* Andamanese, Great Andamanese, Northern.

Aka-Cari [aci] (Cari, Chariar). No known L1 speakers. Andaman Islands, north coast of North Andaman island, Landfall island, other nearby small islands. *Status:* 10 (Extinct). *Class:* Andamanese, Great Andamanese, Northern.

Aka-Jeru [akj] (Jeru, Yerawa). No known L1 speakers. Andaman Islands, interior and south North Andaman island, Sound island. *Status:* 10 (Extinct). *Class:* Andamanese, Great Andamanese, Northern.

Aka-Kede [akx] (Kede). No known L1 speakers. Andaman Islands, central and north central Middle Andaman island. *Status:* 10 (Extinct). *Class:* Andamanese, Great Andamanese, Central.

Aka-Kol [aky] (Kol). No known L1 speakers. Andaman Islands, southeast Middle Andaman island. *Status:* 10 (Extinct). *Class:* Andamanese, Great Andamanese, Central.

Aka-Kora [ack] (Kora). No known L1 speakers. Andaman Islands, northeast and north central coasts of North Andaman island, Smith island. *Status:* 10 (Extinct). *Class:* Andamanese, Great Andamanese, Northern.

Akar-Bale [acl] (Bale, Balwa). No known L1 speakers. Andaman Islands, Ritchie's Archipelago, Havelock island, Neill island. *Status:* 10 (Extinct). *Class:* Andamanese, Great Andamanese, Central.

Allar [all] (Aalan, Alan, Alanmar, Alar, Allan, Chatans). 350 (Shashi and Shri 1994). Kerala, Malappuram district, Perinthalmanna tahsil, Manjeri tahsil, Mannarmala, Aminikadu, and Tazhecode; Palakkad district, Mannarkkad and Ottappalam tahsils. *Status:* 6b (Threatened). *Class:* Dravidian, Unclassified. *Dialects:* None known. Lexical similarity: 61% with Malayalam [mal], 59% with Tamil [tam]. *Lg Use:* Vigorous. All domains. All ages. Very limited bilingual ability in Malayalam [mal]. *Lg Dev:* Literacy rate in L1: Below 1%. *Writing:* Malayalam script. *Other:* Traditional religion, Hindu. *Map:* 360:396.

Amri Karbi [ajz] (Amri). 125,000 (2003). Assam, Kamrup district, south of Brahmaputra river in Chandubi, Loharghat, Rani block, Jalukbari, Pandu, Basbistha, Panikhaith, Jorabat, Sonapur, Khetri, and Kahi Kusi; Meghalaya, Ri-Bhoi district, Nongpoh area, Barni Hat and Umling. *Status:* 5 (Developing). *Class:* Sino-Tibetan, Tibeto-Burman, Sal, Kuki-Chin-Naga, Karbi. *Dialects:* Lower Amri, Upper Amri. Reportedly unintelligible with Karbi [mjw]; intelligibility testing inconclusive regarding whether Guriaghuli area dialect is well understood in Meghalaya. Lexical similarity: 57%–68% with Karbi; 70%–86% between dialects. *Lg Use:* Many ethnic group members no longer use Amri Karbi. Much borrowing from Assamese [asm] (in Assam) and Khasi [kha] (in Meghalaya). Some Amri Karbi villages shifted completely to Assamese due to intermarriage and the perception that Assamese is preferred for children to do well in school. In the remote and isolated border area, the language is still strong. Home, village, religion. All ages. Positive attitudes. Strong feelings of separateness from the dominant Karbi group in Karbi, Anglong District. *Lg Dev:* Literacy rate in L2: 20%—60%. Newspapers. Radio programs. NT: 2010. *Writing:* Latin script. *Other:* Hindu, Christian, traditional religion. *Map:* 356:208.

Anal [anm] (Namfau). 23,200 in India (2001 census). Population total all countries: 23,250. Southeast Manipur, Chandel district, Chandel, Chakpikarong, and Tengnoupal subdivisions, on Chakpi river banks. Possibly in Bangladesh. Also in Myanmar. *Status:* 5 (Developing). *Class:* Sino-Tibetan, Tibeto-Burman, Sal, Kuki-Chin-Naga, Kuki-Chin, Northern. *Dialects:* Laizo, Mulsom. Reportedly most similar to Lamgang [lmk] (Kuki Naga). *Type:* SOV. *Lg Use:* Also use Meitei [mni]. Used as L2 by Moyon Naga [nmo]. *Lg Dev:* Literacy rate in L1: 74% (2001 census). Bible: 2006. *Writing:* Latin script. *Other:* A Scheduled Tribe. Declared themselves Nagas (ethnically) in 1963. Christian. *Map:* 357:273.

Andaman Creole Hindi [hca] (Andaman Hindi). 10,000 (Singh 1994). Andaman and Nicobar Islands, Port Blair, 40 villages south of Port Blair. *Status:* 6a (Vigorous). *Class:* Creole, Hindi based. *Dialects:* None known. A creolization of Hindustani, Bengali [ben], and Malayalam [mal]. *Lg Use:* Home. All ages. Use standard Hindi [hin] with outsiders. Diglossia. *Writing:* Unwritten. *Other:* Spoken as L1 by mixed generations of communities. Contains elements of Indo-Aryan and Dravidian grammar. No literature exists in the creole. Standard Hindi literature is used. *Map:* 361.

Andh [anr] (Andha, Andhi). 100,000 (2007). Ethnic population: 420,000 (2007). Maharashtra, Akola, Aurangabad, Buldana, Nanded, Parbhani, and Yevatmal districts; Andhra Pradesh, Adilabad, Hyderabad; Madhya Pradesh. *Status:* 6b (Threatened). *Class:* Indo-European, Indo-Iranian, Indo-Aryan, Unclassified. *Lg Dev:* Literacy rate in L1: Below 1%. *Writing:* Devanagari script. *Other:* A Scheduled Tribe. Many speak Marathi [mar] as L1. Hindu. *Map:* 358:320.

Angika [anp] (Anga, Angikar, Chhika-Chhiki). 725,000 in India (IMA 1997). Population total all countries: 743,600. Northern Bihar. Also in Nepal. *Status:* 5 (Developing). *Class:* Indo-European, Indo-Iranian, Indo-Aryan, Eastern zone, Unclassified. *Dialects:* None known. 79% inherent intelligibility of Brahmin Maithili. Lexical similarity: 81% (Brahmin) to 87% (non-Brahmin) with Darbhanga Maithili. *Type:* SOV; postpositions; noun head final; content q-word in situ; clause constituents indicated by case-marking; passives and voice; nontonal. *Lg Use:* Use declining (Van Driem 2007). Home, community. All ages. Negative attitudes. Hindi [hin] is used for trading, government, praying. *Lg Dev:* Poetry. Films. *Writing:* Devanagari script. *Other:* Hindu. *Map:* 355:119.

Apatani [apt] (Apa). 28,400 (2001 census). Ethnic population: 35,000. Arunachal Pradesh, Subansiri district, 7 villages in Ziro valley: Hong, Hari, Billa, Dutta, Hija, Mudang-Tage, and Michi Bamin; Assam; Nagaland. *Status:* 6b (Threatened). *Class:* Sino-Tibetan, Tibeto-Burman, Central Tibeto-Burman, Tani. *Dialects:* None known. May be intelligible with Nyishi [njz]. *Lg Use:* Also use Assamese [asm], Hindi [hin], Nefamese [nef]. *Lg Dev:* Literacy rate in L2: 71% (2001 census). Dictionary. Grammar. NT: 2004. *Writing:* Latin script. *Other:* A Scheduled Tribe. Traditional religion. *Map:* 356:205.

A-Pucikwar [apq] (Puchikwar, Pucikwar). No known L1 speakers. *Status:* 10 (Extinct). *Class:* Andamanese, Great Andamanese, Central.

Aranadan [aaf] (Aranatan, Eranadans). 200 (2001 census). Census did not include all people in interior settlements. Kerala, Kozhihkode district, Ernad taluk; Palakkad district; Malappuram district, Nilambur tahsil; Tamil Nadu, Karnataka. *Status:* 6b (Threatened). *Class:* Dravidian, Southern, Tamil-Kannada, Tamil-Kodagu, Tamil-Malayalam, Malayalam. *Dialects:* None known. Lexical similarity: 63%–69% with Malayalam [mal], 53%–55% with Tamil [tam]. *Lg Use:* Vitality in Malappuram District questionable due to small population, no separate settlements, living with Malayalis. Low education level helps keep language stable. Home, village. Negative attitudes. Most have at least basic proficiency in Malayalam [mal], which is used in all the same domains as Aranadan. *Lg Dev:* Literacy rate in L1: Below 1%. Literacy rate in L2: 36%–41% in Kerala, 65% in Tamil Nadu (2001 census). *Other:* A Scheduled Tribe. Traditional religion. *Map:* 360:394.

Assamese [asm] (Asambe, Asami, Asamiya). 12,800,000 in India (2001 census). Population total all countries: 12,828,220. Assam; West Bengal; Meghalaya; Arunachal Pradesh. Also in Bhutan, United States. *Status:* 2 (Provincial). Statutory provincial language in Assam State (1950, Constitution, Schedule VIII). *Class:* Indo-European, Indo-Iranian, Indo-Aryan, Eastern zone, Bengali-Assamese. *Dialects:* Jharwa (Pidgin), Mayang, Standard Assamese, Western Assamese (Kamrupi). *Lg Use:* Used as L2 by Adi [adi], Aiton [aio], Angami Naga [njm], Ao Naga [njo], Apatani [apt], Chang Naga [nbc], Deori [der], Digaro-Mishmi [mhu], Galo Adi [adl], Hajong [haj], Hmar [hmr], Hrangkhol [hra], Hruso [hru], Idu-Mishmi [clk], Kachari [xac], Kamta [rkt], Karbi [mjw], Khamti [kht], Khamyang [ksu], Koch [kdq], Kurmukar [kfv], Lyngngam [lyg], Miji [sjl], Miju-Mishmi [mxj], Mising [mrg], Nocte Naga [njb], Phake [phk], Puroik [suv], Singpho [sgp], Sumi Naga [nsm], Tase Naga [nst], Tiwa [lax], Tutsa Naga [tvt], Wancho Naga [nnp]. *Lg Dev:* Poetry. Magazines. Newspapers. New media. Radio programs. Films. TV. Dictionary. Grammar. Bible: 1833–1995. *Writing:* Bengali script. *Map:* 351.

Asuri [asr] (Ashree, Assur, Asura, Maleta). 7,000 (Van Driem 2007). Jharkhand, southern Palamau, northern Ranchi, Gumla and Lohardaga districts of Chotanagpur Plateau; Chhattisgarh, Raigarh district, Jashpur area; Maharashtra; Odisha, Sambalpur district; West Bengal. *Status:* 6a (Vigorous). *Class:* Austro-Asiatic, Munda, North Munda, Kherwari, Mundari. *Dialects:* Brijia (Birjia, Koranti), Manjhi. *Lg Use:* Also use Bengali [ben], Sadri [sck]. *Lg Dev:* Literacy rate in L1: Below 1%. *Writing:* Devanagari script. *Other:* Asur and Birjia are Scheduled Tribes. Hindu, Christian, traditional religion. *Maps:* 354:98, 355:98.

Atong [aot] (A'tong). 4,600 in India. Population total all countries: 10,000. Meghalaya state, Garo hills; Assam, south Kamrup district. Also in Bangladesh. *Status:* 7 (Shifting). *Class:* Sino-Tibetan, Tibeto-Burman, Sal, Bodo-Garo-Northern Naga, Bodo-Koch, Koch. *Dialects:* None known. Related to Koch [kdq] and Rabha [rah]. *Lg Use:* Also use Garo [grt]. *Lg Dev:* Dictionary. Grammar. *Other:* Traditional religion. *Map:* 355:128 (as A'tong).

Awadhi [awa] (Abadi, Abohi, Ambodhi, Avadhi, Baiswari, Kojali, Kosali). 2,530,000 in India (2001 census). Population total all countries: 3,032,000. Uttar Pradesh,

Kheri, Sitapur, Lucknow, Unnao, Rae-Bareli, Bahraich, Bara-Banki, Pratapgarh, Sultanpur, Gonda, Faizabad, and Allahabad districts; Bihar; Madhya Pradesh; Delhi. Also in Nepal (Avadhi). *Status:* 5 (Developing). *Class:* Indo-European, Indo-Iranian, Indo-Aryan, East Central zone. *Dialects:* Gangapari, Mirzapuri, Pardesi, Uttari. Dialects are generally mutually intelligible. Lexical similarity: with Bhojpuri [bho], Rana Tharu [thr], Maithili [mai], Nepali [npi], Hindi [hin]. Also Sanskrit [san] borrowings. *Type:* SOV; postpositions; noun head final; 2 genders; clause constituents indicated by case-marking; verbal affixation marks person, number and genders of subject and object; no ergativity; tense and aspect; passives and voice; 30 consonant and 8 vowel phonemes; nontonal. *Lg Use:* Also use Hindi [hin]. *Lg Dev:* Literacy rate in L1: 50%–75%. Education is in Hindi. Considerable epic literature. Hindu holy book, Ramcharitmanas, by Tulsi Das. Poetry. Magazines. Newspapers. New media. Radio programs. TV. Videos. Dictionary. Bible: 2000–2005. *Writing:* Devanagari script. *Other:* 'Kosali' is a name used for the Eastern Hindi group. Hindu, Muslim. *Map:* 354:92.

Badaga [bfq] (Badag, Badagu, Baduga, Badugu, Vadagu). 135,000 (2001 census). Tamil Nadu, Nilgiris district, Kunda hills. 200 villages. *Status:* 5 (Developing). *Class:* Dravidian, Southern, Tamil-Kannada, Kannada. *Lg Use:* Used as L2 by Irula [iru], Kota [kfe]. *Lg Dev:* Radio programs. NT: 1999. *Writing:* Badaga script, in development. Kannada script, no longer in use. Latin script. Tamil script, used since 2009. *Other:* Hindu, Christian, traditional religion. *Map:* 360:390.

Bagheli [bfy] (Bagelkhandi, Bhugelkhud, Gangai, Godwani Kawathi, Kenat, Kevat Boli, Kevati, Kewani, Kewat, Kewati, Kewot, Kumhari, Mandal, Mannadi, Riwai). 2,860,000 in India (2001 census). Northeast Madhya Pradesh, Rewa, Satna, Sidhi, Shahdol, Umaria, Anuppur, Jabalpur, Mandla, Chhindwara, Dindori, and Panna districts; Uttar Pradesh, Allahabad, Mirzapur, Banda, and Hamirpur districts; Chhattisgarh, Bilaspur and Koriya districts. Also in Nepal. *Status:* 6a (Vigorous). *Class:* Indo-European, Indo-Iranian, Indo-Aryan, East Central zone. *Dialects:* Godwani, Kumhari, Rewa. Godwani (refers to Bagheli-speaking Gonds), Kumhari (refers to Bagheli-speaking Kumhar). Though geographic and caste variation is found in Bagheli, no dialect is prevalent. Rewa area variety is considered standard. Lexical similarity: 79%–99% between all Bagheli varieties; 72%–91% with Hindi [hin]. *Lg Use:* Vigorous. All domains. All ages. Positive attitudes. 35% of the Bagheli-speaking population is projected to have good general proficiency or more in Hindi [hin]. Hindi use is widespread but does not appear to be completely displacing Bagheli in any of the domains. *Lg Dev:* Literacy rate in L2: 49% in Hindi. Had literature since 16th century. Radio programs. NT: 1821. *Writing:* Devanagari script. *Other:* Hindu. *Map:* 354:104.

Bagri [bgq] (Bagari, Bagria, Bagris, Bahgri, Baorias). 647,000 in India (2001 census). Population total all countries: 847,000. 162,000 monolinguals. Punjab, Firozepur, Rajasthan, Hanumangarh, Sriganganagar, Haryana, Sirsa, and Fatehabad districts. Also in Pakistan. *Status:* 5 (Developing). *Class:* Indo-European, Indo-Iranian, Indo-Aryan, Central zone, Rajasthani, Unclassified. A member of macrolanguage Rajasthani [raj]. *Dialects:* None known. Lexical similarity: 81%–95% between all varietes of Bagri, 58%–63% with Eastern Panjabi [pan], 56%–69% with Hindi [hin], 56%–70% with Haryanvi [bgc], 51%–66% with Marwari [rwr], 58%–69% with Merwari [wry], 69%–76% with Shekhawati [swv], 47%–63% with Godwari [gdx], 63%–65% with Dhundari [dhd], 60%–66% with Mewati [wtm], 74% with Jandavra [jnd]. *Type:* SOV; tonal, 3 tones. *Lg Use:* Vigorous. Home, village, school, market, religion. Positive attitudes. Majority are bilingual in Hindi [hin]. Educated people and men have greater proficiency. *Lg Dev:* Most Bagri live in rural areas and are illiterate. Grammar. *Writing:* Devanagari script. *Other:* A Scheduled Caste. Traditional religion. *Maps:* 352:45, 353:45.

Balochi, Eastern [bgp] (Balochi, Baloci, Baluci). 800 in India (2007). Possibly L2 speakers only. Ethnic population: 95,000. Uttar Pradesh; Gujarat. *Status:* 5 (Developing). *Lg Use:* Also use Urdu [urd]. *Other:* Distinct from Western Balochi [bgn] of Pakistan, Afghanistan, Iran, and Turkmenistan; and Southern Balochi [bcc] of Pakistan, Iran, Oman, and United Arab Emirates. Muslim (Sunni). See main entry on page 266. *Map:* 352:46.

Balti [bft] (Baltistani, Bhoti of Baltistan, Sbalt). 20,000 in India (2001 census). Ethnic population: 38,800. Jammu and Kashmir. *Status:* 6a (Vigorous). *Lg Use:* Many Purik [prx] shifted to Balti. Urdu [urd] reportedly high in some places, except women and uneducated. Also use Shina [scl]. *Lg Dev:* Literacy rate in L2: 62% (2001 census). *Other:* A Scheduled Tribe. Muslim. See main entry on page 266. *Map:* 352:8.

Bantawa [bap] (Bantaba, Bantawa Dum, Bantawa Rai, Bantawa Yong, Bantawa Yüng, Bontawa, Kirat Khambu, Kirat Khambu Rai, Rai). 14,400 in India (2001 census). Few monolinguals. Sikkim State, Rolep, Lingdum and many other parts of the state; West Bengal State, Darjeeling. *Status:* 6b (Threatened). *Lg Use:* Some shift to Nepali [npi] evident, especially among young generation. Home, friends, religion. All ages. Positive attitudes. Hindi [hin] common among ex-soldiers. Most also use some Nepali [npi]. Wide range of proficiency. In some regions, young people prefer Nepali. *Lg Dev:* Taught as an optional subject but not as a medium. *Other:* Traditional religion, Christian, Hindu. See main entry on page 244. *Map:* 355:160.

Bareli, Palya [bpx] (Pali, Palodi, Palya Bareli). 10,000 (2000 V. Varkey). Madhya Pradesh; Barwani district, Rajpur, Barwani tahsils; Khargone district, Jhirniya Tahsil; Maharashtra, Jalgaon district, Yawal, Raver tahsils; Dhule district, Shirpur tahsil. *Status:* 6a (Vigorous). *Class:* Indo-European, Indo-Iranian, Indo-Aryan, Central zone, Bhil. *Dialects:* Dialect center is Madhya Pradesh, Barwani District, Choutharya village of Rajpur tahsil. Lexical similarity 62%–66% with Pauri Bareli [bfb], 67%–73% with Rathwi Bareli [bgd]. *Lg Use:* Vigorous. All domains except education. Positive attitudes. Also use Ahirani [ahr], Hindi [hin], Marathi [mar], Nimadi [noe]. Proficiency in all second languages but Hindi is low. *Lg Dev:* Literacy rate in L2: Below 10%. *Other:* Traditional religion. *Map:* 358:294.

Bareli, Pauri [bfb] (Bareli, Barewali, Barli). 638,000 (2001 census). Maharashtra; Nandurbar district, Dhadgaon, Shahada, and Taloda tahsils; Dhule district, Shirpur tahsil; Madhya Pradesh, Barwani district, Pansemal tahsil, Nivali and Pati blocks. *Status:* 6a (Vigorous). *Class:* Indo-European, Indo-Iranian, Indo-Aryan, Central zone, Bhil. *Dialects:* Pauri Bareli not intelligible with Rathwi Bareli [bgd] or Palya Bareli [bpx]. Dialect center in Maharashtra, Nandurbar district, Dhadgaon tahsil. Lexical similarity: 81%–88% with varieties of Pauri Bareli; 68%–79% with Rathwi Bareli [bgd]; 62%–66% with Palya Bareli [bpx]. *Lg Use:* Vigorous. All domains except education. Positive attitudes. Also use Ahirani [ahr], Hindi [hin], Marathi [mar], Nimadi [noe]. Proficiency in second languages is low. *Lg Dev:* Literacy rate in L2: Below 10%. *Writing:* Devanagari script. *Other:* Traditional religion. *Map:* 358:291.

Bareli, Rathwi [bgd] (Barel, Pauri, Pawari, Pawri, Rathi, Rathia, Rathwi Pauri). 101,000 (2001 census). Madhya Pradesh; Barwani district, Barwani, Sendhwa, and Rajpur tahsils; Khargone district, Bhagawanpura, Jhirniya, and Bhikangaon tahsils; Dewas district, Bagli tahsil; Khandwa district, Burhanpur tahsil; Dhar district; Dahi block; South Jhabua district, Rathia Bhilala; Maharashtra northern Dhule district, Shirpur tahsil; Jalgaon district, Chopda, Raver, and Yawal tahsils. *Status:* 5 (Developing). *Class:* Indo-European, Indo-Iranian, Indo-Aryan, Central zone, Bhil. *Dialects:* Pauri Bareli [bfb] and the Rathwi Pauri dialect not intelligible with Vasavi [vas] or Bhilori [noi]. Dialect center is Madhya Pradesh, Barwani District, Chiklia. Not intelligible with Palya Bareli [bpx] or Pauri Bareli. Understood by Rathia Bhilala of Nimad, Bhilala of Sondhwa block of Jhabua District and Bhils of south Dhar District. Lexical similarity: 81%–93% with Rathwi Bareli dialects; 67%–73% with Palya Bareli [bpx]; 68%–79% with Pauri Bareli [bfb]. *Lg Use:* Vigorous. All domains except education. Positive attitudes. Also use Ahirani [ahr], Hindi [hin], Marathi [mar], Nimadi [noe]. Proficiency in second languages is low. *Lg Dev:* Literacy rate in L2: Below 10%. Bible portions: 1986. *Writing:* Devanagari script. *Other:* A Scheduled Tribe. Ethnonym: Barela and Paura. Traditional religion. *Maps:* 353:82, 358:82.

Bateri [btv]. 800 in India. 200 families. Jammu and Kashmir, near Srinagar. *Status:* 6a (Vigorous). *Other:* Muslim. See main entry on page 266. *Map:* 352:4.

Bauria [bge] (Babri, Badak, Baori, Basria, Bawari, Bawaria, Bhoria, Vaghri). 27,200 (2001 census). Punjab; Himachal Pradesh; Delhi; Haryana; Chandigarh; Rajasthan; Uttar Pradesh. *Status:* 6a (Vigorous). *Class:* Indo-European, Indo-Iranian, Indo-Aryan, Central zone, Bhil. *Lg Use:* Also use Eastern Panjabi [pan]. *Lg Dev:* Literacy rate in L1: Below 1%. *Other:* A Scheduled Caste. Traditional religion, Hindu. *Map:* 352:44.

Bazigar [bfr]. 58,200 (1981 census). Ethnic population: 800,000. Haryana; Chandigarh; Delhi; Gujarat; Himachal Pradesh; Punjab; Jammu and Kashmir; Madhya Pradesh; Karnataka. *Status:* 7 (Shifting). *Class:* Dravidian, Unclassified. *Lg Dev:* Literacy rate in L1: Below 1%. *Other:* Hindu. *Map:* 352:50.

Bellari [brw]. 1,000 (Van Driem 2007). Karnataka; Kerala; Tamil Nadu. *Status:* 7 (Shifting). *Class:* Dravidian, Southern, Tulu. *Dialects:* None known. Related to Tulu [tcy] and Koraga [kfd]. *Lg Dev:* Literacy rate in L1: Below 1%. *Other:* Bellara is a Scheduled Caste in Karnataka, Kerala, and Tamil Nadu. Speak a dialect of Kannada [kan] (Singh 1995). *Map:* 360:380.

Bengali [ben] (Bangala, Bangla, Bangla-Bhasa). 82,500,000 in India (2001 census). West Bengal; Jharkhand, Dhanbad, Manbhum, Singhbhum, and Santal Parganas; Bihar; Assam, Goalpara district; Meghalaya, Garo hills; Mizoram; Nagaland. *Status:* 2 (Provincial). Statutory provincial language in West Bengal, Tripura, Assam states (1950, Constitution, Schedule VIII). *Dialects:* Barik, Bhatiari, Chirmar, Kachari-Bengali, Lohari-Malpaharia, Musselmani, Rajshahi, Samaria, Saraki, Siripuria (Kishanganjia). *Lg Use:* Used as L2 by Asuri [asr], Bishnupriya [bpy], Chakma [ccp], Hajong [haj], Kamta [rkt], Kharia [khr], Kharia Thar [ksy], Koch [kdq], Kudmali [kyw], Kumarbhag Paharia [kmj], Lodhi [lbm], Mahali [mjx], Maithili [mai], Mal Paharia [mkb], Panchpargania [tdb], Pnar [pbv], Rabha [rah], Sadri [sck], Sakachep [sch], Toto [txo]. *Lg Dev:* Literacy rate in L1: 85%. *Other:* Muslim, Hindu. See main entry on page 54. *Map:* 351.

Bhadrawahi [bhd] (Baderwali, Badrohi, Bahi, Bhadarwahi, Bhaderbhai Jamu, Bhaderwali Pahari, Bhadrava, Bhadri). 53,000 (2002). Jammu and Kashmir, Doda district, Bhadarwah town and surrounding villages. *Status:* 6a (Vigorous). *Class:* Indo-European, Indo-Iranian, Indo-Aryan, Northern zone, Western Pahari. *Dialects:* Bhalesi, Padari (Padar). Lexical similarity: 45% with Pangwali [pgg]. *Lg Use:* Vigorous in spite of high bilingualism; L1 seen as important. Home, village, religion. Positive attitudes. Also use Hindi [hin], Kashmiri [kas], Urdu [urd]. Highly multilingual environment. *Lg Dev:* Literacy rate in L2: 70% (84% for males, 53% for females). Poetry. Radio programs. *Writing:* Arabic script. Devanagari script. *Other:* Hindu. *Map:* 352:11.

Bhalay [bhx]. 8,670 (1981 census). Maharashtra, Amravati district. *Status:* 6a (Vigorous). *Class:* Indo-European, Indo-Iranian, Indo-Aryan, Southern zone, Unclassified. *Dialects:* None known. Lexical similarity: 90% with Gowlan [goj]. *Lg Use:* Also use Hindi [hin], Marathi [mar]. *Other:* Bhalay probably an alternate spelling of Balahi (Balai), a Scheduled Caste found in Madhya Pradesh, Maharashtra, Rajasthan, and Uttar Pradesh. Traditional religion. *Map:* 358:297.

Bharia [bha] (Bhar, Bharat, Bhumia, Bhumiya, Paliha). 197,000 (1981 census). Madhya Pradesh, Chhatarpur, Chhindwara, Datia, Jabalpur, Mandla, Panna, Rewa, Sidhi, and Tikamgarh districts; Chhattisgarh, Bilaspur, Durg, and Surguja districts; Uttar Pradesh; West Bengal. *Status:* 6a (Vigorous). *Class:* Dravidian, Unclassified. *Dialects:* None known. They speak a variety of Hindi [hin] (Singh 1993). *Writing:* Devanagari script. *Other:* A Scheduled Tribe. Hindu. *Map:* 354:105.

Bhatola [btl]. 5,050 (2000). Madhya Pradesh. *Status:* 6a (Vigorous). *Class:* Unclassified. *Other:* Bhatola is a subgroup of the Gond Scheduled Tribe in Madhya Pradesh, Maharashtra, and Chhattisgarh. *Maps:* 354:108, 359:108.

Bhatri [bgw] (Basturia, Bhatra, Bhattra, Bhattri, Bhottada, Bhottara). 217,000 (2001 census). Chhattisgarh, Bastar district, Jagdalpur tahsil; Maharashtra; Odisha, Koraput district, Kotpad tahsil. *Status:* 3 (Wider communication). *Class:* Indo-European, Indo-Iranian, Indo-Aryan, Eastern zone, Oriya. *Dialects:* Dialects understand each other at 88% or more. Reportedly similar to Halbi [hlb]. Lexical similarity: 70%–90% between dialects, 58% with Adivasi Oriya [ort]. *Lg Use:* Vigorous. Home, religion. Positive attitudes. Some in Madhya Pradesh use Hindi [hin]. Some in Odisha use Oriya [ory]. Also use Halbi [hlb]. Used as L2 by Duruwa [pci], Halbi [hlb]. *Lg Dev:* Literacy rate in L2: 38% in Chhattisgarh (2001 census). Bible portions. *Writing:* Devanagari script. *Other:* A Scheduled Tribe. Hindu, traditional religion. *Map:* 359:346.

Bhattiyali [bht] (Bhateali, Bhatiali Pahari, Bhatiyali). 102,000 (1991 census). Himachal Pradesh, Chamba district, Bhattiyat tahsil, Sihunta sub-tahsil. *Status:* 6a (Vigorous). *Class:* Indo-European, Indo-Iranian, Indo-Aryan, Northern zone, Western Pahari. *Type:* SOV. *Lg Use:* All ages. Also use Eastern Panjabi [pan], Hindi [hin], Urdu [urd]. *Lg Dev:* Literacy rate in L1: Below 1%. *Other:* Hindu, Buddhist, Christian, Muslim, Sikh. *Map:* 352:14.

Bhilali [bhi] (Bhilala). 681,000 (2001 census). 25,000–50,000 Parya Bhilali. Madhya Pradesh, Khargone (Segaon), Barwani (Rajpur), southern Jhabua and southern Dhar districts; Maharashtra, Dhule district; some in Gujarat; Karnataka; Rajasthan. *Status:* 6a (Vigorous). *Class:* Indo-European, Indo-Iranian, Indo-Aryan, Central zone, Bhil. *Dialect:* Parya Bhilali. *Other:* A Scheduled Tribe. Traditional religion. *Maps:* 353:78, 358:78.

Bhili [bhb] (Bhagoria, Bhil, Bhilbari, Bhilboli, Bhilla, Bhilodi, Lengotia, Vil). 3,310,000 (2001 census). Madhya Pradesh, Jhabua, Dhar, Ratlam, Indore, and Khargone districts; Gujarat, Sabarkantha, Panchmahals, and Dahod districts. *Status:* 5 (Developing). *Class:* Indo-European, Indo-Iranian, Indo-Aryan, Central zone, Bhil. *Dialects:* Ahiri, Anarya (Pahadi), Bhilodi, Bhim, Charani, Habura, Konkani, Kotali (Kotvali, Kotwalia), Labani, Magra Ki Boli, Nahari (Baglani), Naikdi, Panchali, Patelia, Ranawat, Rani Bhil, Siyalgir, Valvi. Bhili of Ratlam District in Madhya Pradesh is inherently intelligible with Wagdi [wbr] and a connecting link between Gujarati [guj] and Rajasthani (Marwari) [mve]. *Lg Use:* Spoken as L1 by the Patelia in Madhya Pradesh. Also use Hindi [hin]. *Lg Dev:* Literacy rate in L1: 1%–5%. Literacy rate in L2: 10%. Radio programs. TV. Videos. Dictionary. Grammar. NT: 1930. *Writing:* Devanagari script. Gujarati script. *Other:* 'Bhil' is an ethnic designation (caste or tribe). Bhili is a Scheduled Tribe in Rajasthan, Gujarat, Maharashtra, Madhya Pradesh, and Tripura; Kotwalia is a Scheduled Tribe in Gujarat and Maharashtra. Dewali (Dehawali) is a cover term for Vasavi and Kotali, among others. Traditional religion. *Maps:* 353:76, 358:76.

Bhojpuri [bho] (Bajpuri, Bhojapuri, Bhozpuri, Bihari, Deswali, Khotla, Piscimas). 37,800,000 in India (2001 census). Population total all countries: 39,716,000. Uttar Pradesh, Gorakhpur, Basti, Deoria, Azamgarh, Ghazipur, Varanasi, Mirzapur, and Ballia districts; Bihar, Champaran, Saran, and Shahabad districts; Jharkhand, Palamau and Ranchi districts; Assam; Delhi; Madhya Pradesh; West Bengal. Also in Mauritius, Nepal. *Status:* 4 (Educational). *Class:* Indo-European, Indo-Iranian, Indo-Aryan, Eastern zone, Bihari. *Dialects:* Bhojpuri Tharu, Domra, Madhesi, Musahari, Northern Standard Bhojpuri (Basti, Gorakhpuri, Sarawaria), Southern Standard Bhojpuri (Kharwari), Western Standard Bhojpuri (Benarsi, Purbi). May be more than 1 language. Extent of dialect variation in India and Nepal not yet determined. The cover term "Bihari" (a pejorative alternate name for Bhojpuri) is also used for Maithili [mai], and Magahi [mag]. Bhojpuri Tharu dialect is spoken by Tharu caste in Nepal and India. Distinct from other Tharu languages. *Type:* SOV; postpositions; final noun head; 2 noun classes or genders; content q-word in situ; 1 prefix, up to 5 suffixes; clause constituents indicated by both case-marking and word order; verbal affixation marks person, number and genders of subject and object; no ergativity; both tense and aspect; nontonal; 34 consonant and 6 vowel phonemes, about 4 diphthongs. *Lg Use:* Used as L2 by Maithili [mai]. *Lg Dev:* Literacy rate in L1: 5%–30%. Literacy rate in L2: 50%–75%. Poetry. Magazines. Newspapers. New media. Radio programs. Films. TV. Videos. Dictionary. Grammar. NT: 1999–2006. *Writing:* Devanagari script. Kaithi script. *Other:* Hindu, Muslim. *Maps:* 354:93, 355:93.

Bhunjia [bhu] (Bhumjiya, Bhunjiya, Bunjia). 6,790 (2000 USCWM). Madhya Pradesh, Hoshangabad district; Chhattisgarh, Raipur district; Odisha, Kalahandi, Koraput, Dhenkanal, Balasore (Baleshwar), and Keonjhar Sambalpur districts, Sunabera Plateau area; Maharashtra. *Status:* 6a (Vigorous). *Class:* Indo-European, Indo-Iranian, Indo-Aryan, Eastern zone, Oriya. *Dialects:* A more divergent dialect of Halbi [hlb]. Lexical similarity: 68%–72% with Kamar [keq]. *Lg Use:* Also use Chhattisgarhi [hne], Hindi [hin]. *Lg Dev:* Literacy rate in L2: 24% in Odisha (2001 census). *Writing:* Devanagari script. *Other:* A Scheduled Tribe. Hindu. *Map:* 359:331.

Biete [biu] (Baite, Bete, Biate). 19,000 (IMA 1997). Northeast Mizoram, Aizawl district, Darlawn, Ratu, and New Vervek villages; Assam, Cachar Hills; Manipur; Meghalaya, Jaintia hills district. *Status:* 5 (Developing). *Class:* Sino-Tibetan, Tibeto-Burman, Sal, Kuki-Chin-Naga, Kuki-Chin, Northern. *Dialects:* None known. Reportedly similar to Hrangkhol [hra], and similar enough to Mizo [lus] and Hmar [hmr] that they can be read with comprehension. *Lg Use:* Home, village, church. Also use Hindi [hin] in Assam. Khasi [kha] in Meghalaya. War Jaintia [aml] in Meghalaya. Also use Mizo [lus]. Used as L2 by Sakachep [sch]. *Lg Dev:* Literacy rate in L1: 56%. Bible: 2005. *Writing:* Latin script. *Other:* A Scheduled Tribe. An ethnic subgroup of the Mizo. Not the same as the Biate dialect of Chin Thado [tcz] (Breton 1997). Christian (Protestant). *Map:* 356:214.

Bijori [bix] (Binjhia, Birijia, Birjia, Brijia, Burja). 25,000 (1998 Gospel Recordings Network). Jharkhand, Cowerdaga, and Ranchi districts; West Bengal, Darjeeling and Jalpaiguri districts; Madhya Pradesh; Odisha. *Status:* 6a (Vigorous). *Class:* Austro-Asiatic, Munda, North Munda, Kherwari. *Lg Use:* Also use Hindi [hin]. *Lg Dev:* Literacy rate in L2: 10% Hindi. *Other:* A Scheduled Tribe. Ethnic group called Birjia. Hindu, Christian. *Maps:* 354:99, 355:99.

Bilaspuri [kfs] (Bilaspuri Pahari, Kahluri, Kehloori Pahari, Kehluri, Pacchmi). 295,000 (1991 census). Himachal Pradesh, Bilaspur district. *Status:* 6a (Vigorous). *Class:* Indo-European, Indo-Iranian, Indo-Aryan, Northern zone, Western Pahari. *Dialects:* None known. 95% intelligibility of Mandeali [mjl], 94% of Kangri [xnr]. Lexical similarity: 90% with Kangri of Palampur, 86% with Mandeali, 84% with Chambeali [cdh]. *Type:* SOV. *Lg Use:* Home, community, agriculture, religion. All ages. Hindi [hin] is used for instruction in school and politics. Middle-aged and older women have limited comprehension of Hindi [hin]. Urdu [urd] is also spoken by middle- aged and older educated people. Also use Eastern Panjabi [pan]. *Lg Dev:* Radio programs. *Other:* 'Kahluri' is based on the old name for the princely state. Hindu. *Map:* 352:43.

Birhor [biy] (Bihor, Birhar, Birhore, Birhul, Mankidi, Mankidia, Mankiria). 2,000 (Van Driem 2007). Nomadic habits make assessment difficult. Some estimates as low as 1,000 (Parkin 1991). Jharkhand, southern Hazaribag, southern Palamau, Singhbhum, and Ranchi districts; Chhattisgarh, Raigarh District; Odisha, Sundargarh, Kalahandi, Keonjhar, Mayurbhanj, and Sambalpur districts; West Bengal, Puruliya District; Maharashtra. *Status:* 6a (Vigorous). *Class:* Austro-Asiatic, Munda, North Munda, Kherwari, Mundari. *Dialects:* None known. Lexical similarity: 55%–72% with Santhali [sat], Ho [hoc], Mundari [unr], and Munda [unx]. *Lg Use:* Vigorous. No indication of language shift. Most domains. Positive attitudes. Also use Hindi [hin], Ho [hoc], Munda [unx], Mundari [unr], Oriya [ory], Sadri [sck], Santhali [sat]. *Lg Dev:* Literacy rate in L1: Below 1%. Literacy rate in L2: 10% Hindi. *Writing:* Devanagari script. *Other:* A Scheduled Tribe. Traditionally nomadic. Hindu, traditional religion. *Map:* 355:136.

Bishnupriya [bpy] (Bishnupria Manipuri, Bishnupuriya, Bisna Puriya). 77,500 in India (2001 census). Population total all countries: 117,500. Assam, Cachar, Hailakandi, and Karimganj districts; north Tripura. Also in Bangladesh. *Status:* 4 (Educational). *Class:* Indo-European, Indo-Iranian, Indo-Aryan, Eastern zone, Bengali-Assamese. *Dialects:* Madai Gang (Leimanai), Rajar Gang (Ningthaunai). Though once regarded as a Bengali-Meitei creole, it retains pre-Bengali features (Masica 1991). Lexical similarity: 81%–85% between dialects in Bangladesh, 41%–45% with Bengali [ben]. *Type:* SOV; postpositions, articles before noun heads, question word before the verb, affixes indicate case of noun phrase; CV, CVC, CVV, CCV, VC, VCV; nontonal. *Lg Use:* Also use Bengali [ben]. *Lg Dev:* Literacy rate in L2: 80%. Taught in primary schools, in Tripura. Poetry. Radio programs. Videos. Dictionary. Bible portions: 1995. *Writing:* Bengali script. *Other:* Reported to also live in three villages in

Myanmar but these villages cannot be identified. Hindu. *Map:* 357:253.

Bodo [brx] (Bara, Bodi, Boro, Boroni, Kachari, Mech, Meche, Mechi, Meci). 1,330,000 in India (2001 census). Population total all countries: 1,334,380. Assam, mainly in Darrang, Nagaon, and Kamrup, Goalpara, Sibsagar, and Lakhimpur districts; West Bengal, Darjeeling, Jalpaiguri, and Cooch-Behar districts; Manipur, Chandel (Tengnoupal) District; Meghalaya, West Garo Hills district, Tikrikilla block, 7 villages, East Khasi Hills district. Also in Nepal (Meche). *Status:* 5 (Developing). Statutory language of provincial identity in Assam (1950, Constitution, Articles 345–347). *Class:* Sino-Tibetan, Tibeto-Burman, Sal, Bodo-Garo-Northern Naga, Bodo-Koch, Bodo-Garo, Bodo. *Dialects:* Chote, Mech. West Bengal dialect reportedly different from Assam. *Lg Use:* Vigorous Bodo language and culture. Assamese [asm] is L1 for most Bodo Mech dialect speakers in Assam (Breton 1997:24). Used as L2 by Koch [kdq]. *Lg Dev:* Literacy rate in L2: 61% Assam (2001 census). Magazines. Radio programs. Dictionary. Grammar. Bible: 1981. *Writing:* Bengali script. Devanagari script. Latin script. *Other:* Traditional religion, Christian. *Map:* 351.

Bodo Parja [bdv] (Bodo Paraja, Harja, Jhaliya, Jharia, Jhodia Parja, Parajhi, Parja, Parjhi, Parji, Paroja, Poroja, Sodia Parja). 50,000 (2001 Indian Bible Translators). Odisha, Koraput district. *Status:* 5 (Developing). *Class:* Indo-European, Indo-Iranian, Indo-Aryan, Eastern zone, Oriya. *Dialects:* None known. Phonology and grammar show Indo-European relationship, not related to Dravidian Duruwa Parji. 86%–96% intelligibility between Bodo and Jhodia caste varieties. Lexical similarity: 76%–86% with Bodo and Jhodia caste varieties, 70%–89% with Desia. *Lg Use:* Most have low proficiency in Adivasi Oriya [ort], which is used in the market. *Lg Dev:* Literacy rate in L2: 15% (2001 census). Bible portions. *Writing:* Oriya script. *Other:* Paroja is a Scheduled Tribe; the name comes from Sanskrit [san] subjects. It is used for a variety of ethnic groups from different language families. Hindu, Christian, traditional religion. *Map:* 359:351.

Bondo [bfw] (Bhonda Bhasha, Bonda, Bondo-Poraja, Nanqa Poroja, Poraja Katha, Remo, Remosum). 9,000 (2002 SIL). 5,570 Upper Bondo and 3,500 Lower Bondo. Few Lower Bondo are monolingual. Odisha, Malkangiri district, Khoirput block, Bondo Hills. *Status:* 6a (Vigorous). *Class:* Austro-Asiatic, Munda, South Munda, Koraput Munda, Gutob-Remo-Geta', Gutob-Remo. *Dialects:* Lower Bondo, Upper Bondo. Bhuksa dialect sometimes mentioned as a dialect of Kanauji [bjj]. Lexical similarity: 70%–94% with other Bondo varieties, 45%–51% with Gutob Gadaba [gbj], 22%–32% with Upper Gata' [gaq] (Didayi). *Lg Use:* Positive attitudes. Many use Adivasi Oriya [ort] for trade and interactions with surrounding communities. Few Upper Bondo are bilingual. *Lg Dev:* Literacy rate in L2: 12% (2001 census). Dictionary. *Writing:* Oriya script. *Other:* A Scheduled Tribe. Traditional religion, Hindu. *Map:* 359:348.

Braj Bhasha [bra] (Antarbedi, Antarvedi, Bijbhasha, Braj, Braj Bhakha, Bri, Brij Bhasha, Briju, Bruj). 574,000 (2001 census). Uttar Pradesh, Agra region; Rajasthan, Bharatpur, and Sawai Madhopur districts; Haryana, Gurgaon district; Bihar; Madhya Pradesh; Delhi. *Status:* 5 (Developing). *Class:* Indo-European, Indo-Iranian, Indo-Aryan, Central zone, Western Hindi, Unclassified. *Dialects:* Antarbedi, Bhuksa, Braj Bhasha, Dangi, Jadobafi, Sikarwari. Bhuksa is sometimes mentioned as a dialect of Kanauji [bjj]. Braj Bhasha is usually considered a dialect of Hindi [hin], and was the predominant literary language before the switch to Hindi in the 19th century. *Lg Dev:* Radio programs. NT: 1824–1999. *Writing:* Devanagari script. *Other:* Hindu, Muslim. *Map:* 354:84.

Brokskat [bkk] (Brokpa, Brokpa of Dah-Hanu, Dokskat, Kyango). 10,000 (Johnstone and Mandryk 2001). Jammu and Kashmir, Ladakh and Kargil districts along Indus river; northern Kashmir, Garkhon area, including Darchiks, Chulichan, Gurgurdo, Batalik, and Dah villages. *Status:* 6a (Vigorous). *Class:* Indo-European, Indo-Iranian, Indo-Aryan, Northwestern zone, Dardic, Shina. *Lg Use:* Also use Ladakhi [lbj]. *Lg Dev:* Literacy rate in L1: Below 1%. Literacy rate in L2: 56% (2001 census). Dictionary. Grammar. *Writing:* Balti script. *Other:* Broq-pa is a Scheduled Tribe. A very divergent variety of Shina [scl]. Minaro is an alternate ethnic name. Ethnonym: Brokpa by Ladakhi. Glossonym: Brokskat, and is the oldest surviving member of the ancient Dardic language. Buddhist, Muslim, traditional religion. *Map:* 352:10.

Bugun [bgg] (Kho, Khoa, Khowa). 900 (2001 Asia Harvest). Arunachal Pradesh, West Kameng district, Singchung and Nafra circles, Wangho, Singchung, New Kaspi, Namphri, Mangopom, Diching, Sachita, Ramu, Situ, Lichini, Dikiang, and Bichom villages on the mountains on both sides of Rupa River, interspersed among the Aka. *Status:* 6a (Vigorous). *Class:* Sino-Tibetan, Tibeto-Burman, Central Tibeto-Burman, Kho-Bwa. *Dialects:* None known. May be mutually intelligible with Puroik [suv] (Chowdhury 1996); Burling (2003) groups it with Puroik and Sherdukpen [sdp] and possibly also with Lish [lsh] and Sartang [onp]. Lexical similarity: low with all neighboring languages. *Lg Use:* Home, village, religion. Also use Hindi [hin], younger people use more Hindi. Also use Sherdukpen [sdp]. Older people use more Sherdukpen. Also use Hruso [hru], Kalaktang Monpa [kkf], Nefamese [nef]. *Lg Dev:* Literacy rate in L2: 24% (1981 census), 35% for men, 12% for women. *Writing:* Latin script. *Other:* Spoken by the Khoa (Khowa) ethnic group. They are culturally like the Hruso, but speak a different language. Traditional religion, Buddhist. *Map:* 356:177.

Buksa [tkb]. 43,000 (IMA 1997). Uttarakhand, southwestern Nainital district, from Ramnagar to Keneshpur. 130 villages in Kichha and Kashipur tahsils, some in Bijnor and Garhwal districts. *Status:* 6a (Vigorous). *Class:* Indo-European, Indo-Iranian, Indo-Aryan, Eastern zone, Unclassified. *Dialects:* None known. 95% intelligibility with Rana Tharu [thr]. Lexical similarity: 58%–79% with western Tharu varieties, 58% with Chitwania Tharu [the], 83% with Hindi [hin]. *Writing:* Devanagari script. *Other:* Traditional religion. *Map:* 352:54.

Bundeli [bns] (Bondili, Bundelkhandi). 3,070,000 (2001 census). Population estimates range up to 20,000,000. Uttar Pradesh, Jalaun, Jhansi, Lalitpur, Hamirpur, and Banda districts; Madhya Pradesh, Balaghat, Chhindwara, Hoshangabad, Sagar, Sehore, Panna, Satna, Chhatarpur, Tikamgarh, Shivpuri, Guna, Bhind, Morena, Gwalior, Narsinghpur, Seoni, Datia districts; Maharashtra, Bhandara, and Nagpur districts; Rajasthan; Gujarat; Andhra Pradesh. *Status:* 5 (Developing). *Class:* Indo-European, Indo-Iranian, Indo-Aryan, Central zone, Western Hindi, Bundeli. *Dialects:* Banaphari, Bhadauri (Towargarhi), Chhindwara Bundeli, Gaoli, Khatola, Kirari, Kundri, Lodhanti (Rathora), Nagpuri Hindi, Nibhatta, Raghobansi, Standard Bundeli, Tirhari. Chhatapur dialect is widely understood. Other dialects are standard Braj of Mathura, Aligarh, western Agra; standard Braj of Bulandshahr; standard Braj of eastern Agra, southern Morena, southern Bharatpur; Braj merging into Kanauji in Etah, Mainpuri, Budaun, and Bareilly; Braj merging into the Bhadauri subdialect in northern Morena; Braj merging into Jaipuri (Rajasthani) in northern Bharatpur and Sawai

Uradhopur; Bhuksa in southern Nainital (Grierson and Konow 1901–1929). Lexical similarity: 41% with Nagpuri Hindi [hin]. *Lg Use:* Home. Positive attitudes toward Chhatapur dialect. Uneducated have low proficiency in Hindi [hin]. *Lg Dev:* Radio programs. Bible portions. *Writing:* Devanagari script. *Other:* Hindu, Buddhist. *Map:* 354:86.

Byangsi [bee] (Bhotia, Byangkho Lwo, Byangkhopa, Byanshi, Byansi, Jaba, Rang, Saukas, Shaukas). 2,830 in India (2000). Population total all countries: 3,310. 0 monolinguals. Uttarakhand, Pithoragarh district, Darchula and Munsyari tahsils, Kuthi Yangti river valley in the Himalayas on Tibet and Nepal borders. Byangs Patti from Budi south to Kuti village in the north; includes Nabi, Gunji, Napalchyu, Rongkang, and Garbyang villages. Also in Nepal. *Status:* 6b (Threatened). *Class:* Sino-Tibetan, Tibeto-Burman, Western Tibeto-Burman, Bodish, West Himalayish, Almora. *Dialects:* Kuti, Pangjungkho Boli, Yerjungkhu Boli. Dialects of Byangs, Chaudangs and Darma valleys are unintelligible to each other (Sharma 1994). Those in Kuti (India) and Tinkar (Nepal) are closely related and quite different from those in other Byangsi villages. Tinkar variety differs from Byangsi, Chaudangsi [cdn], and Darmiya [drd] in forms of agreement affixes and basic vocabulary. Minor dialect differences correspond to geographical divisions (Sharma 2001). *Lg Use:* Home, community. High level of bilingualism in Hindi [hin]. Hindi is education medium. Also use Central Tibetan [bod], Kumaoni [kfy], Nepali [npi]. *Lg Dev:* Dictionary. Grammar. *Writing:* Devanagari script, recently developed. *Other:* Cultural center seems to be India. Ranglo or Rang often used as a cover term for Byangs, Chaudangs, Darmiya and Rongpo. Some borrowing from Indo-Aryan. Hindu. *Map:* 352:58.

Chakma [ccp] (Chakama, Takam, Tsakma). 176,000 in India (2001 census). Other estimates less than 100,000 (2002). Mizoram, southwest along Karnafuli river; Tripura, North Tripura district, Kailashahar subdivision; South Tripura district; Assam, Karbi, Anglong, North Cachar, and Cachar districts; Arunachal Pradesh, Tirap district, Changlang district, Miao subdivision; Lohit district, Chowkham circle; West Bengal; Manipur. *Status:* 5 (Developing). *Lg Use:* Also use Bengali [ben], Mizo [lus]. *Lg Dev:* Taught in primary schools, in Tripura and Mizoram. *Other:* A Scheduled Tribe. Distinct from Chak [ckh]. Buddhist, traditional religion. See main entry on page 54. *Map:* 357:260.

Chamari [cdg] (Chamar, Chambhar Boli, Chambhari). 406,000 (2001 IMB). Madhya Pradesh; Uttar Pradesh, Lucknow; Maharashtra. *Status:* 6a (Vigorous). *Class:* Indo-European, Indo-Iranian, Indo-Aryan, Central zone, Western Hindi, Unclassified. *Lg Dev:* Literacy rate in L1: Below 1%. *Other:* Chamar is a caste name for skin and hide workers. Speakers throughout India (Singh 1995). Traditional religion. *Map:* 359:328.

Chambeali [cdh] (Cameali, Chamaya, Chambiali, Chambiyali, Chamiyali Pahari, Chamya). 130,000 (1991 census). Himachal Pradesh, Chamba district, Chamba tahsil; Jammu and Kashmir. *Status:* 6a (Vigorous). *Class:* Indo-European, Indo-Iranian, Indo-Aryan, Northern zone, Western Pahari. *Dialects:* Bansbali, Bansyari, Gadi Chameali. 91% intelligibility of Mandeali [mjl], 87% of Kangri [xnr]. Lexical similarity: 90% with Palampuri Kangri [xnr], 86% with Bhattiyali [bht], 84% with Bilaspuri [kfs], 83% with Mandeali [mjl], 79% with Gaddi [gbk], 78% with Churahi [cdj]. *Type:* SOV. *Lg Use:* All ages. Also use Eastern Panjabi [pan], Hindi [hin], Urdu [urd]. *Lg Dev:* Radio programs. Bible portions: 1883–1979. *Writing:* Devanagari script. Takri (Tankri, Takari) script, no longer in use. *Other:* Hindu. *Map:* 352:15.

Chamling [rab]. Sikkim, Darjeeling, Regu and other parts of the state. *Status:* 6b (Threatened). See main entry on page 245. *Map:* 355:161.

Changthang [cna] (Byangskat, Byanskat, Changs-Skat, Changtang, Changtang Ladakhi, Rong, Rupshu, Stotpa, Upper Ladakhi). 10,100 (2000). Jammu and Kashmir, Tibet border area, Changthang region east and southeast of Leh. *Status:* 6a (Vigorous). *Class:* Sino-Tibetan, Tibeto-Burman, Western Tibeto-Burman, Bodish, Central Bodish, Western. *Dialects:* 58%–85% intelligibility with Leh dialect of Ladakhi [lbj] with high standard deviation indicating some acquired intelligibility; 94%–95% intelligibility with Stod Bhoti [sbu] from Darcha village. Identify more with Leh Ladakhi culture than with Stod Bhoti despite lack of intelligibility. Related to Rangkas [rgk], Darmiya [drd], Byangsi [bee]. *Lg Use:* Also use English [eng], Hindi [hin], Kashmiri [kas], Ladakhi [lbj], Urdu [urd]. *Lg Dev:* Literacy rate in L2: 37% (2001 census). *Writing:* Tibetan script, Bodhi style. *Other:* Champa is a Scheduled Tribe. Ethnonym: Champas. Buddhist. *Map:* 352:31.

Chaudangsi [cdn] (Bangba Lo, Bangbani, Chanpa Lo, Chaudans Lo, Saukas, Shaukas, Tsaudangsi). 1,830 (2000 USCWM). 0 monolinguals. Uttarakhand, Pithoragarh district, Darchula and Munsyari tahsils, Chaudangs Patti, Kali river west bank facing the Nepal border along Mahakali valley. Villages include Panggu, Rongto, Rimzhim, Waiku, Monggong, Chilla, Song, Sosa, Sirdang, Sirkha, Rung, Zipti, Gala, Tangkul, and Syang Khola. *Status:* 6b (Threatened). *Class:* Sino-Tibetan, Tibeto-Burman, Western Tibeto-Burman, Bodish, West Himalayish, Almora. *Dialects:* None known. Related to Rangkas [rgk], Darmiya [drd], and Byangsi [bee] (Sharma 1989), unintelligible with Darmiya and Byangsi (Sharma 1994). *Lg Use:* Home, community. Negative attitudes. Also use Central Tibetan [bod], Hindi [hin], Kumaoni [kfy], Nepali [npi]. *Lg Dev:* Literacy rate in L1: Below 1%. Hindi used for written communication. *Writing:* Unwritten. *Other:* Ranglo or Rang often used as a cover term for Byangs, Chaudangs, Darmiya, and Rongpo. Hindu, traditional religion. *Map:* 352:60.

Chaura [crv] (Chowra, Tutet). 5,910 (2001 census). Nicobar Islands, Chaura island. *Status:* 6a (Vigorous). *Class:* Austro-Asiatic, Mon-Khmer, Nicobar, Chowra-Teressa. *Other:* Traditional religion. *Map:* 361.

Chenchu [cde] (Chenchucoolam, Chenchwar, Chensulu, Chenswar, Choncharu). 26,000 (2007). Andhra Pradesh, most in Kurnool district, Nallamalla hills; Karnataka; Odisha. *Status:* 6a (Vigorous). *Class:* Dravidian, South-Central, Telugu. *Lg Use:* Also use Telugu [tel]. *Lg Dev:* Literacy rate in L2: 43% among Scheduled Tribes in Kurnool District; 43% among Chenchu in Odisha (2001 census). *Writing:* Telugu script. *Other:* A Scheduled Tribe. Hindu. *Map:* 358:326.

Chetti, Wayanad [ctt] (Chetti, Chetty). 5,000 (2004). Kerala, Wayanad district, Chekadi, Appapara, Panavalli, Pulpalli, Thirunelli, Tholpetti and Kattikkulam villages; Tamil Nadu, Coimbatore, Nilgiri and Periyar districts; Karnataka, Bavali. *Status:* 6a (Vigorous). *Class:* Dravidian, Southern, Tamil-Kannada, Unclassified. *Dialects:* None known. Lexical similarity: 62%–76% with Gowder, 65% with Jennu Kurumba [xuj], 52% with Kannada [kan]. *Other:* 'Chetti', trader, also loosely employed as a caste name (Thurston and Rangachari 1909). 10 groups of Chetti identified in Tamil Nadu. *Map:* 360:383.

Chhattisgarhi [hne] (Khaltahi, Laria). 13,300,000 (2001 census). Chhattisgarh; Bihar; Odisha; possibly in Maharashtra, Uttar Pradesh, and Tripura. Baigani dialect in Madhya Pradesh, Shahdol District. *Status:* 4 (Educational). *Class:* Indo-European, Indo-Iranian, Indo-Aryan, East Central zone. *Dialects:* Baigani (Baiga, Bega, Bhumia, Gowro), Bhulia, Binjhwari, Chhattisgarhi Proper, Kalanga, Kavardi, Khairagarhi, Sadri Korwa. Sadri Korwa spoken by Korwa people in Jashpur tahsil of Raigarh District; Baigani in Balaghat, Raipur, and Bilaspur districts of Chhattisgarh, and Sambalpur District of Odisha; Binjhwari in Raipur and Raigarh districts of Chhattisgarh; Kalanga and Bhulia dialects are spoken in Patna District of Bihar; Chhattisgarhi Proper in Raipur, Durg, Bilaspur, and other districts of Chhattisgarh. Lexical similarity: 66%–69% with Kamar [keq]. *Lg Use:* Nearly all domains. Positive attitudes. Low proficiency in Hindi [hin]. Also use Oriya [ory]. Used as L2 by Bhunjia [bhu], Eastern Muria [emu], Far Western Muria [fmu]. *Lg Dev:* Poetry. Newspapers. Radio programs. TV. NT: 2005. *Writing:* Devanagari script. *Other:* Traditional religion, Hindu, Muslim. *Maps:* 354:110, 355:110, 359:110.

Chin, Bawm [bgr] (Bawm, Bawn, Bawng, Bom). 4,440 in India (2004). Population total all countries: 15,940. Mizoram, Chhimtuipui, Lunglei, and Aizawl districts; Tripura; Assam. Also in Bangladesh, Myanmar. *Status:* 6b (Threatened). *Class:* Sino-Tibetan, Tibeto-Burman, Sal, Kuki-Chin-Naga, Kuki-Chin, Central. *Dialects:* None known. Linguistically and ethnically a subgroup of the Laizou (Anal) [anm] (Matisoff et al. 1996:8). *Type:* SOV. *Lg Use:* Shifting to Assamese [asm] (2007). Also use Mizo [lus]. Used as L2 by Pankhu [pkh]. *Lg Dev:* Radio programs. Bible: 1989. *Writing:* Latin script. *Other:* A Scheduled Tribe. Christian. *Map:* 357:283.

Chin, Falam [cfm] (Fallam, Halam Chin, Hallam, Tipura). 38,300 in India (2001 census). Assam, Karimganj district, south, a few villages in Cachar and North Hills districts; Tripura; Mizoram; West Bengal. *Status:* 5 (Developing). *Dialects:* Chari Chong, Chorei, Halam, Kaipang, Kalai (Koloi), Mursum (Molsom), Rupini, Tapong. *Lg Dev:* Literacy among Kaipeng in Tripura is low. *Other:* Ethnically Halam. A Scheduled Tribe. Many ethnic Halam speak Kok Borok [trp] as L1. Halam is a generic term under which 9 subgroups, each with a distinct dialect, are grouped together: (Sakachep [sch], Chorei, Rupini, Ranglong [rnl], Marcephang (Khochung–dialect of [cfm]), Molsom, Keipang (dialect of [cfm]), Bondcher (dialect of [cfm]), Rangkhol [hra]). Hindu, Christian, traditional religion. See main entry on page 231. *Map:* 357:255.

Chin, Haka [cnh] (Baungshe, "Haka" *pej.*, Lai, Lai Hawlh, Lai Pawi). 25,000 in India (2001 census). Mizoram, Chhimtuipui district, 41 villages, and Aizawi district, Champhai subdivision, southernmost tip; Assam; Meghalaya. *Status:* 4 (Educational). *Dialects:* Klangklang (Thlantlang), Zokhua. *Lg Use:* Used as L2 by Matu Chin [hlt], Zyphe Chin [zyp]. *Lg Dev:* Literacy rate in L2: 54% (1981 census). Most young people can read in Haka. Taught in primary schools. *Other:* Lai Pawi is a Scheduled Tribe. Ethnic autonym in India: Lai. Christian. See main entry on page 231. *Map:* 357:282.

Chin, Khumi [cnk] (Kami, Khami, Khumi, Khuni, Khweymi, Kumi). Mizoram. *Status:* 5 (Developing). *Dialects:* Khami, Khimi. *Other:* Called Khami Chin in India. Traditional religion, Christian. See main entry on page 231. *Map:* 357:285.

Chin, Mara [mrh] (Lakher, Mara, Maram, Mira, Zao). 34,800 in India (2001 census). Population total all countries: 54,800. Mizoram, Chhimtuipui district. 60 villages. Also in Myanmar. *Status:* 4 (Educational). *Class:* Sino-Tibetan, Tibeto-Burman, Sal, Kuki-Chin-Naga, Kuki-Chin, Maraic. *Dialects:* Hlawthai, Tlongsai (Tlosai-Siaha). Reportedly similar to Shendu [shl]. Affiliated with Lai (Haka Chin) [cnh]. Tlosai-Siaha dialect is lingua franca of all Mara (Singh 1994, 1995). *Type:* SOV. *Lg Use:* Also use English [eng], Mizo [lus]. Used as L2 by Zyphe Chin [zyp]. *Lg Dev:* Taught in primary schools since 1978. Bible: 1956–2002. *Writing:* Latin script. *Other:* A Scheduled Tribe. Subgroup of Mizo (Lushai). Christian. *Map:* 357:284.

Chin, Matu [hlt] (Matupi, Nga La). 10,000 in India (2012). Mizoram. *Status:* 5 (Developing). *Dialects:* Haltu, Thui Phum. *Lg Use:* 8,000 also use Haka Chin [cnh]. *Lg Dev:* Literacy rate in L2: 70%. *Other:* Christian. See main entry on page 232. *Map:* 357:279.

Chin, Paite [pck] (Haithe, Paite, Paithe, Parte, Zoukam). 64,100 (2001 census). Manipur, Churachandpur district, Khuga valley, Copur Bazar; Mizoram, Aizawl district, Champhai subdivision, 20 villages; Tripura; Assam. *Status:* 4 (Educational). *Class:* Sino-Tibetan, Tibeto-Burman, Sal, Kuki-Chin-Naga, Kuki-Chin, Northern. *Dialects:* Bukpi (Bukpui), Dapzal (Dapzar), Dim, Dimpi, Lamzang, Lousau, Saizang, Sihzang, Telzang (Teizang), Tuichiap. *Type:* SOV. *Lg Use:* Also use Mizo [lus]. *Lg Dev:* Literacy rate in L1: 75% (2005 BI). Literacy rate in L2: 79% (2001 census). Taught in primary schools. Dictionary. Grammar. Bible: 1971–2005. *Writing:* Latin script. *Other:* A Scheduled Tribe. Paites in Mizoram speak Mizo (Go 1996). Most speak Teizang and Dapzal dialects (Singh 1995). Zomi is a collective ethnic autonym generally used by Tedim Chin of Myanmar, Paite, and Vaiphei of Manipur. Christian. *Map:* 357:264.

Chin, Tedim [ctd] (Tedim, Tiddim). 155,000 in India (1990). Mizoram (north), Manipur (south). *Status:* 5 (Developing). *Dialects:* Kamhau (Kamhao, Kamhow), Sokte. *Other:* Christian, traditional religion. See main entry on page 233. *Map:* 357:278.

Chin, Thado [tcz] (Kuki, Kuki-Thado, Thaadou Kuki, Thado-Pao, Thadou, Thado-Ubiphei). 243,000 in India (2001 census). Population total all countries: 269,200. Manipur, Chandel, Churachandpur, Senapati, and Tamenglong districts; Assam; Mizoram, northeast; Nagaland, Kohima district; Tripura. Also in Myanmar. *Status:* 4 (Educational). *Class:* Sino-Tibetan, Tibeto-Burman, Sal, Kuki-Chin-Naga, Kuki-Chin, Northern. *Dialects:* Changsen, Hawkip, Jangshen, Kaokeep, Khongzai, Kipgen, Langiung, Sairang, Shithlou, Singson (Shingsol), Thangngen. Several varieties, but high mutual intelligibility among dialects. Related to Kamhau (Tedim Chin [ctd] dialect), Ralte [ral], Paite Chin [pck], Zou [zom]. *Type:* SOV. *Lg Use:* Also use Meitei [mni], Nepali [npi]. Used as L2 by Sakachep [sch]. *Lg Dev:* Literacy rate in L2: 57% in Manipur (2001 census). Literacy lower among older people and in villages. Taught in schools in Manipur. Magazines. Radio programs. Dictionary. Grammar. Bible: 1971–1994. *Writing:* Latin script. *Other:* A Scheduled Tribe. Some listed dialects are separate languages. Christian. *Map:* 357:267.

Chin, Zyphe [zyp] (Vawngtu, Zophei, Zoptei, Zyphe). 3,000 in India (2000). Mizoram, Saiha district, Siata and Iana villages. *Status:* 5 (Developing). *Dialects:* Lower Zyphe, Upper Zyphe. *Lg Use:* Also use Haka Chin [cnh], Mara Chin [mrh]. See main entry on page 233. *Map:* 357:281.

Chinali [cih] (Chana, Channali, Chinal, Dagi, Harijan, Shipi). 750 (1996). Himachal Pradesh, Lahul valley, Pattan valley, and Gushal village. *Status:* 6a (Vigorous). *Class:* Indo-European, Indo-Iranian, Indo-Aryan, Unclassified. *Dialects:* None known. Closely related to Sanskrit [san]. *Writing:* Devanagari script. *Other:* Spoken by the Chinal caste. Many are well educated. Hindu. *Map:* 352:29.

Chiru [cdf] (Chhori). 7,000 (2000 A. Khorong). Manipur, Tamenglong district, Lamdangmei and Dolang villages; Senapati, Kangchup, Thangzing, Sadu, Bungte, Nungshai, Dolang Khunou, and Uram villages; Churachandpur district, Charoi Khullen cillage; Thoubal sistrict, Vaithou;

Bishnupur district; Assam, Cachar district, a village near Jirbom; Nagaland. Scattered. *Status:* 5 (Developing). *Class:* Sino-Tibetan, Tibeto-Burman, Sal, Kuki-Chin-Naga, Kuki-Chin, Northern. *Dialects:* None known. Reportedly most similar to Chin Mizo [lus]. *Lg Use:* Educated youth more interested in developing L1 and preserving culture than elders. Community. All ages. Mixed attitudes. Also use English [eng], Meitei [mni]. *Lg Dev:* Literacy rate in L2: 56% in English and Meitei (2000 A. Khorong). *Writing:* Bengali script. Latin script. *Other:* A Scheduled Tribe. Christian. *Map:* 357:250.

Chodri [cdi] (Chaudhari, Chaudri, Chodhari, Choudhara, Choudhary, Chowdhary). 209,000 (2001 census). More speakers in Tapi district. Gujarat, Surat and Tapi districts. *Status:* 5 (Developing). *Class:* Indo-European, Indo-Iranian, Indo-Aryan, Central zone, Bhil. *Lg Use:* Also use Gujarati [guj]. *Lg Dev:* Literacy rate in L2: 63% in Gujarat (2001 census). Radio programs. NT: 2006. *Writing:* Gujarati script. *Other:* A Scheduled Tribe. Ethnically Bhil. Hindu. *Map:* 358:307.

Chug [cvg] (Chug Monpa, Chugpa, Monpa). 850 (2005). Arunachal Pradesh, West Kameng district, Chug village. *Status:* 6a (Vigorous). *Class:* Sino-Tibetan, Tibeto-Burman, Central Tibeto-Burman, Kho-Bwa. *Dialects:* None known. Reportedly most similar to Lish [lsh]. *Lg Use:* High bilingualism expected in Dirang Monpa (Tshangla [tsj]) due to close proximity but no testing done. Also use Hindi [hin]. *Lg Dev:* Literacy rate in L2: 62% for West Kameng District: males 71%, females 49% (2001 census). *Other:* 'Monpa' (Moinba), man of the lower country, refers to several ethnically related peoples which may not be related linguistically. Buddhist. *Map:* 356:172.

Churahi [cdj] (Chaurahi, Churahi Pahari, Churai Pahari). 111,000 (1991 census). Himachal Pradesh, Chamba district, Chaurah and Saluni tahsils, Bhalai sub-tahsil. *Status:* 6a (Vigorous). *Class:* Indo-European, Indo-Iranian, Indo-Aryan, Northern zone, Western Pahari. *Dialects:* None known. 90% intelligibility of Mandeali [mjl], 83% of Kangri [xnr], 85% of Chambeali [cdh]. Lexical similarity: 78% with Chambeali [cdh] (most similar), 70% with Palampuri Kangri [xnr] and Bhattiyali [bht], 67%–69% with Gaddi [gbk], 65% with Mandeali [mjl] and Bilaspuri [kfs], 64% with Pangi. *Type:* SOV; postpositions; genitives after noun heads; adjectives, numerals before noun heads; question word initial; verb suffixes mark person, number, gender of subject. *Lg Use:* All ages. Also use Eastern Panjabi [pan], Hindi [hin], Urdu [urd]. *Other:* Hindu. *Map:* 352:16.

Darlong [dln] (Dalong). 6,000 (1998 T. Darlong). Tripura, North Tripura district, Kailashahar and Kamalpur sub-divisions; Assam, Cachar district. *Status:* 5 (Developing). *Class:* Sino-Tibetan, Tibeto-Burman, Unclassified. *Lg Dev:* Literacy rate in L1: Below 1%. Literacy rate in L2: 45%. NT: 1995. *Writing:* Latin script, used in India. *Other:* Christian. *Map:* 357:257.

Darmiya [drd] (Darimiya, Darmani, Saukas, Shaukas). 1,750 (2006 C. Willis). Ethnic population: 4,000. Uttarakhand, Pithoragarh district, Darchula and Munsyari tahsils, Dhauli valley, from Tawaghat near Dharchula south to Sipoo in the north along Dhauli river. Dar, Bongling, Selachal, Nanglin, Baling, Dugtu, Saung, Baun, Philam, Datu, Gwo, Marchha, Dhakar, Sobla, and Sipoo villages. *Status:* 6b (Threatened). *Class:* Sino-Tibetan, Tibeto-Burman, Western Tibeto-Burman, Bodish, West Himalayish, Almora. *Dialects:* None known. Related to Rangkas [rgk], Chaudangsi [cdn] and Byangsi [bee]. *Lg Use:* Learn Kumaoni [kfy] and Hindi [hin] simultaneously with their mother tongue. Code switching and code mixing very common. Uncertain whether stable bilingualism will continue or whether Kumaoni or Hindi will replace Darmiya. Home, community. High bilingualism Hindi [hin]. Hindi is medium of education at all levels. Also use Central Tibetan [bod], Kumaoni [kfy], Nepali [npi]. *Lg Dev:* Literacy rate in L1: Below 1%. *Writing:* Unwritten. *Other:* Ranglo or Rang often used for Byangs, Chaudangs, Darmiya, and Rongpo. Hindu, traditional religion. *Map:* 352:57.

Deccan [dcc] (Dakini, Deccani, Desi). 12,800,000 (2000). Central Maharashtra, Deccan Plateau; Karnataka, Belgaum and Bijapur districts; Madhya Pradesh, Raisen and Sehore districts; Gujarat. *Status:* 6a (Vigorous). *Class:* Indo-European, Indo-Iranian, Indo-Aryan, Southern zone, Unclassified. *Dialects:* Bijapuri, Kalvadi (Dharwar). *Other:* May be the same as Dakhini dialect of Urdu [urd]. Muslim (Sunni). *Map:* 358:319.

Degaru [dgu] (Dhekaru). 10,000 (2000). Bihar; West Bengal. *Status:* 6a (Vigorous). *Class:* Indo-European, Indo-Iranian, Indo-Aryan, Eastern zone, Unclassified. *Other:* Traditional religion. *Map:* 355:133.

Deori [der] (Chutiya, Dari, Deuri, Dewri, Drori). 28,000 (2001 census). Ethnic population: 50,000. Assam, Lakhimpur, Demaji, Tinsukia, and Jorhat districts. *Status:* 5 (Developing). *Class:* Sino-Tibetan, Tibeto-Burman, Sal, Bodo-Garo-Northern Naga, Bodo-Koch. *Dialects:* May constitute its own subgroup under Bodo-Garo. Reportedly not similar to other languages. Dialect of Lakhimpur District is regarded as purest. Lexical similarity: 77%–93% with Deori varieties, 11%–16% with Bodo [brx]. *Lg Use:* Vigorous among the Dibongya, the only subgroup that has retained the language. Home, village, religion, work. Positive attitudes. Many also use Assamese [asm], but women, older adults and uneducated have less proficiency. *Lg Dev:* Literacy rate in L2: 71%. Poetry. Radio programs. *Writing:* Bengali script. Latin script. *Other:* A Scheduled Tribe. 'Deori', the temple guard. Deori Chutiya is 1 of 4 Chutiya subgroups. Do not call themselves Chutiya. Traditional religion, Buddhist, Hindu. *Map:* 356:196.

Desiya [dso] (Deshia, Desia, Desiya Oriya, Koraput Oriya). 50,000 (2003 Asha Kiran Society). Odisha, Koraput district, Lamtaput block, Nabarangapur district. *Status:* 3 (Wider communication). *Class:* Indo-European, Indo-Iranian, Indo-Aryan, Eastern zone, Oriya. *Dialects:* Intelligible with Adivasi Oriya [ort] but uses different scripts. Lexical similarity: 80%–85% with Adivasi Oriya [ort] dialects in Andhra Pradesh. *Lg Use:* Used as L2 by Bodo Gadaba [gbj], Gata' [gaq], Mirgan [zrg], Pottangi Ollar Gadaba [gdb]. *Lg Dev:* Literacy rate in L2: 6%. Newspapers. *Writing:* Oriya script. *Other:* Traditional religion, Christian. *Map:* 359:337.

Dhanki [dhn] (Dangi, Dangri, Dangs Bhil, Dhanka, Kakachhu-Ki Boli, Tadavi, Tadvi Bhil). 139,000 (2001 census). Gujarat, Dangs district; Maharashtra, Jalgaon district; Karnataka; Rajasthan. *Status:* 3 (Wider communication). *Class:* Indo-European, Indo-Iranian, Indo-Aryan, Central zone, Khandesi. *Dialects:* None known. Reportedly similar to Khandesi [khn]. *Lg Use:* Also use Gujarati [guj]. *Lg Dev:* Literacy rate in L2: 53% in Gujarat (2001 census). *Other:* Dhankia and Tadvi Bhil are Scheduled Tribes. Dhanka of Rajasthan reportedly speak Hindi as L1; Dhanka of Maharashtra use Gujarati as L1; Tadvi Bhil reportedly use Bhili [bhb] as L1. Ethnonym: Dhanka. Traditional religion. *Map:* 358:306.

Dhatki [mki] (Thar). 16,400 in India (2000). Western Rajasthan. *Status:* 6a (Vigorous). *Other:* A Scheduled Tribe. Muslim, Hindu. See main entry on page 267. *Map:* 353:61.

Dhimal [dhi]. 450 in India (2000 K. Cooper). West Bengal, Naxalbari, Chengadhari, and Hatighisha, 16 villages. *Status:* 6a (Vigorous). *Dialect:* Eastern Dhimal. See main entry on page 246. *Map:* 355:135.

Dhodia [dho] (Dhobi, Dhore, Dhori, Dhowari, Doria). 169,000 (2001 census). Gujarat, Surat and Valsad districts, Daman and Diu, Dadra and Nagar Haveli; Madhya Pradesh; Maharashtra; Karnataka; Rajasthan. *Status:* 6a (Vigorous). *Class:* Indo-European, Indo-Iranian, Indo-Aryan, Central zone, Bhil. *Lg Use:* Also use Gujarati [guj]. *Lg Dev:* Literacy rate in L2: 76% in Gujarat (2001 census). Radio programs. *Writing:* Devanagari script. *Other:* A Scheduled Tribe. Traditional religion. *Map:* 358:308.

Dhundari [dhd] (Dhundari-Marwari, Jaipuri). 1,870,000 (2001 census). Rajasthan, Jaipur, Dausa, and Tonk districts. Possibly in Bundi, Kota, Kishangarh, Ajmer, Jhalawar, northern Karauli, and Sawai Madhopur districts. *Status:* 5 (Developing). *Class:* Indo-European, Indo-Iranian, Indo-Aryan, Central zone, Rajasthani, Marwari. A member of macrolanguage Marwari [mwr]. *Dialects:* 54% intelligibility of Marwari [rwr]; 86% of Shekhawati [swv]. Lexical similarity: 75%–89% with dialects; 62%–70% with Merwari [wry], 65%–81% with Shekhawati [swv], 46%–66% with Godwari [gdx], 56%–64% with Mewari [mtr], 64%–73% with Haroti [hoj], 62%–67% with Mewati [wtm], 59% with Hindi [hin]. *Type:* SOV. *Lg Use:* Vigorous. Home, village, market, religion. Positive attitudes. Widespread bilingualism in Hindi [hin] but not all are fluent; educated have more fluency in Hindi. *Writing:* Devanagari script. *Other:* Hindu, Muslim. *Maps:* 353:66, 354:66.

Digaro-Mishmi [mhu] (Darang Deng, Digaro, Digaru, Mishmi, Taaon, Taraon, Taying). 34,000 in India (2001 census). Population total all countries: 34,850. Arunachal Pradesh, Lohit district, Hayuliang, Changlagam, and Goiliang circles, Dibang Valley district; Assam. Also in China (Darang Deng). *Status:* 6a (Vigorous). *Class:* Sino-Tibetan, Tibeto-Burman, Central Tibeto-Burman, Digarish. *Dialects:* None known. May not be in the Tani group, but is related. Lexical similarity: 25% with Idu-Mishmi [clk], 10% with Miju-Mishmi [mxj]. *Type:* SOV; 4 tones which are reported to vary considerably among speakers. *Lg Use:* Also use Assamese [asm], English [eng]. Used as L2 by Miju-Mishmi [mxj]. *Lg Dev:* Literacy rate in L2: 40% for Mishmi (2001 census). Dictionary. Grammar. *Other:* A Scheduled Tribe. Buddhist, Christian, traditional religion. *Map:* 356:189.

Dimasa [dis] (Dimasa Kachari, Hills Kachari). 112,000 (2001 census). Assam, North Cachar district and Cachar hills, Karbi Anglong and Nagaon districts; Nagaland, Haflong district; Meghalaya, Mizoram. *Status:* 5 (Developing). *Class:* Sino-Tibetan, Tibeto-Burman, Sal, Bodo-Garo-Northern Naga, Bodo-Koch, Bodo-Garo, Bodo. *Dialects:* Dimasa, Hariamba. Related to Kachari [xac]. *Lg Use:* Largely assimilated into Bengali [ben] and Assamese [asm] communities (Van Driem 2007). Used as L2 by Sakachep [sch]. *Lg Dev:* Literacy rate in L2: 60% in Assam (2001 census). Dictionary. Grammar. NT: 2005. *Writing:* Bengali script. Latin script. *Other:* A Scheduled Tribe. Some ethnic Dimasa speak other languages as L1: Mikir Karbi [mjw], Bengali [ben], and Assamese [asm]. Hindu, Christian, traditional religion. *Map:* 356:215.

Dogri [dgo] (Dhogaryali, Dogari, Dogri Jammu, Dogri Pahari, Dogri-Kangri, Dongari, Hindi Dogri, Tokkaru). 2,280,000 (2001 census). Jammu and Kashmir, Udhampur, Reasi, Kathua, and Poonch districts. *Status:* 4 (Educational). Statutory language of provincial identity in Jammu and Kashmir (1950, Constitution, Articles 345–347). *Class:* Indo-European, Indo-Iranian, Indo-Aryan, Northern zone, Western Pahari. A member of macrolanguage Dogri [doi]. *Dialects:* Dogri speakers understand each other well. Some reported difficulty understanding Kangri [xnr]. Department of Dogri at Jammu University designated Samba as the standard dialect and published textbooks based on this variety. Lexical similarity: 78% between dialects; excluding the most divergent site, others more than 86%. *Type:* SOV. *Lg Use:* Taught in government schools and as a subject in university. All domains. All ages. Positive attitudes. Panjabi [pan] also used in shops. Hindi [hin] is also used in school and shops. Many know only rudimentary Hindi. Middle-aged and older speakers also use Urdu [urd]. Used as L2 by Gujari [gju]. *Lg Dev:* Literacy rate in L2: 18%–19%. Young people are becoming literate in Dogri. Taught in primary and secondary schools. Radio programs. Films. NT: 1826. *Writing:* Arabic script, Nastaliq style, no longer in use. Devanagari script. Takri (Tankri, Takari) script, no longer in use. *Other:* Dogri formerly considered a Panjabi dialect, but now promoted as a written language in India. Dhogri is a Scheduled Caste in Himachal Pradesh and Punjab who speak Chambeali [cdh] in Himachal and Dogri in Punjab (Singh 1995). Hindu, Muslim. *Map:* 351.

Dogri [doi]. A macrolanguage (see page 9). *Other:* Includes: Dogri [dgo], Kangri [xnr].

Domari [rmt] (Dom, Domra Magu Hiya). 202,000 in India (2000). Bihar, Saran and Champaran districts; Assam; West Bengal; Uttar Pradesh; Punjab; Madhya Pradesh; Jammu and Kashmir; Odisha. *Status:* 6a (Vigorous). *Dialects:* Domaki, Wogri-Boli. *Lg Use:* A Gypsy language partly used for ingroup identification. *Other:* Efforts made to hide meaning of words from outsiders. Similar to Bhojpuri [bho]. Hindu. See main entry on page 202. *Map:* 355:117.

Dotyali [dty]. Uttarakhand, Uttar Pradesh, and Maharastra. *Status:* 6a (Vigorous). See main entry on page 247.

Dubli [dub] (Dubala, Dubla, Rathod, Talavia). 252,000 (2007). Ethnic population: 791,000 (2007). Gujarat, Surat, Valsad, Bharuch (Broach), and Vadodara districts; Maharashtra, Thane District, Talasari and Dahanu areas; Dadra and Nagar Haveli; Daman and Diu; Karnataka; Rajasthan. *Status:* 6b (Threatened). *Class:* Indo-European, Indo-Iranian, Indo-Aryan, Central zone, Bhil. *Dialects:* Dubli of Bharuch District is intelligible with Dungri dialect of Vasavi [vas]. *Lg Use:* Over half the ethnic group uses Gujarati [guj] (2007). *Lg Dev:* Literacy rate in L2: 48% in Gujarat (2001 census). *Other:* A Scheduled Tribe. Glossonym: Dubli. Ethnonym: Dubla. Hindu. *Map:* 358:287.

Dungra Bhil [duh]. 100,000 (2000 IICCC). Gujarat, Vadodara district, Chotaudeyapur and Naswadi tahsils; Madhya Pradesh, Jhabua district, Alirajpur tahsil; Maharashtra, Dedgam tahsil; slopes of Vindhya Satpura mountains drained by Narmada river. 200 villages. *Status:* 5 (Developing). *Class:* Indo-European, Indo-Iranian, Indo-Aryan, Central zone, Bhil. *Dialects:* None known. 84%–89% intelligibility with Bhilori [noi] of Maharashtra. Lexical similarity: 75%–85% between subgroups, 71%–87% with Bhilori and Noiri Bhili, less than 53% with Garasia [gas]. *Lg Dev:* Literacy rate in L2: 3%–5%. NT: 2009. *Writing:* Devanagari script. Gujarati script. *Other:* A Scheduled Tribe in Gujarat. A Bhil subgroup. Dungra Bhil sometimes used as alternate name for Adivasi Garasia [gas] and Rajput Garasia [gra] but probably refers to more than 1 group living in the hills. 'Dungra', hill. Hindu. *Maps:* 353:80, 358:80.

Duruwa [pci] (Dhruva, Dhurwa, Durva, Paraja, Parajhi, Parjhi, Parji, Tagara, Thakara, Tugara). 51,200 (2001 census). Ethnic population: 100,000 (1986). 65% in Bastar, 35% in Koraput. Chhattisgarh, Bastar district, southeast Jagdalpur tahsil; Odisha, Koraput district. *Status:* 6a (Vigorous). *Class:* Dravidian, Central, Parji-Gadaba. *Dialects:* Dharba, Kukanar, Nethanar, Tiriya. Nethanar dialect is central. Lexical similarity: 90%-96% with dialects, 70%-82% with Halbi [hlb]. *Lg Use:* Madiya [mrr] speak Duruwa to communicate with the Dhurwa people. A few also use Bhatri [bgw] in northern Bastar District. Also use Halbi [hlb], Hindi [hin], Oriya [ory]. *Lg Dev:* Literacy rate in L1: Below 1%. Literacy rate in L2: 15%–25%. *Writing:* Devanagari script. Oriya script. *Other:* A Scheduled Tribe. Ethnonym: Dhurwa. Glossonym: Parji. Traditional religion. *Map:* 359:345.

Dzongkha [dzo] (Drukpa, Hloka, Lhoskad). 11,000 in India (2007). West Bengal, Kalimpong and Darjeeling, just inside the Indo-Bhutan border; Sikkim; Assam; Arunachal Pradesh; Nagaland; Manipur; Meghalaya. *Status:* 5 (Dispersed). *Other:* Buddhist. See main entry on page 58. *Map:* 355:162.

English [eng]. 350,000 in India (Crystal 2003). L2 users: 200,000,000 in India (Crystal 2003). *Status:* 1 (National). Statutory national working language (1950, Constitution, Articles 343 and 348(1)). *Other:* Neither British nor American English but a distinct Indian dialect with its own unique vocabulary and style. See main entry on page 319.

Eravallan [era] (Ambuvilluvedar, Villu Vedan, Vilvedan). 5,000 (2001). Ethnic population: 5,440 (2001 census). 3,890 in Kerala and 1,560 in Tamil Nadu. Kerala, Palakkad district, Chittoor taluk; Tamil Nadu, Coimbatore district. *Status:* 6a (Vigorous). *Class:* Dravidian, Southern, Tamil-Kannada, Tamil-Kodagu, Tamil-Malayalam, Tamil. *Dialects:* None known. Lexical similarity: 91% between Eravallan of Coimbatore and of Palakkad, 70%–74% with Tamil [tam], 59%–77% with Irula [iru], 77%–86% with Malasar [ymr]. *Lg Use:* Shifting to Tamil [tam]. Most children learn Tamil first. Also use Tamil [tam]. *Lg Dev:* Literacy rate in L2: 42% in Tamil. Resistant toward literacy in Eravallan. *Other:* Hindu, traditional religion. *Map:* 360:400.

French [fra]. 10,000 in India (2008). *Status:* 2 (Provincial). Statutory language of provincial identity in Puducherry Union Territory (1950, Constitution, Articles 345–347 inclusive), unscheduled language. See main entry on page 320.

Gadaba, Bodo [gbj] (Boi Gadaba, Gadba, Gadwa, Godwa, Gudwa, Gutob, Gutop). 8,000 (2000 IICCC). Odisha, Koraput district, Lamtaput, 40 villages; Malkangiri district, Khoirput block. *Status:* 6b (Threatened). *Class:* Austro-Asiatic, Munda, South Munda, Koraput Munda, Gutob-Remo-Geta', Gutob-Remo. *Dialects:* Birong Raji, Kinda Raji, Koraput, Lamtaput. Dialects mutually intelligible. Speakers in Lamtaput block have 89%–94% intelligibility in Tikrapada and Audipoda villages. Intelligibility of the Hanumal village variety is less. Lexical similarity: 69%–89% among 7 varieties in Odisha, 90% between listed dialects. *Lg Use:* Many speak and are shifting to Desiya [dso] in home and religious domains. Mainly adults. Mixed attitudes. A few also speak Oriya [ory] in Orissa. In Andhra Pradesh, also use Telugu [tel]. Also use Desiya [dso]. *Lg Dev:* Literacy rate in L2: 9% (2000 H. Rajan). Literacy classes in progress. *Writing:* Oriya script. *Other:* A Scheduled Tribe. Some ethnic Gadaba in Madhya Pradesh speak Bhatri [bgw] as L1. Different from Dravidian Mudhili Gadaba [gau] and Pottangi Ollar Gadaba [gdb]. Hindu, Christian, traditional religion. *Map:* 359:349.

Gadaba, Mudhili [gau] (Gadaba, Gol Gadaba, Kondekar, Kondko). 8,000 (2000 IICCC). Andhra Pradesh, Vizianagaram district, Salur and Pachipenta mandals, Vishakhapatnam and Srikakulam districts. *Status:* 5 (Developing). *Class:* Dravidian, Central, Parji-Gadaba. *Dialects:* 93%–98% intelligibility among dialects. Lexical similarity: 84%–94% between dialects. Different from Dravidian Mudhili Gadaba [gau] and Pottangi Ollar Gadaba [gdb]. *Lg Use:* All domains. Positive attitudes. Low proficiency in Telugu [tel]. *Lg Dev:* Literacy rate in L2: 34%–42% (2001 census). *Writing:* Telugu script. *Other:* A Scheduled Tribe. Hindu. *Map:* 359:355.

Gadaba, Pottangi Ollar [gdb] (Allar, Gadba, Hallari, Hollar Gadbas, Konekor, Konekor Gadaba, Mundli, Ollar Gadaba, Ollari, Ollaro, San Gadaba, Sano). 15,000 (2002 M. Kurian). 4,000–7,000 in Koraput District, Pottangi block (1995). Odisha, Koraput district, Pottangi and Nandapur blocks. *Status:* 6a (Vigorous). *Class:* Dravidian, Central, Parji-Gadaba. *Dialects:* None known. Lexical similarity: 69%–80% with 4 varieties in Odisha; 42%–47% with 1 variety in Andhra Pradesh; 52%–62% with Mudhili Gadaba [gau] in Andhra Pradesh. *Lg Use:* Positive attitudes. Desiya [dso] is the main L2. Low proficiency in Telugu [tel]. *Lg Dev:* Literacy rate in L2: 7%. NT: 2012. *Writing:* Oriya script, used in Odisha. Telugu script, used in Andhra Pradesh. *Other:* Gabada is a Scheduled Tribe. Different from Gadaba [gbj] in Munda family, also spoken in Koraput. Traditional religion. *Map:* 359:350.

Gaddi [gbk] (Bharmauri Bhadi, Gaddyali, Gadi, Gadiali, Pahari Bharmauri, Panchi Brahmauri Rajput). 110,000 (2007). Himachal Pradesh, Chamba district, Brahmaur tahsil and Holi sub-tahsils; Uttar Pradesh; Jammu and Kashmir; Madhya Pradesh; Punjab; Delhi. *Status:* 6a (Vigorous). *Class:* Indo-European, Indo-Iranian, Indo-Aryan, Northern zone, Western Pahari. *Dialects:* Bharmauri, Macleod Ganj. 93% intelligibility of Mandeali [mjl], 97% of Kangri [xnr], 83% of Chambeali [cdh]. Lexical similarity: 74%–80% with Palamuri Kangri [xnr], 79% with Chambeali [cdh], 67%–73% with Mandeali [mjl]. *Type:* SOV. *Lg Use:* Hindi [hin] used in school instruction, shops, cities. *Lg Dev:* Literacy rate in L2: 37% for Jammu and Kashmir (2001 census). Radio programs. *Writing:* Devanagari script. Takri (Tankri, Takari) script, no longer in use. *Other:* A Scheduled Tribe. Gaddi is generic for all indigenous populations of Bharmaur area of Chamba District. Hindu. *Map:* 352:24.

Gahri [bfu] (Boonan, Bunan, Erankad, Ghara, Keylong Boli, Lahuli of Bunan, Poonan, Punan). 4,000 (1997). Himachal Pradesh, Gahr Valley along Bhaga river from confluence with the Chandra and upstream, Biling, Kardang, Kyelang, Guskyar, Yurnad, Gumrang, Barbog, Paspara, Pyukar, and Styering villages. *Status:* 6b (Threatened). *Class:* Sino-Tibetan, Tibeto-Burman, Western Tibeto-Burman, Bodish, West Himalayish, Kinauri. *Dialects:* Lexical similarity: 39% with Sunam [ssk], 26%–39% with varieties of Chamba Lahuli (Pattani) [lae], 37% with Tinani [lbf], 26%–34% with some varieties of Central Tibetan [bod], 34% with Jangshung [jna] and Shumcho [scu], 31% with Kinnaur Bhoti [nes], 30% with Chitkuli [cik] and Nesang (Tukpa) [tpq], 24% with Lhasa dialect of Central Tibetan [bod], 23% with Kanauri [kfk]. *Type:* Only singular and plural number; no gender indicated in verbs or pronouns. *Lg Use:* All domains. *Lg Dev:* Literacy rate in L1: Below 1%. Bible portions: 1911–1923. *Writing:* Takri (Tankri, Takari) script, no longer in use. Tibetan script. *Other:* Bodh caste, but speak a different language from Bodhs of Mayar, Khoksar, and Stod valleys. They consider themselves different from Bodhs of the north, whom they call Tibetans. Buddhist. *Map:* 352:23.

Gamit [gbl] (Gamati, Gameti, Gamith, Gamta, Gamti, Gavit). 284,000 (2001 census). Gujarat, Surat district; some in Bharuch, Dangs, and Valsad districts. *Status:* 5 (Developing). *Class:* Indo-European, Indo-Iranian, Indo-Aryan, Central zone, Bhil. *Dialects:* None known. Reportedly similar to Mawchi [mke]. *Lg Dev:* Literacy rate in L2: 53% (2001 census). Most have high school or college education. Radio programs. NT: 1982. *Writing:* Devanagari script. Gujarati script. *Other:* A Scheduled Tribe. Traditional religion, Christian, Hindu. *Map:* 358:288.

Gangte [gnb] (Gante). 14,500 (2001 census). Manipur, south Churachandpur district, 37 villages; Meghalaya; Assam. *Status:* 5 (Developing). *Class:* Sino-Tibetan, Tibeto-Burman, Sal, Kuki-Chin-Naga, Kuki-Chin, Northern. *Dialects:* None known. Related to Thado Chin [tcz]. Differs little from Vaiphei [vap], Paite [pck], or Zou [zom]. *Lg Use:* Under pressure from Meitei [mni] (Van Driem 2007). Also use English [eng], Meitei [mni]. *Lg Dev:* Literacy high among young people and lower among older people. Magazines. Newspapers. Bible: 1991. *Writing:* Latin script. *Other:* A Scheduled Tribe. Christian. *Map:* 357:277.

Garasia, Adiwasi [gas] (Adiwasi Girasia, Adiwasi Gujarati, Girasia). 100,000 (1988 V. Patel). North Gujarat, Banaskantha district, Danta taluk; Sabarkantha district, Poshina taluk. *Status:* 6a (Vigorous). *Class:* Indo-European, Indo-Iranian, Indo-Aryan, Central zone, Bhil. *Dialects:* Understand Rajput Garasia [gra] well. Lexical similarity: 89%–96% between dialects, 75%–93% with dialects of Rajput Garasia; 79%–92% with dialects of Patelia [bhb]; 79%–93% with Wagdi [wbr]; 76%–87% with Marwari [rwr] dialects. *Lg Use:* Low proficiency in Gujarati [guj]. *Lg Dev:* Literacy rate in L2: 15%–25%. Bible portions: 1987. *Other:* Speakers are Bhils. Dungra Bhil is sometimes used as an alternate name for Adiwasi Garasia and Rajput Garasia [gra] but probably refers to more than 1 group living in the hills (Dungra means hill). Traditional religion, Hindu. *Map:* 353:74.

Garasia, Rajput [gra] (Dhungri Garasia, Dungari Garasia, Dungri Grasia, Girasia, Grasia, Nyar, Rajput Garasia). 100,000 (1999 India Evangelical Mission). Rajasthan, Sirchi, Pali, Udaipur districts; Gujarat, Banaskantha district. *Status:* 5 (Developing). *Class:* Indo-European, Indo-Iranian, Indo-Aryan, Central zone, Bhil. *Dialects:* Rajput Garasia do not understand Adiwasi Garasia [gas] but intelligibility is high the other way. Lexical similarity: 94%–99% with Gujarati [guj] and Rajasthani [mve] dialects, 75%–93% with Adiwasi Garasia [gas] dialects; 76%–84% with Patelia [bhb] dialects; 79%–86% with Wagdi [wbr]; 67%–84% with Marwari [rwr] dialects. *Lg Use:* Positive attitudes. Also use Gujarati [guj], Hindi [hin]. Proficiency in second languages is low. *Lg Dev:* Literacy rate in L2: 15%–25%. Bible portions: 1998. *Writing:* Devanagari script. Gujarati script. *Other:* A Scheduled Tribe in Rajasthan, Warrior Caste. Distinct from Dungra Bhil [duh], which is sometimes used as an alternate name for Adiwasi Garasia [gas] and Rajput Garasia but probably refers to more than 1 group living in the hills (Dungra means hill). Traditional religion, Hindu. *Map:* 353:69.

Garhwali [gbm] (Gadhavali, Gadhawala, Gadwahi, Gashwali, Girwali, Godauli, Gorwali, Gurvali, Pahari Garhwali). 2,920,000 (2000 survey). Uttarakhand; Tehri Garhwal, Pauri Garhwal, Uttarkashi, Chamoli, Dehra Dun, Rudraprayag districts; Himachal Pradesh. *Status:* 5 (Developing). *Class:* Indo-European, Indo-Iranian, Indo-Aryan, Northern zone, Garhwali. *Dialects:* Badhani, Bangani, Bhattiani, Chandpuri, Dessaulya, Gangadi (Uttarkashi), Jaunpuri, Lohbya, Majh-Kumaiya, Nagpuriya, Parvati, Rathi, Ravai, Salani (Pauri), Srinagari, Tehri (Gangapariya). Jaunsari [jns] is sometimes referred to as a dialect of Garhwali, but most say they cannot understand it. Parvati dialect also reportedly not mutually intelligible; Srinagari is literary standard; Pauri generally regarded as the sweetest; Srinagari and Pauri are very similar. Lexical similarity: 53%–84% among dialects; 54%–69% with Hindi [hin], 55%–66% with Kumaoni [kfy]. The divergent dialect varieties of Bangani, Parvati, and Ravai are no more similar to Western Pahari varieties than to Garhwali. *Type:* SOV. *Lg Use:* Vigorous. Home, village. All ages. Positive attitudes. Almost everyone uses some Hindi [hin] with more fluency among the men, educated and youth; Hindi used in the market. Used as L2 by Gujari [gju], Jad [jda], Rongpo [rnp]. *Lg Dev:* Literacy rate in L2: 72% for Uttarakhand (2001 census). Older women lack literacy. Poetry. Magazines. Radio programs. NT: 1827–1994. *Writing:* Devanagari script. *Other:* Jaunpuri and Ravai dialects are culturally similar to Jaunsari and distinct from Garhwali. Castes are Brahmin, Rajput, Harijan. Hindu, traditional religion. *Map:* 352:53.

Garo [grt] (Garrow, Mande, Mandi). 889,000 in India (2001 census). Population total all countries: 1,009,000. Meghalaya, Garo Hills district; West Assam, Goalpara, Kamrup, and Karbi Anglong districts; Nagaland, Kohima district; Tripura, South Tripura district, Udaipur subdivision; North Tripura district, Kamalpur, Kailasahar subdivisions; West Tripura district, Sadar subdivision; West Bengal, Jalpaiguri and Koch Bihar districts. Also in Bangladesh. *Status:* 2 (Provincial). Statutory provincial language in Meghalaya State (1950, Constitution, Articles 347), unscheduled language. *Class:* Sino-Tibetan, Tibeto-Burman, Sal, Bodo-Garo-Northern Naga, Bodo-Koch, Bodo-Garo, Garo. *Dialects:* A'beng (A'bengya, Am'beng), A'chick (A'chik, A'we, Chisak, Dual, Matchi), Dacca, Ganching, Kamrup. A'chick is the standardized dialect in India. A'beng dialect used in Bangladesh, but is not mutually intelligible. Reportedly most similar to Koch [kdq]. *Lg Use:* Awe dialect, spoken in Assam, has few remaining speakers. Most use standard Garo. Used as L2 by Atong [aot], Hajong [haj], Koch [kdq], Lyngngam [lyg], Rabha [rah], Ruga [ruh]. *Lg Dev:* Literacy rate in L2: 55% for Meghalaya (2001 census). General level of education is low compared to Khasi [kha]. Taught in primary schools. Radio programs. Films. Dictionary. Grammar. Bible: 1924–1994. *Writing:* Bengali script. Braille script, used since 1998. Latin script. *Other:* A Scheduled Tribe. Christian. *Maps:* 355:127, 356:127.

Gata' [gaq] (Didayi, Didei, Dire, Gataq, Geta', Getaq, Gta', Gta Asa). 3,060 (1991 census). Ethnic population: 7,370 (2001 census). In Odisha. Odisha, Koraput, and Malkangiri districts, Kudumulgumma and Chitrakonda blocks, south of Bondo Hills; some in Khairput block. 47 villages; Andhra Pradesh, East Godavari district. *Status:* 6b (Threatened). *Class:* Austro-Asiatic, Munda, South Munda, Koraput Munda, Gutob-Remo-Geta', Geta'. *Dialects:* Hill Geta', Plains Geta'. Ruhlen treats Plains Geta' and Hill Geta' as separate languages. Lexical similarity: 68%–93% among dialects, 27%–37% with Bondo [bfw] varieties, 22%–28% with Gadaba Gutob [gbj] dialect. *Lg Use:* Also use Desiya [dso], Oriya [ory]. *Lg Dev:* Literacy rate in L2: 10% in Odisha (2001 census). *Other:* A Scheduled Tribe. Traditional religion, Hindu. *Map:* 359:357.

Godwari [gdx]. 3,000,000 (2001 census). Rajasthan, Jhalor, Sirohi, and Pali districts. *Status:* 6b (Threatened). *Class:* Indo-European, Indo-Iranian, Indo-Aryan, Central zone, Rajasthani, Marwari. *Dialects:* Balvi, Khuni, Madahaddi, Sirohi. 88%–92% intelligibility of Marwari [rwr]. Lexical similarity: 70% between dialects; 62%–75% with Merwari [wry], 45%–69% with Shekhawati [swv], 51%–73% with Mewari [mtr], 46%–66% with Dhundari [dhd], 44%–67% with Haroti [hoj], 62%–74% with Marwari [rwr]. *Lg Use:* Vigorous. Home, village, market, religion. All ages. Positive attitudes. Also use Hindi [hin] with very good proficiency among the educated. *Other:* Hindu. *Map:* 353:70.

Gondi [gon]. A macrolanguage (see page 9). *Other:* Includes: Northern Gondi [gno], Southern Gondi [ggo].

Gondi, Northern [gno] (Gaudi, Ghond, Godi, Gondi, Gondiva, Gondu, Gondwadi, Goondile, Goudi, Goudwal). 1,950,000 (1997 Bible Society of India). 2,630,000 all Gondi. Madhya Pradesh, Betul, Chhindwara, Seoni, Mandla, and Balaghat districts; Maharashtra State, Amravati, Wardha, Nagpur, Bhandara, and Yavatmal districts. *Status:* 5 (Developing). *Class:* Dravidian, South-Central, Gondi-Kui, Gondi. A member of macrolanguage Gondi [gon]. *Dialects:* Amravati, Betul, Bhandara, Chhindwara, Mandla, Nagpur, Seoni, Yavatmal. Inherent intelligibility between dialects 94%–97%. Speakers tested in other dialects understood Amravati 94%–97%; Betul 83%–96%, and Seoni 82%–97%. 58%–78% intelligibility of Southern Gondi [ggo]. Different from Muria [hlb], Maria [mrr] of Garhchiroli, Dandami Maria [daq], and Koya [kff]. Lexical similarity: 58%–90% among dialects. *Lg Use:* All ages. Positive attitudes. Use some Hindi [hin] in Madhya Pradesh, with low proficiency. Marathi [mar] in Maharashtra, with low proficiency. Used as L2 by Northwestern Kolami [kfb]. *Lg Dev:* Literacy rate in L1: 1%–5%. Literacy rate in L2: 25%–50%. Radio programs. Films. NT: 1996. *Writing:* Devanagari script. *Other:* Traditional religion, Hindu. *Maps:* 354:107, 358:107, 359:107.

Gondi, Southern [ggo] (Koi Gondi, Telugu Gondi). 100,000 (2004 SIL). Andhra Pradesh, Adilabad district; Maharashtra, south Yavatmal, south Chandrapur and southeast Garhchiroli districts; Chhattisgarh. *Status:* 5 (Developing). *Class:* Dravidian, South-Central, Gondi-Kui, Gondi. A member of macrolanguage Gondi [gon]. *Dialects:* Aheri, Bhamragarh, Etapally Gondi, Nirmal (Adilabad), Rajura, Sironcha, Utnoor. Sironcha dialect understood best by the others, with 73%–98% intelligibility. 49%–58% intelligibility of Northern Gondi [gno]. Lexical similarity: 64%–90% among dialects. *Lg Dev:* Literacy rate in L2: 25%–50%. Dictionary. Bible portions: 1962. *Writing:* Devanagari script. Telugu script. *Other:* Traditional religion, Hindu. *Maps:* 358:323, 359:323.

Gowlan [goj]. 20,200 (2000). Maharashtra, Amravati district, and among Korku [kfq] people. Madhya Pradesh, Hoshangabad district; some in north Karnataka. *Status:* 6a (Vigorous). *Class:* Indo-European, Indo-Iranian, Indo-Aryan, Southern zone, Unclassified. *Dialects:* Dialects in Maharashtra and Karnataka reportedly different. May be more similar to Hindi [hin] (Central zone) than to Marathi [mar] (Southern zone). *Lg Use:* Home. Positive attitudes toward Gowlan and Hindi [hin]. Only some want their children to learn Marathi [mar]. Hindi [hin] bilingualism low in Chikli area. *Other:* Surrounded by Korku. Belong to Gowli caste. Traditional religion, Christian. *Map:* 358:296.

Gowli [gok] (Nand). 35,000 (IMA 1997). Madhya Pradesh; Maharashtra, Amravati district. *Status:* 6a (Vigorous). *Class:* Indo-European, Indo-Iranian, Indo-Aryan, Central zone, Western Hindi, Unclassified. *Dialects:* Khamla, Lingaayat, Nand, Ranya. Nand subdialects have 93% or higher intelligibility with Khamla dialect. Dialect used in Madhya Pradesh appears more similar to Marathi [mar] (Southern zone) than to Hindi [hin] (Central zone). Lexical similarity: 84%–92% between the Ranya and Nand dialects. *Lg Use:* Home. Also use Hindi [hin], Marathi [mar]. *Lg Dev:* Literacy rate in L1: Below 1%. Literacy rate in L2: 5%–15%. *Writing:* Devanagari script. *Other:* Speakers belong to Gowli caste. 1 and a half subgroups; Nand Gowli the highest, Musalman (the half tribe) the lowest. Surrounded by Korku [kfq]. Hindu, traditional religion. *Map:* 358:301.

Great Andamanese, Mixed [gac] (Andamese). 7 (2009 A. Abbi). The last fluent speaker died in 2009 (2009 A. Abbi). Ethnic population: 55. Andaman and Nicobar, Strait island, about 100 km northeast of Port Blair. *Status:* 8b (Nearly extinct). *Class:* Andamanese, Great Andamanese. *Type:* The linguistic system of Mixed Great Andamanese appears to be close to Koineization. It is a mixture of three to four languages spoken once on the island, including Jeru, Khora, Sare and Bo. *Lg Use:* Shifting to Andaman Creole Hindi [hca]. Older adults. *Lg Dev:* Literacy rate in L1: Below 1%. Grammar. *Writing:* Unwritten. *Other:* Mixed Greater Andamanese is used only as a code language in front of outsiders.The seven existing speakers use it occasionally among themselves in day-to-day speech. Other languages in the Central Andamanese group have no remaining speakers. Great Andamanese is a Scheduled Tribe. *Map:* 361.

Groma [gro] (Tromowa). 14,000 in India (2007 Asia Harvest). Sikkim, North district, Chumbi valley. *Status:* 6a (Vigorous). *Dialects:* Lower Groma, Upper Groma. See main entry on page 71. *Map:* 355:152.

Gujarati [guj] (Gujerathi, Gujerati, Gujrathi). 45,700,000 in India (2001 census). Population total all countries: 46,636,510. Gujarat; Maharashtra; Rajasthan; Karnataka; Madhya Pradesh. Also in Bangladesh, Botswana, Canada, Fiji, Kenya, Malawi, Mauritius, Mozambique, Pakistan, Singapore, South Africa, Tanzania, United Kingdom, United States, Zambia, Zimbabwe. *Status:* 2 (Provincial). Statutory provincial language in West Bengal State; union territories Dadra and Nagar Haveli, Daman and Diu (1950, Constitution, Schedule VIII). *Class:* Indo-European, Indo-Iranian, Indo-Aryan, Central zone, Gujarati. *Dialects:* Gamadia (Ahmedabad Gamadia, Anawla, Brathela, Charotari, Eastern Broach Gujarati, Gramya, Patani, Patidari, Surati, Vadodari), Kakari, Kathiyawadi (Bhawnagari, Gohilwadi, Holadi, Jhalawadi, Sorathi), Kharwa, Parsi, Standard Gujarati (Mumbai Gujarati, Nagari, Patnuli, Saurashtra Standard), Tarimuki (Ghisadi). Memoni ethnic group reportedly speak a Kachchi [kfr] variety. *Lg Use:* Used as L2 by Adiwasi Garasia [gas], Chodri [cdi], Dhanki [dhn], Dhodia [dho], Dubli [dub], Indo-Portuguese [idb], Kachchi [kfr], Rajput Garasia [gra], Sansi [ssi], Varli [vav]. *Lg Dev:* Literacy rate in L1: 70% for Gujarat state (2001 census). Fully developed. Bible: 1823–2005. *Writing:* Braille script. Gujarati script, primary usage. Khojki script. *Other:* Hindu, Muslim (Sunni). *Map:* 351.

Gujari [gju] (Gogri, Gojari, Gojri, Gujar, Gujer, Gujjari, Gujuri, Gurjar, Hindki, Kashmir Gujuri, Parimu, Rajasthani Gujuri). 690,000 in India (2000). Population total all countries: 992,000. Ethnic population: 1,600,000 (2002). In Uttar Pradesh, Haryana, Madhya Pradesh, Rajasthan, Maharashtra, Gujarat, Punjab, Delhi. Jammu, line of control border tahsils; Kashmir, Kukernag, Kangan, Tral, Doru, Pahalgam, Shopian, Kulgam, Handwara, Karnah, Kupwara, and Uri tahsils; Himachal Pradesh; Uttarakhand. Also in Afghanistan, Pakistan. *Status:* 5 (Developing). *Class:* Indo-European, Indo-Iranian, Indo-Aryan, Central zone, Rajasthani, Unclassified. A member of macrolanguage Rajasthani [raj]. *Dialect:* Ajiri of Hazara. Poonchi [phr] may be understood by others and form the basis for a standard dialect. In Pakistan, Eastern Gujari appears more similar to Northern Hindko [hno] or Pahari-Potwari [phr]. Western Gujari appear to understand the Eastern dialect better than vice versa. Comparison with India varieties is needed. Lexical similarity: 60% between Uttar Pradesh and Pakistan, 76% with Poonchi. *Lg Use:* In general, Hindu agriculturalists have not retained Gujari language and culture, whereas Muslim Gujari have. Gujars outside Jammu-Kashmir and Himachal Pradesh do not speak Gujari, but regional languages. All domains. Positive attitudes. Also use Dogri [dgo], Garhwali [gbm], Hindi [hin], Jaunsari [jns], Kashmiri [kas], Kullu Pahari [kfx], Kumaoni [kfy], Urdu [urd]. *Lg Dev:* Literacy rate in L2: 5%–15%. Poetry. Magazines. Radio programs. TV. *Writing:* Arabic script, Nastaliq style. Devanagari script, plans for future development using this script. *Other:* A Scheduled Tribe. Muslim, Hindu. *Map:* 352:3.

Gurung, Western [gvr] (Gurung Kura). 33,000 in India (2007). Ethnic population: 112,000. West Bengal, Darjeeling, Sikkim. Possibly in Myanmar. *Status:* 6b (Threatened). *Lg Use:* 77,000 also use Nepali [npi]. See main entry on page 248. *Map:* 355:164.

Hajong [haj] (Haijong, Hazong). 63,000 in India (2001 census). Population total all countries: 71,000. Meghalaya, West Garo Hills district, western side, West and East Khasi hills; Assam, Goalpara, and Nagaon districts; Arunachal Pradesh; West Bengal. Also in Bangladesh. *Status:* 5 (Developing). *Class:* Indo-European, Indo-Iranian, Indo-Aryan, Eastern zone, Bengali-Assamese. *Dialects:* Banai, Dalu. No prestige or standard dialect recognized. Intelligible with Hajong of Bangladesh. Lexical similarity: 82%–91% between Banai dialect of Koch [kdq] and mainstream Hajong varieties, 74%–77% between Dalu dialect and mainstream Hajong varieties, 79% between Banai dialect of Koch [kdq] and Dalu, 54%–64% with Assamese [asm], 63%–67% with Bengali [ben], 74%–85% with Hajong of Bangladesh. *Lg Use:* Vigorous. All domains. Positive attitudes. Also use Assamese [asm]; educated have high fluency in Assamese. Also use Bengali [ben], Garo [grt]. Used as L2 by Koch [kdq]. *Lg Dev:* Literacy rate in L2: 20%–25%; 48% for Meghalaya (2001 census). Radio programs. TV. Bible portions. *Writing:* Bengali script, used in Bangladesh and India. Latin script, used in India. *Other:* A Scheduled Tribe. Jharua may be an alternate name. Though linguistically different, the Banai affiliate themselves with the Koch. Traditional religion, Hindu. *Maps:* 355:129, 356:129.

Halbi [hlb] (Bastari, Halabi, Halba, Halvas, Halvi, Mahari, Mehari). 593,000 (2001 census). L2 users: 200,000 (2001 C. Thomas). Madhya Pradesh, Balaghat district; Chhattisgarh, Bastar district plains; Maharashtra, Gondia district; Odisha, Koraput district; Andhra Pradesh. *Status:* 3 (Wider communication). *Class:* Indo-European, Indo-Iranian, Indo-Aryan, Eastern zone, Bengali-Assamese. *Dialects:* Adkuri, Bastari, Bhunjia, Chandari, Gachikolo, Govari of Balaghat, Kawari, Kunbi, Mahari (Mahara, Mehari), Muri (Muria), Sundi. Bhunjia and Kawari dialects considered more divergent dialects. Reportedly a creole language. Grierson and Konow (1901–1929) called it a dialect of Marathi [mar] for convenience, but noted similarities to Bhatri [bgw], a dialect of Oriya [ory]. *Type:* SOV; postpositions; genitives, articles, adjectives, numerals before noun heads; 2 or 3 affixes per word; word order distinguishes given and new information; noun affixes indicate case; verb affixes mark person, number, gender of subject; passives; causatives; comparatives; CV, CVC, CVV; nontonal. *Lg Use:* Educated men also use Hindi [hin], for trading and common topics. Also use Bhatri [bgw]. Used as L2 by Bhatri [bgw], Duruwa [pci], Eastern Muria [emu], Maria [mrr], Mirgan [zrg]. *Lg Dev:* Literacy rate in L2: 74% for Chhattisgarh plains (2001 census). Government literacy program uses Hindi primers. Bible portions: 1989–1998. *Writing:* Devanagari script. *Other:* A Scheduled Tribe. Traditional religion, Hindu. *Map:* 359:329.

Haroti [hoj] (Hadauti, Hadothi, Hadoti, Harauti). 2,460,000 (2001 census). Rajasthan, Kota, Jhalawar, Bundi, and Baran districts. *Status:* 5 (Developing). *Class:* Indo-European, Indo-Iranian, Indo-Aryan, Central zone, Rajasthani, Unclassified. A member of macrolanguage Rajasthani [raj]. *Dialects:* 45% intelligibility with standard Marwari [rwr], 57%–67% with Merwari [wry], 58%–66% with Shekhawati [swv], 44%–67% with Godwari [gdx], 61%–71% with Mewari [mtr], 64%–73% with Dhundari [dhd], 52%–70% with Mewati [wtm], 55%–62% with Bagri [bgq], 83%–99% between dialects including varieties of Mina [myi], 63%–77% with Hindi [hin]. *Type:* SOV. *Lg Use:* Vigorous. Home, village; market, religion. Positive attitudes. Widespread bilingulism in Hindi [hin] with 40% with very good proficiency, the educated being more proficient. *Lg Dev:* Literacy rate in L2: 75% in Kota District (2001 census). NT: 1822. *Writing:* Devanagari script. *Other:* Hindu, Jain, Muslim. *Maps:* 353:67, 354:67.

Haryanvi [bgc] (Bangaru, Banger, Bangri, Bangru, Chamarwa, Desari, Hariani, Hariyani, Haryani, Jatu). 8,000,000 (2001 census). Ethnic population: 16,000,000 (1992 SIL). Haryana; Rajasthan; Punjab; Karnataka; Delhi; Himachal Pradesh; Uttar Pradesh. *Status:* 6a (Vigorous). *Class:* Indo-European, Indo-Iranian, Indo-Aryan, Central zone, Western Hindi, Unclassified. *Dialects:* Bangaru Proper, Deswali, Khadar. Good intelligibility among dialects, but Haryanvi is not intelligible with Hindi. Reportedly most similar to Braj Bhasha [bra]. Lexical similarity: 92% among dialects. *Lg Use:* Home, religion. All ages. Positive attitudes. Also use Hindi [hin] with proficiency higher among the educated. *Lg Dev:* Literacy rate in L2: 55% Hindi. Dictionary. Grammar. Bible portions: 2001. *Writing:* Devanagari script. *Other:* Ethnonym: Bangru, used for speakers in Jind area; Khadar used by speakers in Jind to refer to the speech of Rohtak and Sonipat. Hindu, Muslim. *Maps:* 352:49, 353:49, 354:49.

Hindi [hin] (Khadi Boli, Khari Boli). 258,000,000 in India (2001 census). Population total all countries: 260,333,620. L2 users: 120,000,000 in India (Wiesenfeld 1999). Widespread in north India: Delhi; Uttar Pradesh; Uttarakhand; Rajasthan; Punjab; Madhya Pradesh; northern Bihar; Himachal Pradesh. Also in Australia, Bangladesh, Belize, Bhutan, Botswana, Canada, Djibouti, Equatorial Guinea, Germany, Guyana, Kenya, Nepal, New Zealand, Philippines, Singapore, Sint Maarten, South Africa, United Arab Emirates, United Kingdom, United States, Yemen, Zambia. *Status:* 1 (National). Statutory national language (1950, Constitution, Article 343), also statutory provincial language in Bihar State and 12 other jurisdictions. *Class:* Indo-European, Indo-Iranian, Indo-Aryan, Central zone, Western Hindi, Hindustani. *Dialects:* None known. Formal vocabulary borrowed from Sanskrit, de-Persianized, de-Arabicized. Literary Hindi, or Hindi-Urdu, has 4 varieties: Hindi (High Hindi, Nagari Hindi, Literary Hindi, standard Hindi); Urdu [urd]; Dakhini; Rekhta. Hindustani, though not listed separately in India, refers here to the unofficial lingua franca of northwest India. Has a lexical mixture in varying proportions of Hindi (vocabulary derived from Sanskrit) and Urdu (vocabulary derived from Persian or Arabic). *Type:* SOV; postpositions; noun head final; 11 noun classes or genders; content q-word in situ; 3 suffixes; clause constituents partially indicated by case-marking, postpositions, and word order; verbal affixation marks person, number, gender, and honorificity of subject; split ergativity; both tense and aspect; passives and voice; nontonal; 28 consonant and 10 vowel phonemes. *Lg Dev:* Fully developed. Bible: 1818–2000. *Writing:* Braille script. Devanagari script, primary usage. Newar (Prachalit Nepal) script, no longer in use, historic usage. *Other:* Hindi, Hindustani, Urdu could be considered co-dialects, but have important sociolinguistic differences. Hindu. *Map:* 351.

Hinduri [hii] (Handuri). 29,700 (2001 census). Himachal Pradesh, Solan district, Ramshahr, Nalagarh and surrounding villages. *Status:* 6a (Vigorous). *Class:* Indo-European, Indo-Iranian, Indo-Aryan, Northern zone, Western Pahari. *Dialects:* Reportedly most similar to Bilaspuri [kfs]. Lexical similarity: 67% with Baghliani dialect of Mahasu Pahari [bfz] spoken in Arki, 60% with Lower Mahasui dialect of Pahari [bfz], 56% with Upper Mahasui dialect of Pahari [bfz] and Sirmauri [srx], 64% with Hindi. *Lg Use:* Home, village. Positive attitudes. Also use Hindi [hin]. *Other:* Hindu. *Map:* 352:42.

Hmar [hmr] (Hamar, Hmari, Mhar). 83,400 (2001 census). Assam, North Cachar and Cachar districts; Manipur, south, Tipaimukh, Churachandpur, 35 villages; Mizoram, Aizawl, Cachar, and North Cachar districts; Tripura. *Status:* 4 (Educational). *Class:* Sino-Tibetan, Tibeto-Burman, Sal, Kuki-Chin-Naga, Kuki-Chin, Central. *Dialects:* None known. Reportedly similar to Zou [zom]. *Lg Use:* Also use Assamese [asm], Meitei [mni], Mizo [lus]. Used as L2 by Sakachep [sch]. *Lg Dev:* Literacy rate in L2: 90%. Taught in primary schools. Dictionary. Grammar. Bible: 1968–2004. *Writing:* Latin script. *Other:* A Scheduled Tribe. Ethnic Hmar living in Mizoram speak Mizo [lus] as L1. Christian. *Map:* 356:240.

Ho [hoc] (Bihar Ho, Lanka Kol). 1,040,000 (2001 census). Jharkhand, Singhbhum district, Kolhan, Seraikella, Dhalbhum areas; Odisha, Mayurbhanj, and Koenjhar districts; West Bengal. *Status:* 5 (Developing). *Class:* Austro-Asiatic, Munda, North Munda, Kherwari, Mundari. *Dialects:* Chaibasa-Thakurmunda, Lohara. Most understand Chaibasa and Thakurmunda dialects well; 90%–92% comprehend narrative discourse. Kherwari (Khanwar, Kharar, Kharoali, Kharwari) is group name for Ho, Mundari [unr], Munda [unx], and Santhali [sat], closely related languages, and other smaller languages or dialects. Lexical similarity: 85% between most dialects, except for 3 on Ho area east and south edges. *Lg Use:* Vigorous. Positive attitudes. Also use Hindi [hin], Oriya [ory], Santhali [sat]. Used as L2 by Birhor [biy]. *Lg Dev:* Literacy rate in L1: 1%–5%. Literacy rate in L2: 25%–50%. Literacy program in progress. Radio programs. Dictionary. Grammar. NT: 1997. *Writing:* Devanagari script, used in Bihar. Oriya script, used in Odisha. Warang Citi script, no longer in use. *Other:* A Scheduled Tribe. Different from Ho (Hani [hni]) of Myanmar, China, Viet Nam, Laos. Traditional religion, Hindu. *Maps:* 355:148, 359:148.

Holiya [hoy] (Gohllaru, Golari-Kannada, Holar, Holari, Hole, Holian, Holu). 500 (2002 survey). Madhya Pradesh, Seoni, Balaghat districts; Maharashtra; Karnataka. *Status:* 6a (Vigorous). *Class:* Dravidian, Southern, Tamil-Kannada, Kannada. *Lg Use:* Also use Kannada [kan]. *Lg Dev:* Literacy rate in L1: Below 1%. Literacy rate in L2: 5% Kannada [kan]. *Other:* A Scheduled Caste in Madhya Pradesh. Hindu, traditional religion. *Map:* 358:318.

Hrangkhol [hra] (Hrangkol, Rangkhol). 18,700 (2000), decreasing. Assam; Tripura; a few in Manipur and Mizoram. *Status:* 5 (Developing). *Class:* Sino-Tibetan, Tibeto-Burman, Sal, Kuki-Chin-Naga, Kuki-Chin, Northern. *Dialect:* Hadem. Reportedly most similar to Biete [biu]. *Type:* SOV. *Lg Use:* Use declining in Mizoram, Manipur and even Assam; shifting to Assamese [asm] or Bengali [ben] (Van Driem 2007). Home, village. Also use Assamese [asm], English [eng], Hindi [hin], Mizo [lus]. Used as L2 by Sakachep [sch]. *Lg Dev:* Literacy rate in L1: Below 1%. Literature committee since 1960. Bible: 2006. *Writing:* Latin script, used in India. *Other:* Christian (Protestant), Hindu, traditional religion. *Map:* 356:239.

Hruso [hru] (Aka, Angka, Angkae, Gusso, Hrusso, Tenae). 3,000 (Van Driem 2007). Arunachal Pradesh, West Kameng district, Thrizino circle, Jamiri, Husigaon, Gohainthan, Buragaon, Karangonia, Raindogonia, Yayom, Gijiri, Dijungonia, Tulu, Polatari, Raghupam, Tania, Khuppi, Bhalukpong, Balipho, and Palizi villages; East Kameng district, Seppa circle, Pisang village. *Status:* 6b (Threatened). *Class:* Sino-Tibetan, Tibeto-Burman, Central Tibeto-Burman, Hrusish. *Dialects:* Hruso, Levai (Bangru). No apparent wider affiliation within Tibeto-Burman. Varieties sometimes grouped under Tibeto-Burman as Hruish. Levai is similar to Miji [sjl] and may be a distinct language. Lexical similarity: 9% between Koro [jkr] and the Hruso dialect [hru]. Both are highly dissimilar to neighboring languages. *Lg Use:* Steady shift away from Hruso, especially among youth educated outside the area. Also use Assamese [asm], English [eng], Hindi [hin], Miji [sjl]. Used as L2 by Bugun [bgg], Miji [sjl]. *Lg Dev:* Literacy rate in L2: 48%: males 58%, females 39% (2001 census). *Writing:* Latin script. *Other:* 'Aka', painted. Has 2 ethnic groups (Kavatsun and Kutsun) and an additional subdivision called Miri-Akas on the other side of Kaya River (known as Khrome) who speak Mising [mrg], not Hruso. Probably not the same as Plains Miri or Hill Miri (Mising) [mrg] (Sinha 1962). Aka in East Kameng District are called Koro Aka [jkr], distinct from Hruso Aka in West Kameng. Traditional religion, Christian. *Map:* 356:178.

Idu-Mishmi [clk] ("Chulikata" *pej.*, "Chulikotta" *pej.*, Ida, Idu, Midhi, Midu, Sulikota, Yidu Luoba). 11,000 in India (2001 census). Population total all countries: 11,080. 2,200 monolinguals. Arunachal Pradesh, Dibang Valley district; Assam; West Bengal. Also in China (Yidu Luoba). *Status:* 6a (Vigorous). *Class:* Sino-Tibetan, Tibeto-Burman, Central Tibeto-Burman, Digarish. *Dialects:* Reportedly most similar to Digaro-Mishmi [mhu]. Different from Adi [adi]. May be a dialect of Mising [mrg]. Lexical similarity: 7% with the Miju-Mishmi dialect of Miju-Mishmi [mxj], 25% with Digaro-Mishmi [mhu]. *Type:* SOV; postpositions; genitives before noun heads; numerals after noun heads, adjective and relatives before noun head; affixes indicate case of noun phrase; comparatives; open syllables; tonal. *Lg Use:* Home, community, religion. All ages. Positive attitudes. Educated use English [eng]. Also use Assamese [asm], Hindi [hin], Nepali [npi]. *Lg Dev:* Literacy rate in L1: Below 1%. Literacy rate in L2: 55% (2001 census). Radio programs. Grammar. *Writing:* Tibetan script, used in China. *Other:* Mishmi Idu is a Scheduled Tribe. May not be in the Tani group, but is related. Buddhist, Hindu. *Map:* 356:188.

Indian Sign Language [ins] (Indo-Pakistani Sign Language, Urban Indian Sign Language). 2,680,000 in India (2003). Widespread. Also in Bangladesh, Pakistan. *Status:* 6a (Vigorous). *Class:* Deaf sign language. *Dialects:* Bangalore-Chennai-Hyderabad Sign Language, Kolkata Sign Language, Mumbai-Delhi Sign Language. Over 75% of signs from all regions are related. Mumbai-Delhi dialect is most influential. Some influence from British Sign Language [bfi] in the fingerspelling system and a few other signs developed indigenously in India. Related to Nepalese Sign Language [nsp]. *Lg Use:* Deaf schools mainly do not use ISL, but vocational programs often do. Nearly all educated deaf are bilingual in a language of wider communication to some degree. *Lg Dev:* Literacy rate in L2: Below 2%. Male literacy rate is higher than female as men more likely to attend school. TV. Videos. Dictionary. *Other:* 2% or less of deaf children attend deaf schools. In 2001, interpretive training courses initiated in Mumbai by the Ali Yavar Jung National Institute for Hearing Handicapped.

Indo-Portuguese [idb]. 4,940 in India (Cardoso 2006). Population total all countries: 4,970. Relatively few monolinguals, even in Korlai (Cardoso 2006). Daman and Diu; Maharashtra, Korlai near Mumbai; Kerala, Kannur. Also in Sri Lanka. *Status:* 6b (Threatened). *Class:* Creole, Portuguese based. *Dialects:* Cannanore, Cochin (Kochi), Diu. *Lg Use:* It is mostly, if not entirely, spoken by multilingual speakers (Cardoso 2006). Some communities in India have no remaining speakers. Few remaining speakers in Cannanore; last speaker in Cochin, Mr. William Rozario, died on Vypeen Island (2010). Some younger speakers. Indo-Portuguese is in competition with standard Portuguese [por] (Cardoso 2006). Also use English [eng], Gujarati [guj], Hindi [hin], Marathi [mar]. *Lg Dev:* NT: 1826–1852. *Writing:* Latin script. *Other:* The term Indo-Portuguese does not stand for 1 language but rather a number of Portuguese-lexified creoles scattered across South Asia (Cardoso 2006). Christian. *Map:* 358:311.

Irula [iru] (Erukala, Irava, Irulan, Irular, Irular Mozhi, Irulavan, Iruliga, Iruligar, Kad Chensu, Korava). 200,000 (2003 E. Udayakumar). Tamil Nadu, Nilgiri, Coimbatore, Periyar districts; Karnataka; Kerala, Palakkad district, Attapady and Walayar panchayats; Andhra Pradesh. *Status:* 5 (Developing). *Class:* Dravidian, Southern, Tamil-Kannada, Tamil-Kodagu, Tamil-Malayalam, Tamil. *Dialects:* Attapady Irula, Irula Urali, Mele Nadu Irula (Malanadu, Southern Irula), Northern Irula (Kasaba, Kasava, Kasuba), Vette Kada Irula (Irula Pallar, Vettakada), Walayar Irula (Urali Irula). Dialects: Vette Kada 73% intelligibility of Mele Nadu; Northern Irula 83% of Mele Nadu; no intelligibility of Tamil [tam] (1993 Irula survey); Vette Kada 94% of Attapady; Walayar 84% of Attapady. (2004 Palakkad survey). Lexical similarity: 78%–86% between Mele Nadu dialect varieties, 67%–70% with Northern Irula, 64%–66% with Vette Kada, 47%–50% with Tamil [tam]. Attapady has 73%–75% with Mele Nadu and 85%–89% with Vette Kada. Walayar has 74%–79% with Attapady, 76% with Vette Kada, and 69% with Mele Nadu. *Type:* SOV; postpositions; nontonal. *Lg Use:* All domains. Positive attitudes. Also use Badaga [bfq], Kannada [kan], Malayalam [mal], Tamil [tam]. Used as L2 by Attapady Kurumba [pkr]. *Lg Dev:* Literacy rate in L1: Below 1%. Literacy rate in L2: 20% among adults, 50% among younger generation. Grammar. Bible portions: 2001–2013. *Writing:* Malayalam script, used in Kerala. Tamil script, used in Tamil Nadu. *Other:* A Scheduled Tribe. Some people called Irula speak Tamil [tam] as mother tongue. Urali Irula (Periyar) is separate from both Betta Kurumba Urali [xub] and Urali [url] in Idukki District, Kerala. Two Urali Irula dialects in Periyar and Palakkad. Traditional religion, Christian. *Map:* 360:399.

Jad [jda] (Bhotia, Dzad, Rongba). 300 (Breton 1997). Uttarakhand, Uttarkashi district, Harsil subdivision, Jadang and Nilang villages in Jad Ganga gorges. *Status:* 6a (Vigorous). *Class:* Sino-Tibetan, Tibeto-Burman, Western Tibeto-Burman, Bodish, Central Bodish, Central, Western. *Dialects:* None known. Reportedly similar to Spiti Bhoti [spt]. *Type:* Does not have pronominalization found in other languages of the area. *Lg Use:* Garhwali [gbm] learned together with Jad. Code switching and code mixing common. Uncertain whether stable bilingualism will continue or whether Jad will be replaced by Garhwali [gbm] or Hindi [hin]. Home, community. All ages. Negative attitudes. Also use Central Tibetan [bod], Garhwali [gbm], Hindi [hin]. *Lg Dev:* Hindi used for all written communication. *Other:* Some borrowing of vocabulary from Hindi [hin] and Garhwali [gbm]. Buddhist. *Map:* 352:40.

Jangshung [jna] (Central Kinnauri, Jangiam, Jangrami, Thebarskad, Thebor, Thebör Skadd, Zangram, Zhang-Zhung). 1,990 (1998 survey). Himachal Pradesh, Kinnaur district, Morang Tahsil, Jangi, Lippa, and Asrang villages. *Status:* 6a (Vigorous). *Class:* Sino-Tibetan, Tibeto-Burman, Western Tibeto-Burman, Bodish, West Himalayish, Kinauri. *Dialects:* None known. Lexical similarity: 70% with Shumcho [scu], 65% with Sunam [ssk], 51% with Chitkuli Kinnauri [cik], 49% with Pahari Kinnauri [kjo]. *Other:* Traditional religion, Buddhist (Lamaist), Hindu. *Map:* 352:36.

Jarawa [anq]. 250 (Abbi 2006). Andaman Islands, interior and south central Rutland island, central interior and south interior South Andaman island, Middle Andaman island, west coast, 70 square km reserve. *Status:* 6a (Vigorous). *Class:* Andamanese, South Andamanese. *Dialects:* None known. Different from Önge [oon] and Sentinel [std]. *Lg Dev:* Literacy rate in L1: Below 1%. Dictionary. Grammar. *Other:* Seminomadic. Traditional religion. *Map:* 361.

Jaunsari [jns] (Jansauri, Jaunsauri, Pahari). 100,000 (2001 USCWM). Uttarakhand, Dehra Dun district, Kalsi, Tiuni, and Chakrata tahsils, Jaunsar-Bawar division. *Status:* 6a (Vigorous). *Class:* Indo-European, Indo-Iranian, Indo-Aryan, Northern zone, Western Pahari. *Dialects:* Jaunsari, Jaunsari-Bawari. 97% intelligibility between dialects. Perceived by some as a Garhwali [gbm] dialect; but users perceive Garhwali as distinct and report lack of intelligibility. Lexical similarity: 70%–77% between dialects, 63%–70% with Garhwali dialects [gbm], 64% with Kumaoni [kfy], 66% with Hindi [hin], 51%–64% with Sirmauri [srx]. *Lg Use:* Vigorous. Home, village, private prayer. Positive attitudes. Also use Hindi [hin] with higher proficiency among the educated. Used as L2 by Gujari [gju]. *Lg Dev:* Literacy rate in L1: Below 1%. Literacy rate in L2: 26%. Hindi preferred for education. Schools officially use Hindi as medium but Jaunsari used among children and by teachers to explain things to primary students. Bible portions: 1895–2009. *Writing:* Devanagari script. Latin script, no longer in use. Takri (Tankri, Takari) script, no longer in use. *Other:* A Scheduled Tribe. Hindu. *Map:* 352:52.

Juang [jun] (Juango, Patra-Saara, Patua, Puttooas). 23,700 (2001 census). 0 monolinguals. Odisha, south Keonjhar, north Angul, east Dhenkanal districts. *Status:* 5 (Developing). *Class:* Austro-Asiatic, Munda, South Munda, Kharia-Juang. *Dialects:* None known. Not closely related to other languages. Lexical similarity: 20%–22% with Kharia [khr]. *Lg Use:* Positive attitudes. Some Oriya [ory] also used with proficiency higher among men and the educated. *Lg Dev:* Literacy rate in L2: 21% (2001 census). Bible portions. *Writing:* Oriya script. *Other:* A Scheduled Tribe. Traditional religion. *Maps:* 355:146, 359:146.

Juray [juy]. 801,000 (2000). Odisha. *Status:* 6a (Vigorous). *Class:* Austro-Asiatic, Munda, South Munda, Koraput Munda, Sora-Juray-Gorum, Sora-Juray. *Dialects:* None known. Reportedly most similar to Sora [srb]. *Other:* Traditional religion. *Map:* 359:342.

Kachari [xac] (Cachari, Plains Kachari). 59,000 (IMA 1997). Assam, North Cachar district, Cachar hills; Nagaland, Kohima district, Dimapur, Dhansiri administrative circles. 16 villages. *Status:* 6b (Threatened). *Class:* Sino-Tibetan, Tibeto-Burman, Sal, Bodo-Garo-Northern Naga, Bodo-Koch, Bodo-Garo, Bodo. *Lg Use:* Some ethnic Kachari speak it as L1. Most speak Assamese [asm] as L1. Rapidly assimilating to Bengali [ben] or Assamese [asm] (Van Driem 2007). Also use Assamese [asm]. *Lg Dev:* Literacy rate in L2: 81% in Assam (2001 census). *Other:* A Scheduled Tribe. *Map:* 356:238.

Kachchi [kfr] (Cuchi, Cutch, Kachchhi, Kachi, Katch,

Katchi, Kautchy, Kutchchi, Kutchie). 823,000 in India (2001 census). Population total all countries: 873,000. Gujarat, Rann of Kachchh area; Andhra Pradesh; Madhya Pradesh; Uttar Pradesh; Assam; Kerala; Tamil Nadu; Maharashtra; Karnataka; Odisha. Also in Malawi, Pakistan, Tanzania. *Status:* 6a (Vigorous). *Class:* Indo-European, Indo-Iranian, Indo-Aryan, Northwestern zone, Sindhi. *Dialect:* Jadeji. Reportedly similar to Sindhi [snd]. *Lg Use:* Almost all are bilingual in Gujarati [guj]. *Lg Dev:* Radio programs. NT: 2013. *Writing:* Devanagari script. *Other:* Hindu, Muslim. *Map:* 353:73.

Kadar [kej] (Kada). 1,960 (2004 survey), decreasing. Kerala, Thrissur district, Palakkad district, Chittoor taluk; Tamil Nadu, Coimbatore district. *Status:* 6b (Threatened). *Class:* Dravidian, Southern, Tamil-Kannada, Tamil-Kodagu, Tamil-Malayalam, Malayalam. *Dialects:* None known. Phonology related to Tamil [tam] and vocabulary related to Malayalam [mal] (Menon 1996). Lexical similarity: 56%–62% with Tamil [tam], 62%–65% with Malayalam [mal], 67% with Mala Malasar [ima], 61%–63 % with Kanikkaran [kev]. *Lg Use:* Some language shift to Malayalam [mal] observed in Kerala. Home, village, religious services. Also use Malayalam [mal], Tamil [tam]. *Lg Dev:* Literacy rate in L1: Below 1%. Literacy rate in L2: 51% in Kerala, 56% in Tamil Nadu (2001 census). *Other:* A Scheduled Tribe. 3 groups named Kadar in Kerala and Tamil Nadu. The Kadar who use the Kadar language live primarily Palakkad and Thrissur hills, and Coimbatore. A second group lives in Wayanad District and use Malayalam [mal]. A third Kadar (Kadir) group is in Tamil Nadu, Triuchirapalli and Tanjavur districts. They have nothing in common with Western Ghats Kadar. Seen as less developed than other tribes of Chittoor. Hindu, traditional religion. *Map:* 360:402.

Kaikadi [kep] (Kaikadia, Kaikai, Kokadi). 23,700 (2001 census). Maharashtra, Jalgaon district; Karnataka. *Status:* 6a (Vigorous). *Class:* Dravidian, Southern, Tamil-Kannada, Tamil-Kodagu, Tamil-Malayalam, Tamil. *Other:* Nomadic. Traditional religion, Hindu. *Map:* 358:300.

Kalanadi [wkl]. 750 (2004 survey). Kerala State, Wayanad district, southwest. *Status:* 6a (Vigorous). *Class:* Dravidian, Southern. *Dialects:* None known. Lexical similarity: 75% with Malayalam [mal], 74% with Paniya [pcg], 72%–75% with Wayanad Kurichiya [kfh], 79%–83% with Mullu Kurumba [kpb], 88% with Pathiya [pty], 81% with Kunduvadi [wku]. *Lg Use:* Continued vitality doubtful, due to small population, no separate settlements, living with Malayalis, and similarity to Malayalam [mal]. Home. Also use Malayalam [mal]. *Lg Dev:* Younger generation reportedly literate in Malayalam. *Other:* Common cultural origin with Kunduvadiyar and Pathiyar. Hindu. *Map:* 360:384.

Kamar [keq]. 40,000 (2003 BI). Madhya Pradesh, Rewa district; Chhattisgarh, Raipur district; Maharashtra. *Status:* 6a (Vigorous). *Class:* Indo-European, Indo-Iranian, Indo-Aryan, East Central zone. *Dialects:* None known. Lexical similarity: 68%–72% with Bhunjia [bhu], 66%–69% with Chhattisgarhi [hne], 68% with Oriya [ory], 61% with Hindi [hin], 27% with Telugu [tel]. *Lg Use:* Chhattisgarhi [hne] used among themselves and Hindi [hin] with others (Singh 1994). *Other:* A Scheduled Tribe. No relationship between the Kamar caste of iron workers in Bengal and Chota Nagpur and this ethnic group. May be an Indo-Aryan language. Traditional religion, Hindu. *Maps:* 354:103, 359:103.

Kamta [rkt] (Goalparia, Kamtapuri, Koch Rajbanshi, Rajbangsi, Rajbanshi, Rajbansi, Rajbongshi). 5,000,000 in India (2007 M. Toulmin). West Bengal, Jalpaiguri, Uttar Dinajpur, Koch Bihar, and Darjeeling districts; Assam, Dhubri and Kokrajhar districts. *Status:* 5 (Developing). *Lg Use:* Strong vitality in West Bengal and parts of Assam near Koch Bihar. Vitality weakens east of Dhubri in Assam. Those farthest east in Assam tend to prefer Assamese over their mother tongue. All ages. Also use Assamese [asm]. Bilingual ability increases with education. Also use Bengali [ben]. Bilingual ability increases with education. *Lg Dev:* Literacy rate in L2: 15%–20% men, lower for women (2007 Word For All). *Other:* Strong language movement and Kamta has been become a symbol of community political aspirations. Hindu, traditional religion. See main entry on page 56 (as Rangpuri). *Maps:* 355:120, 356:120.

Kanashi [xns] (Kanasi, Malani). 1,400 (Chauhan 2002). Himachal Pradesh, Kullu district, Kullu tahsil, glen of Bios valley, Malana (Malani) village area. *Status:* 6a (Vigorous). *Class:* Sino-Tibetan, Tibeto-Burman, Western Tibeto-Burman, Bodish, West Himalayish, Kinauri. *Dialects:* None known. No intelligibility with any Tibeto-Burman languages of Lahul-Spiti and Kinnaur (Chauhan). *Other:* Surrounded by Indo-Aryan languages. Malana village has the oldest surviving democracy in the world. They practice their own parliamentary form of government. Hindu. *Map:* 352:22.

Kanauji [bjj] (Bhakha, Braj, Braj Kanauji, Dehati, Kannauji). 9,500,000 (2001 USCWM). Uttar Pradesh, Kanpur, Farrukhabad, Etawah, Hardoi, Shahjahanpur, Pilibhit, Mainpuri, and Auraiya districts. *Status:* 6b (Threatened). *Class:* Indo-European, Indo-Iranian, Indo-Aryan, Central zone, Western Hindi, Unclassified. *Dialects:* Kanauji Proper, Tirhari, Transitional Kanauji. Transitional Kanauji dialect is between Kanauji and Awadhi [awa]. Grierson and Konow (1901–1929) call it a form of Braj Bhasha [bra]. The variety spoken in Kannauj and Farrukhabad is considered the pure form. Lexical similarity: 84%–97% between all varieties of Kanauji, 72%–76% with Bundeli [bns], 70%–78% with Braj Bhasha [bra], 83%–94% with Hindi [hin]. *Lg Use:* Shifting to Hindi [hin]. Various domains. Negative attitudes. Most also use Hindi [hin], the less-educated having lower proficiency. *Lg Dev:* Literacy rate in L2: 60% (2001 census). NT: 1821. *Writing:* Devanagari script. *Other:* Kanauji may be only a name given by scholars. Language not commonly referred to as Kanauji. Very low identity. Regard their language as a variety of Hindi [hin]. However, a small local group is interested in promoting Kanauji before it dies out. Hindu, Christian. *Map:* 354:87.

Kangri [xnr] (Kangra-Dogri, Pahari, Pahari Kangri). 1,700,000 (1996 Survey). L2 users: Surrounding Pahari dialects have high comprehension of Kangri. Himachal Pradesh, Kangra, Hamirpur, and Una districts. *Status:* 6a (Vigorous). *Class:* Indo-European, Indo-Iranian, Indo-Aryan, Northern zone, Western Pahari. A member of macrolanguage Dogri [doi]. *Dialects:* Hamirpuri, Palampuri. Lexical similarity: Palampuri dialect; 90% with Bilaspuri [kfs] and Chambeali [cdh], 89% with Mandeali [mjl], 83% with Bhattiyali [bht], 80% with the MacLeod Ganj dialect of Gaddi [gbk]. *Lg Use:* Vigorous. Home, work, market. All ages. Positive attitudes. Hindi [hin] used for communicating with outsiders. Also use Eastern Panjabi [pan], English [eng], Urdu [urd]. *Lg Dev:* Literacy rate in L2: 70%. Educators promote Kangri. Acceptability of other Pahari dialects is high. Poetry. Radio programs. *Writing:* Devanagari script. *Other:* Hindu. *Map:* 352:25.

Kanikkaran [kev] (Kanikkar, Kannikan, Kannikaran, Kanikharan, Malampashi). 19,000 (2007). Ethnic population: 19,000. Kerala, Kozhikode, Ernakulam, Koliam, and Trivandrum districts, Neyyattinkara and Nedumangadu taluks; Tamil Nadu, Kanniyakumari and Tirunelveli districts. *Status:* 6a (Vigorous). *Class:* Dravidian, Southern, Tamil-Kannada, Tamil-Kodagu, Tamil-Malayalam, Tamil. *Dialects:* None known. Lexical similarity: 71%–80% between Kanikkaran varieties in Kerala, 67%–71% between Kanikkaran in Kerala and Tamil Nadu, 66%–75% with Malayalam [mal], 59%–65% with Tamil [tam]. *Lg Use:* Almost all in Kerala are shifting to Malayalam [mal], but those in Tamil Nadu use L1. Also use Malayalam [mal], Tamil [tam]. *Lg Dev:* Literacy rate in L2: 71%–80% in Kerala, 59%–68% in Tamil Nadu (2001 census). *Other:* A Scheduled Tribe. Traditional religion, Hindu. *Map:* 360:379.

Kanjari [kft] (Kagari, Kangar Bhat, Kangri, Kanjri). 91,200 (1995). Uttar Pradesh, Aligarh, Farrukhabad, Etawah, Sitapur, and Kheri districts; Rajasthan; Andhra Pradesh; Madhya Pradesh. *Status:* 6a (Vigorous). *Class:* Indo-European, Indo-Iranian, Indo-Aryan, Unclassified. *Dialect:* Kuchbandhi. May be in the Panjabi group. *Other:* Sometimes called a language of Gypsies who reportedly use certain linguistic means of disguising their language to make it unintelligible to outsiders. A Scheduled Caste who speak a dialect of Hindi [hin] in Uttar Pradesh, a dialect of Mewari [mtr] in Rajasthan, and Hindi in Bihar and Madhya Pradesh (Singh 1995). *Map:* 354:88.

Kannada [kan] (Banglori, Canarese, Kanarese, Madrassi). 37,700,000 in India (2001 census). Population total all countries: 37,739,040. L2 users: 9,000,000 in India. Karnataka; Andhra Pradesh; Tamil Nadu; Maharashtra. Also in Canada, United States. *Status:* 2 (Provincial). Statutory provincial language in Karnataka (1950, Constitution, Schedule VIII). *Class:* Dravidian, Southern, Tamil-Kannada, Kannada. *Dialects:* Aine Kuruba, Bellary, Bijapur, Gulbarga, Jeinu Kuruba, Kumta, Nanjangud. About 20 dialects; Badaga [bfq] may be one. *Type:* SOV. *Lg Use:* Used as L2 by Alu Kurumba [xua], Holiya [hoy], Irula [iru], Jennu Kurumba [xuj], Kannada Kurumba [kfi], Kodava [kfa], Kota [kfe], Kudiya [kfg], Lambadi [lmn], Mudu Koraga [vmd], Paniya [pcg], Ravula [yea], Tamil [tam], Tulu [tcy], Vaagri Booli [vaa]. *Lg Dev:* Literacy rate in L1: 60%. Literacy rate in L2: 60%. Fully developed. Bible: 1831–2000. *Writing:* Braille script. Kannada script, primary usage. *Other:* Hindu, Muslim. *Map:* 351.

Karbi [mjw] (Arleng Alam, Karbi Karbak, Manchati, "Mikir" *pej.*, "Mikiri" *pej.*, Nihang, Puta). 420,000 (2001 census). Assam, Karbi Anglong district, Mikir and Rengma hills, Nagaon, Darrang, Marigaon, Sonitpur, Lakhimpur, and North Cachar districts; Arunachal Pradesh, Papumpare district, Balijan circle; Meghalaya, Jaintia district; Nagaland, foothills around Dimapur. *Status:* 5 (Developing). *Class:* Sino-Tibetan, Tibeto-Burman, Sal, Kuki-Chin-Naga, Karbi. *Dialects:* Chingthang (Jynthong), Mirlong, Rong Kethang (Rengkhang, Rongkhang). Lexical similarity: 82%–96% between dialects. *Lg Use:* Other groups speak Karbi as L1, including some Dimasa. Speakers of all ages use Assamese [asm]. Used as L2 by Sakachep [sch]. *Lg Dev:* Literacy rate in L2: 54% in Assam (2001 census). Radio programs. Grammar. Bible: 1952. *Writing:* Latin script. *Other:* A Scheduled Tribe. Hindu, Christian, traditional religion. *Map:* 356:206.

Kashmiri [kas] (Cashmeeree, Cashmiri, Kacmiri, Kaschemiri, Keshur, Koshur). 5,360,000 in India (2001 census). Population total all countries: 5,580,830. Jammu and Kashmir; Punjab; Uttar Pradesh; Delhi; Kashmir valley. Also in Pakistan, United Kingdom, United States. *Status:* 4 (Educational). Statutory language of provincial identity in Jammu and Kashmir (1950, Constitution, Articles 345–347). *Class:* Indo-European, Indo-Iranian, Indo-Aryan, Northwestern zone, Dardic, Kashmiri. *Dialects:* Bakawali, Bunjwali, Kishtwari (Kashtawari, Kashtwari, Kathiawari, Kistwali), Miraski, Poguli, Rambani, Riasi, Shah-Mansuri, Siraji of Doda, Siraji-Kashmiri, Standard Kashmiri, Zayoli, Zirak-Boli. Transitional dialects to Panjabi [pan]. Kashtawari dialect is standard, other dialects are influenced by Dogri [dgo]. *Type:* SVO. *Lg Use:* Most also use Urdu [urd] (Koul 1983). Also use English [eng], Hindi [hin]. Used as L2 by Bhadrawahi [bhd], Changthang [cna], Gujari [gju]. *Lg Dev:* Literacy rate in L1: 88% male; 12% female over 35 years of age (Koul and Schmidt 1983). Literacy rate in L2: 55% for Jammu and Kashmir (2001 census). 83% would prefer use of Kashmiri rather than Urdu as medium in primary school, 48% in middle school (Koul and Schmidt 1983). Newspapers. Radio programs. Films. Dictionary. Grammar. Bible: 1899–2005. *Writing:* Arabic script, Nastaliq style. Devanagari script. Latin script. Sharada script, no longer in use. *Other:* Muslim, Hindu, Sikh. *Map:* 351.

Katkari [kfu] (Katakari, Katari, Kathodi, Katvadi). 12,000 (2007). Ethnic population: 294,000. Kathodi. Maharashtra, Raigad and Thane districts, Sahayadri Range foothills; Rajasthan, northwest, Onga, Samicha Parebati, Mubusha, and Jhadol police station areas; Gujarat, Surat, Bharuch, Sabarkantha, and Dang districts; Dadra and Nagar Haveli, Amboli and Dapada Panchayat areas. *Status:* 6a (Vigorous). *Class:* Indo-European, Indo-Iranian, Indo-Aryan, Southern zone, Konkani. *Dialects:* Central Katkari, Northern Katkari, Southern Katkari. Referred to as a dialect of Marathi [mar]. 89%–96% intelligibility between dialects. Lexical similarity: 67%–75% with Marathi [mar], 77%–90% among dialects. *Lg Use:* Vigorous. Home, community. Also use Marathi [mar]. *Other:* A Scheduled Tribe. L1 in Maharashtra is Marathi [mar], in Dadra and Nagar Haveli is Kukna [kex], in Gujarat is a variety of Marathi [mar], in Rajasthan is Kathodi, a variety of Marathi [mar] (Singh 1994:475–479). Hindu, traditional religion. *Map:* 358:313.

Khaling [klr] (Khael Baat, Khael Bra, Khalinge Rai). Darjeeling and Sikkim area, scattered. *Status:* 5 (Developing). See main entry on page 250. *Map:* 355:166.

Khamba [kbg] (Khamba Khaadi). 1,330 (1991). Arunachal Pradesh, West Siang district, Singa circle, Yang Sang Chu valley, Nyering, Nuykkang, Yortung, Mankota, and Tashigong villages. *Status:* 6a (Vigorous). *Class:* Sino-Tibetan, Tibeto-Burman, Unclassified. *Lg Dev:* Taught in primary schools. *Writing:* Tibetan script, Hingna style. *Other:* Buddhist. *Map:* 356:187.

Khamti [kht] (Hkamti, Khampti, Kham-Tai, Khamti Shan, Khantis, Tai Kham Ti). 5,000 in India (Bradley 2007). Assam, Lakimpur district, Barkhamti, Barigaon, Deotola, Tunijan, Sribhuyan, Barpathar, and Tipling villages, Dibrugarh District; Arunachal Pradesh, Siang and Lohit districts, Chakham, Memong, Barpathar, Mime, Kheram, M. Pong, and Man Khao villages in Namsai subdivision, and Ningro, Nanam, Inten, Nathaw, Mamareng, Mahang villages in Lohit. *Status:* 6b (Threatened). *Dialects:* Assam Khamti, North Burma Khamti, Sinkaling Khamti. *Lg Use:* Many also use Assamese [asm]. All are bilingual (Bradley 2007). *Lg Dev:* Literacy rate in L2: 73% (2001 census). *Other:* A Scheduled Tribe. Buddhist (Hinayana). See main entry on page 236. *Map:* 356:203.

Khamyang [ksu] (Khamiyang, Khamjang, Shyam, Tai Khamyang, Tai Nora). 50 (2003 S. Morey). Ethnic population: 800. Assam, Tinsukia district, Pawaimukh village. *Status:* 8b (Nearly extinct). *Class:* Tai-Kadai, Kam-Tai, Tai, Southwestern. *Dialects:* None known. Reportedly similar to Phake [phk] of Assam and Shan [shn] of Myanmar. *Lg Use:* Shifting to Assamese [asm]. Mainly older adults. Also use Assamese [asm]. *Lg Dev:* Literacy rate in L2: 58% Assamese [asm] (1981 census). *Other:* A Scheduled Tribe. Close affinity to the Khampti of Arunachal. Several thousand Assamese may use their ethnic group name. Buddhist. *Map:* 356:197.

Khandesi [khn] (Dhed Gujari, Khandeshi, Khandeshi Bhili, Khandish, Maharashtra Bhil). 21,900 (2001 census). Maharashtra, Dhule district, Sakri tahsil; Nasik district, Satna tahsil; Nandurbar district, Nandurbar, and Shahada tahsils; Gujarat. *Status:* 6a (Vigorous). *Class:* Indo-European, Indo-Iranian, Indo-Aryan, Central zone, Khandesi. *Dialects:* Dangri, Khandesi, Kotali Bhil, Kunbi (Kunbau), Rangari. All varieties of Khandesi tested at 90% or higher intelligibility with each other. A group of Kukna in Dhule District speak Khandesi. *Lg Use:* Vigorous. A group of Kukna [kex] in Dhule District also use Khandesi. Positive attitudes. Also use Kukna [kex], Marathi [mar]. Used as L2 by Kukna [kex]. *Lg Dev:* Bible portions. *Other:* See also Dhanki [dhn]. Traditional religion, Christian, Hindu. *Map:* 358:304.

Kharia [khr] (Haria, Khadia, Khariya, Kharvi, Khatria, Kheria). 240,000 in India (2001 census). Population total all countries: 241,580. Primarily Jharkhand, Ranchi district, Simdega subdivision, Thethaitangar Anchal and Kolebira Anchal in Khunti subdivision; West Singhbhum, East Singhbhum, Chhattisgarh, Raigarh, Jashpur, Durg, Bilaspur, and Raipur districts; Odisha, Sundargarh, Sambalpur, and Mayurbhanj districts; Assam; Tripura; West Bengal; Andaman and Nicobar Islands. Dhelki dialect mainly in Jashpur, northwest Gangpur (Raigarh) and Sundargarh; Dudh dialect is east and south, in southern Ranchi, Gangpur (Raigarh) and western Sambalpur. Also in Nepal. *Status:* 5 (Developing). *Class:* Austro-Asiatic, Munda, South Munda, Kharia-Juang. *Dialects:* Dhelki Kharia, Dudh Kharia, Mirdha-Kharia. *Lg Use:* Also use Bengali [ben], Hindi [hin], Oriya [ory], Santhali [sat]. *Lg Dev:* Literacy rate in L2: 46% (1991 census). Radio programs. Dictionary. Grammar. NT: 1992. *Writing:* Devanagari script. Latin script. *Other:* A Scheduled Tribe in Bihar, Madhya Pradesh, Odisha, West Bengal. A Scheduled Caste in Tripura. Christian, Hindu. *Maps:* 354:113, 355:113, 359:113.

Kharia Thar [ksy]. 25,000 (2007 SIL). Ethnic population: 25,500 (2007 SIL). West Bengal, Purulia district, Bundwan, Manbazar, Purulia Muffasil, Puncha, Balrampur, Barabazar, and Hura blocks; Bankura district, Raipur, Ranibandh, and Indpur blocks; West Medinipur district, Binpur block; Jharkhand, East Singhbhum district, Potka, Dhalbhumgarh, Ghatsila, Musabani, Dumaria, and Chakulia blocks; a few in West Singhbhum district. *Status:* 6a (Vigorous). *Class:* Indo-European, Indo-Iranian, Indo-Aryan, Eastern zone, Bengali-Assamese. *Dialects:* A Western subdialect of Bengali [ben] (Grierson and Konow 1901–1929). Lexical similarity: 57%–90% among varieties of Kharia Thar, 53%–63% with Bengali [ben], 51%–67% with Oriya [ory], 57%–75% with Lodhi [lbm]. *Lg Use:* Spoken by some Hill Kharia. Ethnic Hill Kharia in Odisha speak Oriya [ory] as L1. Many in Jharkhand and West Bengal speak Bengali [ben] as L1. Home, village, private prayer. Most also use Bengal [ben] in outside domains. Also use Hindi [hin], Oriya [ory], Santhali [sat]. *Other:* Ethnonym: Kheria, Erenga, or Pahari. Ethnic autonym: Sabar. Traditional religion. *Map:* 355:139.

Khasi [kha] (Kahasi, Kassi, Khasa, Khashi, Khasiyas, Khuchia). 843,000 in India (2001 census). Meghalaya, East and West Khasi Hills, and Jaintia Hills districts; Assam, Cachar, Nagaon, North Cachar Hills, Lakhimpur, and Kamrup districts; Manipur; West Bengal; Tripura. Also in Bangladesh. *Status:* 2 (Provincial). Statutory provincial language in Meghalaya State (1950, Constitution, Articles 345–347 inclusive), unscheduled language. *Class:* Austro-Asiatic, Mon-Khmer, Northern Mon-Khmer, Khasian. *Dialects:* Bhoi-Khasi, Khasi (Cherrapunji, Sohra), Khynrium, War. Bhoi Khasi in East Khasi Hills, Nongpoh block, and Nonglung in East Khasi Hills, Umksning block are very different from standard Khasi, with different word order. Many varieties have only partial mutual inherent intelligibility. War dialect is separate from War-Jaintia [aml]. Cherrapunji (Sohra) is the standard. Lexical similarity: 75% between War dialect and standard Khasi. *Type:* SVO. *Lg Use:* Government, courts, mass media in Meghalaya. Used as L2 by Biete [biu], Sakachep [sch], War-Jaintia [aml]. *Lg Dev:* Literacy rate in L2: 63% in Meghalaya (2001 census). Taught in primary schools. Radio programs. TV. Dictionary. Grammar. Bible: 1891. *Writing:* Bengali script, no longer in use. Latin script, used since about 1842. *Other:* A Scheduled Tribe. Christian, Hindu, Muslim. *Map:* 356:210.

Khirwar [kwx] (Kherwari, Khirwara). 34,300. Chhattisgarh, Surguja district, at Madhya Pradesh and Uttar Pradesh borders. *Status:* 6a (Vigorous). *Class:* Dravidian, South-Central, Gondi-Kui, Gondi. *Other:* Khirwar is a subgroup of the Gonds. Hindu, traditional religion. *Map:* 354:101.

Khowar [khw]. 19,200 in India (2000). *Status:* 5 (Developing). *Other:* Muslim. See main entry on page 269.

Kinnauri [kfk] (Kanauri, Kanaury Anuskad, Kanawari, Kanawi, Kanoreunu Skad, Kanorin Skad, Kanorug Skadd, Kinnaura Yanuskad, Kinner, Kinori, Koonawure, Kunawari, Kunawur, Lower Kinnauri, Malhesti, Milchan, Milchanang, Milchang, Tibas Skad). 65,100 (2001 census). L2 users: 15,000. In Kinnaur District. Himachal Pradesh, Kinnaur, Lahul-Spiti districts, Chauhra to Sangla and north along Satluj river to Morang, upper Ropa river valley villages; Shimla and Rampur area; Uttar Pradesh; Punjab; Kashmir. *Status:* 3 (Wider communication). *Class:* Sino-Tibetan, Tibeto-Burman, Western Tibeto-Burman, Bodish, West Himalayish, Kinauri. *Dialects:* Dialect at Nichar has 79% inherent intelligibility of Sangla. Other varieties have functional intelligibility of each other. Related languages: Kanashi [xns], Chitkuli Kinnauri [cik], and Jangshung Tukpa [jna]. Lexical similarity: 76%–90% among varieties. *Lg Use:* Vigorous. Low proficiency in Hindi [hin]. Used as L2 by Chitkuli Kinnauri [cik]. *Lg Dev:* Literacy rate in L2: 37%: men 52%, women 22%. Dictionary. Grammar. Bible portions: 1909–1917. *Writing:* Devanagari script. Takri (Tankri, Takari) script, no longer in use. *Other:* A Scheduled Tribe. Hindu, Buddhist (Lamaist), traditional religion. *Map:* 352:32.

Kinnauri, Bhoti [nes] (Bhotea of Upper Kinnauri, Bod-Skad, Bud-Kat, Myamkat, Myamskad, Nyamkat, Nyamskad, Puh, Sangs-Rgyas, Sangyas). 6,790 (2000 USCWM). Himachal Pradesh, Kinnaur district, Morang tahsil, upper Kinnauri Sutlej river basin where it becomes Spiti river, Morang tahsil, Nesang village, Puh tahsil, Puh village. Possibly in Kuno, Charang villages. *Status:* 6a (Vigorous). *Class:* Sino-Tibetan, Tibeto-Burman, Western Tibeto-Burman, Bodish, West Himalayish, Kinauri. *Dialects:* None known. May be more than 1 language. Lexical similarity: 71% with Tukpa [tpq], 63% with Mane village, 59% with Darcha village, 54% with Tibetan [bod]. *Lg Dev:* Grammar. *Writing:* Unwritten. *Other:* A Scheduled Tribe. Traditional religion, Buddhist (Lamaist), Hindu. *Map:* 352:35.

Kinnauri, Chitkuli [cik] (Chitkhuli, Chitkuli, Kanauri, Kinnauri, Thebarskad, Tsíhuli, Tsitkhuli). 1,060 (1998 survey). Himachal Pradesh, Kinnaur district, Nichar subdivision, Sangla valley, Baspa river area, Chitkul and Rakchham villages. *Status:* 6a (Vigorous). *Class:* Sino-Tibetan, Tibeto-Burman, Western Tibeto-Burman,

Bodish, West Himalayish, Kinauri. *Dialects:* None known. Lexical similarity: 46% with Kinnauri [kfk], 51% with Jangshung [jna], 43% with Shumcho [scu], 38% with Sunam [ssk]. *Lg Use:* Also use Kinnauri [kfk]. *Lg Dev:* Literacy rate in L1: Below 1%. Grammar. *Other:* A Scheduled Tribe. Traditional religion, Buddhist (Lamaist), Hindu. *Map:* 352:37.

Kinnauri, Pahari [kjo] (Boli, Chamang Boli, "Harija" *pej.*, "Harijan Boli" *pej.*, "Kinnauri, Harijan" *pej.*, Lower Kinnauri, Orasi, Ores, Sonar Boli). 6,330 (1998 survey). Himachal Pradesh, throughout Kinnaur district. *Status:* 6a (Vigorous). *Class:* Indo-European, Indo-Iranian, Indo-Aryan, Northern zone, Western Pahari. *Other:* Spoken by Scheduled Castes throughout Kinnaur District. *Map:* 352:38.

Kisan [xis] (Birhor, Koda, Kola, Kora, Kuda, Kunha, Kunhar, Kunna, Kunrukh, Kunuk, Mirdha, Morva, Nagesia, Nageswar). 141,000 (2001 census). Orissa, Sambalpur district and Sundargarh districts; Jharkhand, Palamu district; West Bengal, Jalpaiguri and Darjeeling districts. *Status:* 5 (Developing). *Class:* Dravidian, Northern. *Lg Use:* Home. All ages. Also use Oriya [ory]. *Lg Dev:* Literacy rate in L1: 17% (1981 census). Materials for multilingual education have been prepared in Kisan. Taught in primary schools, in 20 schools in Sambalpur district. *Writing:* Oriya script. *Other:* Kisan is a Scheduled Tribe.

Koch [kdq] (Koc, Kocch, Koce, Kocha, Kochboli, Konch). 30,000 in India (2007 survey), increasing. Includes only the Koch of Garo Hills, Meghalaya, India. Population total all countries: 36,000. 0 monolinguals. Meghalaya, West Garo Hills district; Assam, Goalpara, Nagaon districts; Tripura; West Bengal; Bihar. Also in Bangladesh. *Status:* 6a (Vigorous). *Class:* Sino-Tibetan, Tibeto-Burman, Sal, Bodo-Garo-Northern Naga, Bodo-Koch, Koch. *Dialects:* Harigaya, Margan (Dasgaya), Tintekiya, Wanang. Tintekiya in Meghalaya is intelligible with same dialect in Bangladesh; Tintekiya not intelligible with other Koch dialects; Koch-Rabha and Harigaya are mutually intelligible with Wanang; Dasgaya and Harigaya are mutually intelligible; these form a dialect chain (Koch-Rabha-Wanang-Harigaya-Dasgaya-Tintekiya). Lexical similarity: 90% between Tintekiya Koch of India and Bangladesh; Tintekiya: 44%–55% with other Koch dialects; Kock: 31%–39% with Rongdani Rabha [rah], 13%–17% with Garo [grt]. Lexical borrowing is heavier when it comes to high register vocabulary; Koch has borrowed words from Bangla [ben], Assamese [asm] and Hajong [haj]. *Lg Use:* Vigorous. Non-Koch in Koch villages normally speak Koch. Only 6 of the 8 endogamous groups still speak their mother tongue: Tintekiya, Wanang, Harigaya, Dasgaya, Chapra, and Koch-Rabha. Sankar and Satpariya have no known speakers. All domains. All ages. Positive attitudes. Also use Assamese [asm], Bengali [ben], Bodo [brx], English [eng], Garo [grt], Hajong [haj], Hindi [hin], Nepali [npi], Rabha [rah]. *Lg Dev:* Literacy rate in L2: Approximately 75% in any of the following languages: Assamese [asm], Bangla [ben], Garo [grt], English [eng], Hindi [hin], Rabha [rah], or Bodo [brx]. Show a growing interest toward education (Singh 1994). *Writing:* Bengali script. *Other:* A Scheduled Tribe in Meghalaya. Koch-Rabha belongs to Koch linguistically and ethnically but claims identity with the Rabha for political reasons. Traditional religion, Christian, Hindu. *Map:* 355:123.

Koda [cdz] (Kaora, Kora, Korali, Korati, Kore, Mudi, Mudikora). 43,000 in India (2001 census). Population total all countries: 44,300. West Bengal, Bardhaman and Bankura districts. Also in Bangladesh. *Status:* 6a (Vigorous). *Class:* Austro-Asiatic, Munda, North Munda, Kherwari, Mundari. *Dialects:* None known. Lexical similarity: 49%–55% with Santhali [sat], 61%–67% with Mundari [unr], 57%–60% with Kol [ekl]; wordlist contained 19% Bengali [ben] words. *Writing:* Bengali script. *Map:* 355:134.

Kodaku [ksz] (Koraku). 15,700 (1991 census). Chhattisgarh, Surguja district; Jharkhand, Palamau, Garhwa districts; Uttar Pradesh, Sonbhadra district. *Status:* 6a (Vigorous). *Class:* Austro-Asiatic, Munda, North Munda, Kherwari. *Dialects:* None known. A subgroup of Korwa [kfp] (Parkin 1991). Lexical similarity: 82%–96% between varieties, 50%–70% with Korwa [kfp]. *Lg Use:* Kodaku in Jharkhand shifting to a local variety of Sadri [sck]. Kodaku in Chhattisgarh retaining their mother tongue more. In Chhattisgarh most use Kodaku in home and village and it is used by children with each other. Also use Hindi [hin], Kurux [kru]. *Lg Dev:* Literacy rate in L1: 26% in Chhattisgarh (2001 census). *Other:* Grouped with Korwa on Scheduled Tribes list in Chhattisgarh and Madhya Pradesh. Ethnic autonym: Korwa in Jharkhand, though language used is Kodaku. Traditional religion, Christian, Hindu. *Maps:* 354:100, 355:100.

Kodava [kfa] (Coorge, Kadagi, Khurgi, Kodagu, Kotagu, Kurja, Kurug). 200,000 (2001). Ethnic population: 200,000. 100,000 in Kodagu District; 100,000 in Karnataka District and major cities. Karnataka, Coorg (Kodagu) district, around Mercara, Malayalam border south. *Status:* 5 (Developing). *Class:* Dravidian, Southern, Tamil-Kannada, Tamil-Kodagu, Kodagu. *Dialects:* None known. May be more than 1 language. 66% intelligibility of Malappuram [pcg]. Lexical similarity: 72% with Malappuram Paniya [pcg]. *Lg Use:* Vigorous. L1 of Airi, Male-Kudiya, Meda, Kembatti, Kapal, Maringi, Heggade, Kavadi, Kolla, Thatta, Koleya, Koyava, Banna, Golla, Kanya, Ganiga, and Malaya. Home, community, religion. 50% also use English [eng]. 80% also use Kannada [kan]. Also use Malayalam [mal]. Used as L2 by Kudiya [kfg]. *Lg Dev:* Literacy rate in L2: More than 95% in Kannada [kan]. Newspapers. Radio programs. Films. TV. *Writing:* Kannada script. *Other:* A symbol of identity. 'Kodagu', situated to the west. Northern variety has emerged as standard and is used in Kodava literature (Rajyashree 2001). Hindu, traditional religion. *Map:* 360:367.

Koireng [nkd] (Koirng, Kolren, Koren, Kwoireng, Liangmai, Liangmei, Liyang, Liyangmai, Lyengmai, Quoireng). 3,000 (2002 Baptist Church Association). Manipur, Senapati district, Saikul and Kangpokpi subdivisions, 5 villages; Bishnupur district, 3 villages south of Moirang; Chandel district, 2 villages near Palel; Nagaland. *Status:* 6a (Vigorous). *Class:* Sino-Tibetan, Tibeto-Burman, Sal, Kuki-Chin-Naga, Zeme. *Dialects:* None known. Not intelligible with any related speech varieties (1991 P. Khasung). Lexical similarity: 62%–68% with Aimol [aim], 60%–66% with Purum [pub], 64% with Kharam Naga [kfw]. *Lg Use:* Purest Koireng spoken in Satu and Utonglo (2000 T. Shiekshel). All ages, although children mix Meitei [mni] in with L1. Young people also use English [eng]. 15% also use Kom [kmm]. Also use Meitei [mni]. *Lg Dev:* Literacy rate in L1: Below 1%. Literacy rate in L2: 70%–80%. Older adults read Meitei, the young read English. Bible portions: 1997–2000. *Other:* Different from Liangmai Naga [njn]. A Scheduled Tribe. Assigned under 3 different Naga groups politically. Christian, traditional religion. *Map:* 356:242.

Kok Borok [trp] (Kakbarak, Kokbarak, Tipura, Tripura, Tripuri, Usipi Mrung). 778,000 in India (2001 census). Population total all countries: 783,000. Tripura; Assam. Also in Bangladesh. *Status:* 4 (Educational). Statutory language of provincial identity in Tripura State (1964, Official Languages Act No. 19 (as amended)), not a Schedule VIII language. *Class:* Sino-Tibetan, Tibeto-Burman, Sal, Bodo-Garo-Northern Naga, Bodo-Koch, Bodo-Garo, Bodo. *Dialects:* Debbarma, Jamatia, Noatia (Tipra). Debbarma is spoken by the royal family and is medium of communication with the other dialects; understood by all, but not vice versa. *Lg Dev:* Literacy rate in L1: 74% (2001 census). Taught in primary and secondary schools. Newspapers. Radio programs. Dictionary. Grammar. Bible: 1998. *Writing:* Bengali script. Latin script. *Other:* Traditional religion, Muslim. *Map:* 357:258.

Kolami, Northwestern [kfb] (Kolam, Kolamboli, Kolamy, Kolmi, Kulme). 122,000 (2001 census). Maharashtra, Yavatmal, Wardha, and Nanded districts; Andhra Pradesh; Madhya Pradesh. *Status:* 5 (Developing). *Class:* Dravidian, Central, Kolami-Naiki. *Dialects:* Madka-Kinwat, Maregaon, Pulgaon, Wani. Northwestern [kfb] and Southeastern Kolami [nit] not inherently intelligible. Neither is intelligible of Bodo Parja [bdv], Gadaba [gau], or Pottangi Ollar Gadaba [gdb]. Lexical similarity: 61%–68% with Southeastern Kolami [nit]. *Lg Use:* Home, community. Limited proficiency in Marathi [mar]. Also use Northern Gondi [gno], Telugu [tel]. *Lg Dev:* Literacy rate in L1: 4%. Dictionary. Grammar. NT: 2006. *Writing:* Devanagari script. *Other:* Kolam is a Scheduled Tribe. Traditional religion, Hindu. *Map:* 358:321.

Kolami, Southeastern [nit]. 10,000 (1989 F. Blair). 1,500 speakers of Naiki (Van Driem 2007). Andhra Pradesh, Adilabad district; Maharashtra, Chandrapur, and Nanded districts. *Status:* 6a (Vigorous). *Class:* Dravidian, Central, Kolami-Naiki. *Dialects:* Asifabad, Metla-Kinwat, Naiki, Utnur. Not intelligible with Northwestern Kolami [kfb]. Rao (1950) reports another dialect in Chinnoor and Sirpur taluks of Adilabad District. The Naiki dialect is different from Naikri (Zvelebil 1970:13). Lexical similarity: 85%–88% with Naiki and other Southeastern Kolami dialects, 83% with the Metla-Kinwat and Utnur, 86% with Asifabad and Utnur, 60%–74% with Northwestern Kolami [kfb]. *Lg Dev:* Literacy rate in L2: Low. Bible portions. *Maps:* 358:322, 359:322.

Koli, Kachi [gjk] (Bajania, Kachi, Kachi Gujarati, Katchi, Kohli, Kolhi, Koli, Kori, Kuchi, Kuchikoli, Vagari, Vagaria, Vaghri). 400,000 in India (1998). 100,000 Kachi Koli, 250,000 Rabari, 50,000 or more Vagri Meghwar, Katai Meghwar, and Zalavaria Koli. Gujarat, Rann of Kachchh district, centered around Bhuj. *Status:* 5 (Developing). *Dialects:* Kachi, Kachi Bhil, Katai Meghwar, Rabari (Rahabari), Vagri (Kachi Meghwar), Zalavaria Koli. *Other:* Hindu. See main entry on page 269. *Map:* 353:72.

Koli, Wadiyara [kxp] (Wadaria, Wadhiara). 404,000 in India (2000). Population total all countries: 579,000. Gujarat, near Wadhyar town. Also in Pakistan. *Status:* 6a (Vigorous). *Class:* Indo-European, Indo-Iranian, Indo-Aryan, Central zone, Gujarati. *Dialect:* Tharadari Koli. Mewasi [kxp] and Wadiyara are almost the same linguistically and are converging as a caste. Dialects listed are distinct sociolinguistic endogamous ethnic groups. Lexical similarity: 78% with Kachi Koli [gjk]. *Writing:* Arabic script. *Map:* 353:71.

Kom [kmm] (Kom Rem). 14,700 (2001 census). East and central Manipur, Churachandpur, Tamenglong, and Senapati districts, 22 villages. *Status:* 5 (Developing). *Class:* Sino-Tibetan, Tibeto-Burman, Sal, Kuki-Chin-Naga, Kuki-Chin, Northern. *Dialect:* Kolhreng. Kolhreng may be a distinct language. *Lg Use:* Aimol [aim], Koireng [nkd], and Chiru [cdf] speakers also understand Kom. Fluent in Meitei [mni]. Used as L2 by Koireng [nkd]. *Lg Dev:* Literacy rate in L2: 64% (2001 census). Newspapers. Dictionary. Bible: 1996. *Writing:* Latin script. *Other:* A Scheduled Tribe. Christian. *Map:* 357:251.

Konda-Dora [kfc] (Porja). 20,000 (2007 Word For All). Konda-Dora in Andhra Pradesh, Vizianagaram, Srikakulam, and East Godavari districts; Kubi in Odisha, Koraput district; Assam. *Status:* 5 (Developing). *Class:* Dravidian, South-Central, Gondi-Kui, Konda-Kui, Konda. *Dialects:* Konda-Dora (Konda), Kubi. Konda and Kubi dialects mutually inherently intelligible. Lexical similarity: 83% between Konda-Dora and Kubi dialect, 28%–36% with Telugu [tel]. *Lg Use:* Also use Oriya [ory]. *Lg Dev:* Literacy rate in L2: 35%–44% for Vizianagaram, Srikakulam and E. Godavari districts; 29% among Kubi in Odisha (2001 census). NT: 2006. *Writing:* Telugu script. *Other:* A Scheduled Tribe. Glossonym: Konda-Dora. Ethnonym: Porja. Many ethnic Porja have adopted Telugu as L1. The Porja are well established as two groups: the Pedda Kondalu and Chinna Kondalu. The Pedda Kondalu retain most of their traditional culture; however, the Chinna Kondalu have been heavily influenced by the Telugu. Traditional religion. *Map:* 359:352.

Konkani [knn] (Bankoti, Central Konkan, Concorinum, Cugani, Kathodi, Katvadi, Konkan Standard, Konkanese, Konkani Mangalorean, Kunabi, North Konkan). 2,420,000 in India (2001 census). Population total all countries: 2,423,540. North and central coastal strip of Maharashtra; Karnataka; Dadra and Nagar Haveli; Kerala. Also in Canada. *Status:* 2 (Provincial). Statutory provincial language in Goa State (1992, Constitution, 71st Amendment). *Class:* Indo-European, Indo-Iranian, Indo-Aryan, Southern zone, Konkani. A member of macrolanguage Konkani [kok]. *Dialects:* Agari of Kolaba, Bhandari, Chitapavani, Dhanagari, Ghati (Maoli), Karhadi, Kiristav, Koli, Mahari (Dhed, Holia, Parvari), Parabhi (Damani, Kayasthi), Sangamesvari (Bakoti, Bankoti), Thakuri (Thakari, Thakri, Thakua, Thakura). Dialects closely related; Chitapavani recognized as standard Konkani. Local fishermen use the Koli dialect (Hukkeri). Related to Katkari [kfu] (dialects: Kathodi, Katvadi), Varli [vav], Phudagi [phd], Samvedi [smv], Mangelas. *Lg Use:* Used as L2 by Goan Konkani [gom]. *Lg Dev:* Newspapers. Radio programs. Films. Dictionary. Grammar. Bible: 1997. *Writing:* Devanagari script, primary usage. Kannada script, no longer in use. Latin script, no longer in use. *Other:* Hindu. *Map:* 351.

Konkani [kok]. A macrolanguage (see page 9). *Other:* Includes: Goan Konkani [gom], Konkani [knn].

Konkani, Goan [gom] (Goan, Gomataki, Konknni, Southern Kanara). 3,630,000 in India (2000). Population total all countries: 3,633,900. South coast strip of Maharashtra, Ratnagari district; Goa; Karnataka; Kerala. Also in Kenya, United Arab Emirates. *Status:* 5 (Developing). *Class:* Indo-European, Indo-Iranian, Indo-Aryan, Southern zone, Konkani. A member of macrolanguage Konkani [kok]. *Dialects:* Bardeskari (Gomantaki), Chitpavani (Konkanasths), Daldi (Nawaits), Kudali (Malvani), Mangalore Standard Konkani (Goan), Sarasvat Brahmin. Daldi and Chitapavani [knn] are intermediate varieties between Goan Konkani [gom] and standard Konkani [knn]. *Lg Use:* Also use Konkani [knn]. *Lg Dev:* Bible: 2006. *Writing:* Kannada script. Latin script. *Other:* Christian. *Maps:* 358:327, 360:327.

Koraga, Korra [kfd] (Koragar, Koragara, Korangi, Korra). 14,000 (2007 census). Karnataka, Dakshina Kannada, and Udupi districts; Kerala, Kannur, and Kasargod districts; Tamil Nadu. *Status:* 6b (Threatened). *Class:* Dravidian, Southern, Tulu, Koraga. *Dialects:* Ande, Onti, Tappu. Related to Tulu [tcy], Bellari [brw]. Not intelligible with Mudu Koraga [vmd], Tulu [tcy], or Kannada [kan]. Structural differences in phonology with Mudu Koraga. According to Bhat (1968), there are 4 dialects:

Onti (spoken in Udupi), Tappu (in Hebri), Mudu (in Coondapur), Ande (in Mangalore). *Lg Use:* Also use Tulu [tcy]. *Other:* Koraga is a Scheduled Tribe. Hindu. *Map:* 360:362.

Koraga, Mudu [vmd] (Muudu). Kerala. *Status:* 6b (Threatened). *Class:* Dravidian, Southern, Tulu, Koraga. *Dialects:* None known. Distinct from Korra Koraga [kfd], Tulu [tcy], or Kannada [kan]. Structural differences in phonology with Korra Koraga. *Lg Use:* Also use Kannada [kan]. *Other:* Koraga is a Scheduled Tribe. Hindu. *Map:* 360:363.

Korku [kfq] (Bondeya, Bopchi, Korki, Kuri, Kurku, Kurku-Ruma, Ramekhera). 574,000 (2001 census). South Madhya Pradesh, south Betul district, north, and Betul city area, Hoshangabad district, East Nimar (Khandwa) district; north Maharashtra, Amravati, Buldana, Akola districts. *Status:* 5 (Developing). *Class:* Austro-Asiatic, Munda, North Munda, Korku. *Dialects:* Bondoy, Bouriya, Mawasi (Muasi, Muwasi), Ruma. Dialects in northern Maharashtra and south central Madhya Pradesh constitute one language; 82% to 97% intelligibility among them; Bouriya most widely understood. Lexical similarity: 76%–82% with Laki Bouriya dialects. *Lg Use:* Positive attitudes. Also use Hindi [hin], Marathi [mar]. Used as L2 by Nihali [nll]. *Lg Dev:* Literacy rate in L1: 1%–5%. Literacy program in some villages in Chikaldara field. 50 literates reported. Bible portions: 1900–1981. *Writing:* Devanagari script. *Other:* Different from Koraku [ksz]. A Scheduled Tribe in India. Traditional religion, Hindu. *Maps:* 354:106, 358:106.

Korlai Creole Portuguese [vkp] (Creole Portuguese). 750 (1998 J. Clements). 250 families (2002). Maharashtra, Korlai, 200 km south of Mumbai, west coast. *Status:* 6a (Vigorous). *Class:* Creole, Portuguese based. *Dialects:* None known. A blend of Portuguese [por] and Marathi [mar]. *Lg Use:* L1 of Christian farming community in upper Korlai. Intense cultural pressure from surrounding Marathi-speaking [mar] population. Home. Fluent Marathi [mar] used with outsiders. *Writing:* Devanagari script. Latin script. *Other:* Christian. *Map:* 358:314.

Koro [jkr] (Aka Koro). 1,500 (2011). Arunachal Pradesh, East Kameng district. *Status:* 6b (Threatened). *Class:* Sino-Tibetan, Tibeto-Burman, Unclassified. *Dialects:* None known. Lexical similarity: 9% with Hruso [hru]. Both are highly dissimilar to neighboring languages. *Lg Use:* Home. *Writing:* Unwritten. *Other:* Part of the Aka ethnic group. *Map:* 356:179.

Korwa [kfp] (Ernga, Singli). 34,600 (2001 census). Few monolinguals. Jharkhand, Palamau, Garhwa and Gumla districts; Chhattisgarh, Jashpur, Surguja, Raigarh, Korba, Bilaspur and districts; Odisha, Mayurbhanj and Sundargarh districts; Uttar Pradesh, Mirzapur district; West Bengal; Andhra Pradesh; Maharashtra. *Status:* 6a (Vigorous). *Class:* Austro-Asiatic, Munda, North Munda, Kherwari, Mundari. *Dialect:* Majhi-Korwa. Lexical similarity: 71%–92% between dialects, 50%–70% with Kodaku [ksz], 26%–36% with local Sadri [sck] spoken by Dihari Korwa. Lexical similarity with Sadri (an Indo-Aryan language) shows noticeable influence of Sadri on Korwa. *Lg Use:* Some Pahadi Korwa are shifting to Sadri [sck]. Dihari Korwa of Jashpur speak a local variety of Sadri as mother tongue. Some Korwa speak Chhattisgarhi [hne] as mother tongue. *Lg Dev:* Literacy rate in L1: Below 1%. Literacy rate in L2: 26% for Chhattisgarh (2001 census). *Other:* A Scheduled Tribe in Jharkhand, Chhattisgarh, Madhya Pradesh, Bihar, West Bengal. Also a Scheduled Caste in Uttar Pradesh speaking Hindi as mother tongue (Singh 1995). Korwa divided into two groups: Pahadi (hill dwellers) and Dihari (plains dwellers). No intermarriage. Hindu, Muslim. *Maps:* 354:112, 355:112.

Kota [kfe] (Kother-Tamil, Kotta, Kowe-Adiwasi). 930 (2001 census). Ethnic population: 1,400. Tamil Nadu, Sholur Kokkal, New Kotagiri, Kilkotagiri, Kollimalai, Kundah Kotagiri, Trichicady, and Gudalur settlements; a few in Ooty, Coonoor, Indunagar, Aravankavu, and Wellington; Chennai. *Status:* 5 (Developing). *Class:* Dravidian, Southern, Tamil-Kannada, Tamil-Kodagu, Toda-Kota. *Dialect:* Ko Bashai. Lexical similarity: 35% with Badaga [bfq], 38% with Tamil [tam], 36% with Malayalam [mal], 24% with Toda [tcx]. *Lg Use:* Tamil [tam] used in home and major domains. Language shift taking place. Positive attitudes. Also use Badaga [bfq], Kannada [kan], Tamil [tam]. *Lg Dev:* Literacy rate in L1: Below 1%. Literacy rate in L2: 75% (2001 census). Grammar. *Writing:* Tamil script. *Other:* A Scheduled Tribe. Endogamous within the ethnic group. Hindu. *Map:* 360:388.

Koya [kff] (Kavor, Kaya, Koa, Koi, Koi Gondi, Koitar, Koyato, Koyi, Raj Koya). 362,000 (2001 census). Andhra Pradesh, south of Godavari river, adjoining districts north of the river; Odisha, Koraput district, Malkangiri subdivision; Chhattisgarh, Bastar district; Maharashtra. *Status:* 5 (Developing). *Class:* Dravidian, South-Central, Gondi-Kui, Konda-Kui, Manda-Kui, Kui-Kuvi. *Dialects:* Dorli (Chintoor Koya, Dor Koi, Dora, Dora Koi, Dorla Koitur, Dorla Koya, Korla), Jaganathapuram Koya (Godavari Koya, Gommu Koya), Malkangiri Koya, Podia Koya (Gotte Koya). Linguistic center is Chintoor. Malkangiri and Podia are more divergent. Separate from Northern Gondi [gno] and Southern Gondi [ggo]. *Lg Use:* Some also use Telugu [tel], but proficiency is low. *Lg Dev:* Literacy rate in L2: 7%. NT: 1997–2004. *Writing:* Devanagari script. Latin script, reportedly preferred by Koya leaders. Oriya script. Telugu script. *Other:* A Scheduled Tribe. Traditional religion, Hindu. *Map:* 359:360.

Kudiya [kfg] (Male Kudiya). 2,800 (2007). Karnataka, Kodagu, Dakshina, and Kannada districts; Kerala, Kannur, and Kasargod districts; Tamil Nadu. *Status:* 6a (Vigorous). *Class:* Dravidian, Southern, Tulu. *Lg Use:* Also use Kannada [kan], Kodava [kfa], Malayalam [mal], Tulu [tcy]. *Lg Dev:* Literacy rate in L2: 48% for Scheduled Tribes in Karnataka; 63% for Kudiya in Kerala, 65% in Tamil Nadu (2001 census). *Writing:* Kannada script. Malayalam script. *Other:* A Scheduled Tribe. Traditional religion, Hindu. *Map:* 360:364.

Kudmali [kyw] (Bedia, Dharua, Khotta, Kurmali, Kurmali Thar, Kurumali). 37,000 (IMA 1997). Jharkhand, east side; West Bengal, west Purulia, Bankura Malda, Nadia, and Western Midnapur districts; Odisha, Keonjhar, Mayourbhanj, and Sundargargh districts; Assam, Darrang, Sonitpur, Golaghat, and Jorhat districts. *Status:* 6a (Vigorous). *Class:* Indo-European, Indo-Iranian, Indo-Aryan, Eastern zone, Bihari. *Dialects:* None known. Lexical similarity: 58%–89% between varieties, 61%–86% with Panchpargania [tdb], 58%–72% with Magahi (Khortha) [mag], 51%–73% with Sadri [sck], 46%–53% with Oriya [ory], 41%–55% with Bengali [ben], 44%–58% with Hindi [hin]. *Lg Use:* Vigorous, but most young people in Odisha speak Oriya [ory] among themselves rather than Kudmali. All domains. All ages. Positive attitudes. Also use Bengali [ben], Hindi [hin], Oriya [ory]. *Lg Dev:* There are Pre-degree, Degree, and Masters level programs in Kudmali. *Writing:* Bengali script, used in West Bengal. Devanagari script, used in Jharkhand. Oriya script, used in Odisha. *Other:* Kudmali is spoken by the Kurmi people of Assam brought to the tea gardens from Bihar, Odisha, and West Bengal. Hindu. *Map:* 355:140.

Kui [kxu] (Kanda, Kandh, Khond, Khondi, Khondo, Kodu,

Kodulu, Kuinga, Kuy). 916,000 (2001 census). 410,000 ethnic Kui Khond who speak Kui plus additional ethnic groups. Odisha, Phulbani, Koraput, and Ganjam districts; Ganjam, Udayagiri area; Andhra Pradesh; Madhya Pradesh; Tamil Nadu. *Status:* 6b (Threatened). *Class:* Dravidian, South-Central, Gondi-Kui, Konda-Kui, Manda-Kui, Kui-Kuvi. *Dialects:* Gumsai, Khondi. *Lg Dev:* Radio programs. Bible: 2006. *Writing:* Oriya script. *Other:* Different from Kuvi [kxv] and Koya [kff] (Koi). Kondh is a Scheduled Tribe. Hindu, Christian. *Map:* 359:340.

Kukna [kex] (Kanara, Kanara Konkani, Kokna, Kokni). 111,000 (2001 census). L2 users: 100,000 (1998). Gujarat, Dangs and Valsad districts; Maharashtra, Dhule, Nasik, and Thane districts; Dadra and Nagar Haveli; Karnataka, Dakshina Kannada (Kanara) district; Rajasthan. *Status:* 3 (Wider communication). *Class:* Indo-European, Indo-Iranian, Indo-Aryan, Southern zone, Konkani. *Dialects:* None known. Dhule District Kukna has 98%–100% intelligibility with Khandesi [khn]. *Lg Use:* A group of Kukna in Dhule District also use Khandesi [khn]. Used as L2 by Khandesi [khn]. *Lg Dev:* Literacy rate in L1: 10%–30%. Some literacy work being done. Radio programs. NT: 1977–2002. *Writing:* Devanagari script. Gujarati script. *Other:* May be the same as Dhanki [dhn]. Hindu. *Map:* 358:309.

Kulung [kle] (Kholung, Khulung, Khulunge Rai, Kulu Ring). Sikkim, Assam Lingzey, Zoom and many other places; West Bengal, Jalpaiguri district; Uttarakhand, Dehradun; Assam. *Status:* 6b (Threatened). See main entry on page 251. *Map:* 355:165.

Kumaoni [kfy] (Kamaoni, Kumau, Kumauni, Kumawani, Kumgoni, Kumman, Kunayaoni). 2,360,000 (1998 survey). 472,000 monolinguals (1998 SIL). Uttarakhand, Almora, Nainital, Pithoragarh, Bageshwar, Champawat, and Udhamsingh Nagar districts; Central Kumaoni dialect is in Almora and north Nainital; Northeastern Kumaoni in Pithoragarh; Southeastern Kumaoni in southeast Nainital; Western Kumaoni is west of Almora and Nainital. *Status:* 5 (Developing). *Class:* Indo-European, Indo-Iranian, Indo-Aryan, Northern zone, Central Pahari. *Dialects:* Central Kumaoni, Northeastern Kumaoni, Southeastern Kumaoni, Western Kumaoni. Reportedly, eastern dialects are different. Names sometimes listed for dialects or subgroups are: Askoti, Bhabari of Rampur, Chaugarkhiya, Danpuriya, Gangola, Johari, Khasparjiya, Kumaiya Pachhai, Pashchimi, Phaldakotiya, Kumaoni, Rau-Chaubhaisi, Sirali, Soriyali. Most closely related to Garwhali [gbm] and Nepali [npi]. *Lg Use:* Home, community. All ages. Positive attitudes. Central dialect is most accepted. Hindi [hin] used in towns and markets, mostly by men but also by a few educated women and school-aged children. Used as L2 by Byangsi [bee], Chaudangsi [cdn], Darmiya [drd], Gujari [gju], Rawat [jnl], Rongpo [rnp]. *Lg Dev:* Literacy rate in L2: 72% for Uttarakhand (2001 census). Motivation for literacy not high. Poetry. Magazines. Radio programs. Dictionary. Grammar. Bible portions: 1825–2007. *Writing:* Devanagari script. *Other:* Hindu, traditional religion. *Maps:* 352:55, 354:55.

Kumarbhag Paharia [kmj] (Kumar, Mad, Mal, Maler, Malti, Malto, Maltu, Paharia, Pahariya). 12,500 (Bhaskararao 2006). Jharkhand, central former Santhal Pargana district, Godda district, Sundar Pahardi block, Pakaur district except southernmost block. Reported in West Bengal, Bankura, Barddhaman, and Murshidabad districts; Odisha, Mayurbhanj. *Status:* 6a (Vigorous). *Class:* Dravidian, Northern. *Dialects:* None known. Low comprehension of Mal Paharia [mkb]. Related to Kurux [kru]. Lexical similarity: 80% with Mal Paharia [mkb]. *Lg Use:* Vigorous. All domains. Positive attitudes. Also use Bengali [ben], Hindi [hin]. *Other:* Part of the Malto ethnic group. Traditional religion. *Map:* 355:131.

Kumbaran [wkb]. 10,000 (2004 NLCI). Kerala, Wayanad, Kozhikode, and Malappuram districts; Palakkad, Trissur, Ernakkulam, and Kannur; all states in peninsular India. *Status:* 6b (Threatened). *Class:* Dravidian, Southern. *Dialects:* None known. Reportedly cannot understand Telugu [tel] on Wayanad District radio. Lexical similarity: 48% with Telugu [tel]. *Lg Use:* Fairly vigorous in Wayanad District although Malayalam [mal] is used some in home and village. Positive attitudes in Wayanad District. *Lg Dev:* Literacy rate in L2: below 50% in older adult age group in Kerala. *Other:* Kumbaran are a subcaste of Chettiars (or Adi Andhra) whose caste occupation is pottery or any work with mud or clay. Ethnonym: Adi Andhra (a Scheduled Caste). Ethnic autonym: Kusavan. Kusavan caste also speaks Kumbaran. Hindu, traditional religion. *Map:* 360:393.

Kunduvadi [wku]. 1,000 (2004 SIL). Kerala, Wayanad district, Puthadi, Purakkadi, and Pulpalli villages; Kozhikode district, Vythiri taluk, Cheeyambam, Irulambam, Manaluvayal, Pakkam, and Porakady villages. *Status:* 6a (Vigorous). *Class:* Dravidian, Southern. *Dialects:* Like Malayalam [mal] but with peculiar intonation and dialect virtually unintelligible to others (Shashi 1994; Menon 1996). Lexical similarity: 65% with Malayalam [mal], 61% with Aranadan [aaf], 83% with Pathiya [pty], 81% with Kalanadi [wkl]. *Lg Use:* Continued vitality doubtful, due to small population, no separate settlements, living with Malayalis, and similarity to Malayalam [mal]. Home. Also use Malayalam [mal]. *Other:* Common cultural origin with Kalanadiyar and Pathiyar. Hindu. *Map:* 360:381.

Kupia [key] (Valmiki). 6,600 (2007). Ethnic population: 79,000 (2007). Valmiki. Andhra Pradesh, Vishakhapatnam and East Godavari districts. *Status:* 6b (Threatened). *Class:* Indo-European, Indo-Iranian, Indo-Aryan, Eastern zone, Oriya. *Lg Use:* Home. Speakers use Telegu [tel] in the market, work, travel. *Lg Dev:* Literacy rate in L2: 40% (1991 census). NT: 1983. *Writing:* Telugu script. *Other:* A Scheduled Tribe. Ethnonym: Valmiki. Ethnic Valmiki not the same as L1 Kupia speakers. Traditional religion, Christian, Hindu. *Map:* 359:359.

Kurichiya [kfh] (Kowohans, Kurichchan, Kurichchia, Kurichia, Kurichiyars, Kuruchans). 29,400 (2004 survey). Ethnic population: 32,800 (2001 census). Kerala, Wayanad district, Mananthavady and Vythiri tahsils; Kannur and Kozhikode districts. *Status:* 6b (Threatened). *Class:* Dravidian, Southern. *Dialects:* Kunnam, Wayanad. Lexical similarity: 60%–66% between dialects; Wayanad dialect 67%–71% with Malayalam [mal]. *Lg Use:* Shifting to Malayalam [mal], more in Kunnam than in Wayanad dialect. All are bilingual in Malayalam, but less than half with good proficiency. Many prefer Malayalam over their mother tongue and think children should learn Malayalam first. Possible reluctance to use mother tongue outside of village domain. *Lg Dev:* Literacy rate in L2: 68% (2001 census). Grammar. *Writing:* Malayalam script. *Other:* A Scheduled Tribe. Consider themselves higher caste than Brahmin. An endangered language (Central Institute of Indian Languages). Further study is being done at Annamalai University. Hindu, Christian, traditional religion. *Map:* 360:366.

Kurmukar [kfv] (Kamar, Karmakar, Karmokar, Kumbhakar, Kumhar, Umar). 3,000 (2000 SIL). Assam, Barpeta, Goalpara, and Dhubri districts; Tripura; West Bengal; Bihar; a few in Madhya Pradesh. *Status:* 6a (Vigorous). *Class:* Indo-European, Indo-Iranian, Indo-Aryan, Eastern zone, Bengali-Assamese. *Lg Use:* Also use Assamese [asm],

English [eng], Hindi [hin]. *Writing:* Latin script. *Other:* A dialect of Bengali [ben] which differs a lot from the standard (Singh, Bardoloi, and Athaparia 2003). Hindu. *Map:* 355:124.

Kurumba, Alu [xua] (Alu Kurumba Nonstandard Kannada, Hal Kurumba, Pal Kurumba). 2,500 (1997). Tamil Nadu, east Nilgiri Hills. *Status:* 6a (Vigorous). *Class:* Dravidian, Southern, Tamil-Kannada, Tamil-Kodagu, Kodagu. *Dialects:* None known. Lexical similarity: 80% between Alu Nonstandard Kannada and Pal. *Lg Use:* Vigorous. Some also use standard Kannada [kan] or southern nonstandard Kannada. Also use Tamil [tam]. *Lg Dev:* Literacy rate in L1: Below 1%. Literacy rate in L2: 15%–25%. *Other:* A Scheduled Tribe. Traditional religion, Hindu. *Map:* 360:389.

Kurumba, Attapady [pkr] (Kurumba, Pal Kurumba). 1,370 (1991 census). Kerala State, Palakkad district, Attapady block. *Status:* 6a (Vigorous). *Class:* Dravidian, Southern. *Dialects:* None known. Separate from Alu Kurumba [xua] and Kurumba Kannada [kfi]. Lexical similarity: 82% with Muduga [udg]; 61%–70% with Irula [iru], 50% with Alu Kurumba [xua], 52% with Kurumba Kannada, 55% with Malayalam [mal], 58% with Tamil [tam]. *Lg Use:* Vigorous. Home, village, religion. All ages. Positive attitudes. Despite dissimilarity between Kurumba, Muduga [udg], and Irula [iru], each group uses their mother tongue to communicate with each other. Many use Muduga [udg]. Despite dissimilarity between Kurumba, Muduga, and Irula [iru], each group uses their mother tongue to communicate with each other. Also use Malayalam [mal], Tamil [tam]. *Lg Dev:* Literacy rate in L2: 32% in Attapady; or 23% (27% men, 15% women), including other Kurumba in Wayanad District (1991 census). *Other:* The least developed language group in Attapady. Thudukki variety is reportedly most pure. Hindu, traditional religion. *Map:* 360:397.

Kurumba, Betta [xub] (Kadu Kurumba, Urali Kurumba). 32,000 (2003 NLCI), increasing. Tamil Nadu, Nilgiri district, Gudalur and Panthalur taluks; Karnataka, Kodagu district, Virarajendrapet and Somvarpet taluks; Mysore district, Heggadadevanakote and Piriyapatna taluks; Chamrajnagar district, Gundlupet taluk; Kerala, Wayanad district, S. Bathery, Mananthavady and Vythiri taluks. *Status:* 5 (Developing). *Class:* Dravidian, Southern, Tamil-Kannada, Tamil-Kodagu, Tamil-Malayalam, Tamil. *Dialects:* A nonstandard variety of Tamil [tam] or Kannada [kan]. May be same as Betta Kurumba dialect in Coorg District. Lexical similarity: 59%–77% among groups that are called Betta Kurumba. *Lg Use:* Central Institute of Indian Languages lists Betta Kurumba as endangered. It is being studied by Annamalai University. Home, work, religion. Positive attitudes. *Lg Dev:* Literacy rate in L2: 10%–15% in Tamil Nadu, 15%–20% in Karnataka, 40%–45% in Kerala. Favorable attitude toward literacy. Grammar. *Writing:* Kannada script. Malayalam script. Tamil script. *Other:* 'Kadu Kurumba', jungle shepherds. 'Betta Kurumba', hill shepherds. 3 subdivisions: Ane (elephant) Kurumba, Bevina (neem tree) Kurumba, and Kolli (fire-brand) Kurumba. A Scheduled Tribe. Hindu. *Map:* 360:386.

Kurumba, Jennu [xuj] (Jen Kurumba, Jennu Kurumba, Jennu Nudi, Kattu Nayaka, Naik Kurumba, Naikan, Nonstandard Kannada, Shola Nayakan, Ten Kurumba). 35,000 (IMA 1997). North Nilgiri Hills, Tamil Nadu and Karnataka border, east of Kerala border, Karnataka, Mysore and Kodagu districts; Kerala, Wayanad district. *Status:* 6a (Vigorous). *Class:* Dravidian, Southern, Tamil-Kannada, Tamil-Kodagu, Kodagu. *Dialects:* Possibly the same as Jeinu Kuruba dialect of Kannada [kan]. Lexical similarity: 61%–83% among varieties called Jennu Kurumba, less than 60% with Betta Kurumba [xub] dialects. *Lg Use:* Positive attitudes. Also use Kannada [kan], Malayalam [mal], Tamil [tam]. *Lg Dev:* Literacy rate in L2: 46% in Tamil Nadu (2001 census). Attitudes favorable toward literacy. *Other:* 'Jennu Kurumba', honey shepherds. A Scheduled Tribe. Traditional religion, Hindu. *Map:* 360:382.

Kurumba, Kannada [kfi] (Canarese, Korambar, Kuramwari, Kuremban, Kuruba, Kuruban, Kurubar, Kurubas Kuruma, Kuruman, Kurumans, Kurumar, Kurumba, Kurumban, Kurumbar, Kurumbas, Kurumvari, Palu Kurumba, Southern Nonstandard Kannada). 180,000 (2000). Tamil Nadu, Teni district, Kambam valley; Dindigul district, Sirumalai, Senkuruchi Hillocks, and Palani; Coimbatore district, Pollachi, Western Fields, and Western Gate Hills; Dharmapuri, Vellore, Chingalpattu, and Salem districts; Karnataka; Andhra Pradesh. *Status:* 5 (Developing). *Class:* Dravidian, Southern, Tamil-Kannada, Tamil-Kodagu, Kodagu. *Dialects:* Coimbatore, Dharmapuri, Pudukottai. *Lg Use:* Home. All ages. Also use Kannada [kan], Muduga [udg], Tamil [tam]. *Lg Dev:* Younger generation over 50% literate, older generation less. Radio programs. *Writing:* Tamil script. *Other:* Reportedly 3 groups of Gowda: Okkili, Anuppa, and Kurumba, which may be languages or dialects of 1 language. Sometimes referred to as Alu or Palu Kurumba, but is a different language from Alu Kurumba [xua] in the hills. Kurumba and Kuruman are different Scheduled Tribes. Hindu. *Map:* 360:371.

Kurumba, Mullu [kpb]. 26,000 (2004 survey). 25,000 in Wayanad; 1,000 in Gudalur of Nilgiri. Kerala, east Wayanad district, Sulthan Bathery and Vythiri tahsils; Tamil Nadu, Nilgiri district, west Gudalur tahsil, Erumad and Cherangodu villages, 10 hamlets. *Status:* 6a (Vigorous). *Class:* Dravidian, Southern, Tamil-Kannada, Tamil-Kodagu, Kodagu. *Dialects:* None known. Lexical similarity: 89%–92% between Mullu Kurumba varieties in Tamil Nadu and Kerala, 73%–77% with Malayalam [mal], 56%–65% with Tamil [tam], 22%–36% with Kannada Kurumba [kfi], 29%–41% with other Kurumba languages. *Lg Use:* Use is declining. Home, village, religious services. Positive attitudes. Also use Malayalam [mal]. *Lg Dev:* Literacy rate in L2: 60%. Favorable motivation toward literacy. *Other:* A Scheduled Tribe. Mullukuruman and Mullukurumbar are sometimes referred to as different tribes. Kuruman are in Kerala and Kurumbar in Tamil Nadu. Linguistically can be considered one group. Traditional religion, Hindu. *Map:* 360:391.

Kurux [kru] (Kadukali, Koda, Kola, Kurka, Kurukh, Morva, Oraon, Urang, Uraon). 1,750,000 in India (2001 census). Population total all countries: 1,804,200. Chhattisgarh, Raigarh, and Surguja districts; Jharkhand Ranchi district; West Bengal, Jalpaigiri district; Bihar; Odisha, Sundargarh and Jharsuguda districts; Assam; Tripura. Also in Bangladesh, Bhutan. *Status:* 5 (Developing). *Class:* Dravidian, Northern. *Dialect:* Oraon. Kisan [xis] and the Oraon dialect have 73% intelligibility. Oraon becoming standard. Related to Kumarbhag Paharia [kmj]. Different from Nepali Kurux [kxl]. *Lg Use:* Used as L2 by Kodaku [ksz]. *Lg Dev:* Literacy rate in L1: 62% Oraon in Chhattisgarh, 25% in Bihar (2001 census). Radio programs. Dictionary. Grammar. Bible: 2000. *Writing:* Devanagari script. *Other:* Oraon is a Scheduled Tribe. Hindu, Christian. *Maps:* 354:114, 355:114, 359:114.

Kuvi [kxv] (Jatapu, Khondh, Khondi, Kond, Kuvi Kond, Kuvinga, Kuwi). 158,000 (2001 census). Odisha, Koraput, Kalahandi, Ganjam, and Phulbani districts; Andhra Pradesh, Vishakhapatnam, Vizianagaram, and Srikakulam districts. *Status:* 5 (Developing). *Class:* Dravidian, South-Central, Gondi-Kui, Konda-Kui, Manda-Kui, Kui-Kuvi. *Dialects:* Dongria Khond, Laxmipur, Rayagada. *Lg Use:* Dongria and Kuvi subgroups speak Kuvi as L1. *Lg Dev:* Literacy rate in L2: 34%–42% in for Vishakhapatnam, Vizianagaram, Srikakulam districts (2001 census). Dictionary. Grammar. NT: 1987. *Writing:* Oriya script. *Other:* Kondh is a Scheduled Tribe. Distinct from Kui [kxu] and Koi (Koya). Hindu. *Map:* 359:339.

Ladakhi [lbj] (Ladak, Ladakh Skat, Ladaphi, Ladhakhi, Ladwags). 105,000 in India (2001 census). Population total all countries: 117,000. Jammu and Kashmir, Ladakh district. 250 villages and hamlets. Also in China. *Status:* 5 (Developing). *Class:* Sino-Tibetan, Tibeto-Burman, Western Tibeto-Burman, Bodish, Central Bodish, Western. *Dialects:* Leh (Central Ladakhi), Nubra Ladakhi, Shamma (Lower Ladakhi, Sham, Shamskat). Perhaps 30%–40% intelligibility of Tibetan [bod]. Leh users comprehend 90% of Zangskari [zau] and Changthang [cna]. Nubra and Shamma not adequately intelligible with Leh to use the same educational, literacy, or development materials. Changthang and Zanskar, while understanding Stod Bhoti [sbu] better than Leh dialect, identify more with Leh Ladakhi culture. 58% to 85% intelligibility of Leh by Changthang, 73%–81% by Zanskar. Lexical similarity: 71%–83% with Purik [prx], 53%–60% with Tibetan, 84%–94% among 5 main dialects. *Type:* SOV; postpositions; genitives, relatives before noun heads; articles, adjectives numerals after noun heads; suffixes indicate case of noun phrase; ergative; causatives; comparative; CCVCC or CCCVV maximum; nontonal. *Lg Use:* Vigorous. All ages. Positive attitudes. Also use English [eng], Hindi [hin], Urdu [urd]. Used as L2 by Brokskat [bkk], Changthang [cna], Zangskari [zau]. *Lg Dev:* Literacy rate in L1: 20%–50% (2001 census). Literacy rate in L2: 54%–65% men, 40% women. Percentage of those who can actually read with understanding is lower than census literacy rate indicates. Dictionary. Grammar. Bible: 1948. *Writing:* Tibetan script. *Other:* Written Ladakhi is distinct from spoken forms. Leh dialect is acknowledged as standard spoken Ladakhi. It is the medium of Leh radio broadcasts and standard medium of communication among all Ladakh dialects, including Changthang and Zangskari (Paldan 2002). Buddhist, Muslim. *Map:* 352:9.

Lambadi [lmn] (Bangala, Banjara, Banjari, Banjori, Banjuri, Brinjari, Gohar-Herkeri, Goola, Gormati, Gurmarti, Kora, Labhani, Labhani Muka, Lamadi, Lamani, Lambani, Lambara, Lavani, Lemadi, Lumadale, Singali, Sugali, Sukali, Tanda, Vanjari, Wanji). 4,150,000 (2001 census). Ethnic population: Estimates range up to 40,000,000 for the total group. Andhra Pradesh; Madhya Pradesh; Himachal Pradesh; Gujarat; Tamil Nadu; Maharashtra; Karnataka; Odisha; West Bengal. *Status:* 5 (Developing). *Class:* Indo-European, Indo-Iranian, Indo-Aryan, Central zone, Rajasthani, Unclassified. *Dialects:* Andhra Pradesh Lamani (Telugu Lamani), Karnataka Lamani (Mysore Lamani), Maharashtra Lamani. *Type:* SOV. *Lg Use:* Also use Kannada [kan], Marathi [mar], Telugu [tel]. *Lg Dev:* Literacy rate in L2: 43% for Banjara of Andhra Pradesh. Many sources cite a much lower literacy rate for Banjara, 10%–20% (2001 census). Radio programs. Grammar. NT: 1999. *Writing:* Devanagari script, used in Maharashtra. Kannada script, used in Karnataka. Telugu script, used in Andhra Pradesh. *Other:* A Scheduled Tribe in Odisha, a Scheduled Caste in Karnataka, Haryana, Punjab, Himachal Pradesh. Ethnic autonym: Gormati. Traditional religion, Christian, Hindu. *Maps:* 358:325, 359:325.

Lamkang [lmk] ("Hiroi-Lamgang" *pej.*, "Lamgang" *pej.*, Lamkaang, Lamkang Naga). 10,000 (1999 census). Southeast Manipur, Chandel district, 6 villages to the west, east of Shuganu, 6 villages between Chalong and Mombi New, 18 villages between Palel, Chandel town, Palel and Sibong; Nagaland; Dimapur, Thamlakhuren. *Status:* 5 (Developing). *Class:* Sino-Tibetan, Tibeto-Burman, Sal, Kuki-Chin-Naga, Kuki-Chin, Northern. *Dialects:* None known. Reportedly most similar to Anal Naga [anm]. *Type:* SOV; postpositions; genitives before head nouns; adjectives and numerals after noun heads; noun prefixes mark person, number of possessor; VC, CV, CVC, CCCVC. *Lg Use:* Vigorous, but each successive generation not as knowledgeable about their folksongs and folktales. All ages. Understand Meitei [mni]. Also use English [eng], Hindi [hin]. *Lg Dev:* Literacy rate in L2: 40% Meitei: 10 to 40 year olds (2000 S. Towar). Only 2% can read Latin script. NT: 2002. *Writing:* Latin script. Myanmar (Burmese) script, used in Myanmar. *Other:* A Scheduled Tribe. Christian. *Map:* 357:274.

Lepcha [lep] (Lapche, Nünpa, Rong, Rongke, Rongpa). 50,600 in India (2001 census). Population total all countries: 60,100. Sikkim, Dzongu district; West Bengal, Darjeeling district, Kalimpong. Also in Bhutan, Nepal (Lapcha). *Status:* 6a (Vigorous). *Class:* Sino-Tibetan, Tibeto-Burman, Central Tibeto-Burman, Lepcha. *Dialects:* Ilammu, Rengjongmu, Tamsangmu. Classification uncertain; has been classified both in Himalayan and Naga groups. *Lg Use:* Vigorous. In Sikkim, all ages. *Lg Dev:* Literacy rate in L2: 66% in Sikkim (2001 census). Taught in primary schools. Radio programs. Dictionary. Grammar. NT: 1989. *Writing:* Lepcha (Róng) script. Tibetan script. *Other:* A Scheduled Tribe. Lepcha is both language and name of people. Buddhist, Christian, Hindu. *Map:* 355:155.

Lhomi [lhm] (Lhoket, Shing Saapa, Syingsaaba). 1,320 in India (2000 USCWM). West Bengal, Darjeeling. *Status:* 5 (Developing). *Lg Dev:* Literacy rate in L1: Below 1%. Literacy rate in L2: 5%–25% (men). *Other:* Traditional religion, Buddhist (Lamaist). See main entry on page 252. *Map:* 355:168.

Limbu [lif] (Limbo, Limboo, Lumbu). 37,300 in India (2001 census). Ethnic population: 177,000 (2007). Sikkim, West district; West Bengal, Darjeeling district; Assam. *Status:* 4 (Educational). *Lg Dev:* Taught in primary schools in Sikkim. Taught in secondary schools in Sikkim. *Other:* Traditional religion, Buddhist, Hindu. See main entry on page 252. *Map:* 355:157.

Lish [lsh] (Kishpignag, Lish Monpa, Lishpa, Monpa). 2,340. Arunachal Pradesh, West Kameng district, Lish, Lish Gompache, Lish Gompalok villages. *Status:* 6a (Vigorous). *Class:* Sino-Tibetan, Tibeto-Burman, Central Tibeto-Burman, Kho-Bwa. *Dialects:* None known. Reportedly most similar to Chug [cvg]. *Lg Use:* Also use Tshangla [tsj]. *Lg Dev:* Literacy rate in L2: 62% for West Kameng District, males 71%, females 49% (2001 census). *Other:* The cover term 'Monpa' (Moinba), man of the lower country, used to refer to several ethnically related peoples whose languages may not be related linguistically. Buddhist. *Map:* 356:173.

Lisu [lis]. 2,700 in India (Bradley 2007). Arunachal Pradesh, Changlang district, Miao and Vijoynagar circle in 6 villages. Gandhigram is the largest Lisu village. *Status:* 5 (Developing). *Lg Dev:* Literacy rate in L1: 45%. *Other:* The Lisu people are called Yobin or Yawyin by the Singpho [sgp] people. Christian. See main entry on page 77. *Map:* 356:193.

Lodhi [lbm] (Lodha, Lodi, Lohi, Lozi). 25,000 (2007 survey). Odisha, Mayurbhanj district, Sadar subdivision, Morada and Suliapada; Balasore district, Sora block; West Bengal, West Medinipur district, Binpur, Kharagpur-I blocks; Jharkhand, along West Bengal border. *Status:* 6a (Vigorous). *Class:* Indo-European, Indo-Iranian, Indo-Aryan,

Eastern zone, Bengali-Assamese. *Dialects:* None known. Lexical similarity: 59%–67% with Oriya [ory], 56%–72% with Bangla (Bengali [ben]), 20% with Santhali [sat] and Mundari [unr], 66%–85% between varieties of Lodhi, 57%–75% with Kharia Thar [ksy]. *Lg Use:* Vigorous. All domains. Children are learning Lodhi. Positive attitudes. Also use Bengali [ben], Oriya [ory]. *Lg Dev:* Literacy rate in L2: 22% in Odisha (2001 census). *Other:* Lodha is a Scheduled Tribe. Hindu, Christian. *Maps:* 355:149, 359:149.

Lohar, Gade [gda] (Bagri Lohar, Belani, Bhubaliya Lohar, Chitodi Lohar, Chittoriya Lohar, Dhunkuria, Domba, Dombiali, Gadia Lohar, Gaduliya Lohar, Gara, Kanwar Khati, Lohari, Lohpitta, Panchal Lohar, Rajput Lohar). 1,010 (2000). Rajasthan; Gujarat; Madhya Pradesh; Maharashtra; Uttar Pradesh; Delhi; Haryana; Punjab. *Status:* 6a (Vigorous). *Class:* Indo-European, Indo-Iranian, Indo-Aryan, Central zone, Rajasthani, Unclassified. A member of macrolanguage Rajasthani [raj]. *Dialects:* No significant dialect differences. May be same as Loarki [lrk] in Pakistan. *Lg Dev:* Literacy rate in L2: 40% (1981 census). *Other:* 'Gade Lohar' refers to people who travel in bullock carts and are blacksmiths. Hindu. *Map:* 353:62.

Lohar, Lahul [lhl] (Garas, Lohar). 750 (1996). Himachal Pradesh, Lahul valley. *Status:* 6a (Vigorous). *Class:* Indo-European, Indo-Iranian, Indo-Aryan, Unclassified. *Dialects:* None known. Different from Gade Lohar [gda]. *Lg Use:* Also use Hindi [hin]. *Other:* Lohar is a Scheduled Caste in Himachal Pradesh, not all of whom speak Lahul Lohar. Similar name and occupation to 'Gade Lohar'. *Map:* 352:30.

Lui [lba] (Loi, Looe). No known L1 speakers. *Status:* 10 (Extinct). *Class:* Sino-Tibetan, Tibeto-Burman, Unclassified.

Lyngngam [lyg] (Khasi, Lyngam, Lyngym). 5,000 in India (Singh 1994). Population total all countries: 6,000. Meghalaya; Assam, Kamrup district. Also in Bangladesh. *Status:* 6a (Vigorous). *Class:* Austro-Asiatic, Mon-Khmer, Northern Mon-Khmer, Khasian. *Dialects:* None known. Lexical similarity: 36% with standard Khasi. *Lg Use:* Also use Assamese [asm], Garo [grt], Hindi [hin]. *Lg Dev:* Literacy rate in L2: 10% (Singh 1994). *Other:* Previously listed as dialect of Khasi. Culturally intermediate between the Khasi and the Garo [grt]. Christian. *Map:* 356:209.

Magahi [mag] (Bihari, Magadhi, Magaya, Maghai, Maghaya, Maghori, Magi, Magodhi, Megahi). 14,000,000 in India (2001 census). Population total all countries: 14,035,600. Bihar, Gaya, Bhagalpur, eastern Patna districts; Jharkhand, northern Chotanagpur division, Hazaribagh district; West Bengal, Maldah district. Also in Nepal. *Status:* 4 (Educational). *Class:* Indo-European, Indo-Iranian, Indo-Aryan, Eastern zone, Bihari. *Dialects:* Central Magahi, Khortha, Northern Magahi, Southern Magahi. *Lg Use:* Religion. Positive attitudes. Educated people, city dwellers and those who travel speak Hindi [hin] well. *Lg Dev:* Literacy rate in L1: 30%. Literacy rate in L2: 30% Hindi. Bhojpuri [bho] can use Magahi materials. Magazines. Newspapers. Radio programs. Grammar. NT: 1826. *Writing:* Devanagari script. *Other:* Hindu, Jain, traditional religion. *Map:* 355:118.

Magar, Eastern [mgp] (Magari, Magarkura, Mangari, Manggar). 71,700 in India (2006). Ethnic population: 278,000 (2006 FTT). Sikkim, South district, scattered in East district. *Status:* 6b (Threatened). *Lg Use:* Home. Also use Nepali [npi]. See main entry on page 253. *Map:* 355:156.

Mahali [mjx] (Mahili, Mahle, Mahli). 33,000 in India (2007), decreasing. Population total all countries: 36,000. Ethnic population: 278,000 (2007). Jharkhand, Chotanagpur region, Ranchi, Hazaribagh, Gumla, Santal Pargana, Lohardaga, West Singhbhum, East Singhbhum, Saraikela Kharsawan, and Dhanbad districts; Odisha, Balasore, Mayurbhanj, and Keonjhar districts; West Bengal, Jalpaiguri and West Medinipur districts; Assam, on tea estates. Also in Bangladesh. *Status:* 6b (Threatened). *Class:* Austro-Asiatic, Munda, North Munda, Kherwari, Santali. *Dialects:* Possible dialect of Santhali [sat]. Lexical similarity: 69%–87% between varieties of Mahali, 68%–93% with Santhali [sat], 53%–59% with Mundari [unr]. *Lg Use:* Most in Jharkhand reported Santhali [sat], Sadri [sck] or Mundari [unr] as their mother tongue rather than Mahali. May be a threatened language. Home, village, private prayer for half the L1 speakers in Jharkhand. Also use Bengali [ben], Hindi [hin], Munda [unx], Mundari [unr], Oriya [ory], Santhali [sat]. *Lg Dev:* Literacy rate in L2: 12% for Jharkhand (20% male, 4% female) (1981 census); 32% for Odisha (2001 census). *Other:* Mahli is a Scheduled Tribe, reported to speak Sadri [sck] as L1 in Jharkhand, the Thar dialect of Dhatki [mki] in Odisha, and Bengali in West Bengal. Hindu. *Maps:* 355:143, 359:143.

Maithili [mai] (Apabhramsa, Bihari, Maitili, Maitli, Methli, Tirahutia, Tirhuti, Tirhutia). 30,000,000 in India (2000 SIL). Population total all countries: 33,890,000. 12,000,000 monolinguals (1998). Bihar, from Muzaffarpur on the west, past Kosi on the east to western Purnia district, to Munger and Bhagalpur districts in the south, and Himalayan foothills north. Delhi, Kolkata, Mumbai. Many settled abroad. Cultural and linguistic centers are Madhubani and Darbhanga towns. Janakpur also important culturally and religiously. Also in Nepal. *Status:* 2 (Provincial). Statutory language of provincial identity in Bihar State (1992, Constitution, 71st Amendment). *Class:* Indo-European, Indo-Iranian, Indo-Aryan, Eastern zone, Bihari. *Dialects:* Bajjika, Central Colloquial Maithili (Sotipura), Dehati, Eastern Maithili (Khotta, Kortha, Kortha Bihari), Jolaha, Kisan, Southern Standard Maithili, Standard Maithili, Thetiya, Western Maithili. Caste variation more than geographic variation in dialects. Functional intelligibility among all dialects, including those in Nepal. Reportedly most similar to Magahi [mag]. Lexical similarity: 91% between Brahmin and non-Brahmin dialects. *Type:* SOV; postpositions; noun head final; 11 noun classes or genders; content q-word in situ; genitives, articles, numerals before noun heads, adjectives before and after noun heads; 1 prefix, up to 5 suffixes; clause constituents partially indicated by case-marking and postpositions; verbal affixation marks person, number, gender, and honorificity of subject; split ergativity; object marked by position; person, gender, animate distinguished, obligatory for subject; transitives; both tense and aspect; passives and voice; causatives; comparatives; V, VC, VCC, CV, CVC, CVV, CCV, CVCC, CCVCC; nontonal; 29 consonant and 11 vowel phonemes. *Lg Use:* Used by Brahmin and other high caste or educated Hindus, who influence the culture and language, and other castes. There is a Maithili Academy. Linguistics and literature taught at Patna University and at L. N. Mithila University in Darbhanga. Home, community. Mixed attitudes. Influenced by caste, ranging from superiority to resentment. Non-Brahmin speech viewed as inferior. Hindi [hin] considered superior, Nepali [npi] generally accepted. Also use Bengali [ben], Bhojpuri [bho], English [eng], Hindi [hin], Nepali [npi]. *Lg Dev:* Literacy rate in L1: 25%–50%. Literacy rate in L2: 25%–50%. If they can read Nepali or Hindi, they can read Maithili. The educated read Hindi, Nepali, or English books for pleasure. Some literacy work in India. Poetry. Magazines. Newspapers. Radio programs. Films. TV. Videos. Dictionary. Grammar. NT: 2010. *Writing:* Devanagari script, primary usage.

Kaithi script, used until the turn of the 20th century. Newar (Prachalit Nepal) script, no longer in use, historic usage. Tirhuta script, used until the turn of the 20th century. *Other:* Hindu. *Map:* 351.

Majhi [mjz] (Manjhi). 20,400 in India (2000). Ethnic population: 121,000 (2007). Jharkhand, Gumla district; Sikkim, south district, Majhigaon near Jorethang; east district, Majhitar near Rangpo; West Bengal; Assam. *Status:* 7 (Shifting). *Lg Use:* Rarely used at home; younger generation uses Nepali [npi] in Sikkim. Home. Also use Nepali [npi], Sadri [sck]. *Lg Dev:* Literacy rate in L2: Below 7%. Girls not sent to school. *Other:* Distinct from Majhi dialect of Eastern Panjabi [pan] or Bote (Bote-Majhi) [bmj] of Nepal. Hindu. See main entry on page 254. *Map:* 355:144.

Majhwar [mmj] (Majhvar, Manjhi, Manjhia). 34,300 (1995). Ethnic population: 174,000 (2007). Chhattisgarh, Bilaspur district, Katghora tahsil, Raigarh and Surguja districts; Uttar Pradesh, Allahabad, Varanasi, Mirzapur districts; Sikkim. *Status:* 7 (Shifting). *Class:* Unclassified. *Dialects:* Possibly a dialect of Asuri [asr]. *Other:* A Scheduled Tribe in Chhattisgarh. Reportedly speak Chhattisgarhi [hne] as L1. Hindu. *Map:* 354:115.

Mal Paharia [mkb] (Dehri, Mad, Mader, Mal, Mal Pahariya, Maler, Malpaharia, Malti, Malto, Maltu, Manlati, Mar, Marpaharia, Maw, Mawdo, Mawer, Mawer Nondi, Paharia, Parsi). 51,000 (Bhaskararao 2006). Possibly 40,000 in West Bengal. Ethnic population: 111,000 (2000). Jharkhand, south Santal Pargana district, Ramgarh hills; Dumka district, Pakaur; south Godda, and Deoghar districts; some in Sahibganj district, Borio, Depart village; West Benga, Bankura, Barddhaman, and Murshidabad districts. Possibly in Bangladesh. *Status:* 6b (Threatened). *Class:* Indo-European, Indo-Iranian, Indo-Aryan, Eastern zone, Bengali-Assamese. *Dialects:* Not inherently intelligible with Kumarbhag Paharia [kmj], Sauria Paharia [mjt], Bengali [ben], or Hindi [hin]. Part of the Malto ethnic group. Reportedly speak a variety similar to Kharia Thar [ksy] of Manbhum (Jharkhand). Lexical similarity: 85% between dialects, 59% with Mal Paharia Barmasiya. *Lg Use:* Vigorous. All domains. Positive attitudes. Some shifted to Bengali [ben]. *Lg Dev:* Literacy rate in L2: 13% male, 3% female, average 8% (1981). NT. *Writing:* Devanagari script. *Other:* A Scheduled Tribe. Traditional religion, Christian. *Map:* 355:132.

Mala Malasar [ima] (Maha Malasar, Malai Malasar, Malasir). 1,000 (2004). Kerala, Palakkad district, Parambikulam wildlife sanctuary; Tamil Nadu, Coimbatore district, Annamalai hills. *Status:* 6a (Vigorous). *Class:* Dravidian, Southern, Unclassified. *Dialects:* Lexical similarity: 68%–74% with Malasar [ymr], 70% with Eravallan [era], 70% with Muduga [udg], 65% with Tamil [tam], 61% with Malayalam [mal], 67%–72% with the Attapady dialect of Irula [iru], 75% with the Walayar dialect of Irula. *Lg Use:* Vigorous. Home, village, religion. All ages. Positive attitudes. Also use Malayalam [mal]. *Lg Dev:* Literacy rate in L2: 17% in Kerala, 15% in Tamil Nadu (2001 census). *Other:* A Scheduled Tribe. Mala Malasar means king of the forest. Culturally very distinct from neighboring tribal groups. Hindu, traditional religion. *Map:* 360:403.

Malankuravan [mjo] (Mala Koravan, Malaikuravan, Malakkuravan, Male Kuravan). 18,600 (2001 census). 260 in Kerala, 18,300 in Tamil Nadu. Tamil Nadu, Kanniyakumari district; Kerala, Trivandrum, Kollam, and Kottayam districts, Chittar, Kattachira, and Rajanpara in Ranni Range, Pathanamthitta taluk, Nottakal in Pathanapuram taluk, Pampa river, Neduvanged taluk forest tracks. *Status:* 6a (Vigorous). *Class:* Dravidian, Unclassified. *Dialect:* Malayadiars. *Lg Use:* Also use Tamil [tam]. *Lg Dev:* Literacy rate in L2: 53% for Kerala, 41% for Tamil Nadu (2001 census). *Other:* A Scheduled Tribe. Reported to speak a dialect of Malayalam [mal] with many borrowed words and phrases from Tamil. Traditional religion, Hindu. *Map:* 360:378.

Malapandaram [mjp] (Hill Pantaram, Malapantaram, Malepantaram, Pandaram Basha). 5,850 (2001 census). Kerala, Pathanamthitta and Kollam districts, some in Kottayam and Palakkad districts; Tamil Nadu, Villupuram, Coimbatore and Madurai districts. *Status:* 6a (Vigorous). *Class:* Dravidian, Southern, Tamil-Kannada, Tamil-Kodagu, Tamil-Malayalam, Malayalam. *Dialects:* None known. Lexical similarity: 83%–94% between varieties in Kerala, 63%–68% with Malayalam [mal], 64%–68% with Tamil [tam]. *Lg Use:* Shift toward Malayalam [mal] in Kerala. Home, community. Negative attitudes. Many also use Malayalam [mal], except written. *Lg Dev:* Literacy rate in L2: 48% for Kerala, 59% for Tamil Nadu (2001 census). *Other:* A Scheduled Tribe. Hindu, traditional religion. *Map:* 360:377.

Malaryan [mjq] (Arayans, Karingal, Malai Arayan, Malayarayan, Malayarayar, Male Arayans, Maley Arayan, Vazhiyammar). No known L1 speakers. Ethnic population: 35,000 (2001 census). Kerala, Ernakulam, Idukki, Kottayam, and Thrissur districts; Tamil Nadu. *Status:* 9 (Dormant). *Class:* Dravidian, Southern, Tamil-Kannada, Tamil-Kodagu, Tamil-Malayalam, Malayalam. *Lg Use:* Shifted to Malayalam [mal] in Kerala. *Lg Dev:* Grammar. *Other:* A Scheduled Tribe. Speak a variety of Malayalam [mal] as L1. Malayarayar and Mala Arayan are listed as 2 different communities in the census but are the same group. Though the Kanikkar of Trivandrum District also sometimes call themselves Malayarayar, they are entirely different (Menon 1996:198). Hindu, Christian.

Malasar [ymr] (Malayar). 7,760 (2001 census). Tamil Nadu, Coimbatore district, Pollachi taluk; Kerala, Palakkad district, Chittoor and Palakkad taluks. *Status:* 6a (Vigorous). *Class:* Dravidian, Southern, Unclassified. *Dialects:* None known. Lexical similarity: 68%–74% with Tamil [tam], 79%–83% with Walayar Irula [iru], 77%–86% with Eravallan [era], 57%–61% with Malayalam [mal], 68%–75% with Mala Malasar [ima] (2004 survey); 52%–56% with Malaryan [mjq], 77%–82% between Malasar and Kollimalakkar, Kollimalakkar 80% with Malapulaya (2006 survey). *Lg Use:* Home, village, religion. all ages. Positive attitudes. Bilingual ability in Malayalam [mal] (in Kerala) increases with education but few have higher education. Bilingualism in Tamil [tam] reportedly more widespread even in Kerala. *Lg Dev:* Literacy rate in L2: 36% in Kerala, 22% in Tamil Nadu (2001 census). *Other:* A Scheduled Tribe. Kollimalakkar call themselves Malasar but are different culturally, belonging to the Malayali tribe of Tamil Nadu. They migrated to Nelliyampathy area in Kerala for work many years ago. Traditional religion, Christian, Hindu. *Map:* 360:401.

Malavedan [mjr] (Malai Vedan, Malavetan, Towetan, Veda Bhasha, Vedans, Vettava Bhasha). Ethnic population: 12,600 (2001 census). Total population unknown. 6,190 in Kerala, 6,410 in Tamil Nadu (2001 census). Kerala, Pathanamthitta, Idukki, Ernakulam, Kottayam, Kollam, and Trivandrum districts; Tamil Nadu, Kanniyakumari, Madurai, Dindigul, Nilgiris, Salem, and Tirunelveli districts. *Status:* 6b (Threatened). *Class:* Dravidian, Southern, Tamil-Kannada, Tamil-Kodagu, Tamil-Malayalam, Malayalam. *Dialects:* Vetan, Vettuvan. Lexical similarity: 64%–68% with Malayalam [mal], 48%–52% with Tamil [tam]. *Lg Use:* Dying out in Idukki District, replaced by Malayalam [mal]. Home, village in Pathanamthitta district. Positive attitudes in Pathanamthitta district. Bilingualism in Malayalam [mal] widespread in Kerala. *Lg Dev:* Literacy rate in L2: 67%–78% for Kerala, 56% for Tamil Nadu (2001 census). *Other:* A Scheduled Tribe. Hindu. *Map:* 360:375.

Malayalam [mal] (Alealum, Malayalani, Malayali, Malean, Maliyad, Mallealle, Mopla). 33,000,000 in India (2001 census). Population total all countries: 33,550,900. Kerala, Laccadive Islands, neighboring states. Also in Bahrain, Canada, Fiji, Israel, Malaysia, Qatar, Singapore, United Arab Emirates, United Kingdom, United States. *Status:* 2 (Provincial). Statutory provincial language in Kerala State; union territories Lakshadweep and Puducherry (1950, Constitution, Schedule VIII). *Class:* Dravidian, Southern, Tamil-Kannada, Tamil-Kodagu, Tamil-Malayalam, Malayalam. *Dialects:* Central Kerala, Kasargod, Kayavar, Malabar, Malayalam, Moplah (Mapilla), Nagari-Malayalam, Namboodiri, Nasrani, Nayar, North Kerala, Pulaya, South Kerala. Caste and communal dialects: Namboodiri, Nayar, Moplah, Pulaya, Nasrani. Mapilla is among the most divergent dialects, differing considerably from literary Malayalam. *Lg Use:* Cochin Jews in Kerala speak Malayalam. Used as L2 by Allar [all], Aranadan [aaf], Attapady Kurumba [pkr], Irula [iru], Jennu Kurumba [xuj], Kadar [kej], Kalanadi [wkl], Kanikkaran [kev], Kodava [kfa], Kudiya [kfg], Kunduvadi [wku], Kurichiya [kfh], Mala Malasar [ima], Malapandaram [mjp], Malasar [ymr], Malavedan [mjr], Mannan [mjv], Muduga [udg], Mullu Kurumba [kpb], Muthuvan [muv], Paliyan [pcf], Paniya [pcg], Ravula [yea], Thachanadan [thn], Urali [url]. *Lg Dev:* Fully developed. Bible: 1841–2004. *Writing:* Arabic script. Braille script, used since 1998. Malayalam script, primary usage. *Other:* Hindu, Christian, Jewish, Muslim. *Map:* 351.

Maldivian [div] (Dhivehi, Dhivehi Bas, Divehi, Mahl, Malikh, Malki). 9,500 in India (2012). 9,500 in Minicoy and 5,000 expatriates in Trivandrum. Laccadive Islands, Minicoy island; Kerala, Trivandrum. *Status:* 5 (Dispersed). *Dialect:* Maliku Bas (Minicoy Dialect). *Lg Use:* Those in Minicoy are undergoing acculturation owing to lack of contact with remaining Divehi people and pressure to use other languages (Malayalam [mal], English [eng], and Hindi [hin]). Also use Standard Arabic [arb]. *Lg Dev:* Literacy rate in L1: 95%–100%. Literacy rate in L2: 95%–100%. *Other:* Muslim (Sunni), traditional religion. See main entry on page 228. *Map:* 361.

Malvi [mup] (Malavi, Mallow, Malwada, Malwi, Ujjaini). 5,560,000 (2001 census). 1,110,000 monolinguals. Madhya Pradesh, Ujjain, Indore, Rathlam, Mandsaur, Rajgarh, Dewas, Shajapur, Nimuch, Sehore, Dhar, and Bhopal districts; Rajasthan, Jhalawar district. Sondwari dialect geographically isolated from the others. *Status:* 5 (Developing). *Class:* Indo-European, Indo-Iranian, Indo-Aryan, Central zone, Rajasthani, Unclassified. A member of macrolanguage Rajasthani [raj]. *Dialects:* Rajawadi, Sondwari (Sondhwadi, Soudhwari), Ujjaini (Avanthika, Malvi Proper), Umadwadi. Considered the standard variety, Southeastern Rajasthani Nimadi [noe] is reportedly most similar language with 70% intelligibility. 88%–92% intelligibility of Ujjaini dialect by other dialects. Lexical similarity: 65%–89% among dialects. *Type:* SOV; non-tonal. *Lg Use:* Vigorous. Home, village, religion. Positive attitudes. 55% have high proficiency in Hindi [hin]; 20% have routine proficiency. *Lg Dev:* Literacy rate in L2: 58% for rural Madhya Pradesh (2001 census). Government project discontinued due to low response. Poetry. Radio programs. Dictionary. NT: 1826. *Writing:* Devanagari script. *Other:* Hindu, Muslim. *Maps:* 353:77, 354:77, 358:77.

Manda [mha]. 4,040 (2000). Odisha, Kalahandi district, Thuamul Rampur subdivision. *Status:* 6a (Vigorous). *Class:* Dravidian, South-Central, Gondi-Kui, Konda-Kui, Manda-Kui, Manda-Pengo. *Other:* Hindu. *Map:* 359:338.

Mandeali [mjl] (Mandi, Mandiali, Pahari Mandiyali). 900,000 (1991 census). Himachal Pradesh, Mandi district. *Status:* 5 (Developing). *Class:* Indo-European, Indo-Iranian, Indo-Aryan, Northern zone, Western Pahari. *Dialects:* Preliminary survey suggests speakers have functional intelligibility of Kangri [xnr]. People in southeast Mandi district may have more difficulty understanding Kangri. Standard Mandeali is spoken throughout the broad valley running north and south from Jogindernagar to Sundarnagar. Mandeali Pahari is spoken north around Barot, east of Uhl River. Intelligible with difficulty to standard Mandeali. May be intermediate variety between Mandeali and Kullui [kfx]. Southeast district contains transition to Mahasui [bfz]. In the west, Sarkaghat is also a bit different from standard Mandeali, perhaps forming a transition towards Hamirpur and Bilaspur areas. Lexical similarity: 89% with Palampuri dialect of Kangri [xnr], 83% with Chambeali [cdh]. *Type:* SOV. *Lg Use:* All ages. Also use Eastern Panjabi [pan], Hindi [hin], Urdu [urd]. *Lg Dev:* Newspapers. Radio programs. Grammar. Bible portions: 1970. *Writing:* Devanagari script. Takri (Tankri, Takari) script, no longer in use. *Other:* Hindu. *Map:* 352:26.

Manna-Dora [mju]. Ethnic population: 30,000. Andhra Pradesh, East Godavari, West Godavari, Srikakulam, Vishakhapatnam, and Vizianagaram districts; Tamil Nadu. *Status:* 8b (Nearly extinct). *Class:* Dravidian, South-Central, Telugu. *Lg Use:* It is uncertain if they are speaking Telugu [tel] or a closely related language of their own. *Writing:* Telugu script. *Other:* A Scheduled Tribe. Reportedly speak Telugu [tel] as L1. Hindu. *Map:* 359:354.

Mannan [mjv] (Mannan Pasha, Manne, Mannyod). 7,850 (2001 census). 7,760 in Kerala, 82 in Tamil Nadu. Kerala, Idukki district, Udumpanchola, Devikulam, and Pirmed tahsils; Tamil Nadu, Madurai district. *Status:* 6b (Threatened). *Class:* Dravidian, Southern, Tamil-Kannada, Tamil-Kodagu, Tamil-Malayalam. *Dialects:* Little variation between varieties with 92% intelligibility, 70% intelligibility of Malayalam [mal]. Lexical similarity: 86%–96% between varieties, 57%–61% with Tamil [tam], 56%–64% with Malayalam [mal]. *Lg Use:* Shifting slowly to Malayalam [mal]; still used by some children. Home, village, religion. All ages. Positive attitudes. Interest in language development. Also use Malayalam [mal]; educated and those having contact with outsiders are more bilingual. *Lg Dev:* Literacy rate in L2: 50% for Kerala, 84% for Tamil Nadu (2001 census). Grammar. Bible portions: 2012. *Writing:* Malayalam script. *Other:* A Scheduled Tribe in Kerala and Tamil Nadu. Not the same as the Scheduled Caste Mannan in Trivandrum and other adjoining districts of Kerala and Tamil Nadu who speak Malayalam. Romanized spelling is the same but the Scheduled Caste name is pronounced with retroflex double n. Hindu, traditional religion. *Map:* 360:373.

Marathi [mar] (Maharashtra, Maharathi, Malhatee, Marthi, Muruthu). 71,700,000 in India (2001 census). Population total all countries: 71,780,660. L2 users: 3,000,000 in India. Maharashtra and adjacent states. Also in Canada, Israel, Mauritius, United States. *Status:* 2 (Provincial). Statutory provincial language in Maharashtra State (1950, Constitution, Schedule VIII). *Class:* Indo-European, Indo-Iranian, Indo-Aryan, Southern zone. *Dialects:* Gawdi of Goa, Kasargod, Kosti, Kudali, Nagpuri Marathi. 42 dialects. Complex dialect situation. Dialects bordering other major language areas share many features with those languages. Dialects or closely related languages: Konkani [knn], Goan Konkani [gom], Deccan [dcc], Varhadi-Nagpuri [vah], and Gowlan [goj]. There is a dialect in Thanjavur District and elsewhere in Tamil Nadu influenced lexically by Tamil [tam] and Kannada [kan], with at least 100,000 speakers. *Type:* SOV. *Lg Use:* The Bene Israel are a Marathi-speaking Jewish group in Mumbai. Used as L2 by Ahirani [ahr], Bhalay [bhx], Far Western Muria [fmu], Gowli [gok], Indo-Portuguese [idb], Katkari [kfu], Khandesi [khn], Korku [kfq], Korlai Creole Portuguese [vkp], Lambadi [lmn], Mawchi [mke], Nihali [nll], Noiri [noi], Northern Gondi [gno], Northwestern Kolami [kfb], Palya Bareli [bpx], Pardhan [pch], Pauri Bareli [bfb], Powari [pwr], Rathwi Bareli [bgd], Seraiki [skr], Tulu [tcy], Vaagri Booli [vaa], Varli [vav], Vasavi [vas], Waddar [wbq]. *Lg Dev:* Literacy rate in L1: 77% (2001 census). Literacy rate in L2: 77% (2001 census). Fully developed. Bible: 1821–2002. *Writing:* Braille script. Devanagari script, primary usage. *Other:* The Habshi are Muslim, descended from East African slaves brought to western India. Are is a synonym for a Marathi caste name. Are also refers to Marathi-speaking communities in south India. Hindu, Jewish (Bene Israel), Muslim. *Map:* 351.

Maria [mrr] (Hill Maria, Madi, Madia, Madiya, Modh, Modi). 165,000 (2000). 141,000 Maria and 23,700 Hill Maria. Maharashtra, Garhchiroli (Chanda) district, Etapalli, Bhamragad, and Sironcha tahsils; Chhattisgarh, Bastar district, Narayanpur and Bijapur tahsils. In Narayanpur, an administrative block of 200 villages known as 'Abujhmar block'. *Status:* 6a (Vigorous). *Class:* Dravidian, South-Central, Gondi-Kui, Gondi. *Dialects:* Abujmaria (Abujhmadia, Abujhmaria, Abujmar Maria, Abujmariya, Hill Maria), Adewada, Bhamani Maria (Bhamani), Etapally Maria. Etapally Maria dialect is apparently understood by all. Distinct from Muria, Dandami Maria [daq], Northern Gondi [gno], Southern Gondi [ggo], and Koya [kff]. 76%–77% intelligibility of other Gondi varieties. Muria Gondi [mut] is intelligible of Abujmaria around Narainpur area but not elsewhere. Distinct from Maria dialect of Chanda District in Maharashtra (Natarajan 1985). Intelligibility 90%–100% of Bhamragarh dialect by other Maria speakers. Maria is intelligible to the Gatte Maria, an ethnic group. Lexical similarity: 59%–80% among dialects (1991 survey), 65%–98% (1999 survey). *Lg Use:* All domains. Most men also use a Muria variety or Halbi [hlb]. Also use Hindi [hin]. *Lg Dev:* Literacy rate in L1: Men 5%, women below 1%. Literacy rate in L2: 25%–50%. High interest in literacy. Dictionary. Grammar. *Writing:* Devanagari script. *Other:* A Scheduled Tribe. Hindu, Christian, traditional religion. *Map:* 359:334.

Maria, Dandami [daq] (Bastar Koya, Bison Horn Maria, Dandami Madiya, Dhuru, Madiya, Maria Gond). 200,000 (2000). Chhattisgarh, Bastar and Dantewara districts; Maharashtra, Garhichiroli district. *Status:* 6a (Vigorous). *Class:* Dravidian, South-Central, Gondi-Kui, Gondi. *Dialects:* None known. Those in Geedam and Bailadila have 95%–98% mutual intelligibility, 81% of the Sukma variety, but 18%–21% of Maria [mrr], 18%–45% of Muria in Sukma understood the Geedam variety at 81% or lower; those in Bailadila understood Sukma at 92%. May be more than one language. Distinct from Northern Gondi [gno], Southern Gondi [ggo], Maria of Garhchiroli, and Koya [kff]. *Lg Use:* All ages. *Lg Dev:* Literacy program in progress. Grammar. Bible portions. *Writing:* Devanagari script. *Other:* A Scheduled Tribe. Hindu, traditional religion. *Map:* 359:347.

Marma [rmz] ("Mogh" *pej.*). 30,600 in India (2001 census). Mizoram; Tripura. *Status:* 6a (Vigorous). *Lg Use:* Home, village. *Other:* Buddhist, Christian, Muslim. See main entry on page 55. *Map:* 357:262.

Marwari [mwr]. A macrolanguage (see page 9). *Other:* Includes: Dhundari [dhd], Marwari [rwr], Marwari [mve] (Pakistan), Merwari [wry], Mewari [mtr], Shekhawati [swv].

Marwari [rwr] (Marvadi, Marvari, Marwadi, Rajasthani). 5,600,000 in India (2007 SIL). Population total all countries: 5,622,600. Rajasthan, Jodhpur, Jaisalmer, Barmer, Bikaner, Churu, Pali, and Jalore districts; Gujarat; Madhya Pradesh; Punjab; Delhi; Haryana; Uttar Pradesh; thoughout India. Also in Nepal. *Status:* 5 (Developing). *Class:* Indo-European, Indo-Iranian, Indo-Aryan, Central zone, Rajasthani, Marwari. A member of macrolanguage Marwari [mwr]. *Dialects:* Barmeri, Bikaneri, Jaisalmeri, Standard Marwari (Jodhpuri). The standard form of Marwari. May or may not be different from Marwari of Pakistan [mve]. 67% intelligibility of Shekhawati [swv], 61% of Godwari [gdx], 54% of Mewari [mtr], 54% of Dhundari [dhd], 45% of Haroti [hoj], and 45% of Mewati [wtm]. 53% intelligibility of Shekawati by Marwari. Lexical similarity: 50%–65% with Hindi [hin], 69%–76% with Merwari [wry], 72%–87% between dialects, 62%–74% with Godwari [gdx], 61%–77% with Shekawati [swv]. *Type:* SOV; postpositions; noun head final; content q-word in situ; clause constituents indicated by case-marking; both tense and aspect; 38 consonant and 10 vowel phonemes; nontonal. *Lg Use:* Vigorous. Home, village, market, religion. All ages. Positive attitudes. Educated have very good proficiency in Hindi [hin]. *Lg Dev:* Literacy rate in L1: 5%–10%. Literacy rate in L2: 50%–75%. Poetry. Newspapers. New media. Radio programs. Grammar. NT: 1820–1821. *Writing:* Devanagari script. *Other:* Hindu, Jain, Muslim. *Map:* 353:63.

Mawchi [mke] (Mauchi, Mavchi, Mawachi, Mawchi Bhil, Mowchi). 99,500 (2001 census). Southeast Gujarat; Maharashtra, Dhule district. *Status:* 5 (Developing). *Class:* Indo-European, Indo-Iranian, Indo-Aryan, Central zone, Bhil. *Dialects:* Mawchi, Padvi. *Lg Use:* Also use Marathi [mar]. *Lg Dev:* Literacy rate in L1: 5%–10%. Literacy rate in L2: 25%–50%. Radio programs. NT: 1989. *Writing:* Devanagari script. *Other:* A Scheduled Tribe in Maharashtra. Traditional religion. *Map:* 358:305.

Meitei [mni] (Kathe, Kathi, Manipuri, Meiteilon, Meiteiron, Meithe, Meithei, Menipuri, Mitei, Mithe, Ponna). 1,470,000 in India (2001 census). Population total all countries: 1,485,000. Manipur; Assam, Cachar, Karimganji; Nagaland; Tripura, West and North Tripura districts; Uttar Pradesh; West Bengal. Also in Bangladesh. *Status:* 2 (Provincial). Statutory provincial language in Manipur State (1992, Constitution, 71st Amendment). *Class:* Sino-Tibetan, Tibeto-Burman, Sal, Kuki-Chin-Naga, Meitei. *Dialects:* Loi (Chakpa), Meitei, Pangal (Manipuri Muslim, Panal, Panan). Intelligibility of Meitei in Bangladesh is difficult. Those in Bangladesh may understand India Meitei better than vice versa possibly due to more language change in Bangladesh over the years. India Meitei is more standard. Intelligibility between dialects in Bangladesh definitely sufficient to understand complex and abstract discourse. Lexical similarity: 80%–86% between dialects in Bangladesh, 65%–70% between Bangladesh and India varieties. *Type:* SOV; postpositions; articles before noun heads; CV, CVC, CVV, VC, VCV; nontonal. *Lg Use:* Also use Hindi [hin]. Used as L2 by Aimol [aim], Anal [anm], Chiru [cdf], Chothe Naga [nct], Gangte [gnb], Hmar [hmr], Inpui Naga [nkf], Kharam Naga [kfw], Koireng [nkd], Kom [kmm], Lamkang [lmk], Mao Naga [nbi], Maram Naga [nma], Monsang Naga [nmh], Moyon Naga [nmo], Purum [pub], Tarao Naga [tro], Thado Chin [tcz],

Thangal Naga [nki]. *Lg Dev:* Literacy rate in L1: 73% (2005 BI). Literacy rate in L2: 69% for Manipur (2001 census). Taught in primary schools. Poetry. Radio programs. Videos. Dictionary. Grammar. Bible: 1984–2011. *Writing:* Bengali script. Braille script. Meetei Mayek script. *Other:* Mainly rural. 6 clans (Ningthonia, Luwang, Angom, Moirang, Khabanaganba, Chonglei). Hindu, Christian, Muslim, traditional religion. *Map:* 351.

Merwari [wry] (Ajmeri). 3,900,000 (2001 census). Rajasthan, Ajmer, Nagaur districts. *Status:* 6a (Vigorous). *Class:* Indo-European, Indo-Iranian, Indo-Aryan, Central zone, Rajasthani, Marwari. A member of macrolanguage Marwari [mwr]. *Dialects:* None known. 82%–97% intelligibility of Marwari [mve]. Lexical similarity: 60%–73% between varieties of Merwari in Ajmer and Nagaur districts; 49%–74% with Marwari [rwr], 58%–80% with Shekhawati [swv], 44%–70% with Godwari [gdx], 54%–72% with Mewari [mtr], 62%–70% with Dhundari [dhd], 57%–67% with Haroti [hoj]. *Lg Use:* Vigorous. Home, village, market, religion. All ages. Positive attitudes. Educated have very good proficiency in Hindi [hin]. *Lg Dev:* Radio programs. *Map:* 353:64.

Mewari [mtr] (Mewadi). 5,100,000 (2001 census). Rajasthan, Udaipur, Bhilwara, Chittoaurgarh districts; Gujarat; Haryana; Delhi; Madhya Pradesh; Uttar Pradesh. *Status:* 5 (Developing). *Class:* Indo-European, Indo-Iranian, Indo-Aryan, Central zone, Rajasthani, Marwari. A member of macrolanguage Marwari [mwr]. *Dialect:* Khairari. 54% intelligibility with Marwari [rwr]. Lexical similarity: 81%–97% between dialects, 73%–91% with Marwari, 75%–90% with Wagri-Dhevdi, 72%–89% with Malvi [mup], 54%–72% with Merwari [wry], 57%–66% with Shekhawati [swv], 51%–73% with Godwari [gdx], 56%–64% with Dhundari [dhd], 69%–84% with Haroti [hoj]. *Type:* SOV. *Lg Use:* Home, village. Positive attitudes. 43% also use Hindi [hin]. *Lg Dev:* Literacy rate in L2: 38% (2001 census). Radio programs. Bible portions: 1815. *Writing:* Devanagari script. *Other:* Different from Mewati, dialect of Haryanvi [bgc]. Hindu, traditional religion. *Map:* 353:68.

Mewati [wtm] (Mewathi). 645,000 (2001 census). 51,600 monolinguals (2006). Rajasthan, Alwar, Bharatpur, Dholpur districts; Uttar Pradesh, Madhura district; Haryana, Gurgaon, Faridabad districts. *Status:* 5 (Developing). *Class:* Indo-European, Indo-Iranian, Indo-Aryan, Central zone, Unclassified. *Dialects:* 45% intelligibility of Marwari [rwr]. Over 90% intelligibility of Alwar District dialect throughout Mewati area. Dialect in the Nuh area of Gurgaon is considered purest. Lexical similarity: 72%–77% with Hindi [hin], 63%–68% with Haryanvi [bgc], 57%–70% with Shekhawati [swv], 62%–67% with Dhundari [dhd], 52%–70% with Haroti [hoj], 68%–71% with Braj Bhasha [bra], 86%–99% between all varieties of Mewati. *Lg Use:* Vigorous. Home, village, market, religion. All ages. Positive attitudes. 25% also use Hindi [hin]. An Arabic language or Urdu [urd] also used. *Lg Dev:* Literacy rate in L2: 25% (2006). Taught in primary schools. *Other:* People are called Meo; many Urdu [urd] loanwords. Muslim, Hindu. *Map:* 354:83.

Miji [sjl] (Dammai, Dhammai, Namrei, Sajalong, Sajolang). 6,500 (2001). Arunachal Pradesh, West Kemang district, Nafra circle, Bichom and Pakesa river valley, 25 villages including Debbing, Dichik, Rurang, Nachinghom, Upper Dzang, Naku, Khellong, Dibrick, Nizong, Najang, Zangnaching, Chalang, Nafra, and Lower Dzang; East Kameng district, Bameng and Lada circles, Wakke, Nabolong, Kojo, Rojo, Sekong, Panker, Zarkam, Drackchi, Besai, Naschgzang, Sachung, Gerangzing, Kampaa, Salang, Pego, and Dongko villages. *Status:* 6a (Vigorous). *Class:* Sino-Tibetan, Tibeto-Burman, Central Tibeto-Burman, Hrusish. *Dialects:* None known. Generally considered in the Mirish subgroup. Reportedly completely dissimilar to any surrounding language. Lexical similarity: 54%–65% between varieties of West and East Kameng; 54%–83% between all varieties. *Lg Use:* All ages. Also use Hindi [hin]; educated speak Hindi more fluently than uneducated, but all speakers know some Hindi. Also use Assamese [asm], English [eng], Hruso [hru], Nyishi [njz]. Used as L2 by Hruso [hru], Nyishi [njz]. *Lg Dev:* Literacy rate in L2: 39%, males 48%, females 29% (2001 census). *Writing:* Latin script. *Other:* A Scheduled Tribe. Traditional religion, Christian. *Map:* 356:169.

Miju-Mishmi [mxj] (Eastern Mishmi, Geman Dend, Geman Deng, Kaman, Miji, Miju, Mishmi). 18,000 in India (2006 Arunachal Tourism). Population total all countries: 18,200. Arunachal Pradesh, Lohit district, 25 villages, high altitudes of east, upper Lohit and Dau valleys, east of Haguliang, Billong, and Tilai valleys; Assam. Also in China (Geman Deng). *Status:* 6a (Vigorous). *Class:* Sino-Tibetan, Tibeto-Burman, Central Tibeto-Burman, Mijish. *Dialects:* None known. Conflicting reports about Miju-Mishmi similarity to Idu-Mishmi [clk] and Digaro-Mishmi [mhu]. Reportedly intelligible but recorded lexical similarity is too low for this to be possible. Ethnically related, but may not be linguistically similar. Related to Kachin, Chin and Lepcha [lep] languages (Chowdhury 1996). Some linguists believe the language is similar to Jingpho [kac]. Lexical similarity: 7% with Idu-Mishmi [clk], 10% with Digaro-Mishmi [mhu] (IICCC). *Type:* SOV; tonal, 4 tones which are reportedly has a low functional load. *Lg Use:* Also use Assamese [asm], Digaro-Mishmi [mhu], English [eng], Hindi [hin], Nepali [npi]. *Lg Dev:* Literacy rate in L2: 40% for Mishmi (2001 census). Grammar. *Writing:* Latin script. *Other:* A Scheduled Tribe, subgroup of Mishmi. Different from the Miji [sjl]. Buddhist, traditional religion. *Map:* 356:190.

Mina [myi]. 3,800,000 (IMA 1997). Madhya Pradesh, Gwalior, Shivpuri, Guna, and Rajgarh districts, Vidisha district, Sironj subdivision; Rajasthan, Jaipur, Alwar, Bharatpur, Sawai Madhopur, Tonk, Bundi, and Ajmer districts. *Status:* 6a (Vigorous). *Class:* Indo-European, Indo-Iranian, Indo-Aryan, Unclassified. *Lg Use:* Use a mix of Dhundari [dhd], Mewari [mtr], and Mewati [wtm]. *Other:* A Scheduled Tribe. Reportedly L1 is Dhundari [dhd] in Rajasthjan and Braj Bhasha [bra] in Madhya Pradesh. Not a Bhil tribe, and there is no connection between Mina and Wagdi, who call themselves Mina Bhil. Hindu. *Map:* 354:85.

Mirgan [zrg] (Mirgami, Mirkan, Panika, Panka). 60,000 (1998 N. Lima). Chhattisgarh, Bastar District; Odisha, Koraput, and Nabarangapur districts. *Status:* 6a (Vigorous). *Class:* Indo-European, Indo-Iranian, Indo-Aryan, Eastern zone, Bengali-Assamese. *Dialects:* Batasuna, Jagdal Pur, Kosagumuda, Kotpad, Nabarang Pur, Umerkote. Dialects have good intelligibility. Not functionally intelligible of Halbi [hlb]. Lexical similarity: 83%–95% among dialects. *Lg Use:* Vigorous. Home, religion. Positive attitudes. Deshia [dso] used in Odisha. Halbi [hlb] used in Madhya Pradesh. Hindi [hin] used in Madhya Pradesh. Low proficiency in Oriya [ory]. Oriya used in Odisha. *Lg Dev:* Literacy rate in L2: 10% Oriya [ory]. *Writing:* Oriya script. Telugu script. *Other:* Declared a General Caste by the government. Divided into 2 groups, the larger Kabirpanthi and the smaller Sakta. Traditional religion, Christian, Hindu. *Map:* 359:332.

Mising [mrg] (Miri, Mishing, Takam). 551,000 (2001 census). Assam, North Lakhimpur, Sonitput, Dhemaji, Dibrugarh, Sibsagar, Jorhat, Golaghat, and Tinsukia districts; Arunachal Pradesh, Lower Subansiri district, Ziro subdivision, a few villages near Pasighat, both sides of Kamla river; Upper Subansiri district, Daporizo subdivision. Hill Miri are in Arunachal Pradesh; Plains Miri are in Assam. *Status:* 5 (Developing). *Class:* Sino-Tibetan, Tibeto-Burman, Central Tibeto-Burman, Tani. *Dialects:* Idu-Mishmi [clk] may be a dialect. *Lg Use:* Also use Assamese [asm]. *Lg Dev:* Literacy rate in L2: 53% for Arunachal, 60 % for Assam (2001 census). Radio programs. Grammar. NT: 2001. *Writing:* Bengali script. Devanagari script. Latin script. *Other:* A Scheduled Tribe. Hindu, traditional religion. *Map:* 356:204.

Mizo [lus] (Duhlian Twang, Dulien, Hualngo, Lukhai, Lusago, Lusai, Lusei, Lushai, Lushei, Sailau, Whelngo). 675,000 in India (2001 census). Population total all countries: 687,750. Mizoram; Assam; Manipur, Churachandpur district; Nagaland; Tripura, Jampui Hill range. Also in Bangladesh, Myanmar (Mizo Chin). *Status:* 4 (Educational). Statutory language of provincial identity in Mizoram State (1950, Constitution, Articles 345–347 inclusive), unscheduled language. *Class:* Sino-Tibetan, Tibeto-Burman, Sal, Kuki-Chin-Naga, Kuki-Chin, Central. *Dialects:* Fannai, Mizo, Ngente, Tlau. Related to Hmar [hmr], Pangkhua [pkh], and Falam Chin [cfm] (Zahao dialect). *Type:* SOV. *Lg Use:* Used as L2 by Bawm Chin [bgr], Biete [biu], Chakma [ccp], Hmar [hmr], Hrangkhol [hra], Mara Chin [mrh], Paite Chin [pck], Pankhu [pkh], Pnar [pbv], Ralte [ral]. *Lg Dev:* Literacy rate in L1: 82%. Literacy rate in L2: 74% for Manipur (2001 census). Taught in primary and secondary schools. Magazines. Dictionary. Grammar. Bible: 1959–1995. *Writing:* Bengali script. Braille script. Latin script. *Other:* Mizo is a Scheduled Tribe with subgroups Lushai, Pang, Tlau, and Hualngo. Christian. *Map:* 357:261.

Monpa, Kalaktang [kkf] (Southern Monpa, Tsangla Monpa). 8,000 (2005). Arunachal Pradesh, West Kameng district, Kalaktang administrative center, Khalaktang, Balimu, and Tomko villages. *Status:* 6a (Vigorous). *Class:* Sino-Tibetan, Tibeto-Burman, Western Tibeto-Burman, Bodish. *Dialects:* Reportedly most similar to Dirang dialect of Tshangla [tsj], average 55% intelligibility of Dirang. *Lg Use:* Vigorous. Home, village, religion. Positive attitudes. Also use Hindi [hin]. Used as L2 by Bugun [bgg]. *Lg Dev:* Literacy rate in L2: 62% for West Kameng District, males 71%, females 49% (2001 census). *Writing:* Unwritten. *Other:* 'Monpa' (Moinba), man of the lower country and refers to several ethnically-related peoples which may not be related linguistically. Buddhist. *Map:* 356:174.

Monpa, Tawang [twm] (Brahmi, Cuona Menba, Dwags, Monkit, Northern Monpa, Takpa, Tawan Monba). 8,600 in India. Population total all countries: 9,900. Arunachal Pradesh, Tawang district. Also in China (Cuona Monba). *Status:* 6a (Vigorous). *Class:* Sino-Tibetan, Tibeto-Burman, Western Tibeto-Burman, Bodish, East Bodish. *Type:* Basic SOV. *Lg Use:* Vigorous. Home, village, religion. Positive attitudes. Also use Hindi [hin]. Used as L2 by Sherdukpen [sdp]. *Lg Dev:* Literacy rate in L2: 32% (2001 census). *Writing:* Devanagari script. *Other:* Glossonym: Tawan Monba in Tibet. Monpa (Moinba), 'man of the lower country', refers to several ethnically related peoples, which may not be related linguistically. Buddhist. *Map:* 356:171.

Mru [mro] (Mro, Mrung, Murung, Niopheng). Ethnic population: 2,100. West Bengal, Jalpaiguri, Nadia, and Hoogly districts. *Status:* 5 (Developing). *Other:* Traditional religion, Buddhist. See main entry on page 56. *Map:* 355:122.

Muduga [udg] (Mudugar). 3,370 (1991 census). Kerala, Palakkad district, Mannarkad Taluk, Attapady block, Chundakki, Thazhachundakki, Veeranuru, Karuvare, Ommale, Kallamale, Kottamale, Chitturu, Chandakulam, Koravanpady, Ummathupadiga, Molakambi, Thekkumpanna, Abbannuru, Kottiyuru, Pettikkallu, Kakkuppady, and Mukkali hamlets; Tamil Nadu, Nilgiris, and Coimbatore. *Status:* 6a (Vigorous). *Class:* Dravidian, Southern. *Dialects:* Also influenced by Kannada [kan] and Tulu [tcy]. Has grammatical similarities with Tamil [tam], but cannot be treated as a dialect. It is distinct in the Dravidian family (Menon 1996:274 citing Rajendran). No dialects determined on survey. Lexical similarity: 55%–57% with Malayalam [mal], 59% with Muthuvan [muv], 60% with Tamil [tam], 75% with the Attapady dialect of Irula [iru], 82%–83% with Attapady Kurumba [pkr]. *Lg Use:* Vigorous, children learn it first. Home, village, religion. All ages. Positive attitudes. Education plays major role in determining bilingualism levels, but even some higher educated Muduga are not adequately bilingual in Malayalam [mal]. Used as L2 by Attapady Kurumba [pkr], Kannada Kurumba [kfi]. *Lg Dev:* Literacy rate in L2: 25% (31% men and 17% women) (1991 census). One of the least literate communities in Kerala, but 73% of survey respondents claim to be literate in Malayalam [mal]. *Other:* National census population figures combine Muduga of Attapady with Muthuvan, who, despite the similarity of the spelling of their ethnonym, are entirely different and separated by geographic and cultural distance (Menon 1996). Traditional religion, Hindu. *Map:* 360:398.

Mugom [muk]. 500 in India (2006 SIL). 75 families in India, 60 Mugom and 15 Karmarong. In addition, there are many seasonal workers. Himachal Pradesh, Kullu, Manali; Kinnaur, Dharmshala and Ladakh. *Status:* 6a (Vigorous). *Lg Use:* Youth born in India still use Mugom at home. Home, with friends. All ages. *Other:* Migrate from Nepal temporarily for work, but many stay 20 to 30 years. See main entry on page 255. *Map:* 352:28.

Mukha-Dora [mmk] (Conta-Reddi, Mukha Dhora, Nooka Dora, Nuka-Dora, Reddi, Reddi-Dora, Riddi). 29,700 (1991 census). Andhra Pradesh, Vishakhapatnam, Srikakulam, and Vizianagaram districts. Also scattered in Adivasi Oriya. *Status:* 6a (Vigorous). *Class:* Dravidian, South-Central, Gondi-Kui, Konda-Kui, Konda. *Lg Use:* Use Telugu [tel] as L1 (Singh 1994). Also use Adivasi Oriya [ort]. *Lg Dev:* Literacy rate in L2: 34%–42% for Scheduled Tribes in Vishakhapatnam, Srikakulam, Vizianagaram districts (2001 census). *Other:* A Scheduled Tribe. Hindu, traditional religion. *Map:* 359:353.

Munda [unx] (Heriki, Killi). 469,000 (2001 census). Odisha, Jharkhand; possibly Bihar and West Bengal. *Status:* 6a (Vigorous). *Class:* Austro-Asiatic, Munda, North Munda, Kherwari, Mundari. *Dialects:* None known. Reportedly most similar to Mundari [unr]. *Lg Use:* Used as L2 by Birhor [biy], Mahali [mjx]. *Writing:* Bengali script. Devanagari script. *Other:* Traditional religion, Christian. *Maps:* 355:141, 359:141.

Mundari [unr] (Colh, Horo, Mandari, Mondari, Munari). 1,110,000 in India (2001 census). 1,060,000 Mundari, 47,400 Bhumij. Population total all countries: 1,120,280. Jharkhand, south and west Ranchi district; Odisha; Madhya Pradesh; West Bengal; Himachal Pradesh; Assam; Tripura; Andaman and Nicobar Islands. Also in Bangladesh, Nepal. *Status:* 5 (Developing). *Class:* Austro-Asiatic, Munda, North Munda, Kherwari, Mundari. *Dialects:* Bhumij (Bhumij Munda, Bhumij Thar, Sadar Bhumij), Hasada', Kera', Latar, Naguri. 75% intelligibility of Ho [hoc]. Lexical similarity: 70%–84% with the Bhumij dialect. *Lg Use:* Used as L2 by Birhor [biy], Mahali [mjx]. *Lg Dev:* Literacy rate in L1: 10%–30%. Literacy rate in L2: 50%–75%. Poetry. Magazines. Radio programs. Dictionary. Grammar. Bible: 1910–2002. *Writing:* Bengali script. Devanagari script. Latin script. Oriya script. *Other:* A Scheduled Tribe. There is Bhumij literature. Traditional religion, Hindu. *Map:* 355:142.

Muria, Eastern [emu]. 200,000 (2007). Chhattisgarh, Northeast Bastar district, Keshkal and Kondagaon tahsils; Odisha, Nabarangapur district, Raigarh tahsil. *Status:* 6a (Vigorous). *Class:* Dravidian, South-Central, Gondi-Kui, Gondi. *Dialects:* Lanjoda, Raigarh. 95% intelligibility between dialects; 73%–83% of Western Muria [mut]; 19%–34% of Northern Gondi [gno]; 35% of Dandami Maria [daq]. Lexical similarity: 74%–77% with Western Muria [mut], 65%–75% with Far Western Muria [fmu]. *Lg Use:* Vigorous. Religion, work; mixed use: home, village. All ages. Positive attitudes. Also use Chhattisgarhi [hne], Halbi [hlb], Hindi [hin], Oriya [ory]. *Lg Dev:* Majority are illiterate. *Other:* A Scheduled Tribe. Traditional religion, Hindu. *Map:* 359:336.

Muria, Far Western [fmu] (Gondi, Koitor Boli, Koitori). 400,000 (2007). Maharashtra, north Garhchiroli district, Kurkheda, Korchi, Dhanora, and Armori tahsils; Gondia district, Jamdi tahsil; Chhattisgarh, Rajnandgaon district, Manpur and Mahola tahsils. *Status:* 6a (Vigorous). *Class:* Dravidian, South-Central, Gondi-Kui, Gondi. *Dialects:* None known. 79%–88% intelligibility of other Muria languages; 74% of Dandami Maria [daq], 0% to 34% of Northern Gondi [gno], 6%–50% of Southern Gondi [ggo], 2%–70% of Maria [mrr]. Lexical similarity: 72%–80% with Western Muria [mut]; 65%–75% with Eastern Muria [emu]. *Lg Use:* Vigorous. Home, village, religion. All ages. Positive attitudes. Also use Chhattisgarhi [hne], Marathi [mar]. *Other:* A Scheduled Tribe. Traditional religion, Hindu. *Map:* 359:333.

Muria, Western [mut] (Jhoria, Mudia, Muria Gondi). 400,000 (2000 IICCC). Chhattisgarh, north and west Bastar district. *Status:* 6a (Vigorous). *Class:* Dravidian, South-Central, Gondi-Kui, Gondi. *Dialects:* Banchapai, Dhanora, Sonapal. 80%–96% intelligibility among dialects, 69%–73% of Eastern Muria [emu], 51%–78% of Far Western Muria [fmu]. No intelligibility of Dandami Maria [daq], Northern Gondi [gno], Southern Gondi [ggo], or Maria [mrr]. Lexical similarity: 72%–80% with Far Western Muria [fmu]; 74%–77% with Eastern Muria [emu]. *Lg Use:* All domains. All ages. *Lg Dev:* Literacy rate in L2: 2% (2003 India Church Growth Mission). *Writing:* Devanagari script. *Other:* A Scheduled Tribe. Hindu, traditional religion. *Map:* 359:335.

Muthuvan [muv] (Mudavan, Muduva, Muduvan, Muduvar, Mutuvar). 16,800 (2006 IMB). Kerala, Idukki district, Devikulam tahsil, Devikulam and Adimali blocks; Kozhikode, Kannur, Ernakulam, Kottayam, and Thrissur districts; Tamil Nadu, Coimbatore district, Udumalpet and Valparai tahsils, Anaimalai hills; Madurai district, Cardamom hills; Andhra Pradesh. *Status:* 6a (Vigorous). *Class:* Dravidian, Southern, Tamil-Kannada, Tamil-Kodagu, Tamil-Malayalam, Tamil. *Dialects:* Eastern Muthuvan (Pandi Muthuvan, Tamil Muthuvan), Western Muthuvan (Malayalam Muthuvan, Nattu Muthuvan). Intelligibility 82%–87% between dialects, eastern dialect more intelligible to western than vice versa, 80% intelligibility of Malayalam [mal]. Lexical similarity: 77%–88% between dialects, 62%–67% with Tamil [tam], 58%–68% with Malayalam [mal]. *Lg Use:* Vigorous. Home, village, religion. All ages. Positive attitudes. Youth understand Malayalam [mal] better than Tamil. Older people understand Tamil [tam] better than Malayalam [mal]. *Lg Dev:* Literacy rate in L2: 24% (31% males, 17% females) (1991 census); 40% for Tamil Nadu (2001 census). *Other:* A Scheduled Tribe. Hindu. *Map:* 360:372.

Na [nbt]. 1,500. Arunachal Pradesh, Upper Subansiri district; Taksing circle, Gumsing, Taying, Esnaya, Lingbing, Tongla, Yeja, Reding, Redi, and Dadu villages. *Status:* 6a (Vigorous). *Class:* Sino-Tibetan, Tibeto-Burman, Central Tibeto-Burman, Tani. *Dialects:* None known. Affinity with Tagin [tgj] (Singh 1994). *Lg Use:* Also use English [eng], Hindi [hin]. *Lg Dev:* Literacy rate in L2: 30% (Singh 1995). *Writing:* Devanagari script. Latin script. *Other:* A Scheduled Tribe. Buddhist (Mahayana), traditional religion. *Map:* 356:182.

Naga Pidgin [nag] (Bodo, Kachari Bengali, Naga Creole Assamese, Naga-Assamese, Nagamese). 30,000 (Holm 1989). Nagaland, Kohima district, Dimapur subdivision; Arunachal Pradesh border area. *Status:* 3 (Wider communication). *Class:* Creole, Assamese based. *Dialects:* None known. A variety least similar to Assamese [asm] is spoken by the Yimchenger Naga, and varieties most similar to Assamese by the Angami Naga, and around Dimapur and Kohima. *Lg Use:* L1 for the Kachari in Dimapur area, a small community, and among children of interethnic marriages. Used as L2 by Angami Naga [njm], Chang Naga [nbc], Konyak Naga [nbe], Lotha Naga [njh], Monsang Naga [nmh], Phom Naga [nph], Pochuri Naga [npo], Sakachep [sch], Sangtam Naga [nsa], Southern Rengma Naga [nre], Sumi Naga [nsm], Yimchungru Naga [yim]. *Lg Dev:* Taught in primary schools as language of instruction. Taught in secondary schools. Grammar. *Writing:* Latin script. *Map:* 356:218.

Naga, Angami [njm] (Angamis, Gnamei, Monr, Ngami, Tendydie, Tsanglo, Tsoghami, Tsugumi). 132,000 (2001 census). West Nagaland, Kohima district; Manipur; Maharashtra. *Status:* 3 (Wider communication). Trade language used by about 30,000 Naga of other groups. *Class:* Sino-Tibetan, Tibeto-Burman, Sal, Kuki-Chin-Naga, Angami-Pochuri. *Dialects:* Chakroma (Western Angami), Dzuna, Kehena, Khonoma, Mima, Mozome, Nali, Tengima (Kohima). Tengima (Kohima) dialect is standard. Naga Chokri and Naga Khezha are eastern Angami groups with their own dialects. 2 southern varieties (Viswemal, Jakhama) are not intelligible with dialects listed. Tenyidie is an umbrella term for all the dialects spoken by the Angami people. *Type:* SOV; numerals after head nouns; postpositions; tonal. *Lg Use:* Also use Assamese [asm], English [eng], Hindi [hin], Naga Pidgin [nag]. Used as L2 by Chokri Naga [nri], Khezha Naga [nkh], Sumi Naga [nsm]. *Lg Dev:* Literacy rate in L1: 86% (2001 census). Literacy rate in L2: 86% (2001 census). Most youth read Angami. Literacy among older people is lower. Taught in primary schools. Magazines. Dictionary. Grammar. Bible: 1970. *Writing:* Latin script. *Other:* A Scheduled Tribe. Christian. *Map:* 356:236.

Naga, Ao [njo] (Ao, Aorr, Cholimi, Hatigoria, Nowgong, Paimi, Uri). 261,000 (2001 census). Northeast Nagaland, central Mokokchung district; Assam. *Status:* 4 (Educational). *Class:* Sino-Tibetan, Tibeto-Burman, Sal, Kuki-Chin-Naga, Ao. *Dialects:* Changki, Chongli (Chungli), Dordar (Yacham), Longla, Mongsen Khari. Chongli and Mongsen border on mutual unintelligibility (Burling 2003). *Lg Use:* Also use Assamese [asm], English [eng], Hindi [hin]. Used as L2 by Chang Naga [nbc], Sangtam Naga [nsa], Sumi Naga [nsm]. *Lg Dev:* Literacy rate in L1: 86% (2001 census). Literacy rate in L2: 86% (2001 census). Taught in primary schools. Radio programs. Dictionary. Grammar. Bible: 1964–2004. *Writing:* Latin script. *Other:* A Scheduled Tribe. Christian. *Map:* 356:222.

Naga, Chang [nbc] (Chang, Changyanguh, Machongrr,

Mochumi, Mochungrr, Mojung). 62,400 (2001 census). East central Nagaland, Tuensang district, 36 villages; Assam. *Status:* 5 (Developing). *Class:* Sino-Tibetan, Tibeto-Burman, Sal, Bodo-Garo-Northern Naga, Northern Naga. *Dialects:* Reportedly similar to Wancho Naga [nnp]. Tuensang village dialect is central and intelligible to all. *Lg Use:* Also use Ao Naga [njo], Assamese [asm], English [eng], Hindi [hin], Naga Pidgin [nag]. *Lg Dev:* Dictionary. Bible: 2002. *Writing:* Latin script. *Other:* Christian. *Map:* 356:224.

Naga, Chokri [nri] (Chakhesang, Chakrima Naga, Chakru, Chokri, Eastern Angami). 83,600 (2001 census). Nagaland, Phek district; Cheswezumi is main village. *Status:* 4 (Educational). *Class:* Sino-Tibetan, Tibeto-Burman, Sal, Kuki-Chin-Naga, Angami-Pochuri. *Lg Use:* Also use Angami Naga [njm], English [eng]. *Lg Dev:* Literacy rate in L2: Greater than 40% (2001 census). Taught in primary schools. *Writing:* Latin script. *Other:* An eastern Angami tribe with its own language. Chokri, Khezha [nkh], and Sangtam-Pochuri [nsa] make up the Chakhesang Naga community (see separate entries). Chakhesang Naga is a Scheduled Tribe. Christian, traditional religion. *Map:* 356:233.

Naga, Chothe [nct] (Chawte, Chote, Chothe, Chowte). 3,600 (2001). Ethnic population: 3,600. Southeast Manipur, Chandel district, 15 villages; Bishnupur district, Lamlang Hupi village; Nagaland, near Myanmar border. *Status:* 6a (Vigorous). *Class:* Sino-Tibetan, Tibeto-Burman, Sal, Kuki-Chin-Naga, Kuki-Chin, Northern. *Dialects:* None known. Reportedly most similar to Tarao Naga [tro]. Reported intelligibility of Aimol [aim]. Lexical similarity: less than 60% with any neighboring languages. *Lg Use:* Purest Chothe spoken in Purum Khullen. Home, village, religion. Positive attitudes. Also use English [eng], Meitei [mni]. *Lg Dev:* Literacy rate in L2: 90% in Meitei (Bengali script) (2000). *Writing:* Bengali script. Latin script. *Other:* A Scheduled Tribe. Christian. *Map:* 357:271.

Naga, Inpui [nkf] (Kabui, Kabui Naga, Kapwi, Koboi, Kubai). 29,200 (2001 census). Manipur, Senapati, Tamenglong, and Imphal districts, 16 villages; Nagaland, Dimapur, New Zaluke, Mahei Namchi, and Peren; Assam. *Status:* 6a (Vigorous). *Class:* Sino-Tibetan, Tibeto-Burman, Sal, Kuki-Chin-Naga, Unclassified. *Dialects:* None known. Considered by some to be the same language as Puimei Naga [npu]. Lexical similarity: 68% with Puimei Naga [npu]. *Lg Use:* Home, religion. All ages. Positive attitudes. 80% also use Meitei [mni]. Also use English [eng], Rongmei Naga [nbu]. *Lg Dev:* Literacy rate in L2: 70% in English and in Meitei (Bengali script) (2000). Literacy high among young people in Meitei and English. *Writing:* Latin script. *Other:* 'Kabui' is the government name for Inpui and Rongmei. Kabui recognized as Scheduled Tribe combining Inpui and Rongmei. Christian. *Map:* 357:249.

Naga, Kharam [kfw] (Duisalongmei, Thinglong). 1,400 (2000 SIL). Manipur, Senapati district, Phaijol, Laikot, Thuisenpai, and Kharam Pallen villages. *Status:* 6a (Vigorous). *Class:* Sino-Tibetan, Tibeto-Burman, Sal, Kuki-Chin-Naga, Kuki-Chin, Northern. *Dialects:* None known. Lexical similarity: 71%–73% with Purum [pub], 58%–60% with Kom [kmm], 64% with Koireng [nkd]. *Lg Use:* All ages. Also use English [eng], Meitei [mni], Purum [pub]. *Lg Dev:* Literacy rate in L2: 30% Meitei, English, Hindi. Most 5- to 20-year-olds have learned to read in school. Older people would like to learn to read. *Writing:* Latin script. *Other:* Christian. *Map:* 356:246.

Naga, Khezha [nkh] (Kezami, Khezha, Khezhama). 40,800 (2001 census). East Nagaland, Kohima, Khezhakhonoma, and Phek districts. *Status:* 5 (Developing). *Class:* Sino-Tibetan, Tibeto-Burman, Sal, Kuki-Chin-Naga, Angami-Pochuri. *Dialects:* None known. An east Angami group with its own language. *Lg Use:* Also use Angami Naga [njm]. *Lg Dev:* Taught in primary schools. Grammar. *Other:* Belong to Chakhesang Naga community. Christian. *Map:* 356:228.

Naga, Khiamniungan [kix] (Aoshedd, Kalyokengnyu, Khiamngan, Khiamniungan, Nokaw, Tukhemmi, Welam). 37,800 in India (2001 census). Population total all countries: 47,800. Nagaland, east central Tuensang district. Also in Myanmar. *Status:* 5 (Developing). *Class:* Sino-Tibetan, Tibeto-Burman, Sal, Bodo-Garo-Northern Naga, Northern Naga. *Dialect:* Noklak. Dialects in Myanmar and India somewhat intelligible but have very limited contact. Lexical similarity: 67% with Gongwang dialect of Ponyo-Gongwang Naga [npg], 72%–73% with Ponyo dialect of [npg], 62%–67% with Leinong Naga [lzn], 41% with Lao Naga. Is in Konyak subgroup, but is divergent. They consider Ponyo Naga [npg] a part of Khiamniungan, though lexical similarity is only around 70%. *Type:* SOV. *Lg Dev:* Literacy rate in L1: 30%. Taught in primary schools since 1959. Radio programs. Bible: 2005. *Writing:* Latin script. *Other:* A Scheduled Tribe. Main clans are Lam, Thai, Shiu, and Maya. Christian (Protestant). *Map:* 356:225.

Naga, Khoibu [nkb] (Khoibu, Khoibu Maring, Khoibu Maring Naga). 25,600 (2001). Ethnic population: 25,600. Manipur, southeast, Laiching; north border of Chandel district mountainous regions, Khoibu, Narum, Yangkhul, and Saibol villages. *Status:* 6a (Vigorous). *Class:* Sino-Tibetan, Tibeto-Burman, Sal, Kuki-Chin-Naga, Tangkhul. *Lg Dev:* NT: 1988. *Map:* 357:272.

Naga, Konyak [nbe] (Kanyak, Konyak). 248,000 in India (2001 census). Population total all countries: 250,000. Assam, Sibsagar district, Nagagaon and Bortol villages near Simulguri township; northeast Nagaland, Mon and Tuensang districts. Also in Myanmar. *Status:* 4 (Educational). *Class:* Sino-Tibetan, Tibeto-Burman, Sal, Bodo-Garo-Northern Naga, Northern Naga. *Dialects:* Angphang, Changnyu, Chen, Chingkao, Chinglang, Choha, Gelekidoria, Hopao, Jakphang, Longching, Longkhai (Lungkhai, Lungkhi), Longmein, Longwa, Mon, Mulung, Ngangching, Sang, Shamnyuyanga, Shanlang, Shengha, Shunyuo, Sima, Sowa, Tableng (Angwangku, Kongon, Mohung, Wakching), Tabu, Tamkhungnyuo, Tang, Tobunyuo, Tolamleinyua, Totok. Tableng is standard dialect spoken in Wanching and Wakching. Reportedly similar to Phom Naga [nph]. *Lg Use:* Also use English [eng], Hindi [hin], Naga Pidgin [nag]. *Lg Dev:* Literacy rate in L1: 40% (2001 census). Literacy rate in L2: 40% (2001 census). Taught in primary schools. Radio programs. Dictionary. Bible: 1992. *Writing:* Latin script. *Other:* A Scheduled Tribe. Christian. *Map:* 356:201.

Naga, Liangmai [njn] (Kacha, Liangmai, Liangmei, Liyang, Lyangmay, Lyengmai). 34,200 (2001 census). Nagaland, Kohima district, Jhaluke, Paren, and Medzephima blocks. *Status:* 4 (Educational). *Class:* Sino-Tibetan, Tibeto-Burman, Sal, Kuki-Chin-Naga, Zeme. *Lg Dev:* Taught in primary schools. Bible: 2001. *Writing:* Latin script. *Other:* Merged ethnically with Zeme [nme] and Rongmei [nbu] Naga to form the Zeliangrong community. Liangmai and Zeme are referred to collectively as Zeliang. *Map:* 356:217.

Naga, Lotha [njh] (Chizima, Choimi, Hlota, Kyong, Lhota, Lotha, Lutha, Miklai, Tsindir, Tsontsii). 170,000 (2001 census). Nagaland, west central, Wokha district. *Status:* 5 (Developing). *Class:* Sino-Tibetan, Tibeto-Burman, Sal, Kuki-Chin-Naga, Ao. *Dialects:* Kyo, Kyon, Kyong, Kyou, Live, Ndreng, Tsontsu. *Lg Use:* Also use Naga Pidgin [nag]. Used as L2 by Sumi Naga [nsm]. *Lg Dev:* Literacy rate in L1: High. Taught in primary schools. Dictionary. Grammar. Bible: 1967–2000. *Writing:* Latin script. *Other:* A Scheduled Tribe. Christian. *Map:* 356:220.

Naga, Makuri [jmn] (Makury Naga). 4,000 in India (2007). Nagaland, Phek and Kiphire districts. *Status:* 6a (Vigorous). *Lg Use:* Home, village, market. All ages. See main entry on page 238. *Map:* 356:231.

Naga, Mao [nbi] (Emela, Imemai, Maikel, Mao, Memi, Sopfomo, Sopvoma, Southern Angami, Spowama). 81,000 (1997). Northwest Manipur, Senapati district; Nagaland. *Status:* 5 (Developing). *Class:* Sino-Tibetan, Tibeto-Burman, Sal, Kuki-Chin-Naga, Angami-Pochuri. *Dialect:* Paomata. Paomata dialect and Poumei Naga [pmx] may be the same (Breton 1997). *Lg Use:* Also use Meitei [mni]. *Lg Dev:* Literacy rate in L1: High. Dictionary. Grammar. Bible: 2001. *Writing:* Latin script. *Other:* Mao is a Scheduled Tribe. Christian. *Map:* 356:235.

Naga, Maram [nma] (Maram). 37,300 (2001). North Manipur, Senapati district, 5 villages near Senapati, 26 villages near Maram; Imphal district; Assam. *Status:* 4 (Educational). *Class:* Sino-Tibetan, Tibeto-Burman, Sal, Kuki-Chin-Naga, Zeme. *Dialects:* Maram Khullen Circle, Ngatan, T. Khullen, Willong Circle. *Lg Use:* Home, village, religion. All ages. Men also use Meitei [mni] more than women. *Lg Dev:* Literacy rate in L1: 60% (2003). Literacy rate in L2: 20% (2000) or 40%–50% (2003). All young people can read Latin script. Writing system does not indicate tone. Literacy among older people is lower. Taught in primary and secondary schools. Grammar. NT: 2004. *Writing:* Latin script. *Other:* A Scheduled Tribe. Christian, traditional religion. *Map:* 356:245.

Naga, Maring [nng] (Maring). 22,300 (2001 census). Manipur, southeast, Laiching; Chandel District north border mountainous region, Tengnoupal subdivision. *Status:* 5 (Developing). *Class:* Sino-Tibetan, Tibeto-Burman, Sal, Kuki-Chin-Naga, Tangkhul. *Lg Dev:* Literacy rate in L2: 53% (2001 census). NT: 2001. *Writing:* Bengali script. Latin script. *Other:* A Scheduled Tribe. Christian. *Map:* 357:275.

Naga, Monsang [nmh] (Mawshang, Monshang, Moshang, Mushang). 3,200 (2001). Ethnic population: 3,200. Manipur, Chandel district, Chandel subdivision, Liwchangning, Heibunglok, Liwa Sarei, Japhou, and Monsang Pantha villages; north Nagaland, near Myanmar border. *Status:* 5 (Developing). *Class:* Sino-Tibetan, Tibeto-Burman, Unclassified. *Dialects:* None known. Reportedly most similar to Moyon Naga [nmo] and Anal Naga [anm]. *Lg Use:* Also use English [eng], Hindi [hin], Meitei [mni], Naga Pidgin [nag]. Used as L2 by Moyon Naga [nmo]. *Lg Dev:* Literacy rate in L2: 80% (1988). Many read and write Meitei (Singh 1998). Literacy program in progress by government and church. NT: 2009. *Writing:* Latin script. *Other:* A Scheduled Tribe. Christian. *Map:* 357:269.

Naga, Moyon [nmo] (Mayol, Mayon Naga, Moyon). 3,700 (2001). Ethnic population: 3,700. Nagaland, near Myanmar border; Manipur, Chandel district, 14 villages including Moyon Khullen, Khongjom, Mitong, Komlathabi, Penaching, and Heigru Tampak. *Status:* 5 (Developing). *Class:* Sino-Tibetan, Tibeto-Burman, Sal, Kuki-Chin-Naga, Kuki-Chin, Northern. *Lg Use:* Also use Anal [anm] (Singh 1998). Mostly bilingual in Meitei [mni] (Singh 1998). Also use Monsang Naga [nmh] (Singh 1998). *Lg Dev:* Literacy program in progress (1988). NT. *Writing:* Bengali script. Latin script. *Other:* A Scheduled Tribe. Christian. *Map:* 357:266.

Naga, Mzieme [nme] (Mzieme, Northern Zeme). 29,000 (1997). Southwest Nagaland, Kohima district, Paren area, northeast of Zeme. *Status:* 5 (Developing). *Class:* Sino-Tibetan, Tibeto-Burman, Sal, Kuki-Chin-Naga, Zeme. *Dialects:* None known. Different from Zeme Naga [nzm]. *Lg Dev:* Bible: 1992. *Writing:* Latin script. *Other:* Adopted the designation Northern Zeme because Zeme has government recognition while Mzieme does not. *Map:* 356:237.

Naga, Nocte [njb] (Borduria, Jaipuria, Mohongia, Namsangia, Nocte, Nokte, Paniduria). 33,000 (2001 census). 19,800 monolinguals (2001 census). Southeast Arunachal Pradesh, Tirap district, Khonsa, Namsang, and Laju circles; Changlang district; Assam, Lakhimpur district, Jaipur; North Nagaland, Mon district, Namsang. *Status:* 6a (Vigorous). *Class:* Sino-Tibetan, Tibeto-Burman, Sal, Bodo-Garo-Northern Naga, Northern Naga. *Dialects:* Khapa, Laju, Ponthai (Lamlak). Reportedly similar to Tase Naga [nst]. Ponthai may be an ethnic group, not a dialect. 50% intelligible with Wancho Naga [nnp]. *Type:* SOV; postpositions; genitives before noun heads; articles, adjectives, numerals after noun heads; affixes indicate case of noun phrase; causatives; comparatives; CV, CVC, CVV, CVVC, V; tonal, at least 3 tones. *Lg Use:* Home, village, religion. All ages. Also use Assamese [asm], English [eng], Hindi [hin]. *Lg Dev:* Literacy rate in L2: 47% (2001 census). Radio programs. *Other:* A Scheduled Tribe. Tutsa, Wancho, Laju, Lamlak considered ethnic subgroups of Nocte although Tutsa consider themselves not related to Nocte. Christian, Hindu, traditional religion. *Map:* 356:199.

Naga, Northern Rengma [nnl] (Northern Rengma, Ntenyi, Ntenyi Naga, Nthenyi). 13,000 (1997). Nagaland; Kohima district, north Rengma. *Status:* 5 (Developing). *Class:* Sino-Tibetan, Tibeto-Burman, Sal, Kuki-Chin-Naga, Angami-Pochuri. *Lg Dev:* Bible: 2005. *Writing:* Latin script. *Other:* Christian. *Map:* 356:226.

Naga, Phom [nph] (Assiringia, Chingmengu, Phom, Phon, Tamlu, Tamlu Naga). 123,000 (2001 census). Northeast Nagaland, Tuensang district, Longleng subdivision, 36 villages. *Status:* 4 (Educational). *Class:* Sino-Tibetan, Tibeto-Burman, Sal, Bodo-Garo-Northern Naga, Northern Naga. *Dialect:* Yongyasha. Reportedly similar to Konyak Naga [nbe]. *Type:* Tonal. *Lg Use:* Also use Naga Pidgin [nag]. *Lg Dev:* Literacy rate in L2: 35% adults. Taught in primary schools. Dictionary. Bible: 2005. *Writing:* Latin script. *Other:* A Scheduled Tribe. Christian. *Map:* 356:223.

Naga, Pochuri [npo] (Eastern Rengma, Meluri, Pochuri, Pochury). 16,700 (2001 census). Southeast Nagaland, Phek district, Meluri subdivision, 27 villages. *Status:* 5 (Developing). *Class:* Sino-Tibetan, Tibeto-Burman, Sal, Kuki-Chin-Naga, Angami-Pochuri. *Lg Use:* Also use Naga Pidgin [nag]. *Lg Dev:* Literacy rate in L2: 39% (Singh 1994). NT: 1994. *Writing:* Latin script. *Other:* A Scheduled Tribe. Meluri is a place-name in this region. Pochury is an amalgamation of 3 place-names: Sapo, Kechuri, Khury. Christian. *Map:* 356:232.

Naga, Poumei [pmx] (Paumei, Pomai, Pome, Poumei). 51,000 (1997). Manipur. *Status:* 5 (Developing). *Class:* Sino-Tibetan, Tibeto-Burman, Sal, Kuki-Chin-Naga, Angami-Pochuri. *Dialects:* Similar to Mao Naga [nbi]. Different from Puimei Naga [npu] (Breton 1997:217). Paomata dialect of Mao Naga and Poumei Naga may be the same (Breton 1997). *Lg Dev:* NT: 1992. *Writing:* Latin script. *Map:* 356:234.

Naga, Puimei [npu] (Puimei). 3,000 (2001). Mostly monolingual. Ethnic population: 3,000. Manipur; Assam. *Status:* 6a (Vigorous). *Class:* Sino-Tibetan, Tibeto-Burman, Sal, Kuki-Chin-Naga, Unclassified. *Dialects:* None known. Different from Poumei Naga [pmx] (Breton 1997:217). Not functionally intelligible of any related language (Khasung). Lexical similarity: 68% with Inpui Naga [nkf]. *Writing:* Latin script. *Other:* Were assigned as part of

Rongmei Naga [nbu]. Christian, traditional religion. *Map:* 356:241.

Naga, Rongmei [nbu] (Kabui, Maruongmai, Nruanghmei, Rongmai, Rongmei). 61,200 (2001 census). Northwest Manipur; Nagaland; Assam, Cachar district. 35 villages. *Status:* 4 (Educational). *Class:* Sino-Tibetan, Tibeto-Burman, Sal, Kuki-Chin-Naga, Zeme. *Dialect:* Songbu. *Lg Use:* Used as L2 by Inpui Naga [nkf]. *Lg Dev:* Literacy rate in L1: High. Magazines. Radio programs. Bible: 1989. *Writing:* Latin script. *Other:* Songbu is principal Division of Rongmei. Merged with Zeme and Liangmai Naga to form the Zeliang community. Inpui and Rongmei ethnonym: Kabui by government. Christian, traditional religion. *Map:* 356:244.

Naga, Sangtam [nsa] (Isachanure, Lophomi, Sangtam). 84,300 (2001 census). Southeast Nagaland, Tuensang district, Kiphire subdivision and Chare circle. *Status:* 4 (Educational). *Class:* Sino-Tibetan, Tibeto-Burman, Sal, Kuki-Chin-Naga, Ao. *Dialects:* Kizare, Phelongre, Photsimi, Pirr (Northern Sangtam), Purr (Southern Sangtam), Thukumi (Central Sangtam). Standard based on Tsadanger village dialect. Kizare north of Meluri, and not known how much it differs from other Sangtam. *Lg Use:* Also use Ao Naga [njo], English [eng], Hindi [hin], Naga Pidgin [nag]. *Lg Dev:* Literacy rate in L2: 40% (2001 census). Taught in primary schools. Bible: 1995. *Writing:* Latin script. *Other:* Chokri, Khezha, and a small section of Sangtam make up the Chakhesang Naga community. A Scheduled Tribe. Christian. *Map:* 356:229.

Naga, Southern Rengma [nre] (Injang, Moiyui, Mon, Mozhumi, Nzong, Nzonyu, Rengma, Rengma Naga, Southern Rengma, Unza, Western Rengma). 21,000 (1997). West central Nagaland, Kohima district, Tseminyu subdivision; Assam, Karbi-Anglong district, 15 villages; Manipur. *Status:* 5 (Developing). *Class:* Sino-Tibetan, Tibeto-Burman, Sal, Kuki-Chin-Naga, Angami-Pochuri. *Dialects:* Azonyu (Nzonyu, Southern Rengma), Keteneneyu. Tseminyu principal dialect main center. Southern Rengma and Northern Rengma [nnl] are reportedly inherently unintelligible. *Lg Use:* Also use English [eng], Naga Pidgin [nag]. *Lg Dev:* Literacy in Rengma is higher among older people. Young people are learning English. Bible: 2000. *Writing:* Latin script. *Other:* A Scheduled Tribe. Christian. *Map:* 356:219.

Naga, Sumi [nsm] (Sema, Simi, Sumi). 104,000 (2001 census). Central and south Nagaland, Zunheboto, Kohima, Mokokchung, Tuensang districts; Assam, Tinsukia district, 7 villages. Dayang is near Dayang river. *Status:* 4 (Educational). *Class:* Sino-Tibetan, Tibeto-Burman, Sal, Kuki-Chin-Naga, Angami-Pochuri. *Dialects:* Dayang (Western Sumi), Lazemi, Zhimomi, Zumomi. *Lg Use:* Also use Angami Naga [njm], Ao Naga [njo], Assamese [asm], English [eng], Hindi [hin], Lotha Naga [njh], Naga Pidgin [nag]. *Lg Dev:* Literacy rate in L2: 50% Assamese [asm], English. Taught in primary schools. Dictionary. Grammar. Bible: 2000–2004. *Writing:* Latin script. *Other:* A Scheduled Tribe. Christian. *Map:* 356:227.

Naga, Tangkhul [nmf] (Champhung, Luhuppa, Luppa, Tagkhul, Tangkhul, Thangkhulm). 142,000 (2001 census). Manipur, Ukhrul district, 168 villages; Nagaland; Tripura. *Status:* 4 (Educational). *Class:* Sino-Tibetan, Tibeto-Burman, Sal, Kuki-Chin-Naga, Tangkhul. *Dialects:* Khangoi, Khunggoi, Kupome, Phadang, Ukhrul. Ukhrul is principal dialect. *Lg Dev:* Literacy rate in L1: 73% Meitei, English (2001 census). Literacy rate in L2: 73% Meitei [mni], English (2001 census). Literature is based on the Ukhrul dialect. Taught in primary schools. Magazines. Newspapers. Radio programs. Dictionary. Grammar. Bible: 1976. *Writing:* Latin script. *Other:* A Scheduled Tribe. The most educated group of Manipur. Christian. *Map:* 356:247.

Naga, Tarao [tro] (Tarao, Taraotrong, Tarau). 870 (2000). Manipur, Chandel district, Palel area, Heikakpokpi, Leishokching, Khuringmul Laiminei villages; Ukhrul district, Sinakeithei village. *Status:* 5 (Developing). *Class:* Sino-Tibetan, Tibeto-Burman, Unclassified. *Dialects:* None known. Reportedly most similar to Chothe Naga [nct], 70% intelligibility. Lexical similarity: less than 60% with any neighboring language; 43%–46% with Chothe Naga [nct]. *Type:* Postpositions; genitives, articles, adjectives, numerals, relatives before noun heads; maximum affixes 2; word order distinguishes subjects, objects, and indirect objects; noun affix marks case; verb affixes mark number; no passive; causatives and comparatives; CVC. *Lg Use:* Home, religion. All ages. Positive attitudes. Also use English [eng], Meitei [mni]. *Lg Dev:* Literacy rate in L2: 75% Meitei, English. Literacy program in progress. Older people can read Meitei in Bengali script. Young people prefer Latin script. Most villages have primary and junior schools; attendance is irregular. *Other:* Not recognized as a separate Scheduled Tribe by the government due to its small size. Christian. *Map:* 357:270.

Naga, Tase [nst] (Cham Chang, Rangpan, Tangsa, Tangshang, Tasey). 40,100 in India (2001 census). 400 monolinguals. Southeast Arunachal Pradesh, Changlang district, East hills, Tirap river valley and Namchik area; Assam. *Status:* 5 (Developing). *Dialects:* Have (Havoy), Higsho, Higtsii, Kimsing (Chamchang, Khemsing, Sanke, Sechu, Shangge, Shechu), Longphi (Longkhi), Lungchang, Lungri, Miti, Moklum, Mosang (Hewa), Mungray (Morang), Ngemu, Ponthai, Rongrang, Ronrang (Poerah), Sangche, Sangwal, Taipi, Tikhak, Tonglim (Tangrim), Tutsa, Yogli (Jugli), Yongkuk (Yukok). *Lg Use:* Home, village. All ages. Positive attitudes. Also use Assamese [asm], Burmese [mya], English [eng], Hindi [hin], Singpho [sgp]. *Lg Dev:* Literacy rate in L2: 56% (2001 census). *Other:* 'Tangsa', hill people. A Scheduled Tribe. May be up to 36 subtribes of Tangsa. Kimsing dialect speakers can understand all dialects well. Kimsing is similar to Tutsa. Higsho is similar to Nocte. Kimsing has most speakers and is most influential. Traditional religion, Buddhist, Christian. See main entry on page 239. *Map:* 356:194.

Naga, Thangal [nki] (Khoirao, Khoirao Naga, Koirao, Kolya, Mayangkhang, Miyang-Khang, Ngari, Thangal, Thanggal, Tukaimi). 23,600 (2001). Ethnic population: 23,600. North Manipur, Senapati district, East and West Sadar hills subdivisions, Mapao Thangal, Thangal Surung, Makeng Thangal, Tumnoupokpi, Yaikangpou, Tikhulen, Ningthoubam, Mayangkhang, and Gailongde. Most are east of Barak valley. *Status:* 5 (Developing). *Class:* Sino-Tibetan, Tibeto-Burman, Sal, Kuki-Chin-Naga, Zeme. *Dialects:* None known. Reportedly similar to Maram Naga [nma]. *Type:* Postpositions; genitives, relatives before noun head; articles, adjectives, numerals after noun head; question word initial; case marked by postpositional clitics; comparatives; CV, CVC, CVV, VC, V syllables; nontonal. *Lg Use:* All ages. Also use English [eng], Meitei [mni]. *Lg Dev:* Literacy rate in L2: 90% Meitei, English. Dictionary. NT: 2004. *Writing:* Bengali script. Latin script. *Other:* A Scheduled Tribe. Christian. *Map:* 356:243.

Naga, Tutsa [tvt] (Totcha, Tutsa). 25,000 (2001). 12,500 monolinguals. Arunachal Pradesh, south Changlang and east Tirap districts. *Status:* 6a (Vigorous). *Class:* Sino-Tibetan, Tibeto-Burman, Sal, Bodo-Garo-Northern Naga, Northern Naga. *Dialects:* None known. Reportedly similar to Nocte Naga [njb] and Tase Naga [nst]. *Type:* SOV; postpositions; genitives and articles before noun heads; adjectives and numerals after noun heads; maximum affixes 2; affixes indicate case of noun phrase; ergativity; CV, CVC, VC; may be tonal but it does not carry much functional load. *Lg Use:* Home, village. All ages. Also use Assamese [asm], English [eng], Hindi [hin]. *Lg Dev:* Literacy rate in L2: 5%. Very few with higher education. *Other:* Consider themselves separate from Nocte [njb] and Tase Naga [nst]. Traditional religion. *Map:* 356:198.

Naga, Wancho [nnp] (Banpara Naga, Joboka, Jokoba, Wancho). 49,100 (2001 census). Southeast Arunachal Pradesh, southwest Tirap district, 36 villages; Assam; Nagaland. *Status:* 5 (Developing). *Class:* Sino-Tibetan, Tibeto-Burman, Sal, Bodo-Garo-Northern Naga, Northern Naga. *Dialects:* Bor Muthun (Bor Mutonia), Changnoi, Horu Muthun, Kulung Muthun (Mithan). Significant variation between spoken language in upper and lower regions. Reportedly similar to Chang Naga [nbc] and Konyak Naga [nbe]. *Lg Use:* Also use Assamese [asm], Hindi [hin]. *Lg Dev:* Literacy rate in L2: 25% (2001 census). NT: 2002. *Writing:* Devanagari script. Latin script. *Other:* A Scheduled Tribe. Christian, traditional religion. *Map:* 356:200.

Naga, Yimchungru [yim] (Tozhuma, Yachumi, Yanchunger, Yimchunger, Yimchungre, Yimchungru). 92,100 (2001 census). North Nagaland, Tuensang district, between Namchik and Patkoi. *Status:* 5 (Developing). *Class:* Sino-Tibetan, Tibeto-Burman, Sal, Kuki-Chin-Naga, Ao. *Dialects:* Chirr, Minir, Pherrongre, Tikhir, Wai, Yimchungru. The last 3 dialects listed are in the south. *Lg Use:* Also use English [eng], Hindi [hin], Naga Pidgin [nag]. *Lg Dev:* Taught in primary schools. Bible. *Writing:* Latin script. *Other:* A Scheduled Tribe. Christian. *Map:* 356:230.

Naga, Zeme [nzm] (Arung, Empui, Jeme, Kacha, Kachcha, Kutcha, Mezama, Sangrima, Sengima, Zemi). 34,100 (2001 census). Assam, North Cachar district, upper Barak valley; Manipur, Tamenglong district; Nagaland, Kohima district, Jhaluke, Paren, Medzephima blocks. *Status:* 5 (Developing). *Class:* Sino-Tibetan, Tibeto-Burman, Sal, Kuki-Chin-Naga, Zeme. *Dialects:* Njauna, Paren. *Lg Use:* Used strongly for oral communication but not much in written form. Home, village, church. Positive attitudes. Also use Hindi [hin]. *Lg Dev:* Literacy rate in L2: 59% in Manipur (2001 census). Radio programs. NT: 1978–1992. *Writing:* Latin script. *Other:* Ethnonym: Zeliang, with both Liangmai or Zeliangrong, including Rongmei. A Scheduled Tribe. Christian (Protestant), Hindu. *Map:* 356:212.

Nagarchal [nbg] (Nagar, Nagarchi). No known L1 speakers. Madhya Pradesh, Balaghat, Chhindwara, Mandla, and Seoni districts; Chhattisgarh, Durg district; Maharashtra, Bhandara district; Rajasthan. *Status:* 10 (Extinct). *Class:* Dravidian, South-Central, Gondi-Kui, Gondi. *Lg Use:* Have shifted to Hindi and Northern Gondi [gno]. *Other:* 'Nagarchi' is a people group living in Seoni, Jabalpur, and Mandla districts of Madhya Pradesh who speak Hindi [hin] (Singh 1998).

Nahali [nlx] (Kalto, Nahal, Nahale, Nahalia). 15,000 (2003). Maharashtra, Nandurbar district, Dhadgaon tahsil, 12 villages near Toranmal; Jalgaon district, Chopda tahsil, north of Amalwadi. *Status:* 6a (Vigorous). *Class:* Indo-European, Indo-Iranian, Indo-Aryan, Central zone, Bhil. *Dialects:* None known. 96% intelligibility of Bareli Pauri [bfb]. This may be acquired rather than inherent (1988 S. Watters). Lexical similarity: 58%–68% with Noiri [noi] varieties, 60%–61% with Dungra Bhil [duh], 69%–73% with Bareli Pauri [bfb]. *Other:* A Scheduled Tribe. Reported to speak Nimadi [noe] as L1. (Singh 1994). Nihali [nll] and Nahali are different languages. *Map:* 358:292.

Nahari [nhh] (Nahali). 20,400 (2000). Chhattisgarh, Raipur, Bilaspur districts; Odisha, Sambalpur district. *Status:* 6a (Vigorous). *Class:* Indo-European, Indo-Iranian, Indo-Aryan, Eastern zone, Bengali-Assamese. *Dialects:* None known. A more divergent variety, related to Halbi [hlb]. *Other:* Hindu. *Map:* 359:330.

Nefamese [nef] (Arunamese). Population unknown. May be replaced by Hindi [hin] (2006 Y. Modi). Arunachal Pradesh. *Status:* 8b (Nearly extinct). *Class:* Pidgin, Assamese based. *Lg Use:* Formerly a lingua franca of Arunachal Pradesh. Used as L2 by Apatani [apt], Bugun [bgg], Zakhring [zkr]. *Map:* 356:184.

Nepali [npi] (Eastern Pahari, Gorkhali, Gurkhali, Khaskura, Nepalese, Parbatiya). 2,870,000 in India (2001 census). West Bengal, Darjeeling area; Sikkim; Assam; Arunachal Pradesh; Bihar; Haryana; Himachal Pradesh; Uttar Pradesh; Uttarakhand; Manipur; Mizoram; Nagaland; Meghalaya, Tripura. *Status:* 2 (Provincial). Statutory provincial language in Sikkim, West Bengal state (1992, Constitution, 71st Amendment). *Dialects:* Gorkhali, Nepali, Palpa. *Lg Use:* Used as L2 by Adi [adi], Bantawa [bap], Byangsi [bee], Chaudangsi [cdn], Darmiya [drd], Eastern Magar [mgp], Idu-Mishmi [clk], Koch [kdq], Kullu Pahari [kfx], Maithili [mai], Majhi [mjz], Miju-Mishmi [mxj], Sikkimese [sip], Thado Chin [tcz], Toto [txo], Western Gurung [gvr]. *Lg Dev:* Literacy rate in L1: 30%–100%. Literacy rate in L2: 25%–75%. *Other:* Hindu. See main entry on page 256. *Map:* 351.

Newar [new] ("Newari" *pej.*). 14,000 in India (2007). Ethnic population: 166,000 (2007). Sikkim; West Bengal; Some in Bettiah, Bihar; Andamans. *Status:* 5 (Developing). See main entry on page 256. *Map:* 355:116.

Nicobarese, Car [caq] (Car, Pu). 37,000 (2005). North Nicobar Islands, Car island. *Status:* 3 (Wider communication). Lingua franca for Nicobar Islands. *Class:* Austro-Asiatic, Mon-Khmer, Nicobar, Car. *Lg Dev:* Literacy rate in L2: 46% for Scheduled Tribes in Nicobar District. 72% for Nicobar (2001 census). Dictionary. Bible: 1969. *Writing:* Latin script. *Other:* A Scheduled Tribe. Christian. *Map:* 361.

Nicobarese, Central [ncb] (Muöt, Nicobar). 10,100 (2001 census). 5,310 on Katchal, 3,410 on Kamorta, 930 on Nancowry, 430 on Trinket. Nicobar Islands, Katchal, Camorta, Nancowry, and Trinket islands. *Status:* 5 (Developing). *Class:* Austro-Asiatic, Mon-Khmer, Nicobar, Nancowry. *Dialects:* Camorta (Kamorta), Katchal (Kachel, Tehnu), Nancowry (Nancoury), Trinkut (Trinkat). Central Nicobar once regarded as one language but no longer generally accepted. Dialects now regarded as mutually unintelligible with the exception of Trinket and Katchal. (Parkin 1991). *Lg Dev:* Literacy rate in L2: 46% for Scheduled Tribes in Nicobar District. 72% for Nicobar (2001 census). Bible portions: 1884–1890. *Writing:* Devanagari script. Latin script. *Other:* Christian. *Map:* 361.

Nicobarese, Southern [nik] (Nicobara). 7,500 (2001 census). 350 on Little Nicobar Island, 7,570 total on Great Nicobar, about 400 of these are Shompen. Nicobar Islands, Little Nicobar and outer Great Nicobar islands. *Status:* 6a (Vigorous). *Class:* Austro-Asiatic, Mon-Khmer, Nicobar, Great Nicobar. *Dialects:* Condul (Kondul), Great Nicobar, Little Nicobar, Milo. *Lg Dev:* Literacy rate in L2: 46% for Scheduled Tribes in Nicobar District. 72% for Nicobar (2001 census). *Other:* Hindu, Muslim, traditional religion. *Map:* 361.

Nihali [nll] (Nihal). 2,000 (Parkin 1991). Ethnic population: 5,000 (1987). Maharashtra, Buldana district, Jamod Jalgaon tahsil. *Status:* 6b (Threatened). *Class:* Language isolate. *Dialects:* None known. Lexical similarity: 25% between Nihal in Chikaldara taluk and Akola District and Korku [kfq] (Munda). *Lg Use:* Also use Hindi [hin], Korku

[kfq], Marathi [mar]. *Other:* They live in or near Korku villages in a position of subordination to the Korku people. Possibly belonged to a now extinct speech family of India. Influenced significantly by Munda and Dravidian languages. 60%–70% of vocabulary borrowed. Nihali and Nahali [nlx] are different languages. *Map:* 358:295.

Nimadi [noe] (Nemadi, Nimari, Nimiadi). 2,150,000 (2001 census). Madhya Pradesh, Khandwa, Khargone, Barwani, and south Dhar districts; Uttar Pradesh; Maharashtra. *Status:* 6a (Vigorous). *Class:* Indo-European, Indo-Iranian, Indo-Aryan, Central zone, Rajasthani, Unclassified. *Dialect:* Bhuani. Dialects have 90%–100% mutual inherent intelligibility. Lexical similarity: 74%–94% among dialects, 64%–75% with Malvi [mup], 62%–77% with Hindi [hin], 56%–64% with Gujarati [guj], 49%–58% with Marathi [mar]. *Lg Use:* Vigorous. All domains, except with government officials. Positive attitudes. Low proficiency in Hindi [hin], used in education. Used as L2 by Palya Bareli [bpx], Pauri Bareli [bfb], Rathwi Bareli [bgd]. *Lg Dev:* Literacy rate in L2: 40%. Radio programs. TV. *Writing:* Devanagari script. *Other:* Hindu, Muslim, traditional religion. *Maps:* 353:81, 358:81.

Noiri [noi]. 100,000 (2003 IICCC). Maharashtra, Nandurbar district, Dhadgaon, Akkalkua, and Shahada tahsils; Dhule district, Shirpur tahsil; Jalgaon district, Chopda tahsil; Madhya Pradesh, Badwani district, Pansemal tahsil. *Status:* 6a (Vigorous). *Class:* Indo-European, Indo-Iranian, Indo-Aryan, Central zone, Bhil. *Dialect:* Barutiya. Barutiya people have high acquired intelligibility of Vasavi [vas] and Bareli Pauri [bfb] and Dungra Bhili [duh]. Lexical similarity: 77%–87% with Dungra Bhili [duh], 60%-71% with different Vasavi [vas] varieties, 58%–68% with Nahali [nlx] of Toranmal, 47%–54% with the Kotali dialect of Bhili [bhb]; the Barutiya dialect of Noiri, 64%–70% with Bareli Pauri [bfb]. Noiri-Barutiya variety falls between Vasavi and Bareli Pauri on a dialect continuum. *Lg Use:* Vigorous. Home, village. Positive attitudes to the west. Less positive to the east. Also use Hindi [hin], Marathi [mar]. *Lg Dev:* Literacy rate in L2: 1% in Marathi. *Writing:* Devanagari script. *Other:* A Scheduled Tribe in Maharashtra and Madhya Pradesh. A Bhil subgroup. 'Noira' means people who speak through the nose. Traditional religion, Christian, Hindu. *Map:* 358:293.

Nora [nrr] (Norra, Noza, Nurra). No known L1 speakers. Northeast, near Tibet. *Status:* 10 (Extinct). *Class:* Tai-Kadai. *Dialects:* Byabe, Kizolo, Nora. *Type:* SOV.

Nyishi [njz] (Bangni, Dafla, Daphla, Lel, Nil, Nishi, Nisi, Nissi, Nyising). 230,000 (2001 census). 23,000 speakers of Bangni dialect (Van Driem 2007). Arunachal Pradesh, lower Subansiri district. *Status:* 5 (Developing). *Class:* Sino-Tibetan, Tibeto-Burman, Central Tibeto-Burman, Tani. *Dialects:* Aka Lel, Bangni, Nishang. Reportedly similar to Tagin [tgj]. Apatani [apt] may be a dialect. *Lg Use:* All domains. Also use Miji [sjl]. Used as L2 by Miji [sjl], Puroik [suv]. *Lg Dev:* Literacy rate in L2: 37%—46% (2001 census). NT: 2002. *Writing:* Bengali script. Latin script. *Other:* Nisi is a Scheduled Tribe. Nisi has been used as a cover term for western Tani languages. Traditional religion, Christian, Hindu. *Map:* 356:181.

Oko-Juwoi [okj] (Junoi, Juwoi, Oku-Juwoi). No known L1 speakers. Andaman Islands, west central and southwest interior Middle Andaman island. *Status:* 10 (Extinct). *Class:* Andamanese, Great Andamanese, Central.

Öñge [oon] (Ong). 94 (Abbi 2006). Mainly monolingual. Ethnic population: 110 (1999). South Andaman Islands, Dugong Creek and South Bay islands. *Status:* 6b (Threatened). *Class:* Andamanese, South Andamanese. *Dialects:* None known. Reportedly distinct from Sentinel [std]. *Lg Dev:* Grammar. *Other:* A Scheduled Tribe. Reserved toward outsiders. Traditional religion. *Map:* 361.

Oriya [ory] (Odisha, Odri, Odrum, Oliya, Uriya, Utkali, Vadiya, Yudhia). 32,100,000 in India (2001 census). Population total all countries: 32,137,870. Odisha, Jharkhand, Singhbhum, and Ranchi districts; Chhattisgarh, Raigarh, Raipur, and Bastar districts; West Bengal, Medinipur (Midnapore) district; Assam; Andhra Pradesh, Vishakhapatnam district. Also in Bangladesh, Nepal, United States. *Status:* 2 (Provincial). Statutory provincial language in Odisha State (1950, Constitution, Schedule VIII). *Class:* Indo-European, Indo-Iranian, Indo-Aryan, Eastern zone, Oriya. A member of macrolanguage Oriya [ori]. *Dialects:* Halbi, Midnapore Oriya, Mughalbandi (Oriya Proper, Standard Oriya), North Balasore Oriya, Northwestern Oriya, Southern Oriya, Western Oriya (Sambalpuri). Lexical similarity: 75%–76% with Sambalpuri [spv], 68% with Kamar [keq]. *Lg Use:* Used as L2 by Bhatri [bgw], Birhor [biy], Bodo Gadaba [gbj], Chhattisgarhi [hne], Duruwa [pci], Eastern Muria [emu], Gata' [gaq], Ho [hoc], Juang [jun], Kharia [khr], Kharia Thar [ksy], Kisan [xis], Konda-Dora [kfc], Kudmali [kyw], Lodhi [lbm], Mahali [mjx], Mirgan [zrg], Pengo [peg], Sadri [sck]. *Lg Dev:* Literacy rate in L1: 64% (2001 census). Literacy rate in L2: 64% (2001 census). Fully developed. Bible: 1815–2004. *Writing:* Braille script. Oriya script, primary usage. *Other:* Hindu. *Map:* 351.

Oriya [ori]. A macrolanguage (see page 9). *Other:* Includes: Oriya [ory], Sambalpuri [spv].

Oriya, Adivasi [ort] (Adiwasi Oriya, Kotia Oriya, Kotiya, Tribal Oriya). 200,000 (2011 SIL). L2 users: 200,000 (1998 U. Gustafsson). Andhra Pradesh, Vishakhapatnam district, Araku valley. *Status:* 5 (Developing). *Class:* Indo-European, Indo-Iranian, Indo-Aryan, Eastern zone, Oriya. *Dialects:* None known. Lexical similarity: 38%–42% with standard Oriya [ory], 80%–85% with Desiya [dso] in Odisha. *Lg Use:* Used as L2 by Bodo Parja [bdv], Bondo [bfw], Mukha-Dora [mmk], Parenga [pcj]. *Lg Dev:* Literacy rate in L1: 7%. Literacy rate in L2: 34% for Scheduled Tribes in Vishakhapatnam District (2001 census). Dictionary. NT: 2011. *Writing:* Telugu script. *Other:* Adivasi Oriya is a Scheduled Tribe. Ethnonyms: Kotia in Andra Pradesh, Adivasi, and Desiya in Odisha. Traditional religion, Hindu. *Map:* 359:356.

Pahari, Kullu [kfx] (Kauli, Kullui, Kulu Boli, Kulu Pahari, Kului, Kulvi, Kulwali, Pahari, Pahari Kullu, Phari Kulu). 109,000 (1997). All Pahari 2,170,000 (1997). Himachal Pradesh, Kullu district, Banjar, Balichowk, and Sainj tahsils. *Status:* 6a (Vigorous). *Class:* Indo-European, Indo-Iranian, Indo-Aryan, Northern zone, Western Pahari. *Dialects:* Inner Siragi (Inner Seraji, Saraji, Siragi, Siraji), Kullui, Outer Seraji. Inner Siragi is apparently different from the Siraji-Kashmiri dialect of Kashmiri [kas]. Lexical similarity: 85% or higher among dialects. *Lg Use:* Also use Hindi [hin], Nepali [npi], Tinani [lbf], Urdu [urd]. Used as L2 by Gujari [gju]. *Lg Dev:* Radio programs. Dictionary. Bible portions: 1932–1998. *Writing:* Devanagari script. Takri (Tankri, Takari) script, no longer in use. *Other:* Traditional religion, Hindu. *Map:* 352:27.

Pahari, Mahasu [bfz] (Mahasui). 1,000,000 (2002). Himachal Pradesh, Shimla (Simla) and Solan districts. *Status:* 6a (Vigorous). *Class:* Indo-European, Indo-Iranian, Indo-Aryan, Northern zone, Western Pahari. *Dialects:* Lower Mahasu Pahari (Baghati, Baghliani, Kiunthali), Upper Mahasu Pahari (Rampuri, Rohruri, Shimla Siraji, Sodochi). The Kiunthali variety appears to be understood by others, and their attitude toward it is favorable. Rampuri is also called Kochi; Rohruri is also called Soracholi. Intelligibility among dialects above 85%. Lexical similarity: 74%–82% with upper dialects, 74%–95%

with lower dialects. *Type:* SOV; postpositions; genitives after noun heads; nontonal. *Lg Use:* Home, religion. All ages. The educated are more proficient in Hindi [hin]. *Lg Dev:* Literacy rate in L2: 80% for Shimla District, 82% for Solan (2001 census). Magazines. Newspapers. Radio programs. Dictionary. Bible portions. *Writing:* Devanagari script. *Other:* Hindu. *Map:* 352:41.

Pali [pli]. No known L1 speakers in India. Also in Myanmar. *Status:* 9 (Second language only). *Class:* Indo-European, Indo-Iranian, Indo-Aryan, Unclassified. *Lg Use:* Literary language of Buddhist scriptures. Positive attitudes. *Lg Dev:* NT: 1835. *Writing:* Devanagari script. Myanmar (Burmese) script. Sinhala script. Thai script. *Other:* Buddhist.

Paliyan [pcf] (Makkal, Malai Paliyar, Palani, Palaya, Palayan, Paliyar, Palleyan, Palliyar, Poliyar, Seramar, Tamil). 9,520 (2001 census). Kerala, Idukki district, Pirmed tahsil, Kumily, Vandanmedu, and Chakkupallam panchayats; Ernakulam and Kottayam districts; Tamil Nadu, Dindigul, Madurai, Ramanathapuram, Thanjavur, Pudukkottai, Tirunelveli, and Coimbatore districts; Karnataka. *Status:* 6a (Vigorous). *Class:* Dravidian, Southern, Tamil-Kannada, Tamil-Kodagu, Tamil-Malayalam, Malayalam. *Dialect:* Mala Pulayan (Hill Pulaya, Karavazhi). Lexical similarity: 71%–75% with Tamil [tam], 62%–65% with Malayalam [mal], 79%–85% with Mala Pulayan [pcf]. *Lg Use:* Speakers have high proficiency in Tamil [tam]. Also use Malayalam [mal]. *Lg Dev:* Literacy rate in L2: 44%–62% in Kerala, 50% for Hill Pulaya (2001 census). *Other:* A Scheduled Tribe. Paliya and Mala Pulaya refer to L1 as Tamil [tam], though it differs from standard Tamil. Traditional religion, Christian, Hindu. *Map:* 360:376.

Panchpargania [tdb] (Bedia, Chik Barik, Pan, Pan Sawasi, Tair, Tamara, Tamaria, Tanti, Temoral, Tumariya). 194,000 (2001 census). Jharkhand, Ranchi and Singhbhum districts; Odisha; West Bengal; upper Assam tea gardens. *Status:* 3 (Wider communication). *Class:* Indo-European, Indo-Iranian, Indo-Aryan, Eastern zone, Bihari. *Dialects:* Sonahatu variety considered most pure. Lexical similarity: 77%–94% between dialects, 61%–86% with Kudmali, 68%–76% with Magahi (Khortha) [mag], 61%–70% with Sadri [sck], 48%–52% with Oriya [ory], 45%–58% with Bengali [ben], 50%–60% with Hindi [hin]. *Lg Use:* Vigorous. Home, village, market, religion. All ages. Positive attitudes. Also use Bengali [ben], Hindi [hin]. *Writing:* Bengali script, no longer in use. Devanagari script. Kaithi script, no longer in use. *Other:* Panchpargania means 5 districts, namely Silli, Bundu, Rahe, Baranda, and Tamar parganas of Ranchi (Singh 1995). Hindu, Christian, Muslim, traditional religion. *Map:* 355:138.

Pangwali [pgg] (Pahari, Pangi, Pangwali Pahari). 17,000 (1997). Himachal Pradesh, Chamba district, Pangi tahsil, Lahul-Spiti district, Udaipur on Chenab (Chandra-Bhaga) river to Chamba border at Purthi. Possibly from Tandi to Sach Pass. *Status:* 6a (Vigorous). *Class:* Indo-European, Indo-Iranian, Indo-Aryan, Northern zone, Western Pahari. *Dialects:* 64% inherent intelligibility of Mandeali [mjl], 52% of Kangri [xnr], 44% of Chambeali [cdh], 50% of Bhadrawahi [bhd]; some dialect variation throughout the valley in Chamba District; Purthi reportedly most divergent. Lexical similarity: 55% with Hindi [hin], 77% with Kullu Pahari [kfx]; 45% with Bhadrawahi [bhd]. *Lg Use:* Vigorous. Home, village, religion. Positive attitudes. Also use English [eng], Hindi [hin]. *Lg Dev:* Literacy rate in L2: 9% men, 1% women. In 1981, 9% of the men had a 5th grade education, 1% of the women; 3% of the men had an 8th grade education, fewer than 1% of the women. Poetry. Radio programs. *Writing:* Devanagari script. *Other:* A Scheduled Tribe. Hindu. *Map:* 352:17.

Paniya [pcg] (Nil, Pania, Paniyan, Panyah). 94,000 (2003). Kerala, Wayanad, Kozhikode, Kannur, and Malappuram districts; Tamil Nadu, west of Nilgiris hills; Karnataka, Kodagu district. *Status:* 5 (Developing). *Class:* Dravidian, Southern, Tamil-Kannada, Tamil-Kodagu, Tamil-Malayalam, Malayalam. *Dialects:* Intelligibility of Malappura Paniya by Kodava [kfa] is 66%. Lexical similarity: 79%–88% between dialects and Malappuram Paniya, 71% with Kodaku [ksz] and Kodava [kfa]. *Lg Use:* Home, religion. Also use Kannada [kan], Malayalam [mal], Tamil [tam]. *Lg Dev:* Literacy rate in L2: 41% for Kerala, 26% for Tamil Nadu (2001 census). *Writing:* Kannada script, used in Karnataka. Malayalam script, used in Kerala. Tamil script, used in Tamil Nadu. *Other:* A Scheduled Tribe. Hindu, traditional religion. *Map:* 360:392.

Panjabi, Eastern [pan] (Eastern Punjabi, Gurmukhi, Gurumukhi, Punjabi). 28,200,000 in India (2001 census). Population total all countries: 29,514,770. Punjab, south Firozpur district, Bhatyiana; Rajasthan, north Ganganagar district, Bhatyiana; Haryana; Delhi; Jammu and Kashmir. Majhi dialect in Punjab, Gurdaspur and Amritsar districts. Also in Bangladesh, Canada, Fiji, Kenya, Libya, Malaysia, Mauritius, Singapore, United Arab Emirates, United Kingdom, United States. *Status:* 2 (Provincial). Statutory provincial language in Punjab, West Bengal states; union territories Delhi, Chandigarh (1950, Constitution, Schedule VIII). *Class:* Indo-European, Indo-Iranian, Indo-Aryan, Central zone, Panjabi. *Dialects:* Bathi, Bhatyiana (Bhatneri, Bhatti), Doab, Majhi, Malwa, Panjabi Proper, Powadhi. Western Panjabi [pnb] is distinct from Eastern Panjabi, although there is a chain of dialects to Western Hindi (Urdu) [urd]. Bhatyiana dialect considered a mixture of Panjabi and Marwari [mve]. Majhi considered the purest Panjabi form (Grierson and Konow 1901–1929). *Lg Use:* Used as L2 by Bauria [bge], Bhattiyali [bht], Bilaspuri [kfs], Chambeali [cdh], Churahi [cdj], Dogri [dgo], Kangri [xnr], Mandeali [mjl], Sansi [ssi]. *Lg Dev:* Radio programs. Grammar. Bible: 1959–2002. *Writing:* Arabic script. Gurmukhi script, primary usage. Khojki script. *Other:* Associated with Sikhs. Different from Majhi [mjz] in India and Nepal. Sikh, Muslim (Bhatneri). *Map:* 351.

Panjabi, Mirpur [pmu] (Mirpur, Mirpuri). 1,020,000 in India (2000). Population total all countries: 1,040,000. Kashmir, Mirpur area, near Pakistan border. Possibly in Pakistan. Also in United Kingdom. *Status:* 6a (Vigorous). *Class:* Indo-European, Indo-Iranian, Indo-Aryan, Northwestern zone, Lahnda. A member of macrolanguage Lahnda [lah] (Pakistan). *Dialects:* None known. Distinct from Western Panjabi [pnb], though closely related. *Lg Dev:* Radio programs. *Other:* Hindu, Sikh. *Map:* 352:1.

Panjabi, Western [pnb] (Hindki, Lahanda, Lahnda, Lahndi, Western Punjabi). 1,910,000 in India (2007). Jammu and Kashmir; Delhi; Haryana. *Status:* 5 (Developing). *Other:* Muslim, Christian. See main entry on page 271. *Map:* 352:12.

Pankhu [pkh] (Paang, Pang, Pang Khua, Pangkhu, Pankho, Pankhua, Panko, Pankua). Current population unknown. Ethnic population: 230 (1971). Mizoram, Chhimtuipui and Lunglei districts, 12 villages. *Status:* 6a (Vigorous). *Lg Use:* Also use Bawm Chin [bgr], English [eng], Mizo [lus]. *Other:* Scheduled Tribe. A subgroup of the Mizo [lus]. Christian. See main entry on page 56 (as Pangkhua). *Map:* 357:280.

Pao [ppa] (Pabra). 53,000 (2000). Madhya Pradesh, Satna, Chhatarpur, Datia, Panna, Rewa, Shahdol, Sidhi, and Tikamgarh districts. *Status:* 6a (Vigorous). *Class:* Sino-Tibetan, Tibeto-Burman, Unclassified. *Dialects:* None known. May not be Tibeto-Burman. *Lg Use:* Also use

Hindi [hin]. *Other:* A Scheduled Tribe. Reported to speak Bagheli [bfy] as L1 (Singh 1994). Hindu. *Map:* 354:109.

Pardhan [pch] (Pradhan, Pradhani). 135,000 (2007). Ethnic population: 347,000. Madhya Pradesh, Seoni, Mandla, Chhindwara, Hoshangabad, Betul, Balaghat, and Jabalpur districts; Chhattisgarh, Raipur, Bilaspur, and Surguja districts; Maharashtra, Bhandara, Garhchiroli, Nagpur, Wardha, and Yavatmal districts; Andhra Pradesh, Adilbad district. *Status:* 6b (Threatened). *Class:* Dravidian, South-Central, Gondi-Kui, Gondi. *Lg Use:* Most in Madhya Pradesh also use Hindi [hin]. In Maharashtra also use Marathi [mar]. *Other:* L1 is Gondi [gon] (Singh 1994). Hindu. *Map:* 358:298.

Pardhi [pcl] (Bahelia, Chita Pardhi, Lango Pardhi, Paidia, Paradi, Paria, Phans Pardhi, Takankar, Takia). 49,300 (2001 census). Maharashtra; Andhra Pradesh; Madhya Pradesh; Gujarat; widely scattered. *Status:* 6a (Vigorous). *Class:* Indo-European, Indo-Iranian, Indo-Aryan, Central zone, Bhil. *Dialects:* Haran Shikari, Neelishikari, Pittala Bhasha, Takari. Probably more than 1 language (Lango). Possibly a dialect of Bhili [bhb]. *Other:* A Scheduled Tribe in Gujarat, Karnataka, Madhya Pradesh and Maharashtra, and a Scheduled Caste in Madhya Pradesh. Different than Paradhi, who speak Kachchi [kfr]. Traditional religion. *Map:* 358:317.

Parenga [pcj] (Gorum, Gorum Sama, Pareng, Parenga Parja, Parengi, Parenji, Poroja). Ethnic population: 12,600 (2001 census). In Odisha. Odisha, Koraput district; Andhra Pradesh. *Status:* 8b (Nearly extinct). *Class:* Austro-Asiatic, Munda, South Munda, Koraput Munda, Sora-Juray-Gorum, Gorum. *Lg Use:* Probably extinct. Speakers are shifting to Adivasi Oriya [ort]. *Lg Dev:* Literacy rate in L2: 17% (2001 census). *Writing:* Telugu script. *Other:* A Scheduled Tribe. Ethnonym: Gadaba, erroneously. *Maps:* 355:147, 359:147.

Parsi [prp] (Parsee). 151,000 in India (2000). Population total all countries: 326,000. Gujarat; Maharashtra. Also in China, Pakistan, United Kingdom, United States. *Status:* 6a (Vigorous). *Class:* Indo-European, Indo-Iranian, Iranian, Western, Northwestern, Central Iran. *Dialects:* None known. Reportedly not inherently intelligible with Parsi-Dari [prd], from whom they separated 600–700 years ago. Other reports say they came to India 1,300 years ago. Related to Zoroastrian Dari [gbz] in Iran. *Lg Use:* Also use English [eng]. *Lg Dev:* Literacy rate in L2: 90% in English. Most are well educated. *Other:* Ethnic autonym: Parsee. Distinct from Parsi, a dialect of Gujarati [guj]. Zoroastrian. *Map:* 358:289.

Pathiya [pty]. 1,000 (2004 SIL). Kerala, Wayanad district, Mathamangalam, Thelampatta, Thekkumpatta, Cheramkolli, and Kazhambu villages. *Status:* 6a (Vigorous). *Class:* Dravidian, Southern. *Dialects:* None known. It has been reported that they speak Malayalam [mal] mixed with Kannada [kan] words (Menon 1996:313; Shashi and Shri 1994, Vol. 11). Lexical similarity: 88% with Kalanadi [wkl], 83% with Kunduvadi [wku], 72% with Malayalam [mal], 79% with Paniya [pcg], 76%–80% with Mullu Kurumba [kpb], 70%–74% with Wayanad Kurichiya. *Lg Use:* Continued vitality doubtful, due to small population, no separate settlements, living with Malayalis, and similarity to Malayalam. Home. *Other:* Common cultural origin with Kunduvadiyar and Kalanadikal. Not related to the washerman caste of the same name in Travancore area. (Menon 1996). Jain. *Map:* 360:385.

Pattani [lae] (Chamba, Chamba Lahuli, Changsapa Boli, Lahuli, Manchad, Manchati, Patni, Swangla). 11,000 (1997). Ethnic population: 20,000 (2002). L2 users: 5,000 (1997). Himachal Pradesh, Lahul, Pattan, Chamba-Lahul, and lower Mayar valleys. Some in Kullu, Manali cities. *Status:* 6a (Vigorous). *Class:* Sino-Tibetan, Tibeto-Burman, Western Tibeto-Burman, Bodish, West Himalayish, Kinauri. *Dialects:* Central Pattani, Chamba-Lahuli (Western Pattani), Eastern Pattani. 3 caste dialects exist (Pandit-Rajput, Harijan and Lohar). The lower castes understand Pandit-Rajput, but not vice versa. Lexical similarity: 55%–63% between Western Pattani dialect and Tinani [lbf], 26%–39% with Bunan [bfu], 37% with Shumcho [scu], 35% with Jangshung [jna], 33% with Sunam [ssk], 31% with Chitkuli [cik] and Kinnauri [kfk], 25% with Puh and Kinnaur District varieties (Kinnaur Bhoti [nes]) of Tibetan, 22% with Nesang [tpq], 18% with Tibetan [bod], 14%–15% with the Spiti and Stod varieties of Tibetan. Average of 80% between dialects. *Lg Use:* Home, village, religion. Positive attitudes. Hindi [hin] is used in education and trade; half speak Hindi with good proficiency. Also use English [eng]. Used as L2 by Tinani [lbf]. *Lg Dev:* Literacy rate in L2: 50% for women (even young ones). Over 50% for men. Most young men under 30 can read (2002). Poetry. Bible portions: 1907–1914. *Writing:* Devanagari script. Tibetan script, no longer in use. *Other:* Lahaula and Swangla are both Scheduled Tribes. Hindu. *Map:* 352:18.

Pengo [peg] (Hengo, Pengu). Ethnic population: 350,000 (2000). Odisha, Koraput district, Dasamantapur and Nandapur tahsils; Rayagada district, Kashipur tahsil; Nabarangapur district, Pappadahandi tahsil; Kalahandi district. *Status:* 6a (Vigorous). *Class:* Dravidian, South-Central, Gondi-Kui, Konda-Kui, Manda-Kui, Manda-Pengo. *Dialects:* Awe, Indi. *Lg Use:* Also use Oriya [ory]. *Lg Dev:* Dictionary. *Writing:* Oriya script. *Other:* They consider themselves separate from Jhodia Poraja. Traditional religion, Hindu. *Map:* 359:344.

Phake [phk] (Faake, Phakey, Phakial). 2,000 (Bradley 2007). Assam, Dibrugarh district, Bor-phake, Nam-phake, Tipam-phake, Man-long, Man-po-mung, Pha-neng, Ning-gam, Nong-lai, and Mung-lang villages along Dihing river; Arunachal Pradesh. *Status:* 4 (Educational). *Class:* Tai-Kadai, Kam-Tai, Tai, Southwestern. *Dialects:* None known. Reportedly similar to Aiton [aio]. Similar to Shan [shn] of Myanmar. *Lg Use:* All ages. Also use Assamese [asm]. *Lg Dev:* Taught in primary schools. *Writing:* Myanmar (Burmese) script. *Other:* Buddhist, traditional religion. *Map:* 356:202.

Phudagi [phd] (Vadval). 1,010 (2000). Maharashtra, Thane district. *Status:* 6a (Vigorous). *Class:* Indo-European, Indo-Iranian, Indo-Aryan, Southern zone, Konkani. *Dialects:* A more divergent dialect of, or closely related language to, Konkani [knn]. *Map:* 358:312.

Pnar [pbv]. 243,000 in India (2001 census). Population total all countries: 247,000. Meghalaya, Khasi and Jaintia hills, north of War Jaintia; Mizoram, north Aizawl district; Assam, North Cachar hills, Jatinga, Borolokha, and Dibruchera; Karbi Anglong district, Ulukunchi. Also in Bangladesh. *Status:* 6a (Vigorous). *Class:* Austro-Asiatic, Mon-Khmer, Northern Mon-Khmer, Khasian. *Dialects:* Jaintia (Synteng), Nongtung. Formerly considered a dialect of Khasi [kha]. Jaintia dialect has 12 spoken forms: Jowai, Shangpung, Batau, Raliang, Sutnga, Sumer, Nartiang, Barato, Rymbai, Lakadong, Mynso, and Nongtalang. All are intelligible, except for Nongtalang, which is akin to Central Khmer [khm]. Jowai is standard spoken form. Lexical similarity: 68% with standard Khasi. *Lg Use:* Also use Bengali [ben], English [eng], Hindi [hin], Mizo [lus]. *Lg Dev:* Literacy rate in L2: 62% for Synteng dialect in Meghalaya (2001 census). Radio programs. *Writing:* Latin script. *Other:* A Scheduled Tribe. Christian. *Map:* 356:213.

Portuguese [por]. 250,000 in India. Goa, Daman, Diu,

Dadra, and Nagar Haveli. *Status:* 5 (Dispersed). *Lg Use:* Used as L2 by Indo-Portuguese [idb]. See main entry on page 321.

Powari [pwr]. 426,000 (2001 census). Ethnic population: 2,000,000 (1986 All India Powar Council). Madhya Pradesh, Balaghat, Seoni, Chindwara, and Betul districts; Maharashtra, Wardha, Bhandara, and Gondia districts. *Status:* 6b (Threatened). *Class:* Indo-European, Indo-Iranian, Indo-Aryan, Central zone. *Dialects:* Bhoyar Powari (Bhomiyari, Bhoyari, Bhoyaroo, Bhuiyar, Bhuria, Bohoyeri), Govari of Seoni, Khalari, Koshti, Kumbhari, Lodhi, Marari, Vyneganga Powari. Reported intelligibility between Bhoyar and Vyneganga. Balaghat District dialect considered central among Bhoyar and Vyneganga varieties. Lexical similarity: 60%–87% among dialects; 80%–83% with Koshti, Kumbhari, and Khalari sub-groups; 49%–65% with Bagheli [bfy], 46%–64% with Bundeli [bns]. *Lg Use:* Powari use is decreasing in the Bhoyar and Vyneganga dialect areas. Half the children learn Hindi or Marathi [mar] first. Home. Neutral attitudes. Also use Hindi [hin], Marathi [mar]. *Lg Dev:* Literacy rate in L2: 72% for Powari-speaking districts (2001 census). *Other:* Younger generation is getting education. Hindu. *Maps:* 358:299, 359:299.

Purik [prx] (Burig, Burigskat, Purig, Purigskad, Purik Bhotia, Purki). 37,700 (2001 census). North Kashmir, Kargil district, mainly Suru valley; Dras valley, some in western Himalayas. *Status:* 5 (Developing). *Class:* Sino-Tibetan, Tibeto-Burman, Western Tibeto-Burman, Bodish, Central Bodish, Western. *Dialects:* None known. Reportedly similar to Balti [bft]. *Lg Use:* Dominant language in Kargil District. Many Purik have shifted to Balti [bft]. Low proficiency in Urdu [urd]. Used as L2 by Balti [bft], Shina [scl]. *Lg Dev:* Literacy rate in L2: 61% (2001 census). Grammar. NT: 1950. *Writing:* Arabic script. Tibetan script, no longer in use. *Other:* Ethnonym: Purig-pa. 'Purig', of Tibetan origin. People prefer to be culturally and linguistically identified with Tibet, although religiously with Islam. A Scheduled Tribe. Muslim (Shi'a). *Map:* 352:7.

Puroik [suv] ("Sulung" *pej.*). 20,000 (2011 SIL). Arunachal Pradesh, East Kameng, Papumpare, Kurung Kumey, and Lower Subansiri districts, along Par river, 53 villages. Possibly in China. *Status:* 6a (Vigorous). *Class:* Sino-Tibetan, Tibeto-Burman, Central Tibeto-Burman, Kho-Bwa. *Dialects:* None known. A divergent language which may not be Sino-Tibetan but possibly Austro-Asiatic. Intelligible of Bugun [bgg] (Chowdhury 1996). Burling (2003) groups it with Sherdukpen [sdp] and Bugun; possibly also with Lish [lsh] and Sartang [onp]. Lexical similarity: 54%–67% between varieties; 57%–68% with Chug [cvg]; less than 15% with Bugun [bgg] and Nyishi [njz]. *Lg Use:* Home, village. Positive attitudes. Everyone uses at least some Nyishi [njz]. Also use Assamese [asm], Hindi [hin]. *Lg Dev:* Literacy rate in L2: 2%. Dictionary. *Writing:* Bengali script. Devanagari script. Latin script. *Other:* A satellite relationship to Nyishi and Bangni peoples, bonded economically. A Scheduled Tribe in India. Claim kinship with the Khoa or Bugun. Traditional religion, Christian, Hindu. *Map:* 356:180.

Purum [pub] (Puram, Purum Naga). 500 (2001 census). Manipur, Senapati district, Purumlikli, Purumkhulen, Purumkhunou, Waicheiphai, and Moibunglikli villages; Chandel district, Lamlang Huipi, Chandanpokpi, Khongkhang Chothe, Loirang Talsi, Salemthar, Zat'lang, and New Wangparan. *Status:* 6a (Vigorous). *Class:* Sino-Tibetan, Tibeto-Burman, Sal, Kuki-Chin-Naga, Kuki-Chin, Northern. *Dialects:* None known. 95% intelligibility of Kharam Naga [kfw]. Lexical similarity: 60%–65% with Kom [kmm], 60%–66% with Koireng [nkd], 57%–60% with Aimol [aim], 71%–73% with Kharam Naga [kfw]. *Type:* SOV; postpositions; numerals, adjectives, articles after noun head; question word between subject and object; word order distinguishes subject, object, indirect object; V, CV, CVC, CVV; nontonal. *Lg Use:* Vigorous. Home, village. All ages. Positive attitudes. Use Meitei [mni] with Thangkul Naga [nmf], Thado Chin [tcz], or Kom [kmm] speakers. Used as L2 by Kharam Naga [kfw]. *Lg Dev:* Literacy rate in L2: 30%–40% (2000). *Writing:* Latin script. *Other:* Scheduled Tribe. Christian.

Rabha [rah] (Rava). 165,000 (2001 census). 0 monolinguals. Ethnic population: 374,000 (1993). West Assam, Darrang, Goalpara, and Kamrup districts; Nagaland; West Bengal, Jalpaiguri and Alipurduar subdivisions; Koch Bihar district, Tafangunj subdivision; Meghalaya, East and West Garo hills districts. *Status:* 4 (Educational). *Class:* Sino-Tibetan, Tibeto-Burman, Sal, Bodo-Garo-Northern Naga, Bodo-Koch, Koch. *Dialects:* Maitaria (Maitoria, Maituri), Rangdania (Rongdani). Rongdani is the standard dialect. Lexical similarity: 73% between Maituri and Rongdani. 31%–39% with Koch [kdq]. *Lg Use:* The majority of the ethnic group speaks Assamese [asm] as L1; Rabha spoken only in Rongdani and Maituri. Home, prayer, market, other villages. All ages. Also use Bengali [ben], English [eng], Garo [grt], Hindi [hin]. Used as L2 by Koch [kdq]. *Lg Dev:* Literacy rate in L2: 30%–50%. High interest in language development. Taught in primary schools. Radio programs. TV. Dictionary. Grammar. NT: 2000. *Writing:* Bengali script. Latin script, preferred by Catholics. *Other:* A Scheduled Tribe. Traditional religion, Christian, Hindu. *Maps:* 355:125, 356:125.

Rajasthani [raj]. A macrolanguage (see page 9). *Other:* Includes: Bagri [bgq], Gade Lohar [gda], Gujari [gju], Haroti [hoj], Malvi [mup], Wagdi [wbr].

Ralte [ral]. 900 (2007). Ethnic population: 34,000. Mizoram, mainly Aizawl district, scattered in Lunglei and Chhimtuipui districts; Manipur; Tripura, a few in Jampui hills. *Status:* 7 (Shifting). *Class:* Sino-Tibetan, Tibeto-Burman, Sal, Kuki-Chin-Naga, Kuki-Chin, Northern. *Dialects:* None known. Related to Tedim Chin [ctd], Paite Chin [pck], Thado Chin [tcz], and Zo [zom]. *Type:* SOV. *Lg Use:* Also use Mizo [lus]. *Lg Dev:* Though literacy is high, formal education level is low (in Tripura). *Other:* A Scheduled Tribe. A subgroup of the Mizo [lus]. Spoken only in northern Mizoram villages (Singh 1995). Christian. *Map:* 357:263.

Rangkas [rgk] (Canpa, Chyanam, Johari, Kyonam, Saukas, Saukiya Khun, Shaukas). No known L1 speakers. Ethnic population: 1,010 (2000). 1,420 all countries. Uttarakhand, Pithoragarh district, Johar valley, Darchula and Munsyari tahsils, facing Nepal border along Mahakali valley. *Status:* 9 (Dormant). *Class:* Sino-Tibetan, Tibeto-Burman, Western Tibeto-Burman, Bodish, West Himalayish, Almora. *Lg Use:* Shifted to Kumaoni [kfy]. *Other:* Identity merged with the dominant Kumaoni people. Rangkas sometimes refers to the whole group of Darmiya, Chaudangsi, Byangsi, and the now extinct Johari.

Ranglong [rnl] (Ronglong). 8,000 (2003 BI). Tripura, Joitang village; Assam; Mizoram. *Status:* 5 (Developing). *Class:* Sino-Tibetan, Tibeto-Burman, Unclassified. *Lg Dev:* Literacy rate in L1: 80%. NT: 2003. *Writing:* Latin script. *Other:* Christian, traditional religion. *Map:* 357:259.

Rathawi [rtw] (Bal-La, Kohelia, Rathwi). 451,000 (2006 IMB). Gujarat, Vadodara district, Chhota Udaipur and Kavant taluks, and Panchmahals district; Madhya Pradesh, Jhabua district, Alirajpur taluk. *Status:* 6a (Vigorous). *Class:* Indo-European, Indo-Iranian, Indo-Aryan, Central zone, Bhil. *Dialects:* None known. 76% intelligibility of

Bhilali [bhi]. A chain of related varieties from Bhilali to Rathawa; extremes have limited mutual intelligibility. Lexical similarity: 83% with Bhilali [bhi]. *Lg Dev:* Literacy rate in L2: 37% for Gujarat (2001 census). *Other:* A Scheduled Tribe. Distinct from Rathwi Bareli [bgd] in Madhya Pradesh. Hindu. *Maps:* 353:79, 358:79.

Ravula [yea] (Adiya, Adiyan, Iryavula, Panjiri Yerava, Yerava, Yoruba). 26,900 (2007). Ethnic population: 47,000 (2007). Karnataka, Coorg (Kodagu) district; Kerala, Wayanad district, Mananthavadi tahsil, Kannur district. *Status:* 5 (Developing). *Class:* Dravidian, Southern, Tamil-Kannada, Tamil-Kodagu, Tamil-Malayalam, Malayalam. *Dialects:* Adiya, Pani Yerava, Panjiri Yerava. 93%–94% dialect intelligibility between Yerava and Adiya dialects. Pani Yerava may be a dialect of Ravula or of Paniya [pcg]. Lexical similarity: 83%–98% among Yerava and Adiya varieties, 53%–61% with standard Malayalam [mal], 35%–40% with Badaga [bfq], 32%–42% with colloquial Kannada [kan], 66%–74% Pani Yerava dialect with the Adiya and Yerava dialects. *Lg Use:* Vigorous. Home, village, religion. Positive attitudes. Also use Kannada [kan], Malayalam [mal]. *Lg Dev:* Literacy rate in L2: 40% for Kodagu District, Karnataka; 44% among Adiya in Kerala (2001 census). High motivation for literature, literacy. *Writing:* Kannada script. Malayalam script. *Other:* Glossonym: Ravula or Panjiri Yerava in Karnataka; Ravula or Adiya in Kerala. They prefer Ravula in both places. Adiyan is a Scheduled Tribe in Karnataka and Tamil Nadu. Yerava is a Scheduled Tribe in Karnataka. Pani Yeravas are not the same as the Paniya of Wayanad District. Hindu. *Map:* 360:365.

Rawang [raw] (Chiutse, Ch'opa, Ganung-Rawang, Hkanung, Kiutze, Krangku, Taron). 1,000 in India (2011 SIL). Kunlang dialect is in Arunachal Pradesh, near the Myanmar and Tibet border. *Status:* 5 (Developing). *Dialect:* Kunlang. *Other:* Glossonym: Kiutze or Qiuze by Chinese, Ch'opa by Lisu. See main entry on page 240. *Map:* 356:192.

Rawat [jnl] (Ban Manus, Ban Rauts, Bhulla, Dzanggali, Jangali, Janggali, Jhangar, Raji, Raut). 670 (1998). Uttarakhand, Pithoragarh district, north of Askot Maila, 9 villages. *Status:* 7 (Shifting). *Class:* Sino-Tibetan, Tibeto-Burman, Western Tibeto-Burman, Himalayan, Central Himalayan, Raute-Raji. *Dialects:* None known. Extensive borrowing from areal Indo-Aryan (Kumaoni, Nepali) languages (2011 J. Fortier). Very similar to Raute [rau] and Raji [rji]. *Type:* SOV; postpositions; genitives, articles, adjectives, numerals before noun heads; noun heads both initial and final; no noun classes or genders; content q-word initial; maximum number of suffixes 3; affixes indicate case of noun phrases; verb affixation marks person and number; passives; causatives; comparatives; CV, CVC; nontonal. *Lg Use:* All speakers use a highly mixed variety. Home, religion. Negative attitudes. Due to poor socio-economic status, miniscule number of speakers, fewer domains of language use, attitude of the dominant group and lack of initiative from the state, Rawat is quickly assimilating into Kumaoni [kfy] (Rastogi 2006). *Lg Dev:* Literacy rate in L1: Below 1%. Younger generation taking interest in literacy. *Writing:* Devanagari script. *Other:* A Scheduled Tribe. Government-given ethnonym: Raji now accepted by the people. Many Indo-Aryan loans. Raute are found in Kumaon where they are known as Raji (Gurung 1997). Traditional religion. *Map:* 352:59.

Reli [rei] (Relli). 22,000 (2001 census). Andhra Pradesh, near Adivasi Oriya [ort] language area; Odisha, Koraput district. *Status:* 6a (Vigorous). *Class:* Indo-European, Indo-Iranian, Indo-Aryan, Eastern zone, Oriya. *Dialects:* Possibly a dialect of Oriya [ory]. *Other:* A Scheduled Caste. Hindu. *Map:* 359:358.

Riang [ria] (Kau Bru, Reang, Tipra). 76,500 in India (2001 census). Population total all countries: 77,000. Ethnic population: 144,000. North and central Tripura; Mizoram, Aizawl, Lunglei, and Chhimtuipui districts, Karnafuli river bank area, 30 villages; Assam, Karimganj district. Also in Bangladesh. *Status:* 5 (Developing). *Class:* Sino-Tibetan, Tibeto-Burman, Sal, Bodo-Garo-Northern Naga, Bodo-Koch, Bodo-Garo, Bodo. *Dialects:* Considered dialect of Kok Borok [trp] called Polong-O (Muanthanga). *Lg Dev:* Literacy rate in L2: Very low. School attendance is low. Bible. *Writing:* Latin script. *Other:* A Scheduled Tribe. Different from Riang [ril] of Myanmar, a Mon-Khmer language. Traditional religion, Christian. *Map:* 357:256.

Rongpo [rnp] ("Manchhi Bhassa" *pej.*, "Marchha" *pej.*, "Marchha Pahari" *pej.*, Rang Po Bhasa, Rangkas, Rangpa, "Tolchha" *pej.*). 7,500 (2001 D. Bradley). Uttarakhand, Chamoli district, Joshimath tahsil, Niti valley, Niti, Gamshali, Bampa, and Malari villages; Mana valley, Mana, Indradhara, Gajkoti, Pathiya-Dhantoli, Hanuman Chatti, Benakuli, and Aut. Marchha dialect in Mana and Niti valleys, a few Tolchha in Niti valley. *Status:* 6a (Vigorous). *Class:* Sino-Tibetan, Tibeto-Burman, Western Tibeto-Burman, Bodish, West Himalayish, Kinauri. *Dialects:* Marchha, Tolchha. A Himalayan language distinct from Tibetan [bod]. *Lg Use:* Rongpo speakers learn Garhwali simultaneously with Rongpo. Code switching and code mixing are very common. It is uncertain whether stable bilingualism will continue or whether Rongpo will be replaced by Garhwali or Hindi. Home, community. All ages. Also use Garhwali [gbm], Hindi [hin], Kumaoni [kfy]. *Lg Dev:* Hindi used for all written communication. *Other:* Many Indo-Aryan loanwords. Grierson and Konow (1901–1929) referred to this as the Garhwal dialect of Tibetan. Ranglo or Rang often used as a cover term for Byangs, Chaudangs, Darma, and Rongpo. Hindu. *Map:* 352:56.

Ruga [ruh]. Meghalaya, near the Garo [grt] language area. *Status:* 8b (Nearly extinct). *Class:* Sino-Tibetan, Tibeto-Burman, Sal, Bodo-Garo-Northern Naga, Bodo-Koch, Koch. *Dialects:* None known. Most closely related to Atong [aot], Koch [kdq], and Rabha [rah]. Not inherently intelligible of Garo [grt]. *Lg Use:* Older adults. Garo [grt] used more than Ruga. *Map:* 355:126.

Sadri [sck] (Chota Nagpuri, Dikku Kaji, Ganwari, Gauuari, Gawari, Goari, Jharkhandhi, Nagpuri, Nagpuria, Sadan, Sadana, Sadani, Sadari, Sadati, Sadhan, Sadhari, Sadna, Sadrik, Santri, Siddri, Sradri). 3,290,000 in India (2001 census). 2,050,000 Sadani, 1,243,000 Nagpuria. Population total all countries: 3,291,180. Jharkhand, Ranchi and Palamau districts; West Bengal; Odisha; Assam; Madhya Pradesh; Andaman Islands; Nagaland. Also in Nepal (Kisan). *Status:* 3 (Wider communication). Trade language among tribal groups in Assam. *Class:* Indo-European, Indo-Iranian, Indo-Aryan, Eastern zone, Bihari. *Dialects:* 77% of Sadri [sdr], Oraon of Bangladesh. Speakers name 3 registers of Sadri: Sadani (finer, respectful, formal), Common Sadri (Nagpuri), and Lower Sadri (rough). Lexical similarity: 77%–96% between dialects, 58%–71% with Hindi [hin], 47%–54% with Oriya [ory], 45%–61% with Bengali [ben]. *Lg Use:* 7,000,000 tribals in Assam speak Sadri as language of wider communication. Positive attitudes. Also use Hindi [hin]. Hindi used in the market, with leaders, for prayer and worship, but proficiency is low. Also use Bengali [ben], Oriya [ory]. Used as L2 by Asuri [asr], Birhor [biy], Majhi [mjz]. *Lg Dev:* Literacy rate in L2: 15%–25%. Magazines. Radio programs. Dictionary. Grammar. NT: 1931–1986. *Writing:* Bengali script. Devanagari script. *Other:* Hindu, Christian,

Muslim, traditional religion. *Maps:* 354:97, 355:97.

Sakachep [sch] (Khelma, Sankechep). 25,000 (2003). Assam, Karbi Anglong, N. Cachar Hills and Cachar Hills districts; Nagaland, Kohima district, Khelma village; Meghalaya, Jaintia Hills district, Saithsma, Rumphung, and Mongor villages; Tripura; Mizoram; Manipur. *Status:* 6a (Vigorous). *Class:* Sino-Tibetan, Tibeto-Burman, Unclassified. *Dialects:* Khelma, Sakachep, Thangkachep. Dialects may be simply alternate names for Sakechep depending on the region. *Lg Use:* Home. All ages. Also use Bengali [ben], Biete [biu], Dimasa [dis], Hindi [hin], Hmar [hmr], Hrangkhol [hra], Karbi [mjw], Khasi [kha], Naga Pidgin [nag], Thado Chin [tcz]. *Lg Dev:* Literacy rate in L2: 25%. Radio programs. Bible portions: 2002. *Writing:* Latin script. *Other:* Hindu, Christian. *Map:* 356:216.

Sambalpuri [spv] (Dom, Kosali, Koshal, Koshali, Western Oriya). 519,000 (2001 census). Odisha, Sambalpur, Jharsuguda, Sundargarh, Deogarh, Bargarh, Balangir, Boudh, Sonpur, Nuvapada, and Kalhandi districts; Chhattisgarh, Raipur, Raigarh and Jagdalpur districts. *Status:* 4 (Educational). *Class:* Indo-European, Indo-Iranian, Indo-Aryan, Eastern zone, Oriya. A member of macrolanguage Oriya [ori]. *Dialects:* None known. Lexical similarity: 75%–76% with Oriya [ory]. *Lg Use:* All domains. All ages. Very positive attitudes. *Lg Dev:* Taught in primary and secondary schools. Poetry. Newspapers. Radio programs. TV. *Writing:* Oriya script. *Maps:* 355:145, 359:145.

Samvedi [smv]. Maharashtra. *Status:* 6a (Vigorous). *Class:* Indo-European, Indo-Iranian, Indo-Aryan, Southern zone, Konkani. *Dialects:* A divergent dialect of, or closely related language to Konkani [knn]. Shares many features with Gujarati [guj]. *Map:* 358:316.

Sansi [ssi] (Bhilki, Sansiboli). 60,000 in India (Gusain 2002). Population total all countries: 76,200. Rajasthan; Punjab; Haryana; Delhi; Himachal Pradesh; Jammu and Kashmir; Madhya Pradesh; Karnataka; Uttar Pradesh. Also in Pakistan. *Status:* 7 (Shifting). *Class:* Indo-European, Indo-Iranian, Indo-Aryan, Central zone, Western Hindi, Hindustani, Sansi. *Dialects:* Intermediate between Eastern Panjabi [pan] and Hindustani (see Hindi [hin]). Sometimes identify themselves as Marwari [rwr]. Related to Rajasthani [mwr], Sindhi [snd], Eastern Panjabi. Lexical similarity: 71% with Urdu [urd], 83% with the Sochi dialect of Sansi [ssi](1998). Numerous phonological and morphological borrowings from Eastern Panjabi [pan], Hindi [hin], and Gujarati [guj] (Gusain 2002). *Lg Use:* Not being passed on to the next generation. Much mixing of Hindi, Eastern Panjabi, or Gujarati (Gusain 2002). Home only. Mainly older adults. Also use Eastern Panjabi [pan], Gujarati [guj], Hindi [hin]. *Lg Dev:* Literacy rate in L1: Below 1%. Literacy rate in L2: Below 5%. *Other:* Bhils by caste. Called a Gypsy language. They have an argot called Farsi. Gusain (2002) classifies this as a Rajasthani dialect. Socially separate from surrounding groups. Governed by their own social norms and economy. Losing some tribal characteristics but are not yet integrated into the national mainstream (Gusain 2002). Hindu. *Map:* 352:48.

Sanskrit [san]. 14,100 in India (2001 census). Population total all countries: 15,770. L2 users: 194,000 in India. Also in Nepal. *Status:* 4 (Educational). Statutory language of national identity (1950, Constitution, Schedule VIII). *Class:* Indo-European, Indo-Iranian, Indo-Aryan. *Type:* SOV; both prepositions and postpositions; noun head final; 3 genders; content q-word in situ; up to 3 prefixes, up to 5 suffixes; clause constituents indicated by case-marking; verbal affixation marks person, number and genders of subject and object; non-ergative; tense and aspect; passives and voice; nontonal; 32 consonant and 15 vowel phonemes. *Lg Dev:* Literacy rate in L1: 60%–100%. Literacy rate in L2: 15%–25% literate. Poetry. Magazines. Newspapers. New media. Radio programs. Dictionary. Grammar. Bible: 1822. *Writing:* Devanagari script. Myanmar (Burmese) script. Newar (Prachalit Nepal) script. Sharada script. Sinhala script. *Other:* Classical language of learning and liturgical language. *Map:* 351.

Santhali [sat] (Har, Hor, Samtali, Sandal, Sangtal, Santal, Santali, Santhiali, Satar, Sentali, Sonthal). 5,940,000 in India (2001 census). Population total all countries: 6,228,500. Bihar, Bhagalpur and Munger districts; Jharkhand, Manbhum and Hazaribagh districts; Odisha, Balasore district; West Bengal, Birbhum and Bankura districts; Assam; Mizoram; Tripura. Also in Bangladesh, Bhutan, Nepal. *Status:* 4 (Educational). Statutory language of provincial identity in Jharkhand State (1950, Constitution, Schedule VIII), amended 2003. *Class:* Austro-Asiatic, Munda, North Munda, Kherwari, Santali. *Dialects:* Kamari-Santali, Karmali (Khole), Lohari-Santali, Manjhi, Paharia. Reportedly similar to Ho [hoc], Mundari [unr], and Munda [unx]. *Type:* SOV; postpositions; noun head final; no noun classes or genders; content q-word in situ; 1 prefix, up to 3 suffixes; clause constituents indicated by case-marking; verbal affixation marks person and number; non-ergative; both tense and aspect; passives and voice; nontonal; 33 consonant and 6 vowel phonemes. *Lg Use:* Used as L2 by Birhor [biy], Ho [hoc], Kharia [khr], Kharia Thar [ksy], Mahali [mjx]. *Lg Dev:* Literacy rate in L1: 10%–30%. Literacy rate in L2: 25%–50%. Taught in primary schools. Poetry. Magazines. New media. Radio programs. Videos. Dictionary. Grammar. Bible: 1914–2005. *Writing:* Bengali script. Devanagari script, used in Nepal. Latin script, used in Bangladesh. Ol Chiki (Ol Cemet', Ol, Santali) script. Oriya script. *Other:* A Scheduled Tribe. Language of Santhal tribals of Chota Nagpur Plateau (comprising the states of Jharkhand, Bihar, Odisha, Chhattisgarh). Hindu, traditional religion. *Map:* 351.

Sartang [onp] (Bootpa, But Monpa, But Pa, Matchopa). 1,000 (2005). Arunachal Pradesh, West Kameng district, Nafra and Dirang circles, Jerigaon, Sellary, Khoitam, Rahung, Darbu and Khoina villages. *Status:* 6a (Vigorous). *Class:* Sino-Tibetan, Tibeto-Burman, Central Tibeto-Burman, Kho-Bwa. *Dialects:* None known. Lexical similarity: 49%–60% with Sherdukpen [sdp]. *Lg Use:* Home, village. All ages. Also use Hindi [hin]. *Lg Dev:* Literacy rate in L2: 5% in Hindi. Literature committee formed mid 2003. *Writing:* Devanagari script. Latin script. *Other:* Buddhist. *Map:* 356:170.

Saurashtra [saz] (Palkar, Patnuli, Saurashtri, Sourashtra, Sowrashtra). 185,000 (2001 census). Each listed district has communities of at least 5,000. Tamil Nadu, Madurai, Thanjavur, Dindugul Quaid-E. Milleth, Ramanathapuram, Chengai-Annai, Salem, Tiruchchirappalli, Tirunelveli, and North Arcot districts; Chennai, Deccan, Madurai, Thanjavur, and Salem cities; Karnataka; Andhra Pradesh. *Status:* 5 (Developing). *Class:* Indo-European, Indo-Iranian, Indo-Aryan, Central zone, Gujarati. *Dialects:* Northern Saurashtra, Southern Saurashtra. Indo-Aryan elements reveal Gujarati [guj] relationship; some structure from Dravidian, lexicon from Telugu [tel] and Tamil [tam]. An Indo-European island surrounded by Dravidian languages. The 3 main populations in Salem, Thanjavur, and Madurai cities had between 67% and 97% inherent intelligibility among themselves. Lexical similarity: 77%–96% between all varieties. The 3 main populations: 84%–96%. Southern dialects have 83% or higher lexical similarity with Thanjavur variety. *Lg Use:* Vigorous. Home, prayer. Also use Tamil [tam]. *Lg Dev:* Radio programs. Dictionary.

NT: 2001. *Writing:* Devanagari script. Saurashtra script, a modern version developed in the late 1800s, used for centuries. Tamil script, primary usage. Telugu script. *Other:* Most are weavers; nonweavers are generally better educated. System of exogamous clans. Hindu. *Map:* 360:370.

Sauria Paharia [mjt] (Malatri, Maler, Malti, Malto, Maltu, Sawriya Malto). 54,000 in India (Bhaskararao 2006). Population total all countries: 61,000. Jharkhand, north former Santhal Pargana district, Rajmahal hills; Sahibganj and Godda districts, Pakaur district, Litipara block; West Bengal, Bankura, Barddhaman, and Murshidabad districts. Also in Bangladesh. *Status:* 5 (Developing). *Class:* Dravidian, Northern. *Dialects:* Godda, Hiranpur, Litipara (Chatgam), Sahibganj. Some intelligibility of Kumarbhag Paharia [kmj]. Lexical similarity: 80% with Kumarbhag Paharia [kmj]. *Lg Dev:* Literacy rate in L2: 7%. Literacy classes. Magazines. Newspapers. Radio programs. NT: 1999. *Writing:* Bengali script. Devanagari script. *Other:* Part of Malto ethnic group. A Scheduled Tribe. Traditional religion, Christian. *Map:* 355:130.

Savara [svr]. 253,000 (2001). Andhra Pradesh; Odisha. *Status:* 6a (Vigorous). *Class:* Dravidian, South-Central, Telugu. *Lg Dev:* Radio programs. *Writing:* Oriya script. Savara script. Telugu script. *Other:* Distinct from Sora [srb] (Savara). *Map:* 359:343.

Sentinel [std] (Sentinelese). 150 (Abbi 2006). Southeast Andaman Islands, Sentinel island. *Status:* 6b (Threatened). *Class:* Andamanese, South Andamanese. *Dialects:* None known. Reportedly similar to Önge [oon]. *Other:* A Scheduled Tribe. Reserved toward outsiders. Traditional religion. *Map:* 361.

Seraiki [skr] (Bahawalpuri, Multani, Mutani, Reasati, Riasati, Saraiki, Siraiki, Southern Panjabi). 68,000 in India (2001). Punjab; Rajasthan; Delhi; Gujarat; Maharashtra; Andhra Pradesh; Madhya Pradesh; Uttar Pradesh. *Status:* 5 (Developing). *Dialects:* Bahawalpuri (Bhawalpuri, Reasati, Riasati), Jafri, Jatki, Siraiki Hindki, Thali. *Lg Use:* Also use Marathi [mar], Urdu [urd]. *Lg Dev:* Literacy rate in L1: Below 1%. Literacy rate in L2: 15% Urdu [urd], Marathi [mar]. *Other:* A new literary language based on south Lahnda dialects, especially Multani and Bahawalpuri. Hindu, Sikh. See main entry on page 271. *Map:* 352:47.

Shekhawati [swv] (Shekhawati-Marwari). 3,000,000 (2002 L. Gusain). Rajasthan, Sikar, Jhunjhunun, and Churu districts. *Status:* 5 (Developing). *Class:* Indo-European, Indo-Iranian, Indo-Aryan, Central zone, Rajasthani, Marwari. A member of macrolanguage Marwari [mwr]. *Dialects:* Jhunjhunu-Churu, Sikar. 78% comprehension of Marwari [rwr], 72% intelligibility of Dhundari [dhd]. Lexical similarity: 74%–77% between dialects; 51%–68% with Marwari [rwr], 58%–80% with Merwari [wry], 45%–69% with Godwari [gdx], 57%–66% with Mewari [mtr], 66%–73% with Dhundari [dhd], 58%–66% with Haroti [hoj], 57%–70% with Mewati [wtm], 69%–76% with Bagri [gda], 61%–73% with Haryanvi [bgc], 55%–69% with Hindi [hin]. *Lg Use:* Vigorous. Home, village, market, religion. Positive attitudes. Widespread bilingualism in Hindi [hin]; educated are more proficient in Hindi. *Writing:* Devanagari script. *Other:* Hindu. *Map:* 353:65.

Shendu [shl] (Khieng, Khyen, Sandu, Shandu). Mizoram. *Status:* 6a (Vigorous). *Class:* Sino-Tibetan, Tibeto-Burman, Sal, Kuki-Chin-Naga, Kuki-Chin, Southern. *Map:* 357:286.

Sherdukpen [sdp] (Ngnok). 3,100 (2001). Arunachal Pradesh, West Kameng district, south of Bomdi La Range and Tengapani river valleys, Rupa (Kupa), Shargang (Shergaon), Jigang (Jigaon), and Thungrao villages; Assam. *Status:* 6a (Vigorous). *Class:* Sino-Tibetan, Tibeto-Burman, Central Tibeto-Burman, Kho-Bwa. *Dialects:* None known. Lexical similarity: 49%-60% with Sartang. Burling (2003) groups it with Puroik [suv] and Bugun [bgg] and possibly also with Lish [lsh] and Sartang [onp]. *Lg Use:* Vigorous. Home, village, religion. Also use Hindi [hin], Tawang Monpa [twm]. Used as L2 by Bugun [bgg]. *Lg Dev:* Literacy rate in L2: 15% (20% male, 7% female) (Muanthanga 1998). *Other:* A Scheduled Tribe. Separated from the Sartang by war. Buddhist (Lamaist), traditional religion. *Map:* 356:176.

Sherpa [xsr] (Serwa, Sharpa, Sharpa Bhotia, Xarba, Xiaerba). 18,300 in India (2001 census). West Bengal, Darjeeling district; Sikkim; Arunachal Pradesh. *Status:* 6a (Vigorous). *Other:* A Scheduled Tribe. 'Sharpa', easterner, so the term used in different countries may not always refer to Sherpa. Buddhist (Lamaist). See main entry on page 258. *Map:* 355:158.

Shina [scl] (Shinaki, Sina). 34,400 in India (2001 census). North Kashmir, Dras and Kishenganga valleys, Gurais area. *Status:* 6a (Vigorous). *Dialects:* Drasi, Gurezi. *Lg Use:* Many in Dras Valley also speak Purik [prx], but there are villages in Dras Valley where only Shina is spoken. Used as L2 by Balti [bft]. *Other:* Open to education and jobs outside the area. Distinct from Brokskat [bkk]. Buddhist, Muslim (Shi'a), Muslim (Sunni), traditional religion. See main entry on page 271. *Map:* 352:5.

Sholaga [sle] (Kadu Sholigar, Sholanayika, Sholiga, Sholigar, Solaga, Solanayakkans, Solega, Soliga, Soligar). 24,000 (2006 IMB). Karnataka, Mysore district, Biligiri Rangana hills; Tamil Nadu. *Status:* 6a (Vigorous). *Class:* Dravidian, Southern, Tamil-Kannada, Tamil-Kodagu, Tamil-Malayalam, Tamil. *Dialects:* None known. Lexical similarity: 65% with Kannada [kan]. *Lg Dev:* Literacy rate in L2: 31% for Tamil Nadu. *Other:* A Scheduled Tribe. May be in the Kannada group. Hindu, traditional religion. *Map:* 360:368.

Shom Peng [sii] (Shobang, Shom Pen, Shompen, Shompeng). 400 (2004). Mainly monolingual. Nicobar Islands, interior Great Nicobar island. *Status:* 6a (Vigorous). *Class:* Austro-Asiatic, Mon-Khmer, Nicobar, Shom Peng. *Dialects:* None known. Distinct from other Nicobarese languages. *Other:* A Scheduled Tribe. Seminomadic. Traditional religion. *Map:* 361.

Shumcho [scu] (Central Kinnauri, Shumcu, Sumcho, Sumchu, Sumtsu, Thebarskad, Thebor, Thebör Skadd). 2,170 (1998). Himachal Pradesh, Kinnaur district, Puh tahsil, Kanam, Labrang, Spilo, Shyaso, Taling, and Rushkaling villages. *Status:* 6a (Vigorous). *Class:* Sino-Tibetan, Tibeto-Burman, Western Tibeto-Burman, Bodish, West Himalayish, Kinauri. *Dialects:* None known. Lexical similarity: 70% with Jangshung [jna], 67% with Sunam [ssk], 45% with Pahari Kinnauri [kjo], 43% with Chitkuli Kinnauri [cik]. *Other:* Traditional religion, Buddhist (Lamaist), Hindu. *Map:* 352:33.

Sikkimese [sip] (Dandzongka, Danjongka, Danyouka, Denjong, Denjongkha, Denjongpa, Denjonka, Denjonke, Lachengpa, Lachungpa, Sikami, Sikkim Bhotia, Sikkim Bhutia). 70,300 (2001). Sikkim, all districts; West Bengal, Darjeeling. Possibly in Tibet. *Status:* 4 (Educational). *Class:* Sino-Tibetan, Tibeto-Burman, Western Tibeto-Burman, Bodish, Central Bodish, Central, Southern. *Dialects:* None known. Partially intelligible of Dzongkha [dzo] of Bhutan. Lexical similarity: 65% with Dzongkha [dzo] of Bhutan, 42% with Tibetan [bod]. *Lg Use:* Vigorous. Positive attitudes. Some also use Tibetan [bod] which is viewed as appropriate for religion. Also use Nepali [npi] for education and trade. *Lg Dev:* Literacy rate in L2: 68% for Bhutia in Sikkim (2001 census). Taught in primary schools. *Writing:* Tibetan script. *Other:* Buddhist. *Map:* 355:151.

Simte [smt]. 10,200 (2001 census). Southwest Manipur, Churachandpur district, Mingjang, Tubuong, Simveng, New Bazar, Thanlon, Leikangpai, Zouthang, Shumtuk, Monjon, Pamjal, Sasinoujang, Tallian, Dumsao, Khungung, Lungthul, Singhat, Moijin, Maokot, Suangdai, and Suangpuhmun. *Status:* 5 (Developing). *Class:* Sino-Tibetan, Tibeto-Burman, Sal, Kuki-Chin-Naga, Kuki-Chin, Northern. *Dialects:* None known. An alternate name for Paite [pck] (Singh 1994). *Lg Dev:* Literacy rate in L2: 67% (2001 census). Bible: 1992. *Writing:* Latin script. *Other:* A Scheduled Tribe. Christian. *Map:* 357:252.

Sindhi [snd]. 1,700,000 in India (2001 census). Ethnic population: 3,000,000. Gujarat; Rajasthan; Maharashtra; Andhra Pradesh; Bihar; Delhi; Madhya Pradesh; Odisha; Tamil Nadu; Uttar Pradesh. *Status:* 5 (Developing). Statutory language of provincial identity in Rajasthan State (1950, Constitution, Articles 345–347), Schedule VIII addition, 1961. *Dialects:* Bhatia, Jadeji, Kayasthi, Lari, Lasi, Thareli, Thari, Viccholi, Visholi. *Lg Use:* Many Sindhi do not learn their traditional ethnic language. Mainly women and older adult speakers. Also use Hindi [hin] or other state language. *Other:* Official language of the Sindhi community. Hindu. See main entry on page 272. *Map:* 351.

Singpho [sgp] (Jingphaw, Kachin, Sing-Fo). 2,500 (Morey 2006). Assam, Tinsukia district, Margherita subdivision; Dibrugarh, Sibsagar districts; Arunachal Pradesh, Lohit, and Changlang districts. *Status:* 5 (Developing). *Class:* Sino-Tibetan, Tibeto-Burman, Sal, Jingpho-Luish, Jingpho. *Dialect:* Turung. Lexical similarity: 50% with Jingpho [kac] of Myanmar. *Lg Use:* Home only. Most in Assam are also fluent in Assamese [asm]. Used as L2 by Tase Naga [nst]. *Lg Dev:* Literacy rate in L2: Less than 40%. Bible. *Writing:* Latin script. *Other:* Many loans from Khamti [kht]. Kachin refers to a cultural, rather than a linguistic group. A Scheduled Tribe. Buddhist, traditional religion. *Map:* 356:195.

Sirmauri [srx] (Himachali, Pahari, Sirmouri, Sirmuri). 400,000 (2005 SIL). Himachal Pradesh, Sirmaur district, Shimla district, southeast section. *Status:* 6a (Vigorous). *Class:* Indo-European, Indo-Iranian, Indo-Aryan, Northern zone, Western Pahari. *Dialects:* Dharthi (Giriwari), Giripari. Difficult intelligibility between Dharthi and Giripari; and between Upper Mahasui and Giripar. Dharthi dialect more influenced by Hindi. In south Shimla District, Kiunthali and Sirmauri are used interchangeably. Reportedly a different variety of Sirmauri in Sirmaur District. Lexical similarity: 56%–70% with Dharthi and Giripari, with considerable variation within each dialect; Giripari 67% with Lower Mahasui, 65% with Upper Mahasui, 61% with Jaunsari [jns]. *Lg Use:* Home, village. Positive attitudes. Educated are highly proficient in Hindi [hin], uneducated showing wide range of proficiency in Hindi. Most older, uneducated women have very limited proficiency in Hindi. *Lg Dev:* Literacy rate in L2: 60% for Sirmaur District (2001 census). Newspapers. Radio programs. TV. Videos. Grammar. *Writing:* Devanagari script. Takri (Tankri, Takari) script, special variety used informally (Masica 1991). *Other:* Dharthi is spoken in Giriwar area, Giripari in Giripar area. Hindu. *Map:* 352:51.

Sora [srb] (Sabar, Sabara, Saonras, Saora, Saura, Savara, Sawaria, Shabari, Soura, Swara). 253,000 (2001 census). South Odisha, Ganjam, Koraput, and Phulbani districts; Andhra Pradesh, Srikakulam district; Madhya Pradesh; Bihar; Tamil Nadu; West Bengal; Assam, Plains division. *Status:* 5 (Developing). *Class:* Austro-Asiatic, Munda, South Munda, Koraput Munda, Sora-Juray-Gorum, Sora-Juray. *Lg Dev:* Radio programs. Bible: 1992–2004. *Writing:* Latin script. Oriya script. Sora Sompeng script. Telugu script. *Other:* A Scheduled Tribe. Hindu, Christian. *Map:* 359:341.

Spiti Bhoti [spt] (Nyam, Piti Bhoti). 10,000 (2000). Himachal Pradesh, Lahul-Spiti district, Spiti subdistrict. *Status:* 6a (Vigorous). *Class:* Sino-Tibetan, Tibeto-Burman, Western Tibeto-Burman, Bodish, Central Bodish, Central, Western. *Dialects:* Not intelligible of Ladakhi [lbj]; low intelligibility of Stod Bhoti [sbu]. All areas of Spiti understand each other. Lexical similarity: 41% with the Lhasa Tibetan dialect of Central Tibetan [bod], 57% with Ladakhi (Leh) [lbj], 57% with Stod Bhoti [sbu] from Darcha. *Lg Use:* Home, village. All ages. Also use English [eng], Hindi [hin]. *Lg Dev:* Most literates read Hindi. Some older people and Buddhist monks and nuns, read Tibetan. Radio programs. *Writing:* Unwritten. *Other:* Buddhist. *Map:* 352:19.

Stod Bhoti [sbu] (Lahul Bhoti, Stod, Stod-Kad, Tod, Tod-Kad). 2,500 (1996). Himachal Pradesh, Lahul region, Stod, Khoksar, and upper Mayar valleys. *Status:* 6a (Vigorous). *Class:* Sino-Tibetan, Tibeto-Burman, Western Tibeto-Burman, Bodish, Central Bodish, Central, Western. *Dialects:* Khoksar (Khoksar Bhoti), Mayar (Mayar Bhoti, Mayari), Stod (Kolong). 85% intelligibility of Stod Bhoti by Khoksar, 75% by Mayar, 62% of Khoksar by Mayar, 95% of Khoksar by Stod Bhoti. Lexical similarity: 74% with Spiti Bhoti [spt]. *Lg Use:* Home, community, religion. Positive attitudes toward dialects and Ladakhi [lbj]. Many also use Hindi [hin] for trade, education. Many speak Hindi but are less proficient than those in other Lahul communities. *Lg Dev:* Desire for literacy in Stod Bhoti. *Writing:* Devanagari script. Tibetan script. *Other:* Buddhist. *Map:* 352:20.

Sunam [ssk] (Central Kinnauri, Sangnaur, Sungam, Sungnam, Sunnam, Thebarshad, Thebor, Thebör Skadd). 560 (1998). Himachal Pradesh, Kinnaur district, Puh tahsil, Sunam village. *Status:* 6a (Vigorous). *Class:* Sino-Tibetan, Tibeto-Burman, Western Tibeto-Burman, Bodish, West Himalayish, Kinauri. *Dialects:* None known. Lexical similarity: 67% with Shumcho [scu], 65% with Jangshung [jna], 38% with Pahari Kinnauri [kjo] and Chitkuli Kinnauri [cik]. *Other:* Traditional religion, Buddhist (Lamaist), Hindu. *Map:* 352:34.

Surgujia [sgj] (Suraji, Surguja, Surgujia-Chhattisgarhi, Surjugia). 1,460,000 (2001 census). Chhattigarh, Surguja, Jashpur, and Korea districts; Raigarh and Korba districts' border areas. *Status:* 6a (Vigorous). *Class:* Indo-European, Indo-Iranian, Indo-Aryan, East Central zone. *Dialects:* None known. Lexical similarity: 71%–76% with Chhattisgarhi [hne]. *Lg Use:* Vigorous. All domains. Positive attitudes. *Writing:* Unwritten. *Maps:* 354:111, 355:111.

Surjapuri [sjp] (Sura). 1,220,000 (2001 census). Bihar, Purnia, Kishanganj, Katihar, and Araria districts; West Bengal, Uttar Dinajpur district. *Status:* 6a (Vigorous). *Class:* Indo-European, Indo-Iranian, Indo-Aryan, Eastern zone, Bihari. *Dialects:* None known. Preliminary survey results show intelligibility of Nepali Rajbanshi [rjs]. Lexical similarity: 70%–74% with Hindi [hin], 67%–71% with the western variety of Kamta [rkt] spoken near Dinajpur, 77%–86% with varieties of Surjapuri [sjp]. *Lg Use:* Vigorous. Home, village. All ages. Positive attitudes. Also use Hindi [hin]. *Lg Dev:* Literacy rate in L2: Low (2006 M. Toulmin). Different scripts in Nepal and India. *Writing:* Devanagari script. *Other:* Possible alternate names are Chaupal, Choupal, and Suraji, but surveyors did not find these terms used. Historically more closely related to Kamta [rkt] and Rajbanshi [rjs] than Hindi [hin], a relationship borne out by greater morphological similarity. (2006 M. Toulmin). *Maps:* 354:96, 355:96.

Sylheti [syl] (Bengali of Cachar, Sileti, Siloti, Srihattia, Sylheti Bangla, Sylheti Bengali, Sylhetti, Syloti, Syloty).

3,000,000 in India (2003). South Assam, Barak valley region; Karimganj, Cachar and Hailakandi districts; Nagaland, Kolkata. *Status:* 5 (Developing). *Lg Dev:* Literacy rate in L2: 10%. Educated can read Bengali [ben]. Few women are educated. *Other:* Muslim, Hindu. See main entry on page 56. *Map:* 357:254.

Tagin [tgj] (Nil). 38,200 (2001 census). Arunachal Pradesh, upper Subansiri district. *Status:* 6a (Vigorous). *Class:* Sino-Tibetan, Tibeto-Burman, Central Tibeto-Burman, Tani. *Dialects:* None known. Reportedly similar to Nyishi [njz]. *Lg Use:* Vigorous. Home, cultural activities, market. Very positive attitudes. *Writing:* Unwritten. *Other:* A Scheduled Tribe. Traditional religion, Christian, Hindu. *Map:* 356:183.

Tamang, Eastern [taj]. 17,500 in India (2001 census). Ethnic population: 272,000 (2006 FTT). Sikkim, lower Teesta valley, Rangit valley; West Bengal, Darjeeling; Arunachal Pradesh. *Status:* 4 (Educational). *Lg Dev:* Taught in primary schools in Sikkim. *Other:* Migrate from Nepal. See main entry on page 259. *Map:* 355:159.

Tamil [tam] (Damulian, Tamal, Tamalsan, Tambul, Tamili). 60,700,000 in India (2001 census). Population total all countries: 68,763,360. L2 users: 8,000,000 in India. Tamil Nadu and neighboring states. Also in Bahrain, Belize, Canada, Denmark, Fiji, Germany, Malaysia, Mauritius, Netherlands, Qatar, Réunion, Singapore, South Africa, Sri Lanka, Thailand, United Arab Emirates, United Kingdom, United States. *Status:* 2 (Provincial). Statutory provincial language in Tamil Nadu State; union territories Puducherry, Andaman and Nicobar Islands (1950, Constitution, Schedule VIII). *Class:* Dravidian, Southern, Tamil-Kannada, Tamil-Kodagu, Tamil-Malayalam, Tamil. *Dialects:* Adi Dravida, Aiyangar, Aiyar, Arava, Burgandi, Burma Tamil, Harijan, Hebbar, Kongar, Madrasi, Madurai, Malaya Tamil, Mandyam Brahmin, Pattapu Bhasha, Sanketi, Secunderabad Brahmin, South Africa Tamil, Sri Lanka Tamil, Tamil, Tigalu. Burgandi are nomadic. Aiyar and Aiyangar are Brahmin dialects. Southern dialect around Madurai is literary standard. Eastern dialect is colloquial standard (Zvelebil 1998). Sanketi dialect in Karnataka used by immigrants from Madurai and Shenkotta in Tamil Nadu. Lexicon greatly influenced by Kannada. *Type:* SOV. *Lg Use:* Most also use Kannada [kan]. All are bilingual. (Gowda 1976). Used as L2 by Alu Kurumba [xua], Attapady Kurumba [pkr], Eravallan [era], Irula [iru], Jennu Kurumba [xuj], Kadar [kej], Kanikkaran [kev], Kannada Kurumba [kfi], Kota [kfe], Malankuravan [mjo], Malasar [ymr], Muthuvan [muv], Paliyan [pcf], Paniya [pcg], Saurashtra [saz], Toda [tcx], Vaagri Booli [vaa]. *Lg Dev:* Taught in primary and secondary schools. Fully developed. Bible: 1727–2002. *Writing:* Braille script. Tamil script, primary usage. *Other:* Officially recognized language. Hindu, Muslim. *Map:* 351.

Telugu [tel] (Andhra, Gentoo, Tailangi, Telangire, Telegu, Telgi, Tengu, Terangi, Tolangan). 73,800,000 in India (2001 census). Population total all countries: 74,049,000. L2 users: 5,000,000 in India. Andhra Pradesh and neighboring states. Also in Bahrain, Canada, Fiji, Malaysia, Mauritius, Singapore, South Africa, United Arab Emirates, United States. *Status:* 2 (Provincial). Statutory provincial language in Andhra Pradesh State; Puducherry Union Territory, Andaman and Nicobar islands (1950, Constitution, Schedule VIII). *Class:* Dravidian, South-Central, Telugu. *Dialects:* Berad, Dasari, Dommara, East Godaveri, Golari, Guntur, Kamathi, Komtao, Konda-Reddi, Nellore, Rayalseema, Salewari, Srikakula, Telangana, Telugu, Vadaga, Vadari, Vishakhapatnam, Yanadi (Yenadi). *Type:* SOV. *Lg Use:* Used as L2 by Bodo Gadaba [gbj], Chenchu [cde], Koya [kff], Kupia [key], Lambadi [lmn], Mudhili Gadaba [gau], Northwestern Kolami [kfb], Pottangi Ollar Gadaba [gdb], Vaagri Booli [vaa], Waddar [wbq], Yerukula [yeu]. *Lg Dev:* Taught in primary and secondary schools. Fully developed. Bible: 1854–2002. *Writing:* Braille script. Telugu script, primary usage. *Map:* 351.

Teressa [tef] (Taih-Long). 2,080 (2001 census). Teressa, Bompoka, and Nicobar islands. *Status:* 6a (Vigorous). *Class:* Austro-Asiatic, Mon-Khmer, Nicobar, Chowra-Teressa. *Dialect:* Bompoka (Bompaka, Pauhut). *Lg Dev:* Radio programs. *Map:* 361.

Thachanadan [thn] (Moopan, Thacchanadens, Thachanad Muppans). 3,000 (2004 survey). Kerala, Wayanad district, Kalpetta, Meppadi, Muttil and Ambalavayal panchayats; Malappuram district, Nilambur area. *Status:* 6b (Threatened). *Class:* Dravidian, Southern, Unclassified. *Dialects:* None known. Lexical similarity: 60%–64% with Malayalam [mal], 50%–54% with Tamil [tam], 66%–72% with Mullu Kurumba [kpb]. *Lg Use:* Some use Malayalam in home and village, esp. with children. Use is less among youth. Home, village. All ages. Neutral to positive attitudes. Youth have more negative attitudes. Also use Malayalam [mal]. *Lg Dev:* Literacy rate in L2: 30% (2004 survey). Literacy rate much lower than state literacy rate. *Other:* A Scheduled Tribe. Traditional religion, Hindu. *Map:* 360:395.

Thangmi [thf] (Thami). 500 in India. Sikkim, East district, Aritar Sunua; West Bengal, Darjeeling. *Status:* 6b (Threatened). *Lg Use:* Thangmi culture thriving in Sikkim and Darjeeling area. (Turin 1999). See main entry on page 261. *Map:* 355:154.

Tharu, Chitwania [the]. *Status:* 6a (Vigorous). See main entry on page 261. *Maps:* 354:94, 355:94.

Tharu, Dangaura [thl] (Chaudary, Chaudhari, Chaudhuri, Dang, Dangali, Dangora, Dangura). 174,000 in India (2007). Uttar Pradesh, Kheri district, Nighasan tahsil border; Gonda district, Tulsipur tahsil; Bahraich district. *Status:* 6a (Vigorous). *Lg Use:* Also use Hindi [hin]. *Lg Dev:* Literacy rate in L2: 20%–25% (census). *Other:* A Scheduled Tribe. Traditional religion, Hindu. See main entry on page 261. *Map:* 354:91.

Tharu, Kathariya [tkt] (Kathoriya Tharu, Khatima Tharu). *Status:* 6a (Vigorous). See main entry on page 262. *Map:* 354:90.

Tharu, Kochila [thq] (Saptari). *Status:* 6a (Vigorous). *Dialect:* Morangia. *Other:* Traditional religion, Hindu. See main entry on page 262. *Maps:* 354:95, 355:95.

Tharu, Rana [thr] (Rana Thakur). 150,000 in India (2003). Nepal border, Uttar Pradesh, Lakhimpur Kheri district, Paliakalan tahsil, Chandan Chauki block; Uttarakhand, Udham Singh Nagar district, Khatima tahsil. *Status:* 6a (Vigorous). *Lg Use:* Also use Hindi [hin]. *Lg Dev:* Literacy rate in L2: 20%–25%. *Other:* A Scheduled Tribe. Hindu, traditional religion. See main entry on page 262. *Map:* 354:89.

Thulung [tdh] (Thulunge Rai). Sikkim; West Bengal, Darjeeling district; Uttar Pradesh. *Status:* 5 (Developing). *Lg Use:* Most ethnic Thulungs in Darjeeling do not speak Thulung but Nepali [nep]. *Other:* Hindu. See main entry on page 262. *Map:* 355:163.

Tibetan [bod] (Bhotia, Bod, Central Tibetan, Phoke, Pohbetian, Poke, Skad, Tebilian, Tibate). 85,300 in India (2001 census). Himachal Pradesh, Tibet border; Uttarakhand; Arunachal Pradesh; Assam; Delhi; Sikkim. *Status:* 5 (Developing). *Dialects:* Aba (Batang), Dartsemdo (Tatsienlu), Dru, Gtsang, Hanniu, Kongbo, Nganshuenkuan (Anshuenkuan Nyarong), Panakha-Panags, Paurong. *Lg Use:* Used as L2 by Byangsi [bee], Chaudangsi [cdn], Darmiya [drd], Jad [jda], Sikkimese [sip], Zakhring [zkr]. *Other:* A Scheduled Tribe. In Himalayan countries,

'Bhotiya', people of Tibetan origin, and is applied to various languages. Buddhist (Lamaist). See main entry on page 90 (as Tibetan, Central). *Map:* 355:150.

Tinani [lbf] (Gondhla, Gondla, Lahauli, Lahouli, Lahuli, Rangloi, Teenan, Tinan Lahuli). 22,600 in India (2001). Population total all countries: 23,050. Himachal Pradesh, Lahul and Spiti subdivisions, lower Chandra, Tinan, and Rangloi valleys. Gondhla is main village. Also in China. *Status:* 6a (Vigorous). *Class:* Sino-Tibetan, Tibeto-Burman, Western Tibeto-Burman, Bodish, West Himalayish, Kinauri. *Dialects:* None known. Lexical similarity: 63%–56% with Pattani [lae], 32%–37% with Bunan [bfu], 21% with the Spiti [spt] and Stod [sbu] varieties of central Tibetan [bod], 62% with Tandi village, 34% with Shumcho [scu], 32% with Jangshung [jna], 31% with Kanauri and Sunam [ssk], 13% with Tibetan [bod]. *Lg Use:* Home, village, infrequently in religion. Also use Hindi [hin], Pattani [lae]. Used as L2 by Kullu Pahari [kfx]. *Lg Dev:* Literacy rate in L2: High. Radio programs. Bible portions: 1908–1915. *Writing:* Devanagari script. Tibetan script. *Other:* Lahuli applies to Lahul inhabitants; Spiti refers primarily to a place. Not a tight linguistic designation. Well educated. Buddhist, Hindu. *Map:* 352:21.

Tiwa [lax] (Dowyan, Lalung). 27,100 (2001 census). Ethnic population: 171,000 (2001 census). Assam, Nagaon, Karbi Anglong, Kamrup, Sibsagar, and Lakhimpur districts; Meghalaya, Khasi Hills district. *Status:* 6a (Vigorous). *Class:* Sino-Tibetan, Tibeto-Burman, Sal, Bodo-Garo-Northern Naga, Bodo-Koch, Bodo-Garo, Bodo. *Dialects:* Datiyali, Hajowali. *Lg Use:* Quite a few in Brahmaputra valley adopted Assamese [asm] as L1. Resurgent interest to learn the mother tongue; approved by the state in 2004 to be taught as a subject up to class 4. Home, market. Also use Assamese [asm], English [eng]. *Lg Dev:* Literacy rate in L2: 62% for Assam (2001 census). Literacy rate higher in the plains. In the hills, equally low among men and women. Don Bosco school (Karbi Anglong District) teaches Tiwa up to class 4. Dictionary. Grammar. NT: 1972. *Writing:* Bengali script. Latin script. *Other:* A Scheduled Tribe. Traditional religion, Hindu. *Map:* 356:207.

Toda [tcx] (Todi, Tuda). 1,560 (2001 census). Tamil Nadu, Nilgiri hills, Kunda hills. *Status:* 6a (Vigorous). *Class:* Dravidian, Southern, Tamil-Kannada, Tamil-Kodagu, Toda-Kota. *Dialects:* None known. Lexical similarity: 24% with Kota [kfe], the most similar language. *Lg Use:* Vigorous. All domains. All ages. Positive attitudes. Also use Tamil [tam]. *Lg Dev:* Literacy rate in L2: 66%–79% (2001 census). Dictionary. Grammar. Bible portions: 1897–1910. *Writing:* Tamil script. *Other:* A Scheduled Tribe. Hindu, Christian. *Map:* 360:387.

Toto [txo]. 1,400 (2012 SIL). West Bengal, Jalpaiguri district, Subhapara, Dhunchipara, and Panchayatpara hillocks on Indo-Bhutan border, Totopara village. *Status:* 6a (Vigorous). *Class:* Sino-Tibetan, Tibeto-Burman, Sal, Dhimalish. *Dialects:* None known. Not inherently intelligible of Dhimal [dhi] of Nepal. Lexical similarity: low with Dhimal [dhi]. *Type:* SOV; postpositions; genitives, demonstratives, relatives before noun heads; nontonal. *Lg Use:* Also use Bengali [ben], Hindi [hin], Nepali [npi]. *Writing:* Bengali script. Devanagari script. *Other:* A Scheduled Tribe. Traditional religion, Hindu. *Map:* 355:121.

Tshangla [tsj] (Cangluo Menba, Central Monpa, Dirang, Memba, Menba, Monba, Monpa, Motuo, Sangla, Sharchopkha, Tsangla). 11,200 in India (2007). 8,200 in Kameng District; 3,000 in West Siang. West Arunachal Pradesh, Kameng district, Dirang area, Namsu, Tempang, Sangti, and Bishing villages; West Siang district, former Padma-bkod region, Tuting and Mechuka circles, Mechuka, Opu, Bona, Galling, Korfu, Dorgling Halung, and Tuting villages. *Status:* 5 (Developing). *Lg Use:* Also use Adi [adi], English [eng], Hindi [hin]. Used as L2 by Chug [cvg], Lish [lsh]. *Other:* A Scheduled Tribe. Chowdhury (1996) separates Memba (Tshangla) and Khamba as different tribes in Siang District, both separate from Monpa, in Kameng District. Buddhist. See main entry on page 59. *Map:* 356:175.

Tukpa [tpq] (Nesang, Nyam-kat). 610 (2000). Himachal Pradesh, Kinnaur district, Nesang, Charang, and Kunnu villages. *Status:* 6a (Vigorous). *Class:* Sino-Tibetan, Tibeto-Burman, Western Tibeto-Burman, Bodish, West Himalayish, Kinauri. *Writing:* Unwritten. *Other:* Buddhist. *Map:* 352:39.

Tulu [tcy] (Tal, Tallu, Thalu, Thulu, Tilu, Tullu, Tuluva Bhasa). 1,720,000 (2001 census). Karnataka, South Kanara (Dakshina Kannada) and Udupi districts; Kerala, Kasargod district; scattered in other states. *Status:* 5 (Developing). *Class:* Dravidian, Southern, Tulu. *Dialects:* Brahmin Tulu, Common Tulu, Northeast Tulu (Belthangadi, Kerala), Northwest Tulu (Mangalore, Udipi), South Central Tulu (Bantwal, Puttur), Southeast Tulu (Sullia Subrahmanya), Southwest Tulu (Kasaragod, Manjeswara). *Lg Use:* Also use English [eng], Hindi [hin], Kannada [kan], Marathi [mar]. Used as L2 by Korra Koraga [kfd], Kudiya [kfg]. *Lg Dev:* Literacy rate in L2: 80%–83% in Dakshina Kannada [kan] for Udupi districts. Magazines. Radio programs. Films. Dictionary. Grammar. NT: 1847–2000. *Writing:* Kannada script. Tulu script, philosophical texts and religious verses are sometimes written in this script. *Other:* Hindu, traditional religion. *Map:* 360:361.

Turi [trd]. 2,000 (2007). Ethnic population: 354,000 (2007). Jharkhand, Ranchi, Gumla, and Lohardaga districts, Chotanagpur area; Chhattisgarh, Raigarh district; Odisha, Sambalpur and Sundargarh districts; West Bengal, Birbhum, Nadia, Murshidabad, and Bankura districts. *Status:* 8a (Moribund). *Class:* Austro-Asiatic, Munda, North Munda, Kherwari, Santali. *Other:* A Scheduled Caste. Speak Sadri [sck] as L1 in Jharkhand, Mundari [unr] in West Bengal, Oriya [ory] in Odisha (Singh and Manoharan 1993). Turi spoken only in Chotanagpur (Breton 1997). A Turi caste in Gujarat is not related linguistically. *Map:* 355:137.

Turung [try] (Tai Turung, Tailung, Tairong). No known L1 speakers. Assam, Golaghat district, Titabar and Karbi Anglong. *Status:* 10 (Extinct). *Class:* Sino-Tibetan, Tibeto-Burman, Sal, Jingpho-Luish, Jingpho. *Writing:* Latin script. *Other:* Shifted to a dialect of Singpho [sgp] with borrowed Tai words.

Ullatan [ull] (Katan, Kattalan, Kochuvelan, Ulladan). No known L1 speakers. Ethnic population: 16,700 (2001 census). Kerala, Palakkad, Thrissur, Ernakulam, Kottayam, Idukki, Koliam, Pathanamthitta, Alleppey, and Trivandrum districts. *Status:* 9 (Dormant). *Class:* Dravidian, Southern, Unclassified. *Lg Use:* May have no remaining speakers. Most, if not all, shifted to Malayalam [mal]. *Lg Dev:* Literacy rate in L2: 72–82% (2001 census). *Other:* Prefer to be considered Malayalis rather than Ullatan. Ulladan and Kochu Velan are both Scheduled Tribes. Traditional religion, Hindu.

Urali [url] (Oorazhi, Uraly, Urli). No known L1 speakers. Ethnic population: 6,440 (2001 census). Kerala, Idukki district, Upputhara, Kanchiyar, Vannappuram, Velliyamattom, and Ayyappankovil panchayats. *Status:* 9 (Dormant). *Class:* Dravidian, Southern, Tamil-Kannada, Kannada. *Dialects:* None known. Shares features with Tamil [tam], Irula [iru], and Kannada [kan] (Lal 1991). Lexical similarity: 60%–71% with Malayalam [mal],

54%–58% with Tamil [tam]. *Lg Use:* Mainly older adults. Still exists to some extent in two interior settlements, Memari and Vanchivayal. Being replaced by Malayalam [mal]. *Lg Dev:* Literacy rate in L2: 73% (2001 census). *Other:* A Scheduled Tribe. Irali Urali is a dialect of Irula [iru] in Tamil Nadu. Urali Kurumba is an alternate name for Betta Kurumba [xub] in Wayanad District, Kerala. Traditional religion.

Urdu [urd] (Islami, Undri, Urudu). 51,500,000 in India (2001 census). Jammu and Kashmir; widespread use by Muslims; Dakhini around Hyderabad, Maharashtra. *Status:* 2 (Provincial). Statutory provincial language in Andra Pradesh State; Delhi Union Territory (1950, Constitution, Schedule VIII). Statutory provincial working language in Bihar, Uttar Pradesh states (1950, Constitution, Schedule VIII), limited to official correspondence, notices and other communication. Statutory language of provincial identity in Jammu and Kashmir State (1957, State constitution, Article 145). *Dialects:* Dakhini (Dakani, Dakkhini, Deccan, Desia, Mirgan), Pinjari, Rekhta (Rekhti). *Lg Use:* Used as L2 by Balti [bft], Bhadrawahi [bhd], Bhattiyali [bht], Bilaspuri [kfs], Chambeali [cdh], Changthang [cna], Churahi [cdj], Dogri [dgo], Eastern Balochi [bgp], Gujari [gju], Kangri [xnr], Kashmiri [kas], Kullu Pahari [kfx], Ladakhi [lbj], Mandeali [mjl], Mewati [wtm], Purik [prx], Seraiki [skr]. *Lg Dev:* Taught in primary schools. *Other:* Muslim. See main entry on page 272. *Map:* 351.

Vaagri Booli [vaa] (Guvvalollu, Haki Piki, Hakkipikkaru, Karikkorava, Kuruvikkaran, Marattiyan, Narakureavar, Narikkorava, Rattiyan, Shikarijanam, Wagri Vel, Wogri Boli). 9,300 (2007). Ethnic population: 12,000 (2007). Tamil Nadu, Tiruvannamalai, Vellore, Cuddalore, and Villupuram districts; Andhra Pradesh, Pondicherry, Karnataka, and Maharashtra. *Status:* 6a (Vigorous). *Class:* Indo-European, Indo-Iranian, Indo-Aryan, Unclassified. *Dialects:* None known. Lexical similarity: 36% with Marathi [mar], 40% with Hindi [hin]. *Lg Use:* Also use Kannada [kan], Marathi [mar], Tamil [tam], Telugu [tel]. *Lg Dev:* Literacy rate in L2: Very low. Bible portions: 1975. *Writing:* Tamil script. *Other:* Hakkipikki is a Scheduled Tribe. The people are called by various names meaning bird catchers. Semi-nomadic. Hindu. *Map:* 360:369.

Vaiphei [vap] (Bhaipei, Vaipei, Veiphei). 40,000 (2001 census). South Manipur, Churachandpur district, 30+ villages; Assam; Meghalaya; Tripura. *Status:* 5 (Developing). *Class:* Sino-Tibetan, Tibeto-Burman, Sal, Kuki-Chin-Naga, Kuki-Chin, Northern. *Lg Dev:* Literacy rate in L2: 60% in Manipur (2001 census). NT: 1957–1989. *Writing:* Latin script. *Other:* A Scheduled Tribe. Ethnic Autonym: Zomi is a collective name by which Tedim Chins of Myanmar, Paite and Vaiphei of Manipur generally identify themselves. Christian. *Map:* 357:265.

Varhadi-Nagpuri [vah] (Berar Marathi, Berari, Dhanagari, Kumbhari, Madhya Pradesh Marathi). 6,970,000 (1995). Maharashtra, Amravati, Buldana, and Akola districts; Madhya Pradesh, Chhindwara and Balaghat districts; Andhra Pradesh, Adilabad and Nizamabad districts. *Status:* 5 (Developing). *Class:* Indo-European, Indo-Iranian, Indo-Aryan, Southern zone, Unclassified. *Dialects:* Brahmani, Govari, Jhadpi, Kosti (Rangari), Kunban (Kohli), Kunbi, Mahari (Dhedi), Raipur. Regarded by some as a dialect of Marathi [mar]. *Lg Dev:* Radio programs. Bible portions: 1834. *Writing:* Devanagari script. *Map:* 358:302.

Varli [vav] (Warli). 600,000 (2003). Maharashtra, north Thane district, Dahanu and Talasari taluks; Nasik and Dhule districts; Gujarat, Valsad district, Dharampur taluk; Dadra and Nagar Haveli. Davari dialect is in far north Thane district and south Gujarat. *Status:* 5 (Developing). *Class:* Indo-European, Indo-Iranian, Indo-Aryan, Southern zone, Konkani. *Dialects:* Davari, Eastern Nihiri, Western Nihiri. Sometimes classified as a dialect of Gujarati [guj] or Bhili [bhb]. Lexical similarity: 61%–93% among dialects, 60% with Marathi [mar], 65% with Kukna [kex]. *Lg Use:* Also use Gujarati [guj], Marathi [mar]. *Lg Dev:* Literacy rate in L2: 32% for Gujarat (2001 census). Radio programs. Bible portions: 2009. *Writing:* Devanagari script. Gujarati script. *Other:* Each dialect group is endogamous. Patrilocal. A Scheduled Tribe. Traditional religion. *Map:* 358:310.

Vasavi [vas] (Adiwasi Bhil, Ambodia Bhil, Bhilori, Dhogri Bhil, Keski Bhil, Padwi Bhilori, Vasava, Vasava Bhil, Vasave). 1,200,000 (2002 Friends Missionary Prayer Band). Maharashtra, Nandurbar district, Tapti river area; Gujarat, Surat and Bharuch districts, southern areas of Akkalkuwa and Akrani (Dhadgaon) tahsils, north of Tapti river; Satpudas; central and north Nandurbar and Nawapur tahsils south of Tapti. *Status:* 5 (Developing). *Class:* Indo-European, Indo-Iranian, Indo-Aryan, Central zone, Gujarati. *Dialects:* Ambodi (Ambodia), Dehvali (Kolche), Dogri (Dhogri, Dungri), Khatalia, Kot. Not intelligible of Pauri Bareli [bfb] or Bhili [bhb]. 77%–93% intelligibility between Dogri, Khatali, Dehwali, Dubli, and Kotni varieties. Vasavi Dungri 79% intelligible of Dungra Bhil. *Lg Use:* Low proficiency in Marathi [mar]. *Lg Dev:* Literacy rate in L2: Low. Radio programs. NT: 2006. *Writing:* Devanagari script. Gujarati script. *Other:* Subgroup of Bhil ethnic group. Vasava is the people name. *Map:* 358:290.

Vishavan [vis] (Malankudi, Malarkuti). 150 (Shashi and Shri 1994). Disappearing. Many died in the 1980s from a smallpox epidemic. Kerala, Ernakulam, Kottayam, and Thrissur districts, Parana and Perumuzhi on Idamala river, Idyara range, Moovatupuzha taluk; Chalakudi river near Ittyani. *Status:* 6b (Threatened). *Class:* Dravidian, Unclassified. *Other:* Traditional religion. *Map:* 360:374.

Waddar [wbq] (Od, Orh, Vadari, Vadda Beldar, Werders, Wodde). 172,000 (2001 census). Ethnic population: In India, Pakistan, Nepal, and Sri Lanka about 3 million (2003 IMA). Andhra Pradesh; Karnataka; Maharashtra, Jalgaon district. *Status:* 6a (Vigorous). *Class:* Dravidian, South-Central, Telugu. *Lg Use:* Also use Hindi [hin], Marathi [mar], Telugu [tel]. *Lg Dev:* Some literate in Telugu or Marathi. *Other:* Glossonym: Od in North India and Pakistan. Hindu. *Map:* 358:315.

Wagdi [wbr] (Bhili, Bhilodi, Mina Bhil, Vagadi, Vagari, Vagdi, Vaged, Vageri, Vagi, Wagadi, Wagari, Waghari, Wagholi, Wagri). 2,510,000 (2001 census). L2 users: Merchants and government workers use it as L2. Rajasthan, south Udaipur, Dungarpur, and Banswara districts; Gujarat, Sabarkantha and Panchmahals; Andhra Pradesh, Hyderabad. *Status:* 3 (Wider communication). *Class:* Indo-European, Indo-Iranian, Indo-Aryan, Central zone, Bhil. A member of macrolanguage Rajasthani [raj]. *Dialects:* Adivasi Wagdi, Kherwara, Rewadi, Sagwara. Dialect intelligibility above 95%. Intelligible of Adivasi Garasia [gas] of Bhiloda. Wagdi Banswara highly intelligible of Bhilodi of Gujarat. Wagdi highly intelligible of Patelia [bhb] of Gujarat. Lexical similarity: 84% with Patelia dialects; 75%–80% with Marwari [rwr] dialects; 79%–93% with Adiwasi Garasia dialects; 79%–87% with Rajput Garasia dialects. *Type:* SOV; postpositions; genitives after noun heads; nontonal. *Lg Use:* A regional language in Vagad Desh. Positive attitudes. Some also use Hindi [hin], with proficiency adequate for market. *Lg Dev:* Literacy rate in L1: Below 1%. Literacy rate in L2: 25%–50%. Radio programs. Dictionary. NT: 2000. *Writing:* Devanagari script. *Other:* Vagri is a Scheduled Tribe in Gujarat. *Map:* 353:75.

War-Jaintia [aml] (Amwi, Khasi, War). 25,900 in India (2001 census). Meghalaya, Khasi and Jaintia Hills area; Assam. *Status:* 6a (Vigorous). *Lg Use:* Vigorous. Home, community. All ages. Also use Khasi [kha]. Used as L2 by Biete [biu]. *Other:* Separate from War dialect of Khasi [kha]. Christian, traditional religion. See main entry on page 57. *Map:* 356:211.

Yakkha [ybh] (Yakha, Yakkhaba). 810 in India (2000). Ethnic population: 6,300 (2007). West Bengal, Darjeeling district; Sikkim. *Status:* 7 (Shifting). *Lg Use:* Younger generation uses Nepali [npi] (Singh). *Other:* Buddhist, Hindu. See main entry on page 264. *Map:* 355:153.

Yerukula [yeu] (Erukala, Eruku Bhasha, Korava, Korchi, Kurru Bhasha, Kurutha, Yarukula, Yerkula, Yerukala, Yerukala-Korava, Yerukla, Yerukula-Bhasha). 69,500 (2001 census). Andhra Pradesh, Rayalseema, Telengana and Andhra regions; Tamil Nadu, Nilgiri, Coimbatore, Periyar, Salem, and Chengai Anna; Karnataka; Kerala; Maharashtra. *Status:* 5 (Developing). *Class:* Dravidian, Southern, Tamil-Kannada, Tamil-Kodagu, Tamil-Malayalam, Tamil. *Dialects:* Parikala, Sankara-Yerukala. Lexical similarity: among varieties ranges from 53%–81%, 33%–38% with Irula [iru], 28%–45% with Ravula [yea], 27%–45% with Tamil [tam]. *Lg Use:* Vigorous language use. In Andhra Pradesh: home, community, religion; in Rayalseema and Telengana regions, wider use. Positive attitudes. Some also use Telugu [tel], with higher proficiency in Andhra Pradesh and among educated adults. *Lg Dev:* Literacy rate in L2: 26% (1991 census). *Writing:* Telugu script. *Other:* Some people called Yerukula speak Telugu [tel] as L1. Traditionally nomadic. A Scheduled Tribe. Hindu. *Maps:* 358:324, 360:324.

Zakhring [zkr] (Eastern Mishmi, Meyor, Zaiwa). 300 in India (2002). Arunachal Pradesh, Lohit district, Walong and Kibithoo, Lohit river area. *Status:* 7 (Shifting). *Lg Use:* Also use Central Tibetan [bod], Hindi [hin], Nefamese [nef]. *Other:* Buddhist (Lamaist). See main entry on page 94. *Map:* 356:191.

Zangskari [zau] (Zanskari, Zaskari). 12,000 (2000). Jammu and Kashmir, Zaskar mountains; south end of Kargil district, between the Himalayas and Indus river valley, next to Leh-Ladakhi and Kargil-Purik areas. *Status:* 6a (Vigorous). *Class:* Sino-Tibetan, Tibeto-Burman, Western Tibeto-Burman, Bodish, Central Bodish, Western. *Dialects:* None known. 73%–81% intelligibility of Leh Ladakhi [lbj] with high standard deviation indicating some acquired intelligibility; 90% intelligibility of Stod Bhoti [sbu] of Darcha village. *Lg Use:* Also use Ladakhi [lbj]. *Lg Dev:* Literacy rate in L2: Speakers in Ladakh [lbj] have highest rate. Bible portions: 1945–1951. *Writing:* Tibetan script. *Other:* Buddhist. *Map:* 352:6.

Zou [zom] (Jou, Zo, Zohâm, Zokam, Zoukamz). 20,900 in India (2001 census). Manipur, Chandel district, Singngat subdivision, Sugnu area; Churachandpur district; Assam. *Status:* 5 (Developing). *Lg Use:* Positive attitudes. *Lg Dev:* Literacy rate in L2: 62% in Manipur (2001 census). *Other:* A Scheduled Tribe. Zomi is a collective name by which Tedim Chins [ctd] of Myanmar, Paite [pck] and Vaiphei [vap] of Manipur generally identify themselves. People are known as Zome or Zomi. Christian. See main entry on page 243 (as Zo). *Map:* 357:276.

Indonesia

Republic of Indonesia, Republik Indonesia. 237,642,000 (2010 census). Principal language: Indonesian. Literacy rate: 90% (2009 UNESCO). General references: Adelaar 1995; Barr, Barr, and Salombe 1979; Blust 2003; Fox 1991; Gray, Drummond, and Greenhill 2009; Grimes 1994; Grimes 1995; Grimes, Therik, Grimes, and Jacob 1997; Himmelmann 2001; Hudson 1978; Martens 1989; Noorduyn 1991; Ross 2005; Wumbu et al. 1986; Wurm and Hattori 1981. Deaf population: 2,000,000 or more (1993). Deaf institutions: 94.

The number of individual languages listed for Indonesia is 718. Of these, 705 are living and 13 are extinct. Of the living languages, 18 are institutional, 86 are developing, 261 are vigorous, 265 are in trouble, and 75 are dying. See maps beginning on page 362.

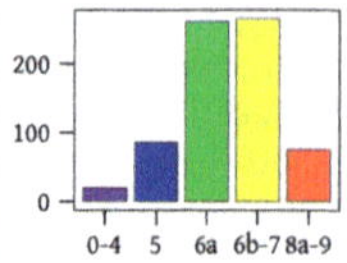

Abinomn [bsa] (Avinomen, "Baso" *pej.*, Foja, Foya). 300 (Clouse, Ma, and Donohue 2002). Papua Province, Sarmi regency, Mamberamo Hulu subdistrict. Lakes plain area, Baso river mouth east of Dabra at Idenburg river, to headwaters in Foya mountains. *Status:* 6a (Vigorous). *Class:* Language isolate. *Type:* SOV. *Lg Use:* Positive attitudes. Also use Foau [flh]. *Lg Dev:* Literacy rate in L1: 10%. Low level of schooling. *Writing:* Latin script. *Other:* Christian, traditional religion. *Map:* 372:197.

Abui [abz] ("Barawahing" *pej.*, Barue, Namatalaki). 16,000. East Nusa Tenggara Province. Western half, Alor island. *Status:* 6a (Vigorous). *Class:* Trans-New Guinea, West, Timor-Alor-Pantar, Alor-Pantar, Alor. *Dialects:* Abui Barat, Abui Selatan, Alakaman, Atimelang. Much dialect diversity. Alakaman may be a dialect of Kamang [woi] (Woisika). May be more than 1 language. *Lg Dev:* Dictionary. Grammar. *Map:* 370.

Abun [kgr] (A Nden, Karon, Manif, Yimbun). 3,000 (1995 SIL). Papua Province, Sorong regency; Ayamaru, Sausapor, and Moraid subdistricts, about 20 villages. North coast, interior of central Bird's Head, north, south of Tamberau mountain range. *Status:* 5 (Developing). *Class:* Language isolate. *Dialects:* Abun Je, Abun Ji (Madik), Abun Tat (Karon Pantai). *Lg Dev:* Literacy rate in L1: 5%–15%. Grammar. NT: 2004. *Writing:* Latin script. *Other:* Christian, traditional religion. *Map:* 371:17.

Aceh [ace] (Acehnese, Achehnese, Achinese). 3,500,000 in Indonesia (2000 census). Population total all countries: 3,500,032. Aceh Province, north tip of Sumatra, coastal areas. Also in United States. *Status:* 5 (Developing). De facto language of provincial identity in Aceh province. *Class:* Austronesian, Malayo-Polynesian, Malayo-Chamic, Chamic, Acehnese. *Dialects:* Banda Aceh, Baruh, Bueng, Daja, Pase, Pidie (Pedir, Timu), Tunong. *Type:* SVO. *Lg Use:* Vigorous. All domains except education and government. All ages. Positive attitudes. Also use Indonesian [ind], mostly in the cities, education. *Lg Dev:* Prefer reading in Indonesian [ind]. Dictionary. Grammar. Bible: 1997. *Writing:* Latin script. *Other:* Muslim. *Map:* 376:1.

Adang [adn] (Alor). 3,000 (2000). East Nusa Tenggara Province. Northwest (Bird's Head), Alor island, northwest of Kalabahi town towards Banda Sea coast. *Status:* 6a (Vigorous). *Class:* Trans-New Guinea, West, Timor-Alor-Pantar, Alor-Pantar, Alor. *Dialect:* Aimoli. Because of linguistic differences and social identity, considered a separate language from Kabola [klz]. *Other:* Christian. *Map:* 370.

Adonara [adr] (Nusa Tadon, Sagu, Vaiverang, Waiwerang). 98,000 (2008 census). East Nusa Tenggara Province. Adonara and east Solor islands, between Flores and Lembata islands. *Status:* 6a (Vigorous). *Class:* Austronesian, Malayo-Polynesian, Central-Eastern Malayo-Polynesian, Bima-Lembata. *Dialects:* East Adonara, East Solor, West Adonara. *Lg Use:* Also use Lamaholot [slp]. *Lg Dev:* Grammar. *Other:* Muslim, Christian. *Map:* 370.

Aghu [ahh] (Djair, Dyair). 3,000 (1987 SIL). Papua Province,

Merauke regency, Jair subdistrict, interior south coast area. Between Mapi and Digul rivers west of Tanamerah town. *Status:* 6b (Threatened). *Class:* Trans-New Guinea, Ok-Awyu, Awyu-Dumut, Awyu. *Lg Dev:* Grammar. *Other:* Different from Aghu-Tharnggala [gtu] of Australia. Christian, traditional religion. *Map:* 373:247.

Airoran [air] (Adora, Aeroran, Iriemkena). 1,000 (1998 SIL). Papua Province, Jayapura regency, Mamberamo Hilir and Pantai Barat subdistricts, Subu, Motobiak, Isirania, and other villages. North coast area, lower Apauwer river. *Status:* 6a (Vigorous). *Class:* Tor-Kwerba, Greater Kwerba, Kwerba, West Coast. *Lg Use:* Religious services. Also use Foau [flh]. Used as L2 by Samarokena [tmj]. *Other:* Christian, traditional religion. *Map:* 372:176.

Alor [aol] (Alorese). 25,000 (Grimes et al. 1997). Nusa Tenggara Province, Coastal Bird's Head of Alor, north Ternate island, pockets along north Pantar and adjacent islands. *Status:* 6a (Vigorous). *Class:* Austronesian, Malayo-Polynesian, Central-Eastern Malayo-Polynesian, Bima-Lembata. *Dialects:* Baranusa, Muna. Not inherently intelligible with Lembata languages or Adonara [adr]. *Lg Use:* Also use Lamaholot [slp]. *Other:* Muslim. *Map:* 370.

Alune [alp] (Patasiwa Alfoeren, Sapalewa). 17,200 (2000). Maluku Province. West Seram island, Seram Barat district, Kairatu, Taniwel districts, 27 villages. *Status:* 5 (Developing). *Class:* Austronesian, Malayo-Polynesian, Central-Eastern Malayo-Polynesian, Central Maluku, East, Seram, Nunusaku, Three Rivers, Amalumute, Northwest Seram, Ulat Inai. *Dialects:* Central East Alune (Buriah-Weth-Laturake), Central West Alune (Niniari-Piru-Riring-Lumoli), Kairatu, North Coastal Alune (Nikulkan-Murnaten-Wakolo), South Alune (Rambatu-Manussa-Rumberu). Rambatu dialect reportedly prestigious. Kawe [kgb] may be a dialect. Lexical similarity: 77%–91% among dialects, 64% with Lisabata-Nuniali [lcs], 63% with Hulung [huk] and Naka'ela [nae]. *Lg Use:* People in the interior, the majority, use it daily. Coastal village usage less vigorous. Southern dialect in Kairatu village has no remaining speakers. Also use Indonesian [ind]. *Lg Dev:* Literacy rate in L1: 50%–65%. Literacy rate in L2: 40%–55%. NT: 2012. *Writing:* Latin script. *Other:* Largest language in west Seram. Christian. *Map:* 367.

Amahai [amq] (Amahei). 50 (Wurm 2007). Maluku Province, 4 villages. Southwest Seram island, near Masohi town. *Status:* 8b (Nearly extinct). *Class:* Austronesian, Malayo-Polynesian, Central-Eastern Malayo-Polynesian, Central Maluku, East, Seram, Nunusaku, Piru Bay, East, Seram Straits, Uliase, Hatuhaha, Elpaputi. *Dialects:* Makariki, Rutah, Soahuku. Lexical similarity: 87% with Makariki and Rutah dialects, probably 2 languages; 59%–69% with Saparua [spr], 59% with Kamarian [kzx], 58% with Kaibobo [kzb], 52% with Luhu [lcq] and Hulung [huk], 50% with Alune [alp], 49% with Naka'ela [nae], 47% with Lisabata-Nuniali [lcs], 45% with Wemale [weo] and Nuaulu, 44% with Boano [bzn] and Saleman [sau]. *Lg Use:* Pressure from Ambon Malay [abs] and Indonesian [ind] (Wurm 2007). *Other:* Muslim, Christian. *Map:* 367.

Amarasi [aaz] (Timor Amarasi, Uab Meto). 70,000 (2011 UBB-GMIT). East Nusa Tenggara Province. Southwest tip, Timor island, 80 villages. Dialect locations: Kotos is central and east, Ro'is is west, Ro'is Tais Nonof is south, Ro'is Hero surrounded by Helong [heg] language area. *Status:* 5 (Developing). *Class:* Austronesian, Malayo-Polynesian, Central-Eastern Malayo-Polynesian, Timor-Babar, Nuclear Timor, Uab Meto. *Dialects:* Kotos, Ro'is, Ro'is Hero (Kopa), Ro'is Tais Nonof. Part of Uab Meto language chain. Reportedly similar to Uab Meto [aoz] but with differences in phonology, vocabulary, and discourse, with semantic shifts, structural differences, intelligibility problems. Ro'is Tais Nonof dialect has intonation like Ro'is dialect, vocabulary like Kotos dialect. *Lg Dev:* Poetry. Newspapers. Bible portions: 2002–2011. *Writing:* Latin script. *Other:* Interspersed with Helong [heg]. Most literature in Kotos dialect. Christian. *Map:* 369.

Ambai [amk] (Ambai-Menawi). 10,100 (2000). Papua Province, Yapen Waropen regency, Yapen Selatan and Yapen Timur subdistricts, 10 villages. On Ambai island in Cenderawasih bay, south of Serui town, along south coast of Serui island. *Status:* 6b (Threatened). *Class:* Austronesian, Malayo-Polynesian, Central-Eastern Malayo-Polynesian, Eastern Malayo-Polynesian, South Halmahera-West New Guinea, West New Guinea, Cenderawasih Bay, Yapen, Central-Western. *Dialects:* Ambai (Wadapi-Laut), Manawi, Randawaya. Lexical similarity: 77% with Serui-Laut [seu], 71% with Wandamen [wad]. *Type:* Serial verbs; complex directional demonstrative system. *Lg Use:* Children use Indonesian [ind]. *Lg Dev:* Literacy rate in L1: 25%–50%. Literacy rate in L2: 50%–75%. Grammar. NT: 2010. *Writing:* Latin script. *Other:* Muslim, Christian. *Map:* 372:94.

Ambelau [amv] (Amblau). 5,700 (1989 SIL). Ethnic population: 5,700. Central Maluku, Ambelau island off southeast coast of Buru island; Buru coast, Wae Tawa village, opposite Ambelau. 8 villages. *Status:* 6a (Vigorous). *Class:* Austronesian, Malayo-Polynesian, Central-Eastern Malayo-Polynesian, Central Maluku, Ambelau. *Dialects:* None known. Not intelligible with Buru [mhs]. *Lg Dev:* Literacy rate in L1: Below 1%. *Other:* Schools through junior high on the island. Wild pigs and rocky terrain on Ambelau make cultivation impossible; that is done in Wae Tawa village on Buru Island. Muslim. *Map:* 367.

Ampanang [apg]. 30,000 (Wurm and Hattori 1981). Southern East Kalimantan Province. West of Mahakam river delta, east of Jambu and Lamper towns. *Status:* 6a (Vigorous). *Class:* Austronesian, Malayo-Polynesian, Greater Barito, Barito-Mahakam. *Other:* Traditional religion. *Map:* 365:1.

Anakalangu [akg] (Anakalang). 16,000. East Nusa Tenggara Province. Sumba island, southwest coast, east of Wanukaka. *Status:* 6a (Vigorous). *Class:* Austronesian, Malayo-Polynesian, Central-Eastern Malayo-Polynesian, Sumba-Hawu, Sumba. *Map:* 369.

Anasi [bpo] (Bapu). 2,000 (1993 R. Doriot). Papua Province, Jayapura regency, Mamberamo Hilir subdistrict. North coast, lower west bank Mamberamo river. *Status:* 6a (Vigorous). *Class:* East Geelvink Bay. *Other:* Christian, traditional religion. *Map:* 372:107.

Andio [bzb] (Andio'o, "Bobongko" *pej.*, Imbao'o, Masama). 1,700 (Busenitz 1991). Central Sulawesi Province, Lamala subdistrict, Tauge and Tangeban villages. Near tip of eastern peninsula. *Status:* 6b (Threatened). *Class:* Austronesian, Malayo-Polynesian, Celebic, Eastern, Saluan-Banggai, Western. *Dialects:* None known. Lexical similarity: 44% with Bobongko [bgb], 60% with Batui [zbt], 62% with Coastal Saluan [loe], 66% with Balantak [blz]. *Lg Use:* Much influence from Indonesian [ind] and neighboring languages, Saluan [loe] and Balantak [blz] (Wurm 2007). *Other:* 'Masama' is preferred local name. Muslim. *Map:* 374:1.

Ansus [and]. 4,600 (1987 SIL). Papua Province, Yapen Waropen regency, Yapen Barat subdistrict, Ansus, Kairawi, Aibondeni, and Yenusi villages. Easternmost Serui island, south coast; Miosnum island to west. *Status:* 6b (Threatened). *Class:* Austronesian, Malayo-Polynesian, Central-Eastern Malayo-Polynesian, Eastern Malayo-Polynesian, South Halmahera-West New Guinea, West New Guinea, Cenderawasih Bay, Yapen, Central-Western. *Di-*

alects: None known. Lexical similarity: 82% with Marau [mvr] and Papuma [ppm], 77% with Wandamen [wad]. *Lg Use:* Used as L2 by Awera [awr]. *Other:* Christian, traditional religion. *Map:* 372:98.

Anus [auq] (Koroernoes, Korur). 320 (2005 SIL). Papua Province, Jayapura regency, Bonggo subdistrict. Podena islands off north coast; coastal area east of Biri river. *Status:* 7 (Shifting). *Class:* Austronesian, Malayo-Polynesian, Central-Eastern Malayo-Polynesian, Eastern Malayo-Polynesian, Oceanic, Western Oceanic, North New Guinea, Sarmi-Jayapura Bay, Sarmi. *Dialects:* None known. Reportedly similar to Podena [pdn]. *Lg Use:* Endangered (2000 S. Wurm). Influence from Kwesten [kwt] on the opposite coast and from Indonesian [ind] (Wurm 2007). Most domains. Used as L2 by Fedan [pdn], Keijar [kdy]. *Other:* Anus and Fedan [pdn] may be the same language. Christian, traditional religion. *Map:* 372:125.

Aoheng [pni] (Penihing). 2,630 (Wurm and Hattori 1981). East Kalimantan Province. Near Sarawak border, western end of province, upper reaches of Kapuas, Barito, and Mahakam rivers. *Status:* 6a (Vigorous). *Class:* Austronesian, Malayo-Polynesian, North Borneo, North Sarawakan, Kayan-Kenyah, Kayanic, Muller-Schwaner 'Punan'. *Dialects:* None known. Lexical similarity: 69% with Kereho [xke], 67% with Hovongan [hov]. *Map:* 364:2.

Aputai [apx] (Ilputih, Opotai, Tutunohan). 150 (Hinton 2000). Southwest Maluku Province, 2 villages. North central Wetar island, Banda Sea coast, Ilputih village; south central Wetar, Wetar strait coast, Lurang village. *Status:* 8b (Nearly extinct). *Class:* Austronesian, Malayo-Polynesian, Central-Eastern Malayo-Polynesian, Timor-Babar, Southwest Maluku, Wetar. *Dialects:* Ilputih, Lurang, Welemur. Welemur dialect has no remaining speakers. Lexical similarity: 93% among dialects, 79% with Perai [wet], 74% with Tugun [tzn], 69% with Ili'uun [ilu], 57% with Galolen [gal]. *Lg Use:* Influence from Galolen [gal] and Indonesian [ind] (Wurm 2007). Ilputih dialect speakers also use Galolen [gal]. Also use Ambonese Malay [abs]. *Lg Dev:* Literacy rate in L1: Below 1%. *Other:* Christian. *Map:* 369.

Aralle-Tabulahan [atq]. 12,000 (1984 SIL). West Sulawesi Province, Mambi subdistrict. Between Mandar and Kalumpang towns. *Status:* 5 (Developing). *Class:* Austronesian, Malayo-Polynesian, South Sulawesi, Northern, Pitu Ulunna Salu. *Dialects:* Aralle, Mambi, Tabulahan. Lexical similarity: 84%–89% with other dialects listed, 75%–80% with Bambam [ptu], Pannei [pnc], and Ulumandak [ulm] dialects. *Lg Dev:* NT: 2004. *Writing:* Latin script. *Other:* Christian, Muslim. *Map:* 375:2.

Arandai [jbj] (Dombano, Jaban, Sebyar, Sumuri, Yaban). 1,000 (1987 SIL). Papua Province, Manokwari regency, Bintuni subdistrict. South Bird's Head, MacCluer Gulf; east and west of Wariaga river, Sebyar (Timoforo) river area. *Status:* 6b (Threatened). *Class:* Trans-New Guinea, South Bird's Head, South Bird's Head Proper, Eastern. *Dialect:* Dombano (Arandai). Lexical similarity: 71% with the Kemberano and Dombano dialects. *Other:* Christian, traditional religion. *Map:* 371:32.

Arguni [agf] (Argoeni). 150 (Wurm 2000). Papua Province, Fak-Fak district. Off northwest coast, Bomberai peninsula on Arguni island in Maccluer gulf. *Status:* 6b (Threatened). *Class:* Austronesian, Malayo-Polynesian, Central-Eastern Malayo-Polynesian, North Bomberai. *Other:* Traditional religion, Christian. *Map:* 371:40.

As [asz]. 230 (Wurm 2000). West Papua Province, Asbakin, Maklaumkarta, and Mega villages. West Bird's Head area, north coast east of Dampler strait, inland towards Warsamson river. *Status:* 6b (Threatened). *Class:* Austronesian, Malayo-Polynesian, Central-Eastern Malayo-Polynesian, Eastern Malayo-Polynesian, South Halmahera-West New Guinea, West New Guinea, Cenderawasih Bay, Raja Ampat. *Dialects:* Lexical similarity: 60% with some dialects on Misool Island. *Lg Use:* Also use Indonesian [ind], Moi [mxn]. *Other:* Reportedly originates from Gag Island, west of Waigeo Island. Traditional religion, Christian. *Map:* 371:6.

Asilulu [asl]. 8,760 (1987 SIL). L2 users: Spoken as L2 in northwest Ambon, north and west Seram, Manipa, Boano, and Kelang islands. Maluku Province, Asilulu, Ureng, and Negeri Lima villages. Northwest Ambon island; some in west Seram island, Hoamoal peninsula, south coast. *Status:* 6b (Threatened). *Class:* Austronesian, Malayo-Polynesian, Central-Eastern Malayo-Polynesian, Central Maluku, East, Seram, Nunusaku, Piru Bay, West, Asilulu. *Dialects:* Asilulu, Negeri Lima (Henalima, Lima), Ureng. Lexical similarity: 88% with Asilulu and the Negeri Lima dialect, 78%–82% with Seit-Kaitetu [hik], 72%–73% with the Wakal dialect of Hitu [htu], 67%–72% with Larike-Wakasihu [alo], 71%–73% with Luhu [lcq] in Seram. *Lg Use:* Also use Indonesian [ind]. *Lg Dev:* Literacy rate in L1: Below 1%. Literacy rate in L2: 15%–25%. *Other:* Muslim. *Map:* 367.

Asmat, Casuarina Coast [asc] (Kaweinag). 9,000 (1991 SIL). 5,200 in Matia and 3,400 in Sapan. Papua Province, Mappi regency, Pantai Kasuari and Edera subdistricts. Casuarina Coast from Ewta river north, to Kuti river south, and inland. *Status:* 6a (Vigorous). *Class:* Trans-New Guinea, Asmat-Kamoro, Asmat. *Dialects:* Matia, Sapan (Safan). *Lg Use:* Home, community. *Other:* Traditional religion, Christian. *Map:* 373:240.

Asmat, Central [cns] (Jas, Manowee, Yas). 7,000 (Roesler 1972). Most are monolingual. Papua Province. Casuarina coast areas. Asmat Regency; Sawa-Erma, Agats, Atsy, and Pantai Kasuari subdistricts. South coast from Owap river northwest to Farec river southwest, inland. Also, Mappi regency, Nambai and Edera subdistricts. Digul river delta area. *Status:* 6b (Threatened). *Class:* Trans-New Guinea, Asmat-Kamoro, Asmat. *Dialects:* Ajam (Ayam), Misman, Simai (Simay). Reportedly similar to Sempan [xse] north of the rivers, Kamoro [kgq] and Citak [txt]. *Lg Use:* Also use Indonesian [ind]. *Lg Dev:* Literacy rate in L2: Less than 5% in Indonesian [ind]. NT: 1985. *Other:* Christian, traditional religion. *Maps:* 372:64, 373:64.

Asmat, North [nks] (Keenok). 1,000 (1991 SIL). Papua Province, Merauke regency, Sawa-Erma subdistrict. Near Pater Le Cocq river headwaters west to Unir river east to the foothills. *Status:* 6a (Vigorous). *Class:* Trans-New Guinea, Asmat-Kamoro, Asmat. *Lg Use:* Most domains. All ages. Positive attitudes. Also use Indonesian [ind]. *Lg Dev:* Literacy rate in L2: 5%. *Other:* Christian, traditional religion. *Map:* 372:65.

Asmat, Yaosakor [asy] (Yaosakor). 2,000 (1991 SIL). Papua Province, Asmat regency, Agats and Atsy subdistricts. South coast, lower Sirac river area. *Status:* 7 (Shifting). *Class:* Trans-New Guinea, Asmat-Kamoro, Asmat. *Lg Dev:* NT: 1995. *Writing:* Latin script. *Other:* Christian, traditional religion. *Map:* 373:237.

Atohwaim [aqm] (Kaugat). 1,000 (1987 SIL). Papua Province, Mappi regency, Pantai Kasuari subdistrict. South coast inland, northeast of Pirimapun town, between Cook and Kronkel rivers. *Status:* 6a (Vigorous). *Class:* Trans-New Guinea, Kayagar. *Lg Use:* Also use Indonesian [ind], Kayagar [kyt], Sawi [saw]. About half are trilingual including Indonesian [ind]. *Other:* Christian, traditional religion. *Map:* 373:241.

Auye [auu] (Auwje). 350 (1995 SIL). Ethnic population: 500 (2012 SIL). Papua Province, Paniai regency, Napan subdistrict. Central highlands southeast of Cenderawasih bay; Siriwo river area. *Status:* 5 (Developing). *Class:* Trans-New Guinea, West, Wissel Lakes. *Dialects:* None known. Related to Ekari [ekg]. *Lg Use:* Influence from Ekari [ekg] and Indonesian [ind] (Wurm 2007). All domains. All ages. Also use Indonesian [ind]. *Lg Dev:* Literacy rate in L1: 25%. Bible portions: 1993–2007. *Writing:* Latin script. *Other:* Distinct from Awyi [auw] (Awye) in Taikat group. Christian, traditional religion. *Map:* 372:79.

Awbono [awh] (Kvolyab). 100 (1999 SIL). 100 monolinguals. Papua Province, Jayawuarar district. Modera river area. *Status:* 6b (Threatened). *Class:* Bayono-Awbono. *Dialects:* None known. Not related to these language families: Ok, Asmat, Awyu-Dumut, Momuna [mqf], or highland languages like Dani [dnw], or Mek family. Lexical similarity: 55% with Bayono [byl]. *Type:* SOV. *Other:* Frequently at war with Kopkaka and Korowai. *Map:* 372:217.

Awera [awr]. 70 (Wurm 2000). Papua Province, Yapen Waropen regency, Waropen Bawah subdistrict,1 village. East side of Cenderawasih bay, Wapoga river mouth. *Status:* 7 (Shifting). *Class:* Lakes Plain, Awera. *Lg Use:* Children prefer Indonesian [ind] (Wurm 2007). Home, community. Also use Ansus [and], Indonesian [ind]. *Other:* Community shared with 100 Ansus [and] speakers. Christian, traditional religion. *Map:* 372:86.

Awyi [auw] (Awje, Awji, Awye, Njao, Nyao). 350 (Wurm 2000). Papua Province, Jayapura regency, Arso subdistrict. Northeast, highland enclave near Papua New Guinea border, south of Jayapura town. *Status:* 8a (Moribund). *Class:* Border, Taikat. *Other:* Distinct from Auye [auu] in Ekari-Wolani-Moni group. Christian, traditional religion. *Map:* 372:157.

Awyu, Asue [psa] (Miaro, Miaro Awyu, Pisa). 6,500 (2002 SIL). Papua Province, South coast area, southwest of Wildeman river, east of Kampong river, inland from Pirimapun. *Status:* 6b (Threatened). *Class:* Trans-New Guinea, Ok-Awyu, Awyu-Dumut, Awyu. *Dialects:* None known. Reportedly similar to Edera Awyu [awy] and South Awyu [aws], but distinct from Central Awyu [awu] and Jair Awyu [awv]. *Lg Use:* All domains. *Lg Dev:* Bible portions: 1985. *Other:* Christian, traditional religion. *Map:* 373:242.

Awyu, Central [awu] (Ajau, Auyu, Avio, Awju, Awya, Nohon). 7,500 (2002 Sohn Myo-sook). Papua Province, Mappi and Boven Digul regencies; Obaa, Citak Mitak, Mandobo, and Bimikia subdistricts. South coast inland, west of Tanahmerah, southwest of Boma town. *Status:* 6a (Vigorous). *Class:* Trans-New Guinea, Ok-Awyu, Awyu-Dumut, Awyu. *Dialects:* 4 dialects. *Lg Use:* Most domains. Also use Indonesian [ind]. *Lg Dev:* Bible portions: 1985. *Other:* Traditional religion. *Map:* 373:246.

Awyu, Edera [awy] (Jenimu, Oser, Siagha, Sjiagha, Syiagha, Yenimu). 3,870 (2002 SIL). Papua Province, Merauke district. Inland, both banks, lower Digul river; north of Keisak town. *Status:* 6b (Threatened). *Class:* Trans-New Guinea, Ok-Awyu, Awyu-Dumut, Awyu. *Lg Use:* All domains. *Other:* Christian, traditional religion. *Map:* 373:253.

Awyu, Jair [awv]. 2,300 (2002 SIL). Papua Province, Merauke district. West of northward bend, Digul river. *Status:* 6a (Vigorous). *Class:* Trans-New Guinea, Ok-Awyu, Awyu-Dumut, Awyu. *Lg Use:* Home, community. *Other:* Christian, traditional religion. *Map:* 373:252.

Awyu, North [yir] (Awyu, Djair, Dyair, Jair, Yair). 1,500 (1987 SIL). Papua Province, Merauke district. West side, Digul river, upstream from Tanamerah town. *Status:* 6a (Vigorous). *Class:* Trans-New Guinea, Ok-Awyu, Awyu-Dumut, Awyu. *Other:* Christian, traditional religion. *Map:* 373:248.

Awyu, South [aws] (Jenimu, Oser, Siagha, Sjiagha, Syiagha, Yenimu). 9,340 (2002 SIL). Papua Province, Merauke district. Both banks, lower Digul river; Bade town area. *Status:* 6b (Threatened). *Class:* Trans-New Guinea, Ok-Awyu, Awyu-Dumut, Awyu. *Lg Use:* All domains. *Other:* Christian, traditional religion. *Map:* 373:254.

Babar, North [bcd]. 1,000 (2007 SIL). South Maluku Province, Ilwiara, Nakarhamto, and Yatoke villages, northeast Babar island east of Timor island. *Status:* 6b (Threatened). *Class:* Austronesian, Malayo-Polynesian, Central-Eastern Malayo-Polynesian, Babar, North. *Dialects:* Dialect variation reported. *Lg Use:* Shifting to a local Malay variety. Home, gardens, ceremonies. Also use a regional Malay variety, probably a dialect of Ambonese Malay [abs], in all domains, more than vernacular. Speakers use Indonesian [ind] primarily in government, Christian religious ceremonies. *Lg Dev:* Literacy rate in L1: Below 1%. *Other:* Christian. *Map:* 368.

Babar, Southeast [vbb]. 4,460 (2007 SIL). South Maluku Province, Kroing, Letwurung, Kokwari, Wakpapai, Ahanari, Analutur, Manuweri, and Tutuwawan villages. Southeast Babar island coast. *Status:* 6a (Vigorous). *Class:* Austronesian, Malayo-Polynesian, Central-Eastern Malayo-Polynesian, Babar, South, Masela-South Babar. *Lg Use:* Vigorous. Also use Ambonese Malay [abs]. *Lg Dev:* Literacy rate in L1: Below 1%. *Other:* Christian. *Map:* 368.

Bada [bhz] (Bada', Tobada'). 6,800 (Martens 1989), increasing. South central Sulawesi Province, Lore Selatan, Pamona Selatan, Poso Pesisir, and Parigi subdistricts, at least 24 villages. Ako dialect in northern Mamuju regency, Pasangkayu subdistrict. Some in Ampibabo subdistrict, Lemusa village. *Status:* 5 (Developing). *Class:* Austronesian, Malayo-Polynesian, Celebic, Kaili-Pamona, Southern, Badaic. *Dialects:* Ako, Bada. Lexical similarity: 85% with Bada and Behoa [bep], 91% with Behoa and Napu [npy], 80% with Bada and Napu [npy]. The 3 are geographically, politically, and culturally separate. *Lg Use:* Vigorous. All domains. Also use Indonesian [ind]. *Lg Dev:* Bible portions: 2011. *Other:* 'Tobada', Bada person. Christian. *Map:* 375:3.

Badui [bac] (Baduy, Bahasa Sunda, Gajebo). 20,000 (2000 census). 12,000 in Kenekes village area. Java, Bantan Province, Rangkasbitung regency, on Ujung river; Pandeglang town, near Mount Kendeng. Separate area in West Java Province, Sukabumi city area. 1 village. *Status:* 6a (Vigorous). *Class:* Austronesian, Malayo-Polynesian, Sundanese. *Dialects:* Sometimes considered a dialect of Sunda [sun]. *Lg Use:* Vigorous. All domains. All ages. Positive attitudes. *Other:* A separate socio-religious group from Sunda [sun]. Inner and outer, Badui refer to location and status within the group religion. Muslim, traditional religion. *Map:* 363.

Bagusa [bqb] (Kapeso, Suaseso). 300 (1987 SIL). Papua Province, Jayapura regency, Mamberamo Tengah subdistrict. East of Mamberamo river, south of Lake Rombebai. *Status:* 6a (Vigorous). *Class:* Tor-Kwerba, Greater Kwerba, Kwerba, Nuclear. *Dialects:* None known. Lexical similarity: 64% with Kwerba [kwe]. *Lg Use:* Vigorous. All ages. *Other:* Traditional religion, Christian. *Map:* 372:177.

Baham [bdw] (Patimuni). 1,100 (1987 SIL). West Papua Province, Fakfak regency, Kaimana, Fakfak, and Kokas subdistricts. Northwest Bomberai peninsula, east of Fakfak city. *Status:* 6b (Threatened). *Class:* Trans-New Guinea, West, West Bomberai, West Bomberai Proper. *Dialects:* None known. Reportedly similar to Iha [ihp]. *Other:* Christian, traditional religion. *Map:* 371:44.

Bahau [bhv]. 19,000 (2007 SIL). East Kalimantan Province, Kutai Barat regency, Long Apari, Long Pahangai, Long Bagun, and Long Hubung subdistricts. Area around confluence of Ratah and Mahakam rivers. *Status:* 6a (Vigorous). *Class:* Austronesian, Malayo-Polynesian, North Borneo, North Sarawakan, Kayan-Kenyah, Kayanic, Kayan Proper. *Map:* 365:3.

Bahonsuai [bsu] (Bahoe-soeaai, Bahonsoewaai). 200 (Mead 1999). Central Sulawesi Province, Bungku Tengah subdistrict, Bahonsuai village on the east coast. *Status:* 7 (Shifting). *Class:* Austronesian, Malayo-Polynesian, Celebic, Eastern, Southeastern, Bungku-Tolaki, Eastern, East Coast. *Dialects:* None known. Lexical similarity: 71% with Tomadino [tdi], 68% with Mori Atas [mzq], Mori Bawah [xmz], and Padoe [pdo]. *Other:* Muslim. *Map:* 375:4.

Bajau, Indonesian [bdl] (Badjaw, Badjo, Bajao, Bajo, Bayo, Gaj, Indonesian Bajaw, Orang Laut, Sama, Taurije'ne'). 150,000 (Mead, Lee, and Neveux 2007). 5,000 or more in North Maluku (Grimes 1982), 8,000 to 10,000 in South Sulawesi (Grimes and Grimes 1987), 7,000 in North Sulawesi and Gorontalo, 36,000 in Central Sulawesi, 40,000 in Southeast Sulawesi (Mead, Lee, and Neveux 2007), and several thousand in Nusa Tenggara (Wurm and Hattori 1981; Verheijen 1986). Widespread throughout Indonesia. Central and South East Sulawesi provinces, islands of the East Sunda Sea. North Maluku Province on Bacan, Obi, Kayoa, and Sula islands. South Sulawesi Province, Selayar, Bone, and Sinjai regencies. Gorontalo Province, Popayato and Tilamuta subdistricts. North Sulawesi Province, Wori, Tumpaan, and Belang subdistricts. *Status:* 6b (Threatened). *Class:* Austronesian, Malayo-Polynesian, Greater Barito, Sama-Bajaw, Sulu-Borneo, Borneo Coast Bajaw. *Dialects:* Jampea, Jaya Bakti, Kajoa, Matalaang, Poso, Roti, Same', Sulamu, Togian 1, Togian 2, Wallace. *Lg Use:* Vigorous in north Maluku and Southeast Sulawesi. Also use Indonesian [ind]. *Other:* Known as Bayo and Taurije'ne' in the Makasar [mak] language. Known as Bajo in Buginese [bug]. Schools in some villages. They live in houses on stilts over water. Other Bajau languages are in Sabah, Malaysia, and the southern Philippines. Muslim, traditional religion. *Maps:* 374:35, 375:35.

Bakati' [bei] (Bakati Nyam, Bakati Riok, Bakatiq, Bekati). 4,000 (1986 UBS). Northwestern West Kalimantan Province. Sambas river headwaters. *Status:* 6b (Threatened). *Class:* Austronesian, Malayo-Polynesian, Land Dayak, Bakati'. *Lg Use:* Also use Kendayan [knx]. *Lg Dev:* Bible portions: 1986. *Map:* 364:4.

Bakati', Rara [lra] (Bekati' Kendayan, Bekati' Nyam-Pelayo, Bekatiq, Lara', Luru). 12,000 in Indonesia (2004 M. Connor). West Kalimantan Province, Pejampi and 2 other villages. Upper Lundu and Sambas rivers, southeast of Sambas town. *Status:* 5 (Developing). *Dialect:* Bina'e. *Lg Use:* Also use Kendayan [knx]. *Other:* Traditional religion. See main entry on page 219. *Map:* 364:53.

Bakati', Sara [sre] (Riok). 4,000 (2004 M. Connor). West Kalimantan Province, near Sanggau-Ledo northeast of Ledo. *Status:* 6a (Vigorous). *Class:* Austronesian, Malayo-Polynesian, Land Dayak, Bakati'. *Dialects:* Some dialect differences. Unidirectional intelligibility of Rara-Bakati' [lra] by Sara. *Lg Use:* Also use Kendayan [knx]. *Lg Dev:* Bible portions: 1986. *Map:* 364:58.

Bakumpai [bkr] (Bakambai, Bara-Jida). 100,000 (2003). Central Kalimantan Province. Kapuas and Barito rivers, northeast of Kuala Kapuas. *Status:* 3 (Wider communication). Used as a LWC in the market in central Kalimantan Province. *Class:* Austronesian, Malayo-Polynesian, Greater Barito, West, South. *Dialects:* Bakumpai, Mengkatip (Mangkatip, Oloh Mengkatip). Lexical similarity: 75% with Ngaju [nij], 45% with Banjar [bjn]. *Lg Use:* Used as L2 by Dusun Deyah [dun], Dusun Witu [duw], Lawangan [lbx], Ma'anyan [mhy]. *Lg Dev:* Dictionary. *Other:* Muslim. *Maps:* 364:5, 365:5.

Balaesang [bls] (Balaesan, Balaisang, Pajo). 3,200 (Himmelmann 2001). Central Sulawesi Province, Balaesang subdistrict, Manimbayu peninsula, Ketong, Kamonji, and Rano villages. *Status:* 7 (Shifting). *Class:* Austronesian, Malayo-Polynesian, Celebic, Tomini-Tolitoli, Tomini, Southern. *Lg Use:* Younger generation prefers Indonesian [ind] (Wurm 2007). *Other:* Muslim. *Map:* 374:5.

Balantak [blz] (Balanta, Kosian). 30,000 (2000 SIL), increasing. 3,000 monolinguals. L2 users: Speakers of other area languages use Balantak as L2. Central Sulawesi Province, Banggai regency, Luwuk, Balantak, Tinangkung, and Lamala subdistricts, at least 49 villages. Eastern peninsular tip, Cape Botok. *Status:* 5 (Developing). *Class:* Austronesian, Malayo-Polynesian, Celebic, Eastern, Saluan-Banggai, Eastern. *Dialects:* None known. Lexical similarity: 66% with Andio [bzb], 51% with Saluan [loe], 39% with Bobongko [bgb]. *Lg Use:* Vigorous. All domains. Positive attitudes. Also use Indonesian [ind]. *Lg Dev:* Literacy rate in L1: 10%. 3,000 can read, 300 can write. Taught in primary schools. Radio programs. Dictionary. Grammar. NT: 2010. *Writing:* Latin script. *Other:* Muslim, Christian. *Map:* 374:6.

Bali [ban] (Balinese). 3,330,000 (2000 census). 7,000 in South Sulawesi. Includes immigrant speakers in west Nusa Tenggara, west Lombok Islands. Java and Bali. Islands of Bali, north Nusa Penida. *Status:* 5 (Developing). *Class:* Austronesian, Malayo-Polynesian, Bali-Sasak-Sumbawa. *Dialects:* Highland Bali ("Bali Aga"), Lowland Bali (Badung, Buleleng, Gianyar, Jembrana, Karangasem, Klungkung, Tabanan), Nusa Penida. Reportedly 2 distinct dialects. High Bali is used in religion, but users are diminishing. Speech strata in several lowland varieties (1989 A. Clynes). *Lg Dev:* Bible: 1990. *Writing:* Balinese script. Javanese script, no longer in use. Latin script, used since early 20th century. *Other:* Nusa Penida Island variety associated with Highland Bali dialect. It is a scattering of villages with minimal influence from the former Majapahit Empire. Hindu. *Maps:* 363, 369.

Bambam [ptu] (Pitu Uluna Salu, Pitu-Ulunna-Salu). 22,000 (Strømme 1987). West Sulawesi Province, west Polmas regency, Mambi subdistrict. Watershed of Maloso and Mapilli rivers; into Majene and Mamuju regencies. *Status:* 5 (Developing). *Class:* Austronesian, Malayo-Polynesian, South Sulawesi, Northern, Pitu Ulunna Salu. *Dialects:* Bambam Hulu, Bumal, Issilita', Matangnga, Mehalaan, Pakkau, Pattae', Salu Mokanam. Complex dialect chain. Lexical similarity: 83%–94% with Bumal; 85%–80% with dialects of Aralle-Tabulahan [atq], Pannei [pnc], and Ulumanda [ulm]. *Lg Use:* Vigorous. All ages. *Lg Dev:* Radio programs. Grammar. NT: 2004–2010. *Writing:* Latin script. *Other:* Christian, Muslim, traditional religion. *Map:* 375:7.

Banda [bnd]. 3,000 (1987 SIL). South Maluku, Kei islands, west and northeast side of Kei Besar island, Banda-Eli and Banda-Elat villages, possibly another village. *Status:* 7 (Shifting). *Class:* Austronesian, Malayo-Polynesian, Central-Eastern Malayo-Polynesian, Central Maluku, East, Banda-Geser. *Dialects:* Elat, Eli. Different from other south Maluku languages. *Lg Use:* All domains. Also use Kei [kei]. Used as L2 by Kei [kei]. *Lg Dev:* Literacy rate in L1: Below 1%. *Other:* The people originally came from the Banda Islands, but the language is no longer spoken there. Muslim. *Map:* 368.

Banggai [bgz] (Aki, Banggaai, Banggaiy, Banggay, Banggaya). 125,000 (2000 census). Central Sulawesi Province, at least 157 villages. Off eastern peninsula, Banggai Islands. *Status:* 7 (Shifting). *Class:* Austronesian, Malayo-Polynesian, Celebic, Eastern, Saluan-Banggai, Eastern. *Dialects:* East Banggai, West Banggai. *Lg Use:* Parental generation or older. *Lg Dev:* Dictionary. Bible: 2002. *Writing:* Latin script. *Other:* Muslim, Christian. *Maps:* 374:8, 375:8.

Bangka [mfb]. 340,000 (2000 census). 50 or less speakers of the Lom dialect (Wurm 2007). Sumatra, Bangka-Belitung Province, Bangka island. *Status:* 6a (Vigorous). *Class:* Austronesian, Malayo-Polynesian, Malayo-Chamic, Malayic, Malay. A member of macrolanguage Malay [msa] (Malaysia). *Dialects:* Capital City Urban Bangka, Central Bangka, Lom (Belom, Mapor), North Bangka, Port Urban Bangka, South Bangka. *Lg Use:* Lom dialect seriously endangered or moribund (2000 S. Wurm). *Other:* A network of dialects with distinct lexical, phonological, and grammatical innovations set Bangka apart from other Malay speech varieties. Muslim, traditional religion. *Map:* 377:2.

Banjar [bjn] (Bandjarese, Banjar Malay, Banjarese, Labuhan). 3,500,000 in Indonesia (2000 census), increasing. Population total all countries: 3,505,000. Kalimantan, around Banjarmasin south and east; East Kalimantan Province, coastal regions of Pulau Laut, Kutai, and Pasir; Central Kalimantan Province as far as Sampit. Also in Malaysia. *Status:* 3 (Wider communication). Banjar became a LWC through trade. LWC in the market, in business, and in media. Banjar, already dominant in South Kalimantan Province, is also growing rapidly in Central and Eastern Kalimantan provinces. *Class:* Austronesian, Malayo-Polynesian, Malayo-Chamic, Malayic, Malay. A member of macrolanguage Malay [msa] (Malaysia). *Dialects:* Hulu, Kuala. Lexically influenced by Javanese [jav]. Lexical similarity: 73% with Indonesian [ind], 66% with Tamuan (Malayic Dayak) [xdy], 45% with Bakumpai [bkr], 35% with Ngaju [nij]. *Lg Use:* Vigorous. Many speakers lack fluency in Indonesian [ind]. *Lg Dev:* Newspapers. New media. TV. Dictionary. *Other:* Muslim. *Maps:* 364:6, 365:6.

Bantik [bnq]. 3,000 (Utsumi 2001), decreasing. North Sulawesi Province, 11 villages. Northern peninsula, northeast section, area around Manado city. *Status:* 8a (Moribund). *Class:* Austronesian, Malayo-Polynesian, Philippine, Sangiric, Southern. *Lg Use:* Under pressure from Manado Malay [xmm]. Fluent users age 50 or older. Positive attitudes. Also use Manado Malay [xmm]. *Other:* Christian.

Barakai [baj] (Workai). 4,450 (2011 SIL). South Maluku Province, Longgar, Apara, Bemun, and Mesiang villages. Southeast Aru chain, Barakai island; some on Gomo-Gomo island northeast of Barakai. *Status:* 6a (Vigorous). *Class:* Austronesian, Malayo-Polynesian, Central-Eastern Malayo-Polynesian, Aru. *Dialects:* Barakai, Mesiang. Reportedly similar to Karey [kyd]. Lexical similarity: 70% with Batuley [bay]. *Lg Use:* Vigorous. *Lg Dev:* Literacy rate in L1: Below 1%. *Other:* Christian, Muslim, traditional religion. *Map:* 368.

Barapasi [brp] (Baropasi). 2,500 (1995 SIL). Papua Province, Yapen Waropen regency, Waropen Atas subdistrict. East Cenderawasih bay, along Barapasi river and tributaries. *Status:* 6b (Threatened). *Class:* East Geelvink Bay. *Dialects:* Marikai, Sipisi. Lexical similarity: 67% with Kofei [kpi], 71% with Sauri [srt], 61% with Tefaro [tfo], 64% with Woria [wor]. *Lg Use:* All domains. Also use Indonesian [ind]. *Lg Dev:* Literacy rate in L2: 15%–25%. *Other:* Traditional religion, Christian. *Map:* 372:92.

Baras [brs] (Ende). 250 (Valkama 1987). 50 households. West Sulawesi Province, Mamuju Regency, Karossa subdistrict, Salubiro village, Baras subdistrict, in and north of Bambaloka village. *Status:* 8a (Moribund). *Class:* Austronesian, Malayo-Polynesian, Celebic, Kaili-Pamona, Northern, Kaili. *Dialects:* Lexical similarity: 84% with Da'a Kaili [kzf], 85% with Inde dialect of Kaili, Da'a [kzf], 80% or more with other Kaili varieties, 64% with Uma [ppk]. *Other:* Some think the language will die out. Muslim. *Map:* 375:10.

Basap [bdb] (Bosap). 15,000 (2007 SIL). East Kalimantan Province, scattered in Bulungan, Sangkulirang, and Kutai regencies. *Status:* 6b (Threatened). *Class:* Austronesian, Malayo-Polynesian, North Borneo, Rejang-Sajau. *Dialects:* Berau, Binatang, Bulungan, Dumaring, Jembayan, Karangan. *Lg Use:* Parents use Indonesian [ind] with children to help prepare them for school (2012 A. Guerrerio). Home, community, religion. *Other:* Traditional religion, Christian. *Map:* 365:7.

Batak Alas-Kluet [btz] (Alas-Kluet Batak). 195,000 (2000 census). Includes 80,000 Alas, 50,000 Kluet, and 65,000 Singkil. Sumatra, southwest Aceh Province, northeast of Tapaktuan and Kutacane. *Status:* 6a (Vigorous). *Class:* Austronesian, Malayo-Polynesian, Northwest Sumatra-Barrier Islands, Batak, Northern. *Dialects:* Alas, Kluet, Singkil (Kade-Kade). Alas dialect may be more similar to Karo Batak [btx], 81% cognate (Soravia 2002), while Kluet and Singkil may be more closely related to Pakpak Dairi [btd]. *Other:* Many reject the label Batak for its cultural connotations. Unclear whether this is a single language. *Map:* 376:3.

Batak Angkola [akb] (Anakola, Angkola). 750,000 (1991 UBS). North Sumatra Province. Sipirok town area; inland from near Sibolga city towards southern provincial border. *Status:* 5 (Developing). *Class:* Austronesian, Malayo-Polynesian, Northwest Sumatra-Barrier Islands, Batak, Southern. *Dialects:* None known. Reportedly similar to Mandailing Batak [btm], but distinct sociolinguistically. *Lg Dev:* Bible: 1991. *Writing:* Batak script. Latin script. *Other:* Christian, Muslim. *Map:* 376:4.

Batak Dairi [btd] (Dairi, Pakpak, Pakpak Dairi). 1,200,000 (1991 UBS). North Sumatra Province. Southwest of Lake Toba; area around Sidikalang town, south to coast. *Status:* 5 (Developing). *Class:* Austronesian, Malayo-Polynesian, Northwest Sumatra-Barrier Islands, Batak, Northern. *Dialects:* Diari and Pakpak dialects are sociolinguistically distinct. *Lg Dev:* Bible: 1998. *Writing:* Batak script. *Other:* Christian. *Map:* 376:5.

Batak Karo [btx] (Karo Batak). 600,000 (1991 UBS). North Sumatra Province. North central area west and northwest of Lake Toba. *Status:* 5 (Developing). *Class:* Austronesian, Malayo-Polynesian, Northwest Sumatra-Barrier Islands, Batak, Northern. *Dialect:* Singkil. *Lg Dev:* Grammar. Bible: 1987–1995. *Writing:* Batak script. Latin script. *Other:* Christian, traditional religion. *Map:* 376:6.

Batak Mandailing [btm] (Batta, Mandailing Batak). 1,100,000 (2000 census). North Sumatra Province. Southern interior area extending across borders with Riau, West Sumatra provinces. *Status:* 6a (Vigorous). *Class:* Austronesian, Malayo-Polynesian, Northwest Sumatra-Barrier Islands, Batak, Southern. *Dialects:* None known. Sociolinguistically different from Angkola Batak [akb]. *Writing:* Batak script. *Other:* A general form of Batak common to a wider area than Angkola. Muslim. *Map:* 376:7.

Batak Simalungun [bts] (Simelungan, Timur). 1,200,000 (2000). North Sumatra Province. Area northeast of Lake Toba; Pematangsiantar town area. *Status:* 5 (Developing). *Class:* Austronesian, Malayo-Polynesian, Northwest Sumatra-Barrier Islands, Batak, Simalungan. *Lg Dev:* Bible: 1976. *Writing:* Batak script. Latin script. *Map:* 376:8.

Batak Toba [bbc] (Batta, Toba Batak). 2,000,000 (1991

UBS). North Sumatra Province. Samosir island; east, south, and west of Lake Toba. *Status:* 5 (Developing). *Class:* Austronesian, Malayo-Polynesian, Northwest Sumatra-Barrier Islands, Batak, Southern. *Dialects:* None known. Reportedly similar to Angkola Batak [akb]. *Lg Dev:* Grammar. Bible: 1894–1989. *Writing:* Batak script, no longer in use. Latin script. *Other:* Christian. *Map:* 376:9.

Bati [bvt] (Gah). 3,500 (Loski and Loski 1989). Maluku Province. East coast, Seram island between Kian Darat and Keleser towns, inland. *Status:* 6b (Threatened). *Class:* Austronesian, Malayo-Polynesian, Central-Eastern Malayo-Polynesian, Central Maluku, East, Banda-Geser, Geser-Gorom. *Dialects:* None known. Related to Geser-Gorom [ges] and Watubela [wah]. *Lg Use:* Also use Geser-Gorom [ges]. *Lg Dev:* Literacy rate in L1: Below 1%. *Other:* Strong separation of ethnolinguistic identity from Geser-Gorom [ges]. Muslim. *Map:* 367.

Batui [zbt] (Baha). 2,900, decreasing. Central Sulawesi Province, Banggai regency, Batui subdistrict, Balantang, Tolando, Sisipan, and Batui villages. Eastern peninsula, mainland across from Peleng island. *Status:* 7 (Shifting). *Class:* Austronesian, Malayo-Polynesian, Celebic, Eastern, Saluan-Banggai, Western, Saluanic. *Dialects:* None known. Lexical similarity: 74% with Saluan [loe], 60% with Andio [bzb], 54% with Bobongko [bgb], 46% with Balantak [blz], 38% with Banggai [bgz]. *Lg Use:* Home, cultural events. Most parents do not pass language on to their children (2006). Positive attitudes. *Other:* Muslim. *Map:* 374:11.

Batuley [bay] (Gwataley, Watulai). 3,640 (2011 SIL). Maluku Province, 7 island villages. Aru islands, east coast, Tanah Besar island. *Status:* 6b (Threatened). *Class:* Austronesian, Malayo-Polynesian, Central-Eastern Malayo-Polynesian, Aru. *Dialects:* None known. Slightly more distant from Dobel [kvo]. Lexical similarity: 70% with Barakai [baj] and Karey [kyd], 81% with Mariri [mqi]. *Lg Use:* Vigorous. *Lg Dev:* Literacy rate in L1: Below 1%. *Other:* Muslim. *Map:* 368.

Bauzi [bvz] (Baudi, Baudji, Baudzi, Bauri). 1,500 (1991 SIL). 1,350 monolinguals. Papua Province, Jayapura and Yapen Waropen regencies, Mamberamo Tengah and Waropen Atas subdistricts, Vakiadi, Noiadi, Danau Bira, Solom, Kustera, Neao, and Itaba villages. Extensive inland area between Mamberamo and Rouffaer rivers. *Status:* 5 (Developing). *Class:* East Geelvink Bay, Bauzi. *Dialects:* Aumenefa, Gesda Dae, Neao. *Lg Use:* Vigorous. Some Aliki speak Bauzi [bvz] due to intermarriage and trading. All domains. Positive attitudes. Also use Eritai [ert], Indonesian [ind]. Used as L2 by Eritai [ert]. *Lg Dev:* Literacy rate in L1: 10%–25%. 230 can read and write it. NT: 2008. *Writing:* Latin script. *Other:* Whistle speech reported. Christian, traditional religion. *Map:* 372:180.

Bayono [byl]. 100 (1999 SIL). Papua Province, Merauke district. Eilanden and Steenboom rivers. *Status:* 6b (Threatened). *Class:* Bayono-Awbono. *Dialects:* None known. Not related to language families like Ok, Asmat, Awyu-Dumut, Momuna, or highlands language families like Dani or Mek. Lexical similarity: 55% with Awbono [awh]. *Type:* SOV. *Maps:* 372:219, 373:219.

Bedoanas [bed]. 180 (Wurm 2000). West Papua Province, Fakfak regency, Kokas subdistrict. Bomberai peninsula. *Status:* 6b (Threatened). *Class:* Austronesian, Malayo-Polynesian, Central-Eastern Malayo-Polynesian, Eastern Malayo-Polynesian, South Halmahera-West New Guinea, West New Guinea, Bomberai. *Lg Use:* Children do not use the language anymore (Wurm 2007). *Other:* Christian, traditional religion. *Map:* 371:39.

Behoa [bep] (Ako, Besoa). 10,000 (2007 SIL), increasing. Central Sulawesi Province, Lore Utara subdistrict, 8 villages. Most speakers in Behoa valley, northwest of Lake Mantana. some in Napu valley. *Status:* 6b (Threatened). *Class:* Austronesian, Malayo-Polynesian, Celebic, Kaili-Pamona, Southern, Badaic. *Dialects:* None known. Geographically, politically, culturally, and lexically distinct from Bada [bhz] and Napu [npy]. *Lg Use:* 70% are speakers. Behoa is passed on to more than 60% of the children. Younger generation now prefers Indonesian [ind] (Wurm 2007). Most domains. Positive attitudes. Nearly everyone can speak Indonesian [ind] at some level. *Lg Dev:* Taught in primary schools. Bible portions: 2004–2008. *Writing:* Latin script. *Other:* Christian, Muslim. *Map:* 375:12.

Beneraf [bnv] (Boneraf, Bonerif). 200 (2005 SIL). Very few monolinguals. Papua Province, Sarmi regency, Pantai Timur subdistrict. North coast area east of Tor river mouth, Beneraf and part of Nenke village. *Status:* 7 (Shifting). *Class:* Tor-Kwerba, Orya-Tor, Tor. *Lg Use:* Home. Children also use Papuan Malay [pmy]. *Other:* Edwas may be the name preferred by the people. Christian, traditional religion. *Map:* 372:169.

Benggoi [bgy] (Bengoi, Isal, Kobi-Benggoi, Uhei Kachlakan, Uhei-Kaclakin, Uhei-Kahlakim). 350 (1989 SIL). Maluku Province, Benggoi, Balakeo, and Lesa villages. Seram island, Werinama and Bula districts, north Seram Sea coast. *Status:* 8a (Moribund). *Class:* Austronesian, Malayo-Polynesian, Central-Eastern Malayo-Polynesian, Central Maluku, East, Seram, Manusela-Seti. *Dialects:* Balakeo, Benggoi, Lesa. Lexical similarity: 70% with dialects; 54%–66% with Liana-Seti [ste], 46%–50% with Salas Gunung dialect [sgu], 32%–46% with Manusela [wha]. *Lg Dev:* Literacy rate in L1: Below 1%. *Other:* Christian, Muslim. *Map:* 367.

Bengkala Sign Language [bqy] (Benkala Sign Language, Kata Kolok). 41 (2007 SIL). More than 1,200 Kata Kolok signers; about 50 of them are deaf (2011 C. de Vos). 40 monolinguals. Java and Bali, Bali island, Buleleng regency, Bengkala village. *Status:* 6b (Threatened). *Class:* Deaf sign language. *Lg Use:* All domains. All ages. Positive attitudes. A school for the deaf 18 km away uses only Indonesian Sign Language [inl]. 2 Bengkala signers now go to this school and have become bilingual. There are 3 bilingual Bengkala signers. *Lg Dev:* Literacy rate in L1: 0%. Literacy rate in L2: About 5% in Indonesian [ind]. In 2007 a local school was set up for deaf children in the village which uses Kata Kolok as a language of instruction. Taught in primary schools. *Other:* In the linguistic literature the language is referred to as Kata Kolok which means deaf language in Balinese [ban]. *Map:* 363.

Bentong [bnu] (Bentong-Dentong, Dentong). 25,000 (1987 SIL). South Sulawesi Province, inland parts of Maros, Bone, Pangkep, and Barru regencies where Bugis [bug], Makassar [mak] and Highland Konjo [kjc] language areas meet. *Status:* 6b (Threatened). *Class:* Austronesian, Malayo-Polynesian, South Sulawesi, Makassar. *Dialects:* None known. Reportedly most similar to Konjo [kjc]. *Lg Use:* Some youth shifting to Indonesian [ind]. *Other:* 'Bentong' and 'Dentong' are Bugis [bug] and Makasarese [mak] exonyms meaning 'nonfluent', but the names do not have negative connotations to speakers themselves. Muslim, Christian. *Map:* 375:13.

Benyadu' [byd] (Balantian, Balantiang, Njadu, Nyadu). 54,000 (2007). West Kalimantan Province, Landak and Bengkayang regencies. Northwest near Sarawak border. *Status:* 6a (Vigorous). *Class:* Austronesian, Malayo-Polynesian, Land Dayak. *Dialects:* Nyadu (Balantian, Balantiang, Njadu), Pandu. *Lg Use:* Also use Kendayan [knx]. *Writing:* Latin script. *Map:* 364:8.

Berik [bkl] (Berick, Berrik, Sewan Teteris, Upper Tor).

1,200 (1994 SIL). Papua Province, Sarmi regency, Tor Atas subdistrict; Bora Bora, Waf, Doronta, Beu, Togonfo, Dangken, Kondirjan, Somanente, Tenwer, Sewan, Safrontani, and Taminambor villages. North coast area along mid and upper Tor river, inland from Sarmi peninsula. *Status:* 6b (Threatened). *Class:* Tor-Kwerba, Orya-Tor, Tor. *Dialects:* None known. Lexical similarity: 45% with Keijar [kdy], 13% with Orya [ury]. *Lg Use:* Also use Papuan Malay [pmy]. Used as L2 by Mander [mqr]. *Lg Dev:* Dictionary. NT: 1993. *Writing:* Latin script. *Other:* Formerly the trade language of Tor area. Christian, traditional religion. *Map:* 372:168.

Betaf [bfe] (Tena). 600 (2005 SIL). Papua Province, Sarmi regency, Pantai Timur subdistrict. North coast area east of Sarmi. *Status:* 6b (Threatened). *Class:* Tor-Kwerba, Orya-Tor, Tor. *Lg Use:* Children more frequently use Papuan Malay [pmy]. Most domains. All ages. Also use Indonesian [ind], Papuan Malay [pmy]. *Other:* Christian, traditional religion. *Map:* 372:120.

Betawi [bew] (Batavi, Batawi, Betawi Malay, Jakarta Malay, Melayu Jakarte). 5,000,000 (2000 census). Population count imprecise due to vague ethnic and linguistic definition of 'Betawi'. Java, Special Capital Territory, Jakarta city. *Status:* 6b (Threatened). *Class:* Creole, Malay based. *Dialects:* None known. A Malay-based creole distinct from both Indonesian [ind] and other Malay-based pidgins and creoles. It evolved mid-19th century. Unique phonological, morphological, and lexical traits. Influences from Peranakan Indonesian [pea] and Bali [ban]. Often not intelligible to Indonesian speakers not familiar with it (1989 R. Allen). *Lg Use:* Functions as a Low variety in a diglossic situation, but has covert prestige when used by the upper class. *Lg Dev:* Poetry. Radio programs. Films. TV. Grammar. Bible portions. *Other:* Muslim. *Map:* 363.

Biak [bhw] (Biak-Numfor, Mafoor, Mafoorsch, Mefoor, Myfoorsch, Noefoor, Noefoorsch, Nufoor). 30,000 (Wurm 2000). L2 users: A few thousand L2 users. West Papua Province, Biak Numfor regency. Biak and Numfor islands north, numerous small islands east and west of Bird's Head, including Mapia island. *Status:* 6b (Threatened). *Class:* Austronesian, Malayo-Polynesian, Central-Eastern Malayo-Polynesian, Eastern Malayo-Polynesian, South Halmahera-West New Guinea, West New Guinea, Cenderawasih Bay, Biakic. *Dialects:* Ariom, Bo'o, Bosnik, Dwar, Fairi, Jenures, Kamer, Korido, Korim, Mandusir, Mapia, Mios Num, Mofu, Monoarfu, Opif, Padoa, Penasifu, Rumberpon, Samberi, Sampori (Mokmer), Sor, Sorendidori, Sorido, Sundei, Vogelkop, Wadibu, Wardo, Wari, Warsa. Some consider Biak and Numfor dialect 2 languages. *Lg Use:* Potentially endangered (2000 S. Wurm). Strong influence from Indonesian [ind]; younger generation losing command of it; many prefer Indonesian (Wurm 2007). *Lg Dev:* NT: 1990. *Writing:* Latin script. *Other:* Christian, traditional religion. *Maps:* 371:4, 372:4.

Bidayuh, Biatah [bth] (Biatah, Bideyu, Landu, Lundu, Pueh, Siburan). 8,480 in Indonesia (2000). Northwestern Kalimantan Province. Area east of Suruh village, near Sarawak border. *Status:* 5 (Developing). *Other:* May be distinct from Biatah [bth] of Sarawak. Christian, traditional religion. See main entry on page 219. *Map:* 364:10.

Bidayuh, Bukar-Sadong [sdo] (Buka, Bukar, Bukar Sadong, Bukar Sadung Bidayah, Sabutan, Sadong, Serian, Tebakang). West Kalimantan Province, Sanggau and Sintang regencies. Mount Cemaru, near Sarawak border. *Status:* 6a (Vigorous). *Dialects:* Bukar Bidayuh (Bidayah, Bidayuh), Bukar Sadong. See main entry on page 219. *Map:* 364:12.

Biga [bhc]. 300 (Remijsen 2001). West Papua Province, Sorong district, Biga village. South of Misool island. *Status:* 6a (Vigorous). *Class:* Austronesian, Malayo-Polynesian, Central-Eastern Malayo-Polynesian, Eastern Malayo-Polynesian, South Halmahera-West New Guinea, West New Guinea, Cenderawasih Bay, Raja Ampat. *Lg Use:* Vigorous. *Map:* 371:12.

Bilba [bpz] (Belubaa, Bilbaa, Eastern Rote, Rote, Rote Timur, Roti, Rotinese). 7,000 (2002 UKAW). Ethnic population: 7,000. East Nusa Tenggara Province. Northeast end of Rote island, west of Rikou. Communities on Semau island and Timor mainland near Kupang. *Status:* 6a (Vigorous). *Class:* Austronesian, Malayo-Polynesian, Central-Eastern Malayo-Polynesian, Timor-Babar, Nuclear Timor, Rote. *Dialects:* Bilba, Diu, Lelenuk. *Lg Use:* Vigorous. All domains. All ages. *Other:* Christian. *Map:* 369.

Bima [bhp] (Bimanese). 500,000 (1989). West Nusa Tenggara Province. Eastern third of Sumbawa island, east of the isthmus; northeast, Sangeang and Banta islands. *Status:* 6a (Vigorous). *Class:* Austronesian, Malayo-Polynesian, Central-Eastern Malayo-Polynesian, Bima-Lembata. *Dialects:* Bima, Kolo, Mbojo, Sangar (Sanggar), Toloweri. *Lg Dev:* Bible portions. *Other:* Muslim. *Map:* 369.

Bintauna [bne] (Bintaoena, Bintawoena, Bitaoena). 11,200 (2000 census). North Sulawesi Province, around Bintauna town. *Status:* 6b (Threatened). *Class:* Austronesian, Malayo-Polynesian, Philippine, Greater Central Philippine, Gorontalo-Mongondow, Gorontalic. *Lg Use:* Younger generation using more Indonesian [ind]. *Other:* Muslim. *Map:* 374:14.

Biritai [bqq] (Aliki, Ati, Biri). 250 (1988 SIL). Papua Province, Puncakjaya district, Biri village. North of mid-Rouffaer river. *Status:* 6a (Vigorous). *Class:* Lakes Plain, Tariku, East. *Dialects:* None known. Lexical similarity: 69% with Obokuitai [afz], 61% with Eritai [ert], 60% with Kwerisa [kkb], 69% with Kaiy [tcq]. *Type:* SOV; tonal. *Other:* Christian, traditional religion. *Map:* 372:185.

Blagar [beu] (Belagar, Kaera, Pura, Tarang). 11,000 (Wurm and Hattori 1981). East Nusa Tenggara Province. East Pantar, north Pura, and south Ternate islands. *Status:* 6a (Vigorous). *Class:* Trans-New Guinea, West, Timor-Alor-Pantar, Alor-Pantar, Pantar. *Dialects:* Apuri, Bakalang, Limarahing, Pura. Retta [ret], spoken on south Pura and nearby islands, is a separate language. *Lg Dev:* Bible portions. *Map:* 370.

Boano [bzl] (Boan-diks, Bolano). 2,700 (Himmelmann 2001). Central Sulawesi Province, Moutong subdistrict, Bolano village. North peninsula, south coast, facing gulf of Tomini. *Status:* 6b (Threatened). *Class:* Austronesian, Malayo-Polynesian, Celebic, Tomini-Tolitoli, Tolitoli. *Dialects:* None known. Lexical similarity: 83% with Totoli [txe]. *Lg Use:* Children are educated in Indonesian [ind] (Wurm 2007). Community. *Other:* Different from Boano [bzn] in Maluku. Muslim. *Map:* 374:15.

Boano [bzn] (Buano). 3,240 (1982). Maluku Province, North Buano main village. Boano island, facing northwest point, Seram island. *Status:* 6a (Vigorous). *Class:* Austronesian, Malayo-Polynesian, Central-Eastern Malayo-Polynesian, Central Maluku, East, Seram, Nunusaku, Piru Bay, West, Hoamoal. *Dialects:* None known. Lexical similarity: 60% with Luhu [lcq], 61% with Lisabata-Nuniali [lcs] (most similar). *Lg Use:* Vigorous in north Boano. South Boano may have no remaining speakers. *Other:* Different from Boano [bzl] in Sulawesi. *Map:* 367.

Bobongko [bgb]. 1,500 (Mead 2001). 1,100 in Lembanato and 400 in Tumbulawa. Central Sulawesi Province, Togian islands, Lembanato village on Kilat bay, north side of Togian island, and Tumbulawa village, northwest coast of Batu Daka island. *Status:* 6a (Vigorous). *Class:* Austronesian, Malayo-Polynesian, Celebic, Eastern, Saluan-Banggai, Western, Saluanic. *Dialects:* None known. Different from Andio [bzb]. Lexical similarity: 53% with Coastal Saluan [loe], 44% with Andio [bzb], and 30% with Gorontalo [gor], 25%–30% with Gorontalo-Mongondow languages. *Other:* Bobongko is not derogatory to its speakers, but it is to the Andio [bzb]. Muslim, Christian. *Map:* 374:16.

Bobot [bty] (Ahtiago, Atiahu, Hatumeten, Ntau, Werinama). 4,500 (1989 SIL). Maluku Province. Southeast Seram, Werinama district, southeast from Atiahu village to Kota Baru; also Tunsai village in Liana area. *Status:* 6b (Threatened). *Class:* Austronesian, Malayo-Polynesian, Central-Eastern Malayo-Polynesian, Central Maluku, East, Seram, Bobot. *Dialects:* None known. Lexical similarity: 44% with Sepa [spb] and Teluti [tlt], 42% with Yalahatan [jal]. *Lg Dev:* Literacy rate in L1: Below 1%. *Other:* Muslim. *Map:* 367.

Bolango [bld] (Atinggola-Bolango, Bolaang Uki, Bolang-Banka, Bulanga, Bulanga-Uki). 23,000 (Sneddon and Usup 1986). Atinggola 16,000, Bolango 7,000. North Sulawesi Province, Bolaang Mongondow Regency. South coast of peninsula, Molibagu area; Gorontalo Province, northeast coast, Atinggola town area. *Status:* 6b (Threatened). *Class:* Austronesian, Malayo-Polynesian, Philippine, Greater Central Philippine, Gorontalo-Mongondow, Gorontalic. *Dialects:* Atinggola (Andagile, Attingola, Diu, Kattinggola), Bolango (Uki). *Lg Use:* Younger generation using more Indonesian [ind]. *Other:* Distinct from Gorontalo [gor] (1974 J. Little). Muslim. *Map:* 374:17.

Bolongan [blj] (Bulungan). 30,000 (Kawi et al. 2002). East Kalimantan Province. Tanjungselor town area, lower Kayan river. *Status:* 6a (Vigorous). *Class:* Austronesian, Malayo-Polynesian, North Borneo, North Sarawakan, Dayic, Murutic, Tidong. *Dialects:* May be a dialect of Tidong [tid] or Segai [sge]. *Other:* Traditional religion. *Map:* 365:11.

Bonerate [bna]. 9,500 (1987 SIL). South Sulawesi Province. Selayer island group; Bonerate, Madu, Kalaotoa, and Karompa islands. *Status:* 6a (Vigorous). *Class:* Austronesian, Malayo-Polynesian, Celebic, Eastern, Southeastern, Muna-Buton, Tukangbesi-Bonerate. *Dialects:* Bonerate, Karompa. Lexical similarity: 79%–81% with Tukang Besi South [bhq], 31% with Kalao [kly], 25% with Laiyolo [lji]. *Other:* Muslim. *Map:* 375:18.

Bonggo [bpg] (Armopa, Bgu, Bogu, Bongo). 790 (2006 SIL). Papua Province, Sarmi regency, Bonggo subdistrict. *Status:* 8a (Moribund). *Class:* Austronesian, Malayo-Polynesian, Central-Eastern Malayo-Polynesian, Eastern Malayo-Polynesian, Oceanic, Western Oceanic, North New Guinea, Sarmi-Jayapura Bay, Sarmi. *Lg Use:* Endangered (2000 D. Tryon). Home. Also use Indonesian [ind], Papuan Malay [pmy]. *Other:* Bgu may be the name preferred by the people. Christian, traditional religion. *Map:* 372:126.

Budong-Budong [bdx] (Bubudong, Tangkou, Tongkou). 70 (Friberg and Laskowske 1989). West Sulawesi Province, Mamuju regency, Budong-Budong subdistrict, Tongkou village. Budong-Budong river area. *Status:* 8a (Moribund). *Class:* Austronesian, Malayo-Polynesian, South Sulawesi, Seko, Panasuan. *Dialects:* None known. Reportedly similar to Aralle-Tabulahan [atq] and Ulumandak [ulm]. Lexical similarity: 56% with Mamuju [mqx] and Seko Padang [skx], 61% with Seko Tengah [sko], 72% with Panasuan [psn]. *Lg Use:* Some intermarriage and bilingualism with Topoiyo [toy] is pressuring vitality (Wurm 2007). *Other:* Muslim. *Map:* 375:19.

Bugis [bug] (Boegineesche, Boeginezen, Bugi, Buginese, De', Rappang Buginese, Ugi). 5,000,000 in Indonesia (2000 census), increasing. Population total all countries: 5,017,800. L2 users: 500,000 in Indonesia. South Sulawesi Province, Kolaka, Wundulako, Rumbia, and Poleang subdistricts, west coast, eastward through to Bone bay; Polmas and Mamuju districts, coastal swamp areas such as Bulukumba, Luwu, and Polewali. Major towns, enclaves in Sulawesi, Kalimantan, Maluku, Papua, and Sumatra provinces. Also in Malaysia. *Status:* 3 (Wider communication). *Class:* Austronesian, Malayo-Polynesian, South Sulawesi, Bugis. *Dialects:* Barru (Nepo, Pare-Pare, Soppeng Riaja, Tanete, Tompo), Bone (Dua Boccoe, Mare, Palakka), Camba, Luwu (Bua Ponrang, Luwu', Malangke-Ussu, Wara), Pangkep (Pangkajene), Pasangkayu (Ugi Riawa), Sawitto (Pinrang), Sidrap (Alitta, Pinrang Utara, Sidenrang), Sinjai (Bulukumba, Enna, Palattae), Soppeng (Kessi), Wajo. Bone and Soppeng dialects are central. *Lg Use:* Vigorous. Two villages of mainly Muslim Geser [ges] and Bugis also use Fordata [frd]. Also use Indonesian [ind]. Used as L2 by Kodeoha [vko], Kodeoha [vko], Lemolang [ley], Moronene [mqn], Rahambuu [raz], Selayar [sly], Wotu [wtw]. *Lg Dev:* Radio programs. Dictionary. Grammar. Bible: 1900–1997. *Writing:* Buginese script, no longer in use. Latin script. *Other:* Muslim. *Maps:* 374:20, 375:20.

Bukat [bvk]. 400 (Wurm and Hattori 1981). West Kalimantan Province, northeast near Sarawak border, Kapuas river, southeast of Mendalam. 3 areas. *Status:* 6a (Vigorous). *Class:* Austronesian, Malayo-Polynesian, North Borneo, North Sarawakan, Kayan-Kenyah, Kayanic, Muller-Schwaner 'Punan'. *Lg Use:* Vigorous. *Map:* 364:13.

Bukitan [bkn] (Bakatan, Bakitan, Beketan, Mangkettan, Manketa, Pakatan). 570 in Indonesia (2000). Population total all countries: 860. Northwestern East Kalimantan Province, Iwan river, Sarawak border. Also in Malaysia. *Status:* 6b (Threatened). *Class:* Austronesian, Malayo-Polynesian, North Borneo, Melanau-Kajang, Kajang. *Dialects:* Punan Busang, Punan Ukit. *Other:* Christian. *Maps:* 364:15, 365:15.

Buli [bzq]. 2,520 (2000). North Maluku Province, 3 villages. Central Halmahera, Buli bay, north shore. *Status:* 6a (Vigorous). *Class:* Austronesian, Malayo-Polynesian, Central-Eastern Malayo-Polynesian, Eastern Malayo-Polynesian, South Halmahera-West New Guinea, South Halmahera, Southeast. *Dialects:* Buli, Wayamli (Jawanli, Wajamli). *Lg Use:* Used as L2 by Sawai [szw]. *Lg Dev:* Literacy rate in L1: Below 1%. *Other:* Several communities of over 100 dwellings. Muslim, Christian. *Map:* 366.

Bunak [bfn] (Buna', Bunake, Bunaq, Gae', Marae). 21,000 in Indonesia (2010). East Nusa Tenggara Province. Timor island, central interior, near border with Timor Leste. Many in Belu district. *Status:* 6a (Vigorous). *Lg Use:* Also use Tetun [tet]. *Other:* Small groups scattered among other languages. Traditional religion. See main entry on page 98. *Map:* 369.

Bungku [bkz] (Ikinyikiusa, Nahina, Tamboeko, Tambuku, Tobuco). 27,000 (2000 census), increasing. Central Sulawesi Province, Bungku Utara, Bungku Tengah, and Bungku Selatan subdistricts, around 45 villages. Northern Southeast Sulawesi Province, Konawe regency, Asera, Soropia, and Lasolo subdistricts; Tulambatu area. *Status:* 6a (Vigorous). *Class:* Austronesian, Malayo-Polynesian, Celebic, Eastern, Southeastern, Bungku-Tolaki, Eastern, East Coast. *Dialects:* Bungku, Landawe, Routa, Torete (To Rete), Tulambatu, Waia. Lexical similarity: 81% with Torete, Waia, Tulambatu, and Landawe dialects; 38% with Pamona dialects [pmf]; 88% with Landawe dialect; 84% with Waia dialect; 82% with Torete dialect; 74% with Wawonii [wow]; 66% with Taloki [tlk], Kulisusu [vkl], and

Koroni [xkq]; 65% with Moronene [mqn]; 54% with the Mori and Tolaki groups; 82% with the Routa dialect. *Lg Use:* LWC before independence. Also use Indonesian [ind]. *Other:* Muslim. *Map:* 375:21.

Buol [blf] (Bual, Bwool, Bwo'ol, Dia). 96,000 (2000 census). Central Sulawesi Province, Paleleh, Bunobogu, Bokat, Momunu, Biau, and Baolan subdistricts, 68 villages. North coast, near Gorontalo Province border. *Status:* 6b (Threatened). *Class:* Austronesian, Malayo-Polynesian, Philippine, Greater Central Philippine, Gorontalo-Mongondow, Gorontalic. *Dialects:* None known. Lexical similarity: 61% with Totoli [txe]. *Writing:* Latin script. *Other:* Muslim. *Map:* 374:22.

Burate [bti]. 100 (Wurm 2000). Papua Province, Yapen Waropen regency, Waropen Bawah subdistrict, 1 village. Near Wapoga river mouth. *Status:* 7 (Shifting). *Class:* East Geelvink Bay. *Dialects:* None known. Lexical similarity: 69% with Demisa [dei], 75% with Tunggare [trt]. *Lg Use:* Endangered (2000 S. Wurm). *Other:* Seminomadic. Traditional religion, Christian. *Map:* 372:81.

Burmeso [bzu] (Boromeso, Borumesso, Burumeso, Manau, Monao, Monau, Taurap). 250 (Donohue 1998). Papua Province, Sarmi regency, Mamberamo Tengah subdistrict,1 village. Middle Mamberamo river, northeast of Lake Holmes. *Status:* 6a (Vigorous). *Class:* East Bird's Head-Sentani, Burmeso. *Dialects:* None known. Lexical similarity: less than 5% with other languages. *Lg Use:* Vigorous. Not spoken by outsiders. All domains. All ages. Positive attitudes. Many also proficient in Indonesian [ind] and neighboring languages. *Lg Dev:* Dictionary. *Other:* Christian, traditional religion. *Map:* 372:181.

Buru [mhs] (Boeroe, Buruese). 33,000 in Indonesia (1989 SIL). 6,620 Wae Sama, 9,600 Masarete, 14,300 Rana, 500 Fogi, and 2,000 in Ambon. Maluku Province, all of Buru island, except northeast corner, 70 villages. Some on Ambon island, in Jakarta. Also in Netherlands. *Status:* 6a (Vigorous). *Class:* Austronesian, Malayo-Polynesian, Central-Eastern Malayo-Polynesian, Central Maluku, Buru. *Dialects:* Central Buru (Rana, Wae Geren, Wae Kabo), Fogi (Li Emteban, Tomahu), Masarete (South Buru), Wae Sama (Waesama). Li Garan is a special taboo dialect spoken by the Rana people (3,000 to 5,000 users). Ethnic population Fogi dialect: 500, but no remaining speakers. Lexical similarity: 90% between Masarete and Wae Sama dialects, 88% between Masarete and Rana, 80% between Wae Sama and Rana, 68% between Lisela [lcl] and Masarete, 48% between Leliali dialect of Kayeli [kzl] and Masarete, 45% between Kayeli [kzl] and Masarete, 44% between Ambelau [amv] and Masarete, 27%–33% between Buru dialects and Sula [szn]. *Type:* SVO; prepositions; genitives before nouns; predominantly head marking; CV, CVC, V, VC; nontonal. *Lg Use:* Vigorous in most areas. Fogi dialect speakers apparently shifted to Ambonese Malay [abs]. All domains. All ages. Also use Ambonese Malay [abs], Indonesian [ind]. *Lg Dev:* Grammar. Bible portions: 1904–1998. *Writing:* Latin script. *Other:* There are word taboos and complex intermarriage patterns on the island. Exogamous. 10 clans. Traditional religion, Christian, Muslim. *Map:* 367.

Burumakok [aip]. 40 (1994 R. Kroneman). Papua Province, Jayawijaya regency, Kurima subdistrict, Burumakok village. *Status:* 8b (Nearly extinct). *Class:* Trans-New Guinea, Ok-Awyu, Ok, Western. *Map:* 372:223.

Burusu [bqr] (Berusuh, Bulusu). 4,350 (2007 SIL). East Kalimantan Province, Bulungan regency, Sesayap subdistrict, Sekatakbunyi town area, west of Kayan river delta. *Status:* 6a (Vigorous). *Class:* Austronesian, Malayo-Polynesian, North Borneo, Rejang-Sajau. *Map:* 365:16.

Buruwai [asi] (Asianara, Asienara, Karufa, Madidwana, Sabakor, Sebakoor). 1,000 (2000). West Papua Province, Fakfak regency, Kaimana subdistrict, Yarona, Kuna, Esania, Marobia, Guriasa, Tairi, Hia, and Gaka villages. South Bomberai peninsula, Kamrau bay southwest. *Status:* 7 (Shifting). *Class:* Trans-New Guinea, Asmat-Kamoro, Sabakor. *Dialects:* None known. Lexical similarity: 60% with Kamberau [irx]. *Other:* Christian, traditional religion. *Map:* 371:47.

Busami [bsm]. 700 (1993 R. Doriot). Papua Province, Yapen Waropen regency, Yapen Barat and Yapen Selatan subdistricts, south and north coast, Serui island, Kamanap, Masiaroti, and Kaonda villages. *Status:* 6b (Threatened). *Class:* Austronesian, Malayo-Polynesian, Central-Eastern Malayo-Polynesian, Eastern Malayo-Polynesian, South Halmahera-West New Guinea, West New Guinea, Cenderawasih Bay, Yapen, Central-Western. *Dialects:* 3 dialects. Lexical similarity: 71% with Ansus [and], 63% with Serui-Laut [seu]. *Other:* Traditional religion, Christian. *Map:* 372:103.

Busoa [bup] (Bosoa). 2,300 (2000 SIL). Southeast Sulawesi Province, Batauga subdistrict, Busoa and Laompo villages. Southwest coast, Buton island. *Status:* 7 (Shifting). *Class:* Austronesian, Malayo-Polynesian, Celebic, Eastern, Southeastern, Muna-Buton, Nuclear Muna-Buton, Munan. *Dialects:* Lexical similarity: 84% with Kambe-Kambero (probably a dialect of Kaimbulawa [zka]), 70%–79% with Muna dialects, 71% with Muna [mnb], 76% with Lantoi [zka]. *Lg Use:* Also use Wolio [wlo]. *Other:* Muslim. *Map:* 375:23.

Campalagian [cml] (Tallumpanuae, Tasing, Tjampalagian). 30,000 (Strømme 1987). West Sulawesi Province, Polewali Mandar regency. South coast, Mandar bay west of Madjene town. *Status:* 6a (Vigorous). *Class:* Austronesian, Malayo-Polynesian, South Sulawesi, Bugis. *Dialects:* Buku, Campalagian. Lexical similarity: 50%–58% with Mandar [mdr], 50%–62% with Bugis [bug], 55% with Bugis Bone [bug], 62% with Bugis Pangkajene [bug], Bugis Sidrap [bug]. *Lg Use:* Vigorous. *Other:* Muslim. *Map:* 375:24.

Chinese, Hakka [hak]. 640,000 in Indonesia (1982). Widespread. Aceh, Bangka-Belitung, Java (5 provinces), Lampung, Maluku (Ambon island), Papua (Jayapura city), Riau islands (Batam island), North Sulawesi, South Suluwesi, North Sumatra, and South Sumatra. Also in West Kalimantan, Singkawang city; South Kalimantan, Banjarmasin city. *Status:* 7 (Shifting). *Lg Use:* Most remaining speakers are of the grandparent generation. See main entry on page 67.

Chinese, Mandarin [cmn]. 460,000 in Indonesia (1982), increasing. Scattered throughout Indonesia. *Status:* 3 (Wider communication). *Lg Use:* Also use Indonesian [ind]. *Other:* Mandarin is sometimes taught in 'National Plus' schools with English and Indonesian. See main entry on page 67.

Chinese, Min Dong [cdo] (Foochow, Hokchiu, Min Dong). Few speakers. Java and Bali. *Status:* 8a (Moribund). *Dialect:* Xinghua (Hsinghua). *Lg Use:* Most remaining speakers are of the grandparent generation. See main entry on page 68.

Chinese, Min Nan [nan] (Min Nan, Minnan). 700,000 in Indonesia (1982). Hokkien: North Sumatra, Pekanbaru, Padang, Jambi, South Sumatra, Bengkulu, Java, Bali (especially Denpasar and Singaraja), Banjarmasin, Kutai, Sumbawa, Manggarai, Kupang, Makassar, Manado, Central Sulawesi, and Kendari. Teochew: North Sumatra, Riau, South Sumatra, and West Kalimantan provinces (especially Pontianak and Ketapang). *Status:* 7 (Shifting). *Dialects:* Hokkien (Fujian), Teochew (Chaochow, Tiu Chiu). *Lg Use:* Most remaining speakers are of the grandparent generation. See main entry on page 68.

Chinese, Yue [yue] (Cantonese, Yue, Yueh). 180,000 in Indonesia (1982). Jakarta, Makassar, and Manado; East Kalimantan, Central Sumatra. *Status:* 8a (Moribund). *Lg Use:* Most remaining speakers of the grandparent generation. See main entry on page 69.

Cia-Cia [cia] (Boetoneezen, Buton, Butonese, Butung, South Buton, Southern Butung). 79,000 (2005 SIL). Extreme Southeast Sulawesi Province. South Buton island, Pasawajo town area; Binongko island; Batu Atas island to the west. *Status:* 6a (Vigorous). *Class:* Austronesian, Malayo-Polynesian, Celebic, Eastern, Southeastern, Muna-Buton, Nuclear Muna-Buton, Buton, West Buton. *Dialects:* Kaesabu, Masiri, Sampolawa (Mambulu-Laporo), Wabula. Lexical similarity: 93% with Masiri dialect, 74% with Kambe-Kambero dialect of Kaimbulawa [zka], 69% with Busoa [bup], 67% with Lontoi dialect of Kaimbulawa [zka], 66% with Liabuku [lix], 61% with Wolio [wlo], 60% with Muna [mnb]. *Lg Use:* Vigorous. All ages. Also use Wolio [wlo]. *Other:* Language name based on the negator, cia (no). Muslim. *Map:* 375:25.

Citak [txt] (Asmat Darat, Cicak, Kaunak, Tjitak, Tjitjak). 8,000 (1985 M. Stringer). Papua Province, Mappi regency, Citak-Mitak subdistrict, 19 villages. South coast area, west of upper Digul river, northeast of Senggo town. *Status:* 5 (Developing). *Class:* Trans-New Guinea, Asmat-Kamoro, Asmat. *Dialects:* Bubis, Esaun, Komasma, Pirabanak, Senggo, Tiau, Vakam. Reportedly similar to Asmat [cns]. *Lg Use:* Vigorous. Also use Indonesian [ind]. *Lg Dev:* NT: 1995. *Writing:* Latin script. *Other:* Christian, traditional religion. *Map:* 373:235.

Citak, Tamnim [tml] (Asmat Darat, Tamnim). 290 (1993 R. Doriot). Papua Province, Mappi,and Asmat regencies, Tamnim, Epem, Zinak, and Wowi villages. Senggo town area. *Status:* 6a (Vigorous). *Class:* Trans-New Guinea, Asmat-Kamoro, Asmat. *Dialects:* None known. May be linguistically more similar to Asmat, but speakers want to be called Citak, not Asmat. *Lg Use:* Vigorous. *Other:* Christian, traditional religion. *Map:* 373:236.

Col [liw] (Cul, Sindang). 145,000 (2000 census). Interior of South Sumatra, Lubuklinggau area and east of Bengkulu; Muaraklingi area, south, east, and north. *Status:* 6a (Vigorous). *Class:* Austronesian, Malayo-Polynesian, Malayo-Chamic, Malayic, Malay. A member of macrolanguage Malay [msa] (Malaysia). *Dialects:* Beliti, Lembak Delapan, Lubuk Linggau, Sindang Kelingi. *Lg Use:* Vigorous. Home, village. All ages. Positive attitudes. Indonesian [ind] used in civic and educational domains. Urban Palembang, a dialect of Musi [mui], used as a trade language with neighboring groups. *Lg Dev:* Not currently a written language. Literacy valued in Indonesian. Taught in primary schools. Grammar. *Other:* The Lembak Delapan dialect of Col in Bengkulu is not to be confused with the Lembak subdialect of the Belide dialect of Musi [mui]. Muslim. *Map:* 377:11.

Dabe [dbe]. 440 (2005 SIL). Papua Province, Sarmi regency, Pantai Timur subdistrict, Dabe village. Tor river valley north to coast. *Status:* 7 (Shifting). *Class:* Tor-Kwerba, Orya-Tor, Tor. *Lg Use:* Home, with friends, in the gardens. Seldom used by young children. Also use Indonesian [ind], Papuan Malay [pmy]. *Other:* Christian, traditional religion. *Map:* 372:116.

Dai [dij]. 820 (2007 SIL). Maluku Province, Sinairusi, 3 other villages. Babar island group, Dai island; north of Babar. *Status:* 6b (Threatened). *Class:* Austronesian, Malayo-Polynesian, Central-Eastern Malayo-Polynesian, Babar, North. *Dialects:* No dialect variation. Lexical similarity: 72% with Dawera-Daweloor (most similar) [ddw], 71% with Nakarahamto, 49% with Masela-South Babar, 48% with Tepa (Luang). *Lg Use:* Vigorous. Home, gardens, village, ceremonies, religion. Positive attitudes. Also use a regional Malay variety, probably a dialect of Ambonese Malay [abs], in the home, garden, ceremonies; children are taught this variety first but become proficient in the vernacular. Speakers also use Indonesian [ind] primarily in government, Christian religious domains. *Lg Dev:* Literacy rate in L1: Below 1%. *Other:* Christian. *Map:* 368.

Dakka [dkk]. 1,500 (Strømme 1987). West Sulawesi Province, Polewali-Mandar regency, Wonomulyo subdistrict. Northwest of Matakali town. *Status:* 7 (Shifting). *Class:* Austronesian, Malayo-Polynesian, South Sulawesi, Northern, Pitu Ulunna Salu. *Dialects:* None known. Lexical similarity: 72%–77% with Pannei [pnc] and Bambam [ptu]. *Lg Use:* Dakka is spoken in a mixed language area including Mandar [mdr], Bugis [bug] and other immigrants. *Other:* Muslim. *Map:* 375:28.

Damal [uhn] (Amung, Amung Kal, Amungme, Amuy, Enggipiloe, Hamung, Oehoendoeni, Uhunduni). 14,000 (Wurm 2000). Papua Province, Paniai Regency, Ilaga and Beoga subdistricts, central highlands west of Western Dani, east of Ekari, southeast of Kemandoga river source, throughout Puncak Jaya, north and south Carstens mountains. *Status:* 6b (Threatened). *Class:* Trans-New Guinea, Damal. *Dialects:* Amongme, Amung, Damal, Enggipilu. Related to Ekari [ekg], Moni [mnz], and Wolani [wod]. *Type:* Tonal. *Lg Use:* Potentially endangered (2000 S. Wurm). Children are beginning to prefer Indonesian [ind] (Wurm 2007). Used as L2 by Nduga [ndx]. *Lg Dev:* NT: 1988. *Other:* Christian. *Map:* 372:62.

Damar, East [dmr] (South Damar). 2,800 (1990 SIL). Southeast Maluku Province, 6 villages. Northeast of Timor island, east of Roma island; Damar island, east side. *Status:* 6a (Vigorous). *Class:* Austronesian, Malayo-Polynesian, Central-Eastern Malayo-Polynesian, Timor-Babar, Southwest Maluku, East Damar. *Dialects:* None known. Not intelligible of West Damar [drn]. *Lg Dev:* Literacy rate in L1: Below 1%. *Map:* 368.

Damar, West [drn] (North Damar). 800 (1987 SIL). Southeast Maluku Province, 2 villages. Northeast of Timor island, east of Roma island; Damar island, north side. *Status:* 6a (Vigorous). *Class:* Austronesian, Malayo-Polynesian, Central-Eastern Malayo-Polynesian, West Damar. *Dialects:* None known. Not intelligible of East Damar [dmr]. *Lg Dev:* Literacy rate in L1: Below 1%. *Map:* 368.

Dampelas [dms] (Dampelasa, Dian). 2,000 (Wurm 2007), decreasing. Ethnic population: 10,000 (Wurm 2007). Central Sulawesi Province, Dampelas, Sojol, and Balaesang subdistricts, 8 villages. Northwesternmost point, north peninsula, Makassar Strait. *Status:* 7 (Shifting). *Class:* Austronesian, Malayo-Polynesian, Celebic, Tomini-Tolitoli, Tomini, Southern. *Lg Use:* Spoken in 8 villages but in 7 there are strong migrant communities and the everyday public language is Indonesian [ind]. Indonesian used increasingly in families who want children to have higher education (Wurm 2007). *Other:* Dampal dialect is extinct. Muslim. *Map:* 374:29.

Dani, Lower Grand Valley [dni]. 20,000 (1996 SIL). Papua Province. Central highlands, Baliem Grand Valley; lower gorge. *Status:* 5 (Developing). *Class:* Trans-New Guinea, West, Dani, Dani Proper. *Dialects:* Lower Bele, Lower Grand Valley Hitigima (Dani-Kurima, Kurima), Lower Kimbin (Kibin), Upper Bele, Upper Pyramid. *Lg Dev:* NT: 1988–1994. *Writing:* Latin script. *Other:* Traditional religion, Christian. *Map:* 372:69.

Dani, Mid Grand Valley [dnt] (Baliem Valley Dani, Central Grand Valley Dani, Tulem). 50,000 (1990 UBS). Papua

Province. Central highlands, Baliem Grand Valley. *Status:* 5 (Developing). *Class:* Trans-New Guinea, West, Dani, Dani Proper. *Lg Dev:* NT: 1990. *Writing:* Latin script. *Other:* Christian, traditional religion. *Map:* 372:70.

Dani, Upper Grand Valley [dna]. 20,000 (1996). Papua Province. Central highlands, Baliem Grand Valley; upper gorge. *Status:* 5 (Developing). *Class:* Trans-New Guinea, West, Dani, Dani Proper. *Lg Dev:* NT: 1992. *Writing:* Latin script. *Other:* Christian, traditional religion. *Map:* 372:71.

Dani, Western [dnw] (Dani Barat, Ilaga Western Dani, Laany, Lani, Oeringoep, Timorini). 180,000 (1993 census). Papua Province. Central highlands, west of Baliem Grand Valley, east from upper Kemandoga river valley. *Status:* 6a (Vigorous). *Class:* Trans-New Guinea, West, Dani, Dani Proper. *Dialects:* Western Dani of Bokondini, Western Dani of Pyramid. Lexical similarity: 65% with Obokuitai [afz], 60% with Wano [wno]. *Lg Use:* Also use Indonesian [ind]. Used as L2 by Wano [wno]. *Lg Dev:* Literacy rate in L2: 10% semiliterate. NT: 1981. *Other:* Christian, traditional religion. *Map:* 372:74.

Dao [daz] (Maniwo, "X-Ray" *pej.*). 250 (1991 SIL). Papua Province, Paniai regency, Napan subdistrict. West central highlands; east of Cenderawasih bay, along Dao river. *Status:* 6a (Vigorous). *Class:* Trans-New Guinea, West, Wissel Lakes. *Dialects:* None known. Lexical similarity: 75% with Auye [auu]. *Lg Use:* Home, community. Also use Papuan Malay [pmy]. *Other:* Traditional religion. *Map:* 372:78.

Dawera-Daweloor [ddw] (Davelor). 1,270 (2007 SIL). Southern Maluku Province. Twin coral islands northeast of Babar island. Daweloor island, to south, Wiratan, Watuwei, and Nurnyaman villages. Dawera island, to north, Welora, Letmasa, and Ilmarang villages. *Status:* 7 (Shifting). *Class:* Austronesian, Malayo-Polynesian, Central-Eastern Malayo-Polynesian, Babar, North. *Dialects:* Minor dialect differences. *Lg Use:* Shifting to a local Malay variety. Home, gardens, village, ceremonies, religion. Also use a regional Malay variety, probably a dialect of Ambonese Malay [abs], in all domains, except for ceremonies; children are taught the Malay variety. Speakers also use Indonesian [ind] primarily in government, Christian religious domains. *Lg Dev:* Literacy rate in L1: Below 1%. *Other:* Christian. *Map:* 368.

Dela-Oenale [row] (Dela, Delha, Oe Nale, Rote, Rote Barat, Roti, Rotinese, Western Rote). 7,000 (2002 UKAW). East Nusa Tenggara Province. Rote island west coast, Dela and Oe Nale domains. *Status:* 6a (Vigorous). *Class:* Austronesian, Malayo-Polynesian, Central-Eastern Malayo-Polynesian, Timor-Babar, Nuclear Timor, Rote. *Dialects:* Dela (Delha), Oenale (Oe Nale). *Lg Use:* Vigorous. All domains. All ages. Also use Indonesian [ind]. *Lg Dev:* Bible portions. *Other:* Christian, traditional religion. *Map:* 369.

Dem [dem] (Lem, Ndem). 1,000 (1987 SIL). Papua Province. Western highlands; along Rouffaer river headwaters; north of Ilaga town. *Status:* 6a (Vigorous). *Class:* Trans-New Guinea, Dem. *Lg Use:* Used as L2 by Wano [wno]. *Other:* Christian, traditional religion. *Map:* 372:76.

Demisa [dei] (Desawa). 400 (Wurm 2000). Papua Province, Waropen Bawah subdistrict, Desawa, Muyere, and Botawa villages. Inland, northeast Canderawasih bay, southeast of Waren town. *Status:* 6a (Vigorous). *Class:* East Geelvink Bay, Bauzi. *Dialects:* None known. Lexical similarity: 69% with Burate [bti], 64% with Kofei [kpi], 60% with Sauri [srt], 65% with Tunggare [trt], 64% with Woria [wor]. *Lg Use:* Home, religious services. *Other:* Christian, traditional religion. *Map:* 372:89.

Dengka [dnk] (Rote, Rote Barat, Roti, Rotinese, Western Rote). 20,000 (2002 UKAW). East Nusa Tenggara Province. Rote island, northwest coast, from Ba'a town west to Tasilo bay near northwest corner of island. *Status:* 6a (Vigorous). *Class:* Austronesian, Malayo-Polynesian, Central-Eastern Malayo-Polynesian, Timor-Babar, Nuclear Timor, Rote. *Dialects:* Eastern Dengka, Lelain, Western Dengka. Western Dengka dialect has marked intonation; some occurrences of, ngg, in Eastern Dengka dialect become, nd, in Western Dengka. Some vocabulary of Western Dengka is like Dhao [nfa]. Dengka and Dela-Oenale [row] are more divergent from other languages on Rote. *Lg Use:* Vigorous. All domains. All ages. Also use Indonesian [ind]. Used as L2 by Helong [heg]. *Lg Dev:* Bible portions: 2004. *Writing:* Latin script. *Other:* Christian, traditional religion. *Map:* 369.

Dera [kbv] (Dra, Kamberataro, Mangguar). 1,000 in Indonesia (1987 SIL). Population total all countries: 1,690. Northeast Papua Province, 13 villages. South of Jayapura town, near Waris. Also in Papua New Guinea. *Status:* 6b (Threatened). *Class:* Senagi. *Other:* Christian, traditional religion. *Map:* 372:142.

Dhao [nfa] (Dao, Kahore, Ndao, Ndaonese, Ndaundau). 5,000 (1997 A. Ranoh). East Nusa Tenggara Province. Ndao island, off western tip of Rote island. Other settlements scattered on Rote and Timor islands. *Status:* 5 (Developing). *Class:* Austronesian, Malayo-Polynesian, Central-Eastern Malayo-Polynesian, Sumba-Hawu, Hawu-Dhao. *Dialects:* None known. Related to Hawu [hvn]. Complex phonology. *Lg Use:* Used as L2 by Helong [heg]. *Lg Dev:* Dictionary. Bible portions: 2000–2011. *Writing:* Latin script. *Other:* Ethnic autonym: Dhao. Rote neighbors refer to them as 'Ndao'. Christian. *Map:* 369.

Diebroud [tbp] (Bok, Dabra, Taburta, Taria, Taworta, Taworta-Aero). 300 (2006 SIL). Papua Province, Sarmi regency, Mamberamo Hulu subdistrict. Area south of Idenburg river, east of Taiyeve town. *Status:* 6a (Vigorous). *Class:* Lakes Plain, East. *Dialects:* None known. Lexical similarity: 35%–40% with Foau [flh]. *Type:* SOV; postpositions; genitives before noun heads; adjectives after noun heads; tonal. *Lg Use:* Potentially endangered (2000 S. Wurm). Under some pressure from Indonesian [ind] (Wurm 2007). Also use Foau [flh], Indonesian [ind]. Used as L2 by Foau [flh]. *Lg Dev:* Literacy rate in L2: 17% in Indonesian [ind]. *Other:* Used as an inter-language. Christian, traditional religion. *Map:* 372:194.

Dineor [mrx] (Maremgi, Marengge). 55 (2006 SIL), decreasing. Papua Province, Jayapura district. North coast; area near Toarim river mouth. *Status:* 8a (Moribund). *Class:* Tor-Kwerba, Orya-Tor, Tor. *Dialects:* None known. Unintelligible to speakers in neighboring settlements including Bonggo. *Lg Use:* Only eleven families live in Tarawasi-Maremgi village, the only place Dineor (Marenggi) language is spoken. Home. Also use Indonesian [ind], Papuan Malay [pmy]. *Other:* Christian, traditional religion. *Map:* 372:127.

Diuwe [diy]. 100 (1999 SIL). Papua Province. Southeast of Wamena city; east of Catalina river. *Status:* 6b (Threatened). *Class:* Trans-New Guinea, Asmat-Kamoro, Diuwe. *Maps:* 372:218, 373:218.

Dobel [kvo] (Doibel, Kobroor, Kobro'or, Sersifar Tannin). 5,680 (2011 SIL), increasing. L2 users: Chinese merchants and other outsiders who live in Dobel villages and residents of Lorang use it as L2. Southeast Maluku Province, Aru islands, entire east coast of Kobror island, 1 village in southeast Wokam island, 4 villages eastern half of Barakai strait (Kobror and Koba islands), 2 villages in central Kobror island. 18 villages; many in Dobo; some in Ambon. *Status:* 5 (Developing). *Class:* Austronesian, Malayo-Polynesian, Central-Eastern Malayo-Polynesian, Aru. *Dialects:* Northern Dobel, Southeast Dobel, Straits

Dobel. At least 3 dialects. Lexical similarity: 78%–86% with Koba [kpd]. *Type:* SVO; prepositions; no adjectives; noun head initial; active verbs and stative verbs; complex reduplication system; 14 consonant phonemes and 5 vowel phonemes; CVC, CV, with CiCiVC, CiCiV patterns occurring only as stressed syllable of a phonological word, when that word is reduplicated; not tonal. *Lg Use:* Vigorous. Some Chinese merchants who speak Dobo Malay dialect of Ambonese Malay [abs] and older Hokkien [nan] learn Dobel. All domains. All ages. Positive attitudes. Also use Dobo Malay, a dialect of Ambonese Malay [abs]. Nearly all school-age speakers of Dobel are bilingual in Ambonese Malay. Also use Indonesian [ind], Manombai [woo]. Used as L2 by Lorang [lrn], Manombai [woo]. *Lg Dev:* Literacy rate in L1: 60%. Bible portions: 1991–2009. *Writing:* Latin script. *Other:* Christian, Muslim. *Map:* 368.

Dondo [dok]. 13,000 (Himmelmann 2001). Central Sulawesi Province. Tolitoli and Buol regencies, Tolitoli Utara, Baolan, Dondo, Galang, and Dampal Utara subdistricts, at least 25 villages. North peninsula, inland from Dondo bay, east and south coasts. *Status:* 6b (Threatened). *Class:* Austronesian, Malayo-Polynesian, Celebic, Tomini-Tolitoli, Tomini, Northern. *Lg Use:* Children receive their education in Indonesian [ind] (Wurm 2007). *Other:* Most of the hill Dondo interact socially with the Dondo coastal population which reinforces the use of Dondo in a variety of functions. Muslim. *Map:* 374:30.

Doutai [tds] (Taori, Taori-So, Tolitai). 70 (Wurm 2000). Ethnic population: 340 (1993 R. Doriot). Papua Province, Toli-Dou village. Area west and south of Taiyeve town. *Status:* 7 (Shifting). *Class:* Lakes Plain, Tariku, East. *Lg Use:* Endangered (2000 S. Wurm). *Other:* Christian, traditional religion. *Map:* 372:191.

Duano [dup] (Desin Dolak, Desin Duano, Duano', Orang Kuala). 15,000 in Indonesia (2006 SIL). Population total all countries: 15,600. Ethnic population: Total ethnic population all countries: 19,000 (2006 E. Seidlitz). Sumatra, Riau Province, west Riau archipelago and Riau Daratan east coast. Also in Malaysia. *Status:* 6a (Vigorous). *Class:* Austronesian, Malayo-Polynesian, Malayo-Chamic, Malayic, Malay. A member of macrolanguage Malay [msa] (Malaysia). *Lg Use:* Vigorous. *Other:* Muslim. *Map:* 377:12.

Duri [mvp] (Masenrempulu, Massenrempulu). 127,000 (2000 census). South Sulawesi Province, north Enrekang regency. Northwest of Enrekang town, west of Sadang river. Also, Makassar city; other communities in province. *Status:* 5 (Developing). *Class:* Austronesian, Malayo-Polynesian, South Sulawesi, Northern, Masenrempulu. *Dialects:* Baraka, Benteng Alla, Cakke-Kalosi. *Type:* VSO; split ergative. *Lg Use:* Vigorous. Prestige language of the Masenrempulu group. *Lg Dev:* NT: 2005. *Writing:* Latin script. *Other:* Muslim. *Map:* 375:31.

Duriankere [dbn] (Duriankari, Esaro, Sailen). 30 (Wurm 2000). Ethnic population: 60. West Papua Province. One island between Salawati island and the west end of Bird's Head. *Status:* 8b (Nearly extinct). *Class:* Trans-New Guinea, South Bird's Head, Inanwatan. *Lg Use:* Seriously endangered (2000 S. Wurm). Elderly speakers. *Other:* Christian, traditional religion. *Map:* 371:10.

Dusner [dsn] (Dusnir). No known L1 speakers. There were 6 elderly speakers in 1978 (Wurm 2007). West Papua Province, Manokwari district. *Status:* 9 (Dormant). *Class:* Austronesian, Malayo-Polynesian, Central-Eastern Malayo-Polynesian, Eastern Malayo-Polynesian, South Halmahera-West New Guinea, West New Guinea, Cenderawasih Bay, Biakic. *Lg Use:* Shifted to Wandamen [wad]. *Other:* Traditional religion, Christian.

Dusun Deyah [dun] (Deah, Dejah). 20,000 (Wurm and Hattori 1981). South Kalimantan Province. Tabalong river northeast of Bongkang town. *Status:* 6a (Vigorous). *Class:* Austronesian, Malayo-Polynesian, Greater Barito, East, Central-South, Central. *Dialects:* None known. Lexical similarity: 53% with Lawangan [lbx], 52% with Tawoyan [twy]. *Lg Use:* Also use Bakumpai [bkr]. *Map:* 365:18.

Dusun Malang [duq]. 4,500 (2003). 2,000 Bayan. Central Kalimantan Province, North Barito regency. One area west of Muarainu town; a second, northeast of Muarateweh town. *Status:* 6b (Threatened). *Class:* Austronesian, Malayo-Polynesian, Greater Barito, East, Central-South, South. *Dialects:* Bayan, Dusun Malang. Lexical similarity: 90% with the 2 dialects. *Maps:* 364:19, 365:19.

Dusun Witu [duw]. 5,000 (2003). Central Kalimantan Province, South Barito regency. Near Pendang and Buntokecil towns; south of Muarateweh town. *Status:* 6b (Threatened). *Class:* Austronesian, Malayo-Polynesian, Greater Barito, East, Central-South, South. *Dialects:* Dusun Pepas, Dusun Witu. Lexical similarity: 75% with Ma'anyan [mhy], 73% with Paku [pku]. *Lg Use:* Also use Bakumpai [bkr]. *Map:* 365:20.

Duvle [duv] (Duvde, Duve, Duvele, Duvre, Wiri). 930 (2000). Papua Province. Area south of Van Daalen river. Eastern dialect along Dagai river, western dialect along Fedide and Wedi rivers. *Status:* 6a (Vigorous). *Class:* Lakes Plain, Tariku, Duvle. *Dialects:* Eastern Duvle, Western Duvle. Few dialect differences. *Lg Use:* Vigorous. Also use Wano [wno]. Used as L2 by Iau [tmu]. *Other:* Christian, traditional religion. *Map:* 372:190.

Edopi [dbf] (Dosobou, Dou, Doufou, Elopi, Foi, Iau, Turu, Urundi, Ururi, Yau). 1,500 (2012 SIL). Papua Province, Yapen Waopen district. Area at Tariku and Kliki rivers confluence. *Status:* 5 (Developing). *Class:* Lakes Plain, Tariku, Central. *Type:* SOV; tonal. *Lg Use:* Also use Indonesian [ind]. Used as L2 by Kirikiri [kiy]. *Lg Dev:* Literacy rate in L1: Below 5%. Literacy rate in L2: Below 5%. Bible portions: 1997–2003. *Writing:* Latin script. *Other:* Christian, traditional religion. *Map:* 372:188.

Eipomek [eip] (Eipo, T-Valley). 3,000 (1987 SIL). Papua Province. Eastern highlands area, Eipo river, east of Naltya town. *Status:* 6a (Vigorous). *Class:* Trans-New Guinea, Mek, Eastern. *Dialects:* None known. Lexical similarity: 75% with Una [mtg]. *Other:* Christian, traditional religion. *Map:* 372:209.

Ekari [ekg] (Ekagi, Kapauku, Me Mana, Mee Mana, Tapiro). 100,000 (1985 M. Doble). Papua Province, Paniai district. West central highlands, inland; Lake Paniai area, south-southwest into West Papua Province. *Status:* 5 (Developing). *Class:* Trans-New Guinea, West, Wissel Lakes. *Dialects:* Mapiya-Kegata, Mee, Simori, Yabi (Jabi). Reportedly most similar to Wolani [wod]. Slight dialect difference with Mapiya-Kegata. *Lg Use:* Also use Indonesian [ind]. *Lg Dev:* NT: 1963–1985. *Writing:* Latin script. *Other:* Ethnonym: Kapauku by southern neighbors. Christian. *Maps:* 371:59, 372:59.

Elseng [mrf] (Djanggu, Janggu, "Morwap" *pej.*, Sawa, Tabu). 300 (1991 SIL). Papua Province, Jayapura and Keerom regencies, Arso, Abepura, Kemtuk Gresi, and Senggi subdistricts. South of Jayapura city; Lake Sentani area, south, southwest. *Status:* 6b (Threatened). *Class:* Language isolate. *Dialects:* None known. Not closely related to any other language. *Lg Use:* Vigorous. Religious services. Minimal ability in Indonesian [ind]. *Other:* Almost no outside influence. 'Morwap' is vigorously rejected as a language name by speakers and government officials. Christian, traditional religion. *Map:* 372:156.

Embaloh [emb] (Malo, Maloh, Matoh, Mbaloh, Memaloh, Palin, Pari, Sangau, Sanggau). 10,000 (1991 NTM). West Kalimantan Province, Kapuas Hulu regency. Upper

Kapuas river, Embaloh, Leboyan, Lauh, Palin, Nyabau, Mandai, and Kalis tributaries. *Status:* 5 (Developing). *Class:* Austronesian, Malayo-Polynesian, South Sulawesi, Bugis, Tamanic. *Dialect:* Kalis (Kalis Dayak, Kalis Maloh). Kalis may be a separate language. *Lg Dev:* NT: 1998. *Writing:* Latin script. *Other:* Complex mix of ethnic groups: Taman of upper Kapuas River, Suai, Taman Mendalem, Taman Sibau, Palin, Lauk, Leboyan, Kalis Dayak. Traditional religion, Christian. *Map:* 364:21.

Emem [enr] (Emumu, Imimkal, Kiamerop). 2,000 (2005 SIL). Some elderly monolinguals. Papua Province. Border area south of Jayapura city. *Status:* 6b (Threatened). *Class:* Pauwasi, Eastern. *Dialects:* None known. Lexical similarity: 25% with Yafi [wfg]. *Lg Use:* Home, community. Positive attitudes. Also use Indonesian [ind], Papuan Malay [pmy]. *Other:* Christian, traditional religion. *Map:* 372:144.

Emplawas [emw]. 250 (2007 SIL). Southern Maluku Province, Emplawas village. Babar island, southern tip, then northwest. *Status:* 8b (Nearly extinct). *Class:* Austronesian, Malayo-Polynesian, Central-Eastern Malayo-Polynesian, Babar, South, Southwest Babar. *Lg Use:* Only the elders. Also use Ambonese Malay [abs], Indonesian [ind]. Almost completely shifted. *Lg Dev:* Literacy rate in L1: Below 1%. *Other:* Christian. *Map:* 368.

Ende [end] (Endeh). 110,000 (2009 census). East Nusa Tenggara Province. South central Flores island. *Status:* 6a (Vigorous). *Class:* Austronesian, Malayo-Polynesian, Central-Eastern Malayo-Polynesian, Bima-Lembata. *Dialects:* Ende (Djau, Endeh, Ja'o), Nga'o (Ngao, West Ende). Some consider Li'o [ljl] to be a dialect of Ende. *Lg Dev:* Bible portions: 2009. *Other:* Christian. *Map:* 370.

Enggano [eno] (Engganese). 1,500 (2000 census), decreasing. Sumatra, Bengkulu Province. Enggano island, southwest of mainland; 4 smaller nearby islands. *Status:* 6b (Threatened). *Class:* Unclassified. *Dialects:* None known. Not closely related to other languages. *Lg Use:* Endangered (2000 S. Wurm). Stable presently; threatened long term if emigration and marriage with other language communities continues. Home, village, market, ceremonies. All ages. Positive attitudes. Indonesian [ind] used in civic, religious and educational areas. *Lg Dev:* Poetry. Dictionary. *Other:* Not conclusively established as an Austronesian language, rather than an isolate with Austronesian loans. Christian, Muslim. *Map:* 377:13.

Enrekang [ptt] (Endekan, Endekan Timur). 50,000 (1986 SIL). South Sulawesi Province, Enrekang and Pinrang regencies. Enrekang town area, west toward head of Mandar bay. *Status:* 6a (Vigorous). *Class:* Austronesian, Malayo-Polynesian, South Sulawesi, Northern, Masenrempulu. *Dialects:* Enrekang, Pattinjo (Letta-Batulappa-Kassa), Ranga. *Other:* Muslim. *Map:* 375:32.

Eritai [ert] (Aliki, Babiruwa, Babrua, Babruwa, Baburiwa, Barua, Editode Edai, Erai, Eri, Haya). 530 (2000). Papua Province, Sarmi regency, Mamberamo Tengah and Mamberamo Hulu subdistricts, Erai, Kustera, and Haya villages. Northwest of confluence of Mamberamo and Rouffaer rivers; area in low mountains, around Kustera airstrip. *Status:* 6a (Vigorous). *Class:* Lakes Plain, Tariku, East. *Dialects:* The dialect in Obogwi village is reportedly similar but not the same. Lexical similarity: 76% with Obokuitai [afz], 86% with Sikaritai [tty]. *Type:* SOV; tonal. *Lg Use:* Vigorous. Also use Bauzi [bvz]. Used as L2 by Bauzi [bvz]. *Lg Dev:* Literacy rate in L1: Below 10%. *Other:* Christian, traditional religion. *Map:* 372:182.

Erokwanas [erw]. 200 (Wurm 2000). Probably fewer than 200 (Wurm 2007). West Papua Province. Bomberai peninsula. *Status:* 8a (Moribund). *Class:* Austronesian, Malayo-Polynesian, Central-Eastern Malayo-Polynesian, Eastern Malayo-Polynesian, South Halmahera-West New Guinea, West New Guinea, Bomberai. *Dialect:* Darembang. Subgroup Darembang may better be considered a separate language. *Lg Use:* Seriously endangered (2000 S. Wurm). Children tend not to use it (Wurm 2007). *Other:* Traditional religion, Christian. *Map:* 371:38.

Fayu [fau] (Sehudate). 1,400 (2012 SIL). Papua Province. Kliki river area, west of its juncture with Tariku river; northwest towards Cenderawasik bay. *Status:* 6a (Vigorous). *Class:* Lakes Plain, Tariku, West. *Lg Use:* Potentially endangered (2000 S. Wurm). Children tend to prefer Indonesian [ind] (Wurm 2007). Used as L2 by Kirikiri [kiy], Tause [tad]. *Other:* 4 nomadic groups. Traditional religion, Christian. *Map:* 372:187.

Fedan [pdn] (Fandanus, Podena). 280 (2005 SIL). Papua Province, Sarmi regency, Bonggo subdistrict, coastal area and island off north coast of Biri river area. *Status:* 8a (Moribund). *Class:* Austronesian, Malayo-Polynesian, Central-Eastern Malayo-Polynesian, Eastern Malayo-Polynesian, Oceanic, Western Oceanic, North New Guinea, Sarmi-Jayapura Bay, Sarmi. *Dialects:* None known. Reportedly similar to Anus [auq]. *Lg Use:* Not used by children. Also use Anus [auq], Indonesian [ind], Papuan Malay [pmy]. *Map:* 372:123.

Foau [flh] (Abawiri, Doa). 350 (2010 SIL), increasing. Papua Province, Mamberamo Raya and Jayapura regencies, Kecamatan subdistrict, 1 village. Mamberamo basin region, bordering on the southwestern edge of the Foja Mountains; on the Dijai river, north of Mamberamo river. *Status:* 6b (Threatened). *Class:* Lakes Plain, East. *Dialects:* None known. Lexical similarity: 35%–49% with Diebroud [tbp]. *Lg Use:* The people want to retain and strengthen their own identity. Home, community, most domains. All ages. Positive attitudes. Some over age 35 understand Diebroud [tbp]. Also use Indonesian [ind] in school. Used as L2 by Abinomn [bsa], Airoran [air], Diebroud [tbp]. *Lg Dev:* Literacy rate in L2: 20% in Indonesian [ind]. *Other:* Ethnic name is Fuau; Abawiri most accepted language name. Christian, traditional religion. *Map:* 372:198.

Fordata [frd] (Larat, Vai Fordata, Vai Sera-Larat-Fordata, Vai Tnebar, Vaidida). 50,000 (Marshall 2000). 25,000 in the language area and 25,000 elsewhere (Marshall 2000). Decreasing use in mixed language towns. 500 monolinguals. Southeast Maluku Province, 30 villages. North Tanimbar islands, Fordata, Larat, and Molu-Maru groups; northwest, Yamdena island west coast. Seira island. Also Jakarta, other cities. *Status:* 6b (Threatened). *Class:* Austronesian, Malayo-Polynesian, Central-Eastern Malayo-Polynesian, Southeast Maluku, Kei-Tanimbar, Kei-Fordata. *Dialects:* Fordata-Larat I, Fordata-Larat II, Molo (Molo-Maru), Sera (Seira). Sera is most divergent dialect. Lexical similarity: 68% with Kei [kei]. *Lg Use:* Vigorous. Some villages have few young people being spoken to in Fordata. All domains, though church context limited. Positive attitudes. 99% also use Ambonese Malay [abs]. Also use Indonesian [ind]. Used as L2 by Bugis [bug], Geser-Gorom [ges]. *Lg Dev:* Literacy rate in L1: 5%–10%. Literacy rate in L2: 50%–75%. 2,500 read; 1,500 can write. Taught in primary schools, as a subject. Taught in secondary schools, as a subject. Poetry. Dictionary. Grammar. Bible portions: 1996–2004. *Writing:* Latin script. *Other:* Primary schools in nearly every village, secondary schools for every 3 or 4 villages. Christian, Muslim. *Map:* 368.

Galela [gbi]. 79,000 (1990 SIL). 41,000 Kadai, 10,000 Kadina, 24,000 Morotai, and 4,000 Sopi. North Maluku Province. Halmahera island; Galela bay, north to northern tip of island, scattered communities, southwest coast. Morotai island except southeast quadrant. Gunage and Moari islands near Kayoa island. Bacan, Obi, Kasiratua, Mandioli, and Labutia islands, coastal areas. *Status:* 5 (Developing). *Class:* West Papuan, North Halmahera, Galela-Loloda. *Dialects:* Kadai, Kadina, Morotai, Sopi. Laba [lau] may be a dialect. 65% intelligibility of Loloda [loa], Loloda 85% of Galela. *Lg Use:* Vigorous. Also use Indonesian [ind]. *Lg Dev:* Literacy rate in L1: 5%–10%. Literacy rate in L2: 50%–75%. Dictionary. Grammar. NT: 2002. *Writing:* Latin script. *Other:* Christian, Muslim. *Map:* 366.

Galolen [gal] (Galoleng, Iliwaki, Ilmedu, Ilwaki, Lir Talo). 680 in Indonesia (1990 SIL). Southwestern Maluku Province, Wetar island, Iliwaki village. *Status:* 6b (Threatened). *Dialects:* Hiay, Ilputih, Ilwaki (Iliwaki). *Lg Use:* Also use Ambonese Malay [abs]. Used as L2 by Aputai [apx]. *Lg Dev:* Literacy rate in L1: Below 1%. *Other:* Immigrants from Kisar learned Galolen. Christian. See main entry on page 98. *Map:* 369.

Gamkonora [gak]. 1,500 (Voorhoeve and Visser 1987). North Maluku Province, a few coastal villages. North Halmahera island, northwest coast, from Baru town inland. *Status:* 6a (Vigorous). *Class:* West Papuan, North Halmahera, Sahu. *Dialects:* None known. Lexical similarity: 81% with Waioli [wli]. *Lg Dev:* Literacy rate in L1: Below 1%. *Other:* Muslim, Christian. *Map:* 366.

Gane [gzn] (Gani, Giman). 2,900 (1982 D. Teljeur). North Maluku Province. Halmahera island, southernmost peninsula. *Status:* 6a (Vigorous). *Class:* Austronesian, Malayo-Polynesian, Central-Eastern Malayo-Polynesian, Eastern Malayo-Polynesian, South Halmahera-West New Guinea, South Halmahera, East Makian-Gane. *Dialects:* Reportedly similar to Kayoa, a dialect of East Makian [mky]. *Lg Use:* Positive attitudes. Used as L2 by Sawai [szw]. *Lg Dev:* Literacy rate in L1: Below 1%. *Other:* Muslim. *Map:* 366.

Gayo [gay] (Gajo). 300,000 (2000 census). Sumatra, Aceh Province, Central Aceh, East Aceh, Gayo Lues, and Southeast Aceh regencies. North Sumatra highland region near Mount Sembuang. *Status:* 6b (Threatened). *Class:* Austronesian, Malayo-Polynesian, Northwest Sumatra-Barrier Islands. *Dialects:* Deret, Lues, Lut, Serbejadi-Lukup. Not closely related to other languages. Some Gayo people consider Alas [btz] a distant Gayo dialect. *Lg Use:* Home, neighborhood, clinic, market, ceremonies, village meetings. All ages. Positive attitudes. *Lg Dev:* Taught in primary schools 2 hours a week called local instruction. Poetry. Newspapers. Dictionary. Grammar. *Other:* Muslim, traditional religion. *Map:* 376:14.

Gebe [gei] (Gebi). 2,650 (2000). North Maluku Province, 4 villages. Papua Province, Halmahera island; Gebe, Yoi'umiyal, and Gag islands between Halmahera's southeastern peninsula and Waigeo island. *Status:* 6b (Threatened). *Class:* Austronesian, Malayo-Polynesian, Central-Eastern Malayo-Polynesian, Eastern Malayo-Polynesian, South Halmahera-West New Guinea, West New Guinea, Cenderawasih Bay, Raja Ampat. *Dialect:* Umera. Lexical similarity: 44% with Patani [ptn]. *Lg Use:* Mining operations started in the area which led to more schooling of children and increasing use of Indonesian [ind] (Wurm 2007). All domains. Also use Indonesian [ind]. *Lg Dev:* Literacy rate in L1: Below 1%. *Other:* A school in each village. Muslim. *Map:* 366.

Geser-Gorom [ges] (Gesa, Geser, Goram, Goran, Gorom, Gorong, Seram, Seran, Seran Laut). 36,500 (1989 SIL). Maluku Province. Seram island, southeast tip, nearby Gorom islands. *Status:* 6a (Vigorous). *Class:* Austronesian, Malayo-Polynesian, Central-Eastern Malayo-Polynesian, Central Maluku, East, Banda-Geser, Geser-Gorom. *Dialects:* Goram Laut, Kelimuri, Mina Mina Gorong. Lexical similarity: 73%–93% among dialects, 51%–61% with Watubela [wah]. *Lg Use:* Two villages of mainly Muslim Geser and Bugis [bug] also use Fordata [frd]. Also use Indonesian [ind]. Used as L2 by Bati [bvt], Masiwang [bnf], Watubela [wah]. *Lg Dev:* Literacy rate in L1: Below 1%. Literacy rate in L2: 50%–75%. *Writing:* Latin script. *Other:* Muslim. *Map:* 367.

Gorap [goq]. 1,000 (1992 SIL). North Maluku Province, Morotai island, Pilowo and Waringin villages; Central Halmahera, Bobane and Igo villages. *Status:* 7 (Shifting). *Class:* Austronesian, Malayo-Polynesian, Unclassified. *Dialects:* None known. A mixed language, with Ternate [tft] and Malay [max] words and different word order from other languages of north Halmahera or Austronesian languages. Lexical similarity: 85% with Indonesian [ind], but comprehension is limited. *Lg Use:* Under strong pressure from the languages from which the majority of its vocabulary seems to have originated (Wurm 2007). All domains. *Other:* Consider Sulawesi their ancestral homeland. *Map:* 366.

Gorontalo [gor] (Gorongtalo, Guarantala, Gunongtello, Holontalo, Hulontalo). 1,000,000 (2000 census). Sulawesi, Gorontalo Province, north peninsula. *Status:* 6b (Threatened). *Class:* Austronesian, Malayo-Polynesian, Philippine, Greater Central Philippine, Gorontalo-Mongondow, Gorontalic. *Dialects:* East Gorontalo, Gorontalo Kota, Limboto (Limbotto), Tilamuta, West Gorontalo (Kwandang). *Lg Use:* Noted shift to Indonesian [ind] in youth. *Lg Dev:* NT: 2000. *Writing:* Latin script. *Other:* Muslim. *Map:* 374:33.

Gresi [grs] (Geresi, Glesi, Gresik, Klesi). 2,500 (1987 SIL). Papua Province, Hawa, Bring, Tabangkwari, Yansu, Ibub, Sunna, and Klaysu villages. West of Lake Sentani, southeast of Genyem town. *Status:* 8a (Moribund). *Class:* Nimboran. *Dialects:* None known. Lexical similarity: 80% with Kemtuik [kmt]. *Lg Use:* Also use Indonesian [ind]. *Other:* Traditional religion, Christian. *Map:* 372:159.

Haji [hji] (Aji). 17,500 (2000 census). Very few monolinguals. South Sumatra Province, Ogan Komering Ulu Selatan regency. *Status:* 6b (Threatened). *Class:* Austronesian, Malayo-Polynesian, Malayo-Chamic, Malayic, Malay. A member of macrolanguage Malay [msa] (Malaysia). *Dialects:* None known. Genetically Malay with approximately one-third Lampung vocabulary. *Lg Use:* Vigorous. Domestic and village life. All ages. Positive attitudes. Indonesian [ind] used in education, religious, and civic domains. *Lg Dev:* Currently not a written language. Grammar. *Other:* Muslim (Sunni). *Map:* 377:15.

Hamap [hmu]. 900. East Nusa Tenggara Province. Alor island, east Kalabahi bay, around Moru town, 2 villages. Area surrounds Kui [kvd] language area. *Status:* 6b (Threatened). *Class:* Trans-New Guinea, West, Timor-Alor-Pantar, Alor-Pantar, Alor. *Dialects:* None known. Said to be intelligible with Adang [adn], but Adang speakers live on Bird's Head area of Alor, while Hamap speakers live geographically separated from Adang speakers, across the bay. Structural and lexical differences with Adang. *Type:* Verb final, contrast between close and open, e; vowel-initial and glottal-initial words. *Other:* Separate sociopolitical history from Adang. Christian. *Map:* 370.

Haruku [hrk]. 18,200 (1989 SIL). Maluku Province. Haruku island, including Lease islands; between Ambon and Seram islands. *Status:* 8a (Moribund). *Class:* Austronesian, Malayo-Polynesian, Central-Eastern Malayo-Polynesian, Central Maluku, East, Seram, Nunusaku, Piru Bay. *Dialects:* Hulaliu, Kabauw, Kailolo, Pelauw, Rohomoni. Each village uses a separate dialect. Lexical similarity: 81%–92% among dialects, 74%–76% with Tulehu [tlu], 67%–71% with Saparua [spr]. *Lg Use:* Also use Ambonese Malay [abs]. *Lg Dev:* Literacy rate in L1: Below 1%. *Other:*

Muslim, Christian. *Map:* 367.

Hatam [had] (Adihup, Atam, Borai, Hattam, Mansim, Miriei, Moi, Tinam, Uran). 16,000 (1993 The Evangelical Alliance Mission). West Papua Province, Manokwari regency. *Status:* 5 (Developing). *Class:* Language isolate. *Dialects:* Adihup, Miriei, Moi (Moire), Tinam, Uran. *Lg Dev:* Bible: 1999. *Writing:* Latin script. *Other:* Christian, traditional religion. *Map:* 371:21.

Hawu [hvn] (Havunese, Sabu, Savu, Savunese, Sawu, Sawunese). 110,000 (1997). About 30,000 outside Sabu Island. East Nusa Tenggara Province. Sawu and Raijua islands; 3 enclaves, 2 on Sumba island, Waingapu and Melolo areas; south central Flores island, Ende area. Others in Kupang city, Timor island. *Status:* 5 (Developing). *Class:* Austronesian, Malayo-Polynesian, Central-Eastern Malayo-Polynesian, Sumba-Hawu, Hawu-Dhao. *Dialects:* Liae, Mesara (Mehara), Raijua (Raidjua), Seba (Heba), Timu (Dimu). *Type:* Complex phonetics with implosives, glottal, long and short vowels, long and short consonants. *Lg Use:* Used as L2 by Helong [heg]. *Lg Dev:* Dictionary. Grammar. NT: 2000. *Writing:* Latin script. *Other:* Christian, traditional religion. *Map:* 369.

Helong [heg] (Helon, Kupang, Semau). 14,000 (Grimes et al. 1997). Ethnic population: 15,000. East Nusa Tenggara Province. Semau island off of Timor island, western tip of Timor, and Kupang city. Interspersed with Amarasi [aaz] and other languages. *Status:* 5 (Developing). *Class:* Austronesian, Malayo-Polynesian, Central-Eastern Malayo-Polynesian, Timor-Babar, Nuclear Timor. *Dialects:* Funai (Land Helong), Helong Darat (Bolok), Helong Pulau (Island Helong, Semau). *Type:* Unlike many surrounding languages, does not inflect V-initial verb roots for person or number; has long and short vowels; glottal stop, metathesis. *Lg Use:* Helong Darat shifting to Kupang Malay [mkn]. Funai dialect endangered through intermarriage and urban contact. Home, community, traditional ceremonies. Also use Dengka [dnk], Dhao [nfa], Hawu [hvn], Indonesian [ind], Kupang Malay [mkn], Uab Meto [aoz]. *Lg Dev:* Dictionary. NT: 2011. *Writing:* Latin script. *Other:* Christian, traditional religion. *Map:* 369.

Hitu [htu]. 16,000 (1987 SIL). Maluku Province, Wakal, Hitu, Mamala, Morela, and Hila villages. Northeast Ambon island, Piru Sea coast, Hitu peninsula. *Status:* 6b (Threatened). *Class:* Austronesian, Malayo-Polynesian, Central-Eastern Malayo-Polynesian, Central Maluku, East, Seram, Nunusaku, Piru Bay, East, Seram Straits, Ambon. *Dialects:* Hila, Hitu, Mamala, Morela, Wakal. Lexical similarity: 67%–82% with Seit-Kaitetu [hik], 74%–82% with Tulehu [tlu]. *Lg Use:* Moderate to vigorous. *Lg Dev:* Literacy rate in L1: Below 1%. *Other:* Muslim, Christian. *Map:* 367.

Hoti [hti]. No known L1 speakers (Wurm 2007). 10 elderly speakers in 1987, but now probably extinct (Wurm 2007). Maluku Province. East Seram island. *Status:* 10 (Extinct). *Class:* Austronesian, Malayo-Polynesian, Central-Eastern Malayo-Polynesian, Central Maluku, East, Seram, East Seram.

Hovongan [hov] (Punan Bungan). 1,000 (1991 NTM). West Kalimantan Province, Kapuas Hulu regency. Far northeast corner; near Sarawak, East Kalimantan province borders. *Status:* 6a (Vigorous). *Class:* Austronesian, Malayo-Polynesian, North Borneo, North Sarawakan, Kayan-Kenyah, Kayanic, Muller-Schwaner 'Punan'. *Dialects:* Hovongan, Penyavung, Semukung Uheng. Lexical similarity: 69% with Kereho [xke], 67% with Aoheng [pni]. *Lg Dev:* Bible portions. *Other:* Traditional religion, Christian. *Map:* 364:22.

Huaulu [hud] (Alakamat, Bahasa Asli). 300 (1987 SIL). Maluku Province, 10 villages. North Seram island, Salemen bay, south end. *Status:* 6b (Threatened). *Class:* Austronesian, Malayo-Polynesian, Central-Eastern Malayo-Polynesian, Central Maluku, East, Seram, Manusela-Seti. *Dialects:* Lexical similarity: 64%–72% with Manusela [wha] dialects. *Other:* Culturally distinct from Manusela. Traditional religion. *Map:* 367.

Hukumina [huw] (Bambaa). No known L1 speakers. Central Maluku, northwest Buru island, Hukumina, Palumata, and Tomahu districts. *Status:* 10 (Extinct). *Class:* Austronesian, Malayo-Polynesian, Central-Eastern Malayo-Polynesian, Hukumina.

Hulung [huk]. No known L1 speakers (Wurm 2007). Spoken by fewer than 10 speakers in 1991, but now probably extinct (Wurm 2007). Central Maluku, west Seram, Hulung village, Sauweli hamlet. *Status:* 10 (Extinct). *Class:* Austronesian, Malayo-Polynesian, Central-Eastern Malayo-Polynesian, Central Maluku, East, Seram, Nunusaku, Three Rivers, Amalumute, Northwest Seram, Hulung. *Dialects:* None known. Lexical similarity: 67% with Lisabata-Nuniali [lcs], 66% with Naka'ela [nae], 63% with Alune [alp], 59% with Wemale [weo].

Hupla [hap] (Soba). 3,000 (1982 WT). Papua Province. Central highlands area, Baliem gorge, east. *Status:* 5 (Developing). *Class:* Trans-New Guinea, West, Dani, Dani Proper. *Dialects:* None known. Reportedly similar to Lower Grand Valley Dani [dni]. *Lg Dev:* NT: 1994. *Writing:* Latin script. *Other:* Christian, traditional religion. *Map:* 372:68.

Iau [tmu] (Foi, Iaw, Turu, Urundi, Ururi, Yau). 600 (2000 J. Bateman), increasing. 500 monolinguals. Ethnic population: 600. Papua Province. Puncak Jaya regency, Barere, Fawi, and Taiyai villages. Area between Rouffaer, upper Van Daalen rivers. Dialects: Poi on Rouffaer river; Turu on Van Daalen river. *Status:* 5 (Developing). *Class:* Lakes Plain, Tariku, Central. *Dialects:* Foi, Iau, Turu. Reportedly similar to Edopi [dbf]. Distinct from Yawa [yva]. Varieties listed as dialects may be separate languages. *Lg Use:* Vigorous. Speakers of other languages in western Lakes Plains area speak basic Iau. All domains. All ages. Positive attitudes. A few also use Duvle [duv] or a Dani variety. Young to middle-aged speakers also use Indonesian [ind]. *Lg Dev:* Literacy rate in L1: 5%–15%. 200 or more can read and write it. Bible portions: 1985–2005. *Writing:* Latin script. *Other:* Christian. *Map:* 372:189.

Iban [iba] (Sea Dayak). 15,000 in Indonesia (Benjamin and Chou 2003). West Kalimantan Province. Upper Kapuas river, north bank, to Sarawak border, from east of Mount Betung, west to Senaning town. *Status:* 5 (Developing). *Dialects:* Batang Lupar, Bugau, Desa, Kantu', Ketungau (Air Tabun, Banjur, Demam, Maung, Sebaru', Sekapat, Seklau, Sesat, Sigarau). *Lg Use:* Used as language of Catholicism by other-language speakers on Rejang river (2004 J. Collins). *Other:* Traditional religion, Christian. See main entry on page 221. *Map:* 364:23.

Ibu [ibu]. 35 (Voorhoeve and Visser 1987). In 1987, there were a few elderly speakers but it is now probably extinct (Wurm 2007). Ethnic population: 50 (1984). North Maluku, north Halmahera island, Ibu river mouth, Gamlamo and Gamici villages. *Status:* 8b (Nearly extinct). *Class:* West Papuan, North Halmahera, Sahu. *Dialects:* None known. May be inherently intelligible with Sahu [saj]. *Lg Use:* Mainly older adults (1987). *Map:* 366.

Iha [ihp] (Kapaur). 5,500 (1987 SIL). West Papua Province, Fakfak regency; Kaimana, Fakfak, and Kokas subdistricts. West Bomberai peninsula. *Status:* 6a (Vigorous). *Class:* Trans-New Guinea, West, West Bomberai, West Bomberai

Proper. *Dialects:* None known. Reportedly similar to Baham [bdw]. *Other:* Christian, traditional religion. *Map:* 371:43.

Iha Based Pidgin [ihb]. No known L1 speakers. West Papua Province. Bomberai peninsula. *Status:* 9 (Second language only). *Class:* Pidgin, Iha based. *Other:* Muslim, Christian.

Ile Ape [ila] (Nusa Tadon). 15,000 (2008 census). East Nusa Tenggara Province. North Lembata island, Ile Ape peninsula; into nearby mainland Lembata island. *Status:* 6b (Threatened). *Class:* Austronesian, Malayo-Polynesian, Central-Eastern Malayo-Polynesian, Bima-Lembata. *Dialects:* North Ile Ape, South Ile Ape. *Lg Use:* Also use Lamaholot [slp]. *Map:* 370.

Ili'uun [ilu] (Erai, Hahutan, Hahutau, Iliun, Ilmaumau, Limera). 1,400 (1990 SIL). Southwest Maluku Province, Telemar, Karbubu, Klishatu, Ilmaumau, Erai, Nabar, Esulit, and Istutun villages. Wetar island west coast, southwest tip; nearby Lirang island. *Status:* 6a (Vigorous). *Class:* Austronesian, Malayo-Polynesian, Central-Eastern Malayo-Polynesian, Timor-Babar, Southwest Maluku, Wetar. *Dialects:* Eray, Esulit, Ilmaumau, Karbubu, Klishatu, Nabar, Telemar, Ustutun. All also use the Ili'uun dialect. Lexical similarity: 93%–97% among dialects, 73% with Tugun [tzn], 69% with Aputai [apx], 67% with Perai [wet], 51% with Galolen [gal]. *Lg Use:* Jeh and Juru have no remaining speakers. Also use Ambonese Malay [abs]. *Lg Dev:* Literacy rate in L1: Below 1%. *Other:* Christian. *Map:* 369.

Imroing [imr] (Imroin). 560 (2007 SIL). Southern Maluku Province, Imroing village. Babar island, southwest. *Status:* 7 (Shifting). *Class:* Austronesian, Malayo-Polynesian, Central-Eastern Malayo-Polynesian, Babar, South, Southwest Babar. *Lg Use:* Shifting to a local Malay variety. Home, gardens, village, ceremonies, religion. Also use a regional Malay variety, probably a dialect of Ambonese Malay [abs], in all domains, except for ceremonies; children are taught the Malay variety. Speakers also use Indonesian [ind] primarily in government, Christian religious domains. *Lg Dev:* Literacy rate in L1: Below 1%. *Other:* Christian. *Map:* 368.

Indonesian [ind] (Bahasa Indonesia). 22,800,000 in Indonesia (2000), increasing. Population total all countries: 23,200,480. L2 users: 140,000,000 in Indonesia. Widespread throughout Indonesia. Also in Netherlands, Philippines, Saudi Arabia, Singapore, Sint Maarten, United States. *Status:* 1 (National). Statutory national language (1945, Constitution, Article 36). *Class:* Austronesian, Malayo-Polynesian, Malayo-Chamic, Malayic, Malay. A member of macrolanguage Malay [msa] (Malaysia). *Dialects:* None known. Lexical similarity: over 80% with Standard Malay [zsm]. *Lg Dev:* Fully developed. Bible: 1974–2000. *Writing:* Arabic script. Braille script. Latin script, primary usage. *Other:* Developed from literary 'Classical Malay' of the Riau-Johor sultanate (Sneddon 2003). Has regional variants. Muslim.

Indonesian Sign Language [inl]. 8,000 (2000). Java and Bali. *Status:* 6a (Vigorous). *Class:* Deaf sign language. *Lg Use:* 94 schools for the deaf use the oral method for instruction. Used as L2 by Bengkala Sign Language [bqy]. *Other:* A blend of Malaysian Sign Language [xml] and indigenous signs. American Sign Language [ase] not used.

Indonesian, Peranakan [pea] (Baba Indonesian, Chinese Indonesian, Peranakan). 20,000 (Wurm and Hattori 1981). East, Central Java provinces; Yogyakarta Special Region; West Java Province, north coastline area towards Pamanukan town. *Status:* 7 (Shifting). *Class:* Creole, Malay based. *Dialects:* None known. Based on Indonesian [ind] and Javanese [jav], with Mandarin [cmn] elements in contrast to Baba Malay [mbf], which has Hokkien (Chinese, Min Nan [nan]) elements. *Lg Use:* Mainly older adults.

Irarutu [irh] (Arguni Bay, Irahutu, Irutu, Kaitero, Kasira). 4,000 (1987 SIL). West Papua Province, 44 villages. East Bomberai peninsula; Arguni bay north to Bintuni bay, southwest. *Status:* 6b (Threatened). *Class:* Austronesian, Malayo-Polynesian, Central-Eastern Malayo-Polynesian, Eastern Malayo-Polynesian, South Halmahera-West New Guinea, South Halmahera. *Dialects:* 6 or 7 dialects. Lexical similarity: 90% with Kuri [nbn]. *Lg Use:* Home, community. Also use Indonesian [ind]. *Lg Dev:* Literacy rate in L2: 15%–25%. Bible portions: 1992–2000. *Writing:* Latin script. *Other:* Christian, Muslim. *Map:* 371:36.

Isirawa [srl] (Okwasar, Saberi, Saweri). 1,800 (Wurm 2000). Papua Province, Jayapura, north coast, Sarmi area and west, Mararena, Kamenawari, Amsira, Siaratesa, Perkami, Martewar, Arsania, Nisero, Arabais, Webro, Wari, Nuerawar, and Waim villages. *Status:* 6b (Threatened). *Class:* Tor-Kwerba, Greater Kwerba, Isirawa. *Dialects:* Eastern Isirawa, Western Isirawa. Reportedly similar to Kwerba [kwe]. Dialects very similar. *Lg Use:* Potentially endangered (2000 S. Wurm). Vigorous, but losing its trade language status to Indonesian [ind]; children are beginning to prefer Indonesian (Wurm 2007). Also use Indonesian [ind]. Used as L2 by Samarokena [tmj]. *Lg Dev:* Literacy rate in L1: 5%–15%. NT: 2005. *Writing:* Latin script. *Other:* Christian, traditional religion. *Map:* 372:171.

Itik [itx] (Betef, Borto, Ittik, Ittik-Tor). 80 (Wurm 2000). Ethnic population: 200. Papua Province. North coast east of Tor river, along upper Biri river. *Status:* 6b (Threatened). *Class:* Tor-Kwerba, Orya-Tor, Tor. *Dialects:* Ittik, Ittik-Tor. *Lg Use:* Potentially endangered (2000 S. Wurm). Under pressure from Indonesian [ind] (Wurm 2007). *Other:* Ethnic group: Borto. 2005 survey data indicates this language may no longer exist or speakers moved to another location. Christian, traditional religion. *Map:* 372:167.

Jangkang [djo]. 37,000 (2007 SIL). West Kalimantan Province, Central Sanggau regency. Between Sanggau and Balai Sebut towns along tributary of Kapuas river. *Status:* 6a (Vigorous). *Class:* Austronesian, Malayo-Polynesian, Land Dayak, Southern. *Dialects:* Jangkang proper, Pompang. *Map:* 364:24.

Javanese [jav] (Djawa, Jawa). 84,300,000 in Indonesia (2000 census). 25,000 in south Sulawesi, and 69,000,000 on Java, 500,000 of them being in Banten region and 2,500,000 in Cirebon region of Java. Population total all countries: 84,308,740. Central Java Province, east third of west Java island, southwest half of east Java, including Banyumas, Cilacap, and Purbalingga regencies. Resettlements in Papua, Sulawesi, Maluku, Kalimantan, and Sumatra. Also in Malaysia, Netherlands, Singapore, United States. *Status:* 2 (Provincial). De facto provincial language in central and eastern Java. *Class:* Austronesian, Malayo-Polynesian, Javanese. *Dialects:* Banten, Banyumas, Cirebon (Cheribon, Tjirebon), Indramayu, Malang-Pasuruan, Manuk, Pasisir, Surabaya, Surakarta (Sawlaw, Solo), Tegal, Tembung. High Javanese (Jawa Halus) is the language of religion, but users diminishing and mostly limited to Central Javanese speakers. Javanese varieties in Suriname and in New Caledonia now only partially intelligible with difficulty. Javanese in New Caledonia reportedly cannot use High Javanese (Koentjaraninggrat 1971). Several dialects in Sabah. *Type:* SVO. *Lg Use:* Also use Musi [mui] in South Sumatra. Used as L2 by Madura [mad], Tengger [tes]. *Lg Dev:* Fully developed. Bible: 1854–1994. *Writing:* Javanese script, no longer in use. Latin script. *Other:* Christian. *Maps:* 363, 376:17, 377:17.

Javindo [jvd] ("Krontjong" *pej.*). No known L1 speakers. May be a few L2 speakers and even a very few L1 speakers (Wurm 2007). Central Java. *Status:* 9 (Dormant). *Class:* Creole, Dutch based. *Dialects:* None known. Derived from Dutch [nld] lexicon and Javanese [jav] grammar.

Jofotek-Bromnya [jbr]. 200 (2007), increasing. Few monolinguals. Papua Province, Sarmi regency, Pantai Timur subdistrict, Biridua village; Bonggo subdistrict, Srum village. Jofotek spoken in Biridua, Bromnya in Srum. *Status:* 6b (Threatened). *Class:* Tor-Kwerba, Orya-Tor, Tor. *Dialects:* Bromnya, Jofotek. *Lg Use:* All domains. All ages. Also use Indonesian [ind], Papuan Malay [pmy]. *Other:* Christian, traditional religion. *Map:* 372:166.

Kabola [klz]. 3,900 (1995 N. Johnston). East Nusa Tenggara Province. Northwest Alor island, eastern half, Bird's Head, north of Kalabahi town. *Status:* 6a (Vigorous). *Class:* Trans-New Guinea, West, Timor-Alor-Pantar, Alor-Pantar, Alor. *Dialects:* Kebun Kopi, Meibuil, Otvai, Pintumbang, Tang'ala. Dialect names and locations in Wurm and Hattori (1981) are disputed by native speakers. May be more than 1 language. Based on linguistic differences and social identity, best considered a separate language from Adang [adn]. *Other:* Christian, Muslim. *Map:* 370.

Kaburi [uka]. 600 (1986 SIL). West Papua Province, Manokwari regency, Merdei and Inanwatan subdistricts. South Bird's Head, inland north of Maccluer bay; west bank lower Kamundan river. *Status:* 6b (Threatened). *Class:* Trans-New Guinea, South Bird's Head, South Bird's Head Proper, Western. *Lg Use:* Home. *Other:* Christian, traditional religion. *Map:* 371:31.

Kadai [kzd]. 350 (2000). North Maluku Province. Sula Islands; Taliabu island, eastern interior mountains. Possible speakers in Mangole island mountains. *Status:* 7 (Shifting). *Class:* Austronesian, Malayo-Polynesian, Central-Eastern Malayo-Polynesian, Central Maluku, Sula, Taliabo. *Dialects:* None known. May be intelligible with Taliabu [tlv]. *Other:* The government wants to resettle them along the coast. Traditional religion. *Map:* 367.

Kafoa [kpu] (Aikoli, Fanating, Jafoo, Pailelang, Ruilak). 1,000 (Wurm and Hattori 1981). Ethnic population: 1,000. East Nusa Tenggara Province. Southwest Alor island, enclave north of Aluben town. *Status:* 6a (Vigorous). *Class:* Trans-New Guinea, West, Timor-Alor-Pantar, Alor-Pantar, Alor. *Other:* The name Kafoa is not known locally. *Map:* 370.

Kaibobo [kzb] (Kaibubu). 500 (Collins 1983). Maluku Province, Kairatu district, Kaibobo, Hatusua, Waisamu, Kamarian, Seruawan, and Tihulale villages. West Seram island, Piru bay area. *Status:* 8b (Nearly extinct). *Class:* Austronesian, Malayo-Polynesian, Central-Eastern Malayo-Polynesian, Central Maluku, East, Seram, Nunusaku, Piru Bay, East. *Dialects:* Hatusua, Kaibobo. Lexical similarity: 82%–88% between Kaibobo and Hatusua dialect, 75% with Kamarian [kzx], 62%–65% with Saparua [spr], 62% with Luhu [lcq], 61% with Naka'ela [nae]. *Lg Use:* May be shifting to Ambonese Malay [abs] in some villages. *Other:* Christian. *Map:* 367.

Kaidipang [kzp] (Dio, Kaidipang-Bolangitang). 26,600 (2000 census). Kaidipang 8,900, Bolaang Itang 17,700. North Sulawesi Province. North coast, west and east of Bolaangitang town. *Status:* 6b (Threatened). *Class:* Austronesian, Malayo-Polynesian, Philippine, Greater Central Philippine, Gorontalo-Mongondow, Gorontalic. *Dialects:* Bolaang Itang (Bolang-Hitam, Bolang-Itam), Kaidipang (Kaidipan, Kodipang). *Lg Use:* Younger generation using more Indonesian [ind]. *Other:* Muslim. *Map:* 374:36.

Kaili, Da'a [kzf] (Binggi, Bunggu, Da'a, Pakawa, Pekava, Pekawa). 55,000 (2007 SIL), increasing. 3,000–5,000 Da'a and Inde in south Sulawesi. Many monolinguals. Central Sulawesi and West Sulawesi provinces in Marawola, Dolo, Sigi-Biromaru, Palolo, and Banawa subdistricts. 'Bunggu' used for Da'a and Inde in West Sulawesi, Mamuju regency, Pasangkayu subdistrict, near Palu. *Status:* 5 (Developing). *Class:* Austronesian, Malayo-Polynesian, Celebic, Kaili-Pamona, Northern, Kaili. *Dialects:* Da'a (Dombu), Inde. Some intelligibility of Ledo dialect of Kaili, Ledo [lew] and other Kaili varieties, but with major sociolinguistic differences. Lexical similarity: 98% between the Da'a and Inde dialects. *Lg Use:* Vigorous. Most children know little Indonesian [ind] when entering school. All domains. Oral use in local administration, commerce, school. Some oral and written use in church. All ages. Positive attitudes. Also use Indonesian [ind] in church. *Lg Dev:* Literacy rate in L1: 45%. NT: 1998. *Writing:* Latin script. *Other:* Christian. *Maps:* 374:27, 375:27.

Kaili, Ledo [lew] (Ledo, Paloesch, Palu). 350,000 (2000 census), increasing. Central Sulawesi Province, coastal area, both sides of neck south of Manimaya peninsula. *Status:* 3 (Wider communication). Ledo is lingua franca in West Toraja area. *Class:* Austronesian, Malayo-Polynesian, Celebic, Kaili-Pamona, Northern, Kaili. *Dialects:* Ado (Pakuli, Sibalaya), Doi (Kayu Malue, Mamboro), Edo (Sidondo), Ija (Sigi), Ledo (Palu), Rai (Sindue-Tawaili, Tawaili-Sindue), Raio (Kori), Ta'a (Dolago-Sausu, Sausu), Taa (Palolo), Tado (Ri Io, To ri Io, Torio, Toriu), Tara (Parigi). Doi dialect is intelligible of Ledo and Edo; Ado next most intelligible; Tado a little less. Some intelligibility of Da'a [kzf], but major sociolinguistic differences. Lexical similarity: 80%–88% between Ledo and the Ado, Edo, Doi, and Lindu dialects. *Lg Use:* Largest and most prestigious of Kaili varieties in Sulawesi. Used as L2 by Uma [ppk]. *Lg Dev:* Dictionary. NT: 1999. *Writing:* Latin script. *Other:* Tado dialect different from Tado, an alternate name for Lindu [klw]. Muslim, Christian. *Maps:* 374:49, 375:49.

Kaili, Unde [unz] (Banava, Banawa). 25,000 (2007 SIL), increasing. Central Sulawesi Province, Banawa, Palu, and Tawaeli subdistricts; from Pulu bay west to Makassar strait shore. Also West Sulawesi Province, Pasangkayu subdistrict. *Status:* 6a (Vigorous). *Class:* Austronesian, Malayo-Polynesian, Celebic, Kaili-Pamona, Northern, Kaili. *Dialects:* Ganti, Lole. *Other:* Lole has negative term, unde. Ganti has negative term, ndepuu. Muslim. *Map:* 374:109.

Kaimbulawa [zka]. 2,200 (2005 SIL). Southeast Sulawesi Province. Siompu island, Kaimbulawa and Lantoi villages; southwest Buton island, southwest of Baubau town, Kambe-kambero village. *Status:* 6b (Threatened). *Class:* Austronesian, Malayo-Polynesian, Celebic, Eastern, Southeastern, Muna-Buton, Nuclear Muna-Buton, Munan, Munic. *Dialects:* Kaimbulawa (Lontoi), Kambe-Kambero. Not a dialect of Muna [mnb] or Cia-Cia [cia]. Lexical similarity: 81% with Kambe-kambero dialect, 75% with Busoa [bup], 64%–74% with Muna [mnb] dialects, 64% with Muna, 70% with Liabuku [lix], 66% with Cia-Cia [cia], 58% with Wolio [wlo], 45% with Kaledupa dialect of Tukang Besi North [khc]; Kambe-kambero dialect is 84% with Busoa [bup], 72% with Muna [mnb], 76% with Liabuku [lix]. *Lg Use:* Vigorous. *Other:* Muslim. *Map:* 375:37.

Kais [kzm] (Aiso, Atori, Kampung Baru, Mintamani). 700 (1993 R. Doriot). West Papua Province, 8 villages. South Bird's Head area; inland along Kais river. *Status:* 7 (Shifting). *Class:* Trans-New Guinea, South Bird's Head, South Bird's Head Proper, Western. *Other:* Christian, traditional religion. *Map:* 371:25.

Kaiy [tcq] (Kai, Taori-Kaiy, Taori-Kei, Todi). 220 (Wurm

2000). Papua Province, Kaiy and Kokou villages. Lakes plain area around Kaiy airstrip on lower Rouffaer river. *Status:* 6a (Vigorous). *Class:* Lakes Plain, Tariku, East. *Dialects:* None known. Lexical similarity: 69% with Biritai [bqq]. *Lg Use:* Potentially endangered (2000 S. Wurm). Under pressure from Indonesian [ind] (Wurm 2007). *Other:* Christian, traditional religion. *Map:* 372:195.

Kalabra [kzz] (Beraur). 3,290 (2000). West Papua Province. West Bird's Head, southeast of Sorong city, along Kalabra river inland. *Status:* 6a (Vigorous). *Class:* West Papuan, West Bird's Head. *Dialects:* None known. Lexical similarity: 60% with Tehit [kps]. *Lg Use:* Religious services. *Other:* Christian, traditional religion. *Map:* 371:14.

Kalao [kly] (Kalaotoa, Lambego). 500 (Friberg and Laskowske 1989). South Sulawesi Province. Selayar islands; Kalao island, west of Bonerate island. *Status:* 7 (Shifting). *Class:* Austronesian, Malayo-Polynesian, Celebic, Wotu-Wolio, Kalao. *Dialects:* None known. Lexical similarity: 76% with Laiyolo [lji] and Wotu [wtw]. *Lg Use:* Under pressure from Bonerate [bna] and Indonesian [ind] (Wurm 2007). *Other:* Muslim. *Map:* 375:38.

Kalumpang [kli] (Galumpang, Maki, Ma'ki, Makki, Mangki, Mangkir). 20,000 (2012 S. Samboy). West Sulawesi Province, southeast Mamuju regency, Kalumpang subdistrict. *Status:* 6a (Vigorous). *Class:* Austronesian, Malayo-Polynesian, South Sulawesi, Northern, Toraja-Sa'dan. *Dialects:* Bone Hau (Ta'da), Karataun (E'da, Makki). Smaller dialects not listed. Lexical similarity: 78% with Mamasa [mqj], 78% with Tae' [rob], 74% with Toraja-Sa'dan [sda]; 82% between Karataun and Bone Hau dialects. *Lg Use:* Vigorous. Used as L2 by Talondo' [tln]. *Other:* Christian, Muslim. *Map:* 375:39.

Kamang [woi] (Kamana-Kamang, Waisika, Woisika). 6,000 (2011 A. Schapper and M. Manimau). East Nusa Tenggara Province. Central Alor island. *Status:* 6a (Vigorous). *Class:* Trans-New Guinea, West, Timor-Alor-Pantar, Alor-Pantar, Alor. *Dialects:* Kamang, Manetaa, Moo, Suboo, Takailubui, Tiee. Probably more than 1 language. *Lg Dev:* Dictionary. *Other:* North central Alor language complex. *Map:* 370.

Kamarian [kzx] (Kamariang, Seruawan). No known L1 speakers (Wurm 2007). Under 10 in 1987; now probably extinct (Wurm 2007). Ethnic population: 6,000 (1987 SIL). Maluku Province. West Seram island. *Status:* 9 (Dormant). *Class:* Austronesian, Malayo-Polynesian, Central-Eastern Malayo-Polynesian, Central Maluku, East, Seram, Nunusaku, Piru Bay, East, Seram Straits, Uliase, Kamarian. *Dialects:* None known. Lexical similarity: 75% with Kaibobo [kzb], 67% with Saparua [spr], 60% with Lisabata-Nuniali [lcs], 59% with Amahai [amq], Luhu [lcq], Naka'ela [nae], and Hulung [huk].

Kamaru [kgx]. 3,500 (2004 SIL). Southeast Sulawesi Province. Southeast Buton island. *Status:* 6b (Threatened). *Class:* Austronesian, Malayo-Polynesian, Celebic, Wotu-Wolio, Wolio-Kamaru. *Dialects:* None known. Lexical similarity: 68% with Lasalimu [llm], 67% with Wolio [wlo], 54% with Cia-Cia [cia], 51% with Pancana [pnp], 49% with Tukang Besi [khc], 45% with Muna [mnb]. *Other:* Muslim. *Map:* 375:40.

Kambera [xbr] (East Sumba, East Sumbanese, Hilu Humba, Humba, Oost-Sumbaas, Sumba, Sumbanese). 240,000 (2009). East Nusa Tenggara Province. Sumba island, eastern half. *Status:* 5 (Developing). *Class:* Austronesian, Malayo-Polynesian, Central-Eastern Malayo-Polynesian, Sumba-Hawu, Sumba. *Dialects:* Kambera, Kanatang, Lewa, Mangili-Waijelo (Rindi, Wai Jilu, Waidjelu, Waijelo), Melolo, Southern Sumba, Uma Ratu Nggai (Umbu Ratu Nggai). Dialect network. Kambera dialect is widely understood. Lewa and Uma Ratu Nggai dialects have difficulty understanding those from Mangili. *Lg Dev:* Dictionary. Grammar. Bible: 1995. *Writing:* Latin script. *Other:* Christian, traditional religion. *Map:* 369.

Kamberau [irx] (Iria, Kambrau, Kamrau). 1,570 (1993 R. Doriot). West Papua Province, Ubia-Seramuku, Bahomia, Waho, Wamoma, Inari, Tanggaromi, Koi, Wamesa, and Coa villages. Southeast Bomberai peninsula, Kamerau bay area. *Status:* 7 (Shifting). *Class:* Trans-New Guinea, Asmat-Kamoro, Sabakor. *Dialects:* None known. Lexical similarity: 60% with Buruwai [asi]. *Other:* Christian, traditional religion. *Map:* 371:48.

Kamoro [kgq] (Kamora, Kaokonau, Lakahia, Mimika, Mukamuga, Nafarpi, Nagramadu, Nefarpi, Neferipi, Umar, Umari). 8,000 (1987 SIL). Papua Province. South coast, Mukamuga river into West Papua Province, Etna bay area. *Status:* 6a (Vigorous). *Class:* Trans-New Guinea, Asmat-Kamoro, Kamoro. *Dialects:* Nanesa, Tarya, Yamur. 4 other dialects. *Lg Use:* Also use Indonesian [ind]. *Other:* Different from Yeretuar (Umari) [gop]. Christian, traditional religion. *Maps:* 371:60, 372:60.

Kangean [kkv]. 110,000 (2000 census). East Java Province. Kangean islands. *Status:* 6a (Vigorous). *Class:* Austronesian, Malayo-Polynesian, Madurese. *Dialects:* None known. Barely intelligible with East Madura [mad]. A separate language (Stevens 1968). Lexical similarity: 75% with Madura [mad]. *Lg Dev:* Poetry. Radio programs. *Map:* 363.

Kanum, Bädi [khd] (Enkelembu, Kenume, Knwne). 10 (1996 M. Donohue). Papua Province, south coast border area, southeast of Merauke city. *Status:* 8b (Nearly extinct). *Class:* South-Central Papuan, Morehead-Upper Maro, Tonda. *Dialects:* None known. Kanum varieties are separate languages, with difficult mutual intelligibility. Reportedly similar to Yei [jei]. Also classified as Australian, Pama-Nyungan. *Lg Use:* Also use Indonesian [ind] as trade language or for official purposes. Also use Morori [mok] as trade language. *Lg Dev:* Literacy rate in L2: 5%. *Other:* One ethnic group with Kanum varieties. Clan marriages common and much ritual exchange. Christian, traditional religion. *Map:* 373:268.

Kanum, Ngkâlmpw [kcd] (Enkelembu, Kenume, Knwne). 150 (1996 M. Donohue). Papua Province, Yanggandur, Tomer, and Onggaya villages. Southernmost point of province, east of Merauke city; along Papua New Guinea border. *Status:* 6b (Threatened). *Class:* South-Central Papuan, Morehead-Upper Maro, Tonda. *Dialects:* None known. Kanum varieties are separate languages, with difficult mutual intelligibility. Reportedly similar to Yei [jei]. Also classified as Australian, Pama-Nyungan. *Lg Use:* Home, hunting camps. All ages. Also use Indonesian [ind] as trade language or for official purposes. Also use Morori [mok] as trade language. *Lg Dev:* Literacy rate in L2: 5%. *Other:* One ethnic group with Kanum varieties. Clan marriages common, and much ritual exchange. Christian. *Map:* 373:266.

Kanum, Smärky [kxq] (Enkelembu, Kenume, Knwne). 80 (1996 M. Donohue). Papua Province, Yanggandur, Tomer, Tomerau, Rawa Biru, and Kondo villages. Southernmost point of province, southeast of Merauke city; bordering Papua New Guinea. *Status:* 6b (Threatened). *Class:* South-Central Papuan, Morehead-Upper Maro, Tonda. *Dialects:* None known. Kanum varieties are separate languages, with difficult mutual intelligibility. Reportedly similar to Yei [jei]. Also classified as Australian, Pama-Nyungan. *Lg Use:* Home, hunting camps. All ages. Also use Indonesian [ind] as trade language or for official purposes. Also use Morori [mok] as trade language. *Lg Dev:* Literacy rate in L2: 5%. *Other:* One ethnic group with Kanum varieties. Clan marriages common, and much ritual exchange. Christian. *Map:* 373:269.

Kanum, Sota [krz] (Enkelembu, Kenume, Knwne). 100

(1996 M. Donohue). Papua Province, Sota village. Southernmost point of province, east northeast of Merauke city; bordering Papua New Guinea. *Status:* 6b (Threatened). *Class:* South-Central Papuan, Morehead-Upper Maro, Tonda. *Dialects:* None known. Kanum varieties are separate languages, with difficult mutual intelligibility. Reportedly similar to Yei [jei]. Also classified as Australian, Pama-Nyungan. *Lg Use:* Home, hunting camps. All ages. Also use Indonesian [ind] as trade language or for official purposes. Also use Morori [mok] as trade language. *Lg Dev:* Literacy rate in L2: 5%. *Other:* One ethnic group with Kanum varieties. Clan marriages common, and much ritual exchange. Christian. *Map:* 373:265.

Kao [kax] (Kau, Ka'u). 400 (2000). North Maluku Province. North Halmahera island; on Kao bay, area near Kao river mouth. *Status:* 7 (Shifting). *Class:* West Papuan, North Halmahera, Sahu. *Dialects:* Could be a marginal dialect of Pagu [pgu], but relates uniquely to other languages in Kao River subbranch. *Lg Use:* Ethnic group membership expressed by knowing the language. Speakers 40 and older. Also use Indonesian [ind]. *Lg Dev:* Literacy rate in L1: Below 1%. Literacy rate in L2: 50%–75%. *Other:* Muslim. *Map:* 366.

Kapauri [khp] (Kapori). 200 (2006 SIL). Papua Province, Pagai village, Kamikaru and Magri hamlets. Upper Idenburg river, north bank; southwest of Jayapura city. *Status:* 6b (Threatened). *Class:* Kaure, Kapore. *Lg Use:* Endangered to seriously endangered (2000 S. Wurm). Most domains. *Other:* Christian, traditional religion. *Map:* 372:200.

Kaptiau [kbi] (Kapitiauw, Kaptiauw). 230 (2006 SIL). Papua Province, Sarmi regency, Bonggo subdistrict, Kaptiau village. North coast west of Jayapura city. *Status:* 7 (Shifting). *Class:* Austronesian, Malayo-Polynesian, Central-Eastern Malayo-Polynesian, Eastern Malayo-Polynesian, Oceanic, Western Oceanic, North New Guinea, Sarmi-Jayapura Bay, Sarmi. *Dialects:* None known. Lexical similarity: with Tarpia [tpf] and Bonggo [bpg] (most). *Lg Use:* Endangered (2000 S. Wurm, 2000 D. Tryon). Private domains, public prayer. Mainly older adults. Also use Indonesian [ind], Papuan Malay [pmy]. *Other:* Christian, traditional religion. *Map:* 372:164.

Karas [kgv]. 240 (1983 SIL). West Papua Province, Antalisa and Mas villages. Karas island off southwest coast of Bomberai peninsula; outside of Sebakor bay. *Status:* 8a (Moribund). *Class:* Trans-New Guinea, West, West Bomberai, Karas. *Lg Use:* Potentially endangered (2000 S. Wurm). Under pressure from Iha [ihp] and Indonesian [ind] (Wurm 2007). *Other:* Christian, traditional religion. *Map:* 371:46.

Karey [kyd] (Kerei, Krei). 610 (2011 SIL). Southern Maluku Province. South Aru Islands, Tarangan island, southeast coast, Karey valley. *Status:* 6a (Vigorous). *Class:* Austronesian, Malayo-Polynesian, Central-Eastern Malayo-Polynesian, Aru. *Dialects:* None known. Lexical similarity: 70% with East Tarangan [tre] and Batuley [bay]. *Lg Use:* Vigorous. *Lg Dev:* Literacy rate in L1: Below 1%. *Other:* Christian, Muslim. *Map:* 368.

Karon Dori [kgw] (Maiyach, Mari, Meon). 5,000 (1987 SIL). West Papua Province, Pef, Asses, Sunopi, and Siakwa villages. Central Bird's Head; area of headwaters of Kamundan river. *Status:* 6a (Vigorous). *Class:* Maybrat. *Dialects:* None known. Reportedly similar to Mai Brat [ayz]. *Lg Dev:* Grammar. *Other:* Christian, traditional religion. *Map:* 371:18.

Kaur [vkk] (Bintuhan, Ka'ur, Mulak). 40,000 (2000 census). Southwest Sumatra, southern Bengkulu Province. Southernmost extent of province. *Status:* 6a (Vigorous). *Class:* Austronesian, Malayo-Polynesian, Malayo-Chamic, Malayic, Malay. A member of macrolanguage Malay [msa] (Malaysia). *Dialects:* Borrowings from Lampung Api [ljp]; reportedly difficult to understand for Central Malay [pse] speakers. Lexical similarity: 70% with Central Malay [pse] dialects Pasemah and Serawai. *Lg Use:* Vigorous. Home, village. All ages. Positive attitudes. Indonesian [ind] used in educational, religious and civic domains. *Lg Dev:* Not currently a written language. *Other:* Muslim, traditional religion. *Map:* 377:18.

Kaure [bpp] (Kaureh). 450 (1995 SIL). Papua, southwest of Lake Sentani, Nawa River, Lereh, Harna, Wes, Masta, Aurina villages. *Status:* 8a (Moribund). *Class:* Kaure, Kaure Proper. *Type:* SOV. *Lg Use:* Religious services. *Lg Dev:* Literacy rate in L1: 10%. Dictionary. Bible portions: 1990–1996. *Writing:* Latin script. *Other:* Christian, traditional religion. *Map:* 372:201.

Kauwera [xau] (Kabera, Kaowerawedj, Kauwerawec, Kauwerawetj, Kawera, Koassa, Tekutameso). 400 (1987 SIL). Papua Province. Middle Mamberamo river, north bank east; southeast of Lake Rombebai. *Status:* 6a (Vigorous). *Class:* Tor-Kwerba, Greater Kwerba, Kwerba, Nuclear. *Lg Use:* Vigorous. *Other:* Traditional religion, Christian. *Map:* 372:175.

Kawe [kgb]. 600 (Remijsen 2001). West Papua Province, Salio, Selepele, Bianci, and Menyefun villages. West coast of Bird's Head, west end of Waigao island and nearby islands. *Status:* 6b (Threatened). *Class:* Austronesian, Malayo-Polynesian, Central-Eastern Malayo-Polynesian, Eastern Malayo-Polynesian, South Halmahera-West New Guinea, West New Guinea, Cenderawasih Bay, Raja Ampat. *Dialects:* None known. Related to Maya [slz], Maden [xmx], and Matbat [xmt]. *Other:* Traditional religion, Christian. *Map:* 371:1.

Kayagar [kyt] (Kajagar, Kaygi, Kaygir, Wiyagar). 10,000 (1993 WT), decreasing. Papua, south coast east of Atohwaim [aqm], south of Awyu Asue [psa] languages. *Status:* 6b (Threatened). *Class:* Trans-New Guinea, Kayagar. *Dialects:* None known. Reportedly most similar to Tamagario [tcg]; related to Atohwaim [aqm]. *Lg Use:* Home, work. Also use Indonesian [ind], Papuan Malay [pmy]. Used as L2 by Atohwaim [aqm]. *Lg Dev:* Literacy rate in L2: 10% somewhat literate in Indonesian [ind]. *Other:* Traditional religion, Christian. *Map:* 373:244.

Kayan Mahakam [xay]. 1,300 (Wurm and Hattori 1981). East Kalimantan Province, West Kutai and Malinau regencies. Area extends from Muller Mountains from south border northward, to within 25 km of Malasia, Sarawak State. *Status:* 6a (Vigorous). *Class:* Austronesian, Malayo-Polynesian, North Borneo, North Sarawakan, Kayan-Kenyah, Kayanic, Kayan Proper. *Other:* Linguistic influences from Ot Danum [otd]. *Maps:* 364:26, 365:26.

Kayan, Busang [bfg] (Busang, Kajan, Kajang). 3,000 (Wurm and Hattori 1981). East Kalimantan Province. Muller Mountains; upper Mahakam, Oga, and Belayan river areas. *Status:* 6a (Vigorous). *Class:* Austronesian, Malayo-Polynesian, North Borneo, North Sarawakan, Kayan-Kenyah, Kayanic, Kayan Proper. *Dialects:* Belayan, Long Bleh, Mahakam Busang. *Other:* Christian, traditional religion. *Maps:* 364:17, 365:17.

Kayan, Kayan River [xkn] (Kajang, Kayan River Kajan). 2,000 (Wurm and Hattori 1981). East Kalimantan Province. 2 Kayan river areas: one downstream, the other larger one, headwaters and south. *Status:* 6a (Vigorous). *Class:* Austronesian, Malayo-Polynesian, North Borneo, North Sarawakan, Kayan-Kenyah, Kayanic, Kayan Proper. *Dialects:* Kayaniyut Kayan, Uma Laran, Uma Leken. *Map:* 365:27.

Kayan, Mendalam [xkd] (Mendalam Kajan). 1,500 (Wurm and Hattori 1981). West Kalimantan Province. Northeast of Putus Sibau town, along Mendalam river. *Status:* 6a (Vigorous). *Class:* Austronesian, Malayo-Polynesian, North Borneo, North Sarawakan, Kayan-Kenyah, Kayanic, Kayan Proper. *Writing:* Latin script, in development. *Map:* 364:41.

Kayan, Wahau [whu] (Wahau Kajan). 500 (Wurm and Hattori 1981). East Kalimantan Province. North of Muara Wahau town, along north tributary of Telen river. *Status:* 6b (Threatened). *Class:* Austronesian, Malayo-Polynesian, North Borneo, North Sarawakan, Kayan-Kenyah, Kayanic, Kayan Proper. *Map:* 365:73.

Kayeli [kzl] (Caeli, Cajeli, Gaeli, Kajeli). No known L1 speakers (Wurm 2007). Last speaker of Liliali dialect died in 1989 (Wurm 2007). Maluku Province. North Buru island. *Status:* 9 (Dormant). *Class:* Austronesian, Malayo-Polynesian, Central-Eastern Malayo-Polynesian, Central Maluku, East, Seram, Nunusaku, Kayeli. *Dialects:* Kayeli, Leliali (Liliali), Lumaete (Lumaiti, Lumara, Mumaite). *Other:* Shifted to Ambonese Malay [abs] or Lisela [lcl] (Wurm 2007). Muslim.

Kayupulau [kzu] (Kajupulau). 50 (Wurm 2000). Used by under 10% of the ethnic group (Wurm 2007). Papua Province. Jayapura harbor. *Status:* 8b (Nearly extinct). *Class:* Austronesian, Malayo-Polynesian, Central-Eastern Malayo-Polynesian, Eastern Malayo-Polynesian, Oceanic, Western Oceanic, North New Guinea, Sarmi-Jayapura Bay, Jayapura Bay. *Dialects:* Not a dialect of Tobati (Yotafa) [tti]. *Lg Use:* Endangered (2000 D. Tryon); seriously endangered (2000 S. Wurm). Mainly adults 50 and older. *Other:* Christian. *Map:* 372:134.

Kedang [ksx] (Dang, Kdang, Kédang, Kedangese). 30,000 (2008 census). East Nusa Tenggara Province. Northeast Lembata island. *Status:* 6a (Vigorous). *Class:* Austronesian, Malayo-Polynesian, Central-Eastern Malayo-Polynesian, Bima-Lembata. *Other:* Christian, Muslim. *Map:* 370.

Kehu [khh]. 200 (2007 SIL). Papua Province, Wapoga river between Auye [auu] and Dao [nfa] in the foothills. *Status:* 6b (Threatened). *Class:* East Geelvink Bay. *Map:* 372:83.

Kei [kei] (Kai, Saumlaki, Veveu Evav). 85,000 (2000 E. Travis). 4,500 monolinguals. L2 users: Also used by outsiders such as ethnic Chinese and Butonese who live in Kei. Southeast Maluku Province, about 207 villages on 10 islands. Kei island group west of Aru islands; Kecil, Besar, and surrounding islands; also, Kur islands, lying west and northwest of Kei group. *Status:* 6a (Vigorous). *Class:* Austronesian, Malayo-Polynesian, Central-Eastern Malayo-Polynesian, Southeast Maluku, Kei-Tanimbar, Kei-Fordata. *Dialects:* Kei Besar, Kei Kecil, Ta'am, Tanimbar Kei (Atnebar), Tayando. Kei Kecil is the prestigious urban dialect. Kei Besar speakers usually also know Kei Kecil, but not vice versa. Kei Besar is reportedly more similar to Fordata [frd] than other Kei dialects. Tanimbar Kei is spoken in only one village. Lexical similarity: 60% with Fordata [frd]. *Lg Use:* Fairly vigorous. All domains. All ages. Positive attitudes. Also use Banda [bnd], Indonesian [ind]. Used as L2 by Banda [bnd], Kur [kuv]. *Lg Dev:* Literacy rate in L1: 100 can read, 10 can write. Literacy rate in L2: 50%–75%. 100 can read, 10 can write. Used informally in school for explanations. Dictionary. Grammar. *Writing:* Latin script. *Other:* Muslim, Christian, traditional religion. *Map:* 368.

Keijar [kdy] (Keder). 370 (2005 SIL). Papua Province. Pacific coast east; north of Tor river mouth. *Status:* 7 (Shifting). *Class:* Tor-Kwerba, Orya-Tor, Tor. *Dialects:* None known. Lexical similarity: 45% with Berik [bkl]. *Lg Use:* Endangered (2000 S. Wurm). Young children seldom speak the language. Also use Anus [auq], Indonesian [ind]. *Other:* Christian, traditional religion. *Map:* 372:115.

Kelabit [kzi] (Apo Duat, Kalabit, Kerabit). 640 in Indonesia (2000). East Kalimantan Province, remote mountains, on Sarawak border, northwest of Longkemuat. *Status:* 6b (Threatened). *Dialects:* Bareo (Bario), Lon Bangag, Long Napir, Pa' Mada, Tring. *Other:* Christian. See main entry on page 222. *Map:* 365:28.

Kemak [kem] (Ema). 10,000 in Indonesia (2010 census). East Nusa Tenggara Province. North central Timor island, East Timor border area. *Status:* 6a (Vigorous). *Dialects:* Kemak, Nogo (Nogo-Nogo). *Other:* Traditional religion, Christian. See main entry on page 98. *Map:* 369.

Kembayan [xem] (Karambai). 11,000 (2007 SIL). West Kalimantan Province. Area from Balaikarangan and Kembayan towns to near Sarawak border, east of Landak river. *Status:* 6a (Vigorous). *Class:* Austronesian, Malayo-Polynesian, Land Dayak, Southern. *Map:* 364:29.

Kemberano [bzp] (Arandai, Barau, Kalitami, Wariagar). 1,500 (1987 SIL). West Papua Province, several villages. Bird's Head, south coast, northwest Bomberai peninsula, south from Kalitami across Bintuni bay, east of Komundan river. *Status:* 6a (Vigorous). *Class:* Trans-New Guinea, South Bird's Head, South Bird's Head Proper, Eastern. *Dialects:* Barau, Weriagar. Lexical similarity: 85% with Arandai [jbj], 60% with Kokoda [xod]. *Other:* Christian, traditional religion. *Map:* 371:33.

Kembra [xkw]. 20 (Wurm 2000). Ethnic population: 50. Papua Province, Jayawijaya regency, Okbibab subdistrict. *Status:* 8b (Nearly extinct). *Class:* Unclassified. *Lg Use:* Moribund (2000 S. Wurm). Home. Used by few children. *Map:* 372:150.

Kemtuik [kmt] (Kamtuk, Kemtuk). 2,500 (1987 SIL). Papua Province, Mamdayawang, Meikari, Merem, Yanim, Braso, Aib, Sabransamon, Mamda, Sabeyap, Sabeyap Kecil, Sekorup, Aimbe, and Sabron Yaru villages. Near southwest shore, Lake Sentani. *Status:* 6b (Threatened). *Class:* Nimboran. *Dialects:* None known. Lexical similarity: 80% with Gresi [grs]. *Lg Use:* All ages. Also use Indonesian [ind]. Used as L2 by Mlap [kja]. *Lg Dev:* Literacy rate in L1: 25%–50%. Literacy rate in L2: 25%–50%. NT: 2008. *Writing:* Latin script. *Other:* Traditional religion, Christian. *Map:* 372:158.

Kendayan [knx] (Baicit, Damea, Kanayatn, Kendayan Dayak, Kendayan-Ambawang, Salako). 321,000 in Indonesia (2007 SIL). Population total all countries: 331,700. West Kalimantan Province, Sambas regency. Northeast of Bengkayang town, Madi and Papan jungle area. Also in Malaysia (Salako). *Status:* 3 (Wider communication). Used as LWC among non-Muslim Dayaks of northwest West Kalimantan province. *Class:* Austronesian, Malayo-Polynesian, Malayo-Chamic, Malayic. *Dialects:* Ahe, Ambawang, Kendayan, Selako. *Lg Use:* Widespread. Used as L2 by Bakati' [bei], Benyadu' [byd], Rara Bakati' [lra], Sanggau [scg], Sara Bakati' [sre], Semandang [sdm]. *Lg Dev:* Radio programs. *Other:* Indonesian [ind] well understood only by a few with at least a 6th-grade education. *Map:* 364:30.

Keninjal [knl] (Dayak Kaninjal, Kaninjal, Kaninjal Dayak). 32,000 (2007 SIL). West Kalimantan Province; areas near Nangapinoh, Nangaella, Nangasayan, and Gelalak towns; along Sayan and Melawi rivers. *Status:* 6a (Vigorous). *Class:* Austronesian, Malayo-Polynesian, Malayo-Chamic, Malayic. *Dialect:* Kubing. Lexical similarity: more than 80% with other "Malayic Dayak" dialects in Melawi Basin like Barai, Nanga Nuak, Kebahan, Ransa, Kenyilu, Limbai and Kubin. *Other:* Keninjal is one of many ill-defined "Malayic Dayak" varieties. *Map:* 364:31.

Kenyah, Mainstream [xkl] (Highland Kenyah, Usun Apau Kenyah). 12,000 in Indonesia (2007 A. Soriente), decreasing. Population total all countries: 52,000. 0 monolinguals. East Kalimantan Province, Malinau regency, Kayan, Mahakam, Upper Baram, Bahau, Upper

Balui, Malinau, Belayan, Segah, Kelai, and Telen river areas, Pimping, Long Setulang, Batu Kajang, Long Uli, and Long Belua villages. Also in Malaysia. *Status:* 6b (Threatened). *Class:* Austronesian, Malayo-Polynesian, North Borneo, North Sarawakan, Kayan-Kenyah, Kenyah. *Dialects:* Badeng, Bakung, Lepo' Bem, Lepo' Ke, Lepo' Kuda, Lepo' Maut, Lepo' Ndang, Lepo' Tau, Lepo' Tepu', Uma' Jalan, Uma' Tukung. *Lg Use:* Vigorous. Used as L2 by Uma' Lasan [xky], Uma' Lung [ulu], Wahau Kenyah [whk]. *Lg Dev:* NT: 1978. *Maps:* 364:39, 365:39.

Kenyah, Wahau [whk] (Lebu' Kulit, Wahau Kenya). 8,000 in Indonesia (2007 A. Soriente), decreasing. Population total all countries: 9,000. 0 monolinguals. East Kalimantan Province, Batu Majang, Buluk Sen, Uma' Dian, Muara Pedohon, Kampung Baru, Uma' Bekuai, and Tabang Lama villages. Upper Mahakam river area. Also in Malaysia. *Status:* 6b (Threatened). *Class:* Austronesian, Malayo-Polynesian, North Borneo, North Sarawakan, Kayan-Kenyah, Kenyah, Kayanic Kenyah. *Dialects:* Lebu' Kulit, Uma Timai, Uma' Ujok. *Lg Use:* Vigorous. Neutral attitudes. Indonesian [ind] used in education. Also use Mainstream Kenyah [xkl]. *Map:* 365:74.

Ke'o [xxk] (Nage-Keo). 40,000 (2001 L. Baird). Ethnic population: 40,000. East Nusa Tenggara Province, 4 villages. South central Flores island, south and southeast of Ebu Lobo volcano. *Status:* 6a (Vigorous). *Class:* Austronesian, Malayo-Polynesian, Central-Eastern Malayo-Polynesian, Bima-Lembata. *Dialects:* None known. Reportedly distinct from but most similar to Nage [nxe]. *Type:* SVO; isolating language; 4-way phonemic stop distinction. *Lg Use:* All domains, ceremonies, personal letter-writing. All ages. *Lg Dev:* Literacy rate in L2: 20% Indonesian. Literacy program by government for adults and in schools. Grammar. *Other:* People and language are both called Ke'o. Muslim, Christian, traditional religion. *Map:* 370.

Kepo' [kuk] (Kepoq). 6,000 (2010). East Nusa Tenggara Province. 2 separate areas, Central Flores island; between Manggarai [mqy], Rembong [reb], and Wae Rana [wrx] language areas. *Status:* 6b (Threatened). *Class:* Austronesian, Malayo-Polynesian, Central-Eastern Malayo-Polynesian, Bima-Lembata. *Map:* 370.

Kereho [xke] (Keriau Punan). 500 (2003). West Kalimantan Province, far east Kapuas Hulu regency. Near Sarawak border, Kereho river. *Status:* 6b (Threatened). *Class:* Austronesian, Malayo-Polynesian, North Borneo, North Sarawakan, Kayan-Kenyah, Kayanic, Muller-Schwaner 'Punan'. *Dialects:* Seputan, Uheng (Kereho-Uheng). Lexical similarity: 69% with Hovongan [hov], 69% with Aoheng [pni]. *Map:* 364:32.

Kerinci [kvr] (Kerinchi, Kinchai). 260,000 in Indonesia (2000 census). Population total all countries: 285,000. Sumatra, Jambi Province, western mountains, Sungaipenuh area, and north and west. Also in Bahrain. *Status:* 6b (Threatened). *Class:* Austronesian, Malayo-Polynesian, Malayo-Chamic, Malayic, Malay. A member of macrolanguage Malay [msa] (Malaysia). *Dialects:* High dialect diversity in a small area, shading into Jambi Malay [zlm] east and Minangkabau [min] north. Distinct from Kerinci-Minangkabau dialect of Minangkabau. *Writing:* Kaganga script. *Other:* Muslim. *Maps:* 376:19, 377:19.

Ketengban [xte] (Kupel, Oktengban). 9,970 (2000). Papua Province. Near Papua New Guinea border, east highland slopes; scattered. *Status:* 5 (Developing). *Class:* Trans-New Guinea, Mek, Western. *Dialects:* Bime, Okbap, Omban, Onya. Lexical similarity: 69% with Una [mtg]. *Lg Use:* All domains. Used as L2 by Lepki [lpe]. *Lg Dev:* Literacy rate in L1: 30%–40%. Dictionary. NT: 1997. *Writing:* Latin script. *Other:* Christian, traditional religion. *Map:* 372:210.

Ketum [ktt] (Kitum, Wambon-Ketum). 900 (2003 SIL). Papua Province. Foothills of Eastern Highlands, east of East Digul river, about 40 km west of Papua New Guinea border. *Status:* 6a (Vigorous). *Class:* Trans-New Guinea, Ok-Awyu, Awyu-Dumut, Dumut. *Dialects:* None known. Related to Wambon [wms] and Mandobo. *Lg Use:* Home, community. *Other:* Traditional religion, Christian. *Maps:* 372:231, 373:231.

Kimaghima [kig] (Kaladdarsch, Kimaama, Kimaghama, Teri-Kalwasch). 3,000 (1987 SIL). Southeast Papua Province. Kolopom island, interior, east of Merauke city. *Status:* 6b (Threatened). *Class:* Trans-New Guinea, Kolopom. *Lg Use:* Home. *Other:* Christian, traditional religion. *Map:* 373:257.

Kimki [sbt] (Aipki, Kimgi, Sukubatom, Sukubatong). 500 (2004 SIL). Papua Province, Pegunungan Bintang regency, Batom subdistrict. Border area where Sepik river enters Papua New Guinea. *Status:* 6b (Threatened). *Class:* Unclassified. *Lg Use:* Most domains. Also use Indonesian [ind], Papuan Malay [pmy]. Used as L2 by Murkim [rmh]. *Other:* Christian, traditional religion. *Map:* 372:148.

Kioko [ues]. 1,000 (1991 SIL). Southeast Sulawesi Province, North Buton regency, Bonegunu and Kambowa subdistricts. Buton island. *Status:* 6b (Threatened). *Class:* Austronesian, Malayo-Polynesian, Celebic, Eastern, Southeastern, Muna-Buton, Nuclear Muna-Buton, Munan, Munic, Western. *Dialects:* Kambowa, Kioko. Possibly dialect of the Pancana [pnp] language. Lexical similarity: 82% with Kambowa dialect, 81% with Laompo dialect of Muna [mnb], 74% with Muna, 75% with Liabuku [lix] and Busoa [bup]. *Other:* Muslim. *Map:* 375:41.

Kirikiri [kiy] (Kirira). 250 (1982 SIL). Papua Province, Dofu Wahuka and Paniai villages. On Papua New Guinea border, west of confluence of Tariku and Kliki rivers. *Status:* 6a (Vigorous). *Class:* Lakes Plain, Tariku, West. *Dialects:* Faia, Kirikiri. *Type:* SOV; tonal. *Lg Use:* Vigorous. All ages. Also use Edopi [dbf], Fayu [fau], Papuan Malay [pmy]. *Lg Dev:* Literacy rate in L1: Below 5%. Literacy rate in L2: 5% in Papuan Malay [pmy]. Dictionary. *Other:* No schools in the area. Traditional religion, Christian. *Map:* 372:186.

Kisar [kje] (Meher, Yotowawa). 20,000 (1995 SIL). Southern Maluku Province, over 20 villages total. Kisar island, northeast of Timor island, 19 villages; nearby Roma and Wetar islands, Hila, Likagraha, Amau, Naumatan, and Hi'ai villages. Some in Ambon, Dili, and Kupang cities. *Status:* 5 (Developing). *Class:* Austronesian, Malayo-Polynesian, Central-Eastern Malayo-Polynesian, Timor-Babar, Southwest Maluku, Kisar-Roma. *Dialects:* Not related to Oirata [oia], which has sometimes been called a dialect. *Lg Use:* Also use Indonesian [ind]. Used as L2 by Luang [lex], Oirata [oia]. *Lg Dev:* Literacy rate in L1: Below 1%. Literacy rate in L2: 25%–50%. NT: 2008. *Writing:* Latin script. *Other:* Called Yotowawa or Meher locally. Christian. *Map:* 369.

Klon [kyo] (Kalong, Kelon, Kelong, Kolon). 5,000 (2008 L. Baird). East Nusa Tenggara Province. Southwest, Alor island, Halerman, Margera, Manatang, Probur, Probur Utara, and Tribur villages. *Status:* 6b (Threatened). *Class:* Trans-New Guinea, West, Timor-Alor-Pantar, Alor-Pantar, Alor. *Dialects:* Klon Bring, Klon Paneia. *Map:* 370.

Koba [kpd]. 870 (2011 SIL). Southeast Maluku Province, at least 3 villages. Aru island group, Baun and Fukarel islands southeast of Kobroor island, mouth of Barakai strait. *Status:* 6a (Vigorous). *Class:* Austronesian, Malayo-Polynesian, Central-Eastern Malayo-Polynesian, Aru. *Dialect:* Southeast Koba. Low comprehension of Dobel [kvo]. Lexical similarity: 78%–86% with Dobel [kvo]. *Map:* 368.

Kodeoha [vko] (Kondea, Kondeha). 1,500 (Mead 1999). Southeast Sulawesi Province, North Kolaka regency, Lasusua subdistrict, 4 villages. Upper Bone bay, east coast. *Status:* 6a (Vigorous). *Class:* Austronesian, Malayo-Polynesian, Celebic, Eastern, Southeastern, Bungku-Tolaki, Western, West Coast. *Dialects:* Lexical similarity: 75% with Rahambuu [raz]; 70% with the Mekongga dialect of Tolaki [lbw], and Waru [wru]; 54% with the several Mori and Bungku [bkz] groups. *Lg Use:* Also use the Mekongga dialect of Tolaki [lbw]. Also use Bugis [bug], Bugis [bug]. *Other:* Muslim. *Map:* 375:42.

Kodi [kod] (Kudi). 20,000. East Nusa Tenggara, West Sumba. *Status:* 6a (Vigorous). *Class:* Austronesian, Malayo-Polynesian, Central-Eastern Malayo-Polynesian, Sumba-Hawu, Sumba. *Dialects:* Kodi Bangedo, Kodi Bokol, Nggaro (Nggaura). May be most similar to Wejewa [wew]. *Other:* Traditional religion, Christian. *Map:* 369.

Kofei [kpi]. 100 (Wurm 2000). Papua Province. East side of Geelvink bay. *Status:* 7 (Shifting). *Class:* East Geelvink Bay. *Dialects:* None known. Lexical similarity: 67% with Barapasi [brp], 64% with Demisa [dei], 76% with Sauri [srt], 63% with Woria [wor]. *Lg Use:* Endangered (2000 S. Wurm). *Other:* Christian, traditional religion. *Map:* 372:91.

Kohin [kkx] (Bahasa Seruyan, Seruyan). 8,000 (2003). Central Kalimantan Province, Kotawaringin Timur regency, 10 villages. Central and north Seruyan river area. *Status:* 6b (Threatened). *Class:* Austronesian, Malayo-Polynesian, Greater Barito, West, North. *Dialects:* None known. Lexical similarity: 60%–65% with Ot Danum [otd], 50%–69% with Ngaju [nij]. *Map:* 364:33.

Kokoda [xod] (Kasuweri, Komudago, Nebes, Oderago, Samalek, Tarof). 3,700 (1991 SIL). West Papua Province, Sorong district. Bird's Head, northwest coast of Maccluer Gulf, east of Inanwatan city. *Status:* 6b (Threatened). *Class:* Trans-New Guinea, South Bird's Head, South Bird's Head Proper, Central. *Dialects:* Kasuweri (Komudago), Negri Besar (Negeri Besar), Tarof. Wurm and Hattori (1981) list Kasuweri and Tarof as separate languages. Komudago and Tarof dialects are most similar. Lexical similarity: 60% with Kemberano [bzp]; Kasuweri dialect 86% with Tarof dialect; Negri Besar 82% with Tarof. *Lg Use:* Home. *Map:* 371:30.

Kola [kvv] (Kulaha, Marlasi, Warilau). 7,400 (2011 SIL). Southeast Maluku, 22 villages. North Aru islands, Kola island, widespread, to adjacent islands. *Status:* 6a (Vigorous). *Class:* Austronesian, Malayo-Polynesian, Central-Eastern Malayo-Polynesian, Aru. *Dialects:* Intelligibility test showed Marlasi dialect intelligible of Kompane [kvp]. Lexical similarity: 77% with Kompane [kvp], 70% with Ujir [udj]. *Lg Use:* Vigorous. Outsiders want to learn it. Home, garden. All ages. Positive attitudes. Also use Indonesian [ind]. *Lg Dev:* Literacy rate in L1: Below 1%. Literacy rate in L2: 25%–50%. Bible portions: 2004–2010. *Writing:* Latin script. *Other:* Muslim, Christian. *Map:* 368.

Kombai [tyn] (Komboy). 4,000 (1991 SIL). Papua Province. Interior south coast area; on plain between upper Wideman and Digul rivers, east of Senggo city. *Status:* 6b (Threatened). *Class:* Trans-New Guinea, Ok-Awyu, Awyu-Dumut, Dumut. *Dialects:* Central Kombai, Tayan. Reportedly most similar to Wanggom [wng]. *Other:* Christian, traditional religion. *Map:* 373:234.

Komering [kge] (Kumoring). 470,000 (2000 census). 20,000 in Jakarta (1992). L2 users: Some immigrants from other ethnic groups. South Sumatra Province. Separate areas along Komering river from Lake Ranau to near Palembang city. *Status:* 6b (Threatened). *Class:* Austronesian, Malayo-Polynesian, Lampung. *Dialects:* Downstream Komering, Kayu Agung, Kayu Agung Asli, Komering, Upstream Komering. Lexical similarity: 70% with the Kalianda dialect of Lampung Api [ljp]; 74% with Sungkai dialect of Lampung Api (most similar). *Lg Use:* Vigorous. Home, village. All ages. Positive attitudes. 90% also use Indonesian [ind]. Palembang Musi [mui] is market language. *Lg Dev:* Radio programs. Videos. Dictionary. *Other:* Muslim (Shafi Sunni). *Map:* 377:20.

Komodo [kvh]. 700 (2000). East Nusa Tenggara Province. Komodo island, west coast, Flores island. *Status:* 6b (Threatened). *Class:* Austronesian, Malayo-Polynesian, Central-Eastern Malayo-Polynesian, Bima-Lembata. *Dialects:* None known. A separate language from Manggarai [mqy] (1982 J. Verheijen). *Lg Dev:* Dictionary. Grammar. *Map:* 369.

Kompane [kvp] (Komfana, Kongampani). 330 (1995 SIL). South Maluku Province, Kompane village. Northeast Aru islands, Kongan island east of Wokam island. *Status:* 6b (Threatened). *Class:* Austronesian, Malayo-Polynesian, Central-Eastern Malayo-Polynesian, Aru. *Dialects:* None known. Similar to Kola [kvv], linguistically between Kola and Batuley [bay]. Good intelligibility of Kola. *Lg Use:* Vigorous. *Other:* Muslim. *Map:* 368.

Komyandaret [kzv]. 300 (2000 SIL). Papua Province. Headwaters of Sungai river, west bank. *Status:* 6a (Vigorous). *Class:* Trans-New Guinea, Ok-Awyu, Ok, Ngalum. *Dialects:* None known. May be mutually intelligible with Tsaukambo [kvz]. *Other:* Traditional religion. *Maps:* 372:221, 373:221.

Konda [knd] (Ogit, Yabin, Yabin-Konda). 500 (1988 SIL). Papua Province, Teminabuan subdistrict, Konda village. Southwest Bird's Head area facing Seram Sea; lower Waromge river, south of Teminabuan city. *Status:* 6b (Threatened). *Class:* Trans-New Guinea, South Bird's Head, Konda-Yahadian. *Dialects:* None known. Lexical similarity: 61% with Yahadian [ner]. *Other:* Christian, traditional religion. *Map:* 371:26.

Koneraw [kdw] (Konorau). 1,200 (2001 SIL). Southeast Papua Province. Kolopom island, south coast. *Status:* 7 (Shifting). *Class:* Trans-New Guinea, Mombum. *Lg Use:* Potentially endangered (2000 S. Wurm). Under pressure from Kimaghima [kig] and Indonesian [ind] (Wurm 2007). *Other:* Christian, traditional religion. *Map:* 373:258.

Konjo, Coastal [kjc] (Kondjo, Tiro). 125,000 (1990 SIL). 50,000 Kajang, 10,000 Tiro. South Sulawesi Province, Sinjai, Bulukumba, and Bantaeng regencies. Southeasternmost corner of peninsula; Salayer strait. *Status:* 6b (Threatened). *Class:* Austronesian, Malayo-Polynesian, South Sulawesi, Makassar. *Dialects:* Bantaeng (Bonthain), Konjo Pesisir (Ara, Bira), Tana Toa (Black Konjo, Kadjang, Kajang, Tana Towa). Tana Toa is north end of dialect subgroup. Lexical similarity: 76% with Makassar [mak]; Tana Toa dialect: 10% with other coastal dialects. *Lg Use:* Youth increasingly use Indonesian [ind]. *Writing:* Latin script. *Other:* Tana Towa resist modern ways, contact with outsiders. Muslim, traditional religion. *Map:* 375:26.

Konjo, Highland [kjk] (Konjo Pegunungan, Konyo). 150,000 (1991 SIL). South Sulawesi Province, Sinjai, Bone, Gowa, and Bulukumba regencies. Southern peninsula interior; Mount Lompobatang area northwest, past Makassar city. *Status:* 6b (Threatened). *Class:* Austronesian, Malayo-Polynesian, South Sulawesi, Makassar. *Dialects:* None known. Lexical similarity: 75% with Coastal Konjo [kjc]. *Other:* Muslim, Christian. *Map:* 375:34.

Kopkaka [opk] (Kopka). 400 (2002 SIL). 400 monolinguals. Papua Province, Jayawijaya regency, Kurima subdistrict, Siradala, and Burungmakok villages. In lowlands south of the main ranges; headwaters area, several tributaries of upper Sirac river. *Status:* 6a (Vigorous). *Class:* Trans-New Guinea, Ok-Awyu, Ok, Western. *Dialects:* Marub, Tokuni.

Reportedly similar to Kwer [kwr]. *Other:* Christian, traditional religion. *Map:* 372:216.

Koroni [xkq] (Oengsongi). 500 (Mead 1999). Central Sulawesi Province, Bungku Tengah subdistrict, Unsongi village. On Tolo bay, east coast, south of Bungku town. *Status:* 7 (Shifting). *Class:* Austronesian, Malayo-Polynesian, Celebic, Eastern, Southeastern, Bungku-Tolaki, Eastern, East Coast, Kulisusu. *Dialects:* Lexical similarity: 75% with Taloki [tlk] and Kulisusu [vkl], 66% with Wawonii [wow], Bungku [bkz], Tulambatu dialect of Bungku [bkz]; 65% with Moronene [mqn]. *Lg Use:* Under pressure from Indonesian [ind] (Wurm 2007). *Other:* Muslim. *Map:* 375:43.

Korowai [khe] (Kolufaup). 3,500 (2007 P. de Vries). 3,000 monolinguals. Papua Province. Southeast inland area, northeast of Senggo town; between upper Sirac and Digul rivers. *Status:* 6a (Vigorous). *Class:* Trans-New Guinea, Ok-Awyu, Awyu-Dumut, Korowai. *Dialects:* North Korowai, South Korowai. Dialects have high mutual intelligibility. Lexical similarity: 90% with dialects. *Lg Use:* Vigorous. All domains. All ages. Neutral to positive attitudes. Younger village speakers also use Indonesian [ind]. *Lg Dev:* Literacy rate in L1: Below 1% (2007 P. de Vries). Literacy rate in L2: Less than 1% in Indonesian (2007 P. de Vries). *Writing:* Latin script. *Other:* Traditional religion. *Maps:* 372:220, 373:220.

Korupun-Sela [kpq] (Kimyal of Korupun, Korapun). 8,000 (1996 E. Young). Papua Province, Jayawijaya regency, Kurima subdistrict. Eastern highlands, on upper reaches of Erok river. *Status:* 5 (Developing). *Class:* Trans-New Guinea, Mek, Eastern. *Dialects:* Dagi, Deibula, Korupun (Duram), Sela, Sisibna (Gobugdua). Lexical similarity: 60% with Nipsan [nps]. *Lg Use:* Religious services. Also use Nipsan [nps]. *Lg Dev:* NT: 2010. *Other:* Traditional religion, Christian. *Map:* 372:212.

Kosare [kiq] (Kosadle). 250 (1993 R. Doriot). Papua Province. West of Nawa and Idenburg rivers confluence; south of Jayapura city. *Status:* 6a (Vigorous). *Class:* Kaure, Kaure Proper. *Lg Use:* Most domains. All ages. Positive attitudes. *Other:* Christian, traditional religion. *Map:* 372:202.

Kowiai [kwh] (Adi, Aiduma, Kaiwai, Kajumerah, Kayumerah, Koiwai, Kuiwai, Namatota, Namatote). 600 (2000 SIL). West Papua Province, Keroi, Adijaya, Namatota, and Kayumerah villages. Bomberai peninsula, southwest coast; Kamrau bay area; Kaimana. Namatote, and Adi islands, smaller islands in bay. *Status:* 6b (Threatened). *Class:* Austronesian, Malayo-Polynesian, Central-Eastern Malayo-Polynesian, South Bomberai. *Dialects:* Adijaya, Keroi, Namatota. *Lg Use:* Potentially endangered (2000 S. Wurm) but also not endangered. Positive attitudes. Also use Indonesian [ind], Papuan Malay [pmy]. Used as L2 by Mairasi [zrs]. *Writing:* Latin script. *Other:* Muslim. *Map:* 371:49.

Kubu [kvb] (Anak Dalam, Orang Hutan, Orang Rimba). 10,000 (1989). Sumatra, Jambi Province. Eastern swamp region; possibly some in Riau and South Sumatra provinces. *Status:* 6b (Threatened). *Class:* Austronesian, Malayo-Polynesian, Malayo-Chamic, Malayic, Malay. A member of macrolanguage Malay [msa] (Malaysia). *Dialects:* Bajat, Dawas, Jambi, Lalang, Nomadic Kubu, Ridan, Supat, Tungkal, Tungkal Ilir, Ulu Lako. Related to Lubu [lcf]. *Lg Use:* For Kubu living in settled villages, L1 already replaced in all domains outside the home; for Kubu in Jambi areas (more isolated and less sedentary), the vitality is higher. Home. All ages. Positive attitudes. Villagers use Indonesian [ind] or another trade language for education, religion, civic, with other ethnic groups. *Other:* Territory rapidly shrinking, somewhat due to deforestation. Traditional religion, Muslim. *Map:* 377:21.

Kui [kvd] (Lerabain). 1,900. Ethnic population: 1,900. East Nusa Tenggara Province. Alor island; Kui dialect on south coast in Lerabaing and Buraga villages, also in Moru in Kalabahi bay interspersed with Hamap [hmu]; Batulolong dialect: Sibera and Kapebang villages. *Status:* 6b (Threatened). *Class:* Trans-New Guinea, West, Timor-Alor-Pantar, Alor-Pantar, Alor. *Dialects:* Batulolong, Kiramang (Kramang), Kui (Buraga, Lerabaing). *Other:* Muslim, Christian. *Map:* 370.

Kula [tpg] (Kola, Lamtoka, Lantoka, Tanglapui). 5,000 (Grimes et al. 1997). East Nusa Tenggara Province, Alor island, central eastern mountains, between Kamang [woi] and Sawila [swt] language areas; also on northeast coast, Maukuru, Takala, Koilela, Peisaka, and Kiralela villages. *Status:* 6a (Vigorous). *Class:* Trans-New Guinea, West, Timor-Alor-Pantar, Tanglapui. *Dialects:* Arumaka, Iramang, Kula, Kula Watena, Kulatela, Larena, Sumang, Watena. Reportedly structurally similar to Sawila [swt], but intelligibility is marginal. *Writing:* Latin script. *Other:* Christian, traditional religion. *Map:* 370.

Kulisusu [vkl] (Kalisusu, Kolensusu, Kolinsusu). 22,000 (Mead 1999), increasing. Southeast Sulawesi Province, North Buton regency, Kulisusu Utara, Kulisusu Induk, Kulisusu Barat, and Bonegunu subdistricts. Northernost Buton island. *Status:* 6a (Vigorous). *Class:* Austronesian, Malayo-Polynesian, Celebic, Eastern, Southeastern, Bungku-Tolaki, Eastern, East Coast, Kulisusu. *Dialects:* Lexical similarity: 81% between dialects, 77% with Tolaki [lbw], 75% with Koroni [xkq], 66% with Wawonii [wow] and Bungku [bkz] group, 65% with Moronene [mqn], 54% with the Mori languages. *Lg Use:* Positive attitudes. *Writing:* Latin script. *Other:* Muslim. *Map:* 375:44.

Kumbewaha [xks] (Kumberaha, Umbewaha). 3,400 (2004 SIL). Southeast Sulawesi Province, Buton regency, Lasalimu subdistrict, Kumbewaha and Wajah Jaya villages. Buton island, southeast; west of Wangiwangi island. *Status:* 6a (Vigorous). *Class:* Austronesian, Malayo-Polynesian, Celebic, Eastern, Southeastern, Muna-Buton, Nuclear Muna-Buton, Buton, East Buton. *Lg Use:* All domains. All ages. Also use Indonesian [ind], Lasalimu [llm], Tukang Besi North [khc], Tukang Besi South [bhq]. *Lg Dev:* Literacy rate in L2: 20%. *Other:* Muslim. *Map:* 375:45.

Kur [kuv]. 3,180 (2000). Southeast Maluku Province, West Kei Kecil district. Kur and surrounding islands. *Status:* 6a (Vigorous). *Class:* Austronesian, Malayo-Polynesian, Central-Eastern Malayo-Polynesian, Teor-Kur. *Dialects:* Different from Kei [kei]. Boundaries of intelligibility with dialects north and the central dialect, and with Teor [tev] need further investigation. Lexical similarity: 47%–50% with Kei [kei], 71%–83% with Teor [tev], 41% with Watubela [wah], 38% with Geser [ges]. *Lg Use:* Vigorous. Also use Kei [kei]. *Other:* Muslim. *Map:* 368.

Kuri [nbn] (Modan, Nabi). 500 (1982 SIL). West Papua Province, 16 villages. Southwest Bomberai peninsula; area south of Bituni bay, northeast of Arguni bay. *Status:* 7 (Shifting). *Class:* Austronesian, Malayo-Polynesian, Central-Eastern Malayo-Polynesian, Unclassified. *Dialects:* None known. Lexical similarity: 90% with Irarutu [irh]. *Lg Use:* Home. *Other:* Traditional religion, Christian. *Map:* 371:54.

Kurudu [kjr]. 2,180 (1993 R. Doriot). Papua Province, Kaipuri and Poiwai villages. Kurudu islands between east tip of Serui (Yapen) island and northwest mainland. *Status:* 6b (Threatened). *Class:* Austronesian, Malayo-Polynesian, Central-Eastern Malayo-Polynesian, Eastern Malayo-Polynesian, South Halmahera-West New Guinea, West New Guinea, Cenderawasih Bay, Yapen, East. *Dialects:* Lexical similarity: 71% with Wabo [wbb],

46% with Western Serui. Kaipuri dialect has highest lexical similarity with Yapen group. *Lg Use:* Vigorous. Religious services. *Other:* Christian. *Map:* 372:106.

Kwer [kwr]. 100 (1998 M. Donohue). Papua Province, Jayawijaya regency, Kurima subdistrict, Kwer village. Lowlands area south of main ranges; headwaters of Sirac river tributaries, northeast of Senggo town. *Status:* 6b (Threatened). *Class:* Trans-New Guinea, Ok-Awyu, Ok, Western. *Dialects:* None known. Reportedly similar to Kopkaka [opk]; may be considered the same language. *Lg Use:* All ages. *Map:* 372:222.

Kwerba [kwe] (Airmati, Armati, Koassa, Mataweja, Naibedj, Segar Tor, Serikenam, Tekutameso). 2,500 (1996 SIL). Papua Province, Aurime, Munukania, Wamariri, Tatsewalem, and Apiaweti villages. Northeast mainland interior; headwaters of Apauwer river. *Status:* 5 (Developing). *Class:* Tor-Kwerba, Greater Kwerba, Kwerba, Nuclear. *Dialects:* Nogukwabai, Sasawa, Serikenam. Lexical similarity: 64% with Bagusa [bqb]. *Lg Use:* Used as L2 by Samarokena [tmj]. *Lg Dev:* Literacy rate in L1: Below 5%. Bible portions: 1986–2001. *Writing:* Latin script. *Other:* Traditional religion, Christian. *Map:* 372:172.

Kwerba Mamberamo [xwr] (Napok, Nobuk, Nogukwabai, Nopuk, Nopukw, Tatsewalem). 300 (1993 R. Doriot). Papua Province, Kwerba, Edifalen, and Marinafalen villages. East bank, Mamberamo river, into highlands; southeast of Kasonaweja town. *Status:* 6a (Vigorous). *Class:* Tor-Kwerba, Greater Kwerba, Kwerba, Nuclear. *Lg Use:* Vigorous. All ages. *Other:* 'Nopukw', language, in the Kwerba family, and does not distinguish a particular variety. Traditional religion, Christian. *Map:* 372:174.

Kwerisa [kkb] (Taogwe). 15 (Wurm 2000). Ethnic population: 130. Papua Province. Lower Rouffaer river. *Status:* 8b (Nearly extinct). *Class:* Lakes Plain, Tariku, East. *Dialects:* None known. Lexical similarity: 60% with Biritai [bqq]. *Lg Use:* Moribund (2000 S. Wurm). Most of the ethnic group shifted to Kaiy [tcq]. Home. Older adults. *Other:* Traditional religion, Christian. *Map:* 372:192.

Kwesten [kwt]. 2,000 (1987 SIL). Papua Province, Holmhaven, Mafenter, Arare, and Omte villages. Pacific coast area east of Sarmi town; lower Tor river area. *Status:* 7 (Shifting). *Class:* Tor-Kwerba, Orya-Tor, Tor. *Dialects:* None known. Lexical similarity: 40% with Berik [bkl]. *Other:* Christian, traditional religion. *Map:* 372:170.

Kwinsu [kuc] (Ansudu). 500 (2007). Papua Province, Sarmi regency, Pantai Timur subdistrict, Ansudu village. *Status:* 7 (Shifting). *Class:* Tor-Kwerba, Orya-Tor, Tor. *Lg Use:* Children seldom speak it. Only adults are fluent. Also use Indonesian [ind], Papuan Malay [pmy]. *Map:* 372:121.

Laba [lau] (Kedi, South Loloda). 2,000 (1991 SIL). North Maluku Province, south end of Loloda district, 4 villages. North Halmahera island, interior from northwest coast. *Status:* 6a (Vigorous). *Class:* West Papuan, North Halmahera, Galela-Loloda. *Dialects:* None known. Phonology like Galela [gbi], 70% intelligibility, 75% of Loloda [loa]. Lexical similarity: 75% with Galela [gbi], 78% with Loloda [loa]. *Other:* Christian. *Map:* 366.

Laha [lhh] (Central Ambon). 3,890 (1987 SIL). Maluku Province, Laha and other villages. Ambon island, south central coast. *Status:* 6a (Vigorous). *Class:* Austronesian, Malayo-Polynesian, Central-Eastern Malayo-Polynesian, Central Maluku, East, Seram, Nunusaku, Piru Bay, East, Seram Straits, Ambon. *Dialects:* None known. Distinct from Manusela [wha]. Lexical similarity: 64%–66% with Asilulu [asl] and Seit-Kaitetu [hik] (most similar). *Lg Use:* Parents encourage children to speak Laha. All ages. Also use Ambonese Malay [abs]. *Other:* Muslim, Christian. *Map:* 367.

Laiyolo [lji] (Barang-Barang, Da'ang). 800 (1997 SIL). 250 Laiyolo, 550 Barang-Barang. South Sulawesi Province, Laiyolo, Barang-Barang, Lowa, and other villages. Selayar island south tip. *Status:* 6b (Threatened). *Class:* Austronesian, Malayo-Polynesian, Celebic, Wotu-Wolio, Kalao. *Dialects:* Barang-Barang (Loa, Loa', Lowa), Laiyolo (Lajolo, Layolo). Lexical similarity: 86% between Laiyolo and Barang-Barang dialect, 76% with Kalao [kly], 65% with Wolio [wlo], 53% with Wotu [wtw], 39% with Muna [mnb]. *Lg Use:* Vigorous in Barang-Barang dialect. Mainly adults in Laiyolo; all ages in Barang-Barang. Little Indonesian [ind] used. Selayar [sly] is main L2. *Other:* Muslim, Christian. *Map:* 375:46.

Lamaholot [slp] (Solor, Solorese). 180,000 (2010). L2 users: Many L2 users. East Nusa Tenggara Province. East tip Flores, west Solor islands; in pockets on north Pantar coast, northwest Alor, surrounding islands. *Status:* 3 (Wider communication). *Class:* Austronesian, Malayo-Polynesian, Central-Eastern Malayo-Polynesian, Bima-Lembata. *Dialects:* Lamaholot (Ile Mandiri, Larantuka, Lewolaga, Ritaebang, Taka, Tanjung Bunda), West Lamaholot (Muhang, Pukaunu), West Solor. *Lg Use:* The area around Larantuka is multiethnic and some people have shifted to Malay [lrt]. Used as language of wider communication. Used as L2 by Adonara [adr], Alor [aol], Ile Ape [ila], Lamalera [lmr], Lamatuka [lmq], Levuka [lvu], Lewo Eleng [lwe], Lewotobi [lwt], South Lembata [lmf], West Lembata [lmj]. *Lg Dev:* Dictionary. Grammar. *Other:* 'Lamaholot-Alor' is used to refer to both a lingua franca and also to any of several Austronesian varieties spoken from eastern Flores to Alor. Alor [aol] is part of a chain which includes Lamaholot. Traditional religion, Christian, Muslim. *Map:* 370.

Lamalera [lmr] (Kawela, Lebatukan, Mulan). 4,000 (2008 census). East Nusa Tenggara Province. South coast, Lembata island. At least 3 villages. *Status:* 6a (Vigorous). *Class:* Austronesian, Malayo-Polynesian, Central-Eastern Malayo-Polynesian, Bima-Lembata. *Lg Use:* Also use Lamaholot [slp]. *Lg Dev:* Grammar. *Map:* 370.

Lamatuka [lmq] (Lamatoka). 4,000 (2008 census). East Nusa Tenggara Province. Central Lembata island, between Ile Ape [ila] and Lewo Eleng [lwe] language areas. Several villages. *Status:* 6a (Vigorous). *Class:* Austronesian, Malayo-Polynesian, Central-Eastern Malayo-Polynesian, Bima-Lembata. *Dialects:* None known. Lewo Eleng [lwe] is probably most closely related. *Lg Use:* Also use Lamaholot [slp]. *Other:* Christian, traditional religion. *Map:* 370.

Lamboya [lmy]. 25,000 (Grimes et al. 1997). East Nusa Tenggara Province. Sumba island, southwest coast, southwest of Waikabubak city. *Status:* 6a (Vigorous). *Class:* Austronesian, Malayo-Polynesian, Central-Eastern Malayo-Polynesian, Sumba-Hawu, Sumba. *Dialects:* Lamboya, Nggaura. *Map:* 369.

Lampung Api [ljp] (Api, Lampong, Lampung, Lampung Pesisir). 827,000 (2000 census). Sumatra, west, central, and south Lampung Province; south Benkulu Province around Krui, Sanggi, and Kotajawa; South Sumatra Province, south of Muaradua, near headwaters of Kanan river. *Status:* 6b (Threatened). *Class:* Austronesian, Malayo-Polynesian, Lampung. *Dialects:* Daya, Krui (Kroe, Kru'i, Njo, Western Lampung), Pubian, Ranau, Southern Pesisir, Sungkai. *Lg Use:* Outside of the city, home and village everyday. All ages. Positive attitudes. Also use Indonesian [ind]. *Lg Dev:* Grammar. NT: 2002. *Writing:* Latin script. Kaganga script. *Other:* Teachers must use L1, especially in lower grades. Muslim. *Map:* 377:22.

Lampung Nyo [abl] (Abung, Lampong). 180,000 (2000 census). Sumatra, east Lampung Province. 3 enclaves situated between Kanan and Seputih rivers. *Status:* 6a (Vigorous). *Class:* Austronesian, Malayo-Polynesian, Lampung. *Dialects:* Abung, Melinting, Sukadana, Tulang-bawang. Many differences in vocabulary and phonology with Lampung Api [ljp]. Lexical similarity: 72% between the Menggala dialect and the Kalianda dialect of Lampung Api [ljp], 77% among dialects. *Lg Use:* Home. All ages. Positive attitudes. Indonesian [ind] used in education, religion, and civil domains. *Lg Dev:* Taught in primary schools, as an auxiliary medium. *Writing:* Kaganga script. *Other:* Muslim. *Map:* 377:23.

Larike-Wakasihu [alo]. 12,600 (1987 SIL). Maluku Province, Larike, Wakasihu, Tapi, Allang, and Lai villages. Southwesternmost Ambon island coast, Hitu peninsula. *Status:* 6b (Threatened). *Class:* Austronesian, Malayo-Polynesian, Central-Eastern Malayo-Polynesian, Central Maluku, East, Seram, Nunusaku, Piru Bay, West, Hoamoal. *Dialects:* Allang, Larike, Wakasihu. The western end of the Ambon dialect subgroup. Lexical similarity: 81% among Allang, and Larike, and Wakasihu dialects; 92% between Larike and Wakasihu; 68%–71% with Asilulu [asl], 67%–72% with Negeri Lima dialect of Asilulu [asl]. *Lg Use:* Vigorous use in Larike and Wakasihu, weak in Allang. Only older adults in Allang, Allang Asaude, Uraur, and Urusana still know Allang, but apparently do not use it. Younger generation prefers regional or national language. Also use Indonesian [ind]. *Lg Dev:* Literacy rate in L1: 1%–5%. Literacy rate in L2: 50%–75%. Dictionary. Grammar. *Writing:* Latin script. *Other:* Muslim, Christian. *Map:* 367.

Lasalimu [llm]. 1,700 (1999 SIL). Southeast Sulawesi Province, Lasalimu subdistrict, Lasalimu and Malaoge villages. Buton island, southeast; Lasalima town area. *Status:* 6b (Threatened). *Class:* Austronesian, Malayo-Polynesian, Celebic, Eastern, Southeastern, Muna-Buton, Nuclear Muna-Buton, Buton, East Buton. *Dialects:* None known. Lexical similarity: 68% with Kamaru [kgx], 64% with Cia-Cia [cia], 48% with Tukang Besi North [khc], 49% with Tukang Besi South [bhq], 51% with Pancana [pnp], 50% with Wolio [wlo] and Muna [mnb]. *Lg Use:* Used as L2 by Kumbewaha [xks]. *Other:* Muslim. *Map:* 375:47.

Latu [ltu]. 2,130 (1982 SIL). Maluku Province, Latu village. Seram island southwest, Elpaputih bay, Point Latu. *Status:* 7 (Shifting). *Class:* Austronesian, Malayo-Polynesian, Central-Eastern Malayo-Polynesian, Central Maluku, East, Seram, Nunusaku, Piru Bay, East, Seram Straits, Uliase, Hatuhaha, Saparua. *Dialects:* Lexical similarity: 82%–84% with Saparua [spr] dialects. *Map:* 367.

Lauje [law] (Laudje, Tinombo). 44,000 (Himmelmann 2001). 6,000 use Ampibabo dialect (Himmelmann 2001). Central Sulawesi Province, Dampelas Sojol, Dondo, Tinombo, Tomini, and Ampibabo subdistricts. Northwest coast along Tomini bay, Sidoan river area. *Status:* 6b (Threatened). *Class:* Austronesian, Malayo-Polynesian, Celebic, Tomini-Tolitoli, Tomini, Northern. *Dialect:* Ampibabo (Ampibabo-Lauje). Ampibabo dialect may be a separate language. *Lg Dev:* Bible portions. *Other:* Christian, Muslim, traditional religion. *Map:* 374:48.

Laura [lur] (Laora). 10,000 (Grimes et al. 1997). East Nusa Tenggara Province. Northwest Sumba island, from Mamboru town west to Cape Karosso. *Status:* 6a (Vigorous). *Class:* Austronesian, Malayo-Polynesian, Central-Eastern Malayo-Polynesian, Sumba-Hawu, Sumba. *Dialects:* Laura, Mbukambero (Bukambero). Not intelligible with Kodi [kod]. *Map:* 369.

Lawangan [lbx] (Luwangan, Northeast Barito). 100,000 (Wurm and Hattori 1981). Central East Kalimantan Province. Karau river area. *Status:* 6a (Vigorous). *Class:* Austronesian, Malayo-Polynesian, Greater Barito, East, North. *Dialects:* Ajuh, Bakoi (Lampung), Bantian (Bentian), Banuwang, Bawu (Bawo), Benua, Kali, Karau (Beloh), Lawa, Lolang, Mantararen, Njumit, Pasir, Purai, Purung, Taboyan, Tuwang. At least 17 dialects. Tawoyan [twy] may be inherently intelligible. Lexical similarity: 77% with Tawoyan [twy], 53% with Dusun Deyah [dun]. Benua (population 25,000, six subdialects) may be distinct enough to be considered a separate language. (Nikolić 2008). *Lg Use:* Also use Bakumpai [bkr]. *Map:* 365:35.

Legenyem [lcc] (Laganyan). 250 (Wurm 2000). Papua Province, Raja Ampat Islands, Waigeo island in northwest end of main bay and on south coast, Beo, Lempintol, and Wawiai villages. *Status:* 6a (Vigorous). *Class:* Austronesian, Malayo-Polynesian, Central-Eastern Malayo-Polynesian, Eastern Malayo-Polynesian, South Halmahera-West New Guinea, West New Guinea, Cenderawasih Bay, Raja Ampat. *Lg Use:* Vigorous. *Other:* Muslim, Christian, traditional religion. *Map:* 371:2.

Lembata, South [lmf]. 7,000 (2008 census). East Nusa Tenggara Province. South Lembata island, between Lamalera [lmr] and Lamatuka [lmq] language areas. *Status:* 6a (Vigorous). *Class:* Austronesian, Malayo-Polynesian, Central-Eastern Malayo-Polynesian, Bima-Lembata. *Lg Use:* Also use Lamaholot [slp]. *Map:* 370.

Lembata, West [lmj] (Labalekan, Mingar). 8,000 (2008 census). East Nusa Tenggara Province. Lembata island, western end. *Status:* 6a (Vigorous). *Class:* Austronesian, Malayo-Polynesian, Central-Eastern Malayo-Polynesian, Bima-Lembata. *Lg Use:* Also use Lamaholot [slp]. *Map:* 370.

Lemolang [ley] (Baebunta, Limola, Limolang). 2,000 (Vail 1991), decreasing. South Sulawesi Province, Luwu Utara regency, Sassa and Salassa villages. Inland from northeast coast, Bone bay; middle Rongko river area. Scattered in Sabbang, possibly Baebunta areas. *Status:* 8a (Moribund). *Class:* Austronesian, Malayo-Polynesian, South Sulawesi, Lemolang. *Dialects:* None known. Lexical similarity: 41% with Mori Bawah [xmz], 39% with Mori Atas [mzq], 38% with Bungku [bkz], 39% with Wolio [wlo], 31% with Seko Padang [skx], 30% with Rampi [lje], 29% with Toraja-Sa'dan [sda], 26% with Muna [mnb], 25% with Wotu [wtw], 24% with Bugis [bug]. *Lg Use:* Youth shifted to Bugis [bug]. Also use Bugis [bug], Indonesian [ind], Tae' [rob]. *Other:* Muslim. *Map:* 375:50.

Lengilu [lgi]. 3 (Wurm 2000). Northeast Kalimantan, between Sa'ban and Lundayeh. *Status:* 8b (Nearly extinct). *Class:* Austronesian, Malayo-Polynesian, North Borneo, North Sarawakan, Dayic, Kelabitic. *Lg Use:* Moribund (2000 S. Wurm). *Map:* 365:36.

Lepki [lpe]. 530 (1991 SIL). Papua Province, Jayawijaya regency, Okbibab subdistrict. Near middle Sogber river, north of Apmisibil town. *Status:* 6a (Vigorous). *Class:* Unclassified. *Dialects:* None known. Possible genetic similarities with Murkim [rmh]. *Type:* SOV; head and dependent marking; tonal. *Lg Use:* Home, religious services, market. Some at Luban also use Ketengban [xte]. *Other:* Traditional religion, Christian. *Map:* 372:149.

Leti [lti]. 7,500 (1995 SIL). Maluku Province, Leti island. *Status:* 7 (Shifting). *Class:* Austronesian, Malayo-Polynesian, Central-Eastern Malayo-Polynesian, Timor-Babar, Southwest Maluku, Luang. *Dialects:* None known. Marginal intelligibility and difficulty with written Luang [lex]. Lexical similarity: 89% with Luang [lex]. *Lg Use:* No longer spoken by younger generations (Hajek 2006). Also use Indonesian [ind]. Used as L2 by Luang [lex]. *Lg Dev:* Literacy rate in L1: Below 1%. Literacy rate in L2: 25%–50%. *Other:* Matrilineal. They share historical and cultural heritage with Luang [lex], but maintain their own identity and local pride. Christian. *Maps:* 368, 369.

Levuka [lvu] (Lembata, Lewokukun, Lewuka, Painara). 4,000 (2008 census). East Nusa Tenggara Province.

West central Lembata island between Ile Ape [ila] and Lamalera [lmr] language areas. *Status:* 6a (Vigorous). *Class:* Austronesian, Malayo-Polynesian, Central-Eastern Malayo-Polynesian, Bima-Lembata. *Dialects:* Kalikasa, Levuka. *Lg Use:* Also use Lamaholot [slp]. *Other:* Christian, traditional religion. *Map:* 370.

Lewo Eleng [lwe]. 4,000 (2008 census). East Nusa Tenggara Province. Central eastern Lembata island, between Lamatuka [lmq] and Kedang [ksx] language areas, several villages. North coastal plains villages are from recent government-induced migrations. *Status:* 6a (Vigorous). *Class:* Austronesian, Malayo-Polynesian, Central-Eastern Malayo-Polynesian, Bima-Lembata. *Dialects:* None known. Lamatuka [lmq] probably most closely related. *Lg Use:* Also use Lamaholot [slp]. *Other:* Christian, traditional religion. *Map:* 370.

Lewotobi [lwt] (Southwest Lamaholot). 6,000. East Nusa Tenggara Province. Southeastern Flores island across from Solor island, Lewotobi volcano area. *Status:* 6a (Vigorous). *Class:* Austronesian, Malayo-Polynesian, Central-Eastern Malayo-Polynesian, Bima-Lembata. *Lg Use:* Also use Lamaholot [slp]. *Map:* 370.

Liabuku [lix]. 75 (2004 SIL), decreasing. Southeast Sulawesi, Bungi subdistrict, south Buton island, part of Liabuku village north of Bau-Bau. *Status:* 8a (Moribund). *Class:* Austronesian, Malayo-Polynesian, Celebic, Eastern, Southeastern, Muna-Buton, Nuclear Muna-Buton, Munan, Munic, Western. *Dialects:* Quite divergent from other Muna varieties. Lexical similarity: 82% with the Burukene dialect of Muna [mnb], 72%–76% with other Muna dialects, 72% with Muna, 75% with Kioko [ues]. *Lg Use:* All users are older adults. Also use Indonesian [ind], Wolio [wlo]. *Other:* Muslim. *Map:* 375:51.

Liana-Seti [ste] (Liambata-Kobi, Liana, Lianan, Teula, Uhei Kachlakan, Uhei Kaclakin, Uhei Kahlakim). 3,000 (1989 SIL). Central Maluku Province, Bula, Werinama, and Tehoru districts, 8 villages. Seram island, from east Teluti bay north to Seram Sea coast. *Status:* 6b (Threatened). *Class:* Austronesian, Malayo-Polynesian, Central-Eastern Malayo-Polynesian, Central Maluku, East, Seram, Manusela-Seti. *Dialects:* Kobi, Seti, Wahakaim. Lexical similarity: 66%–74% between Seti (westernmost and interior) and Wahakaim (near coast) dialects, 69%–78% between Kobi and Seti, 70% between Kobi and Wahakaim, 42%–61% between Kobi and Manusela [wha], 54%–66% between Kobi and Benggoi [bgy], 48%–58% between Kobi and Salas [sgu]. *Lg Use:* Vigorous. Seti also use Teluti [tlt]. *Lg Dev:* Literacy rate in L1: Below 1%. Literacy rate in L2: 25%–50%. *Writing:* Latin script. *Other:* Speakers use Liana. Christian. *Map:* 367.

Liki [lio] (Moar). 11 (2005 SIL), decreasing. Ethnic population: 320. Papua Province, Sarmi regency, Sarmi subdistrict, Islands off north coast of Sarmi. *Status:* 8a (Moribund). *Class:* Austronesian, Malayo-Polynesian, Central-Eastern Malayo-Polynesian, Eastern Malayo-Polynesian, Oceanic, Western Oceanic, North New Guinea, Sarmi-Jayapura Bay, Sarmi. *Dialects:* None known. Reportedly similar to Sobei [sob]. *Lg Use:* Not used by youth. Adults more. Also use Indonesian [ind], Papuan Malay [pmy]. *Map:* 372:112.

Lindu [klw] (Lindoe, Linduan, Tado). 2,400 (2000 census), increasing. Central Sulawesi Province, Lindu subdistrict, Anca, Tomado, and Langko villages. Area near Lake Lindu. *Status:* 5 (Developing). *Class:* Austronesian, Malayo-Polynesian, Celebic, Kaili-Pamona, Northern, Kaili. *Dialects:* Lindu is reportedly very similar to Moma [myl]; considered by some a Moma dialect. *Lg Dev:* 50 Lindu speakers enrolled in the literacy program (2013 A. Eastwood). Used in 50% of the schools one hour per week for literacy. *Other:* 'Tado' (alternate for Lindu) is different from Tado dialect of Kaili Ledo [lew]. Christian. *Map:* 374:52.

Li'o [ljl] (Aku, Lio, Lionese, Tanah Kunu). 105,000 (2009 census). East Nusa Tenggara Province. East central Flores island, bi-coastal, between Sika [ski] and Ende [end] language areas. *Status:* 6a (Vigorous). *Class:* Austronesian, Malayo-Polynesian, Central-Eastern Malayo-Polynesian, Bima-Lembata. *Dialects:* Dialect subgroup with Ende [end]. *Other:* Christian. *Map:* 370.

Lisabata-Nuniali [lcs] (Lisabata, Noniali, Nuniali). 1,830 (1982). Maluku Province, 5 villages. West and north Seram island, across north coast. *Status:* 6a (Vigorous). *Class:* Austronesian, Malayo-Polynesian, Central-Eastern Malayo-Polynesian, Central Maluku, East, Seram, Nunusaku, Three Rivers, Amalumute, Northwest Seram. *Dialects:* Kawa, Lisabata-Timur, Nuniali, Sukaraja. Lexical similarity: between Kawa (far western) and Lisabata Timur (far eastern) dialects is 85%, 72% with Naka'ela [nae], 67% with Hulung [huk], 63% with Alune [alp]. *Lg Use:* Vigorous, except in Kawa. Also use Ambonese Malay [abs]. *Other:* Muslim, Christian (Nuniali). *Map:* 367.

Lisela [lcl] (Buru, Li Enyorot, Liet Enjorot, North Buru, Wayapo). 11,900 (1989 SIL). Maluku Province. Buru island, west of Manipa, Seram islands. 4 separate areas; largest area: northeast coast, lower inland Wae and Apo river valleys west of Kajeli town; other 3 areas westward across north Seram Sea coast. Some in Ambon. *Status:* 7 (Shifting). *Class:* Austronesian, Malayo-Polynesian, Central-Eastern Malayo-Polynesian, Central Maluku, Buru. *Dialects:* Lisela (Licela, Licella), Tagalisa. *Lg Use:* Shifting to Ambonese Malay [abs]. *Other:* Muslim, traditional religion. *Map:* 367.

Lola [lcd]. 900 (2011 SIL). Southeast Maluku Province, Lola, Warabal, and Jambuair villages. Aru island group; 3 islands east of Kobroor and Baun islands. *Status:* 6b (Threatened). *Class:* Austronesian, Malayo-Polynesian, Central-Eastern Malayo-Polynesian, Aru. *Dialects:* Lola, Warabal. Reportedly linguistically between Batuley [bay] and Dobel [kvo]; similar to Koba [kpd]. *Lg Use:* Most vigorous in Warabal. Also use Ambonese Malay [abs]. *Other:* Muslim. *Map:* 368.

Lolak [llq]. 3,000 (2004 SIL). North Sulawesi Province, Bolaang Mongondow regency, Lolak subdistrict, Lolak, Mongkoinit, and Motabang villages. Inland area watershed of lower Mongodow river. *Status:* 8b (Nearly extinct). *Class:* Austronesian, Malayo-Polynesian, Philippine, Greater Central Philippine, Gorontalo-Mongondow, Gorontalic. *Dialects:* None known. Structurally related to Gorontalo [gor], but with heavy lexical borrowing from Mongondow [mog]. Lexical similarity: 79% with Mongondow [mog], 66% with Ponosakan [pns], 63% with Kaidipang [kzp]. *Lg Use:* Children mostly or exclusively use Indonesian [ind] (1990). Also use Indonesian [ind], Mongondow [mog]. *Other:* Muslim. *Map:* 374:53.

Lole [llg] (Ba'a, Baä, Central Rote, Loleh, Rote, Rote Tengah, Roti, Rotinese). 20,000 (2002 UKAW). Ethnic population: 20,000. East Nusa Tenggara Province. West central Rote island, from northern coast Ba'a town to south coast. North Lole dialect covers north and central regions of Lole domain. *Status:* 6a (Vigorous). *Class:* Austronesian, Malayo-Polynesian, Central-Eastern Malayo-Polynesian, Timor-Babar, Nuclear Timor, Rote. *Dialects:* Ba'a, North Lole, South Lole. North Lole, na-hina, becomes South Lole, ni-hina. *Lg Use:* Vigorous. All domains. All ages. Also use Indonesian [ind], Kupang Malay [mkn]. *Lg Dev:* Bible portions: 2004. *Writing:* Latin script. *Other:* Christian. *Map:* 369.

Loloda [loa] (Loda, North Loloda). 15,000 (1991 SIL). 2,000

Bakun. North Maluku Province. North Halmahera island, northwest coast, nearby islands. *Status:* 5 (Developing). *Class:* West Papuan, North Halmahera, Galela-Loloda. *Dialect:* Bakun. Intelligibility of Laba [lau] very limited. 85% intelligibility of Galela [gbi], Galela [gbi] has 65% intelligibility of Loloda. *Lg Use:* Vigorous. Also use Indonesian [ind]. *Lg Dev:* Literacy rate in L1: Below 1%. Literacy rate in L2: 50%–75%. Grammar. Bible portions: 1915. *Writing:* Latin script. *Other:* Christian, Muslim. *Map:* 366.

Lorang [lrn]. 220 (2011 SIL). Southeast Maluku Province. Central Aru island group, Koba island, northwest coast. *Status:* 6a (Vigorous). *Class:* Austronesian, Malayo-Polynesian, Central-Eastern Malayo-Polynesian, Aru. *Dialects:* None known. Reportedly similar to Koba [kpd] and, to a lesser extent, Dobel [kvo]. Some similarities with Manombai [woo], but intelligibility is lower than might be expected. *Lg Use:* Vigorous. Also use Dobel [kvo]. *Other:* Christian. *Map:* 368.

Loun [lox]. No known L1 speakers. Central Maluku, north central Seram. *Status:* 10 (Extinct). *Class:* Austronesian, Malayo-Polynesian, Central-Eastern Malayo-Polynesian, Central Maluku, East, Seram, Nunusaku, Three Rivers, Amalumute, Northwest Seram, Loun. *Lg Use:* Shifted to Ambon Malay [abs] and Indonesian [ind].

Luang [lex] (Letri Lgona, Lgona, Literi Lagona). 18,000 (1995 SIL). 200 monolinguals. Maluku Province. East of Timor island; entire Wetan island, across Wetan strait to northwest Babar island. *Status:* 5 (Developing). *Class:* Austronesian, Malayo-Polynesian, Central-Eastern Malayo-Polynesian, Timor-Babar, Southwest Maluku, Luang. *Dialects:* Lakor, Luang, Moa, Wetan (Wetang). Low comprehension of Leti [lti]. Lexical similarity: 89% with Leti [lti]. *Lg Use:* Positive attitudes. Also use Ambonese Malay [abs], Indonesian [ind], Kisar [kje], Leti [lti]. *Lg Dev:* Literacy rate in L1: 15%. Literacy rate in L2: 15%–25%. NT: 2005. *Writing:* Latin script. *Other:* Matrilineal. Christian. *Map:* 368.

Lubu [lcf]. 30,000 (Wurm and Hattori 1981). Sumatra, West Sumatra Province. *Status:* 6a (Vigorous). *Class:* Austronesian, Malayo-Polynesian, Malayo-Chamic, Malayic, Malay. A member of macrolanguage Malay [msa] (Malaysia). *Dialects:* None known. Related to Kubu [kvb]. *Other:* Muslim. *Map:* 376:24.

Luhu [lcq] (Piru). 6,500 (Collins 1983). Maluku Province, western Seram island, Hoamoal peninsula, Luhu village. Boano and Kelang islands, west of Seram island. *Status:* 6b (Threatened). *Class:* Austronesian, Malayo-Polynesian, Central-Eastern Malayo-Polynesian, Central Maluku, East, Seram, Nunusaku, Three Rivers, Amalumute, Northwest Seram. *Dialects:* Batu Merah, Kelang, Luhu. Lexical similarity: 72% with Luhu dialect, 71%–73% with Asilulu [asl]. *Lg Use:* Vigorous. Batu Merah dialect spoken on Ambon Island has few remaining speakers. Also use Ambonese Malay [abs]. *Other:* Muslim, Christian. *Map:* 367.

Lun Bawang [lnd] (Lun Daya, Lun Dayah, Lun Daye, Lun Dayoh, Lundaya Putuk, Lundayeh, Southern Murut). 23,000 in Indonesia (2007 SIL). Population total all countries: 47,500. East Kalimantan Province; mountainous area where Sesayap River tributaries arise. 2 enclaves in western Sabah State. Also in Brunei, Malaysia. *Status:* 5 (Developing). *Class:* Austronesian, Malayo-Polynesian, North Borneo, North Sarawakan, Dayic, Kelabitic. *Dialects:* Lun Bawang (Long Bawan, Sarawak Murut), Lun Daye, Papadi. Not Murutic, although sometimes called Southern Murut. *Lg Dev:* Radio programs. Bible: 1982. *Writing:* Latin script. *Other:* Christian, traditional religion. *Map:* 365:37.

Ma'anyan [mhy] (Ma'anjan, Maanyak Dayak). 150,000 (2003). Central Kalimantan Province, Barito Selatan regency, Dusun Hilir, Karau Kuala, Dusun Selatan, Dusun Utara, Gunung Bintang Awai, Dusun Tengah, Awang, and Patangkep Tutui subdistricts. South Tamianglayang town area, Patai river watershed. *Status:* 6b (Threatened). *Class:* Austronesian, Malayo-Polynesian, Greater Barito, East, Central-South, South. *Dialects:* Dusun Balangan, Samihim (Buluh Kuning), Sihong (Siong). Related to Malagasy languages in Madagascar. Lexical similarity: 77% with Paku [pku], 75% with Dusun Witu [duv]. *Lg Use:* Also use Bakumpai [bkr]. *Lg Dev:* Grammar. NT: 1999. *Writing:* Latin script. *Other:* Traditional religion. *Map:* 365:38.

Maba [mqa] (Bicoli, Bitjoli, Ingli). 6,620 (2000). North Maluku Province. Halmahera island, southeast peninsula, north coast facing Buli bay; Wasilei area. *Status:* 6a (Vigorous). *Class:* Austronesian, Malayo-Polynesian, Central-Eastern Malayo-Polynesian, Eastern Malayo-Polynesian, South Halmahera-West New Guinea, South Halmahera, Southeast. *Lg Use:* Also use Indonesian [ind]. Used as L2 by Sawai [szw]. *Lg Dev:* Literacy rate in L1: Below 1%. Literacy rate in L2: 25%–50%. *Other:* Muslim. *Map:* 366.

Maden [xmx] (Palamul, Saparan, Sapran). 600 (Remijsen 2001). West Papua Province. Raja Ampat islands; western Salawati island. *Status:* 6b (Threatened). *Class:* Austronesian, Malayo-Polynesian, Central-Eastern Malayo-Polynesian, Eastern Malayo-Polynesian, South Halmahera-West New Guinea, West New Guinea, Cenderawasih Bay, Raja Ampat. *Dialect:* Kawait. *Other:* Possibly the same as Maya [slz]. Christian, traditional religion. *Map:* 371:9.

Madura [mad] (Basa Mathura, Madhura, Madurese). 6,770,000 in Indonesia (2000 census), decreasing. 86,000 Bawean. 2000 census reports large population decrease. Due to intermarriage, language attitudes, and other socioeconomic issues, the Madurese population is likely underreported. Population total all countries: 6,770,900. East Java Province, Madura island, Sapudi islands; coastal area of Java island, south and west of Surabaja city, southwest of Madura island. Also in Singapore. *Status:* 5 (Developing). *Class:* Austronesian, Malayo-Polynesian, Madurese. *Dialects:* Bangkalan (Bangkalon), Bawean (Babean, Bhebien, Boyanese), Pamekesan (Pamekasan), Sampang, Sapudi, Sumenep. Dialect continuum. Reports differ about inherent intelligibility among dialects: some Sumenep and Sampang report they cannot understand Pamekasan or Sumenep. Difficult intelligibility with Kangean [kkv]. Bawean may be a separate language. Lexical similarity: 75% with Kangean [kkv]. *Type:* SVO; nontonal; partial reduplication. *Lg Use:* Vigorous on Madura Island and East Java. All domains. All ages. Also use Indonesian [ind], Javanese [jav]. *Lg Dev:* Literacy rate in L2: 40%. Literacy higher among Bangkalon. Taught in primary schools (religious education). Taught in secondary schools, (religious education). Poetry. Newspapers. New media. Radio programs. Films. Videos. Dictionary. Grammar. Bible: 1994. *Writing:* Latin script. *Other:* Mainly rural. Bawean consider their language separate from Madurese. East Madurese, especially Sumenep, is considered high, or standard Madurese. Sumenep is isolated culturally and geographically. Bangkalon, spoken in Surabaya, is important economically because that city is highly urbanized and is most affected by Bahasa Indonesia. Muslim. *Map:* 363.

Mai Brat [ayz] (Ajamaru, Atinjo, Ayamaru, Brat, Maibrat, Maite, Majbrat, Maybrat, Mey Brat). 20,000 (1987 SIL). West Papua Province, about 40 villages. Central Bird's Head, area around Ayamaru lakes. *Status:* 5 (Developing). *Class:* Maybrat. *Dialects:* Maimaka, Maisawiet, Maisefa,

Maite, Maiyah. Lexical similarity: 10% with Tehit [kps], Mpur [akc], Abun [kgr], and its most similar neighbors. *Type:* SVO; heavy verb serialization. *Lg Use:* Religious services. All ages. High bilingualism among those in cities, highly educated. Used as L2 by Tehit [kps]. *Lg Dev:* Literacy rate in L1: 25%–50%. Literacy rate in L2: 25%–50%. Dictionary. Grammar. NT: 2004–2007. *Writing:* Latin script. *Other:* Ethnic autonym: Ayamaru. Traditional religion. *Map:* 371:24.

Mairasi [zrs] (Faranyao, Kaniran). 3,300 (1996 SIL). Papua Province, Bomberai peninsula, southwest coast facing Arafura Sea; area from Arguni bay east, southeast toward Triton bay on south coast. *Status:* 5 (Developing). *Class:* Mairasi. *Dialect:* Northeastern Mairasi. Reportedly similar to Semimi [etz]. Northeastern Mairasi may be a separate language. Lexical similarity: 69% with Semimi [etz], 61% with Mer [mnu]. *Lg Use:* Also use Indonesian [ind], Kowiai [kwh]. *Lg Dev:* Literacy rate in L2: 15%–25%. Dictionary. NT: 2004. *Writing:* Latin script. *Other:* Christian, traditional religion. *Map:* 371:50.

Maiwa [wmm] (Masenrempulu). 50,000 (1990 SIL). South Sulawesi Province, Enrekang and Sidenrang-Rappang regencies. Interior highlands east of Enrekang town; both sides of Boya river. *Status:* 6a (Vigorous). *Class:* Austronesian, Malayo-Polynesian, South Sulawesi, Northern, Masenrempulu. *Other:* Muslim. *Map:* 375:54.

Makasar [mak] (Goa, Macassar, Macassarese, Makassa, Makassaarsche, Makassar, Makassarese, Mangasara, Mengkasara, Taena, Tena). 2,130,000 (2000 census). L2 users: 400,000. Ethnic Chinese speakers. Many ethnic Chinese speak Makassar dialect as L1. South Sulawesi Province, southwest corner of the peninsula, most of Pangkep, Maros, Gowa, Bantaeng, Jeneponto, and Takalar regencies. *Status:* 6b (Threatened). *Class:* Austronesian, Malayo-Polynesian, South Sulawesi, Makassar. *Dialects:* Gowa (Goa, Lakiung), Maros-Pangkep, Turatea (Jeneponto). Gowa dialect is prestigious. Dialects form a chain. *Lg Use:* Vigorous. *Lg Dev:* Dictionary. Grammar. Bible: 1900–1999. *Writing:* Buginese script, no longer in use. Latin script. *Other:* Muslim. *Map:* 375:55.

Makian, East [mky] (Makian Dalam, Makian Timur). 20,000. 18,000 or more in East Makian, 2,000 or more in Kayoa (1983 SIL). North Maluku Province. South Halmahera island, west coast; nearby east Makian and south Mori islands; Kayoa, Bacan, and Obi islands. Transmigration project near Kao. *Status:* 6b (Threatened). *Class:* Austronesian, Malayo-Polynesian, Central-Eastern Malayo-Polynesian, Eastern Malayo-Polynesian, South Halmahera-West New Guinea, South Halmahera, East Makian-Gane. *Dialects:* East Makian, Kayoa (Kajoa). Similar to Gane [gzn]. *Lg Use:* Positive attitudes. Also use Indonesian [ind]. *Lg Dev:* Literacy rate in L1: Below 1%. Literacy rate in L2: 25%–50%. *Other:* A volcanic eruption on Makian Island, transmigrations, speakers of other languages in the area and pressure from those languages have taken a toll on vitality. Muslim. *Map:* 366.

Makian, West [mqs] (Makian Barat, Makian Luar). 12,000 (Voegelin and Voegelin 1977). 7,000 on Makian Island, 5,000 on Kayoa Islands. North Maluku Province. South Halmahera island, southwest coast near Gita town; west Makian island, some Kayoa islands. *Status:* 6a (Vigorous). *Class:* West Papuan, North Halmahera, West Makian. *Dialects:* None known. Language isolate within north Halmahera. Formerly classified as Austronesian. *Lg Use:* Also use Indonesian [ind]. *Lg Dev:* Literacy rate in L1: Below 1%. Literacy rate in L2: 25%–50%. *Other:* Muslim. *Map:* 366.

Maklew [mgf] (Makleu). 120. Papua Province, south coast area, east side of Marianne strait, west of Marind [mrz] and east of Yelmek [jel] language areas. *Status:* 6b (Threatened). *Class:* South-Central Papuan, Yelmek-Maklew. *Dialects:* None known. Reportedly similar to Yelmek [jel]. *Lg Use:* Home, friends. *Other:* Christian, traditional religion. *Map:* 373:262.

Malay [zlm] (Bahasa Daerah, Bahasa Melayu, Malayu). 4,910,000 in Indonesia (2000 census). 3,970,000 in Sumatra (100,000 in Belitung, 1,830,000 in Riau, 2,000,000 Deli, Asahan, etc. in North Sumatra and 40,000 Tamiang in Aceh), and 940,000 in Kalimantan (primarily Pontianak, Sambas and Ketapang). Primarily coastal regions of central and north Sumatra and western Kalimantan. *Status:* 6a (Vigorous). De facto language of provincial identity in Sumatra. *Dialects:* Akit, Belitung, coastal Jambi, Deli, Kapuas Hulu, Ketapang, Landak, Pontianak, Riau islands (Sea Tribe dialects), Riau Mainland, Sakai, Sambas, Sanggau, Sekadau, Sintang, Sukadana, Tamiang. *Lg Use:* Vigorous. Home, trade, some religion. All ages. Positive attitudes. Also use Indonesian [ind] for education, religion, government activities. *Other:* This entry refers to numerous, local or vernacular, Malay varieties not well differentiated from each other, as well as varieties for which further research is required to clarify differentiation from more mainstream dialects. Distinguished from court-Malay-derived Standard Malay [zsm] and Indonesian [ind]. Muslim (Sunni), Christian, traditional religion. See main entry on page 223. *Maps:* 363, 364:25, 376:25, 377:25.

Malay, Ambonese [abs] (Ambonese, Ambong, Malayu Ambon, Moluccan (Maluku) Malay). 200,000 in Indonesia (1987 J. Collins). Population total all countries: 245,020. L2 users: 1,400,000 in Indonesia (2013 M. Connor). Maluku Province. Central area: Ambon, Haruku, Nusa Laut, and Saparua islands; coastal areas of Seram island. Southern area: northwest Aru island group, Wamar island. Also in Netherlands, United States. *Status:* 3 (Wider communication). Became an LWC through trade, and is used in inter-cultural ommunication, market, and some media. *Class:* Creole, Malay based. *Dialect:* Dobo Malay. Marginal intelligibility with Indonesian [ind]. Difficult intelligibility with North Moluccan Malay [max]; speakers switch to Indonesian. Lexical similarity: 81% with Indonesian [ind]. Banda Malay [bpq] may best be considered a dialect of Moluccan Malay [max]. *Lg Use:* Also use Dutch [nld], Indonesian [ind]. Used as L2 by Aputai [apx], Buru [mhs], Dai [dij], Dawera-Daweloor [ddw], Dobel [kvo], Emplawas [emw], Fordata [frd], Galolen [gal], Haruku [hrk], Ili'uun [ilu], Imroing [imr], Laha [lhh], Lisabata-Nuniali [lcs], Lola [lcd], Luang [lex], Luhu [lcq], North Babar [bcd], Perai [wet], Seit-Kaitetu [hik], Southeast Babar [vbb], Tela-Masbuar [tvm], Tugun [tzn], Wemale [weo], West Masela [mss], West Tarangan [txn], Yamdena [jmd]. *Lg Dev:* Literacy rate in L1: 1%–5%. Literacy rate in L2: 50%–75%. New media. Dictionary. Grammar. Bible portions: 2007–2012. *Writing:* Latin script. *Other:* Developed from Sabah Malay [msi] and still reflects some archaic forms. Further diverged by adapting to the vernaculars of central Maluku. Many varieties of trade Malay are considered Malay-based creoles (Grimes 1988, 1991; Holm 1989) and as Austronesian with contact features (Collins 1980; Gil 2001; Wolff 1988). Christian, Muslim. *Maps:* 367, 368.

Malay, Bacanese [btj] (Bacan, Batjan). 6 (2012 SIL). North Maluku Province, at least 2 villages. Bacan island west of southern Halmahera island, Labuha Area; some on Mandioli Island. *Status:* 8b (Nearly extinct). *Class:* Austronesian, Malayo-Polynesian, Malayo-Chamic, Malayic, Malay. A member of macrolanguage Malay [msa] (Malaysia). *Lg Dev:* Literacy rate in L1: 1%–5%. Literacy rate in L2: 50%–75%. *Other:* No evidence of an earlier indigenous language (1987 J. Collins). Muslim. *Map:* 366.

Malay, Balinese [mhp]. 25,000 (2000 census). Bali Province, Bali island. *Status:* 6b (Threatened). *Class:* Creole, Malay based. *Other:* Balinese Malay arose as L1 in the Muslim community of Western Bali among immigrants from Southern Sulawesi (2007 S. Paauw). *Map:* 363.

Malay, Banda [bpq]. 3,690 (2000). Maluku Province. Banda islands; south, off southeast coast of Seram island. *Status:* 6a (Vigorous). *Class:* Creole, Malay based. *Dialects:* May better be considered a dialect of Moluccan (Ambonese) Malay [abs]. *Other:* Muslim. *Maps:* 367, 368.

Malay, Berau [bve] (Berau, Merau Malay). 11,200 (2007 SIL). East Kalimantan Province. Central coastal area; north, Cape Pandan, Tanjungreder, and Muaramalinau towns on lower Segah river; south along Celebes Sea coast past Sepinang town to Cape Batube area. *Status:* 6a (Vigorous). *Class:* Austronesian, Malayo-Polynesian, Malayo-Chamic, Malayic, Malay. A member of macrolanguage Malay [msa] (Malaysia). *Other:* Shares phonological innovations with Kutai Malay [vkt], Banjar [bjn], and Brunei [xkd]. *Maps:* 365:9, 374:9.

Malay, Bukit [bvu] (Bukat, Bukit, Meratus). 59,000 (2007 SIL). South Kalimantan Province. Central interior; Sampanahan river area, northwest of Limbungan town. *Status:* 6a (Vigorous). *Class:* Austronesian, Malayo-Polynesian, Malayo-Chamic, Malayic, Malay. A member of macrolanguage Malay [msa] (Malaysia). *Dialects:* None known. A variant of Banjar Malay [bjn] (Collins 2001). *Other:* Traditional religion. *Map:* 365:14.

Malay, Central [pse] (Bengkulu, Besemah, Enim, Lintang, Midden Maleisch, Ogan, Pasemah, Semendo, Serawai). 590,000 (2000 census). South Sumatra Province. East down Lematang and Ogan river valleys; south of Muaraenim town, east and southeast of Lahat town. Bengkulu Province; central Bukit Barisan highlands west to Indian Ocean along Bengkulu coast. *Status:* 6a (Vigorous). *Class:* Austronesian, Malayo-Polynesian, Malayo-Chamic, Malayic, Malay. A member of macrolanguage Malay [msa] (Malaysia). *Dialects:* Benakat, Bengkulu, Enim, Kikim, Kisam, Lematang Ulu, Lintang, Ogan, Pasemah, Rambang, Semenda, Serawai. Lexical similarity: 75% with Kaur [vkk], 80% between Pekal [pel] and some dialects such as Pasemah and Bengkulu. *Lg Use:* Vigorous. Home, village, commerce, religion. All ages. Positive attitudes. Also use Indonesian [ind], Musi [mui]. *Lg Dev:* Indonesian [ind] preferred for educational and religious materials, but L1 for cultural stories and songs. Mixed preference for health and agricultural materials. Not currently used as a written language in most dialects. Taught in primary schools. Dictionary. Grammar. NT: 1995. *Other:* Muslim. *Map:* 377:10.

Malay, Jambi [jax] (Batin, Djambi). 1,000,000 (2000 census). Southeast Sumatra, Jambi Province. Widespread. *Status:* 6a (Vigorous). *Class:* Austronesian, Malayo-Polynesian, Malayo-Chamic, Malayic, Malay. A member of macrolanguage Malay [msa] (Malaysia). *Dialects:* Downstream Jambi Malay, Upstream Jambi Malay. Forms a network of related varieties with Minangkabau [min] west, Riau Malay [zlm] north, and Musi [mui] south (Anderbeck 2008). *Lg Use:* As with many Malay varieties, gradually becoming more like Indonesian [ind]. Home, village. All ages. Positive attitudes. Also use Indonesian [ind]. *Other:* Muslim. *Map:* 377:16.

Malay, Kota Bangun Kutai [mqg]. 80,000 (Wurm and Hattori 1981). East Kalimantan Province. Lakes Semajang and Melintang areas, north along Belayen river; westward then south, central Mahakam river basin. *Status:* 6a (Vigorous). *Class:* Austronesian, Malayo-Polynesian, Malayo-Chamic, Malayic, Malay. A member of macrolanguage Malay [msa] (Malaysia). *Dialects:* Not intelligible with mainstream Tenggarong Kutai Malay [vkt], but may be with one of its dialects (Northern Kutai). *Map:* 365:34.

Malay, Kupang [mkn] (Basa Kupang, Kupang). 200,000 (1997 M. Jacob). L2 users: 100,000. East Nusa Tenggara Province, west end,Timor island, Kupang city area. *Status:* 3 (Wider communication). Regional L2. *Class:* Creole, Malay based. *Dialects:* Air Mata, Kupang. *Lg Use:* Vigorous. All domains. All ages. Used as L2 by Helong [heg], Lole [llg], Termanu [twu], Tii [txq]. *Lg Dev:* Poetry. Newspapers. Radio programs. Videos. Dictionary. NT: 2007. *Writing:* Latin script. *Other:* Loanwords from several Rote and Chinese languages, Portuguese [por], Uab Meto [aoz], Sabu [hvn], Spanish [spa], Dutch [nld], English [eng]. Christian, Muslim. *Map:* 369.

Malay, Larantuka [lrt] (Bahasa Nagi, Ende Malay, Melayu Larantuka, Nagi). 20,000 (2007). East Nusa Tenggara Province. East end, Flores island, Larantuka city area. *Status:* 6b (Threatened). *Class:* Creole, Malay based. *Map:* 370.

Malay, Makassar [mfp] (Macassarese Malay, Makassarese Malay, Sulsel Indonesian, Ujung Pandang Indonesian). L2 users: 1,880,000 (2000). South Sulawesi, Makassar port area. *Status:* 3 (Wider communication). *Class:* Austronesian, Malayo-Polynesian, Malayo-Chamic, Malayic, Malay. *Lg Use:* Second language only. *Lg Dev:* Dictionary.

Malay, Manado [xmm] (Manadonese Malay, Minahasan Malay). 850,000 (2001). L2 users: 1,500,000. In North Sulawesi. North Sulawesi Province, throughout Minahasa regency; other areas in North Sulawesi and Gorontalo provinces. *Status:* 3 (Wider communication). An important, growing lingua franca in many parts of Sulawesi. *Class:* Creole, Malay based. A member of macrolanguage Malay [msa] (Malaysia). *Dialects:* None known. Reportedly most similar to North Moluccan Malay [max]. Also similar to Sri Lankan Malay [sci]. *Lg Use:* Also use Indonesian [ind]. Used as L2 by Bantik [bnq]. *Lg Dev:* Dictionary. Bible portions: 2003–2012. *Writing:* Latin script. *Other:* Influences from Portuguese [por] and Ternate [tft]. Christian, Muslim. *Map:* 374:59.

Malay, North Moluccan [max] (Ternate Malay). 700,000 (2001 SIL). 100,000 monolinguals. L2 users: 300,000 (2001 R. Whisler). North Maluku Province. Islands off of southern tip of Halmahera island; Sula and Obi island groups to south and west. *Status:* 3 (Wider communication). Became LWC through trade, also used in daily life, inter-ethnic contact. *Class:* Creole, Malay based. A member of macrolanguage Malay [msa] (Malaysia). *Dialects:* None known. Different meaning of particles from Manado Malay [xmm]. Reportedly more similar to Manado Malay than to Ambonese Malay [abs]. *Lg Use:* A few communities use it as L1. Used orally between speakers of different languages. 600,000 also use Indonesian [ind]. Used as L2 by Sawai [szw], Tabaru [tby], Tidore [tvo], Tobelo [tlb]. *Lg Dev:* Literacy rate in L1: 1%–5%. Literacy rate in L2: 50%–75%. Bible portions: 2005–2012. *Writing:* Latin script. *Other:* Muslim, Christian. *Map:* 366.

Malay, Papuan [pmy]. 500,000 (2007 SIL), increasing. L1 and L2 speakers combined. L2 users: 500,000 L1 and L2 speakers combined. Papua Province. *Status:* 3 (Wider communication). LWC in Papua Province. Used in market, some business, and in situations where ethnic groups are mixed (market, sports, etc.) and in government offices. Became an LWC through trade. *Class:* Creole, Malay based. *Dialects:* None known. Reportedly similar to both Ambonese Malay [abs] and Manado Malay [xmm]. *Lg Use:*

Growing number of L1 speakers, who express a strong preference for their Malay variety over Indonesian [ind] or other regional varieties. All domains except religion, government or education. All ages. Positive attitudes. Most also use Indonesian [ind] or a vernacular language or both. Used as L2 by Beneraf [bnv], Berik [bkl], Betaf [bfe], Bonggo [bpg], Dabe [dbe], Dao [daz], Dineor [mrx], Emem [enr], Fedan [pdn], Jofotek-Bromnya [jbr], Kaptiau [kbi], Kayagar [kyt], Kimki [sbt], Kirikiri [kiy], Kowiai [kwh], Kwinsu [kuc], Liki [lio], Mawes [mgk], Mo [wkd], Morori [mok], Nakai [nkj], Namla [naa], Nimboran [nir], Orya [ury], Skou [skv], Sobei [sob], Sowari [dmy], Sunum [ymn], Tangko [tkx], Tarpia [tpf], Tebi [dmu], Tobati [tti], Towei [ttn], Usku [ulf], Viid [snu], Vitou [vto], Warembori [wsa], Yei [jei], Zorop [wfg]. *Lg Dev:* Papuan Malay used unofficially in many school settings. Films.

Malay, Tenggarong Kutai [vkt] (Kutai, Tenggarong). 210,000 (Wurm and Hattori 1981). 100,000 in Tenggarong, 60,000 in Ancalong, 50,000 in Northern Kutai. East Kalimantan Province. East central coastal area, from Mahakam river basin east to Celebes Sea coast, north from Cape Pandan along coast south to Samarinda city area. *Status:* 6a (Vigorous). *Class:* Austronesian, Malayo-Polynesian, Malayo-Chamic, Malayic, Malay. A member of macrolanguage Malay [msa] (Malaysia). *Dialects:* Ancalong Kutai, Northern Kutai, Tenggarong Kutai. Many dialects. Tenggarong and Kota Bangun (Malay, Kota Bangun Kutai [mqg]) are not inherently intelligible. Shares phonological innovations with Berau Malay [bve], Banjar [bjn], and Brunei [xkd]. *Map:* 365:68.

Malayic Dayak [xdy] (Bamayo, Bumayoh). 520,000 (Wurm and Hattori 1981). 300 Tapitn, 100,000 Banana', 100,000 Kayung, 200,000 Delang, 10,000 Semitau, 10,000 Suhaid, 20,000 Mentebah-Suruk. Widespread. Eastern West Kalimantan and west Central Kalimantan provinces. Semitau, Suhaid, and Mentebah-Suruk dialects: southeast of Kapuas river, from Sintang to Putus Sibau towns; Banana and Tapitn dialects: area bounded by Singakawang, Bengkayang, Darit, and Sungairaya towns; Kayung and Delang dialects: area bounded by Sandai, Muarakayang, Pembuanghulu, Sukamara, and Sukaraja towns. *Status:* 6a (Vigorous). *Class:* Austronesian, Malayo-Polynesian, Malayo-Chamic, Malayic. *Dialects:* Arut (Sukarame), Banana', Belantikan (Sungkup), Delang, Kayung (Kayong), Lamandau (Landau Kantu), Melahui, Mentebah-Suruk, Pangin, Payak, Riam (Nibung Terjung), Sekakai, Semitau, Serawai, Silat, Suhaid, Sukamara (Kerta Mulya), Tamuan, Tapitn, Tebidah, Tomun, Undau. Listed dialects form a chain and may constitute 3 or more languages. Related to Keninjal [knl]. *Other:* Serawai dialect different from the Serawai dialect of Central Malay [pse] in Sumatra. The term Malayic Dayak is misleading (would better be termed Dayak Malayic (Collins 2003) and not linguistically based. However, it is not yet clear what linguistic label(s) should replace it. *Map:* 364:40.

Malimpung [mli]. 5,000 (1986 SIL). South Sulawesi Province, Pinrang regency, Patampanua subdistrict, Malimpung, Sulili (part), and Urung villages. Northward bend of Sadang river, northwest of Maiwa town. *Status:* 6a (Vigorous). *Class:* Austronesian, Malayo-Polynesian, South Sulawesi, Northern, Masenrempulu. *Dialects:* None known. Lexical similarity: 80% with Maiwa [wmm], 70% with Enrekang [ptt]. *Other:* They view themselves as distinct from Bugis [bug] and Enrekang [ptt]. Muslim. *Map:* 375:56.

Mamasa [mqj] (Mamasa Toraja). 100,000 (1991 SIL). West Sulawesi Province, Mamasa regency, along Mamasa river. *Status:* 6a (Vigorous). *Class:* Austronesian, Malayo-Polynesian, South Sulawesi, Northern, Toraja-Sa'dan. *Dialects:* Central Mamasa, Northern Mamasa, Pattae' (Binuang, Binuang-Paki-Batetanga-Anteapi, Patta' Binuang, Southern Mamasa, Tae'). Lexical similarity: 78% with Toraja-Sa'dan [sda]. *Lg Use:* Vigorous. *Lg Dev:* NT: 2011. *Writing:* Latin script. *Other:* Christian, Muslim (Pattae'). *Map:* 375:57.

Mamboru [mvd] (Memboro). 10,000 (2007). East Nusa Tenggara Province. Northwest Sumba island, coastal area, Memboro town. *Status:* 6a (Vigorous). *Class:* Austronesian, Malayo-Polynesian, Central-Eastern Malayo-Polynesian, Sumba-Hawu, Sumba. *Map:* 369.

Mamuju [mqx] (Mamoedjoe, Mamoedjoesch, Mamudju, Udai). 60,000 (1991 SIL). 50,000 in Mamuju dialect. West Sulawesi Province, Mamuju regency, Mamuju, Kalukku, and Budong-Budong subdistricts on Makassar strait coast. *Status:* 6b (Threatened). *Class:* Austronesian, Malayo-Polynesian, South Sulawesi, Northern, Mamuju. *Dialects:* Mamuju, Padang, Sinyonyoi, Sumare-Rangas. Mamuju dialect is prestigious. *Lg Use:* Positive attitudes. *Writing:* Latin script. *Other:* Muslim. *Map:* 375:58.

Mandar [mdr] (Andian, Mandharsche, Manjar). 475,000 (2000 census). West Sulawesi Province, Majene, Polewali Mandar, and Mamuju regencies. Main area near Cape Mandar and Majene city; 3 coastal enclaves north of Majene city; northernmost point of province, coastal area between Parangkayu and Simajo towns. Also, south Sulawesi Province, Pangkep regency, Pabbring islands near Makassar city, other areas. *Status:* 5 (Developing). *Class:* Austronesian, Malayo-Polynesian, South Sulawesi, Northern, Mandar. *Dialects:* Balanipa (Napo-Tinambung), Majene, Malunda, Pamboang, Sendana (Cenrana, Tjendana). A complex dialect grouping. May be more dialects than those listed. Balanipa and Sendana may each be more than 1 dialect. Balanipa is prestige dialect. Mandar, Mamuju [mqx], and Bambam [ptu] are separate languages in a language chain. *Lg Dev:* Dictionary. *Writing:* Buginese script, no longer in use. Latin script. *Other:* Muslim. *Maps:* 374:60, 375:60.

Mander [mqr]. 20 (1991 SIL). Papua Province. North coast area; upper Tor river tributary of upper Bu river. *Status:* 8b (Nearly extinct). *Class:* Tor-Kwerba, Orya-Tor, Tor. *Lg Use:* Seriously endangered (2000 S. Wurm). Home. Adults only. Also use Berik [bkl]. *Other:* Nomadic. Christian, traditional religion. *Map:* 372:173.

Mandobo Atas [aax] (Dumut, "Kaeti" *pej.*, Kambon, Kwem, Mandobbo, Nub, Wambon). 10,000 (2002 SIL). Papua Province. Area south of Digul river headwaters, between Tanahmerah and Mindiptanah towns, extending towards Fly River border, Papua New Guinea. *Status:* 6a (Vigorous). *Class:* Trans-New Guinea, Ok-Awyu, Awyu-Dumut, Dumut. *Other:* Christian, traditional religion. *Map:* 373:249.

Mandobo Bawah [bwp] (Dumut, "Kaeti" *pej.*, Kambon, Mandobbo, Nub). 20,000 (2002 SIL). Papua Province, Getentiri, Anggai, Butiptiri, Subur, Aiwat, and Kaisah villages. Area east of Digul river south of Tanahmerah and Mindiptanah towns, to Fly River on Papua New Guinea border. *Status:* 6b (Threatened). *Class:* Trans-New Guinea, Ok-Awyu, Awyu-Dumut, Dumut. *Other:* Christian, traditional religion. *Map:* 373:251.

Manem [jet] (Jeti, Skofro, Wembi, Yeti). 400 in Indonesia (1978 SIL). Papua Province, Wembi, Yeti, and Kiba villages. Northeast border area, south of Jayapura. *Status:* 6a (Vigorous). *Lg Use:* Also use Indonesian [ind]. *Lg Dev:* Literacy rate in L2: Significant level. *Other:* Christian, traditional religion. See main entry on page 321. *Map:* 372:138.

Manggarai [mqy]. 900,000. East Nusa Tenggara Province. Flores island, western third. *Status:* 6a (Vigorous). *Class:* Austronesian, Malayo-Polynesian, Central-Eastern Malayo-Polynesian, Bima-Lembata. *Dialects:* Central

Manggarai (Ruteng), Eastern Manggarai, West-Central Manggarai, Western Manggarai. Around 43 subdialects. Reportedly similar to Riung [riu]. *Lg Dev:* Poetry. Dictionary. Grammar. NT: 2013. *Other:* Christian, Muslim. *Maps:* 369, 370.

Mangole [mqc] (Mangoli, Sula Mangoli). 7,280 (2000). North Maluku Province. Sula islands; Mangole island, south coast; south to Sulabesi island, south tip. *Status:* 6a (Vigorous). *Class:* Austronesian, Malayo-Polynesian, Central-Eastern Malayo-Polynesian, Central Maluku, Sula. *Other:* Muslim. *Map:* 367.

Manikion [mnx] (Mantion, Sogh, Sougb). 12,000 (1987 SIL). Papua Province, about 50 villages. Bird's Head area, east; southeast from the Anggi lakes to Momi town on northwest Cenderawasih bay. *Status:* 5 (Developing). *Class:* East Bird's Head-Sentani, East Bird's Head, Mantion. *Dialects:* 4 dialects. *Lg Dev:* NT: 1997. *Writing:* Latin script. *Other:* Christian, traditional religion. *Map:* 371:22.

Manipa [mqp] (Soow Huhelia). 1,500 (Voorhoeve and Collins 1981). Maluku Province, 4 villages. Manipa island, west of Seram island. *Status:* 6a (Vigorous). *Class:* Austronesian, Malayo-Polynesian, Central-Eastern Malayo-Polynesian, Central Maluku, East. *Dialects:* None known. Lexical similarity: 64% with Luhu [lcq], 60%–62% with Hitu [htu], 60%–61% with Tulehu [tlu] and Asilulu [asl], 58%–61% with Seit-Kaitetu [hik], 55%–60% with Larike-Wakasihu [alo], 56% with Boano [bzn] and Kaibobo [kzb]. *Other:* Muslim. *Map:* 367.

Manombai [woo] (Manobai, Wamar, Wokam). 9,110 (2011 SIL). Southeast Maluku, Aru islands, Manombai strait (Sungai) area as far as Wakua, west coast of Wokam island, from Wokam village south, 21 villages; Kobror island, Benjina; west end of Barakai strait, Maikor island, Gardakau; east coast of Wokam island, Kobamar village. May no longer be spoken on Wamar island. *Status:* 6a (Vigorous). *Class:* Austronesian, Malayo-Polynesian, Central-Eastern Malayo-Polynesian, Aru. *Dialects:* None known. Not inherently intelligible with Dobel [kvo]. Lexical similarity: 76% with Lorang [lrn]. *Lg Use:* Vigorous. Also use Dobel [kvo]. Used as L2 by Dobel [kvo]. *Writing:* Latin script. *Other:* Christian, Muslim. *Map:* 368.

Manusela [wha] (Wahai, Wahinama). 7,000 (1989 SIL). Maluku Province, 30 villages. Seram island, north, Mansuela mountain area; south, area along Teluti bay. *Status:* 6a (Vigorous). *Class:* Austronesian, Malayo-Polynesian, Central-Eastern Malayo-Polynesian, Central Maluku, East, Seram, Manusela-Seti. *Dialects:* Hatuolu, Kanikeh, Maneo, South Manusela. Lexical similarity: 66%–74% between the Kanikeh dialect and other varieties, 67%–75% with Hatuolo, 64%–86% with Maneo, 66%–86% with Maneoratu, 67%–80% with South Manusela; 64%–72% with Huaulu [hud], 42%–61% with Liana Seti [ste], 45% with Saleman [sau]. *Lg Use:* Vigorous. Also use Teluti [tlt]. *Lg Dev:* Grammar. *Other:* Traditional religion, Christian, Hindu. *Map:* 367.

Mapia [mpy] (Mapian). No known L1 speakers. Ethnic population: The ethnic group emigrated to Micronesia and probably now speak either Palauan [pau], Sonsorol [sov], or Tobian [tox]. Papua Province. Mapia islands, about 290 km north of Manokwari town. *Status:* 10 (Extinct). *Class:* Austronesian, Malayo-Polynesian, Central-Eastern Malayo-Polynesian, Eastern Malayo-Polynesian, Oceanic, Central-Eastern Oceanic, Remote Oceanic, Micronesian, Micronesian Proper, Ponapeic-Trukic, Trukic. *Lg Use:* Shifted to Biak [bhw] (Wurm 2007).

Marau [mvr]. 1,700 (1987 SIL). Papua Province, 5 villages. South coast, eastern Serui island fronting Cenderawasih bay. *Status:* 6a (Vigorous). *Class:* Austronesian, Malayo-Polynesian, Central-Eastern Malayo-Polynesian, Eastern Malayo-Polynesian, South Halmahera-West New Guinea, West New Guinea, Cenderawasih Bay, Yapen, Central-Western. *Dialect:* Warabori (Natabui, Warembori). Probably the same language as Munggui [mth] (96% lexically similar). Lexical similarity: 82% or more with Pom [pmo], Munggui [mth], Papuma [ppm], and Ansus [and]. *Other:* Christian. *Map:* 372:101.

Marind [mrz] (Gawir, Holifoersch, Southeast Marind, Tugeri). 7,000 (1987 SIL). Papua Province, Merauke regency. South coast area; north and west of Merauke city. Also enclave at southernmost extreme of province. *Status:* 6b (Threatened). *Class:* Trans-New Guinea, Marind, Nuclear Marind. *Dialects:* Gawir, Halifoersch, Southeast Marind, Tugeri. Significant differences between inland and coastal dialects, but speakers report intelligibility. *Lg Use:* Vigorous. Home, market. Children in towns have passive ability. Positive attitudes. Used as L2 by Morori [mok], Yei [jei]. *Lg Dev:* Dictionary. Grammar. Bible portions. *Other:* Christian, traditional religion. *Map:* 373:261.

Marind, Bian [bpv] (Bian, Boven-Mbian, Northwest Marind). 2,900 (2002 Sohn Myo-sook). Papua Province, Merauke regency, Muting subdistrict, Sanayu village. Upper Bian river area. *Status:* 7 (Shifting). *Class:* Trans-New Guinea, Marind, Nuclear Marind. *Dialects:* None known. Not inherently intelligible with Marind [mrz]. *Lg Use:* Home. *Other:* Traditional religion, Christian. *Map:* 373:263.

Mariri [mqi] (Mairiri). 280 (2011 SIL). Southeast Maluku Province,1 village. Aru island group; Mariri island, east of Kobroor island. *Status:* 6a (Vigorous). *Class:* Austronesian, Malayo-Polynesian, Central-Eastern Malayo-Polynesian, Aru. *Dialects:* None known. Lexical similarity: 81% with Batuley [bay]. *Lg Use:* Vigorous. *Other:* Muslim. *Map:* 368.

Masela, Central [mxz] (Central Marsela, Marsela-South Babar). 510 (1980 N. de Jonge). Maluku Province, 3 villages. Marsela island southwest of Babar island, Marsela town area. *Status:* 8a (Moribund). *Class:* Austronesian, Malayo-Polynesian, Central-Eastern Malayo-Polynesian, Babar, South, Masela-South Babar. *Lg Dev:* Literacy rate in L1: Below 1%. *Other:* Christian. *Map:* 368.

Masela, East [vme] (East Marsela). 520 (1980 N. de Jonge). Maluku Province south, 3 villages. Marsela island southwest of Babar island, east central area across island. *Status:* 8a (Moribund). *Class:* Austronesian, Malayo-Polynesian, Central-Eastern Malayo-Polynesian, Babar, South, Masela-South Babar. *Lg Dev:* Literacy rate in L1: Below 1%. *Other:* Christian. *Map:* 368.

Masela, West [mss] (West Marsela). 850 (2007 SIL). Maluku Province south, 5 villages. Marsela island southwest of Babar island, western tip. *Status:* 6b (Threatened). *Class:* Austronesian, Malayo-Polynesian, Central-Eastern Malayo-Polynesian, Babar, South, Masela-South Babar. *Lg Use:* Vigorous. Home, gardens, village, ceremonies, religion. Also use a regional Malay variety, probably a dialect of Ambonese Malay [abs], in all domains, except home and cultural domains. Also use Indonesian [ind] primarily in government and Christian religious domains. *Lg Dev:* Literacy rate in L1: Below 1%. *Other:* Christian. *Map:* 368.

Masimasi [ism]. 10 (2005 SIL). Papua Province, Sarmi regency, Pantai Timur subdistrict, island off north coast east of Tor river mouth. *Status:* 8b (Nearly extinct). *Class:* Austronesian, Malayo-Polynesian, Central-Eastern Malayo-Polynesian, Eastern Malayo-Polynesian, Oceanic, Western Oceanic, North New Guinea, Sarmi-Jayapura Bay, Sarmi. *Other:* Christian, traditional religion. *Map:* 372:117.

Masiwang [bnf] (Bonfia). 1,000 (1989 SIL). Maluku Province, Bula district. Seram island; area along northeast coast, up from Waru bay. *Status:* 6a (Vigorous). *Class:* Austronesian, Malayo-Polynesian, Central-Eastern Malayo-Polynesian, Central Maluku, East, Seram, Masiwang. *Dialects:* None known. Lexical similarity: 44% with Bobot [bty], 43% with Salas [sgu], 39% with Sepa [spb] and Teluti [tlt], 36% with Liana Seti [ste] and Yalahatan [jal]. *Lg Use:* Also use Geser-Gorom [ges]. Used as L2 by Salas [sgu]. *Lg Dev:* Grammar. *Map:* 367.

Massep [mvs] (Masep, Potafa, Wotaf). 25 (Wurm 2000). Ethnic population: 85. Papua Province, north coast east of Mamberamo river mouth and west of Sarmi, near Apauwer river. *Status:* 8b (Nearly extinct). *Class:* Language isolate. *Lg Use:* Seriously endangered (2000 S. Wurm). Under pressure from Isirawa [srl], Samarokena [tmj] and Indonesian [ind] (Wurm 2007). Home, religious services. *Other:* Christian, traditional religion. *Map:* 372:110.

Matbat [xmt] (Me). 1,250 (Remijsen 2001). West Papua Province. Raja Ampat archipelago; Misool and Segaf islands. *Status:* 6b (Threatened). *Class:* Austronesian, Malayo-Polynesian, Central-Eastern Malayo-Polynesian, Eastern Malayo-Polynesian, South Halmahera-West New Guinea, West New Guinea, Cenderawasih Bay, Raja Ampat. *Dialects:* Magey, Tomolol. *Type:* Tonal; 5 tones. *Other:* Traditional religion, Christian. *Map:* 371:11.

Mawes [mgk]. 850 (2006 SIL). Papua Province, Sarmi regency, Bonggo subdistrict, Mawes Wres, Mawes Dai, and Mawes Mukti villages. Northeast coastal area, southeast of Sarmi town; west bank of Buri river inland. *Status:* 6b (Threatened). *Class:* Tor-Kwerba, Greater Kwerba, Mawes. *Lg Use:* Home; with friends. All ages. Also use Indonesian [ind], Papuan Malay [pmy]. *Other:* Christian, traditional religion. *Map:* 372:122.

Ma'ya [slz] (Sailolof, Salawati, Samate). 4,000 (Remijsen 2001). West Papua Province. Raja Ampat islands; central Waigeo, Salawati islands. *Status:* 6b (Threatened). *Class:* Austronesian, Malayo-Polynesian, Central-Eastern Malayo-Polynesian, Eastern Malayo-Polynesian, South Halmahera-West New Guinea, West New Guinea, Cenderawasih Bay, Raja Ampat. *Dialects:* Banlol, Batanta Island, Ma'ya. *Lg Use:* Vigorous in some villages, shifting in others due to influx of outsiders (Remijsen 2001). *Other:* Christian, traditional religion. *Map:* 371:8.

Mekwei [msf] (Demenggong-Waibron-Bano, Menggei, Menggwei, Moi, Mooi, Munggai, Mungge, Munkei, Waipu). 1,200 (1987 SIL). Papua Province, Maribu, Waibrong, Kendate, and Sabron Dosay villages. Area west of Lake Sentani. *Status:* 8a (Moribund). *Class:* Nimboran. *Dialect:* Moi. Lexical similarity: 60% with Kemtuik [kmt]. *Lg Use:* Also use Indonesian [ind]. *Other:* Different from Moi (Mosana) [mxn]. Christian, traditional religion. *Map:* 372:128.

Mentawai [mwv] (Mentawei, Mentawi). 58,000 (2000 census). West Sumatra Province. Mentawai islands, across from Padang city. *Status:* 5 (Developing). *Class:* Austronesian, Malayo-Polynesian, Northwest Sumatra-Barrier Islands. *Dialects:* North Siberut, Pagai, Sakalagan, Saumanganja, Silabu, Simalegi, Sipura, South Siberut, Taikaku. *Lg Dev:* NT: 1987–1996. *Writing:* Latin script. *Other:* Christian, traditional religion. *Map:* 376:26.

Meoswar [mvx] (War). 250 (1993 R. Doriot). West Papua Province. Meoswar island, west Cenderawasih bay. *Status:* 6a (Vigorous). *Class:* Austronesian, Malayo-Polynesian, Central-Eastern Malayo-Polynesian, Eastern Malayo-Polynesian, South Halmahera-West New Guinea, West New Guinea, Cenderawasih Bay, Biakic. *Other:* Traditional religion, Christian. *Map:* 371:55.

Mer [mnu] (Miere, Muri). 85 (2000). West Papua Province. Central Bird's Head area; headwaters of Wosimi and Uremo rivers. *Status:* 6b (Threatened). *Class:* Mairasi. *Dialects:* None known. Lexical similarity: 63% with Semimi [etz], 61% with Mairasi [zrs]. *Other:* Christian, traditional religion. *Maps:* 371:52, 372:52.

Meyah [mej] (Arfak, Mansibaber, Meah, Meax, Mejach, Mejah, Meyach). 14,800 (2000). West Papua Province. Eastern Bird's Head; northeast coast, west of Manokwari town. *Status:* 5 (Developing). *Class:* East Bird's Head-Sentani, East Bird's Head, Meax. *Dialects:* None known. Reportedly most similar to Manikion [mnx]. *Lg Use:* Also use Indonesian [ind]. *Lg Dev:* Literacy rate in L1: 25%–50%. Literacy rate in L2: 25%–50%. Grammar. NT: 1997. *Writing:* Latin script. *Other:* Christian, traditional religion. *Map:* 371:20.

Minangkabau [min] (Minang, Padang). 5,530,000 (2007). 500,000 in Jakarta. Widespread in the Indonesian Archipelago; west central Sumatra Province, Padang area. Nearly half live outside central Sumatra; South Sumatra, west coast Mukomuko area. *Status:* 5 (Developing). *Class:* Austronesian, Malayo-Polynesian, Malayo-Chamic, Malayic, Malay. A member of macrolanguage Malay [msa] (Malaysia). *Dialects:* Agam, Aneuk Jamee (Jamee), Batu Sangkar-Pariangan, Kerinci-Minangkabau, Orang Mamak, Pajokumbuh, Pancuang Soal (Muko-Muko), Penghulu, Si Junjung, Singkarak, Tanah, Ulu. Not intelligible with Indonesian [ind]. Pekal [pel] may be intelligible with Minangkabau. *Type:* SVO. *Lg Use:* Vigorous. Positive attitudes. *Lg Dev:* Taught in primary schools in grades 1 and 2. Newspapers. Radio programs. NT: 1996. *Writing:* Latin script. *Other:* Muslim (Sunni). *Maps:* 376:27, 377:27.

Mlap [kja] (Kuangsu-Bonggrang, Kwangsu-Bonggrang, Kwansu, Kwansu-Bonggrang, Malf). 300 (Wurm 2000). Papua Province. Northwest coast, west of Lake Sentani. *Status:* 8b (Nearly extinct). *Class:* Nimboran. *Dialects:* None known. Lexical similarity: 60% with Kemtuik [kmt]. *Lg Use:* Potentially endangered (2000 S. Wurm). Also use Indonesian [ind], Kemtuik [kmt]. *Other:* Much intermarriage with Kemtuik [kmt] speakers. Kwansu is an obsolete village name. Christian, traditional religion. *Map:* 372:161.

Mo [wkd] (Wakde). 550 (2005 SIL). Papua Province, Sarmi regency, Pantai Timur subdistrict. Coastal area of Wakde island, off the north coast, just east of Tor river. *Status:* 7 (Shifting). *Class:* Austronesian, Malayo-Polynesian, Central-Eastern Malayo-Polynesian, Eastern Malayo-Polynesian, Oceanic, Western Oceanic, North New Guinea, Sarmi-Jayapura Bay, Sarmi. *Lg Use:* Mo is often mixed with Indonesian [ind] and Papuan Malay [pmy]. Home, community. Seldom used by children. Also use Indonesian [ind], Papuan Malay [pmy]. *Other:* Christian, traditional religion. *Map:* 372:114.

Modang [mxd]. 15,300 (Wurm and Hattori 1981). East Kalimantan Province. 5 enclaves, upper reaches of the Mahakam, Segah, Kelinjau, and Belayan rivers. *Status:* 6a (Vigorous). *Class:* Austronesian, Malayo-Polynesian, North Borneo, North Sarawakan, Kayan-Kenyah, Kayanic, Modang. *Dialects:* Benehes, Kelingan (Long Wai, Long We), Liah Bing, Long Bento', Long Glat, Nahes. *Map:* 365:42.

Modole [mqo] (Madole). 2,000 (1983 SIL). North Maluku Province. Interior north Halmahera island, Kao river headwaters. *Status:* 6a (Vigorous). *Class:* West Papuan, North Halmahera, Galela-Loloda. *Dialects:* North Modole, South Modole. Minimal differences between north and south Modole. *Lg Use:* Positive attitudes. *Other:* Some intermarriage with the Tabaru [tby]. Christian. *Map:* 366.

Moi [mxn] (Mekwei, Mooi, Mosana, Waipu). 4,600 (1993 R. Doriot). West Papua Province, 9 villages. West Bird's Head area; eastern Salawati island around to Sorong city east and southeast. *Status:* 6b (Threatened). *Class:* West Papuan, West Bird's Head. *Dialect:* Mosemah. *Lg Use:* Used as L2 by As [asz]. *Other:* Different from Mekwei [msf] (Moi) dialect. Christian, traditional religion. *Map:* 371:7.

Moksela [vms] (Maksela, Opselan). No known L1 speakers. Last speaker died in 1974. Central Maluku Province, possibly east Buru island, near Kayeli. *Status:* 10 (Extinct). *Class:* Austronesian, Malayo-Polynesian, Central-Eastern Malayo-Polynesian, Central Maluku, Buru.

Molof [msl] (Poule). 230 (2005 SIL). Papua Province, 9 villages. Around 100 km south of Jayapura city, west of Senggi town. *Status:* 6a (Vigorous). *Class:* Unclassified. *Dialects:* None known. Not closely related to any other language. *Other:* Stronger use in Molof than in Waley. Christian, traditional religion. *Map:* 372:154.

Moma [myl] (Kulawi). 5,500 (Barr, Barr, and Salombe 1979). Central Sulawesi Province, Kulawi subdistrict. Primarily Kulawi and Toro town areas. *Status:* 5 (Developing). *Class:* Austronesian, Malayo-Polynesian, Celebic, Kaili-Pamona, Northern, Kaili. *Dialects:* None known. Reportedly historically a variety of Kaili [lew], but strong lexical influences from Uma [ppk]. *Lg Dev:* 550 Moma speakers enrolled in the literacy program (2013 A. Eastwood). Used in 50% of the schools one hour per week for literacy. Bible portions: 1939–2013. *Writing:* Latin script. *Other:* Christian. *Maps:* 374:61, 375:61.

Mombum [mso] (Kemelom, Kemelomsch, Komolom). 250 (1993 R. Doriot). Papua Province. Island next to southeast coast of Kolopom island; west of Marauke city across Arafura Sea. *Status:* 8a (Moribund). *Class:* Trans-New Guinea, Mombum. *Dialects:* None known. Reportedly most similar to Koneraw [kdw]. *Other:* Christian, traditional religion. *Map:* 373:259.

Momina [mmb]. 200 (1998 M. Donohue). Papua Province, Samboka village. Low hills just south of main ranges; headwaters area of Brazza and Einladen rivers. *Status:* 6b (Threatened). *Class:* Somahai. *Dialects:* None known. May be the same language as Momuna [mqf]. *Map:* 372:215.

Momuna [mqf] (Somage, Somahai, Sumohai). 2,000 (Wurm 2000). Papua Province, lowlands just south of main ranges, from south of Silimo east to south of Korupun-Sela [kpq] language area. *Status:* 6b (Threatened). *Class:* Somahai. *Dialects:* None known. May be the same language as Momina [mmb]. *Lg Use:* Potentially endangered (2000 S. Wurm). Losing its status as a contact language; being replaced by Indonesian [ind] (Wurm 2007). *Lg Dev:* Literacy rate in L1: 5%–15%. Bible portions: 1985–1991. *Writing:* Latin script. *Other:* They have contact with Dani who are learning Momuna. Christian, traditional religion. *Maps:* 372:214, 373:214.

Mongondow [mog] (Bolaang Mongondow, Bolang-Mogondo, Minahassa, Mongondou). 230,000 (2000 census). North Sulawesi Province. North peninsula, both coasts; north side from Poigar town west to Bijaj river; south side, between Pinolosian town and west of Belang town. *Status:* 7 (Shifting). *Class:* Austronesian, Malayo-Polynesian, Philippine, Greater Central Philippine, Gorontalo-Mongondow, Mongondowic. *Dialects:* Dumoga, Lolayan, Passi. *Lg Use:* Used as L2 by Lolak [llq]. *Lg Dev:* Dictionary. Grammar. Bible portions: 1932–1939. *Writing:* Latin script. *Other:* Traditional religion, Christian, Muslim. *Map:* 374:62.

Moni [mnz] (Djonggunu, Jonggunu, Migani). 20,000 (1991 SIL). Papua Province, central highlands, northeast Lake Paniai area. *Status:* 5 (Developing). *Class:* Trans-New Guinea, West, Wissel Lakes. *Dialect:* Awembak (Awembiak). *Lg Use:* Used as L2 by Nduga [ndx], Wano [wno]. *Lg Dev:* NT: 1990. *Writing:* Latin script. *Other:* Christian, traditional religion. *Map:* 372:61.

Mor [mhz] (Austronesian Mor). 700 (1987 SIL). Papua Province, Mor islands, east Cenderawasih bay near Nabire. *Status:* 7 (Shifting). *Class:* Austronesian, Malayo-Polynesian, Central-Eastern Malayo-Polynesian, Eastern Malayo-Polynesian, South Halmahera-West New Guinea, West New Guinea, Cenderawasih Bay, Mor. *Type:* Tonal. *Other:* Different from Trans-New Guinea Mor [moq]. Traditional religion, Christian. *Map:* 372:85.

Mor [moq] (Mor2). 30 (2012 H. Hammarström). 70 semi-speakers (2012 H. Hammarström). Papua Province, northwest Bomberai peninsula, Bintuni bay coast. *Status:* 8b (Nearly extinct). *Class:* Trans-New Guinea, Mor. *Lg Use:* Seriously endangered (2000 S. Wurm). Under pressure from Baham [bdw], Iha [ihp], and Indonesian [ind] (Wurm 2007). Home. Used by few or no children. *Other:* Distinct from Austronesian Mor [mhz]. Christian, traditional religion. *Map:* 371:37.

Moraid [msg]. 1,000 (1988 SIL). Papua Province, West Bird's Head. *Status:* 6a (Vigorous). *Class:* West Papuan, West Bird's Head. *Lg Use:* Religious services. *Other:* Christian, traditional religion. *Map:* 371:16.

Mori Atas [mzq] (Aikoa, Berg-Tomori, Boven-Mori, Upper Mori, West Mori). 14,000 (1988 D. Mead). Central Sulawesi Province, Mori Atas, Lembo, and Petasia subdistricts, 25 villages. Southeast peninsula neck, southeast of Lake Paso; into South Sulawesi Province, Nuha subdistrict. *Status:* 6b (Threatened). *Class:* Austronesian, Malayo-Polynesian, Celebic, Eastern, Southeastern, Bungku-Tolaki, Western, Interior. *Dialects:* Impo, Molio'a, Molongkuni, Tambee (Ajo, South Mori, Tambee, Zuid-Mori), Ulu Uwoi. Lexical similarity: 73%–86% with Mori Bawah [xmz] and Padoe [pdo]. *Lg Dev:* NT: 1948. *Writing:* Latin script. *Other:* Christian. *Map:* 375:63.

Mori Bawah [xmz] (Beneden-Tomori, East Mori, Lower Mori, Nahina, Oost-Mori, Petasia). 14,000 (1988 D. Mead). Central Sulawesi Province, Petasia, Lembo, and Bungku Tengah subdistricts, 24 villages. Southeast peninsula neck, Lake Towuti area. Also, South Sulawesi Province. *Status:* 6b (Threatened). *Class:* Austronesian, Malayo-Polynesian, Celebic, Eastern, Southeastern, Bungku-Tolaki, Eastern, East Coast. *Dialects:* Karunsi'e (Karonsie, Korongsi, Sinongko), Moiki (Tomoiki), Nuha (Soroako), Tinompo (Mokole, Soroako), Tiu (Tioe), Watu (Towatoe). Lexical similarity: 73%–86% with Mori Atas [mzq], 75% with Padoe [pdo]. *Lg Dev:* Grammar. NT: 1948. *Writing:* Latin script. *Other:* Christian, Muslim. *Map:* 375:64.

Moronene [mqn] (Maronene). 37,000 (2000 D. Andersen), increasing. Wita Ea 23,000, Tokotu'a 14,000. Includes about 3,500 living in cities. Second or third generations in cities no longer speak Moronene. 1,850 monolinguals. Southeast Sulawesi Province, Bombana regency. Southeast mainland, Rumbia mountains area. Kabaena island, Tokotu'a village; on the mainland portion opposite Kabaena; Wita Ea village. Wita Ea dialect: Rumbia, Poleang, and Poleang Timur subdistricts. Also Kolaka regency, Watubangga subdistrict. *Status:* 6b (Threatened). *Class:* Austronesian, Malayo-Polynesian, Celebic, Eastern, Southeastern, Bungku-Tolaki, Eastern, Southwest. *Dialects:* Tokotu'a (Kabaena), Wita Ea (Poleang, Rumbia). Lexical similarity: Wita Ea dialect 80% with Tokotu'a dialect; 68% with Menui dialect of Wawonii [wow], 66% with Kulisusu [vkl], 65% with Taloki [tlk], Koroni [xkq], Tulambatu dialect of Bungku [bkz], 64% with Bungku [bkz], and 57% with Tolaki [lbw]. *Lg Use:* Vigorous in many villages. Occasional oral use in church, letter writing. All ages. Positive attitudes. In Poleang many also use Bugis [bug]. In some villages, some parents speak Indonesian [ind] to their children; some children are not proficient in Moronene. *Lg Dev:* Taught as an oral and written subject in both elementary and secondary schools. Radio programs. Bible portions: 2003. *Writing:*

Latin script. *Other:* Formerly a kingdom. Muslim. *Map:* 375:65.

Morop [iwo] (Iwoer, Iwur). 6,900 (2011 J. Elliot). Papua Province, Iwur river valley border area, Ok Iwur, east to Ok Denom. Dintere dialect: 22 villages; Dinmane dialect: Dewok; Upper Dintere dialect: Aurarin hamlet. *Status:* 6a (Vigorous). *Class:* Trans-New Guinea, Ok-Awyu, Ok, Lowland. *Dialects:* Dinmane, Dintere, Nemah/Nehayah, Upper Dintere. *Other:* Ethnonym: Morop. Dintere most widespread dialect. The previous language name 'Iwur' came from a single village within the Morop group. Relationship between Nemah and Dintere is unclear, and may constitute more than one language. Christian, traditional religion. *Map:* 372:227.

Morori [mok] (Marori, Moaraeri, Moraori, Morari). 50 (1998 M. Donohue). Ethnic population: 250 (1998 M. Donohue). Papua Province, south coast border area 20 km east of Merauke, east of Marind, west of Kanum. *Status:* 8b (Nearly extinct). *Class:* Trans-New Guinea, Moraori. *Dialects:* Menge dialect remembered as the language of ceremony, though the last Menge speaker died in 1997. *Lg Use:* Endangered (2000 S. Wurm). Under pressure from Marind [mrz], a language group which surrounds the Morori, and from Indonesian [ind] (Wurm 2007). Mainly older adults. 100% also use Indonesian [ind]. 100% also use Papuan Malay [pmy]. Also use Marind [mrz]. Used as L2 by Bädi Kanum [khd], Ngkâlmpw Kanum [kcd], Smärky Kanum [kxq], Sota Kanum [krz]. *Other:* Christian, traditional religion. *Map:* 373:267.

Moskona [mtj] (Meninggo, Meningo, Meyah, Sabena). 8,000 (1996 SIL). Papua Province, southeast Bird's Head, south of Meyah, west of Manikion. *Status:* 5 (Developing). *Class:* East Bird's Head-Sentani, East Bird's Head, Meax. *Dialects:* None known. Lexical similarity: 85% with Meyah [mej]. Also related to Manikion [mnx]. *Lg Dev:* NT: 2001. *Writing:* Latin script. *Other:* Christian, traditional religion. *Map:* 371:23.

Mpur [akc] (Amberbaken, Dekwambre, Ekware, Kebar). 7,000 (1993 R. Doriot). Papua Province, north coast of Bird's Head, west of Manokwari, and Kebar valley. *Status:* 6b (Threatened). *Class:* Language isolate. *Dialects:* Ajiw, Sirir. *Lg Use:* Also use Indonesian [ind]. *Lg Dev:* Literacy rate in L2: 15%–25%. Bible portions: 1998–2012. *Writing:* Latin script. *Other:* Christian, traditional religion. *Map:* 371:19.

Mualang [mtd]. 40,000 (Tjia 2007). West Kalimantan Province, Belitang Hilir, Belitang, and Belitang Hulu Sekadau subdistricts. Area along Ayak and Belitang rivers, about 320 km upstream from Pontianak. *Status:* 5 (Developing). *Class:* Austronesian, Malayo-Polynesian, Malayo-Chamic, Malayic, Ibanic. *Dialects:* Mualang Ili', Mualang Ulu. Reportedly similar to Iban [iba]; however only one-way intelligibility from Mualang to Iban. *Lg Use:* Language shift reportedly taking place in the younger generation. Positive attitudes. *Lg Dev:* Taught in primary schools. Grammar. *Other:* Christian. *Map:* 364:43.

Muna [mnb] (Wuna). 300,000 (2007 R. Van den Berg). Southwest South Sulawesi Province, Muna island; northwest coast, Buton island. Also, central Maluku Province, Ambon city. *Status:* 6b (Threatened). *Class:* Austronesian, Malayo-Polynesian, Celebic, Eastern, Southeastern, Muna-Buton, Nuclear Muna-Buton, Munan, Munic, Western. *Dialects:* Burukene, Gu, Kadatua, Kapontori, Katobengke, Lakudo, Laompo, Mawasangka, Siompu, Standard Muna (Northern Muna), Tiworo (Eastern Muna). Subvarieties of standard Muna are: Tungkuno, Kabawo, Lawa, Katobu, Tobea Besar; of Gulamas are: Gu, Mawasangka, Lakudo, Wale-Ale, Lawama, Kadatua, Lowu-Lowu, Kalia-Lia, Katobengke, Topa, Salaa, Lawela, Laompo, and Burukene. Lexical similarity: 71% with Pancana [pnp], 62% with Cia-Cia [cia], 52% with Wolio [wlo], 50% with Lasalimu [llm], 47% with Tukang Besi [khc] or [bhq], 45% with Kamaru [kgx]. *Lg Use:* Vigorous. Also use Indonesian [ind]. Used as L2 by Taloki [tlk]. *Lg Dev:* Taught in primary schools. Dictionary. Grammar. NT: 2004. *Writing:* Latin script. *Other:* Muslim. *Map:* 375:66.

Munggui [mth] (Natabui). 800 (1982 SIL). Papua Province, north coast of Serui island, 1 village. *Status:* 6a (Vigorous). *Class:* Austronesian, Malayo-Polynesian, Central-Eastern Malayo-Polynesian, Eastern Malayo-Polynesian, South Halmahera-West New Guinea, West New Guinea, Cenderawasih Bay, Yapen, Central-Western. *Dialects:* None known. Probably the same language as Marau [mvr], reportedly 96% lexically similar (Price and Donohue 2009). Lexical similarity: 82% with Papuma [ppm]. *Other:* Traditional religion, Christian. *Map:* 372:102.

Murkim [rmh]. 290 (2004 SIL). Papua Province, Pegunungan Bintang regency, Batom subdistrict, southeast of Yetfa [yet] language area, Mot and Milki villages. *Status:* 6a (Vigorous). *Class:* Unclassified. *Dialects:* None known. Possible genetic relationship to Lepki [lpe]. *Lg Use:* Home, community. All ages. Also use Kimki [sbt], Yetfa [yet]. *Map:* 372:147.

Musi [mui] (Palembang, Palembangnese, Sekayu). 3,105,000 (2000 census). South Sumatra Province, Musi river upstream to Bukit Barisan mountains, downstream to eastern coastal swamplands. *Status:* 3 (Wider communication). Much of the population from other language groups in South Sumatra Province learn enough Urban Palembang dialect to use it as a trade language. *Class:* Austronesian, Malayo-Polynesian, Malayo-Chamic, Malayic, Malay. A member of macrolanguage Malay [msa] (Malaysia). *Dialects:* Belide, Burai, Coastal Malay, Kelingi, Lematang Ilir, Meranjat, Musi Sekayu, Palembang Lama, Pegagan, Penesak, Penukal, Rawas. A mutually-intelligible dialect chain stretching along the Musi River with 2 subgroups: Musi and Palembang. *Lg Use:* Home, village, market, religion. All ages. Positive attitudes. Also use English [eng], Indonesian [ind]. Used as L2 by Central Malay [pse], Col [liw], Javanese [jav], Komering [kge]. *Lg Dev:* Not currently a written language. Preference is for Indonesian for educational and religious materials. Preference is for L1 for cultural stories and songs. Mixed preference for health and agricultural materials. Radio programs. TV. Dictionary. Grammar. *Other:* Muslim. *Map:* 377:28.

Muyu, North [kti] (Kataut, Kati-Ninanti, Niinati, Ninatie, North Kati, North Moejoe, Yonggom, Yongkom, Yongom). 8,000 (2002 SIL). Papua Province, south coast border area, north of South Muyu [kts] and east of Wambon [wms] language areas. *Status:* 6a (Vigorous). *Class:* Trans-New Guinea, Ok-Awyu, Ok, Lowland. *Dialects:* Kanggewot, Toemoetoe (Are). *Maps:* 372:228, 373:228.

Muyu, South [kts] (Digoel, Digul, Kati Metomka, Metomka, Moejoe, Ok Bari, South Kati, Yonggom, Yongkom, Yongom). 4,000 (2002 SIL). Papua Province, south coast, just north of Fly river border with Papua New Guinea. *Status:* 6a (Vigorous). *Class:* Trans-New Guinea, Ok-Awyu, Ok, Lowland. *Dialect:* Metomka. *Map:* 373:250.

Nafri [nxx]. 1,630 (1975 SIL). Papua Province, Jayapura area, southeast end of Yotafa bay, Nafri village. *Status:* 8a (Moribund). *Class:* East Bird's Head-Sentani, Sentani, Sentani Proper. *Other:* Christian, traditional religion. *Map:* 372:136.

Nage [nxe] (Nagé, Nage-Keo). 50,000 (Forth 1993). East Nusa Tenggara Province. Central Flores island, Ebu Lobo volcano north, west slopes. Northeast of Ngad'a [nxg] language area. *Status:* 6a (Vigorous). *Class:* Austronesian,

Malayo-Polynesian, Central-Eastern Malayo-Polynesian, Bima-Lembata. *Map:* 370.

Naka'ela [nae]. No known L1 speakers. Central Maluku Province, northwest Seram, Kairatu village. *Status:* 10 (Extinct). *Class:* Austronesian, Malayo-Polynesian, Central-Eastern Malayo-Polynesian, Central Maluku, East, Seram, Nunusaku, Three Rivers, Amalumute, Northwest Seram, Ulat Inai. *Dialects:* None known. Lexical similarity: 71% with Lisabata-Nuniali [lcs], 66% with Hulung [huk], 63% with Alune [alp]. *Other:* Formerly lived in mountains then moved down to Kairatu.

Nakai [nkj] (Na'ai, Nagai, Na'i). 700 (1999 M. Donohue). Papua Province, east of upper Digul river, Awimbom village in the center of 5 other villages extending toward Ok Sibil northeast, and southwest toward Iwur [iwo]. *Status:* 6a (Vigorous). *Class:* Trans-New Guinea, Ok-Awyu, Ok, Mountain. *Dialects:* They report Indonesian [ind] and Papuan Malay [pmy] difficult to understand. Probably 3 dialects, two of these may constitute a separate language called Nagi. Not the same as Larantuka Malay [lrt] (Nagi) in Nusa Tenggara. *Lg Use:* Home, local government. Also use Indonesian [ind], Papuan Malay [pmy]. *Other:* Traditional religion. *Map:* 372:225.

Nalca [nlc] (Hmanggona, Hmonono, Kimjal, Kimyal, Naltje, Naltya). 16,000 (2013 R. Doriot). Papua Province, northeast of Korupun [kpq] language area and southeast of Nipsan [nps] language area, north slopes, east highlands area. *Status:* 5 (Developing). *Class:* Trans-New Guinea, Mek, Eastern. *Dialects:* None known. Lexical similarity: 59% with Kosarek Yale [kkl]. *Lg Use:* Also use Indonesian [ind]. *Lg Dev:* Literacy rate in L2: Below 1% semiliterate. NT: 2001. *Writing:* Latin script. *Other:* Distinct from Korupun (Kimyal) dialect of Korupun-Sela [kpq]. Christian, traditional religion. *Map:* 372:208.

Namla [naa]. 30 (2005 SIL). Papua Province, Senggi subdistrict, Keerom regency, Namla village. *Status:* 8b (Nearly extinct). *Class:* Unclassified. *Dialects:* None known. Possible genetic relationship to Tofanma [tlg]. *Lg Use:* 30 also use Papuan Malay [pmy]. More Tofanma [tlg] speakers than Namla in their village. *Other:* Christian. *Map:* 372:153.

Napu [npy] (Pekurehua). 6,100 (2000 R. Hanna), increasing. Central Sulawesi Province, Lore Utara subdistrict, 10 villages. Napu valley. *Status:* 6b (Threatened). *Class:* Austronesian, Malayo-Polynesian, Celebic, Kaili-Pamona, Southern, Badaic. *Dialects:* None known. Reportedly most similar to Behoa [bep]. *Lg Use:* 60% of parents pass it on to the children. Young people tend to use Indonesian [ind] (Wurm 2007). Some domains, hymns, work announcements. Mildly positive attitudes. Nearly all also use Indonesian [ind]. *Lg Dev:* High interest in Napu literature. NT: 2000. *Writing:* Latin script. *Other:* Christian. *Maps:* 374:67, 375:67.

Narau [nxu]. Papua Province, Jayapura area, Kecamatan Kaureh. *Status:* Unattested. *Class:* Kaure, Kaure Proper. *Other:* 2006 survey data indicates language may not exist and could possibly be merged with Kosare [kiq]. Christian, traditional religion. *Map:* 372:203.

Nasal [nsy]. 3,000 (2008 K. Anderbeck). Very few monolinguals. Sumatra, Bengkulu Province, Kaur regency, Tanjung Betuah, Gedung Menung, and Tanjung Baru villages. Nasal river area. *Status:* 6a (Vigorous). *Class:* Austronesian, Malayo-Polynesian, Nasal. *Dialects:* None known. Not closely related to surrounding languages, but heavy loans from Lampung [ljp]. *Lg Use:* Vigorous. All domains. All ages. Positive attitudes. *Lg Dev:* Dictionary. *Other:* Muslim. *Map:* 377:29.

Ndom [nqm]. 1,200 (2002 SIL). Papua Province, Kolopom (Frederik Hendrik) island. *Status:* 6a (Vigorous). *Class:* Trans-New Guinea, Kolopom. *Dialects:* None known. Reportedly most similar to Kimaghima [kig] and Riantana [ran]. *Other:* Christian, traditional religion. *Map:* 373:260.

Nduga [ndx] (Dauwa, Dawa, Ndauwa, Ndugwa, Pesecham, Pesechem, Pesegem). 10,000 (1985 M. Owen). Papua Province, Jayawijaya regency, Tiom, central highlands, south of high ranges, south of Western Dani, north of Asmat. Scattered. *Status:* 5 (Developing). *Class:* Trans-New Guinea, West, Dani, Ngalik. *Dialects:* Hitadipa Nduga, Sinak Nduga. *Lg Use:* Also use Damal [uhn], Indonesian [ind], Moni [mnz]. *Lg Dev:* NT: 1984. *Writing:* Latin script. *Other:* Christian, traditional religion. *Map:* 372:66.

Nedebang [nec] (Balungada, Klamu, Nédebang). 1,500. East Nusa Tenggara Province. North central Pantar island, south, southwest of Kabir town. *Status:* 6a (Vigorous). *Class:* Trans-New Guinea, West, Timor-Alor-Pantar, Alor-Pantar, Pantar. *Map:* 370.

Ngad'a [nxg] (Badjava, Bajava, Bajawa, Nad'a, Ngada, Nga'da, Ngadha, Rokka). 60,000 (1995). East Nusa Tenggara Province. South central Flores island, between Manggarai [mqy], Ende [end], and Li'o [ljl] language areas. *Status:* 6a (Vigorous). *Class:* Austronesian, Malayo-Polynesian, Central-Eastern Malayo-Polynesian, Bima-Lembata. *Dialects:* Bajawa, Central Ngada, South Ngada. Dialect diversity. *Lg Dev:* Grammar. *Other:* Christian. *Map:* 370.

Ngad'a, Eastern [nea] (Southeast Ngada). 5,000 (1994). East Nusa Tenggara Province. South central Flores, Kabupaten Ngada and Kecamatan Golewa between Ngad'a [nxg] and Nage [nxe] language areas, Sara Sedu, Taka Tunga, and Sanga Deto administrative villages; Desa Rowa, Kecamatan Boawae. *Status:* 6a (Vigorous). *Class:* Austronesian, Malayo-Polynesian, Central-Eastern Malayo-Polynesian, Bima-Lembata. *Dialects:* Minor dialect variation. *Other:* Christian. *Map:* 370.

Ngaju [nij] (Biadju, Dayak Ngaju, Ngadju, Ngaja, Ngaju Dayak, Southwest Barito). 890,000 (2003). Central Kalimantan Province. Upper reaches or headwaters of Kapuas, Kahayan, Katingan, and Mentaya rivers. *Status:* 3 (Wider communication). Widely used as LWC for trade in much of Kalimantan, from Barito to Sampit rivers. Used in many domains (church, school, village-level government, market, etc.). *Class:* Austronesian, Malayo-Polynesian, Greater Barito, West, South. *Dialects:* Ba'amang (Bara-Bare, Sampit), Kahayan, Kahayan Kapuas, Katingan Ngaju, Katingan Ngawa, Mantangai (Oloh Mangtangai), Pulopetak. Lexical similarity: 75% with Bakumpai [bkr], 62% with Kohin [kkx], 50% with Ot Danum [otd], 35% with Banjar [bjn]. *Lg Dev:* Taught in primary schools. Taught as a subject in Palangkaraya since 1988 (Masinambow and Haenen 2002). Dictionary. Grammar. Bible: 1858–2005. *Writing:* Latin script. *Map:* 364:44.

Ngalum [szb] (Sibil). 10,000 in Indonesia (1987 SIL). Population total all countries: 18,000. Papua Province, northeast of Nakai [nkj] language area, Ok Sibil, Ok Tsop, and perhaps Ok Bon valleys, main range border area north of Muyu [kts] (Yongkom) and Morop [iwo] language areas. Also in Papua New Guinea. *Status:* 6a (Vigorous). *Class:* Trans-New Guinea, Ok-Awyu, Ok, Ngalum. *Dialects:* Apmisibil, Ngalum, Sibil. *Lg Dev:* NT: 1992–2000. *Other:* Christian, traditional religion. *Map:* 372:226.

Nggem [nbq]. 4,400 (2005). Papua Province, north of Wamena, middle Hablifoeri river. *Status:* 5 (Developing). *Class:* Trans-New Guinea, West, Dani, Dani Proper. *Dialects:* None known. Lexical similarity: 67% with Yali [yac] (Pass Valley), 62% with Walak [wlw], and 50% with Western Dani [dnw]. *Type:* SOV; clause chaining. *Lg Dev:* Bible portions: 1982–2003. *Writing:* Latin script. *Other:* Christian, traditional religion. *Map:* 372:73.

Nias [nia] (Batu, Nias Selatan). 770,000 (2000 census). North Sumatra Province. Nias, Batu islands off west coast. Northwest dialect: Alasa area, west in Sirombu and Mandrehe areas; Central dialect: Gomo area, south in Teluk Dalam and Batu islands. *Status:* 5 (Developing). *Class:* Austronesian, Malayo-Polynesian, Northwest Sumatra-Barrier Islands, Nias. *Dialects:* Central Nias, North Nias (Gunung Sitoli), Northwest Nias, South Nias, West Nias. *Lg Use:* Vigorous. Positive attitudes. Limited proficiency in Indonesian [ind]. *Lg Dev:* Bible: 1911. *Writing:* Latin script. *Other:* North dialect (particularly Gunung Sitoli) has high prestige and is a lingua franca in Nias. The South dialect (particularly Teluk Dalam variety) has lower prestige, especially in northern Nias, and is considered by many Nias speakers from other areas as unrefined. Christian. *Map:* 376:30.

Nila [nil]. No known L1 speakers. Central Maluku Province, south central Seram island transmigration area. 6 villages. (Originally Nila island in south central Maluku). *Status:* 10 (Extinct). *Class:* Austronesian, Malayo-Polynesian, Central-Eastern Malayo-Polynesian, Timor-Babar, Southwest Maluku, Teun-Nila-Serua, Nila-Serua. *Dialects:* None known. Reportedly similar to Serua [srw]. Not intelligible with Teun [tve]. *Lg Use:* Shifted to Ambon Malay [abs].

Nimboran [nir] (Nambrong). 2,000 (1987 SIL). Ethnic population: 3,500 (1987 SIL). North Papua Province, due west of Lake Sentani. About 26 villages. *Status:* 8a (Moribund). *Class:* Nimboran. *Dialects:* None known. Lexical similarity: 40% with Kemtuik [kmt]. *Lg Use:* Older adults. Children learn Papuan Malay [pmy] exclusively. Also use Papuan Malay [pmy]. *Lg Dev:* Bible portions: 1982–1985. *Map:* 372:162.

Ninggerum [nxr] (Kasiwa, Kativa, Muyu, Ninggeroem, Ninggirum, Ninggrum, Orgwo). 1,000 in Indonesia. Papua Province, border area. *Status:* 6a (Vigorous). *Other:* 2002–2003 survey data indicates probably all live in Papua New Guinea, but have land on the Indonesia side where they temporarily migrate to gather food. Christian, traditional religion. See main entry on page 321. *Maps:* 372:229, 373:229.

Nipsan [nps] (Southern Jale, Yale-Nipsan). 2,500 (1993 R. Doriot). Papua Province, Jayawijaya regency, Kurima subdistrict, just west of Hmanggona. *Status:* 6a (Vigorous). *Class:* Trans-New Guinea, Mek, Eastern. *Dialects:* None known. Lexical similarity: 78% with Kosarek Yale [kkl], 59% with Nalca [nlc]. *Lg Use:* Religious services. Used as L2 by Korupun-Sela [kpq]. *Lg Dev:* Bible portions: 1982. *Other:* Distinct from Yali of Ninia [nlk], Yali of Angguruk [yli], and Yali of Pass Valley [yac]. Christian, traditional religion. *Map:* 372:204.

Nisa [njs] (Bonefa, Kerema). 500 (1987 SIL). Papua Province, east side of Geelvink bay inland, Danau Nisa area. *Status:* 6b (Threatened). *Class:* East Geelvink Bay. *Lg Use:* Vigorous. *Other:* Christian, traditional religion. *Map:* 372:178.

Nuaulu, North [nni] (Fatakai, Nuaulu, Patakai). 500 (1990 SIL). Maluku Province, 2 villages. Seram island, central north coast, inland from west shore, Saleman bay. *Status:* 6a (Vigorous). *Class:* Austronesian, Malayo-Polynesian, Central-Eastern Malayo-Polynesian, Central Maluku, East, Seram, Sawai-Nuaulu. *Dialects:* None known. Lexical similarity: 67% with South Nuaulu [nxl], 64% with Saleman [sau]. *Other:* Distinct from Huaulu [hud]. *Map:* 367.

Nuaulu, South [nxl] (Fatakai, Nuaulu, Patakai). 1,500 (1995 SIL). Maluku Province, Amahai district, 6 villages. Seram island, upland from south coast. *Status:* 6a (Vigorous). *Class:* Austronesian, Malayo-Polynesian, Central-Eastern Malayo-Polynesian, Central Maluku, East, Seram, Sawai-Nuaulu. *Dialects:* None known. Lexical similarity: 67% with North Nuaulu [nni]; 50% with South Wemale [weo], Hulung [huk], and Naka'ela [nae]; 48% with Saleman [sau]. *Lg Use:* Vigorous. Also use Indonesian [ind], Sepa [spb]. *Lg Dev:* Literacy rate in L1: Below 1%. Literacy rate in L2: 5%–15%. Dictionary. Bible portions: 1991–2004. *Writing:* Latin script. *Other:* Different from Huaulu [hud]. Christian, traditional religion. *Map:* 367.

Nusa Laut [nul] (Nusalaut). No known L1 speakers. Ethnic population: 2,230 (1989 SIL). Central Maluku Province, Lease islands, Nusa Laut island, Titawai village. *Status:* 9 (Dormant). *Class:* Austronesian, Malayo-Polynesian, Central-Eastern Malayo-Polynesian, Central Maluku, East, Seram, Nunusaku, Piru Bay, East, Seram Straits, Uliase, Hatuhaha, Elpaputi. *Dialects:* None known. Lexical similarity: 69% with Saparua [spr], 65% with Amahai [amq]. *Lg Use:* Shifted to Malay [abs]. *Other:* Christian.

Obokuitai [afz] (Aliki, Ati, Obogwitai). 120 (Wurm 2000). Papua Province, Lakes plain just north of mid-Rouffaer river, Obogwi village. *Status:* 6b (Threatened). *Class:* Lakes Plain, Tariku, East. *Dialects:* None known. Lexical similarity: 78% with Eritai [ert], 69% with Biritai [bqq]. *Type:* SOV; tonal. *Lg Use:* Potentially endangered (2000 S. Wurm). Children influenced by Indonesian [ind] (Wurm 2007). *Lg Dev:* Literacy rate in L1: 15%. Bible portions: 1994. *Writing:* Latin script. *Other:* 'Ati', language. *Map:* 372:184.

Oirata [oia] (Maaro). 1,220 (1987 SIL). Southwestern Maluku Province, southeast Kisar island, east and west Oirata. 2 villages; Ambon city. *Status:* 7 (Shifting). *Class:* Trans-New Guinea, West, Timor-Alor-Pantar. *Dialects:* None known. Not related to other languages on Oirata or to central Maluku languages. Not closely related to languages in East Timor. *Type:* SOV. *Lg Use:* A few on Kisar island also use Kisar [kje]. *Lg Dev:* Literacy rate in L1: Below 1%. *Other:* Christian. *Map:* 369.

Okolod [kqv] (Kolod, Kolour, Kolur, Okolod Murut). 3,390 in Indonesia (2000). Population total all countries: 4,970. East Kalimantan Province. Along Sabah border, northwestern corner of province; east of Lumbis town, north of Lundayeh town. Also in Malaysia. *Status:* 6a (Vigorous). *Class:* Austronesian, Malayo-Polynesian, North Borneo, North Sarawakan, Dayic, Murutic, Murut. *Dialects:* Lexical similarity: 82% with Okolod variety in Sabah, 70% with Pensiangan Murut dialect of Tagal Murut [mvv], 34% with Lun Bawang [lnd]. *Other:* Traditional religion, Christian. *Map:* 365:45.

Onin [oni] (Onim, Sepa). 500 (Wurm 2000). Papua Province, north and northwest Bomberai peninsula. *Status:* 6b (Threatened). *Class:* Austronesian, Malayo-Polynesian, Central-Eastern Malayo-Polynesian, North Bomberai. *Dialects:* Nikuda, Ogar, Patipi, Sepa. *Lg Use:* Potentially endangered (2000 S. Wurm). Under pressure from Iha [ihp] and Indonesian [ind] (Wurm 2007). *Other:* Traditional religion, Christian. *Map:* 371:42.

Onin Based Pidgin [onx]. No known L1 speakers. Papua Province, Onin peninsula. *Status:* 9 (Second language only). *Class:* Pidgin, Onin based.

Ormu [orz]. 500 (Wurm 2000). Papua Province, north coast area just west of Jayapura, north of Cyclops mountains, Ormu Besar and Ormu Kecil villages. *Status:* 7 (Shifting). *Class:* Austronesian, Malayo-Polynesian, Central-Eastern Malayo-Polynesian, Eastern Malayo-Polynesian, Oceanic, Western Oceanic, North New Guinea, Sarmi-Jayapura Bay, Jayapura Bay. *Lg Use:* Endangered (2000 D. Tryon); potentially endangered (Wurm 2000). Largely bilingual in

Indonesian [ind] (Wurm 2007). *Other:* Traditional religion, Christian. *Map:* 372:132.

Orya [ury] (Oria, Uria, Warpok, Warpu). 1,600 (1985 P. Fields). 900 in Unurum-Guay, 100 in Bonggo subdistrict, 600 in Lereh subdistrict. 0 monolinguals. L2 users: Some store owners and police have learned Orya. Papua Province, Unurum-Guay, Bonggo, and Lereh subdistricts, Taja, Witi, and Wamho (formerly of Orya) villages. *Status:* 6b (Threatened). *Class:* Tor-Kwerba, Orya-Tor, Orya. *Dialects:* Barat (West Orya), Timur (East Orya), Yapsi-Taja. Slight dialect differences. *Lg Use:* Children learn Orya in most cases. All domains. Positive attitudes. Also use Indonesian [ind], Papuan Malay [pmy], Sause [sao]. *Lg Dev:* Literacy rate in L1: 5%–15%. Some adult literacy classes. NT: 2005. *Writing:* Latin script. *Other:* Uria is a misspelling used earlier. Glossonym: Warpok by the Nimboran. Traditional religion, Christian. *Map:* 372:160.

Osing [osi] (Banyuwangi). 300,000 (2000 census). East Java Province, Banyuwangi regency area, east coast Java island, west side, Bali strait. *Status:* 6a (Vigorous). *Class:* Austronesian, Malayo-Polynesian, Javanese. *Lg Use:* Vigorous. All children are learning and use the language at home. *Writing:* Javanese script. *Other:* Muslim. *Map:* 363.

Ot Danum [otd] (Dohoi, Malahoi, Uud Danum, Uut Danum). 78,800 (2007 SIL). Central Kalimantan Province, 7 villages. Remote area, upper reaches of south Kapuas river, large area south of Schwaner range. West Kalimantan Province. *Status:* 6a (Vigorous). *Class:* Austronesian, Malayo-Polynesian, Greater Barito, West, North. *Dialects:* Dohoi, Kadorih, Kuhin, Ot Balawan, Ot Banu'u, Ot Murung 1 (Murung 1, Punan Ratah), Ot Olang, Ot Tuhup, Sarawai (Melawi), Sebaung, Ulu Ai' (Da'an). Lexical similarity: 70% with Siang [sya], 65% with Kohin [kkx], 60% with Katingan dialect of Ngaju [nij], 50% with Ngaju (main dialect) [nij]. *Lg Dev:* Grammar. NT: 1998. *Other:* Dohoi and Murung 1 dialects may be separate languages. Traditional religion, Christian. *Maps:* 364:46, 365:46.

Padoe [pdo] (Alalao, Pado-e, Padoé, South Mori). 5,000 (1991 P. Vuorinen). South Sulawesi Province, east Luwu Utara regency, Nuha, Malili, and Mangkutana subdistricts, 9 villages. Inland betwen Lake Mantana and Usu arm of north Bone bay. Central Sulawesi Province, Morowali regency, Mori Atas and Pamona Utara subdistricts, 4 villages. *Status:* 6b (Threatened). *Class:* Austronesian, Malayo-Polynesian, Celebic, Eastern, Southeastern, Bungku-Tolaki, Western, Interior. *Dialects:* Central Padoe, Western Padoe. 2 dialects. Lexical similarity: 73%–86% with Mori Atas [mzq], 75% with Mori Bawah [xmz]. *Lg Use:* Vigorous. Also use Indonesian [ind]. *Lg Dev:* Dictionary. *Writing:* Latin script. *Other:* Christian, Muslim. *Map:* 375:68.

Pagu [pgu] (Pago, Pagoe). 3,310 (2000). North Maluku Province. Interior northern Halmahera south of Modole [mqo] language area, to mouth of Kao river. *Status:* 7 (Shifting). *Class:* West Papuan, North Halmahera, Galela-Loloda. *Dialects:* Isam, Pagu, Toliwiku (Toliliko). *Lg Use:* Also use Indonesian [ind]. *Lg Dev:* Literacy rate in L1: Below 1%. Literacy rate in L2: 25%–50%. *Other:* Muslim, Christian. *Map:* 366.

Paku [pku] (Bakau). 3,500 (2003), decreasing. Few monolinguals. Central Kalimantan Province, East Barito regency. South of Ampah town. *Status:* 8a (Moribund). *Class:* Austronesian, Malayo-Polynesian, Greater Barito, East, Central-South, South. *Dialects:* None known. Lexical similarity: 77% with Ma'anyan [mhy], 73% with Dusun Witu [duv]. *Lg Use:* Mainly older adults. *Map:* 365:47.

Palu'e [ple] (Lu'a, Palue, Paluqe). 10,000 (Grimes et al. 1997). East Nusa Tenggara Province. Palu'e island, north of central Flores island. North coast, Flores mainland, northwest of Maumere, Nangahure village. *Status:* 6a (Vigorous). *Class:* Austronesian, Malayo-Polynesian, Central-Eastern Malayo-Polynesian, Bima-Lembata. *Dialects:* None known. Possible grouping with Ende [end] and Li'o [ljl] languages; marginal intelligibility of Li'o. *Other:* Christian, traditional religion. *Map:* 370.

Palumata [pmc] (Balamata, Palamata). No known L1 speakers. Central Maluku, northwest Buru island. *Status:* 10 (Extinct). *Class:* Austronesian, Malayo-Polynesian, Central-Eastern Malayo-Polynesian, Central Maluku, Buru.

Pamona [pmf] (Baree, Bare'e, Poso). 137,000 (Lauder et al. 2000). Central and South Sulawesi provinces, total 193 villages. Central Sulawesi Province, Poso regency, Poso Kota, Poso Pesisir, Parigi, Lage, Pamona Utara, Pamona Selatan, Tojo, Ulubongko, Ampana Kota, Ampanatete, Una-Una, Mori Atas, Petasia, Bungku Utara, and Bungku Tengah subdistricts; South Sulawesi Province, Luwu Utara district, Mangkutana, north Wotu, and Bone-Bone subdistricts. *Status:* 6b (Threatened). *Class:* Austronesian, Malayo-Polynesian, Celebic, Kaili-Pamona, Northern, Pamona. *Dialects:* Laiwonu (Iba), Pamona, Rapangkaka (Aria), Taa (Topotaa, Wana), Tobau (Bare'e, Tobalo, Tobao), Tokondindi, Tomoni, Topada. Laiwonu and Rapangkaka dialects may be separate languages. Lexical similarity: 76% (Taa)–90% among dialects, except for Tombelala [ttp], which has 66%–76% with other Bungku Tengah dialects, and is considered a separate language. *Lg Use:* Also use Indonesian [ind]. *Lg Dev:* Dictionary. Grammar. NT: 1933–1992. *Writing:* Latin script. *Other:* Pamona speakers in Bungku Utara recognize 5 ethnic groups with minor dialect differences: Pusangke, Kajumorangka, Tokasiala, Burangas, and Topotaa. The first 4 are interior mountain dwellers; the Topotaa are coastal. Bungku Tengah recognize 5 varieties: Topotaa (same as Taa), Tobau, Tokondindi, and Topada. Christian. *Maps:* 374:69, 375:69.

Panasuan [psn] (To Pamosean, To Panasean). 800 (2004 SIL). Ethnic population: 800. West Sulawesi Province, Mamuju regency, Kalumpang and Seko subdistricts. 2 villages. *Status:* 6b (Threatened). *Class:* Austronesian, Malayo-Polynesian, South Sulawesi, Seko, Panasuan. *Dialects:* None known. Lexical similarity: 67% with Seko Tengah [sko], 63% with Seko Padang [skx], 72% with Tangkou [tkx]. *Lg Use:* Some pressure from Kalumpang [kli], Seko Tengah [sko] and Indonesian [ind] (Wurm 2007). Home, church announcements, sermons, village government, at school, trade. All ages. Very positive attitudes. *Other:* Christian. *Map:* 375:70.

Pancana [pnp] (Pantjana). 6,000 (2005 D. Andersen). South Sulawesi Province, central Buton island. *Status:* 6a (Vigorous). *Class:* Austronesian, Malayo-Polynesian, Celebic, Eastern, Southeastern, Muna-Buton, Nuclear Muna-Buton, Munan, Munic, Western. *Dialects:* Kalende (Lawele), Kapontori (Akido), Labuandiri. Dialect names are also place names. May be more than 1 language. Lexical similarity: 71% with Muna [mnb], 57% with Cia-Cia [cia]. *Lg Use:* Also use Wolio [wlo]. *Other:* Muslim. *Map:* 375:71.

Pannei [pnc] (Tapango). 9,000 (1983). West Sulawesi Province, Polewali Mandar regency, Wonomulyo subdistrict. *Status:* 6a (Vigorous). *Class:* Austronesian, Malayo-Polynesian, South Sulawesi, Northern, Pitu Ulunna Salu. *Dialects:* Bulo, Tapango. Lexical similarity: 87%–93% between the Bulo dialect and other varieties, 75%–80% with dialects of Ulumanda' [ulm], Bambam [ptu], and Aralle-Tabulahan [atq]. *Other:* Muslim. *Map:* 375:72.

Pantar, Western [lev] (Lamma, Lamma', Lemma, Mauta,

Pantar Barat). 10,000. Ethnic population: 10,000. Nusa Tenggara Province, west Pantar island. *Status:* 6a (Vigorous). *Class:* Trans-New Guinea, West, Timor-Alor-Pantar, Alor-Pantar, Pantar. *Dialects:* Lamma', Mauta, Tubbe. *Lg Dev:* Dictionary. Grammar. *Map:* 370.

Papasena [pas]. 400 (1982 SIL). Papua Province, Lakes plain area, lower Idenburg river just east of Rouffaer river juncture. *Status:* 6a (Vigorous). *Class:* Lakes Plain, Tariku, East. *Dialects:* None known. Lexical similarity: 23% with Sikaritai [tty]. *Other:* Christian, traditional religion. *Map:* 372:196.

Papuma [ppm]. 600 (1982 SIL). Papua Province, Serui island south coast, Papuma village. *Status:* 6b (Threatened). *Class:* Austronesian, Malayo-Polynesian, Central-Eastern Malayo-Polynesian, Eastern Malayo-Polynesian, South Halmahera-West New Guinea, West New Guinea, Cenderawasih Bay, Yapen, Central-Western. *Dialects:* None known. Lexical similarity: 82% with Munggui [mth], Marau [mvr], and Ansus [and]. *Lg Use:* Shifting to Ansus [and]. *Other:* Christian, traditional religion. *Map:* 372:97.

Patani [ptn]. 10,600 (2000). North Maluku Province, 9 villages. Halmahera island, narrow tip, southeast peninsula, west along the coast. *Status:* 6a (Vigorous). *Class:* Austronesian, Malayo-Polynesian, Central-Eastern Malayo-Polynesian, Eastern Malayo-Polynesian, South Halmahera-West New Guinea, South Halmahera, Southeast. *Lg Use:* Vigorous. Also use Indonesian [ind]. Used as L2 by Sawai [szw]. *Lg Dev:* Literacy rate in L1: Below 1%. Literacy rate in L2: 25%–50%. *Other:* Schools. Muslim. *Map:* 366.

Paulohi [plh]. 50 (1982). Central Maluku Province, west Seram, south central Seram island, Elpaputih bay west shore. 2 villages, Kecamatan Amahai. *Status:* 8b (Nearly extinct). *Class:* Austronesian, Malayo-Polynesian, Central-Eastern Malayo-Polynesian, Central Maluku, East, Seram, Nunusaku, Piru Bay, East, Seram Straits, Solehua. *Other:* Experienced a severe earthquake and tidal wave in 2009. *Map:* 367.

Pekal [pel]. 30,000 (2000 census). South Sumatra and Bengkulu provinces. West coast, near northern provincial border; northeast of Ipuh town to Tembesi river, to near Argamakmur town south. *Status:* 6a (Vigorous). *Class:* Austronesian, Malayo-Polynesian, Malayo-Chamic, Malayic, Malay. A member of macrolanguage Malay [msa] (Malaysia). *Dialects:* None known. Related to Minangkabau [min] with Rejang influences [rej]. *Lg Use:* Vigorous. Home, village. All ages. Positive attitudes. Use Indonesian [ind] for civics and religion. *Writing:* Unwritten. *Other:* See themselves as Malay culturally and linguistically, not Minangkabau [min], though Pekal has Minangkabau influences. Neither Minangkabau nor Malay readily understand Pekal, due to lexical and phonological distinctiveness. Muslim. *Map:* 377:31.

Pendau [ums] (Ndaoe, Ndau, "Umalasa" *pej.*). 4,500 (Quick 2007). Central Sulawesi Province, centered in Balaesang district, Walandano, Sibayu, and other villages. Scattered settlements as far north as Dampal Utara district. *Status:* 6b (Threatened). *Class:* Austronesian, Malayo-Polynesian, Celebic, Tomini-Tolitoli, Tomini, Southern. *Lg Use:* Pendau is the everyday language in their settlements. They use Indonesian [ind] with outside officials. Children's education is in Indonesian (2007). *Lg Dev:* Grammar. Bible portions: 2002–2005. *Writing:* Latin script. *Other:* "Umalasa" is a Bugis [bug] exonym meaning 'the sick ones' with negative connotations. Muslim, Christian. *Map:* 374:73.

Perai [wet] (Tutunohan). 280 (Hinton 2000). Southwestern Maluku Province, Wetar island northeast coast, north of Timor, Uhak and Moning villages. *Status:* 6b (Threatened). *Class:* Austronesian, Malayo-Polynesian, Central-Eastern Malayo-Polynesian, Timor-Babar, Southwest Maluku, Wetar. *Dialects:* Moning, Uhak. Lexical similarity: 93% among dialects, 79% with Aputai [apx], 76% with Tugun [tzn], 67% with Ili'uun [ilu], 51% with Galolen [gal]. *Lg Use:* Also use Ambonese Malay [abs]. *Lg Dev:* Literacy rate in L1: Below 1%. *Other:* Intermarry with the Kisar [kje]. Christian. *Map:* 369.

Petjo [pey] (Peco', Pecok, Petjoh). There are some L1 speakers (Wurm 2007). Java, Jakarta Special Capital Region. Urban area. *Status:* 8b (Nearly extinct). *Class:* Creole, Dutch based. *Dialects:* None known. Influences from Dutch [nld], Javanese [jav], and Betawi [bew]. *Other:* Predominantly Malay and Dutch [nld] vocabulary, with Malay and Sundanese elements. *Map:* 363.

Pom [pmo]. 2,000 (1987 SIL). Papua Province, Miosnum island, west Serui island, Pom, Serewen, and Mias Endi villages. *Status:* 6b (Threatened). *Class:* Austronesian, Malayo-Polynesian, Central-Eastern Malayo-Polynesian, Eastern Malayo-Polynesian, South Halmahera-West New Guinea, West New Guinea, Cenderawasih Bay, Yapen, Central-Western. *Dialect:* Jobi. *Other:* Christian, traditional religion. *Map:* 372:100.

Ponosakan [pns] (Ponasakan). 3,000 (Wurm and Hattori 1981). North Sulawesi Province. North peninsula, south coast, Belang town area. *Status:* 8a (Moribund). *Class:* Austronesian, Malayo-Polynesian, Philippine, Greater Central Philippine, Gorontalo-Mongondow, Mongondowic. *Dialects:* None known. Lexical similarity: 75% with Mongondow [mog], 66% with Lolak [llq]. *Other:* Muslim. *Map:* 374:74.

Punan Aput [pud] (Aput). 370 (Wurm and Hattori 1981). East Kalimantan Province. South of Kayan river, northwest of Mount Menyapa. *Status:* 6b (Threatened). *Class:* Austronesian, Malayo-Polynesian, North Borneo, North Sarawakan, Kayan-Kenyah, Kayanic, Muller-Schwaner 'Punan'. *Dialects:* None known. Allegedly unintelligible of other Penan languages (Soriente 2003). *Map:* 365:48.

Punan Merah [puf]. 140 (Wurm and Hattori 1981). East Kalimantan Province. Mahakam river, east of Ujohhilang town. *Status:* 6b (Threatened). *Class:* Austronesian, Malayo-Polynesian, North Borneo, North Sarawakan, Kayan-Kenyah, Kayanic, Muller-Schwaner 'Punan'. *Other:* Distinct from Punan Merap [puc]. *Map:* 365:49.

Punan Merap [puc]. 200 (Wurm and Hattori 1981). East Kalimantan Province. Upper Malinau river, east of Longkemuat town. *Status:* 6b (Threatened). *Class:* Austronesian, Malayo-Polynesian, North Borneo, Rejang-Sajau. *Other:* Distinct from Punan Merah [puf]. *Map:* 365:50.

Punan Tubu [puj]. 2,000 (Wurm and Hattori 1981). East Kalimantan Province. Malinau, Mentarang, and Sembakung river areas. *Status:* 6a (Vigorous). *Class:* Austronesian, Malayo-Polynesian, North Borneo, North Sarawakan, Punan Tubu. *Other:* Not a Kenyah language (2003 A. Soriente). Penan is generic, nonagricultural peoples (Blust 1974). There are no Penan languages as a distinguishable subgroup. *Map:* 365:51.

Puragi [pru] (Mogao). 700 (1991 SIL). Papua Province, southwest Bird's Head along Maccluer Gulf, inland Matamani river area. *Status:* 6b (Threatened). *Class:* Trans-New Guinea, South Bird's Head, South Bird's Head Proper, Western. *Other:* Christian, traditional religion. *Map:* 371:29.

Putoh [put] (Putuk). 6,000 (Wurm and Hattori 1981). East Kalimantan Province. Area on both sides of Mentarang river; Longberang, Mensalong, and Bangalan town areas. *Status:* 6b (Threatened). *Class:* Austronesian, Malayo-Polynesian, North Borneo, North Sarawakan,

Dayic, Kelabitic. *Dialects:* Abai, Pa Kembaloh. May be the same as Lun Bawang [lnd]. *Map:* 365:52.

Rahambuu [raz] (Lellewao, Lellewau, Noihe, Wiaoe, Wiau). 5,000 (Mead 1999). Southeast Sulawesi Province, North Kolaka Regency, Pakue subdistrict. West coast, upper Bone bay, north of Kodeoha [vko] language area to Central Sulawesi Province border. Some in Central Sulawesi Province. *Status:* 6b (Threatened). *Class:* Austronesian, Malayo-Polynesian, Celebic, Eastern, Southeastern, Bungku-Tolaki, Western, West Coast. *Dialects:* Lexical similarity: 87% between dialects, 75% with Kodeoha [vko], 70% with Tolaki [lbw], Mekongga dialect of Tolaki [lbw], and Waru [wru]; 54% with Mori [mzq] or [xmz] and Bungku [bkz] groups. *Lg Use:* Also use Bugis [bug] (Wurm 2007). *Other:* Muslim. *Map:* 375:75.

Rajong [rjg] (Razong). 6,000 (2010). East Nusa Tenggara Province. 2 enclaves on Central Flores island. Area near Mount Watuweri; also, south of northern Kepo' [kuk] language area. *Status:* 6a (Vigorous). *Class:* Austronesian, Malayo-Polynesian, Central-Eastern Malayo-Polynesian, Bima-Lembata. *Map:* 370.

Rampi [lje] (Ha'uwa, Leboni, Rampi-Leboni). 10,000 (2006). South Sulawesi Province, Luwu Utara regency, Rampi district, 6 isolated mountain villages; also scattered in Sabbang, Limbong, Wotu, and Mangkutana districts. Also, Central Sulawesi Province. *Status:* 6b (Threatened). *Class:* Austronesian, Malayo-Polynesian, Celebic, Kaili-Pamona, Southern. *Dialects:* Rampi (Lambu), Rato. Leboni is prestige dialect. *Lg Use:* Vigorous in some villages. Used as L2 by Uma [ppk]. *Lg Dev:* Bible portions: 2011. *Writing:* Latin script. *Other:* Christian, Muslim. *Map:* 375:76.

Rasawa [rac]. 200 (1987 SIL). Papua Province, Waropen Bawah subdistrict, south coast. 2 villages. *Status:* 6b (Threatened). *Class:* Lakes Plain, Rasawa-Saponi. *Lg Use:* Home. *Other:* Christian, traditional religion. *Map:* 372:88.

Ratahan [rth] (Bentenan, Pasan, Toratan). 500 (Himmelmann and Wolff 1999), decreasing. Ethnic population: 30,000 (1989). North Sulawesi Province. Northeast section of peninsula, southwest of Lake Tondano to northeast coast. *Status:* 8b (Nearly extinct). *Class:* Austronesian, Malayo-Polynesian, Philippine, Sangiric, Southern. *Lg Use:* Under pressure from Manado Malay [xmm]. Most are 60 and older. *Other:* Traditional religion, Christian. *Map:* 374:77.

Rejang [rej] (Djang, Redjang). 350,000 (2000 census). Sumatra, north Bengkulu Province. Southwest highlands; areas near Arga Makmur, Muara Aman, Curup, and Kapahiang towns; South Sumatra Province, Musi Rawas Ulu. *Status:* 6a (Vigorous). *Class:* Austronesian, Malayo-Polynesian, Rejang. *Dialects:* Kepahiang (Kebanagung), Lebong, Musi (Curup), Pasisir, Rawas. Lebong recognized as central dialect. *Lg Use:* Vigorous language vitality. Very positive attitudes. Low bilingualism in Indonesian [ind]. *Lg Dev:* Literacy rate in L2: 45%. Dictionary. Grammar. *Writing:* Kaganga script. *Other:* 85% live in remote rural areas. Different from Rejang-Baram group of languages on Borneo. Musi and Rawas dialects (named after rivers they are on) not to be confused with Malay varieties of the same name. Muslim. *Map:* 377:32.

Rembong [reb]. 5,000 (2010 C. Grimes). East Nusa Tenggara Province. North central Flores island, between eastern Manggarai [mqy] and Riung [riu] language areas. *Status:* 6a (Vigorous). *Class:* Austronesian, Malayo-Polynesian, Central-Eastern Malayo-Polynesian, Bima-Lembata. *Dialects:* Namu, Rembong, Wangka. *Map:* 370.

Reta [ret] (Retta). 800. East Nusa Tenggara Province. South Pura island; south Ternate island. *Status:* 6b (Threatened). *Class:* Trans-New Guinea, West, Timor-Alor-Pantar, Alor-Pantar, Pantar. *Dialects:* None known. Not intelligible of languages on north Pura. *Map:* 370.

Riantana [ran] (Kimaam). 1,100 (Voegelin and Voegelin 1977). Papua Province, Frederik Hendrik island. *Status:* 6a (Vigorous). *Class:* Trans-New Guinea, Kolopom. *Lg Use:* Home. *Other:* Christian, traditional religion. *Map:* 373:256.

Ribun [rir]. 45,000 (Wurm and Hattori 1981). West Kalimantan Province, Kapuas Hulu regency, Tayan Hulu subdistrict. Landak river area west of Kembayan town. *Status:* 6a (Vigorous). *Class:* Austronesian, Malayo-Polynesian, Land Dayak, Southern. *Dialects:* Bekidoh, Ribun. *Map:* 364:54.

Rikou [rgu] (Eastern Rote, Ringgou, Rote, Rote Timur, Roti, Rotinese). 12,000 (2011). East Nusa Tenggara Province. East Rote island, Rikou, Landu, and Oe Pao domains. *Status:* 6a (Vigorous). *Class:* Austronesian, Malayo-Polynesian, Central-Eastern Malayo-Polynesian, Timor-Babar, Nuclear Timor, Rote. *Dialects:* Landu, Oe Pao (Oepao), Rikou. *Lg Use:* Vigorous. All domains. All ages. Also use Indonesian [ind]. *Lg Dev:* Bible portions: 2004. *Other:* 'Ringgou' is the pronunciation in some other Rote languages. Ethnic autonym: Rikou. Christian. *Map:* 369.

Riung [riu] (Far Eastern Manggarai). 14,000 (Wurm and Hattori 1981). East Nusa Tenggara Province, North central Flores island, Kabupaten Ngada, Kecamatan Riung. *Status:* 6a (Vigorous). *Class:* Austronesian, Malayo-Polynesian, Central-Eastern Malayo-Polynesian, Bima-Lembata. *Dialects:* None known. Reportedly similar to Manggarai [mqy], but marginal intelligibility. *Map:* 370.

Roma [rmm] (Romang). 1,700 (1991 SIL). Southwestern Maluku Province, Jerusu village. Roma island east of Wetar island. *Status:* 6a (Vigorous). *Class:* Austronesian, Malayo-Polynesian, Central-Eastern Malayo-Polynesian, Timor-Babar, Southwest Maluku, Kisar-Roma. *Lg Use:* Also use Indonesian [ind]. *Lg Dev:* Literacy rate in L1: Below 1%. Literacy rate in L2: 25%–50%. *Other:* Christian. *Maps:* 368, 369.

Rongga [ror]. 4,000 (2005 W. Arka). East Nusa Tenggara Province. South central Flores island, between Manggarai [mqy] and Ngad'a [nxg], and south of Wae Rana [wrx] language areas. *Status:* 6a (Vigorous). *Class:* Austronesian, Malayo-Polynesian, Central-Eastern Malayo-Polynesian, Bima-Lembata. *Map:* 370.

Roon [rnn] (Ron). 1,100 (1993 R. Doriot). Papua Province, Roon island west of Cenderawasih bay, north of Wandamen peninsula. *Status:* 6a (Vigorous). *Class:* Austronesian, Malayo-Polynesian, Central-Eastern Malayo-Polynesian, Eastern Malayo-Polynesian, South Halmahera-West New Guinea, West New Guinea, Cenderawasih Bay, Yapen, Central-Western. *Other:* Traditional religion, Christian. *Map:* 371:56.

Sa'ban [snv] (Merau). 850 in Indonesia (2000). East Kalimantan Province, Nunukan regency. East of Sarawak border, south of Benuang town. *Status:* 6b (Threatened). *Lg Use:* Some Sa'ban parents use Indonesian [ind] with their children. See main entry on page 226. *Map:* 365:55.

Sahu [saj] (Sahu'u, Sau, Sa'u). 7,500 (Voorhoeve and Visser 1987). 3,500 in Tala'i, 4,000 in Pa'disua. North Maluku Province. North Halmahera island, southwestern coast, Jailolo town area. *Status:* 5 (Developing). *Class:* West Papuan, North Halmahera, Sahu. *Dialects:* Pa'disua (Palisua), Tala'i. Reportedly similar to Waioli [wli] and Gamkonora [gak]. *Lg Use:* Vigorous. Also use Indonesian [ind]. *Lg Dev:* Literacy rate in L1: Below 1%. Literacy rate in L2: 25%–50%. Dictionary. Bible portions: 2002–2007. *Writing:* Latin script. *Other:* Christian, Muslim. *Map:* 366.

Sajau Basap [sjb] (Sajau, Sujau). 6,000 (Wurm and Hattori 1981). East Kalimantan Province, Berau, and Bulungan regencies. Northeast of Muaramalinau town. *Status:* 6a (Vigorous). *Class:* Austronesian, Malayo-Polynesian, North

Borneo, Rejang-Sajau. *Dialects:* Punan Basap, Punan Batu 2, Punan Sajau. *Map:* 365:56.

Salas [sgu] (Lenkaitahe, Liambata, Salas Gunung). 50 (1989 SIL). Central Maluku Province, Seram island, Gunung village. *Status:* 8b (Nearly extinct). *Class:* Austronesian, Malayo-Polynesian, Central-Eastern Malayo-Polynesian, Central Maluku, East, Seram, Manusela-Seti. *Dialects:* None known. Lexical similarity: 48%–58% with Liana-Seti [ste], 46%–50% with Benggoi [bgy], 35%–46% with Manusela [wha]. *Lg Use:* Shifting to Masiwang [bnf] (Wurm 2007). Also use Masiwang [bnf]. *Other:* Christian. *Map:* 367.

Saleman [sau] (Hatue, Sawai, Seleman, Wahai). 4,800 (1989 SIL). Maluku Province, Saleman, Pasanea, Sawai, Besi, and Wahai villages. North central Seram island, Saleman bay. *Status:* 6b (Threatened). *Class:* Austronesian, Malayo-Polynesian, Central-Eastern Malayo-Polynesian, Central Maluku, East, Seram, Sawai-Nuaulu. *Dialects:* None known. Lexical similarity: 64% with North Nuaulu [nni], 48% with South Nuaulu [nxl]. *Lg Use:* Vigorous except in Wahai. *Other:* Muslim. *Map:* 367.

Saluan [loe] (Loinang, Loindang, Madi, Mondono). 76,000 (1978). East Central Sulawesi Province, Batui, Batui, Kintom, Luwuk, East Luwuk, Boalemo, Pagimana, Bunta, and Nuhon subdistricts, 136 villages. *Status:* 6b (Threatened). *Class:* Austronesian, Malayo-Polynesian, Celebic, Eastern, Saluan-Banggai, Western, Saluanic. *Dialects:* Kintom-Pagimana-Boalemo, Loinang (Baloa', Kohumama', Lingketeng), Luwuk. Lexical similarity: 74% with Batui [zbt], 53% with Bobongko [bgb], 62% with Andio [bzb], 51% with Balantak [blz]. *Lg Use:* Some children only use Indonesian [ind]. *Lg Dev:* Bible: 2002. *Other:* Users prefer Saluan over Loinang. Muslim, Christian, traditional religion. *Maps:* 374:78, 375:78.

Samarokena [tmj] (Karfasia, Samarkena, Tamaja, Tamaya). 400 (1982 SIL). Papua Province, north coast inland just east of Apauwar river, west of Sarmi, Karfasia, Samarkena, Maseb, and Tamaya villages. *Status:* 6b (Threatened). *Class:* Tor-Kwerba, Greater Kwerba, Kwerba, West Coast. *Lg Use:* Also use Airoran [air], Isirawa [srl], Kwerba [kwe]. *Other:* Christian, traditional religion. *Map:* 372:111.

Sanggau [scg]. 45,000 (Wurm and Hattori 1981). West Kalimantan Province, Sanggau regency. Kapuas river, both sides, west, south of Sanggau town. *Status:* 6a (Vigorous). *Class:* Austronesian, Malayo-Polynesian, Land Dayak. *Dialects:* Dosan, Mayau, Sanggau. Very heterogenous dialects, probably more than 1 language in this group. Not all Sanggau isolects mutually intelligible. Koman and Semerawai could be in this group. *Lg Use:* Also use Kendayan [knx]. *Map:* 364:57.

Sangir [sxn] (Sangi, Sangih, Sangihé, Sangirese). 200,000 in Indonesia (Maryott 1993), increasing. 50,000 Siau, 10,000 Tagulandang. Population total all countries: 255,000. North Sulawesi Province. Northwest of east end of peninsula, Great Sangir island. Also in Philippines. *Status:* 5 (Developing). *Class:* Austronesian, Malayo-Polynesian, Philippine, Sangiric, Northern. *Dialects:* Manganitu (Tamako), Siau (Sjauw), Tabukang (Tabukan), Tagulandang (Tahulandang), Taruna (Tahuna). *Lg Use:* Positive attitudes. *Lg Dev:* Dictionary. Grammar. NT: 1883–1994. *Writing:* Latin script. *Other:* Christian, Muslim. *Map:* 374:79.

Saparua [spr]. 10,200 (1989 SIL). 4,520 in Iha. Maluku Province, Kulur, Iha, Siri-Sori, Iha, Kulur, Latu, Hualoy, Tomalehu, and Kairatu villages. Saparua, nearby Seram islands. *Status:* 8a (Moribund). *Class:* Austronesian, Malayo-Polynesian, Central-Eastern Malayo-Polynesian, Central Maluku, East, Seram, Nunusaku, Piru Bay, East, Seram Straits, Uliase, Hatuhaha, Saparua. *Dialects:* Iha-Saparua, Iha-Seram, Kulur, Siri-Sori. Each village has its own dialect. Lexical similarity: 86%–89% among dialects; 82%–84% with Latu [ltu], 69% with Amahai [amq], 67% with Kamarian [kzk], 68%–71% with Haruku [hrk], 65% with Kaibobo [kzb], 62%–66% with Tulehu [tlu], 49% with Luhu [lcq], 54% with Naka'ela [nae]. *Lg Use:* Shifting to Ambon Malay [abs] (Wurm 2007). *Lg Dev:* Literacy rate in L1: Below 1%. *Other:* Spoken by hundreds of Latu [ltu] people in Kairatu village. Muslim, Christian. *Map:* 367.

Saponi [spi]. No known L1 speakers. Papua Province, interior Waropen Bawah subdistrict, Botawa village. *Status:* 10 (Extinct). *Class:* Lakes Plain, Rasawa-Saponi. *Lg Use:* Moribund (2000 S. Wurm). Shifting to Rasawa [rac] and Indonesian [ind].

Sarudu [sdu] (Doda'). 4,000 (Grimes and Grimes 1987). West Sulawesi Province, north Mamuju regency, south Pasangkayu subdistrict. Enclaves on Makassar strait north coast. *Status:* 6b (Threatened). *Class:* Austronesian, Malayo-Polynesian, Celebic, Kaili-Pamona, Southern. *Dialects:* Kulu (Lariang), Nunu'. Lexical similarity: 75% with Uma [ppk], 80% with Benggaulu dialect of Uma [ppk]. *Other:* Contact with Bugis [bug] and Kaili Ledo [lew] speakers. Muslim. *Maps:* 374:80, 375:80.

Sasak [sas] (Lombok). 2,100,000 (1989). West Nusa Tenggara Province, Lombok island. *Status:* 5 (Developing). *Class:* Austronesian, Malayo-Polynesian, Bali-Sasak-Sumbawa, Sasak-Sumbawa. *Dialects:* Kuto-Kute (North Sasak), Meno-Mene (Central Sasak), Mriak-Mriku (Central South Sasak), Ngeno-Ngene (Central East Sasak, Central West Sasak), Ngeto-Ngete (Northeast Sasak). Complex dialect network. Some varieties have low mutual intelligibility. *Lg Dev:* Dictionary. NT. *Writing:* Balinese script, extended. Latin script. *Other:* Subgroups: Waktu Lima, Waktu Telu. Most Waktu Telu own farms; most Waktu Lima are landless, travel more, and have diverse occupations. Muslim, traditional religion. *Map:* 369.

Sauri [srt]. 100 (1987 SIL). Papua Province, east side of Cenderawasih bay near Waropen [wrp] language area, Sauri-Sirami village, near Sirami river. *Status:* 6b (Threatened). *Class:* East Geelvink Bay. *Dialects:* None known. Lexical similarity: 71% with Barapasi [brp], 60% with Demisa [dei], 76% with Kofei [kpi], 63% with Tefaro [tfo]. *Lg Use:* Under some pressure from Waropen [wrp] and Indonesian [ind] (Wurm 2007). *Other:* Christian, traditional religion. *Map:* 372:93.

Sause [sao] (Seuce). 250 (Wurm 2000). Papua Province, southwest of Sentani, northwest of Lereh, Ures, Mubararon, Sause-Bokoko, Witti-Yadow, Lidya, and Puaral villages. *Status:* 6a (Vigorous). *Class:* Tor-Kwerba, Orya-Tor, Sause. *Lg Use:* Endangered (2000 S. Wurm). Under pressure from Indonesian [ind] (Wurm 2007). Used as L2 by Orya [ury]. *Other:* Christian, traditional religion. *Map:* 372:199.

Sawai [szw] (Weda, Weda-Sawai, Were). 12,000 (2000 SIL), increasing. Few monolinguals. North Maluku Province, Gane Timur and Weda districts,13 villages. Halmahera island, southeast peninsula, Weda bay, both coasts. *Status:* 6b (Threatened). *Class:* Austronesian, Malayo-Polynesian, Central-Eastern Malayo-Polynesian, Eastern Malayo-Polynesian, South Halmahera-West New Guinea, South Halmahera, Southeast. *Dialects:* Faya-Mafa, Kobe, Messa-Dote, Sawai, Weda. Lexical similarity: 64% with North Nuaulu [nni]. *Lg Use:* Some domains, local commerce. Youth are taught Indonesian [ind] first; then learn to understand Sawai. Positive attitudes. Also use Buli [bzq], Gane [gzn], Indonesian [ind], Maba [mqa], North Moluccan Malay [max], Patani [ptn], Ternate [tft], Tidore [tvo], Tobelo [tlb]. *Lg Dev:* Literacy rate in L1: field: 5,000 can read, 1,000 can write. Literacy rate in L2: 25%–50%. 5,000 can read it, 1,000 can write it. Bible portions: 1994–2005. *Writing:* Latin script. *Other:* Different from Saleman [sau]. Muslim, Christian. *Map:* 366.

Saweru [swr] (Sarwar Use). 300 (1991 SIL). Papua Province, Serui Waropen regency, Yapen Selatan subdistrict, central Serui island, an island south of Yapen island near Serui. *Status:* 6b (Threatened). *Class:* West Papuan, Yapen. *Other:* Christian, traditional religion. *Map:* 372:95.

Sawi [saw] (Aejauroh, Sawuy). 3,500 (1993 R. Doriot). Papua Province, Asmat Regency, Pantai Kasuari and Fayit subdistricts, near south coastal lowland, between Kronkel and Ayip rivers and upper Fayit river area, Kamur, Esebor, Wiagas, Minahai, and Comoro villages. *Status:* 8a (Moribund). *Class:* Trans-New Guinea, Ok-Awyu, Awyu-Dumut, Sawi. *Lg Use:* Also use Indonesian [ind]. Used as L2 by Atohwaim [aqm]. *Lg Dev:* Literacy rate in L2: 5% semiliterate. NT: 1973–1994. *Other:* Christian, traditional religion. *Map:* 373:239.

Sawila [swt] (Tanglapui). 3,000 (Grimes et al. 1997). East Nusa Tenggara Province. Southeast Alor island, between Kula [tpg] and Wersing [kvw] language areas. *Status:* 6a (Vigorous). *Class:* Trans-New Guinea, West, Timor-Alor-Pantar, Tanglapui. *Dialects:* Lalamana, Lona, Salimana, Sawila, Sileba. Marginal intelligibility but reportedly structurally similar to Kula [tpg]; distinct historical ethnic identities. *Other:* Many current village locations are the result of recent migrations from older locations. Christian, traditional religion. *Map:* 370.

Seberuang [sbx]. 37,000 (2007 SIL). West Kalimantan Province. Kapuas river area from Nanga Silat town to Selimbau town, on Belimbing, Lebang, Belitang, Seauk, Tempunak, Selimbau, and Silat rivers. *Status:* 6a (Vigorous). *Class:* Austronesian, Malayo-Polynesian, Malayo-Chamic, Malayic, Ibanic. *Dialects:* Quite similar to Desa, a dialect of Iban [iba] (2004 M. Connor). *Type:* SVO. *Other:* Traditional religion, Christian. *Map:* 364:59.

Sedoa [tvw] (Baria, Tawaelia, Tawailia, Topobaria). 900 (2009 S. Shore). 900 in Sedoa village; 3,000 ethnic Sedoa also live outside the area, but most do not speak Sedoa. Ethnic population: 4,000. Central Sulawesi Province, Lore Utara subdistrict, Sedoa village; Poso Pesisir subdistrict, parts of Tambarona and Pinedapa villages. *Status:* 5 (Developing). *Class:* Austronesian, Malayo-Polynesian, Celebic, Kaili-Pamona, Northern, Kaili. *Dialects:* Not a dialect of nearby Napu [npy] or of Kaili languages. Most closely related to Moma [myl] in Palolo Valley. *Lg Use:* Vigorous. *Lg Dev:* Bible portions: 2011. *Writing:* Latin script. *Other:* Christian. *Map:* 374:81.

Segai [sge] (Ga'ay, Segayi). 2,000 (Wurm and Hattori 1981). East Kalimantan Province, Berau regency. Kelai river area around Longlaai town. *Status:* 6a (Vigorous). *Class:* Austronesian, Malayo-Polynesian, North Borneo, North Sarawakan, Kayan-Kenyah, Kayanic, Modang. *Dialects:* Kelai, Segah. Called Segayi by the Berau, Ga'ay by the Kenyah and Kayan. *Map:* 365:60.

Seget [sbg]. 1,200 (1988 SIL). Papua Province, west Bird's Head southwest of Sorong, west and southwest of Moi [mxn] language area, Walian, Sailolof, Segum, and Seget villages. *Status:* 6a (Vigorous). *Class:* West Papuan, West Bird's Head. *Other:* Christian, traditional religion. *Map:* 371:13.

Seit-Kaitetu [hik] (Hila-Kaitetu). 10,200 (1987 SIL). Maluku Province, Seit and Kaitetu villages. Ambon island, north coast. *Status:* 6b (Threatened). *Class:* Austronesian, Malayo-Polynesian, Central-Eastern Malayo-Polynesian, Central Maluku, East, Seram, Nunusaku, Piru Bay, West, Asilulu. *Dialects:* Kaitetu, Seit (Seith). Lexical similarity: 85% between Kaitetu and Seit dialects. Lexical similarity: 78%–82% with Asilulu [asl], 67%–74% with Tulehu [tlu]. *Lg Use:* Vigorous. Also use Ambonese Malay [abs]. *Other:* Muslim, Christian. *Map:* 367.

Sekak [lce] (Lonchong, Loncong, Lontjong, Orang Laut, Sawang, Seka, Sekah). 420 (2000), decreasing. Sumatra, Bangka-Belitung Province. 2 coastal enclaves, northeast Bangka island; Lepar, Liat, Mendanau, and others between Bangka and Belitung. Some possible on nearby coast, South Sumatra Province. *Status:* 6b (Threatened). *Class:* Austronesian, Malayo-Polynesian, Malayo-Chamic, Malayic, Malay. A member of macrolanguage Malay [msa] (Malaysia). *Dialects:* Lexically and phonologically distinct from the Belitung dialect of Malay [zlm] and other Sea Tribe varieties. Lexically most similar to Bintan Orang Laut Malay [zlm] dialect. *Other:* Ethnic autonym: Orang Sawang, sea people. Southernmost of dozens of Malayic-speaking Orang Laut, sea tribe, groups ranging from the waters of Thailand through the Riau archipelago and Bangka and Belitung. Traditional religion. *Map:* 377:33.

Sekar [skz] (Seka). 450 (Voegelin and Voegelin 1977). Papua Province, northwest Bomberai peninsula coast and one small island. *Status:* 6b (Threatened). *Class:* Austronesian, Malayo-Polynesian, Central-Eastern Malayo-Polynesian, North Bomberai. *Dialects:* None known. Lexical similarity: highest with Arguni [agf]. *Other:* Christian, traditional religion. *Map:* 371:41.

Seko Padang [skx] (Seko, Wono). 5,000 (1985 SIL). 2,300 in the Seko area. South Sulawesi Province, North Luwu regency, northeast Limbong subdistrict. Northwestern corner of province. Also, Central Sulawesi Province, Palolo valley. *Status:* 6a (Vigorous). *Class:* Austronesian, Malayo-Polynesian, South Sulawesi, Seko. *Dialects:* Hono' (Wono), Lodang. *Lg Use:* Vigorous. Also use Indonesian [ind]. Used as L2 by Uma [ppk]. *Lg Dev:* Bible portions: 2000–2013. *Writing:* Latin script. *Other:* Many primary schools. Christian, Muslim. *Map:* 375:82.

Seko Tengah [sko] (Pewanean, Pewaneang, Pohoneang, Seko). 2,500 (Laskowske and Laskowske 1987). Northern South Sulawesi Province, west Limbong subdistrict. Area along Betue river. *Status:* 6a (Vigorous). *Class:* Austronesian, Malayo-Polynesian, South Sulawesi, Seko. *Dialects:* None known. Lexical similarity: 71% with Seko Padang [skx], 67% with Panasuan [psn]. *Lg Use:* Also use Indonesian [ind]. *Other:* Christian, Muslim. *Map:* 375:83.

Selaru [slu] (Salaru). 8,000 (2001 SIL). Southest Maluku Province, at least 6 villages. Tanimbar island group; Selaru island off southwest tip of main island Yamdena; Yamdena island itself; Nuswotar island off Yamdena west coast. Some in Saumlake, Ambon towns. *Status:* 6b (Threatened). *Class:* Austronesian, Malayo-Polynesian, Central-Eastern Malayo-Polynesian, Southeast Maluku, Southern. *Dialect:* Kandar. Slight dialect differences. Not closely related to nearby languages. Lexical similarity: 56% with Seluwasan [sws]. *Lg Use:* Vigorous. Also use Indonesian [ind]. *Lg Dev:* Literacy rate in L1: Below 1%. Literacy rate in L2: 25%–50%. Grammar. Bible portions: 1997–2010. *Writing:* Latin script. *Other:* Christian. *Map:* 368.

Selayar [sly] (Salajar, Salayar, Salayer, Saleier, Siladja, Silajara). 128,000 (2000 census). South Sulawesi Province. Selayar island. *Status:* 6a (Vigorous). *Class:* Austronesian, Malayo-Polynesian, South Sulawesi, Makassar. *Dialects:* None known. Lexical similarity: 69% with Makassar [mak]. *Lg Use:* Vigorous. All ages. Positive attitudes. Also use Bugis [bug], Indonesian [ind]. Used as L2 by Laiyolo [lji]. *Other:* Muslim, Christian. *Map:* 375:84.

Selungai Murut [slg] (Murut). 640 in Indonesia (2000). Population total all countries: 1,240. East Kalimantan Province, Nunukan regency. East of Lumbis town; upper reaches of Sembakung river. Also in Malaysia. *Status:*

6b (Threatened). *Class:* Austronesian, Malayo-Polynesian, North Borneo, North Sarawakan, Dayic, Murutic, Murut. *Map:* 365:61.

Seluwasan [sws] (Selvasa, Selwasa). 2,840 (Florey 2005). 740 in Makatian, 2,100 in Seluwasan. Southeast Maluku Province, Wermatang, Batu Putih, Marantutu, and Makatian villages. Tanimbar island group, Yamdena island, southwest coast. *Status:* 6b (Threatened). *Class:* Austronesian, Malayo-Polynesian, Central-Eastern Malayo-Polynesian, Southeast Maluku, Southern. *Dialects:* Makatian, Seluwasan. Makatian dialect quite different from others. *Lg Use:* Possibly endangered (Florey 2005). *Other:* Christian (Protestant). *Map:* 368.

Semandang [sdm] (Kualan-Semandang). 20,000 (2004 M. Connor). West Kalimantan Province, Ketapang regency. Kualan and Semandang river areas. *Status:* 6a (Vigorous). *Class:* Austronesian, Malayo-Polynesian, Land Dayak, Southern. *Dialects:* Beginci, Bihak, Gerai, Komi, Semandang. *Lg Use:* Also use Kendayan [knx]. *Lg Dev:* Literacy rate in L1: Reportedly low (2004 M. Connor). Bible portions: 1982. *Other:* Traditional religion, Christian. *Map:* 364:62.

Sembakung Murut [sbr] (Sembakoeng, Sembakong, Simbakong, Tingalun, Tinggalan, Tinggalum). 3,180 in Indonesia (2000). East Kalimantan Province, Nunukan regency. Sembakung river mouth; west of Alang town. Also in Malaysia. *Status:* 6a (Vigorous). *Class:* Austronesian, Malayo-Polynesian, North Borneo, North Sarawakan, Dayic, Murutic, Tidong. *Map:* 365:63.

Semimi [etz] (Etna Bay, Muri, Wesrau). 1,000 (1991 SIL). Papua Province, Bomberai peninsula near Kaniran, south end extending west to Triton bay. *Status:* 7 (Shifting). *Class:* Mairasi. *Dialects:* None known. Lexical similarity: 69% with Mairasi [zrs], 63% with Mer [mnu]. *Lg Use:* Many children do not speak it (1991 L. Peckham). *Other:* Christian, traditional religion. *Maps:* 371:51, 372:51.

Sempan [xse] (Nararapi). 1,000 (1987 SIL). Papua Province, middle south coast, between Kokonao and Agats, east of Kamoro [kgq] and west of Asmat language areas. *Status:* 6a (Vigorous). *Class:* Trans-New Guinea, Asmat-Kamoro, Sempan. *Dialects:* None known. Reportedly similar to Kamoro [kgq]. *Other:* Christian, traditional religion. *Map:* 372:63.

Sentani [set] (Buyaka). 30,000 (1996 SIL), increasing. Few monolinguals. Papua Province, Lake Sentani area, about 30 villages. Scattered in Papua and other parts of Indonesia. *Status:* 5 (Developing). *Class:* East Bird's Head-Sentani, Sentani, Sentani Proper. *Dialects:* Central Sentani, East Sentani, West Sentani. Lexical similarity: 30% with Tabla [tnm]. *Lg Use:* Vigorous use in most families. All domains. Positive attitudes. Also use Indonesian [ind]. *Lg Dev:* Literacy rate in L1: 16%. Literacy rate in L2: 50%–75%. About 5,000. Schools are beginning to use Sentani grades 1 to 6. Dictionary. Grammar. NT: 1997. *Writing:* Latin script. *Other:* Ethnic autonym: Buyaka. Traditional religion, Christian. *Map:* 372:130.

Sepa [spb] (Tamilouw). 2,600 (1989 SIL). Maluku Province, Sepa village. Seram island, several enclaves along southwest coast between Elapaputih and Teluti bays. *Status:* 6a (Vigorous). *Class:* Austronesian, Malayo-Polynesian, Central-Eastern Malayo-Polynesian, Central Maluku, East, Seram, Nunusaku, Piru Bay, East. *Dialects:* None known. Lexical similarity: 69%–78% with Teluti [tlt], 50% with Yalahatan [jal]. *Lg Use:* Used as L2 by South Nuaulu [nxl]. *Map:* 367.

Serili [sve]. 330 (1980 N. de Jonge). Southern Maluku Province. Babar island group, Marsela island, northeast tip. *Status:* 8a (Moribund). *Class:* Austronesian, Malayo-Polynesian, Central-Eastern Malayo-Polynesian, Babar, South, Masela-South Babar. *Lg Use:* Under pressure from Masela and Indonesian [ind] (Wurm 2007). *Lg Dev:* Literacy rate in L1: Below 1%. *Other:* Christian. *Map:* 368.

Serua [srw]. No known L1 speakers. Central Maluku Province, south central Seram island, transmigration area. 4 villages. *Status:* 10 (Extinct). *Class:* Austronesian, Malayo-Polynesian, Central-Eastern Malayo-Polynesian, Timor-Babar, Southwest Maluku, Teun-Nila-Serua, Nila-Serua. *Dialects:* None known. Reportedly similar to Nila [nil]. Not intelligible with Teun [tve]. *Lg Use:* Shifted to Ambon Malay [abs]. *Other:* Government had moved them from Serua Island, south central Maluku, to Seram due to volcanic activity on their island.

Serui-Laut [seu] (Arui). 1,200 (1987 SIL). Papua Province, south central Serui island, Nau island south of Serui. 5 villages. *Status:* 6b (Threatened). *Class:* Austronesian, Malayo-Polynesian, Central-Eastern Malayo-Polynesian, Eastern Malayo-Polynesian, South Halmahera-West New Guinea, West New Guinea, Cenderawasih Bay, Yapen, Central-Western. *Dialects:* None known. Lexical similarity: 82% with Ansus [and], 77% with Ambai [amk]. *Lg Use:* Vigorous. *Other:* Christian. *Map:* 372:96.

Siang [sya] (Ot Siang). 60,000 (Wurm and Hattori 1981). Central Kalimantan Province, Murung Raya regency. Northern bend area, Barito river, north along tributary. *Status:* 6a (Vigorous). *Class:* Austronesian, Malayo-Polynesian, Greater Barito, West, North. *Dialects:* Murung 2, Siang. *Maps:* 364:64, 365:64.

Sika [ski] (Krowe, Maumere, Sara Sikka, Sikka, Sikkanese). 175,000 (Lewis and Grimes 1995). East Nusa Tenggara Province. East Flores island, between Li'o [ljl] and Lamaholot [slp] language areas. *Status:* 6a (Vigorous). *Class:* Austronesian, Malayo-Polynesian, Central-Eastern Malayo-Polynesian, Bima-Lembata. *Dialects:* Sara Krowe (Central Sikka), Sikka Natar (Kangaé, South Coast Sikka), Tana Ai. Wide linguistic and cultural variation. *Lg Dev:* Grammar. *Other:* Christian. *Maps:* 369, 370.

Sikaritai [tty] (Aikwakai, Araikurioko, Ati, Sikari, Tori, Tori Aikwakai). 800 (1993 R. Doriot). Papua Province, Lakes plain area, Idenburg and Rouffaer river junctions north, Mamberamo river, Sikari, Haya, and Iri villages. *Status:* 5 (Developing). *Class:* Lakes Plain, Tariku, East. *Dialects:* None known. Lexical similarity: 86% with Eritai [ert]. *Lg Use:* Vigorous. *Lg Dev:* Bible portions: 1992. *Writing:* Latin script. *Other:* Christian, traditional religion. *Map:* 372:183.

Sikule [skh] (Sichule, Sikhule, Wali Banuah). 20,000. Sumatra, Aceh Province. Simeulue archipelago; central portion, Simeulue island. *Status:* 6a (Vigorous). *Class:* Austronesian, Malayo-Polynesian, Northwest Sumatra-Barrier Islands, Nias. *Dialects:* Lekon, Tapah. Reportedly similar to Nias [nia]. *Map:* 376:34.

Silimo [wul] (Paiyage, South Ngalik, Usak, Wulik). 5,000 (1987 SIL). 2,500 monolinguals. Papua Province, central highlands south of the range immediately west of Baliem River, Amo and Kiniage valleys. *Status:* 5 (Developing). *Class:* Trans-New Guinea, West, Dani, Ngalik. *Dialect:* Lower Samenage. *Lg Dev:* NT: 1992. *Writing:* Latin script. *Other:* Traditional religion, Christian. *Map:* 372:67.

Simeulue [smr] (Long Bano, Simalur, Simeuloë, Simulul). 30,000. Sumatra, Aceh Province. West and east ends of Simeulue island; Babi and Banjak islands. *Status:* 6a (Vigorous). *Class:* Austronesian, Malayo-Polynesian, Northwest Sumatra-Barrier Islands. *Other:* Muslim. *Map:* 376:35.

Skou [skv] (Sekol, Sekou, Sko, Skouw, Skow, Sukou, Te Mawo, Tumawo). 700 (1999 M. Donohue). Papua Province, east of Jayapura, north coast border area, Tami river mouth, Sko-Yambe, Sko-Mabu, and Sko-Sai villages.

Status: 6a (Vigorous). *Class:* Skou, Skou-Serra-Piore, Nuclear Skou, Skou. *Lg Use:* All domains. All ages. Also use Indonesian [ind], Papuan Malay [pmy], Vanimo [vam], Wutung [wut]. *Lg Dev:* Literacy rate in L1: 10%. Literacy rate in L2: 10% Indonesian. Literacy motivation high, program in progress. Dictionary. *Writing:* Latin script. *Other:* Christian, traditional religion. *Map:* 372:135.

So'a [ssq] (Soa). 10,000 (1994). East Nusa Tenggara Province. Central Flores island, central Kabupaten Ngada, between Ngad'a [nxg] and Riung [riu] language areas. *Status:* 6a (Vigorous). *Class:* Austronesian, Malayo-Polynesian, Central-Eastern Malayo-Polynesian, Bima-Lembata. *Dialects:* None known. Reportedly similar to Ngad'a [nxg]. *Other:* Christian. *Map:* 370.

Sobei [sob] (Biga, Imasi, Liki). 1,000 (Wurm 2000). Ethnic population: 1,850 (2000 D. Tryon). Papua Province, Sarmi regency, Sarmi subdistrict, north coast area east of Sarmi. *Status:* 7 (Shifting). *Class:* Austronesian, Malayo-Polynesian, Central-Eastern Malayo-Polynesian, Eastern Malayo-Polynesian, Oceanic, Western Oceanic, North New Guinea, Sarmi-Jayapura Bay, Sarmi. *Dialects:* None known. Reportedly comprehension of Liki [lio]. *Lg Use:* Endangered (2000 D. Tryon; 2000 S. Wurm). Sobei speakers are beginning to shift to Papuan Malay [pmy]. Children are bilingual in Indonesian [ind] and tend to prefer it. Also use Papuan Malay [pmy] with people of other language areas. *Lg Dev:* Dictionary. Grammar. *Writing:* Latin script. *Other:* Government schools through entire area. Increasing intermarriage with other groups. Christian. *Map:* 372:113.

Sowanda [sow] (Waina, Waina-Sowanda, Wanja, Wanya, Wina). 210 in Indonesia (2002 SIL). Papua Province, south of Jayapura, northeast border area. *Status:* 6a (Vigorous). *Other:* Christian, traditional religion. See main entry on page 322. *Map:* 372:140.

Sowari [dmy] (Demta, Muris). 1,300 (2000), decreasing. Papua Province, north coast west of Tanahmerah bay, Muris Besar, Muris Kecil, Ambora, and Yougafsa villages. *Status:* 8a (Moribund). *Class:* East Bird's Head-Sentani, Sentani, Demta. *Lg Use:* Seldom used. Also use Indonesian [ind], Papuan Malay [pmy]. *Other:* Traditional religion, Christian. *Map:* 372:129.

Suabo [szp] (Iagu, Inanwatan, Mirabo, Suabau). 1,100 (1987 SIL). Papua Province, south Bird's Head along Maccluer bay. 15 villages. *Status:* 6a (Vigorous). *Class:* Trans-New Guinea, South Bird's Head, Inanwatan. *Dialects:* None known. Reportedly most similar to Duriankere [dbn]. *Other:* Christian, traditional religion. *Map:* 371:28.

Sula [szn] (Sanana). 20,000 (1983 SIL). North Maluku Province. Sula islands; Sulabesi island, widespread, scattered on Mangole island, east and west ends, north coast, Buru island, northeast coast. *Status:* 6a (Vigorous). *Class:* Austronesian, Malayo-Polynesian, Central-Eastern Malayo-Polynesian, Central Maluku, Sula. *Dialects:* Facei (Facé), Fagudu, Falahu. Reportedly similar to Mangole [mqc]. *Lg Use:* Vigorous. *Lg Dev:* Literacy rate in L1: Below 1%. *Other:* Muslim. *Map:* 367.

Sumbawa [smw] (Semawa, Sumbawarese). 300,000 (1989). West Nusa Tenggara Province. Sumbawa island, west of the isthmus, Moyo island off northern coast. *Status:* 6a (Vigorous). *Class:* Austronesian, Malayo-Polynesian, Bali-Sasak-Sumbawa, Sasak-Sumbawa. *Map:* 369.

Sunda [sun] (Priangan, Sundanese). 34,000,000 (2000 census). West Java and Banten provinces. Western third of the island. *Status:* 5 (Developing). De facto language of provincial identity in western Java. *Class:* Austronesian, Malayo-Polynesian, Sundanese. *Dialects:* Bogor (Krawang), Cirebon, Pringan. *Lg Use:* All domains. All ages. Positive attitudes. 5% also use Dutch [nld]. Also use Indonesian [ind]. *Lg Dev:* Poetry. Magazines. Newspapers. Radio programs. Bible: 1891–1991. *Writing:* Arabic script, used since 12th or 13th century. Javanese script, used until 17th century. Latin script, used since mid-19th century. Sundanese script, no longer in use. *Other:* Muslim, traditional religion. *Map:* 363.

Sunum [ymn] (Yamna). 560 (2005 SIL). Papua Province, Sarmi regency, Pantai Timur subdistrict, coastal area and an island off north coast, east of Tor river. *Status:* 6b (Threatened). *Class:* Austronesian, Malayo-Polynesian, Central-Eastern Malayo-Polynesian, Eastern Malayo-Polynesian, Oceanic, Western Oceanic, North New Guinea, Sarmi-Jayapura Bay, Sarmi. *Lg Use:* More vigorous on mainland than on island. Mainly older adults. Also use Indonesian [ind], Papuan Malay [pmy]. *Other:* Christian, traditional religion. *Map:* 372:119.

Suwawa [swu] (Bonda, Bone, Bunda, Bune, Suvava, Toewawa). 5,000 (2012 Y. Kitada). Sulawesi, Gorontalo Province. Bunda river valley, east of Gorontalo city. *Status:* 7 (Shifting). *Class:* Austronesian, Malayo-Polynesian, Philippine, Greater Central Philippine, Gorontalo-Mongondow, Gorontalic. *Other:* Separate language from Gorontalo [gor]. Muslim. *Map:* 374:85.

Tabaru [tby] (Tobaru). 15,000 (1991 SIL). North Maluku Province, Ibu, Jailolo, and Oba districts. North Halmahera island. *Status:* 5 (Developing). *Class:* West Papuan, North Halmahera, Galela-Loloda. *Dialects:* Adu, Nyeku. Northern dialect is the main one. Dialects mutually inherently intelligible. *Lg Use:* Also use Indonesian [ind], North Moluccan Malay [max]. *Lg Dev:* Literacy rate in L1: Below 1%. Literacy rate in L2: 25%–50%. NT: 2008. *Writing:* Latin script. *Other:* Christian. *Map:* 366.

Tabla [tnm] (Jakari, Tabi, Tanah Merah, Tanahmerah 2, Tepera). 3,750 (1990 UBS). Papua Province, Jayapura, Demta, Depapre, 13 villages on north coast east and west of Tanahmerah bay. *Status:* 8a (Moribund). *Class:* East Bird's Head-Sentani, Sentani, Sentani Proper. *Dialects:* Tepera, Yewena-Yongsu, Yokari. Yokari dialect understood by other dialects at 80% to 95%, others have 95%–100% mutual intelligibility. Lexical similarity: 30% with Sentani [set]. *Lg Use:* Also use Indonesian [ind]. *Lg Dev:* Bible portions: 1986–1991. *Writing:* Latin script. *Other:* Distinct from Tanahmerah [tcm] (Sumeri) of Bomberai Peninsula. Ethnic autonym: Tepera. Christian, traditional religion. *Map:* 372:131.

Tae' [rob] (East Toraja, Luwu', Luwu-Rongkong, Rongkong, Rongkong-Luwu, Tae' Tae', Taeq, "Toala'", Toraja Timur, Toware). 340,000 (2000 census), increasing. South Sulawesi Province, Luwu and North Luwu regencies. Main area along the northwest coast; Bone bay; west in Bastem subdistrict, along Rongkong river valley past Salutallang village; Seko Lemo subdialect spoken in its own enclave in Uro valley, northwest of Sallutallang; enclave of Rongkong speakers in East Luwu regency, Nuha subdistrict near Soroako. *Status:* 5 (Developing). *Class:* Austronesian, Malayo-Polynesian, South Sulawesi, Northern, Toraja-Sa'dan. *Dialects:* Bua, Northeast Luwu (Bone-Bone, Masamba), Rongkong, South Luwu. Dialect chain throughout Tae' area east into Toraja-Sa'dan [sda]. Lexical similarity: 82% or greater among dialects, 82% with Toraja-Sa'dan [sda]. *Lg Use:* Vigorous. Written use for ancestral stories. All domains. Positive attitudes. Also use Indonesian [ind]. Used as L2 by Lemolang [ley]. *Lg Dev:* Literacy rate in L1: 20%–30%. About 10%–20% write. *Writing:* Latin script. *Other:* Different from Toraja-Sa'dan (Tae') [sda]. Different from the Bugis-Luwu dialect of Bugis [bug]. Different from the Bugis-speaking "Toala" identified by P. and F. Sarasin (1903). "Toala'" is a pejorative Bugis exonym meaning forest people.

Rongkong dialect has Seko Lemo, Rongkong Atas (Rongkong-Kanandede) and Rongkong Bawah (Sabbang) subdialects. Bua dialect has Bajo (Palili') and Bastem ("Toala'") subdialects. Muslim. *Map:* 375:86.

Tagal Murut [mvv] (Semambu, Semembu, Sumambu, Sumambuq, Sumambu-Tagal). 2,000 in Indonesia. East Kalimantan Province, Nunukan regency. *Status:* 6b (Threatened). *Dialects:* Alumbis (Loembis, Lumbis), Maligan (Bol Murut, Bole Murut, Mauligan, Meligan), Pensiangan Murut (Lagunan Murut, Pentjangan, Taggal, Tagul), Rundum (Arundum), Sapulot Murut (Sapulut Murut), Sumambu (Semembu, Sumambuq), Tagal (North Borneo Murut, Sabah Murut, Tagol), Tawan, Tolokoson (Telekoson), Tomani (Tumaniq). See main entry on page 227. *Map:* 365:65.

Taikat [aos] (Arso, Tajkat). 500 (Wurm 2000). Papua Province, due south of Jayapura, northeast border area. *Status:* 6a (Vigorous). *Class:* Border, Taikat. *Dialects:* None known. Reportedly most similar to Awyi [auw]. *Lg Use:* Potentially endangered (2000 S. Wurm). Under strong pressure from Indonesian [ind] (Wurm 2007). *Other:* Christian, traditional religion. *Map:* 372:137.

Taje [pee] (Andje, Lole, Petapa). 350 (Himmelmann 2001), decreasing. Central Sulawesi Province, Parigi Tengah, and Ampibabo subdistricts. *Status:* 8b (Nearly extinct). *Class:* Austronesian, Malayo-Polynesian, Celebic, Tomini-Tolitoli, Tomini, Southern. *Lg Use:* Except for one elderly man, most speakers do not know the language well. Most have been resettled (Wurm 2007). *Other:* Different from the Lole dialect of Kaili Unde [unz]. Muslim. *Map:* 374:87.

Tajio [tdj] (Adjio, Kasimbar, Ta'adjio, Tadjio). 12,000 (Himmelmann 2001). Central Sulawesi Province, Ampibabo, Tinombo, and Sindue subdistricts, 21 villages. Western shore, Tomini bay. *Status:* 7 (Shifting). *Class:* Austronesian, Malayo-Polynesian, Celebic, Tomini-Tolitoli, Tomini, Southern. *Dialects:* Central Tajio, Northern Tajio, Western Tajio. *Other:* Ethnic autonym: Tajio. Kasimbar is the main town. Muslim. *Map:* 374:88.

Talaud [tld] (Talaur, Talaut, Talodda). 82,000 (2000 census). North Sulawesi Province. Talaud islands, northeast of Sangir islands. *Status:* 6a (Vigorous). *Class:* Austronesian, Malayo-Polynesian, Philippine, Sangiric, Northern. *Dialects:* Arangka'a, Awit, Beo, Dapalan (Riung), Essang, Kaburuang, Lirang (Salebabu, Salibabu), Nenusa-Maingas, South Karakelong (Karakelang, Karakelong). *Lg Dev:* NT: 1993. *Other:* Christian. *Map:* 374:89.

Taliabu [tlv] (Taliabo). 4,520 (2000). 500–1,500 in Mangei. North Maluku Province. Sula island group; Taliabu island, northwest coast; some on Mangole island. *Status:* 6a (Vigorous). *Class:* Austronesian, Malayo-Polynesian, Central-Eastern Malayo-Polynesian, Central Maluku, Sula, Taliabo. *Dialects:* Mananga, Mangei (Mang, Mange, Mange'e, Sobojo, Soboyo), Padang (Samada). Dialects 90% or more lexically similar. *Lg Use:* Positive attitudes. *Other:* Talo, Seho, Biha, and Bono (Mbono) are place names. Traditional religion, Christian. *Map:* 367.

Taloki [tlk] (Talloki, Taluki). 550 (2005 R. Van den Berg). 400 in Maligano, 150 in Wakalambe. South East Sulawesi Province, Buton island. Wakorumba subdistrict, Maligano village; northwest coast; Kapontori subdistrict, Wakalambe village, in southern island area. *Status:* 7 (Shifting). *Class:* Austronesian, Malayo-Polynesian, Celebic, Eastern, Southeastern, Bungku-Tolaki, Eastern, East Coast, Kulisusu. *Dialects:* Lexical similarity: 77% with Kulisusu [vkl]; 75% with Koroni [xkq]; 66% with Wawonii [wow], Bungku [bkz], and Tulambatu dialect of Bungku [bkz]; 65% with Moronene [mqn]. *Lg Use:* Under pressure from Indonesian [ind] (Wurm 2007). High level of bilingualism in Muna [mnb] (Wurm 2007). *Other:* Muslim. *Map:* 375:90.

Talondo' [tln] (Talondo Kondo). 1,200 (2011 A. Tadollo), increasing. West Sulawesi Province, Mamuju regency, Bonehau subdistrict, part of Bonehau village. *Status:* 6a (Vigorous). *Class:* Austronesian, Malayo-Polynesian, South Sulawesi, Northern, Toraja-Sa'dan. *Dialects:* None known. May be in the Seko subgroup (Padang [skx] or Tengah [sko]). Lexical similarity: 80% with Kalumpang [kli]. *Lg Use:* Home, playing field. All ages. Also use Indonesian [ind] for trade and in education. Also use Bone Hau dialect of Kalumpang [kli], but Kalumpang speakers do not understand Talondo. *Other:* Muslim, Christian. *Map:* 375:91.

Tamagario [tcg] (Buru, Tamaraw, Wagow, Wiyagar). 3,500 (1987 SIL). Papua Province, south coast area, south and east of Kayagar [kyt] and west of Yaqay [jaq] language areas. *Status:* 6a (Vigorous). *Class:* Trans-New Guinea, Kayagar. *Dialects:* None known. Reportedly most similar to Kayagar [kyt], also related to Atohwaim [aqm]. *Lg Use:* Home, community. *Other:* Christian, traditional religion. *Map:* 373:243.

Taman [tmn] (Dayak Taman, Taman Dayak). 30,000 (2007 SIL). West Kalimantan Province, Kapuas Hulu regency. Upper Kapuas river; upriver from Putussibau town. South of Mount Lawit. *Status:* 6a (Vigorous). *Class:* Austronesian, Malayo-Polynesian, South Sulawesi, Bugis, Tamanic. *Lg Use:* Language and culture are still vital. *Other:* Traditional religion, Christian. *Map:* 364:66.

Tanahmerah [tcm] (Sumeri, Sumerine). 500 (1978 SIL). Papua Province, north Bomberai peninsula, Gondu and Bapai rivers. *Status:* 6b (Threatened). *Class:* Trans-New Guinea, Tanah Merah. *Other:* Distinct from Tanahmerah (Tabla) of Sentani [set] branch. Christian, traditional religion. *Map:* 371:35.

Tandia [tni]. No known L1 speakers. Papua Province, Bird's Head neck area just south of Wandamen peninsula and Wohsimi river. *Status:* 9 (Dormant). *Class:* Austronesian, Malayo-Polynesian, Central-Eastern Malayo-Polynesian, Eastern Malayo-Polynesian, South Halmahera-West New Guinea, West New Guinea, Cenderawasih Bay, Tandia. *Lg Use:* Shifted to Wandamen [wad]. *Other:* Traditional religion, Christian.

Tangko [tkx]. 100 (2000 SIL). Papua Province, west of Nakai [nkj] language area, Kawemaot village. *Status:* 6b (Threatened). *Class:* Trans-New Guinea, Ok-Awyu, Ok, Tangko. *Lg Use:* Most domains. Also use Indonesian [ind], Papuan Malay [pmy]. *Other:* Christian, traditional religion. *Map:* 372:224.

Tarangan, East [tre] (East Trangan, Tarangan Timur). 6,110 (2011 SIL). Population counted in the 12 villages only. Southeastern Maluku Province, south Aru islands, Tarangan island east coast, and villages in Maikor strait (Sungai Maikor). 12 villages. *Status:* 6a (Vigorous). *Class:* Austronesian, Malayo-Polynesian, Central-Eastern Malayo-Polynesian, Aru. *Dialects:* North East Tarangan, South East Tarangan. Lexical similarity: 71% with West Tarangan [txn]. *Lg Use:* Vigorous. *Lg Dev:* Literacy rate in L1: Below 1%. *Other:* Christian, Muslim. *Map:* 368.

Tarangan, West [txn] (Tarangan Barat, West Trangan). 7,910 (2011 SIL), increasing. 0 monolinguals. L2 users: Used as L2 on Aru Islands, especially to the south. Southeastern Maluku Province, south Aru islands, Tarangan island west coast. *Status:* 5 (Developing). *Class:* Austronesian, Malayo-Polynesian, Central-Eastern Malayo-Polynesian, Aru. *Dialects:* North Central Tarangan, Southwestern Tarangan. 2 sharply distinct dialect groups with minor variation within them. Lexical similarity: 70% with East Tarangan [tre] and Manombai [woo]. *Type:* SVO;

prepositions; noun head Initial; 2 maximum prefixes, 2 maximum suffixes; clause constituent marked by word order; verb agreement; no passive; 15 lexical consonants; 7 vowel phonemes; nontonal. *Lg Use:* Vigorous. Home, community. All ages. Positive attitudes. 100% also use Ambonese Malay [abs]. Dobo Malay dialect. 90% also use Indonesian [ind]. *Lg Dev:* Literacy rate in L1: 10%–70%. Literacy rate in L2: 90% in Indonesian [ind]. Poetry. New media. Bible portions: 1997–2008. *Writing:* Latin script. *Other:* Largest language group in Aru Islands. Christian, Muslim. *Map:* 368.

Tarpia [tpf] (Sufrai, Tarfia). 630 (2006 SIL). Papua Province, Jayapura regency, Demta subdistrict, Tarfia village. *Status:* 8a (Moribund). *Class:* Austronesian, Malayo-Polynesian, Central-Eastern Malayo-Polynesian, Eastern Malayo-Polynesian, Oceanic, Western Oceanic, North New Guinea, Sarmi-Jayapura Bay, Sarmi. *Dialects:* None known. Reportedly most similar to Kaptiau [kbi] and Bonggo [bpg]. *Lg Use:* Endangered (2000 D. Tryon; 2000 S. Wurm). Under pressure from Sentani [set] and Indonesian [ind] (Wurm 2007). Private domains. Mainly older adults. Also use Indonesian [ind], Papuan Malay [pmy]. *Other:* Christian. *Map:* 372:163.

Tause [tad] (Darha, Doa). 300 (Wurm 2000). Papua Province, west Lakes plain (Paniai), southwest of Danau Bira, Deraposi area, northeast of Fayu [fau] and northwest of Edopi [dbf] language areas. *Status:* 6b (Threatened). *Class:* Lakes Plain, Tariku, West. *Dialects:* Deirate, Tause, Weirate. *Lg Use:* Potentially endangered (2000 S. Wurm). No Indonesian [ind] spoken. Also use Fayu [fau]. *Other:* First contact with outside world in 1982. Christian, traditional religion. *Map:* 372:84.

Tausug [tsg] (Joloano Sulu, Moro Joloano, Sooloo, Sulu, Suluk, Taosug, Tausog, Taw Sug). 12,000 in Indonesia (Wurm and Hattori 1981). Coastal settlements in Northeast Kalimantan Province, immigrants from Sulu Archipelago in the Philippines. *Status:* 5 (Developing). *Other:* Muslim. See main entry on page 291.

Tawoyan [twy] (Tabojan, Tabojan Tongka, Taboyan, Tabuyan, Tawoyan Dayak, Tewoyan). 20,000 (Wurm and Hattori 1981). Eastern Central Kalimantan Province. Near border of southern East Kalimantan Province; area around Palori town. *Status:* 5 (Developing). *Class:* Austronesian, Malayo-Polynesian, Greater Barito, East, North. *Dialects:* None known. Lexical similarity: 77% with Lawangan [lbx], 52% with Dusun Deyah [dun]. *Lg Dev:* Grammar. Bible portions: 1985. *Writing:* Latin script. *Map:* 365:67.

Tebi [dmu] (Dubu). 220 (2005 SIL). Papua Province, border area south of Jayapura, south of Zorop [wfg], east of Emem [enr], and north of Towei [ttn] language areas, Dubu, Jembatan Web, and Affi villages. *Status:* 7 (Shifting). *Class:* Pauwasi, Western. *Lg Use:* Potentially endangered (2000 S. Wurm). Home only. Mainly older adults. Also use Indonesian [ind], Papuan Malay [pmy]. *Other:* Christian, traditional religion. *Map:* 372:143.

Tefaro [tfo] (Demba). 100 (1987 SIL). Papua Province, east side of Cenderawasih bay, Tefaro and Demba villages. *Status:* 6b (Threatened). *Class:* East Geelvink Bay. *Dialects:* None known. Lexical similarity: 61% with Barapasi [brp], 63% with Sauri [srt], 70% with Tunggare [trt]. *Lg Use:* Home. *Other:* Traditional religion, Christian. *Map:* 372:90.

Tehit [kps] (Kaibus, Tahit, Tehid, Teminabuan). 10,000 (2000 R. Hesse). 500 monolinguals. Papua Province, southwest Bird's Head, Sorong regency, most of Teminabuan subdistrict, half of Sawiat subdistrict. About 31 villages. *Status:* 6b (Threatened). *Class:* West Papuan, West Bird's Head. *Dialects:* Fkar, Imyan, Mbol Fle, Saifi, Sawiat Salmeit, Sfa Riere, Tehit Jit. Lexical similarity: 60% with Kalabra. *Lg Use:* Vigorous. Parents in villages in the interior pass Tehit on to children. In villages bordering towns, Indonesian [ind] used with children. Users of neighboring languages learn Tehit. All domains. Positive attitudes. Also use Indonesian [ind]. Schools in Indonesian, although most teachers speak Tehit. Indonesian is the LWC. Also use Dutch [nld], English [eng], Mai Brat [ayz]. *Lg Dev:* Literacy rate in L1: 5%. Literacy rate in L2: 15%–25%. Taught in primary schools. Bible portions: 1998. *Writing:* Latin script. *Other:* Christian, traditional religion. *Map:* 371:15.

Teiwa [twe] (Tewa). 4,000 (Klamer and Klamer 2010). East Nusa Tenggara Province, 6 villages. Central Pantar island. *Status:* 6a (Vigorous). *Class:* Trans-New Guinea, West, Timor-Alor-Pantar, Alor-Pantar, Pantar. *Dialects:* Deing, Lebang, Madar. Deing (Diang) may be a separate language. *Lg Dev:* Grammar. *Map:* 370.

Tela-Masbuar [tvm] (Masbuar-Tela, Tela'a). 1,050 (2007 SIL). Maluku Province south, Tela and Masbuar villages. Southwest Babar island. *Status:* 6b (Threatened). *Class:* Austronesian, Malayo-Polynesian, Central-Eastern Malayo-Polynesian, Babar, South, Southwest Babar. *Lg Use:* Vigorous. Home, gardens, village, ceremonies, religion. Also use a regional Malay variety, probably a dialect of Ambonese Malay [abs], in all domains, except for home and cultural domains; children are taught the Malay variety first. Speakers also use Indonesian [ind] primarily in government and Christian religious domains. *Lg Dev:* Literacy rate in L1: Below 1%. *Other:* Christian. *Map:* 368.

Teluti [tlt] (Silen, Taluti, Tehoru, Tihoru, Wolu). 17,000 (1989 SIL). Maluku Province. South Seram island, Teluti bay. *Status:* 6a (Vigorous). *Class:* Austronesian, Malayo-Polynesian, Central-Eastern Malayo-Polynesian, Central Maluku, East, Seram, Nunusaku, Piru Bay, East. *Dialects:* Laha Serani, West Teluti (Haya, Tehoru, Tehua, Wolu). Lexical similarity: 74%–89% among dialects, 69%–78% with Sepa [spb], 50% with Yalahatan [jal]. *Lg Use:* Used as L2 by Liana-Seti [ste], Manusela [wha]. *Other:* Muslim, Christian. *Map:* 367.

Tengger [tes] (Tenggerese). 80,000 (2000 census). East Java Province. South of Pasuran regency. Area near Mount Bromo. *Status:* 6a (Vigorous). *Class:* Austronesian, Malayo-Polynesian, Javanese. *Dialects:* None known. May be marginally intelligible with Javanese [jav]. *Lg Use:* 20% also use Indonesian [ind]. Also use Javanese [jav]. *Lg Dev:* Literacy rate in L2: 20%. *Writing:* Javanese script. *Other:* Ethnically distinct from Javanese. Hindu. *Map:* 363.

Teor [tev] (Tio'or). 1,100 (1986 SIL). Maluku Province. Watubela archipelago, Teor and Ut islands. *Status:* 6a (Vigorous). *Class:* Austronesian, Malayo-Polynesian, Central-Eastern Malayo-Polynesian, Teor-Kur. *Dialects:* Gaur Kristen, Ut. Self-report to understand Kur [kuv]. Lexical similarity: 79% with Gaur Kristen and Ut, 71%–83% with Kur [kuv], 41% with Watubela [wah], 38% with Geser [ges]. *Other:* Muslim, Christian. *Map:* 368.

Tereweng [twg]. 800 (Grimes et al. 1997). East Nusa Tenggara Province, 2 villages on Tereweng island off southeast coast of Pantar island, and one village on Pantar. *Status:* 6a (Vigorous). *Class:* Trans-New Guinea, West, Timor-Alor-Pantar, Alor-Pantar, Pantar. *Other:* Distinct ethnic identity from Blagar. *Map:* 370.

Termanu [twu] (Central Rote, Pa'da, Rote, Rote Tengah, Roti, Rotinese). 30,000 (2002 UKAW). East Nusa Tenggara Province. Termanu, Keka, Talae, Korbafo, and Bokai domains. Central Rote island. *Status:* 6a (Vigorous). *Class:* Austronesian, Malayo-Polynesian, Central-Eastern Malayo-Polynesian, Timor-Babar, Nuclear Timor, Rote. *Dialects:* Bokai, Korbafo (Korbaffo), Pa'da (Termanu),

Pa'da Kona (Keka-Talae, Southern Termanu). Reportedly seems more similar to Lole [llg] than to other varieties on Rote. Korbafo and Bokai may need to be separated for sociolinguistic reasons. *Lg Use:* Vigorous. All domains. All ages. Some older people educated in Dutch [nld]. Also use Indonesian [ind], Kupang Malay [mkn]. *Lg Dev:* Dictionary. Grammar. Bible portions: 1895–2004. *Writing:* Latin script. *Other:* Christian. *Map:* 369.

Ternate [tft]. 42,000 (Wurm and Hattori 1981). L2 users: 20,000. North and northeast Halmahera. North Maluku Province. Ternate island. Kayoa islands on north end of Lapan bay; islands between Bacan and Kasiruta islands. Halmahera island; Damar, Yoronge islands off of southeasternmost point, some communities on western north coast. *Status:* 6b (Threatened). *Class:* West Papuan, North Halmahera, Ternate-Tidore. *Dialects:* None known. Reportedly similar to Tidore [tvo]. *Lg Use:* Former trade language, now shifting to North Moluccan Malay [max]; weaker in core area, stronger in periphery (2012 J. Bowden). Also use Indonesian [ind]. Used as L2 by Sawai [szw]. *Lg Dev:* Literacy rate in L1: 1%–5%. Literacy rate in L2: 25%–50%. *Other:* Muslim. *Map:* 366.

Ternateño [tmg] (Ternatenyo). No known L1 speakers. North Maluku Province. Ternate island. *Status:* 10 (Extinct). *Class:* Creole, Portuguese based. *Dialects:* Spanish [spa] relexification. Historical relationship with Chavacano and dialects, still spoken in the Philippines. *Lg Use:* The Jakarta variety of creole Portuguese survived in Tugu until recent times (Wurm and Hattori 1981). Varieties also spoken in Larantuka, Flores; Adonara (Vure), Solor; as well as Sumatra, Kalimantan, Sulawesi, and Maluku. Varieties of creole Portuguese were also spoken in Banda and Ambon.

Tetun [tet] (Belo, Belu, Fehan, Teto, Tettum, Tetu, Tetum, Tetun Belu, Tetung). 400,000 in Indonesia (2011). Population total all countries: 463,500. L2 users: Additional 50,000 L2 speakers in both East Timor and Indonesia. East Nusa Tenggara Province. Central Timor island, bi-coastal. Also in East Timor. *Status:* 5 (Developing). De facto language of provincial identity in portions of Timor Island, East Nusa Tenggara province. *Class:* Austronesian, Malayo-Polynesian, Central-Eastern Malayo-Polynesian, Timor-Babar, Nuclear Timor. *Dialects:* Eastern Tetun (Lakluta, Natarbora, Soibada, Tetun Loos, Tetun Los, Tetun Terik), Northern Tetun (Belu Utara, Foho, Hill Tetun, Lia Foho, North Belu, Tasi Feto, Tetun Terik, Tetun Therik), Southern Tetun (Belu Selatan, Fehan, Lia Fehan, Plains Tetun, South Belu, South Tetun, Tasi Mane). *Lg Use:* Used as L2 by Bunak [bfn]. *Lg Dev:* Poetry. New media. Radio programs. TV. Videos. Dictionary. Grammar. NT: 2013. *Writing:* Latin script. *Other:* Different language from Tetun Dili [tdt]. Christian, traditional religion. *Map:* 369.

Te'un [tve]. No known L1 speakers. Central Maluku Province, south central Seram island transmigration area. 4 villages. *Status:* 10 (Extinct). *Class:* Austronesian, Malayo-Polynesian, Central-Eastern Malayo-Polynesian, Timor-Babar, Southwest Maluku, Teun-Nila-Serua, Teun. *Lg Use:* Shifted to Ambon Malay [abs]. *Other:* Government moved them from Teun Island, south central Maluku, due to volcanic activity on their island.

Tidong [tid] (Camucones, Tedong, Tidoeng, Tidung, Tiran, Tirones, Tiroon, Zedong). 27,000 in Indonesia (2007 SIL). East Kalimantan Province, Bulungan regency. Sembakung and Sibuka river deltas; Tarakan, Bunyu, Baru, Tibi, and nearby islands; coastal areas north to Point Sida; interior, Malinau river. Also in Malaysia. *Status:* 6a (Vigorous). *Class:* Austronesian, Malayo-Polynesian, North Borneo, North Sarawakan, Dayic, Murutic, Tidong. *Dialects:* Nonukan (Nunukan), Penchangan, Sedalir (Sadalir, Salalir, Saralir, Selalir), Sesayap (Sesajap), Sibuku, Tarakan (Terakan), Tidung. *Lg Use:* Vigorous. Home, village, traditional ceremonies. *Map:* 365:69.

Tidore [tvo]. 26,000 (Wurm and Hattori 1981). L2 users: 20,000. North Maluku Province. Tidore island. Ternate, Mare, and northern Moti islands. Also Halmahera island, west coast areas, facing in turn Tidore, Moti, and Kayaa islands. *Status:* 6a (Vigorous). *Class:* West Papuan, North Halmahera, Ternate-Tidore. *Dialects:* None known. Reportedly similar to Ternate [tft]. *Lg Use:* Positive attitudes. Also use Indonesian [ind], North Moluccan Malay [max]. Used as L2 by Sawai [szw]. *Lg Dev:* Literacy rate in L1: 1%–5%. Literacy rate in L2: 25%–50%. *Writing:* Latin script. *Other:* Muslim. *Maps:* 366, 374:92.

Tii [txq] (Rote, Rote Barat, Roti, Rotinese, Thie, Ti, Western Rote). 20,000 (2002 UKAW). East Nusa Tenggara Province. Rote island, southwest. East of Dela-Oenale [row], west of Lole [llg], and south of Dengka [dnk] language areas. *Status:* 6a (Vigorous). *Class:* Austronesian, Malayo-Polynesian, Central-Eastern Malayo-Polynesian, Timor-Babar, Nuclear Timor, Rote. *Dialects:* Minor variation, third singular verb prefix, na-fa'da, varies with, i-fa'da. *Lg Use:* Vigorous. All domains. All ages. Also use Indonesian [ind], Kupang Malay [mkn]. *Lg Dev:* Bible portions: 2004–2011. *Other:* Christian. *Map:* 369.

Tobati [tti] (Enggros, Humboldt Jotafa, Jayapura, Jotafa, Tobwadic, Yautefa, Yotafa). 100 (Wurm 2007). Papua Province, Jayapura bay, near Jayapura, Tobati, Enggros, Entrop, Kota Raja, and Tanah Hitam villages. *Status:* 8b (Nearly extinct). *Class:* Austronesian, Malayo-Polynesian, Central-Eastern Malayo-Polynesian, Eastern Malayo-Polynesian, Oceanic, Western Oceanic, North New Guinea, Sarmi-Jayapura Bay, Jayapura Bay. *Dialects:* None known. Formerly classified as Papuan. *Lg Use:* Endangered (2000 D. Tryon); seriously endangered (2000 S. Wurm). Mainly assimilated to Indonesian [ind] language and culture. Also use Papuan Malay [pmy]. *Other:* Christian. *Map:* 372:133.

Tobelo [tlb]. 27,700 (2000). North Maluku Province, Tubelo, Kao, and Jailolo districts, North Halmahera; Maba and Wasile districts, Central Halmahera. Halmahera island, west coast, contiguous area surrounding Kao bay, inland. Morotai island, east coast central. Communities on Patani, Weda, Gane, Bacan, Obi, Ambon, and Raja Ampat islands. Papua Province, Sorong area. *Status:* 5 (Developing). *Class:* West Papuan, North Halmahera, Galela-Loloda. *Dialects:* Boëng, Dodinga, Tobelo (Heleworuru). *Lg Use:* Positive attitudes. Also use Indonesian [ind], North Moluccan Malay [max]. Used as L2 by Sawai [szw]. *Lg Dev:* Literacy rate in L1: 1%–5%. Literacy rate in L2: 25%–50%. Dictionary. Grammar. Bible: 2002. *Other:* Taught in middle school in Tobelo town. Traditional religion, Christian. *Map:* 366.

Tofanma [tlg] (Tofamna). 250 (2005 SIL). Papua Province, south Jayapura border area, Keerom regency, Senggi subdistrict, Tofanma Satu, Tofanma Dua, and most of Namla villages. *Status:* 6a (Vigorous). *Class:* Unclassified. *Dialects:* None known. Not closely related to any other language. *Lg Use:* Potentially endangered (2000 S. Wurm). Home, religion. All ages. Used as L2 by Namla [naa]. *Other:* Christian, traditional religion. *Map:* 372:151.

Tolaki [lbw] (Laki, Lolaki, Tokia, Tololaki, To'olaki). 331,000 (2000 census). 298,000 Tolaki (Konawe), 33,000 Mekongga and 200 Wiwirano. Asera and Laiwui not separately listed, but less than 1,000. South East Sulawesi Province, North Konawe, Konawe, South Konawe, Kolaka, and North Kolaka regencies; Mekongga district, west coast. Broad area from Point Kolono, southeast peninsula, extending northwest across plains up to highlands; along west coast, past Klaka town towards Bone bay narrows. *Status:* 6b (Threatened). *Class:* Austronesian, Malayo-Polynesian, Celebic, Eastern, Southeastern, Bungku-Tolaki, Western, West Coast. *Dialects:* Asera (Asera Wanua, Noie), Konawe (Kendari, Kioki, Tambuoki), Laiwui, Mekongga (Bingkokak, Kolaka, Konio, Norio, Tamboki), Wiwirano (Nohina). Lexical similarity: 88% with Asera, 84% with Konawe, 85% with Mekongga, 81% with Laiwui, 78% with Waru, 70% with Rahambuu and Kodeoha, 54% with the Mori and Bungku groups. Mekongga has 86% with Konawe, 80% with Laiwui. *Lg Use:* Vigorous in many villages. Some parents speak Indonesian [ind] to their children, and some children are not proficient in Tolaki. Used as L2 by Kodeoha [vko]. *Lg Dev:* Taught in primary and secondary schools. Radio programs. Dictionary. Bible portions: 2000. *Writing:* Latin script. *Other:* Language names based on negative forms are no longer in use. Muslim. *Map:* 375:93.

Tomadino [tdi]. 600 (Mead 1999). Central Sulawesi Province, Bungku Tengah subdistrict, Sakita village. On east coast, Tolo bay, near Bungku town. *Status:* 8a (Moribund). *Class:* Austronesian, Malayo-Polynesian, Celebic, Eastern, Southeastern, Bungku-Tolaki, Western, Interior. *Dialects:* None known. Lexical similarity: 71% with Bahonsuai [bsu], 68% with Mori Atas [mzq], Mori Bawah [xmz], and Padoe [pdo]. *Lg Use:* Shifting to Bungku [bkz]. *Other:* Muslim. *Map:* 375:94.

Tombelala [ttp] (Baria, Belala, Mbelala). 1,100 (Mead and Mead 1991). Central Sulawesi Province, Bungku Tengah subdistrict, 4 villages. On west coast, Tolo bay, south of Bungku town. *Status:* 6b (Threatened). *Class:* Austronesian, Malayo-Polynesian, Celebic, Kaili-Pamona, Northern, Pamona. *Dialects:* None known. Lexical similarity: 66%–76% with Pamona [pmf] varieties and 38% with Bungku [bkz]. *Lg Use:* Also use Indonesian [ind]. *Other:* Consider themselves Pamona. Muslim. *Map:* 375:95.

Tombulu [tom] (Minahasa, Minhasa, Tombalu, Tombula, Tombulu', Toumbulu). 60,000 (Wurm and Hattori 1981), decreasing. North Sulawesi Province. Northeast coast, near Manado city, Tanawangko and Tomohon areas. *Status:* 7 (Shifting). *Class:* Austronesian, Malayo-Polynesian, Philippine, Minahasan, North, Northeast. *Dialects:* Taratara, Tomohon. Reportedly most similar to Tondano [tdn] and Tonsea [txs]. *Lg Use:* Under pressure from Manado Malay [xmm]. *Lg Dev:* Bible portions: 1933–2012. *Writing:* Latin script. *Other:* Traditional religion, Christian. *Map:* 374:96.

Tomini [txm] (Mouton, Moutong, Tiadje, Tialo). 30,000 (Himmelmann 2001). Central Sulawesi Province, Moutong, Tomini, and Tinombo subdistricts, 42 villages. Northeast coast along Tomini bay, inland. Southwest corner of Gorontalo Province. *Status:* 6b (Threatened). *Class:* Austronesian, Malayo-Polynesian, Celebic, Tomini-Tolitoli, Tomini, Northern. *Other:* Muslim. *Map:* 374:97.

Tondano [tdn] (Tolou, Tolour, Tondanou, Toulour). 92,000 in Indonesia (Wurm and Hattori 1981), decreasing. North Sulawesi Province, Toulour regency. North peninsula, Lake Tondano area southeast and east. Also in United States. *Status:* 7 (Shifting). *Class:* Austronesian, Malayo-Polynesian, Philippine, Minahasan, North, Northeast. *Dialects:* Kakas (Ka'kas), Remboken, Tondano. Reportedly most similar to Tombulu [tom] and Tonsea [txs]. *Lg Use:* Under pressure from Manado Malay [xmm]. *Lg Dev:* Grammar. NT: 1996. *Writing:* Latin script. *Other:* Christian. *Map:* 374:98.

Tonsawang [tnw] (Tombatu). 20,000 (Wurm and Hattori 1981), decreasing. North Sulawesi Province. Landlocked area southwest of Lake Manado; near Tombatu town. *Status:* 7 (Shifting). *Class:* Austronesian, Malayo-Polynesian, Philippine, Minahasan. *Lg Use:* Under pressure from Manado Malay [xmm]. *Other:* Christian. *Map:* 374:99.

Tonsea [txs] (Tonsea'). 90,000 (1989), decreasing. North Sulawesi Province, northeasternmost tip. *Status:* 6b (Threatened). *Class:* Austronesian, Malayo-Polynesian, Philippine, Minahasan, North, Northeast. *Dialects:* Airmadidi, Kalabat Atas, Kauditan, Likupang, Maumbi. *Lg Use:* Under pressure from Manado Malay [xmm]. *Lg Dev:* Bible portions: 2005–2006. *Writing:* Latin script. *Other:* Traditional religion, Christian. *Map:* 374:100.

Tontemboan [tnt] (Pakewa, Tompakewa, Tountemboan). 150,000 (1990 J. Merrifield). North Sulawesi Province. Minahasa peninsula, northeast coast, southern shore, Amurang bay inland. *Status:* 6b (Threatened). *Class:* Austronesian, Malayo-Polynesian, Philippine, Minahasan, North. *Dialects:* Sonder (Matanai, Matana'i-Maore'), Tompaso (Makelai, Makela'i-Maotow). *Lg Use:* Under pressure from Manado Malay [xmm]. *Lg Dev:* Dictionary. Grammar. NT: 1933. *Writing:* Latin script. *Other:* Christian. *Map:* 374:101.

Topoiyo [toy]. 450 (Yamaguchi and Nakashima 2001), decreasing. West Sulawesi Province, Mamuju regency, Budong-Budong subdistrict. Inland along Budong-Budong river. *Status:* 8a (Moribund). *Class:* Austronesian, Malayo-Polynesian, Celebic, Kaili-Pamona, Northern, Kaili. *Dialects:* Lexical similarity: 66% with Sarudu [sdu] and Da'a [kzf], 56% with Ledo [lew], 54% with the Parigi dialect of Kaili [lew]. *Lg Use:* Most speakers are over age 40. *Other:* Recent settlers from elsewhere and rubber plantation development brought new language contacts. Muslim. *Map:* 375:102.

Toraja-Sa'dan [sda] (Sada, Sadan, Sa'dan, Sadang, Sa'dansche, South Toraja, Tae', Taeq, Toradja, Toraja). 750,000 (2000 census), increasing. South Sulawesi Province, Tana Toraja and Luwu regencies; South East Sulawesi Province, Kolaka and Wundulako subdistricts; west coast. Some in Makassar city. *Status:* 5 (Developing). *Class:* Austronesian, Malayo-Polynesian, South Sulawesi, Northern, Toraja-Sa'dan. *Dialects:* Makale (Tallulembangna), Rantepao (Kesu'), Toraja Barat (Mappa-Pana, West Toraja). Rantepao is prestige dialect. *Lg Use:* Vigorous. All ages. Positive attitudes. *Lg Dev:* Dictionary. Bible: 1960–1995. *Writing:* Latin script. *Other:* Christian, Muslim, traditional religion. *Map:* 375:103.

Totoli [txe] (Gage, Tolitoli, Tontoli). 25,000 (Himmelmann 2001). Central Sulawesi Province, Tolitoli Utara, Galang, Baolan, and Dondo subdistricts, 29 villages. Northernmost portion of province; west coast, Dondo bay; Kabetan island; area southwest of Point Arus. *Status:* 7 (Shifting). *Class:* Austronesian, Malayo-Polynesian, Celebic, Tomini-Tolitoli, Tolitoli. *Lg Use:* Many also use Indonesian [ind] (Wurm 2007). *Other:* Muslim. *Map:* 374:104.

Towei [ttn] (Towe). 120 (1975 SIL). Papua Province, border area south of Jayapura, Towe Hitam village, south of Dubu [dmu] and west of Emem [enr] language areas. *Status:* 8a (Moribund). *Class:* Pauwasi, Western. *Lg Use:* Also use Indonesian [ind], Papuan Malay [pmy], Yetfa [yet]. *Other:* Christian, traditional religion. *Map:* 372:145.

Trimuris [tip]. 300 (1999 SIL). Papua Province, Jayapura regency, Mamberamo Tengah subdistrict, Mamberamo river east bank, between Kauwera [xau] and Bagusa [bqb] language areas. *Status:* 6a (Vigorous). *Class:* Tor-Kwerba, Greater Kwerba, Kwerba, Nuclear. *Dialects:* None known. Low intelligibility of Kwerba [kwe]. Lexical similarity: 70% with Kauwera [xau] and 60% with Kwerba [kwe]. *Lg Use:* Vigorous. All ages. *Other:* Traditional religion, Christian. *Map:* 372:179.

Tsaukambo [kvz] (Kotogüt, Tsakwambo, Tsokwambo). 780 (2000 SIL). Papua Province, west side of upper Digul river, north of Wanggom, south of Komyandaret. *Status:* 6a (Vigorous). *Class:* Trans-New Guinea, Ok-Awyu, Ok, Ngalum. *Dialects:* None known. Reportedly most similar to Komyandaret [kzv]. *Lg Use:* Home. *Other:* Traditional religion, Christian. *Map:* 373:232.

Tugun [tzn] (Mahuan, Tutunohan). 1,200 (1990 SIL). 10 monolinguals. L2 users: Those who marry into group learn the language. Southwestern Maluku Province, Mahuan, Masapun, Tomliapat, Ilpokil, Kahailin, Ilway, and Arwala villages. Wetar island west of Barat Daya archipelago; southeast end of island. *Status:* 6a (Vigorous). *Class:* Austronesian, Malayo-Polynesian, Central-Eastern Malayo-Polynesian, Timor-Babar, Southwest Maluku, Wetar. *Dialects:* Arwala, Ilpokil, Kahailin Ilway, Mahuan, Masapua, Tomliapat. Lexical similarity: 92%–97% among dialects, 76% with Perai [wet], 74% with Aputai [apx], 73% with Ili'uun [ilu], 52% with Galolen [gal]. *Lg Use:* Vigorous. Home, local commerce, oral tradition. Positive attitudes. Also use Ambonese Malay [abs], Indonesian [ind]. *Lg Dev:* Literacy rate in L1: Below 1%. Literacy rate in L2: 15%–25%. *Writing:* Latin script. *Other:* Christian (Protestant). *Map:* 369.

Tugutil [tuj]. 2,590 (2000). North Maluku Province, Tobelo, Kao, Wasile, and Maba districts, Miaf, Bebseli, and Marasibno villages. North Halmahera island, inland around Kusuri, inland in Tobelo district, Taboulamo area in Kao district, the pass between Lolobata and Buli in Wasilei district, Dodaga, Tutuling, Akelamo, and Mabulan rivers in Maba district. A few on Lili, Waisango, and Afu rivers. *Status:* 6a (Vigorous). *Class:* West Papuan, North Halmahera, Galela-Loloda. *Dialects:* Kusuri, Teluk Lili. Possibly several dialects separated by large distances. Inadequate intelligibility with Tobelo [tlb] variety. *Lg Use:* Positive attitudes. Also use Indonesian [ind]. *Lg Dev:* Literacy rate in L1: Below 1%. Literacy rate in L2: 5%–15%. *Other:* Forest people who have contact with village people when selling copra and purchasing supplies. Traditional religion, Christian. *Map:* 366.

Tukang Besi North [khc] (Buton, Wakatobi). 120,000 in Indonesia (1995 SIL). 60,000 in Maluku. South East Sulawesi Province,Tukang Besi archipelago north, Kaledupa and Wangiwangi islands; also, Runduma islands, to east. Maluku, Bacan, Taliabu, Mongole, Buru, Sulabesi, Seram, and Ambon islands. Also, Baubau and Sumbawa cities. Also in Singapore. *Status:* 6a (Vigorous). *Class:* Austronesian, Malayo-Polynesian, Celebic, Eastern, Southeastern, Muna-Buton, Tukangbesi-Bonerate. *Dialects:* Kaledupa (Kahedupa), Wanci (Wangi- Wangi, Wanje, Wanji, Wantji). Lexical similarity: 80% with Kaledupa and Wanci, and may be separate languages. 70%–75% with Tukang Besi South [bhq], 48% with Lasalimu [llm], 47% with Cia-Cia [cia], 40% with Kamaru [kgx], an average of 35% with other nearby languages. *Lg Use:* Vigorous. All ages, even in communities away from the main islands. Used as L2 by Kumbewaha [xks]. *Lg Dev:* Grammar. *Other:* Most in Nusa Tenggara and Maluku are mixed with Tukang Besi South. Muslim. *Map:* 375:105.

Tukang Besi South [bhq] (Buton, Tukang-Besi, Wakatobi). 130,000 (1995 SIL), increasing. 100,000 in Maluku. South East Sulawesi Province. Tukang Besi archipelago, south islands; northern Binongko and Tomea islands; South Sulawesi Province, Selayar regency, Madu, Kalaotoa, Bonerate, and Karompa islands. Maluku, Taliabu, Mongole, Sulabesi, Buru, Seram, Ambon, and Alor islands. Settlements throughout western Papua Province. *Status:* 6a (Vigorous). *Class:* Austronesian, Malayo-Polynesian, Celebic, Eastern, Southeastern, Muna-Buton, Tukangbesi-Bonerate. *Dialects:* Binongko, Bonerate, Tomea (Tomia). Lexical similarity: 70%–75% with Tukang Besi North [khc], 48% with Cia-Cia [cia], 49% with Lasalimu [llm], average of 35% with other nearby languages. Lexical similarity 85% with Binongko and Tomea, 81% with Bonerate, 79% with Tomea and Bonerate. *Type:* Pronominal indexing; grammatical status of subject; morphological case; causative; Philippine and Oceanic type language features. *Lg Use:* Vigorous. All ages, even in communities away from the main islands. Also use Wolio [wlo]. Used as L2 by Kumbewaha [xks]. *Lg Dev:* Grammar. *Other:* Muslim. *Map:* 375:106.

Tulehu [tlu] (Northeast Ambon, Sou Amana Teru). 18,800 (1987 SIL). Maluku Province, 4 villages. Ambon island, northeast coast. *Status:* 7 (Shifting). *Class:* Austronesian, Malayo-Polynesian, Central-Eastern Malayo-Polynesian, Central Maluku, East, Seram, Nunusaku, Piru Bay, East, Seram Straits, Ambon. *Dialects:* Liang, Tengah-Tengah, Tial, Tulehu. Each dialect is in a separate village. Eastern end of Ambon dialect chain. Lexical similarity: 84%–90% among dialects, 74%–82% with Hitu [htu], 72%–76% with Haruku [hrk]. *Lg Use:* Most over 30 years old. *Other:* Muslim, Christian. *Map:* 367.

Tunggare [trt] (Tarunggare, Turunggare). 500 (1993 R. Doriot). North central Papua Province, west of Mamberamo river, east Geelvink bay near Nabire, inland from Waropen [wrp] language area. *Status:* 6b (Threatened). *Class:* East Geelvink Bay. *Dialects:* None known. Lexical similarity: 70% with Bauzi [bvz], 75% with Burate [bti], 65% with Demisa [dei], 70% with Tefaro [tfo], 69% with Woria [wor]. *Other:* May be better considered a dialect of Burate [bti]. Christian, traditional religion. *Map:* 372:80.

Tunjung [tjg] (Tunjung Dayak). 50,000 (Nikolic 2008). East Kalimantan Province, Kutai regency. Area between Adas, Dempar, and Melak towns; then down the Mahakam rivers, east around Djempang lake; area south of Muntaiwan town. *Status:* 6b (Threatened). *Class:* Austronesian, Malayo-Polynesian, Greater Barito, Barito-Mahakam. *Dialects:* Pahu, Tunjung (Tunjung Tengah), Tunjung Linggang, Tunjung Londong. *Map:* 365:70.

Uab Meto [aoz] (Atoni, "Dawan" *pej.*, Meto, Orang Gunung, "Rawan" *pej.*, Timol, Timor, "Timor Dawan" *pej.*, Timoreesch, Timoreezen, Timorese, Uab Atoni Pah Meto, Uab Pah Meto). 700,000 (2009 census). East Nusa Tenggara Province. Most of west Timor island. *Status:* 5 (Developing). *Class:* Austronesian, Malayo-Polynesian, Central-Eastern Malayo-Polynesian, Timor-Babar, Nuclear Timor, Uab Meto. *Dialects:* Amanuban-Amanatun (Amanatun, Amanuban, Amanubang), Amfoan-Fatule'u-Amabi (Amabi, Amfoan, Amfuang, Fatule'u), Biboki-Insana (Biboki, Insanao), Kusa-Manlea (Kusa, Manea, Manlea), Mollo-Miomafo (Miomafo, Mollo). Much dialect variation. Ethnological and linguistic differences in nearly every valley. Same language chain as Amarasi [aaz] and Baikeno [bkx]. *Lg Use:* Used as L2 by Helong [heg]. *Lg Dev:* Dictionary. Bible: 2000. *Writing:* Latin script. *Other:* Christian, traditional religion. *Map:* 369.

Ujir [udj] (Udjir). 1,030 (2011 SIL). Southeast Maluku Province. Northwest Aru islands, Ujir and Wokam islands west peninsula tip. *Status:* 7 (Shifting). *Class:* Austronesian, Malayo-Polynesian, Central-Eastern Malayo-Polynesian, Aru. *Dialects:* None known. Lexical similarity: 75% with Kola [kvv] in north Aru, and slightly less with Kola on the west coast of Kola Island. *Lg Use:* Use declining in Ujir because Malay [abs] used increasingly by outsiders. Use reportedly less in Samang than in Ujir. *Other:* Muslim. *Map:* 368.

Ulumanda' [ulm] (Awo-Sumakuyu, Botteng-Tappalang, Kado, Oeloemanda, Tubbi, Ulumandak, Ulunda). 30,000 (1986 SIL). 18,000 in Polmas and Majene. West Sulawesi Province, Majene, Mamuju, and Polewali-Mandar regencies. Mostly interior area north of Majene town. *Status:* 6a (Vigorous). *Class:* Austronesian, Malayo-Polynesian, South Sulawesi, Northern, Pitu Ulunna Salu. *Dialects:* Botteng, Sondoang, Tappalang. About 6 dialects. Lexical similarity: 75%–80% with dialect of Bambam [ptu], Aralle-Tabulahan [atq], and Pannei [pnc]. *Other:* Muslim. *Map:* 375:107.

Uma [ppk] (Koro, Oema, Pipikoro). 20,000 (1990 M. Martens), increasing. 15,000 in the region, 5,000 outside (1990 SIL), 500 in Benggaulu. Central Sulawesi Province, Donggala regency, South Kulawi and Pipikoro subdistricts, 32 villages. Along Lariang river and tributaries. South Sulawesi Province, North Luwu regency, Bana in enclave within the Seko Padang language area; south Pasangkayu regency, Mamuju subdistrict. Gimpu and Palolo valleys, other areas north of Palu. *Status:* 5 (Developing). *Class:* Austronesian, Malayo-Polynesian, Celebic, Kaili-Pamona, Southern. *Dialects:* Bana, Benggaulu (Bingkolu), Kantewu (Central Uma), Southern Uma (Aria), Tobaku (Dompa, Ompa, Western Uma), Tolee' (Eastern Uma), Winatu (Northern Uma). Literature exists in Kantewu dialect, but many would prefer to read their own dialect. *Lg Use:* Use vigorous in the Uma homeland. Kantewu is prestige dialect. Among those living outside (e.g., in Palu, Palolo, Gimpu), use is vigorous among adults. For those who move away as adults, Uma remains language of the home. For those who move away as children, half retain Uma as home language. Daily work, local administration, religious services. All ages. Positive attitudes. Also use Indonesian [ind] (2000 SIL). Also use Ledo Kaili [lew] (2000 SIL). Also use Rampi [lje] (2000 SIL). Also use Seko Padang [skx] (2000 SIL). *Lg Dev:* Taught in primary schools. Grammar. NT: 1996. *Writing:* Latin script. *Other:* Christian, Muslim. *Maps:* 374:108, 375:108.

Uma' Lasan [xky] (Western Kenyah). 1,500 in Indonesia (Soriente 2005). East Kalimantan Province, Malinau regency, Long Pujungan, Long Jelet Mesahan, and Long Pejalin (Uma Alim dialect) villages. *Status:* 6a (Vigorous). *Dialects:* Uma' Alim, Uma' Baka, Uma' Lasan. *Lg Use:* Also use Mainstream Kenyah [xkl]. *Other:* Christian. See main entry on page 228. *Map:* 365:71.

Uma' Lung [ulu] (Oma Longh). 3,000 (Soriente 2006), decreasing. East Kalimantan Province, Malinau regency, Pimping, Long Setulang, Batu Kajang, Long Uli, and Long Belua villages. Middle Malinau river. *Status:* 6b (Threatened). *Class:* Austronesian, Malayo-Polynesian, North Borneo, North Sarawakan, Kayan-Kenyah, Kenyah, Upper Pujungan. *Dialects:* None known. Marginally intelligible of Uma Lasan [xky]. *Lg Use:* Decreasing due to mixed marriage and urbanization. All domains. Also use Mainstream Kenyah (Lepo Tau' dialect) [xkl]. *Map:* 365:72.

Una [mtg] (Goliath, Langda, Mt. Goliath, Oranje-Gebergte). 5,600 (2006 SIL), increasing. Papua Province, east highlands on south slopes of main ranges east of Sela valley, west of Ngalum, Bidabuh, east Weip valley, Yay valley, around Langda, Bomela, and Sumtamon. *Status:* 4 (Educational). *Class:* Trans-New Guinea, Mek, Eastern. *Dialects:* None known. Lexical similarity: 75% with Eipomek [eip], 69% with Ketengban [xte]. *Type:* SOV; clause chaining; switch reference; split ergative. *Lg Use:* All domains. All ages. *Lg Dev:* Literacy rate in L1: 40%. Dictionary. NT: 2007. *Writing:* Latin script. *Other:* Christian, traditional religion. *Map:* 372:211.

Uruangnirin [urn] (Faur, Tubiruasa). 400 (1983 SIL). Papua Province, Karas island and 2 small islands between Karas island and mainland of southwest Bomberai peninsula. *Status:* 6b (Threatened). *Class:* Austronesian, Malayo-Polynesian, Central-Eastern Malayo-Polynesian, North Bomberai. *Other:* Blust (1991) says this appears to be Central Malayo-Polynesian. Christian, traditional religion. *Map:* 371:45.

Usku [ulf] (Afra). 110 (2004 SIL). Population estimates range from 20 to 160 (Wurm 2007). Few monolinguals. Papua Province, south of Jayapura, Usku village; west of Namla [naa] and south of Molof [msl] language areas. *Status:* 8a (Moribund). *Class:* Unclassified. *Dialects:* None known. Not closely related to any other language. *Lg Use:* Seriously endangered (2000 S. Wurm). Home, friends. Mainly older adults. Positive attitudes. Also use Indonesian [ind], Papuan Malay [pmy]. *Lg Dev:* Literacy rate in L2: Under 5% in Indonesian [ind]. *Other:* Afra may be the name preferred by the people. *Map:* 372:152.

Viid [snu] (Senggi). 250 (2005 SIL). 0 monolinguals. Papua Province, border area south of Jayapura, Senggi village. *Status:* 8a (Moribund). *Class:* Border, Waris. *Lg Use:* Endangered (2000 S. Wurm). Frequently mix Viid with Indonesian [ind], Papuan Malay [pmy]. Also use Indonesian [ind], Papuan Malay [pmy]. *Other:* Christian, traditional religion. *Map:* 372:155.

Vitou [vto] (Takar). 630 (2007). Papua Province, Sarmi regency, Pantai Timur subdistrict, Takar village. *Status:* 7 (Shifting). *Class:* Tor-Kwerba, Orya-Tor, Tor. *Dialects:* None known. Lexical similarity: 63% with Betaf [bfe]. *Lg Use:* Mainly older adults. Also use Indonesian [ind], Papuan Malay [pmy]. *Other:* Christian, traditional religion. *Map:* 372:118.

Wabo [wbb] (Nusari, Woriasi). 1,500 (1987 SIL). Papua Province, Serui island, north and south coast of east end. 6 villages. *Status:* 7 (Shifting). *Class:* Austronesian, Malayo-Polynesian, Central-Eastern Malayo-Polynesian, Eastern Malayo-Polynesian, South Halmahera-West New Guinea, West New Guinea, Cenderawasih Bay, Yapen, East. *Dialects:* None known. Lexical similarity: 71% with Kurudu [kjr], 46% with Western Serui [seu]. *Other:* Traditional religion, Christian. *Map:* 372:105.

Wae Rana [wrx] (Waerana). 3,000 (2010). East Nusa Tenggara Province. South central Flores island, 2 separate enclaves between Manggarai [mqy] and Ngad'a [nxg] language areas. *Status:* 6a (Vigorous). *Class:* Austronesian, Malayo-Polynesian, Central-Eastern Malayo-Polynesian, Bima-Lembata. *Map:* 370.

Waigeo [wgo] (Ambel, Amber, Amberi, Waigiu). 300 (1978 SIL). Papua Province, north central Waigeo island off western Bird's Head, Sorong regency, Waigeo Selatan subdistrict, Warsanbin, Selegop, Waifoi, Go, Kabilol, Kabare, and Nyandesawai villages. *Status:* 6b (Threatened). *Class:* Austronesian, Malayo-Polynesian, Central-Eastern Malayo-Polynesian, Eastern Malayo-Polynesian, South Halmahera-West New Guinea, West New Guinea, Cenderawasih Bay, Raja Ampat. *Dialects:* Metnyo, Metsam. *Other:* Christian, traditional religion. *Map:* 371:3.

Waioli [wli] (Wajoli, Wayoli). 3,000 (Voorhoeve and Visser 1987). North Maluku Province. Northwest Halmahera island, Coastal area, from Sasu town, inland to highland interior. *Status:* 6a (Vigorous). *Class:* West Papuan, North Halmahera, Sahu. *Dialects:* None known. Lexical similarity: 81% with Gamkonora [gak]. *Other:* Christian, Muslim. *Map:* 366.

Walak [wlw] (Lower Pyramid, Wodo). 20,000 (2007 P. Seow). Papua Province, Ilugwa, Wodo, Bugi, Mogonik, and Wurigelebut villages. *Status:* 6a (Vigorous). *Class:* Trans-New Guinea, West, Dani, Dani Proper. *Writing:* Latin script. *Other:* Traditional religion, Christian. *Map:* 372:72.

Wambon [wms]. 3,000 (1987 SIL). Papua Province, south coast area north of Mandobo language area.

Status: 6a (Vigorous). *Class:* Trans-New Guinea, Ok-Awyu, Awyu-Dumut, Dumut. *Dialects:* Kenon, Kenyam. *Lg Use:* Home. *Writing:* Latin script. *Other:* Christian, traditional religion. *Maps:* 372:230, 373:230.

Wandamen [wad] (Bentoeni, Bentuni, Bintuni, Wamesa, Wandamen-Windesi, Windesi, Windessi). 5,000 (1993 R. Doriot). Papua Province, Wasior, Manokwari, west Cenderawasih bay along Wandamen bay extending west to east end of Bintuni bay. *Status:* 5 (Developing). *Class:* Austronesian, Malayo-Polynesian, Central-Eastern Malayo-Polynesian, Eastern Malayo-Polynesian, South Halmahera-West New Guinea, West New Guinea, Cenderawasih Bay, Yapen, Central-Western. *Dialects:* Aibondeni, Ambumi, Bintuni, Dasener, Steenkool, Wamesa (Ubu), Waruritinao, Wasior, Windesi. *Lg Use:* Also use Indonesian [ind]. *Lg Dev:* Literacy rate in L1: 25%. Literacy rate in L2: 50%. Dictionary. Bible portions: 1937–1994. *Writing:* Latin script. *Other:* Christian. *Map:* 371:34.

Wanggom [wng] (Wanggo, Wangom). 1,180 (2002 SIL). Papua Province, upper Digul river area. East of Kombai [tyn] and west of Wambon [wms] language areas. *Status:* 6a (Vigorous). *Class:* Trans-New Guinea, Ok-Awyu, Awyu-Dumut, Dumut. *Dialects:* None known. Reportedly most similar to Kombai [tyn]. *Lg Use:* Home. *Map:* 373:233.

Wano [wno] (Waano). 1,000 (2011), decreasing. 200 monolinguals. Ethnic population: 1,000. L2 users: 0. Papua Province, central highlands area, upper Rouffaer river basin north of Damal [uhn], northwest of Dem [dem], south of Kirikiri [kiy], Iau [tmu], and Duvle [duv], east of Moni [mnz], west of Western Dani [dnw] language areas. *Status:* 6b (Threatened). *Class:* Trans-New Guinea, West, Dani, Wano. *Dialects:* Central Wano, East Wano, West Wano. Reportedly similar to Nggem [nbq], and Walak [wlw]. Lexical similarity: 65% with Western Dani [dnw]. *Type:* SOV; postpositions; possessor before noun head; articles, adjectives, numerals, and relatives after noun head; question words initial in VP, final with demonstratives; 2 prefixes, 5 suffixes; bare-root with complex verbal morphology, switch reference and (or) delayed vs. immediate sequential, tail-head linkage; (C)V(C); final stress; nontonal. *Lg Use:* Under pressure from Western Dani [dnw] and Indonesian [ind] (Wurm 2007). Religious services, home, field, community, oral. Most ages. Negative attitudes. Little interest in language revival, low prestige, considered inferior to Western Dani [dnw] and Indonesian [ind]. Also use Dem [dem], Indonesian [ind], Moni [mnz], Western Dani [dnw]. Used as L2 by Duvle [duv]. *Lg Dev:* Bible portions: 1979–1989. *Other:* Traditional religion, Christian. *Map:* 372:75.

Wanukaka [wnk] (Wanokaka). 10,000 (Wurm and Hattori 1981). East Nusa Tenggara Province. West Sumba island, southwest coast, southeast of Waikabubak city. *Status:* 6a (Vigorous). *Class:* Austronesian, Malayo-Polynesian, Central-Eastern Malayo-Polynesian, Sumba-Hawu, Sumba. *Dialects:* Rua, Wanukaka. *Map:* 369.

Warembori [wsa] (Waremboivoro, Warenbori). 600 (1998 SIL). L2 users: 20. Papua Province, north coast, Mamberamo river mouth and west to Poiwai, Warembori, Tamakuri, and Bonoi villages. *Status:* 7 (Shifting). *Class:* Lower Mamberamo. *Dialect:* Bonoi Buroro. Lexical similarity: 33% with Yoke [yki]. 30% Austronesian vocabulary. *Type:* Typology resembles Austronesian: SVO; prepositions; genitives before noun heads; articles, adjectives, numerals, relatives after noun heads; 1 prefix, 6 or more suffixes on a word; word order distinguishes subject, object, indirect object; topic (SVO) is for pragmatic salience; CV; nontonal. *Lg Use:* Home. Mainly adults. Indonesian [ind] also used. Yoke [yki] also used. Also use Papuan Malay [pmy]. Used as L2 by Yoke [yki]. *Lg Dev:* Literacy rate in L2: 30% in Indonesian. Dictionary. Grammar. *Other:* Traditional religion, Christian. *Map:* 372:108.

Wares [wai]. 200 (1993 R. Doriot). Papua Province, north coast area inland from Kwesten [kwt] language area on upper Biri river, south side, Maweswares village. *Status:* 7 (Shifting). *Class:* Tor-Kwerba, Orya-Tor, Tor. *Other:* 2005 survey data indicates language may not exist or speakers have moved. Maweswres village now inhabited by Mawes [mgk] speakers. Christian, traditional religion. *Map:* 372:165.

Waris [wrs] (Walsa). 1,500 in Indonesia. Northeastern Papua Province, Keerom regency, Waris subdistrict, south of Jayapura. *Status:* 6b (Threatened). *Other:* Christian, traditional religion. See main entry on page 323. *Map:* 372:139.

Waritai [wbe] (Wari, Weretai). 150 (Wurm 2000). Papua Province, Lakes plain area around Taiyeve. *Status:* 6b (Threatened). *Class:* Lakes Plain, Tariku, East. *Lg Use:* Endangered (2000 S. Wurm). Under pressure from Indonesian [ind] (Wurm 2007). *Other:* Different from Waris [wrs] or Wares [wai]. Christian, traditional religion. *Map:* 372:193.

Warkay-Bipim [bgv] (Bipim, Bipim As-So). 300 (1993 R. Doriot). Papua Province, south coast area bordering Asmat languages to east and Sawi [saw] language to west, lower Eilanden river. 3 villages. *Status:* 6b (Threatened). *Class:* Trans-New Guinea, Marind, Yaqay. *Lg Use:* Half also use some Indonesian [ind] or an Asmat variety. *Other:* Traditional religion, Christian. *Map:* 373:238.

Waropen [wrp] (Aropen, Wonti, Worpen). 6,000 (1987 SIL). Papua Province, south coast of Serui island, east Cenderawasih bay. *Status:* 7 (Shifting). *Class:* Austronesian, Malayo-Polynesian, Central-Eastern Malayo-Polynesian, Eastern Malayo-Polynesian, South Halmahera-West New Guinea, West New Guinea, Cenderawasih Bay, Waropen. *Dialects:* Mo'or, Napan, Waropen Kai. *Lg Use:* Children have a passive understanding (2012 Y. Sawaki). Also use Indonesian [ind]. *Lg Dev:* Literacy rate in L2: 25%. *Other:* Christian. *Map:* 372:82.

Waru [wru] (Mapute, Mopute). 350 (Mead 1999). South East Sulawesi Province, North Konawe regency, Asera subdistrict, Mopute village. Interior area; north of confluence of Solo and Lindu rivers. *Status:* 6b (Threatened). *Class:* Austronesian, Malayo-Polynesian, Celebic, Eastern, Southeastern, Bungku-Tolaki, Western, West Coast. *Dialects:* Lalomerui, Waru. Lexical similarity: 86% with the Waru and Lalomerui dialects, 79% with Mekongga and other Tolaki [lbw] dialects, 70% with Rahambuu [raz] and Kodeoha [vko], 54% with the Mori [mzq] or [xmz] and Bungku [bkz] groups. *Lg Use:* Under pressure from larger neighboring languages and from Indonesian [ind] (Wurm 2007). *Other:* Muslim. *Map:* 375:110.

Watubela [wah] (Esiriun, Kasiui, Kasui, Kesui, Matabello, Snabi Watubela, Wesi). 4,000 (1990 SIL). East central Maluku Province. Watubela islands, north of Kur island. *Status:* 6a (Vigorous). *Class:* Austronesian, Malayo-Polynesian, Central-Eastern Malayo-Polynesian, Central Maluku, East, Banda-Geser, Geser-Gorom. *Dialects:* Sulmelang, Tamher Timur. Lexical similarity: 77% between dialects, 51%–61% with Geser-Gorom [ges], 41% with Teor [tev] and Kur [kuv], 37% with Bobot [bty], 34% with Masiwang [bnf]. *Lg Use:* Also use Geser-Gorom [ges]. *Other:* Muslim, Christian. *Map:* 368.

Wauyai [wuy]. 300 (Remijsen 2001). Papua Province, southwest Waigeo island, Wauyai village. *Status:* 7 (Shifting). *Class:* Austronesian, Malayo-Polynesian, Central-Eastern Malayo-Polynesian, Eastern Malayo-Polynesian, South

Halmahera-West New Guinea, West New Guinea, Cenderawasih Bay, Raja Ampat. *Lg Use:* Dormant on Friwen Island (the original village), vigorous in the one village on the bay (2012 Y. Sawaki). *Other:* Christian, traditional religion. *Map:* 371:5.

Wawonii [wow] (Wowonii). 30,000 (2004 D. Andersen), increasing. 22,500 Wawonii, 7,500 Menui. South East Sulawesi Province. West coast, Wawonii and Menui islands near Kendari port. *Status:* 6a (Vigorous). *Class:* Austronesian, Malayo-Polynesian, Celebic, Eastern, Southeastern, Bungku-Tolaki, Eastern, East Coast. *Dialects:* Menui (Manoei), Wawonii. Lexical similarity: 75% with Bungku [bkz] and Tulambatu dialect of Bungku [bkz], 66% with Taloki [lbw], Kulisusu [vkl], and Koroni [xkq], 65% with Moronene [mqn]. *Other:* Muslim. *Map:* 375:111.

Wejewa [wew] (Veveva, Waidjewa, Wajewa, West Sumbanese, Wewewa, Wewjewa, Weyewa). 55,000 (2011). East Nusa Tenggara Province. West Sumba island, interior. *Status:* 6a (Vigorous). *Class:* Austronesian, Malayo-Polynesian, Central-Eastern Malayo-Polynesian, Sumba-Hawu, Sumba. *Dialects:* Lauli (Loli), Tana Righu, Weyewa. *Lg Dev:* NT: 1971. *Writing:* Latin script. *Other:* Christian, traditional religion. *Map:* 369.

Wemale [weo] (Honitetu, Oemale, Tala). 6,000 (2000 census). 0 monolinguals. Ethnic population: 7,500. Maluku Province, at least 14 villages. Seram island north coast, from Taniwel to Walakone towns; southwest Seram, northeast of Kairatu town. *Status:* 6a (Vigorous). *Class:* Austronesian, Malayo-Polynesian, Central-Eastern Malayo-Polynesian, Central Maluku, East, Seram, Nunusaku, Three Rivers, Wemale. *Dialects:* East Wemale, South Wemale, West Wemale, West-Central Wemale. Lexical similarity: 84% with east and west dialects, 70% with South Wemale dialect. *Lg Use:* Vigorous. Home, neighborhood, traditional ceremonies. All ages. Positive attitudes. 100% also use Ambonese Malay [abs]. *Lg Dev:* Literacy rate in L1: 0%. Literacy rate in L2: 90% Indonesian [ind]. *Writing:* Latin script. *Other:* Christian, Muslim. *Map:* 367.

Wersing [kvw] (Kolana, Kolana-Wersin, Warsina, Wersin). 3,700 (Grimes et al. 1997). East Nusa Tenggara Province. Alor island. East coast area, southeast coast, Pietoko and Pureman, 2 enclaves on central north coast. *Status:* 6a (Vigorous). *Class:* Trans-New Guinea, West, Timor-Alor-Pantar. *Dialects:* Kolana, Langkuru (Mademang, Pureman), Maneta. *Other:* Cultural and historical relationship with Liquisa area in East Timor. Christian, traditional religion. *Map:* 370.

Woi [wbw] (Wo'oi). 1,800 (2012 Y. Sawaki). Papua Province, Miosnum and west Serui islands, Wooi and Wainap villages. *Status:* 6b (Threatened). *Class:* Austronesian, Malayo-Polynesian, Central-Eastern Malayo-Polynesian, Eastern Malayo-Polynesian, South Halmahera-West New Guinea, West New Guinea, Cenderawasih Bay, Yapen, Central-Western. *Dialects:* None known. Lexical similarity: 77% with Pom [pmo], Marau [mvr], and Ansus [and]. *Other:* Christian. *Map:* 372:99.

Wolani [wod] (Woda, Woda-Mo, Wodani). 5,000 (1992 UBS). Papua Province, west central highlands, Kemandoga and Mbiyandogo rivers, north of Ekari [ekg] language area, northeast of Lake Paniai, north of Wissel Lakes and northwest of Moni [mnz] language area. *Status:* 5 (Developing). *Class:* Trans-New Guinea, West, Wissel Lakes. *Lg Dev:* Bible portions: 1984–1995. *Writing:* Latin script. *Other:* Traditional religion, Christian. *Map:* 372:77.

Wolio [wlo] (Baubau). 65,000 in Indonesia (2004 D. Andersen). Population does not include those in other provinces. Southeast Sulawesi Province. Buton island, southwest coast towards Buntung strait; Baubau city, adjacent areas northeast and east. Also in Malaysia. *Status:* 6b (Threatened). *Class:* Austronesian, Malayo-Polynesian, Celebic, Wotu-Wolio, Wolio-Kamaru. *Dialects:* Lexical similarity: 61% with Cia-Cia [cia]; 60% with Masiri dialect of Cia-Cia and Lantoi dialect of Kaimbulawa [zka]. *Lg Use:* Former court language of Baubau Sultanate, and surrounding communities; formerly used by nobility in the region. Wolio is declining in the urban center, but being maintained at the rural periphery. Children in villages use Wolio, but city children primarily use Indonesian. Also use Indonesian [ind]. Used as L2 by Busoa [bup], Cia-Cia [cia], Liabuku [lix], Pancana [pnp], Tukang Besi South [bhq]. *Lg Dev:* Dictionary. *Writing:* Arabic script. *Other:* 'Buton' usually used generically inside Southeast Sulawesi to refer to Wolio; outside Southeast Sulawesi it refers to people from Southeast Sulawesi, or is sometimes confused with Bajau people as sailors. Muslim. *Map:* 375:112.

Woria [wor]. 5 (2000 R. Doriot). Papua Province, interior Waropen Bawah, Botawa village. *Status:* 8b (Nearly extinct). *Class:* East Geelvink Bay. *Dialects:* None known. Lexical similarity: 64% with Barapasi [brp], 64% with Demisa [dei], 63% with Kofei [kpi], 69% with Tunggare [trt]. *Lg Use:* Moribund (2000 S. Wurm). *Other:* Botawa is a Demisa and Waropen [wrp]-speaking village. *Map:* 372:87.

Wotu [wtw] (Wadu). 500 (2009 Masruddin and Wahibah), decreasing. Ethnic population: 4,000 (2009). South Sulawesi Province, East Luwu regency, Wotu subdistrict, Lampenai, and Bawalipu villages. Northern end of Bone bay; coast near mouth of Kalaena river between Wotu and Angkona villages. *Status:* 6b (Threatened). *Class:* Austronesian, Malayo-Polynesian, Celebic, Wotu-Wolio. *Dialects:* None known. Lexical similarity: 58% with Wolio [wlo], 53% with Laiyolo [lji], average 43% with South Sulawesi Group, 43% with Kaili-Pamona Subgroup, 41% with Seko Padang [skx], 39% with Tae' Luwu [rob], 36%–43% with Bungku-Tolaki Subgroup, 37% with Toraja-Sa'dan [sda], 33% with Bugis [bug], 31% with Rampi [lje], 25% with Lemolang [ley]. *Lg Use:* Parents no longer pass Wotu on to their children (2009). Also use the Bugis-Luwu dialect of Bugis [bug]. Also use Indonesian [ind]. *Other:* Muslim. *Map:* 375:113.

Yahadian [ner] (Jahadian, Nerigo, Yabin Yahadian). 500 (1991 SIL). Papua Province, south Bird's Head, along Maccluer bay between lower Mintamani and Sekak rivers. *Status:* 6b (Threatened). *Class:* Trans-New Guinea, South Bird's Head, Konda-Yahadian. *Dialects:* None known. Lexical similarity: 60% with Konda [knd]. *Other:* Christian, traditional religion. *Map:* 371:27.

Yalahatan [jal] (Atamanu, Awaiya, Jahalatan, Jahalatane). 1,700 (2004 SIL). Maluku Province, south central Seram island, coastal area west of Teluti bay. *Status:* 6b (Threatened). *Class:* Austronesian, Malayo-Polynesian, Central-Eastern Malayo-Polynesian, Central Maluku, East, Seram, Nunusaku, Three Rivers. *Dialects:* Slight dialect differences reported between the 2 villages. Lexical similarity: 50%–52% with Sepa [spb], 49%–50% with Teluti [tlt]. *Lg Use:* Also use Indonesian [ind]. *Lg Dev:* Literacy rate in L1: Below 1%. Literacy rate in L2: 15%–25%. *Writing:* Latin script. *Other:* The name Atamanu is not currently known. *Map:* 367.

Yale, Kosarek [kkl] (In-lom, Kosarek, Wanam, Yale-Kosarek). 2,300 (1993 R. Doriot). 2,300 monolinguals. Nearly 100% are monolingual. Ethnic population: 2,300. Papua Province, eastern highlands, just east of Yali of Ninia, northwest of Nipsan, east of Dani, north of Yali [yli] of Angguruk. *Status:* 5 (Developing). *Class:* Trans-New Guinea, Mek, Eastern. *Dialects:* Gilika (Kilika), Kosarek, Tiple. Lexical similarity: 78% with Nipsan [nps], 59%

with Nalca [nlc]. *Lg Use:* Vigorous. All domains. Negative attitudes. Also use Indonesian [ind]. *Lg Dev:* Literacy rate in L2: Below 5%. Bible portions: 1992–1996. *Writing:* Latin script. *Other:* The name In-lom refers to only half the group. Christian, traditional religion. *Map:* 372:207.

Yali, Angguruk [yli] (Angguruk, Northern Yali, Yalimo). 15,000 (1991 J. Wilson). Papua Province, central highlands area northwest of Nalca [nlc] and east of Grand Valley Dani language areas. *Status:* 5 (Developing). *Class:* Trans-New Guinea, West, Dani, Ngalik. *Lg Dev:* NT: 1988. *Writing:* Latin script. *Other:* Christian, traditional religion. *Map:* 372:205.

Yali, Ninia [nlk] (Jalè, Jaly, Ninia, North Ngalik, Southern Yali, Yali Selatan). 10,500 (1999 J. Wilson). Papua Province, central highlands area south of Angguruk, east of Soba, west of Korupun, Ninia, Holuwon, and Lolat villages; Elelim, transmigrated by government in 1989 following earthquake. More than 50 villages. *Status:* 5 (Developing). *Class:* Trans-New Guinea, West, Dani, Ngalik. *Dialects:* None known. Different from Yali of Pass Valley [yac], Yali of Angguruk [yli], and Hupla [hap]. *Lg Use:* Also use Indonesian [ind]. *Lg Dev:* Literacy rate in L1: 20%–25%. Literacy rate in L2: 15%–20%. Bible: 2000. *Writing:* Latin script. *Other:* Christian, traditional religion. *Map:* 372:213.

Yali, Pass Valley [yac] (Abendago, North Ngalik, Pass Valley, Western Yali, Yaly). 5,000 (1988 SIL). Papua Province, central highlands, east of Angguruk and northwest of Naltya, Jayawijaya, Kurulu, and Kurima regencies. *Status:* 6a (Vigorous). *Class:* Trans-New Guinea, West, Dani, Ngalik. *Dialects:* Apahapsili, Landikma, Pass Valley. *Lg Dev:* NT: 1977. *Other:* Christian, traditional religion. *Map:* 372:206.

Yamdena [jmd] (Jamden, Jamdena, Tanemprar lirin). 25,000 (1991 SIL), decreasing. Ethnic population: 35,000 (1991 SIL). Southeast Maluku Province, 35 villages. Tannembar islands; east coast Yamdena island, down to north tip of Selaru island. Latdalam village, southwest Yamdena. *Status:* 5 (Developing). *Class:* Austronesian, Malayo-Polynesian, Central-Eastern Malayo-Polynesian, Southeast Maluku, Kei-Tanimbar, Yamdena. *Dialects:* North Yamdena (Nus Das), South Yamdena (Nus Bab). A chain of related varieties from north to south with 90% lexical similarity between extremes, but with morphological and phonological differences. Southern dialect thought more prestigious. Lexical similarity: 90% among the north and south dialects, 47% with Fordata [frd]. *Lg Use:* Vigorous except for some northern villages. Strong users mostly over 30 years old. All domains, very limited use in religion. Also use Ambonese Malay [abs], Indonesian [ind]. *Lg Dev:* Literacy rate in L1: 2%–5%. Literacy rate in L2: 80%. Taught in primary schools, as a subject. Taught in secondary schools, as a subject. Poetry. Dictionary. Bible portions. *Writing:* Latin script. *Other:* Christian (Roman Catholic), Christian (Protestant). *Map:* 368.

Yaqay [jaq] (Jakai, Jaqai, Mapi, Sohur, Yaqai). 10,000 (1987 SIL). Papua Province, south coast Obaa river area, southeast of Kayagar [kyt] and southwest of Central Awyu [awu] language areas. *Status:* 6b (Threatened). *Class:* Trans-New Guinea, Marind, Yaqay. *Dialects:* Bapai, Nambiomon-Mabur, Oba-Miwamon. *Lg Use:* Home, religious services. Also use Indonesian [ind]. *Other:* Traditional religion, Christian. *Map:* 373:245.

Yarsun [yrs]. 200 (1991 SIL). Papua Province, Sarmi regency, Bonggo subdistrict, island off north coast east of Biri river. *Status:* 8a (Moribund). *Class:* Austronesian, Malayo-Polynesian, Central-Eastern Malayo-Polynesian, Eastern Malayo-Polynesian, Oceanic, Western Oceanic, North New Guinea, Sarmi-Jayapura Bay, Sarmi. *Other:* Yarsun may not exist or speakers may have moved (2005 SIL). Christian, traditional religion. *Map:* 372:124.

Yaur [jau] (Jaur). 350 (1978 SIL). Papua Province, lower end of Cenderawasih bay, west of Yeresiam [ire] language area. *Status:* 7 (Shifting). *Class:* Austronesian, Malayo-Polynesian, Central-Eastern Malayo-Polynesian, Eastern Malayo-Polynesian, South Halmahera-West New Guinea, West New Guinea, Cenderawasih Bay, Yaur. *Other:* Traditional religion, Christian. *Maps:* 371:57, 372:57.

Yawa [yva] (Mantembu, Mora, Turu, Unat, Yapanani, Yava, Yawa Unat). 10,000 (2011 SIL). Papua Province, Yapen island: 8 north coast villages, 2 interior villages, and 18 south coast villages, all in the central portion of the island. *Status:* 5 (Developing). *Class:* West Papuan, Yapen. *Dialects:* Central Yawa (Mora), East Yawa, North Yawa, South Yawa, West Yawa. *Lg Use:* Home, market, religious services, school. *Lg Dev:* Literacy rate in L1: 40%–50%. Taught in the lower grades in some village schools. Dictionary. NT: 2011. *Writing:* Latin script. *Other:* Christian, traditional religion. *Map:* 372:104.

Yei [jei] (Je, Jei, Yei-Nan, Yey). 2,390 (2001 SIL). Papua Province, south coast border area, east of Marind along Maro river. 6 villages. *Status:* 7 (Shifting). *Class:* South-Central Papuan, Morehead-Upper Maro, Yey. *Dialects:* Lower Yei, Upper Yei. Dialects mutually inherently intelligible only with difficulty. *Lg Use:* Home. Also use Marind [mrz], Papuan Malay [pmy]. *Other:* Different cultural group from Marind. Christian, traditional religion. *Map:* 373:264.

Yelmek [jel] (Jab, Jabsch, Jelmek, Jelmik). 400 (1978 SIL). Papua Province, south coast area, east side of Marianne strait between Kolopom (Frederik Hendrik) island and mainland. *Status:* 8a (Moribund). *Class:* South-Central Papuan, Yelmek-Maklew. *Dialects:* None known. Reportedly most similar to Maklew [mgf]. *Other:* Christian, traditional religion. *Map:* 373:255.

Yeresiam [ire] (Beduba, Iresim). 70 (Wurm 2000). Papua Province, south Cenderawasih bay, west of Nabire and around Yamur lake. *Status:* 7 (Shifting). *Class:* Austronesian, Malayo-Polynesian, Central-Eastern Malayo-Polynesian, Eastern Malayo-Polynesian, South Halmahera-West New Guinea, West New Guinea, Cenderawasih Bay, Iresim. *Lg Use:* Endangered (2000 S. Wurm). Shifting to Indonesian [ind] (Wurm 2007). *Other:* Traditional religion, Christian. *Maps:* 371:58, 372:58.

Yeretuar [gop] (Goni, Umar, Umari). 350 (2000). Papua Province, lower Cenderawasih bay, south of Wandamen [wad] language area. *Status:* 7 (Shifting). *Class:* Austronesian, Malayo-Polynesian, Central-Eastern Malayo-Polynesian, Eastern Malayo-Polynesian, South Halmahera-West New Guinea, West New Guinea, Cenderawasih Bay, Yeretuar. *Lg Use:* Two of three villages have shifted mostly to Wandamen [wad]. *Other:* Distinct from Kamoro [kgq]. Christian, traditional religion. *Maps:* 371:53, 372:53.

Yetfa [yet] (Biaksi, Biksi, Inisine). 1,000 (1996). L2 users: 400 (2013 M. Donohue). Papua Province, Pegunungan Bintang regency, Okbibab subdistrict, border area east and north of Sobger river, south of Ji mountain. *Status:* 3 (Wider communication). Trade language in the area, extending to Papua New Guinea border. *Class:* Unclassified. *Dialects:* None known. Yetfa and Biksi are 2 ethnic groups, speaking the same language. *Lg Use:* Home, market, religious services. Used as L2 by Murkim [rmh], Towei [ttn]. *Other:* Christian, traditional religion. *Map:* 372:146.

Yoke [yki] (Bitovondo, Jauke, Pauwi, Yauke, Yoki). 200 (1998 M. Donohue). Papua Province, Sarmi regency, east of Warembori, east of Mamberamo river, Mantarbori village. Recently moved to coast from interior. *Status:* 6b (Threatened). *Class:* Lower Mamberamo. *Dialects:* None known. Lexical similarity: 33% with Warembori [wsa]. *Lg Use:* Vigorous. Religious services. All ages. Also use Indonesian [ind], Warembori [wsa]. Used as L2 by Warembori [wsa]. *Other:* Traditional religion, Christian. *Map:* 372:109.

Zorop [wfg] (Jafi, Jafi Wagarindem, Wagarindem, Wargarindem, Warlef, Yaffi, Yafi). 230 (2005 SIL). 0 monolinguals. Northeastern Papua Province, border area south of Jayapura, Warlef village, Yabanda Satu. *Status:* 7 (Shifting). *Class:* Pauwasi, Eastern. *Dialects:* None known. Lexical similarity: 25% with Emem [enr]. *Lg Use:* Home, community. Mainly older adults. 100% also use Indonesian [ind]. 100% also use Papuan Malay [pmy]. *Other:* Christian, traditional religion. *Map:* 372:141.

Iran

Islamic Republic of Iran. 75,150,000 (2011 census). Principal language: Iranian Persian. Literacy rate: 81% (2008 UNESCO). Immigrant languages: Dari (1,000,000), Hulaulá (350), Turkish (2,570). General references: Drower 1937; Oberling 1974; Sebeok 1970. Deaf population: 3,978,100. Deaf institutions: 50.

The number of individual languages listed for Iran is 78. Of these, 76 are living and 2 are extinct. Of the living languages, 5 are institutional, 8 are developing, 27 are vigorous, 31 are in trouble, and 5 are dying.

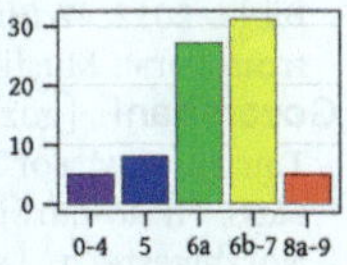

Aimaq [aiq]. 170,000 in Iran (Johnstone 1993). Mazanderan Province. *Status:* 6a (Vigorous). *Dialect:* Teimuri (Teimurtash). *Other:* Barbari and Berberi are also applied to Hazara people in Mashad. See main entry on page 47.

Alviri-Vidari [avd]. Near Saveh, Markazi Province. *Status:* 7 (Shifting). *Class:* Indo-European, Indo-Iranian, Iranian, Western, Northwestern, Talysh. *Dialects:* Alvir (Alviri), Vidar (Vidari). Related to Gozarkhâni [goz] and Vafsi [vaf]. *Other:* Muslim.

Arabic, Gulf Spoken [afb] (Gulf Arabic, Khaliji). 200,000 in Iran (1993). South coast and islands; Khamseh nomads in east Fars Province; other Arab nomadic groups in several south central provinces. *Status:* 6a (Vigorous). *Dialects:* Al-Hasâ, Khamseh. *Lg Use:* The largest of 5 Khamseh clans uses Iranian Persian [pes] as L1. Also use Iranian Persian [pes]. Used as L2 by Lari [lrl]. See main entry on page 213.

Arabic, Mesopotamian Spoken [acm] (Arabi, Mesopotamian Gelet Arabic). 1,200,000 in Iran. Khuzestan Province, southwest side of Zagros mountains, Shatt al Arab river bank. *Status:* 6a (Vigorous). *Lg Use:* Used as L2 by Mandaic [mid]. *Other:* Muslim (Sunni), Muslim (Shi'a). See main entry on page 206.

Armenian [hye] (Armani, Armjanski, Erâmani, Ermenice, Haieren, Somekhuri). 171,000 in Iran (1993). North, Azerbaijan provinces, Khoi, Shahpur, Ahar, Tabriz, Tehran, Isfahan, and Shiraz areas. *Status:* 4 (Educational). *Dialects:* Agulis, Astrakhân, Eastern Armenian, Jolfâ (Dzhulfa), Karabagh Shamakhi, Khoi-Salmst (Khvoy), Urmia-Maragheh. *Lg Use:* Vigorous. Home, church. All ages. Also use Iranian Persian [pes], South Azerbaijani [azb]. *Lg Dev:* Literacy rate in L2: 80%. Taught in Armenian private schools. *Other:* Christian. See main entry on page 51.

Ashtiani [atn] (Ashtiyani, Astiani). 21,100 (2000). Markazi Province, Ashtiyan and Tafresh. *Status:* 7 (Shifting). *Class:* Indo-European, Indo-Iranian, Iranian, Western, Northwestern, Central Iran. *Dialects:* Ashtiani, Tafresh. Transitional between central Iranian dialects and Talysh [tly]. Dialects may be separate languages. Reportedly very similar to Vafsi [vaf]. *Lg Use:* Also use Iranian Persian [pes]. *Other:* Muslim.

Assyrian Neo-Aramaic [aii]. 15,000 in Iran (1994). Ethnic population: 80,000 (1994). Most in Tehran; Reza'iyeh (Rizaiye, Urmia, Urmi). *Status:* 6b (Threatened). *Dialect:* Iranian Koine (General Urmi). *Other:* Religious separation of Assyrian from Chaldean happened in the 16th century. Christian (Nestorian). See main entry on page 206.

Avestan [ave] (Avesta, Pazend). No known L1 speakers. *Status:* 10 (Extinct). *Class:* Indo-European, Indo-Iranian, Iranian. *Dialects:* Old Avestan (Gathic), Younger Avestan. *Lg Use:* The language of Zoroastrian scriptures. *Writing:* Arabic script. Avestan script, used until 7th century. Gujarati script.

Azerbaijani [aze]. A macrolanguage (see page 9). *Other:* Includes: North Azerbaijani [azj] (Azerbaijan), South Azerbaijani [azb].

Azerbaijani, South [azb] (Torki). 15,500,000 in Iran (2010). Population total all countries: 16,913,280. Ethnic population: 18,700,000. L2 users: Used as L2 in Northwestern Iran. East and West Azerbaijan provinces, Ardebil, Zanjan, and part of Markazi provinces; Tehran districts; Fars Province and scattered. Also in Azerbaijan, Iraq, Jordan, Syria, Turkey, United States. *Status:* 3 (Wider communication). *Class:* Altaic, Turkic, Southern, Azerbaijani. A member of macrolanguage Azerbaijani [aze]. *Dialects:* Afshari (Afsar, Afshar), Aynallu (Inallu, Inanlu), Baharlu (Kamesh), Bayat, Karapapakh, Moqaddam, Nafar, Pishagchi, Qajar, Qaragozlu, Shahsavani (Shahseven), Tabriz. *Lg Use:* Vigorous. All ages. Also use Iranian Persian [pes]. Also use English [eng]. Used as L2 by Armenian [hye], Iranian Persian [pes]. *Lg Dev:* Fully developed. *Writing:* Arabic script, used in Iraq and Iran. *Other:* Muslim (Shi'a).

Bakhtiâri [bqi] (Lori, Lori-ye Khaveri). 1,000,000 (2001). 350,000 monolinguals. Ethnic population: 1,000,000 (2001). Southwest, west Chahar-Mahal va Bakhtiâri, east Khuzestan, east Lorestan, and west Isfahan provinces. Masjed-e Soleiman, Shahr-e Kord, Dorud. *Status:* 6a (Vigorous). *Class:* Indo-European, Indo-Iranian, Iranian, Western, Southwestern, Luri. *Dialects:* Aligudarz, Chelgerd/Kuhrang, Haftgel, Ize, Masjed-e Soleiman, Shahr-e Kord. Bakhtiâri is on a continuum of related varieties between Northern Luri [lrc] and Southern Luri [luz]. Farsi dialects in Chaharmahâl va Bakhtiâri Province are mutually intelligible with Bakhtiâri. Lexical similarity: 75% with Southern Luri (Mamasani) [lrc], 86% with Southern Luri (Boyerahmadi) [luz], 73% with Northern Luri (rural), 78% with Northern Luri (Khorramabadi), 76% with Iranian Persian [pes]. *Lg Use:* Vigorous. Home, commerce. All ages. Positive attitudes. Also use English [eng], Iranian Persian [pes]. Women and older people have lower levels of bilingualism. Used as L2 by Dezfuli [def], Domari [rmt]. *Lg Dev:* Poetry. Dictionary. Grammar. *Writing:* Arabic script. *Other:* Little contact with Southern Luri [luz], some contact with Northern Luri [lrc]. Muslim (Shi'a).

Balochi, Southern [bcc] (Baloci, Baluchi, Baluci). 405,000 in Iran. Baluchistan Province, South Sistan; west Hormozgan Province coastal areas; Fars Province, scattered communities. *Status:* 5 (Developing). *Dialects:* Koroshi, Makrani (Lotuni). *Other:* Muslim (Sunni). See main entry on page 266.

Balochi, Western [bgn] (Baloci, Baluchi, Baluci). 451,000 in Iran (1986). North Sistan and Baluchistan Province. Half in cities and villages, half nomadic. *Status:* 5

(Developing). *Dialects:* Rakhshani (Raxshani), Sarawani. *Lg Use:* Also use Iranian Persian [pes]. Used as L2 by Brahui [brh]. *Other:* Distinct from Eastern Balochi [bgp] and Southern Balochi [bcc]. Ethnic group: Yarahmadza. Muslim (Shi'a), Muslim (Sunni). See main entry on page 266.

Bashkardi [bsg] (Bashaka). 7,030 (2000). East Hormozgan, South Kerman, possibly southwest Sistan va Baluchistan provinces. *Status:* 7 (Shifting). *Class:* Indo-European, Indo-Iranian, Iranian, Western, Northwestern, Balochi. *Dialects:* Northern Bashaka, Southern Bashaka. *Other:* Muslim.

Brahui [brh] (Barahui, Birahui, Brahudi, Kur Galli). 20,000 in Iran (2007), increasing. Central Sistan and Baluchistan provinces, including Zahedan. *Status:* 6b (Threatened). *Dialects:* Jharawan (Jhalawan), Kalat, Sarawan. *Lg Use:* Neutral attitudes. Also use Iranian Persian [pes], Western Balochi [bgn]. *Other:* Muslim. See main entry on page 266.

Dari, Zoroastrian [gbz] ("Gabar" *pej.*, "Gabri" *pej.*, "Yazdi" *pej.*). 8,000 (1999). Yazd and Kerman areas. *Status:* 7 (Shifting). *Class:* Indo-European, Indo-Iranian, Iranian, Western, Northwestern, Central Iran. *Dialects:* None known. Related to Parsi-Dari [prd] and Nâyini [nyq]. *Lg Use:* Used by Persian Zoroastrians in personal communications as a private language. Also use Iranian Persian [pes]. *Other:* Different from Dari dialect of Eastern Farsi [prs] of Afghanistan, though both names refer to Darius, the ancient Persian Emperor ('dar' is Classical Persian for court). Many Zoroastrians speak Parsi-Dari and do not know Zoroastrian Dari [gbz]. Zoroastrian.

Dezfuli [def] (Dizfuli). Dezful and Shushtar, north Khuzestan Province. *Status:* 6a (Vigorous). *Class:* Indo-European, Indo-Iranian, Iranian, Western, Northwestern, Unclassified. *Dialects:* Dezfuli, Shushtari. *Lg Use:* Also use Bakhtiâri [bqi], Iranian Persian [pes]. *Lg Dev:* Grammar. *Other:* Muslim.

Domari [rmt] (Gypsy, Luti, Mehtar, Middle Eastern Romani, Tsigene). 1,340,000 in Iran (2000). Population total all countries: 3,952,810. Kurbat and Luti in west; Mehtar and Ghorbat in Fars and Kohgiluyeh va Boyerahmad Province; Karachi in north. Also in Afghanistan, Egypt, India, Iraq, Israel, Jordan, Libya, Palestine, Russian Federation, Sudan, Syria, Turkey, Uzbekistan. *Status:* 6a (Vigorous). *Class:* Indo-European, Indo-Iranian, Indo-Aryan, Central zone, Dom. *Dialects:* Karachi, Koli, Kurbati (Ghorbati), Luli, Maznoug, Nawar, Qinati, Yürük. Dialects in Iran may be highly divergent from one another. Not intelligible to Romani speakers. *Lg Use:* Vigorous. Home and in communication with other gypsies. All ages. Also use Bakhtiâri [bqi], Iranian Persian [pes], Kashkay [qxq], Northern Luri [lrc], Southern Luri [luz]. *Lg Dev:* Grammar. *Writing:* Unwritten. *Other:* Influenced by Arabic, as well as languages of host ethnic groups with which any Domari group is associated. Muslim.

Dzhidi [jpr] (Djudi, Judeo-Persian, Judi). *Status:* 7 (Shifting). *Other:* Jewish. See main entry on page 208.

Eshtehardi [esh]. Markazi Province, Karaj District, Eshtehard area. *Status:* 7 (Shifting). *Class:* Indo-European, Indo-Iranian, Iranian, Western, Northwestern, Talysh. *Dialects:* Reportedly similar to Takestani [tks]. May be the same language as some dialects spoken southwest of Qazvin. *Other:* Muslim.

Fars, Northwestern [faz]. 7,500 (2006). Fars Province, scattered pockets. *Status:* 7 (Shifting). *Class:* Indo-European, Indo-Iranian, Iranian, Western, Northwestern, Central Iran. *Dialects:* None known. Reportedly similar to Sivandi [siy]. *Other:* Distinct from Farsi [prs] or [pes]. Muslim.

Fars, Southwestern [fay] ("Tajik" *pej.*). 100,000 (2012). Central Fars Province: Somghun, Papun, Masarm, Buringun, Kondazi, Davani, and others. *Status:* 7 (Shifting). *Class:* Indo-European, Indo-Iranian, Iranian, Western, Southwestern, Fars. *Dialects:* None known. Related to Iranian Persian [prs] or [pes] and Lari [lrl]. *Other:* Distinct from Iranian Persian [prs] or [pes]. Muslim.

Gazi [gzi]. 7,030 (2000). Gaz. *Status:* 7 (Shifting). *Class:* Indo-European, Indo-Iranian, Iranian, Western, Northwestern, Central Iran. *Other:* Muslim.

Georgian [kat] (Gruzin, Kartuli). 60,000 in Iran. Fereydan and Fereydunshahr provinces, Isfahan, Najaf Abad, Shahin Shahr, Yazdanshahr. *Status:* 5 (Dispersed). *Dialect:* Fereydan (Ferejdan). *Other:* Muslim. See main entry on page 99.

Gilaki [glk] (Gelaki, Gilani, Guilaki, Guilani). 3,270,000 (1993), decreasing. 2,000 Galeshi. Gilan region, coastal plain, south of Talish. Galeshi is a mountain dialect. *Status:* 4 (Educational). *Class:* Indo-European, Indo-Iranian, Iranian, Western, Northwestern, Caspian. *Dialects:* Bandar Anzali, Fumani, Galeshi, Lahijani, Langerudi, Rashti, Rudbari, Rudsari, Some'e Sarai. Reportedly similar to Mâzanderâni [mzn]. *Lg Use:* Home, market, work. All ages. Positive attitudes. Also use Iranian Persian [pes]. *Lg Dev:* Magazines. Radio programs. TV. Dictionary. Grammar. Bible: 2012. *Writing:* Arabic script. *Other:* Heavy influence from Farsi. Muslim (Shi'a).

Gozarkhani [goz]. Gozarkhan, northwest of Qazvin; Tajrish, north of Tehran; Alamut area. *Status:* 7 (Shifting). *Class:* Indo-European, Indo-Iranian, Iranian, Western, Northwestern, Talysh. *Dialects:* None known. Reportedly similar to Maraghei [vmh] and Semnani [smy]. *Other:* Muslim.

Harzani [hrz]. 28,100 (2000). East Azerbaijan Province, between Marand and Jolfa, northwest of Tabriz; related varieties in Galin Qaya, Babra, and Dizmar. *Status:* 7 (Shifting). *Class:* Indo-European, Indo-Iranian, Iranian, Western, Northwestern, Talysh. *Dialects:* None known. Reportedly similar to Karingani [kgn] and Talysh [tly]. *Other:* Muslim.

Hawrami [hac] (Awromani, Gorani, Gurani, Hawramani, Hewrami, Howrami). 200,000 in Iran (Paul 2007). West Kurdestan Province, near Iraq border, Hewraman, east of Sanandaj, north of Kermanshah. *Status:* 7 (Shifting). *Dialects:* Gawhara, Gurani (Gorani), Hawraman i Luhon, Hawraman i Taxt, Kakai (Macho), Kandula. *Lg Use:* Also use Central Kurdish [ckb], Iranian Persian [pes]. *Other:* Muslim, Ahl-e Haqq. See main entry on page 207 (as Gurani).

Hazaragi [haz] (Hazara, Hezareh, Hezare'i). 283,000 in Iran (1993). Population increased significantly due to influx of Hazaragi-speaking refugees from Afghanistan. Widespread, especially urban centers. *Status:* 6a (Vigorous). *Lg Use:* Also use Iranian Persian [pes]. *Other:* Ethnic group names are (Central) Dai Kundi, Dai Zangi, Behsud, Yekaulang, (Southern) Polada, Urusgani, Jaguri, Ghazni Hazaras, Dai Miradad. Muslim (Imami Shi'a), Muslim (Ismaili), Muslim (Sunni). See main entry on page 48.

Jadgali [jdg] (Jat, Jatgali, Jatki). 10,000 in Iran (2012). *Status:* 6a (Vigorous). *Other:* Different from Jakati [jat] of Afghanistan and Ukraine, and Russian Central Asia. Muslim. See main entry on page 268.

Kabatei [xkp]. Gilan Province, Rudbar district. *Status:* 7 (Shifting). *Class:* Indo-European, Indo-Iranian, Iranian, Western, Northwestern, Talysh. *Dialects:* Kabate, Kalas. Reportedly similar to Upper Taromi [tov]. *Other:* Muslim.

Kajali [xkj]. East Azerbaijan Province, Kaqazkonan district, Kajal. *Status:* 7 (Shifting). *Class:* Indo-European, Indo-Iranian, Iranian, Western, Northwestern, Talysh.

Dialects: None known. Reportedly similar to Shahrudi [shm] and Koresh-e Rostam [okh]. *Other:* Muslim.

Karingani [kgn] (Keringani). 17,600 (2000). East Azerbaijan Province, Dizmar district, Keringan village; Hasanu district, northeast of Tabriz. *Status:* 7 (Shifting). *Class:* Indo-European, Indo-Iranian, Iranian, Western, Northwestern, Talysh. *Dialects:* Various dialects. Reportedly very similar to Harzani [hrz]. *Other:* Muslim.

Kashkay [qxq] (Kashkai, Qashqa'i, Qashqay). 1,500,000 (1997). Southwest, Fars and South Kohgiluyeh va Boyerahmad provinces. Shiraz, Gachsaran, and Firuzabad are centers. *Status:* 6a (Vigorous). *Class:* Altaic, Turkic, Southern. *Dialects:* None known. Reportedly similar to Azerbaijani [azb]. *Lg Use:* Vigorous. Home, commerce. All ages. Also use Iranian Persian [pes], Southern Luri [luz]. Used as L2 by Domari [rmt]. *Lg Dev:* Many can read Farsi well. *Writing:* Arabic script. *Other:* Nomadic. Muslim (Shi'a).

Kazakh [kaz] (Gazaqi, Kazak, Kazakhi). 3,000 in Iran (1982). Mazanderan Province, Gorgan city. *Status:* 5 (Dispersed). *Other:* Muslim. See main entry on page 212.

Khalaj [kjf]. 42,100 in Iran (2000). *Status:* 6a (Vigorous). *Other:* Pronounced with 2 short or front a's. Different from Turkic Khalaj [klj] in Iran. See main entry on page 52.

Khalaj, Turkic [klj] (Khalaj). 42,100 (2000). Central Province, northeast of Arak. *Status:* 6a (Vigorous). *Class:* Altaic, Turkic, Southern. *Dialects:* Not a dialect of Azerbaijani [azb], as previously supposed. Distinct from other extant Turkish languages (Doerfer et al 1971). Different from Indo-Iranian Khalaj [kjf]. *Lg Use:* All ages. Also use Iranian Persian [pes]. *Other:* Muslim.

Kho'ini [xkc]. Zanjan Province, Kho'in district. *Status:* 7 (Shifting). *Class:* Indo-European, Indo-Iranian, Iranian, Western, Northwestern, Talysh. *Dialects:* Various dialects. Related to Kabatei [xkp] and Takestani [tks]. Closely related varieties spoken in nearby villages of Balbavin, Sefidkamar, Halab, and Sa'dabad. *Other:* Muslim.

Khorasani Turkish [kmz] (Quchani). 400,000 (1977 G. Doerfer). Northeast, north Khorasan Province, northwest of Mashhad. West dialect in Bojnurd area; north in Quchan area (probably largest), south in Soltanabad area near Sabzevar. *Status:* 6a (Vigorous). *Class:* Altaic, Turkic, Southern, Turkish. *Dialects:* North Quchani (Northeast Quchani), South Quchani, West Quchani (Northwest Quchani). Midway linguistically between Azerbaijani and Turkmen [tuk], but not a dialect of either. The Oghuz-Uzbek dialect of Uzbek, Northern [uzn] in Uzbekistan is reportedly a dialect. Different from Khorasani, a local Persian dialect in Khorasan. *Lg Use:* Also use Iranian Persian [pes]. *Lg Dev:* Radio programs. *Other:* Muslim.

Khunsari [kfm]. 21,100 (2000). Isfahan Province, Kashan and Isfahan areas. *Status:* 7 (Shifting). *Class:* Indo-European, Indo-Iranian, Iranian, Western, Northwestern, Central Iran. *Dialects:* May be one of a large complex of dialects in Esfahan Province. Other Northwestern closely related dialects include Vonishun, Qohrud, Keshe, Zefre, Sedeh, Gaz, Kafran, Mahallat, So, Mejme, and Djaushaqan. Distinct from Kumzari [zum] of Oman. *Other:* Muslim.

Koresh-e Rostam [okh]. East Azerbaijan Province, Koresh-e Rostam district. *Status:* 7 (Shifting). *Class:* Indo-European, Indo-Iranian, Iranian, Western, Northwestern, Talysh. *Other:* Muslim.

Koroshi [ktl]. 160. 40–50 families. Fars Province. *Status:* 8b (Nearly extinct). *Class:* Indo-European, Indo-Iranian, Iranian, Western, Northwestern, Balochi. *Other:* Appears to be Baluchi with some features of Farsi. They work for the Qashqa'i people.

Kumzari [zum]. 600 in Iran (Anonby and Yousefian 2011). Hormozgan Province, Larak island. *Status:* 8a (Moribund). See main entry on page 265.

Kurdish, Central [ckb] (Kordi, Korkora, Kurdi, Kurdy, Mokri, Mukri, Sine'i, Sorani, Wawa). 3,250,000 in Iran. Northwest, primarily Kurdestan and west Azerbaijani provinces, areas north of Kermanshah. Mukri dialect: Mahabad area; Sineyi (Sine'i) dialect: Sanandaj (Sine) area. *Status:* 3 (Wider communication). De facto provincial working language in northwest. *Dialects:* Mukri (Kordi, Mokri), Pijdari, Sanandaji (Sina'i, Sine'i, Sineyi), Southern Jafi. *Lg Use:* Mukri dialect also used as literary language similar to Central Kurdish (Sorani) literary language used in Iraqi Kurdistan (Hajo 1994). Used as L2 by Hawrami [hac]. *Lg Dev:* Taught at 2 universities. *Other:* 90% in cities or villages, 10% nomadic. Kordi may also refer to Northern Kurdish varieties (such as in Khorasan Province), and Southern Kurdish [sdh] varieties, such as Kermanshahi [sdh]. Muslim (Sunni). See main entry on page 207.

Kurdish, Northern [kmr] (Eastern Kurmanji, Kordi, Kurdi, Kurmancî, Kurmanji). 350,000 in Iran (Stanzer 1988). North and west of Lake Urmia. Some in Kalardast region, Mazandaran Province. Northern Kurdish variety of Khorasani Kurmanji is east of the Caspian Sea, in north Khorassan Province, Quchan and Bojnurd towns. *Status:* 5 (Developing). *Dialects:* Khorassani Kurmanji, Northern Kurdish (Kurmanji). *Lg Dev:* Teaching Kurdish is prohibited in Iranian schools. *Other:* Muslim (Shi'a), Muslim (Sunni). See main entry on page 305.

Kurdish, Southern [sdh]. 3,000,000 in Iran (Fattah 2000). West, Kermanshah and Ilam provinces; Eastern Iraq border provinces, including Xanaqin. Also in Iraq. *Status:* 6a (Vigorous). *Class:* Indo-European, Indo-Iranian, Iranian, Western, Northwestern, Kurdish. A member of macrolanguage Kurdish [kur] (Iraq). *Dialects:* Bayray, Feyli, Garrusi (Bijari), Kalhori, Kermanshahi (Kermanshani), Kolyai, Kordali, Luri, Malekshahi (Maleksh ay), Sanjabi. *Lg Use:* Home. Also use Persian [pes]. Also use Northern Luri [lrc]. *Lg Dev:* Bible portions: 1894–1900. *Writing:* Arabic script. *Other:* Muslim (Shi'a).

Laki [lki] (Alaki, Leki). 1,000,000 (Fattah 2000). 150,000 monolinguals. Ilam Province, western Lorestan, Aleshtar, Kuhdasht, Nurabad-e Dolfan, and Khorramabad. *Status:* 6a (Vigorous). *Class:* Indo-European, Indo-Iranian, Iranian, Western, Northwestern, Kurdish. *Dialects:* Lexical similarity: 70% with Iranian Persian [pes], 78% with Luristani (Khorramabadi), 69% with Northern Luri [lrc] (central rural dialects). *Lg Use:* Vigorous. Home. All ages. Positive attitudes. 85% also use Iranian Persian [pes]. 85% also use Northern Luri [lrc]. Used as L2 by Northern Luri [lrc]. *Lg Dev:* Poetry. Dictionary. *Writing:* Arabic script. *Other:* Muslim (Shi'a), Ahl-e Haqq.

Lari [lrl] (Larestani). 80,000, increasing. Ethnic population: 100,000. South Fars Province, Lar district; Shiraz; some in United Arab Emirates. *Status:* 6a (Vigorous). *Class:* Indo-European, Indo-Iranian, Iranian, Western, Southwestern, Fars. *Dialect:* Lari. Verbal system distinct from Iranian Persian [pes]. *Lg Use:* Vigorous. Home, commerce. Also use Gulf Spoken Arabic [afb], Iranian Persian [pes]. *Lg Dev:* Dictionary. *Other:* Muslim (Sunni), Muslim (Shi'a).

Lasgerdi [lsa] (Läsgerdi, Lasjerdi, Läsjerdi). 1,000 (2006 census). Semnan Province, southwest of Semnan, Lasjerd. *Status:* 6a (Vigorous). *Class:* Indo-European, Indo-Iranian, Iranian, Western, Northwestern, Semnani. *Lg Use:* All ages. Also use Iranian Persian [pes]. *Lg Dev:* Literacy rate in L2: 72%. Dictionary. *Other:* Muslim.

Luri, Northern [lrc] (Lori, Luristani). 1,500,000 (2001).

Ethnic population: 1,700,000 (2001). West: central and south Lorestan, north Khuzestan, and south Hamadan provinces, southern edge of Markazi Province, some regions of Ilam Province; Khorramabad, Borujerd, and Andimeshk; possibly eastern Iraq. *Status:* 6a (Vigorous). *Class:* Indo-European, Indo-Iranian, Iranian, Western, Southwestern, Luri. *Dialects:* Andimeshki, Bala-Gariva'i, Borujerdi, Cagani, Khorramabadi, Mahali (Rural Mahali), Nahavandi. Major Northern Luri dialects (Khorramabadi, Borujerdi) are found in Lorestan and Khuzestan. Some areas in Ilam Province (Posht-e Kuh) reportedly speak Northern Luri dialects. A few villages in Iraq, using a dialect of Northern Luri (Fattah 2000). Reportedly similar to Kumzari [zum]. Lexical similarity: Mahali dialect: 80% with Iranian Persian [pes], 69% with Laki [lki], and 73% with Bakhtiâri [bqi] (Haflang); Khorramabadi dialect: 85% with Iranian Persian [pes], 78% with Laki, and 75% with Bakhtiâri (Haflang). Similarity to Iranian Persian [pes] is due to lexical borrowing and language shift. *Lg Use:* Vigorous. Home, commerce. All ages. Also use Iranian Persian [pes], Laki [lki]. Used as L2 by Domari [rmt], Iranian Persian [pes], Laki [lki], Southern Kurdish [sdh]. *Lg Dev:* Poetry. Radio programs. TV. Dictionary. Grammar. *Writing:* Arabic script. *Other:* Ethnic groups: Pish-e Kuh, some parts of Posht-e Kuh. Muslim (Shi'a).

Luri, Southern [luz] (Lor, Lori, Lori-ye Jonubi, Lur). 875,000 (1999), increasing. 300,000 monolinguals. Ethnic population: 900,000. Kohgiluyeh va Boyerahmad Province. Boyerahmadi dialect: Yasuji. Kohgiluyeh dialect: east Khuzestan Province, Dehdasht; northwest Fars Province. Mamasani dialect: Nurabad. Shuli dialect: Shul, Shiraz. *Status:* 6a (Vigorous). *Class:* Indo-European, Indo-Iranian, Iranian, Western, Southwestern, Luri. *Dialects:* Boyerahmadi, Kohgiluyeh, Mamasani, Shuli, Yasuji (Yasichi). Southern Luri is on a continuum between Bakhtiari [bqi] and Iranian Persian [pes] dialects such as Bushehri and Southwestern Fars [fay]. A non-Lur tribe in Fars Province called Kurdshuli reportedly speaks a Southern Luri dialect. Their winter quarters are at Qasr-e Dasht near Sivand, 70 km from Sharaz on Shiraz-Esfahan road. Reportedly similar to Kumzari [zum]. Lexical similarity: 75% with Iranian Persian [pes], 80% with Bushehri dialect of Iranian Persian; Mamasani dialect 75% with Bakhtiâri [bqi], Boyerahmadi dialect 86% with Bakhtiâri. *Type:* SOV. *Lg Use:* Vigorous. Home, commerce, some media. All ages. 70% also use Iranian Persian [pes]. Used as L2 by Domari [rmt], Iranian Persian [pes], Kashkay [qxq]. *Lg Dev:* Literacy rate in L1: 0%. Literacy rate in L2: 60%. Poetry. Radio programs. Dictionary. Grammar. *Other:* Muslim (Shi'a).

Mandaic [mid] (Mandaean, Mandi, Mandini, Modern Mandaic, Neo-Mandaic, Sabean, Sabe'in, Subbi). 500 in Iran (2001). Ethnic population: 23,000. Khuzestan, Hoveiseh, other towns. *Status:* 7 (Shifting). *Dialects:* Ahwaz (Ahvaz), Iraqi Neo-Mandaic, Shushtar (Shustar). *Lg Use:* Ethnic group of 5,000 in Khuzestan, Iran, speak Iranian Persian [pes] (1994 H. Mutzafi). Iraqi Neo-Mandaic became extinct during the 20th century. Shushtar dialect may have no remaining speakers. Mainly older adults. Also use Iranian Persian [pes], Mesopotamian Spoken Arabic [acm]. *Other:* Ethnic Mandaeans in Iraq now speak Arabic (1994 H. Mutzafi). Assyrians in the United States report Mandaic speakers there, whom they call Yokhananaye. Mandaean. See main entry on page 207.

Mandaic, Classical [myz] (Classical Mandaean). No known L1 speakers. Also used liturgically in Iraq (Basrah) and small communities in the United States (New York) and Australia (300 Mandaeans in Sydney in 1995). *Status:* 9 (Dormant). *Class:* Afro-Asiatic, Semitic, Central, Aramaic, Eastern, Mandaic. *Dialects:* None known. Appears to be the direct ancestor of Modern Mandaic [mid]. *Lg Use:* Liturgical language used by followers of the Mandaean religion. *Writing:* Mandaic script.

Maraghei [vmh]. Upper Rudbar area (Rudbar-e Alamut). *Status:* 7 (Shifting). *Class:* Indo-European, Indo-Iranian, Iranian, Western, Northwestern, Talysh. *Dialect:* Dikini. Various other dialects. Reportedly similar to Gozarkhani [goz]. *Other:* Muslim.

Mazanderani [mzn] (Gilaki, Mazandarani, Tabri). 3,270,000 (1993), decreasing. Some monolinguals in rural areas. North near Caspian Sea, south half of Mazanderan Province. *Status:* 7 (Shifting). *Class:* Indo-European, Indo-Iranian, Iranian, Western, Northwestern, Caspian. *Dialects:* Gorgani, Mazanderani. *Lg Use:* Reportedly increased interest, but increasing desire for children to be educated and therefore be taught Iranian Persian [pes] as first language to better their opportunities. Home, market, work. Mainly adults. Neutral to positive attitudes. Many young people speak Iranian Persian [pes] as their first language; if one non-Mazandarani speaker is present, Iranian Persian is used. *Lg Dev:* Literacy rate in L1: Very low. Literacy rate in L2: Very high in Persian. The educated can read Farsi [pes] well. Radio programs. Films. TV. Grammar. *Writing:* Arabic script. *Other:* Muslim (Shi'a).

Natanzi [ntz]. 7,030 (2000). Isfahan Province, Natanz, on Isfahan-Kashan road. *Status:* 6a (Vigorous). *Class:* Indo-European, Indo-Iranian, Iranian, Western, Northwestern, Central Iran. *Dialects:* Farizandi, Natanzi, Yarani (Yarandi). *Other:* Muslim.

Nayini [nyq] (Biyabanak). 7,030 (2000). Isfahan Province, Nayin and Anarak, east of Isfahan; Khuri dialect in Khur (Khvor) and Mehrjan, northeast of Isfahan. *Status:* 6a (Vigorous). *Class:* Indo-European, Indo-Iranian, Iranian, Western, Northwestern, Central Iran. *Dialects:* Anarak, Khuri, Nayini. Dialects listed may be separate languages. Khuri distinct from other dialects. Related to Zoroastrian Dari [gbz]. *Other:* Muslim.

Parsi-Dari [prd] (Parsee, Parsee-Dari, Parsi). 350,000 (1999). Very few monolinguals. *Status:* 6a (Vigorous). *Class:* Indo-European, Indo-Iranian, Iranian, Western, Northwestern, Central Iran. *Dialects:* None known. Reportedly not inherently intelligible with Parsi [prp] of India, Pakistan, and other countries, but linguistically and ethnically related. They diverged 600 to 700 years ago or more. Related to Dari [gbz]. *Lg Use:* Little use of other languages. *Writing:* Arabic script. *Other:* 'Parsee' is ethnic group name. Zoroastrian.

Pashto, Southern [pbt] ("Afghani" *pej.*, Paktu, Pashtu). 113,000 in Iran (1993). Population does not include refugees. Khorasan on Afghanistan border east of Qa'en. *Status:* 5 (Dispersed). *Lg Use:* Also use Iranian Persian [pes]. *Other:* Different from Northern Pashto [pbu] of Pakistan and India. Muslim (Sunni). See main entry on page 50.

Persian [fas]. A macrolanguage (see page 9). *Other:* Includes: Dari [prs] (Afghanistan), Iranian Persian [pes].

Persian Sign Language [psc]. *Status:* 6a (Vigorous). *Class:* Deaf sign language. *Lg Dev:* Dictionary.

Persian, Iranian [pes] (New Persian, Parsi, Persian, West Persian). 45,000,000 in Iran (2011), increasing. 800,000 Eastern Farsi in Khorasan speak dialects which are transitional with Iranian Persian. Population total all countries: 47,045,100. Widespread. Most concentrated in central, south central, and northeast. Also in Australia, Austria, Azerbaijan, Bahrain, Canada, Denmark, France, Germany, Greece, India, Iraq, Israel, Netherlands, Oman, Qatar, Saudi Arabia, Spain, Sweden, Syria, Tajikistan,

Turkey, Turkmenistan, United Arab Emirates, United Kingdom, United States, Uzbekistan. *Status:* 1 (National). Statutory national language (1979, Constitution, Article 15). *Class:* Indo-European, Indo-Iranian, Iranian, Western, Southwestern, Persian. A member of macrolanguage Persian [fas]. *Dialects:* Abadani, Araki, Bandari, Basseri, Esfahani, Kashani, Kermani, Ketabi, Mahalhamadani, Mashadi (Meshed), Old Shirazi, Qazvini, Sedehi, Shahrudi Kazeruni, Shirazi, Shirazjahromi, Tehrani, Yazdi. Literary language virtually identical in Iran and Afghanistan, with very minor lexical differences. Dialect shading into Dari [prs] in Afghanistan and Tajiki [tgk] in Tajikistan. Many dialects may be separate languages. *Type:* SOV. *Lg Use:* Vigorous. All domains. All ages. Also use English [eng], Northern Luri [lrc], South Azerbaijani [azb], Southern Luri [luz]. *Lg Dev:* Taught in primary and secondary schools. Fully developed. Bible: 1838–1995. *Writing:* Arabic script. *Other:* Muslim (Shi'a), Baha'i, Christian.

Razajerdi [rat]. Qazvin and Kuhpayeh area, Razajerd. *Status:* 7 (Shifting). *Class:* Indo-European, Indo-Iranian, Iranian, Western, Northwestern, Talysh. *Dialects:* Various dialects. Related to Takestani [tks]. *Other:* Muslim.

Romani, Balkan [rmn]. *Status:* 7 (Shifting). *Other:* Muslim. See main entry on page 322.

Rudbari [rdb]. Sefid Rud valley. *Status:* 7 (Shifting). *Class:* Indo-European, Indo-Iranian, Iranian, Western, Northwestern, Talysh. *Dialects:* Various dialects. Transitional to Caspian languages. Related to Vafsi [vaf]. *Other:* Muslim.

Salchuq [slq]. No known L1 speakers. *Status:* 10 (Extinct). *Class:* Altaic, Turkic, Southern, Azerbaijani. *Dialects:* Probably a dialect of Azerbaijani [azb].

Sangisari [sgr] (Mahdi Shahri, Mehdishahri, Sangesari, Sängesäri, Sangsari, Sängsari, Sängsäri, Sengiseri, Sengsari). 36,000 (2006 census). Semnan Province. Shahmirzadi dialect: Shamirzad north of Mehdi. *Status:* 6a (Vigorous). *Class:* Indo-European, Indo-Iranian, Iranian, Western, Northwestern, Semnani. *Dialect:* Shahmirzadi. *Lg Use:* All ages. Positive attitudes. Also use Iranian Persian [pes]. *Lg Dev:* Literacy rate in L2: 89%. Dictionary. Grammar. *Other:* Muslim, Baha'i.

Semnani [smy] (Simnani). 60,000 (2007). Semnan Province. *Status:* 6a (Vigorous). *Class:* Indo-European, Indo-Iranian, Iranian, Western, Northwestern, Semnani. *Dialects:* Biyabunaki might be a dialect of Semnani. *Lg Use:* All ages. Positive attitudes. Also use Iranian Persian [pes]. *Lg Dev:* Literacy rate in L2: 93%. Dictionary. *Other:* Muslim.

Senaya [syn] (Christian Neo-Aramaic, Lshan Sray, Senaaya, Shan Gyanan, Shan Sray, Soray, Sray). 60 in Iran (1997 H. Mutzafi). Population total all countries: 460. Tehran and Qazvin. Originally in Kurdestan Province, Sanandaj. Also in United States. *Status:* 8b (Nearly extinct). *Class:* Afro-Asiatic, Semitic, Central, Aramaic, Eastern, Central, Northeastern. *Dialects:* None known. Qazvin variety slightly different from that spoken by Sanandaj-born people. *Lg Use:* Shifting to Assyrian Neo-Aramaic [aii]. *Writing:* Syriac script. *Other:* Christian (Chaldean).

Shahmirzadi [srz]. Semnan Province, Shahmirzad. *Status:* 6a (Vigorous). *Class:* Indo-European, Indo-Iranian, Iranian, Western, Northwestern, Caspian. *Dialects:* None known. Reportedly similar to Mazanderani [mzn] and Gilaki [glk]. *Lg Dev:* Dictionary.

Shahrudi [shm]. East Azerbaijan Province, Khalkhal district, Shahrud district, Shal, Kolur, Lerd. *Status:* 7 (Shifting). *Class:* Indo-European, Indo-Iranian, Iranian, Western, Northwestern, Talysh. *Dialects:* Reportedly similar to Kajali [kjf] and Koresh-e Rostam [okh]. Different from Sharudi, an Iranian Persian [pes] dialect. *Other:* Muslim.

Sivandi [siy]. 7,030 (2000). Fars Province, Sivand, northwest of Shiraz on Shiraz-Isfahan Road. *Status:* 7 (Shifting). *Class:* Indo-European, Indo-Iranian, Iranian, Western, Northwestern, Central Iran. *Other:* Muslim.

Soi [soj]. 7,030 (2000). *Status:* 6a (Vigorous). *Class:* Indo-European, Indo-Iranian, Iranian, Western, Northwestern, Central Iran. *Other:* Muslim.

Sorkhei [sqo]. 10,000 (2006 census). Semnan Province, Sorkheh, southwest of Semnan. *Status:* 6a (Vigorous). *Class:* Indo-European, Indo-Iranian, Iranian, Western, Northwestern, Semnani. *Dialect:* Aftari. *Lg Use:* All ages. Also use Iranian Persian [pes]. *Lg Dev:* Literacy rate in L2: 86%. Dictionary. *Other:* Muslim.

Takestani [tks] (Takistani). 220,000. Zanjan, Qazvin, and Markazi provinces, from Khalkhal to Saveh, Takestan, south and southeast. *Status:* 7 (Shifting). *Class:* Indo-European, Indo-Iranian, Iranian, Western, Northwestern, Talysh. *Dialects:* Khalkhal, Kharaqan, Ramand (Takestan), Tarom, Zanjan. Khalkhal dialect is reportedly similar to Talysh [tly]. Transitional between Talysh and Semnani [smy] languages. Similar to Eshtehardi [esh]. *Lg Use:* Also use Iranian Persian [pes]. *Other:* Different from Tat [ttt] of the Russian Federation, Azerbaijan, and Iran. Muslim.

Talysh [tly] (Talesh, Taleshi, Talish, Talishi, Talyshi). 112,000 in Iran (1993). Northwest Gilan Province, Caspian coastal plain and mountain areas from Masuleh, Masal, and Kapur-Chal (Kepri-Chal) to Azerbaijan border. Northern Talyshi dialect: Azerbaijan, Astara and the Caspian littoral areas. Central Talyshi dialect: Gilan Province, Asalem-Hashtpar area along Caspian littoral. Southern Talyshi dialect: Gilan Province, Shandermen, Masal, Masuleh, and surrounding mountainous areas. *Status:* 5 (Developing). *Dialects:* Central Talyshi, Northern Talyshi, Southern Talyshi. *Lg Use:* Also use Iranian Persian [pes]. *Other:* Muslim. See main entry on page 53.

Taromi, Upper [tov]. Zanjan Province, upper Tarom, Hazarrud, Siavarud. *Status:* 7 (Shifting). *Class:* Indo-European, Indo-Iranian, Iranian, Western, Northwestern, Talysh. *Dialects:* Various dialects. Reportedly similar to Kabatei [xkp]. *Other:* Muslim.

Tat, Muslim [ttt] (Mussulman Tati). 8,000 in Iran. *Status:* 8a (Moribund). *Other:* Different from Takestani [tks] of Iran. Muslim (Shi'a). See main entry on page 53.

Turkmen [tuk] (Torkomani). 2,000,000 in Iran (1997). Northeast, Mazanderan Province, Turkmenistan border area, Gonbad-e Kavus and Pahlavi Dezh. *Status:* 5 (Dispersed). *Dialects:* Anauli, Chavdur, Esari (Esary), Goklen (Goklan), Khasarli, Nerezim, Nokhurli (Nohur), Salyr, Saryq, Teke (Tekke), Trukmen, Yomud (Yomut). *Lg Use:* Also use Iranian Persian [pes]. *Other:* Not a literary language in Iran. Many are seminomadic. Ethnic groups: Yomut, Goklan. Muslim (Hanafi Sunni), Muslim (Shi'a). See main entry on page 307.

Vafsi [vaf]. 18,000 (2003). Markazi Province, Arak district, Vafs, near Tafresh. *Status:* 7 (Shifting). *Class:* Indo-European, Indo-Iranian, Iranian, Western, Northwestern, Central Iran. *Dialects:* Various dialects. Transitional between central Iranian dialects and Talysh [tly]; reportedly very similar to Ashtiani [atn]. *Lg Use:* Also use Iranian Persian [pes]. *Other:* Muslim.

Iraq

Republic of Iraq. 32,405,000 (2009 UNSD). Principal languages: Mesopotamian Spoken Arabic, Standard Arabic. Literacy rate: 71% (2010 UNESCO). Immigrant languages:

Egyptian Spoken Arabic (450,000), Turkish (3,000), Turkmen (227,000), Turoyo (3,000). General references: Fischer and Jastrow 1980; Jastrow 1978; Johnstone 1967; Kloss and McConnell 1974; Sebeok 1963. Deaf population: 200,000. Deaf institutions: 5.

The number of individual languages listed for Iraq is 22. All are living languages. Of these, 4 are institutional, 3 are developing, 5 are vigorous, 8 are in trouble, and 2 are dying. See map on page 350.

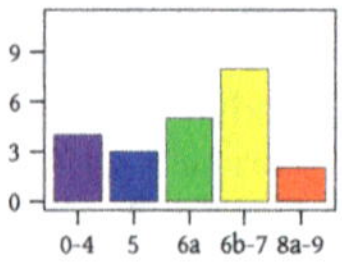

Adyghe [ady] (Adygey, West Circassian). 19,000 in Iraq (1993). *Status:* 5 (Developing). *Other:* Muslim (Sunni). See main entry on page 319.

Arabic, Gulf Spoken [afb] (Gulf Arabic, Khaliji). 40,000 in Iraq. Basra. *Status:* 6a (Vigorous). *Dialect:* Zubair-Faau Arabic. See main entry on page 213. *Map:* 350.

Arabic, Judeo-Iraqi [yhd] (Arabi, Iraqi Judeo-Arabic, Jewish Iraqi-Baghdadi Arabic, Yahudic). 120 in Iraq (1992 H. Mutzafi). *Status:* 8a (Moribund). *Lg Use:* Older adults only. *Other:* Jewish. See main entry on page 208.

Arabic, Mesopotamian Spoken [acm] (Arabic, Baghdadi, Furati, Iraqi Arabic, Mesopotamian Gelet Arabic, Mesopotamian Qeltu Arabic). 11,500,000 in Iraq. Population total all countries: 15,100,000. Tigris and Euphrates area. Also in Iran, Jordan, Syria, Turkey. *Status:* 3 (Wider communication). De facto national working language. *Class:* Afro-Asiatic, Semitic, Central, South, Arabic. A member of macrolanguage Arabic [ara] (Saudi Arabia). *Dialects:* Anatolian Cluster, Euphrates Cluster, Tigris Cluster. Geographical and sectarian divisions correlate with Iraqi dialects. The vernacular standard based on Baghdad speech. Also Bedouin dialects. Nearly unintelligible to speakers of certain other vernacular Arabic varieties. Anatolian Cluster in Turkey. *Type:* SVO. *Lg Dev:* Radio programs. TV. *Writing:* Arabic script. *Other:* Muslim (Shi'a), Christian, Jewish, Muslim (Sunni), Yezidi. *Map:* 350.

Arabic, Najdi Spoken [ars]. 900,000 in Iraq. Central Najdi dialect in western desert, used by Bedouin; North Najdi is south between the rivers up to the Syrian border. *Status:* 6a (Vigorous). *Dialects:* Central Najdi, North Najdi (Shammar). See main entry on page 293. *Map:* 350.

Arabic, North Mesopotamian Spoken [ayp] (Mesopotamian Qeltu Arabic, Moslawi, Syro-Mesopotamian Vernacular Arabic). 5,400,000 in Iraq (1992). Population total all countries: 6,300,000. Tigris, some Euphrates valleys north of Baghdad. Also in Jordan, Syria, Turkey. *Status:* 6a (Vigorous). De facto language of provincial identity in Kurdistan Region. *Class:* Afro-Asiatic, Semitic, Central, South, Arabic. A member of macrolanguage Arabic [ara] (Saudi Arabia). *Dialects:* None known. Reportedly very similar to Judeo-Iraqi Arabic [yhd], but has important sociolinguistic differences. *Writing:* Arabic script. *Other:* Muslim, Christian. *Map:* 350.

Arabic, Standard [arb]. Widespread. *Status:* 1 (National). Statutory national language (2005, Constitution, Article 4(1)). *Lg Use:* Education, official purposes. See main entry on page 293.

Armenian [hye]. 60,000 in Iraq. *Status:* 7 (Shifting). Recognized language (2005, Constitution, Article 4(1)). *Dialect:* Western Armenian. *Other:* Christian. See main entry on page 51.

Assyrian Neo-Aramaic [aii] (Aisorski, Assyrian, Assyrianci, Assyriski, Lishana Aturaya, Neo-Syriac, Sooreth, Suret, Sureth, Suryaya Swadaya). 30,000 in Iraq (1994). Population total all countries: 232,300. Ethnic population: 4,250,000 (1994). Northern Iraq, Baghdad, Basrah, Karkuk, Arbil. Also in Armenia, Austria, Azerbaijan, Belgium, Brazil, Canada, Cyprus, France, Georgia, Germany, Greece, Iran, Italy, Lebanon, Netherlands, New Zealand, Russian Federation, Sweden, Switzerland, Syria, Turkey, United Kingdom, United States. *Status:* 6b (Threatened). Recognized language (2005, Constitution, Article 4(1)), constitutional term: Syriac. Unevenly recognized except in Kurdistan Region. *Class:* Afro-Asiatic, Semitic, Central, Aramaic, Eastern, Central, Northeastern. A member of macrolanguage Syriac [syr]. *Dialects:* Central Assyrian (Anhar, Mar Bishu, Nochiya, Shamezdin, Tergawar), Northern Assyrian (Baz, Dez, Gavar, Jilu, Qudshanis, Salamas, Upper Barwari, Van), Sapna (Aradhin, Benatha, Daudiya, Inishke, Tina), Urmi Assyrian (Sipurghan, Solduz, Urmi), Western Assyrian (Lewin, Lower Barwari, Tal, Tkhuma). Similar linguistically to other Northeastern Aramaic varieties. Inherent intelligibility is difficult to estimate due to extensive exposure throughout the Assyrian diaspora to many dialects, especially Urmi and Iraqi Koine. As a result, intelligibility between dialects is as high as 80%–90%. Urmian group subdialects: Urmi, Sipurghan, Solduz; Northern Group: Salamas, Van, Jilu, Gavar, Qudshanis, Upper Barwari, Dez, Baz; Central Group: Mar Bishu, Nochiya (Shamezdin), Tergawar, Anhar; Western Group: Tkhuma, Lower Barwari, Tal, Lewin; Sapna Group: Aradhin, Tina, Daudiya, Inishke, Benatha. Standard literary Assyrian is based on Urmi. Many left original areas and developed a common spoken and written form based on the prestigious Urmi dialect as spoken in Baghdad, the United States, and elsewhere (Iraqi Koine). Most Christians understand it. This Urmi variety is different from Lishán Didán Urmi variety. All dialects of Western, Northern, and Central Assyrian are spoken in Syria. *Lg Dev:* Radio programs. Bible: 1852–1919. *Writing:* Syriac script. *Other:* Religious separation of Assyrian and Chaldean happened in the 16th century. Christian (Nestorian). *Map:* 350.

Azerbaijani, South [azb]. 600,000 in Iraq (1982). Kirkuk City, Arbil, Rowanduz; southeast from Kirkuk as far as Al Miqdadiyah, Khanaqin, and Mandali; some in Mosul area. *Status:* 5 (Developing). Recognized language (2005, Constitution, Article 4(1)), constitutional term: Turkmen. Unevenly recognized except in Kurdistan Region. *Dialect:* Kirkuk. *Lg Use:* Home. *Lg Dev:* Many read Arabic or Kurdish. Low literacy rate in South Azerbaijani. *Other:* Ethnonym: Turkmen or Turks in Iraq and Syria. Little literature. Muslim. See main entry on page 201. *Map:* 350.

Bajelani [bjm] (Bajalani, Bajoran, Bejwan, Chichamachu, Gurani). 20,000 (1976 S. Sara). Qasr-e Shirin, Zohâb, Bin Qudra, Quratu, north of Khanaqin; Mosul Province. Kurdish areas. *Status:* 7 (Shifting). *Class:* Indo-European, Indo-Iranian, Iranian, Western, Northwestern, Zaza-Gorani. *Dialects:* In the Gurani and Zaza group. Closely related to other Gurani varieties, such as Shabak, Sarli (less closely to Zaza dialects). Contact with Kurdish. *Other:* Many displaced since late 1980s. Muslim.

Chaldean Neo-Aramaic [cld] (Chaldean, Fallani, Fellihi, Kaldaya, Kildani, Lishana Kaldaya, Modern Chaldean, Neo-Chaldean, Soorath, Soorith, Suras, Sureth). 100,000 in Iraq (1994 H. Mutzafi). Population total all countries: 206,000. Mosul, Baghdad, Basrah, southeast Iraqi Kurdistan. Also in Belgium, Canada, Germany, Lebanon, Netherlands, Syria, Turkey, United States. *Status:* 7 (Shifting). Recognized language (2005, Constitution, Article 4(1)), constitutional term: Syriac. Unevenly recognized except in Kurdistan Region. *Class:* Afro-Asiatic, Semitic, Central, Aramaic, Eastern, Central, Northeastern. A member of macrolanguage Syriac [syr]. *Dialects:* Alqosh, Bartille, Dihok, Mangesh, Shirnak-Chizre (Bohtan), Tel

Kepe, Tisqopa. High intelligibility of Lishana Deni [lsd] and Ashirat [aii] (western dialect group of Assyrian Neo-Aramaic); little or no intelligibility with other Northeastern Aramaic varieties. *Lg Dev:* NT: 2006. *Writing:* Syriac script. *Other:* Ethnic group distinct religiously from other Northeastern Aramaic varieties; separated from the Assyrian in 16th century. The names Chaldean and Assyrian sometimes used in a popular sense to include both groups. Originally located in central western and northern Iraqi Kurdistan and some in bordering Turkey. Christian. *Map:* 350.

Domari [rmt] (Middle Eastern Romani). 22,900 in Iraq (2000). *Status:* 8a (Moribund). *Other:* Muslim. See main entry on page 202.

Gurani [hac] (Gorani, Hawramani, Hawrami, Hewrami, Macho, Macho-Zwani). Speakers in Iran and Iraq: 200,000–300,000 (2007 S. Paul). Population total all countries: 200,000. Near Halabja, east of Silemani (Sulaimaniya), Topzawa near Tawuq, pockets from Mosul to Khanaqin. Also in Iran (Hawrami). *Status:* 7 (Shifting). *Class:* Indo-European, Indo-Iranian, Iranian, Western, Northwestern, Zaza-Gorani. *Dialects:* Bajelani, Gorani, Kakai, Shabaki, Zengana. Zaza-Gurani group includes Southern Zazaki [diq] (Zaza) (Turkey), and Gurani [hac], Bajelani [bjm] (Bajalani), Shabak [sdb], and Sarli [sdf] (Iraq); Hawrami [hac] (Iran). *Lg Use:* Positive attitudes. Some also use Central Kurdish [ckb] (Sorani) or Arabic. *Lg Dev:* Poetry. Dictionary. *Writing:* Arabic script. *Other:* Very old literary tradition since A.D. 1300's. Muslim, Ahl-e Haqq.

Koy Sanjaq Surat [kqd] (Koi Sanjaq Soorit, Koi-Sanjaq Sooret, Koy Sanjaq Sooret, Koy Sanjaq Soorit). 800 (1995 H. Mutzafi). North, Koi-Sanjaq, Armota. *Status:* 6a (Vigorous). *Class:* Afro-Asiatic, Semitic, Central, Aramaic, Eastern, Central, Northeastern. *Dialects:* None known. Related in certain morphological and lexical respects to Senaya [syn]. *Writing:* Syriac script. *Other:* Christian. *Map:* 350.

Kurdish [kur]. A macrolanguage (see page 9). *Other:* Includes: Central Kurdish [ckb], Northern Kurdish [kmr] (Turkey), Southern Kurdish [sdh] (Iran).

Kurdish, Central [ckb] (Kurdi, Sorani). 3,500,000 in Iraq (2009). Population total all countries: 6,750,000. South of Great Zab river, Silemani (Sulaimaniya), Arbil, Kirkuk, Khanaqin, and Mandali provinces. Diaspora communities elsewhere, including western Europe and the United States. Also in Iran. *Status:* 2 (Provincial). Statutory provincial language in Kurdistan Region (2005, Constitution, Article 4(1)). *Class:* Indo-European, Indo-Iranian, Iranian, Western, Northwestern, Kurdish. A member of macrolanguage Kurdish [kur]. *Dialects:* Bingird, Garmiyani, Hewleri (Arbili), Kerkuki, Mukri, Pizhdar, Rewandiz, Suleimani (Silemani), Warmawa, Xoshnaw. In Sulaimaniya, Hewleri and Kerkuki dialects seen as mutually intelligible. *Type:* SOV; no grammatical gender or case; noun head initial; tense-split ergative pattern; 9 vowel phonemes, 31 consonant phonemes (McCarus 2009). *Lg Use:* All domains. Children learn it first. Positive attitudes. Used as L2 by Gurani [hac]. *Lg Dev:* Literary standard is based on Sorani (from Suleimaniye) variety. Taught in primary and secondary schools. Fully developed. NT: 1994–2011. *Writing:* Arabic script. *Other:* Christian, Yezidi. *Map:* 350.

Kurdish, Northern [kmr] (Badinani, Bahdini, Behdini, Kirmanciya Jori, Kurmanji). 2,800,000 in Iraq (2004). North of Great Zab river, Dohuk and Mosul provinces; Surchi dialect near Great Zab river. *Status:* 2 (Provincial). Statutory provincial language in Kurdistan Region (2005, Constitution, Article 4(1)). *Dialects:* Akre, Amadiye, Barwari Jor, Gulli, Sheikhan, Surchi, Zakho. *Lg Use:* Positive attitudes. *Other:* Surchi dialect shares elements of both Northern and Central Kurdish. Many displaced since late 1980s. Muslim (Sunni), Yezidi. See main entry on page 305. *Map:* 350.

Kurdish, Southern [sdh]. South of Xanaqin, Kirind, and Qorwaq. *Status:* 6a (Vigorous). *Dialects:* Bayray, Feyli, Kalhori, Kermanshahi (Kermanshani), Kolyai, Kordali, Luri, Maleksh ahi (Maleksh ay), Sanjabi. *Lg Use:* Home. Also use Arabic. *Other:* Muslim (Shi'a). See main entry on page 203. *Map:* 350.

Mandaic [mid] (Mandaean, Mandi, Mandini, Modern Mandaic, Neo-Mandaic, Sabean, Sabe'in, Subbi). 5,000 in Iraq (2006). Population total all countries: 5,500. Ethnic population: 30,000. Baghdad, Basra. Also in Iran, United States. *Status:* 7 (Shifting). *Class:* Afro-Asiatic, Semitic, Central, Aramaic, Eastern, Mandaic. *Dialect:* Iraqi Neo-Mandaic. *Lg Use:* Ethnic Mandaeans have shifted to Arabic as their L1 (Dimmendaal and Voeltz 2007). *Writing:* Mandaic script. *Other:* Mandaean.

Persian, Iranian [pes] (Persian). 227,000 in Iraq (1993). *Status:* 5 (Dispersed). *Other:* Muslim. See main entry on page 204.

Sarli [sdf] (Sarliya). Fewer than 20,000. Kirkuk Province, north of Mosul; many displaced. *Status:* 7 (Shifting). *Class:* Indo-European, Indo-Iranian, Iranian, Western, Northwestern, Zaza-Gorani. *Dialects:* None known. In the Gurani [hac] (Gorani) and Zaza group. Reportedly most similar to Bajelani [bjm]. *Other:* Muslim.

Shabak [sdb]. 10,000 (Blau 1989). North of Mosul, Ali Rach, Yangija, Khazna, Talara villages; many displaced since 1980s. *Status:* 7 (Shifting). *Class:* Indo-European, Indo-Iranian, Iranian, Western, Northwestern, Zaza-Gorani. *Dialects:* None known. In the Gurani [hac] (Gorani) and Zaza group. *Other:* Muslim.

Syriac [syr]. A macrolanguage (see page 9). *Other:* Includes: Assyrian Neo-Aramaic [aii], Chaldean Neo-Aramaic [cld].

Israel

State of Israel. 7,552,000 (2008 census). Principal languages: Hebrew, South Levantine Spoken Arabic, Standard Arabic. About half the Jewish people are Sephardi and half Ashkenazi. Literacy rate: 97% (2011 USDS). Immigrant languages: Egyptian Spoken Arabic (25,000), French (40,000), Italian (7,250), Levantine Bedawi Spoken Arabic (50,000), Malayalam (8,000), Marathi (8,000), North Levantine Spoken Arabic (100,000), Spanish (60,000), Standard German (200,000), Turkish (30,000). General references: Comrie 1987; Fischer and Jastrow 1980; Fishman 1985; Gold 1974; Paper 1978; Saenz-Badillos 1993. Deaf population: 4,500–306,000 (1998). Deaf institutions: 31.

The number of individual languages listed for Israel is 34. All are living languages. Of these, 6 are institutional, 7 are developing, 4 are vigorous, 12 are in trouble, and 5 are dying.

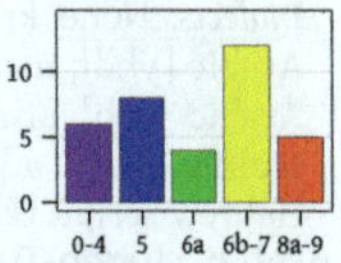

Adyghe [ady] (Adygey, West Circassian). 3,000 in Israel (1987). Kafr Kama and Rehaniya, small border villages. *Status:* 5 (Developing). *Lg Use:* Also use South Levantine Spoken Arabic [ajp]. *Other:* Came about 100 years ago from the Caucasus (now the Russian Federation). Very slight dialect differences between the 2 villages. Understand radio programs in Adyghe from Jordan. Muslim (Sunni). See main entry on page 319.

Al-Sayyid Bedouin Sign Language [syy] (ABSL). 140

(Sandler et al. 2005). L2 users: Also used by many of the 3,500 hearing people in the village; Members of the community generally recognize ABSL as L2 of the village. Negev District, Al-Sayyid village. *Status:* 6a (Vigorous). *Class:* Deaf sign language. *Dialects:* None known. Those who have any familiarity with Israeli Sign Language (ISL) [isr], including those who have attended schools for the deaf outside the village, recognize that the two sign languages are distinct. ISL signers outside the village do not understand ABSL. ABSL signers do not understand Jordanian Sign Language [jos] used on Jordanian television programs received in the area. *Lg Use:* Siblings and children of deaf individuals, and other members of a household (which may include several wives and their children) often become fluent signers. Hearing people there routinely assess their own proficiency, praising those with greater facility in the language. Positive attitudes.

Amharic [amh] ("Falasha" *pej.*). 40,000 in Israel (1994 H. Mutzafi). *Status:* 5 (Dispersed). *Lg Use:* Also use Hebrew [heb]. Used as L2 by Tigrigna [tir]. *Other:* Spoken by Jews of Ethiopian origin. Jewish. See main entry on page 319.

Arabic, Judeo-Iraqi [yhd] (Arabi, Iraqi Judeo-Arabic, Jewish Iraqi-Baghdadi Arabic, Yahudic). 100,000 in Israel (1994). Population total all countries: 151,820. Also in India, Iraq, United Kingdom. *Status:* 7 (Shifting). *Class:* Afro-Asiatic, Semitic, Central, South, Arabic. A member of macrolanguage Judeo-Arabic [jrb]. *Dialects:* None known. Reportedly not intelligible with Judeo-Tripolitanian Arabic [yud], Judeo-Tunisian Arabic [ajt], or Judeo-Moroccan Arabic [aju]. Reportedly similar to Baghdadi Arabic and North Mesopotamian Arabic [acm]. *Lg Use:* Mainly older adults. Also use Hebrew [heb]. *Writing:* Hebrew script. *Other:* The term Yahudic is used by a few scholars to denote all Judeo-Arabic languages. Jewish.

Arabic, Judeo-Moroccan [aju]. 250,000 in Israel (1992 H. Mutzafi). Population total all countries: 258,930. Also in Canada, France, Morocco. *Status:* 7 (Shifting). *Class:* Afro-Asiatic, Semitic, Central, South, Arabic. A member of macrolanguage Judeo-Arabic [jrb]. *Dialects:* Many dialects. Much intelligibility with Tunisian Judeo-Arabic [aeb], some with Judeo-Tripolitanian Arabic [yud], none with Judeo-Iraqi Arabic [yhd]. May be inherently intelligible with Moroccan Arabic [ary]. *Lg Use:* Also use Hebrew [heb]. *Lg Dev:* Radio programs. *Writing:* Hebrew script. *Other:* Many borrowings from Spanish [spa], Ladino [lad] and French [fra]. Jewish.

Arabic, Judeo-Tripolitanian [yud] (Jewish Tripolitanian-Libyan Arabic, Tripolita'it, Tripolitanian Judeo-Arabic, Yudi). 30,000 in Israel (1994 H. Mutzafi). Population total all countries: 35,000. Also in Italy. *Status:* 7 (Shifting). *Class:* Afro-Asiatic, Semitic, Central, South, Arabic. A member of macrolanguage Judeo-Arabic [jrb]. *Dialects:* None known. Not intelligible with Judeo-Iraqi Arabic [yhd]; medium intelligibility with Judeo-Tunisian Arabic [aeb] and Judeo-Morocco Arabic [aju]. *Lg Use:* Mainly older adults. Also use Hebrew [heb]. *Writing:* Hebrew script. *Other:* Jewish.

Arabic, Judeo-Tunisian [ajt]. 45,000 in Israel (1995 H. Mutzafi). Population total all countries: 45,500. Also in France, Italy, Spain, Tunisia. *Status:* 7 (Shifting). *Class:* Afro-Asiatic, Semitic, Central, South, Arabic. A member of macrolanguage Judeo-Arabic [jrb]. *Dialects:* None known. Medium intelligibility with Judeo-Moroccan Arabic [aju] and Judeo-Tripolitanian Arabic [yud], but none with Judeo-Iraqi Arabic [yhd]. A lexicon of 5,000 words in 1950 had 79% words of Arabic origin, 15% Romance loanwords, 5% Hebrew loanwords, 2% others (Cohen 1985). *Lg Use:* Mainly older adults. Also use Hebrew [heb]. *Lg Dev:* Bible portions: 1897–1937. *Writing:* Arabic script. Hebrew script, no longer in use. *Other:* Jewish.

Arabic, Judeo-Yemeni [jye] (Judeo-Yemeni, Yemenite Judeo-Arabic). 50,000 in Israel (1995 Y. Kara). Population total all countries: 51,000. Also in Yemen. *Status:* 6a (Vigorous). *Class:* Afro-Asiatic, Semitic, Central, South, Arabic. A member of macrolanguage Judeo-Arabic [jrb]. *Dialects:* 'Aden, Be:da, Habban, San'a. Jewish varieties markedly different from their coterritorial Muslim counterparts. *Writing:* Hebrew script. *Other:* Jewish.

Arabic, South Levantine Spoken [ajp] (Levantine, Palestanian-Jordanian Arabic). 910,000 in Israel. *Status:* 3 (Wider communication). De facto language of national identity. *Dialects:* Fellahi, Madani. *Lg Use:* Also use Hebrew [heb]. Used as L2 by Adyghe [ady], Armenian [hye], Domari [rmt]. *Lg Dev:* Literacy rate in L2: 90% in Arabic [arb], 60% in Hebrew [heb]. *Other:* A few hundred are of Gypsy origin. Muslim, Christian, Druze, Jewish. See main entry on page 212.

Arabic, Standard [arb]. Widespread. *Status:* 1 (National). Statutory national language (1922, Palestine Order in Council, Article 82, 10 October). *Lg Use:* Education and communication among Arabic-speaking countries. See main entry on page 293.

Armenian [hye] (Armjanski, Ermenice, Haieren, Somkhuri). 3,000 in Israel (1971). Jerusalem. *Status:* 7 (Shifting). *Dialect:* Western Armenian. *Lg Use:* Also use South Levantine Spoken Arabic [ajp]. *Other:* The Eastern Armenian dialect of Armenian [hye] is spoken in Armenia, Turkey, and Iran; Western Armenian in other countries, including Israel. Christian. See main entry on page 51.

Barzani Jewish Neo-Aramaic [bjf] (Bijil Neo-Aramaic, Lishan Didan, Lishan Dideni). 20 (2004 H. Mutzafi). In 1951, it was spoken among the 8 Jewish families of Bijil, a village in Iraqi Kurdistan. (1998 H. Mutzafi). Speaker who died in 1998 was over 80. Last Bijil dialect speaker died in 1998. *Status:* 8b (Nearly extinct). *Class:* Afro-Asiatic, Semitic, Central, Aramaic, Eastern, Central, Northeastern. *Dialects:* Barzan, Bijil, Shahe. Sandu is a Jewish Neo-Aramaic dialect closely related to Barzani, but several isoglosses link it with Lishana Deni [lsd]. *Lg Use:* All older than 70 years. Some passive users in their 50s. Also use Hebrew [heb], some also speak other Neo-Aramaic languages. Also use Kurdish [kur]. *Other:* Originally spoken in 3 villages near Aqra, Iraq. Also in Nerim village perhaps as a separate dialect.

Bukharic [bhh] (Bokharan, Bokharic, Bukharan, Bukharian, Judeo-Tajik). 50,000 in Israel (1995 H. Mutzafi). Population total all countries: 110,000. Also in United States, Uzbekistan. *Status:* 7 (Shifting). *Class:* Indo-European, Indo-Iranian, Iranian, Western, Southwestern, Persian. *Dialects:* None known. May be easily intelligible of Tajiki or Farsi [pes]. Similar to Dzhidi [jpr]. *Lg Dev:* Radio programs. *Writing:* Cyrillic script, primary usage. Hebrew script. Latin script, no longer in use. *Other:* Many recent immigrants (1995). Jewish.

Domari [rmt] (Nawari, Near-Eastern Gypsy). 2,000 in Israel (1997 Y. Matras). Mainly Jerusalem (old city), Bir Zeit near Ramallah, and Gaza. *Status:* 6a (Vigorous). *Dialect:* Nawari. *Lg Use:* All ages. Also use South Levantine Spoken Arabic [ajp]. *Other:* Many loanwords from Arabic [arb], Kurdish, and other Iranian languages. Muslim. See main entry on page 202.

Dzhidi [jpr] (Judeo-Persian). 60,000 in Israel (1995). Also in Iran. *Status:* 7 (Shifting). *Class:* Indo-European, Indo-Iranian, Iranian, Western, Southwestern, Persian. *Dialects:* None known. Reportedly similar to Bukharic [bhh] and Iranian Persian [pes]. *Lg Use:* Also use Iranian

Persian [pes]. *Writing:* Hebrew script. *Other:* Jewish.

English [eng] (Anglit). 100,000 in Israel (1993). *Status:* 3 (Wider communication). See main entry on page 319.

Hebrew [heb] (Israeli, Ivrit). 4,850,000 in Israel (1998). Spoken by all Israelis as L1 or L2. Some who use it as L1 now in Israel learned it as L2 originally. Population total all countries: 5,302,770. Also in Australia, Canada, Germany, Palestine, Panama, United Kingdom, United States. *Status:* 1 (National). Statutory national language (1922, Palestine Order in Council, Article 82, 10 October). *Class:* Afro-Asiatic, Semitic, Central, South, Canaanite. *Dialects:* Oriental Hebrew (Arabized Hebrew, Yemenite Hebrew), Standard Hebrew (Europeanized Hebrew, General Israeli). An amalgamation of different Hebrew strata plus intrinsic linguistic evolution; not a direct offspring from Biblical or other varieties of Ancient Hebrew. *Type:* SVO. *Lg Dev:* Fully developed. Bible: 1599–1877. *Writing:* Braille script. Hebrew script, primary usage. *Other:* Jewish.

Hebrew, Ancient [hbo] (Old Hebrew). No known L1 speakers. *Status:* 9 (Dormant). *Class:* Afro-Asiatic, Semitic, Central, South, Canaanite. *Lg Use:* Liturgical language; Jewish Bible text. *Lg Dev:* OT: c. 2000–400 B.C. *Writing:* Hebrew script. *Other:* Jewish.

Hulaulá [huy] ('Aramit, Galiglu, Hula Hula, Jabali, Judeo-Aramaic, Kurdit, Lishana Axni, Lishana Noshan). 10,000 in Israel (1999 H. Mutzafi). Population total all countries: 10,350. Also in Iran, United States. *Status:* 8a (Moribund). *Class:* Afro-Asiatic, Semitic, Central, Aramaic, Eastern, Central, Northeastern. *Dialects:* Kerend, Sanandaj, Saqiz, Suleimaniya. Very different and not intelligible with Senaya [syn] or Lishana Deni [lsd]. 60%–70% intelligibility of Lishanan and Lishanid Noshan [aij]. *Lg Use:* Older people also use Kurdish [kur]. Also use Hebrew [heb]. *Writing:* Hebrew script. *Other:* Originally from Iranian Kurdistan and adjoining areas of Iraq. Jewish.

Hungarian [hun]. 70,000 in Israel (1998 H. Mutzafi). *Status:* 5 (Dispersed). *Lg Use:* Older adults prefer Hungarian. Also use Hebrew [heb]. *Other:* Jewish. See main entry on page 320.

Israeli Sign Language [isr] (ISL). L2 users: 5,000 (Van Cleve 1986). Including some hearing persons. *Status:* 5 (Developing). *Class:* Deaf sign language. *Dialects:* Not derived from and relatively little influenced by other sign languages. No special signs introduced from outside by educators. Minor dialect variation. *Type:* A finger-spelling system developed in 1976. *Lg Use:* Not all deaf use ISL. Interpreters provided in courts. Some interpretation for college students. Sign language instruction for parents of deaf children. Many sign language classes for hearing people. Committee on national sign language; organization for sign language teachers. Classroom sign language and that used by deaf adults outside are different. *Lg Dev:* Films. TV. Videos. Dictionary. Grammar. *Other:* The first deaf school was established in Jerusalem in 1934. Jewish.

Jewish Babylonian Aramaic [tmr] (Babylonian Talmudic Aramaic). No known L1 speakers. *Status:* 9 (Dormant). *Class:* Afro-Asiatic, Semitic, Central, Aramaic, Eastern, Central, Northeastern. *Lg Use:* Used widely in Jewish culture and life. *Other:* Extinct around 11th or 12th century. Language of Babylonian Talmud and other sacred Jewish works. Familiar to students of Judaism in religious and scholarly realms; studied diligently by most Orthodox Jewish young men.

Judeo-Arabic [jrb]. A macrolanguage (see page 9). *Lg Use:* Used as L2 by Judeo-Berber [jbe]. *Other:* Includes: Judeo-Iraqi Arabic [yhd], Judeo-Moroccan Arabic [aju], Judeo-Tripolitanian Arabic [yud], Judeo-Tunisian Arabic [ajt], Judeo-Yemeni Arabic [jye].

Judeo-Berber [jbe]. 2,000 (1992 B. Podolsky). Formerly High Atlas range, Tifnut, other communities. *Status:* 7 (Shifting). *Class:* Afro-Asiatic, Berber, Northern, Atlas. *Lg Use:* Older adults. Also formerly used Judeo-Arabic [jrb] (Fishman 1985). *Writing:* Hebrew script. *Other:* Migrated to Israel from 1950 to 1960. Jewish.

Judeo-Georgian [jge]. 59,800 in Israel (2000). Population total all countries: 79,800. Also in Georgia. *Status:* 6a (Vigorous). *Class:* Kartvelian, Georgian. *Dialects:* Oriental and Ashkenazic Jews in Georgia live separately; Judeo-Georgian speakers live separately from non-Jewish Georgian [kat] speakers. May not be a separate language from Georgian, but a dialect using various Hebrew loanwords. *Other:* Some migrated to the Russian Federation and other countries. Jewish.

Judeo-Tat [jdt] (Bik, Dzhuhuric, Jewish Tat, Judeo-Tatic, Juhuri, "Tati" *pej.*). 70,000 in Israel (1998). Sderot, Haderah, and Or Akiva. *Status:* 5 (Developing). *Dialect:* Derbend. *Other:* 2,000 speakers a year, called Bik, emigrate from the Caucasus Mountains to Israel. Jewish. See main entry on page 321.

Ladino [lad] (Dzhudezmo, Haquetiya, Judeo Spanish, Judezmo, Sefardi, Spanyol). 100,000 in Israel (1985). Population total all countries: 112,130. Also in Greece, Puerto Rico, Turkey, United States. *Status:* 4 (Educational). *Class:* Indo-European, Italic, Romance, Italo-Western, Western, Gallo-Iberian, Ibero-Romance, West Iberian, Castilian. *Dialects:* Haquetiya (Haketia, Haketiya, Hakitia), Judezmo (Jidyo, Judyo), Ladino. The Balkan dialect is more influenced by Turkish [tur] and Greek [ell]. The North African dialect is more influenced by Arabic [arb]and French [fra]. *Lg Use:* Not the dominant language for most. Formerly the main language of Sephardic Jewry. Also use Hebrew [heb]. *Lg Dev:* New Media. Newspapers. Radio programs. Bible: 1829. *Writing:* Cyrillic script, used by Sephardic speakers in the Balkans. Hebrew script. Latin script, used in Turkey. *Other:* The name Dzhudezmo is used by Jewish linguists and Turkish Jews, Judeo-Spanish by Romance philologists, Ladino by laymen (especially in Israel), Hakitia by Moroccan Jews, Spanyol by some others. Different from Ladin [lld] in the Rhaeto-Romansch group. Jewish.

Lishán Didán [trg] (Galihalu, Lakhlokhi, Lishanán, Lishanid Nash Didán, Persian Azerbaijan Jewish Aramaic). 4,230 in Israel (2001). Population total all countries: 4,450. Jerusalem, Tel-Aviv area. Also in Azerbaijan, Georgia. *Status:* 7 (Shifting). *Class:* Afro-Asiatic, Semitic, Central, Aramaic, Eastern, Central, Northeastern. *Dialects:* Northern Cluster Lishán Didán (Anatolia, Salmas, Urmi), Southern Cluster Lishán Didán (Mahabad, Naghada, Ushno). 60%-70% intelligibility of Hulaulá [huy] and Lishanid Noshan [aij], but not of other Aramaic languages. The Urmi variety of Lishán Didán is different from the Urmi variety of Assyrian Neo-Aramaic. *Lg Use:* Older adults. Hebrew [heb] is L2. Some multilingual; many married nonspeakers. *Lg Dev:* OT. *Writing:* Hebrew script. *Other:* Many loanwords from Kurdish, Turkish [tur], Arabic, Eastern Farsi [prs] or Western Farsi [pes], Hebrew [heb], and several European languages. Glossonym: Judeo-Kurdish or Azerbaijani Kurdish, both erroneous. Originally from Iranian Azerbaijan and southeast Turkey. Jewish.

Lishana Deni [lsd] (Judeo-Aramaic, Kurdit, Lishan Hozaye, Lishan Hudaye). 7,500 (1999 H. Mutzafi). Ethnic population: 9,060. Jerusalem and vicinity, including Maoz Tsiyon. *Status:* 7 (Shifting). *Class:* Afro-Asiatic, Semitic, Central, Aramaic, Eastern, Central, Northeastern. *Dialects:*

Amadiya, Atrush, Barashe, Bétanure, Dohuk, Nerwa, Shukho, Zakho. Resembles Chaldean Neo-Aramaic [cld], but with differences in morphology and other features. Inherent intelligibility is high between them. Low intelligibility with Ashirat dialects of Assyrian New-Aramaic [aii]; not intelligible with other Neo-Aramaic varieties. *Lg Use:* The Shukho dialect probably has no remaining speakers. Older adults. *Lg Dev:* Bible portions. *Writing:* Hebrew script. *Other:* Jewish.

Lishanid Noshan [aij] (Galigalu, Hulani, Hula'ula, Jbeli, Kurdit, Lishana Didán). 2,200 (1994 H. Mutzafi). *Status:* 7 (Shifting). *Class:* Afro-Asiatic, Semitic, Central, Aramaic, Eastern, Central, Northeastern. *Dialects:* Arbel (Arbil), Dobe, Koy Sanjaq, Qaladze, Ranye, Rustaqa, Rwanduz, Shaqlawa. 60%–70% inherent intelligibility with Lishanan [lsd] and Hulaulá [huy]. Very different and not inherently intelligible with Christian Aramaic languages and Lishana Deni. Western cluster subdialects are Arbil, Dobe. Eastern cluster subdialects are Southeastern varieties: Koy Sanjaq, Qaladze. Northeastern varieties: Rwanduz, Rustaqa. *Lg Use:* Older adults. *Writing:* Hebrew script. *Other:* Jewish.

Polish [pol] (Polski). 100,000 in Israel (1992 H. Mutzafi). *Status:* 5 (Dispersed). *Lg Use:* Also use Hebrew [heb]. *Other:* Jewish. See main entry on page 321.

Romanian [ron]. 250,000 in Israel (1993 Statistical Abstract of Israel). *Status:* 5 (Dispersed). *Lg Use:* Also use Hebrew [heb]. *Other:* Jewish. See main entry on page 322.

Russian [rus] (Russit, Russki). 750,000 in Israel (1999 H. Mutzafi). *Status:* 5 (Dispersed). *Lg Use:* Also use Hebrew [heb]. *Other:* Jewish. See main entry on page 322.

Tigrigna [tir] ("Falashas" *pej.*, Tigrinya). 10,000 in Israel (1994 H. Mutzafi). *Status:* 7 (Shifting). *Lg Use:* Also use Amharic [amh], Hebrew [heb]. *Other:* The liturgy is written in Geez [gez]. Jewish. See main entry on page 323.

Yevanic [yej] (Judeo-Greek, Yevanitika). 35 in Israel. Population total all countries: 50. Also in United States. *Status:* 8b (Nearly extinct). *Class:* Indo-European, Greek, Attic. *Lg Use:* A few semispeakers in 1987 and may be none now. *Other:* Possibly also a handful of older adults in Turkey. Jewish.

Yiddish [yid]. A macrolanguage (see page 9). *Other:* Includes: Eastern Yiddish [ydd], Western Yiddish [yih] (Germany).

Yiddish Sign Language [yds]. *Status:* Unattested. *Class:* Deaf sign language. *Other:* Apparently spurious. No reliable attestation, and several knowledgeable linguists have never heard of it except in past editions of Ethnologue (2013 B. Spolsky). Jewish.

Yiddish, Eastern [ydd] (Judeo-German, Yiddish). 215,000 in Israel (1986). Population total all countries: 1,505,030. Southeastern dialect in Ukraine and Romania, Mideastern dialect in Poland and Hungary, Northeastern dialect in Lithuania and Belarus. Also in Argentina, Australia, Belarus, Belgium, Canada, Costa Rica, Latvia, Lithuania, Moldova, Panama, Poland, Puerto Rico, Romania, Russian Federation, South Africa, Sweden, Ukraine, United States, Uruguay. *Status:* 4 (Educational). *Class:* Indo-European, Germanic, West, High German, Yiddish. A member of macrolanguage Yiddish [yid]. *Dialects:* Mideastern Yiddish, Northeastern Yiddish, Southeastern Yiddish. Many loans from Hebrew [heb] and local languages. Eastern and Western [yih] Yiddish have difficult inherent intelligibility due to differing histories and influences from other languages. Some Western Yiddish [yih] in Israel (1977 M. Herzog). *Type:* SVO. *Lg Use:* Used as L2 by Western Yiddish [yih]. *Lg Dev:* Magazines. Radio programs. Bible: 1821–1936. *Writing:* Hebrew script. *Other:* Jewish.

Japan

Nipponkoku. 128,057,000 (2010 census). Principal language: Japanese. Literacy rate: 99% (2011 USDS). Immigrant languages: Chinese (150,000), English (70,000). General references: Shibatani 1990; Wurm and Hattori 1981. Deaf population: 24,000–300,000. Deaf institutions: 131.

The number of individual languages listed for Japan is 12. All are living languages. Of these, 1 is institutional, 1 is developing, 1 is vigorous, 8 are in trouble, and 1 is dying. See map on page 378.

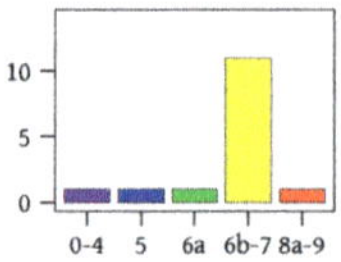

Ainu [ain] (Ainu Itak). 10 (Bradley 2007). Ethnic population: 15,000. Kuril islands (Tsishima), Hokkaido. *Status:* 8b (Nearly extinct). *Class:* Language isolate. *Dialects:* Hokkaido (Ezo, Yezo), Kuril (Shikotan, Tsishima), Sakhalin (Saghilin), Taraika. There were at least 19 dialects. *Type:* SOV. *Lg Use:* Shifting to Japanese [jpn]. Small numbers of young people are learning Ainu in classes; revival efforts underway (Bradley 2007). Fluent speakers are 80 and older; some additional semi-speakers are 60 and older (2012). *Lg Dev:* Newspapers. New media. Dictionary. NT: 1897. *Writing:* Katakana script, primary usage. Latin script. *Other:* Ainu [aib] in China is a different, unrelated language.

Amami-Oshima, Northern [ryn] (Northern Amami-Osima, Oosima, Oshima, Osima). 10,000 (2004). Northwest Okinawa; north Amami-Oshima island. *Status:* 7 (Shifting). *Class:* Japonic, Ryukyuan, Amami-Okinawan, Northern Amami-Okinawan. *Dialects:* Naze, Sani. Inherent intelligibility generally impossible, or very difficult, with Ryukyuan languages and Japanese [jpn]. *Lg Use:* Adults only. The younger the generation, the more fluently they speak Japanese [jpn] (Wurm and Hattori 1981). Those under 20 mostly monolingual in Japanese (1989 T. Fukuda). *Map:* 378.

Amami-Oshima, Southern [ams] (Southern Amami-Osima). 1,800 (2004). North Okinawa; south Amami-Oshima, Kakeroma, Yoro, and Uke islands. *Status:* 7 (Shifting). *Class:* Japonic, Ryukyuan, Amami-Okinawan, Northern Amami-Okinawan. *Dialects:* None known. Inherent intelligibility low with other Ryukyuan languages and Japanese [jpn]. *Lg Use:* Those over 50 use vernacular at home, but understand and use standard Japanese. Those 20–50 understand the vernacular, but mainly speak Japanese. Mainly older adults. *Map:* 378.

Japanese [jpn]. 121,000,000 in Japan (1985). Population figure may include other ethnic groups. Population total all countries: 122,056,940. L2 users: 1,000,000 in Japan. Widespread. Also in American Samoa, Argentina, Australia, Belize, Brazil, Canada, Hong Kong, Taiwan, Dominican Republic, Germany, Guam, Mexico, Micronesia, Mongolia, New Zealand, Northern Mariana Islands, Palau, Panama, Paraguay, Philippines, Singapore, Thailand, United Arab Emirates, United Kingdom, United States. *Status:* 1 (National). De facto national language. *Class:* Japonic. *Dialects:* Eastern Japanese, Western Japanese, Zu-zu-ben. Possibly related to Korean [kor]. Kagoshima dialect is 84% cognate with Tokyo dialect. Zu-zu-ben dialects unintelligible to other Japanese, and dying out as standard Tokyo Japanese takes over. *Type:* SOV; postpositions; demonstrative, numeral, adjective, possessive, relative clause, proper noun precedes noun head; adverb precedes verb; sentence final question particle; CV. *Lg Dev:* Taught in primary and secondary schools. Fully developed. Bible: 1883–1987. *Writing:* Braille script. Han,

Hiragana, and Katakana scripts, primary usage. *Other:* Buddhist, Shintoist. *Map:* 378.

Japanese Sign Language [jsl] (Shuwa, Temane). 317,000 (Van Cleve 1986). *Status:* 6a (Vigorous). *Class:* Deaf sign language. *Dialects:* None known. Related to Taiwanese [tss] and Korean [kvk] sign languages. *Lg Use:* Over 95% of the deaf understand Japanese Sign Language. 107 deaf schools. The first school opened in Kyoto in 1878. *Lg Dev:* TV. *Other:* 'Temane' is the former name. Pidgin Signed Japanese is distinct, and used often in formal situations, lectures, speeches, and for interaction with hearing people. 80% of the deaf understand finger spelling.

Kikai [kzg]. Ethnic population: 13,100 (2000). Those under 20 are mainly monolingual in Japanese (1989 T. Fukuda). Northeast Okinawa; Kikai island. *Status:* 7 (Shifting). *Class:* Japonic, Ryukyuan, Amami-Okinawan, Northern Amami-Okinawan. *Dialect:* Onotsu. Inherent intelligibility generally impossible or very difficult with Ryukyuan languages and Japanese [jpn]. *Lg Use:* Mainly older adults. The younger the generation, the more fluently they speak Japanese [jpn] (Wurm 1981). *Map:* 378.

Korean [kor]. 905,000 in Japan (2011 census). *Status:* 5 (Dispersed). *Lg Use:* Also use Japanese [jpn]. *Other:* Buddhist, Christian. See main entry on page 294.

Kunigami [xug]. 5,000 (2004). Central Okinawa, central and north Okinawa island; Iheya, Izena, Ie-jima, Sesoko islands. *Status:* 7 (Shifting). *Class:* Japonic, Ryukyuan, Amami-Okinawan, Southern Amami-Okinawan. *Dialect:* Nago. Inherent intelligibility generally impossible, or very difficult, of Ryukyuan languages and Japanese [jpn]. Ryukyuan languages are 62%–70% cognate with Tokyo dialect of Japanese. Lexical similarity: Ryukyu languages: 62%–70% with Tokyo dialect of Japanese. *Lg Use:* Those under 20 are mainly monolingual in Japanese (1989 T. Fukuda). Mainly older adults. The younger the generation, the more fluently they speak Japanese [jpn] (Wurm 1981). *Map:* 378.

Miyako [mvi]. Ethnic population: 67,700 (2000). Southern Okinawa; Miyako, Ogami, Ikema, Kurima, Irabu, Tarama, Minna islands. *Status:* 7 (Shifting). *Class:* Japonic, Ryukyuan, Sakishima. *Dialects:* Irabu-Jima, Miyako-Jima (Hirara, Ogami), Tarama-Minna. Not intelligible of Ryukyuan languages and Japanese [jpn]. Dialects listed have noticeable differences, but communication is not impossible. *Lg Use:* Mainly older adults. The younger the generation, the more fluently they speak Japanese [jpn] (Wurm and Hattori 1981). Those under 20 are mainly monolingual in Japanese (1989 T. Fukuda). *Lg Dev:* Dictionary. Grammar. *Map:* 378.

Okinawan, Central [ryu] (Luchu, Okinawan). 984,000 (2000). Ethnic population: 1,200,000 (2000 Yukio Uemura). Central Okinawa; southern Okinawa island, Kerama Islands, Kume-jima, Tonaki, Aguna islands, islands east of Okinawa island. *Status:* 7 (Shifting). *Class:* Japonic, Ryukyuan, Amami-Okinawan, Southern Amami-Okinawan. *Dialects:* Kudaka, Naha, Shuri, Torishima. Inherent intelligibility generally impossible, or very difficult, with Ryukyuan languages and Japanese [jpn]. Ryukyu languages are 62%–70% cognate with Tokyo dialect of Japanese [jpn]. *Lg Use:* Mainly adults. Also use Japanese [jpn]. *Lg Dev:* Dictionary. Bible portions: 1855–1858. *Writing:* Katakana script. *Map:* 378.

Oki-No-Erabu [okn]. 3,200 (2004). North central Okinawa; Oki-no-erabu island. *Status:* 7 (Shifting). *Class:* Japonic, Ryukyuan, Amami-Okinawan, Southern Amami-Okinawan. *Dialects:* East Oki-No-Erabu, West Oki-No-Erabu. Inherent intelligibility generally impossible, or very difficult, with Ryukyuan languages and Japanese [jpn]. Dialect differences noticeable, but communication not impossible. Ryukyuan languages are 62%–70% cognate with Tokyo dialect of Japanese. Ryukyu languages are 62%–70% cognate with Tokyo dialect of Japanese [jpn]. *Lg Use:* Mainly adults. Also use Japanese [jpn]. *Map:* 378.

Toku-No-Shima [tkn]. 5,100 (2004). Northern Okinawa; Toku-no-shima island. *Status:* 7 (Shifting). *Class:* Japonic, Ryukyuan, Amami-Okinawan, Northern Amami-Okinawan. *Dialect:* Kametsu. Inherent intelligibility generally impossible, or very difficult, with Ryukyuan languages and Japanese [jpn]. *Lg Use:* Younger generation has passive understanding but cannot speak it (Okamura 2010). Also use Japanese [jpn]. *Map:* 378.

Yaeyama [rys] (Yayeyama). Ethnic population: 47,600 (2000). Southern Okinawa; Ishigaki, Iriomote, Hatoma, Kohama, Taketomi, Kuroshima, Hateruma, Aregusuku islands. *Status:* 7 (Shifting). *Class:* Japonic, Ryukyuan, Sakishima. *Dialects:* Hateruma, Hatoma, Ishigaki, Kabira, Kohama, Kuroshima, Shiraho, Sonai, Taketomi. Inherent intelligibility generally impossible, or very difficult, of Ryukyuan languages and Japanese [jpn]. *Lg Use:* Mainly adults. Also use Japanese [jpn]. *Map:* 378.

Yonaguni [yoi]. 800 (2004). Southern Okinawa; Yonaguni island. *Status:* 7 (Shifting). *Class:* Japonic, Ryukyuan, Sakishima. *Dialects:* None known. Inherent intelligibility generally impossible, or very difficult, with Ryukyuan languages and Japanese [jpn]. *Lg Use:* Mainly adults. Also use Japanese [jpn]. *Map:* 378.

Yoron [yox]. 950 (2004). North central Okinawa; Yoron island. *Status:* 7 (Shifting). *Class:* Japonic, Ryukyuan, Amami-Okinawan, Southern Amami-Okinawan. *Dialects:* Inherent intelligibility generally impossible, or very difficult, with Ryukyuan languages and Japanese [jpn]. Lexical similarity: Ryukyu languages 62%–70% with Tokyo dialect of Japanese [jpn]. *Lg Use:* Mainly adults. Also use Japanese [jpn]. *Map:* 378.

Jordan

Hashemite Kingdom of Jordan. 5,104,000 (2004 census). Principal languages: South Levantine Spoken Arabic, Standard Arabic. Literacy rate: 89% (2010 UNESCO). Immigrant languages: Egyptian Spoken Arabic (10,000), Mesopotamian Spoken Arabic (500,000), North Mesopotamian Spoken Arabic (200,000), Northern Kurdish (4,000), South Azerbaijani (4,000). General references: Fischer and Jastrow 1980; Ingham 1982; Johnstone 1967; Sebeok 1963. Deaf population: 240,200. Deaf institutions: 2.

The number of individual languages listed for Jordan is 10. All are living languages. Of these, 2 are institutional, 3 are developing, 2 are vigorous, 2 are in trouble, and 1 is dying. See map on page 379.

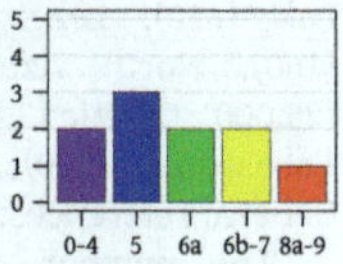

Adyghe [ady] (Adygey, West Circassian). 44,300 in Jordan (1986). *Status:* 5 (Developing). *Other:* City dwellers. Muslim (Sunni). See main entry on page 319. *Map:* 379.

Arabic, Levantine Bedawi Spoken [avl] (Bedawi). 700,000 in Jordan. Widespread but especially east. *Status:* 6a (Vigorous). *Dialects:* Eastern Egyptian Bedawi Arabic, North Levantine Bedawi Arabic, South Levantine Bedawi Arabic. *Other:* The language of Jordan before Palestinian refugees arrived. Remains the language of the army. Muslim (Sunni), Christian. See main entry on page 319 (as Arabic, Eastern Egyptian Bedawi Spoken). *Map:* 379.

Arabic, Najdi Spoken [ars]. 50,000 in Jordan. Small towns, settlements in far eastern Jordan. *Status:* 6a (Vigorous). See main entry on page 293. *Map:* 379.

Arabic, South Levantine Spoken [ajp] (Arabic, Levantine Arabic, Palestinian-Jordanian, South Levantine Arabic). 3,500,000 in Jordan (1996). Population total all countries: 6,200,000. Also in Argentina, Egypt, Israel, Kuwait, Libya, Palestine, Puerto Rico, Syria. *Status:* 3 (Wider communication). De facto national working language. *Class:* Afro-Asiatic, Semitic, Central, South, Arabic. A member of macrolanguage Arabic [ara] (Saudi Arabia). *Dialects:* Fellahi, Madani. Village to village difference of which speakers are aware. Newly emerging urban standard dialect based on Amman. *Lg Use:* Drama. *Lg Dev:* Radio programs. TV. Bible portions: 1940–1973. *Writing:* Arabic script. *Other:* Muslim, Christian. *Map:* 379.

Arabic, Standard [arb]. Widespread. *Status:* 1 (National). Statutory national language (1952, Constitution, Article 2). *Lg Use:* Use promoted for students. Regional varieties used less in schools. Official purposes, print publications, communication in Arabic-speaking countries. *Lg Dev:* Taught in primary schools. See main entry on page 293.

Armenian [hye]. 8,000 in Jordan (1971). *Status:* 7 (Shifting). *Dialect:* Western Armenian. *Other:* Christian. See main entry on page 51.

Chechen [che]. 3,000 in Jordan (Johnstone 1993). 2 or 3 villages mixed among Adyghey [ady] and Arabic speakers. *Status:* 5 (Developing). *Other:* Muslim (Sunni), Muslim (Sufi). See main entry on page 319.

Domari [rmt] (Barake, Gypsy, Kurbat, Middle Eastern Romani, Nawar, Tsigene). 4,910 in Jordan (2000). *Status:* 8a (Moribund). *Dialects:* Barake, Kurbat, Nawar. *Other:* Arabic influence. Muslim. See main entry on page 202.

Jordanian Sign Language [jos] (LIU, Lughat il-Ishaarah il-Urduniyyah). *Status:* 5 (Developing). *Class:* Deaf sign language. *Lg Dev:* Grammar.

Kabardian [kbd]. 56,000 in Jordan (2005 Circassian Association). Amman, Jerash, Sweileh, Russeifa, Zarqa. *Status:* 6b (Threatened). *Other:* Muslim (Sunni). See main entry on page 321.

Kazakhstan

Republic of Kazakhstan. 16,036,000 (2009 census). Principal languages: Kazakh, Russian. Literacy rate: 100% (2010 UNESCO). Immigrant languages: Armenian (19,000), Avar (960), Bashkort (21,400), Belarusan (183,000), Chuvash (22,900), Dargwa (640), Eastern Mari (9,090), Erzya (34,400), Georgian (7,700), Greek (47,000), Karachay-Balkar (1,460), Korean (107,000), Kumyk (550), Kyrgyz (9,610), Lak (620), Lezgi (2,570), Lithuanian (11,000), Nogai (160), North Azerbaijani (90,000), Northern Kurdish (25,000), Ossetic (3,490), Polish (61,400), Romanian (33,000), Tabassaran (220), Turkmen (3,270), Udmurt (15,800). General references: Sebeok 1963.

The number of individual languages listed for Kazakhstan is 14. All are living languages. Of these, 2 are institutional, 9 are developing, 2 are in trouble, and 1 is dying. See map on page 380.

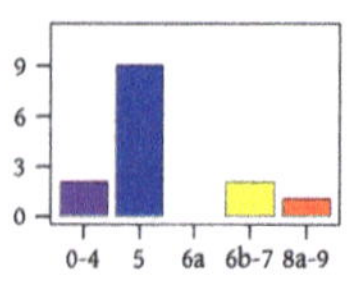

Dungan [dng]. *Status:* 7 (Shifting). *Dialect:* Shaanxi. *Other:* Came from China over 100 years ago. See main entry on page 213. *Map:* 380.

German, Standard [deu]. 958,000 in Kazakhstan. Population excludes Plautdietsch [pdt]. *Status:* 5 (Dispersed). Recognized language (1997, Language Law, No. 151-1, 11 July, Articles 4,6,7). *Lg Dev:* Found in minority schools. See main entry on page 320.

Ili Turki [ili] (Tuerke, T'urk). *Status:* 8a (Moribund). *Lg Use:* Mainly older adults. *Other:* May be none in Kazakhstan. See main entry on page 73.

Ingush [inh]. 16,900 in Kazakhstan (1999 census). *Status:* 5 (Developing). See main entry on page 321.

Kazakh [kaz] (Kaisak, Kazak, Kosach, Qazaq). 5,290,000 in Kazakhstan (1979 census). Population total all countries: 8,077,770. Also in China, Germany, Iran, Kyrgyzstan, Mongolia, Russian Federation, Tajikistan, Turkey, Turkmenistan, Ukraine, United States, Uzbekistan. *Status:* 1 (National). Statutory national language (1995, Constitution, Article 7(1)). *Class:* Altaic, Turkic, Western, Aralo-Caspian. *Dialects:* Northeastern Kazakh, Southern Kazakh, Western Kazakh. Minor dialect differences. *Type:* SOV. *Lg Use:* 98% speak Kazakh as L1. Positive attitudes. Increasing ethnic pride and feelings of Islamic brotherhood. Also use Northern Uzbek [uzn], Russian [rus]. *Lg Dev:* Increasing education in Kazakh. Newspapers. Radio programs. TV. Bible: 1820–2010. *Writing:* Arabic script, used in China and Iran. Braille script. Cyrillic script, used in Kazakhstan and Mongolia. Latin script, used in Turkey. *Other:* Seminomadic. Eastern Kirghiz and Western Kirghiz erroneously applied to Kazakh. Muslim (Sunni). *Map:* 380.

Plautdietsch [pdt] (Low German). 50,000 in Kazakhstan (1986). Alma Ata near the China border, beyond Tashkent. *Status:* 7 (Shifting). *Lg Use:* In Central Asia, the transmission of the language to children has all but stopped (Salminen 2007). 50% also use Russian [rus]. *Other:* Christian. See main entry on page 321.

Romani, Sinte [rmo] (Manouche, Manuche, Sinti, Tsigane). *Status:* 5 (Developing). *Other:* Ethnic group: Sasítka Romá. Christian. See main entry on page 322.

Russian [rus]. 6,230,000 in Kazakhstan. *Status:* 1 (National). Statutory national language (1995, Constitution, Article 7(2)). See main entry on page 322. *Map:* 380.

Tajiki [tgk]. 26,000 in Kazakhstan. *Status:* 5 (Dispersed). Recognized language (1997, Language Law, No. 151-1, 11 July, Articles 4,6,7). *Lg Dev:* Found in minority schools. See main entry on page 299.

Tatar [tat]. 328,000 in Kazakhstan. Yamal-Nenets Autonomous area. *Status:* 5 (Developing). Recognized language (1997, Language Law, No. 151-1, 11 July, Articles 4,6,7). *Lg Dev:* Found in minority schools. See main entry on page 322.

Turkish [tur]. *Status:* 5 (Dispersed). Recognized language (1997, Language Law, No. 151-1, 11 July, Articles 4,6,7). See main entry on page 306.

Ukrainian [ukr]. 898,000 in Kazakhstan. *Status:* 5 (Dispersed). Recognized language (1997, Language Law, No. 151-1, 11 July, Articles 4,6,7). *Lg Dev:* Found in minority schools. See main entry on page 323.

Uyghur [uig] (Novouygur, Uighur, Uiguir, Uygur). 300,000 in Kazakhstan (1993). Taranchi dialect in Kazakhstan; Kashgar-Yarkand in Uzbekistan. *Status:* 5 (Developing). Recognized language (1997, Language Law, No. 151-1, 11 July, Articles 4,6,7). *Dialects:* Kashgar-Yarkand, Taranchi (Kulja). *Lg Use:* 86% speak it as L1. *Lg Dev:* Found in minority schools. *Other:* Muslim (Sunni). See main entry on page 92. *Map:* 380.

Uzbek, Northern [uzn]. 332,000 in Kazakhstan. *Status:* 5 (Dispersed). Recognized language (1997, Language Law, No. 151-1, 11 July, Articles 4,6,7). *Lg Use:* Used as L2 by Kazakh [kaz]. *Lg Dev:* Found in minority schools. See main entry on page 308.

Kuwait

State of Kuwait. 3,328,000 (2008 census). Principal languages: Gulf Spoken Arabic, Standard Arabic. Literacy rate: 92% (2008 UNESCO). Immigrant languages: Egyptian Spoken Arabic (20,000), Najdi Spoken Arabic (200,000), South Levantine Spoken Arabic (85,000). General references: Holes 1990; Ingham 1982; Johnstone 1967. Deaf population: 110,300. Deaf institutions: 1.

The number of individual languages listed for Kuwait is 3. All are living languages. Of these, 2 are institutional and 1 is in trouble.

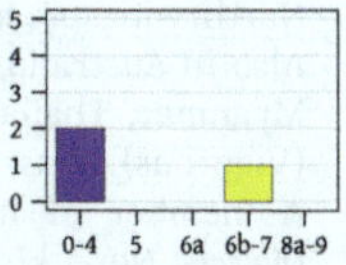

Arabic, Gulf Spoken [afb] (Khaliji). 500,000 in Kuwait (1986). Population total all countries: 2,339,000. Also in Bahrain, Iran, Iraq, Oman, Qatar, Saudi Arabia, United Arab Emirates, Yemen. *Status:* 3 (Wider communication). De facto national working language, widely used in public administration. *Class:* Afro-Asiatic, Semitic, Central, South, Arabic. A member of macrolanguage Arabic [ara] (Saudi Arabia). *Dialects:* Kuwaiti Bedouin Arabic, Kuwaiti Hadari Arabic. *Writing:* Arabic script. *Other:* Muslim.

Arabic, Standard [arb]. Widespread. *Status:* 1 (National). Statutory national language (1962, Constitution, Article 3). *Lg Use:* Education, official purposes. See main entry on page 293.

Mehri [gdq] (Mahri). 14,400 in Kuwait (2000). Scattered individuals. *Status:* 6b (Threatened). *Other:* Muslim. See main entry on page 317.

Kyrgyzstan

Kyrgyz Republic, Kyrgyzskaja Respublika. 5,327,000 (2009 census). Principal languages: Kyrgyz, Russian. Literacy rate: 99% (2009 UNESCO). Immigrant languages: Armenian (3,290), Bashkort (3,250), Belarusan (7,680), Chuvash (2,090), Crimean Tatar (38,000), Dargwa (1,420), Erzya (5,390), Georgian (1,000), Karachay-Balkar (2,460), Kazakh (37,000), Korean (18,000), Lak (260), Lezgi (1,600), Lithuanian (430), North Azerbaijani (17,200), Northern Kurdish (14,000), Romanian (1,380), Standard German (101,000), Tatar (70,000), Turkmen (350), Ukrainian (109,000), Uyghur (37,000). General references: Sebeok 1963.

The number of individual languages listed for Kyrgyzstan is 5. All are living languages. Of these, 2 are institutional, 2 are developing, and 1 is in trouble. See map on page 381.

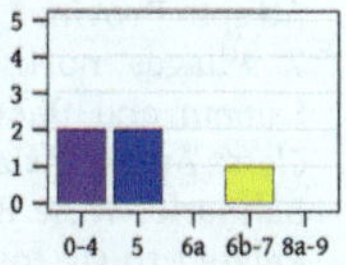

Dungan [dng] (Dzhunyan, Kwuizwu, Tungan, Zwn'jan). 40,000 in Kyrgyzstan (Johnstone and Mandryk 2001). Population total all countries: 41,900. Ethnic population: 100,000. Gansu mainly in Prschewalsk and Osh; Shaanxi in Kazakhstan, and Fergana, Uzbekistan. Also in Kazakhstan, Russian Federation, Tajikistan, Turkmenistan, Uzbekistan. *Status:* 7 (Shifting). *Class:* Sino-Tibetan, Chinese. *Dialects:* Ganzu (Gansu), Shaanxi (Shensi), Yage. Shaanxi and Ganzu varieties have difficult mutual inherent intelligibility. Debate over whether Dungan has 3 tones (a merging of 2 standard Mandarin tones) or 4 tones (with only a partial merging of the 2 standard Mandarin tones). Different from Mandarin [cmn] in phonology and lexicon. *Lg Use:* Those under 50–55 speak Russian [rus] as L1. *Lg Dev:* Bible portions: 2002–2011. *Writing:* Cyrillic script. *Other:* Came from China over 100 years ago. Muslim (Sunni). *Map:* 381.

Kyrgyz [kir] (Kara-Kirgiz, Kirghiz, Kirgiz). 2,450,000 in Kyrgyzstan (1993 UBS). Population total all countries: 2,941,930. Widespread. Also in Afghanistan, China, Kazakhstan, Russian Federation, Tajikistan, Turkey, United States, Uzbekistan. *Status:* 1 (National). Statutory national language (2010, Constitution, Art 10(1)). *Class:* Altaic, Turkic, Western, Aralo-Caspian. *Dialects:* Northern Kyrgyz, Southern Kyrgyz. *Type:* SOV. *Lg Use:* L1 for 98% of Kyrgyz. The Ichkilik are a Kyrgyz-speaking people of non-Kyrgyz origin. Also use Russian [rus]. *Lg Dev:* Schools in Kyrghyz. Newspapers. Radio programs. Films. TV. Bible: 1995–2004. *Writing:* Arabic script, used in China. Cyrillic script, not used in Afghanistan. Latin script, used in Turkey. *Other:* The names Eastern Kyrghyz and Western Kyrghyz have been erroneously applied to Kazakh. Increasing education. Muslim (Sunni), Buddhist (Lamaist). *Map:* 381.

Russian [rus]. 1,410,000 in Kyrgyzstan (1996). *Status:* 1 (National). Statutory national language (2010, Constitution, Article 10(2)). *Other:* Christian. See main entry on page 322. *Map:* 381.

Tajiki [tgk]. 34,000 in Kyrgyzstan. *Status:* 5 (Dispersed). Recognized language (2010, Constitution, Article 10(3)). See main entry on page 299.

Uzbek, Northern [uzn]. 657,000 in Kyrgyzstan (1996). *Status:* 5 (Dispersed). Recognized language (1997, Constitution, Article 10(3)). See main entry on page 308.

Laos

Lao People's Democratic Republic. 6,514,000 (2012 census). Principal language: Lao. Literacy rate: 73% (2005 UNESCO). Immigrant languages: Central Khmer (10,400), Sedang (520), Vietnamese (76,000). General references: Bradley 2007; Edmondson and Solnit 1997; Lebar, Hickey, and Musgrave 1964; Matisoff, Baron, and Lowe 1996; Thomas and Headley 1970; Wurm and Hattori 1981.

The number of individual languages listed for Laos is 86. All are living languages. Of these, 1 is institutional, 10 are developing, 50 are vigorous, 23 are in trouble, and 2 are dying. See map on page 382.

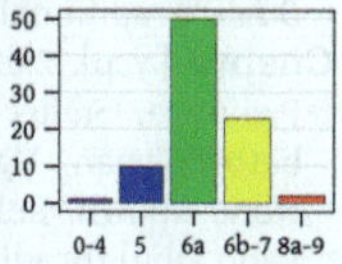

Aheu [thm] (Kha Tong Luang, Phon Soung, Phonsung, So, Thavung). 250 in Laos (Bradley 2007). Ethnic population: 500 (Bradley 2007). Bolikhamxai Province, Khamkeut district, near Lak Sao. *Status:* 6b (Threatened). *Other:* Traditional religion. See main entry on page 299. *Map:* 383:1.

Akeu [aeu] (Aki, Akui). 1,000 in Laos (1996). Phongsali Province, Gnot Ou district. *Status:* 7 (Shifting). See main entry on page 62.

Akha [ahk] (Ahka, Aini, Aka, Ak'a, Ekaw, Hka Ko, Ikaw, Ikor, Kaw, Khako, Khao Kha Ko, Ko, Yani). 66,100 in Laos (Bradley 2007). Phongsali and Loungnamtha provinces. *Status:* 5 (Developing). *Lg Use:* Used as L2 by Phana' [phq]. *Other:* Traditional religion, Christian. See main entry on page 230. *Map:* 382:2.

Alak [alk] (Harak, Hrlak). 4,000 (Bradley 2007). South, mainly Salavan and Xekong provinces. *Status:* 6a (Vigorous). *Class:* Austro-Asiatic, Mon-Khmer, Eastern Mon-Khmer, Bahnaric, Central Bahnaric. *Dialects:* None known. Reportedly similar to Bahnar [bdq], Tampuan [tpu], and Romam [rmx]. *Other:* Traditional religion. *Map:* 383:3.

Arem [aem] (Chombrau, Chomrau, Umo). 20 in Laos. Ethnic population: 500 (1995). West central, Khammouan Province, both sides of the Viet Nam-Laos border, west of Phuc Trach. *Status:* 8b (Nearly extinct). See main entry on page 309. *Map:* 383:4.

Bit [bgk] (Buxinhua, Khabit, Khbit, Pasing, Phsin, Phsing). 1,960 in Laos (2005 census). Population total all countries: 2,160. Near China border, Loungnamtha Province, northeast of Namtha district, and south of Boun Neua; Phongsali Province, Boun-Tai, Mai and Khua districts, 8 villages; Oudomxai Province, Nama district. Also in China (Buxinhua). *Status:* 6b (Threatened). *Class:* Austro-Asiatic, Mon-Khmer, Northern Mon-Khmer, Khmuic, Khao. *Dialects:* None known. Not Khmuic, but Palaungic (1990 J. Svantesson). Related to Khao [xao] in Viet Nam. *Type:* SVO; complex morphology (prefixing); attributives follow noun heads; adverbials precede verb heads; simple syllable structure; nontonal. *Other:* Traditional religion. *Map:* 382:5.

Bo [bgl]. 2,950 (2000). Central, inland from Mekong and Nhang rivers, Bolikhamxai Province, Lak Sao area; Khammouan Province, Hinboun district, Nape area. *Status:* 6a (Vigorous). *Class:* Austro-Asiatic, Mon-Khmer, Viet-Muong, Muong. *Other:* Traditional religion. *Map:* 383:6.

Bru, Eastern [bru] (Bru Tri). 26,700 in Laos (2005 census). Population total all countries: 82,300. East Savannahkhet Province, Sepone district; southeast Khammouan Province, Boulapha district. Also in Viet Nam. *Status:* 5 (Developing). *Class:* Austro-Asiatic, Mon-Khmer, Eastern Mon-Khmer, Katuic, West Katuic, Brou-So. *Dialects:* Leun (Kaleu, Leung), Tri (Chali, So Tri, So Trii). Partially intelligible with Western Bru [brv] of Thailand. The Mangkong dialect in Viet Nam and eastern Laos is a dialect of Eastern Bru, different linguistically from the Mangkong that are the same as So [sss] of Thailand. Mangkong is also an ethnic group. *Lg Use:* Also use Lao [lao]. *Lg Dev:* Literacy rate in L1: 1%–5%. Literacy rate in L2: 15%–25%. Radio programs. Dictionary. NT: 1981–2009. *Writing:* Lao script. Latin script. Thai script. *Other:* Traditional religion. *Map:* 383:10.

Chepya [ycp]. 2,000 (Bradley 2007). Northwest Phongsali Province. *Status:* 7 (Shifting). *Class:* Sino-Tibetan, Tibeto-Burman, Ngwi-Burmese, Ngwi, Southern. *Dialects:* None known. Related to Akeu [aeu]. *Lg Use:* Shifting to Lahu [lhu] (Bradley 2007).

Chut [scb] (May, Ruc, Sach, Salang). 200 in Laos (Bradley 2007). 50 May, 150 Ruc (Bradley 2007). Ethnic population: 400 (Bradley 2007). Khammouan Province, Boualapha district, near Viet Nam border. *Status:* 7 (Shifting). *Dialects:* May, Ruc. *Other:* Seminomadic. Traditional religion. See main entry on page 310. *Map:* 383:8.

Con [cno]. 1,000 (Wurm and Hattori 1981). Bokeo Province, Tonpheung district; Loungnamtha Province, southwest of Vieng Pou Kha. *Status:* 6a (Vigorous). *Class:* Austro-Asiatic, Mon-Khmer, Northern Mon-Khmer, Palaungic, Eastern Palaungic, Lametic. *Map:* 382:9.

Halang Doan [hld] (Doan, Duan, Halang Duan). 2,350 in Laos (2000). Xekong Province, Dakcheung district; Attapu Province, Kasseng plateau, Sanxai district, Kamane and Dak Robay rivers' left banks, near Viet Nam border. *Status:* 6a (Vigorous). *Other:* Traditional religion. See main entry on page 310. *Map:* 383:11.

Hani [hni] (Hanhi, Haw). 1,120 in Laos (1995). Phongsali Province, Yunnan border. *Status:* 6b (Threatened). *Other:* An official nationality in China. Traditional religion. See main entry on page 72. *Map:* 382:12.

Hmong Daw [mww] (Bai Miao, Hmong Der, Hmoob Dawb, Meo Kao, White Hmong, White Lum, White Meo, White Miao). 170,000 in Laos (1995 census). North, widespread; co-extensive with Hmong Njua [hnj]. *Status:* 5 (Developing). *Dialect:* Hmong Gu Mba (Hmong Qua Mba, Striped Hmong). *Other:* Traditional religion. See main entry on page 72. *Map:* 382:13.

Hmong Njua [hnj] (Blue Hmong, Blue Meo, Ching Miao, Green Hmong, Green Meo, Hmong Leng, Hmong Nzhua, Hmoob Leeg, Lu Miao, Meo Dam, Meo Lai, Mong Leng, Mong Ntsua, Qing Miao, Tak Miao). 100,000 in Laos (Hattaway 2000). Population total all countries: 312,020. North, widespread; co-extensive with Hmong Daw [mww]. Also in Australia, Canada, China, France, French Guiana, Myanmar, Thailand, United States, Viet Nam. *Status:* 6a (Vigorous). *Class:* Hmong-Mien, Hmongic, Chuanqiandian. A member of macrolanguage Hmong [hmn] (China). *Dialects:* None known. Speakers in Myanmar understand well border speakers in China. *Lg Dev:* Bible: 2011. *Writing:* Lao script. Latin script, primary usage. Miao (Pollard) script, used in China. Pahawh Hmong script. Thai script, used in Thailand. *Map:* 382:14.

Hung [hnu]. 2,000 in Laos (Ferlus 1996). Population total all countries: 2,700. Bolikhamxai Province, Khamkeut district; Toum dialect is northeast of Nape and south of Phong river. Also in Viet Nam. *Status:* 7 (Shifting). *Class:* Austro-Asiatic, Mon-Khmer, Viet-Muong, Cuoi. *Dialects:* Phong (Pong, Pong 1, Pong 2, Poong), Toum (Tum). *Other:* Traditional religion. *Map:* 382:15.

Ir [irr] (In, Yiir, Yir). 4,420 (2000). Salavan Province, east of Salavan town. *Status:* 6a (Vigorous). *Class:* Austro-Asiatic, Mon-Khmer, Eastern Mon-Khmer, Katuic, Central Katuic, Ta'oih. *Dialects:* None known. Reportedly most similar to Ong [oog]. *Other:* Traditional religion. *Map:* 383:16.

Iu Mien [ium] (Highland Yao, Man, Mien, Myen, Yao). 20,300 in Laos (2000). Loungnamtha, Xiagnabouli, Phongsali, and Bokeo provinces. *Status:* 5 (Developing). *Lg Use:* Some language shift. Used as L2 by Kim Mun [mji]. *Other:* Almost all Western refugees came from Laos. Daoist, traditional religion. See main entry on page 73. *Map:* 382:17.

Jeh [jeh] (Die, Gie, Yeh). 10,600 in Laos (2005 census). South, Xekong Province, Dakchung district; Attopeu Province, Sanxai district, basin of Poko, Kamane, and Dak Main rivers. *Status:* 5 (Developing). *Dialects:* Jeh Bri La, Jeh Mang Ram. *Lg Use:* Also use Lao [lao]. *Lg Dev:* Literacy rate in L1: 1%–5%. Literacy rate in L2: 15%–25%. *Other:* Traditional religion. See main entry on page 311. *Map:* 383:18.

Jeng [jeg] (Cheng, Chiengceng). 4,540 (Bradley 2007). Attapu Province, Samakkhixai and Sanamxai districts, 7 villages north of Attopeu town; Xekong Province, Lamam and Dakcheung districts. *Status:* 6a (Vigorous). *Class:* Austro-Asiatic, Mon-Khmer, Eastern Mon-Khmer, Bahnaric, West Bahnaric, Oi-The. *Dialects:* None known. Related to Oy [oyb], Sapuan [spu], and Sok [skk]. *Other:* Traditional religion. *Map:* 383:19.

Kaduo [ktp] (Khatu). 5,000 in Laos (Wurm and Hattori 1981). On China border, Phongsali Province, north of Mong Ou Tay. *Status:* 6a (Vigorous). *Other:* Different from Kadu [zkd], Western Katu [kuf]. See main entry on page 74. *Map:* 382:20.

Kang [kyp] (Tai Khang). 47,600 in Laos (1995 census). Population total all countries: 81,700. Houaphan Province, Xam-Tai district; Xiangkhoang Province, Nonghet district. Also in China. *Status:* 6a (Vigorous). *Class:* Tai-Kadai, Kam-Tai, Kam-Sui.

Kasseng [kgc] (Kaseng, Koseng, Kraseng). 1,200 (2000 D. Bradley). Ethnic population: 6,000 (2000). South, Xekong Province near Viet Nam border, Boloven plateau area and between Jeh [jeg], Alak [alk], Laven [lbo], and Tareng [tgr] language areas; into Attapu Province. *Status:* 6b (Threatened). *Class:* Austro-Asiatic, Mon-Khmer, Eastern Mon-Khmer, Katuic, East Katuic, Kaseng. *Other:* Also classified as West Bahnaric. Traditional religion. *Map:* 383:21.

Kataang [kgd] (Katang). 118,000 (2005 census). South, Savannahkhet Province, Phin and Nong districts; Salavan Province, centered in Toumlan district;. *Status:* 6a (Vigorous). *Class:* Austro-Asiatic, Mon-Khmer, Eastern Mon-Khmer, Katuic, Central Katuic, Ta'oih. *Lg Use:* Also use Lao [lao]. *Lg Dev:* Literacy rate in L1: Below 1%. Literacy rate in L2: 25%–50%. Dictionary. *Writing:* Lao script. Thai script. *Map:* 383:22.

Katu, Western [kuf]. 22,800 (2005 census). Xekong Province, upper Xe Kong river, high basin of Song Boung river watershed along the border. *Status:* 6a (Vigorous). *Class:* Austro-Asiatic, Mon-Khmer, Eastern Mon-Khmer, Katuic, East Katuic, Katu-Pacoh. *Dialects:* None known. A different language, Eastern Katu [ktv], and orthography from Viet Nam. *Writing:* Lao script. Tai Le script. *Other:* Traditional religion. *Map:* 383:71.

Khlor [llo] (Klor, Lor). 6,000 (Wurm and Hattori 1981). Salavan Province, Laongam district, south of Ir and Ong; into Xekong Province. *Status:* 6b (Threatened). *Class:* Austro-Asiatic, Mon-Khmer, Eastern Mon-Khmer, Katuic, East Katuic, Ngeq-Nkriang. *Dialects:* None known. Reportedly most similar to Ngeq [ngt]. *Lg Use:* People tending toward Lao [lao] use (2011). *Other:* Traditional religion. *Map:* 383:23.

Khmu [kjg] (Kamhmu, Kammu, Kamu, Khamu, Khamuk, Khmu', Khomu, Kmhmu, Lao Terng, Mou, Pouteng, Pu Thenh, Tenh, Theng). 614,000 in Laos (2005 census). Population total all countries: 704,000. Scattered in the north. Also in China, France, Thailand, United States, Viet Nam. *Status:* 5 (Developing). *Class:* Austro-Asiatic, Mon-Khmer, Northern Mon-Khmer, Khmuic, Mal-Khmu', Khmu'. *Dialects:* Hat, Khroong (Krong), Luang Prabang, Lyy, Rok, Sayabury, U, Yuan. There are two subgroups of Khmu in China (Damaile and Damailao), which may differ in dialect. *Type:* SVO. *Lg Dev:* Radio programs. Dictionary. Bible portions: 1918. *Writing:* Duota script, used in a small collection of villages well away from the rest of the language group, also used in China. Lao script. Latin script. *Other:* Traditional religion. *Map:* 382:24.

Khua [xhv]. 2,000 in Laos (1981). Khammouan Province, Bouarapha district, northwest of Boualapha. *Status:* 6a (Vigorous). *Other:* Different from Cua [cua]. Traditional religion. See main entry on page 312. *Map:* 383:25.

Khuen [khf] (Khouen, Khween, Kween). 8,000 in Laos (1995 L. Chazee). Population total all countries: 9,000. Loungnamtha Province, Nale, Sing, and Viangphoukha districts, near the Lamet [lbn] language area. Also in China, United States. *Status:* 6a (Vigorous). *Class:* Austro-Asiatic, Mon-Khmer, Northern Mon-Khmer, Khmuic, Mal-Khmu', Khmu'. *Writing:* Thai script. *Other:* Distinct from Kuan [uan], Khmu Keun [kjg]. Buddhist. *Map:* 382:26.

Khün [kkh]. 600 in Laos (Schliessinger 2003). Louangphabang Province, sacred temple area. *Status:* 6a (Vigorous). See main entry on page 236.

Kim Mun [mji] (Jim Mun, Lan Tin, Lanten, Lowland Yao, Man Lan-Tien, Mun). 4,500 in Laos (1995 L. Chazee). *Status:* 6a (Vigorous). *Lg Use:* Also use Iu Mien [ium], Lahu [lhu], Lao [lao]. *Other:* Daoist. See main entry on page 75.

Kiorr [xko] (Col, Con, Saamtaav, Samtao, Samtao 2). 2,360 (1985 F. Proschan). Loungnamtha and Oudomxai provinces, 6 villages. *Status:* 6a (Vigorous). *Class:* Austro-Asiatic, Mon-Khmer, Northern Mon-Khmer, Palaungic, Eastern Palaungic, Angkuic. *Other:* Buddhist. *Map:* 382:27.

Kuan [uan]. 2,500 (1995 census). Bolikhamxai Province, Viangthong district, near Muang river. *Status:* 6a (Vigorous). *Class:* Tai-Kadai, Kam-Tai, Tai. *Dialects:* None known. Not easily classified, possibly due to migration. *Other:* Traditional religion.

Kuy [kdt] (Aouei, Cuoi, Dui, Khamen-Boran, Kui, Kuoy, Old Khmer, Soai, Suai, Suay, Suei, Sui, Suoi). 42,800 in Laos (2005 census). 34,200 monolinguals. South, Savannahkhet, Salavan, and Champasak provinces; both sides of the Mekong. *Status:* 6b (Threatened). *Dialects:* Antra, Na Nhyang. *Lg Use:* Also use Lao [lao]. *Lg Dev:* Literacy rate in L1: 1%–5%. Literacy rate in L2: 37%. *Other:* Traditional religion. See main entry on page 301. *Map:* 383:28.

Lahu [lhu] (Muhso, Museu, Musso, Mussuh). 8,700 in Laos (1995 census). Bokeo Province, Peung, Tonpheung, and Houayxay districts; Loungnamtha Province, Long district. *Status:* 6a (Vigorous). *Dialects:* Na (Black Lahu, Loheirn, Musser Dam, Northern Lahu), Nyi (Luhishi, Luhushi, Musseh Daeng, Red Lahu, Southern Lahu), Shehleh. *Lg Use:* Vigorous. Used as L2 by Kim Mun [mji], Phana' [phq]. *Other:* Traditional religion, Christian. See main entry on page 76. *Map:* 382:29.

Lahu Shi [lhi] (Kui). 3,000 in Laos (2007). Bokeo Province, Kentung. *Status:* 6a (Vigorous). *Other:* Traditional religion. See main entry on page 76.

Lamet [lbn] (Kha Lamet, Khamed, Khamet, Lemet, Rmeet). 19,800 in Laos (2005 census). Population total all countries: 19,932. Northwest, Oudomxai, Loungnamtha, and Bokeo provinces. Also in Thailand, United States. *Status:* 6a (Vigorous). *Class:* Austro-Asiatic, Mon-Khmer, Northern Mon-Khmer, Palaungic, Eastern Palaungic, Lametic. *Dialects:* Lower Lamet, Upper Lamet. *Lg Use:* Also use Lao [lao]. *Lg Dev:* Literacy rate in L1: Below 1%. Literacy rate in L2: 25%–50%. *Writing:* Lao script. Latin script. *Other:* Glossonym: Lamet in Laos, Khamet in Thailand. Traditional religion. *Map:* 382:30.

Lao [lao] (Eastern Thai, Lào, Lao Kao, Lao Wiang, Lao-Lum, Lao-Noi, Lao-Tai, Laotian, Laotian Tai, Lum Lao, Phou Lao, Rong Kong, Tai Lao). 3,070,000 in Laos (2005 census). Population total all countries: 3,273,180. L2 users: 800,000 in Laos. Mekong river valley, Luang Prabang south to the Cambodia border. Lao-Khrang dialect is in Nakhonsawan and Nakhon Pathom areas. Also in Australia, Cambodia, Canada, France, Thailand, United States, Viet Nam. *Status:* 1 (National). Statutory national language (2003, Constitution, Article 89). *Class:* Tai-Kadai, Kam-Tai, Tai, Southwestern. *Dialects:* Lao-Kao, Lao-Khrang, Luang Prabang, Pakse, Savannakhet (Suwannakhet), Vientiane (Wiang Jan). Dialect subgroup with Northeastern Tai [tts] of Thailand. *Type:* SOV. *Lg Use:* Also use Lao [lao]. *Lg Dev:* Literacy rate in L1: 30%–60%. Literacy rate in L2: 50%–75%. Grammar. Bible: 1932–2012. *Writing:* Lao script. *Other:* The Lao Kao migrated to Thailand and are in Nan, Loei, Saraburi, and elsewhere. Buddhist, Christian, traditional religion. *Maps:* 382:31, 383:31.

Laopang [lbg] (Laopa). 9,550 (2000). Bokeo Province. *Status:* 6a (Vigorous). *Class:* Sino-Tibetan, Tibeto-Burman, Ngwi-Burmese, Ngwi, Unclassified. *Type:* SOV.

Laos Sign Language [lso]. *Status:* 6a (Vigorous). *Class:* Deaf sign language. *Other:* Possibly more than one language.

Lave [brb] (Brao, Braou, Brau, Brou, Laveh, Love, Proue, Rawe). 22,800 in Laos (2005 census). Population total all countries: 32,235. Attapu and Champasak provinces, Laos-Cambodia border. Also in Cambodia (Brao), France (Brao), United States (Brao), Viet Nam (Brao). *Status:* 5 (Developing). *Class:* Austro-Asiatic, Mon-Khmer, Eastern Mon-Khmer, Bahnaric, West Bahnaric, Brao-Kravet. *Dialect:* Palau. Reportedly similar to Kru'ng 2 [krr], Kavet [krv], and Sou [sqq]. *Lg Dev:* Poetry. Radio programs.

Bible portions: 2007–2011. *Writing:* Lao script. Latin script. *Other:* Glossonym: Lave in Laos. Traditional religion. *Map:* 383:32.

Laven [lbo] (Boloven, Boriwen, Jaru, Jru', Jruq, Laweenjru, Loven). 28,100 in Laos (Bradley 2007). Southwest, Champasak, Salavan, Xekong, and Attapu provinces, Boloven plateau. Also in United States. *Status:* 6a (Vigorous). *Class:* Austro-Asiatic, Mon-Khmer, Eastern Mon-Khmer, Bahnaric, West Bahnaric, Laven. *Other:* Different from Brao [brb]. Traditional religion. *Map:* 383:33.

Lü [khb] (Lu, Lue, Pai-I, Shui-Pai-I). 123,000 in Laos (2005 census). North, Phongsali, Loungnamtha, Bokeo, Oudomxai, Xiagnabouli, and Louangphabang provinces. *Status:* 6b (Threatened). *Other:* Traditional religion, Buddhist. See main entry on page 78. *Map:* 382:35.

Mal [mlf] (Htin, Khatin, Thin, Tin, T'in). 23,200 in Laos (1995 census). Population total all countries: 26,200. Xiagnabouli Province, Phiang district, west of the Mekong. Also in Thailand, United States. *Status:* 5 (Developing). *Class:* Austro-Asiatic, Mon-Khmer, Northern Mon-Khmer, Khmuic, Mal-Khmu', Mal-Phrai. *Dialects:* None known. Not intelligible with Lua' [prb], Prai [prt], or Pray 3 [pry]. *Lg Dev:* NT: 1994. *Writing:* Latin script. Thai script. *Other:* Ethnic autonym: Mal and Madl; T'in in Thailand. Traditional religion. *Map:* 382:36.

Maleng [pkt] (Malang, Malieng). 500 in Laos (Bradley 2007). Population total all countries: 700. Ethnic population: Less than 1,000 (Bradley 2007). Khammouan Province, Nakay district, Nam Theun valley, near Theun river banks. Also in Viet Nam. *Status:* 6b (Threatened). *Class:* Austro-Asiatic, Mon-Khmer, Viet-Muong, Chut. *Dialects:* Hareme, Malang, Maleng, Pakatan (Kha Pakatan). *Other:* Traditional religion. *Map:* 383:37.

Mlabri [mra] (Ma Ku, Mabri, Mla, Mla-Bri, Mrabri, Yellow Leaf, Yumbri). 24 in Laos (1985 F. Proschan). Xiagnabouli Province, Phiang district, near Thailand border. *Status:* 8a (Moribund). *Other:* Nomadic. Different from Kha Tong Luang (Phi Tong Luang, Yellow Leaf), which are Western Viet-Muong (Wurm and Hattori 1981). Traditional religion. See main entry on page 302. *Map:* 382:38.

Ngeq [ngt] (Kriang, Ngae, Nge', Ngeh, Nkriang). 12,900 (2005 census). 9,030 monolinguals. Xekong and Salavan provinces, 25 villages. *Status:* 6a (Vigorous). *Class:* Austro-Asiatic, Mon-Khmer, Eastern Mon-Khmer, Katuic, East Katuic, Ngeq-Nkriang. *Dialects:* None known. Reportedly most similar to Khlor [llo]. *Lg Use:* Also use Lao [lao]. *Lg Dev:* Literacy rate in L1: Below 1%. Literacy rate in L2: 15%–25%. Dictionary. *Writing:* Lao script. Latin script. *Other:* Ethnic autonym: Nkriang. Traditional religion, Christian. *Map:* 383:39.

Nung [nut] (Nong). A few in Laos. *Status:* 5 (Developing). *Other:* Different from Chinese Nung [yue] (Cantonese in Viet Nam). See main entry on page 313.

Nyaheun [nev] (Hin, Hoen, Hun, Nha Heun, Nia Hoen, Niahon, Nyah Heuny, Nyahön, Yaheun). 3,960 (Bradley 2007). Champasak Province, east Boloven plateau near Sekong and Paksong. *Status:* 6a (Vigorous). *Class:* Austro-Asiatic, Mon-Khmer, Eastern Mon-Khmer, Bahnaric, West Bahnaric, Nyaheun. *Lg Use:* Also use Lao [lao]. *Lg Dev:* Literacy rate in L1: Below 1%. Literacy rate in L2: 15%–25%. *Other:* Traditional religion. *Map:* 383:41.

O'du [tyh] ("Haat" *pej.*, "Hat" *pej.*, 'Iduh, Oedou, "Tay Hat" *pej.*). 650 in Laos (2005 census). Xiangkhoang Province, Khouone district, 2 villages. *Status:* 7 (Shifting). *Lg Use:* Middle-aged and older. *Other:* An official ethnic community in Viet Nam. Traditional religion. See main entry on page 313. *Map:* 382:42.

Ong [oog] (Hantong, Tong). 10,300 (2000). Champasak Province; into Salavan Province, north of Salavan town. *Status:* 7 (Shifting). *Class:* Austro-Asiatic, Mon-Khmer, Eastern Mon-Khmer, Katuic, Central Katuic, Ta'oih. *Dialects:* None known. Reportedly most similar to Ir [irr]. *Other:* Traditional religion. *Map:* 383:43.

Oy [oyb] (Huei, Oi). 11,200 (Bradley 2007). 8,960 monolinguals. Attapu Province, at the foot of Bolaven plateau, and near Pakse; Xekong Province, Thateng district. *Status:* 6a (Vigorous). *Class:* Austro-Asiatic, Mon-Khmer, Eastern Mon-Khmer, Bahnaric, West Bahnaric, Oi-The. *Dialects:* Inn Tea, Kranyeu, Riyao, Tamal Euy. Related to Jeng [jeg], Sapuan [spu], Sok [skk], and The [thx]. *Other:* Traditional religion. *Map:* 383:44.

Pacoh [pac] (Bo River Van Kieu, Pokoh). 16,500 in Laos (2005 census). 15,800 in Salavan Province. 11,600 monolinguals. Salavan Province, Samouay district; Xekong Province, Kaleum district. *Status:* 6a (Vigorous). *Dialects:* Ka'do, Pahi. *Lg Use:* Also use Lao [lao]. *Lg Dev:* Literacy rate in L1: Below 1%. Literacy rate in L2: 15%–25%. *Other:* 'Koh' in Pacoh, mountain. Traditional religion. See main entry on page 314. *Map:* 383:45.

Phana' [phq] (Bana', Pana'). 350 (1995 census). Ethnic population: Included within the Ahka [ahk] ethnic group (Bradley 2007). Phongsali Province, east of Moung Ou Tail; Loungnamtha Province, Namtha district, Bopiet and Namtoung villages; Bokeo Province, Houayxay district, 1 village. *Status:* 6a (Vigorous). *Class:* Sino-Tibetan, Tibeto-Burman, Ngwi-Burmese, Ngwi, Southern. *Dialects:* None known. Very similar to Sila [slt] (Bradley 2007). *Lg Use:* Being replaced by Lahu [lhu] in Houayxay District, by Akha [ahk] in Namtha Province (Bradley 2007). Also use Akha [ahk], Lahu [lhu]. *Other:* A larger population may be in China under Han nationality. *Map:* 382:46.

Phong-Kniang [pnx] (Keneng, Kenieng, Khaniang, Lao Phong, Pong 3). 1,000 (Wurm and Hattori 1981). South Houaphan Province, Xieng Khor and Aet districts, near Neun river; north Xiangkhoang Province. *Status:* 6a (Vigorous). *Class:* Austro-Asiatic, Mon-Khmer, Northern Mon-Khmer, Khmuic, Xinh Mul. *Lg Dev:* Many are educated. *Other:* A Phong exonym of Kniang and not to be confused with Kha Phong, a dialect of Maleng [pkt], nor with the autonym Pong as a dialect of Hung [hnu] (Ferlus 1996). Traditional religion. *Map:* 382:47.

Phu Thai [pht] (Phutai, Putai, Puthay). 187,000 in Laos (2005 census). Mainly in Bolikhamxai, Savannahkhet, and Khammouan provinces; Salavan Province, centered in Toumlan district; Xiangkhoang and Champasak provinces. *Status:* 6a (Vigorous). *Lg Use:* Also use Lao [lao]. *Other:* Traditional religion. See main entry on page 303. *Maps:* 382:48, 383:48.

Phuan [phu] (Lao Phuan, Phu Un). 106,000 in Laos (2000). Xiangkhoang Province, Phookood, Kham, and Pek districts. *Status:* 6a (Vigorous). *Other:* Name also used for Lao in Thailand. Buddhist. See main entry on page 303. *Map:* 382:49.

Phunoi [pho] (Phounoy, Phu Noi, Punoi, Sinsali). 35,600 (1995 census). North central, Phongsali Province. *Status:* 6b (Threatened). *Class:* Sino-Tibetan, Tibeto-Burman, Ngwi-Burmese, Ngwi, Southern, Bisoid. *Dialects:* Black Khoany, Hwethom, Khaskhong, Mung, White Khoany. Reportedly similar to Bisu [bzi], Pyen [pyy], and Mpi [mpz]. Listed dialects may be separate languages. *Writing:* Lao script. *Other:* Glossonym: Phunoi or Phounoy in Laos, Côông in Viet Nam. Traditional religion, Buddhist. *Map:* 382:50.

Prai [prt] (Lao Mai). 21,900 in Laos (2005 census). Xiagnabouli Province, Hongsa, Xaignabouli, Xiang Hon, and Phiang districts. *Status:* 6a (Vigorous). *Other:* Distinct from Mal [mlf]. Traditional religion. See main entry on page 303. *Map:* 382:51.

Pu Ko [puk] (Poko). Xiagnabouli Province, 2 villages. *Status:* 6b (Threatened). *Class:* Tai-Kadai, Kam-Tai, Tai, Southwestern.

Puoc [puo] (Kha Niang, Kha Puhoc, Ksing Mul, Lao Muh, Pou Hok, Puhoc, Puok, Xin Mul, Xing Mun, Xingmoun, Xinh Mul). 8,570 in Laos (2005 census). Northeast, Houaphan Province, Xiangkho district; Xieng Khouang Province, Het river, along Viet Nam border. *Status:* 6a (Vigorous). *Other:* Buddhist. See main entry on page 314. *Map:* 382:52.

Rien [rie]. 5,280 (2000). Viangchan Province. *Status:* 6a (Vigorous). *Class:* Tai-Kadai, Kam-Tai, Tai.

Saek [skb] (Sek, Set, Tai Sek). 3,730 in Laos (2005 census). Population total all countries: 14,730. Central, near Viet Nam border; Khammouan Province, Upper Nam Noy and Nam Pheo areas; Bolikhamxai Province, Khamkeut district, Na Kadok village. Also in Thailand. *Status:* 7 (Shifting). *Class:* Tai-Kadai, Kam-Tai, Tai, Northern. *Dialects:* Khammouan, Na Kadok. Reportedly similar to Tai Mène [tmp]. *Lg Use:* Also use Lao [lao]. *Other:* The Saek of Na Kadok claim to have come from Phu Quan, Ban Pho Quang, Duc Tho District, in what is now Ha Tinh Province, Viet Nam. Khammouan dialect speakers are originally from Nakai District, and it is still spoken in Toeng, Nam Meo, Na Moey, and Beuk. Traditional religion. *Map:* 383:53.

Salang [hal] (Halang). 4,000 in Laos. South, Attapu Province. *Status:* 6b (Threatened). *Lg Use:* Also use Lao [lao]. *Lg Dev:* Literacy rate in L1: 5%–10%. Literacy rate in L2: 25%–50%. *Other:* Traditional religion. See main entry on page 310 (as Halang). *Map:* 383:54.

Samtao [stu] (Samtau, Samtuan). 3,530 in Laos (2005 census). Bokeo Province, Houay Xai district. *Status:* 6a (Vigorous). See main entry on page 241. *Map:* 382:...

Sapuan [spu] (Sapouan). 2,400 (1981). South, Xekong and Champasak provinces, Se Kong and Se Kamane rivers' banks. *Status:* 6a (Vigorous). *Class:* Austro-Asiatic, Mon-Khmer, Eastern Mon-Khmer, Bahnaric, West Bahnaric, Oi-The. *Other:* Traditional religion. *Map:* 383:55.

Sila [slt] (Asong, "Kha Pai" *pej.*, Sida). 1,770 in Laos (1995 census). Most members of the ethnic group speak the language (Bradley 2007). Population total all countries: 2,480. Oudomxai Province, Namo district; Phongsali Province, Samphan, Boun Neua, and Ngot Ou. Also in Viet Nam. *Status:* 6b (Threatened). *Class:* Sino-Tibetan, Tibeto-Burman, Ngwi-Burmese, Ngwi, Southern. *Lg Use:* Negative attitudes. *Other:* Traditional religion. *Map:* 382:56.

Sô [sss] (Bru, Kah So, Makong, Mang Cong, Mangkong, Mang-Koong, Mankoong, So Makon, Thro). 118,000 in Laos (2005 census). Population total all countries: 188,000. Savannahkhet, Khammouan, and Bolikhamxai provinces. Also in Thailand. *Status:* 6a (Vigorous). *Class:* Austro-Asiatic, Mon-Khmer, Eastern Mon-Khmer, Katuic, West Katuic, Brou-So. *Dialects:* So Phong, So Slouy, So Trong. Reportedly similar to Bru [bru]. *Lg Use:* Also use Lao [lao]. *Lg Dev:* Literacy rate in L1: Below 1%. Literacy rate in L2: 15%–25%. Dictionary. Grammar. Bible portions: 1980–2004. *Writing:* Thai script. *Other:* Glossonym: Mangkong and Bru in Laos. Traditional religion. *Map:* 383:57.

Sok [skk] (Sawk, Sork). 1,600 (1981). Xekong, Champasak, and Attapu provinces. *Status:* 6a (Vigorous). *Class:* Austro-Asiatic, Mon-Khmer, Eastern Mon-Khmer, Bahnaric, West Bahnaric, Oi-The. *Map:* 383:58.

Sou [sqq] (Sawk, Souk, Su, Su', Suq). 2,360 (2000). South, Attapu Province, Phouvong and Sanamxai districts. *Status:* 6a (Vigorous). *Class:* Austro-Asiatic, Mon-Khmer, Eastern Mon-Khmer, Bahnaric, West Bahnaric, Brao-Kravet. *Other:* Traditional religion. *Map:* 383:59.

Tai Daeng [tyr] (Daeng, Red Thai, Tai Deng, Thai Dang, Thai Do). 25,000 in Laos (1991). Northeast, Houaphan Province, near Viet Nam border. *Status:* 6b (Threatened). *Other:* Part of the official Thai ethnic community in Viet Nam. Traditional religion. See main entry on page 315. *Map:* 382:60.

Tai Dam [blt] (Black Tai, Tai Noir, Thai Den). 50,000 in Laos (1995). Scattered across northern Laos to Khammouan Province. *Status:* 5 (Developing). *Dialect:* Tai Muoi (Meuay, Tai Muei, Tay Mueai). *Lg Use:* Used as L2 by Tai Dón [twh]. See main entry on page 315. *Map:* 382:61.

Tai Dón [twh] (Tai Blanc, Tai Kao, Tai Lai, Thái Tráng, White Tai). 200,000 in Laos (1995 census). Northeast, Houaphan Province; also in Phongsali Province. *Status:* 6a (Vigorous). *Lg Use:* A large influential group. Also use Tai Dam [blt]. *Other:* Traditional religion. See main entry on page 315. *Map:* 382:62.

Tai Loi [tlq] (Loi, Monglwe, Tailoi, Wakut). 500 in Laos (1995 census). Loungnamtha Province, Long district; possibly in China. *Status:* 7 (Shifting). *Dialects:* Doi, Tai Loi. *Other:* Traditional religion. See main entry on page 241. *Map:* 382:63.

Tai Long [thi]. 4,800 (2004). Louangphabang Province. *Status:* 6a (Vigorous). *Class:* Tai-Kadai, Kam-Tai, Tai, Southwestern.

Tai Mène [tmp] (Tai Maen, Tai Man, Tai Men, Tai Mene, Tai-Maen, Tay Mènè). 7,200 (1995 census). Bolikhamxai Province, Vieng Thong district; Khamkeut district, Lak Xao, Khamkeut, Na Heuang, Nam Sak, Sop Chat, Ka'ane, Phon Thoen, Sop Pone, and Tha Veng. *Status:* 6a (Vigorous). *Class:* Tai-Kadai, Kam-Tai, Tai, Northern. *Dialects:* None known. Reportedly similar to Saek [skb]. *Other:* They claim to have come from Xieng Lip and Ban Pot in Nghe An, Viet Nam. *Map:* 383:64.

Tai Nüa [tdd] (Chinese Shan, Tai Neua, Tai Nuea). 35,000 in Laos (1995 L. Chazee). Northwest, Xiangkhoang, Viangchan, Houaphan, and Bolikhamxai provinces. *Status:* 6b (Threatened). *Other:* Glossonym: Dehong Dai or Shan in China. A different dialect from that in China. Traditional religion. See main entry on page 89. *Map:* 382:65.

Tai Pao [tpo]. 3,300 (1995 census). Bolikhamxai Province, Viangthong, Khamkeut, and Pakkading districts. *Status:* 6a (Vigorous). *Class:* Tai-Kadai, Kam-Tai, Tai. *Other:* Classification unclear, possibly due to migration. Traditional religion. *Map:* 382:66.

Talieng [tdf] (Taliang, Tariang, Triang). 29,100 (2005 census). Savannahkhet Province, Phine district. *Status:* 6a (Vigorous). *Class:* Austro-Asiatic, Mon-Khmer, Eastern Mon-Khmer, Bahnaric, North Bahnaric, West. *Dialects:* None known. May be the same language as Trieng [stg]. *Other:* Apparently different from Tareng [tgr], which is East Katuic. 'Tariang', headhunters. Traditional religion. *Map:* 383:67.

Ta'oih, Lower [tto] (Tong). 15,800 (2000). Xekong Province, Kaleum district; Salavan Province, northwest of Saravan town. *Status:* 6a (Vigorous). *Class:* Austro-Asiatic, Mon-Khmer, Eastern Mon-Khmer, Katuic, Central Katuic, Ta'oih. *Dialects:* Hantong', Tong. Not intelligible of Upper Ta'oih [tth]. *Lg Use:* Also use Upper Ta'oih [tth]. *Writing:* Lao script. *Map:* 383:34.

Ta'oih, Upper [tth] (Kantua, Ta Hoi, Ta-Oi, Ta-Oy, Tau Oi). 30,900 in Laos (1995 census). Population total all countries: 49,900. 21,500 monolinguals. Salavan Province, Ta-Oy district; also in Xekong and Savannahkhet provinces. Also in United States, Viet Nam. *Status:* 6a (Vigorous). *Class:* Austro-Asiatic, Mon-Khmer, Eastern

Mon-Khmer, Katuic, Central Katuic, Ta'oih. *Dialects:* Ha'aang (Sa'ang), Kamuan', Leem, Palee'n, Pasoom. Not inherently intelligible of Lower Ta'oih [tto]. Intelligibility can be acquired after at least 2 weeks' contact. *Lg Use:* Used as L2 by Lower Ta'oih [tto]. *Writing:* Lao script. *Other:* Traditional religion. *Map:* 383:70.

Tareng [tgr] (Tariang). 5,000 (Wurm and Hattori 1981). Xekong Province, west of Viet Nam border, east of Kayong, north of Chavane and Thia. *Status:* 6a (Vigorous). *Class:* Austro-Asiatic, Mon-Khmer, Eastern Mon-Khmer, Katuic, East Katuic, Katu-Pacoh. *Other:* Distinct from Talieng [tdf], which is North Bahnaric. *Map:* 383:68.

Tay Khang [tnu]. 200. Bolikhamxai Province. *Status:* 6b (Threatened). *Class:* Tai-Kadai, Kam-Tai, Tai. *Other:* Some problem in classification and confusion with Kháng [kjm] of Viet Nam. *Map:* 382:69.

Thai, Northern [nod] (Lan Na, Lanatai, Lanna, Lannatai, Muang, Myang, "Youanne" *pej.*, "Youon" *pej.*, "Yuan" *pej.*). 29,500 in Laos (2005 census). Oudomxai and Xiagnabouli provinces. *Status:* 6a (Vigorous). *Dialect:* Nan. See main entry on page 304. *Map:* 382:40.

The [thx] (Thae). 2,920 (2000). Attapu Province. *Status:* 6a (Vigorous). *Class:* Austro-Asiatic, Mon-Khmer, Eastern Mon-Khmer, Bahnaric, West Bahnaric, Oi-The.

Yoy [yoy] (Dioi, Jui, Yoi, Yooi, Yooy). 1,000 in Laos (1995 census). Khammouan Province. *Status:* 6a (Vigorous). *Lg Use:* 100% also use Lao [lao]. *Other:* May be same as Tai Yo of Khammouan Province, a Northern Tai language. Buddhist. See main entry on page 305. *Map:* 383:72.

Lebanon

Lebanese Republic. 4,140,000 (2012 World Factbook). Principal languages: Armenian, French, North Levantine Spoken Arabic, Standard Arabic. Literacy rate: 87% (2007 UNESCO). Immigrant languages: Assyrian Neo-Aramaic (1,000), Chaldean Neo-Aramaic (18,000), Turoyo (18,000). General references: Fischer and Jastrow 1980; Fleisch 1974; Sebeok 1963. Deaf population: 12,000. Deaf institutions: 13.

The number of individual languages listed for Lebanon is 6. All are living languages. Of these, 4 are institutional and 2 are developing.

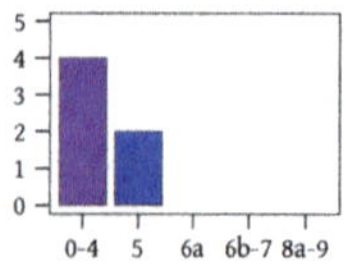

Arabic, North Levantine Spoken [apc] (Lebanese-Syrian Arabic, Levantine Arabic, Syro-Lebanese Arabic). 3,900,000 in Lebanon (1991). Widespread. *Status:* 3 (Wider communication). De facto national working language. *Dialects:* Beqaa Arabic, Iqlim-Al-Kharrub Sunni Arabic, Jdaideh Arabic, North Lebanese Arabic, North-Central Lebanese Arabic (Mount Lebanon Arabic), Saida Sunni Arabic, South Lebanese Arabic (Metuali, Shii), South-Central Lebanese Arabic (Druze Arabic), Standard Lebanese Arabic, Sunni Beiruti Arabic. *Other:* Muslim, Christian, Druze. See main entry on page 296.

Arabic, Standard [arb]. Widespread. *Status:* 1 (National). Statutory national language (1943, Constitution, Article 11). *Lg Use:* Education, print publications, official purposes, communication among Arabic speaking countries. See main entry on page 293.

Armenian [hye] (Armanski, Ermenice, Haieren, Somkhuri). 235,000 in Lebanon (1986). *Status:* 5 (Dispersed). De facto language of national identity. *Dialect:* Western Armenian. *Other:* Christian. See main entry on page 51.

English [eng]. 3,300 in Lebanon (2004). *Status:* 3 (Wider communication). *Lg Use:* Used to some extent since American University of Beirut founded in 1866. Many English language publications. Language of instruction in some schools and universities. Not spoken on the street or in Lebanese homes. See main entry on page 319.

French [fra]. 16,600 in Lebanon (2004). *Status:* 3 (Wider communication). De facto national working language. *Lg Use:* About 20% of the population speak French in their daily lives, and up to 65% of the population can read and converse in French. A number of government and private universities teach in French. *Lg Dev:* Language of instruction in many schools. Taught in primary and secondary schools. See main entry on page 320.

Kurdish, Northern [kmr]. 75,000 in Lebanon (Meho 2002). Ethnic population: 215,000. Beirut; Sidon, Tripoli, and Biqa Valley. *Status:* 5 (Developing). *Lg Dev:* Literacy rate in L1: 40%. *Other:* Muslim (Sunni). See main entry on page 305.

Macao

Macao Special Administrative Region of the People's Republic of China, Aomen Tebie Xingzhengqu, Região Administrativa Especial de Macau. As a Special Administrative Region, Macao has a significant amount of autonomy in all areas except defence and foreign affairs. 503,000 (2006 census). Principal language: Chinese. Literacy rate: 91% (2006 UNESCO. Immigrant language: English (2,790).

The number of individual languages listed for Macao is 5. All are living languages. Of these, 3 are institutional, 1 is vigorous, and 1 is dying.

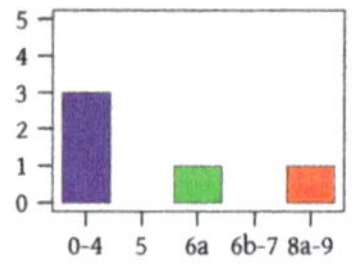

Chinese, Mandarin [cmn]. 6,660 in Macao (2001 census). *Status:* 1 (National). See main entry on page 67.

Chinese, Min Nan [nan]. 18,900 in Macao (2001 census). *Status:* 6a (Vigorous). See main entry on page 68.

Chinese, Yue [yue] (Macau Cantonese). 373,000 in Macao (2001 census). *Status:* 2 (Provincial). De facto provincial language in Macao. See main entry on page 69.

Macanese [mzs] (Macaense, Macao Creole Portuguese, Makista, Patuá). 50 in Macao (Bradley 2007). Ethnic population: 5,000 (Bradley 2007). Also in Hong Kong. *Status:* 8b (Nearly extinct). *Class:* Creole, Portuguese based. *Lg Use:* A small number of older adult women in Macau use as L1 (1996). Ages 70 and older. *Other:* A creole that blends Portuguese [por] with Cantonese [yue] and Malay, plus traces of Hindi [hin], Japanese [jpn] and the languages of other stops on Portuguese trade routes during the past few centuries.

Portuguese [por]. 2,810 in Macao (2001 census). *Status:* 2 (Provincial). Statutory provincial working language in Macao (1999, Basic Law, Article 9). See main entry on page 321.

Malaysia

Malaysia. 28,334,000 (2011 census). Principal languages: English, Mandarin Chinese, Standard Malay, Tamil. Literacy rate: 91% (2010 UNESCO). Immigrant languages: Eastern Panjabi (56,400), Malayalam (35,800), Rohingya (100,000), Sinhala (1,640), Sylheti, Telugu (39,000), Western Cham (12,000). General references: Boutin 1986; Boutin and Boutin 1985; Hudson 1978; King and King 1984; Kroeger 1985, 1986; Moody and Walton 1984; Omar 1983; Prentice 1971, 1987; Rensch 2006; Rensch et al. 2006; Salleh 2006; Soriente 2005; Wurm and Hattori 1981. Deaf population: 29,500. Deaf institutions: 5.

The number of individual languages listed for Malaysia is 95. Of these, 93 are living and 2 are extinct. Of the living languages, 9 are institutional, 5 are developing, 3 are vigorous, 65 are in trouble, and 11 are dying. See maps beginning on page 384.

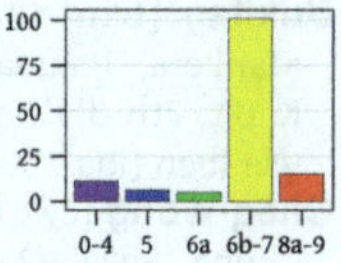

Abai Sungai [abf]. Ethnic population: 500 (2000 SIL). Sabah, lower reaches of Kinabatangan river. *Status:* 7 (Shifting). *Class:* Austronesian, Malayo-Polynesian, North Borneo, Sabahan, Paitanic. *Dialects:* None known. Distinct from other Paitanic languages (Upper Kinabatangan [dmg], Tombonuo [txa]). *Lg Use:* Shifting to Standard Malay [zsm]. Neutral attitudes. Also use Sabah Malay [msi] (Wurm 2007). *Writing:* Unwritten. *Other:* Muslim. *Map:* 386:112.

Bajau, West Coast [bdr] (Land Bajaw, West Coast Bajao, West Coast Bajaw). Ethnic population: 55,000 (2000 SIL). West coast of Sabah, Kuala Penyu to Kudat, north, some east areas. *Status:* 6b (Threatened). *Class:* Austronesian, Malayo-Polynesian, Greater Barito, Sama-Bajaw, Sulu-Borneo, Borneo Coast Bajaw. *Dialects:* Banggi, Kawang, Kota Belud, Papar, Pitas Bajau, Putatan, Sandakan Bajau. More structural diversity than other Borneo languages. Related to but distinct from East Coast Bajau languages of Malaysia and the Philippines, and Indonesian Bajau [bdl] (1977 K. Pallesen). Less than 65% intelligibility with Southern Sama [ssb]. Papar dialect used in national broadcasting. May be more than 1 language. *Lg Use:* Used as L2 by Papar [dpp]. *Lg Dev:* Radio programs. Grammar. *Writing:* Latin script, developed in about 1998. *Map:* 386:114.

Bakati', Rara [lra] (Luru). 11,300 in Malaysia (2000). Population total all countries: 23,300. Sarawak, 1st division, Lundu, Pasir river, 2 small villages. Also in Indonesia. *Status:* 6b (Threatened). *Class:* Austronesian, Malayo-Polynesian, Land Dayak, Bakati'. *Dialects:* None known. Most closely related to other Bakati' languages spoken in Kalimantan. Lexical similarity: 46%–50% with Bidayuh languages. *Lg Use:* Some young people, all adults. *Lg Dev:* Bible portions: 1989. *Writing:* Latin script. *Map:* 387:30.

Balau [blg] (Bala'u). 5,000 (Wurm and Hattori 1981). Southwest Sarawak, southeast of Simunjan. *Status:* 6b (Threatened). *Class:* Austronesian, Malayo-Polynesian, Malayo-Chamic, Malayic, Ibanic. *Dialects:* May be a dialect of Iban [iba]. *Writing:* Unwritten. *Other:* View themselves as a distinct ethnic group. *Map:* 387:36.

Banjar [bjn] (Bandjarese, Banjar Malay, Banjarese). 5,000 in Malaysia (2013 SIL). Sabah State, Tawau district. *Status:* 7 (Shifting). *Lg Use:* All adults. See main entry on page 153.

Batek [btq] (Bateg, Bateq, Batok, Kleb, Nong, Tomo). 1,000 (2006 JHEOA), decreasing. Ethnic population: 1,160 (2008 JHEOA). Peninsular, North Pahang State, Kelantan, and Terengganu. *Status:* 6b (Threatened). *Class:* Austro-Asiatic, Mon-Khmer, Aslian, North Aslian, Eastern. *Dialects:* Batek De' (Deq), Batek Iga, Batek Nong (Nong), Batek Teq (Teq). Deq and Nong dialects may be separate languages. *Lg Use:* Vigorous. All ages. Many also use Temiar [tea] (Bradley 2007). Also use Malay [msa]. *Writing:* Unwritten. *Map:* 385:10.

Belait [beg] (Lemeting, Meting). Sarawak. *Status:* 7 (Shifting). *Lg Use:* Shifting to Brunei Malay [kxd]. See main entry on page 59.

Berawan, Central [zbc] (Batu Belah, Long Teru). 1,500 (2010 SIL). North Sarawak, Batu Belah (Tutoh river) and Long Teru (Tinjar river) villages. *Status:* 8a (Moribund). *Class:* Austronesian, Malayo-Polynesian, North Borneo, North Sarawakan, Berawan-Lower Baram, Berawan, Central-East Berawan. *Dialects:* Batu Belah Berawan, Long Teru Berawan. *Lg Use:* Home, village. Older adults and elderly. *Writing:* Unwritten. *Map:* 387:60.

Berawan, East [zbe] (Long Jegan Berawan). 1,100 (2010 SIL). Sarawak, Long Jegan, Long Taveng, Long Takong, and Long Teran Batu villages. *Status:* 6b (Threatened). *Class:* Austronesian, Malayo-Polynesian, North Borneo, North Sarawakan, Berawan-Lower Baram, Berawan, Central-East Berawan. *Lg Use:* Home, village. *Writing:* Unwritten. *Map:* 387:59.

Berawan, West [zbw] (Berawan, Long Terawan). 1,000 (2010 SIL). Sarawak, Long Terawan village, Mulu town. *Status:* 6b (Threatened). *Class:* Austronesian, Malayo-Polynesian, North Borneo, North Sarawakan, Berawan-Lower Baram, Berawan. *Lg Use:* Home, church, village. *Lg Dev:* Bible portions: 2011. *Writing:* Latin script, developed in about 2003. *Map:* 387:68.

Bidayuh, Bau [sne] (Bau-Jagoi, Jaggoi, Jagoi, Sarawak Dayak). 29,200 (2000 census). Sarawak, Bau, 1st Division, Sadong, Samarahan, and Lundu rivers. About 50 villages. *Status:* 6b (Threatened). *Class:* Austronesian, Malayo-Polynesian, Land Dayak, Bidayuh, Core, Western. *Dialects:* Assem, Dongay, Empawa, Grogo (Grogoh), Gumbang, Krokong, Serambau (Serambo, Serambu), Singai (Bisingai, Singgai, Singgi, Singgie, Singhi), Stenggang Jagoi, Suti, Taup (Tahup), Tengoh. Gumbang may be more closely related to Tringgus-Sembaan [trx]. Lexical similarity: 69% with Bukar Sadong [sdo], 53% between Bukar Sadong and Singai dialect. *Lg Use:* Some young people, all adults. *Lg Dev:* Community-run play schools. Radio programs. *Writing:* Latin script, developed in about 2005. *Map:* 387:31.

Bidayuh, Biatah [bth] (Bikuab, Kuap, Quop, Sentah). 63,900 in Malaysia (2000 census). Population total all countries: 72,380. Sarawak, 1st Division, Kuching district. 10 villages. Also in Indonesia. *Status:* 6b (Threatened). *Class:* Austronesian, Malayo-Polynesian, Land Dayak, Bidayuh, Core, Central. *Dialects:* Siburan, Stang (Bisitaang, Sitaang), Tibia. Not intelligible with Bukar-Sadong Bidayuh [sdo], Salako [knx], or other Bidayuh varieties from Indonesia. Siburan is the prestige dialect. Lexical similarity: 71% with Singai dialect of Bau Bidayuh [sne]. *Lg Use:* Some young people, all adults. *Lg Dev:* Literacy rate in L2: 45%. Radio programs. NT: 1963–2003. *Writing:* Latin script, developed in about 1995. *Other:* 'Bidayuh' is a cover term for all Sarawak Land Dayak groups, plus Salako. Ethnic autonym: Siburan. *Map:* 387:33.

Bidayuh, Bukar-Sadong [sdo] (Buka, Bukar, Bukar Sadung Bidayah, Sadung, Serian, Tebakang). 49,100 in Malaysia (2000 census). Sarawak, Serian 1st division. 30 or more villages. Also in Indonesia. *Status:* 6b (Threatened). *Class:* Austronesian, Malayo-Polynesian, Land Dayak, Bidayuh, Eastern. *Dialects:* Bukar Bidayuh (Bidayah, Bidayuh, Bideyu), Bukar Sadong, Bukar Sadung Bidayuh, Mentuh Tapuh. Lexical similarity: 57% with Standard Malay [zsm]. *Lg Use:* Some young people, all adults. Used as L2 by Remun [lkj]. *Lg Dev:* Radio programs. *Writing:* Latin script, developed in about 2005. *Map:* 387:34.

Bidayuh, Tringgus-Sembaan [trx] (Tringus). 850 in Malaysia (2007 Z. Akter). Sarawak, southwest of Kuching, south of the Bau Bidayuh [sne] language area, on Kalimantan border. Also in Indonesia. *Status:* 6b (Threatened). *Class:* Austronesian, Malayo-Polynesian, Land Dayak, Bidayuh, Core, Sembaan. *Dialects:* Mbaan (Bimbaan, Sembaan), Tringgus. Each dialect has a few villages. Reportedly more similar to Biatah Bidayuh [bth] than to Bau Bidayuh [sne]. Gumbang [sne] may be a Tringgus-Sembaan Bidayuh [trx] dialect rather than a Bau Bidayuh [sne] dialect. *Writing:* Unwritten. *Other:* A different language from Tring [tgq]. *Map:* 387:32.

Bintulu [bny]. 4,200 (Wurm and Hattori 1981). Sarawak, northeast coast, Sibuti area, west of Niah; Bintulu area, and 2 enclaves west. *Status:* 6b (Threatened). *Class:* Austronesian, Malayo-Polynesian, North Borneo, North Sarawakan, Bintulu. *Dialects:* None known. Could also be classified as a Baram-Tinjar subgroup or as an isolate within the Rejang-Baram Group. *Writing:* Unwritten. *Other:* Blust classifies it as an isolate with North Sarawakan. Not similar to other languages (Blust 1974). *Map:* 387:43.

Bisaya, Brunei [bsb] (Bekiau, Bisaya Bukit, Bisayah, Lorang Bukit, Visayak). 20,000 in Malaysia (2007 SIL). Sarawak, Limbang, and Lawas districts. *Status:* 6b (Threatened). *Dialects:* Sarawak Bisaya (Bisaya'), Tutong 1. See main entry on page 59. *Map:* 387:66.

Bisaya, Sabah [bsy] (Basaya, Besaya, Bisaia, Bisayah, Jilama Bawang, Jilama Sungai). Ethnic population: 15,800 (2000). Sabah, north Brunei Bay coast area, mainly west Beaufort along Padas river, south of Weston; south Kuala Penyu district to the coast. *Status:* 6b (Threatened). *Class:* Austronesian, Malayo-Polynesian, North Borneo, Sabahan, Dusunic, Bisaya. *Dialects:* 90% intelligibility of Tatana [txx]. Lexical similarity: with dialects of Brunei Bisaya [bsb]: 58% with Sarawak dialect and 57%–59% with Brunei dialect. *Lg Use:* Neutral attitudes. Used as L2 by Papar [dpp]. *Lg Dev:* Bible portions: 1938. *Writing:* Latin script, no longer in use. *Map:* 386:77.

Bonggi [bdg] (Bangay, Banggi, Banggi Dusun). Ethnic population: 1,400 (1990 UBS). Sabah, Kudat district, Banggi island. 15 villages. *Status:* 6b (Threatened). *Class:* Austronesian, Malayo-Polynesian, North Borneo, Sabahan, Dusunic, Bisaya. *Dialects:* Reportedly most similar to Molbog [pwm] of the Philippines. Lexical similarity with dialects of Brunei Bisaya [bsb]: 58% with Sarawak dialect and 57%–59% with Brunei dialect. *Lg Use:* Also use Sabah Malay [msi]. *Lg Dev:* Bible portions: 1992. *Writing:* Latin script, used from about 1987 to 2001. *Map:* 386:103.

Bookan [bnb] (Baukan, Baukan Murut). Ethnic population: 1,700 (2000 SIL). Sabah, Keningau and Kinabatangan districts, Sook and Kinabatangan rivers' headwaters area. *Status:* 6b (Threatened). *Class:* Austronesian, Malayo-Polynesian, North Borneo, North Sarawakan, Dayic, Murutic, Northern. *Dialects:* Baukan (Baokan, Bokan, Boken, Bokon, Bokun, Bookan, Bukun, Pingas, Ulun-No-Bokan, Ulun-No-Bokon), Kokoroton Murut, Tengara (Kinabatangan Murut, Tangara', Tanggaraq, Tenggaraq, Tingara, Tungara). Reportedly similar to Keningau Murut [kxi], Timugon [tih], and Tagal [mvv]. *Writing:* Latin script, developed in about 2003 till about 2005. *Map:* 386:80.

Brunei [kxd] (Brunei-Kadaian, Orang Bukit). 51,000 in Malaysia (2013 SIL). Sarawak, 4th, 5th divisions, Upper Balait and Tutau rivers, north coast; Sabah, Beaufort, Kuala Penyu, Putatan, and Kota Kinabalu districts; Labuan, Labuk-Sugut, Papar, Sipitang, Sandakan, and Tenom districts. *Status:* 7 (Shifting). *Dialects:* Brunei, Kadaian (Kadayan, Kadian, Kadien, Kadyan, Karayan, Kedayan, Kedien, Kedyan, Kerayan). *Lg Use:* All adults. Also use Malay [zlm]. Used as L2 by Papar [dpp]. *Other:* Regional, not ethnic, dialect variations. See main entry on page 59. *Maps:* 386:63, 387:63.

Bugis [bug] (Buginese). 17,800 in Malaysia (2000 SIL). Sabah. *Status:* 7 (Shifting). *Lg Use:* All adults. See main entry on page 156.

Bukitan [bkn] (Bakatan, Bakitan, Beketan, Mangkettan, Manketa, Pakatan). 290 in Malaysia (2000). Sarawak, Kapit, 7th division. *Status:* 6b (Threatened). *Lg Use:* Also use Iban [iba]. See main entry on page 156. *Map:* 387:45.

Cheq Wong [cwg] (Beri, Ceq Wong, Che Wong, Che'wong, Chuba, Siwang). 460 (2008 JHEOA). Peninsular, Pahang State, just south of Semai. *Status:* 6b (Threatened). *Class:* Austro-Asiatic, Mon-Khmer, Aslian, North Aslian, Chewong. *Lg Use:* Increasing exposure to Standard Malay [zsm], schooling in Standard Malay for the children. Also use Malay [zlm]. *Writing:* Unwritten. *Map:* 385:13.

Chinese, Hakka [hak]. 1,090,000 in Malaysia (2000). Peninsular. *Status:* 6b (Threatened). *Lg Use:* Stronger in Sabah, weakening in Semenanjung. See main entry on page 67.

Chinese, Mandarin [cmn]. Recent census figures do not detail the number of Mandarin speakers. Peninsular, Sabah, and Sarawak. *Status:* 1 (National). Statutory national working language (1996, Education Act, No. 550, Articles 2 and 18). *Lg Use:* Positive attitudes. *Lg Dev:* Taught in primary and secondary schools. *Other:* Primarily urban, in commerce. See main entry on page 67.

Chinese, Min Dong [cdo]. 252,000 in Malaysia (2004). Sarawak, mostly in Sibu, Sarikei, Bintangor towns. *Status:* 6b (Threatened). *Dialect:* Foochow (Fuzhou). *Lg Use:* Some young people, all adults. See main entry on page 68.

Chinese, Min Nan [nan] (Min Nan, Minnan). 2,660,000 in Malaysia (2000). 497,000 Teochew, 141,000 Hainanese, 2,020,000 Hokkien (2000). The population figures given here are for Peninuslar Malaysia only. The corresponding figures for Sabah and Sarawak are not currently available. Peninsular. *Status:* 6a (Vigorous). *Dialects:* Hainanese, Hokkien (Amoy, Fujianese, Fukienese), Teochew (Chaochow, Teochow). See main entry on page 68.

Chinese, Pu-Xian [cpx]. 24,700 in Malaysia (Salleh 2006). Ethnic population: 24,700 (2000 census). In Peninsular Malaysia. Peninsular. *Status:* 6b (Threatened). *Dialect:* Xinghua (Hinghua, Hsinghua). See main entry on page 68.

Chinese, Yue [yue] (Cantonese, Yue, Yueh). 1,070,000 in Malaysia (2000 census). Peninsular; largest community in Johor State. *Status:* 2 (Provincial). De facto provincial language in Johor State. *Dialects:* Cantonese, Toishanese. See main entry on page 69.

Duano [dup] (Desin Dolak, Desin Duano, Orang Kuala, Orang Laut). 600 in Malaysia (2007 SIL). 0 monolinguals. Ethnic population: 3,010 (2008 JHEOA). Peninsular, Johor state west coast, Pontian Kecil area, Muar, Batu Pahat, and Pontian districts, Lenga, Semerah, Minyak Beku, Senggarang, Rengit, Kuala Benut, Pontian Besar, and Sungai Layau settlements. *Status:* 8a (Moribund). *Lg Use:* Only older people. Shifting to Malay [zlm] (Bradley 2007). Social interactions. Older adults. *Lg Dev:* Literacy rate in L1: 0%. Literacy rate in L2: 50%. See main entry on page 160. *Map:* 385:25.

Dumpas [dmv] (Doompas). Ethnic population: 1,100 (2000). Sabah, Labuk-Sugut district, Perancangan village. *Status:* 6b (Threatened). *Class:* Austronesian, Malayo-Polynesian, North Borneo, Sabahan, Dusunic, Unclassified. *Dialects:* None known. May be Paitanic. Comprehension of Tombonuo [txa] 87%, of Labuk-Kinabatangan Kadazan [dtb] 57%, of Coastal Kadazan [kzj] 44%. *Lg Use:* Language dying out due to intermarriage with other groups. Also use Tombonuo [txa]. *Writing:* Unwritten. *Map:* 386:109.

Dusun, Central [dtp] (Central Kadazan, Dusan, Dusum, Dusun, Dusur, Kadasan, Kadayan, Kedayan). 141,000 (1991 SIL). 50,000 Ranau (1989 UBS), 70,000 Bundu (1990 UBS), perhaps 500 Kuala Monsok Dusun (Wurm and

Hattori 1981). Sabah, Labuk-Sugut district, Perancangan village. *Status:* 6b (Threatened). *Class:* Austronesian, Malayo-Polynesian, North Borneo, Sabahan, Dusunic, Dusun, Central. *Dialects:* Beaufort, Bundu (Taginambur), Dusun Sinulihan (Sinulihan), Kadazan-Tagaro (Tagaro), Kiundu, Kuala Monsok Dusun, Luba, Menggatal (Kiulu, Telipok), Pahu', Ranau, Sokid, Tindal. *Lg Use:* Used as L2 by Gana [gnq], Ida'an [dbj], Kuijau [dkr], Sugut Dusun [kzs], Tampias Lobu [low]. *Lg Dev:* Taught in primary and secondary schools. Dictionary. Bible: 2000. *Writing:* Latin script. *Map:* 386:95.

Dusun, Sugut [kzs] (Dusun, Kadayan, Sugut, Sugut Kadazan, Tanggal, Tilau-Ilau). Ethnic population: 12,200 (2000). Sabah, Labuk-Sugut district, Sugut river headwaters. *Status:* 6b (Threatened). *Class:* Austronesian, Malayo-Polynesian, North Borneo, Sabahan, Dusunic, Dusun, Central. *Dialects:* Talantang, Tinagas. *Lg Use:* Also use Central Dusun [dtp]. *Writing:* Unwritten. *Map:* 386:108.

Dusun, Tambunan [kzt] (Tambunan). Ethnic population: 15,600 (2000). Sabah, Tambunan district, parts of Keningau. *Status:* 6b (Threatened). *Class:* Austronesian, Malayo-Polynesian, North Borneo, Sabahan, Dusunic, Dusun, Central. *Writing:* Latin script. *Map:* 386:85.

Dusun, Tempasuk [tdu] (Kedamaian Dusun, Tampasok, Tampassuk, Tampasuk, Tempasok, Tindal). Ethnic population: 6,000 (Wurm 1981). Sabah, Tempasuk village area, Kota Belud. *Status:* 6b (Threatened). *Class:* Austronesian, Malayo-Polynesian, North Borneo, Sabahan, Dusunic, Dusun, Central. *Writing:* Unwritten. *Map:* 386:99.

English [eng]. 380,000 in Malaysia (Crystal 2003), increasing. L2 users: 7,000,000 in Malaysia (Crystal 2003). Peninsular. *Status:* 1 (National). Statutory national working language (1957, Constitution, Articles 152(2) through 152(5)). *Lg Use:* Nearly all domains. All ages. Positive attitudes. *Lg Dev:* Taught in primary and secondary schools. See main entry on page 319.

Gana [gnq] (Gana', Ganaq, Keningau Dusun, Minansut). Ethnic population: 1,000 (2000 SIL). Sabah, Keningau district, Minusut and Kuangoh, along Baiaya river, a tributary of Pegalan river, north of Keningau town. *Status:* 7 (Shifting). *Class:* Austronesian, Malayo-Polynesian, North Borneo, Sabahan, Dusunic, Dusun. *Lg Use:* People seldom use Gana. Also use Central Dusun [dtp], Malay [zlm], Sabah Malay [msi]. *Writing:* Unwritten. *Map:* 386:88.

Iban [iba] (Sea Dayak). 752,000 in Malaysia (2013 SIL). Population total all countries: 788,400. L2 users: 700,000 in Malaysia (2013 SIL). Sarawak, Sadong river north to Bintulu, Sibu; Sabah, Tawau district, 1 village. Also in Brunei, Indonesia. *Status:* 3 (Wider communication). Spoken from Sri Aman Division in the south west to Miri Division in the north east in the domains of market, church, business, and media. *Class:* Austronesian, Malayo-Polynesian, Malayo-Chamic, Malayic, Ibanic. *Dialects:* Batang Lupar, Bugau, Dau, Lemanak, Skrang, Ulu Ai, Undup. *Type:* SVO. *Lg Use:* Positive attitudes. Used as L2 by Bukitan [bkn], Kajaman [kag], Kiput [kyi], Narom [nrm], Remun [lkj]. *Lg Dev:* Taught in primary schools. Radio programs. Dictionary. Grammar. Bible: 1988–2011. *Writing:* Latin script. *Other:* Largest language group in Sarawak. *Maps:* 386:42, 387:42.

Ida'an [dbj] (Bulud Upi, Eraans, Idaan, Idahan, Idan, Idayan). 10,000 (2013 SIL). Population includes 1,500 Begak. East coast of Sabah, Lahad Datu, Kinabatangan, and Sandakan districts. *Status:* 6b (Threatened). *Class:* Austronesian, Malayo-Polynesian, North Borneo, Sabahan, Ida'an. *Dialects:* Begak (Bagahak, Begahak), Ida'an, Subpan (Sungai, Supan). Not closely related to other languages. *Lg Use:* Some young people, all adults. Also use Central Dusun [dtp], Malay [zlm], Sabah Malay [msi]. *Lg Dev:* Grammar. Bible portions: 1987–2011. *Writing:* Arabic script, no longer in use. Latin script. *Map:* 386:115.

Iranun [ill] ("Ilanun" *pej.*, Illanoan, Illanoon, Illanos, Illanun, Iranon Maranao, Iranum, Lanoon, Lanun, Ylanos). 15,000 in Malaysia (2000 SIL). Sabah, Lahad Datu and Kota Belud districts, 17 villages; also reportedly in Kudat and Marudu. *Status:* 6b (Threatened). *Lg Use:* Some young people, all adults. See main entry on page 281. *Map:* 386:98.

Jah Hut [jah] (Jah Het). Ethnic population: 3,760 (2008 JHEOA). Peninsular, Pahang State, just south of main body of Semai [sea] language area and Kuala Krau. *Status:* 6a (Vigorous). *Class:* Austro-Asiatic, Mon-Khmer, Aslian, Jah Hut. *Dialects:* Kerdau, Ketiar Krau (Tengganu), Krau, Kuala Tembeling, Pulau Guai, Ulu Ceres (Cheres), Ulu Tembeling. *Lg Use:* All ages. 100% also use Malay [zlm]. *Lg Dev:* Bible portions: 2011. *Writing:* Latin script, developed in about 2003. *Map:* 385:14.

Jakun [jak] (Djakun, Jakoon, Jaku'd, Jakud'n, Orang Hulu). Ethnic population: 25,000 (2008 JHEOA). Peninsular, Pahang and Johor states, Pekan district south along east coast to south of Johor river. *Status:* 6b (Threatened). *Class:* Austronesian, Malayo-Polynesian, Malayo-Chamic, Malayic, Malay. A member of macrolanguage Malay [msa]. *Writing:* Unwritten. *Other:* Perhaps better considered a dialect of Malay [zlm]. *Map:* 385:26.

Javanese [jav] (Jawa). Ethnic population: 300,000 (Wurm 1981). Sabah. *Status:* 8a (Moribund). *Lg Use:* Older adults and elderly. See main entry on page 164.

Jehai [jhi] (Jahai, Pangan). 1,000 in Malaysia (2006). Ethnic population: 1,660 (2008 JHEOA). Peninsular, Northeast Perak and west Kelantan states. Also in Thailand. *Status:* 6b (Threatened). *Class:* Austro-Asiatic, Mon-Khmer, Aslian, North Aslian, Eastern. *Dialects:* Batek Teh, Jehai. *Lg Use:* Southern Jehai are beginning to settle down and intermarry with Temiars [tea]. 100% also use Malay [zlm]. *Writing:* Unwritten. *Map:* 385:5.

Kadazan, Coastal [kzj] (Kadazan Tangaa', Membakut Kadazan, Papar Kadazan, Penampang Kadazan). Ethnic population: 60,000 (1986 SIL). West coast of Sabah, Penampang, and Papar districts. *Status:* 8a (Moribund). *Class:* Austronesian, Malayo-Polynesian, North Borneo, Sabahan, Dusunic, Dusun. *Type:* VSO. *Lg Use:* Older adults and elderly. *Lg Dev:* Newspapers. Radio programs. Dictionary. Bible portions: 1986. *Writing:* Latin script. *Map:* 386:92.

Kadazan, Klias River [kqt]. 1,000 (1984 SIL). Ethnic population: 1,000 (1984 SIL). Sabah, Klias river area, Beaufort district. *Status:* 6b (Threatened). *Class:* Austronesian, Malayo-Polynesian, North Borneo, Sabahan, Dusunic, Dusun. *Dialects:* None known. Low intelligibility with Coastal Kadazan [kzj]. Lexical similarity: 77% with Tatana [txx]. *Writing:* Unwritten. *Map:* 386:89.

Kadazan, Labuk-Kinabatangan [dtb] (Eastern Kadazan, Labuk Kadazan, Sogilitan, Tindakon, Tompulung). Ethnic population: 20,600 (2000 SIL). 14,000–16,000 Labuk (1987 SIL); 7,000–8,000 Sungai (1982 SIL). Northeast Sabah, Sandakan, Labuk-Sugut, and Kinabatangan districts. *Status:* 6b (Threatened). *Class:* Austronesian, Malayo-Polynesian, North Borneo, Sabahan, Dusunic, Dusun, Eastern. *Dialects:* Labuk, Lamag Sungai (Sungei), Mangkaak (Mangkahak, Mangkak, Mangkok), Sukang. *Type:* VSO; prepositions; genitives after nouns; question word initial; nontonal. *Lg Use:* Children may learn Sabah Malay [msi] first. Standard Malay [zsm] used in church, school, and official settings. Home, market, village. 95% of the children are not learning the language and using it in the home. Positive attitudes. 10,000 also use Sabah Malay [msi]. Also use Standard Malay [zsm]. *Lg Dev:* Literacy rate in L2: 85% in Standard Malay [zsm]. Literacy is highly valued. Dictionary. NT: 1996. *Writing:* Latin script. *Other:* Cross-cultural marriage and migration. *Map:* 386:84.

Kajaman [kag] (Kayaman, Kejaman). 500 (Wurm and Hattori 1981). Central Sarawak, 7th Division, near Belaga on Balui river. *Status:* 6b (Threatened). *Class:* Austronesian, Malayo-Polynesian, North Borneo, Melanau-Kajang, Kajang. *Lg Use:* Limited comprehension of Iban [iba]. *Writing:* Unwritten. *Map:* 387:56.

Kalabakan [kve] (Kalabakan Murut, Tawau Murut, Tidung). Ethnic population: 2,230 (2000). Sabah, Tawau district along Kalabakan river. *Status:* 6b (Threatened). *Class:* Austronesian, Malayo-Polynesian, North Borneo, North Sarawakan, Dayic, Murutic, Tidong. *Writing:* Unwritten. *Map:* 386:118.

Kayan, Baram [kys] (Baram Kajan). 4,150 (Wurm and Hattori 1981). Northern Sarawak, Baram river area. *Status:* 6b (Threatened). *Class:* Austronesian, Malayo-Polynesian, North Borneo, North Sarawakan, Kayan-Kenyah, Kayanic, Kayan Proper. *Dialects:* Long Akahsemuka, Long Atip. *Lg Use:* Some young people, all adults. *Lg Dev:* Bible: 1990. *Writing:* Latin script. *Map:* 387:71.

Kayan, Rejang [ree] (Rejang Kajan). 3,030 (Wurm and Hattori 1981). Sarawak, Rejang, Balui river areas. *Status:* 6b (Threatened). *Class:* Austronesian, Malayo-Polynesian, North Borneo, North Sarawakan, Kayan-Kenyah, Kayanic, Kayan Proper. *Dialects:* Lemena, Lisum, Long Badan, Long Geng, Long Kehobo (Uma Poh), Long Murun, Ma'aging, Uma Daro, Uma Juman. Limited comprehension of Baram Kayan [kys]. *Writing:* Unwritten. *Other:* Different from Rejang [rej] in Sumatra. *Map:* 387:48.

Kelabit [kzi] (Kalabit, Kerabit). 4,000 in Malaysia (2011 SIL). Population total all countries: 4,640. Ethnic population: 5,000. North Sarawak, highest and most remote Borneo mountains, Bario highlands. Also in Indonesia. *Status:* 6b (Threatened). *Class:* Austronesian, Malayo-Polynesian, North Borneo, North Sarawakan, Dayic, Kelabitic. *Dialects:* Brung, Lepu Potong, Libbung, Long Lellang, Long Peluan, Pa' Dalih, Pa' Umor (spoken in Bario), Tabun. *Lg Use:* Decreasingly used by the youth. All domains in the village. Positive attitudes. *Lg Dev:* Community mother-tongue based play school started in 2007 in Bario. Taught in primary schools. Dictionary. Bible portions: 1965. *Writing:* Latin script, developed in about 2009. *Other:* Strongly independent. Most live outside language area. *Maps:* 386:73, 387:73.

Keningau Murut [kxi] (Central Murut). 1,000 to 1,200 Dusun Murut (1985 SIL). Ethnic population: 7,000 (2000). Sabah, Keningau district, area north of Keningau town, Pegalan river. *Status:* 6b (Threatened). *Class:* Austronesian, Malayo-Polynesian, North Borneo, North Sarawakan, Dayic, Murutic, Murut. *Dialects:* Ambual, Dusun Murut, Nabay (Dabai, Dabay, Nabai, Nebee, Rabai, Rabay). Reportedly similar to Bookan [bnb] and Timugon [tih]. *Lg Use:* Young people prefer Sabah Malay [msi], Standard Malay [zsm]. *Lg Dev:* NT: 2010. *Writing:* Latin script. *Map:* 386:87.

Kensiu [kns] (Kenseu, Kensieu, Kensiw, Mendi, Monik, Moniq, Ngok Pa, Orang Bukit, Orang Liar). Ethnic population: 200 (2013 SIL). Peninsular, northeast Kedah State, near Thai border; into Perak State, Hulu Perak district. Also in Thailand. *Status:* 5 (Developing). *Class:* Austro-Asiatic, Mon-Khmer, Aslian, North Aslian, Western. *Dialects:* Bong, Ijoh (Ijok), Jarum, Jeher (Sakai Tanjong of Temongoh), Kedah (Quedah), Kensiu Batu (Batuq), Kensiu Siong (Siong), Kentaq Nakil (Nakil), Maniq, Plus, Ulu Selama. *Lg Use:* Numerous other extinct dialects further west (Bradley 2007). All ages. All also use Malay (Bradley 2007). *Writing:* Latin script. Thai script. *Map:* 385:3.

Kenyah, Mainstream [xkl] (Bakong, Bakung, Bakung Kenya, Bakung Kenyah). 40,000 in Malaysia (2013 SIL). South central Sarawak, near Kalimantan border, villages along Baram and Balui rivers and some tributaries; 1 village on Kakus river; Sungai Asap area. *Status:* 6b (Threatened). *Dialects:* Badeng (Madeng), Bakung, Leppo' Aga, Leppo' Ga, Leppo' Jamok, Leppo' Jengan, Leppo' Ke', Leppo' La'ang, Leppo' Tau, Leppo' Teppu', Sambup, Uma' Ake, Uma' Jalan. *Lg Use:* Some young people, all adults. See main entry on page 168. *Map:* 387:44.

Kenyah, Wahau [whk]. 1,000 in Malaysia (2007 A. Soriente). Sarawak. *Status:* 6b (Threatened). See main entry on page 169. *Map:* 387:52.

Kimaragang [kqr] (Kimaragan, Kimaragangan, Maragang, Marigang). Ethnic population: 25,000 (2007 SIL). Sabah, Kota Marudu and Pitas districts. *Status:* 6b (Threatened). *Class:* Austronesian, Malayo-Polynesian, North Borneo, Sabahan, Dusunic, Dusun. *Dialects:* Pitas Kimaragang, Sandayo, Sonsogon, Tandek (Garo). *Lg Use:* Children don't learn it in many areas, at least not well. Neutral attitudes. Used as L2 by Kota Marudu Talantang [grm]. *Lg Dev:* Literacy rate in L1: 5%. Literacy rate in L2: 85%. Poetry. Bible portions: 1996. *Writing:* Latin script. *Map:* 386:106.

Kinabatangan, Upper [dmg] (Sungai Milian). Ethnic population: 5,000 (2000 SIL). Sabah, primarily upper reaches of Kinabatangan river; Lahad Datu and Sandakan districts, Maligatan, Minusu, and Tongud. *Status:* 6b (Threatened). *Class:* Austronesian, Malayo-Polynesian, North Borneo, Sabahan, Paitanic, Upper Kinabatangan. *Dialects:* Dusun Segama (Saga-i, Segai, Soghai), Kalabuan (Kolobuan), Makiang, Sinabu' (Sinabu). Dialects have approximately 87% mutual intelligibility. Lexical similarity: over 90% among all dialects, 80% with Makiang and Sinabu'. *Lg Dev:* Bible portions: 1984–1995. *Writing:* Latin script, developed in about 1984 till 2004. *Other:* Traditional religion, Christian, Muslim. *Map:* 386:113.

Kintaq [knq] (Bong, Kenta, Kintak, Kintaq Bong). 110 in Malaysia (2008 JHEOA). Population total all countries: 111. Ethnic population: 240 (Bradley 2007). Peninsular, Kedah-Perak border area, Thai border. Also in Thailand. *Status:* 6b (Threatened). *Class:* Austro-Asiatic, Mon-Khmer, Aslian, North Aslian, Western. *Lg Use:* All also use Malay (Bradley 2007). *Writing:* Unwritten. *Map:* 385:4.

Kiput [kyi]. 2,460 (Wurm and Hattori 1981). Sarawak, south of Marudi, Benawa and Kuala Tutoh villages. *Status:* 6b (Threatened). *Class:* Austronesian, Malayo-Polynesian, North Borneo, North Sarawakan, Berawan-Lower Baram, Lower Baram, Central, A. *Dialects:* Long Kiput, Long Tutoh (Kuala Tutoh). Related to Narom [nrm], Lelak [llk], Tutong [ttg], Belait [beg], and Berawan languages. *Lg Use:* Also use Iban [iba]. *Writing:* Unwritten. *Map:* 387:61.

Kota Marudu Talantang [grm]. Ethnic population: 1,800 (2000). Sabah, Kota Marudu district, Talantang 1 and Talantang 2. *Status:* 6b (Threatened). *Class:* Austronesian, Malayo-Polynesian, North Borneo, Sabahan, Dusunic, Dusun. *Lg Use:* Also use Kimaragang [kqr]. *Writing:* Unwritten. *Map:* 386:97.

Kota Marudu Tinagas [ktr]. Ethnic population: 1,250 (1985 SIL). Sabah, south Kota Marudu and Parong, and a migrant village in north Kota Marudu. *Status:* 6b (Threatened). *Class:* Austronesian, Malayo-Polynesian, North Borneo, Sabahan, Dusunic, Dusun, Central. *Writing:* Unwritten. *Map:* 386:96.

Kuijau [dkr] (Hill Dusun, Kijau, Koijoe, Kuiyow, Kujau, Kuliow, Kuriyo, Kwijau, Menindal, Menindaq, Minansut, Tidung, Tindal). Ethnic population: 7,910 (2000). Sabah,

Keningau district, Keningau town area north and west. *Status:* 6b (Threatened). *Class:* Austronesian, Malayo-Polynesian, North Borneo, Sabahan, Dusunic, Dusun. *Lg Use:* Also use Central Dusun [dtp]. *Writing:* Unwritten. *Map:* 386:86.

Lahanan [lhn] (Lanan, Lanun). 350 (Wurm and Hattori 1981). Central Sarawak, east of Belaga, southwest of Long Murum. *Status:* 6b (Threatened). *Class:* Austronesian, Malayo-Polynesian, North Borneo, Melanau-Kajang, Kajang. *Dialects:* None known. Reportedly most similar to Kajaman [kag]. *Writing:* Unwritten. *Other:* Different from Iranun [ill] of Sabah or Iranun (Maguindanao) [mdh] of the Philippines. *Map:* 387:55.

Lanoh [lnh] (Jengjeng). Ethnic population: 240 (2008 JHEOA). Peninsular, north central Perak State. *Status:* 6b (Threatened). *Class:* Austro-Asiatic, Mon-Khmer, Aslian, Senoic. *Lg Use:* 100% also use Malay [zlm]. Many also use Temiar [tea] as lingua franca (Bradley 2007). *Writing:* Unwritten. *Other:* Lanoh includes Sabüm and Semnam as subgroups (Burenhult and Wegener 2009). *Map:* 385:7.

Lelak [llk]. No known L1 speakers. Sarawak, Long Teru and Sungai Bunen at Loagan Bunut lake, on Tinjar river. *Status:* 10 (Extinct). *Class:* Austronesian, Malayo-Polynesian, North Borneo, North Sarawakan, Berawan-Lower Baram, Lower Baram, Central, B. *Dialects:* None known. Related to Narom [nrm]. *Lg Use:* Shifted to Central Berawan [zbc]. *Writing:* Unwritten.

Lobu, Lanas [ruu] (Keningau Lobu). Ethnic population: 2,800 (1986 SIL). 2,000 in Lobu, 800 in Rumanau. Sabah, Keningau district, Lobu near Lanas, Rumanau in Masaum, Mangkawagu, Minusu, and Kinabatangan District. *Status:* 6b (Threatened). *Class:* Austronesian, Malayo-Polynesian, North Borneo, Sabahan, Paitanic, Upper Kinabatangan. *Dialects:* Lobu, Rumanau (Romanau, Roomarrows, Rumanau Alab). May be a dialect of Upper Kinabatangan [dmg]. *Writing:* Unwritten. *Map:* 386:81.

Lobu, Tampias [low]. Ethnic population: 1,800 (1985 SIL). Sabah, Tampias area, Ranau. 3 villages. *Status:* 6b (Threatened). *Class:* Austronesian, Malayo-Polynesian, North Borneo, Sabahan, Paitanic, Upper Kinabatangan. *Dialects:* None known. High intelligibility of Upper Kinabatangan [dmg]. Lexical similarity: 73% with Lanas Lobu [ruu]. *Lg Use:* Also use Central Dusun [dtp]. *Writing:* Unwritten. *Map:* 386:83.

Long Wat [ttw] (Tutoh Kenya, Tutoh Kenyah). 600 (Wurm and Hattori 1981). Northeast Sarawak, Tutoh river. *Status:* 6b (Threatened). *Class:* Austronesian, Malayo-Polynesian, North Borneo, North Sarawakan, Kayan-Kenyah, Kenyah, Kayanic Kenyah. *Dialects:* Long Labid, Long Wat, Lugat. Not closely related to other languages. *Writing:* Unwritten. *Map:* 387:69.

Lotud [dtr] (Dusun Lotud, Suang Lotud). Ethnic population: 5,000 (1985 SIL). Sabah State, Tuaran District, just north of Kota Kinabalu, Tuaran town area. *Status:* 6b (Threatened). *Class:* Austronesian, Malayo-Polynesian, North Borneo, Sabahan, Dusunic, Dusun. *Lg Use:* Home, market, village. All ages. Positive attitudes. Also use Sabah Malay [msi], Standard Malay [zsm]. *Lg Dev:* Bible portions: 1992. *Writing:* Latin script, developed in about 1987. *Map:* 386:94.

Lun Bawang [lnd] (Lun Daya, Lun Dayah, Lun Daye, Lun Dayeh, Lun Dayoh, Lun Lod, Lun-Bawang, Lundaya, Lundayeh, Southern Murut). 24,000 in Malaysia (1982 SIL). Sarawak 21,000, Sabah 3,000–4,000. Southwest border of Sabah and Sarawak. *Status:* 6b (Threatened). *Dialects:* Kolur, Lepu Potong, Lun Bawang (Sarawak Murut), Lun Dayah, Padas, Trusan (Lawas, Limbang). *Lg Use:* Some young people, all adults. *Other:* Not Murutic, although sometimes called Southern Murut. See main entry on page 175. *Maps:* 386:74, 387:74.

Mah Meri [mhe] (Besisi, Cellate). 2,990 (2003 Center for Orang Asli Concerns). Ethnic population: 3,680 (2008 JHEOA). Peninsular, coastal areas of Selangor, Putrajaya, and Negeri Sembilan; also islands near such coasts. *Status:* 6b (Threatened). *Class:* Austro-Asiatic, Mon-Khmer, Aslian, South Aslian. *Dialects:* Betise' (Betisek), Kuala Langot Besisi, Malakka Besisi, Selangor Sakai, Sisi, Ulu Langat Orang Bukit. *Lg Use:* One dialect became extinct late 19th century, others have become extinct. 100% also use Malay [zlm]. *Lg Dev:* NT: 1933. *Map:* 385:20.

Malaccan Creole Malay [ccm] (Chitties Creole Malay). Ethnic population: 300. Peninsular, Malacca straits, Kampung Tujung, Gajah Berang, and Melaka. *Status:* 8a (Moribund). *Class:* Creole, Malay based. *Dialects:* None known. May be historically related to Sri Lankan Creole Malay [sci]. *Lg Use:* Shifting to Baba Malay [mbf] or Malay [zlm]. Additionally, intermarriage and out-migration are shrinking the community (Mohammed 2009). *Lg Dev:* Dictionary. *Writing:* Unwritten. *Other:* Spoken since the 16th century by descendants of Tamil merchants who intermarried with other groups. Speakers are called Chitties (Lim 1981; Holm 1989). *Map:* 385:23.

Malaccan Creole Portuguese [mcm] (Bahasa Geragau, Bahasa Serani, Kristang, Luso-Malay, Malaccan, Malaqueiro, Malaquenho, Malaquense, Malaquês, Malayo-Portuguese, Malaysian Creole Portuguese, Papia Cristao, Papia Kristang, Português de Malaca, Portuguese Patois, Serani). 2,150 (Bradley 2007). Ethnic population: 10,000 (Bradley 2007). L2 users: Also spoken as L2 by some Chinese shopkeepers in Hilir. Peninsular, Straits of Malacca,Trankera and Hilir, Melaka. Related varieties in parts of Kuala Lumpur and Singapore. *Status:* 8a (Moribund). *Class:* Creole, Portuguese based. *Lg Use:* English [eng] is rapidly becoming the dominant language among the younger generation. Mainly adults 50 and older, about one-third of young adults, some children (Bradley 2007). Some older women use some English [eng]. Most also use local varieties of Malaysian English. Most also use local varieties of market Malay [zlm]. *Lg Dev:* Dictionary. Grammar. Bible portions: 1884. *Other:* Ethnic autonym: Kristang (or Papia Cristao), also name for religion. Variety in Pulau Tikus spoken more in 1997 than in 1987. *Map:* 385:24.

Malay [zlm] (Bahasa Malayu, Colloquial Malay, Informal Malay, Local Malay, Malayu). 10,500,000 in Malaysia (2004 census). 10 million in Peninsular Malaysia, 506,000 in Sarawak, and 30,000 in Labuan. Population total all countries: 15,848,500. L2 users: 3,000,000 in Malaysia. Widespread in Peninsular Malaysia; also in Sarawak State, Kuching, Samarahan, Sri Aman, and Belong districts. Also in Canada, Indonesia, Singapore, Sint Maarten, United Arab Emirates, United States. *Status:* 3 (Wider communication). *Class:* Austronesian, Malayo-Polynesian, Malayo-Chamic, Malayic, Malay. A member of macrolanguage Malay [msa]. *Dialects:* Akit, Belitung, coastal Jambi, Coastal Terengganu, Deli, Inland Terengganu, Jugra-Muar-Melaka-Johor, Kelantan, Lubu, Northwestern Kalimantan, Orang Hulu, Orang Kuala, Pahang, Riau islands, Riau Mainland, Sakai, Sarawak (Sarawak Malay), Southeast Island, Southwestern Coastal Kalimantan, Tamiang, Upstream Western Kalimantan. Kedah Malay [meo], Negeri Sembilan Malay [zmi], Jakun [jak], Orang Kanaq [orn], Orang Seletar [ors], Temuan [tmw], Sabah Malay [msi], and Brunei [kxd], are so closely related that they may one day be included as dialects of Malay [zlm]. Coastal Terengganu, inland Terengganu, Kelantan most aberrant but evidently mutually intelligible with Patani [ptn]. *Lg Use:* Also use English [eng], Standard Malay [zsm]. Used as L2 by Brunei [kxd], Central Melanau [mel], Cheq Wong [cwg], Gana [gnq], Ida'an [dbj], Jah Hut [jah], Jehai [jhi], Lanoh [lnh], Mah Meri [mhe], Malaccan Creole Portuguese [mcm], Minokok [mqq], Minriq [mnq], Remun [lkj], Salako [knx], Selungai Murut [slg], Semai [sea], Semelai [sza], Southern Sama [ssb], Tamil [tam], Temiar [tea]. *Writing:* Arabic script. Latin script. *Other:* This entry refers to, local or vernacular, Malay varieties not well differentiated from each other, and other varieties for which further research is needed to clarify differentiation from mainstream dialects. Distinguished from court-Malay-derived Standard Indonesian [ind] or Standard Malay [zsm] by sociolinguistic status as vernaculars, and other linguistic features. *Maps:* 385:22, 387:22.

Malay [msa]. A macrolanguage (see page 9). *Lg Use:* Used as L2 by Batek [btq]. *Other:* Includes: Bacanese Malay [btj] (Indonesia), Bangka [mfb] (Indonesia), Banjar [bjn] (Indonesia), Berau Malay [bve] (Indonesia), Brunei [kxd] (Brunei), Bukit Malay [bvu] (Indonesia), Central Malay [pse] (Indonesia), Cocos Islands Malay [coa], Col [liw] (Indonesia), Duano [dup] (Indonesia), Haji [hji] (Indonesia), Indonesian [ind] (Indonesia), Jakun [jak], Jambi Malay [jax] (Indonesia), Kaur [vkk] (Indonesia), Kedah Malay [meo], Kerinci [kvr] (Indonesia), Kota Bangun Kutai Malay [mqg] (Indonesia), Kubu [kvb] (Indonesia), Lubu [lcf] (Indonesia), Malay [zlm], Manado Malay [xmm] (Indonesia), Minangkabau [min] (Indonesia), Musi [mui] (Indonesia), Negeri Sembilan Malay [zmi], North Moluccan Malay [max] (Indonesia), Orang Kanaq [orn], Orang Seletar [ors], Pattani Malay [mfa] (Thailand), Pekal [pel] (Indonesia), Sabah Malay [msi], Sekak [lce] (Indonesia), Standard Malay [zsm], Temuan [tmw], Tenggarong Kutai Malay [vkt] (Indonesia), Urak Lawoi' [urk] (Thailand).

Malay, Baba [mbf] (Chinese Malay, Straits Malay). 2,000 in Malaysia (Salleh 2006). Peninsular, Malacca Straits, Pulau Pinang State, Pinang island; Melaka City area and nearby coast, central Melaka State. *Status:* 8a (Moribund). *Lg Use:* Monolinguals are over 70 years old. *Other:* Developed since the 15th century from Low Malay with many Hokkien Chinese borrowings. Lim (1981) and Holm (1989) treat it as a Malay-based creole. See main entry on page 294. *Map:* 385:21.

Malay, Cocos Islands [coa]. Ethnic population: 4,000 (2000 SIL). Sabah, Tawau and Lahad Datu districts; 1 village northwest of Beluran. Also in Australia. *Status:* 6b (Threatened). *Class:* Creole, Malay based. A member of macrolanguage Malay [msa]. *Lg Use:* Home, market, village meetings. All ages. Positive attitudes. *Writing:* Unwritten. *Other:* From the Cocos Islands (Keeling Islands), an Australian territory. *Map:* 386:116.

Malay, Kedah [meo] (Satun Malay). 2,600,000 in Malaysia (2004). Peninsular, Kedah, Perak, Perlis, and Pulau Pinang states. Also in Thailand (Satun Malay). *Status:* 3 (Wider communication). *Class:* Austronesian, Malayo-Polynesian, Malayo-Chamic, Malayic, Malay. A member of macrolanguage Malay [msa]. *Dialects:* None known. Distinct from Pattani Malay [mfa] and Standard Malay [zsm]. *Lg Use:* Also use Thai [tha]. *Writing:* Latin script. *Other:* More use Thai [tha] than Pattani Malay. Most outside contacts are with Thai population centers in Songkhla, Phattalung, and Haad Yai; with west coast Malay states of Perlis and Kedah. Culturally Malay. May be a dialect of Malay [zlm]. *Map:* 385:1.

Malay, Sabah [msi] (Bazaar Malay, Pasar Malay). L2 users: 3,000,000 (2013 SIL). Mostly second-language speakers, but growing number of L1 speakers. Sabah. *Status:* 3 (Wider communication). Used throughout the state of Sabah in virtually all non-formal domains. *Class:* Austronesian, Malayo-Polynesian, Malayo-Chamic, Malayic, Malay. A member of macrolanguage Malay [msa]. *Type:* SVO. *Lg Use:* A few L1 speakers in urban areas, especially children of parents who have other first languages. Used mainly as contact language in Sabah, so not yet fully developed. Speakers shift to other languages to fill in expressions in domains where Sabah Malay is lacking. If the only form of Malay a person knows is Sabah Malay, there will be difficulty understanding Standard Malay [zsm] in other domains. Used as L2 by Abai Sungai [abf], Bonggi [bdg], Gana [gnq], Ida'an [dbj], Labuk-Kinabatangan Kadazan [dtb], Lotud [dtr], Minokok [mqq], Molbog [pwm], Rungus [drg]. *Lg Dev:* Dictionary. *Writing:* Unwritten. *Other:* May be a dialect of Brunei [kxd]. Bazaar Malay, refers to many regional nonstandard Malay varieties.

Malay, Standard [zsm] (Bahasa Malayu, Formal Malay, Informal Malay, Malay, Malayu, Melayu, Melayu Baku). Few L1 speakers. L2 includes most Malaysian population. Widespread in Peninsular Malaysia, Sabah, and Sarawak. Also in Brunei, Singapore. *Status:* 1 (National). Statutory national language (1963, Constitution (amended), Article 153A(1)). *Class:* Austronesian, Malayo-Polynesian, Malayo-Chamic, Malayic, Malay. A member of macrolanguage Malay [msa]. *Dialects:* None known. Lexical similarity: more than 80% with Indonesian [ind]. *Type:* SVO. *Lg Use:* Also use English [eng], Mandarin Chinese [cmn], Tamil [tam]. *Lg Dev:* Used through secondary education and in some tertiary institutions. Fully developed. Bible: 1733–1996. *Writing:* Arabic script. Braille script. Latin script. *Other:* On Peninsular Malaysia, Standard Malay [zsm] exists in a diglossic relationship with Local Malay [zlm]. Standard Malay (derived from court Malay), both in terms of its linguistic structure as well as its sociolinguistic function, has its closest counterpart not in a particular Local Malay dialect but in Standard Indonesian [ind].

Malaysian Sign Language [xml] (Bahasa Isyarat Malaysia). 24,000. Peninsular. *Status:* 5 (Developing). *Class:* Deaf sign language. *Dialects:* Variations found in every state, but are mutually intelligible with the possible exception of some places in Terengganu state. The status of the sign language in Terengganu is not yet clear. *Lg Use:* Under development by Ministry of Education since 1978. Used in government programs. Used by most deaf in Malaysia, especially those who have gone to school. All ages. Positive attitudes. Used as L2 by Penang Sign Language [psg], Selangor Sign Language [kgi]. *Lg Dev:* Literacy rate in L1: 0%. Literacy rate in L2: 40%–50% in Malay; 30%–40% in English. Dictionary. *Writing:* Unwritten.

Mapun [sjm] (Bajau Kagayan, Cagayan de Sulu, Cagayanon, Jama Mapun, Kagayan, Orang Cagayan, Sama Mapun). 15,000 in Malaysia (2011 SIL). East coast of Sabah, Sandakan; west coast of Sabah, Banggi, Marudu, Kudat, and Kota Kinabalu. 9 villages. *Status:* 6b (Threatened). *Lg Use:* All adults. Used as L2 by Molbog [pwm]. See main entry on page 287. *Map:* 386:101.

Melanau, Central [mel] (Belana'u, Milanau, Milano). 113,000 in Malaysia (2000 census). Population total all countries: 113,280. Sarawak, 3rd division, Rejang delta coastal area to Balingian river. Also in Brunei. *Status:* 6b (Threatened). *Class:* Austronesian, Malayo-Polynesian, North Borneo, Melanau-Kajang, Melanau. *Dialects:* Balingian, Bruit, Dalat (Dalad), Igan, Mukah-Oya (Muka, Mukah, Oga, Oya, Oya'), Prehan, Sarikei, Segahan, Segalang, Siteng. Balingian dialect is linguistically quite distinct from others. *Lg Use:* Positive attitudes. Also use Malay [zlm]. *Lg Dev:* Literacy rate in L2: above 50%. Grammar. *Writing:* Unwritten. *Map:* 387:38.

Melanau, Daro-Matu [dro]. 7,600 (Wurm and Hattori 1981). 4,800 Matu, 2,800 Daro. Sarawak, Matu river from north channel of Rejang river to the sea, Daro and Matu areas. *Status:* 6b (Threatened). *Class:* Austronesian, Malayo-Polynesian, North Borneo, Melanau-Kajang, Melanau. *Dialects:* Daro, Matu (Langle-Tamtlaih, Ngaleng, Phaneng). *Writing:* Unwritten. *Map:* 387:39.

Melanau, Kanowit-Tanjong [kxn]. 200 (Wurm 2000). Ethnic population: 500. Sarawak, 3rd Division, middle stretch Rejang River. Kanowit dialect downstream from Tanjong dialect. *Status:* 6b (Threatened). *Class:* Austronesian, Malayo-Polynesian, North Borneo, Melanau-Kajang, Melanau. *Dialects:* Kanowit, Tanjong. *Lg Use:* Endangered (2000 S. Wurm). Being absorbed by Iban [iba]. Home. Few or no children use Kanowit dialect. Neutral attitudes. *Writing:* Unwritten. *Map:* 387:41.

Melanau, Sibu [sdx] (Seduan-Banyok, Sibu, Siduan, Siduani). 420 (Wurm and Hattori 1981). Sarawak, Sibu, 3rd division, Rejang river. *Status:* 7 (Shifting). *Class:* Austronesian, Malayo-Polynesian, North Borneo, Melanau-Kajang, Melanau. *Dialects:* Banyok, Seduan. May be intelligible with Central Melanau [mel]. *Lg Use:* Shifting to Central Melanau [mel]. *Writing:* Unwritten. *Map:* 387:40.

Minokok [mqq]. 1,200 (2007 SIL). Sabah, Kinabatangan river headwaters. *Status:* 6b (Threatened). *Class:* Austronesian, Malayo-Polynesian, North Borneo, Sabahan, Dusunic, Dusun, Central. *Dialects:* None known. Reportedly most similar to Labuk-Kinabatangan Kadazan [dtb], Kimaragang [kqr] and Tobilung [tgb]. *Lg Use:* Also use Malay [zlm], Sabah Malay [msi], Standard Malay [zsm]. *Writing:* Unwritten. *Map:* 386:82.

Minriq [mnq] (Mendriq, Menraq, Menrik, Menriq). Ethnic population: 270 (2008 JHEOA). Peninsular, Southeast Kelantan State; 2 villages. *Status:* 6b (Threatened). *Class:* Austro-Asiatic, Mon-Khmer, Aslian, North Aslian, Eastern. *Lg Use:* Many also use Temiar [tea] (Bradley 2007). Also use Malay [zlm]. *Writing:* Unwritten. *Map:* 385:9.

Mintil [mzt] (Mitil). 180 (2005 Lye Tuck-Po). Peninsular, Pahang State, Tamun river, 3 villages. *Status:* 8a (Moribund). *Class:* Austro-Asiatic, Mon-Khmer, Aslian, North Aslian, Eastern. *Writing:* Unwritten. *Other:* May have no remaining speakers. *Map:* 385:11.

Molbog [pwm]. 7,000 in Malaysia (2013 SIL). Sabah, Banggi island. *Status:* 5 (Developing). *Lg Use:* Also use Mapun [sjm], Sabah Malay [msi]. See main entry on page 287. *Map:* 386:104.

Murik [mxr]. 1,120 (Wurm and Hattori 1981). Sarawak, below Long Miri (Banyok) and below Lio Mato (Semiang) on Baram river. *Status:* 8a (Moribund). *Class:* Austronesian, Malayo-Polynesian, North Borneo, North Sarawakan, Kayan-Kenyah, Kayanic, Murik Kayan. *Dialects:* Long Banyok (Banyok), Long Semiang (Semiang). *Lg Use:* Shifting to Malay [zlm]. Speakers over 30. *Writing:* Unwritten. *Map:* 387:58.

Narom [nrm] (Narum). Ethnic population: 4,000. Population includes about 1,000 Bakong, 1,000 Dali', and 1,000 Miri' (2012 SIL). Sarawak, south of Baram river mouth, Miri area and south; Bakong dialect is near Beluru and Bekenu, in Kuala Nusah and Tanjung Beliput Niah area; Dali' dialect is in Bekenu, Rancha-Rancha, Benkenu Asli, Rambai Asli, Menjelin, and Jengalas villages; Miri dialect is in Miri City, Bakam, Pengkalan, Pujut, and Lopeng villages. *Status:* 6b (Threatened). *Class:* Austronesian, Malayo-Polynesian, North Borneo, North Sarawakan, Berawan-Lower Baram, Lower Baram, Central, B. *Dialects:* Bakong, Dali', Miri', Narom. Bakong, Dali', and Miri' may be distinct languages. *Lg Use:* Also use Iban [iba]. *Writing:* Unwritten. *Map:* 387:62.

Negeri Sembilan Malay [zmi] (Malaysian Minangkabau, Ulu Muar Malay). Used as L1 by many inhabitants of Negeri Sembilan State (2011 K. Anderbeck). Ethnic population: 508,000 (2004). Peninsular, Southeast of Kuala Lumpur, Negeri Sembilan State, Ulu Muar district. *Status:* 6b (Threatened). *Class:* Austronesian, Malayo-Polynesian, Malayo-Chamic, Malayic, Malay. A member of macrolanguage Malay [msa]. *Lg Use:* Shifting to Malay [zml]. *Writing:* Unwritten. *Other:* People call Minangkabau immigrants, who have come during the last 60 to 80 years, Minang. May be a dialect of Malay [zlm]. *Map:* 385:18.

Okolod [kqv] (Kolod, Kolour, Kolur, Okolod Murut). 1,580 in Malaysia (2000). 1,000 in Sarawak, 100 to 200 in Sabah. Sarawak; Kalimantan; Sabah, southwest of Tenom and Sipitang districts on plantation estates; Padas river headwater area. *Status:* 6b (Threatened). See main entry on page 184. *Maps:* 386:76, 387:76.

Orang Kanaq [orn] (Kanaq). Ethnic population: 160 (2008 JHEOA). Peninsular, eastern Johor State, northeast of Mawai (Kota Tinggi). *Status:* 8b (Nearly extinct). *Class:* Austronesian, Malayo-Polynesian, Malayo-Chamic, Malayic, Malay. A member of macrolanguage Malay [msa]. *Writing:* Unwritten. *Other:* May be better considered a dialect of Malay [zlm]. Originally from Sumatra, previously a sea tribe which settled on the land in the mid-19th century (Musa 2011). *Map:* 385:27.

Orang Seletar [ors] (Orang Laut). Ethnic population: 1,250 (2008 JHEOA). Peninsular, Johor State, southeast coast around Kukuo, Johore Bahru, east and north. Also in Singapore. *Status:* 6b (Threatened). *Class:* Austronesian, Malayo-Polynesian, Malayo-Chamic, Malayic, Malay. A member of macrolanguage Malay [msa]. *Writing:* Unwritten. *Other:* May be better considered a dialect of Malay [zlm]. Named after Seletar Island in Singapore from which they were removed in 1986. *Map:* 385:28.

Paluan [plz]. 5,500 (2000 SIL). 3,000 Paluan, 1,000 to 2,000 Pandewan. Sabah, Tenom, Keningau, and Pensiangan districts, Padas river tributaries; Dalit, Keramatoi, Nabawan, Pamentarian, and Mesopo rivers; lower Sook river valley; Talankai and Sapulut rivers' headwaters. *Status:* 6b (Threatened). *Class:* Austronesian, Malayo-Polynesian, North Borneo, North Sarawakan, Dayic, Murutic, Murut. *Dialects:* Dalit Murut, Makaheeliga (Makialiga), Paluan (Peluan), Pandewan (Pandewan Murut), Sook Murut, Takapan. Reportedly most similar to Tagal Murut [mvv]. *Lg Use:* Also fluent in Tagal Murut [mvv]. *Writing:* Unwritten. *Map:* 386:79.

Papar [dpp] (Bajau Bukit). Ethnic population: 1,000 (2000). Sabah, Kuala Penyu district. *Status:* 6b (Threatened). *Class:* Austronesian, Malayo-Polynesian, North Borneo, Sabahan, Dusunic, Dusun. *Lg Use:* Also use Brunei [kxd], Sabah Bisaya [bsy], Standard Malay [zsm], Tatana [txx], West Coast Bajau [bdr]. *Writing:* Unwritten. *Map:* 386:91.

Penan, Bah-Biau [pna] (Bah-Biau, Punan). 450 (Wurm and Hattori 1981). Central Sarawak, 7th division, Merit and Rejang rivers areas. *Status:* 6b (Threatened). *Class:* Austronesian, Malayo-Polynesian, North Borneo, Rejang-Sajau. *Dialects:* Punan Bah (Punan Ba), Punan Biau. *Writing:* Unwritten. *Other:* Nomadic. They get salt from the Kayan. *Map:* 387:46.

Penan, Eastern [pez] ("Punan" *pej.*). 10,000 in Malaysia (2011 SIL). Population total all countries: 10,055. Sarawak, Apoh river district, east of Baram river. Also in Brunei. *Status:* 6b (Threatened). *Class:* Austronesian, Malayo-Polynesian, North Borneo, North Sarawakan, Kayan-Kenyah, Penan. *Dialect:* Penan Apoh. Not intelligible of Western

Penan [pne] and Uma Lasan [xky]. *Lg Dev:* NT: 1978–2009. *Writing:* Latin script. *Map:* 387:70.

Penan, Western [pne] (Nibon, Nibong, "Punan" *pej.*). 3,400 (2007 SIL). Sarawak, 4th to 7th divisions, upper Baram and Balui rivers, Mount Dulit area, 3 villages; Nibong branch of Lobong river, a tributary of Tinjar river. *Status:* 6b (Threatened). *Class:* Austronesian, Malayo-Polynesian, North Borneo, North Sarawakan, Kayan-Kenyah, Penan. *Dialects:* Bok Penan (Bok), Jelalong Penan, Nibong, Penan Apo, Penan Gang (Gang), Penan Lanying, Penan Lusong (Lusong), Penan Silat, Sipeng (Speng). Not closely related to other languages. *Lg Dev:* NT: 1974. *Writing:* Latin script. *Other:* Traditionalists are nomadic and seminomadic. *Map:* 387:54.

Penang Sign Language [psg]. 1,000, decreasing. 150 monolinguals. Ethnic population: 2,000. Peninsular, Penang. *Status:* 8a (Moribund). *Class:* Deaf sign language. *Lg Use:* Home. Mainly older adults. Neutral attitudes. Also use Malaysian Sign Language [xml]. *Lg Dev:* Literacy rate in L1: 0%. Literacy rate in L2: Up to 50% in English. *Writing:* Unwritten. *Other:* Deaf school established 1954, with only oral method. Sign language evolved outside the classroom. Use declined late 1970s due to spread of other sign languages.

Punan Batu 1 [pnm]. 30 (Wurm 2000). L2 users: L2 used for most of the key domains. Central Sarawak, west of Long Geng, southeast of Belaga. *Status:* 8b (Nearly extinct). *Class:* Austronesian, Malayo-Polynesian, North Borneo, Melanau-Kajang, Kajang. *Lg Use:* Seriously endangered (2000 S. Wurm). A few to half the children speak it. *Writing:* Unwritten. *Other:* Different from Punan Batu 2, a dialect of Sajau Basap [sjb] in Kalimantan. Nomadic. They get salt from the Kayan. *Map:* 387:53.

Remun [lkj] (Milikin, Millikin). 3,500 (2000 SIL). Sarawak, Serian district, Kuching division, southeast of Serian to Balai Ringin. 13 villages. *Status:* 6b (Threatened). *Class:* Austronesian, Malayo-Polynesian, Malayo-Chamic, Malayic, Ibanic. *Lg Use:* Strong identity centered around the Remun isolect. All ages. Also use Bukar-Sadong Bidayuh [sdo], English [eng], Iban [iba], Malay [zlm]. *Writing:* Unwritten. *Other:* Ethnic autonym: Remun Iban. *Map:* 387:35.

Rungus [drg] (Dusun Dayak, Melobong Rungus, Memagun, Memogun, Momogun, Roongas, Rungus Dusun). 55,000 (2009 Protestant Church in Sabah). Ethnic population: 60,000. Sabah, Kudat and Bengkoka peninsulas surrounding Marudu bay; Marudu district south of Marudu bay; Labuk-Sugut district southeast of Marudu bay. *Status:* 6b (Threatened). *Class:* Austronesian, Malayo-Polynesian, North Borneo, Sabahan, Dusunic, Dusun. *Dialects:* Gandahon, Gonsomon, Nuluw, Pilapazan (Central Rungus, Rungus Tanga). Gonsomon and Nuluw most distinctive dialects. Gandahon is less distinct. Lexical similarity among dialects within 86%–96%. *Lg Use:* 90% L1 speakers. All domains. All ages. Positive attitudes. Also use Sabah Malay [msi], Standard Malay [zsm]. *Lg Dev:* Literacy rate in L1: low for those over 45; much higher for those under 30. Literacy in L2: Standard Malay [zsm] literacy higher than Rungus; school language is Standard Malay [zsm]. Dictionary. NT: 1981. *Writing:* Latin script. *Other:* Reside on 2 peninsulas surrounding a bay and identify themselves by which side of the bay they come from. Self-identify as Momogun and have complex internal social and ethnic relationships (Appell 1965). There is a strong sense of Rungus ethnic identity across all dialect groups. *Map:* 386:102.

Sa'ban [snv] (Merau). 1,110 in Malaysia (2000). Population total all countries: 1,960. Northeast Sarawak on Kalimantan border, 4th Division, south of Ramudu, Upper Baram, Long Banga', Long Puak, Long Peluan. Also in Indonesia. *Status:* 6b (Threatened). *Class:* Austronesian, Malayo-Polynesian, North Borneo, North Sarawakan, Dayic, Kelabitic. *Lg Use:* Vigorous. All ages. *Lg Dev:* Bible portions: 1969. *Map:* 387:72.

Sabüm [sbo]. No known L1 speakers. Peninsular, North central Perak State. *Status:* 9 (Dormant). *Class:* Austro-Asiatic, Mon-Khmer, Aslian, Senoic. *Dialects:* None known. Reportedly most similar to Lanoh [lnh] and Semnam [ssm]. *Writing:* Unwritten.

Salako [knx] (Kenayatn, Kendayan, Salakau, Selakau, Selako, Silakau). 10,700 in Malaysia (2000 census). Sarawak, 1st division, Saak and Lundu. 22 villages. *Status:* 6a (Vigorous). *Lg Use:* Gradually being adopted by Lara' [lra] youth. Home, village. All ages. Positive attitudes. Also use Malay [zlm]. *Other:* Sarawak census data for Lundu Bidayuhs; Salako are not linguistically Bidayuh, but are referred to as Bidayuh. See main entry on page 168 (as Kendayan). *Map:* 387:29.

Sama, Balangingih [sse] (Baangingi', Balagnini, Balangingi, Balangingi Bajau, Balanian, Balanini, Balignini, Banadan, Bangingih Sama, Binadan, Northern Sinama, Sama, Sama Bangingih). 5,000 in Malaysia (2013 SIL). East coast of Sabah. *Status:* 5 (Developing). See main entry on page 288. *Map:* 386:105.

Sama, Central [sml] (Badjaw, Sinama). 15,000 in Malaysia (2000 C. Soderberg). Sabah, Semporna and Kunak districts. *Status:* 5 (Developing). See main entry on page 289.

Sama, Southern [ssb] (Southern Bajau). 15,000 in Malaysia (2005 C. Soderberg). 0 monolinguals. Ethnic population: 119,000 (2000 SIL). 6,000 Sikubung, 15,000 Bajau Laut, 13,000, Bajau Ubian, 700 Bajau Banaran, 9,000 Sibutu, 14,500 Bajau Simunul, 61,000 Bajau Kubang (or Bajau Semporna). Sabah, east, north, and west coasts; Banggi, Kota Belud, Gaya Island, Kuala Penyu; Semporna district, Sandakan, Kota Kinabalu. *Status:* 6b (Threatened). *Dialects:* Bajau Banaran, Bajau Darat, Bajau Laut (Mandelaut, Pala'au, Sama Laut, Sama Mandelaut, Sama Pala'au, Sea Bajau, Sea Gypsies), Bajau Semporna (Bajau Asli, Kubang, Sama Kubang), Laminusa (Laminusa Sinama), Sama (A'a Sama, Sama', Samah, Samal, Samar), Sibutu (Sama Sibutu, Samah Lumbuh, Samah-Samah, Sibutuq), Sikubung (Kubung, Sama Kubung), Simunul (Sama Simunul), Ubian (Obian, Sama Ubian, Tau Ubian). *Lg Use:* Also use Malay [zlm], Tausug [tsg]. See main entry on page 289. *Map:* 386:93.

Sebop [sib] (Cebop, Sabup, Sebob, Sibop). 1,730 (Wurm and Hattori 1981). North Sarawak, 4th division, upper Tinjar river, between Rejang and Baram rivers. *Status:* 6b (Threatened). *Class:* Austronesian, Malayo-Polynesian, North Borneo, North Sarawakan, Kayan-Kenyah, Kenyah, Kayanic Kenyah. *Dialects:* Bah Malei (Ba Mali), Lirong, Long Atun, Long Ekang (Long Ikang), Long Luyang, Long Pokun, Tinjar Sibop. *Writing:* Unwritten. *Other:* Cebop used on the Indonesian side of the border, Sebop in Sarawak. *Map:* 387:57.

Sebuyau [snb] (Sabuyan, Sabuyau, Sibuian, Sibuyan, Sibuyau). 9,000 (Wurm and Hattori 1981). Sarawak, Lundu, 1st division, Lupa river mouth, Sebuyau west bank area. *Status:* 6b (Threatened). *Class:* Austronesian, Malayo-Polynesian, Malayo-Chamic, Malayic, Ibanic. *Writing:* Unwritten. *Map:* 387:37.

Sekapan [skp] (Sekepan). 750 (Wurm and Hattori 1981). Sarawak, Belaga, 7th division. *Status:* 6b (Threatened). *Class:* Austronesian, Malayo-Polynesian, North Borneo, Melanau-Kajang, Kajang. *Writing:* Unwritten. *Map:* 387:49.

Selangor Sign Language [kgi] (KLSL, Kuala Lumpur Sign Language). 500. Peninsular, Selangor, elsewhere.

Status: 8a (Moribund). *Class:* Deaf sign language. *Lg Use:* Home. Not used much by youth. May die out in the next generation. Positive attitudes. Also use Malaysian Sign Language [xml]. *Lg Dev:* Literacy rate in L1: 0%. Literacy rate in L2: 50% in English. *Other:* Uses many American signs with mostly English word order.

Selungai Murut [slg]. 600 in Malaysia (2000). Ethnic population: 600 (2000 SIL). Sabah, Pensiangan district, Sapulut river confluence with Pensiangan river south to Indonesia border. 1 village. *Status:* 6b (Threatened). *Lg Use:* Also use Malay [zlm] or other Sama variety. Also use Tausug [tsg] or other Sama variety. See main entry on page 189. *Map:* 386:120.

Semai [sea] ("Central Sakai" *pej.*, Sengoi, Seng'oi, Senoi). Ethnic population: 42,400 (2008 JHEOA). Peninsular, Northwest Pahang and south Perak states, north Selangor State. *Status:* 3 (Wider communication). The lingua franca of the Malaysian Aslian military armed forces unit (Bradley 2007). *Class:* Austro-Asiatic, Mon-Khmer, Aslian, Senoic. *Dialects:* Betau, Bidor, Bil, Cameron (Cameron Highlands), Gopeng, Jelai, Lipis, Parit, Perak I, Perak II, Tanjung Malim, Tapah (Jalan Pahang), Telom, Ulu Kampar (Kampar). Some dialects not mutually intelligible (2006 T. Phillips). *Lg Use:* Cameron Highlands dialect is used on radio and is a school language (Bradley 2007). Vigorous. Home, church, village. All ages. Positive attitudes. 100% also use Malay [zlm]. Some also use Temiar [tea] (Bradley 2007). *Lg Dev:* Literacy rate in L1: 5%. Literacy rate in L2: 60%. Literacy in Semai growing. Taught in primary schools. Dictionary. Bible portions: 1951–2011. *Writing:* Latin script. *Other:* 'Sakai', slave. 'Sengoi', people, in Semai. West Semai more acculturated to Malay society than east Semai. *Map:* 385:12.

Semaq Beri [szc] (Semaq Bri, Semoq Beri). 2,000 (Bradley 2007). Ethnic population: 3,970 (2008 JHEOA). Peninsular, Pahang, Terengganu, and Kelantan states. *Status:* 6a (Vigorous). *Class:* Austro-Asiatic, Mon-Khmer, Aslian, South Aslian. *Dialects:* 2 dialects. *Lg Use:* All ages. All also use Malay (Bradley 2007). *Writing:* Unwritten. *Map:* 385:15.

Sembakung Murut [sbr] (Sembakoeng, Sembakong, Simbakong, Tidoeng, Tidong, Tidung, Tingalun, Tinggalan, Tinggalum). Ethnic population: 2,000 (2000 SIL). 2,000–3,000 in Sabah. Along Sembakung river, from the mouth upstream into Sabah. *Status:* 6b (Threatened). See main entry on page 190. *Map:* 386:119.

Semelai [sza]. 4,100 (Kruspe 2009). Ethnic population: 6,270 (2008 JHEOA). Peninsular, southwest Pahang and northwest Negeri Sembilan states, Tasek Bera shores area, along Bera, Teriang, and Serting rivers; northwest Johore, Muar river. *Status:* 6b (Threatened). *Class:* Austro-Asiatic, Mon-Khmer, Aslian, South Aslian. *Type:* 32 consonant and 20 vowel phonemes. *Lg Use:* 100% also use Malay [zlm]. *Writing:* Unwritten. *Map:* 385:17.

Semnam [ssm]. 670 (2000). Peninsular, North central Perak State. *Status:* 6b (Threatened). *Class:* Austro-Asiatic, Mon-Khmer, Aslian, Senoic. *Dialects:* None known. Reportedly similar to Lanoh [lnh] and Sabüm [sbo]. *Writing:* Unwritten. *Map:* 385:6.

Seru [szd]. No known L1 speakers. Sarawak State. *Status:* 10 (Extinct). *Class:* Austronesian, Malayo-Polynesian, North Borneo, Melanau-Kajang, Melanau. *Writing:* Unwritten.

Serudung Murut [srk] (Serudong, Tawau Murut, Tidung). Ethnic population: 350 (2000 SIL). Sabah, Tawau district along Serudung river; Tawau town area. 1 village. *Status:* 6b (Threatened). *Class:* Austronesian, Malayo-Polynesian, North Borneo, North Sarawakan, Dayic, Murutic, Tidong. *Writing:* Unwritten. *Map:* 386:117.

Sian [spg] (Sihan). 50 (Wurm 2000). Sarawak, Belaga, 7th division. *Status:* 7 (Shifting). *Class:* Austronesian, Malayo-Polynesian, North Borneo, Melanau-Kajang, Kajang. *Dialects:* None known. May be intelligible of Bukitan [bkn], Ukit [umi], and Punan Batu 1 [pnm]. *Lg Use:* Endangered (2000 S. Wurm). A few to half the children speak Sian. *Writing:* Unwritten. *Map:* 387:47.

Tagal Murut [mvv]. Ethnic population: 13,000 (2000 SIL). Mainly in southwest Sabah State, Pensiangan, south Keningau, Tenom, Sipitang, and Nabawa districts; smaller area in Sarawak State, Limbang district. Also in Indonesia. *Status:* 6b (Threatened). *Class:* Austronesian, Malayo-Polynesian, North Borneo, North Sarawakan, Dayic, Murutic, Murut. *Dialects:* Alumbis (Loembis, Lumbis), Maligan (Bol Murut, Bole Murut, Mauligan, Meligan), Pensiangan Murut (Lagunan Murut, Pentjangan), Rundum (Arundum), Salalir (Sadalir, Saralir, Sedálir), Sapulot Murut (Sapulut Murut), Sumambu (Semambu, Semembu, Sumambuq), Tagal (North Borneo Murut, Sabah Murut, Taggal, Tagol, Tagul), Tawan, Tolokoson (Telekoson), Tomani (Tumaniq). Reportedly most similar to Paluan [plz]. *Lg Use:* Used as L2 by Paluan [plz]. *Lg Dev:* Bible: 1998. *Writing:* Latin script, developed in about 1987. *Maps:* 386:75, 387:75.

Tamil [tam]. 3,780,000 in Malaysia (Salleh 2006). Does not include 8,730 Sri Lankan Tamil. Peninsular. *Status:* 4 (Educational). Statutory language of national identity (1996, Education Act, No. 550, Articles 2 and 18). *Lg Use:* Also use English [eng], Malay [zlm]. Used as L2 by Standard Malay [zsm]. *Lg Dev:* Taught in primary and secondary schools. See main entry on page 145.

Tatana [txx] (Tatana', Tatanaq). Ethnic population: 5,500 (1982 SIL). Sabah, Kuala Penyu district. *Status:* 6b (Threatened). *Class:* Austronesian, Malayo-Polynesian, North Borneo, Sabahan, Dusunic, Bisaya. *Lg Use:* Positive attitudes. Used as L2 by Papar [dpp]. *Lg Dev:* Grammar. *Writing:* Latin script, developed in about 1983 till about 1989. *Map:* 386:90.

Tausug [tsg] (Joloano, Joloano Sulu, Moro, Sooloo, Sulu, Suluk, Taosug, Tausog, Taw Sug). 150,000 in Malaysia (2000 SIL). Sabah, Sempurna, Sandakan, Tawau, Lahad Datu, Labuk-Sugut, and Kudat districts. *Status:* 5 (Developing). *Lg Use:* All ages. Used as L2 by Selungai Murut [slg], Southern Sama [ssb]. *Other:* Immigrants from Sulu Archipelago in the Philippines. Glossonym: Suluk in Sabah. See main entry on page 291. *Map:* 386:110.

Temiar [tea] (Northern Sakai, Pie, Seroq, Temer). 15,000 (Bradley 2007). Ethnic population: 24,900 (2008 JHEOA). Peninsular, Perak, Kelantan, and Pahang states. *Status:* 3 (Wider communication). Used as a lingua franca by many northern Aslian groups (Bradley 2007). *Class:* Austro-Asiatic, Mon-Khmer, Aslian, Senoic. *Dialects:* Grik, Kenderong, Kenering, Lanoh Kobak, Po-Klo (Sakai Bukit of Temongoh), Sakai of Plus Korbu, Sungai Piah, Tanjong Rambutan, Tembe' (Tembi), Ulu Kinta (Kinta Sakai). *Lg Use:* The most secure Aslian language, but losing domains (Bradley 2007). 100% also use Malay [zlm]. Used as L2 by Batek [btq], Lanoh [lnh], Minriq [mnq], Semai [sea]. *Lg Dev:* Grammar. *Writing:* Unwritten. *Other:* Seminomadic. *Map:* 385:8.

Temoq [tmo]. Peninsular, southeast Pahang State, Jeram river. *Status:* 8b (Nearly extinct). *Class:* Austro-Asiatic, Mon-Khmer, Aslian, South Aslian. *Writing:* Unwritten. *Map:* 385:16.

Temuan [tmw] (Benua, Niap). Ethnic population: 22,700 (2008 JHEOA). Peninsular, south half of the peninsula, Negeri Sembilan, Selangor, Johor, and Putrajaya states, Kuala Langat and scattered settlements. *Status:* 6b (Threatened). *Class:* Austronesian, Malayo-Polynesian, Malayo-Chamic, Malayic, Malay. A member of macrolanguage Malay [msa]. *Dialects:* Beduanda (Biduanda), Belanda (Belana, Belanas, Belandas, Blanda, Landa), Berembun (Birmun), Mantra (Mentera, Mintra), Temuan, Udai. *Writing:* Unwritten. *Other:* Also classified as Malacca group of Austro-Asiatic phylum. Beduanda sometimes considered a separate language. May be a dialect of Malay [zlm]. *Map:* 385:19.

Tidong [tid] (Camucones, Nonukan, Tedong, Tidoeng, Tiran, Tirones, Tiroon, Zedong). Ethnic population: 20,000 (2000 SIL). In Sabah. Sabah, Kota Marudu and Kota Belud districts, Kota Kinabalu towns, others. *Status:* 6a (Vigorous). *Dialects:* Sesayap (Sesajap), Tarakan (Terakan). *Lg Use:* Home, market, village. All ages. Positive attitudes. *Lg Dev:* Standard Malay [zsm] used in school and formal settings. See main entry on page 194. *Map:* 386:111.

Timugon Murut [tih] (Temogun, Tenom Murut, Timigan, Timigun, Timogon, Timogun, Timugon, Tumugun). Ethnic population: 7,000 (2000 SIL). 1,200–1,700 in Beaufort Murut (1982 SIL). Sabah, Tenom district, Padas river from Melalap to Batu; Beaufort district, Bukau and lower Padas rivers. *Status:* 6b (Threatened). *Class:* Austronesian, Malayo-Polynesian, North Borneo, North Sarawakan, Dayic, Murutic, Murut. *Dialects:* Beaufort Murut (Binta'), Bukau (Bukow), Dabugus, Kapagalan, Lower Murut, Murut Padas, Poros, Sandiwar (Sandewar), Timugon. *Lg Dev:* Dictionary. NT: 1998. *Writing:* Latin script, developed in about 1984. *Map:* 386:78.

Tobilung [tgb] (Tabilong, Tebilung, Tobilang). Ethnic population: 8,850 (2007 A. Ripau). Sabah, Kota Marudu and Kota Belud districts; Kota Kinabalu and other towns. *Status:* 6b (Threatened). *Class:* Austronesian, Malayo-Polynesian, North Borneo, Sabahan, Dusunic, Dusun. *Dialects:* None known. Low intelligibility with Coastal Kadazan [kzj]; moderate intelligibility with Kimaragang [kqr] and Rungus [drg]. *Lg Use:* Stronger in villages in the interior. Home, market, village. 95% of the children are not learning the language or using it at home. Positive attitudes. L2 used in school. *Lg Dev:* L2 used in school. Dictionary. *Writing:* Latin script, developed in about 2004. *Map:* 386:100.

Tombonuo [txa] (Lobu, Paitan, Sungai, Sungei, Tambanua, Tambanuo, Tambanuva, Tambanwas, Tambenua, Tambunwas, Tembenua, Tombonuva, Tombonuwo, Tumbunwha, Tunbumohas). Ethnic population: 10,000 (2000 SIL). 3,000 Lingkabau. Sabah, Labuk-Sugut, Kota Marudu, and Pitas districts. *Status:* 6b (Threatened). *Class:* Austronesian, Malayo-Polynesian, North Borneo, Sabahan, Paitanic. *Dialect:* Lingkabau Sugut (Linkabau). *Lg Use:* Used as L2 by Dumpas [dmv]. *Lg Dev:* Dictionary. NT: 2002. *Writing:* Latin script, developed in about 1984. *Map:* 386:107.

Tonga [tnz] (Mos Tean-ean). 15 in Malaysia (2007). Peninsular, Perlis State, northwest tip north of Kaki. *Status:* 6b (Threatened). *Dialect:* Satun. *Other:* This small group crosses back and forth between the Malaysia and Thailand. See main entry on page 304. *Map:* 385:2.

Tring [tgq]. 550 (2000). Sarawak, Lower Tutoh river, Long Terawan village. *Status:* 6b (Threatened). *Class:* Austronesian, Malayo-Polynesian, North Borneo, North Sarawakan, Dayic, Kelabitic. *Writing:* Unwritten. *Other:* Distinct from Tringgus-Sembaan Bidayuh [trx]. *Map:* 387:67.

Ukit [umi]. 120 (Wurm and Hattori 1981). Sarawak, 7th division, upper Rajom and Tatau rivers, Baleh. *Status:* 6b (Threatened). *Class:* Austronesian, Malayo-Polynesian, North Borneo, Melanau-Kajang, Kajang. *Writing:* Unwritten. *Other:* Different from the Punan Ukit dialect of Bukitan [bkn]. *Map:* 387:50.

Uma' Lasan [xky] (Kanyay, Kenja, Kindjin, Kinjin, Western Kenya, Western Kenyah). 1,250 in Malaysia (Wurm and Hattori 1981). Population total all countries: 2,750. Sarawak, Balui, Belaga, Kalua, Kemena rivers. Sungai Asap resettlement camp. Also in Indonesia. *Status:* 6b (Threatened). *Class:* Austronesian, Malayo-Polynesian, North Borneo, North Sarawakan, Kayan-Kenyah, Kenyah, Upper Pujungan. *Dialects:* Uma' Alim, Uma' Baka, Uma' Lasan. Lexical similarity: 80% with Badeng and Lepu Kulit dialects of Mainstream Kanyah [xkl]. *Writing:* Unwritten. *Map:* 387:51.

Wolio [wlo] (Buton, Butonese, Butung). Ethnic population: 520 (1999 SIL). Sabah. *Status:* 6b (Threatened). *Other:* 'Buton' often used generically outside southeast Sulawesi for people from southeast Sulawesi, or is confused with Bajau people as sailors. Sabah varieties may be Cia-Cia [cia], Tukang Besi [bhq], Indonesian Bajau [bdl], or some other. See main entry on page 199.

Maldives

Republic of Maldives. 316,000 (2006 UNSD). Principal languages: English, Maldivian. 1,200 islands; 203 inhabited. Literacy rate: 98% (2006 UNESCO). Immigrant language: Arabic (300). Deaf population: 15,280.

The number of individual languages listed for Maldives is 2. All are living languages. Of these, 2 are institutional.

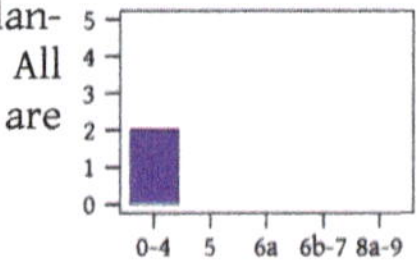

English [eng]. *Status:* 3 (Wider communication). De facto national working language. *Lg Use:* Used as L2 by Maldivian [div]. See main entry on page 319.

Maldivian [div] (Dhivehi, Divehi, Divehi Bas, Divehli, Mali, Malikh, Malki). 331,000 in Maldives (2012). Population total all countries: 340,500. Widespread. Also in India. *Status:* 1 (National). Statutory national language (2008, Constitution, Article 11). *Class:* Indo-European, Indo-Iranian, Indo-Aryan, Sinhalese-Maldivian. *Dialects:* Addu, Fuvah Mulaku, Huvadu, Malé, Maliku Bas. Southern dialects mutually intelligible but not with Male'. Southerners understand Male' by acquired intelligibility. Users of Male' cannot understand the others. *Type:* SOV. *Lg Use:* Vigorous. All domains. All ages. Positive attitudes. Also use English [eng]. English is education medium in most schools. Also use Hindi [hin], Urdu [urd]. Also use Arabic varieties. *Lg Dev:* Literacy rate in L2: 94%. Literacy rate is for those 6 years and older. English is educational medium of instruction in all government schools. Fully developed. Bible portions. *Writing:* Thaana script. *Other:* Muslim (Sunni).

Mongolia

Mongol uls. 2,648,000 (2010 census). Principal language: Halh Mongolian. Literacy rate: 98% (2010 UNESCO). General references: Poppe 1955; Sebeok 1967. Deaf population: 10,000–147,330.

The number of individual languages listed for Mongolia is 11. All are living languages. Of these, 2 are institutional, 4 are developing, 3 are vigorous, 1 is in trouble, and 1 is dying.

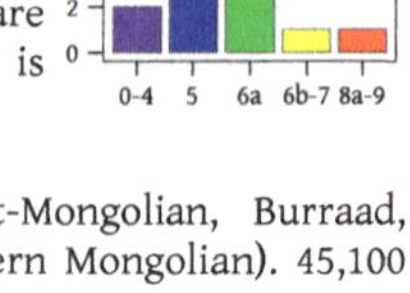

Buriat, Mongolia [bxm] (Buriat-Mongolian, Burraad, Buryat, Mongolian Buriat, Northern Mongolian). 45,100

(2010 census), decreasing. Northeast, especially Russian (Republic of Buryatia) border. *Status:* 6a (Vigorous). *Class:* Altaic, Mongolic, Eastern, Oirat-Khalkha, Khalkha-Buriat, Buriat. A member of macrolanguage Buriat [bua] (Russian Federation). *Dialects:* Aga, Khori. Buriat in Mongolia is a variety of Khori and differs considerably from Buriat [bxu] of China and the Russian Federation. Influenced by and mutually intelligible with standard (Halh) Mongolian [khk]. *Lg Use:* Also use Halh Mongolian [khk] as literary language. *Lg Dev:* Literacy rate in L2: High in Halh Mongolian [khk]. Films. Videos. Grammar. Bible portions: 2004. *Writing:* Cyrillic script. Latin script, used in 1930s. Mongolian script, used until 1917. *Other:* Some books in Buriat. Not a literary language in Mongolia. Traditional religion, Buddhist (Lamaist).

Chinese, Mandarin [cmn] (Hoton, Hui, Hui-Zu, Hytad, Khoton, Mandarin, Northern Chinese, Qotong, Xui). 35,000 in Mongolia (Johnstone 1993). 11,300 ethnic Khoton speak a form of Mandarin Chinese [cmn]. Northwest, Uvs Aimag. *Status:* 5 (Dispersed). *Lg Use:* Also use Halh Mongolian [khk]. *Lg Dev:* Literacy rate in L2: High literacy rate in Halh, or Mandarin. *Other:* Traditional religion. See main entry on page 67.

Daur [dta] (Daguor, Dagur, Dawar, Dawo'er, Tahuerh, Tahur). *Status:* 6a (Vigorous). *Dialects:* Buteha (Bataxan), Haila'er (Hailar), Qiqiha'er (Qiqihar, Tsitsikhar). See main entry on page 69.

Evenki [evn] (Khamnigan, Solon, Tungus). 1,000 in Mongolia (Krauss 1992). May be no longer spoken in Mongolia (Bradley 2007). North, Selenge Aimag. *Status:* 8b (Nearly extinct). *Lg Use:* Also use Halh Mongolian [khk]. *Other:* Traditional religion, Buddhist (Lamaist). See main entry on page 71.

Kazakh [kaz] (Kaisak, Kazakhi, Kazax, Kosach, Qazaq, Qazaqi). Ethnic population: 106,000 (2010 census). Northwest, Bayan-Olgiy Aimag, mining communities east of the capital; far east Choibalsan area. *Status:* 5 (Dispersed). *Lg Use:* Also use Halh Mongolian [khk]. *Other:* Muslim, traditional religion. See main entry on page 212.

Mongolian [mon]. A macrolanguage (see page 9). *Other:* Includes: Halh Mongolian [khk], Peripheral Mongolian [mvf] (China).

Mongolian Sign Language [msr]. Unknown number of users out of 10,000–147,330 deaf (1998). *Status:* 6a (Vigorous). *Class:* Deaf sign language. *Other:* Different from Russian Sign Language [rsl] and other sign languages.

Mongolian, Halh [khk] (Central Mongolian, Halh, Khalkha Mongolian, Mongol). 2,350,000 in Mongolia (1995). 32,300 Dariganga, 20,400 Darkhat. Population total all countries: 2,376,590. Widespread. Also in Taiwan, Czech Republic, Kyrgyzstan, Russian Federation, United States. *Status:* 1 (National). Statutory national language (1992, Constitution, Article 8(1)). *Class:* Altaic, Mongolic, Eastern, Oirat-Khalkha, Khalkha-Buriat, Mongolian Proper. A member of macrolanguage Mongolian [mon]. *Dialects:* Dariganga, Darkhat (Darhad, Darkhad), Halh (Khalkha), Khotogoit, Sartul, Tsongol. *Lg Use:* Vigorous. All domains. All ages. *Lg Dev:* Taught in all schools. Taught in primary and secondary schools. Poetry. Magazines. Newspapers. New media. Radio programs. TV. Videos. Dictionary. Grammar. NT: 1990. *Writing:* Braille script. Cyrillic script. Mongolian script, used prior to 1941 with a resurgence since the 1990s. Phags-pa script, no longer in use. Tibetan script, no longer in use. *Other:* Buddhist, traditional religion.

Mongolian, Peripheral [mvf] (Southern-Eastern Mongolian). *Status:* 5 (Developing). *Dialects:* Jirim (Khorchin), Jostu (Kharachin, Kharchin), Ordos, Tumut (Tumet), Ujumchin (Ujumuchin, Uzemchin), Urat. *Lg Use:* Also use Halh Mongolian [khk]. *Lg Dev:* Literacy is in Halh [khk]. See main entry on page 81.

Oirat [xal] (Kalmyk-Oirat, Western Mongol). 150,000 in Mongolia (Salminen 2007). Mainly in Kobdo and Ubsu leagues. *Status:* 6b (Threatened). *Dialects:* Bayit, Jakhachin, Khoshut (Khoshuud), Khoton (Hoton), Mingat, Olot (Eleuth, Elyut, Ööld), Uriankhai. *Lg Use:* Continues to be used as a community language in most areas (Salminen 2007). *Other:* Khoton (Hoton) originally of Turkic origin (Kara 1990), and were Muslim. Different from Chinese-speaking Qotong (Hoton) [cmn]. See main entry on page 321 (as Kalmyk-Oirat).

Russian [rus] (Russki). 4,000 in Mongolia (Johnstone 1993). *Status:* 3 (Wider communication). *Other:* 'Mectny Oros', permanent Russian residents. Widely taught in schools and higher education. See main entry on page 322.

Tuva [tyv] (Diba, Kök Mungak, Soyod, Soyon, Soyot, Tannu-Tuva, Tuba, Tuvan, Tuva-Uriankhai, Tuvia, Tuvin, Tuvinian, Tuwa-Uriankhai, Uriankhai, Uryankhai-Monchak). 27,000 in Mongolia (Johnstone 1993). North and west, Hövsgöl and Hovd Aimags. *Status:* 5 (Developing). *Dialects:* Khöwsögöl Uigur, Kokchulutan. *Lg Use:* Also use Halh Mongolian [khk]. *Lg Dev:* Literacy is in Halh [khk]. *Other:* Buddhist. See main entry on page 323.

Uyghur [uig] (Uighuir, Uighur, Uiguir, Uigur, Uygur). 1,000 in Mongolia (1982). North, Khovd and Bayan-Ölgii provinces. *Status:* 5 (Developing). *Lg Dev:* Literacy is in Halh [khk] in Mongolia; the Uyghur are generally assimilated to Halh culture. *Other:* Muslim (Sunni). See main entry on page 92.

Myanmar

Republic of the Union of Myanmar. 52,171,000 (2002 census). Principal language: Burmese. Literacy rate: 90% (2010 UNESCO). Immigrant language: Chinese (1,015,000). General references: Burling 2003; Bradley 1997, 2005, 2007; Comrie 1987; Hale 1982; Jones 1988; Lebar, Hickey, and Musgrave 1964; Manson 2010, 2011; Matisoff, Baron, and Lowe 1996; Thurgood and LaPolla 2003; van Bik 2006. Deaf population: 2,684,500. Deaf institutions: 2.

The number of individual languages listed for Myanmar is 117. Of these, 116 are living and 1 is extinct. Of the living languages, 11 are institutional, 34 are developing, 49 are vigorous, 18 are in trouble, and 4 are dying. See maps beginning on page 388.

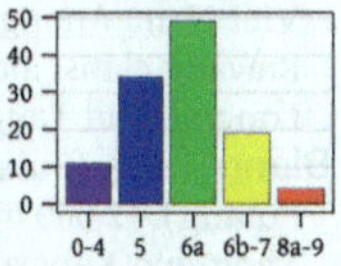

Achang [acn] (Acang, Anchan, Atsang, Chung, Manmaw, Mönghsa, Ngac'ang, Ngachang, Ngochang, Tai Sa'). 35,000 in Myanmar (2007). L2 users: Also used by Tai Sa blacksmiths among northern Shan. Kachin State, Waimaw and Japhwi townships, west of Ayeyarwaddy river near Bhamo (locally known as Manmaw), scattered among the Lashi [lsi] language area; China border. *Status:* 5 (Developing). *Dialect:* Maingtha. *Lg Use:* Also used by Tai Sa blacksmiths among northern Shan. Most domains. All ages. Positive attitudes. *Lg Dev:* Literacy rate in L1: Below 1%. Literacy rate in L2: 5%–15%. *Other:* Burmese glossonym: Maingtha, Chinese glossonym: Achang. Christian. See main entry on page 62. *Map:* 389:30.

Akeu [aeu] (Akheu, Aki, Akui). 1,000 in Myanmar (2004). Shan State, Kengtung and Mongla townships. *Status:* 6a (Vigorous). *Lg Use:* Vigorous. All domains. All ages. Positive attitudes. *Lg Dev:* Some communities have literacy classes. See main entry on page 62. *Map:* 391:97.

Akha [ahk] (Ahka, Aini, Aka, Ak'a, Ekaw, Ikaw, Ikor, Kaw, Kha Ko, Khako, Khao Kha Ko, Ko, Yani). 200,000 in Myanmar (Bradley 2007). Population total all countries: 563,960. L2 users: Other minority people who live among them use Ahka as L2. Shan State, east Kengtung district. Also in China, Laos, Thailand, Viet Nam. *Status:* 3 (Wider communication). *Class:* Sino-Tibetan, Tibeto-Burman, Ngwi-Burmese, Ngwi, Southern. *Dialects:* Much dialectal variation; some do not understand each other. *Type:* SOV; 5 tones. *Lg Use:* Vigorous. All domains. All ages. Positive attitudes. *Lg Dev:* Literacy classes in some communities. Dictionary. Bible: 2001. *Writing:* Latin script, used at least since 1950, used in China, Myanmar, and Thailand. Myanmar (Burmese) script, used in Myanmar. Thai script, used in Thailand. *Map:* 391:98.

Anal [anm] (Namfau). 50 in Myanmar (2010). Sagaing Region, Tamu town, 10 households. Possibly in Bangladesh. *Status:* 6b (Threatened). *Lg Use:* Vigorous. Positive attitudes. *Other:* Christian. See main entry on page 102.

Anong [nun] (Anoong, Anu, Anung, Fuchve, Fuch'ye, Khingpang, Kwingsang, Kwinp'ang, Naw, Nawpha, Nu). 400 in Myanmar (2000 D. Bradley), decreasing. Population total all countries: 450. Ethnic population: 10,000 (Bradley 2007). Northern Kachin State, mainly Kawnglangphu township. Also in China. *Status:* 8a (Moribund). *Class:* Sino-Tibetan, Tibeto-Burman, Central Tibeto-Burman, Nungish. *Dialects:* Slightly different dialects of Anong spoken in China and Myanmar, although no reported difficulty communicating with each other. Low inherent intelligibility with the Matwang variety of Rawang [raw]. Lexical similarity: 87%–89% with Anong in Myanmar and Anong in China, 73%–76% with T'rung [duu], 77%–83% with Matwang variety of Rawang [raw]. *Type:* SOV. *Lg Use:* Shifting to Lisu [lis] in all domains, except with very elderly. Ages 40 and over. Neutral attitudes; majority are indifferent that Anong is disappearing (Sun Hong Kai 2005). Highly bilingual in Lisu [lis]; most Anong speak Lisu as their first and best language. *Lg Dev:* Literacy rate in L1: Below 1%. Some community literacy classes. Dictionary. Grammar. NT: 1981. *Writing:* Latin script. *Other:* Different from Nung (Tai family) of Viet Nam, Laos, and China, and from Chinese Nung (Cantonese) of Viet Nam. Anong is one of the five principal divisions of Rawang clans, along with Matwang [raw], Daru-Jerwang, Longmi, and Tangsar (Morse 1989:240). Christian.

Blang [blr] (Bulang, K'ala, Kawa, Kontoi, Plang, Pula, Pulang). 12,000 in Myanmar (1994). East Shan State, Mong Yang and Kengtung townships. *Status:* 6a (Vigorous). *Lg Use:* Vigorous. All domains. All ages. Positive attitudes. Also use Awa [vwa]. *Other:* Some urbanized in Myanmar, Thailand, and China. An official nationality in China. Buddhist, Christian. See main entry on page 64. *Map:* 391:100.

Burmese [mya] (Bama, Bamachaka, Myanmar, Myen). 32,000,000 in Myanmar (2000 D. Bradley), increasing. 250,000 Beik, 20,000 Yaw (Bradley 2007). Population total all countries: 32,035,300. L2 users: 10,000,000 in Myanmar. Minority peoples throughout the country. Widespread in central Myanmar. Also in Malaysia, Thailand, United States. *Status:* 1 (National). Statutory national language (1974, Constitution, Articles 102, 152(b), 198). *Class:* Sino-Tibetan, Tibeto-Burman, Ngwi-Burmese, Burmish, Southern. *Dialects:* Beik (Merguese, Mergui), Mandalay Burmese, Yangon Burmese, Yaw. Diglossic high and low varieties. Bangladesh speakers use a non-standard variety called Bomang. *Type:* SOV. *Lg Use:* Many Mon, some Shan, some Karen are monolingual in Burmese. All domains. All ages. Positive attitudes. Also use English [eng], Mandarin Chinese [cmn]. *Lg Dev:* Taught in primary and secondary schools. Fully developed. Bible: 1835–2006. *Writing:* Braille script. Myanmar (Burmese) script, primary usage. *Other:* The official language name is Myanmar. Educated speech has many Pali borrowings. Buddhist. *Maps:* 389:35, 390:35, 391:35, 392:35.

Chak [ckh] (Ashah, Sak, Thet). 1,000 in Myanmar (Bradley 2007). Population total all countries: 4,000. Ethnic population: 1,600 (Bradley 2007). Northwest Rakhine State, 17 villages. Also in Bangladesh. *Status:* 6b (Threatened). *Class:* Sino-Tibetan, Tibeto-Burman, Sal, Jingpho-Luish, Luish. *Lg Use:* 1,000 also use Rakhine [rki]. *Other:* Distinct from Chakma [ccp]. Buddhist. *Map:* 390:63.

Chakma [ccp] (Daingnet, Sangma). North Rakhine State, Buthidaung, Maungdaw, Punnakyun, and Kyauktaw (main concentration) townships; south Chin State, Paletwa township, a few villages. *Status:* 6a (Vigorous). *Lg Use:* Vigorous. All ages. 10,000 also use Rakhine [rki]. Also use Burmese [mya]. *Other:* Dialect variation by township. A variety of Bangla, not to be confused with Chak [ckh]. Buddhist. See main entry on page 54. *Map:* 390:66.

Chin, Anu-Hkongso [anl] (Kaungso, Kaungtso, Khaungtso, Khawngso, Khong, Khongso, No). 4,000 (2008), decreasing. 0 monolinguals. Chin State, Paletwa township, between Kaladan and Michaung rivers. *Status:* 6b (Threatened). *Class:* Sino-Tibetan, Tibeto-Burman, Ngwi-Burmese, Mru. *Dialects:* Anu, Hkongso. Lexical similarity: 96%–98% and high intelligibility between Anu and Hkongso dialects, 72%–76% with Mru [mro] but intelligibility is low, 23%–37% lexical similarity with all neighboring Chin languages, but bilingualism is high. *Type:* SVO; negation is marked before the verb. *Lg Use:* Fairly strong vitality in Anu and Hkongso majority villages. But in mixed villages and intermarried families, Khumi [cnk] and Eastern Khumi [cek] varieties are now used. Most domains. All ages. Positive attitudes. 4,000 also use Rakhine [rki]. Also use Burmese [mya], Eastern Khumi Chin [cek], Khumi Chin [cnk]. *Lg Dev:* Anu and Hkongso have separate literature efforts. Some literacy classes. *Writing:* Latin script. *Other:* Although the Anu and Hkongso varieties are not part of the Kuki-Chin-Naga branch, these groups consider themselves to be Chin. Christian, Buddhist, traditional religion. *Map:* 390:59.

Chin, Asho [csh] (Asho, Ashu, Khamaw, Khamoe, Khyang, Kyang, Qin, Saingbaung, Sho, Shoa). 30,000 in Myanmar (2011 SIL). Population total all countries: 34,000. Ayeyarwaddy river lowlands; Rakhine State mountain areas. Also in Bangladesh. *Status:* 5 (Developing). *Class:* Sino-Tibetan, Tibeto-Burman, Sal, Kuki-Chin-Naga, Kuki-Chin, Southern. *Dialects:* Also related to Shendu [shl] and Chinbon [cnb]. Khyang dialect in Bangladesh is likely a separate language. *Type:* SOV; negation is marked after the verb. *Lg Use:* Vigorous. All domains. All ages. Positive attitudes. Also use Burmese [mya]. *Lg Dev:* Bible: 2009. *Writing:* Myanmar (Burmese) script. *Other:* Buddhist, Christian. *Map:* 390:70.

Chin, Bawm [bgr] (Bawm, Bawn, Bawng, Boam, Bom, Laisaw, Langkay). 1,500 in Myanmar (2010), decreasing. Chin State, Paletwa township, south Chin hills, Pi Taung, Ton Balay, and Bahun Taung villages. *Status:* 6b (Threatened). *Lg Use:* Vigorous. All domains. All ages. Positive attitudes. *Other:* Christian. See main entry on page 108. *Map:* 390:58.

Chin, Bualkhaw [cbl] (Bualkhaw-Chin). 2,500 (2006). Chin State, Falam township, north of Falam town. *Status:* 5 (Developing). *Class:* Sino-Tibetan, Tibeto-Burman, Sal, Kuki-Chin-Naga, Kuki-Chin, Central. *Dialects:* None known. Reportedly most similar to Falam Chin [cfm]. *Type:* SOV; negation is marked after the verb. *Lg Use:* Vigorous. All domains. All ages. Positive attitudes. *Lg Dev:* NT: 2011.

Writing: Latin script. *Other:* Christian. *Map:* 390:41.

Chin, Chinbon [cnb] (Chindwin Chin, Chinpon, Oo-pu, Sho, Tuishiip, Tuiship, Uppu, Ütbü). 19,600 (1983 census). Chin State, Kanpetlet and Paletwa townships; Magway region, Saw and Sidoktaya townships; Rakhine State, Minbya township. *Status:* 6a (Vigorous). *Class:* Sino-Tibetan, Tibeto-Burman, Sal, Kuki-Chin-Naga, Kuki-Chin, Southern. *Dialects:* None known. Lexical similarity: 50% with Asho Chin [csh]. *Type:* SOV; negation is marked after the verb. *Lg Use:* Vigorous. All domains. All ages. Positive attitudes. *Writing:* Latin script, recently developed, has a small user community. *Other:* Traditional religion, Buddhist, Christian. *Map:* 390:68.

Chin, Daai [dao] (Dai, Khyo, Kkhyou). 37,000 (2010). Chin State, Matupi, Paletwa, Kanpetlet, and Mindat townships, 142 villages. *Status:* 5 (Developing). *Class:* Sino-Tibetan, Tibeto-Burman, Sal, Kuki-Chin-Naga, Kuki-Chin, Southern. *Dialects:* Kanpetlet Daai (Nghngilo/Yang, Yindu), Matupi Daai (Ma-Tu, Shiip), Mindat Daai (Duk-Msang, Kheng, Mkui), Paletwa Daai (Ngxang, Vet, Yet). Intelligibility among Nghngilo (Yang), Yindu, and Mkui subgroups is high, but is lower among other subgroups. Lexical similarity: more than 90% with Yindu, Yang, Mkui, Duk, and Msang Daai, 81%–88% with Ngxang Daai (Paletwa Township) and Kheng Daai, 80% with Shiip Daai (Matupi Township), 91%–94% with Ng-Gha (part of Müün [mwq]), and 81%–87% with Müün. *Type:* SOV; negation is marked before the verb. *Lg Use:* Vigorous. All domains. All ages. Positive attitudes. Also use Burmese [mya], Müün Chin [mwq]. Used as L2 by Kaang Chin [ckn]. *Lg Dev:* Grammar. NT: 1996. *Writing:* Latin script. *Other:* Ethnic autonym: Khyo. The name Nghmoye is used by both Yang and Yindu to refer to each other. Matupi Daai may be a separate language. Christian. *Map:* 390:56.

Chin, Eastern Khumi [cek] (Ta-aw, Ta-oo). 12,000 (2009 SIL). Chin State, eastern Paletwa township, Sami subtownship, 85 villages. *Status:* 6a (Vigorous). *Class:* Sino-Tibetan, Tibeto-Burman, Sal, Kuki-Chin-Naga, Kuki-Chin, Southern. *Dialects:* Asang (Kasang, Sangtha), Khenlak, Khongtu, Lemi (Akelong, Aki Along, Kaja, Kajauk), Likhy (Likhaeng), Nideun (Amlai, Ghu, Laungtha, Maru, Paru, Tahaensae, Taheunso, Uiphaw), Nisay (Nise, Palyng, Tao Cha), Rengsa (Namboi, Nangbwe). High degree of intelligibility among the dialect groups, although strong attitudes against sharing the same literature. Lexical similarity: Nisay, Nideun, and Khongtu dialects share 92%–97%; Khenlak and Asang dialects also share 92%–97%; all dialects share at least 74% with each other; 75%–87% with Khumi Chin [cnk]; Likhy variety shares 86%–90% with Mro-Khimi Chin [cmr]. *Type:* SOV; negation is marked after the verb. *Lg Use:* Vigorous. All domains. All ages. Positive attitudes. 100% also use Rakhine [rki]. Or another Khumi variety. Used as L2 by Anu-Hkongso Chin [anl]. *Lg Dev:* Literacy classes are being taught in some communities. Preliminary orthographies and primers have been developed by many of the dialect groups. Poetry. Bible portions: 2007–2010. *Writing:* Latin script. *Other:* These dialect groups do not have a unified identity or overarching name for themselves. However, because their speech varieties are highly intelligible with each other and because they are referred to as Nisay - eastern groups - by the Khumi, the term Eastern Khumi is used here as a cover term to refer to these groups. The Likhy people live among the other Eastern Khumi peoples, but their language is very similar to the Aroeng variety of Mro-Khimi [cmr]. Christian. *Map:* 390:57.

Chin, Falam [cfm] (Falam, Fallam, Halam, Hallam Chin). 69,000 in Myanmar (1983). 9,000 Tashon, 16,000 Zanniat, 7,000 Khualshim, 4,000 Lente, 14,400 Zahao, 18,600 in Laizao (1983). Population total all countries: 107,300. Chin State, Falam township. Also in India. *Status:* 5 (Developing). *Class:* Sino-Tibetan, Tibeto-Burman, Sal, Kuki-Chin-Naga, Kuki-Chin, Central. *Dialects:* Hualngo, Khualshim (Kwelshin), Laizo (Laiso, Laizao, Laizo-Shimhrin), Lente (Gunte, Lyente), Ngawn, Sim, Taisun (Shunkla, Sunkhla, Taishon, Tashom, Tashon), Tapong, Zahao (Lyen-Lyem, Yahow, Zahau, Zahau-Shimhrin, Za-How), Zanniat (Zahnyiet, Zanniet). The Chorei dialect (in India) and Zanniat may be separate languages. Collectively called Baro Halam. Rupini and Koloi reportedly quite different from the others; Tapong reportedly has difficult intelligibility for other dialect speakers. 75% lexical similarity with Zanniat dialect. *Type:* SOV; negation is marked after the verb. *Lg Use:* Vigorous. All domains. All ages. Positive attitudes. *Lg Dev:* Most youth and some older people, if educated, can read Falam. Radio programs. Bible: 1991–2011. *Writing:* Bengali script. Latin script. *Other:* Christian. *Map:* 390:42.

Chin, Haka [cnh] (Baungshe, Hakha, Lai). 100,000 in Myanmar (1991 UBS). Population total all countries: 125,000. L2 users: 40,000 in Myanmar (2013 SIL). Chin State, Hakha township. Also in India. *Status:* 3 (Wider communication). Used as an LWC in church, market, business, and some media in parts of Chin State: Hakha Township, Thantlang Township, and parts of Matupi Township. *Class:* Sino-Tibetan, Tibeto-Burman, Sal, Kuki-Chin-Naga, Kuki-Chin, Central. *Dialects:* Klangklang (Thlantlang), Zokhua. *Type:* SOV; negation is marked after the verb. *Lg Use:* Vigorous. All domains. All ages. Positive attitudes. Used as L2 by Lautu Chin [clt], Matu Chin [hlt], Senthang Chin [sez], Thaiphum Chin [cth], Zyphe Chin [zyp]. *Lg Dev:* Lower for older people. Bible: 1978–2005. *Writing:* Latin script. *Other:* Christian. *Map:* 390:43.

Chin, Kaang [ckn] (Kang, Makaang, Mgan, M'kaang, Mkan). 1,000 (2010 SIL). Chin State, Mindat township, 3 villages. *Status:* 6a (Vigorous). *Class:* Sino-Tibetan, Tibeto-Burman, Sal, Kuki-Chin-Naga, Kuki-Chin, Southern. *Dialects:* Some dialectal variation among Kaang villages. Lexical similarity: 73%–80% with Rawngtu Chin [weu], 77%–79% with Müün Chin [mwq], 67%–80% with Daai [dao] varieties. *Type:* SOV; negation is marked before the verb. *Lg Use:* Vigorous. All domains. All ages. Positive attitudes. Also use Burmese [mya], Daai Chin [dao], Müün Chin [mwq]. *Lg Dev:* Literacy classes in some communities. *Writing:* Latin script. *Other:* Christian. *Map:* 390:55.

Chin, Khumi [cnk] (Common Khumi, Kaladan Khumi, Khami, Khimi, Khumi, Khweymi, Yangpan). 60,000 in Myanmar (2006). Population total all countries: 62,090. Chin State, Paletwa township, Kaladan river area; Rakhine State, Kyauktaw township, a few villages. Also in Bangladesh, India. *Status:* 5 (Developing). *Class:* Sino-Tibetan, Tibeto-Burman, Sal, Kuki-Chin-Naga, Kuki-Chin, Southern. *Dialects:* Eastern Kaladan, Kaladan, Pi Chaung, Southern Paletwa. Little dialect variation within Khumi. Lexical similarity: 76%–87% with Eastern Khumi varieties, 78%–81% with Mro-Khimi. *Type:* SOV; genitives, articles, adjectives, numerals after noun heads; negation is marked after the verb. *Lg Use:* Vigorous. All domains. All ages. Positive attitudes. 60,000 also use Rakhine [rki]. Used as L2 by Anu-Hkongso Chin [anl]. *Lg Dev:* Literacy rate in L2: 60%. Some community literacy classes. Radio programs. NT: 1959–1999. *Writing:* Latin script. *Other:* Christian, Buddhist, traditional religion. *Map:* 390:60.

Chin, Laitu [clj] (Daitu, Hio Bei, Hle-tu, Laikhy, Laitu Kheu, Ledu, Leitu). 15,000 (2007 SIL). Rakhine State, Sittwe district, Minpya, Mrauk-U, and Myepung townships. *Status:* 6a (Vigorous). *Class:* Sino-Tibetan, Tibeto-Burman, Sal, Kuki-Chin-Naga, Kuki-Chin, Southern. *Dialects:* Dalet Stream (Doitu, Ekai, Khulai), Kanni Stream, Panmyaunggyi River (Kongtu), Phuntha Stream (Daaitu), Yaw Stream. Dialects tend to differ by stream. High intelligibility within the main dialect area along the Kanni Stream (Nyuan Net Khuasung, Ahongdong, Pharphyaw, Pheithapyin villages). Lower intelligibility with more distant dialect areas, such as Dalet Stream and Yaw Stream. Intelligibility to some extent with Sumtu Chin [csv]. Reportedly somewhat similar to Chinbon Chin [cnb]. Low intelligibility with Songlai [csj]. Lexical similarity: 91%–96% with Sumtu Chin [csv] and Songlai Chin [csj], 85%–89% with Chinbon Chin [cnb], 82%–84% with Asho [csh]. *Lg Use:* Vigorous. All domains. All ages. Positive attitudes. 15,000 also use Rakhine [rki]. *Lg Dev:* Literacy classes are being taught in some communities. *Writing:* Latin script, preliminary orthography developed in 2009. *Other:* Buddhist. *Map:* 390:67.

Chin, Lautu [clt] (Lawhtu). 15,000 (2005 SIL). Chin State, Matupi and Thantlang townships, 17 villages. *Status:* 6a (Vigorous). *Class:* Sino-Tibetan, Tibeto-Burman, Sal, Kuki-Chin-Naga, Kuki-Chin, Maraic. *Dialects:* None known. High intelligibility within Lautu. Some differences between the northern Surngen variety and the southern varieties. Lexical similarity: 90%–97% within Lautu Chin, 87%–94% with Mara Chin [mrh], 82%–85% with Zophe Chin [zyp], 80%–86% with Senthang Chin [sez]. *Lg Use:* Vigorous. All domains. All ages. Positive attitudes. 7,000 also use Haka Chin [cnh]. Also use Burmese [mya]. *Writing:* Latin script, developed in the 1960s. *Other:* Christian. *Map:* 390:49.

Chin, Mara [mrh] (Lakher, Mara, Maram, Mira, Miram, Zao). 20,000 in Myanmar (1994). Chin State, Paletwa, Matupi, and Thantlang townships, border area with Mizoram in India, 70 villages. *Status:* 5 (Developing). *Dialects:* Hlawthai, Sabeu, Tlongsai. *Lg Use:* Vigorous. All domains. All ages. Positive attitudes. Used as L2 by Zyphe Chin [zyp]. *Other:* Christian. See main entry on page 108. *Map:* 390:47.

Chin, Matu [hlt] (Nga La). 30,000 in Myanmar (2012). Population total all countries: 40,000. Chin State, Matupi township. Also in India. *Status:* 5 (Developing). *Class:* Sino-Tibetan, Tibeto-Burman, Sal, Kuki-Chin-Naga, Kuki-Chin, Southern. *Dialects:* Ciing (Langle-Tamtlaih, Ngaleng, Phaneng, Siing, Vuitu), Doem (Ngatu, Valang), Langle-Tamtlaih, Ngala (Batu), Ngaleng, Phaneng, Thlangpang (Changpyang). Not intelligible with Haka Chin [cnh]. Mizoram Matu reportedly not intelligible with Myanmar varieties. There are many Matu varieties in Myanmar, all intelligible to some extent with each other. Lexical similarity: 78%–89% within Matu varieties in Myanmar, 65%–76% with Rawngtu Chin [weu], 66%–71% with Thaiphum Chin [cth]. *Type:* SOV; negation is marked after the verb. *Lg Use:* Vigorous. All domains. All ages. Positive attitudes. Also use Burmese [mya], Haka Chin [cnh]. Used as L2 by Thaiphum Chin [cth]. *Lg Dev:* Dictionary. NT: 1999–2000. *Writing:* Latin script. *Other:* The Chin in Mindat Township refer to all the Matu as Batu, but the Matu use this name only for the area around Matupi Town. Christian. *Map:* 390:48.

Chin, Mizo [lus] (Haulngo, Hualngo, Ka-Lin-Kaw, Le, Lusai, Lushai, Lushay, Lushei, Mizo, Whelngo). 12,500 in Myanmar (1983 census). Chin State, northwest Falam, western Tedim and Tonzang townships, near India border. *Status:* 5 (Developing). *Dialects:* Dulien, Mizo, Ngente. *Lg Use:* Vigorous. All domains. All ages. Positive attitudes. Used as L2 by Zyphe Chin [zyp]. *Lg Dev:* Some community literacy classes. *Other:* Christian. See main entry on page 131 (as Mizo). *Map:* 390:38.

Chin, Mro-Khimi [cmr] (Awa Khami, Khimi, Khumi Awa, "Kwe Myi" *pej.*, Mro, Mro Chin, Vakung, Wakun, Wakung). 75,000 (2012 SIL). Rakhine State, Kyauktaw, Buthidaung, Ponnagyun, Pauktaw, Mrauk U, and Maungdaw townships; Chin State, Paletwa township. *Status:* 6b (Threatened). *Class:* Sino-Tibetan, Tibeto-Burman, Sal, Kuki-Chin-Naga, Kuki-Chin, Southern. *Dialects:* Arang (Ahraing Khami, Areung, Aroeng), Vakung (Wakung), Xata, Xengna (Hrengna). Generally high comprehension of Vakung dialect among other dialect speakers. Vakung is the largest dialect and basis of literature. Lexical similarity: 91%–98% within Mro-Khimi varieties, 86%-90% with Likhy variety of Eastern Khumi [cek], 81%–85% with Lemi variety of Eastern Khumi [cek], 77%–81% with Kaladan Khumi [cnk]. *Type:* SOV; negation is marked after the verb. *Lg Use:* Vigorous. All domains. All ages. Positive attitudes. 138,000 also use Rakhine [rki]. *Lg Dev:* Some literacy classes. Bible portions: 2007–2010. *Writing:* Latin script. *Other:* Buddhist, Christian, traditional religion. *Map:* 390:65.

Chin, Müün [mwq] (Cho, K'cho Chin, Mindat, Mün, Müün). 15,000 (2011). Chin State, Mindat township. *Status:* 5 (Developing). *Class:* Sino-Tibetan, Tibeto-Burman, Sal, Kuki-Chin-Naga, Kuki-Chin, Southern. *Dialects:* Hngiyung, Ng'men (Hletlong, Hmong-K'cha, Nitu). Related to Daai Chin [dao]. Daai usually understand Müün due to contact, but Müün have difficulty understanding Daai. *Type:* SOV; negation is marked before the verb. *Lg Use:* Vigorous. All domains. All ages. Positive attitudes. Also use Burmese [mya]. Used as L2 by Daai Chin [dao], Kaang Chin [ckn], Rawngtu Chin [weu]. *Lg Dev:* Some literacy classes. Dictionary. Bible: 2000–2012. *Writing:* Latin script. *Other:* The ethnonyms Yawdwin, Chinbok, Tsinbok, Chinme, and Chinbe are old colonial names referring to people groups of current south Chin State and neighboring Yaw Valley and not to distinct languages. Christian, Buddhist, traditional religion. *Map:* 390:52.

Chin, Ngawn [cnw] (Ngawn, Ngon, Ngorn). 15,000 (1984). Chin State, north Falam township. *Status:* 5 (Developing). *Class:* Sino-Tibetan, Tibeto-Burman, Sal, Kuki-Chin-Naga, Kuki-Chin, Central. *Type:* SOV; negation is marked after the verb. *Lg Use:* Vigorous. All domains. All ages. Positive attitudes. *Lg Dev:* NT: 2006. *Writing:* Latin script. *Other:* Christian. *Map:* 390:40.

Chin, Rawngtu [weu] (Rongtu, Shimi, Welaung). 5,000 (2008). Chin State, Mindat township; Magway region, Htilin township, 2 villages. *Status:* 6a (Vigorous). *Class:* Sino-Tibetan, Tibeto-Burman, Sal, Kuki-Chin-Naga, Kuki-Chin, Southern. *Dialects:* Boishi, Kyonnam, Shitwanu, Welaung. Most Rawngtu in Mindat Township adequately comprehend the Kyonnam variety, but nearby Matu [hlt] villages in Matupi Township do not. These villages also do not consider themselves Rawngtu. Lexical similarity: more than 90% within Rawngtu; 84%-89% with Matupi Daai [dao], 67%–74% with Kaang Chin [ckn], 71%–83% with Matu varieties [hlt], less than 70% with Rungtu [rtc]. *Type:* SOV; negation is marked after the verb. *Lg Use:* Vigorous. All domains. All ages. Positive attitudes. Also use Burmese [mya], Müün Chin [mwq]. *Lg Dev:* Literacy rate in Burmese [mya] highest; very low literacy rate in Müün [mwq]. *Writing:* Latin script. *Other:* Christian (Protestant). *Map:* 390:53.

Chin, Rungtu [rtc] (Thaungtha). 0 monolinguals. Magway Region, Htilin, and Kyaukhtu townships, 25 villages. *Status:* 6b (Threatened). *Class:* Sino-Tibetan, Tibeto-Burman, Sal, Kuki-Chin-Naga, Kuki-Chin, Southern. *Dialects:* Central Rungtu, Northern Rungtu, Southern Rungtu.

Lexical similarity: 94%–96% within Rungtu, 60%–66% with Rawngtu Chin [weu]. *Type:* SOV; negation is marked after the verb. *Lg Use:* Shifting to Burmese [mya]. Only older adults. *Writing:* Unwritten. *Other:* Buddhist, traditional religion. *Map:* 390:51.

Chin, Senthang [sez] (Hsemtang, Sentang). 33,000 (2007 SIL). Chin State, Hakha township; Thantlang township, 2 villages; Magway region, Gangaw township, 15 villages; Sagaing region, Kaleymyo township, 2 villages. *Status:* 6b (Threatened). *Class:* Sino-Tibetan, Tibeto-Burman, Sal, Kuki-Chin-Naga, Kuki-Chin, Maraic. *Dialects:* Central Senthang (Bungzung, Khuapi, Lei-Um, Phaipha), Sakta, Shoneshi (Shonshe), Shonshe, Surkhua/Lungrang. High intelligibility among all Senthang villages, except possibly outlying dialects of Shoneshi, Surkhua (Lungrang), and Sakta. Lexical similarity: 79%–95% within Senthang. *Type:* SOV; negation is marked after the verb. *Lg Use:* Vigorous in Hakha township villages; lower use in Magway division, Gangaw township. All domains in Hakha township villages. All ages. Positive attitudes. Younger generation also use Burmese [mya]. 15,000 also use Haka Chin [cnh]. Mostly older generation. *Lg Dev:* Some community literacy classes (2011). *Writing:* Latin script. *Other:* Preliminary orthography developed and primers designed: 2007–2010. Christian, Buddhist. *Map:* 390:45.

Chin, Siyin [csy] (Siyang, Siyin, Sizang). 10,000 (1991 UBS). Chin State, south Tedim township. *Status:* 5 (Developing). *Class:* Sino-Tibetan, Tibeto-Burman, Sal, Kuki-Chin-Naga, Kuki-Chin, Northern. *Dialects:* None known. Reportedly similar to Tedim Chin [ctd] and Paite Chin [pck]. *Type:* SOV; negation is marked after the verb. *Lg Use:* Vigorous. All domains. All ages. Positive attitudes. *Lg Dev:* Bible: 2004. *Writing:* Latin script. *Other:* Christian. *Map:* 390:39.

Chin, Songlai [csj] (Hio). 7,300 (2012 SIL). Chin State, Paletwa township (Mang Um, Doitu, and Hettui dialects); Rakhine State, Mrauk-U township (Lai dialect); along the Laymyo or Phunglaung river. *Status:* 6a (Vigorous). *Class:* Sino-Tibetan, Tibeto-Burman, Sal, Kuki-Chin-Naga, Kuki-Chin, Southern. *Dialects:* Doitu, Hettui, Lai, Mang Um (Song). Reportedly closely related to Laitu Chin [clj]; lexical similarity over 90% but not intelligible. *Lg Use:* Vigorous. All domains. All ages. *Other:* Traditional religion, Buddhist, Christian.

Chin, Sumtu [csv] (Ahmyo, Chang, Hmyo, Settu, Settu Hmyo, Sungtu). 14,000 (2007 SIL). Rakhine State, Minbya, Myebon, and Ann townships. *Status:* 6a (Vigorous). *Class:* Sino-Tibetan, Tibeto-Burman, Sal, Kuki-Chin-Naga, Kuki-Chin, Southern. *Dialects:* Some variation between Minbya and Myebon townships, more variation with Ann township. High intelligibility within Sumtu. Lexical similarity: 91%–96% with Laitu Chin [clj], 96%–97% with Dalet Stream variety of Laitu Chin, 84%–87% with Chinbon Chin [cnb]. *Type:* SOV; negation is marked after the verb. *Lg Use:* Vigorous. All domains. All ages. Positive attitudes. 14,000 also use Rakhine [rki]. *Writing:* Latin script, preliminary orthography developed in 2010. *Other:* Buddhist, Christian. *Map:* 390:69.

Chin, Tawr [tcp] (Tawr, Torr). 700 (1996 D. van Bik). Chin State, Haka township, Lamthok and Rovan villages. *Status:* 6a (Vigorous). *Class:* Sino-Tibetan, Tibeto-Burman, Sal, Kuki-Chin-Naga, Kuki-Chin, Central. *Type:* SOV; negation is marked after the verb. *Lg Use:* Vigorous. All domains. All ages. Positive attitudes. *Writing:* Latin script. *Other:* Included in official ethnic list as Torr. Not the same as Chintaw, a dialect of Achang [acn], a Northern Burmic language spoken in Yunnan, China. Christian. *Map:* 390:44.

Chin, Tedim [ctd] (Hai-Dim, Tedim, Tiddim). 189,000 in Myanmar (1990). Population total all countries: 344,000. L2 users: Used as L2 in Tiddim political subdivision. Chin State, Tedim, Tonzang, and Cikha townships; Kalay area. Also in India. *Status:* 5 (Developing). *Class:* Sino-Tibetan, Tibeto-Burman, Sal, Kuki-Chin-Naga, Kuki-Chin, Northern. *Dialects:* Kamhau (Kamhao, Kamhow), Sokte. Other area Chin languages or dialects are Saizang [pck], Teizang [pck], and Zou [zom]. *Type:* SOV; negation is marked after the verb. *Lg Use:* Vigorous. All domains. All ages. Positive attitudes. *Lg Dev:* Bible: 1977–2010. *Writing:* Latin script. *Other:* Zomi may refer to Tedim [ctd] or to all Chin groups. Christian. *Maps:* 389:37, 390:37.

Chin, Thado [tcz] (Kuki, Kuki-Thado, Thado-Pao, Thadou, Thado-Ubiphei). 26,200 in Myanmar (1983 census). Sagaing Region, Khamti, Homalin, Layshi, and Tamu townships, India border area. *Status:* 5 (Developing). *Dialects:* Baite, Changsen, Hawkip, Jangshen, Kaokeep, Khongzai, Kipgen, Langiung, Paite, Sairang, Thangngen. *Lg Use:* Vigorous. All domains. All ages. Positive attitudes. *Other:* Christian. See main entry on page 108. *Map:* 389:21.

Chin, Thaiphum [cth] (Thui Phum). 1,000 (2005 SIL). Chin State, Matupi township, 4 villages. *Status:* 6a (Vigorous). *Class:* Sino-Tibetan, Tibeto-Burman, Sal, Kuki-Chin-Naga, Kuki-Chin. *Dialects:* Very little dialectal variation among the Thaiphum villages. Thaiphum is intelligible to some extent with neighboring languages, such as the Eastern Khumi [cek] varieties of Khenlak, Asang, and Rengsa. Lexical similarity: 72%–75% with Eastern Khumi [cek], 69%–71% with Khumi [cnk], 65%–68% with Mro-Khimi [cmr], 66%–71% with Matu Chin [hlt]. *Type:* SOV; negation is marked after the verb. *Lg Use:* Vigorous. All domains. All ages. Positive attitudes. The older generation also uses Haka Chin [cnh]. Also use Matu Chin [hlt]. Also use Burmese [mya]. *Writing:* Unwritten. *Other:* Christian. *Map:* 390:54.

Chin, Zotung [czt] (Yotun, Zo Mingphuin, Zobya, Zotung). 40,000 (1990 UBS). Chin State, Reizwa subtownship. *Status:* 5 (Developing). *Class:* Sino-Tibetan, Tibeto-Burman, Sal, Kuki-Chin-Naga, Kuki-Chin, Maraic. *Dialects:* None known. Reportedly intelligible with Haka Chin [cnh]. *Type:* SOV; negation is marked after the verb. *Lg Use:* Vigorous. All domains. All ages. Positive attitudes. *Lg Dev:* NT: 2004. *Writing:* Latin script. *Other:* Christian. *Map:* 390:50.

Chin, Zyphe [zyp] (Zo-pe, Zophei, Zoptei, Zyphe). 17,000 in Myanmar (1994). Population total all countries: 20,000. Chin State, Thantlang township. Also in India. *Status:* 5 (Developing). *Class:* Sino-Tibetan, Tibeto-Burman, Sal, Kuki-Chin-Naga, Kuki-Chin, Maraic. *Dialects:* Lower Zyphe, Upper Zyphe. Reportedly similar to Mara Chin [mrh]. Myanmar and India varieties reportedly mutually intelligible. *Lg Use:* Vigorous. All domains. All ages. Positive attitudes. 10,000 also use Haka Chin [cnh]. Also use Mara Chin [mrh], Mizo [lus]. *Lg Dev:* Some community literacy classes. NT: 2010. *Writing:* Latin script, developed in 1997. *Other:* Christian. *Map:* 390:46.

Chinese, Mandarin [cmn] (Tayok). 500,000 in Myanmar (1994). North Shan State; small groups around the country. *Status:* 5 (Dispersed). *Dialect:* Kokang (Kokant). *Lg Use:* Vigorous. All domains. All ages. Positive attitudes. Also use Burmese [mya]. Used as L2 by Burmese [mya], Drung [duu], Parauk Wa [prk], Rumai Palaung [rbb], Tai Loi [tlq], Tai Nüa [tdd]. *Other:* The Kokang have been given a Self-Administered Zone. The Kokang dialect in Myanmar is most similar to the dialect spoken in Yunnan Province, China. Buddhist, Daoist. See main entry on page 67. *Maps:* 389:32, 391:32.

Danau [dnu] (Danaw). 1,000 (Robinne 2000). Ethnic population: 5,000 (Robinne 2000). Southwest Shan State, Kalaw township, Ang Pan area, just west of

Inle lake, on road to Heho. *Status:* 6b (Threatened). *Class:* Austro-Asiatic, Mon-Khmer, Northern Mon-Khmer, Palaungic, Western Palaungic, Danau. *Dialects:* None known. Reportedly most similar to Riang-Lang [ril]. *Lg Use:* Endangered. Also use Pa'o [blk]. *Lg Dev:* Literacy rate in L1: Below 1%. *Other:* Not the same as Danu [dnv], a Southern Burmic language. Buddhist, traditional religion. *Map:* 391:91.

Danu [dnv] (Taruw). 100,000 (Bradley 2007). Shan State, Danu self-administered zone, Ywa Ngan and Pindaya townships; Taunggyi, Yak Sauk, Ye Oo, Aung Ban, and Kalaw townships. *Status:* 6a (Vigorous). *Class:* Sino-Tibetan, Tibeto-Burman, Ngwi-Burmese, Burmish, Southern. *Dialects:* Some dialect variation between Danu villages; however, intelligilibility is quite high. Lexical similarity: 93% with standard Burmese [mya], 93% with Intha [int], 91% with Taungyo [tco], 85%–94% with Rakhine [rki]. *Lg Use:* Vigorous. All domains. All ages. Positive attitudes. Also use Burmese [mya]. *Writing:* Unwritten. *Other:* Officially considered a Burmese dialect. Not the same as Danau [dnu], a Palaungic language. Buddhist. *Maps:* 390:92, 391:92.

Drung [duu] (Derung, Dulong, Qiu, Rawang, Tarong, Thrung, Trung, T'rung, Tulung). 225 in Myanmar. Far north Kachin State, Pannandin township, Talatu and Khraung villages. *Status:* 6a (Vigorous). *Lg Use:* Vigorous. All domains. All ages. Positive attitudes. High bilingualism in the Jerwang variety of Rawang [raw]. Also use Burmese [mya], Lisu [lis], Mandarin Chinese [cmn]. *Lg Dev:* Literacy rate in L1: Very low. *Other:* Geographically isolated from the Drung in China. Christian (Protestant). See main entry on page 70. *Map:* 389:2.

Hmong Njua [hnj] (Blue Hmong, Blue Meo, Ching Miao, Green Hmong, Green Meo, Hmong Leng, Hmong Nzhua, Hmoob Leeg, Lu Man Zi, Meo Dam, Meo Lai, Miao Tsi, Mong Leng, Mong Ntsua, Qing Miao, Tak Miao). 10,000 in Myanmar (2000). Shan State, Kunlong township, 6 villages; Hseni, and Namtu townships. *Status:* 6a (Vigorous). *Lg Use:* Vigorous. All domains. All ages. Positive attitudes. *Other:* Christian. See main entry on page 214. *Maps:* 389:29, 391:29.

Hpon [hpo] (Hpön, Megyaw, Phon, Phön, Phun, Samong). No known L1 speakers (Bradley 2007), decreasing. Southern dialect extinct; northern dialect moribund; some older people remember lexical items but none can speak it (Bradley 2007). Ethnic population: 1,500 (Bradley 2007). Kachin State, Upper Ayeyarwady gorges, north of Bhamo. *Status:* 9 (Dormant). *Class:* Sino-Tibetan, Tibeto-Burman, Ngwi-Burmese, Burmish, Northern. *Dialects:* North Hpon, South Hpon. *Writing:* Unwritten. *Map:* 389:27.

Intha [int] (Inntha, Insa, Naung Ma). 90,000 (2000 D. Bradley). South Shan State, Taunggyi district, Inle lake area, Shwe Nyaung township. Important Intha-speaking villages: Heha Ywama (largest), In Chan, Tha Lay, Nan Pan, and Paw Kon. *Status:* 6a (Vigorous). *Class:* Sino-Tibetan, Tibeto-Burman, Ngwi-Burmese, Burmish, Southern. *Dialects:* Well-known nonstandard variety of Burmese [mya] with major pronunciation and vocabulary differences. Some dialect variation between Intha villages; however, intelligibility reportedly high. Some comprehension of Danu [dnv] and Taungyo [tco]. Lexical similarity: 95% with standard Burmese [mya], 93% with Danu [dnv], 89% with Taungyo [tco], 90% with Rakhine [rki]. *Type:* SOV. *Lg Use:* Vigorous. All domains except education and formal contexts. All ages. Positive attitudes. Also use Burmese [mya]. *Writing:* Unwritten, informal and non-standardized use of Myanmar script. *Other:* Officially viewed as a Burmese dialect. Pa-O people call them Naung Ma, people who live on the lake. Buddhist. *Map:* 391:88.

Jingpho [kac] (Chingpaw, Chingp'o, Jinghpaw, Kachin). 900,000 in Myanmar (Johnstone and Mandryk 2001). Population total all countries: 940,000. Kachin State; northwest Shan State. Also in China. *Status:* 3 (Wider communication). Lingua franca for Zaiwa [atb], Lashi [lsi], and Lhao Vo [mhx]. *Class:* Sino-Tibetan, Tibeto-Burman, Sal, Jingpho-Luish, Jingpho. *Dialects:* Dulong (Dalaung, Duleng), Dzili (Jili), Hkaku (Hka-Hku), Kauri (Gauri, Guari, Hkauri). Dzili may be a separate language. Hkaku and Kauri are only slightly different. Lexical similarity: 50% with Singhpo [sgp] of India. *Type:* SOV; adjectives and numbers follow nouns; singular, dual, plural pronouns; tense-lax vowel distinction; 4 tones. *Lg Use:* Most domains. All ages. Positive attitudes. Also use Burmese [mya]. Used as L2 by Khamti [kht], Lashi [lsi], Lhao Vo [mhx], Lisu [lis], Rawang [raw], Rumai Palaung [rbb], Zaiwa [atb]. *Lg Dev:* Literacy rate in L1: 60%–100%. Literacy rate in L2: 50%–75%. Some community literacy classes. Newspapers. Radio programs. Films. Dictionary. Bible: 1927–2009. *Writing:* Latin script. *Other:* Kachin refers to a cultural, not linguistic, group. Glossonym: Aphu or Phu by Rawang [raw] people. Christian. *Maps:* 389:9, 391:9.

Kadu [zkd] (Gadu, Ka'do, Kadu-Ganaan, Kantu', Kato, Kudo, Maw, Mawteik, Puteik, Thet). 30,000 (2007 SIL), decreasing. Over 30 villages in Mawteik dialect (nearly extinct); over 30 villages in Settaw dialect; 5 villages in Mawkhwin dialect. 0 monolinguals. Sagaing Region, Katha district, Banmauk and Indaw townships; also in Homalin, Paungbyin, Pinlebu, and Wuntho townships. *Status:* 6b (Threatened). *Class:* Sino-Tibetan, Tibeto-Burman, Sal, Jingpho-Luish, Luish. *Dialects:* Mawkhwin, Mawteik, Settaw. Each Kadu dialect distinct with low comprehension between the Mawkhwin, Settaw, and Mawteik Kadu varieties. All Kadu (except possibly Mawkhwin Kadu) have low comprehension of Kanan [zkn]. Lexical similarity: 95%–98% with Settaw and Mawteik Kadu, 91%–93% with Mawkhwin Kadu and other Kadu varieties, 84%–89% with Kadu varieties and Kanan [zkn]. *Lg Use:* Vigorous in Banmauk Township (Settaw and Mawkhwin dialects), almost extinct in Indaw and Pinlebu townships (Mawteik dialect) where speakers have shifted to Burmese [mya]. All domains. All ages in Banmauk Township; only over 80 years old in Indaw Township. Positive attitudes. Also use Burmese [mya]. *Lg Dev:* Literacy rate in L1: Below 1%. *Writing:* Latin script, in development. *Other:* Different from Kaduo [ktp], a Sino-Tibetan language of China and Laos. The Kadu say they are descended from the Thet, also known as Sak (see Chak [ckh]). Buddhist. *Map:* 389:26.

Kanan [zkn] (Ganaan, Ganan, Ganon, Genan, Kana). 9,000 (2007 SIL). 0 monolinguals. Sagaing Region, Katha district, Banmauk township, along Mu river, southwest of Kadu [zkd] language area, 24 villages; Homalin, Indaw, and Pinlebu townships, a few villages. *Status:* 6a (Vigorous). *Class:* Sino-Tibetan, Tibeto-Burman, Sal, Jingpho-Luish, Luish. *Dialects:* None known. High comprehension within all the Kanan villages. Low comprehension of, but reportedly similar to, Kadu [zkd]. Lexical similarity: 95%–99% within Kanan varieties, 84%–89% with Kadu varieties. *Lg Use:* Vigorous. All domains. All ages. Positive attitudes. Also use Burmese [mya]. *Writing:* Unwritten. *Other:* Buddhist. *Map:* 389:25.

Karen, Bwe [bwe] (Baghi, Bghai Karen, Blimaw, Bwe, Dareh, Manaw). 17,200 (1997 F. Bennett), decreasing. 0 monolinguals. Kayin State, Thandaung township, about 100 villages; Kayah State, Hpruso township. *Status:* 6b (Threatened). *Class:* Sino-Tibetan, Tibeto-Burman, Karenic, Central. *Dialects:* Eastern Bwe Karen, Western

Bwe Karen. Most comprehend Western Bwe Karen dialect; some comprehend Geba [kvq] and Kayaw [kvl]; no inherent intelligibility with Kayah [eky] or Geko [ghk]. Lexical similarity: 82%–100% with Geba Karen [kvq]. *Type:* SVO. *Lg Use:* Some shift to S'gaw Karen [ksw] or Burmese [mya]. Most domains, except church. All ages. Positive attitudes. 10,000 also use S'gaw Karen [ksw]. S'gaw Karen used in church. Also use Burmese [mya]. *Lg Dev:* Literacy rate in L1: Below 1%. Some S'gaw Karen [ksw] literacy classes held. Bible portions: 1857–1862. *Writing:* Myanmar (Burmese) script. *Other:* Western Bwe Karen more widely understood, more prestigious. Bwe is sometimes used as an overarching cover term for all high-dwelling Central Karennic groups, who are not S'gaw Karen or Pwo Karen. Bwe people are very similar to the Mobwa people in lifestyle and culture. Christian (Roman Catholic), Christian (Protestant). *Map:* 391:77.

Karen, Geba [kvq] (Daneh, Geba, Kaba, Karenbyu, Kayinbyu, Kono, Koo-ong, Northern Bwe). 40,000 (2010 Geba Literature and Culture Committee). North Kayin State, Thandaunggyi township, 140 villages; Bago Region; Mandalay Region, Pyinmana township; Shan State, Pekon and Pinlong townships; Kayah State. *Status:* 6a (Vigorous). *Class:* Sino-Tibetan, Tibeto-Burman, Karenic, Central. *Dialects:* Gerkho-Geba, Sawkho, Thamitaik (Sawkeepho). May be same subgroup with Bwe Karen [bwe] and Kayaw [kvl]. Some comprehension of Bwe Karen [bwe]. Sawkho and Gerkho-Geba varieties slightly divergent. Lexical similarity: 82%–100% with Bwe Karen [bwe]. *Lg Use:* Vigorous. All domains. All ages. Positive attitudes. Catholics, Baptists and Anglicans also use Burmese [mya]. 10,000 also use S'gaw Karen [ksw]. Baptists and Anglicans use S'gaw Karen. *Lg Dev:* Radio programs. Dictionary. Grammar. Bible portions: 1870–2001. *Writing:* Latin script, used since 1870, used by Roman Catholics. Myanmar (Burmese) script, used since 2002, used by Anglicans and Baptists. *Other:* Geko Karen [ghk] and Geba Karen are grouped together in the local Baptist Association administration and are often considered to be the same language (Geko-Geba), although they are distinct. Christian (Roman Catholic), Christian (Protestant). *Map:* 391:81.

Karen, Geko [ghk] (Gaikho, Gekho, Gek'o, Ghekhol, Ghekhu, Gheko, Kakhau, Kayan, Kayan Kakhau, Kekaungdu, Kekhong, Keku, Yathu Gekho). 17,000 (Manson 2010). North Kayin State, Thandaunggyi township; south Shan State, Pekon township; Mandalay Region, Yamethin District; Bago Region, Toungoo district. *Status:* 6a (Vigorous). *Class:* Sino-Tibetan, Tibeto-Burman, Karenic, Central. *Dialects:* Geker, Gekho, Thaidai (Htideh). *Type:* SVO. *Lg Use:* Vigorous. All domains. All ages. Positive attitudes. 5,000 also use S'gaw Karen [ksw]. Also use Burmese [mya]. *Writing:* Unwritten. *Other:* Geko Karen is often considered a sub-variety or clan of Kayan [pdu]. Geko Karen and Geba Karen [kvq] are grouped together in the local Baptist Association administration and are often considered to be the same language (Geko-Geba), although they are distinct. Christian. *Map:* 391:86.

Karen, Mobwa [jkm] (Bilichi, Blimaw, Dermuha, Maleh, Monpwa, Mopwa, Palachi, Palakhi, Palaychi, Pa-Le-Chi). 4,000 (2010 SIL). Also live mixed with Bwe Karen [bwe] and Paku Karen [jkp] in some villages. Karen State, Thandaung township, western foot of Thandaung mountains. 9 villages. *Status:* 6b (Threatened). *Class:* Sino-Tibetan, Tibeto-Burman, Karenic, Southern. *Dialects:* Dermuha (Southern Mobwa), Palaychi (Southern Mobwa). Reportedly similar to Paku Karen [jkp]. *Lg Use:* Shifting to S'gaw Karen [ksw] and Burmese [mya]. Home. All ages. Positive attitudes. 2,000 also use S'gaw Karen [ksw]. Also use Burmese [mya]. *Writing:* Unwritten. *Other:* Similar to Bwe Karen [bwe] in lifestyle and culture. Christian. *Map:* 391:78.

Karen, Paku [jkp] (Mogpha, Mogwa, Monebwa, Monnepwa, Mopaga, Mopha, Pagu, Paku, Thalwepwe). 5,300 (1983 census). North Kayin State, hills southeast of Taungoo in east Bago Region bordering Kayin State; south Kayah State. *Status:* 6a (Vigorous). *Class:* Sino-Tibetan, Tibeto-Burman, Karenic, Southern. *Dialects:* Bawgali, Kyauk Gyi, Mawchi, Shwe Kyin. Dialects based on villages: Kyauk Gyi and Shwe Kyin are spoken in east Bago Region, Taungoo District near Kayin State border; Mawchi is spoken in Kayah State; Bawgali is spoken in north Kayin State. Some Paku dialects are reportedly quite similar to S'gaw Karen [ksw], while others are more similar to Bwe [bwe] and Geba [kvq]. *Type:* SVO. *Lg Use:* Vigorous. All domains. All ages. Positive attitudes. 5,000 also use S'gaw Karen [ksw]. Also use Burmese [mya]. *Lg Dev:* The Paku Karen use S'gaw Karen [ksw] literature and consider it to be their own. S'gaw Karen literacy classes in some Christian communities through the churches. *Writing:* Unwritten. *Other:* Christian. *Map:* 391:73.

Karen, Pwo Eastern [kjp] (Moulmein Pwo Karen, Phlong, Phlou, Pho). 1,000,000 in Myanmar (1998). Population total all countries: 1,050,000. Kayin State, Mon State, Tanintharyi Region. Also in Thailand (Pwo West-Central Thailand Karen). *Status:* 5 (Developing). *Class:* Sino-Tibetan, Tibeto-Burman, Karenic, Peripheral. *Dialects:* Kawkareik (Eastern Border Pwo Karen), Pa'an (Inland Eastern Pwo Karen, Moulmein), Tavoy (Southern Pwo Karen). Not intelligible with Pwo Karen [pwo]. Reportedly fairly high comprehension among Eastern Pwo Karen dialects. Lexical similarity: 91%–97% among dialects; 63%–65% with Pwo Karen [pwo]. *Type:* SVO. *Lg Use:* Vigorous. All domains. All ages. Positive attitudes. Also use Burmese [mya]. Used as L2 by S'gaw Karen [ksw]. *Lg Dev:* Bible portions: 2002. *Writing:* Leke (Chicken-Scratch) script, developed between 1830–1860, used by adherents to the Leke Millenarian sect. Myanmar (Burmese) script, primary usage, a variety of orthographies are in use. Thai script, developed by expatriates around 2000, used by West Central Thailand Pwo Karen community, limited usage. *Other:* Buddhist, Christian (Protestant). *Maps:* 391:74, 392:74.

Karen, Pwo Western [pwo] (Bassein Pwo Karen, Delta Pwo Karen, Mon Karen, Mutheit, Pathein Pwo Karen, Phlong, Phlong Sho, Pho, Shu, Talaing Karen). 210,000, decreasing. Ayeyarwaddy Region, Delta area, Pathein, Twante, Ma Ubin, Ein Meh, Kyone Pyaw, Hinthada, and Yangon. *Status:* 6b (Threatened). *Class:* Sino-Tibetan, Tibeto-Burman, Karenic, Peripheral. *Dialects:* Very little dialectal variation among Western Pwo Karen. *Type:* SVO. *Lg Use:* Vigorous in villages; lessening in towns. All domains. All ages. Positive attitudes. Also use Burmese [mya]. Used as L2 by S'gaw Karen [ksw]. *Lg Dev:* Summer and church literacy classes in many communities; used and taught in Bible schools. Dictionary. Bible: 1883–1885. *Writing:* Myanmar (Burmese) script. *Other:* Buddhist, Christian. *Maps:* 390:71, 391:71, 392:71.

Karen, S'gaw [ksw] (Burmese Karen, Kanyaw, Kayinpyu, Kyetho, Paganyaw, Pchcknya, Pwakanyaw, S'gau, S'gaw, S'gaw Kayin, White Karen, Yang Khao). 1,280,000 in Myanmar (1983 census). Population total all countries: 1,480,000. L2 users: 80,000 in Myanmar (2013 SIL). Ayeyarwaddy delta area, Tanintharyi Region, the Pegu range between Irrawaddy and Sittang rivers; Kayin State east hills; Mon State. Delta dialect: Ayeyarwaddy delta area, Yangon, up to Mandalay; scattered in Kachin State, Shan State; Eastern dialect: south Kayin and Mon states, and Mawlamyine; Southern dialect: Tanintharyi Region. Also in Thailand. *Status:* 3 (Wider communication). S'gaw Karen used in the church domain for many Karen languages. *Class:* Sino-Tibetan, Tibeto-Burman, Karenic, Southern. *Dialects:* Delta dialect of S'gaw Karen, Eastern dialect of S'gaw Karen (Pa'an), Southern dialect of Western Kayah (Dawei). Reportedly similar to Paku Karen [jkp]. *Type:* SVO. *Lg Use:* Most communities vigiorous; some shift toward Burmese [mya]. All domains. All ages. Positive attitudes. Also use Burmese [mya], Pwo Eastern Karen [kjp], Pwo Western Karen [pwo]. Used as L2 by Bwe Karen [bwe], Eastern Kayah [eky], Geba Karen [kvq], Geko Karen [ghk], Kayan [pdu], Kayaw [kvl], Manumanaw [kxf], Mobwa Karen [jkm], Paku Karen [jkp], Western Kayah [kyu], Yintale [kvy]. *Lg Dev:* Some literacy classes. Magazines. Dictionary. Grammar. Bible: 1853–1995. *Writing:* Latin script, no longer in use. Myanmar (Burmese) script. *Other:* Buddhist, Christian (Protestant), traditional religion. *Maps:* 390:72, 391:72, 392:72.

Kayah, Eastern [eky] (Karenni, Karennyi, Kayah Li, Kayay, Red Karen). 8,000 in Myanmar (2007). Population total all countries: 26,000. Kayah State, Shadaw township, east of Thanlwin river. Also in Thailand. *Status:* 6a (Vigorous). *Class:* Sino-Tibetan, Tibeto-Burman, Karenic, Central. *Dialects:* Lower Eastern Kayah, Upper Eastern Kayah. Upper Eastern Kayah and Lower Eastern Kayah are mutually intelligible; Huai Sua Thaw village (Lower Eastern) is prestigious in both dialect groups. Difficulty understanding Western Kayah [kyu]. *Lg Use:* Vigorous. All domains. All ages. Positive attitudes. Also use Burmese [mya] among Buddhists and Roman Catholics. 5,000 also use S'gaw Karen [ksw]. Also use Central Thai [tha] in education of Kayah in permanent villages. Western Kayah [kyu] used in education in refugee camps. Also use Shan [shn]. *Lg Dev:* Literacy rate in L1: Below 1%. Dictionary. *Writing:* Kayah Li script. *Other:* Buddhist, Christian, traditional religion. *Map:* 391:76.

Kayah, Western [kyu] (Karenni, Karennyi, Karieng Daeng, Kayah Li, Red Karen, Yang Daeng). 150,000 (2007). 2,000 refugees in Thailand. Kayah and Kayin states, east of Thanlwin river; south Shan State, Pekon township. Northern dialect: Shan State, north of Loikaw; Southern dialect: Hpruso and Dimawso townships, south of Loikaw. *Status:* 5 (Developing). *Class:* Sino-Tibetan, Tibeto-Burman, Karenic, Central. *Dialects:* Chi Kwe, Dawnnyjekhu, Dawtama, Northern dialect of Western Kayah, Sounglog, Southern dialect of Western Kayah, Wan Cheh. Part of a dialect continuum of Central Karen varieties stretching from Thailand (Eastern Kayah [eky]) to western Kayah State. *Lg Use:* Vigorous. All domains. All ages. Positive attitudes. Also use Burmese [mya] among Baptists; others also use Burmese. 20,000 also use S'gaw Karen [ksw]. Used as L2 by Eastern Kayah [eky]. *Lg Dev:* Literacy rate in L1: 10%. Literacy classes in some communities. Dictionary. NT: 2010. *Writing:* Kayah Li script. Latin script, preferred by Catholics. Myanmar (Burmese) script. *Other:* Buddhist, Christian, traditional religion. *Map:* 391:75.

Kayan [pdu] (Kayang, Ka-Yun, Lahwi, "Long-Necked Karen" *pej.*, "Padaung" *pej.*, "Padaung Karen" *pej.*). 133,000 in Myanmar (2005 E. Phan). Population total all countries: 133,180. South Shan State, Pekon township; northwest Kayah State; Kayin State, Thandaung township; Mandalay Region, Pyinmana township. Kayan Lahwi dialect: Kayah State, Lahwi and northwest Dimawso; Shan State, south Pekon. Kayan Kangan dialect: northwest Kayah State, Dimawso area. Also in Thailand. *Status:* 6a (Vigorous). *Class:* Sino-Tibetan, Tibeto-Burman, Karenic, Northern. *Dialects:* Kayan Kangan (Yeinbaw, Yinbaw), Kayan Lahwi, Standard Pekon. Significant dialectal variation. Most seem to understand standard Pekon (prestige) dialect. Lexical similarity: more than 90% among dialects, 71%–76% with Lahta [kvt]. *Lg Use:* Vigorous in most areas, but in some larger towns, children are no longer learning it. All domains. All ages. Positive attitudes. Other religions also use Burmese [mya]. 15,000 also use S'gaw Karen [ksw]. Used as L2 by Lahta [kvt], Zayein [kxk]. *Lg Dev:* Literacy rate in L2: Below 5%. Literacy classes in some communities. Poetry. Dictionary. Grammar. Bible portions: 2009–2011. *Writing:* Latin script. *Other:* Christian (Roman Catholic), Buddhist, Christian (Protestant). *Map:* 391:80.

Kayaw [kvl] ("Bre" *pej.*, "Brec" *pej.*, "Brek" *pej.*, Deleh, Ka-yaw, "Kayaw Brek" *pej.*, Laku, "Paret" *pej.*, Pramano, "Pre" *pej.*, "Pret" *pej.*). 16,600 (1983 census). East Kayah State, 30 villages; northeast Kayin State, Yado area; south Shan State, Pekon township. *Status:* 6a (Vigorous). *Class:* Sino-Tibetan, Tibeto-Burman, Karenic, Central. *Dialects:* Bwe-Kayaw, Lowe Kayaw, Upper Kayaw. Upper Kayaw dialect is the basis for Kayaw literature. Some intelligibility with Bwe Karen [bwe], though some Kayaw who speak with the Bwe Karen may use S'gaw Karen [ksw] to communicate. *Lg Use:* Vigorous. All domains. All ages. Positive attitudes. 2,000 also use S'gaw Karen [ksw]. Also use Burmese [mya]. *Lg Dev:* Literacy rate in L1: Below 1%. Bible portions: 1990–1999. *Writing:* Latin script, used by Roman Catholics and Baptists. *Other:* Brek and Bwe are variant names of a dialect continuum extending from southwest Kayah State to northeast Kayin (Karen) State. Bwe-Kayaw is a mixed variety spoken in the middle of this continuum. See also Karen, Bwe [bwe]. Christian. *Map:* 391:79.

Khamti [kht] (Hkamti, Kam Ti, Khampti, Khampti Shan, Khamti Shan, Khandi Shan, Tai Kam Ti, Tai-Khamti). 8,000 in Myanmar (2000). Population total all countries: 13,000. Kachin State, Putao district (4,500) and Myitkyina area (3,500); north Sagaing Region. Also in India. *Status:* 5 (Developing). *Class:* Tai-Kadai, Kam-Tai, Tai, Southwestern. *Dialects:* Assam Khamti, North Burma Khamti, Sinkaling Hkamti. *Type:* SOV; postpositional case-marking particle. *Lg Use:* Vigorous. All domains. All ages. Positive attitudes. Also use Burmese [mya]. All are bilingual (Bradley 2007). Also use Jingpho [kac]. All are bilingual (Bradley 2007). *Lg Dev:* Dictionary. *Writing:* Myanmar (Burmese) script. *Other:* Buddhist. *Map:* 389:5.

Khün [kkh] (Gon Shan, Hkun, Khuen, Khun Shan, Khyn, Tai Khun, Tai-Khuen). 100,000 in Myanmar (Diller and Juntanamalaga 1990). Population total all countries: 106,880. East Shan State, Kentung valley area. Also in Laos, Thailand. *Status:* 5 (Developing). *Class:* Tai-Kadai, Kam-Tai, Tai, Southwestern. *Dialects:* Kang Muang, Muang Lang. Khün, Northern Thai [nod] and Lü [khb] traditionally all use the same ancient script. Lexical similarity: 93%–100% with Khün varieties; Khün varieties: 90%–95% with Northern Thai [nod], 92%–95% with Lü [khb], 93%–97% with Shan [shn], 80%–83% with standard Thai [tha]. *Lg Use:* Vigorous. All domains. All ages. Positive attitudes. Also use Burmese [mya], Shan [shn]. *Lg Dev:* Literacy rate in L1: 95% among males; 50% among females. Promoted through monastery education. Bible portions: 1938. *Writing:* Tai Tham (Lanna) script. *Other:* Different from Khuen [khf], a Mon-Khmer language of Laos. Buddhist. *Map:* 391:99.

Lahta [kvt] (Kayan Lahta, Khahta, Lahta Karen, Peu, Taru, Tarulakhi, Yan Wohta). 9,550 (2000). South Shan State, Pekon and Pinlaung townships; Mandalay Region, Pyinnmana township. *Status:* 6a (Vigorous). *Class:*

Sino-Tibetan, Tibeto-Burman, Karenic, Northern. *Dialects:* Socially related to Kayan [pdu] but not intelligible. Zayein [kxk] may be a dialect of Lahta. *Lg Use:* Vigorous. All domains. All ages. Positive attitudes. Young people also use Burmese [mya]. Also use Kayan [pdu], Pa'o [blk]. *Writing:* Unwritten. *Other:* Officially recognized as part of Kayan [pdu]. Much dialect variation. Called Yan Wohta by the Shan [shn]. Buddhist, Christian, traditional religion. *Map:* 391:87.

Lahu [lhu] (Lahuna, Launa, Lohei, Muhso, Museu, Musso, Mussuh). 200,000 in Myanmar (2012 D. Bradley), increasing. Shan State, Kentung district. *Status:* 3 (Wider communication). *Dialects:* Na (Black Lahu, Lohei, Musser Dam, Northern Lahu), Nyi (Luhishi, Luhushi, Musseh Daeng, Red Lahu, Southern Lahu), Shehleh. *Lg Use:* Vigorous. All domains. All ages. Positive attitudes. Formerly most also used Shan [shn]. Also use Burmese [mya]. Used as L2 by Lahu Shi [lhi], Parauk Wa [prk], Pyen [pyy]. *Lg Dev:* Literacy classes in some communities. *Other:* Christian, traditional religion. See main entry on page 76. *Map:* 391:94.

Lahu Shi [lhi] (!Kwi). 60,000 in Myanmar (2007). Shan State, Kentung district. *Status:* 6a (Vigorous). *Lg Use:* Vigorous. All domains. All ages. Positive attitudes. Also use Lahu [lhu]. *Lg Dev:* Literacy classes taught in some communities. *Other:* Little dialect variation between Lahu Shi spoken in Myanmar and Thailand. They live among the Lahu Na [lhu]. Christian (Protestant). See main entry on page 76. *Map:* 391:96.

Lashi [lsi] (Ac'ye, Chashan, La Chit, Lachikwaw, Lacid, Lacik, Lashi-Maru, Lasi, Lechi, Leqi, Letsi). 30,000 in Myanmar (2000 D. Bradley). Population total all countries: 31,800. Kachin State, east border area. Also in China. *Status:* 5 (Developing). *Class:* Sino-Tibetan, Tibeto-Burman, Ngwi-Burmese, Burmish, Northern. *Type:* SOV; final nasals and stops; vowel length and tense-lax contrasts; tonal, 4 tones. *Lg Use:* Vigorous. Most domains. All ages. Positive attitudes. Also use Jingpho [kac]. *Lg Dev:* Literacy rate in L1: Below 1%. Literacy rate in L2: 5%–15%. Bible: 2009. *Writing:* Latin script. *Other:* Glossonym: Lashi by the Jingpho and Burmese, Lachi by the Chinese. Christian. *Map:* 389:8.

Lhao Vo [mhx] (Diso, Lang, Langsu, Laungaw, Laungwaw, Lawgore, Lawng, Lhaovo, Malu, "Maru" *pej.*, Mulu, Zi). 100,000 in Myanmar (Bradley 1997). Population total all countries: 103,500. Kachin State, east border area, Waimaw, Chiphwe, and Sawlaw townships, widely dispersed; north Shan State, Kutkai township. Also in China (Lhaovo). *Status:* 5 (Developing). *Class:* Sino-Tibetan, Tibeto-Burman, Ngwi-Burmese, Burmish, Northern. *Dialects:* Dago' Lawng Bit, Gawan Naw', Hlo'lan, Laking, Lawng Hsu, Wa Khawk, Zagaran Mran. Lawng Hsu may have difficult intelligibility with the other dialects. *Type:* SOV; tense-lax vowel distinction; loans from Jingpho [kac], Daai Chin[dao], Burmese [mya], and Chinese [cmn]; 3 tones. *Lg Use:* Vigorous. Most domains. All ages. Positive attitudes. Also use Jingpho [kac]. *Lg Dev:* Literacy rate in L1: Below 1%. Literacy rate in L2: 25%–50%. Bible: 2009. *Writing:* Latin script. *Other:* Different from Mru [mro] and Mro-Khimi [cmr] of northwest Rakhine State and Paletwa Township, South Chin State. Culturally similar to Kachin. Glossonym: Maru by Jingpho [kac] and Burmese [mya], Liangsu by Chinese [cmn]. Christian. *Map:* 389:6.

Lisu [lis] (Central Lisu, Li-Hsaw, Lisaw, Li-Shaw, Lu-Tzu, Southern Lisu, Yao Yen, Yaw Yin, Yaw-Yen, Yeh-Jeh). 300,000 in Myanmar (Bradley 2007). Shan State, Lashio and Loilem areas; Kachin State, Myitkyina. Bhamo, Putao area toward Assam border. *Status:* 3 (Wider communication). Many use Lisu as L2. *Dialects:* Black Lisu, Hwa Lisu (Flowery Lisu), Lu Shi Lisu. *Lg Use:* Vigorous. All domains. All ages. Positive attitudes. Also use Burmese [mya], Jingpho [kac], Rawang [raw], Thai [tha]. Used as L2 by Anong [nun], Drung [duu], Nusu [nuf], Rawang [raw]. *Lg Dev:* Literacy rate in L1: 30%–60%. Literacy rate in L2: 50%–75%. Literacy classes in some communities. *Other:* All 3 dialects are found in Myanmar. Black Lisu is most distinct. The Lisu in Myanmar and Thailand have difficulties in communicating due to dialect differences. Christian (Protestant). See main entry on page 77. *Maps:* 389:4, 390:4, 391:4.

Lü [khb] (Lue, Pai-I, Shu-Ai-I, Tai Lu). 60,000 in Myanmar (2013). East Shan State, Muang Yong township. *Status:* 5 (Developing). *Dialect:* Muang Yong. *Lg Use:* Vigorous. All domains. All ages. Positive attitudes. Used as L2 by Ruching Palaung [pce], Tai Loi [tlq]. *Other:* Buddhist. See main entry on page 78. *Map:* 391:101.

Manumanaw [kxf] (Kayah-Munu, Kayàw, Manö, Manu, Manu Manaw, Manumanaw Karen, Monu). 10,000 (2000 D. Bradley). Ethnic population: 10,000 (2000 D. Bradley). Kayah State, West Kyèbogyi area, border of Bawlake and Hpruso townships. 23 villages. *Status:* 6a (Vigorous). *Class:* Sino-Tibetan, Tibeto-Burman, Karenic, Central. *Dialects:* Doloso, Tawkhu. Reports of comprehension difficulty between the 2 dialects. Reportedly similar to Western Kayah [kyu]. *Lg Use:* Vigorous. All domains. All ages. Positive attitudes. 3,000 also use S'gaw Karen [ksw]. Also use Burmese [mya]. Used as L2 by Yintale [kvy]. *Lg Dev:* Literacy rate in L1: Below 1%. *Writing:* Latin script, used by Roman Catholics. Myanmar (Burmese) script, used since 2011. *Other:* Christian. *Map:* 391:84.

Moken [mwt] (Basing, Chau Ko', Lawta, Mawken, Orang Laut, Salon, Salong, Selong, Selung). 4,000 in Myanmar (Bradley 2007). Population total all countries: 6,000. South. Tanintharyi Region, Mergui archipelago, Dung, and other islands. Also in Thailand. *Status:* 6b (Threatened). *Class:* Austronesian, Malayo-Polynesian, Moklen. *Dialects:* Dung, Jait (Ja-It), L'be. Reportedly most similar to Moklen [mkm]. *Type:* SVO. *Lg Use:* All ages. Also use Burmese [mya], Thai [tha]. *Lg Dev:* NT: 2002. *Writing:* Myanmar (Burmese) script. *Other:* Primarily live on boats, but occasionally settle on area islands. Traditional religion, Christian. *Map:* 392:105.

Mon [mnw] (Aleng, Mou, Mun, Peguan, Raman, Rman, Rmen, Takanoon, Talaing, Taleng, Teguan). 743,000 in Myanmar (2004), decreasing. Population total all countries: 851,000. Ethnic population: 1,000,000. Mon and Kayin states, Tanintharyi, Bago, Yangon, and Mandalay regions. Also in Thailand. *Status:* 5 (Developing). *Class:* Austro-Asiatic, Mon-Khmer, Monic. *Dialects:* Martaban-Moulmein (Central Mon, Mon Te), Pegu (Mon Tang, Northern Mon), Ye (Mon Nya, Southern Mon). Intelligibility between Mon varieties high; between Mon in Thailand and Myanmar 99% (Huffman 1976). Varieties in Myanmar and Thailand "mutually intelligible" (Bauer 1990) but lexical borrowings from Thai and Burmese may cause miscommunication (Guillon 1999). Lexical similarity: 69% with Mon and Nyah Kur [cbn] (Huffman 1976). *Type:* SVO. *Lg Use:* Vigorous in some rural areas and in Three Pagodas border area. Low or no usage in urban centers. Many domains in some communities; only among the elderly, in the monastery, or not at all in other communities. All ages. Positive attitudes. Widespread bilingualism; some language shift. Also use Burmese [mya]. *Lg Dev:* Literacy rate in L1: Some literacy among the older generation; very low literacy rates among those under 40. Taught in some Buddhist monasteries in both Myanmar and Thailand. Some literacy efforts made on Thailand-Myanmar border. Poetry. Dictionary. Grammar.

Bible: 1928. *Writing:* Myanmar (Burmese) script. *Other:* Remnants of a nation that once spread over south Myanmar and west Thailand. Preferred names: Mon or Raman. Buddhist. *Map:* 392:103.

Mru [mro] (Dak, Launghu, Mro, Mrucha, Mrung, Mrusa, Murung, Niopreng, Taung Mru). 20,000 in Myanmar (1999 Association of Baptists for World Evangelization). Rakhine State, Buthidaung, Maungdaw, and Ponnagyun townships. *Status:* 5 (Developing). *Dialects:* Anok, Dowpreng (Doumrong, Pongmi, Tamsa), Launghu, Sungma. *Lg Use:* Vigorous. All domains. All ages. Positive attitudes. 20,000 also use Rakhine [rki]. *Lg Dev:* Literacy rate in L1: Below 1%. *Other:* Christian. See main entry on page 56. *Map:* 390:61.

Naga, Akyaung Ari [nqy] (Ngachan). 1,000 (2004 SIL). Sagaing Region, south Layshi township, Heinkut, Jagram, and Ngachan villages. *Status:* 6a (Vigorous). *Class:* Sino-Tibetan, Tibeto-Burman, Sal, Kuki-Chin-Naga, Unclassified. *Dialects:* Very little (if any) dialect variation within Akyaung Ari Naga. Lexical similarity: 52% with Tanghkul Naga of Somra [ntx], 23% with Tangkhul Naga of Ukhrul in India [nmf], 23% with Koki Naga [nxk]. *Lg Use:* Vigorous. All domains. All ages. Positive attitudes. Also use Tangkhul Naga [ntx]. *Writing:* Unwritten. *Other:* Tribally, the Akyaung Ari are included as part of Tangkhul Naga, but their language is very distinct. Christian. *Map:* 389:20.

Naga, Khiamniungan [kix] (Makware, Nokaw, Para, Tukhemmi, Welam). 10,000 in Myanmar (2010). Sagaing Region, Khamti district, Lahe and Khamti townships. About 30 villages. *Status:* 5 (Developing). *Dialects:* Nokhu, Ponso, Thang, Wolam. *Lg Use:* Vigorous. All domains. All ages. Positive attitudes. Used as L2 by Ponyo-Gongwang Naga [npg]. *Lg Dev:* Literacy rate in L1: Below 1%. *Other:* This group is sometimes called Para by other groups, but the Para [pzn] are a different Naga group. Christian (Protestant). See main entry on page 133. *Map:* 389:15.

Naga, Koki [nxk] (Konke). 2,000 (2004 SIL). Sagaing Region, south Layshi township. 10 villages. *Status:* 6a (Vigorous). *Class:* Sino-Tibetan, Tibeto-Burman, Sal, Kuki-Chin-Naga, Unclassified. *Dialects:* Very little (if any) dialect variation within Koki. Lexical similarity within Koki: 98%. Lexical similarity: 19%–32% with Tangkhul Naga [ntx] in Myanmar, 23% with Akyaung Ari Naga [nqy], 22%–24% with Para Naga [pzn]. *Lg Use:* Vigorous. All domains. All ages. Positive attitudes. Older generation also uses Tangkhul Naga [ntx]. *Writing:* Unwritten. *Other:* Tribally, the Koki are included as part of Tangkhul Naga, but their language is very distinct. Not the same as Kuki Chin (Chin, Thado [tcz]). Buddhist, Christian, traditional religion. *Map:* 389:22.

Naga, Konyak [nbe]. 2,000 in Myanmar (2010). Sagaing Region, Khamti district, Lahe township. *Status:* 5 (Developing). *Dialects:* Kun, Lonwa. *Lg Use:* Vigorous. All domains. All ages. Positive attitudes. Some also use Burmese [mya] or standard Konyak Naga dialect from India. *Lg Dev:* Literacy rate in L2: Below 1%. Use Konyak Naga literature from India. *Other:* Christian. See main entry on page 133. *Map:* 389:11.

Naga, Kyan-Karyaw [nqq] (Chen, Kaiyaw, Karyaw, Kayaw, Kayu, Kyan). 9,000 (2012 SIL). Sagaing Region, Khamti district, Lahe township, 13 villages. Along the border with India. *Status:* 6a (Vigorous). *Class:* Sino-Tibetan, Tibeto-Burman, Sal, Bodo-Garo-Northern Naga, Northern Naga. *Dialects:* Karyaw, Kyan. The 2 dialects are closely related. Karyaw is reportedly similar to the Chuyo and Gakat dialects of Tase Naga [nst]. *Lg Use:* Vigorous. All domains. All ages.

Naga, Lao [nlq] (Law, Loh). 1,000 (2012 SIL). Sagaing Region, Khamti district, Lahe township, along the border with India. *Status:* 6a (Vigorous). *Class:* Sino-Tibetan, Tibeto-Burman, Sal, Bodo-Garo-Northern Naga, Northern Naga. *Dialects:* Reportedly most similar to Kyan-Karyaw Naga [nqq] and the Chuyo and Gakat dialects of Tase Naga [nst]. *Lg Use:* Vigorous. All domains. All ages. Also use Leinong Naga [lzn].

Naga, Leinong [lzn] (Htang Ngan, Htangan, Lainong Naga, Lenaung Naga). 7,000 (2008). Sagaing Region, Khamti district, Lahe township. About 25 villages. *Status:* 6a (Vigorous). *Class:* Sino-Tibetan, Tibeto-Burman, Sal, Bodo-Garo-Northern Naga, Northern Naga. *Dialects:* Southern Leinong, Yao Dyang (Northern Leinong, Zau Dyang). High intelligibility in Leinong villages. Lexical similarity: within Leinong Naga 89%–100%. Lexical similarity: 69%–75% with Ponyo-Gongwang Naga [npg], 62%–67%with Khiamniungan Naga [kix], 37%–41% with Lao variety of Konyak Naga [nbe]. *Lg Use:* Vigorous. All domains. All ages. Positive attitudes. Also use Burmese [mya]. Used as L2 by Lao Naga [nlq], Makyan Naga [umn], Ponyo-Gongwang Naga [npg]. *Lg Dev:* Literacy rate in L1: Below 1%. Some literacy classes. Dictionary. Bible portions: 2005–2010. *Writing:* Latin script. *Other:* The majority group within Lahe Township. Buddhist, Christian, traditional religion. *Map:* 389:12.

Naga, Long Phuri [lpn] (Amimi Naga, Longpfuri, Longpfuru, Mimi). 1,000 (2004). Sagaing Region, Khamti district, Layshi township. 6 villages. Some across the border in India. *Status:* 6a (Vigorous). *Class:* Sino-Tibetan, Tibeto-Burman, Sal, Kuki-Chin-Naga, Unclassified. *Dialects:* Little (if any) dialect variation within Long Phuri. Lexical similarity: 30%–37% with Makuri Naga [jmn], 23%–25% with Para Naga [pzn]. *Lg Use:* Vigorous. All domains. All ages. Positive attitudes. Also use Burmese [mya], especially youth. Many bilingual in Makuri Naga [jmn], especially older generation. *Writing:* Unwritten. *Other:* Christian, Buddhist, traditional religion. *Map:* 389:17.

Naga, Makuri [jmn] (Makury). 2,500 in Myanmar (2004). Population total all countries: 6,500. Sagaing Region, Khamti district, Layshi, Homalin, and Lahe townships. Also in India. *Status:* 6a (Vigorous). *Class:* Sino-Tibetan, Tibeto-Burman, Sal, Kuki-Chin-Naga, Unclassified. *Dialects:* Arale, Kyaungphuri (Shu), Kyile, Makhwale, Saingphule (Saingpuri), Shera (Shaera). Lexical similarity: 93% with Makuri Naga, 30%–37% with Long Phuri Naga [lpn], 17%–19% with Para Naga [pzn]. *Lg Use:* Vigorous. All domains. All ages. Positive attitudes. Also use Burmese [mya]. Used as L2 by Long Phuri Naga [lpn]. *Writing:* Latin script. *Other:* Christian (Protestant), Buddhist, traditional religion. *Map:* 389:16.

Naga, Makyan [umn] (Lasam, Macham Naga, Makyam, Pongnyun). 4,000 (2008 SIL). Sagaing Region, Khamti district, northeast Lahe township. 13 villages. *Status:* 6a (Vigorous). *Class:* Sino-Tibetan, Tibeto-Burman, Sal, Bodo-Garo-Northern Naga, Northern Naga. *Dialects:* Main dialect variation is between western Makyan villages and Kuku villages. Lexical similarity: 99% with western Makyan, 31%–35% with Ponyo-Gongwang Naga [npg], 29%–36% with Leinong Naga [lzn], 27%–28% with Lao variety of Konyak Naga [nbe]. *Lg Use:* Vigorous. All domains. All ages. Positive attitudes. Youth also use Burmese [mya]. Older generation also uses Leinong Naga [lzn]. *Writing:* Unwritten. *Other:* Endoglossonym: Makyam. Distinct language from Leinong Naga [lzn], although culturally and geographically related. Christian, Buddhist, traditional religion. *Map:* 389:13.

Naga, Para [pzn] (Bara Naga, Jejara Naga, Parasar). 1,500 (2004). Sagaing Region, Khamti district, Layshi township. 7 villages. *Status:* 6a (Vigorous). *Class:* Sino-Tibetan, Tibeto-Burman, Sal, Kuki-Chin-Naga, Unclassified. *Dialects:* Very little dialect variation within Para. Lexical similarity: 83%–93% with Para Naga, 23%–25% with Long Phuri Naga [lpn], 17%–19% with Makuri Naga [jmn]. *Lg Use:* Vigorous. All domains. All ages. Positive attitudes. Also use Burmese [mya]. *Lg Dev:* Literacy rate in L1: Below 1%. Dictionary. *Writing:* Latin script. *Other:* Christian, Buddhist, traditional religion. *Map:* 389:18.

Naga, Ponyo-Gongwang [npg] (Gongvan, Gongwang, Manauk, Mannok, Ponyo, Pounyu, Saplow, Solo, Tsawlaw). 4,500 (2008 SIL). Sagaing Region, Khamti district, Lahe township. 19 villages. *Status:* 6a (Vigorous). *Class:* Sino-Tibetan, Tibeto-Burman, Sal, Bodo-Garo-Northern Naga, Northern Naga. *Dialects:* Gongwang, Ponyo. Very little dialect variation within Gongwang and within Ponyo, but between these 2 dialects, there are differences. Comprehension seems to be high between Ponyo and Gongwang speakers. Lexical similarity: 89%–91% between Ponyo and Gongwang, 69%–75% with Leinong Naga [lzn], 67%–73% with Khiamniungan Naga [kix]. *Lg Use:* Vigorous. All domains. All ages. Positive attitudes. Also use Khiamniungan Naga [kix], Leinong Naga [lzn]. *Writing:* Unwritten. *Other:* They feel culturally and linguistically related to both Leinong Naga [lzn] and Khiamniungan Naga [kix]. Christian, Buddhist, traditional religion. *Map:* 389:14.

Naga, Tangkhul [ntx] (Somara, Somra). 4,000 (2004 SIL). Sagaing Region, south Layshi township, Somra tract; Homalin township. *Status:* 6a (Vigorous). *Class:* Sino-Tibetan, Tibeto-Burman, Sal, Kuki-Chin-Naga, Tangkhul. *Dialect:* Somra. Very little dialect variation within Tangkhul (Somra) Naga. Somra village is the prestige dialect. Lexical similarity: 93%–94% with Tangkhul (Somra) Naga, 31% with Tangkhul Naga [nmf] in India, 51%–52% with Akyaung Ari Naga [nqy], 29%–32% with Koki Naga [nxk]. *Lg Use:* Vigorous. All domains. All ages. Positive attitudes. Also use Burmese [mya]. Used as L2 by Akyaung Ari Naga [nqy], Koki Naga [nxk]. *Lg Dev:* Literacy rate in L1: Below 1%. Bible: 1989. *Writing:* Latin script, based on the Somra village dialect. *Other:* Included in official ethnic group list as Tangkhul. The Koki Naga [nxk] and Akyaung Ari Naga [nqy] in Myanmar are included tribally within Tangkhul, but their languages are quite distinct. The Tangkhul (Somra) Naga [ntx] language in Myanmar is very different from Tangkhul (Ukhrul) Naga [nmf] in India. Christian, Buddhist, traditional religion. *Map:* 389:19.

Naga, Tase [nst] (Haimi, Hawa, Heimi, Kuwa, Pangmi, Pangwa, Rangpan, Rangpang, Tangshang, Tangwa). 60,000 in Myanmar (2010). Population total all countries: 100,100. Sagaing Region, Khamti district, Nanyun, Pangsau, Lahe, and Khamti townships; Kachin State, Myitkyina district, Shinbwiyan and Tanai townships. Also in India. *Status:* 5 (Developing). *Class:* Sino-Tibetan, Tibeto-Burman, Sal, Bodo-Garo-Northern Naga, Northern Naga. *Dialects:* Asen (Aasen, Hansin, Raqsa, Yasa), Bote (Bongtai, Butay, Hteinpa, Nokpa, Nukpa), Chamchang (Kimsing), Chamkok (Tamko, Thamkok), Champhang (Thamphang), Cholim (Tawlum, Tulim, Tulum), Chuyo (Wanggu, Wangoo), Gaha (Halum), Gakat (Wakka, Wanga), Gaqchan (Gashan), Gawkchung (Kochong), Hacheng (Hakyai), Hachum (Chumnyu, Chumsa, Gachung), Hakhü (Gakhi, Hachi, Hakhii, Hatse), Hakhun (Gakhun), Haman (Gaman), Hapaw, Hasik (Awla, Awlay, Laju), Henchin (Sanching, Shangchein), Hokuq, Jöngi (Dongai, Donghee, Dongi), Kaisan (Kyetsan), Khalak (Hkalak), Kon (Chawang, Kyawan, Yawngkon, Yongkon), Kotlum (Kawlum), Kumka (Kum Ga, Kumga), Lakki (Lakai), Lama, Lochang (Lanchein, Langshin), Lonyung (Galawn, Galun), Lumnu, Lungkhi (Longkhai), Lungri, Maitai (Meitei, Mitay), Miku (Maihku), Mitay (Maitai), Moshang (Mawshang), Mungre (Mawrang, Morang), Nahen (Nahim, Nahin), Ngaimong (Maimong, Ngaimau), Pingku (Pyengoo), Ranchi (Rangchein), Ranu, Rara, Rasa, Rera (Ronrang), Riha (Lulum), Ringkhu (Rangkhu), Sansik (Sheiknyo, Siknyo, Sikpo), Shangti (Sangtai, Shangthi), Shangwan (Changwan, Shangwal, Shawvel), Shekyü (Sangche, Sanke, Shaekjeng, Shaekyeu), Shokra (Sawkrang, Shaukra, Shograng), Toke (Tawkay), Yangno. A group of many Naga speech varieties, some of which are separate languages. Intelligibility high between some speech varieties; low between others. Intelligibility between varieties is higher in the north and fairly low in the south. Wide range of lexical similarity within dialects, from 35%–97%. *Type:* SOV; postpositions; genitives, articles before noun heads; numerals, adjectives after head nouns; question word final; word order distinguishes subject, object, and indirect object; ergative-absolutive marked, particles indicate case after the noun; passives; tonal. *Lg Use:* Vigorous in remote areas; lessening in town areas. Shifting to Burmese [mya] in town areas. All domains in remote areas. All ages. Positive attitudes. Also use Burmese [mya]. *Lg Dev:* Literacy rate in L1: Below 1%. Radio programs. NT: 1992–2007. *Writing:* Latin script. *Other:* This group is called Tangshang in Myanmar and Tangsa in India. Tase is the Chamchang (Kimsing) pronunciation of the name. Christian, Buddhist. *Map:* 389:10.

Nusu [nuf] (Nang Tsu, "Naw" *pej.*, "No" *pej.*, "No Pha" *pej.*, "No Shi" *pej.*, No Tso, No Tsu, "Nu" *pej.*). 670 in Myanmar (2011), decreasing. 0 monolinguals. Ethnic population: 1,500. Northeast Kachin State near China border, Myitkyina, Chipwi, and Tsawlaw townships. About 22 villages. *Status:* 6b (Threatened). *Dialects:* Central Nusu (Miangu/Laomudeng), Northern Nusu (Wawa, Yuoduoluo), Southern Nusu (Puluo, Tuoping). *Lg Use:* Vigorous in remote areas, but most communities are shifting toward Lisu [lis]. Nusu is not used at all in some communities. Home. All ages in some areas; only elderly in others. Positive attitudes. 100% also use Burmese [mya]. Most also use Lisu [lis], many ethnic Nusu people use Lisu as L1. *Lg Dev:* Literacy rate in L1: High literacy rates in Lisu [lis]. Some literacy classes. *Other:* Christian (Protestant). See main entry on page 84. *Map:* 389:7.

Palaung, Ruching [pce] (Da'ang, Di-Ang, Ngwe Palaung, Palay, Silver Palaung). 258,000 in Myanmar (2000). Population total all countries: 272,000. South Shan State, near Kalaw; north Shan State, Kyawkme area; Lashio to the China border; Lashio east to the Salween; Kokaing area villages east of Salween river. Also in China, Thailand (Pale Palaung). *Status:* 6a (Vigorous). *Class:* Austro-Asiatic, Mon-Khmer, Northern Mon-Khmer, Palaungic, Western Palaungic, Palaung. *Dialects:* Pale, Rulai. Rulai dialect near Lashio has regular phonological changes and some lexical difference from Ruching. *Type:* SVO. *Lg Use:* Vigorous. Home, village, market, religion. All ages. Positive attitudes. Also use Burmese [mya], Lü [khb], Shan [shn], Thai [tha]. Used as L2 by Rumai Palaung [rbb]. *Lg Dev:* Literacy rate in L2: Below 5%. Strong literacy program. Grammar. Bible: 2013. *Writing:* Myanmar (Burmese) script. *Other:* Kalaw dialect tends toward loss of final consonants, could be moving to develop tones. Tense vowels change into glides with a palatal final in the Pale variety. Buddhist, traditional religion. *Map:* 391:90.

Palaung, Rumai [rbb] (Humai, Ngwe Palaung, Rumai, Rumai Humai, Shan Rumai, Silver Palaung, Ta'ang, Ta'ang Rumai, Tai Rumai). 137,000 in Myanmar. Population total all countries: 140,600. North Shan State, Lashio area; the road north to the border, Nam Kham and Muse, Mantong, North Hsenwi, and Tawngpeng (the ancient Palaung State). Also in China. *Status:* 6a (Vigorous). *Class:* Austro-Asiatic, Mon-Khmer, Northern Mon-Khmer, Palaungic, Western Palaungic, Palaung. *Dialects:* Nam Kham Rumai is a different dialect from Lashio Rumai but comprehension is still good. *Type:* SVO. *Lg Use:* Vigorous. Home, village, market. All ages. Positive attitudes. Also use Burmese [mya], Jingpho [kac], Mandarin Chinese [cmn], Nepali [npi], Ruching Palaung [pce], Shan [shn]. Used as L2 by Parauk Wa [prk]. *Lg Dev:* Literacy rate in L1: Below 1%. Dictionary. Grammar. *Writing:* Myanmar (Burmese) script. *Other:* Buddhist, traditional religion. *Map:* 389:31.

Palaung, Shwe [pll] (Golden Palaung, Liang, Red Da'ang, Shwe Palaung, Ta-Ang Palaung, Ta'ang Samlung). 148,000 in Myanmar (1982). Population total all countries: 150,000. North Shan State, centered in Nam Hsan. Also in China. *Status:* 6a (Vigorous). *Class:* Austro-Asiatic, Mon-Khmer, Northern Mon-Khmer, Palaungic, Western Palaungic, Palaung. *Dialect:* Ywama. 15 Palaung dialects in Myanmar. Ruching Palaung [pce] and Rumai Palaung [rbb] are related, but distinct languages. *Type:* SVO. *Lg Use:* Vigorous. Home, village. All ages. Positive attitudes. Also use Shan [shn]. *Lg Dev:* Literacy rate in L1: Below 1%. *Writing:* Myanmar (Burmese) script, initial development in the 1930s with revisions in the 1980s. *Other:* Ywama is a prestige dialect. Buddhist, traditional religion. *Map:* 391:93.

Pali [pli]. No known L1 speakers in Myanmar. *Status:* 9 (Second language only). *Lg Use:* Literary language of Buddhist Scriptures. *Lg Dev:* Taught in Buddhist monasteries. See main entry on page 138.

Pa'o [blk] (Black Karen, Northern Taungthu, Pa Oh, Pa-O, Pa'o Karen, Pa-U). 560,000 in Myanmar (1983 census). Population total all countries: 560,740. Southwest Shan State; Kayah State, Loikaw; Kayin State areas near Shan State border; Mon State near Thaton. Also in Thailand. *Status:* 5 (Developing). *Class:* Sino-Tibetan, Tibeto-Burman, Karenic, Peripheral. *Dialects:* Northern Pa'o, Southern Pa'o. Reportedly fairly high comprehension among dialects. *Type:* SVO. *Lg Use:* Vigorous. All domains. All ages. Positive attitudes. Also use Burmese [mya], Shan [shn]. Used as L2 by Danau [dnu], Lahta [kvt], Zayein [kxk]. *Lg Dev:* Literacy classes in some communities, especially at Buddhist monasteries. Dictionary. NT: 2009. *Writing:* Myanmar (Burmese) script. *Other:* Buddhist. *Map:* 391:82.

Pyen [pyy] (Hpinba, Hpyin, Misu, Pyin). 600 (2013 Pyen Language Committee). East Shan State, Mong Yang township, Namt Theun and Yaw Tan villages. *Status:* 5 (Developing). *Class:* Sino-Tibetan, Tibeto-Burman, Ngwi-Burmese, Ngwi, Southern, Bisoid. *Dialects:* None known. Reportedly similar to Phunoi [pho], Bisu [bzi], and Mpi [mpz]. Lexical similarity: 36% with Hani [hni], 32% with Lahu [lhu], 31% with Lisu [lis]. *Type:* SVO; simple syllable structure; syllables may be closed by stop or nasal; modifiers follow heads; loanwords from Shan [shn] and Lahu [lhu]; 3 contrastive tones. *Lg Use:* Small population but vigorous use. All domains. All ages. Positive attitudes. Also use Lahu [lhu], Shan [shn]. *Lg Dev:* Orthography revision planned in preparation for literacy classes. Grammar. Bible portions: 2011. *Writing:* Latin script. *Other:* Christian. *Map:* 391:95.

Rakhine [rki] (Arakanese, Mogh, Rakhain, Rakhaing, Rakkhaine). 800,000 in Myanmar (2013 SIL). Population total all countries: 1,000,000. L2 users: 1,020,000 in Myanmar (2013 SIL). Minority peoples in Rakhine and Chin states, Paletwa Township. Throughout Rakhine State; Chin State, Paletwa township. Also in Bangladesh. *Status:* 3 (Wider communication). Throughout Rakhine State and in Paletwa Township, Chin State. Especially in market, business, oral language at school, and in some media. Rakhine is the largest ethnic group and dominant language in the area and Rakhine people control most business, transport, and trade. *Class:* Sino-Tibetan, Tibeto-Burman, Ngwi-Burmese, Burmish, Southern. *Dialects:* Chaungtha, Kyaukphyu, Man Aung (Chebuda Island), Mrauk-U, Sittwe (Akyab), Yangbye (Rambree, Yanbe, Yanbye, Yangye). Intelligibility in Rakhine State of prestigious Sittwe dialect seems fairly high. Slight variations in north Rakhine speech in Sittwe, Kyauktaw, Mrauk-U, Minpya, Ponnagyun, Buthidaung, and Maungdaw townships. The variety spoken in south Rakhine State townships of Kyauk Phyu, Yangbye, Thandwe, and Toungup noticeably different from the northern variety. The southern variety, particularly in Thandwe Township, is more similar to standard Burmese [mya]. Lexical similarity: among Rakhine and Marma varieties in both Myanmar and Bangladesh is over 85%. Lexical similarity: 91% with standard Burmese [mya]. *Type:* SOV. *Lg Use:* Vigorous, but some shift toward Burmese [mya], especially in south Rakhine State. All except formal domains. All ages. Positive attitudes. Also use Rohingya [rhg] in Buthidaung and Maungdaw townships. Also use Burmese [mya]. Used as L2 by Anu-Hkongso Chin [anl], Chak [ckh], Chakma [ccp], Eastern Khumi Chin [cek], Khumi Chin [cnk], Laitu Chin [clj], Mro-Khimi Chin [cmr], Mru [mro], Rohingya [rhg], Sumtu Chin [csv]. *Lg Dev:* ". . .the literary (written) languages of Rakhine and standard Burmese are largely identical" (Leider 2008:453). Rakhine pronunciation is closer to the literary language than modern spoken Burmese. Some Rakhine spell words according to Rakhine usage, but most use standard Burmese [mya] for writing. Newspapers. New media. Films. *Writing:* Myanmar (Burmese) script, informal and non-standardized use. *Other:* Buddhist. *Maps:* 390:64, 392:64.

Rawang [raw] (Chiutse, Ch'opa, Ganung-Rawang, Hkanung, Kiutze, Nung, Nung Rawang). 62,000 in Myanmar (2000). Population total all countries: 63,000. North Kachin State, Putao district, Putao, Machanbaw, Naungmaw, Kawnglangphu, and Pannandin townships. Also in India. *Status:* 3 (Wider communication). Matwang dialect is L2 or church language used by other dialect speakers. *Class:* Sino-Tibetan, Tibeto-Burman, Central Tibeto-Burman, Nungish. *Dialects:* Daru-Jerwang, Khrangkhu/Thininglong (Southern Lungmi), Kyaikhu (Dangraq-Mashang, Northern Lungmi), Matwang, Tangsar East (Changgong), Tangsar West (Langdaqgong, Renyinchi), Thaluq. Most reportedly understand Matwang, a central, written dialect. Part of a chain of related varieties with the Drung [duu] people of Nu nationality in China. Dialects near Tibet border more divergent. Lungmi varieties of Mashang and Dangraq are especially divergent. Rawang speakers from the Kunglang variety of Daru live in Arunachal Pradesh, India. Some Rawang dialects, especially Kyaikhu Lungmi and Changgong Tangsar, have less intelligibility with the standard written dialect of Matwang. Anong (Khingpang) [nun] and Drung (Thrung) [duu] are related to Rawang and are sometimes included as Rawang varieties (Morse 1989). Lexical similarity: 82%–99% among Matwang-related dialects. Lexical similarity between Matwan and the following varieties or languages: 74% with Drung [duu], 79%–80% with Anong [nun], 81%–87% with Renyinchi (Langdaqgong Tangsar), 77% with Changgong Tangsar,

74%–85% with Lungmi, 74%–80% with Daru-Jerwang. *Type:* SOV. *Lg Use:* Vigorous. All domains. Rawang literature used mainly in church. All ages. Positive attitudes. Most young people also use Burmese [mya]. Also use Jingpho [kac], Lisu [lis]. Used as L2 by Drung [duu], Lisu [lis]. *Lg Dev:* Literacy rate in L1: 30%–60%. Literacy rate in L2: 75%–100%. Older generation is more literate in Rawang; younger generation literacy rate in Rawang is declining. Magazines. Newspapers. Grammar. Bible: 1986. *Writing:* Latin script. *Other:* Glossonym: Kiutze or Qiuze by Chinese, Ch'opa by Lisu. Traditionally, Rawang is made up of five major clan divisions (plus subclans): Lungmi, Matwang, Daru-Jerwang, Tangsar, and Anong [nun] (Morse 1989). Christian. *Map:* 389:3.

Riang [ril] (Black Karen, Black Riang, Black Yang, Liang Sek, Riang-Lang, Yang, Yang Wan Kun, Yanglam, Yin, Yin Kya, Yin Net, Yinnet). 12,500 in Myanmar (2008). Population total all countries: 15,500. Northeast. Shan State, near southern Shan town of Pang Long. Also in China. *Status:* 6b (Threatened). *Class:* Austro-Asiatic, Mon-Khmer, Northern Mon-Khmer, Palaungic, Western Palaungic, Riang. *Dialects:* Black Riang, Red Riang, Yinja. Not related to Tripuri [trp]-speaking Riang of India and Bangladesh or to Pa'o [blk], which is Sino-Tibetan. Red and Black Riang difference unknown but these have been treated as separate languages; traditionally, the two groups occupy different social and geographic space, and wear different traditional clothing styles. May be the same language as Shwe Palaung [pll]. *Type:* SVO. *Lg Use:* Endangered. Also use Shan [shn]. *Lg Dev:* Literacy rate in L1: Below 1%. Bible portions: 1950. *Writing:* Latin script. *Other:* Different from Riang [ria] of India, a Tibeto-Burman language. Buddhist, traditional religion.

Rohingya [rhg] (Rohinja). 800,000 in Myanmar (2012). Due to unrest, numbers are very uncertain. Population total all countries: 1,800,000. North Rakhine State, Maungdaw and Buthidaung townships; Sittwe and Rathedaung townships. Also in Bangladesh, China, Malaysia, Pakistan, Saudi Arabia, Thailand. *Status:* 6a (Vigorous). *Class:* Indo-European, Indo-Iranian, Indo-Aryan, Eastern zone, Bengali-Assamese. *Dialects:* Not much contact between dialect groups living in different townships; intelligibility situation is not clear. Dialects differ by river valleys. *Lg Use:* Vigorous. All domains. All ages. Positive attitudes. Those with education are literate in Burmese [mya]. 750,000 also use Rakhine [rki]. Used as L2 by Rakhine [rki]. *Lg Dev:* Literacy rate in L1: Below 1%. *Writing:* Arabic script. Latin script. Rohingya Hanifi script, some development in immigrant communities for all three scripts. *Other:* About 1,000,000 refugees went to Bangladesh in recent years, the majority of whom have dispersed to other countries. Most refugees in UNHCR-controlled camps in Bangladesh were repatriated back to Myanmar, but many of these have returned to Bangladesh unofficially. *Map:* 390:62.

Samtao [stu] (Samtau, Samtuan). 9,550 in Myanmar (2000). Population total all countries: 13,180. East Shan State. Also in China, Laos, Thailand. *Status:* 6a (Vigorous). *Class:* Austro-Asiatic, Mon-Khmer, Northern Mon-Khmer, Palaungic, Eastern Palaungic, Angkuic. *Lg Use:* Vigorous. Home, village, community affairs. All ages. Positive attitudes. *Lg Dev:* Literacy rate in L1: Below 1%. *Other:* Samtao is used among the Palaungic peoples to refer to unintelligible dialects of Plang [blr]. In China, Samtao refers to Plang in Burma and occasionally to Plang from other China-based varieties with low intelligibility. 'Samtao', also refers to south Mong La area in East Shan State between the China border and Nam Lwe River. A third meaning refers to Plang who live in the Samtao area. Wan Phii Plang is a Samtao variety similar to and intelligible with Wan Sen and Wan Nyet, ancient Plang villages along Mong La-Kentung Road further west. A fourth meaning of 'Samtao' refers to Palaungic varieties more similar to Wa, such as the Wa, Pangloh, who also refer to themselves as Samtao. 1 Samtao village in Veng Phu Kha insists they speak the ancient Samtao language, but lexically it is Lao [lao] with Mon-Khmer phonology. Traditional religion.

Shan [shn] (Burmese Shan, Great Thai, "Ngeo" *pej.*, "Ngiao" *pej.*, "Ngiaw" *pej.*, "Ngio" *pej.*, "Ngiow" *pej.*, Sam, Sha, Shan Bama, Shan Gyi, Tai Long, Tai Luang, Tai Shan, Tai Yai, Tai-Lon, Thai Yai). 3,200,000 in Myanmar (Johnstone and Mandryk 2001). 350,000 Tai Mao (1990 A. Diller). Population total all countries: 3,295,000. L2 users: Minority speakers in Shan State. Shan state. Tai Mao is on Myanmar-Yunnan border, centered at Mu'ang Mao Long or Namkham. Also in China, Thailand. *Status:* 3 (Wider communication). *Class:* Tai-Kadai, Kam-Tai, Tai, Southwestern. *Dialects:* Northern Shan State, Southern Shan State, Tai Mao (Mao Shan, Tai Khe). Regional dialect differences. Low intelligibility of Lü [khb]. *Lg Use:* Vigorous. All domains. All ages. Positive attitudes. Also use Burmese [mya], Thai [tha]. Used as L2 by Eastern Kayah [eky], Khün [kkh], Lahu [lhu], Pa'o [blk], Parauk Wa [prk], Pyen [pyy], Riang [ril], Ruching Palaung [pce], Rumai Palaung [rbb], Shwe Palaung [pll], Yinchia [yin]. *Lg Dev:* Bible: 1892–1995. *Writing:* Myanmar (Burmese) script. *Other:* Tai Mao (Mao Shan, Tai Khe) is linguistically closer to Tai Nüa [tdd] but political and cultural factors lead them to identify with Shan. Buddhist. *Maps:* 389:24, 391:24.

Tai Laing [tjl] (Red Tai, Shan Bamar, Shan Kalee, Shan Ni, Tai Laeng, Tai Lai, Tai Lang, Tai Nai, Tai Naing). 100,000 (2010 SIL). Kachin State, from Myitkyina to Bamaw township; Sagaing Region, Homalin township, along the Irrawaddy, Chindwin, and Uru rivers. *Status:* 6b (Threatened). *Class:* Tai-Kadai, Kam-Tai, Tai, Southwestern. *Dialects:* Tai Lai, Tai Nai. Two subgroups: Those who live along the railway line between Myitkyina and Mandalay and call themselves Tai Nai; Those who live along the river south of Myitkyina who call themselves Tai Lai. However, apart from the sound shift l to n among the first group, there do not seem to be any major differences in language between these 2 subgroups. Reportedly similar to Khamti [kht]. *Lg Use:* Shifting to Burmese [mya] in some areas. *Writing:* Myanmar (Burmese) script, historical usage with some recent revival of the script. *Other:* The name Tai Laing means Red Tai. Buddhist. *Map:* 389:23.

Tai Loi [tlq] (Aw-aak, Bulang-Su, Doi, Khabe, Kon Doi, Kon Loi, Loi, Monglwe, Muak Sa-aak, Tailoi, Tai-Loi, Wakut). 4,460 in Myanmar (2008). Population total all countries: 4,960. East Shan State, north Mong Yawng township and into China. Also in Laos. *Status:* 6a (Vigorous). *Class:* Austro-Asiatic, Mon-Khmer, Northern Mon-Khmer, Palaungic, Eastern Palaungic, Angkuic. *Dialect:* Saneung Muak. Considerable dialectal variation between villages. Lexical similarity: 42% with U [uuu] of China; 40% with Pang Pung Plang [blr]; 25% with standard Wa [prk]. *Type:* SVO. *Lg Use:* Vigorous. All domains. All ages. Positive attitudes. Educated young people also use Burmese [mya]. Adults also use Tai Lue [khb]. Also use Mandarin Chinese [cmn]. *Lg Dev:* Literacy rate in L1: Below 1%. *Writing:* Latin script. *Other:* Tai Loi means 'mountain Tai' and is a cover term for multiple Palaungic groups in the area, some of which are Angkuic and some of which are Waic. Buddhist, Christian (Protestant). *Map:* 391:102.

Tai Nüa [tdd] (Chinese Shan, Tai Kong, Tai Neua). 72,400 in Myanmar (1983 census). North Shan State; east Kachin State. *Status:* 5 (Developing). *Dialects:* Mang Shi, Ruili (Meng Mao). *Lg Use:* Vigorous. All domains. All ages. Positive attitudes. Also use Mandarin Chinese [cmn]. *Other:* Mang Shi is the prestige dialect. Tai Nüa in Laos is probably a distinct but related language. Buddhist. See main entry on page 89. *Map:* 389:28.

Taman [tcl]. No known L1 speakers. Last Taman speaker died in 1990s. Descendants intermarried and now speak other languages. Sagaing Region, Khamti deistrict, Homalin township, Tamanthi area. *Status:* 9 (Dormant). *Class:* Sino-Tibetan, Tibeto-Burman, Sal, Jingpho-Luish, Jingpho. *Type:* SOV. *Lg Use:* Very limited usage. Only very elderly adults. 100% also use Taman [tcl]. Used as L2 by Taman [tcl]. *Writing:* Unwritten.

Taungyo [tco] (Taru, Taung-yo, Toru, Twing Reu, Twinreu). 40,000 (2000 D. Bradley). East central Shan State, Taunggyi district, Kalaw, and Pinlong townships. *Status:* 6a (Vigorous). *Class:* Sino-Tibetan, Tibeto-Burman, Ngwi-Burmese, Burmish, Southern. *Dialects:* None known. Nonstandard variety of Burmese [mya]. Intelligibility low between distant villages; low comprehension of Intha [int]; high comprehension of Danu [dnv]. Lexical similarity: 89% with standard Burmese [mya] and Intha [int], 91% with Danu [dnv], 84%–92% with Rakhine [rki]. *Type:* SOV. *Lg Use:* Vigorous. All except formal domains. All ages. Positive attitudes. Also use Burmese [mya]. *Writing:* Unwritten, informal and non-standardized use of Myanmar script. *Other:* Officially viewed as a Burmese dialect. Buddhist. *Map:* 391:89.

Tavoyan [tvn] (Dawai, Dawe, Dawei, Tavoya, Tawe-Tavoy). 400,000 (2000 D. Bradley). Southeast, Tanintharyi Region. *Status:* 6a (Vigorous). *Class:* Sino-Tibetan, Tibeto-Burman, Ngwi-Burmese, Burmish, Southern. *Dialects:* None known. A well-known nonstandard Burmese with profound pronunciation and vocabulary differences from Burmese [mya]. *Type:* SOV. *Lg Use:* Vigorous. All except formal domains. All ages. Positive attitudes. Also use Burmese [mya]. *Writing:* Unwritten, informal and non-standardized use of Myanmar script. *Other:* Officially viewed as a Burmese dialect [mya]. Buddhist. *Map:* 392:104.

Tibetan, Khams [khg]. 300 in Myanmar (2010 D. Bradley). Far north Kachin State, Da On Dam, San Dam, Mading, and Dahom Dam villages. *Status:* 6a (Vigorous). *Lg Use:* All ages. *Other:* Buddhist (Lamaist). See main entry on page 91. *Map:* 389:1.

Wa, Parauk [prk] (Baraog, Phalok, Praok, Standard Wa, Wa). 400,000 in Myanmar (2000 census). Population total all countries: 805,700. Northeast Shan State, upper Salween river area; East Shan State, Kengtung area; resettling since 2000 in southeast Shan State, Mong Hsat and Mong Ton townships, especially Mong Yawn, Pong Pa Kyin, and Mong Kyut town areas. Also in China, Thailand. *Status:* 2 (Provincial). De facto provincial language in Shan State. *Class:* Austro-Asiatic, Mon-Khmer, Northern Mon-Khmer, Palaungic, Eastern Palaungic, Waic, Wa. *Dialects:* Ai Cheung, Ai Swa, Ang Krax, Awm Plawk, Bible Wa, Caong Naong, Cuan, Hom, Ien, Kang Seu, Kaung Sang, Kawn Cawng, Kawn Jiem, Kawn Mau, Kawn Poih, Kawn Rao, Kawng Lang, Kha Lax, Khui Ma, Kok Lah, La Dah, La Kong, Lah Kreum, Lhax Tiah, Lung Kua, Man Leen, Man Shiang, Man Teu (Jo Phyu, Man Teey, Man Ton, Man Tong), Man Tong, Meung, Meung Kun, Meung Mao, Meung Yum, Muik Lhang, Muik Lhax, Muik Nghawng, Muik Nu, Muik Raix, Muik Sime, Nawng Plawx, Nom Tum, Pa Tah, Pang Vai, Pang Yang (Muik Khaox), Panglao, Rho Mawng, Rok Tong, Sau Hin, Savaik, Sheeiem, Shiem Tum, Shiiem Ceeim, Si Gang Rai, Si Nawk, Si Nga, Si Viex, Simung, Taoh Mie, Toi Lawng, Veng Ngeen, Vui Sai, Yaong Brex, Yaong Khrum, Yaong Krak, Yaong Kua, Yaong Leen, Yaong Lung, Yaong Nong, Yaong O, Yaong Peng, Yaong Raok, Yaong Riex, Yaong Sang, Yaong Soi, Yaong Ting, Ying Phang (Sigang). Over 70 varieties of Wa in Myanmar; 300 varieties in China (2006 Institute of Nationalities, Sun Hong Kai). Wa official nationality standard form in China based on Yong Shuai, one of many Parauk varieties. Bible Wa, a composite language, based on the Yong Shuai, Yong Rauk, Mang Toei, and Toilawng varieties, forms the standard for Myanmar. *Lg Use:* Vigorous. Females in rural areas tend to be monolingual in local Parauk varieties. Males tend to be more bilingual. All domains. All ages. Positive attitudes. Also use other varieties of Parauk and Palaungic. Also use Burmese [mya], Lahu [lhu], Mandarin Chinese [cmn], Shan [shn]. *Lg Dev:* Literacy rate in L2: Burmese 8% (mostly males); Chinese 5% in border areas (mostly males); Shan 2% (males). Literacy classes. Dictionary. Bible: 2006–2012. *Writing:* Latin script. *Other:* Traditional religion, Buddhist, Christian. *Maps:* 389:33, 391:33.

Wa, Vo [wbm] (Meung Hom, Peung Sux, Vhax). 700 in Myanmar (2012). Shan State, Hopang township, five villages. *Status:* 6b (Threatened). *Other:* Traditional religion, Buddhist, Christian. See main entry on page 93.

Wewaw [wea] (Wewau). No known L1 speakers. Karen hills, near Taungoo; Bago Yoma range between Ayeyawaddy and Sittang rivers. *Status:* 10 (Extinct). *Class:* Sino-Tibetan, Tibeto-Burman, Karenic, Southern. *Dialects:* Reportedly similar to and may be a dialect of S'gaw Karen [ksw]. *Type:* SOV. *Lg Use:* Shifted to S'gaw Karen [ksw]. *Writing:* Unwritten.

Yinbaw [kvu] (Yeinbaw, Yinbaw Karen). 7,300 (1983). East Shan State; Kayah State. *Status:* 6a (Vigorous). *Class:* Sino-Tibetan, Tibeto-Burman, Karenic, Northern. *Dialects:* None known. Consider themselves part of Kayan ethnic group. Reportedly similar to Kayan [pdu] and Geko [ghk]. *Lg Use:* All ages. *Writing:* Unwritten. *Other:* Buddhist, Christian, traditional religion. *Map:* 391:85.

Yinchia [yin] (Black Riang, Ranei, Striped Karen, Yin Kya, Yin Net, Yinnet). 12,000 (2008), decreasing. South Shan State. *Status:* 6b (Threatened). *Class:* Austro-Asiatic, Mon-Khmer, Northern Mon-Khmer, Palaungic, Western Palaungic, Riang. *Type:* SVO. *Lg Use:* Endangered. Also use Shan [shn] (southern dialect). Also use Burmese [mya]. *Lg Dev:* Literacy rate in L1: Below 1%. *Other:* Belha. Buddhist, traditional religion.

Yintale [kvy] (Taliak, Yangatalet, Yangtadai, Yintale Karen, Yintalet). 1,000 (2000 D. Bradley), decreasing. Wa Awng village is main village, with 100 households. Ethnic population: 10,000 (2000 D. Bradley). Kayah State, Bawlakhè district, Hpasawng township. 3 villages. *Status:* 6b (Threatened). *Class:* Sino-Tibetan, Tibeto-Burman, Karenic, Northern. *Dialects:* Bawlake, Wa Awng. Reportedly a variety of Western Kayah [kyu]. *Lg Use:* Used in 3 villages; in other villages not used at all. Elderly and young children, not youth. Neutral attitudes. Some in the older generation also use Manumanaw [kxf]. The youth also use Sgaw Karen [ksw]. *Lg Dev:* Literacy rate in L1: Below 1%. Some language development activity at Wa Awng village monastery. *Writing:* Unwritten. *Other:* Buddhist. *Map:* 391:83.

Zaiwa [atb] (Aci, Atshi, Atsi, Atzi, Azi, Zi). 30,000 in Myanmar (1997). Kachin State, Waimaw township, Sedan area; Shan State, Kentung district. *Status:* 5 (Developing). *Lg Use:* Vigorous. Most domains. All ages. Positive attitudes. Also use Jingpho [kac]. *Lg Dev:* Literacy rate in L1: 5%–10%. Literacy rate in L2: 50%–75%. Literacy classes in some communities. *Other:* The Chinese name is Tsaiwa, Jingpho is Atsi, Burmese is Zi. Christian. See main entry on page 94. *Map:* 389:34.

Zayein [kxk] (Gaungtou, Khaungtou, Zayein Karen). 9,300 (1983 census). Population including Lahta [kvt] and Zayein: 13,500 (Manson 2010). South Shan State, between Mobyè and Phekon towns. *Status:* 6a (Vigorous). *Class:* Sino-Tibetan, Tibeto-Burman, Karenic, Northern. *Dialects:* None known. May be subgroup of Latha [kvt]. *Lg Use:* All domains. All ages. Positive attitudes. Also use Burmese [mya], Kayan [pdu], Pa'o [blk]. *Writing:* Unwritten. *Other:* Reportedly, Zayein is an area name where many Latha [kvt] live. Buddhist, traditional religion.

Zo [zom] (Jou, Kuki Chin, Yo, Yos, Yote, Zau, Zome, Zomi, Zou). 61,000 in Myanmar (2012 T. Philipzo). Population total all countries: 81,900. Chin State, Tonzang, Hakha, and Tedim townships; Sagaing Region, Kalay, Khampat, and Tamu townships. Also in India (Zou). *Status:* 5 (Developing). *Class:* Sino-Tibetan, Tibeto-Burman, Sal, Kuki-Chin-Naga, Kuki-Chin, Northern. *Dialects:* None known. Reportedly similar to Tedim [ctd], Paite Chin [pck], Vaiphei [vap], and Simte [smt]. *Type:* SOV. *Lg Use:* Vigorous. All domains. All ages. Positive attitudes. *Lg Dev:* Bible: 1983–1995. *Writing:* Latin script, used in India. *Other:* Ethnic autonym: Zomi or Zome, also a collective name by Tedim Chin [ctd] of Myanmar, Paite [pck], and Vaiphei [vap] of Manipur. Christian. *Maps:* 389:36, 390:36.

Nepal

Federal Democratic Republic of Nepal. 26,494,000 (2011 census). Principal language: Nepali. Literacy rate: 48% (2010 UNESCO). Immigrant languages: English (2,030), Magahi (35,600), Oriya (580), Sindhi (520). General references: Bista 1967, 1973, 1996; Burling 2003; Ebert 1994; Hale 1982; Hansson 1991; Hugoniot 1970; Matisoff, Baron, and Lowe 1996; Thurgood and LaPolla 2003; Toba 1976, 1983, 1991; Toba, Toba and Rai 2002, 2005; Van Driem 2001, 2007. Deaf population: 192,000. Deaf institutions: 3. Recognized nationalities: The government of Nepal officially recognizes 59 indigenous nationalities, or "Adibasi Janajatis" as they are called in Nepali. They are enumerated in the 2002 legislation that created the National Foundation for Development of Indigenous Nationalities, Act 20, Section 2a. Furthermore, the Interim Constitution of 2007 states in Article 5 that all languages spoken as mother tongues in Nepal are considered national languages.

The number of individual languages listed for Nepal is 119. Of these, 117 are living and 2 are extinct. Of the living languages, 7 are institutional, 21 are developing, 28 are vigorous, 55 are in trouble, and 6 are dying. See maps beginning on page 393.

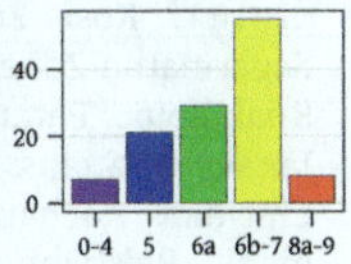

Angika [anp] (Anga, Angikar, Chhika-Chhiki). 18,600 in Nepal (2011 census), decreasing. Kosi Zone, Morang and Sunsari districts. *Status:* 6b (Threatened). *Lg Use:* Also use Hindi [hin], Maithili [mai], Nepali [npi]. *Other:* Hindu, Muslim. See main entry on page 102. *Map:* 397:96.

Athpariya [aph] (Arthare, Athapre, Athpare, Athpre, Sanango Ring). 5,530 (2011 census), decreasing. Kosi Zone, Dhankuta district, north of the Tamur, between the Dhankuta khola west, and the Tangkhuwa east; Dhankuta municipality and Bhirgau VDC. *Status:* 6b (Threatened). Recognized language (2002, Education Plan, Section 1.1.3). Language of recognized indigenous nationality: Rai. *Class:* Sino-Tibetan, Tibeto-Burman, Western Tibeto-Burman, Himalayan, Kiranti, Eastern. *Dialects:* None known. Athpare and Belhariya [byw] are very similar, but not mutually intelligible (Bickel 1996). *Type:* SOV; postpositions; genitives, adjectives, numerals before noun heads; polar questions marked with a suffix attached to the verb sentence final; noun head final; no noun classes or genders; content q-word in situ; content questions can have the same word order as assertive sentences, or the question word occurs directly before the verb; up to 2 prefixes, up to 9 suffixes; clause constituents indicated by case-marking; affixes indicate case of noun phrase; verbal affixation marks person, number, object—obligatory; split ergative; comparatives with Nepali, Bhanda; both tense and aspect; no passives or voice; CV, CVC, CVCC; 24 consonant and 5 vowel phonemes; nontonal. *Lg Use:* Shifting to Nepali [npi]. Home, religion; mixed use: Friends. All ages. Positive attitudes. Also use Nepali [npi]. *Lg Dev:* Literacy rate in L2: 2%. Taught in 5 mother-tongue multilingual education schools since 2008. Taught in primary schools. Poetry. Magazines. Newspapers. Radio programs. Videos. Dictionary. Grammar. *Writing:* Devanagari script. *Other:* Communities prefer to be called Kirati rather than Kirant. Traditional religion, Buddhist, Hindu. *Map:* 397:90.

Avadhi [awa] (Abadhi, Abadi, Abohi, Ambodhi, Awadhi, Dehati, Deshi, Gawnaru, Koseli). 502,000 in Nepal (2011 census), increasing. L2 users: 20,000 in Nepal (1991 census). Lumbini Zone, Nawalparasi, Rupandehi and Kapilvastu districts; Bheri Zone, Banke and Bardia districts; Rapti Zone, Dang district; Seti Zone, Kailali district; Mahakali Zone, Kanchanpur district. *Status:* 4 (Educational). Language of recognized indigenous nationality: Kushwadiya. *Dialects:* Baiswari, Chhatisgadhi. *Lg Use:* Strongly vital, vigorous. Home, friends; mixed use: Religion, work, education. All ages. Positive attitudes. Also use Hindi [hin], Nepali [npi]. Used as L2 by Bhojpuri [bho]. *Lg Dev:* Taught in primary and secondary schools. *Other:* Hindu, Buddhist, Christian, Muslim, Sikh. See main entry on page 102 (as Awadhi). *Maps:* 394:17, 395:17.

Bagheli [bfy] (Bagelkhandi, Bhugelkhud, Gangai, Kawathi, Kenat, Kevat Boli, Kevati, Kewani, Kewat, Kewati, Kewot, Mandal, Mannadi, Riwai). Ethnic population: 137,000 (2001 census). Kewat. Kosi Zone, Morang district. *Status:* 6a (Vigorous). Language of recognized indigenous nationality: Gangai. *Other:* Further research is needed to identify whether Bagheli in Nepal is linked with Gangai (and Rajbanshi [rjs] or with Avadhi [awa]) as is Bagheli in India. Hindu. See main entry on page 103.

Bahing [bhj] (Baying, Bayung, Kiranti-Bayung). 11,700 (2011 census). Sagarmatha Zone, northeast Okhaldhunga district, Harkapur, Ragdip, Bigutar, Baruneswor, Okhaldhunga, Rumjatar, Barnalu, Mamkha, Ratmate, Serna, Diyale, and Bhadaure VDCs (Rumdali dialect); mid southeastern Okhaldhunga district, Ketuke, Moli, Waksa, and Ubu VDCs (Tolocha dialect); Solukhumbu district south tip, Necha Batase and Sallyan VDCs; Khotang district; Kathmandu. *Status:* 6a (Vigorous). Language of recognized indigenous nationality: Rai. *Class:* Sino-Tibetan, Tibeto-Burman, Western Tibeto-Burman, Himalayan, Kiranti, Western. *Dialects:* Hangu, Moblocha, Nechali, Rumdali, Tolacha. 85% or above intelligibility among all dialects. Rumdali is best understood among all Bahing dialects (Lee et al 2005); Bahing is more homogeneous than most Kiranti languages. Related to Sunwar [suz]. Lexical similarity: 83%–95% with dialects, 48% with Sunwar [suz] (Lee et al 2005). *Type:* SOV. *Lg Use:* Reportedly still used often by younger generation. Shift to Nepali [npi] relatively low (Winter and Hanson 1991); High vitality (Lee et al. 2005). Home, friends, religion, work. All ages. Positive attitudes. 40% have inadequate Nepali [npi] proficiency to understand or discuss complicated or abstract concepts. (Lee et al 2005).

Used as L2 by Bantawa [bap], Nepali [npi], Thulung [tdh], Wambule [wme]. *Lg Dev:* Bahing orthography introduced through community-based development efforts. Two books published (2009). Bahing orthography being promoted for use by the whole Bahing community. Poetry. Magazines. Radio programs. Dictionary. *Writing:* Devanagari script. Latin script. *Other:* Traditional religion, Christian, Hindu. *Map:* 397:107.

Bantawa [bap] (Bantaba, Bantawa Dum, Bantawa Rai, Bantawa Yong, Bantawa Yüng, Bontawa). 133,000 in Nepal (2011 census). Population total all countries: 166,600. 6,000 monolinguals. Kosi Zone, Morang, Dhankuta, Bhojpur, and Sunsari districts; Sagarmatha Zone, Khotang, Okhaldunga, and Udayapur districts; Mechi Zone, Ilam, Jhapa, Panchthar, and Taplejung districts. Amchoke dialect: Limbu area, especially Ilam district. Homeland is Eastern hills but many migrated to the Tarai. Also in Bhutan, India. *Status:* 6b (Threatened). Language of recognized indigenous nationality: Rai. Some varieties are used as traditional lingua franca among Rai minorities in eastern Nepal, Sikkim, India, and Bhutan, and as L1 among Rai of other origin. (Bradley 1996). *Class:* Sino-Tibetan, Tibeto-Burman, Western Tibeto-Burman, Himalayan, Kiranti, Eastern. *Dialects:* Amchoke (Western Bantawa), Dhankuta (Eastern Bantawa), Dilpali (Northern Bantawa), Hatuwali (Southern Bantawa). Dialects are reportedly mutually inherently intelligible. Rungchenbung and Yangma are subvarieties of Dilpali. Eastern dialect is most divergent. Lexical similarity: Bantawa dialects and closely related languages form a continuum. Differences are primarily in meaning shifts and usage. *Type:* SOV; postpositions; noun heads initial; no noun classes or genders; content q-word in situ; genitives, adjectives, numerals before noun heads; polar questions marked only with rising intonation; content questions same word order as assertive sentences or question word directly before the verb; up to 2 prefixes, 10 suffixes; clause constituents indicated by word order; affixes indicate case of noun phrases; verbal affixation mark person, number, object—obligatory; tense and aspect; no passives or voice; split ergative; comparatives use Nepali word, bhanda; 25 consonant and 6 vowel phonemes; numbers above 3 are borrowed from Nepali [npi]; CV, CVC, CVCC; nontonal. *Lg Use:* Some shift to Nepali [npi] evident, especially among northern dialect speakers (2003 SIL). Home, religion; mixed use: Friends, work. All ages. Positive attitudes. Also use Bahing [bhj]. Hindi [hin] common among ex-soldiers. Most also use some Nepali [npi]. Wide range of proficiency. In some regions, young people prefer Nepali. Used as L2 by Chhintang [ctn], Chhulung [cur], Dungmali [raa], Puma [pum]. *Lg Dev:* Nepali literacy rapidly increasing. Taught in some primary schools. Poetry. Magazines. Newspapers. New media. Radio programs. Films. Videos. Dictionary. Grammar. *Writing:* Devanagari script. *Other:* Traditional religion, Christian. *Maps:* 396:84, 397:84.

Baram [brd] (Baraamu, Baramu). 160 (2011 census), decreasing. Ethnic population: 7,380 (2001 census). Gandaki Zone, Central and southern Gorkha district, Dandagaun and Mailung VDCs, Takhu village up the Doraundi Khola, east side above Chorgate, near Kumhali. About 7 villages. May be in Dhading district. *Status:* 8b (Nearly extinct). Language of recognized indigenous nationality: Baramou. *Class:* Sino-Tibetan, Tibeto-Burman, Western Tibeto-Burman, Himalayan, Central Himalayan, Thangmi-Baraamu. *Dialects:* Dandagaun, Mailung. Related to Thangmi [thf] (Grierson-Konow). *Type:* SOV; postpositions; noun head final; 2 noun classes (animate and inanimate); genitives, adjectives, numerals before noun heads; content q-word in situ; maximum number of prefixes 3, 1 suffix; clause constituents indicated by case-marking; affixes indicate case of noun phrase; verb affixation does not mark person or number—obligatory; ergative; both tense and aspect; no passives or voice; causatives, comparatives; simple syllable patterns: V, CV, VC, CVC; nontonal; 21 consonant and 6 vowel phonemes. *Lg Use:* Shifting to Nepali [npi]. Home, religion; mixed use: Friends, work. Older adults and elderly. Positive attitudes. Also use Nepali [npi]. *Lg Dev:* Literacy rate in L1: Low. Literacy rate in L2: 49% in Nepali [npi]. Newspapers. Radio programs. Dictionary. Grammar. *Writing:* Devanagari script, recently developed. *Other:* Traditional religion, Christian, Hindu. *Map:* 395:37.

Belhariya [byw] (Athpagari, Athpahariya, Athpare, Athpariya, Belhare). 600 (2011 census), decreasing. Kosi Zone, Dhankuta district, Belhara village and hill west of Dhankuta Bajar. *Status:* 6b (Threatened). Language of recognized indigenous nationality: Rai. *Class:* Sino-Tibetan, Tibeto-Burman, Western Tibeto-Burman, Himalayan, Kiranti, Eastern. *Dialects:* None known. Different from Athpariya [aph], although also called and closely related to it (Winter 1991). Not intelligible with Athpariya although Athpariya speakers claim full intelligibility (Bickel 1996:21). *Type:* SOV; postpositions; noun head final; no genders; content q-word in situ; up to 3 prefixes, up to 10 suffixes, and several clitics; clause constituents indicated by case-marking; verbal affixation marks person and number; ergativity; passives and voice; nontonal; 22 consonant and 8 vowel phonemes. *Lg Use:* Many parents only use Nepali [npi] with their children, citing advantages for economic and social success. Religion; mixed use: Home, friends, work. Adults and elderly. Some use among children and adolescents. Negative attitudes. Also use Nepali [npi]. *Lg Dev:* About 5 speakers are literate in their mother tongue. Dictionary. Grammar. *Writing:* Devanagari script, recently developed. *Other:* Athpare refers to the ethnic group made up of Belhare and Athpariya which have close cultural ties, but who recognize their linguistic differences. They clarify by calling the Dhankuta people Noupagari and the Belhare people Athpagari (Bickel 1996). Traditional religion, Hindu. *Map:* 397:91.

Bengali [ben] (Bangala, Bangla, Bangla-Bhasa). 21,100 in Nepal (2011 census), increasing. Mechi Zone, Jhapa district; Kosi Zone, Morang and Sunsari districts; Sagarmatha Zone, Saptari district. Some in Kathmandu, Bhaktapur, Patan, Birgunj, Bhairawa, Nepalguni, and Janakpur. *Status:* 5 (Dispersed). *Dialects:* Barik, Bhatiari, Chirmar, Kachari-Bengali, Lohari-Malpaharia, Musselmani, Rajshahi, Samaria, Saraki, Siripuria. *Lg Use:* Vigorous use if both parents are of Bengali origin. Home, friends; mixed use: Religion, work. All ages. Positive attitudes. Used as L2 by Maithili [mai], Meche [brx], Rajbanshi [rjs]. *Other:* Classified as a cultural group (2001 census). Hindu, Christian, Muslim. See main entry on page 54.

Bhojpuri [bho] (Bajpuri, Bhojapuri, Bhozpuri). 1,580,000 in Nepal (2011 census), increasing. L2 users: 74,100 in Nepal (1991 census). Narayani Zone, Rautahat, Bara, Parsa, and Chitwan districts; Lumbini Zone, Nawalparasi and Rupandehi districts; Janakpur Zone, Sarlahi district. *Status:* 4 (Educational). *Dialects:* Banarsi Boli, Bangar Boli, Bhojpuri Tharu, Kashika, Mallika, Purbi Boli, Sheikh Boli. *Lg Use:* Home, friends, work; mixed use: Religion, education. All ages. Positive attitudes. Also use Hindi [hin]. Literate in Hindi. Also use Nepali [npi]. Literate in Nepali. Also use Awadhi [awa], Maithili [mai]. Used as L2 by Bote [bmj], Chitwania Tharu [the], Maithili [mai],

Nepali Kurux [kxl], Southwestern Tamang [tsf]. *Lg Dev:* Literacy rate in L2: 50%–75%. Literate in Nepali [npi], Hindi [hin]. Taught as a subject in secondary schools. *Other:* Hindu, Muslim. See main entry on page 105. *Maps:* 395:50, 396:50.

Bhujel [byh] (Bujal, Bujhel, Bujheli, Bujhyal, "Gharti" *pej.*, Pukhgyal Ngur, Western Chepang). 21,700 (2011 census), decreasing. 0 monolinguals. Ethnic population: 7,200 (Regmi 2007). Gandaki Zone, Tanahun district, Kulmun, Arthumpka, Andimul, and Baniyatar; Gorkha district, Beltar; Lumbini Zone, Nawalparasi district, Dhodeni; Narayani Zone, Chitwan district, Chanaute. Separated from Chepang [cdm] language areaby Trisuli river. *Status:* 7 (Shifting). Language of recognized indigenous nationality: Bhujel. *Class:* Sino-Tibetan, Tibeto-Burman, Western Tibeto-Burman, Himalayan, Central Himalayan, Chepang-Bhujel. *Dialects:* Andimul, Arthumpka, Baniyatar, Beltar, Chanaute, Dhodeni, Kulmun. More than 80% intelligibility among all the dialects. Pronominal affix differences hinder intelligibility with Chepang [cdm]. Lexical similarity: Between 34% (2011 D. Regmi) and 98% (2004 R. Caughley) with Chepang [cdm]. *Type:* SOV; postpositions; genitives, adjectives, numerals, before noun heads; relatives before or without noun heads; noun head final; content q-word in situ; question word final; no noun classes or genders; 1 prefix, up to 5 suffixes; clause constituents indicated by case-marking; consistently ergative; anti-dative marking; affixes indicate case of noun phrase; verb affixation marks person, number and direct relations; no passives or voice; causatives; comparatives; CV to CCCVCCC with certain restrictions; non-tonal; 31 consonant and 16 vowel (including 6 diphthongs) phonemes. *Lg Use:* Shifting to Nepali [npi] (Van Driem 2007). Home; mixed use: Work, education. Older adults and elderly. Positive attitudes. Youth use some Nepali [npi]. Used as L2 by Sunwar [suz]. *Lg Dev:* Literacy rate in L2: 15% in Nepali [npi]. Grammar. *Writing:* Devanagari script, recently developed. *Other:* Similar culturally to Magar and Gurung living near the Bhujel. Gharti is a sub-caste name associated with former slavery. Bhujels reject the name, but outsiders often use it. Hindu, Buddhist, Christian. *Map:* 395:44.

Bote [bmj] (Bote-Majhi, Pakhe-Bote, Pani-Bote). 8,770 (2011 census), decreasing. 0 monolinguals (2002 UNESCO). Ethnic population: 7,970. Gandaki Zone,Tanahu district; Lumbini Zone, Nawalparasi district; Narayani Zone, Chitwan district. Along the rivers, especially the Gandaki. *Status:* 6b (Threatened). Language of recognized indigenous nationality: Bote. *Class:* Indo-European, Indo-Iranian, Indo-Aryan, Eastern zone, Unclassified. *Type:* SOV; postpositions; final noun head; no noun classes or genders; content q-word in situ; 1 prefix, up to 2 suffixes; clause constituents indicated by case-marking; verbal affixation marks person and number; ergativity; both tense and aspect; passives and voice; nontonal; 29 consonant and 6 vowel phonemes. *Lg Use:* Use is mostly local. Rapid shift to Nepali [npi] (Van Driem 2007). Mixed use: Home, friends, religion, work. Elderly. Some use among children, adolescents, younger and older adults. Positive attitudes. Growing language activism. Also use Bhojpuri [bho], Nepali [npi]. *Lg Dev:* Literacy rate in L1: None. Generally, literacy programs are conducted in Nepali [npi]. Newspapers. *Writing:* Devanagari script, recently developed. *Other:* 2 groups of Bote: Pani (water) Bote and Pakhe (land) Bote. Hindu. *Map:* 395:46.

Byangsi [bee] (Byangkho Lwo, Byanshi, Byansi, Byasi, Sauka, Shauka). 480 in Nepal (2011 census), decreasing. 0 monolinguals (2002 UNESCO). Ethnic population: 2,100. L2 users: 160 in Nepal (1991 census). Mahakali Zone, Darchula district, Byas valley. 9 villages. *Status:* 6b (Threatened). Language of recognized indigenous nationality: Byasi. *Dialects:* Byansi, Pang Sungkhu Boli, Rang, Sauka, Yerjungkhu Boli. *Lg Use:* Home, friends. Also use Hindi [hin], Kumaoni [kfy], Nepali [npi]. *Lg Dev:* Literacy rate in L2: 26% in Nepali [npi]. See main entry on page 107. *Map:* 394:1.

Chamling [rab] (Camling, Chamlinge Rai, Rodong). 76,800 in Nepal (2011 census), decreasing. Very few monolinguals. East, Sagarmatha Zone, mainly central Khotang district and northern Udayapur districts. Also in India. *Status:* 6b (Threatened). Language of recognized indigenous nationality: Rai. *Class:* Sino-Tibetan, Tibeto-Burman, Western Tibeto-Burman, Himalayan, Kiranti, Eastern. *Dialects:* Balamtali, Halesi, Ratanchhali. Ratanchhali and Halesi dialects are similar to each other but Balamtali is very different. Reportedly most similar to Bantawa [bap] and Puma [pum] linguistically. Many speak a variety mixed with Nepali [npi]. *Type:* SOV; postpositions; noun head final; no noun classes or genders; content q-word in situ; up to 2 prefixes, up to 7 suffixes; clause constituents indicated by case-marking; verbal affixation marks person and number; split and inverse ergativity; mixed tense-aspect; no passives or voice; nontonal; 28 consonant and 5 vowel phonemes. *Lg Use:* Home, religion; mixed use: friends, work. All ages. Used as L2 by Puma [pum]. *Lg Dev:* Poetry. Magazines. Radio programs. Films. Videos. Dictionary. Grammar. *Writing:* Devanagari script, recently developed. *Other:* Many ethnic subgroups, but linguistically homogeneous. Traditional religion, Hindu. *Maps:* 396:63, 397:63.

Chantyal [chx] (Chantel, Chantel Kham, Chentel, Chhantel, Chhantyal, Khamkura). 4,280 (2011 census), decreasing. 0 monolinguals. Ethnic population: 9,820 (2001 census). Dhawalagiri Zone, Myagdi district, Kali Gandaki river valley. Ethnic Chantel in Baglung district. *Status:* 6b (Threatened). Language of recognized indigenous nationality: Chhantyal. *Class:* Sino-Tibetan, Tibeto-Burman, Western Tibeto-Burman, Bodish, West Bodish, Gurung-Tamang, Gurungic. *Dialects:* None known. Related to Gurung [ggn], Manangba [nmm], Tamang [tdg], and Thakali [ths] (Noonan 1996). *Lg Use:* Home, villages (Noonan 1996). Not used for singing. Also use Nepali [npi]. *Lg Dev:* Dictionary. Grammar. *Writing:* Devanagari script, recently developed. *Other:* Some believe Chantyal will be replaced soon. Outsiders often regard it as Magar, but they claim a Thakuri origin (de Sales 1993). Much lexical borrowing from Nepali. Sometimes called Khamkura as are Kham languages, which can have a general meaning of local non-Nepali dialect. (Watters 2002). Traditional religion, Buddhist. *Maps:* 394:23, 395:23.

Chepang [cdm] (Praja Bhasa, Tsepang). 48,500 (2011 census), decreasing. 0 monolinguals. Ethnic population: 52,200. Narayani Zone, Makwanpur, Chitwan districts; Bagmati Zone, southern Dhading district; Gandaki Zone, southern Gorkha district. *Status:* 6b (Threatened). Language of recognized indigenous nationality: Chepang. *Class:* Sino-Tibetan, Tibeto-Burman, Western Tibeto-Burman, Himalayan, Central Himalayan, Chepang-Bhujel. *Dialects:* Eastern Chepang, Western Chepang. Bhujel [byh] has difficult intelligibility with Chepang due to different pronominal suffix morphology. Dialects of Chepang differ in verb forms. Reportedly similar in morphology to Kirati languages. Lexical similarity: 98% with Bhujel [byh] (2004 R. Caughley, based on 100-item word list). *Type:* SOV; postpositions; noun head final; no noun classes or genders; relatives before or without noun heads; content q-word in situ; no prefixes, up to 8 suffixes; clause constituents indicated by case-marking; affixes indicate case of noun phrase; verbal affixation marks person and number; ergative; tense and aspect; voice; causatives; comparatives; CV to CCCVCCC with certain restrictions; 18 consonant and 6 vowel phonemes; nontonal (not phonemic, but phonetic pitch). Whistle speech. *Lg Use:* Home; mixed use: Friends, religion, work. Young adults and older. Some use among children and adolescents. Positive attitudes. Speakers over 5 know some Nepali [npi]. It is often learned in school. Men can talk about most common topics and political affairs. Women know greetings and vocabulary for trade. Young people may sometimes speak Nepali to each other. *Lg Dev:* Literacy rate in L1: 1%–5%. Literacy rate in L2: 40% men, 15% women in Nepali [npi]; 14% ethnic group (1991 census). Difficulties in reading Chepang: long words, consonant clusters. Written Chepang has lower prestige than Nepali. Motivation high for Nepali. Newspapers. Radio programs. Films. Videos. Dictionary. Grammar. NT: 1993. *Writing:* Devanagari script. *Other:* Traditional religion, Christian. *Maps:* 395:42, 396:42.

Chhintang [ctn] (Chhintange, Chintang, Chintang Rûng, Teli). 3,710 (2011 census), decreasing. 0 monolinguals. Ethnic population: 5,000. East, Kosi Zone, Dhankuta district, Chhintang and Aahale VDCs. *Status:* 6b (Threatened). Language of recognized indigenous nationality: Rai. *Class:* Sino-Tibetan, Tibeto-Burman, Western Tibeto-Burman, Himalayan, Kiranti, Eastern. *Dialects:* Mulgaun, Sambhugaon. Probably not intelligible with Bantawa [bap], but sometimes considered a dialect of it due to reportedly ethnic similarities. Only a few lexical items and grammatical markers are different between the two dialects. *Type:* SOV; postpositions; noun head final; no noun classes or genders; content q-word in situ; up to 4 prefixes (in free order), up to 7 suffixes; clause constituents indicated by case-marking; verbal affixation marks person and number; ergativity; both tense and aspect; no passives or voice; nontonal; 29 consonant and 6 vowel phonemes. *Lg Use:* Home, religion, work; mixed use: Friends. Young adults and older. Some use among children and adolescents. Neutral attitudes. Almost all are bilingual in Bantawa [bap]. *Lg Dev:* Videos. Dictionary. Grammar. *Writing:* Devanagari script, recently developed. *Other:* Traditional religion, Christian. *Map:* 397:93.

Chhulung [cur] (Chhiling, Chhilling, Chholung, Chhûlûng Rûng, Chiling, Chulung, Chülüng). 2,050 (2011 census), decreasing. L1 speakers dwindling (Van Driem 2007). Kosi Zone, Dhankuta district, Ankhisalla VDC. *Status:* 7 (Shifting). Language of recognized indigenous nationality: Rai. *Class:* Sino-Tibetan, Tibeto-Burman, Western Tibeto-Burman, Himalayan, Kiranti, Eastern. *Type:* SOV; postpositions; verbal affixation marks person and number; tense; nontonal. *Lg Use:* Home; mixed use: Friends, religion, work. Older adults and elderly. Some use among children, adolsecents, and young adults. Also use Bantawa [bap], Nepali [npi]. *Writing:* Unwritten. *Other:* Traditional religion. *Map:* 397:92.

Chukwa [cuw] (Cukwa Ring, Pohing, Pohing Kha). 100 (2011 SIL), decreasing. Only 5 fluent speakers (2011). Kosi Zone, Bhojpur district, Kulung VDC, Jimigau. *Status:* 8a (Moribund). Language of recognized indigenous nationality: Rai. *Class:* Sino-Tibetan, Tibeto-Burman, Western Tibeto-Burman, Himalayan, Kiranti, Eastern. *Dialects:* None known. A noticeable number of shared nouns with Northern Lohorung [lbr] (2011 J. Eppele). *Type:* SOV; postpositions; verbal affixation marks person and number; tense; nontonal. *Lg Use:* Shifting to Nepali [npi] and English [eng]. Religion; mixed use: Home. Elderly. *Writing:* Unwritten. *Other:* Linguistically between Kulung-Nachering-Sangpang and Meohang-Saam (Hansson 1991), but there is no supporting data. The Chukwa claim a close linguistic and ethnic affiliation with Saam [raq]; they say that their language is very different from Kulung [kle], although Van Driem (2001) lists Chukwa as a subgroup of Kulung. Traditional religion, Hindu. *Map:* 396:77.

Danuwar [dhw] (Danuwar Rai, Danwar, Denwar, Dhanvar, Dhanwar). 45,800 (2011 census), decreasing. 0 monolinguals (Toba, Toba, and Rai 2005). Ethnic population: 53,200. Narayani Zone, Makwanpur; Janakpur Zone, Sindhuli; Bagmati Zone, Kabhrepalanchok and Lalitpur Districts. *Status:* 7 (Shifting). Language of recognized indigenous nationality: Danuwar. *Class:* Indo-European, Indo-Iranian, Indo-Aryan, Unclassified. *Dialects:* Bakultar Danuwar, Dukuchhap Danuwar, Judigaon Danuwar, Kamala Khonch Danuwar, Panchkhal Danuwar, Sindhuli Danuwar. Danuwar Kachariya in Rautahat and elsewhere is probably distinct from Danuwar [dhw]. The dialects spoken in Bakultar, Panchkhal, Judigaon (Kabhrepalanchok) district are mutually intelligible, whereas the dialects spoken in Dukuchhap (Lalitpur district) and Sindhuli are different. *Type:* SOV; postpositions; noun head final; 2 noun classes or genders; content q-word in situ; 1 prefix, up to 4 suffixes; clause constituents indicated by case-marking; verbal affixation marks person, number and gender of subject; ergativity; both tense and aspect; no passives and voice; nontonal; 29 consonant and 6 vowel phonemes. *Lg Use:* Rapidly assimilating to Nepali [npi] (Van Driem 2007). Home, religion; mixed use: Friends, work. Older adults and elderly. Some use among children, adolescents, and young adults. Neutral attitudes. Also use Eastern Tamang [taj] at work and with friends in Kabhre district. Also use Nepali [npi] at work and with friends in Kabhre district. *Lg Dev:* Although some people are writing in Danuwari, no data is available on L1 literacy. Radio programs. Dictionary. *Writing:* Devanagari script. *Other:* Hindu, traditional religion. *Map:* 396:58.

Darai [dry]. 11,700 (2011 census), decreasing. Very few monolinguals. Ethnic population: 14,900. Narayani Zone, Chitwan district, Bharatpur municipality, Mangalpur, Kathar, Jagatpur, and Chainpur VDCs; Gandaki Zone, Tanahun district, Vyas municipality, Kyamin and Ramjakot VDCs. *Status:* 6b (Threatened). Language of recognized indigenous nationality: Darai. *Class:* Indo-European, Indo-Iranian, Indo-Aryan, Unclassified. *Dialects:* Chitwan, Tanahun. Lexical similarity: 85%–90% with Bote [bmj]. *Type:* SOV; postpositions; noun head final; 2 noun classes or genders; 1 prefix, up to 4 suffixes; clause constituents indicated by case-marking; verbal affixation marks for person and number; nominal-based split ergativity; both tense and aspect; passives and voice; nontonal; 29 consonant and 6 vowel phonemes; head-marking of noun in genitive construction. *Lg Use:* Rapidly assimilating to Nepali [npi] (Van Driem 2007). Home; mixed use: Friends, religion, work. Young adults and older. Some use among children and adolescents. Positive attitudes. Most know Nepali [npi] very well, well enough to understand complex subjects. *Lg Dev:* Magazines. Newspapers. Radio programs. Films. Videos. Dictionary. *Writing:* Devanagari script. *Other:* Darai do not have social subdivisions found in most other Nepali groups. They do not organize communities into social, religious, economic, or political organizations (Bista 1996). Hindu. *Map:* 395:48.

Dhimal [dhi] (Dhemal). 19,300 in Nepal (2011 census), decreasing. Population total all countries: 19,750. Ethnic population: 19,500. L2 users: 410 in Nepal (1991 census).

Mechi Zone, Jhapa district, 24 villages; Kosi Zone, Morang and Sunsari districts, 51 villages; eastern and western dialects are separated by Kankai river in Jhapa. Also in India. *Status:* 6b (Threatened). Language of recognized indigenous nationality: Dhimal. *Class:* Sino-Tibetan, Tibeto-Burman, Sal, Dhimalish. *Dialects:* Eastern Dhimal, Western Dhimal. 75%–80% intelligibility between eastern and western dialect speakers. Lexical similarity: 80%–82% with dialects. *Type:* SOV; postpositions; noun head final; no noun classes or genders; content q-word in situ; genitives, demonstratives, relatives before noun heads; 1 prefix, up to 3 suffixes; clause constituents indicated by case-marking; verbal affixation marks person; non-ergative; tense and aspect; passives and voice; nontonal; 31 consonant and 16 vowel phonemes (includes 5 basic vowels, 5 long vowels and 5 nasalized vowels); honorificity is marked for 1st person when speaking with in-laws. *Lg Use:* Home, friends, religion; mixed use: Work. Adolescents and older. Some use among children. Positive attitudes. Also use Hindi [hin], Nepali [npi], Rajbanshi [rjs]. *Lg Dev:* Literacy rate in L2: 39% (1991 census). Poetry. Magazines. New media. Radio programs. Dictionary. Grammar. Bible portions: 2000. *Writing:* Devanagari script. *Other:* Traditional religion, Christian, Hindu. *Map:* 397:95.

Dolpo [dre] (Dolkha, Dolpa Tibetan, Dolpali, Dolpike, Phoke Dolpa). 1,670 (2011 census). Ethnic population: 8,000 (2010 K. Kopp). Karnali Zone, Dolpa district, Barbung river valley, villages north and east of Kag; Tarap river valley, Lang village and north; beyond mountains west of upper Kali Gandaki river valley; confined by the Dhaulagiri Himal south and Tibet north; Suligag river valley, north of Rengi village and the lake area; headwaters of Karnali river; many small villages in Nangong, Panzang, Tarap, and Barbung river valleys. *Status:* 5 (Developing). Language of recognized indigenous nationality: Dolpo. *Class:* Sino-Tibetan, Tibeto-Burman, Western Tibeto-Burman, Bodish, Central Bodish, Central, gTsang. *Dialects:* None known. Phoksumdo Lake, Barbung River, and Charka areas are slightly different, but intelligibility is good. The central valleys of Nankong and Dho Tarap are well understood by other varieties. Lexical similarity: 78% with Loke [loy], 69% with Lhomi [lhm], 68% with Lhasa Tibetan [bod], Walungge [ola], and Kyerung (Kyirong) [kgy], 67% with Nubri [kte], 66% with Helambu Sherpa [scp], 62% with Jirel [jul] and Sherpa [xsr] (2010 K. Kopp). *Type:* SOV; postpositions; noun head initial; no noun classes or genders; content q-word in situ; 1 prefix, up to 3 suffixes; clause constitutents indicated by case-marking; conjunct or disjunct verbal agree with subject with evidential marking in the verbal auxiliary; gender is marked explicitly in the noun phrase; ergativity; tense and aspect (aspect marked overtly as a verbal suffix); no passives or voice; 36 consonant and 7 vowel phonemes; tonal. *Lg Use:* Vigorous. Home, friends, religion, work. All ages. Positive attitudes. Also use Central Tibetan [bod], Loke [loy], Nepali [npi]. Used as L2 by Kaike [kzq]. *Lg Dev:* Literacy rate in L1: Below 10%. Literacy materials have been produced and are being tested. Non-formal classes are being planned (2010). Poetry. Dictionary. *Writing:* Tibetan script. *Other:* Buddhist (Lamaist). *Maps:* 394:4, 395:4.

Dotyali [dty] (Dotali, Doteli). 788,000 in Nepal (2011 census). Mahakali Zone, Baitadi, Dadeldhura, north Kanchanpur, south Daichula districts; Seti Zone, Doti, north Kailali, southwest Bajhang districts. Small area in Bheri Zone. Also in India. *Status:* 5 (Developing). *Class:* Indo-European, Indo-Iranian, Indo-Aryan, Northern zone, Eastern Pahari. A member of macrolanguage Nepali [nep]. *Dialects:* None known. Reportedly similar to Nepali [npi] and Kumaoni [kfy]. *Lg Use:* Vigorous. All domains. All ages. Very positive attitudes. *Lg Dev:* Poetry. Magazines. Radio programs. TV. Dictionary. Grammar. *Writing:* Devanagari script. *Map:* 394:11.

Dumi [dus] (Dumi Bo'o, Dumi Bro, Hopupo Bro, Lsi Rai, Ro'do Bo', Sotmali). 7,640 (2011 census), decreasing. 0 monolinguals. Ethnic population: 12,000. Sagarmatha Zone, north Khotang district, Makpa, Jalapa, Baksila, Sapteshwor, and Kharmi VDCs. *Status:* 7 (Shifting). Language of recognized indigenous nationality: Rai. *Class:* Sino-Tibetan, Tibeto-Burman, Western Tibeto-Burman, Himalayan, Kiranti, Western. *Dialects:* Kharbari, Lamdija, Makpa. Reportedly most similar to Khaling [klr] and Koi [kkt]. Makpa dialect is markedly divergent. *Type:* SVO; postpositions; noun head final; no noun classes or genders; content q-word in situ; 1 prefix, unknown number of suffixes; verbal affixation marks person and number; ergativity; nontonal; 25 consonant and 14 vowel phonemes. *Lg Use:* Pressure to shift to Nepali [npi] in education and communication with outsiders is strong. Few parents teach Dumi to their children or encourage their children to use their language. Home, religion. Mixed use: Friends, work. Young adults and older. Some use among children and adolescents. Most are bilingual in neighboring local languages, then in Nepali [npi]. *Lg Dev:* Poetry. Magazines. Dictionary. Grammar. *Writing:* Devanagari script. *Other:* Efforts have been made by some to preserve the language by creating written materials. Traditional religion, Christian, Hindu. *Map:* 396:64.

Dungmali [raa] (Arthare, Arthare-Khesang, Dungmali Pûk, Dungmali-Bantawa, Khesange). 6,260 (2011 census), decreasing. 150 monolinguals. Ethnic population: 10,000. Kosi Zone; east Bhojpur district, Thulo Dungma, Sano Dungma, and Bastim VDCs, east border is Arun river. *Status:* 6b (Threatened). Language of recognized indigenous nationality: Rai. *Class:* Sino-Tibetan, Tibeto-Burman, Western Tibeto-Burman, Himalayan, Kiranti, Eastern. *Dialect:* Khesang (Khesange). 82% cognate with Bantawa [bap] but morphology and phonology differ (Winter 1991). Lexical similarity: 80% with Bantawa [bap], 65% with Puma [pum]. *Type:* SOV; postpositions; noun head final; content q-word in situ; 1 prefix; clause constituents indicated by case-marking; verbal affixation marks person and gender; split ergativity; tense; no passives or voice; tonal; 18 consonant and 6 vowel phonemes. *Lg Use:* Home, religion. Mixed use: Friends, work. Young adults and older. Some use among children and adolescents. Also use Bantawa [bap]. *Lg Dev:* Poetry. Newspapers. Dictionary. *Other:* Local names which may not be dialects: Chhinamkhang, Chhichhangchha, Hangbang, Khandung, Pungwai, Roktulung, Tuncha, Waitpang. Traditional religion. *Map:* 397:86.

Dura [drq]. Ethnic population: 2,160 (2011 census). Gandaki Zone, Lamjung district, Dura Danda. *Status:* 9 (Dormant). Language of recognized indigenous nationality: Dura. *Class:* Sino-Tibetan, Tibeto-Burman, Western Tibeto-Burman, Bodish, West Bodish. *Type:* SOV; postpositions; noun head final; no noun classes or genders; content q-word in situ; 1 prefix, up to 3 suffixes; clause constituents indicated by case-marking; ergativity; tense (2) and aspect; no passives or voice; nontonal; 37 consonant and 6 vowel phonemes. *Lg Use:* Shifting to Nepali [npi]. *Writing:* Unwritten. *Other:* Tandrange may be a dialect of Dura. Hindu, Buddhist.

Ghale, Northern [ghh] (Lila, Ril-Lila). 4,440 (2006 SIL). 400 monolinguals. Gandaki Zone, Gorkha district, Buri Gandaki valley. *Status:* 6b (Threatened). *Class:* Sino-Tibetan, Tibeto-Burman, Western Tibeto-Burman,

Bodish, West Bodish, Ghale. *Dialects:* Jagat, Khorla, Nyak, Philim, Uiya. Nyak is most diverse dialect. Philim has 94% intelligibility of Uiya. 75%–79% intelligibility of Barpak in Southern Ghale [ghe]. Dialect chain runs north and south. Lexical similarity: 73%–89% among dialects, 65%–81% with Southern Ghale [ghe], 45%–61% with Kuke [ght], 29%–37% with Western Tamang [tdg], 21%–27% with Nubri [kte], 22%–25% with Tsum [ttz], 19%–23% with Kyerung (Kyirong) [kgy], 19%–21% with Tibetan [bod]. *Lg Use:* Vigorous. Home, friends, religion, work. Young adults and older. Some use among children and adolescents. Positive attitudes. Speakers in Philim, Lho, and Bihi have no more than basic bilingual proficiency in Nepali [npi]. *Writing:* Unwritten. *Other:* Buddhist, Christian, Hindu. *Maps:* 395:31, 396:31.

Ghale, Southern [ghe] (Galle Gurung, Lila, Ril-Lila). 21,500 (2006 SIL). Gandaki Zone, Gorkha district, hills south of Macha Khola. *Status:* 6a (Vigorous). *Class:* Sino-Tibetan, Tibeto-Burman, Western Tibeto-Burman, Bodish, West Bodish, Ghale. *Dialects:* Barpak, Kyaura, Laprak. Some intelligibility between Northern [ghh] and Southern Ghale. Dialect subgroup. Glover (1974:8–12) identifies a Ghale branch under Bodish intermediate between Tibetan and Gurung branches. Lexical similarity: 75%–78% among dialects, 65%–81% with Northern Ghale, 39%–49% with Kuke [ght], 27%–30% with Western Gurung [gvr], 31% with Western Tamang [tdg], 20% with Nubri [kte] and Tsum [ttz], 18% with Tibetan [bod]. *Type:* SOV; postpositions; noun head both initial and final; no noun classes or genders; content q-word in situ; up to 2 prefixes, 1 suffix; clause constituents indicated by case-marking; no verbal affixation; no passives or voice; tonal; 18 consonant and 6 vowel phonemes. *Lg Use:* Vigorous. Home, religion; mixed use: Friends, work. All ages. Positive attitudes. Also use English [eng], Hindi [hin], Nepali [npi]. *Lg Dev:* Dictionary. NT: 1992. *Writing:* Devanagari script. *Other:* Hindu, Christian. *Map:* 395:38.

Ghandruk Sign Language [gds]. 20 (2011 SIL). Gandaki Zone, Kaski district, Ghandruk. *Status:* 8b (Nearly extinct). *Class:* Deaf sign language. *Dialects:* Similar to Kathmandu and Pokhara dialects of Nepalese Sign Language [nsp]. *Lg Use:* All domains. *Writing:* Unwritten. *Map:* 395:33.

Gurung, Eastern [ggn] (Daduwa, Gurung, Tamu Kyi). 227,000 (2007), decreasing. 326,000 all Gurung languages in Nepal (2011 census). 23,000 monolinguals. Ethnic population: 544,000. L2 users: 18,918 L2 speakers of all Gurung languages. Mainly occupational castes who live in and serve the Gurung communities (1991 census). Gandaki Zone, Lamjung, Tanahu, and west Gorkha districts. Possibly Manang district. *Status:* 6b (Threatened). Language of recognized indigenous nationality: Gurung. *Class:* Sino-Tibetan, Tibeto-Burman, Western Tibeto-Burman, Bodish, West Bodish, Gurung-Tamang, Gurungic. *Dialects:* Gorkha Gurung, Lamjung Gurung, Tamu Kyi. Eastern and Western Gurung [gvr] do not have adequate intelligibility to handle complex and abstract discourse. Daduwa town in Lamjung District seems central linguistically. *Type:* SOV; postpositions; noun head final; genitives, adjectives, relative clause precede noun heads; numerals after noun heads; rising intonation in bipolar questions; no noun classes or genders; content q-word in situ; 1 prefix on negative verbs; up to 2 suffixes; clause constituents indicated by case-marking; case of noun phrase shown by preposition; no subject or object referencing in verbs; split ergative system according to tense; causatives; benefactives; aspect; no passives or voice; 24 consonant and 5 vowel phonemes; CV, CCV, CCCV; tonal: voice quality or register is part of tone system. *Lg Use:* Children and young people use Gurung less frequently than those who are older. Passed down only a little from generation to generation (UNESCO). Mixed use: Home, friends, religion, work, education. Some use among all ages. School graduates use some English [eng]. Also use Lhomi [lhm], Nepali [npi]. *Lg Dev:* Literacy rate in L1: 30%. Literacy rate in L2: 30%. Radio programs. Bible portions: 1994. *Writing:* Devanagari script. Latin script. *Other:* Buddhist, Hindu. *Map:* 395:36.

Gurung, Western [gvr] (Gurung, Tamu Kyi). 125,000 in Nepal (2007), increasing. 326,000 all Gurung languages in Nepal (2011 census). Population total all countries: 158,000. 12,000 monolinguals. Ethnic population: 544,000. L2 users: 18,918 L2 speakers of all Gurung languages. Mainly occupational castes who live in and serve the Gurung communities (1991 census). Gandaki Zone, Kaski and Syangja districts; Dhawalagiri Zone, Parbat district. Possibly in Myanmar. Also in Bhutan, India. *Status:* 6b (Threatened). Language of recognized indigenous nationality: Gurung. *Class:* Sino-Tibetan, Tibeto-Burman, Western Tibeto-Burman, Bodish, West Bodish, Gurung-Tamang, Gurungic. *Dialects:* Northwestern Gurung (Kaski Gurung), Southern Gurung (Syangja Gurung). Dialect speakers may have enough mutual intelligibility to understand complex and abstract discourse, but not enough with Eastern Gurung [ggn]. Related to Thakali [ths]. *Type:* SOV; postpositions; genitives, adjectives, relative clauses precede noun heads; numerals after noun heads; noun head final; no noun classes or genders; content q-word in situ; rising intonation marks bipolar questions; one negative prefix on verbs; up to 2 suffixes; clause constituents indicated by case-marking; case of noun phrases is indicated by postpositions; no subject or object referencing in verbs; split ergative system according to tense; causatives; benefactives; aspect; no passives or voice; 24 consonant and 5 vowel phonemes; CV, CCV, CCCV; tonal: voice quality or register is part of the tone system. *Lg Use:* Children and young people use Gurung less frequently than those who are older. Passed down only a little from generation to generation (2002 UNESCO). Home; mixed use: Friends, religion, work. Some use among all ages. Positive attitudes. School graduates speak some English [eng]. Also use Lhomi [lhm], Nepali [npi]. *Lg Dev:* Literacy rate in L1: 30%. Literacy rate in L2: 30%. Poetry. Magazines. Newspapers. New media. Radio programs. Films. TV. Videos. Dictionary. Grammar. NT: 1982. *Writing:* Devanagari script. *Other:* Buddhist, Christian, Hindu. *Map:* 395:35.

Helambu Sherpa [scp] (Hyolmo, Yholmo, Yohlmu Tam, Yolmo). 10,200 (2011 census). Very few monolinguals. Bagmati Zone, northern Nuwakot and northwestern Sindhupalchok districts. *Status:* 6a (Vigorous). Language of recognized indigenous nationality: Hyolmo. *Class:* Sino-Tibetan, Tibeto-Burman, Western Tibeto-Burman, Bodish, Central Bodish, Central, gTsang. *Dialects:* Eastern Helambu Sherpa, Lamjung Yohlmo, LangDang Yohlmo, Western Helambu Sherpa. Melamchi river divides dialects. Understand other dialects even for abstract and complex subjects, including possibly Tarke Ghyang, Kahng-Kharka, Pahndang, but not Kagate [syw]. Lexical similarity: 66% with Dolpo [dre] and Walungge [ola]; 65% with Lhasa Tibetan [bod], Jirel [jul], and Kyerung (Kyirong) [kgy]; 63% with Loke [loy] and Sherpa [xsr]; 61% with Nubri [kte]; 60% with Lhomi [lhm]. *Type:* SOV; postpositions; head noun initial; genitives, relatives before noun heads; articles, adjectives, numerals mostly after noun heads; no noun classes or genders; content q-word is usually the second word in the clause; maximum number of prefixes 1; maximum number of suffixes 4; clause constituents indicated primarily by case-marking, but word order distinguishes subject, object, indirect object some, but normally marked by postpositions; case of noun phrase indicated by postposition; split ergativity; rich system of tense and aspect; no passives or voice; causatives; comparatives; CV, CVC, CVV, CCV, CCVV, CVVC; tonal (4 tones); 36 consonant and 10 vowel phonemes. *Lg Use:* Home; mixed use: Friends, religion, work. Older adults and elderly. Some use among children, adolescents, and young adults. Helambu Sherpa more prestigious and has more original culture preserved than Kagate [syw]. Shermathang-Chhimi area and east is prestigious. Many lamas live there. Not much contact with Kagate. Also use Nepali [npi], viewed as useful. Also use Central Tibetan [bod], Hindi [hin]. *Lg Dev:* Literacy rate in L1: Below 1%. Literacy rate in L2: 15%–25%. Literacy motivation not high, except in English [eng]. Radio programs. Dictionary. Grammar. NT: 2000. *Writing:* Devanagari script. *Other:* They go to northern India as laborers or resettle in Kathmandu or in India. Buddhist (Lamaist), Christian, traditional religion. *Map:* 396:54.

Hindi [hin] (Dakhini, Hindi-Urdu, Hindustani, Khariboli). 77,600 in Nepal (2011 census), increasing. L2 users: 490,000 in Nepal (1991 census). South, Tarai region; Kathmandu valley. *Status:* 3 (Wider communication). *Lg Use:* Home, friends, religion, education; mixed use: Work. All ages. Used as L2 by Angika [anp], Avadhi [awa], Bantawa [bap], Bhojpuri [bho], Byangsi [bee], Chitwania Tharu [the], Dangaura Tharu [thl], Dhimal [dhi], Helambu Sherpa [scp], Jumli [jml], Kathariya Tharu [tkt], Maithili [mai], Marwari [rwr], Mugom [muk], Newar [new], Rajbanshi [rjs], Raji [rji], Rana Tharu [thr], Raute [rau], Southern Ghale [ghe]. *Lg Dev:* Also taught at higher levels of education. Taught in primary and secondary schools. *Other:* Hindu, Buddhist, Christian, Muslim. See main entry on page 114.

Humla [hut] (Dangali, "Humla Bhotia" *pej.*, Humli Khyampa, Phoke). 4,000 (Sharma and Gautam 1999). Seti Zone, Bajura district; Karnali Zone, Humla district, villages northwest from Simikot towards China border, villages slightly northeast of Simikot; Kathmandu. *Status:* 6a (Vigorous). *Class:* Sino-Tibetan, Tibeto-Burman, Western Tibeto-Burman, Bodish, Central Bodish, Central, gTsang. *Dialects:* Humli Khyampa, La Yakba, Limi, Nyinba, Upper Humla. Nyinba is nearly unintelligible to other Humla Tibetans but speakers report all dialects are mutually intelligible (Wilde 2001). *Type:* SOV; postposition; noun head initial; noun classes or genders; content q-word in situ; 1 prefix, up to 3 suffixes; case-marking and word order; verbal affixation marks person (conjunct vs. disjunct distinction); tense and aspect; no passives or voice; 35 consonants (Limi variety) and 7 vowel phonemes; tonal. *Lg Use:* Home, friends, religion, work. All ages. Positive attitudes. Also use Central Tibetan [bod]. *Lg Dev:* Literacy rate in L2: 10%–15% Tibetan [bod]. Some schools using English [eng] medium, some Tibetan [bod] instruction. *Writing:* Unwritten. *Other:* Buddhist. *Map:* 394:2.

Jerung [jee] (Jero, Jero Mala, Jerum, Jerunge, Jherung, Zero, Zero Mala, Zerum). 1,760 (2011 census). Janakpur Zone, Sindhuli district, Bahadur Khola west bank villages, Sunkosi river south to Mohangar village; Sagarmatha Zone, Okhaldhunga district, Maulang Khola river area, north of Sunkosi river. *Status:* 6b (Threatened). Language of recognized indigenous nationality: Rai. *Class:* Sino-Tibetan, Tibeto-Burman, Western Tibeto-Burman, Himalayan, Kiranti, Western. *Dialects:* Balkhu-Sisneri, Madhavpur, Ratnawati (Sindhuli). Reportedly most similar to Wambule [wme]. Alternate dialect analysis: Northern dialect spoken in Okhaldhunga District, Southern dialect in Sindhuli District. (2004 J. Opgenort). *Type:* SOV; postpositions; noun head final; 2 genders (non-productive); content q-word can appear anywhere in the phrase, often in initial position; 1 prefix, up to 4 suffixes (word-internal) and 4 phrasal affixes; clause constituents indicated by case-marking; verbal affixation marks person and number; ergativity; aspect; no passives or voice; nontonal; 31 consonant and 11 vowel phonemes. *Lg Use:* Home, friends, religion; mixed use: Work, education. Young adults and older. Also use Nepali [npi]. Used as L2 by Wambule [wme]. *Lg Dev:* Magazines. Dictionary. Grammar. *Other:* 'Chaurasia' is the name for the linguistic unit combining Jerung and Wambule [wme]. Traditional religion, Hindu. *Map:* 397:108.

Jhankot Sign Language [jhs]. Karnali Zone, Dolpa district, Jhankot village. *Status:* Unattested. *Class:* Deaf sign language. *Lg Use:* Reportedly used by deaf and hearing alike throughout the village. *Other:* Existence attested only by a single source (Taylor 1997). *Maps:* 394:7, 395:7.

Jirel [jul] (Jiri, Jirial, Ziral). 4,830 (2011 census), decreasing. Janakpur Zone, Dolakha district, Jiri (main area) and Sikri valleys, eastern hills; Chhyatrapa; Lumbini Zone, Nawalparasi district; Bagmati Zone, Sindhupalchok district; Narayani Zone, Parsa district. *Status:* 6b (Threatened). Language of recognized indigenous nationality: Jirel. *Class:* Sino-Tibetan, Tibeto-Burman, Western Tibeto-Burman, Bodish, Central Bodish, Central, gTsang. *Dialects:* Accent differences, but not real dialects. Some comprehension of Lhasa Tibetan [bod] and some Tibetan dialects. Lexical similarity: 67% with Sherpa [xsr], 65% with Helambu Sherpa [scp], 62% with Dolpo [dre] and Loke [loy], 60% with Kyerung (Kyirong) [kgy], 57% with Nubri [kte], Lhomi [lhm], and Walungge [ola], 54% with Lhasa Tibetan [bod]. *Type:* SOV; postpositions; genitives, demonstratives, adjectives before noun heads; numerals after noun heads; relatives before and without noun heads; content q-word in situ; polar question word final; maximum number of prefixes 1, maximum number of suffixes 4; clause constituents indicated by case-marking; affixes indicate case of noun phrases; ergative; causatives; no passives or voice; CV, CVC, V, VC; tonal. *Lg Use:* Home, friends. Young adults and older. Some use among children and adolescents. Also use Eastern Tamang [taj], Nepali [npi], Sherpa [xsr], Sunwar [suz]. *Lg Dev:* Literacy rate in L2: 25%–30% adults, 60% younger people (1991 census). People literate in Nepali [npi] can read Jirel. Dictionary. NT: 1992. *Writing:* Devanagari script. *Other:* Buddhist, Christian, traditional religion. *Map:* 397:103.

Jumla Sign Language [jus]. 8 (2005 International Nepal Fellowship). 8 monolinguals. Karnali Zone, Jumla district, Jumla town. *Status:* 6b (Threatened). *Class:* Deaf sign language. *Dialects:* None known. Lexical similarity: 45%–49% with Nepalese Sign Language [nsp]. *Writing:* Unwritten. *Other:* Deaf children in the Nepalese Sign Language school in Jumla come from 1 or 2 days walk away and do not know Jumla Sign Language. *Maps:* 394:9, 395:9.

Jumli [jml] (Central Nepali, Jumla, Jumleli, Khas Kura, Sijali, Singja, Sinjali). 850 (2011 census). Karnali Zone, Jumla, Humla, Kalikot, Mugu districts; Seti Zone, Bajura district, east Bajhang, Achham districts. Small area in Bheri Zone. *Status:* 6a (Vigorous). *Class:* Indo-European, Indo-Iranian, Indo-Aryan, Northern zone, Eastern Pahari. *Dialects:* Asi, Chaudhabis, Paanchsai, Sinja. 73%–89% intelligible with standard Nepali [npi]. Not sufficient to understand complex and abstract discourse. Lexical similarity: 73%–80% with standard Nepali [npi] (Bandhu

1971). *Type:* SOV; postpositions; noun head final; 2 genders; content q-word in situ; 1 prefix, up to 5 suffixes; clause constituents indicated by case-marking; verbal affixation marks person and number; ergativity; aspect; passives and voice; nontonal; 31 consonant and 6 vowel phonemes. *Lg Use:* Home, friends, religion, work. All ages. Mixed attitudes. Some embarrassed by their own speech when speaking to Standard Nepali [npi] speakers. Also use Hindi [hin], Nepali [npi]. *Lg Dev:* Poetry. Magazines. Newspapers. Radio programs. Dictionary. Grammar. *Writing:* Devanagari script. *Other:* Traditional religion, Buddhist (Lamaist), Christian, Hindu. *Maps:* 394:10, 395:10.

Kagate [syw] ("Kagate Bhote" *pej.*, Shuuba, Shyuuba, Syuuba, Syuwa, Yholmo, Yholmoli, Yholmu). 100 (2011 census). Very few monolinguals. Janakpur Zone, Ramechhap district, a Likhu Khola ridge. *Status:* 6a (Vigorous). *Class:* Sino-Tibetan, Tibeto-Burman, Western Tibeto-Burman, Bodish, Central Bodish, Central, gTsang. *Dialects:* Differs from Helambu Sherpa [scp] by less use of the honorific system in verbs, which makes intelligibility more of a problem for the Kagate. It could be considered a dialect of Helambu Sherpa. *Type:* SOV; postpositions; genitives, adjectives, relatives before noun heads; numerals after noun heads; noun head initial; no noun classes or genders; content q-word early in the clause; 1 prefix, up to 4 suffixes; subject, object, indirect object, case of noun phrase indicated by postpositions; clause constituents indicated by both case-marking and word order; split ergativity; rich tense and aspect system; no passives or voice; impersonal voice; causatives; comparatives; CV, CVC, CVV, CCV, CCVV, CVVC; 26 consonant and 5 vowel phonemes; tonal (4 tones). *Lg Use:* Home, friends; mixed use: Religion, work. Older adults and elderly. Some use among children, adolescents, and young adults. Positive attitudes. Some also use Nepali [npi] at home. Used as L2 by Helambu Sherpa [scp]. *Lg Dev:* Literacy rate in L2: Few. Literates in Nepali [npi] have very little trouble reading Kagate in Devanagari script. Poetry. Dictionary. Bible portions: 1977. *Writing:* Devanagari script. *Other:* Buddhist (Lamaist), Christian, Muslim, traditional religion. *Map:* 397:106.

Kaike [kzq] (Tarali Kham). 50 (2011 census), decreasing. 0 monolinguals. Ethnic population: 2,000 (2011 A. Regmi). Karnali Zone, Dolpa district, Shahartara VDC, Shahartara, Tupatara, Tarakot, and Belawa villages. *Status:* 6a (Vigorous). *Class:* Sino-Tibetan, Tibeto-Burman, Western Tibeto-Burman, Bodish, West Bodish. *Type:* SOV; postpositions; noun head final; no noun classes or genders; content q-word in situ; 1 prefix, up to 2 suffixes; clause constituents indicated by case-marking; consistently ergative; no passives or voice; semi-tonal; 29 consonant and 10 vowel phonemes; complex conjunct-disjunct system, and nominalization. *Lg Use:* Vigorous. Home, friends, religion, work; mixed use: Education. All ages. Positive attitudes. Also use Dolpo [dre] for trade and commerce when speaking to Dolpo. Also use Dolpo [dre], Nepali [npi]. *Writing:* Unwritten. *Other:* Kaike sometimes known as Tarali Kham, though quite different from Kham, a Himalayan language of western Nepal. (Bradley 1997:11). Kaike is both the ethnonym and the glossonym, as the fairy language (kai - fairy, ke - language). Buddhist, Hindu. *Maps:* 394:6, 395:6.

Kayort [kyv]. 22,000 (2002). Kosi Zone, Morang district, Dakuwa Danga, near Rajbanshi [rjs] language area. *Status:* 6a (Vigorous). *Class:* Indo-European, Indo-Iranian, Indo-Aryan, Eastern zone, Bengali-Assamese. *Dialects:* None known. Ostensibly related to Bengali [ben]. *Writing:* Unwritten. *Other:* No known published or survey-based attestation for this as a separate language variety.

Khaling [klr] (Khaling Kura). 14,500 in Nepal (2011 census), decreasing. 0 monolinguals. Ethnic population: 20,000. Sagarmatha Zone, Solukhumbu district, Kanku, Basa, Waku, Buksa, Jubing, and Phuleli villages; Khotang district, Buipa and Kharmi villages; Kosi Zone, Sankhuwasabha district, Tungkhaling village; Sunsari district, Dharan; Mechi Zone, Ilam district, Pang, Sumbek, and Mai Pokhari villages. Also in India. *Status:* 6a (Vigorous). Language of recognized indigenous nationality: Rai. *Class:* Sino-Tibetan, Tibeto-Burman, Western Tibeto-Burman, Himalayan, Kiranti, Western. *Dialects:* Northern Khaling, Southern Khaling. Reporteldy most similar to Dumi [dus] and Koi [kkt]. *Type:* SOV; postpositions; adjectives, numerals, relatives before noun heads; content q-word initial; no noun classes or genders; 1 prefix, up to 2 suffixes; clause constituents indicated by case-marking; affixes indicate case of noun phrase; verbal affixation marks person and number of subject—obligatory; ergative; causatives; comparatives; passives and voice; CV, V, CCCV; nontonal; 23 consonant and 9 vowel phonemes. *Lg Use:* Vigorous. Home, religion; mixed use: Friends, work. Young adults and older. Some use among children and adolescents. Positive attitudes. Most also use Nepali [npi]. Older women are less bilingual and may comprehend Nepali minimally. Also use Lhomi [lhm]. *Lg Dev:* Literacy rate in L2: 20% Nepali [npi]. Poetry. New media. Radio programs. Dictionary. Bible: 2011. *Writing:* Devanagari script. *Other:* Traditional religion, Christian, Hindu. *Maps:* 396:66, 397:66.

Kham, Eastern Parbate [kif] (Eastern Parbate, Nisel, Nishel Kham, Nisi, Nisi Kham). 7,500 (2003 SIL), decreasing. 27,100 all Kham languages in Nepal (2011 census). No adult monolinguals. Dhawalagiri Zone, Baglung district. Nishel dialect: Nisi, Bhalkot, and Budhathok; Bhujel dialect: Kuku, Diza, Kang, Masbang, Musuri, and Sukurdung villages. *Status:* 6b (Threatened). *Class:* Sino-Tibetan, Tibeto-Burman, Western Tibeto-Burman, Himalayan, Central Himalayan, Kham-Magar, Kham. *Dialects:* Bhujel Kham, Nishel Kham. Partially intelligible with Western Parbate [kjl] dialects. Lexical similarity: 79% between dialects, 71% with Western Parbate [kjl], 55% with Gamale [kgj], 44% with Sheshi [kip]. *Lg Use:* Young adults and older. Also use Nepali [npi]. *Lg Dev:* Literacy rate in L2: Below 5%. Dictionary. Grammar. *Writing:* Unwritten. *Other:* Traditional religion, Hindu. *Maps:* 394:22, 395:22.

Kham, Gamale [kgj] (Gamale). 13,100 (2000), increasing. 27,100 all Kham languages in Nepal (2011 census). Rapti Zone, Rolpa district, Dhawalagiri Zone, Baglung district. Gam Khola, western hills, Gam, Jhyalgung, Chalbang, Tamali, Dangadhara, Sheram, Ghusbang, Huiching, Guwakholagau, Maulabang, and Kuipadhara villages. *Status:* 6a (Vigorous). *Class:* Sino-Tibetan, Tibeto-Burman, Western Tibeto-Burman, Himalayan, Central Himalayan, Kham-Magar, Kham. *Dialects:* Ghusbanggi, Tamali. Only 30% intelligibility with Western Parbate [kjl] due to radical differences in verbal morphology. Lexical similarity: 71% with Western Parbate (most similar) [kjl], 55% with Eastern Parbate [kif] and Sheshi [kip], 45% with Bhujel [kif]. *Type:* SOV; postpositions; clause constituents indicated by case-marking; verbal affixation marks person and gender; passives and voice; tonal. *Lg Use:* Vigorous in the villages. Home, friends, work; mixed use: Religion. All ages. Positive attitudes. Younger generation uses some Nepali [npi]. *Lg Dev:* Literacy rate in L2: 5%–15%. *Writing:* Devanagari script. *Other:* Traditional religion, Christian. *Maps:* 394:21, 395:21.

Kham, Sheshi [kip] (Sheshi). 20,000 (2003), decreasing.

27,100 all Kham languages in Nepal (2011 census). Rapti Zone, Rukum district, western hills, Jangkot, Kotgaon (Tapnang), Rimsek, Korcabang, Dangdung, Hwama, Dhangsi, Bhabang, and Ghapa villages. *Status:* 6b (Threatened). *Class:* Sino-Tibetan, Tibeto-Burman, Western Tibeto-Burman, Himalayan, Central Himalayan, Kham-Magar, Kham. *Dialects:* Jangkoti, Tapnanggi. 30% intelligibility levels with Gamale Kham [kgj], and even less with Western Parbate [kjl]. Lexical similarity: 55% with Gamale Kham [kgj] (most similar), 51% with Western Parbate [kjl], 46% with Eastern Parbate [kif]. *Lg Use:* 100% also use Nepali [npi]. *Lg Dev:* Literacy rate in L1: Below 1%. Literacy rate in L2: Below 5%. Dictionary. Grammar. *Writing:* Devanagari script. *Other:* Traditional religion, Hindu. *Maps:* 394:19, 395:19.

Kham, Western Parbate [kjl] (Kham-Magar, Takale, Takale Kham, Western Parbate). 24,500 (2003 SIL), increasing. 27,100 all Kham languages in Nepal (2011 census). Rapti Zone, Rukum and Rolpa districts. Taka-Shera is center. Karnali Zone, Dolpa district. *Status:* 5 (Developing). *Class:* Sino-Tibetan, Tibeto-Burman, Western Tibeto-Burman, Himalayan, Central Himalayan, Kham-Magar, Kham. *Dialects:* Lukumel, Mahatale, Maikoti, Takale, Thabangi, Wale. Reportedly greatest similarities between Eastern [kif] and Western Parbate [kjl]. Parbate, Sheshi, and Gamale groups are all inherently unintelligible. Position of Mahatale and Miruli within the Kham linguistic group is undecided. Lexical similarity: 71% with Gamale Kham [kgj] and Eastern Parbate [kif]; 58% with Bhujel Kham, 51% with Sheshi [kip]. 25% with Magar and Gurung, slightly below 25% with the Tibetan group, 15% with the Rai and Limbu groups. *Type:* SOV; postpositions; genitives, adjectives, numerals, relatives before noun heads; noun heads final; no noun classes or genders; maximum number for nouns: 1 prefix, 8 suffixes; for verbs: 5 prefixes, 7 suffixes; clause constituents indicated by case-marking; case marked on NPs by affixes; verbal affixation marks person and number of subject and object—obligatory; split ergative; detransitivization common, some of which is passive-like; a kind of semantic inverse marked in verb morphology; passives and voice; causatives; applicatives; (C)V(V)(C) where the second V is a dipthong or long vowel; tonal. *Lg Use:* Vigorous in the villages in Rukum. Home, friends, religion, work. All ages. Speakers use Nepali [npi] only when outside their homeland. Young men are most proficient, older adult women the least. Most can discuss common topics in Nepali. *Lg Dev:* Literacy rate in L1: Some. Literacy rate in L2: Some. Poetry. Radio programs. Dictionary. Grammar. NT: 1985. *Writing:* Devanagari script. *Other:* Different from the Khams of eastern Tibet as spoken by the Khampa. Previously migrated in summer to the foot of glaciers on west end of Dhaulagiri massif, and in winter to Rolpa District southern hills. Traditional religion, Buddhist. *Maps:* 394:20, 395:20.

Kharia [khr] (Khariya). 1,580 in Nepal (2001 census). Mechi Zone, Jhapa district, India border. Small area, Kosi Zone, Morang district. *Status:* 6b (Threatened). Language of recognized indigenous nationality: Bankariya. See main entry on page 119. *Map:* 397:97.

Kisan [sck] (Sadri). 1,180 in Nepal (2011 census). Mechi Zone, Jhapa district, Bahundangi, Dhaijan, Shantinagar, and Anarmani VDCs, Damak municipality. *Status:* 6a (Vigorous). Language of recognized indigenous nationality: Kisan. See main entry on page 141 (as Sadri). *Map:* 397:100.

Koi [kkt] (Kohi, Koyee, Koyi, Koyu). 1,270 (2011 census). L2 users: Some lower caste people and Sherpa speak Koi in northern Sungdel. Sagarmatha Zone, northeast Khotang district, Sungdel VDC near Rawakhola headwaters, Sungdel and Dipsung. *Status:* 6a (Vigorous). Language of recognized indigenous nationality: Rai. *Class:* Sino-Tibetan, Tibeto-Burman, Western Tibeto-Burman, Himalayan, Kiranti, Western. *Dialects:* Behere, Sungdel. Reportedly most similar to Dumi [dus] and Khaling [klr]. *Type:* SOV; postpositions; noun head final. *Lg Use:* Home, friends, religion; mixed use: Work. All ages. Positive attitudes. Also use Nepali [npi]. *Lg Dev:* Poetry. Magazines. New media. Dictionary. *Other:* Ethnonym: Koi, live scattered in other language areas, speak only Nepali [npi]. Traditional religion, Christian, Hindu. *Map:* 396:74.

Kuke [ght] (Bhotte, Kutang, Kutang Ghale). 29 (2011 census). Gandaki Zone, north Gorkha district, Bihi VDC, Dyang, Rana, Bihi, Ghap, Chak, Kwak, and Krak villages. *Status:* 6a (Vigorous). *Class:* Sino-Tibetan, Tibeto-Burman, Western Tibeto-Burman, Bodish, West Bodish, Ghale. *Dialects:* Bihi, Chak, Rana. Varieties spoken in Chhak and Kwak villages are reportedly similar to each other and different from all other villages. Lexical similarity: 62%–76% among dialects, 39%–49% with Southern Ghale [ghe], 45%–61% with Northern Ghale [ghh], 18% with Western (Banspur) Gurung [gvr], 16%–23% with Tamang varieties, 13%–31% with Nubri [kte], 23%–27% with Tsum [ttz], 22%–27% with Kyerung (Kyirong) [kgy], 19%–24% with Tibetan [bod]. *Type:* SOV. *Lg Use:* Some Tibetan religious books translated into Kuke by priests. Home, friends; mixed use: Work. All ages. Positive attitudes. Speakers in Bihi village have minimal bilingual proficiency in Tibetan [bod]. Minimal proficiency in Bihi village in Nepali [npi]. Nepali used to communicate with Northern [ghh] and Southern Ghale [ghe] speakers. Many are bilingual in Nubri [kte]. Nubri is used since many Nubri speakers do not use Kuke. *Lg Dev:* Literacy rate in L1: Some can read Kuke in Tibetan script. Literacy rate in L2: 5%. *Writing:* Tibetan script. *Other:* Referred to as thieves' language, a mixture of nearby languages. Buddhist (Lamaist), Hindu. *Map:* 395:29.

Kulung [kle] (Kulu Ring, Kulunge). 33,200 in Nepal (2011 census). Sagarmatha Zone, Solukhumbu district, in Hungu river valley, Bung, Pelmang, Chhemsing, Chheskam, Lucham, Chachalung, Satdi, Gudel, Namlung, Sotang, and Chekma villages; Kosi Zone, Sankhuwasabha district, Mangtewa, Yaphu, and Seduwa VDCs; Bhojpur district, Phedi, Limkhim, Khartanga, and Wasepla VDCs. Also in India. *Status:* 6b (Threatened). Language of recognized indigenous nationality: Rai. *Class:* Sino-Tibetan, Tibeto-Burman, Western Tibeto-Burman, Himalayan, Kiranti, Eastern. *Dialect:* Sotto Ring. 100% intelligibility between Kulung and Sotto Ring; only a few words pronounced differently. Related to Sampang [rav] and Nachering [ncd]. *Type:* SOV; postpositions; noun head final; no noun classes or genders; content q-word initial; 1 prefix, up to 3 suffixes; clause constituents indicated by case-marking; verbal affixation marks person and number; ergativity; tense; no passives or voice; nontonal; 22 consonant and 6 vowel phonemes. *Lg Use:* Home, friends, religion. Some use among children and adolescents. Almost all can understand some Nepali [npi] at a basic level. Used as L2 by Eastern Mewahang [emg], Nepali [npi], Western Mewahang [raf]. *Lg Dev:* High motivation for literacy. Poetry. Magazines. New media. Dictionary. Grammar. Bible portions: 1976. *Writing:* Devanagari script. *Other:* Exogamous clan marriage. The high number of Kulung reflect the tendency of smaller groups to consider themselves Kulung, but are not Kulung by origin. The Kulung possibly absorb smaller groups. Traditional religion. *Map:* 396:67.

Kumhali [kra] (Kumal, Kumali, Kumbale, Kumhale,

Kumkale). 12,200 (2011 census), decreasing. 0 monolinguals. Ethnic population: 99,400. Lumbini Zone, Nawalparasi district, south of Darai [dry] language area; Arghakhanchi and Palpa districts; Gandaki Zone, Gorkha and Tanahun districts; Rapti Zone, Dang district. *Status:* 7 (Shifting). Language of recognized indigenous nationality: Kumal. *Class:* Indo-European, Indo-Iranian, Indo-Aryan, Unclassified. *Dialects:* Arghakhanchi, Gorkha, Nawalparasi, Palpa. All four dialects are mutually intelligible, with Arghakhanchi being the most different. *Type:* SOV; postpositions; noun head final; 2 noun classes or genders; content q-word in situ; 1 prefix, up to 3 suffixes; clause constituents indicated by case-marking; verbal affixation marks person and number; ergativity; both tense and aspect; passives and voice; nontonal; 29 consonant and 6 vowel phonemes. *Lg Use:* Religion; mixed use: Home, friends, work. Older adults and elderly. Some use among adolescents. Increasingly positive attitudes, though not reflected in their language choices. All are bilingual in Nepali [npi], even the elderly are speaking Nepali half the time with each other. Most children do not speak Kumal at all. (UNESCO). *Lg Dev:* Poetry. Magazines. Newspapers. Films. Videos. Dictionary. *Writing:* Devanagari script. *Other:* Hindu. *Map:* 395:43.

Kurux, Nepali [kxl] (Dhangar, Jangad, Janghard, Jhangad, Jhanger, Oraon, Orau, Uraon, Uraw). 28,600 (2001 census), decreasing. 0 monolinguals (2002 UNESCO). Ethnic population: 41,800. Dhagar (Jhagar). Kosi Zone, Sunsari district. *Status:* 6b (Threatened). *Class:* Dravidian, Northern. *Dialects:* None known. Some differences from Kurux [kru] in India and Bangladesh, but mutually intelligible. *Type:* SOV; postpositions; noun head final; 2 noun classes (human, non-human); content q-word initial; 1 prefix, up to 6 suffixes; clause constituents indicated by case-marking; verbal affixation marks person, number and genders of subject and object; ergativity; tense and aspect; passives and voice; nontonal; 29 consonant and 10 vowel phonemes. *Lg Use:* Home, religion. Mixed use: Friends, work, education. Older adults and elderly. Some use among children, adolescents, and young adults. Also use Assamese [asm], Bhojpuri [bho], Maithili [mai], Marathi [mar], Nepali [npi]. *Lg Dev:* Taught in primary schools. Poetry. Newspapers. New media. Radio programs. Videos. Dictionary. Bible portions: 1977. *Writing:* Devanagari script. *Other:* The alternate names are used for the people. Hindu. *Map:* 396:61.

Kusunda [kgg] (Kusanda). 3 (2014 M. Donohue), decreasing. 87 reported in 2001 census, living in Pyuthan, Dang and Tanahun. 0 monolinguals. Ethnic population: 160. Gandaki Zone, Tanahu district, west hills, Satto Bhatti west of Chepetar, possibly the jungle south of Ambhu; Rapti Zone, Dang district, Ambapur and Deukhuri; Rolpa district, Tunibot; Lumbini Zone, Argakhachi district. *Status:* 8b (Nearly extinct). Language of recognized indigenous nationality: Kushunda. *Class:* Language isolate. *Dialects:* Gorkha, Rolpa-Dang, Tanahun. The Kusunda speakers of Rolpa, Dang and possibly Arghakhanchi districts of Midwestern Nepal belong to the same family. For this reason, their historical dialects (created by generation and geographical separation) are mutually intelligible. *Type:* SOV; postpositions; noun head final; 1 prefix, up to 2 suffixes; clause constituents indicated by case-marking; verbal affixation marks person and number; verb pronominalization with subject agreement; 31 consonant and 6 vowel phonemes. *Lg Use:* Most Kusunda speakers live separately and are married to non-Kusunda speakers. Older adults and elderly. Positive attitudes. 100% also use Nepali [npi]. *Lg Dev:* Dictionary. Grammar. *Writing:* Unwritten. *Other:* Traditional religion.

Kyirong [kgy] (Gyirong, Kyerung, Kyirung). 500 in Nepal (2013 M. Hedlin). Bagmati Zone, Rasuwa district, Setang, Bongswadi, Lingling, Bridhim, Khangjim, Thangmpuchet, Khangim, and Shaphrubesi villages; Kathmandu valley, Swoyambhu, Thulo Barang, Thamel, and Boudha. *Status:* 6a (Vigorous). *Other:* Ethnonym: Kyirong-nga. Buddhist (Lamaist), traditional religion. See main entry on page 75 (as Kyerung). *Map:* 396:53.

Lapcha [lep] ("Lapche" *pej.*, Lepcha, Nünpa, Rong, Rongke, Rongpa). 7,500 in Nepal (2011 census), decreasing. 0 monolinguals. Ethnic population: 3,660. Mechi Zone, Ilam district. *Status:* 7 (Shifting). Language of recognized indigenous nationality: Lepcha. *Dialects:* Ilammu, Rengjongmu, Tamsangmu. *Lg Use:* Many youth speak Nepali [npi] as L1 and do not speak Lepcha. Older adults and elderly. *Other:* Linguistic position within Tibeto-Burman still under discussion. Buddhist, Christian. See main entry on page 125 (as Lepcha). *Map:* 396:85.

Lhomi [lhm] ("Bho Te bhasha" *pej.*, "Kar Bhote" *pej.*, "Kath Bhote" *pej.*, Lhoket). 810 in Nepal (2011 census), increasing. Population total all countries: 3,130. Ethnic population: 15,000. Kosi Zone, north Sankhuwasabha district to the border, Chepuwa VDC, Chepuwa, Chyamtang, Gumba, Chhumusur, and Rukuma villages; Hatiya VDC, Hatiya, Hungung, Pharang, Syaksila, Simbung, Namase, and Shiprung villages; southernmost village is Seksum in Arun valley; some in Kathmandu. Also in China, India. *Status:* 5 (Developing). Language of recognized indigenous nationality: Lhomi (Shingsawa). *Class:* Sino-Tibetan, Tibeto-Burman, Western Tibeto-Burman, Bodish, Central Bodish, Central, gTsang. *Dialects:* None known. Lexical similarity: 69% with Dolpo [dre], 68% with Loke [loy], 66% with Walungge [ola], 65% with Lhasa Tibetan [bod] and Kyerung (Kyirong) [kgy], 64% with Nubri [kte], 60% with Helambu Sherpa [scp], 58% with Sherpa [xsr], 57% with Jirel [jul]. *Type:* SOV; postpositions; noun head initial; masculine and feminine (limited class); content q-word precedes the main verb; 1 prefix, up to 3 suffixes; clause constituents indicated by case-marking; split ergativity; aspect; no passives or voice; tonal (tense-lax); 23 consonant and 8 vowel phonemes; evidentiality is a salient feature of Lhomi syntax. *Lg Use:* Vigorous. Home, friends, religion; mixed use: Work. All ages. Positive attitudes. 90% of men have functional trade level in Nepali [npi]. Women increasingly use Nepali. Educated Lhomis are fluent Nepali speakers. Also use Central Tibetan [bod]. Used as L2 by Eastern Gurung [ggn], Eastern Tamang [taj], Khaling [klr], Naaba [nao], Thudam [thw], Western Gurung [gvr]. *Lg Dev:* Literacy rate in L1: 25%. Literacy rate in L2: 30%. Bilingual literacy campaign should impact adult (and women's) literacy rate in Lhomi and Nepali [npi]. Poetry. Newspapers. New media. Videos. NT: 1995. *Writing:* Devanagari script. *Other:* Traditional religion, Buddhist (Lamaist), Christian. *Map:* 396:70.

Limbu [lif]. 344,000 in Nepal (2011 census), increasing. Population total all countries: 381,300. Relatively few monolinguals. Eastern hills, east of Arun river; Kosi Zone, Dhankuta, Sankhuwasabha, Terhathum, Dhankuta, and Morang districts; Mechi Zone, Taplejung, Panchthar, Ilam, and Jhapa districts. Also in Bhutan, India. *Status:* 5 (Developing). Language of recognized indigenous nationality: Limbu. *Class:* Sino-Tibetan, Tibeto-Burman, Western Tibeto-Burman, Himalayan, Kiranti, Eastern. *Dialects:* Chaubise (Charkhole), Chhatthare (Chatthare, Chhathar), Panthare, Phedappe, Tamorkhole (Taplejunge), Yanggrokke (Yanggruppe). Yanggrokke, Chaubise and Charkhole are minor variants of the Panthare dialect; Phedappe and Tamorkhole are similar. Chattare is less well understood by other dialect speakers. The dialect spoken in Sikkim, India, is same as Panthare. Intelligibility among all varieties 84% and higher. *Type:* SOV; postpositions; genitives, articles, adjectives, numerals before noun heads; noun head final; content question word in situ; bipolar question word final; maximum of 3 prefixes, 6 suffixes; affixes indicate case of noun phrases; verb affixes mark subjects, objects, indirect objects—obligatory; verbal affixation marks person and number; split ergativity; reflexes conjugated intransitively can be used as a kind of passive; passives and voice; antipassives; causatives; comparatives; 16 consonant and 13 vowel phonemes; V, CV, CVC, CCV, CCVC; nontonal. *Lg Use:* Vigorous. A main group in eastern Nepal. Home, religion; mixed use: Friends, work, education. Older adults and elderly. Some use among children, adolescents, and young adults. Positive attitudes. Panthare dialect is dominant in size, prestige, and language development. People prefer their own dialect, but are not negative toward others. Many adult speakers completed 5 years of school, and have good proficiency in Nepali [npi]. Nepali used often, especially among youth. Limbu is not replaced in any domain, though children now speak more Nepali than Limbu (UNESCO 2002). Some women also use Yakkha [ybh] due to intermarriage. *Lg Dev:* Motivation for development is high among all. Literacy programs in progress to teach Sirijonga script (Salminen 2007). Poetry. Magazines. Newspapers. New media. Radio programs. Films. TV. Videos. Dictionary. Grammar. NT: 2009. *Writing:* Devanagari script, primary usage. Limbu (Kiranti, Sirijonga) script, dating to early 18th century. *Other:* Priestly high language, known by some older people and priests, is called Mundumban. Traditional religion. *Maps:* 396:83, 397:83.

Lingkhim [lii] (Saam). Mechi Zone, Ilam district, Phikkal VDC. *Status:* Unattested. *Class:* Sino-Tibetan, Tibeto-Burman, Western Tibeto-Burman, Himalayan, Kiranti, Eastern. *Other:* Little information exists to support Lingkhim's identification as a distinct language. It may be a part of Saam [raq] (Hansson 1988:20–21; Hansson 1991:61, 85). The 2001 census reports 97 speakers of Lingkhim. Van Driem (2001:704) points out that Limkhim is a village in northern Bhojpur district, suggesting that this is an alternate name for Saam.

Lohorung [lbr] (Lohorong, Lohrung, Lohrung Khanawa, Lorung, Northern Lorung). 3,720 (2011 census). Kosi Zone, central Sankhuwasabha district, between middle Arun valley and the Sabhakhola, Pangma, Angala, Higuwa, Khorande, Bardeu, Gairiaula, Malta, Sitalpati, and Dhupu. *Status:* 6b (Threatened). Language of recognized indigenous nationality: Rai. *Class:* Sino-Tibetan, Tibeto-Burman, Western Tibeto-Burman, Himalayan, Kiranti, Eastern. *Dialect:* Biksit (Bikshi). 44% intelligibility of Yamphu [ybi]. A Kirat Rai group. Lexical similarity: 88%–99% between dialects, 64%–67% with Yamphu [ybi], 65%–68% with Southern Yamphu [lrr]. *Type:* SOV; postpositions; verbal affixation marks person and number; tense; nontonal. *Lg Use:* Lohorung is an endangered language, picking up Nepali [npi] influences (2002 T. P. Neupane). Home, religion; mixed use: Friends, work. All ages. Positive attitudes. Nearly all speak at least some Nepali [npi]. Used as L2 by Eastern Mewahang [emg], Western Mewahang [raf]. *Lg Dev:* Radio programs. Dictionary. *Writing:* Devanagari script. *Other:* Hansson claims that the Biksit dialect is spoken in Dhupu VDC (Hansson 1991). Traditional religion, Christian, Hindu. *Map:* 396:81.

Loke [loy] (Glo Skad, Lhopa, Lo Montang, Loba, Lopa, Lowa, Loyu, Mustangi). 3,030 (2011 census). Dhawalagiri Zone, Mustang district, north central upper Kali Gandaki river area; high valleys north of middle-range Thakali, Gurung and Magar areas. Bahragaun dialect: Kagbeni, Muktinath, and Dzong VDCs; Upper Mustang dialect: Ghimi, Tsarang, Lo Monthang, Surkhang, Chhosher, Chunnup VDCs, and Samar village in Chuksang VDC; Karnali Zone, Dolpa district. *Status:* 6a (Vigorous). Language of recognized indigenous nationality: Bahragaunle, Lhopa. *Class:* Sino-Tibetan, Tibeto-Burman, Western Tibeto-Burman, Bodish, Central Bodish, Central, gTsang. *Dialects:* Baragaunle (Baragaon, Baragaun, Bhoti Gurung), Upper Mustang (Loke). High intelligibility between dialects reported. Lexical similarity: 79%–88% between dialects, 59%–71% with Dolpo [dre], 54%–57% with Lhasa Tibetan [bod], 58%–67% with Mugom [muk]. *Type:* SOV; postpositions; noun head initial; 5 noun classes and 3 genders; content q-word in situ; at least 2 suffixes; no passives or voice; tonal; 44 consonant and 8 vowel phonemes. *Lg Use:* Some youth totally educated outside language area and may not be able to speak Loke. Tibetan [bod] is used in religious domain. Home, friends. All ages. Positive attitudes. Also use Central Tibetan [bod], Nepali [npi]. Used as L2 by Dolpo [dre], Seke [skj]. *Lg Dev:* Literacy rate in L2: 41% for whole district, includes Thakalis, Nepalis. (males 57%, females 28%). Non-formal education. Grammar. *Writing:* Devanagari script. Tibetan script. *Other:* Distinct from Lhoba in China and India, a Mirish language. Lo inhabitants are called Lopa or Lowa. Their capital is Manthang, called Mustang by outsiders. Manthang has 200 houses, many monasteries. Buddhist, traditional religion. *Map:* 395:25.

Lumba-Yakkha [luu] (Yakkhaba Cea). 1,200 (2000). Kosi Zone, North Dhankuta district, Arkhoule Jitpur and Marek Kathar VDCs. *Status:* 6b (Threatened). *Class:* Sino-Tibetan, Tibeto-Burman, Western Tibeto-Burman, Himalayan, Kiranti, Eastern. *Type:* SOV; postpositions; noun head final; verbal affixation marks person and number; both tense and aspect, nontonal. *Lg Use:* Language retained among some youth (Hansson 1991). Home. *Writing:* Unwritten. *Other:* Traditional religion, Christian, Hindu. *Map:* 397:87.

Magar, Eastern [mgp] (Magari, Manggar). 462,000 in Nepal (2001 census), decreasing. 789,000 all Magar in Nepal (2011 census). The identification of Magars is complicated by the fact that a number of other ethnic groups (Chantyal, Kham, Kaike, Kusunda, Raute, Raji) have claimed to be Magars to outsiders. Population total all countries: 533,700. Isolated enclaves of monolinguals are found in Nawalparasi and southern Tanahu districts. Ethnic population: 1,620,000 (2001 census). Includes Eastern and Western Magar. Gandaki Zone, Tanahu and south Gorkha districts; Lumbini Zone, Palpa and Nawalparasi districts, east of Bagmati river, central mountains; Janakpur Zone, Sindhuli district. Kosi Zone scattered, Bhojpur, Terhathum, Dhankuta districts; Sagarmatha Zone, Okhaldhunga district; Mechi Zone, Taplejung, Ilam districts. Also in Bhutan, India. *Status:* 6b (Threatened). Language of recognized indigenous nationality: Magar. *Class:* Sino-Tibetan, Tibeto-Burman, Western Tibeto-Burman, Himalayan, Central Himalayan, Kham-Magar, Magar. *Dialects:* Gorkha, Nawalparasi, Tanahu. Also long-extant migrant communities scattered throughout the Eastern Development Region speak a different variety from those west of Kathmandu. Reports of intelligibility between these varieties vary. *Lg Use:* Also use Nepali [npi]. *Lg Dev:* Literacy rate in L2: 25%–50%. Poetry. Dictionary. NT: 1991. *Writing:* Akkha script. Devanagari script. *Other:* Traditional religion, Buddhist, Christian, Hindu. *Maps:* 395:45, 396:45, 397:45.

Magar, Western [mrd] (Magar, Magari, Mangar, Mangari).

308,000 (2001 census), decreasing. 789,000 all Magar in Nepal (2011 census). Census statistics likely include non-ethnic Magars and many that do not speak Magar. Ethnic population: 1,620,000 (2001 census). Includes Eastern and Western Magar. Lumbini Zone, Palpa district; Gandaki Zone, Syangja and Tanahu districts; isolated in Bheri Zone, Surkhet, Jajarkot, and Dailekh districts. Small area in Dhawalagiri Zone, Parbat district. *Status:* 6b (Threatened). Language of recognized indigenous nationality: Magar. *Class:* Sino-Tibetan, Tibeto-Burman, Western Tibeto-Burman, Himalayan, Central Himalayan, Kham-Magar, Magar. *Dialects:* Palpa, Syangja. Some differences between dialects, yet reportedly high intellligibility. *Type:* SOV; postpositions, but mostly case clitics; noun head final; alienable and inalienable noun classes; content q-word in situ; up to 3 prefixes, up to 7 suffixes; clause constituents indicated by case-marking; verbal affixation marks person and number; ergativity; tense and aspect; passives; nontonal; 33 to 37 consonant and 6 vowel phonemes. *Lg Use:* Fewer people becoming fluent in Nepali [npi] than before, i.e. the older generation speaks better Nepali. Magar language continues to thrive. Mixed use: Home, friends, work. Elderly. Some use among children, adolescents, young and older adults. Mixed attitudes. Rhetoric is positive but language conservation is generally not implemented. Almost all also use at least some Nepali [npi]. *Lg Dev:* Poetry. Magazines. Newspapers. New media. Radio programs. Films. Videos. Dictionary. Grammar. *Writing:* Devanagari script. *Other:* Traditional religion, Buddhist, Christian, Hindu. *Map:* 395:34.

Maithili [mai] (Apabhramsa, Bihari, Dehati, Maitili, Maitli, Methli, Tirahutia, Tirhuti, Tirhutia). 3,890,000 in Nepal (2011 census), increasing. 793,000 Bajjika, 3,090,000 Maithili (2011 census). Narayani Zone, Rautahat district; Janakpur Zone, Sarlahi, Mahottari, and Dhanusa districts; Sagarmatha Zone, Siraha and Saptari districts; Kosi Zone, Sunsari and Morang districts. *Status:* 5 (Developing). *Dialects:* Bajjika, Bantar, Barei, Barmeli, Dehati, Kawar, Kyabrat, Makrana, Musar, Tati, Thenthi. *Lg Use:* Spoken by a wide variety of castes. Long literary tradition. A Maithili Academy in Patna; Bihar Maithili taught at L. N. Mithila University in Darbhanga, Patna University, and Janakpur campus of Tribhuvan University. Home, friends. All ages. Also use Bengali [ben], Bhojpuri [bho], English [eng], Hindi [hin], Nepali [npi]. Used as L2 by Angika [anp], Bhojpuri [bho], Kochila Tharu [thq], Nepali Kurux [kxl], Rajbanshi [rjs], Santhali [sat], Southwestern Tamang [tsf]. *Lg Dev:* Literacy rate in L1: 20%. Literacy rate in L2: 25%–50%. Educated read Hindi [hin], Nepali [npi], or English [eng]. If they can read Hindi or Nepali, they can read Maithili.Mother-tongue multilingual education and adult literacy programs have been carried out in Maithili communities throughout the Rajbanshi area. *Other:* Written variety considered standard. Hindi [hin] and its speakers considered close, culturally similar; Nepali [npi] accepted. Hindu, Christian. See main entry on page 126. *Maps:* 396:59, 397:59.

Majhi [mjz] (Manjhi). 24,400 in Nepal (2011 census), decreasing. Population total all countries: 44,800. Ethnic population: 72,600. Janakpur Zone, Ramechhap district, Chisapani, Bhatauli, Pagarbas, Bhaluwajor, and Rakathum VDCs. Also in India. *Status:* 6b (Threatened). Language of recognized indigenous nationality: Majhi. *Class:* Indo-European, Indo-Iranian, Indo-Aryan, Eastern zone, Bihari. *Dialects:* Manthali, Rajgaun, Sitkha. *Type:* SOV; postpositions; noun head final; no noun classes or genders; content q-word in situ; 1 prefix, up to 2 suffixes; clause constituents indicated by case-marking; verbal affixation marks person and number; split ergativity based on nominal hierarchy (the first and second person pronouns do not code ergativity but the third person pronouns do); passives and voice; nontonal; 29 consonant and 6 vowel phonemes. *Lg Use:* Being replaced by Nepali [npi] (UNESCO). Religion. 100% also use Nepali [npi]. *Lg Dev:* Radio programs. *Writing:* Devanagari script, used in India. *Other:* Distinct from Majhi in Panjabi group or Bote [bmj]. Majhi, Bote, and Kushar all are used by hill peoples. Hindu, Christian. *Map:* 396:56.

Manangba [nmm] (Manang, Manang Ke, "Manangbhot" *pej.*, Manange, Manangi, Nyeshang, Nyeshangte, Nyishang). 390 (2011 census), decreasing. Gandaki Zone, Manang district, Upper Manang, Pisang, Dhukur Pokhari, Humde, Ghyaru, Ngawal, Braka, Manang, Tengki, and Khangsar villages; Kathmandu. *Status:* 6b (Threatened). *Class:* Sino-Tibetan, Tibeto-Burman, Western Tibeto-Burman, Bodish, West Bodish, Gurung-Tamang, Gurungic. *Dialects:* Manang, Pisang. Very high intelligibility of Manang dialect by Pisang residents. Very different from Eastern Gurung [ggn]. Lexical similarity: 94% or greater with all varieties of Manangba. *Type:* SOV; postpositions; noun head both initial and final; no noun classes or genders; content q-word initial; 1 prefix, up to 2 suffixes; clause constituents indicated by case-marking; verbal affixation marks person (not strictly person, but aligns with evidentiality); ergativity; aspect; no passives or voice; tonal; 30 consonant and 6 (plus nasalized) vowel phonemes. *Lg Use:* Fairly strong vitality. Some community involvement in language and culture preservation activities both in home area and in Kathmandu. Mixed use: Home, friends, work. Older adults and elderly. Some use among children, adolescents, and young adults. Positive attitudes. Tibetan [bod] for some religious domains. English [eng] used in local government schools. Nepali [npi] used for business, and in local government schools. *Lg Dev:* Poetry. New media. TV. Dictionary. Grammar. *Writing:* Unwritten. *Other:* Language has Tibetan influence. Most speakers have the surname Gurung or Ghale, but they do not claim to be a part of these distinct ethnolinguistic groups. Buddhist. *Map:* 395:32.

Marwari [rwr] (Marwadi). 22,600 in Nepal (2001 census). Ethnic population: 44,000. L2 users: 930 in Nepal (1991 census). Mechi Zone, Jhapa district; Kosi Zone, Morang and Sunsari districts; Narayani Zone, Parsa district; Kathmandu and other urban areas. *Status:* 5 (Developing). *Lg Use:* Home, friends; mixed use: Religion, work. All ages. Positive attitudes. Also use Hindi [hin], Nepali [npi]. *Lg Dev:* Literacy rate in L2: 88%. *Other:* Hindu. See main entry on page 129.

Meche [brx] (Bara, Bodi, Bodo, Boro, Boroni, Mache, Mech, Mechi, Meci). 4,380 in Nepal (2011 census). 0 monolinguals. Ethnic population: 3,760 (2001 census). Mechi Zone, Jhapa district. *Status:* 6b (Threatened). Language of recognized indigenous nationality: Meche (Bodo). *Lg Use:* Also use Bengali [ben], Nepali [npi]. *Other:* Traditional religion. See main entry on page 106 (as Bodo). *Map:* 397:101.

Mewahang, Eastern [emg] (Eastern Meohang, Mewahang, Newahang, Newahang Jimi, Newang, Newange Rai). 4,650 all Mewahang (2011 census). Almost no monolinguals. Ethnic population: 3,000. Kosi Zone, Sankhuwasabha district, Mangtewa, Yaphu, and Choyang VDCs; upper Arun valley east of the river. Sunsari dialect: Sunsari district, Bhaludhunga and Bishnupaduka VDC; Dibum (Dibung) dialect: Mangtewa VDC; Mulgaon-Wangtang dialect: Yaphu VDC. *Status:* 6b (Threatened). Language of recognized indigenous nationality: Rai. *Class:* Sino-Tibetan, Tibeto-Burman, Western Tibeto-Burman, Himalayan, Kiranti, Eastern. *Dialects:* Dibum, Mulgaon-Wangtang,

Sunsari. Structurally different from Western Mewahang [raf]. *Type:* SOV; postpositions; noun head final; verbal affixation marks person and number; tense and aspect. *Lg Use:* Shifting to Nepali [npi]. Home, religion; mixed use: Friends, work. Older adults and elderly. Some use among children, adolescents, and young adults. Also use Kulung [kle], Lohorung [lbr], Nepali [npi]. *Lg Dev:* Poetry. Dictionary. *Writing:* Devanagari script. *Other:* The language is regarded as a dialect of Western Mewahang [raf]. Traditional religion, Hindu. *Map:* 396:68.

Mewahang, Western [raf] (Mewahang, Newahang, Newahang Jimi, Newang, Newange Rai, Western Meohang). 4,650 all Mewahang (2011 census). Few monolinguals. Ethnic population: 3,000. Kosi Zone, Sankhuwasabha district, upper Arun valley west of Arun river, Bala, Yamdang, Tamku, and Sisuwa. Bala dialect: Bala village, Sankhuwasabha VDC; Bumdemba dialect: Sishuwakhola VDC. *Status:* 6b (Threatened). Language of recognized indigenous nationality: Rai. *Class:* Sino-Tibetan, Tibeto-Burman, Western Tibeto-Burman, Himalayan, Kiranti, Eastern. *Dialects:* Bala (Balali), Bumdemba. Structurally different from Eastern Mewahang [emg]. *Type:* SOV; postpositions; 24 consonant and 14 vowel phonemes. *Lg Use:* The language is nearly extinct in the village of Tamku, the largest settlement in the area, where many ex-Gurkha pensioners live. Home; mixed use: Friends, religion, work. Young adults and older. Some use among children and adolescents. Positive attitudes. Also use Kulung [kle], Lohorung [lbr], Nepali [npi]. *Lg Dev:* Poetry. Dictionary. *Writing:* Devanagari script. *Other:* Traditional religion, Hindu. *Map:* 396:76.

Mugali [lmh] (Lambicchong, Lambichhong, Lambichong, Lambitshong, Phangduwali Mugali). 1,500 (2010 I. Rai), decreasing. Very few monolinguals. Kosi Zone, Dhankuta district, Arun river east bank, between Mugakhola and Sinuwakhola; Muga, Pakhribas and Phalate VDCs. *Status:* 7 (Shifting). Language of recognized indigenous nationality: Rai. *Class:* Sino-Tibetan, Tibeto-Burman, Western Tibeto-Burman, Himalayan, Kiranti, Eastern. *Dialect:* Phangdhuwali. Reportedly similar to Chhulung [cur], Belhariya [byw], and Chhintang [ctn]. *Type:* SOV; postpositions; no gender; verbal affixation marks person and number; split ergativity; tense; no passives or voice; nontonal; 23 consonant and 5 vowel phonemes. *Lg Use:* Older adults and elderly. *Writing:* Unwritten. *Other:* Traditional religion. *Map:* 397:89.

Mugom [muk] (Mugali, Mugu, Mugum). 6,500 in Nepal (2006 SIL). Population total all countries: 7,000. 1,630 monolinguals (2002 UNESCO). Ethnic population: 6,500. Karnali Zone, Mugu district, Mugu, Mangri, Pulu, Kimri, and Dolphu VDCs; Jumla district, Jumla; Kathmandu. Also in India. *Status:* 6a (Vigorous). Language of recognized indigenous nationality: Mugali. *Class:* Sino-Tibetan, Tibeto-Burman, Western Tibeto-Burman, Bodish, Central Bodish, Central, gTsang. *Dialects:* Karmarong (Karani, Kar-ket, Karmai-kat), Mugom (Moe-ket, Mugali, Mugomba, Mumbai-kat). Intelligibility 89%–93% between dialect speakers (possibly higher). Definitely sufficient to understand complex and abstract discourse. Reportedly similar to Humla [hut], Dolpo [dre], and Loke [loy]. Lexical similarity: more than 85% between dialects, 75% with Tibetan [bod]. *Type:* SOV; postpositions; content q-word in situ; clause constituents indicated by case-marking; ergativity; no passives or voice; tonal. *Lg Use:* Vigorous. Home, friends; mixed use: Religion, work, education. All ages. Positive attitudes. Some children are being introduced to English [eng]. Some men also use Hindi [hin]. Also use Central Tibetan [bod], Nepali [npi]. *Lg Dev:* Literacy rate in L2: Up to 22% in Nepali [npi]; men 30%, women 5%. Mugu District ranks very low in literacy among Nepal districts, especially among children and women. Strong affinity felt towards Tibetan [bod] and its writing system because of high lexical similarity. Poetry. Newspapers. *Writing:* Tibetan script. *Other:* Karanis want recognition as a separate ethnic group. Mugalis may not accept materials written in Karani, and vice versa. Mugom value Nepali and English as a way to higher education. Mugalis see themselves a bit higher than Karanis, and are more influential as they travel and trade more. Buddhist (Lamaist). *Map:* 394:3.

Mundari [unr] (Horo, Mandari, Mondari, Munari, Munda, Santhali, Satar). 7,780 in Nepal (2006). Mechi Zone, southern Jhapa district; Koshi Zone, Morang district. *Status:* 5 (Developing). Language of recognized indigenous nationality: Jhangad. Could be a separate language. *Dialects:* Hasada, Kera, Latar, Naguri, Santhai, Satar. *Lg Use:* Home; mixed use: Friends, religion, work, education. All ages. Positive attitudes. *Lg Dev:* Used as subject of instruction in basic education. *Other:* Hindu, Christian. See main entry on page 131. *Map:* 397:99.

Musasa [smm] (Musahar, Rishaidep). 50,000 (2003). 20,000 Musasa and 30,000 Musasa Bantar. Ethnic population: 172,000. Janakpur Zone, Sindhuli, Dolakha, Mahotari, and Dhanusa districts; Kosi Zone, Morang and Sunsari districts; Sagarmatha Zone, Siraha and Saptari districts. *Status:* 6b (Threatened). *Class:* Indo-European, Indo-Iranian, Indo-Aryan, Eastern zone, Bihari. *Dialect:* Bantar. Reportedly similar to Kochila (Saptari) Tharu [thq]. *Lg Use:* Speakers have high proficiency in Nepali [npi]. *Writing:* Unwritten. *Other:* Dalit caste. It has been suggested but not documented that they may speak a sociolect of the larger language groups they live among: Maithili [mai], Bhojpuri [bho], Avadhi [awa], and Kochila Tharu [thq]. Not listed in the 2001 Nepal census. Hindu.

Naaba [nao] (Naapa, Naapaa, Naba, Nawa Sherpa). 770 (2006). Kosi Zone, Sankhuwasabha district, Kimathanka VDC, Kimathanka village; Hatiya VDC, Dangok and Pharang villages; Piibu, Chumusur, and Ridak villages; Tsanga village, across the border in China. *Status:* 6a (Vigorous). *Class:* Sino-Tibetan, Tibeto-Burman, Western Tibeto-Burman, Bodish, Central Bodish, Unclassified. *Type:* SOV; postpositions; clause constituents indicated by case-marking; ergativity; no passives or voice; tonal. *Lg Use:* All ages. Inhabitants of Pharang and Dangok also use Lhomi [lhm]. *Writing:* Unwritten. *Other:* The Lhomi [lhm] consider the Naaba people a distinct group. The Naaba have learned Lhomi as a language of wider communication, but are more culturally and linguistically similar to Sherpa [xsr] and Thudam [thw] than to Lhomi. Buddhist. *Map:* 396:71.

Nachering [ncd] (Bangdale, Bangdel Tûm, Bangdile, Mathsereng, Nacchhering, Nacering Ra, Nachering Tûm, Nachiring, Nasring). 10,000 (2011 census), decreasing. Sagarmatha Zone, upper northeast Khotang district near Rawakhola calley, Lidim Khola river slopes area, headwaters and tributaries to Aiselukharke south, Rakha, Bangdel, Dipsun, Para, Badel, Patel, Bakacho, and Aiselukharka VDCs; Solukhumbu district, Waddu and Sotang VDCs. *Status:* 7 (Shifting). Language of recognized indigenous nationality: Rai. *Class:* Sino-Tibetan, Tibeto-Burman, Western Tibeto-Burman, Himalayan, Kiranti, Eastern. *Dialects:* Bangdele (Achero, Hachero, Hangkula), Parali, Rakhali, Sotange. High comprehension of Kulung among northern Nachering and Sampang among southern Nachering. *Type:* SOV. *Lg Use:* Degree of Nepalization is very high. Language retention among the younger generation appears to be limited to Bakachol, Rakha, and Bangdel VDCs. (Hansson 1991:73; 2011 J. Rai).

Religion; mixed use: Home. Older adults and elderly. Some use among children, adolescents, and young adults. Positive attitudes. Almost all also use Nepali [npi]. *Lg Dev:* Poetry. *Writing:* Unwritten. *Other:* Different from Sampang, although sometimes called Sangpang or Sampang. Traditional religion, Christian, Hindu. *Map:* 396:73.

Nar Phu [npa] (Nar-Phu). 600 (2011 K. Hildebrandt). 200 Phu speakers, 400 Nar speakers. Gandaki Zone, Manang district, Nar valley north of Manang valley, Nar (Nargaon, Chhuprung) and Phu (Phugaon, Nartwe) villages. *Status:* 6a (Vigorous). *Class:* Sino-Tibetan, Tibeto-Burman, Western Tibeto-Burman, Bodish, West Bodish, Gurung-Tamang, Gurungic. *Dialects:* Nar (Lower Nar, Nar-Mä), Phu (Nar-Tö, Upper Nar). In a dialect continuum with Manangba [nmm] and possibly intelligible with it. *Type:* SOV; postpositions; noun head initial; no noun classes or gender; content q-word in situ; 1 prefix, up to 2 suffixes; clause constituents primarily indicated by case-marking; tense and aspect; no passives or voice; tonal; 25 consonants, 8 simple vowels and 5 diphthongs. *Lg Use:* If work is locally oriented, then Nar-Phu used; Tibetan [bod] is the liturgical language, but one can hear Nar-Phu in certain contexts during religious festivals. All ages. Many men are fluent in Tibetan [bod]. *Lg Dev:* Many men are literate in Classical Tibetan. Poetry. Dictionary. *Writing:* Unwritten. *Other:* See themselves as separate from Manangba and Gurung. Used as a secret language to confound Manangis and Gurungs who might otherwise understand their conversation (2002 M. Noonan). Buddhist. *Map:* 395:27.

Nepalese Sign Language [nsp] (Nepali Sign Language). 5,740 (2001 census). Most are monolingual. Central and east. *Status:* 5 (Developing). *Class:* Deaf sign language. *Dialects:* Kathmandu, Pokhara. Developed from local and introduced signs. Related to Indian [ins] and Pakistan [pks] sign languages. *Lg Use:* Used by United States Peace Corps. All domains. All ages. Some comprehension of Nepali [npi] by those who have become literate. *Lg Dev:* Taught in primary and secondary schools. Magazines. Films. TV. Videos. Dictionary. *Other:* The Nepal Federation of the Deaf and Hard of Hearing starts schools for the deaf in the larger towns. A few other smaller organizations also work with the deaf and have Nepalese Sign Language [nsp] classes for the hearing. Hindu, Buddhist, Christian, Muslim.

Nepali [npi] (Eastern Pahadi, Gorkhali, Gurkhali, Khaskura, Nepalese, Parbate). 12,300,000 in Nepal (2011 census), increasing. 143,000 Achhami, 273,000 Baitadeli, 67,600 Bajhangi, 10,700 Bajureli, 490 Dadeldhuri, 3,100 Dailekhi, 5,930 Darchuleli, and 11,800,000 Nepali (2011 census). Population total all countries: 15,360,100. East and adjacent south central regions. Also in Bhutan, Brunei, India, United States. *Status:* 1 (National). Statutory national language (1990, Interim Constitution, 2063, Article 5(2)). *Class:* Indo-European, Indo-Iranian, Indo-Aryan, Northern zone, Eastern Pahari. A member of macrolanguage Nepali [nep]. *Dialects:* Acchami, Baitadeli (Baitadi), Bajhangi, Bajurali (Bajura, Bajureli), Bheri, Dadeldhuri, Dailekhi, Darchulali (Darchuleli, Darjula), Darchuli (Darjula), Gandakeli, Humli, Purbeli, Soradi. Reportedly similar to Dotyali [dty]. Dialects listed may be quite distinct from standard Nepali. Intelligibility is also low among Baitadeli, Bajhangi, Bajurali (Bajura), Humli, and Acchami. *Type:* SOV; postpositions; noun head final; 11 noun classes or genders; content q-word in situ; 1 prefix, up to 5 suffixes; clause constituents indicated by case-marking; verbal affixation marks person, number and gender of subject; split ergativity; both tense and aspect; passives and voice; nontonal; 29 consonant and 11 vowel phonemes. *Lg Use:* All domains. All ages. Positive attitudes. A few Nepali-speaking families from the tailor caste (Damai) and blacksmith caste (Kami) have an active command of Kulung [kle] in Chheskam. Many lower caste Nepali speakers in Mukli VDC speak Thulung [tdh]. Also use Bahing [bhj]. *Lg Dev:* Taught at all levels of education. Fully developed. Bible: 1914–2004. *Writing:* Braille script. Devanagari script, primary usage. *Other:* Hindu, Buddhist. *Maps:* 394:8, 395:8, 396:8, 397:8.

Nepali [nep]. A macrolanguage (see page 9). *Other:* Includes: Dotyali [dty], Nepali [npi].

Newar [new] (Nepal Bhasa, Newaah Bhaaye, Newal Bhaye, "Newari" *pej.*). 847,000 in Nepal (2011 census), decreasing. Population total all countries: 861,000. Many women are monolingual. Ethnic population: 1,260,000. Includes 1,245,000 Newar and 11,500 Pahari. Bagmati Zone, Kathmandu valley; many other urban areas. Fewer far west. Also in India. *Status:* 4 (Educational). Language of recognized indigenous nationality: Newar. *Class:* Sino-Tibetan, Tibeto-Burman, Western Tibeto-Burman, Himalayan, Central Himalayan, Newar. *Dialects:* Badikhel Pahari, Baglung, Balami, Bhaktapur, Citlang, Dolkhali (Dolakha), Gopali, Kathmandu-Patan-Kirtipur, Pyang Gaon, Sindhupalchok Pahri (Pahari, Pahri), Totali. The Dolakhae dialect of Dolakha has complex person-number verb agreement with residue reflex in the Pahari dialect of Badikhel. These two dialects are not fully intelligible to the speakers of Kathmandu Valley where the language has a simple conjunct-disjunct agreement. Kirtipur and Lalitpur are reportedly similar to Kathmandu. Bhaktapur people mostly understand Kathmandu despite some lexical differences. The Eastern Newar dialects, including at least Dolakha and Tauthali, are mutually unintelligible with the dialects of the Kathmandu Valley. The same may also be true of Pahri of Sindhupalchok and other varieties. Some vocabulary differences between Hindus and Buddhists. *Type:* SOV; postpositions; genitives, adjectives, demonstratives before noun heads; noun heads final; 4 noun classes: animate, inanimate, common, honored; content q-word in situ; relatives before and without noun heads; in polar questions there is a particle sentence finally; 1 prefix, up to 3 suffixes; clause constituents indicated by case-marking; verbal affixation marks person and number (in Dolakha and Badikhel dialects); affixes or clitics indicate case of noun phrases; ergative; causatives; comparatives; tense and aspect; no passives or voice; V, VC, CV, CVC, CCV, CCVC; nontonal; 28 consonant and 6 vowel phonemes. *Lg Use:* Language shift greater among Hindus than Buddhists. Home, religion; mixed use: Friends, work, education. Children, young adults and older. Some use among adolescents. Also use Central Tibetan [bod], English [eng], Hindi [hin], Nepali [npi]. *Lg Dev:* Literacy rate in L1: 60% (1991 census). Literacy rate in L2: 60% (1991 census). Youth more literate than older; men more than women. Taught in primary and secondary schools. Poetry. Magazines. Newspapers. New media. Radio programs. Films. TV. Videos. Dictionary. Grammar. NT: 1986. *Writing:* Devanagari script, primary usage. Newar (Prachalit Nepal) script, in common use during the Malla period and earlier, recent efforts to revive usage. Ranjana (Lantsa, Wartu) script, no longer in use. *Other:* One of the principal languages of Nepal; historically an official language of the Newar Malla Kings of the three cities of Kathmandu Valley. Kathmandu is the prestige dialect with most published materials. English [eng] highly valued; mixed feelings about Hindi [hin]; Tibetan [bod] does not have high prestige. People learn whichever language will help them economically: Nepali [npi], English [eng], Hindi [hin], and others. Hindu, Buddhist, traditional religion. *Maps:* 395:52, 396:52.

Nubri [kte] (Kutang, Kutang Bhotia, Larkye). 2,000 (2001 census). 500 monolinguals. Gandaki Zone, North Gorkha district, upper Buri Gandaki river, from Namrung to Samdo and Prok. *Status:* 6a (Vigorous). Language of recognized indigenous nationality: Larke. *Class:* Sino-Tibetan, Tibeto-Burman, Western Tibeto-Burman, Bodish, Central Bodish, Central, gTsang. *Dialects:* Lho, Namrung, Prok, Sama. Only moderately intelligible of Kyirong Tibetan [kgy] (74%). The most distinct variety reportedly spoken in Samdo village. Sama is somewhat divergent. Tsum [ttz] reportedly not intelligible with Nubri. The language spoken in the Kutang area is not intelligible with Nubri, although most who live in this area reportedly can speak and understand Nubri. Lexical similarity: 78%–93% among dialects. Prok is more distinct. 71%–78% with Tsum [ttz]; 66%–74% with Kyirong Tibetan [kgy]; 67% with Dolpo [dre]; 65% with Loke [loy]; 59%–64% with Lhasa Tibetan [bod]; 64% with Olangchung Gola [ola] (Walungge) and Lhomi [lhm]; 61% with Helambu Sherpa [scp]; 57% with Jirel [jul]; 55% with Sherpa [xsr]; 21%–27% with Northern Ghale [ghh]; 20%–23% with Southern Ghale [ghe]; 14%–31% with Kuke [ght]; 14% with Eastern Gorkha Tamang [tge], Western Gurung [gvr], and Banspur Tamang. *Type:* SOV; postpositions; content q-words in situ. *Lg Use:* Vigorous. Most domains. Positive attitudes. 1,500 also use Central Tibetan [bod]. Speakers have minimal proficiency in Tibetan. 1,500 also use Nepali [npi]. Minimal proficiency in Nepali, which is used with outsiders. Used as L2 by Kuke [ght]. *Lg Dev:* Literacy rate in L2: Below 10%. *Writing:* Unwritten. *Other:* Nubri marry within their community and from the Kutang community. People trade in Gorkha District and also with Tibet. Ethnonym: Bhotia or Bhote, refers to people of Tibetan origin; in some contexts derogatory. Ethnic identity is closely affiliated between the Nubri and the Kuke [ght]. Buddhist (Lamaist). *Map:* 395:28.

Palpa [plp] (Pahari-Palpa). No known L1 speakers. Lumbini Zone, Palpa town. *Status:* 10 (Extinct). *Class:* Indo-European, Indo-Iranian, Indo-Aryan, Northern zone, Eastern Pahari. *Dialects:* Palpa stands midway between Nepali [npi] (Eastern Pahari) and Kumaoni [kfy] (Central Pahari). Might be considered a dialect of Kumaoni or Nepali. *Lg Dev:* NT: 1827. *Writing:* Devanagari script. *Other:* Pahari, of the hills, also refers to a dialect of Newar [new]. Identification of Palpa as a separate language has been questioned.

Phangduwali [phw] (Phangduvali, Phangduwali Poti). 290 (2011 census). Kosi Zone, Dhankuta district, Pakhribas VDC, above Mugakhola headwaters. *Status:* 7 (Shifting). Language of recognized indigenous nationality: Rai. *Class:* Sino-Tibetan, Tibeto-Burman, Western Tibeto-Burman, Himalayan, Kiranti, Eastern. *Dialects:* None known. Linguistically between Yakkha [ybh] and Belhariya [byw]. The language spoken by the Phangduwali people is well-understood by Mugali [lmh] people and vice versa except for a few lexical items and accents. *Type:* SOV; postpositions; 23 consonant and 5 vowel phonemes. *Writing:* Unwritten. *Other:* Van Driem (2001) claims that the Phangduwali are actually Yakkha [ybh], whereas I.P. Rai (forthcoming) suggests these two languages are distinct. Both assert that Phangduwali and Mugali [lmh] are the same language. Traditional religion. *Map:* 397:88.

Puma [pum] (Puma Kala, Puma La, Puma Pima). 6,690 (2011 census), decreasing. L2 users: Adults use L2 as much as L1 (Toba, Toba, and Rai 2005). Sagarmatha Zone, south Khotang district, Diplung, Chisapani, Devisthan, Mauwabote, and Pauwasera VDCs; Udayapur district, Beltar, and Saunechour VDCs; Ruwa Khola valley to Buwa Khola across the Dudh Koshi southward. *Status:* 6b (Threatened). Language of recognized indigenous nationality: Rai. *Class:* Sino-Tibetan, Tibeto-Burman, Western Tibeto-Burman, Himalayan, Kiranti, Eastern. *Type:* SOV; postpositions; noun head final; content q-word in situ; clause constituents indicated by both case-marking and word order; verbal affixation marks person and number; ergativity; tense and aspect; no passive or voice, but antipassive is a remarkable feature; nontonal. *Lg Use:* Home, religion, work; mixed use: Friends. Older adults and elderly. Some use among children, adolescents, and young adults. Positive attitudes, especially among younger generation. Also use Bantawa [bap], Chamling [rab], Nepali [npi]. *Lg Dev:* Poetry. Magazines. Films. Videos. Dictionary. *Writing:* Devanagari script. *Other:* Traditional religion, Christian, Hindu. *Map:* 396:62.

Rajbanshi [rjs] (Gangai, Koch, Koche, Rajbangsi, Rajbansi, Tajpuria). 143,000 (2011 census), increasing. 2,080 Koche, 122,000 Rajbanshi, 18,800 Tajpuriya. L2 users: 3,220 (1991 census). Mechi Zone, Jhapa district; Kosi Zone, Morang and Sunsari districts. *Status:* 5 (Developing). Language of recognized indigenous nationality: Rajbanshi (Koch). *Class:* Indo-European, Indo-Iranian, Indo-Aryan, Eastern zone, Bengali-Assamese. *Dialects:* Central Rajbanshi, Eastern Rajbanshi, Western Rajbanshi. Intelligibility is fairly high throughout the area (2001 J. Eppele and J. Grimes). Lexical similarity: 77%–95% with all varieties in Nepal (2001 J. Eppele and J. Grimes). *Type:* SOV; postpositions; noun head final; 2 noun classes or genders; content q-word in situ; 1 prefix, up to 4 suffixes; clause constituents indicated by both case-marking and word order; verbal affixation marks person and number; non-ergative; tense and aspect; passives and voice (no morphological passive, but 2 analytical passives); nontonal; 32 consonant and 6–7 vowel phonemes. *Lg Use:* Vigorous. Home, friends, religion, work; mixed use: Education. All ages. Positive attitudes. Also use Bengali [ben], Hindi [hin], Maithili [mai], Nepali [npi]. Used as L2 by Dhimal [dhi]. *Lg Dev:* Literacy rate in L2: 38% (1991 census). Mother-tongue multilingual education and adult literacy programs have been carried out in villages throughout the Rajbanshi area. Taught in primary schools. Poetry. Newspapers. Radio programs. Films. Videos. Dictionary. Grammar. NT: 2009. *Writing:* Devanagari script. *Other:* Hindu, Christian, Muslim, traditional religion. *Map:* 397:94.

Raji [rji] (Ban Raji, Janggali, Rajibar, Rawati, Rjya). 3,760 (2011 census), decreasing. Ethnic population: 4,000. Bheri Zone, Surkhet, Banke and Bardiya districts; Seti Zone, Kailali district; Mahakali Zone, Kanchanpur district. *Status:* 6b (Threatened). Language of recognized indigenous nationality: Rajhi. *Class:* Sino-Tibetan, Tibeto-Burman, Western Tibeto-Burman, Himalayan, Central Himalayan, Raute-Raji. *Dialects:* Barh Bandale, Naukule, Purbiya. Reportedly similar to Rawat [jnl]. Speakers of Barh Bandale and Purbiya have difficulty in understanding the Naukule variety. Lexical similarity: From 84% and 86% between the three varieties; 55% with Raute [rau]. *Lg Use:* In one village in Kailali District, Khailad VDC, speakers under 6 years of age and over 60 years old are monolingual. Religion; mixed use: Home, friends, work. Some use among all ages. Negative attitudes. Also use Hindi [hin], Nepali [npi]. *Lg Dev:* Literacy rate in L2: 22% (1991 census). Literacy in Nepali [npi] is increasing since parents have started sending their children to school. Poetry. Dictionary. *Writing:* Devanagari script. *Other:* The Raji were a nomadic group, but now settled. Sharma (1990) identifies Raji in India (perhaps Bodo Gadaba [gbj]) as a Munda language with borrowings from Tibeto-Burman and Indo-Aryan. Barh Bandale dialect is the most prestigious. May be the same as Rawat [jnl] in India. Traditional religion, Buddhist. *Maps:* 394:18, 395:18.

Raute [rau] (Boto boli, Khamchi, Raji, Rajwar, Rautya, Rautye). 460 (2011 census), decreasing. All nomadic Raute are monolingual. Mahakali Zone, Dadeldhura district, Jogbudha and Sirsa VDCs, in Karnali and Mahakali (Kali) rivers watershed regions (800 settled). Bheri Zone, Surkhet district, former nomadic camp; midwest and far west forest regions (about 25 nomads). *Status:* 6a (Vigorous). Language of recognized indigenous nationality: Raute. *Class:* Sino-Tibetan, Tibeto-Burman, Western Tibeto-Burman, Himalayan, Central Himalayan, Raute-Raji. *Dialects:* None known. There are reportedly many similarities with Raji [rji], but the relationship of Raute with and intelligibility between Rawat [jnl] and Raji [rji] needs further investigation. Lexical similarity: 80% with Rawat [jnl], 60% with Chepang [cdm], 25% with Kham. *Type:* SOV; postpositions; noun head final; no noun classes or gender; content q-word in situ; clause constituents indicated by case-marking; verbal affixation marks person and number; ergativity; both tense and aspect; nontonal; 35 consonant and 7 vowel phonemes. *Lg Use:* Vigorous. Home, friends, religion, work. Children, older adults, and elderly. Some use among adolescents and young adults. Some youth also use Hindi [hin]. Settled Raute also use some Nepali [npi] with outsiders. Some youth also use Nepali [npi]. Among nomadic Raute, only the headman is allowed to speak with outsiders. *Lg Dev:* Literacy rate in L1: 0%. Dictionary. *Writing:* Unwritten. *Other:* Ethnic autonym: Ra'te. The name may be of Tibeto-Burman origin, from ra- meaning human plus a person marker, -to or -te. Other scholars suggest it derives from the Sanskrit Indo-Aryan word raut from Sanskrit, rajaputra, prince. Rautes deem their language sacred and are linguistically conservative toward adopting non-Raute words or grammatical features. Traditional religion. *Maps:* 394:12, 395:12.

Saam [raq] (Saam Rai, Saama Kha, Samakha). 530 (2011 census). 130 Lingkhim, 400 Saam (2011 census). Kosi Zone, northern Bhojpur district, Dobhane and Khatamma (Khartangma) VDCs, straddling Irkhuwa river, in Dangmaya, Okharbote, Khartangma, and Dobhane settlements between Phedi and Irkhuwa rivers. *Status:* 8b (Nearly extinct). Language of recognized indigenous nationality: Rai. *Class:* Sino-Tibetan, Tibeto-Burman, Western Tibeto-Burman, Himalayan, Kiranti, Eastern. *Dialects:* Bungla, Lingkhim (Lingkhim Kulung, Lingkhim Rai, Linkhim), Sambya. *Lg Use:* Shifting to Nepali [npi]. Some use among older adults. *Writing:* Unwritten. *Other:* Almost no study or documentation has been done on the languages spoken in northern Bhojpur district. Other groups called Saam may be Kulung [kle] or Lingkhim [lii]. Hindu, traditional religion. *Map:* 396:75.

Sampang [rav] (Sampang Gun, Sampang Gung, Sampang Kha, Sampange Rai, Sangpang, Sangpang Gîn, Sangpang Gun, Sangpang Kha). 18,300 (2011 census), decreasing. Phali dialect spoken by a few elderly speakers. 0 monolinguals. Khotang dialect: Sagarmatha Zone, Khotang district, Tap Khola river upriver villages, Baspani, Khartamcha, Phedi, and Patheka; Koshi Zone, Bhojpur district, Lahure Khola river headwaters, Okharbote; Syam Khola area, Kimalung, Nigale, Talakharka, and Surke; Dingla bazaar area. Phali dialect: Kosi Zone, Bhojpur district, Sangpang, a few elderly speakers. *Status:* 6b (Threatened). Language of recognized indigenous nationality: Rai. *Class:* Sino-Tibetan, Tibeto-Burman, Western Tibeto-Burman, Himalayan, Kiranti, Eastern. *Dialects:* Khotang, Phali. Mutual intelligibility between the Khartamcha variety and the Patheka variety of the Khotang dialect is high. Mutual intelligibility between the Khotang and Phali Sampang dialect is difficult to estimate but appears to be low. *Type:* SOV; postpositions; noun head final; noun classes or gender; content q-word in situ; 1 prefix, up to 6 suffixes; word-order clause constituents; verbal affixation marks person and number; split ergativity; tense and aspect; passives and voice; nontonal; 28 consonant and 20 vowel phonemes; distinctive pitch-accent, nasal vowel phonemes and syllabic nasals; a prominent role is played in the grammar by an imperfective nominalizing suffix; in nominal morphology, the ergative structure is breaking down through the introduction of the Nepali [npi] oblique case marker. *Lg Use:* Shifting to Nepali [npi]. Mixed use: Home, friends, religion, work. Young adults and older. Some use among children and adolescents. Positive attitudes. Most speak some Nepali [npi] but men, educated and younger people have higher proficiency. Nepali is valued as language of education. *Lg Dev:* Literacy rate in L2: 80%. Dictionary. NT: 2008. *Writing:* Devanagari script. *Other:* Traditional religion, Christian, Hindu. *Map:* 396:72.

Sanskrit [san] (Deva Bhasha, Deva vani, Sanskrit bhasha). L2 users: 1,670 in Nepal (2011 census). Use as an L2 is decreasing. Widely dispersed. *Status:* 9 (Dormant). *Lg Use:* Religion, education; mixed use: Home, friends, work. Positive attitudes. *Lg Dev:* Mahayana Buddhist schools use Sanskrit. Taught in primary and secondary schools. *Other:* Hindu, Buddhist. See main entry on page 142.

Santhali [sat] (Har, Hor, Sainti, Sandal, Sangtal, Santal, Santali, Santhal, Satar, Sentali, Sonthal). 49,900 in Nepal (2011 census), increasing. Very few monolinguals. Ethnic population: 42,700. L2 users: 1,900 in Nepal (1991 census). 1,339 L2 Satar speakers; 559 L2 Santhal speakers (1991 census). Kosi Zone, Morang and Sunsari districts; Mechi Zone, Jhapa district. *Status:* 5 (Developing). Language of recognized indigenous nationality: Satar (Santhal). *Lg Use:* Migration, seasonal labor, illiteracy, lack of educational facilities are all threats to vitality. UNESCO). Home, friends, religion, work; mixed use: Education. All ages. Positive attitudes. Also use Nepali [npi]. At least 25,420 Santali speakers report speaking another language, Nepali (2001 census). Also use Maithili [mai]. *Lg Dev:* Literacy rate in L1: Very low. Taught in primary schools (mother-tongue multilingual education). *Other:* Traditional religion, Christian, Hindu. See main entry on page 142. *Map:* 397:98.

Seke [skj]. 700 (2002 SIL). Dhawalagiri Zone, Mustang district, Chuksang, Tsaile, Tangbe, Tetang, and Gyakar villages; Jomsom and Pokhara. *Status:* 6a (Vigorous). Language of recognized indigenous nationality: Tangbe. *Class:* Sino-Tibetan, Tibeto-Burman, Western Tibeto-Burman, Bodish, West Bodish, Gurung-Tamang, Gurungic. *Dialects:* Chuksang, Tangbe, Tetang. Reportedly similarities with Thakali [ths] and Manangba [nmm]. Very different from Loke [loy]. Tangbe dialect speakers do not understand the Chuksang dialect very well, but the Chuksang understand Tangbe. Reportedly understand Gurung but Gurung do not understand Seke. *Lg Use:* All ages. Use Nepali [npi] with the Gurung. Also use Loke [loy]. *Writing:* Unwritten. *Other:* Seke villages are surrounded by Baragaunle [loy] speaking villages. Buddhist. *Map:* 395:26.

Sherpa [xsr] (Serwa, Sharpa, "Sharpa Bhotia" *pej.*, Xiaerba). 145,000 in Nepal (2011 census), decreasing.

Population total all countries: 168,800. A few elderly monolinguals in remote villages (UNESCO). Ethnic population: 155,000 (2001 census). L2 users: Some non-Sherpas who work in the trekking trade learn some Sherpa. Sagarmatha Zone, Solu Khumbu district; Janakpur Zone, Dolakha and Ramechhap districts; Bagmati Zone, northeast Sindhupalchok district. Also in Bhutan, China, India, United States. *Status:* 5 (Developing). Language of recognized indigenous nationality: Sherpa. *Class:* Sino-Tibetan, Tibeto-Burman, Western Tibeto-Burman, Bodish, Central Bodish, Central, gTsang. *Dialects:* Central Sherpa (Solu, South Sherpa), East Sherpa (Dolakha, Ramechhap), North Sherpa (Khumbu), West Sherpa. 95% comprehension of Solu dialect by Western and Khumbu. Lexical similarity: 90% between Solu and Khumbu dialects; 67% with Jirel [jul]; 65% with Helambu Sherpa [scp]; 62% with Loke [loy] and Dolpo [dre]; 58% with Lhomi [lhm] and Lhasa Tibetan [bod]; 57% with Kyerung (Kyirong) [kgy]; 55% with Nubri [kte] and Walungge [ola]. *Type:* SOV; postpositions; noun head initial; no noun classes or genders; content q-word in situ; 1 prefix, up to 3 suffixes; clause constituents indicated by case-marking; verbal affixation marks person; split ergativity; tense and aspect; no passive forms; tonal; 31 consonant and 6 vowel phonemes (also 6 diphthongs). *Lg Use:* Vigorous in villages but not in urban areas where there is some shift towards Nepali [npi]. Mixed use: Home, friends, religion, work, education. Older adults and elderly. Some use among children, adolescents, and young adults. Positive attitudes. In schools children are teased if they use Sherpa. In Kathmandu parents use Nepali [npi] with school-age children. Also use Central Tibetan [bod], English [eng], French [fra], Korean [kor], Nepali [npi], Standard German [deu]. Guides learn languages of trekkers. Used as L2 by Jirel [jul], Tibetan [bod]. *Lg Dev:* Literacy rate in L1: 8%–9%. The Mountain Institute and the Curriculum Development Centre have published some primary education materials. Lack of language development is source of embarrassment for some. Poetry. Newspapers. Radio programs. Dictionary. Bible portions: 1975–2008. *Writing:* Devanagari script. Tibetan script. *Other:* Tourism and increased wealth have given Sherpas the financial means to send their children to Kathmandu and abroad for education contributing to language shift. Buddhist (Lamaist), Christian. *Maps:* 396:55, 397:55.

Sonha [soi] (Sonaha, Sonahaa, Sunah, Sunha). 580 (2011 census), decreasing. 0 monolinguals. Seti Zone, Kailali District, along Karnali River; Bheri Zone, Surkhet district along Bheri river; Bardia district, Daulatpur VDC, Murgawagaon; Mahakali Zone, along Mahakali river; Kanchanpur district, Bhimadatta VDC, Odaligaon, Mahendranagar tahsil. *Status:* 7 (Shifting). *Class:* Indo-European, Indo-Iranian, Indo-Aryan, Central zone, Unclassified. *Dialects:* None known. Reportedly similar to Avadhi [awa]. Lexical similarity: 69% with Rana Tharu [thr], 73% with Kathariya Tharu [tkt], 72% with Dangaura Tharu [thl]. Sonha and Kathoriya [tkt] form a lexical bridge with Rana and Dangaura varieties of Tharu. *Type:* SOV; postpositions; noun head final; content q-word in situ; clause constituents indicated by case-marking; verbal affixation marks number; split ergativity; passives and voice; nontonal. *Lg Use:* Home; mixed use: Friends, religion, work. Young adults and older. Some use among children and adolescents. *Writing:* Unwritten. *Other:* 'Sonha' is an occupational caste (gold panners). Hindu, Christian, traditional religion. *Map:* 394:13.

Sunwar [suz] (Bhujuwar, Kirati-Koits, Koits Lo, Mukhiya, Pirthwar, Sunuwar, Sunwari). 38,200 (2011 census). 37,900 Sunwar, 290 Surel (2011 census). Very few monolinguals. Ethnic population: 95,300 (2001 census). Janakpur Zone, Ramechhap, Dolakha districts, east hills; Sagarmatha Zone, northwest Okhaldhunga district. *Status:* 6b (Threatened). Language of recognized indigenous nationality: Surel. Sunuwar. *Class:* Sino-Tibetan, Tibeto-Burman, Western Tibeto-Burman, Himalayan, Kiranti, Western. *Dialect:* Surel. Lexical similarity: more than 80% with Surel dialect. *Type:* SOV; postpositions; genitives after noun heads; relatives before noun heads; noun heads both initial and final; 5 noun classes; content q-word initial and in situ; up to 2 prefixes and 3 suffixes; clause constituents indicated by split-case marking; verbal affixation marks person and number; causatives; comparatives; passives and voice; CV, CVC CVV, CCV, CCVC, V, VC; tonal; 24 consonant and 6 vowel phonemes; nasal contrastive pairs. *Lg Use:* Mixed use: Home, friends, religion, work. Adolescents and older. Some use among children. Language is passed down to children only in village areas (Toba, Toba, and Rai 2002). Positive attitudes. Younger people speak Nepali [npi] for trade, official purposes with low proficiency (1998 SIL). Most speak 2 or more languages, including Nepali (2002 UNESCO). Also use Bhujel [byh], Eastern Tamang [taj]. Used as L2 by Jirel [jul]. *Lg Dev:* Literacy rate in L1: 20% (2010 L. Rapacha). Literacy rate in L2: Males 15% in villages, 20% in Kathmandu. Poetry. Magazines. Newspapers. New media. Radio programs. Videos. Dictionary. Grammar. Bible: 2011. *Writing:* Devanagari script. *Other:* Traditional religion, Christian, Daoist, Hindu. *Map:* 397:105.

Tamang, Eastern [taj] ("Bhotia" *pej.*, Ishang, Murmi, Sei). 1,180,000 in Nepal (2001 census), increasing. Population for all Tamang varieties: 1,350,000 (2011 census). Population total all countries: 1,197,500. In some remote communities, particularly women, children and elderly people are monolingual. Ethnic population: 1,290,000 (2001 census). L2 users: 23,600 in Nepal (1991 census). L2 speakers of all Tamang. Kathmandu; Janakpur Zone, Sindhuli, Ramechhap, and Dolkha districts; Bagmati Zone, Kavre Palanchok district; west Sindhupalchowk, Lalitpur, Bhaktapur, and east Nuwakot districts; Narayani Zone, Makwanpur and Chitwan districts; Sagarmatha Zone, Okhaldhunga, west Khotang, and Udayapur districts. Also in Bhutan, India. *Status:* 4 (Educational). Language of recognized indigenous nationality: Tamang. *Class:* Sino-Tibetan, Tibeto-Burman, Western Tibeto-Burman, Bodish, West Bodish, Gurung-Tamang, Tamang. *Dialects:* Central-Eastern Tamang (Temal Tamang), Outer-Eastern Tamang (Sailung Tamang), Southwestern Tamang. Central-Eastern most widely understood among all tested to date: 85% by both Trisuli and Rasuwa Western Tamang [tdg], 93%–98% by Outer-Eastern, 87% by Southwestern Tamang [tsf]. Comprehension of Outer-Eastern 58% by Western Rasuwa Tamang [tdg], 64%–75% by Western Trisuli Tamang [tdg], 67%–54% by Southwestern Tamang [tsf], 88%–93% by Central-Eastern Tamang [taj], and 90%–98% among its own varieties. Southwestern Tamang [tsf] may be a bridge between Eastern and Western Tamang (Varenkamp 1996). Lexical similarity: 88%–99% with Outer Eastern varieties; 89%–100% with Central Eastern; 79%–93% with Outer Eastern and Central Eastern, 77%–82% with Southwestern Tamang [tsf], 86%–93% with Southwestern and Central-Eastern, 74%–80% with Eastern and Western Trisuli Tamang [tdg], 69%–81% with Western Rasuwa Tamang [tdg], 72%–80% with Northwestern Dhading Tamang [tmk], 63%–77% with

Eastern Gorkha Tamang [tge] (Varenkamp 1996). *Type:* SOV; postpositions, genitives after nouns; noun head final; no noun classes or genders; content q-word in situ; 1 prefix, up to 3 suffixes; clause constituents indicated by case-marking; ergative; aspect and tense; no passives or voice; 34 consonant and 16 vowel phonemes; CV, CVC, CCV, V, CCVC; tonal; vowel phonemes include 5 basic, 5 long, 6 diphthongs; aspiration and length are phonemic. *Lg Use:* Vigorous. Home, friends, religion; mixed use: Work, education. All ages. Those who have been to school or traveled often speak Nepali [npi]; others have limited proficiency, especially women, older adults, children. Also use Lhomi [lhm]. Used as L2 by Danuwar [dhw], Jirel [jul], Sunwar [suz]. *Lg Dev:* Literacy rate in L1: 1%–5%. Literacy rate in L2: 25%–50%. Some non-formal and formal literacy materials, textbooks and classes. Taught in primary schools, up to class 3 as medium of instruction; to class 5 as subject. Poetry. Magazines. Newspapers. New media. Radio programs. Films. TV. Videos. Dictionary. Grammar. NT: 2011. *Writing:* Devanagari script. Tibetan script, Tamhig style. *Other:* Traditional religion, Buddhist, Christian, Hindu. *Maps:* 395:51, 396:51, 397:51.

Tamang, Eastern Gorkha [tge]. 3,980 (2000). Population for all Tamang varieties: 1,350,000 (2011 census). Gandaki Zone, north Gorkha district, south and east of Jagat. *Status:* 6a (Vigorous). Language of recognized indigenous nationality: Tamang. *Class:* Sino-Tibetan, Tibeto-Burman, Western Tibeto-Burman, Bodish, West Bodish, Gurung-Tamang, Tamang. *Dialects:* Kasigaon, Kerounja. Lexical similarity: 89% with dialects, 76%–77% with Northwestern (Dhading) Tamang [tmk], 77%–79% with Western (Trisuli) Tamang [tdg], 72%–73% with Western (Rasuwa) Tamang [tdg], 70%–73% with Southwestern Tamang [tsf], 63%–73% with Eastern Tamang [taj] dialects (Varenkamp 1996), 50% with Western (Banspur) Gurung [gvr], 31%–37% with Northern [ghh] and Southern Ghale [ghe], 18%–23% with Kuke [ght], 14%–16% with Nubri [kte], Tsum [ttz], and Kyerung (Kyirong) [kgy], 12%–14% with Tibetan [bod] (1992 J. Webster). *Lg Use:* Also use Nepali [npi]. *Lg Dev:* Literacy rate in L2: Below 10%. *Writing:* Devanagari script. *Other:* Refer to themselves as Gurung, but recognize their language is different. Traditional religion, Buddhist, Hindu. *Maps:* 395:39, 396:39.

Tamang, Northwestern [tmk] (Kath-Bhotiya, Lama Bhote, Murmi, Rongba, Sain, Tamang Gyoi, Tamang Lengmo, Tamang Tam). 55,000 (1991 census), increasing. Population for all Tamang varieties: 1,350,000 (2011 census). Bagmati Zone, Nuwakot district, central mountainous strip. *Status:* 6a (Vigorous). Language of recognized indigenous nationality: Tamang. *Class:* Sino-Tibetan, Tibeto-Burman, Western Tibeto-Burman, Bodish, West Bodish, Gurung-Tamang, Tamang. *Dialect:* Dhading. All Western Tamang varieties have high mutual intelligibility. Lexical similarity: 94% with Western Trisuli Tamang [tdg], 82%–83% with Western Rasuwa Tamang [tdg], 76%–78% with Southwestern Tamang [tsf], 76%–77% with Eastern Gorkha Tamang [tge], 72%–80% with Eastern Tamang [taj]. *Type:* SOV; postpositions; noun head both initial and final; no noun classes or gender; no prefixes, up to 4 suffixes; clause constituents indicated by case-marking; ergativity; genitives after noun head; relatives before noun head; question word medial; tense and aspect; no passives or voice; CV, CVC, CCV, V, CCVC, CVCCC; tonal; 25 consonant and 5 vowel phonemes. *Lg Use:* Home; mixed use: Friends, religion, work, education. All ages. Positive attitudes. Also use Tibetan [bod] in religious contexts. Also use Nepali [npi] in official contexts. *Lg Dev:* Literacy rate in L1: 1%–10%. Literacy rate in L2: 25%–75%. Taught in primary schools. Poetry. Magazines. Newspapers. New media. Radio programs. Dictionary. *Writing:* Devanagari script. *Other:* Traditional religion, Buddhist. *Maps:* 395:41, 396:41.

Tamang, Southwestern [tsf] (Kath-Bhotiya, Lama Bhote, Murmi, Rongba, Sain, Tamang Gyoi, Tamang Lengmo, Tamang Tam). 109,000 (1991 census), increasing. Population for all Tamang varieties: 1,350,000 (2011 census). Bagmati Zone, southern Dhading district; Narayani Zone, Chitwan, northwest Makwanpur, Bara, Parsa, and Rautahat districts; west and northwest Kathmandu district area. *Status:* 6a (Vigorous). Language of recognized indigenous nationality: Tamang. *Class:* Sino-Tibetan, Tibeto-Burman, Western Tibeto-Burman, Bodish, West Bodish, Gurung-Tamang, Tamang. *Dialects:* Preliminary results: 86% intelligibility of Western Trisuli Tamang [tdg], 87% by Central-Eastern Tamang [taj], 54%–67% by Outer-Eastern Tamang [taj]. Relationship within Tamang needs evaluation. Southwestern Tamang has 80% lexical similarity with Western Trisuli Tamang [tdg], 76%–78% with Western Rasuwa dialect [tdg], 78% with Northwestern Tamang [tmk], 70%–73% with Eastern Gorkha Tamang [tge], 77%–93% with Eastern Tamang [taj]. *Type:* SOV; postpositions; noun head both initial and final; no noun classes or gender; content q-word initial; up to 4 suffixes; clause constituents indicated by case-marking; genitives after nouns; relatives before nouns; question word medial; ergativity; tense and aspect; no passives or voice; CV, CVC, CCV, V, CCVC, CVCCC; tonal; 24 consonant and 5 vowel phonemes. *Lg Use:* Home; mixed use: Friends, religion, work, education. All ages. Positive attitudes. Also use Tibetan [bod] in religious contexts. Also use Nepali [npi] in official contexts. Also use Bhojpuri [bho], Maithili [mai]. *Lg Dev:* Literacy rate in L1: 1%–10%. Literacy rate in L2: 25%–75%. Taught in primary schools. Poetry. Magazines. Newspapers. New media. Radio programs. Films. Dictionary. *Writing:* Devanagari script. *Other:* Buddhist, traditional religion. *Maps:* 395:49, 396:49.

Tamang, Western [tdg] (Murmi, Sain). 323,000 (2000), increasing. Population for all Tamang varieties: 1,350,000 (2011 census). Mostly monolingual below school age or over 60 years of age. Bagmati Zone, west Nuwakot, Rasuwa, and Dhading districts; northeast Sindhupalchok district, Bhote Namlan, and Bhote Chaur, on Trishuli river west bank toward Budhi Gandaki river; Narayani Zone, northwest Makwanpur district, Phakel, Chakhel, Khulekhani, Markhu, Tistung, and Palung; north Kathmandu, Jhor, Thoka, and Gagal Phedi. *Status:* 5 (Developing). Language of recognized indigenous nationality: Tamang. *Class:* Sino-Tibetan, Tibeto-Burman, Western Tibeto-Burman, Bodish, West Bodish, Gurung-Tamang, Tamang. *Dialects:* Northwestern dialect of Western Tamang (Dhading), Rasuwa, Southwestern dialect of Western Tamang, Trisuli (Nuwakot). Preliminary results showed 86% intelligibility of Rasuwa dialect, 81%–88% of Central-Eastern [taj], 78%–88% of Outer-Eastern [taj], 86% of Southwestern [tsf]; 80% of Rasuwa with Trisuli, up to 70% of Outer-Eastern [taj]. Lexical similarity: 94% between Trisuli dialect and Northwestern Tamang [tmk], 82%–83% with Rasuwa, 80% with Southwestern Tamang [tsf], 77%–79% with Eastern Gorkha Tamang [tge], 82%–83% between Rasuwa and Northwestern [tmk], 78% with Southwestern [tsf], 72% with Eastern Gorkha [tge], 69%–81% between Western varieties and Eastern Tamang varieties. *Type:* SOV; postpositions; noun head both initial and final; genitives after nouns, relatives before nouns; no noun classes or genders; content q-word initial; up to 2 prefixes, up to

11 suffixes; clause constituents indicated by word order; ergativity; no passives or voice; 24 consonant and 5 vowel phonemes; CV, CVC, CCV, V, CCVC, CVCCC; tonal. *Lg Use:* Home, friends, religion; mixed use: Work, education. All ages. Younger population also uses Nepali [npi] due to education in the national language. *Lg Dev:* Literacy rate in L2: 25%–75%. Taught in primary schools, primary mother-tongue multilingual education program since 2007. Poetry. Magazines. Newspapers. Radio programs. Videos. Dictionary. NT: 1990. *Writing:* Devanagari script. Tibetan script. *Other:* Murmi is the ethnonym used by the Lepcha and Kirati communities and Sain by the Newar. Traditional religion, Buddhist, Christian. *Maps:* 395:40, 396:40.

Thakali [ths] (Barhagaule, Panchgaunle, Thaksya). 5,240 (2011 census), decreasing. Ethnic population: 13,000 (2001 census). L2 users: 1,060 (1991 census). Dhawalagiri Zone, Mustang district, Thak Khola, mid Kali Gandaki valley, with Annapurna Himal on one side and Dhawalagiri Himal on the other, Tatopani village in the south to Jomsom north. Tukuche dialect: Tukuche to Thaksatsae, in 13 villages: Tukuche, Khanti, Kobang, Larjung, Dampu, Naurikot, Bhurjungkot, Nakung, Tithi, Kunjo, Taglung, Lete, Ghansa. Many live outside the area. *Status:* 7 (Shifting). Language of recognized indigenous nationality: Thakali, Chhairotan, Marphali Thakali, Tieengaule Thakali. *Class:* Sino-Tibetan, Tibeto-Burman, Western Tibeto-Burman, Bodish, West Bodish, Gurung-Tamang, Gurungic. *Dialects:* Marpha (Puntan Thakali), Syang (Yhulkasom), Tukuche (Tamhang Thakali, Thaksaatsaye, Thaksatsae). Thakali dialects have 91%–97% inherent intelligibility. Tukuche dialect most easily understood by others. Tukuche is cultural center and the most prestigeous dialect. Lexical similarity: 41%–46% with Gurung languages, 46%–51% with Tamang languages (1994 J. Webster). Thakali dialects in 4 villages have 75%–86% lexical similarity. *Type:* SOV; postpositions; noun head both initial and final; no noun classes or genders; content q-word final; verbal affixation marks number; tense; no passives or voice; tonal; 27 consonant and 6 vowel phonemes. *Lg Use:* Youth in Tukuche maintain Thakali strongly. Elsewhere youth use less Thakali, but develop it more fully as they grow older (1994 J. Webster). Religion; mixed use: Home, friends, religion, work. Older adults and elderly. Some use among children, adolescents, and young adults. *Lg Dev:* Taught in primary schools. Poetry. Videos. Dictionary. Grammar. *Writing:* Devanagari script. *Other:* Marpha dialect is in an endogamous village. People of Marpha, Syang, Thini, Chhairo, and Chimang villages are sometimes collectively known as Panchgaunle (5 villages), the name used for both the ethnic group and language. Buddhist, Christian, traditional religion. *Map:* 395:24.

Thangmi [thf] (Thami, Thangmi Kham, Thangmi Wakhe, Thani). 23,200 in Nepal (2011 census), decreasing. Population total all countries: 24,000. 100 monolinguals (2002 UNESCO). Ethnic population: 35,000 (Turin 2007). L2 users: Some occupational castes and other ethnic groups in Thangmi-dominant areas speak Thangmi also. Janakpur Zone, Dolakha district, villages north and west; Ramechhap district, villages on Sailung Khola; Bagmati zone, Sindhupalchok district, villages east; Kathmandu. Also in China, India. *Status:* 6b (Threatened). Language of recognized indigenous nationality: Thami. *Class:* Sino-Tibetan, Tibeto-Burman, Western Tibeto-Burman, Himalayan, Central Himalayan, Thangmi-Baraamu. *Dialects:* Eastern Thangmi (Dolakha), Western Thangmi (Sindhupalchok). Related to Baram [brd] (Grierson-Konow). Some cognates with Dolakha dialect of Newar [new]. Dolakha and Sindhupalchok dialects are not mutually intelligible. Differ in phonology, nominal and verbal morphology and lexicon. *Type:* SOV; both prepositions and postpositions; noun head both initial and final; gender, only some animate nouns; content q-word in situ; up to 3 prefixes, up to 4 suffixes; clause constituents indicated by case-marking; verbal affixation marks person; no ergativity; tense; passives and voice; nontonal; 33 consonant and 13 vowel phonemes. *Lg Use:* Ethnic Thangmi outside Dolakha and Sindhupalchok no longer speak Thangmi. Religion; mixed use: Home, friends. Older adults and elderly. Some use among children, adolescents, and young adults. Negative attitudes, but changing to more neutral and positive. *Lg Dev:* Literacy rate in L1: Below 10%. Taught in primary schools. Poetry. Magazines. Newspapers. New media. Radio programs. Films. TV. Videos. Dictionary. Grammar. *Writing:* Devanagari script. *Other:* Traditional religion, Buddhist, Christian, Hindu. *Map:* 397:102.

Tharu, Chitwania [the] (Chitoniya Tharu, Chitwan Tharu, Chitwaniya). 285,000 in Nepal (2001 census), increasing. Population for all Tharu varieties: 1,530,000 (2011 census). L2 users: 46,600 L2 speakers for all Tharu languages (1991 census). Narayani Zone, Chitwan, Bara, Parsa, Rautahat, and Makwanpur districts; Lumbini Zone, Nawalparasi district; Gandaki Zone, Tanahu district. Also in India. *Status:* 5 (Developing). Language of recognized indigenous nationality: Tharu. *Class:* Indo-European, Indo-Iranian, Indo-Aryan, Eastern zone, Unclassified. *Dialect:* Nawalpuriya Tharu (Laulpuriya Tharu). *Type:* SOV; postpositions; noun head final; 2 genders; content q-word in situ; up to 3 suffixes; clause constituents indicated by case-marking; verbal affixation marks person and number; tense and aspect; no passive or voice; nontonal; 34 consonant and 6 vowel phonemes (5 of the vowels can be nasalized). *Lg Use:* Vigorous within the language community. Home, friends, religion; mixed use: Work, education. All ages. Neutral or negative attitudes. Also use Bhojpuri [bho], Hindi [hin], Nepali [npi]. *Lg Dev:* Literacy rate in L1: Below 1%. Taught in primary schools, in 2 schools in Chitwan District only. Poetry. Magazines. Newspapers. New media. Radio programs. Films. Videos. Bible portions: 1977. *Writing:* Devanagari script. *Other:* Traditional religion. *Map:* 395:47.

Tharu, Dangaura [thl] (Dangaha, Dangali, Dangauli, Dangora, Dangura). 500,000 in Nepal (2003), increasing. Population for all Tharu varieties: 1,530,000 (2011 census). Population total all countries: 674,000. 28,500 monolinguals. L2 users: 46,600 L2 speakers for all Tharu languages (1991 census). Rapti Zone, Dang district; Bheri Zone, Bardiya, Banke, and Surkhet districts; Seti Zone, Kailali district; Mahakali Zone, Kanchanpur district; Lumbini Zone, Rupandehi and Kapilvastu districts. Also in India. *Status:* 5 (Developing). Language of recognized indigenous nationality: Tharu. *Class:* Indo-European, Indo-Iranian, Indo-Aryan, Central zone, Unclassified. *Dialect:* Dangaha (Dang). 68%–91% intelligibility of Rana Tharu [thr], 95% to 97% of Kathoriya [tkt]. Some intelligibility difficulty with speakers from India. Possibly Eastern Hindi Group. Lexical similarity: 85% with Deukhuri, 83% with Malhoriya, 72%–74% with Sonha [soi], 63%–72% with Rana Tharu [thr], 76% with Desauriya, 61%–67% with Chitwania [the], 70% with Kathariya Tharu [tkt], 58%–65% with Hindi [hin], 46%–52% with Kochila Tharu [thq]. *Type:* SOV; postpositions; noun head initial; genitives after noun heads; adjectives, numerals before noun heads; content q-word initial (usually); clause constituents indicated by case-marking; verbal affixation marks person and number; tense-aspect; passives and voice; CV, CVC, CCV; nontonal; 30 consonant and 8 vowel phonemes. *Lg Use:* High vitality but increasing Nepali [npi] loanwords. Home, friends, religion. All ages. Hindi [hin] is also used. Educated people tend to use more Nepali [npi], men more than women, young people more than older people. *Lg Dev:* Literacy rate in L2: All Tharu as an ethnic group 28% (1991 census). Poetry. Magazines. Radio programs. Dictionary. Grammar. Bible portions: 2010. *Writing:* Devanagari script. *Other:* Traditional religion, Christian, Hindu. *Maps:* 394:15, 395:15.

Tharu, Kathariya [tkt] (Kathariya, Kathoriya Tharu). 106,000 in Nepal (2006). Population for all Tharu varieties: 1,530,000 (2011 census). L2 users: 46,600 L2 speakers for all Tharu languages (1991 census). Seti Zone, Kailali district, Hasuliya, Udasipur, Pahalmanpur, Lalbojhi, Thapapur, Joshipur, Munuwa, Durgauli, Patharaiya, and Chauha VDCs. Also in India. *Status:* 6a (Vigorous). Language of recognized indigenous nationality: Tharu. *Class:* Indo-European, Indo-Iranian, Indo-Aryan, Central zone, Unclassified. *Dialects:* Speech differences between Nepal and India dialects. Lexical similarity: 70%–76% with Dangaura Tharu [thl] and Rana Tharu [thr], 66% with Hindi [hin], 66%–69% with Buksa [tkb], 63% with Chitwania [the], 51%–59% with Kochila Tharu [thq]. *Type:* SOV; postpositions; noun head final (unmarked). *Lg Use:* Some shifting to Hindi [hin]. Also use Hindi [hin], Nepali [npi]. *Lg Dev:* Literacy rate in L2: All Tharu as an ethnic group 28% (1991 census). *Writing:* Devanagari script. *Other:* Hindu, Christian. *Map:* 394:16.

Tharu, Kochila [thq] (Saptariya Tharu). 258,000 in Nepal (2003), increasing. Population for all Tharu varieties: 1,530,000 (2011 census). Mostly illiterate older women are monolingual. L2 users: 46,600 L2 speakers for all Tharu languages (1991 census). Kosi Zone, Morang and Sunsari districts; Sagarmatha Zone, Saptari and Udayapur districts. Also in India. *Status:* 5 (Developing). Language of recognized indigenous nationality: Tharu, Dhanuk. *Class:* Indo-European, Indo-Iranian, Indo-Aryan, Eastern zone, Unclassified. *Dialects:* Dhanusa, Mahottari, Morangiya, Saptari, Sarlahi, Siraha, Sunsari, Udayapur. Each district has a different variety. Dialect names refer to districts. Lexical similarity: 51%–59% with Kathariya Tharu, 46%–52% with Dangaura Tharu. *Type:* SOV; postpositions; noun head final; no gender; content q-word in situ; 1 prefix, up to 3 suffixes; clause constituents indicated by case-marking; verbal affixation marks person; tense and aspect; passives (syntactic, not morphological); nontonal; 32 consonant and 8 vowel phonemes. *Lg Use:* Vigorous. Home, friends, religion; mixed use: Work, education. All ages. Positive attitudes. Also use Maithili [mai], Nepali [npi]. *Lg Dev:* Literacy rate in L1: Below 1%. Mother-tongue multilingual education introduced in one school. Literacy increasing. Taught in primary schools. Radio programs. Films. Videos. Dictionary. *Writing:* Devanagari script. *Other:* Tharu from each district usually take the district name as a more specific name or identity. Other Tharu in Siraha, Udayapur, and Saptari districts who call themselves Kochila but speak Sapatariya Tharu. Traditional religion, Christian. *Maps:* 396:60, 397:60.

Tharu, Rana [thr]. 336,000 in Nepal (2006), increasing. Population for all Tharu varieties: 1,530,000 (2011 census). Population total all countries: 486,000. L2 users: 46,600 L2 speakers for all Tharu languages (1991 census). Mahakali Zone, Kanchanpur district; Seti Zone, Kailali district. Also in India. *Status:* 5 (Developing). Language of recognized indigenous nationality: Tharu. *Class:* Indo-European, Indo-Iranian, Indo-Aryan, Eastern zone, Unclassified. *Dialects:* 96%–99% intelligibility among dialects, 90% of Kathariya [tkt], 51%–88% reported of Dangaura [thl]. Differences with dialects in India. Reportedly similar to Awadhi (Avadhi) [awa]. Lexical similarity: 83%–97% among dialects, 73%–79% with Buksa, 74%–79% with Kathariya [tkt], 70%–73% with Sonha [soi], 63%–71% with Dangaura [thl], 56%–60% with Chitwania [the], 68%–72% with Hindi [hin]. *Type:* SOV; postpositions; noun head final; 2 genders; content q-word in situ; 1 prefix, up to 2 suffixes; clause constituents indicated by case-marking; verbal affixation marks person and number; ergativity; tense (4 tenses: past, present, imminent future, irrealis future); passives and voice; nontonal; 28 consonant and 11 vowel phonemes. *Lg Use:* Vigorous. Home, friends, religion; mixed use: Work, education. All ages. Positive attitudes. Also use Hindi [hin], Nepali [npi]. *Lg Dev:* Mother-tongue multilingual education up to grade three in Kanchanpur. Taught in primary schools. Poetry. Magazines. Radio programs. Films. Videos. *Writing:* Devanagari script. *Other:* Hindu, Christian. *Map:* 394:14.

Thudam [thw] ("Thudam Bhote" *pej.*). 1,800 (2000). Kosi Zone, Sankhuwasabha district, Chepuwa VDC, Thudam village. *Status:* 6a (Vigorous). Language of recognized indigenous nationality: Thudam. *Class:* Sino-Tibetan, Tibeto-Burman, Western Tibeto-Burman, Bodish, Central Bodish, Unclassified. *Dialects:* None known. Similar to Walungge [ola] in Nepal and to the varieties spoken in the villages of Kudo and Sar in Tibet (von Furer-Haimendorf 1975). *Type:* SOV; postpositions; content q-word in situ; clause constituents indicated by case-marking; ergativity; no passives or voice; tonal. *Lg Use:* Some older people also speak Lhomi [lhm]. Also use Nepali [npi]. *Writing:* Unwritten. *Other:* Culturally akin to the Walungs. Buddhist, Christian. *Map:* 396:78.

Thulung [tdh] (Tholong Lo, Thulu Luwa, Thululoa, Thulung Jemu, Thulung La, Thulunge Rai, Toaku Lwa). 20,700 in Nepal (2011 census). Thulung communities also in Bhojpur and Sankhuwasabha districts, scattered in Udayapur, Morang, Panchthar, and Ilam districts. Migrants may not speak Thulung as L1. A few elderly monolinguals. Sagarmatha Zone, southeast Solukhumbu district, Deusa, Lokhim, Mukli, Jubu, Tingla, Salyan, Panchan, and Necha VDCs; Khotang district, Salle, Jaleswori, and Maheswori VDCs; Okhaldhunga district, Tuintar VDC, 6 or 7 villages; Koshi Zone, Bhojpur district, 1 village; west of the slopes' highest ridges to Dudhkosi, north of Nechedanda and Halesidanda ranges, east of upper Solu river, and south of the Kakukhola and the confluence of Ingkhukhola and Dudhkosi. Also in India. *Status:* 5 (Developing). Language of recognized indigenous nationality: Rai. *Class:* Sino-Tibetan, Tibeto-Burman, Western Tibeto-Burman, Himalayan, Kiranti, Western. *Dialects:* Central Thulung (Mukli Lwa), Eastern Thulung (Jubu Lwa, Lokhim Lwa), Northern Thulung (Deusa Lwa), Southern Thulung (Necha Lwa). Many cognates with Khaling [klr]. *Type:* SOV; postpositions; noun head final; content q-word in situ; no prefixes, up to 4 suffixes; clause constituents indicated by case-marking; verbal affixation marks person and number; ergativity; tense; passives and voice, but rare; tonal; 29 consonant and 16 vowel phonemes. *Lg Use:* Language retention high compared to other Rai languages (Winter and Hanson 1991). Home, friends, religion. All ages. Neutral attitudes. Do not believe each other's dialect is 'pure' Thulung. Also use Bahing [bhj]. Women speak less Nepali [npi] than men. Most men speak Nepali well. Used as L2 by Nepali [npi]. *Lg Dev:* Poetry. Magazines. Newspapers. New media. Radio programs. Videos. Dictionary. Bible portions: 2006. *Writing:* Devanagari script. *Other:* Interest in development among cultural associations (Thulung Rai Society). Traditional religion, Buddhist, Christian, Hindu. *Maps:* 396:65, 397:65.

Tibetan [bod] (Bhotia, Bod Skad, Central Tibetan, Phoke, Poke, Zang Wen). 4,450 in Nepal (2011 census), increasing. Mainly Kathmandu and Pokhara. Sagarmatha Zone, two small areas in Solukhumbu district. Scattered refugee communities along China border. *Status:* 4 (Educational). Spoken as a trade language among Bodish groups in Nepal. *Dialects:* Diaspora Tibetan, Utsang. *Lg Use:* Home, religion; mixed use: Friends, work, education. All ages. Positive attitudes. Tibetan speakers who move into Khumbu often learn to speak Sherpa [xsr]. Also use Nepali [npi]. Used as L2 by Dolpo [dre], Helambu Sherpa [scp], Humla [hut], Kaike [kzq], Kuke [ght], Lhomi [lhm], Loke [loy], Manangba [nmm], Mugom [muk], Nar Phu [npa], Newar [new], Northwestern Tamang [tmk], Nubri [kte], Sherpa [xsr], Southwestern Tamang [tsf]. *Lg Dev:* The written and spoken languages are in a diglossic relationship. There is no literacy based on the spoken variety. Taught in primary and secondary schools. *Other:* Buddhist (Lamaist), Christian. See main entry on page 90 (as Tibetan, Central). *Map:* 397:104.

Tichurong [tcn] (Ticherong). 2,420 (2000). Karnali Zone, Dolpa district, Thuli Bheri river basin. *Status:* 6a (Vigorous). *Class:* Sino-Tibetan, Tibeto-Burman, Western Tibeto-Burman, Bodish, Central Bodish, Central, gTsang. *Dialects:* None known. Reportedly similar to Dolpo [dre]. *Type:* SOV; postpositions; noun head final. *Writing:* Unwritten. *Other:* Culturally distinct from Dolpo. Buddhist. *Maps:* 394:5, 395:5.

Tilung [tij] (Tiling, Tilling, Tilung Blama). 1,420 (2011 census), decreasing. Sagarmatha Zone, southern Khotang district, Chyasmitar VDC, on Halesi Range last ridge, on Sunkosi river bank. *Status:* 8a (Moribund). Language of recognized indigenous nationality: Rai. *Class:* Sino-Tibetan, Tibeto-Burman, Western Tibeto-Burman, Himalayan, Kiranti, Western. *Dialects:* Choskule, Dorunkecha. Choskule and Dorungkecha dialects may be related languages. *Type:* SOV; postpositions. *Lg Use:* Mixed use: Religion. Elderly. Some use among young and older adults. *Writing:* Unwritten. *Other:* Geographically isolated community. Traditional religion, Hindu. *Map:* 397:110.

Tsum [ttz] (Tsumge). 4,790 (2000). Gandaki Zone, north Gorkha district, Tsum valley, the region drained by the Shiar Khola north of Ganesh Himal. Chekampar (Chokong) is prestige village. *Status:* 6a (Vigorous). Language of recognized indigenous nationality: Siyar. *Class:* Sino-Tibetan, Tibeto-Burman, Western Tibeto-Burman, Bodish, Central Bodish, Central, gTsang. *Dialects:* None known. 71%–78% intelligibility of Nubri [kte], 66% of Kyerung (Kyirong) [kgy]; 60%–66% of Lhasa Tibetan [bod]; 22%–25% of Northern Ghale [ghh], 14%–22% of Southern Ghale [ghe], 23%–27% of Kuke [ght]; 6% of Eastern Gorkha Tamang [tge], 14% of Western Gurung [gvr], 15% of Banspur Tamang. Divided into upper region, Yarba, and lower region, Ushug. *Type:* SOV. *Lg Use:* Vigorous. Home, friends. All ages. Very positive attitudes. Tibetan [bod] viewed very favorably in religious domain; Nepali [npi] viewed fairly positively as language of education and potential advancement. Minimal bilingualism in Nepali [npi], used only with those who do not understand Tsum. *Lg Dev:* Literacy rate in L2: 10% or less. A few primary schools. *Writing:* Unwritten. *Other:* Ethnonym: Tsumba, Glossonym: Tsumge by Tibetans in Kathmandu. Buddhist (Lamaist). *Map:* 395:30.

Urdu [urd]. 692,000 in Nepal (2011 census). L2 users: 22,900 in Nepal (1991 census). Southeast districts: Jhapa, Morang, Sunsari, Saptari, Siraha, Dhanusa, Mahottari, Sarlahi, and Rautahat, on India border; some in Banke district west. *Status:* 5 (Dispersed). *Other:* Muslim. See main entry on page 272.

Waling [wly] (Walung, Walüng). No known L1 speakers. Kosi zone, Bhojpur district, Khairang panchayat. *Status:* 10 (Extinct). *Class:* Sino-Tibetan, Tibeto-Burman, Western Tibeto-Burman, Himalayan, Kiranti, Eastern. *Lg Use:* Shifted to Bantawa [bap] in the late 1800s. *Writing:* Unwritten.

Walungge [ola] (Halung, Halungge, Walongchung Gola, Walung, Walungchung Gola, Walunggi Keccya). 1,500 in Nepal (2001 census), decreasing. 1,200 in the original language area. High language loss among those who have left the language area. Mechi Zone, Taplejung district, upper Tamar and Gunsa valleys. Small area in Kosi Zone. Also in China, India. *Status:* 6b (Threatened). Language of recognized indigenous nationality: Walung, Topkegola. *Class:* Sino-Tibetan, Tibeto-Burman, Western Tibeto-Burman, Bodish, Central Bodish, Unclassified. *Dialects:* Ghunsa River, Olangchung Gola (Upper Tamar River), Topke Gola (Mewa River). High intelligibility of Thudam [thw]. Reportedly similar to Tibetan dialect in Tingay District of Tibet. Lexical similarity: 71% with Lhasa Tibetan [bod], 68% with Dolpo [dre], Loke [loy], and Kyerung (Kyirong) [kgy], 66% with Lhomi [lhm] and Helambu Sherpa [scp], 64% with Nubri [kte], 57% with Jirel [jul], 55% with Sherpa [xsr]. *Lg Use:* Positive attitudes. *Writing:* Tibetan script. *Other:* Cut off from the Lhomi, with more links to Tibet. Some intermarriage with Lhomi and Tibetan. The people call themselves Sherpa. They do not have a specific language name which groups all varieties of the language together and distinguishes the language from other Tibetan languages. The word "Walungge" comes from a name of one of the main villages in the language area. Buddhist. *Map:* 396:79.

Wambule [wme] (Ambule, Caurasia, Chaurasia, Chaurasya, Chourase, Chourasia, Ombule, Tsaurasya, Umbule, Vambucauras Raduyor, Vambule). 13,500 (2011 census). A few elderly monolinguals. Sagarmatha Zone, south Okhaldhunga district, Wamdyal dialect: Rikdum, Lukuvapani, Wamdyal (Ubu), Huku, Sikapu, Tarkomdada, Salle, Dhepti, Dhaircaur, Khayapu, Lorphe, Thulacaur, Moli, Vaksa, Leva, Sinju, Gairigau, Dhemdalu, Kopsepu, Phasku, and Serankhu; Hilepane dialect: Pipale, Bhadare, Hilepani, Thakle, Mandhare, Sokma Tar, Dundunma, Jakma, Jerun, Ricuva, and Lambole; Udayapur dialect: Udayapur, Phedigau, Barasi, Ghiramdi, Simkaku, and Peku; west Khotang district, Jhappali dialect: Kurleghat, Majhkhani, Byanditar, Rupatar, Kharka, Cuvabot, Jhapa, Lurkhudada, Vaitar, Balui, Thumka, Pakauci, Goviar, Gurdum, Jayaram Gha, Bahuni Dada, Todke, Limlun, Damli, Vetagau, and Temtuku; Sagarmatha Zone, north Udaypur district and Janakpur Zone, northeast Sindhuli district, Hilepane dialect: Lekhani, Ghurmi, Salle, Sorun, Salleni, Pallo Salleni, Sindure, Majhkhani, Bhirpani, Kusumtar, and Jortighat. *Status:* 5 (Developing). Language of recognized indigenous nationality: Rai. *Class:* Sino-Tibetan, Tibeto-Burman, Western Tibeto-Burman, Himalayan, Kiranti, Western. *Dialects:* Bonu, Hilepane, Jhappali, Udaipure, Wamdyal. Dialects appear adequately mutually inherently intelligible. Jerung [jee] and Wambule are mutually intelligible (Opgenort 2004). Lexical similarity: 93% with Jerung [jee] (Opgenort 2005). *Type:* SOV; postpositions; noun head final; no noun classes or genders; content q-word in situ; 1 prefix, up to 4 (word-internal) suffixes and 4 phrasal affixes; clause constituents indicated by case-marking (and verbal marking for agent and patient); verbal affixation marks person and number; ergativity, but an expression of volitionality causes the intransitive subject to have ergative marking; both tense and aspect; no passives or voice; nontonal; 33 consonant and 9 vowel phonemes; ingressive laterals. *Lg Use:* Vigorous. Home, friends, religion; mixed use: Work, education. All ages. Also use Bahing [bhj], Jerung [jee], Nepali [npi]. *Lg Dev:* Taught in primary schools. Poetry. Magazines. New media. Videos. Dictionary. Grammar. *Writing:* Devanagari script. *Other:* Traditional religion, Christian, Hindu. *Map:* 397:109.

Wayu [vay] (Bayu, Hayu, Vayu, Wayo). 1,520 (2011 census), decreasing. 0 monolinguals. Ethnic population: 1,800 (2001 census). Janakpur Zone, Ramechhap district, Mudajor and Sukajor villages; Sindhuli district, Manedihi village. Sun Koshi valley across Mahabharat range south. *Status:* 7 (Shifting). Language of recognized indigenous nationality: Hayu. *Class:* Sino-Tibetan, Tibeto-Burman, Western Tibeto-Burman, Himalayan, Kiranti, Western. *Dialects:* Marin Khola, Sindhuli. *Type:* SOV; postpositions; noun head final; no noun classes or genders; content q-word in situ; clause constituents indicated by case-marking; verbal affixation marks person and number; ergativity; tense; no passives or voice; nontonal; 27 consonant and 8 vowel phonemes. *Lg Use:* Ethnic Wayu live on the hills on both sides of the Sun Kosi River but the language is only spoken in the villages listed. In 1995 many children in Mudajor were not learning Wayu but the language was alive and well in Manedihi (2002 UNESCO). A growing interest in language preservation. Religion; mixed use: Home, friends. Older adults and elderly. Some use among young adults. Negative attitudes among some Wayu who feel the language is an obstacle to progress; a minority would like to keep speaking it. 100% also use Nepali [npi]. *Writing:* Devanagari script. *Other:* Strong Nepali [npi] influences in phonology, lexicon, and grammar (Matisoff 1991). Traditional religion, Hindu. *Maps:* 396:57, 397:57.

Yakkha [ybh] (Dewansala, Yakha, Yakkhaba, Yakkhaba Cea, Yakkhaba Sala, Yakthomba). 19,600 in Nepal (2011 census), decreasing. Population total all countries: 20,410. Very few monolinguals. Ethnic population: 17,000. Kosi Zone, south Sankhuwasabha and east Dhankuta districts, east to Arun river between Hinuwankhola north and Leguwakhola south. Northern Yakkha dialect: south Sankhuwasabha district and adjoining extreme north Dhankuta district; Southern Yakkha dialect: Dhankuta district. Also in India. *Status:* 6b (Threatened). Language of recognized indigenous nationality: Yakkha. *Class:* Sino-Tibetan, Tibeto-Burman, Western Tibeto-Burman, Himalayan, Kiranti, Eastern. *Dialects:* Eastern Yakkha (Ilam, Panchthar), Northern Yakkha (Sankhuwasabha), Southern Yakkha (Dhankuta). Dialects have minimal diversity. Lexical similarity: with Athpariya [aph], Limbu [lif], and Yamphu [ybi]. *Type:* SOV; postpositions; noun head final; no noun classes or genders; content q-word in situ; 1 prefix, up to 10 suffixes (depending on analysis); clause constituents indicated by case-marking; verbal affixation marks person and number; ergativity; tense and aspect; passives and voice; nontonal; 22 consonant and 5 vowel phonemes. *Lg Use:* Home, friends, religion; mixed use: Work, education. Children and elderly. Some use among adolescents, young and older adults (Toba, Toba, and Rai 2005). Also use Nepali [npi]. Used as L2 by Limbu [lif]. *Lg Dev:* Literacy rate in L2: 10% in Nepali [npi]. There are attempts to teach Yakkha at school, and textbooks are published up to grade 3, but not widely used. Poetry. Dictionary. *Writing:* Unwritten. *Other:* Considered by many a distinct group of Kirati not fitting neatly into either Rai or Limbu groups (Bista 1996:39); in terms of mythology and people's own judgment, they seem closer to Limbu than to Rai groups. Traditional religion, Buddhist, Hindu. *Maps:* 396:82, 397:82.

Yamphu [ybi] (Yamphe, Yamphu Kha, Yamphu Rai). 9,210 (2011 census), decreasing. Kosi Zone, Sankhuwasabha district, Hedangna, Num, Seduwa, Peppuwa, Mangsimma, Karmarang, Tungkhaling, Uwa, Ala, Uling, and Walung villages. Eastern hills, upper Arun valley, Matsayapokhari VDC, extreme north Lorung area, directly southwest of Jaljale Mountains; Kosi Zone, Bhojpur district. *Status:* 6b (Threatened). Language of recognized indigenous nationality: Rai. *Class:* Sino-Tibetan, Tibeto-Burman, Western Tibeto-Burman, Himalayan, Kiranti, Eastern. *Dialects:* The Yamphu Rai are most closely related to Lohorung [lbr] and Mewahang. 61% intelligibility of Lohorung [lbr]. Lexical similarity: 84%–90% between dialects, 74%–84% with Southern Yamphu [lrr], 64%–67% with Lohorung [lbr]. *Lg Use:* Language passed on to children but being steadily replaced by Nepali (Toba, Toba, and Rai 2005). Religion. Almost all are bilingual in Nepali [npi] (2002 UNESCO). *Lg Dev:* Poetry. Dictionary. Grammar. *Writing:* Unwritten. *Other:* Traditional religion, Christian, Hindu. *Map:* 396:69.

Yamphu, Southern [lrr] (Lohorong, Lohrung, Lohrung Khap, Lohrung Khate, Southern Lohorung, Southern Lorung, Yakkhaba Lorung, Yamphu). 2,500 (2011 SIL), decreasing. Kosi Zone, Dhankuta district, Bodhe, Mounabudhuk, Bhedetar, and Rajarani; north Sankhuwasabha district, Devitar and Matsya Pokhari. South of the Tamorkhola, between the Jaruwakhola east and the Raghuwkhola west. *Status:* 6b (Threatened). Language of recognized indigenous nationality: Rai. *Class:* Sino-Tibetan, Tibeto-Burman, Western Tibeto-Burman, Himalayan, Kiranti, Eastern. *Dialects:* Gessa, Yamphe (Newahang Yamphe, Yakkhaba, Yakkhaba Khap, Yamphe Kha). 61% intelligibility of Lohorung [lbr], 43%–58% (depending on site) intelligibility of Yamphu [ybi]. A Rai group, most closely related to Yamphu [ybi], but distinct in grammar and phonology (Hansson 1991). Lexical similarity: 84%–89% between Southern Yamphu varieties, 74%–83% with Yamphu [ybi], 65%–68% with Lohorung [lbr]. *Type:* SOV; postpositions; verbal affixation marks person and number; tense; nontonal. *Lg Use:* Home, religion, work; mixed use: Friends. Young adults and older. Some use among children and adolescents. Positive attitudes. *Lg Dev:* Dictionary. *Writing:* Devanagari script. *Other:* Speakers of the language identify themselves ethnically as 'Yamphu'. Hansson (1991) described this group as two separate languages, "Yamphu" and "Southern Lorung" (cf. Ethnologue, 16th edition and earlier). Traditional religion, Christian, Hindu. *Maps:* 396:80, 397:80.

Korea, North

Democratic People's Republic of Korea. 23,350,000 (2008 census). Principal language: Korean. Literacy rate: 100% (2008 UNESCO). Immigrant language: Chinese (51,000). General references: Comrie 1987.

Only 1 language is listed for Korea, North. It is living and institutional.

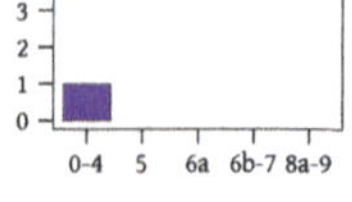

Korean [kor]. 23,300,000 in Korea, North (2008). *Status:* 1 (National). De facto national language. *Dialects:* Hamgyongdo (North Hamgyongdo, South Hamgyongdo),

Hwanghaedo, P'yong'ando (North P'yong'ando, South P'yong'ando). *Other:* Buddhist, Christian, Confucianist. See main entry on page 294.

Oman

Sultanate of Oman. 2,773,000 (2010 census). Principal language: Standard Arabic. Literacy rate: 87% (2008 UNESCO). Immigrant language: Urdu (30,000). General references: Holes 1988, 1990; Johnstone 1967. Deaf population: 103,100.

The number of individual languages listed for Oman is 16. All are living languages. Of these, 1 is institutional, 3 are developing, 5 are vigorous, 4 are in trouble, and 3 are dying. See map on page 398.

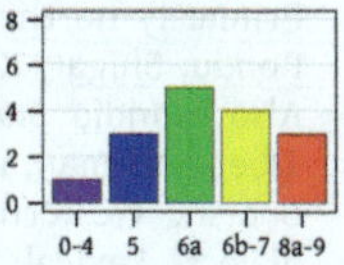

Arabic, Baharna Spoken [abv]. 10,000 in Oman (1995). *Status:* 6a (Vigorous). See main entry on page 53. *Map:* 398.

Arabic, Dhofari Spoken [adf] (Dhofari, Zofari). 70,000 (1996). Salala and nearby coastal regions. *Status:* 6a (Vigorous). *Class:* Afro-Asiatic, Semitic, Central, South, Arabic. A member of macrolanguage Arabic [ara] (Saudi Arabia). *Dialects:* None known. Related to Hadrami Spoken Arabic [ayh], Gulf Spoken Arabic [afb], and Omani Spoken Arabic [acx]. *Other:* Different from Omani Spoken Arabic [acx]. *Map:* 398.

Arabic, Gulf Spoken [afb] (Bedawi, Gulf Arabic, Khaliji, Omani Bedawi Arabic). 441,000 in Oman (1995). Inland Dhofar Governorate, on Saudi Arabia border, to the southeast coast; United Arab Emirates border regions. *Status:* 5 (Developing). *Other:* Muslim. See main entry on page 213. *Map:* 398.

Arabic, Omani Spoken [acx] (Omani Hadari Arabic). 720,000 in Oman (1996). Population total all countries: 853,900. Mainly in Hajar mountains highlands; a few coastal regions. Also in Djibouti, Kenya, Tanzania, United Arab Emirates. *Status:* 6a (Vigorous). *Class:* Afro-Asiatic, Semitic, Central, South, Arabic. A member of macrolanguage Arabic [ara] (Saudi Arabia). *Type:* SVO. *Map:* 398.

Arabic, Shihhi Spoken [ssh]. 22,000 in Oman (2000). *Status:* 6a (Vigorous). See main entry on page 308. *Map:* 398.

Arabic, Standard [arb]. Widespread. *Status:* 1 (National). Statutory national language (1996, Basic Law, Article 3). *Lg Use:* Education, official purposes, formal speeches. See main entry on page 293.

Balochi, Southern [bcc] (Baloci, Baluchi, Baluci). 130,000 in Oman (1993). Ethnic population: 312,000 (1993). Dispersed on the coast. *Status:* 6b (Threatened). *Dialects:* Barahuwi, Bashgaadi, Huuti, Makrani (Lotuni, Zadgaali). *Lg Use:* Ethnic Baloch who immigrated long ago are Omani citizens, but no longer speak Balochi. *Other:* From Pakistan. The majority are not Omani citizens. Muslim (Sunni). See main entry on page 266. *Map:* 398.

Bathari [bhm] (Batahari, Bathara). 200 in Oman (2011). Dhofar Governorate, coastal towns, from Al Jazeer to Shweymia. Also in Yemen. *Status:* 8b (Nearly extinct). *Class:* Afro-Asiatic, Semitic, South, South Arabian. *Dialects:* Reportedly very similar to Mehri [gdq], some considering it a dialect of Mehri. *Other:* Muslim. *Map:* 398.

Harsusi [hss] (Harsi 'Aforit, Hersyet). 600 (2011). South central Oman, Dhofar Governorate, Jiddat al-Harasis. *Status:* 7 (Shifting). *Class:* Afro-Asiatic, Semitic, South, South Arabian. *Dialects:* None known. Reportedly similar to Mehri [gdq], but usually considered a separate language. *Lg Use:* Increasing use and proficiency in Mehri [gdq]. *Other:* Spoken by the Harasis and 'Ifar ('Afar). *Map:* 398.

Hobyót [hoh] (Hewbyót, Hobi, Kalam Rifi). 100 in Oman (1998 H. Mutzafi). Near Yemen border. Also in Yemen. *Status:* 8a (Moribund). *Class:* Afro-Asiatic, Semitic, South, South Arabian. *Dialects:* None known. Related to and possibly a mixed language with Mehri [gdq] and Shehri [shv]. *Other:* Define themselves as Mahra tribe members. Muslim. *Map:* 398.

Kumzari [zum] (Kumzai). 1,700 in Oman (1993 census). Population total all countries: 2,300. North Oman, Musandam peninsula. Also in Iran. *Status:* 8a (Moribund). *Class:* Indo-European, Indo-Iranian, Iranian, Western, Southwestern, Luri. *Other:* Distinct from Khunsari [kfm] of Iran. Muslim. *Map:* 398.

Luwati [luv] (Khojki, Lawatiyya). 30,000 (Salman 2012). Mostly in Muscat city and coastal towns of Saham, Barka, Khabura, and Musana. *Status:* 6a (Vigorous). *Class:* Indo-European, Indo-Iranian, Indo-Aryan, Northwestern zone, Sindhi. *Dialects:* None known. Related to Kachchi [kfr]. *Type:* 37 consonants. *Other:* Ethnonym: Lawatiya, Khoja or Hyderabadi. Ancestors reportedly migrated from Iran to Hyderabad, then to Mutrah. Muslim (Shi'a). *Map:* 398.

Mehri [gdq] (Mahri). 50,800 in Oman (2000). South Oman near Yemen border. *Status:* 6b (Threatened). *Dialect:* Nagdi. *Lg Use:* Used as L2 by Harsusi [hss]. *Other:* Muslim. See main entry on page 317. *Map:* 398.

Persian, Iranian [pes] (Persian). 25,000 in Oman (1993). Scattered coastal cities. Mutrah area, Jabroo community, toward Ruwi. *Status:* 5 (Dispersed). *Lg Use:* Many women speak only Farsi. Men who go outside the community speak Arabic as L2, and many know 2 or 3 other languages. *Other:* Muslim (Shi'a). See main entry on page 204.

Shehri [shv] (Ehkili, Geblet, Jibali, Jibbali, Qarawi, Sehri, Shahari, Sheret). 25,000 (1993 census). Dhofar mountains and coastal plain. *Status:* 6b (Threatened). *Class:* Afro-Asiatic, Semitic, South, South Arabian. *Dialects:* Central Jibbali, Eastern Jibbali, Western Jibbali. Eastern Jibbali includes Kuria Muria (Baby Jibbali). Reportedly increasingly bilingual in Dhofari Arabic [adf]. *Other:* Spoken by Qara (Ehkeló, Ahkló), Shahra (Sheró, Shahara), Barahama, Bait Ash-Shaik, and some Batahira. Muslim. *Map:* 398.

Swahili [swh]. 22,000 in Oman. *Status:* 5 (Dispersed). See main entry on page 322.

Pakistan

Islamic Republic of Pakistan. 180,150,000 (2011 census). Principal languages: English, Urdu. Literacy rate: 41% (2009 UNESCO). Immigrant languages: Arabic (122,000), Chinese (6,000), Parsi (20,000), Rohingya (200,000), Southern Uzbek (50,000), Uyghur. General references: Addleton 1986; Bashir 2003; Decker and Decker 1992; Decker, Hallberg and Rensch 1992; Masica 1991; Morgenstierne 1974; Payne 1987; Shackle 1979, 1980; Strand 1973, 2001; Van Driem 2007. Deaf population: 244,000. Deaf institutions: 31.

The number of individual languages listed for Pakistan is 71. All are living languages. Of these, 5 are institutional, 18 are developing, 38 are vigorous, 8 are in trouble, and 2 are dying. See maps beginning on page 400.

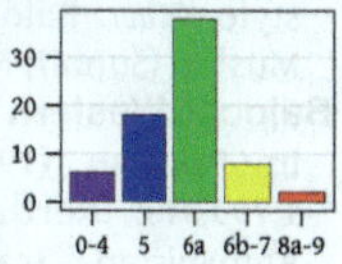

Aer [aeq]. 100 (1998). Women monolingual. Ethnic population: 330 Aer in Deh area. Lower Sindh, Jikrio Goth near Kunri, Deh area, Hyderabad, Jamesabad. *Status:* 6b (Threatened). *Class:* Indo-European, Indo-Iranian, Indo-Aryan, Central zone, Gujarati. *Dialects:* Jamesabad Aer, Jikrio Goth Aer. Lexical similarity: 78% with Katai Meghwar and Kachi Bhil–both dialects of Kachi Koli [gjk], 75%–77% with the Rabari dialect of Kachi Koli [gjk], 76% with Kachi Koli [gjk]. *Lg Use:* All ages. Also use Sindhi [snd] (adult men for common topics). 100% of boys and 25% of girls attend Sindhi medium schools. Also use Western Panjabi [pnb] (adult men of Jikrio Goth, only for common topics). Also use Gujarati [guj]. *Lg Dev:* Literacy rate in L2: 15% in Sindhi. *Writing:* Arabic script. *Other:* Unusual interrogative word suggests possible historical connection with Western Rajasthani group. Speakers in Pakistan running out of marriage possibilities and may have to move to India. The Indian group is most influential. Other Aer people in Nawabshah, Sindh reportedly speak a different language, dress differently, and do not intermarry with this group. Hindu. *Map:* 401.

Badeshi [bdz] (Badakhshi). No known L1 speakers. No known speakers for three or more generations. Ethnic population: 2,830 (2000). Bishigram valley upper reaches, east of Madyan, Swat Kohistan; small groups in Swat, Tirat and Pooran Chakesar valleys; Alai. *Status:* 9 (Dormant). *Class:* Indo-European, Indo-Iranian, Unclassified. *Lg Use:* Also use Pashto. *Other:* Only dominant area languages now used: Torwali [trw], Pashto or Ushojo [ush]. Muslim (Sunni).

Bagri [bgq] (Bagari, Bagria, Bagris, Bahgri, Baorias, Bawri). 200,000 in Pakistan. 100,000 in Sindh Province (1998). Sindh Province; Punjab. *Status:* 6a (Vigorous). *Lg Use:* Also use Sindhi [snd], Urdu [urd]. *Lg Dev:* Literacy rate in L1: Below 1%. Literacy rate in L2: Below 5%. *Other:* Distinct from Vaghri [vgr]. Nomadic. See main entry on page 103. *Map:* 401.

Balochi, Eastern [bgp] (Baloci, Baluchi, Baluci, Eastern Hill Balochi). 1,800,000 in Pakistan (1998). 5,000,000 including L2 users of all Balochi languages. Population total all countries: 1,800,800. Northeast Balochistan Province, northwest Sindh, southwest Punjab. Also in India. *Status:* 5 (Developing). *Class:* Indo-European, Indo-Iranian, Iranian, Western, Northwestern, Balochi. A member of macrolanguage Baluchi [bal]. *Lg Dev:* Literacy rate in L1: Below 1%. Literacy rate in L2: 5%–15%. Radio programs. Bible portions: 1815–1906. *Writing:* Arabic script, Nastaliq style. *Other:* Balochi is the official spelling in Pakistan. A major language in Pakistan. Distinct from Western Balochi [bgn] and Southern Balochi [bcc]. A small body of literature. Muslim (Sunni). *Map:* 401.

Balochi, Southern [bcc] (Baloci, Baluchi, Baluci, Makrani). 2,770,000 in Pakistan (1998). Population total all countries: 3,405,000. South Balochistan, south Sindh, Karachi. Also in Iran, Oman, United Arab Emirates. *Status:* 5 (Developing). *Class:* Indo-European, Indo-Iranian, Iranian, Western, Northwestern, Balochi. A member of macrolanguage Baluchi [bal]. *Dialects:* Coastal Balochi, Kechi (Keci), Makrani (Lotuni). Distinct from Eastern Balochi [bgp] and fairly distinct from Western Balochi [bgn]. *Lg Dev:* Literacy rate in L1: Below 1%. Literacy rate in L2: 5%–15%. Radio programs. NT: 1999. *Writing:* Arabic script, Nastaliq style. *Other:* Balochi is the official spelling in Pakistan. Muslim (Sunni), Muslim (Zikri). *Map:* 401.

Balochi, Western [bgn] (Baloci, Baluchi, Baluci). 1,116,000 in Pakistan (1998). Population total all countries: 1,799,840. Northwest Baluchistan Province. Also in Afghanistan, Iran, Tajikistan, Turkmenistan. *Status:* 5 (Developing). *Class:* Indo-European, Indo-Iranian, Iranian, Western, Northwestern, Balochi. A member of macrolanguage Baluchi [bal]. *Dialects:* Lashari, Rakhshani (Raxshani), Sarawani. Strongly influenced by Farsi, but not intelligible with Farsi [prs]. *Lg Use:* Used as L2 by Brahui [brh]. *Lg Dev:* Literacy rate in L1: 1%–5%. Literacy rate in L2: 5%–15%. Newspapers. Radio programs. Dictionary. Bible portions: 1984–2005. *Writing:* Arabic script, Nastaliq style, used in Afghanistan. *Other:* Balochi is the official spelling in Pakistan. A small body of literature. Muslim (Sunni). *Map:* 401.

Balti [bft] (Baltistani, Bhotia of Baltistan, Sbalti). 270,000 in Pakistan (1992). Population total all countries: 290,000. Primarily northeast Pakistan, Baltistan district, Skardu, Rondu, Shigar, Khapalu, Kharmang, and Gultari valleys. Also in India. *Status:* 5 (Developing). *Class:* Sino-Tibetan, Tibeto-Burman, Western Tibeto-Burman, Bodish, Central Bodish, Western. *Dialects:* Chorbat is most divergent dialect. Lexical similarity: 87%–100% among dialects, 78%–85% with Purik [prx]. *Lg Use:* Also use Shina [scl], Urdu [urd]. *Lg Dev:* Literacy rate in L2: 3%–5% in Urdu. Dictionary. Grammar. Bible portions: 1903–1940. *Writing:* Arabic script, used since the 17th century. Balti script, no longer in use. Devanagari script, used since the 1970s. Tibetan script, used between 8th and 17th century, recent efforts to revive usage. *Other:* Muslim (Shi'a). *Map:* 400:7.

Baluchi [bal]. A macrolanguage (see page 9). *Other:* Includes: Eastern Balochi [bgp], Southern Balochi [bcc], Western Balochi [bgn].

Bateri [btv] (Batera Kohistani, Baterawal, Baterawal Kohistani, Bateri Kohistani). 28,300 in Pakistan (2000). Population total all countries: 29,100. Extreme south, Kohistan district, Indus River east bank, some north of Besham; Batera area. Also in India. *Status:* 6a (Vigorous). *Class:* Indo-European, Indo-Iranian, Indo-Aryan, Northwestern zone, Dardic, Kohistani. *Dialects:* None known. Reportedly more similar to Indus Kohistani [mvy] than to Kohistani Shina [plk], but distinct from both. Lexical similarity: 58%–61% with Indus Kohistani, 60% with Gowro [gwf], 54% with Chilisso [clh], 29% with Kohistani Shina [plk] and Torwali [trw], 27% with Kalami [gwc]. *Lg Use:* Vigorous. Also use Pashto or Kohistani Shina [plk]. *Writing:* Devanagari script. *Map:* 400:21.

Bhaya [bhe]. 70 (1998). Lower Sindh Province, Kapri Goth near Samaro, Khipro area, Jamesabad, Mirke goth, Mirpurkhas, Phuladia, and a few in Hyderabad. Possibly in India. *Status:* 6b (Threatened). *Class:* Indo-European, Indo-Iranian, Indo-Aryan, Central zone, Western Hindi, Unclassified. *Dialects:* Similarity of key morphemes: The possessive postposition with, g-, contrasts with all other languages in the area. Gender endings match Marwari [mve]. May be the same as Bhoyari dialect of Malvi [mup] in India. May be in Western Hindi group. Lexical similarity: 84% with Marwari [mve], 75% with Malhi dialect of Dhatki [mki], 73% with Bhat, 72%–73% with Goaria [gig], 70%–73% with Sindhi Meghwar dialect of Sindhi Bhil [sbn], 63%–72% with Mogi, 63%–71% with Sindhi Bhil [sbn], 70% with Urdu [urd]. *Map:* 401.

Brahui [brh] (Birahui, Brahuidi, Brahuigi, Kur Galli). 4,000,000 in Pakistan (2011). Population total all countries: 4,220,000. South central, Quetta and Kalat region, east Baluchistan and Sind provinces. Also in Afghanistan, Iran, Turkmenistan. *Status:* 5 (Developing). *Class:* Dravidian, Northern. *Dialects:* Jharawan, Kalat, Sarawan. Kalat is standard dialect, Jharawan is lowland. Low percentage of lexical similarity with surrounding languages. *Lg Use:* Also use Western Balochi [bgn]. *Lg Dev:* Literacy rate in L1: Below 1%. Literacy rate in L2: Below 5%. Poetry. Newspapers. Dictionary. Grammar. NT: 1998.

Writing: Arabic script, Nastaliq style. *Other:* Muslim. *Map:* 401.

Burushaski [bsk] (Biltum, Brushaski, Burucaki, Burucaski, Burushaki, Burushki, Khajuna, Kunjut). 87,000 in Pakistan (2000), increasing. North Gilgit district areas, Hunza-Nagar and Yasin areas; scattered in Gilgit, Kashmir, and various cities. Also in India. *Status:* 6a (Vigorous). *Class:* Language isolate. *Dialects:* Hunza, Nagar (Nagir), Yasin (Werchikwar). Yasin is geographically separated from other dialects. Lexical similarity: 91%–94% between Nagar and Hunza dialects, 67%–72% between Yasin and Hunza, 66%–71% between Yasin and Nagar. *Type:* SOV. *Lg Use:* Vigorous, but acquiring Urdu [urd] borrowings. Positive attitudes. Yasin speakers also use Khowar [khw]. Women also use Urdu [urd]. Used as L2 by Domaaki [dmk], Khowar [khw], Wakhi [wbl]. *Lg Dev:* Literacy rate in L2: 20% in Hunza, less in Nagar. *Writing:* Arabic script, Nastaliq style, no longer in use, plans for future development using this script. Arabic script, Naskh style. Latin script. *Other:* Muslim (Shi'a), Muslim (Sunni). *Map:* 400:4.

Chilisso [clh] (Chiliss, Galos). 1,000 (1992 SIL). Ethnic population: 1,600. Indus river east bank, Indus Kohistan, Koli, Palas area. *Status:* 6a (Vigorous). *Class:* Indo-European, Indo-Iranian, Indo-Aryan, Northwestern zone, Dardic, Kohistani. *Dialects:* None known. Lexical similarity: 70% with Indus Kohistani [mvy], 65%–68% with Gowro [gwf], 54% with Bateri [btv], 48%–56% with Kohistani Shina [plk], 26% with Torwali [trw], 25% with Kalami [gwc]. *Lg Use:* Socially integrated with the Kohistani Shina [plk]. Almost all use Kohistani Shina [plk] as an L1 or L2. *Map:* 400:22.

Dameli [dml] (Damedi, Damel, Damia, Damiabaasha, Gidoji, Gudoji). 5,000 (Cacopardo and Cacopardo 2001), increasing. Kunar river east side, south Chitral district, south of Drosh, Damel valley. 4 main and several smaller villages. *Status:* 6a (Vigorous). *Class:* Indo-European, Indo-Iranian, Indo-Aryan, Northwestern zone, Dardic, Kunar. *Dialects:* 2 groups: Shinteri-Dondideri and Swati-Aspar, but no significant dialect variation. Lexical similarity: 44% with Gawar-Bati [gwt], Savi [sdg], and Palula [phl]; 33% with Kamviri [xvi]; 29% with Kati [bsh]. *Lg Use:* Vigorous. Home, community. All ages. A few men also use Urdu [urd]; a few women also use Pashto. *Lg Dev:* Literacy rate in L1: 0%. Urdu [urd] is used in schools. Poetry. *Other:* Speakers probably of mixed origin. Language influenced by Nuristani languages. Muslim (Sunni). *Map:* 400:12.

Dari [prs] (Afghan Persian, Badakhshi, Madaglashti, Tajik). 1,000,000 in Pakistan. 2,000–3,000 in Madaglasht (Chitral), and many Afghan refugees (1992 SIL). Southeast Chitral, Shishi Koh Valley, Madaglasht village; Peshawar, Rawalpindi, Lahore, Karachi, and other large cities. *Status:* 5 (Dispersed). *Lg Use:* Used as L2 by Hazaragi [haz]. *Other:* Madaglasht community in Chitral came from Badakhshan, Afghanistan 200 years ago. Other communities in Pakistan are primarily refugees or settlers from Afghanistan. Muslim. See main entry on page 48.

Dehwari [deh] (Deghwari). 13,000 (1998). Central Balochistan, Kalat, and Mastung. *Status:* 6a (Vigorous). *Class:* Indo-European, Indo-Iranian, Iranian, Western, Southwestern, Persian. *Lg Dev:* Literacy rate in L1: Below 1%. Literacy rate in L2: Below 5%. *Other:* Influenced by Brahui [brh]. *Map:* 401.

Dhatki [mki] (Dhati). 132,000 in Pakistan (2000). 100,000 in Sind (1987). Population total all countries: 148,400. Lower Sindh, Tharparkar, and Sanghar districts. Also in India. *Status:* 5 (Developing). *Class:* Indo-European, Indo-Iranian, Indo-Aryan, Central zone, Rajasthani, Marwari. *Dialects:* Barage, Central Dhatki, Eastern Dhatki, Malhi, Southern Dhatki. Varies considerably from northern Marwari [mve], though they claim to understand one another. Lexical similarity: 80%–83% with Marwari [mve] dialects, 88% with Dhatki of Rajasthan and Dhatki of Thar. *Lg Use:* Also use Sindhi [snd], Urdu [urd]. Used as L2 by Sindhi Bhil [sbn]. *Lg Dev:* Literacy rate in L1: Below 5%. Literacy rate in L2: Below 5%. Radio programs. Bible portions: 1999. *Writing:* Arabic script. *Other:* Hindu, Christian, Muslim. *Map:* 401.

Domaaki [dmk] (Doma, Dumaki). 340 (Matthias 2011), decreasing. Concentrated mostly in one village (Van Driem 2007). Gilgit district, areas north, mainly Hunza valley, Mominabad village; Big Nagar, Punyal; Shishkat; Gilgit, Shishkat; Oshkandas east of Gilgit, and Bakor village. *Status:* 8a (Moribund). *Class:* Indo-European, Indo-Iranian, Indo-Aryan, Central zone. *Dialects:* None known. Loanwords from Shina [scl] and Burushaski [bsk], but not mutually intelligible. Lexical similarity: 40% with Gilgit Shina [scl]. *Lg Use:* Home. Elderly only. Bilingualism is fairly high in Burushaski [bsk], especially among young people. Also use Shina [scl], Urdu [urd]. *Lg Dev:* Grammar. *Other:* Ethnonyms: Bericho, Dom, or Doma. Not all Doms speak Domaaki; most speakers concentrated in Mominabad and Hunza. Muslim. *Map:* 400:6.

English [eng]. L2 users: 17,000,000 in Pakistan (Crystal 2003). *Status:* 1 (National). Statutory national language (1973, Constitution, Article 251(2)). See main entry on page 319.

Gawar-Bati [gwt] (Arandui, Gowar-Bati, Gowari, Narisati, Narsati, Satre). 1,500 in Pakistan (1992). South Chitral, Arandu; along Kunar river south of Arandu. *Status:* 6a (Vigorous). *Lg Use:* Vigorous. All domains. Also use Northern Pashto [pbu]. *Other:* Refer to themselves as Kohistani, as do other ethnolinguistic groups in the region. Muslim (Sunni). See main entry on page 48. *Map:* 400:13.

Ghera [ghr] (Bara, Sindhi Ghera). 10,000 (1998). Hyderabad, 1 colony, between main bus stop and railway station. Speakers say more than 90% remained in Surat and Ahmedabad, India. *Status:* 6a (Vigorous). *Class:* Indo-European, Indo-Iranian, Indo-Aryan, Central zone, Western Hindi, Unclassified. *Dialects:* None known. Quite different grammatically from Gurgula [ggg]; reportedly similar to Urdu [urd]. Lexical similarity: 87% with Gurgula [ggg], 70% with Urdu [urd]. *Lg Use:* Also use Sindhi [snd], Urdu [urd]. *Lg Dev:* Literacy rate in L2: 20% Sindhi. *Other:* Almost totally urbanized. Hindu. *Map:* 401.

Goaria [gig]. 25,400 (2000). Widespread in Sindh Province (except Karachi), Larkana, Sukkur, Moro, Badin, and Umerkot. *Status:* 6a (Vigorous). *Class:* Indo-European, Indo-Iranian, Indo-Aryan, Central zone, Rajasthani, Marwari. *Dialects:* Maybe the same as Sadri (Gawari) [sck] in India. Lexical similarity: 75%–83% with Jogi, 76%–80% with Marwari [mve] sweeper caste, 72%–78% with Marwari (Meghwar dialect) [mve], 70%–78% with Loarki [lrk]. *Lg Use:* All domains except religion. All ages. Hindi [hin] used for worship. Adults also use Sindhi [snd]. *Lg Dev:* Literacy rate in L2: Below 1% in Sindhi. *Writing:* Arabic script. *Other:* Hindu.

Gowro [gwf] (Gabar Khel, Gabaro). 200 (1990), decreasing. Indus Kohistan east bank, Kolai area, Mahrin village. *Status:* 6b (Threatened). *Class:* Indo-European, Indo-Iranian, Indo-Aryan, Northwestern zone, Dardic, Kohistani. *Dialects:* None known. Lexical similarity: 65%–68% with Chilisso [clh], 62% with Indus Kohistani [mvy], 60% with Bateri [btv], 40%–43% with Kohistani Shina [plk], 25% with Torwali [trw], 24% with Kalami [gwc]. *Lg Use:* Most, if not all, also use Kohistani Shina [plk]. *Other:* Ancestral language of the Gabar Khel, a clan residing primarily in Mahrin (Indus Kohistan). Different from Gawri, an alternate name for Kalami [gwc]. *Map:* 400:23.

Gujarati [guj]. Lower Punjab, Sindh. *Status:* 5 (Developing). *Lg Use:* Used by all Parsi (5,000), many Ismaili Muslims, and many Hindu sweepers (10,000–100,000). Many Parsi and Ismaili Muslims are literate. Seemingly many Gujarati-speaking sweepers are shifting to Urdu [urd]. Used as L2 by Aer [aeq], Gurgula [ggg], Memoni [mby], Parkari Koli [kvx], Vaghri [vgr]. See main entry on page 113.

Gujari [gju] (Gogri, Gojari, Gojri, Gujer, Gujjari, Gujuri, Gujuri Rajasthani, Kashmir Gujuri). 300,000 in Pakistan (1992). 2,910 in Chitral (1969), 20,000 in Swat Kohistan (1987), 200,000–700,000 in Azad Jammu and Kashmir (1989). Widespread in the north, east Hazara district, NWFP, Kaghan valley, Azad Kashmir; scattered in south Chitral, Swat Kohistan; Dir Kohistan, NWFP; Gilgit. *Status:* 5 (Developing). *Dialects:* Eastern Gujari, Western Gujari. *Lg Use:* Most Gujars in Pakistani Punjab may have shifted to Panjabi [pnb]. Spoken in some pockets of Punjab by immigrants from elsewhere. *Other:* Some move seasonally with herds. Muslim. See main entry on page 113. *Maps:* 400:11, 401.

Gurgula [ggg] (Marwari Ghera). 35,300 (2000). Sindh Province, Bhens colony, Karachi; smaller urban centers of Mirpur Khas, Shahdadpur, Panj, Moro, Sabura and Tando Allahyar. *Status:* 6a (Vigorous). *Class:* Indo-European, Indo-Iranian, Indo-Aryan, Central zone, Rajasthani, Unclassified. *Dialects:* None known. Ghera [ghr] is quite different grammatically. Lexical similarity: 87% with Ghera [ghr]. *Lg Use:* All domains. Positive attitudes. Widespread multilingualism in Sindhi [snd] and Urdu [urd]. Also use Gujarati [guj], Urdu [urd]. *Lg Dev:* Literacy rate in L2: 5% in Urdu. *Writing:* Arabic script. *Other:* Hindu.

Hazaragi [haz] (Azargi, Hazara, Hezareh). 157,000 in Pakistan (2000). Many recent refugees from Afghanistan. Baluchistan, Qunduz area, Quetta, Karachi and Islamabad, some villages in rural Sindh. *Status:* 6a (Vigorous). *Lg Use:* Also use Dari [prs], Urdu [urd]. *Lg Dev:* Literacy rate in L1: Below 10%. Literacy rate in L2: 10%–30% Urdu [urd], Dari [prs], or Farsi. *Other:* Alternate names listed refer to the people. Group or regional names are (Central) Dai Kundi, Dai Zangi, Behsud, Yekaulang, (Southern) Polada, Urusgani, Jaguri, Ghazni Hazaras, Dai Miradad, Kabul. Muslim (Imami Shi'a). See main entry on page 48. *Map:* 401.

Hindko, Northern [hno] (Hazara Hindko, Hindki, Kagani, Kaghani). 1,880,000 (1981 census). Total Hindko in Pakistan 3,000,000 (1993). Hazara division, Mansehra and Abbotabad districts, Indus and Kaghan valleys and Indus valley tributaries, NWFP. *Status:* 5 (Developing). *Class:* Indo-European, Indo-Iranian, Indo-Aryan, Northwestern zone, Lahnda. A member of macrolanguage Lahnda [lah]. *Dialects:* Also related to Panjabi [pnb], Seraiki [skr], and Pahari-Potwari [phr]; which have all been called Greater Panjabi, forming part of Lahnda [lah]. Lexical similaritiy: 82%–92% with Northern Hindko dialects, 67%–82% with Northern and Southern Hindko [hnd] varieties. *Lg Use:* The educated also use Urdu [urd] with varied proficiency. Also use Pashto, Western Panjabi [pnb] with low proficiency. Used as L2 by Kundal Shahi [shd]. *Lg Dev:* Literacy rate in L2: Below 20%. Poetry. Radio programs. TV. NT: 1991. *Writing:* Arabic script. *Other:* Muslim (Sunni). *Maps:* 400:20, 401.

Hindko, Southern [hnd]. 625,000 (1981 census). Punjab Province, Attock district, to south Hazara division, NWFP; Kohat and Peshawar districts, NWFP. *Status:* 5 (Developing). *Class:* Indo-European, Indo-Iranian, Indo-Aryan, Northwestern zone, Lahnda. A member of macrolanguage Lahnda [lah]. *Dialects:* Attock Hindko (Attock-Haripur Hindko), Kohat Hindko (Kohati), Peshawar Hindko (Peshawari), Rural Peshawar Hindko. The dialect in Dera Ismail Khan, sometimes called, Hindko, is reportedly more similar to Seraiki [skr]. *Lg Use:* Also use Urdu [urd], Western Panjabi [pnb]. *Lg Dev:* Radio programs. TV. *Writing:* Arabic script. *Other:* Muslim (Sunni). *Maps:* 400:19, 401.

Jadgali [jdg] (Jat, Jatgali, Jatki). 100,000 in Pakistan (1998). Population total all countries: 110,000. Southeast Balochistan Province, southwest Sind. Also in Iran. *Status:* 6a (Vigorous). *Class:* Indo-European, Indo-Iranian, Indo-Aryan, Northwestern zone, Sindhi. *Lg Dev:* Literacy rate in L1: Below 1%. Literacy rate in L2: Below 5%. *Other:* Different from Jakati [jat] of Afghanistan and Ukraine. Muslim. *Map:* 401.

Jandavra [jnd] (Jhandoria). 5,000 (1998). South Sindh Province, Hyderabad to east of Mirpur Khas. Reportedly also in Jodhpur, Rajasthan, India. *Status:* 6a (Vigorous). *Class:* Indo-European, Indo-Iranian, Indo-Aryan, Central zone, Gujarati. *Dialects:* Lexical similarity: 74% with Bagri [bgq] and the Katai Meghwar dialect of Kachi Koli [gjk], 68% with Kachi Koli [gjk]. *Lg Use:* All ages. Also use Sindhi [snd], Urdu [urd]. *Lg Dev:* No literates. *Other:* Hindu. *Map:* 401.

Kabutra [kbu] (Nat, Natra). 1,000 (1998). Sindh, Umerkot, Kunri, and Nara Dhoro areas. Speakers say 90% of the people remain in Zal area of Marwar, India. *Status:* 6a (Vigorous). *Class:* Indo-European, Indo-Iranian, Indo-Aryan, Central zone, Western Hindi, Hindustani, Sansi. *Dialects:* Reported inherent intelligibility with Sansi [ssi] and the Sochi dialect of Sansi, and use Kabutra when speaking to them. Lexical similarity: 74% with the Sochi [ssi] language variety. *Lg Use:* Also use Sindhi Bhil [sbn], Urdu [urd]. *Lg Dev:* Literacy rate in L2: 5% in Urdu. *Other:* Hindu.

Kachchi [kfr] (Cuchi, Cutch, Kachchhi, Kachi, Katch, Katchi, Kautchy, Kutchchi, Kutchie). 50,000 in Pakistan (1998). Karachi. *Status:* 6a (Vigorous). *Dialect:* Jadeji. See main entry on page 116.

Kalami [gwc] (Bashgharik, Bashkarik, Baskarik, Dir Kohistani, Diri, Dirwali, Gaawro, Garwa, Garwi, Gawri, Gowri, Kalami Kohistani, Kohistana, Kohistani). 100,000 (Baart and Sagar 2004), increasing. Upper Swat Kohistan, between Peshmal and Kalam north to Kalam area upper valleys; Dir Kohistan in Thal, Lamuti, Biar, and Rajkot villages. *Status:* 6b (Threatened). *Class:* Indo-European, Indo-Iranian, Indo-Aryan, Northwestern zone, Dardic, Kohistani. *Dialects:* Dashwa, Kalam, Lamuti (Lamti), Rajkoti (Patrak), Thal, Ushu. Dialect differences do not hinder communication, except speakers of other dialects have difficulty with Rajkot. Lexical similarity: 90%–93% among main dialects; Rajkoti has 75% with Kalami; Dashwa has 77% with Kalami [gwc], and 74% with Rajkoti. *Lg Use:* Apparently few remaining speakers of Dashwa dialect. Men have routine proficiency in Pashto, women more limited; Rajkoti men are highly proficient in Pashto. Uneducated have low proficiency in Urdu [urd]. Used as L2 by Kalkoti [xka], Khowar [khw]. *Writing:* Arabic script, Nastaliq style. *Other:* Most widely understood indigenous language in north Swat and Dir Kohistan. Muslim. *Map:* 400:28.

Kalasha [kls] (Kalash, Kalashamon). 5,000 (Heegård Petersen 2006). 3,200 in Northern Kalasha area; unknown and decreasing number in Southern Kalasha area. South Chitral district. Southern Kalasha dialect: Urtsun valley; Northern Kalasha: Rumbur, Bumboret, and Birir valleys.

Status: 6a (Vigorous). *Class:* Indo-European, Indo-Iranian, Indo-Aryan, Northwestern zone, Dardic, Chitral. *Dialects:* Northern Kalasha (Birir, Bumboret, Rumbur), Southern Kalasha (Urtsun). Very little contact between northern and southern dialects of Kalasha, so there are difficulties in communication now. Lexical similarity: 75% southern dialect with northern dialects. *Type:* SOV. *Lg Use:* In the south, Kalasha is being supplanted by Khowar [khw] or Kati [bsh]. Home, in-group communication in the north. In the south Kati [bsh] sometimes used in the home for in-group communication. Speakers have proficiency in Khowar [khw]; in Birir, some men do not speak Khowar. Women are learning Khowar. In the south Khowar sometimes used in the home for in-group communication. Women are learning some Urdu [urd]. *Lg Dev:* Poetry. Dictionary. *Writing:* Arabic script. *Other:* Originally Kalasha was the language of most of the southern Chitral district. Now Khowar [khw] is the predominant language, with earlier languages just used in villages of the side valleys. Traditional religion, Muslim. *Map:* 400:8.

Kalkoti [xka]. 6,000 (2006). Khyber-Pakhtunkhwa Province, Dir Kohistan, Kalkot village. *Status:* 6a (Vigorous). *Class:* Indo-European, Indo-Iranian, Indo-Aryan, Northwestern zone, Dardic, Shina. *Dialects:* None known. Lexical similarity: 69% with Kalami [gwc], 59% with Palula [phl], 60% with Savi [sdg]. Kalkoti, Palula and Savi form a cluster of closely related varieties within the Shina group. *Lg Use:* Also use Kalami [gwc]. *Other:* Muslim. *Map:* 400:29.

Kamviri [xvi] (Kamdeshi, Kamik, Lamertiviri, Shekhani). 2,000 in Pakistan (2004). South Chitral district, Langorbat, Lamerot, Badrugal, and Urtsun valley. *Status:* 6a (Vigorous). *Dialects:* Kamviri, Shekhani. See main entry on page 48. *Map:* 400:10.

Kashmiri [kas] (Cashmeeree, Cashmiri, Kacmiri, Kaschemiri, Keshuri). 105,000 in Pakistan (1993). Azad Kashmir, south of Shina. *Status:* 5 (Developing). *Lg Use:* Negative attitudes. *Lg Dev:* Literacy rate in L1: 0%. See main entry on page 118. *Map:* 400:18.

Kati [bsh] (Bashgali, Kativiri, Nuristani). 3,700 in Pakistan (1992). Eastern Kativiri dialect: Chitral district, Gobar in Lutkuh valley, Kunisht in Rumbur valley, Shekhanan Deh in Bumboret valley and Urtsun valley. *Status:* 6a (Vigorous). *Dialects:* Eastern Kativiri (Shekhani), Mumviri, Western Kativiri. *Lg Use:* Used as L2 by Kalasha [kls]. *Other:* Eastern Kativiri dialect often called Shekhani in Pakistan, but different from Kamviri [xvi] dialect also called Shekhani in Southern Chitral. See main entry on page 48. *Map:* 400:1.

Khetrani [xhe]. 4,000. Northeast Balochistan Province. *Status:* 6a (Vigorous). *Class:* Indo-European, Indo-Iranian, Indo-Aryan, Northwestern zone, Lahnda. A member of macrolanguage Lahnda [lah]. *Dialects:* None known. Related to Siraiki [skr]. *Lg Dev:* Literacy rate in L1: Below 1%. Literacy rate in L2: Below 5%. *Other:* Influenced by Balochi. Muslim. *Map:* 401.

Khowar [khw] (Arniya, Chitrali, Chitrari, Citrali, Kashkari, Khawar, Patu, Qashqari). 223,000 in Pakistan (1992). Population total all countries: 242,200. Chitral; Ghizr valley, Shandur pass to Gupis; Gilgit district, Yasin and Ishkhoman valleys, north Swat valley, Ushu; Peshawar and Rawalpindi. Also in India. *Status:* 3 (Wider communication). *Class:* Indo-European, Indo-Iranian, Indo-Aryan, Northwestern zone, Dardic, Chitral. *Dialects:* East Khowar, North Khowar, South Khowar, Swat Khowar. Northern dialect considered more pure. Related to Kalasha [kls] but different. Lexical similarity: 86%–98% among dialects. *Type:* SOV. *Lg Use:* The most important language of Chitral. Also use Burushaski [bsk] in the Gilgit District. Also use English [eng] among the educated. Also use Shina [scl] in Gilgit District. Urdu [urd] used among the educated, and in schools. Also use Kalami [gwc]. Used as L2 by Burushaski [bsk], Kalasha [kls], Palula [phl], Yidgha [ydg]. *Lg Dev:* Literacy rate in L2: 15%–20% men, 1% women. Urdu used in schools. Newspapers. Radio programs. *Writing:* Arabic script. *Other:* Muslim (Sunni), Muslim (Ismaili). *Map:* 400:3.

Kohistani, Indus [mvy] (Khili, Kohistani, Kohiste, Mair, Maiyã, Maiyon, Shuthun). 200,000 (1992). Indus Kohistan district, west bank Indus river. *Status:* 6a (Vigorous). *Class:* Indo-European, Indo-Iranian, Indo-Aryan, Northwestern zone, Dardic, Kohistani. *Dialects:* Duber-Kandia (Khili, Manzari), Indus (Jijal, Mani, Pattan, Seo). A separate language from nearby varieties: Bateri [btv], Chilisso [clh]. Lexical similarity: 88%–92% between dialects, 69%–71% with Chilisso [clh], 61%–63%% with Gowro [gwf], 58%–61% with Bateri [btv], 36%–41% with Kohistani Shina [plk], 26%–28% with Kalami [gwc] and Torwali [trw]. *Writing:* Arabic script. *Other:* Mani and Manzari are not used for dialects, but are said to refer to brothers whose descendants settled in the 2 dialect areas. *Map:* 400:25.

Koli, Kachi [gjk] (Kachi, Kachi Gujarati, Katchi, Kohli, Kolhi, Koli, Kori, Kuchi, Vagari, Vagaria). 170,000 in Pakistan (1998). 80,000–100,000 Kachi Koli, 5,000–6,000 Rabari, 10,000 Kachi Bhil, 50,000 Vagri, 10,000 Katai Meghwar, 1,000 Zalavaria Koli. Population total all countries: 570,000. Lower Sindh, an area bordered by Sakrand and Nawabshah north, Matli south, and east beyond Mirpur Khas and Jamesabad, Tando Allahyar, and Tando Adam town areas. Also in India. *Status:* 5 (Developing). *Class:* Indo-European, Indo-Iranian, Indo-Aryan, Central zone, Gujarati. *Dialects:* Kachi, Kachi Bhil, Katai Meghwar, Rabari (Rahabari), Vagri (Kachi Meghwar), Zalavaria Koli. Becoming more like Sindhi [snd]. Lexical similarity: Kachi dialect; 89% with Kachi and Rabari, 96% with Kachi Bhil, 86% with Vagri, 92% with Katai Meghwar, 88% with Zalavaria Koli, 78% with Gujarati [guj], 76% with Wadiyara Koli [kxp]. *Lg Dev:* Literacy rate in L1: Below 1%. Literacy rate in L2: Below 5%. Grammar. NT: 2002. *Writing:* Arabic script. Gujarati script, used by older people. *Other:* People with basically the same language are socially quite distinct. Hindu. *Map:* 401.

Koli, Parkari [kvx] (Parkari). 250,000 (1995). Sindh, southeast tip bordering India, Tharparkar District, Nagar Parkar. Most lower Thar Desert, west as far as Indus River, bordered north and west by Hyderabad, to south and west of Badin. *Status:* 5 (Developing). *Class:* Indo-European, Indo-Iranian, Indo-Aryan, Central zone, Gujarati. *Dialects:* None known. Lexical similarity: 77%–83% with Marwari Bhil [mve], 83% with Wadiyara Koli [kxp]. *Lg Use:* Also use Gujarati [guj], Sindhi [snd], Urdu [urd]. *Lg Dev:* Literacy rate in L1: Below 1%. Literacy rate in L2: Below 5%, mostly in Sindhi, a few in Urdu, very few in Gujarati. NT: 1996. *Writing:* Arabic script. *Other:* Hindu. *Map:* 401.

Koli, Wadiyara [kxp] (Wadaria, Wadhiara). 175,000 in Pakistan (1998). 75,000 Wadiyara, 5,000 Mewasi and Nairya, 30,000 Tharadari, 45,000 Hasoria, 20,000 Rardro. Sindh, bounded by Hyderabad, Tando Allahyar and Mirpur Khas north, Matli and Jamesabad south. *Status:* 6a (Vigorous). *Dialects:* Hasoria Bhil, Hasoria Koli, Mewasi (Mayvasi Koli), Nairya Koli, Rardro Bhil, Tharadari Bhil, Tharadari Koli, Wadiyara Koli. *Lg Dev:* Literacy rate in L1: Below 1%. Literacy rate in L2: Below 5%. *Other:* Some strict caste rules about intermarriage and interdining are changing; possibly 'lower' groups wishing to move up, and barriers in closed castes breaking down. See main entry on page 121. *Map:* 401.

Kundal Shahi [shd] ("Rawri" *pej.*). 700 (Rehman and Baart 2005). Azad Kashmir, Neelam district, Kundal Shahi village, 72 km from Muzaffarabad. *Status:* 7 (Shifting). *Class:* Indo-European, Indo-Iranian, Indo-Aryan, Northwestern zone, Dardic, Shina. *Dialects:* None known. Lexical similarity: 50% with Shina [scl]. *Lg Use:* Home. Most speakers are over 40 years old. The language is being replaced by Hindko [hno] among the younger generations. *Writing:* Unwritten. *Other:* The language is spoken by the Qureshi ethnic group. *Map:* 400:17.

Lahnda [lah]. A macrolanguage (see page 9). *Other:* Includes: Khetrani [xhe], Mirpur Panjabi [pmu] (India), Northern Hindko [hno], Pahari-Potwari [phr], Seraiki [skr], Southern Hindko [hnd], Western Panjabi [pnb].

Lasi [lss] (Lassi). 15,000 (1998). Southeast Balochistan Province, Las Bela district, north-northwest of Karachi. *Status:* 6a (Vigorous). *Class:* Indo-European, Indo-Iranian, Indo-Aryan, Northwestern zone, Sindhi. *Lg Dev:* Literacy rate in L1: Below 1%. Literacy rate in L2: Below 5%. *Other:* Influenced by Balochi. Muslim. *Map:* 401.

Loarki [lrk]. 20,000 (1998). Sindh Province, rural. *Status:* 6a (Vigorous). *Class:* Indo-European, Indo-Iranian, Indo-Aryan, Central zone, Rajasthani, Marwari. *Dialects:* None known. Probably the same as Gade Lohar [gda] in Rajasthan, India, a Rajasthani language. Lexical similarity: 82% with Jogi, 80% with Marwari [mve]. *Lg Use:* All domains. All ages. Educated also use Urdu [urd]. Also use Sindhi [snd]. *Lg Dev:* Literacy rate in L2: 25% boys, some older men, no girls or women in Sindhi, some Urdu. *Other:* Alternate people names are: Loar, Lohar, Gadlia, Gadolia Rajput, Gadolia Rajput Loar, Karia, Sisudia Rajput, Sisudia Loar. Hindu.

Marwari [mve] (Jaiselmer, Marawar, Marwari Bhil, Marwari Meghwar, Merwari, Rajasthani). 220,000. 100,000 Northern Marwari, 120,000 or more Southern Marwari (1998). The latter 100,000 Marwari Bhil, 10,000 Marwari Meghwar, 12,000 to 13,000 Marwari Bhat. Northern Marwari dialect: south Punjab and north Sindh, north of Dadu and Nawabshah; Southern Marwari: Sindh and south Punjab provinces, between Tando Mohammed Khan and Tando Ghulam Ali south, Dadu and Nawabshab north. *Status:* 4 (Educational). *Class:* Indo-European, Indo-Iranian, Indo-Aryan, Central zone, Rajasthani, Marwari. A member of macrolanguage Marwari [mwr] (India). *Dialects:* Marwari Bhat, Marwari Bhil, Marwari Meghwar, Northern Marwari, Southern Marwari. Northern and Southern Marwari mutually inherently intelligible. Lexical similarity: 79%–83% with Dhatki [mki], 87% between Southern and Northern Marwari, 78% with Marwari Meghwar and Marwari Bhat dialects. *Lg Use:* One sweeper community of 10,000–100,000 identifies itself as Marwari, but is undergoing rapid shift to Urdu [urd]. Marwari is not usually written. Hindi [hin] is literary language in Rajasthan. Speakers are moderately bilingual in Sindhi [snd], educated speakers also use Sindhi. Educated speakers also use Urdu [urd]. *Lg Dev:* Literacy rate in L1: Below 1%. Literacy rate in L2: Below 5% in Sindhi or Urdu. Newspapers. Bible portions: 1969–1991. *Writing:* Arabic script, Nastaliq and Naskh styles. *Other:* 'Rajasthani' is a linguistic cover term for a group of languages. Speakers tend to be urban and educated. Northern Bhil tribes: Marwari-Thori, Gulguli, Shikari, Jogi, Sochi. Hindu, Christian, Muslim. *Map:* 401.

Memoni [mby]. Karachi. *Status:* 7 (Shifting). *Class:* Indo-European, Indo-Iranian, Indo-Aryan, Unclassified. *Dialects:* None known. Reportedly similar to Sindhi [snd] and Gujarati [guj]. *Lg Use:* Mainly adults. Also use Gujarati [guj], Sindhi [snd], Urdu [urd]. *Lg Dev:* Most are highly educated. *Other:* Reportedly 500–600 years ago Memoni speakers moved from a Sindhi-speaking area to a Gujarati-speaking area. Muslim.

Od [odk] (Oad, Odki). 50,000 (1998). Widespread in Sindh; a few in south Punjab. Possibly in Rajasthan, India. *Status:* 6a (Vigorous). *Class:* Indo-European, Indo-Iranian, Indo-Aryan, Unclassified. *Dialects:* Resembles Marathi [mar] with Gujarati [guj] features and borrowings from Marwari [mve] and Panjabi. Lexical similarity: 86%–88% among dialects in Dadu, Shikarpur, and Pithoro, 70%–78% with Marwari [mve], Dhatki [mki] and Bagri [bgq]. *Lg Use:* 80% also use Sindhi [snd]. Also use Urdu [urd]. *Writing:* Arabic script. *Map:* 401.

Ormuri [oru] (Baraki, Baraks, Bargista, Ormui, Ormur, Urmuri). 6,000 in Pakistan (2004 R. Burki). Population total all countries: 6,050. Kaniguram, a pocket in Mahsud Pashto area northwest of Dera Ismail Khan, Wazirstan. Also in Afghanistan. *Status:* 6a (Vigorous). *Class:* Indo-European, Indo-Iranian, Iranian, Western, Northwestern, Ormuri-Parachi. *Dialects:* Kanigurami, Logar. Lexical similarity: 27% with Waneci [wne], 25%–33% with Pashto dialects. *Lg Use:* Kanigurami retain the language. *Lg Dev:* Poetry. Dictionary. Grammar. *Writing:* Arabic script. *Map:* 401.

Pahari-Potwari [phr] (Chibhali, Dhundi-Kairali, Pothohari, Potohari, Potwari). 2,500,000 (Lothers and Lothers 2007). Pahari: Rawalpindi, Murree Hills, and east in Azad Kashmir (Poonchi (Punchhi) and Chibhali); north in the lower half of the Neelum Valley. Potwari: Pothwar Plateau, from Rawalpindi to Gujar Khan and south to Jhelum. Mirpuri: southern Azad Kashmir. *Status:* 6a (Vigorous). *Class:* Indo-European, Indo-Iranian, Indo-Aryan, Northwestern zone, Lahnda. A member of macrolanguage Lahnda [lah]. *Dialects:* Chibhali, Mirpuri, Pahari (Dhundi-Kairali), Pothwari (Potwari), Punchhi (Poonchi). 'Pahari', hill language; Potwari is the language of the Pothwar Plateau. A chain of related varieties with Punjabi [pnb], Hindko [hno] [hnd], and Saraiki [skr], also called Greater Panjabi. Degree of similarity to Western Pahari varieties in India unknown. Lexical similarity: 76%–84% among varieties called, Pahari, Potwari, and some called Hindko in Mansehra, Muzzaffarabad, and Mirpuri in Jammu. *Writing:* Arabic script, Nastaliq style. *Other:* Muslim. *Maps:* 400:16, 401.

Pakistan Sign Language [pks] (Isharon Ki Zubann). *Status:* 5 (Developing). *Class:* Deaf sign language. *Dialects:* Some regional variation in vocabulary. Related to Nepalese Sign Language [nsp]; may be identical to Indian Sign Language [ins]. *Lg Use:* Used in urban centers. The National Institute of Special Education encourages a total communication approach, including the teaching of PSL. *Lg Dev:* Dictionary. Grammar.

Palula [phl] (Biyori, Dangarikwar, Palola, Phalulo, Phalura). 10,000 (Liljegren 2008). Population of Ashret and Biori Valleys is almost completely monolingual (Liljegren 2008). L2 users: Used and understood by many other-tongue speakers in Badrugal and Kalkatak. Lower east Chitral river, Ashret and Biori, 12 villages; some in main valley, Kalkatak, and Shishi Koh valley, Purigal; reportedly some in Dir Kohistan. Ashreti dialect: Ashret Valley; Northern Palula dialect: Biori Valley, Kalkatak, and Purigal. *Status:* 6a (Vigorous). *Class:* Indo-European, Indo-Iranian, Indo-Aryan, Northwestern zone, Dardic, Shina. *Dialects:* Ashreti, Northern Palula. No, or limited, intelligibility of Kalkoti [xka] and Savi [sdg]. Lexical similarity: 92% with Ashreti and Northern Palula dialects,

56%–58% with Savi [sdg] in Afghanistan, 38%–42% with Kohistani Shina [plk]. Palula, Kalkoti [xka] (spoken in Dir Kohistan) and Savi [sdg] (spoken in Afghanistan) form a cluster of closely related varieties within the Shina group (Liljegren 2008). *Lg Use:* Vigorous within Ashret and Biori valleys. Reluctant to use Palula when speakers of other languages are present. Home, community. All ages. Positive attitudes. Also use Khowar [khw], Northern Pashto [pbu]. *Lg Dev:* 2-year mother-tongue multilingual education program (bridging from Palula to Urdu) now tested in two locations (2012). Taught in primary schools, but limited. Poetry. Dictionary. *Writing:* Arabic script. *Other:* Muslim (Sunni). *Map:* 400:9.

Panjabi, Western [pnb] (Lahanda, Lahnda, Lahndi, Lahori, Majhi, Western Punjabi). 60,600,000 in Pakistan (2000). Population total all countries: 62,613,000. Mainly in Punjab. Also in Canada, India, United Arab Emirates, United Kingdom, United States. *Status:* 5 (Developing). *Class:* Indo-European, Indo-Iranian, Indo-Aryan, Northwestern zone, Lahnda. A member of macrolanguage Lahnda [lah]. *Dialects:* A continuum of related varieties between Eastern Panjabi [pan] in India and Western Panjabi, and 'Lahnda'. Lahnda (originally called Western Panjabi by Grierson) is a label for the dialect continuum between Hindko [hno] [hnd], Pahari-Potwari [phr], and Saraiki [skr]; Lahnda varieties are 70%–85% lexically similar to Punjabi [pan]. Lexical similarity: 70%–85% with Punjabi [pan]. *Lg Use:* Educated younger generations living in cities opt to use Urdu [urd] and English [eng], and parents also encourage them to use Urdu or English even at home. Home, community, religious settings. All ages. Positive attitudes. Used as L2 by Aer [aeq], Northern Hindko [hno], Sansi [ssi], Southern Hindko [hnd]. *Lg Dev:* Newspapers. Radio programs. Films. TV. Videos. Grammar. NT: 1819–2000. *Writing:* Arabic script. Khojki script. Lahnda (Landa) script, no longer in use. *Other:* Muslim (Sunni), Christian. *Map:* 401.

Pashto, Central [pst] (Mahsudi, Waziri). 6,520,000 (2013 SIL). Wazirstan, Bannu, Karak, southern ethnic group territories and adjacent areas. *Status:* 6a (Vigorous). *Class:* Indo-European, Indo-Iranian, Iranian, Eastern, Southeastern, Pashto. A member of macrolanguage Pushto [pus]. *Dialects:* Bannuchi (Bannochi, Bannu), Waciri (Waziri). Lexical comparison and interviews indicate this is distinct from Northern Pashto [pbu] and Southern Pashto [pbt]. *Lg Use:* Used as L2 by Savi [sdg], Ushojo [ush]. *Lg Dev:* Dictionary. Grammar. *Writing:* Arabic script. *Other:* Muslim (Sunni). *Map:* 401.

Pashto, Northern [pbu] (Pakhto, Pashtu, Pushto, Yousafzai Pashto, Yusufzai Pashto). 18,700,000 in Pakistan (2013 SIL). Population total all countries: 20,540,000. Ethnic population: Possibly 49,600,000 Pashto in all countries. Afghanistan border, most of NWFP, Yusufzai, and Peshawar. Also in Afghanistan, Canada, India, United Arab Emirates, United Kingdom, United States. *Status:* 4 (Educational). *Class:* Indo-European, Indo-Iranian, Iranian, Eastern, Southeastern, Pashto. A member of macrolanguage Pushto [pus]. *Dialects:* Eastern Afghan Pashto, Ningraharian Pashto, Northeastern Pashto. Much similarity with Northwestern Pashto in Afghanistan. Subdialects of Northeastern Pashto are Kohat (Khatak), Yusufzai (Peshawar), Afridi, Shinwari, Mohmand, Shilmani. Lexical similarity: 80% between Northeastern and Southwestern Pashto. *Lg Use:* Rich literary tradition. The Powinda are a nomadic Pashto-speaking group. Used as L2 by Gawar-Bati [gwt], Palula [phl]. *Lg Dev:* Literacy rate in L2: Low. Taught in primary schools. Poetry. Magazines. Newspapers. New media. Radio programs. Films. TV. Videos. Dictionary. Grammar. Bible: 1895. *Writing:* Arabic script, Nastaliq and Naskh styles. *Other:* Muslim (Sunni), Muslim (Shi'a). *Maps:* 400:14, 401.

Pashto, Southern [pbt] (Pashtu, Pushto, Pushtu, Quetta-Kandahar Pashto). 4,580,000 in Pakistan (2013 SIL). Balochistan, Quetta area. *Status:* 5 (Dispersed). *Dialects:* Quetta Pashto, Southeastern Pashto. *Lg Use:* Some Pashto educated in Urdu [urd] medium schools mix the languages. Used as L2 by Torwali [trw]. *Other:* Muslim. See main entry on page 50. *Map:* 401.

Pushto [pus]. A macrolanguage (see page 9). *Other:* Includes: Central Pashto [pst], Northern Pashto [pbu], Southern Pashto [pbt] (Afghanistan).

Sansi [ssi] (Bhilki). 16,200 in Pakistan (2000). North Sindh Province, Karachi. Sochi dialect: throughout Sindh Province. *Status:* 6b (Threatened). *Dialect:* Sochi. *Lg Use:* Also use Seraiki [skr], Sindhi [snd], Urdu [urd], Western Panjabi [pnb]. *Lg Dev:* Literacy rate in L1: Below 1%. Literacy rate in L2: Below 5%. *Other:* Bhils by caste. Immigrated from India in 1947. Hindu, Muslim. See main entry on page 142. *Map:* 401.

Savi [sdg] (Sau, Sauji, Sawi). Sau, Kunar valley; Dir, many in refugee camps near Timargarha; Chitral, near Drosh; a few in Jalalabad. *Status:* 6a (Vigorous). *Lg Use:* Also use Central Pashto [pst]. *Lg Dev:* Literacy rate in L1: Below 1%. Literacy rate in L2: 5%–15%. *Other:* Muslim. See main entry on page 50.

Seraiki [skr] (Bahawalpuri, Multani, Riasiti, Saraiki, Siraiki, Southern Panjabi). 13,900,000 in Pakistan (1998 census). Population total all countries: 13,968,000. South Punjab and north Sind, Indus river valley, Jampur area. Derawali dialect: Dera Ismail Khan, Tank, Bannu, and Dera Ghazi Khan; Jangli dialect: Sahiwal area. Also in India, United Kingdom. *Status:* 5 (Developing). *Class:* Indo-European, Indo-Iranian, Indo-Aryan, Northwestern zone, Lahnda. A member of macrolanguage Lahnda [lah]. *Dialects:* Bahawalpuri (Reasati, Riasati), Derawali, Jangli, Jatki, Multani (Khatki). Dialects blend together into Panjabi east and Sindhi [snd] south. Until recently it was considered a dialect of Panjabi. 80% intelligibility of Dogri [dgo]. Lexical similarity: 85% with Sindhi [snd]; 68% with Dhatki [mki], Od [odk], and Sansi [ssi]. *Lg Use:* Used as L2 by Sansi [ssi]. *Lg Dev:* Literacy rate in L1: Below 1%. Literacy rate in L2: 5%–15%. Radio programs. TV. Dictionary. Grammar. NT: 1819. *Writing:* Arabic script, primary usage. Devanagari script, no longer in use. Gurmukhi script, no longer in use. Khojki script. *Other:* Muslim, Hindu. *Map:* 401.

Shina [scl] (Brokpa, Shinaki, Sina). 337,000 in Pakistan (1998 census), increasing. Population total all countries: 371,400. North, Gilgit District, scattered villages in Yasin and Ishkoman valleys, Punial, Gilgit, Haramosh, lower Hunza Valley; Diamer district, Chilas area, Darel and Tangir valleys, Astor Valley; scattered in Baltistan district, Satpara, Kharmang, Kachura, and other small valleys; NWFP, east Kohistan district, Sazin, Harban. Also in India. *Status:* 6a (Vigorous). *Class:* Indo-European, Indo-Iranian, Indo-Aryan, Northwestern zone, Dardic, Shina. *Dialects:* Astori (Astor, Dras, Gurezi, Kharmangi, Satpara), Chilasi Kohistani (Chilas, Darel, Harban, Sazin, Tangir), Gilgiti (Bagrote, Bunji, Gilgit, Haramosh, Hunza-Nagar, Punial, Rondu). Gilgit functions as the language standard. Shina is the primary language in Gilgit and Diamer districts. Lexical similarity: 79%–99% within Gilgiti (Northern) dialect subgroup, 81%–96% with Astori (Eastern) subgroup, 84%–98% with Chilas (Diamer) subgroup. *Lg Use:* Vigorous. All domains. All ages. Positive attitudes. Also use Urdu [urd]. Used as L2 by Balti [bft], Domaaki [dmk], Khowar [khw]. *Lg Dev:* Literacy rate in L1: 0%. Bible portions: 1929. *Writing:* Arabic script. *Other:*

Ethnonym: Brokpa in Baltistan and Ladakh. Glossonym: Brokskat, name also used semiofficially in India to refer to a highly divergent variety of Shina spoken by Buddhists. Muslim (Sunni), Muslim (Shi'a). *Map:* 400:15.

Shina, Kohistani [plk] (Kohistani, Kohistyo, Palasi-Kohistani). 200,000 (1981 census), increasing. Kohistan district, NWFP, east bank Indus river, Jalkot, Palas, and Kolai valley areas. *Status:* 6a (Vigorous). *Class:* Indo-European, Indo-Iranian, Indo-Aryan, Northwestern zone, Dardic, Shina. *Dialects:* Jalkoti, Kolai, Palasi. A somewhat divergent variety of Shina linguistically and socially. Reportedly similar to Shina [scl] of Chilas, but more distant from Gilgit [scl] dialect. *Lg Use:* Vigorous. All domains. All ages. Positive attitudes. Used as L2 by Bateri [btv], Chilisso [clh], Gowro [gwf]. *Lg Dev:* Literacy rate in L1: 0%. *Other:* Muslim (Sunni). *Map:* 400:24.

Sindhi [snd]. 18,500,000 in Pakistan (Johnstone and Mandryk 2001). Population total all countries: 20,270,500. Sindh. Possibly also United Arab Emirates. Also in Belize, Canada, India, Nepal, Philippines, Singapore, United Kingdom, United States. *Status:* 2 (Provincial). De facto provincial language in Sindh. *Class:* Indo-European, Indo-Iranian, Indo-Aryan, Northwestern zone, Sindhi. *Dialects:* Dukslinu (Hindu Sindhi), Kachchi, Katiawari Kachi, Lari, Lasi, Macharia, Shikari Bhil, Sindhi Musalmani (Muslim Sindhi), Thareli, Vicholo (Central Sindhi, Viccholi, Vicholi). Some southern Bhil groups speak dialects of Sindhi. 100,000 in rural Sindh originally from Kathiawar Peninsula in India are Muslims, exhibit widespread bilingualism in Sindh, and are almost completely assimilated with the Sindhi people. *Lg Use:* Used as L2 by Aer [aeq], Bagri [bgq], Dhatki [mki], Ghera [ghr], Goaria [gig], Gurgula [ggg], Jandavra [jnd], Loarki [lrk], Marwari [mve], Memoni [mby], Od [odk], Parkari Koli [kvx], Sansi [ssi], Sindhi Bhil [sbn], Vaghri [vgr]. *Lg Dev:* Radio programs. Dictionary. Grammar. Bible: 1954. *Writing:* Arabic script, Nastaliq style. Devanagari script. Gurmukhi script, used in India. *Other:* Shikari (hunter) Bhils are a nomadic group of 2,000 to 3,000 who live in south Sindh Province, centered around Badin, and have adopted the Sindhi language. Muslim, Hindu. *Map:* 401.

Sindhi Bhil [sbn]. 56,500 (2000). Sindh Province, Mohrano, Badin-Matli-Thatta, and Ghorabari (on west). Sindhi Meghwar scattered from Badin-Matli to Tando Allahyar area. *Status:* 6a (Vigorous). *Class:* Indo-European, Indo-Iranian, Indo-Aryan, Northwestern zone, Sindhi. *Dialects:* Badin, Mohrano, Sindhi Bhil, Sindhi Meghwar. Badin dialect is reportedly similar to Sindhi [snd]. Lexical similarity: 82% between the Mohrani dialect and Sindhi; 89% between Sindhi Bhil [sbn] and Sindhi Meghwar. *Lg Use:* Positive attitudes. Also use Dhatki [mki], Sindhi [snd]. Used as L2 by Kabutra [kbu]. *Other:* Sindhi or Dhatki orthographies are acceptable. Hindu, Muslim. *Map:* 401.

Torwali [trw] (Torwalak, Torwali Kohistani, Turvali). 80,000 (Lunsford 2001). Bahrain dialect: Upper Swat district, both sides of Swat river, from just north of Madyan up to Asret (located between Mankjal and Peshmal); Chail dialect: Primarily 2 villages in the Chail valley, 5–8 km east of Madyan. *Status:* 6a (Vigorous). *Class:* Indo-European, Indo-Iranian, Indo-Aryan, Northwestern zone, Dardic, Kohistani. *Dialects:* Bahrain, Chail. Lexical similarity: 44% with Kalkoti [xka] and Kalami [gwc], 89% with Bahrain and Chail dialects. *Lg Use:* Home, community. All ages. Very positive attitudes. Also use Southern Pashto [pbt], Urdu [urd]. Used as L2 by Ushojo [ush]. *Lg Dev:* Curriculum was developed for a 2-year multilingual education program that bridges children from Torwali to Urdu [urd]. Taught in primary schools, but only to a limited extent. Poetry. Dictionary. *Writing:* Arabic script. *Other:* Muslim (Sunni). *Map:* 400:27.

Urdu [urd] (Bihari). 10,000,000 in Pakistan (1998 census). Population total all countries: 63,948,800. L2 users: 94,000,000 in Pakistan (1999). Widespread. Also in Bahrain, Bangladesh (Bihari), Botswana, Canada, Denmark, Fiji, Germany, India, Malawi, Mauritius, Nepal, Norway, Oman, Qatar, Saudi Arabia, Singapore, South Africa, Thailand, United Arab Emirates, United Kingdom, United States, Zambia. *Status:* 1 (National). Statutory national language (1973, Constitution, Article 251(1)). *Class:* Indo-European, Indo-Iranian, Indo-Aryan, Central zone, Western Hindi, Hindustani. *Dialects:* Intelligible with Hindi, but formal vocabulary borrowed from Arabic and Persian. Dakhini dialect of Urdu [urd] in India has fewer Persian and Arabic loans than Urdu. Rekhta is a form of Urdu used in poetry. *Lg Use:* All domains. All ages. *Lg Dev:* Taught in primary and secondary schools. Fully developed. Bible: 1843–1998. *Writing:* Arabic script, Nastaliq style, primary usage. Braille script. *Other:* Muslim (Sunni). *Map:* 401.

Ushojo [ush] (Ushuji). 2,000 (1992). Swat Kohistan, upper reaches of Bishigram valley, east of Madyan. 12 villages. *Status:* 6a (Vigorous). *Class:* Indo-European, Indo-Iranian, Indo-Aryan, Northwestern zone, Dardic, Shina. *Dialects:* None known. Lexical similarity: 50% with Kolai Shina [plk], 48% with Palas Shina [plk], 42% with Gilgiti Shina [scl], 35% with Chail Torwali [trw], 31% with Palula [phl], 27% with Bateri [btv], 23% with Kalami [gwc], 22% with Kalkoti [xka]. *Type:* SOV. *Lg Use:* All ages. Also use Central Pashto [pst], Torwali [trw], Urdu [urd]. *Other:* Not known by linguists until 1989. Reportedly came from Kolai, Indus Kohistan several hundred years ago via Ushu, Swat, hence the name Ushojo. Muslim (Sunni). *Map:* 400:26.

Vaghri [vgr] (Bavri, Salavta, Vaghri Koli). 10,000 (1998). Sindh, in Sukkur, Karachi, Nawabshah, Sakrand, Hala, Sanghar, Tando Adam, Tando Mohammed Khan, Badin, Matli, Tando Ghulam Ali, Digri, Noakot, Jang Sai, Mirpur Khas, and Tando Allahyar. Possibly 90,000 in India. *Status:* 6a (Vigorous). *Class:* Indo-European, Indo-Iranian, Indo-Aryan, Central zone, Gujarati. *Dialects:* None known. Reportedly related to Kukar people's language who live near Chanesar Halt, Mehmoodabad in Karachi. Lexical similarity: 78% with Wadiyari Koli [kxp]. *Lg Use:* Also use Gujarati [guj], Sindhi [snd], Urdu [urd]. *Lg Dev:* Literacy rate in L1: Below 1%. Literacy rate in L2: Below 5%. *Other:* Urbanized. Hindu.

Wakhi [wbl] (Khikwar, Vakhan, Wakhani, Wakhigi). 20,000 in Pakistan (2008), increasing. 4,500–6,000 Gojal, 2,000 Ishkoman, 200 Yasin, 900 Yarkhun (1992), plus refugees. Northeasternmost Chitral, Baroghil area, in glacier area. Gojal dialect: upper Hunza valley, Gulmit to Chinese and Afghanistan borders, Shimshal and Chupursan valleys, upper Yarkhun valley of Chitral, and upper Ishkoman valley. *Status:* 6a (Vigorous). *Dialects:* Gojal, Ishkoman, Yarkhun, Yasin. *Lg Use:* Home, villages. All ages. Positive attitudes. Older people and those who live in mixed villages in Gojal also use Burushaski [bsk]. Men and young people also use Urdu [urd]; fewer than half the women and few older people in remote areas speak Urdu. *Lg Dev:* Literacy rate in L2: Quite high in Gojal. Literacy is primarily in Urdu [urd] and English [eng]. Some are now using an English-Roman based alphabet to write, especially on social network websites. *Other:* Muslim (Ismaili). See main entry on page 51. *Map:* 400:5.

Waneci [wne] (Chalgari, Tarino, Vanechi, Wanechi, Wanetsi). 95,000 (1998). Northeastern Balochistan Province, Harnai area. *Status:* 6a (Vigorous). *Class:* Indo-European, Indo-Iranian, Iranian, Eastern, Southeastern, Pashto. *Dialects:* None known. Lexical similarity: 71%–75% with Southern Pashto [pbt], 63%–72% with other Pashto varieties, 27% with Ormuri [oru]. *Lg Dev:* Literacy rate in L1: Below 1%. Literacy rate in L2: Below 5%. *Other:* Muslim. *Map:* 401.

Yidgha [ydg] (Lutkuhwar, Yidga, Yudga, Yudgha). 6,150 (2000). Chitral, Upper Lutkuh valley, west of Garam Chishma. *Status:* 6b (Threatened). *Class:* Indo-European, Indo-Iranian, Iranian, Eastern, Southeastern, Pamir. *Dialects:* No significant dialect variation. Lexical similarity: 56%–80% with Munji [mnj] in Afghanistan. *Lg Use:* Home. Positive attitudes. Also use Khowar [khw]. *Other:* Muslim (Ismaili). *Map:* 400:2.

Palestine

State of Palestine. 4,283,000 (2012 census). Principal language: Standard Arabic. Recognized by the United Nations during the interim period, based on the Israeli-Palestinian Declaration of Principles of 1993 (also known as the Oslo Accords), and the Interim agreement of 1995. Literacy rate: 41% (2010 UNESCO). Immigrant language: Hebrew (200,000). General references: Fischer and Jastrow 1980.

The number of individual languages listed for Palestine is 6. All are living languages. Of these, 1 is institutional, 1 is developing, 2 are vigorous, and 2 are dying.

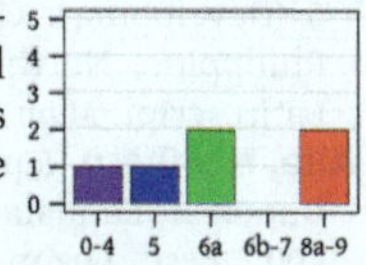

Arabic, Levantine Bedawi Spoken [avl] (Bedawi). 10,000 in Palestine (1996). Judean desert and along Jordan River. *Status:* 6a (Vigorous). *Dialects:* Eastern Egyptian Bedawi Arabic, North Levantine Bedawi Arabic, South Levantine Bedawi Arabic. *Other:* Muslim (Sunni). See main entry on page 319 (as Arabic, Eastern Egyptian Bedawi Spoken).

Arabic, South Levantine Spoken [ajp] (Bedawi). 1,600,000 in Palestine (1996). *Status:* 5 (Developing). *Dialects:* Fellahi, Madani. *Lg Use:* Also use Hebrew [heb]. Used as L2 by Domari [rmt]. *Other:* Distinct from North Levantine (Lebanese-Syrian) Arabic [apc]. Muslim, Christian. See main entry on page 212.

Arabic, Standard [arb]. Widespread. *Status:* 1 (National). De facto national language. *Lg Use:* Education, official purpose, formal speeches. See main entry on page 293.

Domari [rmt] (Nawari, Near-Eastern Gypsy). 2,000 in Palestine (1997). Gaza and Bir Zeit near Ramallah. *Status:* 6a (Vigorous). *Dialect:* Nawari. *Lg Use:* All ages. Also use South Levantine Spoken Arabic [ajp]. *Other:* Many loanwords from Arabic [arb], Kurdish, and some other Iranian languages. Muslim. See main entry on page 202.

Samaritan [smp] (Samaritan Hebrew). No known L1 speakers in Palestine. Ethnic population: 620 (1999 H. Mutzafi). West Bank near Nablus, Tel Aviv, Israel. Also in Israel. *Status:* 9 (Dormant). *Class:* Afro-Asiatic, Semitic, Central, South, Canaanite. *Lg Use:* Samaritan Hebrew and Samaritan Aramaic [sam] secondarily mainly used as liturgical languages. About 30% live near Nablus and speak Palestinian Arabic [ajp] as L1. Others live near Tel Aviv and speak Hebrew [heb] as L1. Religion. *Lg Dev:* Bible: 1853. *Writing:* Arabic script. Hebrew script, no longer in use. Samaritan script. *Other:* Jewish (Samaritan).

Samaritan Aramaic [sam]. No known L1 speakers in Palestine. Ethnic population: 620 (1999 H. Mutzafi). West Bank near Nablus; Tel Aviv, Israel. Also in Israel. *Status:* 9 (Dormant). *Class:* Afro-Asiatic, Semitic, Central, Aramaic, Western. *Lg Use:* Ceased as L1 for daily functions in 10th–12th centuries A.D. Samaritan Hebrew and Samaritan Aramaic [sam] secondarily mainly used as liturgical languages. About 30% live near Nablus and speak Palestinian Arabic [ajp] as L1. Others live near Tel Aviv and speak Hebrew [heb] as L1. Religion. *Writing:* Hebrew script. Samaritan script.

Philippines

Republic of the Philippines, Republika ng Pilipinas. 92,340,000 (2010 census). Principal languages: English, Filipino, Tagalog. Literacy rate: 96% (2008 UNESCO). Immigrant languages: French (700), Hindi (2,420), Indonesian (2,580), Japanese (2,900), Sindhi (20,000), Standard German (960). General references: Crystal 2003; Lobel 2004, 2005, 2012; Reid 1971; Wurm 2007; Zorc 1977. Deaf population: 2,914,600. Deaf institutions: 17.

The number of individual languages listed for Philippines is 184. Of these, 180 are living and 4 are extinct. Of the living languages, 40 are institutional, 71 are developing, 46 are vigorous, 13 are in trouble, and 10 are dying. See maps beginning on page 402.

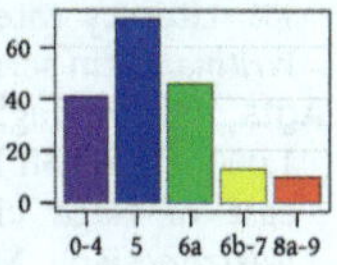

Adasen [tiu] (Addasen, Addasen Tinguian, Itneg Adasen). 4,000 (NTM). Ethnic population: 5,720. Luzon, northeast Abra Province. *Status:* 5 (Developing). *Class:* Austronesian, Malayo-Polynesian, Philippine, Northern Luzon, Northern Cordilleran, Cagayan Valley, Isnag. *Dialects:* Eastern Addasen, Western Addasen. Comprehension of Isnag [isd] 74%. *Lg Use:* Young people tend to prefer Ilocano [ilo] (Wurm 2007). Some domains. Young adults and older. Mildly positive attitudes. High proficiency in Ilocano [ilo] (among the young in most key domains). *Lg Dev:* NT: 1990. *Writing:* Latin script. *Map:* 403:5.

Agta, Alabat Island [dul] (Alabat Island Dumagat). 30 (Wurm 2000). Ethnic population: 75. Luzon, east of Quezon Province. *Status:* 8b (Nearly extinct). *Class:* Austronesian, Malayo-Polynesian, Philippine, Greater Central Philippine, Umiray Dumaget. *Lg Use:* Seriously endangered (2000 S. Wurm). Most shifted to Tagalog [tgl] (Wurm 2007). Home. Used by a few children. Neutral attitudes. High bilingualism in Tagalog [tgl] (Wurm 2007). *Maps:* 403:51, 404:51.

Agta, Casiguran Dumagat [dgc] (Casiguran Dumagat). 610 (Headland 1989). Luzon east coast, Aurora Province. *Status:* 5 (Developing). *Class:* Austronesian, Malayo-Polynesian, Philippine, Northern Luzon, Northern Cordilleran, Northeastern Luzon, Northern. *Dialects:* None known. Intelligibility: 83% of Paranan [prf]. *Lg Use:* All ages. Also use Filipino [fil]. Used as L2 by Arta [atz]. *Lg Dev:* Literacy rate in L1: 2%. Literacy rate in L2: 2%. Dictionary. NT: 1979. *Writing:* Latin script. *Other:* Negrito. Pressure from Filipino homesteaders moving into the area. Traditional lands now used by homesteaders for agriculture. *Map:* 403:29.

Agta, Central Cagayan [agt] (Labin Agta). 780 (2000). Ethnic population: 820. Northeast Luzon. *Status:* 5 (Developing). *Class:* Austronesian, Malayo-Polynesian, Philippine, Northern Luzon, Northern Cordilleran, Cagayan Valley, Ibanagic, Gaddangic. *Lg Use:* All domains. All ages. Positive attitudes. Also use Filipino [fil] in school. Also use Ilocano [ilo] with all non-Agta speakers. *Lg Dev:* Literacy rate in L1: 6%. Literacy rate in L2: 6%. Grammar. NT: 1992. *Writing:* Latin script. *Other:* Negrito. Christian. *Map:* 403:11.

Agta, Dicamay [duy] (Dicamay Dumagat). No known L1 speakers. Luzon, Isabela Province, near Jones.

Status: 10 (Extinct). *Class:* Austronesian, Malayo-Polynesian, Philippine, Northern Luzon, Northern Cordilleran, Northeastern Luzon, Northern.

Agta, Dupaninan [duo] (Dupaningan Agta, Eastern Cagayan Agta). 1,200 (1986 SIL). Ethnic population: 1,500 (2007 L. Reid). Northeast Luzon, from below Divilacan bay south to Palaui island north. *Status:* 6b (Threatened). *Class:* Austronesian, Malayo-Polynesian, Philippine, Northern Luzon, Northern Cordilleran, Northeastern Luzon, Northern. *Dialects:* Barongagunay, Bolos Point, Camonayan, Palaui Island, Peñablanca, Roso (Southeast Cagayan), Santa Ana-Gonzaga, Santa Margarita, Tanglagan, Valley Cove, Yaga. Intelligibility of Yaga dialect 83%. Yaga and Central Cagayan Agta [agt] are 63% intelligible. Lexical similarity: 51% between Central Cagayan Agta [agt] and Tanglagan dialect, 66% between Central Cagayan Agta [agt] and Yaga dialect. *Lg Dev:* Literacy rate in L1: Below 1%. Literacy rate in L2: Below 1%. Grammar. NT: 2001. *Writing:* Latin script. *Map:* 403:12.

Agta, Isarog [agk]. 5 (Wurm 2000). Ethnic population: 1,000 (1984 SIL). Luzon, Bicol region, mount Isarog east of Naga city. *Status:* 8b (Nearly extinct). *Class:* Austronesian, Malayo-Polynesian, Philippine, Greater Central Philippine, Central Philippine, Bikol, Coastal, Naga. *Lg Use:* Home. Negative attitudes. Also use Central Bikol [bcl]. *Maps:* 403:72, 404:72.

Agta, Mt. Iraya [atl] (Inagta of Mt. Iraya, Itbeg Rugnot, Lake Buhi, Rugnot of Lake Buhi East). 150 (Wurm 2000). Ethnic population: 380. Luzon, Bicol region, east of Lake Buhi. *Status:* 7 (Shifting). *Class:* Austronesian, Malayo-Polynesian, Philippine, Greater Central Philippine, Central Philippine, Bikol, Coastal, Naga. *Dialects:* 54%–86% comprehension of Naga dialect of Central Bikol [bcl], 94% comprehension of Mt. Iriga Agta [agz], Iriga City dialect. Lexical similarity: 85%–90% with Bikol; 70% with Mt. Iriga Agta, Iriga City dialect, 93% among four dialects. *Lg Use:* Home. Used by a few children. Negative attitudes. Also use Filipino [fil]. *Other:* Heavy borrowing from Legaspi dialect of Central Bikol [bcl]. *Map:* 404:75.

Agta, Mt. Iriga [agz] (Lake Buhi West, Mt. Iriga Negrito, San Ramon Inagta). 1,500 (1979 SIL). Luzon, Bicol region, east of Iriga city, west of Lake Buhi. *Status:* 6a (Vigorous). *Class:* Austronesian, Malayo-Polynesian, Philippine, Greater Central Philippine, Central Philippine, Bikol, Inland. *Dialects:* 86% intelligibility of Rinconada Bikol [bto], 82% of Mt. Iraya Agta [atl], 72% of Central Bikol [bcl] (Naga dialect). Intelligibility of Naga Bikol for Mt. Iriga Agta doubtful. Lexical similarity: 76% with Iriga City Bikol [bto], 66% with Mt. Iraya Agta [atl], 66% with Central Bikol [bcl] (Naga dialect). *Lg Use:* Also use Filipino [fil]. *Map:* 404:76.

Agta, Pahanan [apf] (Palanan Agta). 1,700 (2009 J. Lobel), increasing. Luzon, Isabela province east coast, between Divilacan bay and Dinapigue town, inland to San Mariano. *Status:* 5 (Developing). *Class:* Austronesian, Malayo-Polynesian, Philippine, Northern Luzon, Northern Cordilleran, Northeastern Luzon. *Dialects:* None known. Reportedly similar to Paranan [prf]. *Lg Use:* Home, church, village meetings. All ages. Positive attitudes. 90% also use Filipino [fil]. 10% also use Ilocano [ilo]. *Lg Dev:* Literacy rate in L1: 20%. Literacy rate in L2: 20%. Taught in grades 1–2. Poetry. Bible portions: 1988–2006. *Writing:* Latin script. *Other:* Traditional religion, Christian. *Map:* 403:14.

Agta, Umiray Dumaget [due] (Umiray Agta, Umirey Dumagat). 3,000 (1994 SIL), decreasing. Luzon, Quezon Province. *Status:* 5 (Developing). *Class:* Austronesian, Malayo-Polynesian, Philippine, Greater Central Philippine, Umiray Dumaget. *Dialects:* Anglat Agta, Polillo Island Agta. *Lg Use:* Some parents passing the language on to children. All domains. Mostly adults. Neutral attitudes. Most also use Filipino [fil]. Most also use Ilocano [ilo]. *Lg Dev:* Literacy rate in L1: 5%–10%. Literacy rate in L2: 5%–10%. NT: 1977. *Writing:* Latin script. *Map:* 403:49.

Agta, Villa Viciosa [dyg]. No known L1 speakers. Luzon, Abra Province. *Status:* 10 (Extinct). *Class:* Austronesian, Malayo-Polynesian, Philippine. *Lg Use:* Shifted to Ilocano [ilo].

Agutaynen [agn] (Agutayno, Agutaynon). 15,000 (2007 SIL). Agutaya island, 5 surrounding islands; Roxas, San Vicente, and Brooke's Point, Palawan municipalities; Mindoro, Taytay, Linapacan, and Manila. *Status:* 5 (Developing). *Class:* Austronesian, Malayo-Polynesian, Philippine, Kalamian. *Dialects:* None known. Lexical similarity: 52% with Cuyonon [cyo], 71% with Calamian Tagbanwa [tbk]. *Lg Use:* Mostly spoken in group. All ages. Neutral attitudes. Also use some Cuyonon [cyo]. Also use English [eng], Filipino [fil]. *Lg Dev:* Literacy rate in L1: 90%. Literacy rate in L2: 90% in Filipino [fil] or English [eng]. Videos. Dictionary. NT: 2004. *Writing:* Latin script. *Other:* Culturally lowland. Christian (Roman Catholic). *Maps:* 404:119, 405:119.

Alangan [alj]. 7,690 (2000). North central Mindoro. *Status:* 5 (Developing). *Class:* Austronesian, Malayo-Polynesian, Philippine, North Mangyan. *Lg Dev:* NT: 1989. *Writing:* Latin script. *Map:* 404:112.

Alta, Northern [aqn] (Baler Negrito, Ditaylin Alta, Ditaylin Dumagat, Edimala). 200 (Wurm 2000). Ethnic population: 400. East Luzon, Aurora Province, Bayanihan, and San Luis; Diteki. *Status:* 7 (Shifting). *Class:* Austronesian, Malayo-Polynesian, Philippine, Northern Luzon, Meso-Cordilleran, Alta. *Dialects:* None known. Reportedly not similar to other languages (1992 L. Reid). Lexical similarity: 34% with Southern Alta [agy]. *Lg Use:* Home. Some children. Neutral attitudes. *Map:* 403:48.

Alta, Southern [agy] (Ita, Kabulowan, Kabuluen, Kabuluwan, Kabuluwen). 1,000 (1982 SIL). Luzon, Quezon Province coastal areas, east Nueva Ecija, Sierra Madre, and San Miguel town; Bulacan Province, a large community in remote San Miguel. North of the Umiray Dumaget [due] language area. *Status:* 6a (Vigorous). *Class:* Austronesian, Malayo-Polynesian, Philippine, Northern Luzon, Meso-Cordilleran, Alta. *Dialects:* None known. Reportedly not similar to other languages. Lexical similarity: 34% with Northern Alta [aqn]. *Lg Use:* Also use Filipino [fil]. *Lg Dev:* Bible portions: 1970. *Map:* 403:47.

Arta [atz]. 11 (2013 Y. Kimoto). 35–45 have some knowledge of the language, but cannot speak properly (2013 Y. Kimoto). Ethnic population: 150. Luzon, Quirino Province, Nagtipunan municipality, Disimungal, San Ramos. *Status:* 8b (Nearly extinct). *Class:* Austronesian, Malayo-Polynesian, Philippine, Northern Luzon, Arta. *Dialects:* None known. Not similar to any other language (1992 L. Reid). *Lg Use:* Elderly, all over 50 years of age. Neutral attitudes. Also use Casiguran Dumagat Agta [dgc], Ilocano [ilo]. *Other:* Negrito. *Map:* 403:31.

Ata [atm]. 2 (Wurm 2000). In 1973, only a few families of speakers were reported. Probably extinct (Wurm 2007). Central Visayas, Negros Oriental province, Mabinay. *Status:* 8b (Nearly extinct). *Class:* Austronesian, Malayo-Polynesian, Philippine, Greater Central Philippine, Central Philippine. *Lg Use:* Shifted to Hiligaynon [hil]. Negative attitudes. Also use Cebuano [ceb]. *Other:* Different from Ata Manobo [atd] or Atta languages.

Ati [atk] (Inati). 1,500 (1980 SIL). Western Visayas, Panay island, small groups in all provinces. *Status:* 6a (Vigorous). *Class:* Austronesian, Malayo-Polynesian,

Philippine, Greater Central Philippine, Central Philippine, Bisayan, Central, Peripheral. *Dialects:* Barotac Viejo Nagpana, Malay. Barotac Viejo Nagpana is the prestige dialect. *Lg Use:* Home, community. Also use Hiligaynon [hil] for school, contact with outsiders, outside culture topics, jobs, religion. Malay people mostly use Malaynon [mlz]. Also use Kinaray-a [krj]. *Other:* Negrito. *Map:* 404:104.

Atta, Faire [azt] (Southern Atta). 300 (Wurm 2000). Ethnic population: 600. Luzon, Cagayan Province, near Faire-Rizal. *Status:* 6b (Threatened). *Class:* Austronesian, Malayo-Polynesian, Philippine, Northern Luzon, Northern Cordilleran, Cagayan Valley, Ibanagic. *Dialects:* None known. Lexical similarity: 81% with Pudtol Atta [atp], 60% with Isnag [isd], 66% with Central Cagayan Agta [agt], 82% with Pamplona Atta [att], 90% with Rizal Atta, 72% with Ibanag [ibg]. *Lg Use:* Home. Some children. Neutral attitudes. Also use Ibanag [ibg], Pamplona Atta [att]. *Other:* Negrito. *Map:* 403:10.

Atta, Pamplona [att] (Northern Cagayan Negrito). 1,000 (1998 SIL). Ethnic population: 1,000. Luzon, Northwest Cagayan Province. *Status:* 5 (Developing). *Class:* Austronesian, Malayo-Polynesian, Philippine, Northern Luzon, Northern Cordilleran, Cagayan Valley, Ibanagic. *Dialects:* None known. Comprehension of Ibanag North [ibg] 97%, of Itawit [itv] 52%. Lexical similarity: 91% with Ibanag North, 63% with Ilocano [ilo], 69% with Itawit. *Lg Use:* Also use Ilocano [ilo]. Used as L2 by Faire Atta [azt], Pudtol Atta [atp]. *Lg Dev:* Literacy rate in L1: 20%–25%. Literacy rate in L2: 20%–25%. NT: 1996. *Writing:* Latin script. *Map:* 403:8.

Atta, Pudtol [atp]. 710 (2000). Luzon, Apayao Province, Pudtol, and Abulog river south of Pamplona. *Status:* 6a (Vigorous). *Class:* Austronesian, Malayo-Polynesian, Philippine, Northern Luzon, Northern Cordilleran, Cagayan Valley, Ibanagic. *Dialects:* None known. Lexical similarity: 86% with Pamplona Atta [att], 75% with Ibanag [ibg], 63% with Isnag [isd], 81% with Faire Atta [azt], 42% with Ilocano [ilo]. *Lg Use:* Also use Ibanag [ibg], Pamplona Atta [att]. *Other:* Negrito. *Map:* 403:9.

Ayta, Abellen [abp] (Abenlen, Aburlen Negrito, Ayta Abellen Sambal). 3,000 (2008 SIL), decreasing. 45 monolinguals. Ethnic population: 5,000. Luzon, Tarlac Province, San Jose, Maamot; Station Juliana, Mayantoc, and Capas. *Status:* 5 (Developing). *Class:* Austronesian, Malayo-Polynesian, Philippine, Central Luzon, Sambalic. *Dialects:* None known. Lexical similarity: 66% with Botolan Sambal [sbl], 49% with Sambal [xsb], 38%–44% with Ilocano [ilo], Pangasinan [pag], Filipino [fil], Pampangan [pam]. *Lg Use:* In some remote areas, children still learn it first. Home, community, church. Mainly younger adults. Neutral attitudes. A few in remote areas are nearly monolingual, otherwise speakers generally acquire and use L2's at home, community, or school, trying to negotiate multiple linguistic identities. Also use Botolan Sambal [sbl]. Used as L2 by Botolan Sambal [sbl], Ilocano [ilo]. *Lg Dev:* Literacy rate in L1: 3%. Literacy rate in L2: 3%. Bible portions: 2006–2011. *Writing:* Latin script. *Other:* Traditional religion, Christian. *Map:* 403:40.

Ayta, Ambala [abc] (Ambala Agta, Ambala Sambal). 1,660 (1986 SIL). Luzon, Zambales Province, San Marcelino, Subic city, Olongapa, Castillejos barrios; Luzon, Bataan province, Dinalupinan barrio. *Status:* 6a (Vigorous). *Class:* Austronesian, Malayo-Polynesian, Philippine, Central Luzon, Sambalic. *Dialects:* None known. Ambala Ayta speakers' comprehension of Botolan Sambal [sbl] is 60%, of Mag-Indi Ayta [blx] is 54%, of Mag-antsi Ayta [sgb] is 60%, of Magbukun Ayta [ayt] is 70%. Lexical similarity: 70% with Botolan Sambal, 55% with Filipino [fil]. *Lg Use:* Also use Filipino [fil]. *Lg Dev:* Literacy rate in L1: 25%. Literacy rate in L2: 25%. *Other:* Do not mix with other Ayta groups. Affected by Mount Pinatubo eruption. Traditional religion, Christian. *Map:* 403:45.

Ayta, Mag-antsi [sgb] (Ayta, Mag-Anchi, Mag-Anchi Sambal). 8,200 (1992 SIL). Central Luzon, Mount Pinatubo east side, Botolan Sambal area, near Tarlac-Pampanga border, Capas, Tarlac, Bamban, San Marcelino, Zambales, 2 of Castillejos, Zambales, 2 of Mabalacat, Pampanga, Sapang Bato, and Angeles city barrios. *Status:* 5 (Developing). *Class:* Austronesian, Malayo-Polynesian, Philippine, Central Luzon, Sambalic. *Dialects:* None known. 77% intelligibility of Mag-Indi Ayta [blx], 65% of Ambala Ayta [abc], 46% of Pampangan [pam]. Lexical similarity: 76% with Botolan Sambal [sbl], 50% with Filipino [fil], 46% with Pampangan. *Lg Dev:* Literacy rate in L1: 10%. Literacy rate in L2: 10%. Dictionary. NT: 2006. *Writing:* Latin script. *Other:* People scattered due to Mount Pinatubo eruption. *Map:* 403:43.

Ayta, Magbukun [ayt] (Bataan Ayta, Bataan Sambal, Mariveles Ayta). 1,000 (2011 SIL). Ethnic population: 1,000. Luzon, Bataan Province, Mariveles. *Status:* 6b (Threatened). *Class:* Austronesian, Malayo-Polynesian, Philippine, Central Luzon, Sambalic. *Dialects:* None known. Lexical similarity: 63% with Botolan Sambal [sbl] and Filipino [fil]. *Lg Use:* A few key domains. All ages. Mildly positive attitudes. Also use Filipino [fil]. *Other:* Negrito. *Map:* 403:46.

Ayta, Mag-Indi [blx] (Indi Ayta, Mag-Indi Sambal). 5,000 (1998 SIL), increasing. Ethnic population: 30,000. All Ayta in Zambales, Pampanga, and Tarlac regions. Luzon, Pampanga Province, barrios and communities in Florida Blanca and Porac; Zambales Province, San Marcelino. *Status:* 5 (Developing). *Class:* Austronesian, Malayo-Polynesian, Philippine, Central Luzon, Sambalic. *Dialects:* None known. 46% comprehension of Botolan Sambal [sbl], 50% of Ambala Ayta [abc], 59% of Pampangan [pam], 32% of Mag-antsi Ayta [sgb]. Lexical similarity: 75% with Botolan Sambal [sbl], 38% with Filipino [fil], 83% with Mag-Anchi [sgb], 71% with Ayta Abellen [abp], 51% with Kapampangan [pam]. *Lg Use:* Stable. Home, community. All ages. Positive attitudes. 4,000 also use Filipino [fil]. 3,000 also use Pampangan [pam]. *Lg Dev:* Literacy rate in L1: Below 10%. Literacy rate in L2: Below 10%. Bible portions: 2002–2010. *Writing:* Latin script. *Map:* 403:44.

Ayta, Sorsogon [ays]. 15 (Wurm 2000). Ethnic population: 180. Luzon, Sorsogon Province, Prieto Diaz. *Status:* 8b (Nearly extinct). *Class:* Austronesian, Malayo-Polynesian, Philippine, Greater Central Philippine, Central Philippine. *Lg Use:* Home. Mainly adults. Negative attitudes. *Other:* Frequent intermarriage with other groups. *Map:* 404:82.

Ayta, Tayabas [ayy]. No known L1 speakers. Luzon, Quezon Province, Tayabas. *Status:* 10 (Extinct). *Class:* Austronesian, Malayo-Polynesian, Philippine, Greater Central Philippine, Central Philippine. *Lg Use:* Shifted to Filipino [fil]. *Other:* Negrito.

Balangao [blw] (Balangao Bontoc, Balangaw, Farangao). 21,300 (2000), decreasing. 0 monolinguals. Luzon, east Mountain Province. *Status:* 4 (Educational). *Class:* Austronesian, Malayo-Polynesian, Philippine, Northern Luzon, Meso-Cordilleran, South-Central Cordilleran, Central Cordilleran, North Central Cordilleran, Nuclear Cordilleran, Balangaw. *Lg Use:* Vigorous. All domains. All ages. Positive attitudes. Children in school also speak English [eng]. Also use Filipino [fil], Ilocano [ilo]. *Lg Dev:* Literacy rate in L1: 42%. Literacy rate in L2: 42%. Teachers use Balangao to explain questions. Grammar. NT: 1982. *Writing:* Latin script. *Other:* Traditional religion,

Christian. *Map:* 403:65.

Bantayanon [bfx]. 71,600 (2007 J. Lobel). Central Visayas, Cebu Province, Bantayan and surrounding islands. *Status:* 6a (Vigorous). *Class:* Austronesian, Malayo-Polynesian, Philippine, Greater Central Philippine, Central Philippine, Bisayan, Central. *Dialects:* None known. Reportedly similar to Hiligaynon [hil]. *Map:* 404:88.

Bantoanon [bno]. 75,000 (2011 Governor's Office, Romblon Province), decreasing. 500 monolinguals. Ethnic population: 75,000. Romblon Province. *Status:* 5 (Developing). *Class:* Austronesian, Malayo-Polynesian, Philippine, Greater Central Philippine, Central Philippine, Bisayan, Banton. *Dialects:* Banton, Calatravanhon, Odionganon, Sibalenhon (Sibale), Simaranhon. 63% intelligibility with Hiligaynon [hil]; 92% with Inonhan [loc]. Odionganon dialect preferred for literature. Lexical similarity: 83% with Romblomanon [rol] (Zorc 1977). *Lg Use:* Home, community. All ages. Positive attitudes. Used for politics, education, church in main towns, and with non-Bantoanon speakers. Also use English [eng], Inonhan [loc], Romblomanon [rol]. *Lg Dev:* Literacy rate in L1: 80%–90%. Literacy rate in L2: 80%–90%. Taught in primary schools, occasional use only. Taught in secondary schools, occasional use only. Dictionary. Bible portions: 1992–1996. *Writing:* Latin script. *Other:* Christian (Roman Catholic), Buddhist, Christian (Protestant), Muslim. *Map:* 404:109.

Batak [bya] (Babuyan, Palawan Batak, Tinitianes). 200 (Wurm 2000), decreasing. Ethnic population: 2,040 (1990 census). North-central Palawan island. *Status:* 7 (Shifting). *Class:* Austronesian, Malayo-Polynesian, Philippine, Greater Central Philippine, Palawanic. *Type:* VOS. *Lg Use:* Heavy influence from Palawano and Tagbanwa (Wurm 2007). Few domains. Somewhat positive attitudes. Also use Filipino [fil]. *Lg Dev:* Bible portions: 1972. *Writing:* Latin script. *Other:* Negrito. Traditional religion, Christian. *Map:* 404:123.

Baybayanon [bvy] (Leyte, Utudnon). 10,000 (2009 J. Lobel). Eastern Viscayas, Leyte island, Baybay town in Pangasugan river area, Guadalupe (Utod), Gabas, Kilim, Patag and Pangasugan villages. *Status:* 6a (Vigorous). *Class:* Austronesian, Malayo-Polynesian, Philippine, Greater Central Philippine, Central Philippine, Bisayan, Central, Warayan. *Dialects:* None known. Reportedly similar to Waray-Waray [war]. *Map:* 404:90.

Bikol [bik]. A macrolanguage (see page 9). *Other:* Includes: Buhi'non Bikol [ubl], Central Bikol [bcl], Libon Bikol [lbl], Miraya Bikol [rbl], Northern Catanduanes Bikol [cts], Rinconada Bikol [bto], Southern Catanduanes Bikol [bln], West Albay Bikol [fbl].

Bikol, Buhi'non [ubl] (Bikol Buhi, Boîn?n, Buhi, Buhi'non, Buhi-non). 73,600 (2009 SIL). Speakers of all Bikol languages: 4,580,000 (2000 census). 0 monolinguals. Luzon, Camarines Sur Province, Buhi town. *Status:* 6a (Vigorous). *Class:* Austronesian, Malayo-Polynesian, Philippine, Greater Central Philippine, Central Philippine, Bikol, Inland. A member of macrolanguage Bikol [bik]. *Dialects:* None known. Reportedly similar to Rinconada Bikol [bto]. *Writing:* Latin script. *Other:* Christian. *Map:* 404:77.

Bikol, Central [bcl] (Bikol, Central Bicolano). 2,500,000 (1990 census), increasing. Speakers of all Bikol languages: 4,580,000 (2000 census). L2 users: Also used by migrants and those who marry into the area as L2. Luzon, Camarines Norte, Camarines Sur, southern Catanduanes, northern Sorsogon, and Albay provinces. *Status:* 3 (Wider communication). Statutory language of provincial identity in Camarines Norte, 4 other provinces (1991, ACFLC Section 3(f)). *Class:* Austronesian, Malayo-Polynesian, Philippine, Greater Central Philippine, Central Philippine, Bikol, Coastal, Naga. A member of macrolanguage Bikol [bik]. *Dialects:* Legaspi, Naga. *Lg Use:* All domains. All ages. Positive attitudes. Also use English [eng], Tagalog [tgl]. Second languages acquired through schooling, media, and travel. Used as L2 by Inabaknon [abx], Isarog Agta [agk], Northern Sorsoganon [bks], Rinconada Bikol [bto], Southern Sorsoganon [srv]. *Lg Dev:* Taught in primary schools. Bible: 1915. *Writing:* Braille script. Latin script, primary usage. *Other:* Christian (Roman Catholic). *Maps:* 403:71, 404:71.

Bikol, Libon [lbl] (Libongeño). 68,800 (2009 SIL). Speakers of all Bikol languages: 4,580,000 (2000 census). 0 monolinguals. Luzon, Albay Province, Libon town. *Status:* 6a (Vigorous). *Class:* Austronesian, Malayo-Polynesian, Philippine, Greater Central Philippine, Central Philippine, Bikol, Inland. A member of macrolanguage Bikol [bik]. *Dialects:* None known. Reportedly similar to Rinconada Bikol [bto]. *Other:* Christian. *Map:* 404:79.

Bikol, Miraya [rbl] (Bikol, Daraga). 300,000 (2009 SIL). Speakers of all Bikol languages: 4,580,000 (2000 census). 0 monolinguals. Luzon, Albay Province, Guinobatan, Camalig, Daraga, and Jovellar towns; Sorsogon Province, Donsol town. *Status:* 6a (Vigorous). *Class:* Austronesian, Malayo-Polynesian, Philippine, Greater Central Philippine, Central Philippine, Bikol, Inland. A member of macrolanguage Bikol [bik]. *Dialects:* None known. Reportedly similar to West Albay Bikol [fbl]. *Other:* Christian. *Map:* 404:81.

Bikol, Northern Catanduanes [cts] (Northern Catanduanes Bicolano, Pandan). 77,500 (2000 census). Speakers of all Bikol languages: 4,580,000 (2000 census). L2 users: Used by those intermarrying with local speakers and for business purposes. Luzon, Catanduanes Province, Pandan, Caramonan, Viga, Panganiban, and Bato. *Status:* 6a (Vigorous). *Class:* Austronesian, Malayo-Polynesian, Philippine, Greater Central Philippine, Central Philippine, Bikol, Pandan. A member of macrolanguage Bikol [bik]. *Dialects:* 68% comprehension of Naga dialect of Central Bikol [bcl], 66% comprehension of Filipino [fil] narrative. *Lg Use:* All domains. All ages. Positive attitudes. *Other:* Proud of language and culture. People who identify with this language are negotiating multiple identities. *Map:* 404:73.

Bikol, Rinconada [bto] (Bicolano, Iriga, Rinconada Bicolano, Rinconada Bikol). 234,000 (2000 census), increasing. Speakers of all Bikol languages: 4,580,000 (2000 census). 2,300 monolinguals. Monolingual speakers are elderly; boast of their identity as Rinconada. Ethnic population: 320,000. L2 users: Used by those intermarrying with locals. Luzon, Camarines Sur Province, Rinconada district, Iriga city, Baao, Bato, Balatan, Bula, and Nabua. *Status:* 6a (Vigorous). *Class:* Austronesian, Malayo-Polynesian, Philippine, Greater Central Philippine, Central Philippine, Bikol, Inland, Iriga. A member of macrolanguage Bikol [bik]. *Lg Use:* All domains. All ages. Positive attitudes. Also use Central Bikol [bcl], English [eng], Tagalog [tgl]. *Lg Dev:* Taught in primary schools. Poetry. Newspapers. Radio programs. *Writing:* Latin script. *Other:* Iriga City inhabitants regard Naga [bcl] dialect as true Bicolano; proud of their language and culture. Christian (Roman Catholic). *Map:* 404:78.

Bikol, Southern Catanduanes [bln] (Southern Catanduanes Bikolano, Virac). 135,000 (2000 census). Speakers of all Bikol languages: 4,580,000 (2000 census). Luzon, Catanduanes Province, southern municipalities: Virac, San Miguel, San Andres, Gigmoto, Bato, and Baras. *Status:* 6a (Vigorous). *Class:* Austronesian, Malayo-Polynesian, Philippine, Greater Central Philippine, Central Philippine, Bikol, Coastal, Virac. A member of macrolanguage Bikol

[bik]. *Dialects:* Samples had 85% comprehension of Central Bikol [bcl] and Filipino [fil] narrative. Intelligibility of Northern Catanduanes [cts] 91%. Prefer Virac dialect for literature. *Other:* Christian (Roman Catholic). *Map:* 404:74.

Bikol, West Albay [fbl] (Bicol, Bikol, Ligaoeño, Oasnun, Oasnün, Polanguinon). 260,000 (2009 SIL). Speakers of all Bikol languages: 4,580,000 (2000 census). 0 monolinguals. Luzon, Albay Province, Polangui, Oas, Ligao, and Pio Duran towns. *Status:* 6a (Vigorous). *Class:* Austronesian, Malayo-Polynesian, Philippine, Greater Central Philippine, Central Philippine, Bikol, Inland. A member of macrolanguage Bikol [bik]. *Dialects:* None known. Reportedly similar to Miraya Bikol [rbl]. *Writing:* Latin script. *Other:* Christian. *Map:* 404:80.

Binukid [bkd] (Binokid, Binukid Manobo, Bukidnon). 100,000 (1987 SIL). North Central Mindanao, Agusan del Sur, south Bukidnon and northeast Cotabato provinces. *Status:* 5 (Developing). *Class:* Austronesian, Malayo-Polynesian, Philippine, Greater Central Philippine, Manobo, North. *Dialects:* None known. Reportedly similar to Higaonon [mba]. *Type:* VSO, VOS; prepositions; genitives after noun heads; articles, adjectives, numerals all before noun heads; relatives after noun heads or without noun heads; question word in sentence-initial position; maximum number of affixes: 3 prefixes, 2 suffixes; affixes do not indicate case of noun phrase; non-obligatory verb affixes indicate number; passives; causatives; comparatives; CV, CVC, CVV, CVVC; nontonal. *Lg Dev:* Literacy rate in L1: 63%. Literacy rate in L2: 63%. Dictionary. NT: 1986. *Writing:* Latin script. *Map:* 405:172.

Binukidnon, Northern [kyn] (Karolanos). 15,100 (2000). Negros Occidental Province, Kabankalan. *Status:* 6a (Vigorous). *Class:* Austronesian, Malayo-Polynesian, Philippine, Greater Central Philippine, Central Philippine. *Dialects:* None known. Reportedly similar to Southern Binukidnon [mtw].

Binukidnon, Southern [mtw] (Bukidnon, "Magahat" *pej.*). 7,570 (2000). Negros Oriental Province, Mount Arniyo near Bayawan, upper Tayaban, Bayawan, Tanjag, Santa Catalina, and Siaton municipalities. *Status:* 6a (Vigorous). *Class:* Austronesian, Malayo-Polynesian, Philippine, Greater Central Philippine, Central Philippine. *Dialects:* None known. Reportedly similar to Northern Binukidnon [kyn]. Reportedly includes a heavy mixture of Cebuano [ceb] and Hiligaynon [hil]. *Other:* Tend to live in high elevations. *Map:* 404:98.

Blaan, Koronadal [bpr] (Baraan, Bilanes, Biraan, Koronadal Bilaan, Tagalagad). 150,000 (2007 SIL). 40,000 monolinguals. Mindanao, South Cotabato and Sarangani provinces. *Status:* 5 (Developing). *Class:* Austronesian, Malayo-Polynesian, Philippine, Bilic, Blaan. *Type:* VSO; prepositions; genitives before noun heads; articles, adjectives, numerals all before noun heads; no relative markers; question word in sentence-final position; maximum number of affixes: 1 prefix, 1 suffix; word order distinguishes subject, object and direct objects, topic and comment; affixes indicate case of noun phrase; non-obligatory verb affixes indicate number; passives; causatives; comparatives; C, CV, CVC; nontonal. *Lg Use:* All ages. Positive attitudes. Also use Cebuano [ceb], Kalagan [kqe], Tboli [tbl]. *Lg Dev:* Literacy rate in L1: 35% (2007 SIL). Literacy rate in L2: 35% (2007 SIL). Ongoing non-formal literacy teaching (2007 SIL). Radio programs. Videos. Grammar. NT: 1995. *Writing:* Latin script. *Other:* Traditional religion, Christian. *Map:* 405:151.

Blaan, Sarangani [bps] (Balud, Bilaan, Tumanao). 90,800 (2000). Mindanao, south Cotabato, Sarangani, and Davao Del Sur provinces. *Status:* 5 (Developing). *Class:* Austronesian, Malayo-Polynesian, Philippine, Bilic, Blaan. *Type:* VSO; prepositions; genitives before noun heads; articles, adjectives, numerals all before noun heads; no relative markers; question word in sentence-final position; maximum number of affixes: 1 prefix, 1 suffix; word order distinguishes subject, object and direct objects, given and new information, topic and comment; affixes indicate case of noun phrase; non-obligatory verb affixes indicate number; passives; causatives; comparatives; C, CV, CVC; nontonal. *Lg Use:* Also use Cebuano [ceb], English [eng], Filipino [fil], Maguindanaon [mdh], Sangil [snl], Sangir [sxn], Sarangani Manobo [mbs], Tboli [tbl]. *Lg Dev:* Literacy rate in L1: 28%. Literacy rate in L2: 28%. Videos. NT: 1981–1998. *Writing:* Latin script. *Other:* Traditional religion, Christian. *Map:* 405:152.

Bolinao [smk] (Bino-Bolinao, Binubolinao, Binubulinao, Bolinao Sambal, Bolinao Zambal, Bulinaw, Sambal Bolinao). 51,200 (2007 census), decreasing. 510 monolinguals. Ethnic population: 104,000. L2 users: 5,000. Used by outsiders for marketing, politics, some teachers. Luzon, West Pangasinan Province, Bolinao and Anda municipalities. *Status:* 6b (Threatened). *Class:* Austronesian, Malayo-Polynesian, Philippine, Central Luzon, Sambalic. *Type:* VSO; verb affixation indicates relationships of constituents and directions; gender not marked. Initial content question word; no obligatory yes-no question marker; rhetorical or emotional question word, verb phrase medially; 14 unique consonants and 4 vowels in the non-borrowed words. *Lg Use:* Shifting to Filipino [fil]. All ages, especially in the islands. Positive attitudes. English [eng] acquired in school. Filipino [fil] used at home, school, and community; Filipino is acquired through intermarriage and community relations. Used as L2 by Cebuano [ceb], Ilocano [ilo], Tagalog [tgl]. *Lg Dev:* Literacy rate in L1: Over 90%. Literacy rate in L2: Over 90% in Filipino (Tagalog); 40% in English. Pilot project in one school. Taught as a course in some secondary schools. Poetry. Dictionary. NT: 2012. *Writing:* Latin script. *Other:* Christian (Roman Catholic), Christian (Protestant). *Map:* 403:38.

Bontok [bnc]. A macrolanguage (see page 9). *Other:* Includes: Central Bontok [lbk], Eastern Bontok [ebk], Northern Bontok [rbk], Southern Bontok [obk], Southwestern Bontok [vbk].

Bontok, Central [lbk] (Bontoc, Bontoc Igorot, Bontoc, Central). 19,600 (2007 census). Luzon, Mountain Province, Bontoc municipality, Bontoc ili, Caluttit, Dalican, Guina-ang, Ma-init, Maligcong, Samoki, and Tocucan villages. *Status:* 5 (Developing). *Class:* Austronesian, Malayo-Polynesian, Philippine, Northern Luzon, Meso-Cordilleran, South-Central Cordilleran, Central Cordilleran, North Central Cordilleran, Nuclear Cordilleran, Bontok-Kankanay, Bontok. A member of macrolanguage Bontok [bnc]. *Dialects:* None known. Reportedly similar to Northern Bontok [rbk], Southwestern Bontok [vbk], Southern Bontok [obk], and Eastern Bontok [ebk]. *Lg Use:* The great majority of older people are also bilingual in English [eng]. Youth use Ilocano [ilo] when speaking together, especially in high school and college contexts. The great majority of older people are also bilingual in Ilocano [ilo]. Youth also use Tagalog [tgl] when speaking together, especially in high school and college. Fewer older people speak Tagalog. Used as L2 by Northern Bontok [rbk], Southwestern Bontok [vbk]. *Lg Dev:* Literacy rate in L1: 35%. Literacy rate in L2: 35%. Dictionary. NT: 1992. *Writing:* Latin script. *Map:* 403:67.

Bontok, Eastern [ebk] (Eastern Bontoc, Finallig, Southern Bontoc). 6,170 (2007 census). Luzon, east Mountain Province, Barlig municipality, Barlig, Kadaklan, and Lias villages. *Status:* 5 (Developing). *Class:* Austronesian, Malayo-Polynesian, Philippine, Northern Luzon, Meso-Cordilleran, South-Central Cordilleran, Central Cordilleran, North Central Cordilleran, Nuclear Cordilleran, Bontok-Kankanay, Bontok. A member of macrolanguage Bontok [bnc]. *Dialects:* None known. Reportedly similar to Central Bontok [lbk], Northern Bontok [rbk], Southwestern Bontok [vbk], and Southern Bontok [obk]; intelligibility of Ilocano [ilo] 53%, of Balangao [blw] 49%. *Lg Use:* Also use Ilocano [ilo]. *Lg Dev:* Literacy rate in L1: 67%. Literacy rate in L2: 67%. NT: 2004. *Writing:* Latin script. *Other:* Traditional religion. *Map:* 403:66.

Bontok, Northern [rbk] (Bontoc, Bontoc, Central, Bontoc, Northern). 9,700 (2007 census). Luzon, northern Mountain Province, Sadanga municipality, Anabel, Bekigan, Belwang, Betwagan, Demang, Sacasacan, Saclit, and the municipal center, Sadanga Poblacion. *Status:* 8a (Moribund). *Class:* Austronesian, Malayo-Polynesian, Philippine, Northern Luzon, Meso-Cordilleran, South-Central Cordilleran, Central Cordilleran, North Central Cordilleran, Nuclear Cordilleran, Bontok-Kankanay, Bontok. A member of macrolanguage Bontok [bnc]. *Dialects:* None known. Reportedly similar to Central Bontok [lbk], Eastern Bontok [ebk], Southwestern Bontok [vbk], and Southern Bontok [obk]. *Lg Use:* Mostly older speakers. Also use Ilocano [ilo]. Young, educated people use Ilocano. Young, educated people use Tagalog [tgl]. Also use Central Bontok [lbk]. *Other:* Various Sadanga municipality residents do not identify their language as Bontok. They identify with their community dialect, and label it distinctively. *Map:* 403:63.

Bontok, Southern [obk] (Bontoc, Southern Bontoc). 2,760 (2007 census). Luzon, Mountain Province, south of Bontoc municipality, Talubin, Bayyo, and Can-eo towns. *Status:* 6a (Vigorous). *Class:* Austronesian, Malayo-Polynesian, Philippine, Northern Luzon, Meso-Cordilleran, South-Central Cordilleran, Central Cordilleran, North Central Cordilleran, Nuclear Cordilleran, Bontok-Kankanay, Bontok. A member of macrolanguage Bontok [bnc]. *Dialects:* None known. Reportedly similar to Northern Bontok [rbk], Central Bontok [lbk], Southwestern Bontok [vbk], and Eastern Bontok [ebk]. *Lg Use:* Also use Ilocano [ilo]. *Writing:* Unwritten. *Other:* Traditional religion. *Map:* 403:68.

Bontok, Southwestern [vbk] (Bontoc). 2,470 (2007 census). Luzon, Mountain Province, Bontoc municipality, Alab, Balili, Gonogon and villages in Chico river valley, southwest of municipal capital Bontoc, along Halsema Highway. *Status:* 8a (Moribund). *Class:* Austronesian, Malayo-Polynesian, Philippine, Northern Luzon, Meso-Cordilleran, South-Central Cordilleran, Central Cordilleran, North Central Cordilleran, Nuclear Cordilleran, Bontok-Kankanay, Bontok. A member of macrolanguage Bontok [bnc]. *Dialects:* None known. Reportedly similar to Central Bontok [lbk], Northern Bontok [rbk], Southern Bontok [obk], and Eastern Bontok [ebk]. *Lg Use:* Home. Mostly older speakers. Also use Central Bontok [lbk]. Also use Ilocano [ilo], Kankanaey [kne]. *Other:* Various municipality residents do not identify their language as Bontok. They identify with their community dialect, and label it distinctively: Alab (Ina-ab), Balili (Binalili), Gonogon (Ginonogon); however, they maintain a sense of community with other Southwestern Bontok speakers based on perceived phonological and other linguistic differences from Central Bontok [lbk]. *Map:* 403:69.

Buhid [bku] (Bangon, Batangan, Bukil). 8,000 (1991 OMF). South Mindoro island. *Status:* 5 (Developing). *Class:* Austronesian, Malayo-Polynesian, Philippine, Greater Central Philippine, South Mangyan, Buhid-Taubuid. *Lg Dev:* NT: 1988. *Writing:* Buhid script. Latin script, primary usage. *Map:* 404:115.

Butuanon [btw]. 34,500 (1990 census). Mindanao, Agusan del Norte Province, Butuan city. *Status:* 7 (Shifting). *Class:* Austronesian, Malayo-Polynesian, Philippine, Greater Central Philippine, Central Philippine, Bisayan, South, Butuan-Tausug. *Dialects:* None known. Lexical similarity: 70% with Kamayo [kyk]; 69% with Surigaonon [sgd]. *Lg Use:* Also use Cebuano [ceb]. *Maps:* 404:95, 405:95.

Caluyanun [clu] (Caluyanen, Caluyanhon). 30,000 (1994 SIL). Very few monolinguals. Western Visayas, Antique Province, Caluya Islands. *Status:* 5 (Developing). *Class:* Austronesian, Malayo-Polynesian, Philippine, Greater Central Philippine, Central Philippine, Bisayan, West. *Dialect:* Semirara. 69% comprehension of Hiligaynon [hil], 62% of Cuyonon [cyo]. *Lg Use:* All domains. All ages. Positive attitudes. 100% also use Hiligaynon [hil]. 100% also use Tagalog [tgl]. *Lg Dev:* Literacy rate in L1: 67%. Literacy rate in L2: 67%. Occasional use in primary and secondary schools. Poetry. NT: 1990. *Writing:* Latin script. *Other:* Christian. *Map:* 404:106.

Capiznon [cps] (Capisano, Capiseño). 639,000 (2000). Western Visayas, Capiz Province, northeast Panay. *Status:* 6a (Vigorous). *Class:* Austronesian, Malayo-Polynesian, Philippine, Greater Central Philippine, Central Philippine, Bisayan, Central, Peripheral. *Dialects:* None known. Sample had 91% comprehension of Hiligaynon [hil] narrative. *Lg Use:* Also use Filipino [fil]. *Map:* 404:102.

Cebuano [ceb] (Binisaya, Bisayan, Sebuano, Sugbuanon, Sugbuhanon, Visayan). 15,800,000 in Philippines (2000 census). Population total all countries: 15,810,000. Negros, Cebu, Bohol, Leyte, Biliran, and south Masbate provinces; parts of Mindanao. Also in United States. *Status:* 3 (Wider communication). Statutory language of provincial identity in Cebu Province, 4 other areas (1991, ACFLC Section 3(f), may not be subject to population threshold). *Class:* Austronesian, Malayo-Polynesian, Philippine, Greater Central Philippine, Central Philippine, Bisayan, Cebuan. *Dialects:* Boholano, Cebu, Leyte, Mindanao Visayan. Boholano sometimes considered a separate language. *Lg Use:* Also use Bolinao [smk]. Used as L2 by Ata [atm], Butuanon [btw], Central Sama [sml], Central Subanen [syb], Chavacano [cbk], Cotabato Manobo [mta], Davawenyo [daw], Giangan [bgi], Higaonon [mba], Ilianen Manobo [mbi], Inabaknon [abx], Kagan Kalagan [kll], Kalagan [kqe], Kamayo [kyk], Kinamiging Manobo [mkx], Kolibugan Subanon [skn], Koronadal Blaan [bpr], Mandaya [mry], Matigsalug Manobo [mbt], Northern Subanen [stb], Obo Manobo [obo], Porohanon [prh], Rajah Kabunsuwan Manobo [mqk], Sangil [snl], Sarangani Blaan [bps], Southern Subanen [laa], Surigaonon [sgd], Tagakaulo [klg], Tandaganon [tgn]. *Lg Dev:* Dictionary. Grammar. Bible: 1917–1981. *Writing:* Braille script. Latin script, primary usage. *Other:* Christian. *Maps:* 404:97, 405:97.

Chavacano [cbk] (Chabacano, Chabakano, Zamboangueño). 1,200,000 (Quilis 1996). 155,000 Zamboangueño (Holm 1989); 359,000 Zamboangueño (Rubino 2008); 27,800 Caviteño; 3,750 Ternateño (1975 census); 5,470 Cotabato Chavacano (Wurm and Hattori 1981). Mindanao, Zamboanga and Basilan provinces, Kabasalan, Siay, Margosatubig, Ipil, Malangas, Lapuyan, Buug, Tungawan, Alicia, Isabela, Lamitan, Maluso, Malamawi, and Cotabato city; Cavite, Ternate, and Ermita near Manila. Speakers in 60 of 66 provinces (1970 census). *Status:* 4 (Educational). *Class:* Creole, Spanish based. *Dialects:* Caviteño, Cotabato Chavacano (Cotabateño), Davaweño

Zamboangueño (Abakay Spanish, Davao Chavacano, Davaoeño, Davaweño), Ermitaño (Ermiteño), Ternateño (Ternateño Chavacano), Zamboangueño (Chavacano). *Type:* Accusative actancy structure. *Lg Use:* Davaweño Zamboangueño dialect may have no remaining speakers. Ermiteño is extinct; Zamboangueño, Caviteño, and Cotabateño are still used. Most domains. All ages. Positive attitudes. Nearly all also use Filipino [fil]. Also use Cebuano [ceb], Tausug [tsg]. Used as L2 by Balangingih Sama [sse], Central Sama [sml], Yakan [yka]. *Lg Dev:* Literacy rate in L1: 80%. Literacy rate in L2: 80%. Taught in primary schools. Poetry. Radio programs. Films. TV. Dictionary. Grammar. NT: 1981. *Writing:* Braille script. Latin script, primary usage. *Other:* A creole with predominantly Spanish vocabulary and Philippine-type grammatical structure. Christian. *Map:* 405:136.

Chinese, Mandarin [cmn]. 500 in Philippines. Ethnic population: All ethnic Chinese are 53,300 (1990 census). *Status:* 3 (Wider communication). *Lg Use:* Used as L2 by Ibatan [ivb]. See main entry on page 67.

Chinese, Min Nan [nan] (Min Nan). 592,000 in Philippines (1982). 99% of Chinese population in the Philippines (1982). *Status:* 5 (Developing). *Lg Use:* Used as L2 by Ibatan [ivb]. See main entry on page 68.

Chinese, Yue [yue]. 9,780 in Philippines (2000). *Status:* 5 (Developing). See main entry on page 69.

Cuyonon [cyo] (Cuyo, Cuyono, Cuyunon, Kuyonon, Kuyunon). 123,000 (1990 census). Palawan coast, Cuyo Islands between Palawan and Panay. *Status:* 5 (Developing). *Class:* Austronesian, Malayo-Polynesian, Philippine, Greater Central Philippine, Central Philippine, Bisayan, West, Kuyan. *Dialects:* None known. Reportedly similar to Ratagnon [btn]. *Lg Use:* 2,000 also use Calamian Tagbanwa [tbk]. Cuyonon married to or who live near Tagbanwas. Used as L2 by Agutaynen [agn], Central Tagbanwa [tgt], Kagayanen [cgc]. *Lg Dev:* NT: 1982. *Writing:* Latin script. *Map:* 404:120.

Davawenyo [daw] (Davaoeño, Davaweño, Matino). 147,000 (1990 census). Mindanao, Davao Oriental and Davao del Sur provinces. *Status:* 6a (Vigorous). *Class:* Austronesian, Malayo-Polynesian, Philippine, Greater Central Philippine, Central Philippine, Mansakan, Davawenyo. *Dialects:* Synthesis of Filipino [fil], Cebuano [ceb], other Visayan dialects. Some Spanish [spa] words. Not a Spanish creole. Different from Davawenyo dialect of Chavacano [cbk]. 2 dialects: East Coast (90% of speakers), and Davao City area (Whinnom 1956). Lowland Davawenyo have 89% intelligibility of Kamayo [kyk]. *Lg Use:* Lowland Davawenyo also use Cebuano [ceb]. Highland Davawenyo have low comprehension of Cebuano. *Map:* 405:159.

Dumagat, Remontado [agv] (Hatang-Kayey, Remontado Agta, Sinauna, Sinauna Tagalog). 2,530 (2000). Luzon, Rizal Province, Santa Inez; Quezon Province, General Nakar, Paimohuan. *Status:* 8a (Moribund). *Class:* Austronesian, Malayo-Polynesian, Philippine, Central Luzon, Sinauna. *Dialects:* None known. Lexical similarity: 73% with Filipino [fil], 37% with Umiray Dumaget Agta [due]. *Lg Use:* Also use Filipino [fil]. *Other:* Reportedly highly endangered; possibly no longer in use (2006 SIL). Reportedly high levels of bilingualism (1989 SIL). Previously erroneously identified as a variety of Agta. *Map:* 403:50.

English [eng]. 20,000 in Philippines (Crystal 2003). L2 users: 40,000,000 in Philippines (Crystal 2003). *Status:* 1 (National). Statutory national working language (1987, Constitution, Article 14(7)). See main entry on page 319.

Filipino [fil]. L2 users: 45,000,000 (2013). Widely spoken as L2. Widespread. *Status:* 1 (National). Statutory national language (1987, Constitution, Article 14(6)), not used in all official domains. *Class:* Austronesian, Malayo-Polynesian, Philippine, Greater Central Philippine, Central Philippine, Tagalog. *Lg Dev:* Taught in primary and secondary schools. Bible: 1905. *Writing:* Latin script. Tagalog script, no longer in use. *Other:* Primarily based on Tagalog [tgl] with some terminology imported from other regional languages. Christian.

Ga'dang [gdg] (Baliwon, Gaddang, Ginabwal). 6,000 (2002 SIL). Very few monolinguals. Luzon, Mountain Province, Paracelis; Ifugao Province, Potia. *Status:* 5 (Developing). *Class:* Austronesian, Malayo-Polynesian, Philippine, Northern Luzon, Northern Cordilleran, Cagayan Valley, Ibanagic, Gaddangic. *Dialects:* None known. Lexical similarity: 80% with Gaddang [gad]. *Lg Use:* Also use Ilocano [ilo]. *Lg Dev:* Literacy rate in L1: 60%–80%. Literacy rate in L2: 60%–80%. NT: 2000. *Writing:* Latin script. *Other:* Traditional religion, Christian. *Map:* 403:18.

Gaddang [gad] (Cagayan). 30,000 (1984 SIL). Luzon, central Isabela Province; Nueva Vizcaya Province, Bagabag, Bayombong, and Solano municipalities. *Status:* 6a (Vigorous). *Class:* Austronesian, Malayo-Polynesian, Philippine, Northern Luzon, Northern Cordilleran, Cagayan Valley, Ibanagic, Gaddangic. *Dialects:* None known. Less than 80% intelligibility of Ga'dang [gdg]. Lexical similarity: 80% with Ga'dang [gdg]. *Lg Use:* Also use Ilocano [ilo]. *Lg Dev:* Dictionary. Grammar. *Other:* A lowland group. Ethnonym: Gaddang for those in Nueva Vizcaya; Cagayan, for those in central Isabela. Christian. *Map:* 403:26.

Giangan [bgi] (Atto, Bagobo, Clata, Eto, Guanga, Gulanga, Jangan). 55,000 (1990 census). Mindanao, Davao City; Davao del Sur Province, east slopes of Mount Apo. *Status:* 7 (Shifting). *Class:* Austronesian, Malayo-Polynesian, Philippine, Bilic. *Dialects:* None known. 69% comprehension of Tagabawa [bgs]; 79% of Obo Manobo [obo]. Lexical similarity: 34% with Tagabawa [bgs], 35% with Obo Manobo [obo], 43% with Blaan [bpr]. *Lg Use:* Marginally bilingual in Cebuano [ceb]. *Other:* Different from Manobo. *Map:* 405:158.

Hanunoo [hnn] (Hanonoo). 13,000 (2000). South Oriental Mindoro Province. *Status:* 5 (Developing). *Class:* Austronesian, Malayo-Polynesian, Philippine, Greater Central Philippine, South Mangyan, Hanunoo. *Dialects:* Binli, Bulalakawnon, Gubatnon (Gubat, Sorsogonon), Kagankan, Waigan, Wawan. *Lg Dev:* NT: 1985. *Writing:* Hanunoo script, used in love songs and correspondence. Latin script, primary usage. *Map:* 404:116.

Higaonon [mba] (Higaunon, Misamis Higaonon Manobo). 30,000 (1996 NTM). North central Mindanao, Misamis Oriental Province, south of Ginoog city. *Status:* 5 (Developing). *Class:* Austronesian, Malayo-Polynesian, Philippine, Greater Central Philippine, Manobo, North. *Dialects:* None known. Related to Binukid [bkd] with 77%–81% intelligibility. *Lg Use:* Also use Cebuano [ceb]. *Lg Dev:* NT: 2009. *Writing:* Latin script. *Map:* 405:171.

Hiligaynon [hil] (Hiligainon, Illogo, Ilonggo). 5,770,000 in Philippines (2000 census). Western Visayas, Panay, Iloilo and Capiz provinces; Negros Occidental Province. Also in United States. *Status:* 3 (Wider communication). Statutory language of provincial identity in Iloilo, 4 other provinces (1991, ACFLC Section 3(f), may not be subject to population threshold). *Class:* Austronesian, Malayo-Polynesian, Philippine, Greater Central Philippine, Central Philippine, Bisayan, Central, Peripheral. *Dialects:* Hiligaynon, Kari, Kawayan. *Lg Use:* Also use Filipino [fil]. Used as L2 by Ati [atk], Caluyanun [clu], Central Subanen [syb], Cotabato Manobo [mta], Inakeanon [akl], Inonhan [loc], Kagayanen [cgc], Kinaray-a [krj], Tagakaulo [klg]. *Lg Dev:* Grammar. Bible: 1912–2002. *Writing:* Braille script. Latin script, primary usage. *Other:* Christian. *Maps:* 404:99, 405:99.

Ibaloi [ibl] (Benguet-Igorot, Ibadoy, Ibaloy, Igodor, Inibaloi, Nabaloi). 111,000 (1990 census). Luzon, central and south Benguet Province, west Nueva Vizcaya Province. *Status:* 5 (Developing). *Class:* Austronesian, Malayo-Polynesian, Philippine, Northern Luzon, Meso-Cordilleran, South-Central Cordilleran, Southern Cordilleran, West Southern Cordilleran, Nuclear Southern Cordilleran, Ibaloy. *Dialects:* Bokod, Daklan, Kabayan. *Lg Use:* Used as L2 by Karao [kyj]. *Lg Dev:* Literacy rate in L1: 75%–100%. Literacy rate in L2: 75%–100%. NT: 1978. *Writing:* Latin script. *Map:* 403:35.

Ibanag [ibg] (Ybanag). 500,000 (1990 SIL). Luzon, Isabela and Cagayan provinces. *Status:* 4 (Educational). De facto language of provincial identity in Cagayan and Isabela provinces. *Class:* Austronesian, Malayo-Polynesian, Philippine, Northern Luzon, Northern Cordilleran, Cagayan Valley, Ibanagic. *Dialects:* North Ibanag, South Ibanag. Intelligibility with Itawit [itv] 69%. *Type:* VSO; genitives after noun heads; adjectives and numerals before noun heads; CV, CVC; nontonal. *Lg Use:* Positive attitudes. Also use Filipino [fil], Ilocano [ilo]. Used as L2 by Faire Atta [azt], Pudtol Atta [atp]. *Lg Dev:* Literacy rate in L1: 75%–100%. Literacy rate in L2: 75%–100%. Taught in primary schools, in Cayagan and Isabela provinces. NT: 1911–1989. *Writing:* Latin script. *Map:* 403:15.

Ibatan [ivb] (Babuyan, Ibataan, Ivatan). 1,240 (2007 National Commission for Indigenous Peoples). 0 monolinguals. Ethnic population: 1,400 (2008 SIL). North of Luzon, Babuyan Islands, Ibatan tribe ancestral domain. *Status:* 4 (Educational). *Class:* Austronesian, Malayo-Polynesian, Philippine, Bashiic, Ivatan. *Dialects:* None known. Intelligibility of Itbayaten Ivatan [ivv] 64%; Basco Ivatan [ivv] 31%. Lexical similarity: 72% with Itbayaten Ivatan [ivv], 74% with Basco Ivatan [ivv] (1974–1975 SIL survey). *Lg Use:* Shifting to Ilocano [ilo]. All domains as well as religious services and ceremonies, and local commerce. All ages. Positive attitudes. Increasingly bilingual in Ilocano [ilo]. Code switching common between Ilocano and Ibatan (2007 SIL). Also use English [eng], Filipino [fil], Mandarin Chinese [cmn], Min Nan Chinese [nan]. Used as L2 by Ilocano [ilo]. *Lg Dev:* Literacy rate in L1: 90%. Literacy rate in L2: 80% (2007 SIL). All school-aged children are literate. Schooling is in Filipino [fil] or English [eng]. Taught in primary schools, but only if instructions not understood in English (2007 SIL). Taught in secondary schools. Grammar. NT: 1996. *Writing:* Latin script. *Other:* Since 1978, speakers have increased from 450 to 1,220. On June 1, 2007, the Ibatan were awarded title to their island home of Babuyan Claro with all collective rights to natural resources, including 5 km of ocean around the island. The ancestral domain was established with the help of the National Commission on Indigenous Peoples of the Philippines and based on the Indigenous Peoples Rights Act of 1997 (2007 SIL). Christian. *Map:* 403:3.

Ifugao, Amganad [ifa] (Amganad, Ifugaw). 27,100 (2000 SIL). 168,000 all Ifugao (1990 census). 10,000 monolinguals. L2 users: A few speakers of other languages speak Ifugao in school, market, commerce. Luzon, central Ifugao Province. *Status:* 5 (Developing). *Class:* Austronesian, Malayo-Polynesian, Philippine, Northern Luzon, Meso-Cordilleran, South-Central Cordilleran, Central Cordilleran, North Central Cordilleran, Nuclear Cordilleran, Ifugaw. *Dialects:* Banaue Ifugao, Burnay Ifugao. Intelligibility of Burnay dialect 81%. Lexical similarity: 83% with Burnay dialect. *Lg Use:* Many Ifugao parents raising children in non-Ifugao-speaking areas do not teach Ifugao to their children (2007 SIL). All domains as well as religious services, traditional ceremonies, administration, and commerce. All ages. Positive attitudes. Also use English [eng], Filipino [fil], Ilocano [ilo]. Used as L2 by Tuwali Ifugao [ifk]. *Lg Dev:* Literacy rate in L1: 20%. Literacy rate in L2: 60% (2007 SIL). 17,550 read it and 14,000 write it (2007 SIL). Videos. NT: 1980–2002. *Writing:* Latin script. *Other:* Christian, traditional religion. *Map:* 403:22.

Ifugao, Batad [ifb] (Ayangan Ifugao, Batad, Ifugaw). 43,000 (1987 SIL). Luzon, Ifugao Province. *Status:* 5 (Developing). *Class:* Austronesian, Malayo-Polynesian, Philippine, Northern Luzon, Meso-Cordilleran, South-Central Cordilleran, Central Cordilleran, North Central Cordilleran, Nuclear Cordilleran, Ifugaw. *Dialect:* Ducligan Ifugao. Intelligibility of Ayangan Batad Ifugao: Mayoyao [ifu] 86%–94%. Lexical similarity: 89% with Ducligan dialect, 79% with Mayoyao [ifu]. *Lg Dev:* Literacy rate in L1: 55%–60%. Literacy rate in L2: 55%–60%. Dictionary. Bible: 2010. *Writing:* Latin script. *Other:* Traditional religion, Christian. *Map:* 403:20.

Ifugao, Mayoyao [ifu] (Ifugaw, Mayaoyaw, Mayoyao). 30,000 (2007 SIL). L2 users: 0. Luzon, Ifugao Province. *Status:* 4 (Educational). *Class:* Austronesian, Malayo-Polynesian, Philippine, Northern Luzon, Meso-Cordilleran, South-Central Cordilleran, Central Cordilleran, North Central Cordilleran, Nuclear Cordilleran, Ifugaw. *Dialects:* None known. 86%–94% intelligibility of Batad Ifugao [ifb]. Grammatical markers are different. Lexical similarity: 54% with Batad Ifugao [ifb]. *Lg Use:* Home and personal interaction; in school for bridging; some churches. All ages. Positive attitudes. Also use English [eng], Ilocano [ilo]. *Lg Dev:* Literacy rate in L1: more than 60%. Literacy rate in L2: 50%–60%. Taught in primary schools. Poetry. New media. NT: 2004. *Writing:* Latin script. *Other:* Traditional religion, Christian. *Map:* 403:19.

Ifugao, Tuwali [ifk] (Gilipanes, Ifugaw, Kiangan Ifugao, Quiangan). 30,000 (2000 SIL), increasing. Only those below grade-school age are monolingual. L2 users: Occasionally speakers of other languages will use Tuwali, mostly in trading or because of intermarriage. Luzon, south Ifugao Province. *Status:* 4 (Educational). *Class:* Austronesian, Malayo-Polynesian, Philippine, Northern Luzon, Meso-Cordilleran, South-Central Cordilleran, Central Cordilleran, North Central Cordilleran, Nuclear Cordilleran, Ifugaw. *Dialects:* Hapao Ifugao, Hungduan Ifugao, Lagawe Ifugao. 77% intelligibility of Amganad Ifugao [ifa], 78% of Batad Ifugao [ifb]. Hapao dialect has 88% intelligibility of Hungduan dialect. Lexical similarity: 80% with Amganad Ifugao [ifa], 72% with Batad Ifugao [ifb], 78% with Hapao dialect, 86% with Hungduan dialect. *Type:* VSO; prepositions; genitives, relatives after noun heads; articles, adjectives, numerals before noun heads; question word initial; 1 suffix, 2 infixes; passives; causatives; comparatives; V, CV, CVC. *Lg Use:* Vigorous. Used by other language speakers in trading and in exogamous marriages. High bilingualism; all are bilingual by the time they are in elementary school. All domains. Court, religion, commerce. All ages. Positive attitudes. 100% also use Amganad Ifugao [ifa]. 100% also use English [eng]. Those over 40 use more English than others. 100% also use Filipino [fil]. 100% also use Ilocano [ilo]. Used as L2 by Keley-i Kallahan [ify]. *Lg Dev:* Literacy rate in L1: 25,000 can read and write. Literacy rate in L2: 60%. Taught in primary schools. Bible: 2005. *Writing:* Latin script. *Other:* Kiangan is the place, Tuwali the language. Christian. *Map:* 403:27.

Ilocano [ilo] (Ilokano, Iloko). 6,920,000 in Philippines (2000 census). Population total all countries: 7,016,400. Northwest Luzon, La Union and Ilocos provinces; Babuyan islands; Cagayan valley, Mindoro, Mindanao areas. Also in

Canada, United States. *Status:* 3 (Wider communication). Statutory language of provincial identity in northwest Luzon Island, other areas (1991, ACFLC Section 3(f), may not be subject to population threshold). *Class:* Austronesian, Malayo-Polynesian, Philippine, Northern Luzon, Ilocano. *Dialects:* None known. A pidginized form is used in northern Luzon highlands. *Lg Use:* Also use Bolinao [smk]. Ilocano migrants to the islands also use Ibatan [ivb]. Also use Abellen Ayta [abp]. Used as L2 by Abellen Ayta [abp], Adasen [tiu], Amganad Ifugao [ifa], Arta [atz], Balangao [blw], Banao Itneg [bjx], Binongan Itneg [itb], Butbut Kalinga [kyb], Central Bontok [lbk], Central Cagayan Agta [agt], Eastern Bontok [ebk], Ga'dang [gdg], Gaddang [gad], Ibanag [ibg], Ibatan [ivb], Inlaod Itneg [iti], Isinai [inn], Isnag [isd], Itawit [itv], Karao [kyj], Kayapa Kallahan [kak], Keley-i Kallahan [ify], Limos Kalinga [kmk], Lubuagan Kalinga [knb], Maeng Itneg [itt], Majukayang Kalinga [kmd], Masadiit Itneg [tis], Mayoyao Ifugao [ifu], Moyadan Itneg [ity], Northern Bontok [rbk], Pahanan Agta [apf], Pamplona Atta [att], Paranan [prf], Sambal [xsb], Southern Bontok [obk], Southern Kalinga [ksc], Southwestern Bontok [vbk], Tanudan Kalinga [kml], Tuwali Ifugao [ifk], Umiray Dumaget Agta [due], Yogad [yog]. *Lg Dev:* Bible: 1909–1996. *Writing:* Braille script. Latin script, primary usage. Tagalog script, no longer in use. *Other:* Christian. *Map:* 403:2.

Ilongot [ilk] (Bugkalut, Bukalot, Lingotes). 50,800 (1990 census). Luzon, east Nueva Vizcaya and west Quirino provinces. *Status:* 5 (Developing). *Class:* Austronesian, Malayo-Polynesian, Philippine, Northern Luzon, Meso-Cordilleran, South-Central Cordilleran, Southern Cordilleran, Ilongot. *Dialects:* Abaka (Abaca), Egongot, Ibalao (Ibilao), Italon, Iyongut. *Lg Use:* Used as L2 by Tboli [tbl]. *Lg Dev:* NT: 1982. *Writing:* Latin script. *Map:* 403:32.

Inabaknon [abx] (Abaknon, Abaknon Sama, Capuleño, Kapul, Sama). 26,400 (2010 M. Jacobson). Population increases 300–500 yearly. About 500 leave annually to find opportunities elsewhere. 3,000 monolinguals. Almost all children. North Samar Province, east Visayas region, San Bernardino strait, Capul island, west Samar coast facing the island; Manila. *Status:* 4 (Educational). *Class:* Austronesian, Malayo-Polynesian, Greater Barito, Sama-Bajaw, Abaknon. *Lg Use:* Vigorous. New inhabitants of Capul Island tend to learn the language or leave. All domains. All ages. Also use Cebuano [ceb], Central Bikol [bcl], English [eng], Filipino [fil]. *Lg Dev:* Literacy rate in L1: 11,000 can read and write. Literacy rate in L2: 90%–95%. Written form used in village health education, song books, some event programs, and religious ceremonies. Taught in primary schools. NT: 1996. *Writing:* Latin script. *Other:* Ethnic autonym: Abaknon, Capul is the island and Sama the language family. Heteroglossonym: Capuleño. Christian (Roman Catholic). *Map:* 404:85.

Inakeanon [akl] (Aklan, Aklano, Aklanon, Aklanon-Bisayan, Panay). 435,000 in Philippines (2000 census). Population total all countries: 458,600. Aklan Province, west Visayas, north Panay. Also in United States. *Status:* 4 (Educational). De facto language of provincial identity in Aklan and Capiz provinces. *Class:* Austronesian, Malayo-Polynesian, Philippine, Greater Central Philippine, Central Philippine, Bisayan, West, Aklan. *Dialects:* None known. 66% intelligibility with Hiligaynon [hil]. Lexical similarity: 68% with Hiligaynon [hil]. *Lg Use:* Also use Hiligaynon [hil]. *Lg Dev:* Literacy rate in L1: 70%. Literacy rate in L2: 70%. Taught in primary schools, in Aklan and Capiz. Bible portions: 1990–1996. *Writing:* Latin script. *Map:* 404:103.

Inonhan [loc] (Loocnon, Looknon, "Unhan" *pej.*). 85,800 (2000). Romblon Province, South Tablas island; Mindoro Oriental and Mindoro Occidental provinces. *Status:* 5 (Developing). *Class:* Austronesian, Malayo-Polynesian, Philippine, Greater Central Philippine, Central Philippine, Bisayan, West, North Central. *Dialects:* Alcantaranon, Bulalakaw, Dispoholnon, Looknon. Lexical similarity: 70% with Odionganon [bno] (Bantuanon), 93% with Aklanon [akl], 86% with Caluyanun [clu]. *Lg Use:* Also use Hiligaynon [hil]. Used as L2 by Bantoanon [bno]. *Lg Dev:* NT: 2000. *Writing:* Latin script. *Other:* Loocnon is a town name. *Map:* 404:107.

Iranun [ill]. 241,000 in Philippines (1981 SIL). Population total all countries: 256,000. Mindanao, Maguindanao, North Cotabato, South Cotabato, Sultan Kuderat, Zamboanga del Sur, and Bukidnon provinces. Also in Malaysia. *Status:* 6a (Vigorous). *Class:* Austronesian, Malayo-Polynesian, Philippine, Greater Central Philippine, Danao, Maranao-Iranon. *Dialects:* Ilanon, Ilanum, Illanon, Iranon. 85% intelligibility of Maranao [mrw] of the Philippines. Most closely related to Maranao. Related to, but distinct from, Maguindanaon [mdh]. Different from Lahanan [lhn] of Sarawak. *Writing:* Latin script, developed in about 2000. *Map:* 405:144.

Iraya [iry]. 10,000 (1991 OMF). North Mindoro island. *Status:* 5 (Developing). *Class:* Austronesian, Malayo-Polynesian, Philippine, North Mangyan. *Dialects:* Abra-De-Ilog, Alag-Bako, Pagbahan, Palauan-Calavite, Pambuhan, Santa Cruz. *Lg Use:* Many also use Filipino [fil] in the home. *Lg Dev:* NT: 1991. *Writing:* Latin script. *Map:* 404:113.

Isinai [inn] (Inmeas, Insinai, Isinay, Isnay). 5,520 (1990 census). Luzon, Nueva Vizcaya Province, Bambang, Dupax, and Aritao municipalities. *Status:* 6b (Threatened). *Class:* Austronesian, Malayo-Polynesian, Philippine, Northern Luzon, Meso-Cordilleran, South-Central Cordilleran, Central Cordilleran, Isinai. *Dialects:* None known. Not similar to other languages. Lexical similarity: 47% with Ilocano [ilo]. *Lg Use:* Positive attitudes. Basic proficiency in Ilocano [ilo]. *Map:* 403:33.

Isnag [isd] (Dibagat-Kabugao-Isneg, Isneg, Maragat). 30,000 (1994 SIL). Luzon, north Apayao Province. *Status:* 4 (Educational). *Class:* Austronesian, Malayo-Polynesian, Philippine, Northern Luzon, Northern Cordilleran, Cagayan Valley, Isnag. *Dialects:* Bayag, Calanasan, Dibagat-Kabugao, Karagawan (Daragawan), Talifugu-Ripang (Tawini). Calanasan dialect 94% intelligibility of Dibagat dialect, 88% of Ilocano [ilo]; Talifugu-Ripang 89% of Dibagat, 71% of Ilocano. *Lg Use:* Also use Ilocano [ilo]. *Lg Dev:* Literacy rate in L1: 50%. Literacy rate in L2: 50%. NT: 1980–2005. *Writing:* Latin script. *Map:* 403:7.

Itawit [itv] (Itawes, Itawis, Tawit). 134,000 (1990 census). 120,000 Itawit, 14,500 Malaweg. Luzon, south Cagayan Province. *Status:* 5 (Developing). *Class:* Austronesian, Malayo-Polynesian, Philippine, Northern Luzon, Northern Cordilleran, Cagayan Valley, Ibanagic. *Dialects:* Itawis, Malaweg (Malaueg). Related to Ibanag languages; 72% intelligibility of South Ibanag [ibg]; 68% of Ilocano [ilo]. Lexical similarity: 53% with Ilocano [ilo]. *Lg Use:* Also use Ilocano [ilo]. *Lg Dev:* NT: 1992. *Writing:* Latin script. *Other:* Malaweg may be reclassified as a separate language. *Map:* 403:16.

Itneg, Banao [bjx] (Banao, Banaw, Itneg, Timggian, Tinguian). 3,500 (2003 SIL). Unknown number in Malibcong dialect area. Luzon, east Abra Province. *Status:* 6a (Vigorous). *Class:* Austronesian, Malayo-Polynesian, Philippine, Northern Luzon, Meso-Cordilleran, South-Central Cordilleran, Central Cordilleran, North Central Cordilleran, Kalinga-Itneg, Kalinga. *Dialects:* Banao Pikekj, Gubang Itneg, Malibcong Banao. Lexical similarity: Malibcong Banao 58% with Ilocano [ilo], 81%

with Lubuagan Kalinga [knb], 73% with Limos Kalinga [kmk]; Banao Pikek (Daguioman) dialect 62% with Ilocano, 83% with Masadiit and Boliney Itneg [tis], 79% with Masadiit and Sallapadan Itneg [tis], 78% with the Banao dialect of Malibcong, and 73% with Binongan Itneg [itb]. *Lg Use:* Moderate vitality. Home, community. All ages. Positive attitudes. Also use English [eng], Filipino [fil], Ilocano [ilo]. *Other:* High value placed on education. Traditional religion, Christian (Roman Catholic). *Map:* 403:58.

Itneg, Binongan [itb] (Tingguian, Tinguian). 7,500 (2003 SIL). 46,400 in all Itneg varieties (1990 census). Luzon, Abra Province, Licuan-Baay. *Status:* 6a (Vigorous). *Class:* Austronesian, Malayo-Polynesian, Philippine, Northern Luzon, Meso-Cordilleran, South-Central Cordilleran, Central Cordilleran, North Central Cordilleran, Kalinga-Itneg, Itneg. *Dialects:* None known. Lexical similarity: 69% with Ilocano [ilo], 79% with Masadiit Itneg [tis]. *Lg Use:* Vigorous. Home, community. All ages. Also use English [eng], Filipino [fil], Ilocano [ilo]. *Lg Dev:* Grammar. Bible portions: 1967. *Writing:* Latin script. *Other:* Christian. *Map:* 403:57.

Itneg, Inlaod [iti] (Tinggian, Tinguian). 9,000 (2003 SIL). Northern Luzon, Abra Province, a few villages in Penarubia, Lagangilang, Danglas, and Langiden municipalities; southwest of Binongan Itneg [itb] and northwest of Masadiit Itneg [tis] language areas. *Status:* 6b (Threatened). *Class:* Austronesian, Malayo-Polynesian, Philippine, Northern Luzon, Meso-Cordilleran, South-Central Cordilleran, Central Cordilleran, North Central Cordilleran, Kalinga-Itneg, Itneg. *Dialects:* None known. Lexical similarity: Inlaod of Langiden 73% with Ilocano [ilo]; Inlaod of Danglas 71% with Ilocano, 75%–77% with Binongan Itneg [itb], 75%–76% with Masadiit [tis] of Sallapadan, 74%–75% with Moyadan Itneg [ity]. Inlaod of Langiden and Inlaod of Danglas 86% with each other. *Lg Use:* Vigorous in some communities. Home, community. Use among children decreasing. Also use English [eng], Filipino [fil], Ilocano [ilo]. *Other:* Christian. *Map:* 403:4.

Itneg, Maeng [itt] (Luba-Tiempo Itneg, Southern Itneg). 18,000 (2003 SIL). Ethnic population: 18,000. Luzon, south Abra Province, Luba, Tubo, and Villavisciosa municipalities. *Status:* 6a (Vigorous). *Class:* Austronesian, Malayo-Polynesian, Philippine, Northern Luzon, Meso-Cordilleran, South-Central Cordilleran, Central Cordilleran, North Central Cordilleran, Kalinga-Itneg, Itneg. *Dialects:* None known. Lexical similarity: Tubo area 60% with Ilocano [ilo], 68% with Northern Kankanaey [kne]; Villavisciosa area 76% with Ilocano, 61% with Northern Kankanaey. *Lg Use:* Vigorous. Home, community. All ages. Also use English [eng], Filipino [fil], Ilocano [ilo]. *Other:* Christian. *Map:* 403:56.

Itneg, Masadiit [tis]. 7,500. 45,000 all Itnegs in Abra Province. Luzon, Abra Province, Sallapadan, Bucloc, and Boliney municipalities. *Status:* 6a (Vigorous). *Class:* Austronesian, Malayo-Polynesian, Philippine, Northern Luzon, Meso-Cordilleran, South-Central Cordilleran, Central Cordilleran, North Central Cordilleran, Kalinga-Itneg, Itneg. *Dialects:* Masadiit Boliney, Masadiit Sallapadan. Lexical similarity: 62% with Ilocano [ilo], 70% with Guinaang Kalinga [knb], 86% with Binongan Itneg [itb]. *Lg Use:* Vigorous. Home, community. All ages. Also use English [eng], Filipino [fil], Ilocano [ilo]. *Other:* Christian (Roman Catholic), Christian (Protestant). *Map:* 403:55.

Itneg, Moyadan [ity] (Tinggian, Tinguian). 12,000 (2003 SIL). Luzon, Abra Province. *Status:* 6a (Vigorous). *Class:* Austronesian, Malayo-Polynesian, Philippine, Northern Luzon, Meso-Cordilleran, South-Central Cordilleran, Central Cordilleran, North Central Cordilleran, Kalinga-Itneg, Itneg. *Dialects:* None known. Lexical similarity: 68% with Ilocano [ilo], 85% with Masadiit Sallapadan [tis], 80% with Masadiit Boliney [tis], 76% with Binongan Itneg [itb], 75% with Inlaod Danglas [iti], 74% with Inlaod Langiden [iti], 73% with Maeng [itt] of Tubo. *Lg Use:* Vigorous. Home, community. All ages. Positive attitudes. Also use Filipino [fil], Ilocano [ilo], Spanish [spa]. *Other:* Christian (Roman Catholic). *Map:* 403:54.

Ivatan [ivv]. 35,000 (1998 SIL), increasing. 3,450 Itbayatan (1996 census). North of Luzon, Batanes Islands. Many relocated to Mindanao near Bukidnon, Lanao del Sur, and Cotabato; Manila, Luzon, and Palawan. *Status:* 4 (Educational). De facto language of provincial identity in Batanes province. *Class:* Austronesian, Malayo-Polynesian, Philippine, Bashiic, Ivatan. *Dialects:* Basco Ivatan, Itbayaten, Southern Ivatan. *Type:* VSO. *Lg Use:* Vigorous. Only very young and very old are monolingual. Not used in schools. Home, administration, religion, commerce, labor relations, letters. All ages. Positive attitudes. 34,300 also use English [eng]. 92% also use Filipino [fil]. *Lg Dev:* Literacy rate in L1: 92%. Literary tradition of laji (old songs) and folklore. Letters, hymnbooks. Taught in primary schools, in the Batanes. Poetry. New media. Radio programs. Dictionary. Grammar. NT: 1984. *Writing:* Latin script. *Other:* Christian (Roman Catholic). *Map:* 403:1.

I-wak [iwk] (Iwaak). 3,260 (2000). Luzon, Benguet Province, east Itogon, Tojongan, Bakes, Lebeng, Domolpos, Bujasjas, Kayo-ko, and Salaksak (in Kayapa) villages; also in Nueva Ecija, Capintalan, but speak only Kallahan [kak]. *Status:* 6a (Vigorous). *Class:* Austronesian, Malayo-Polynesian, Philippine, Northern Luzon, Meso-Cordilleran, South-Central Cordilleran, Southern Cordilleran, West Southern Cordilleran, Nuclear Southern Cordilleran, Ibaloy. *Dialects:* None known. Related to Karao [kyj], Ibaloi [ibl], and Kallahan [kak]. *Other:* Less acculturated to outside culture than other mountain groups. *Map:* 403:36.

Kagayanen [cgc] (Cagayano, Kagay-anen, Kinagayanen). 30,000 (2007 SIL), increasing. Few monolinguals. Ethnic population: 30,000 (2007 SIL). L2 users: Government workers or church workers, teachers. Palawan Province, Cagayan island between Negros and Palawan; Palawan coastal communities; south Palawan, Balabac island, Quezon and Rizal areas; north Palawan, Busuanga, Coron municipality; Iloilo Province, Silay, Negros, and Manila. *Status:* 4 (Educational). *Class:* Austronesian, Malayo-Polynesian, Philippine, Greater Central Philippine, Manobo, North. *Dialect:* Calamian Kagayanen. *Type:* VSO; prepositions; genitives after noun heads; articles, adjectives, numerals all before noun heads; relatives (and relative clauses) after noun heads; question word in sentence-initial position; 2 maximum number of suffixes, 1 prefix; word order distinguishes subjects, objects and indirect objects, given and new information, topic and comment; affixes do not indicate case of noun phrases; passives; causatives; comparatives; ergativity; CV, CCV, CVC, CCVC (V and VC with glottal initial); nontonal. *Lg Use:* Vigorous. All domains. Some oral use in local administration, commerce, religion, some schools. Letters, oral literature. All ages. Positive attitudes. Also use Cuyonon [cyo], English [eng], Filipino [fil], Hiligaynon [hil]. *Lg Dev:* Literacy rate in L1: 85%. Literacy rate in L2: 75% Hiligaynon, Filipino, Cuyunon, Kinaray-a, Cebuano. Tendency to believe reading is in Filipino [fil] or English [eng]. Kagayanen used for speaking (2007 SIL). Taught in primary and secondary schools. Poetry. Newspapers. Radio programs. Videos. Dictionary. NT: 2007. *Writing:* Latin script. *Other:* A growing number are moving to cities for economic improvement, education. Christian, traditional religion. *Maps:* 404:122, 405:122.

Kalagan [kqe] (Kaagan, Kalagan, Minuslim, Kinalagan). 70,000 (2002 census), decreasing. 7,000 monolinguals. Ethnic population: 70,000. L2 users: Used by those intermarrying with local speakers. Mindanao, Davao del Sur and Davao, Compostela Valley, and Davao Oriental provinces, east and west shores of Davao gulf. Isamal dialect: Samal Island; Western dialect: Davao Oriental Province, Lupon along the gulf down to Hagonoy and Guihing near Digos city; Eastern dialect: mainly Davao Oriental Province. *Status:* 5 (Developing). *Class:* Austronesian, Malayo-Polynesian, Philippine, Greater Central Philippine, Central Philippine, Mansakan, Western. *Dialects:* Eastern Kalagan, Isamal, Western Kalagan. Lexical similarity: 72% with Kagan [kll], 74% with Mansaka [msk], 83% with Mandaya [mry]. *Type:* VOS, VSO; prepositions; articles before adjectives, before numerals, before noun heads; question word in sentence-initial position; 3 maximum prefixes, 2 maximum suffixes. *Lg Use:* Strong in communities that are mainly Kalagan, but in mixed communities speakers tend to use Cebuano [ceb]. Youth bilingual in Cebuano, some are losing Kalagan ability. Home, neighborhood, religion. Adults; youth only in solid Kalagan communities. Sample scored 87% on Cebuano [ceb] narrative text. Also use English [eng], Tagalog [tgl]. Used as L2 by Koronadal Blaan [bpr], Tausug [tsg]. *Lg Dev:* Literacy rate in L1: 80%. Literacy rate in L2: 80% in Cebuano, 50% in Tagalog; English. Bible portions: 1989–2011. *Writing:* Latin script. *Other:* Muslim. *Map:* 405:157.

Kalagan, Kagan [kll] (Kaagan, Kagan Kalagan). 6,000 (1981 SIL). Mindanao, Davao del Sur Province near Digos city. *Status:* 5 (Developing). *Class:* Austronesian, Malayo-Polynesian, Philippine, Greater Central Philippine, Central Philippine, Mansakan, Western. *Dialects:* 82% intelligibility with Kalagan [kqe] dialect. *Type:* VOS, VSO; prepositions; genitives before noun heads; articles before adjectives, before and after numerals, before noun heads; relatives after noun heads; question word in sentence-initial position; 3 maximum prefixes, 2 maximum suffixes; word order distinguishes subjects, objects and indirect objects when case does not, word order distinguishes given and new information, topic and comment; affixes do not indicate case of noun phrases; verb affixes mark number; ergativity; passives; causatives; comparatives; CV, CVC, CVV, CVVC; nontonal. *Lg Use:* Positive attitudes. Also use Cebuano [ceb]. *Lg Dev:* Literacy rate in L2: Perhaps 60%. *Writing:* Latin script. *Map:* 405:162.

Kalinga, Butbut [kyb] (Butbut). 15,000 (2008), increasing. 1,000 monolinguals. Northern Luzon, Kalinga Province, Cordillera Region, Tinglayan and Butbut; Buscalan, Bugnay, Loccong, and Ngibat; Tabuk city, Lucnang, Pakak, Kataw, and Dinongsay; Rizal Province, Annenang, Malapiat, Andaraya, and Bua. *Status:* 4 (Educational). *Class:* Austronesian, Malayo-Polynesian, Philippine, Northern Luzon, Meso-Cordilleran, South-Central Cordilleran, Central Cordilleran, North Central Cordilleran, Kalinga-Itneg, Kalinga. *Dialects:* None known. 72% intelligibility of Limos Kalinga [kmk]; 44% of Ilocano [ilo]; 70% of Guinaang [knb], 47% of Tanudan [kml], 74% of Bangad (Southern) Kalinga [ksc]. Lexical similarity: 82% with Southern Kalinga, 78% with Guinaang and Tanudan. *Type:* VSO; prepositions; genitives before noun heads; articles normally before adjectives, numerals, and noun heads; question word in sentence-initial position; 3 maximum suffixes; word order distinguishes subjects, objects and indirect objects, given and new information, topic and comment; affixes do not indicate case of noun phrases; verb affixes mark number; passives; causatives; comparatives; CV, CVC; nontonal. *Lg Use:* Home, community, church. All ages. Positive attitudes. 14,000 also use Ilocano [ilo]. Acquired through school, travel, media, and use in church. *Lg Dev:* Literacy rate in L2: 98%. Taught in primary schools. Poetry. Newspapers. Radio programs. TV. Videos. Dictionary. Grammar. Bible portions: 2012. *Writing:* Latin script. *Other:* Christian, traditional religion. *Map:* 403:62.

Kalinga, Limos [kmk] (Limos-Liwan Kalinga, Northern Kalinga). 12,700 (2007 census), increasing. L2 users: Used by those intermarrying with local speakers and by outsiders living in the area. Luzon, Kalinga Province, Pinukpuk, Tabuk, and Rizal municipalities. *Status:* 4 (Educational). *Class:* Austronesian, Malayo-Polynesian, Philippine, Northern Luzon, Meso-Cordilleran, South-Central Cordilleran, Central Cordilleran, North Central Cordilleran, Kalinga-Itneg, Kalinga. *Dialects:* None known. Intelligibility: Lubuagan Kalinga [knb] 65%, Southern Kalinga [ksc] 66%, Tanudan Kalinga 67% [kml], Ilocano [ilo] 84%. *Type:* VOS; prepositions; genitives before noun heads; articles, adjectives and numerals before noun heads; relatives after noun heads; question word in sentence-initial position; 3 maximum prefixes, 2 maximum suffixes; word order does not distinguish subjects, objects and indirect objects; word order does not distinguish given and new information, topic and comment; affixes do not indicate case of noun phrases; verb affixes mark number; passives; causatives; comparatives; CV, CVC. *Lg Use:* All domains. All ages. Positive attitudes. Also use English [eng], Ilocano [ilo], Tagalog [tgl]. Used as L2 by Mabaka Valley Kalinga [kkg]. *Lg Dev:* Literacy rate in L1: 70%. Literacy rate in L2: 80%. Taught in secondary schools. Radio programs. Videos. Grammar. NT: 2004. *Writing:* Latin script, used since 1976. *Other:* Lowland teachers and church leaders use other languages which Limos Kalinga speakers find difficult to understand, and it forces the Limos Kalinga speakers to shift to the other languages. Christian. *Map:* 403:17.

Kalinga, Lubuagan [knb]. 30,000 (2008 V. Dumatog), increasing. L2 users: Used by those intermarrying with local speakers and by business people. Northern Luzon, Kalinga Province, Cordillera Region, Lubuagan; Tabuk city; Manila; Baguio city. *Status:* 4 (Educational). *Class:* Austronesian, Malayo-Polynesian, Philippine, Northern Luzon, Meso-Cordilleran, South-Central Cordilleran, Central Cordilleran, North Central Cordilleran, Kalinga-Itneg, Kalinga. *Dialects:* Ableg-Salegseg, Balatok-Kalinga (Balatok-Itneg), Balbalasang, Guinaang, Lubuagan. Intelligibility of Balbalasang dialect 81%, Sumadel [ksc] 82%, Limos [kmk] 70%, 48% comprehension of Ilocano [ilo] narrative. Lexical similarity: 81% with Balbalasang and Limos. *Type:* VSO; prepositions; genitives before noun heads; articles, adjectives, and numerals normally before noun heads; relatives after noun heads; question word in sentence-initial position; 3 maximum suffixes; word order distinguishes subjects, objects, and indirect objects, and given and new information, topic and comment; affixes do not indicate case of noun phrases; verb affixes mark number; passives; causatives; comparatives; CV, CVC; nontonal. *Lg Use:* All domains. All ages. Positive attitudes. Also use English [eng], Ilocano [ilo], Tagalog [tgl]. *Lg Dev:* Literacy rate in L1: 90%. Literacy rate in L2: 80%. Taught in primary schools. Dictionary. Grammar. Bible portions: 1970–2005. *Writing:* Latin script. *Other:* Traditional religion, Christian (Roman Catholic). *Map:* 403:60.

Kalinga, Mabaka Valley [kkg] (Kal-Uwan, Mabaka,

Mabaka Itneg). Luzon, southeast Kalinga Province. *Status:* 6a (Vigorous). *Class:* Austronesian, Malayo-Polynesian, Philippine, Northern Luzon, Meso-Cordilleran, South-Central Cordilleran, Central Cordilleran, North Central Cordilleran, Kalinga-Itneg, Kalinga. *Dialects:* None known. 79% comprehension of Limos Kalinga [kmk]. *Lg Use:* Also use Limos Kalinga [kmk]. *Map:* 403:6.

Kalinga, Majukayang [kmd] (Kalinga, Madukayang, Majukayong). 1,500 (1990 SIL), increasing. L2 users: Used by those intermarrying with local speakers. Northern Luzon, south Mountain Province, Cordillera Region, Majukayong. *Status:* 6a (Vigorous). *Class:* Austronesian, Malayo-Polynesian, Philippine, Northern Luzon, Meso-Cordilleran, South-Central Cordilleran, Central Cordilleran, North Central Cordilleran, Kalinga-Itneg, Kalinga. *Dialects:* None known. 83% intelligibility of Limos Kalinga [kmk] and Balangao [blw], 86% of Tanudan Kalinga [kml]; 68% of Ilocano [ilo]. Lexical similarity: 80% with Tanudan Kalinga [kml], 68% with Limos Kalinga [kmk], 65% with Balangao [blw]. *Lg Use:* Home, community, church. All ages. Positive attitudes. Also use English [eng], Ilocano [ilo], Tagalog [tgl]. *Other:* Traditional religion, Christian. *Map:* 403:64.

Kalinga, Southern [ksc] (Madlango Kalinga, Tinglayan Kalinga). 13,000 (2000 SIL), increasing. 7,540 monolinguals. L2 users: Used by those intermarrying with local speakers and by outsiders living in the area. Luzon, Kalinga Province. 13 villages; some in Tabuk. *Status:* 4 (Educational). *Class:* Austronesian, Malayo-Polynesian, Philippine, Northern Luzon, Meso-Cordilleran, South-Central Cordilleran, Central Cordilleran, North Central Cordilleran, Kalinga-Itneg, Kalinga. *Dialects:* Bangad, Mallango, Sumadel, Tinglayan. Intelligibility of Guinaang Kalinga [knb] 63%, Tanudan Kalinga [kml] 51%. *Lg Use:* Vigorous. All domains. Written use in religious services. All ages. Positive attitudes. Also use English [eng], Ilocano [ilo]. *Lg Dev:* Literacy rate in L1: 65%. Literacy rate in L2: 65%. Language of instruction. Grammar. NT: 1986. *Writing:* Latin script, used since 1979. *Other:* Traditional religion, Christian. *Map:* 403:61.

Kalinga, Tanudan [kml] (Lower Tanudan, Lower Tanudan Kalinga, Mangali Kalinga). 11,200 (1998 SIL), increasing. 1,120 monolinguals. L2 users: Used by those intermarrying with local speakers and by outsiders living in the area. Luzon, south Kalinga Province, south end of Tanudan valley. *Status:* 5 (Developing). *Class:* Austronesian, Malayo-Polynesian, Philippine, Northern Luzon, Meso-Cordilleran, South-Central Cordilleran, Central Cordilleran, North Central Cordilleran, Kalinga-Itneg, Kalinga. *Dialects:* Dacalan, Lubo, Minangali (Mangali), Pinangol (Pangul), Tinaloctoc (Taluctoc). Intelligibility: 79% of Limos Kalinga [kmk], 66% of Guinaang dialect of Lubuagan Kalinga [knb]. Lexical similarity: 97% with Pinangol dialect, 80% with Madukayang Kalinga [kmd]. *Lg Use:* All domains. All ages. Positive attitudes. Also use English [eng], Filipino [fil], Ilocano [ilo]. *Lg Dev:* Literacy rate in L1: 82%. Literacy rate in L2: 70%–82%. Bible portions: 1980–1987. *Writing:* Latin script. *Other:* Christian, traditional religion. *Map:* 403:59.

Kallahan, Kayapa [kak] (Ikalahan, Kalangoya, Kalangoya-Ikalahan, Kalanguya). 15,000 (1991 UBS), increasing. Luzon, west Nueva Vizcaya, northeast Pangasinan, west Ifugao provinces. *Status:* 5 (Developing). *Class:* Austronesian, Malayo-Polynesian, Philippine, Northern Luzon, Meso-Cordilleran, South-Central Cordilleran, Southern Cordilleran, West Southern Cordilleran, Nuclear Southern Cordilleran, Kallahan. *Dialects:* Central Kalanguya (Kayapa), Northern Kalanguya (Ambaguio), Southern Kalanguya (Santa Fe). *Lg Use:* Vigorous. Home, church, community affairs. All ages. Positive attitudes. 98% also use Ilocano [ilo]. 98% also use Tagalog [tgl]. Used as L2 by Karao [kyj]. *Lg Dev:* Literacy rate in L2: 85%. Mother-tongue multilingual education has been implemented in primary schools. Taught in primary schools. Poetry. Radio programs. Films. Videos. Grammar. NT: 1983. *Writing:* Latin script. *Other:* Intermarriage with Ilocanos and other groups. Children in such marriages tend to adapt a somewhat different language which is a combination of their parents' languages. Christian, traditional religion. *Map:* 403:34.

Kallahan, Keley-i [ify] (Antipolo Ifugao, Hanalulo, Keley-i, Keley-i Kalanguya, Keleyqiq Ifugao). 8,000 (2000 SIL). Only children under 5 are monolingual. Luzon, Ifugao Province, Kiangan municipality, Aritao municipality. *Status:* 4 (Educational). *Class:* Austronesian, Malayo-Polynesian, Philippine, Northern Luzon, Meso-Cordilleran, South-Central Cordilleran, Southern Cordilleran, West Southern Cordilleran, Nuclear Southern Cordilleran, Kallahan. *Dialects:* Bayninan, Ya-Tuka. *Lg Use:* Vigorous. All domains. All ages. Positive attitudes. Also use English [eng], Ilocano [ilo], Tuwali Ifugao [ifk]. *Lg Dev:* Literacy rate in L1: 4,000–5,000 can read and write. Literacy rate in L2: 70%–75%. Taught in primary schools. Bible: 2008. *Writing:* Latin script. *Other:* Traditional religion, Christian. *Map:* 403:24.

Kallahan, Tinoc [tne] (Tinoc Kalangoya). Luzon, Ifugao Province, Hungduan municipality, Tinoc barrio. *Status:* 6a (Vigorous). *Class:* Austronesian, Malayo-Polynesian, Philippine, Northern Luzon, Meso-Cordilleran, South-Central Cordilleran, Southern Cordilleran, West Southern Cordilleran, Nuclear Southern Cordilleran, Kallahan. *Map:* 403:21.

Kamayo [kyk] (Davaweño, Davawenyo, Kadi, Kinadi, Kinamayo). 363,000 (2000 census). Estimated population for Caraga, Davao Oriental, and Surigao del Sur regions. Mindanao, Surigao del Sur Province, between Marihatag and Lingig. *Status:* 6a (Vigorous). *Class:* Austronesian, Malayo-Polynesian, Philippine, Greater Central Philippine, Central Philippine, Mansakan, Northern. *Dialects:* North Kamayo, South Kamayo. Lexical similarity: 66% with Surigaonon [sgd], 70% with Butuanon [btw]. *Lg Use:* Vigorous. Home, friends, some in government. All ages. Positive attitudes. 100% also use Cebuano [ceb]. Also use English [eng], Tagalog [tgl]. *Lg Dev:* Literacy rate in L2: 80% in Cebuano. Taught in a few primary schools. New media. Films. Dictionary. *Other:* Stable diglossia; high bilingualism in Cebuano [ceb]. Christian (Roman Catholic), Christian (Protestant). *Map:* 405:169.

Kankanaey [kne] (Central Kankanaey, Kankanai, Kankanay). 150,000 (1991 SIL). All Kankanai 218,000 (1990 census). Luzon, north Benguet, southwest Mountain, southeast Ilocos Sur, and northeast La Union provinces. *Status:* 5 (Developing). *Class:* Austronesian, Malayo-Polynesian, Philippine, Northern Luzon, Meso-Cordilleran, South-Central Cordilleran, Central Cordilleran, North Central Cordilleran, Nuclear Cordilleran, Bontok-Kankanay, Kankanay. *Dialects:* Bakun-Kibungan, Guinzadan, Kapangan, Mankayan-Buguias. *Lg Use:* Used as L2 by Southwestern Bontok [vbk]. *Lg Dev:* Literacy rate in L1: 75%. Literacy rate in L2: 78%. NT: 1990–2000. *Writing:* Latin script. *Other:* Traditional religion, Christian. *Map:* 403:23.

Kankanay, Northern [xnn] (Sagada Igorot, Western Bontoc). 70,000 (1987 SIL). Luzon, west Mountain and southeast Ilocos Sur provinces. *Status:* 5 (Developing). *Class:* Austronesian, Malayo-Polynesian, Philippine, Northern Luzon, Meso-Cordilleran, South-Central Cordilleran, Central Cordilleran, North Central Cordilleran, Nuclear Cordilleran, Bontok-Kankanay, Kankanay. *Lg Dev:* Literacy rate in L1: 65%–70%. Literacy rate in L2: 65%–70%. Grammar. NT: 1984. *Writing:* Latin script. *Map:* 403:53.

Karao [kyj] (Karaw). 2,000 (2011 SIL). Luzon, east Benguet Province, Karao, Ekip, and Bokod areas. *Status:* 5 (Developing). *Class:* Austronesian, Malayo-Polynesian, Philippine, Northern Luzon, Meso-Cordilleran, South-Central Cordilleran, Southern Cordilleran, West Southern Cordilleran, Nuclear Southern Cordilleran, Karaw. *Dialects:* None known. Limited comprehension testing showed 85% comprehension of Kayapa Kallahan [kak]; 78% of Ilocano [ilo]. Lexical similarity: 90% with Ibaloi [ibl]. *Lg Use:* Vigorous. All domains. All ages. Positive attitudes. Also use English [eng], Ibaloi [ibl], Ilocano [ilo], Kayapa Kallahan [kak]. *Lg Dev:* Literacy rate in L1: 80%–90%. Literacy rate in L2: 80%–90%. Taught in primary schools. *Writing:* Latin script. *Map:* 403:25.

Kasiguranin [ksn] (Casiguranin). 10,000 (1975 SIL). Luzon, Aurora Province, Casiguran municipality. *Status:* 6a (Vigorous). *Class:* Austronesian, Malayo-Polynesian, Philippine, Northern Luzon, Northern Cordilleran, Northeastern Luzon, Northern. *Dialects:* None known. 82% intelligibility of Paranan [prf]. Lexical similarity: 52% with Filipino [fil], 75% with Paranan [prf]. *Lg Use:* Also use Filipino [fil]. *Map:* 403:30.

Katabaga [ktq]. No known L1 speakers. Luzon, Quezon Province, Bondoc peninsula. *Status:* 10 (Extinct). *Class:* Austronesian, Malayo-Polynesian, Unclassified. *Lg Use:* Shifted to Filipino [fil]. *Other:* Negrito.

Kinabalian [cbw] (Bisaya', Cabalian). 14,000 (2009 J. Lobel). Leyte island, southern Leyte Province, 6 villages in San Juan (Cabalian) town. *Status:* 6a (Vigorous). *Class:* Austronesian, Malayo-Polynesian, Philippine, Greater Central Philippine, Central Philippine, Bisayan, Central, Warayan. *Dialects:* None known. Reportedly similar to Waray-Waray [war]. *Map:* 404:91.

Kinaray-a [krj] (Antiqueño, Ati, Hamtiknon, Hinaray-a, Karay-a, Kiniray-a, Panayano, Sulud). 378,000 (1994 SIL), increasing. 1,000 monolinguals. L2 users: Business people, intermarriage. Western Panay, Iloilo and Antique provinces; Mindanao; national capital region. *Status:* 4 (Educational). *Class:* Austronesian, Malayo-Polynesian, Philippine, Greater Central Philippine, Central Philippine, Bisayan, West, Kinarayan. *Dialects:* Anini-y, Guimaras Island (Gimaras), Hamtik, Lambunao, Miag-Ao, Pandan, Pototan. Antique area has 75% comprehension of Filipino [fil]; 90% of Hiligaynon [hil]; Iloilo area, 95% of Hiligaynon; 90% of Antique. *Lg Use:* All domains. All ages. Positive attitudes. Also use Hiligaynon [hil]; L2 acquired through school, travel, and media; L2 used in church and school. Used as L2 by Ati [atk]. *Lg Dev:* Literacy rate in L1: 95%. Literacy rate in L2: 90% in Hiligaynon [hil]. Taught in primary and secondary schools. Poetry. Radio programs. TV. Videos. Dictionary. NT: 2009. *Writing:* Latin script. *Other:* Christian (Roman Catholic). *Map:* 404:100.

Maguindanaon [mdh] (Magindanaon, Magindanaw, Magindanawn, Maguindanaw). 1,100,000 (2010 SIL). Mindanao, Maguindanao, Cotabato, South Cotabato, Sultan Kuderat, and Zamboanga del Sur provinces. *Status:* 3 (Wider communication). Statutory language of provincial identity in North Cotabato and 3 other Mindanao provinces (1991, ACFLC Section 3(f)). *Class:* Austronesian, Malayo-Polynesian, Philippine, Greater Central Philippine, Danao, Magindanao. *Dialects:* Biwangan, Ilud, Laya, Sibugay, Tagakawanan. Intelligibility 60% of Maranao [mrw], 96% of Iranun [ill]. *Type:* VSO; prepositions; genitives after noun heads; articles, adjectives, and numerals before noun heads; relatives after noun heads; question word in sentence-initial position; markers that relate to the affixation of the verb, or the form of the pronoun, make the verbal complements obvious; affixes do not indicate case of noun phrases; verb affixes mark number; ergativity; passives; causatives; comparatives; CV, CVC; nontonal. *Lg Use:* Value English [eng] proficiency as an aid to employment. Home, neighborhood. Positive attitudes. Comprehension of Filipino [fil] is low. Used as L2 by Ilianen Manobo [mbi], Sarangani Blaan [bps]. *Lg Dev:* Literacy rate in L2: 60%. Taught in selected Grade 1 classrooms. New media. Videos. Dictionary. Bible portions: 1991–2010. *Writing:* Latin script. *Other:* Muslim. *Map:* 405:147.

Malaynon [mlz]. 8,500 (1973 SIL). Panay, lowland, northwest Aklan Province, Malay municipality. *Status:* 6a (Vigorous). *Class:* Austronesian, Malayo-Polynesian, Philippine, Greater Central Philippine, Central Philippine, Bisayan, West, Aklan. *Dialects:* None known. Lexical similarity: 93% with Aklanon [akl]. *Lg Use:* Vigorous. Used as L2 by Ati [atk]. *Map:* 404:105.

Mamanwa [mmn] (Mamanwa Negrito, Minamanwa). 5,150 (1990 census). Mindanao, Agusan del Norte and Surigao provinces. *Status:* 5 (Developing). *Class:* Austronesian, Malayo-Polynesian, Philippine, Greater Central Philippine, Central Philippine, Mamanwa. *Type:* VSO, VOS; prepositions; genitives before noun heads; articles, adjectives, numerals all before noun heads; relatives are formed by juxtaposing two clauses without a relative marker; question word in sentence-initial position; maximum number of affixes: 3 prefixes, 1 suffix; word order distinguishes given and new information, topic and comment; affixes do not indicate case of noun phrase; non-obligatory verb affixes indicate number; causatives; comparatives formed by juxtaposition of two clauses; CV, CVC; nontonal. *Lg Dev:* Literacy rate in L1: 7%. Literacy rate in L2: 7%. Grammar. NT: 1982. *Writing:* Latin script. *Map:* 404:92.

Mandaya [mry] (Davawenyo). 250,000 (2010). Mindanao, Davao Oriental Province, Manay, Caraga, Baganga, and Cateel municipalities; Davao del Norte Province. *Status:* 6a (Vigorous). *Class:* Austronesian, Malayo-Polynesian, Philippine, Greater Central Philippine, Central Philippine, Mansakan, Eastern. *Dialects:* Carraga Mandaya, Cateelenyo, Karaga, Manay Mandayan, Mandaya, Cataelano, Mangaragan Mandaya, Sangab. 77% intelligibility of Mansaka [msk]. Lexical similarity: 89% with Mansaka [msk], 83% with Kalagan [kqe]. *Lg Use:* Home, neighborhood. Adults, youth. 80% also use Cebuano [ceb]. Also use Mansaka [msk]. *Lg Dev:* Poetry. Dictionary. *Other:* Many Mandaya will say they are Davawenyo; "Mandaya" can be a derogatory term, meaning uneducated people from the hills. Christian, traditional religion. *Map:* 405:161.

Manide [abd] (Abiyan, Camarinas Norte Agta). 3,800 (Lobel 2010). Luzon, Camarines Norte Province, Santa Elena and Labo municipalities. *Status:* 6a (Vigorous). *Class:* Austronesian, Malayo-Polynesian, Philippine, Greater Central Philippine, Umiray Dumaget. *Dialects:* None known. Lexical similarity: 67% with Alabat Agta [dul], 35% with Mt. Iriga Agta [agz]. *Lg Use:* Young people tend to prefer Tagalog [tgl] (Wurm 2007). Home. Used by a few children. Mildly positive attitudes. Bilingualism in Tagalog [tgl] is prevalent (Wurm 2007). *Maps:* 403:70, 404:70.

Manobo, Agusan [msm] (Agusan). 60,000 (2002 SIL). 157,000 all Manobo (1990 census). Mindanao, Agusan del Norte, Agusan del Sur, and Surigao del Sur provinces. *Status:* 5 (Developing). *Class:* Austronesian, Malayo-Polynesian, Philippine, Greater Central Philippine, Manobo, Central, East. *Dialects:* Adgawan, Omayamnon, Surigao,

Umayam. 83% intelligibility of Dibabawon [mbd]. Lexical similarity: 80% with Omayamnon dialect and other dialects, 85% with Dibabawon Manobo [mbd]. *Type:* VSO; prepositions; genitives after noun heads; articles before noun heads, adjectives, numerals before and after noun heads; relatives after noun heads or without noun heads; question word in sentence-initial position, final as tag; maximum number of affixes: 4 prefixes, 1 suffix; word order distinguishes subject, object and direct objects, when noun marker is the same; affixes do not indicate case of noun phrase; verb affixes sometimes mark number; passives; causatives; comparatives; CV, CVC; nontonal. *Lg Use:* Used as L2 by Rajah Kabunsuwan Manobo [mqk]. *Lg Dev:* Literacy rate in L1: 54%. Literacy rate in L2: 55%–60%. Dictionary. NT: 1999–2001. *Writing:* Latin script. *Other:* Ethnic autonym: Manobo. Christian (Roman Catholic), traditional religion. *Map:* 405:170.

Manobo, Ata [atd] (Ata of Davao, Atao Manobo, Langilan). 26,700 (2000 census). Mindanao, northwest Davao del Norte Province. *Status:* 5 (Developing). *Class:* Austronesian, Malayo-Polynesian, Philippine, Greater Central Philippine, Manobo, Central, South, Ata-Tigwa. *Lg Dev:* Literacy rate in L1: 25%. Literacy rate in L2: 25%–30%. NT: 2000. *Writing:* Latin script. *Other:* Different from Ata [atm] of Mabinay, Negros Oriental, and Atta languages. A Negrito people. *Map:* 405:166.

Manobo, Cotabato [mta] (Dulangan Manobo). 30,000 (2007 SIL), increasing. 5,000 monolinguals. Ethnic population: 30,000. Mindanao, Sultan Kudarat, Experanza, Kalamansig, Lebak, Palimbang, Sen. Ninoy Aquino, and south Cotabato Province. *Status:* 5 (Developing). *Class:* Austronesian, Malayo-Polynesian, Philippine, Greater Central Philippine, Manobo, South. *Dialects:* Blit, Tasaday. *Type:* VSO; prepositions; articles, adjectives, numerals all before noun heads; relatives after noun heads or without noun heads; question word in sentence-initial position; maximum number of affixes: 3 prefixes, 2 suffixes; word order distinguishes subject, object and direct objects, given and new information, topic and comment; affixes do not indicate case of noun phrase; passives; causatives; comparatives; CV, CVC; nontonal. *Lg Use:* Vigorous. All domains. All ages. Positive attitudes. Also use Cebuano [ceb], Filipino [fil], Hiligaynon [hil]. Second languages acquired in school and community and used in schools, trade with non-Manobos, and government. Used as L2 by Tiruray [tiy]. *Lg Dev:* Literacy rate in L1: 25%. Literacy rate in L2: 5%–10%. Radio programs. Dictionary. Grammar. NT: 1988–2005. *Writing:* Latin script. *Other:* Christian, traditional religion. *Map:* 405:149.

Manobo, Dibabawon [mbd] (Debabaon, Dibabaon, Mandaya). 10,000 (1978 SIL). Mindanao, Davao del Norte Province, Manguagan. *Status:* 5 (Developing). *Class:* Austronesian, Malayo-Polynesian, Philippine, Greater Central Philippine, Manobo, Central, East. *Type:* Prepositions; genitives after noun heads; articles, adjectives, numerals all before noun heads; relatives after noun heads; question word in sentence-initial position; maximum number of affixes: 3 prefixes, 1 suffix; word order distinguishes given and new information; affixes do not indicate case of noun phrase; non-obligatory verb affixes indicate number; passives; causatives; comparatives; CV, CVC, CVV, CVVC; nontonal. *Lg Use:* Used as L2 by Rajah Kabunsuwan Manobo [mqk]. *Lg Dev:* Literacy rate in L1: 23%. Literacy rate in L2: 23%. NT: 1978. *Writing:* Latin script. *Map:* 405:167.

Manobo, Ilianen [mbi] (Ilianen). 14,600 (2000). Few monolinguals. Mindanao, northern Cotabato Province. *Status:* 5 (Developing). *Class:* Austronesian, Malayo-Polynesian, Philippine, Greater Central Philippine, Manobo, Central, West. *Dialects:* Arakan, Livunganen, Pulangiyan. *Lg Use:* Vigorous. All domains. Positive attitudes. Also use Cebuano [ceb], Filipino [fil], Maguindanaon [mdh]. *Lg Dev:* Literacy rate in L1: 15%–20%. Literacy rate in L2: 15%–20%. NT: 1989. *Writing:* Latin script. *Other:* Unable to enforce traditional land claims. Traditional religion. *Map:* 405:145.

Manobo, Kinamiging [mkx] (Cinamiguin, Kamigin, Kinamigin, Kinamiguin, Manobo, Cinamiguin). 26,700 (2000 census). Camiguin Island, north of Mindanao. *Status:* 6b (Threatened). *Class:* Austronesian, Malayo-Polynesian, Philippine, Greater Central Philippine, Manobo, North. *Type:* VOS, VSO; prepositions; genitives after noun heads; articles, adjectives, and numerals before noun heads; relatives after noun heads; question word in sentence-initial position; word order distinguishes subjects, objects and indirect objects in some structures, word order distinguishes given and new information, topic and comment; affixes do not indicate case of noun phrases; verb affixes mark number; passives; causatives; comparatives; CV, CVC, CVV, CCV; nontonal. *Lg Use:* Also use Cebuano [ceb]. *Map:* 404:96.

Manobo, Matigsalug [mbt] (Matig-Salug Manobo). 50,000 (2010 SIL), increasing. 5,000 monolinguals. Mindanao, Davao del Norte and southeast Bukidnon provinces. *Status:* 5 (Developing). *Class:* Austronesian, Malayo-Polynesian, Philippine, Greater Central Philippine, Manobo, Central, South, Ata-Tigwa. *Dialect:* Kulamanen. Tigwa has marginal intelligibility of Matigsalug. Tala Ingod may have adequate intelligibility of Matigsalug. *Type:* VSO; prepositions; genitives after noun heads; articles, adjectives, and numerals before noun heads; question word in sentence-initial position; 3 maximum prefixes, 2 maximum suffixes; ergativity; passives; causatives; comparatives; CV, CVC; nontonal. *Lg Use:* Home, neighborhood, church. All ages. Positive attitudes. Increasingly use Cebuano [ceb]. *Lg Dev:* Literacy rate in L1: 10%. Literacy rate in L2: 25%. Poetry. New media. Radio programs. Films. Videos. Dictionary. NT: 2010. *Writing:* Latin script. *Other:* Christian, traditional religion. *Map:* 405:165.

Manobo, Obo [obo] (Bagobo, Kidapawan Manobo, Obo Bagobo). 60,000 (2007 SIL). 20,000 monolinguals. L2 users: Used by those intermarrying with local speakers. Mindanao, northeast slope of Mount Apo, between Davao del Sur and North Cotabato provinces. *Status:* 4 (Educational). *Class:* Austronesian, Malayo-Polynesian, Philippine, Greater Central Philippine, Manobo, Central, South, Obo. *Dialects:* Arakan Manobo, Kidapawan Manobo, Magpet Manobo, Marilog. 69% intelligibility of Tigwa (Matigsalug Manobo [mbt] reportedly most similar) and 60% of Tagabawa [bgs]. Lexical similarity: 63% with Tagabawa [bgs] and Ilianen Manobo [mbi], 35% with Cebuano [ceb]. *Type:* VSO, VOS; prepositions; genitives after noun heads; articles, adjectives, and numerals before noun heads; question word in sentence-initial position; 2 maximum prefixes, 1 maximum suffix; ergativity; passives; causatives; comparatives; CV, CVC, CVV. CVVC; nontonal. *Lg Use:* Home, market, church. All ages. Positive attitudes. Also use Cebuano [ceb], Tagabawa [bgs]. *Lg Dev:* Literacy rate in L1: 65%–70%. Literacy rate in L2: 95% in Cebuano [ceb]. Literacy work ongoing. Taught in 3 primary schools (2007 SIL). Taught in 1 secondary school (2007 SIL). New media. Radio programs. Videos. Dictionary. Grammar. NT: 2011. *Writing:* Latin script. *Other:* Christian, traditional religion. *Map:* 405:163.

Manobo, Rajah Kabunsuwan [mqk] (Rajah Kabungsuan Manobo). 7,560 (2000). Mindanao, south Surigao del Sur,

Lingig, Rajah Cabungsuan. *Status:* 6a (Vigorous). *Class:* Austronesian, Malayo-Polynesian, Philippine, Greater Central Philippine, Manobo, Central, East. *Dialects:* Intelligibility of Dibabawon Manobo [mbd] 80%, San Miguel Calatugan Agusan [msm] 81%. Lexical similarity: 82% with Dibabawon Manobo [mbd], 76% with Sagunto dialect of Agusan Manobo [msm] and San Miguel Calatugan dialect of Agusan Manobo. *Lg Use:* Low bilingualism in Cebuano [ceb]. Also use Agusan Manobo [msm], Dibabawon Manobo [mbd]. *Other:* Christian, traditional religion. *Map:* 405:168.

Manobo, Sarangani [mbs]. 58,000 (2000 census). Mindanao, Davao del Sur and Davao Oriental provinces. *Status:* 5 (Developing). *Class:* Austronesian, Malayo-Polynesian, Philippine, Greater Central Philippine, Manobo, South. *Dialect:* Governor Generoso Manobo. *Type:* VSO; prepositions; genitives after noun heads; articles, adjectives, numerals all before noun heads; relatives after noun heads; question word in sentence-initial position; maximum number of affixes: 3 prefixes, 2 suffixes; word order distinguishes subject, object and direct objects, but is also determined by case marking; affixes do not indicate case of noun phrase; non-obligatory verb affixes indicate number; ergatives; passives; causatives; comparatives; CV, CVC, CCV; nontonal. *Lg Use:* Used as L2 by Sarangani Blaan [bps]. *Lg Dev:* Literacy rate in L1: 44%. Literacy rate in L2: 44%. NT: 1982. *Writing:* Latin script. *Map:* 405:155.

Manobo, Western Bukidnon [mbb]. 15,000 (2008 SIL). Ethnic population: 15,000. Mindanao, south Bukidnon Province. *Status:* 5 (Developing). *Class:* Austronesian, Malayo-Polynesian, Philippine, Greater Central Philippine, Manobo, Central, West. *Dialects:* Ilentungen, Kiriyenteken, Pulangiyen. *Type:* VSO; prepositions; genitives after noun heads; articles, adjectives, numerals all before noun heads; relatives after noun heads; question word in sentence-initial position; maximum number of affixes: 5 prefixes, 1 suffix; word order distinguishes subject, object and direct objects, given and new information, topic and comment; affixes do not indicate case of noun phrase; causatives; comparatives; CV, CVC; nontonal. *Lg Use:* Home, church, and community. All ages. Positive attitudes. L2 is acquired through the community and used in school, community. *Lg Dev:* Literacy rate in L1: 45%. Literacy rate in L2: 45%. Dictionary. NT: 1978–2003. *Writing:* Latin script. *Map:* 405:164.

Mansaka [msk] (Mandaya Mansaka). 57,800 (2000). Mindanao, Davao Oriental Province. *Status:* 5 (Developing). *Class:* Austronesian, Malayo-Polynesian, Philippine, Greater Central Philippine, Central Philippine, Mansakan, Eastern. *Dialects:* Lexical similarity: 80% with Bislig-Mati, 89% with Mandaya [mry], 84% with Mati, 74% with Piso dialect of Kalagan [kqe]. *Type:* VSO, VOS; prepositions; genitives after noun heads; articles, adjectives, and numerals before noun heads; relatives without noun heads; question word in sentence-initial position; 3 maximum prefixes, 2 maximum suffixes; word order distinguishes given and new information, topic and comment; affixes do not indicate case of noun phrases; verb affixes mark number; passives; causatives; comparatives; CV, CVC, CVV; nontonal. *Lg Use:* Used as L2 by Mandaya [mry]. *Lg Dev:* Dictionary. Grammar. NT: 1975. *Writing:* Latin script. *Map:* 405:160.

Mapun [sjm] (Bajau Kagayan, Cagayan, Cagayan de Sulu, Cagayanen, Cagayano, Cagayanon, Jama Mapun, Kagayan, Orang, Sama Mapun). 43,000 in Philippines (2011 SIL). Population total all countries: 58,000. 4,000 monolinguals. Ethnic population: 43,000. Muslim Mindinao autonomous region, Tawi-Tawi, Cagayan de Sulu (Mapun) island. Also in Malaysia. *Status:* 5 (Developing). *Class:* Austronesian, Malayo-Polynesian, Greater Barito, Sama-Bajaw, Sulu-Borneo, Borneo Coast Bajaw. *Dialects:* None known. Intelligibility of Central Sama [sml] 59%, intelligibility of Sama Pangutaran [sml] 61%. *Type:* VSO; stress is on the penultimate syllable; verbal affixations can mark actor-experiencer, instrument, object-undergoer-patient, beneficiary, location, passive, imperative, abilitative, causative, non-volitional, reciprocal, multiple actors, intransitive, etc; 3 prepositions used primarily to indicate special and temporal relationships. *Lg Use:* Home, neighborhood, work. All ages. Positive attitudes. 37,000 also use Tausug [tsg]. Also use English [eng]. Used as L2 by Molbog [pwm], Southern Sama [ssb]. *Lg Dev:* Literacy rate in L1: 65%–70%. Literacy rate in L2: 30% in English; 60% in Tausug [tsg]. Many older women are illiterate. Used some at school. Poetry. Videos. Dictionary. Bible portions: 1979–1998. *Writing:* Latin script. *Other:* The center of the ethnic group is on Mapun island (pop. 20,000), also known as Cagayan de Sulu, Cagayan Sulu, and Cagayan de Tawi-Tawi. The Mapun people only refer to it as Mapun. Many people from the island go to Sabah, Malaysia to find work. Many have settled there over the past century. There are approximately 15,000 Mapun people in Malaysia. There are approximately 5,000 to 10,000 Mapun people on the island of Palawan in the Philippines. Muslim. *Map:* 405:129.

Maranao [mrw] (Maranaw, Ranao). 776,000 (1990 census). Mindanao, Lanao del Norte and Lanao del Sur provinces. *Status:* 4 (Educational). De facto language of provincial identity in Lanao del Sur. *Class:* Austronesian, Malayo-Polynesian, Philippine, Greater Central Philippine, Danao, Maranao-Iranon. *Dialects:* None known. Intelligibility of Iranun [ill] 87%, of Maguindanaon [mdh] 52%. *Lg Dev:* Literacy rate in L2: 20%. Taught in primary schools, in Lanao provinces. Dictionary. NT: 1981. *Writing:* Latin script. *Other:* Muslim. *Map:* 405:143.

Masbatenyo [msb] (Masbateño, Minasbate). 350,000 (2002 SIL), increasing. 50,000 monolinguals. Mostly children. Ethnic population: 700,000. L2 users: 250,000 (2002 SIL). Masbate Province, 3 islands. *Status:* 3 (Wider communication). Statutory language of provincial identity in Masbate Province (1991, ACFLC Section 3(f)). *Class:* Austronesian, Malayo-Polynesian, Philippine, Greater Central Philippine, Central Philippine, Bisayan, Central, Peripheral. *Dialects:* None known. Lexical similarity: 79% with Capiznon [cps], 76% with Hiligaynon [hil]. *Lg Use:* Home, market, work. All ages. Used as L2 by Southern Sorsoganon [srv]. *Lg Dev:* Literacy rate in L1: 65%. Literacy rate in L2: 50%. Taught in primary and secondary schools. Newspapers. Radio programs. Dictionary. Grammar. NT: 1993. *Writing:* Latin script. *Other:* Christian (Roman Catholic), Christian (Protestant). *Map:* 404:86.

Molbog [pwm] (Balabak, Molbog Palawan). 6,680 in Philippines (1990 census). Population total all countries: 13,680. Ethnic population: 13,400. L2 users: Immigrants to Balabac Island. Palawan Province, Palawan, Bataraza, Balabac, Banggi, Ramos, and Balambangam islands. Also in Malaysia. *Status:* 5 (Developing). *Class:* Austronesian, Malayo-Polynesian, Philippine, Greater Central Philippine, Palawanic. *Dialects:* Balabac Island, Banggi Island, Southern Palawan. Intelligibility of Brooke's Point Palawano [plw] is 27%, of South Palawano is 55%. Lexical similarity: 69% with Quezon Palawano [plc] (Central). *Lg Use:* Home, at school, informal and formal community. All ages. Positive attitudes. Also use Filipino [fil]. L2 acquired through community, trade, school and travel. L2 used in school, government, travel and trade. Also use Mapun [sjm]. L2 acquired through community, trade, school and travel. L2 used in school, government, travel and trade. Also use Sabah Malay [msi]. L2 acquired through community, trade, school and travel. L2 used in school, government, travel and trade. *Lg Dev:* Literacy rate in L1: 5%. Literacy rate in L2: 7%. Bible portions: 1977. *Writing:* Latin script. *Other:* Muslim. *Map:* 405:128.

Palawano, Brooke's Point [plw] (Brooke's Point Palawan, Palawan, Palawanun, Palaweño). 14,400 (2000). Southeast Palawan Island, south of Abu Abu to Bataraza, mostly along upland rivers, some along the coast. *Status:* 5 (Developing). *Class:* Austronesian, Malayo-Polynesian, Philippine, Greater Central Philippine, Palawanic. *Dialect:* South Palawano (Bugsuk Palawano). Intelligibility of Central Palawano [plc] 76%; of Southwest Palawano [plv] 68%. Lexical similarity: 82% with Quezon Palawano [plc] (Central), 85% with Southwest Palawano [plv], 83% with South Palawano. *Lg Use:* Low comprehension of Filipino [fil]. *Lg Dev:* Literacy rate in L1: 10%. Literacy rate in L2: 10% in Filipino [fil] (2007 SIL). Bible portions: 1992–2000. *Writing:* Latin script. *Map:* 405:125.

Palawano, Central [plc] (Palawanen, Palaweño, Quezon Palawano). 12,000 (1981 UBS). 40,500 all Palawano (1990 census). Southwest Palawan Island, north of Quezon to north of Rizal; east Abu Abu area, mostly along upland rivers, some along the coast. *Status:* 5 (Developing). *Class:* Austronesian, Malayo-Polynesian, Philippine, Greater Central Philippine, Palawanic. *Dialects:* None known. Lexical similarity: 82% with Brooke's Point Palawano [plw], 78% with Southwest Palawano [plv]. *Lg Use:* Low comprehension of Filipino [fil]. *Lg Dev:* NT: 1964. *Writing:* Latin script. *Map:* 405:126.

Palawano, Southwest [plv]. 12,000 (2005 W. Davis). Southwest Palawan Island, north of Rizal to the south tip, east side from Bataraza south, mostly along upland rivers, some along the coast. *Status:* 6a (Vigorous). *Class:* Austronesian, Malayo-Polynesian, Philippine, Greater Central Philippine, Palawanic. *Dialects:* None known. Intelligibility of Central Palawano [plc] 75%, of Brooke's Point Palawano [plw] 76%. Lexical similarity: 85% with Brooke's Point Palawano [plw], 78% with Central Palawano [plc]. *Lg Use:* Low comprehension of Filipino [fil]. *Lg Dev:* Bible portions. *Map:* 405:127.

Pampangan [pam] (Kapampangan, Pampango, Pampangueño). 1,900,000 in Philippines (1990 census). Population total all countries: 1,905,430. Luzon, Pampanga, Tarlac, and Bataan provinces. Also in United States. *Status:* 3 (Wider communication). Statutory language of provincial identity in Pampanga and 2 other Luzon provinces (1991, ACFLC Section 3(f)). *Class:* Austronesian, Malayo-Polynesian, Philippine, Central Luzon, Pampangan. *Lg Use:* Dominant language in Pampanga Province. Used as L2 by Mag-Indi Ayta [blx]. *Lg Dev:* New media. Bible: 1917–1994. *Writing:* Braille script. Latin script, primary usage. *Map:* 403:42.

Pangasinan [pag]. 1,160,000 in Philippines (1990 census). Population total all countries: 1,162,140. Luzon, Pangasinan Province. Also in United States. *Status:* 3 (Wider communication). Statutory language of provincial identity in Pangasinan Province (1991, ACFLC Section 3(f)). *Class:* Austronesian, Malayo-Polynesian, Philippine, Northern Luzon, Meso-Cordilleran, South-Central Cordilleran, Southern Cordilleran, West Southern Cordilleran. *Lg Dev:* Grammar. Bible: 1915–1983. *Writing:* Braille script. Latin script, primary usage. *Map:* 403:37.

Paranan [prf] (Palanan, Palanenyo). 15,000 (2009 J. Lobel). Luzon, Isabela Province east coast, between Divilacan bay and Dinapigue town and inland to San Mariano. *Status:* 4 (Educational). *Class:* Austronesian, Malayo-Polynesian, Philippine, Northern Luzon, Northern Cordilleran, Northeastern Luzon. *Dialects:* None known. Reportedly similar to Pahanan Agta [apf]. *Lg Use:* Home, community meetings, some churches. All ages. Positive attitudes. Also use Filipino [fil], Ilocano [ilo]. *Lg Dev:* Literacy rate in L1: 75%. Literacy rate in L2: 50%. Taught in primary and secondary schools. Poetry. Films. Videos. NT: 2012. *Writing:* Latin script. *Other:* Christian. *Map:* 403:13.

Philippine Sign Language [psp] (Filipino Sign Language, FSL, Local Sign Language). 100,000 deaf persons (Van Cleve 1986). *Status:* 5 (Developing). *Class:* Deaf sign language. *Dialects:* None known. Reportedly similar to American Sign Language [ase]. *Lg Use:* Total communication used in deaf schools, with teachers both speaking and signing. Used by United States Peace Corps. American Sign Language [ase] well known as L2.

Porohanon [prh] (Camotes). 23,000. Central Visayas, Camotes Islands. *Status:* 6a (Vigorous). *Class:* Austronesian, Malayo-Polynesian, Philippine, Greater Central Philippine, Central Philippine, Bisayan, Central, Peripheral. *Dialects:* None known. Barely intelligible with Cebuano [ceb] (1967 J. Wolff). Reportedly more similar to Masbatenyo [msb] and Hiligaynon [hil]. Lexical similarity: 87% with Cebuano [ceb] (1967 J. Wolff). *Lg Use:* Also use Cebuano [ceb]. *Map:* 404:89.

Ratagnon [btn] (Aradigi, Datagnon, Lactan, Latagnun, Latan). 2 (Wurm 2000). Ethnic population: 2,000 (1997 SIL). Occidental Mindoro Province, south tip. *Status:* 8b (Nearly extinct). *Class:* Austronesian, Malayo-Polynesian, Philippine, Greater Central Philippine, Central Philippine, Bisayan, West, Kuyan. *Dialects:* Ratagnon, Santa Teresa. Reportedly similar to Cuyonon [cyo]. *Lg Use:* Moribund (2000 S. Wurm). Shifting to Filipino [fil]. Adults only. Negative attitudes. *Map:* 404:117.

Romblomanon [rol] (Romblon). 94,000 (2011 SIL). Romblon and Sibuyan Islands, northeast of Tablas Island (San Agustin), north of Panay. *Status:* 5 (Developing). *Class:* Austronesian, Malayo-Polynesian, Philippine, Greater Central Philippine, Central Philippine, Bisayan, Central, Romblon. *Dialects:* Bisaya', Romblon, Sibuyanon. Sibuyan Island has 70% intelligibility of Inakeanon [akl], 73% of Hiligaynon [hil], 94% of the Romblon dialect. *Lg Use:* Positive attitudes. Also use Filipino [fil]. Used as L2 by Bantoanon [bno]. *Lg Dev:* New media. Dictionary. Grammar. Bible portions: 1992–2011. *Writing:* Latin script. *Map:* 404:108.

Sama, Balangingih [sse] (Baangingi', Balanguingui, Bangingi, Bangingih Sama, Northern Sama, Sama Bangingih, Samal). 80,000 in Philippines (2007). Population total all countries: 85,000. Western Mindanao, Sulu archipelago northeast of Jolo, Zamboanga coast peninsula and islands and Basilan island. Northern Sama dialect: Luzon, White Beach near Subic bay; Lutangan dialect: Olutangga island. Possibly on Luzon and Palawan. Also in Malaysia. *Status:* 5 (Developing). *Class:* Austronesian, Malayo-Polynesian, Greater Barito, Sama-Bajaw, Sulu-Borneo, Inner Sulu Sama. *Dialects:* Balangingi, Daongdung, Kabinga'an, Lutangan (Lutango), Sibuco-Vitali (Sibuku), Sibuguey (Batuan). Most Lutangan understand Bangingih Sama, the prestige dialect. Intelligibility of Central Sama [sml] 71%, 83% of Lutangan, 85% of Sibuco-Vitali. Lexical similarity: 77% with Lutangan, 75% with Sibuco-Vitali. *Type:* SVO to introduce a topic, thereafter VSO; prepositions; gender not marked; ergative; nontonal; CVC, CV, VC; 17 consonant phonemes and 5 vowel phonemes. *Lg Use:* Vigorous. Home, community. All ages. Positive attitudes. Also use Chavacano [cbk], English [eng], Filipino [fil], Tausug [tsg]. *Lg Dev:* Literacy rate in L2: 40%–45%. Most urban men are literate. Videos. Grammar. Bible portions: 1979–2009. *Writing:* Arabic script, plans for future development using this script. Latin script. *Other:* Balangingi is the prestige dialect of Northern Sama. Muslim. *Map:* 405:134.

Sama, Central [sml] ("Bajaw" *pej.*, Central Sinama, Orang Laut, Sama Dilaut, Samal, Siasi Sama, Sinama). 90,000 in Philippines (2000). Population total all countries: 105,000. 30,000 monolinguals. Ethnic population: 105,000. Muslim Mindinao autonomous region, Sulu andTawi-Tawi provinces, Siasi, Tabawan, Bonggao Sitangkai, Cagayan de Sulu island; Basilan island, Maluso, Malamawi, Bohe' Lobbong; Zamboanga del Sur Province, Rio Hondo, Batuan Lumbayaw, Taluk Sangay, Sanggali; Zamboanga del Norte Province, Olutangga; Davao City, Isla Verde, and Sasa; Cagayan de Oro; Visayas, Cebu and Tagbilaran; Palawan, Puerto Princesa; Batangas. Also in Malaysia. *Status:* 4 (Educational). *Class:* Austronesian, Malayo-Polynesian, Greater Barito, Sama-Bajaw, Sulu-Borneo, Inner Sulu Sama. *Dialects:* Sama Deya, Sama Dilaut, Sama Laminusa, Sama Siasi, Sama Tabawan. Intelligibility of Bangingih Sama [sse] 79%. Lexical similarity: 47% with Inabaknon [abx], 62% with Yakan [yka], 76% with Pangutaran Sama [slm], 77% with Balangingi [sse], 72–78% with Southern Sama [ssb], 59% with West Coast Bajau [bdr], 66% with Mapun [sjm], 48–51% with Indonesian Bajau [bdl], 25% with Cebuano [ceb], 45% with Tausug [tsg] (Pallesen 1985). *Lg Use:* Vigorous. All domains. All ages. Positive attitudes. Also use Cebuano [ceb], Chavacano [cbk], Malay [zlm], Tagalog [tgl], Tausug [tsg]. Used as L2 by Southern Sama [ssb]. *Lg Dev:* Literacy rate in L1: 15%. Literacy rate in L2: 15%. Taught in primary schools, as a language of instruction, but only in Davao and Zamboanga in a few classes run by non-governmental organizations. New media. Films. Videos. NT: 1987–2008. *Writing:* Latin script. *Other:* Muslim, Christian, traditional religion. *Map:* 405:132.

Sama, Pangutaran [slm] (Siyama). 35,200 (2000). Western Mindanao, west central Sulu, Pangutaran island, west of Jolo; south Palawan, Cagayan de Tawi-Tawi. *Status:* 5 (Developing). *Class:* Austronesian, Malayo-Polynesian, Greater Barito, Sama-Bajaw, Sulu-Borneo, Western Sulu Sama. *Dialects:* None known. Intelligibility of Central Sama [sml] 65%. *Lg Use:* Vigorous. All domains. Oral use in education for explanations. Market. Some written use in communications. Positive attitudes. 20% also use Filipino [fil]. Some who have been to Malaysia also speak Malay [zlm]. 80% also use Tausug [tsg]. Used as L2 by Southern Sama [ssb]. *Lg Dev:* Literacy rate in L1: 25%–30%. Literacy rate in L2: 25%–35%. Dictionary. NT: 1994. *Writing:* Latin script. *Other:* Muslim. *Map:* 405:130.

Sama, Southern [ssb] (Sama Tawi-Tawi, Southern Sinama). 200,000 in Philippines (2007 SIL), increasing. Population total all countries: 215,000. 20,000 monolinguals. Muslim Mindanao autonomous region, southern Sulu, Tawi-Tawi Island Province, Tawi-Tawi, Simunul, Sibutu, and other major islands. Also in Malaysia. *Status:* 5 (Developing). *Class:* Austronesian, Malayo-Polynesian, Greater Barito, Sama-Bajaw, Sulu-Borneo, Inner Sulu Sama. *Dialects:* Balimbing, Bongao, Languyan, Obian, Sama Sibutu, Sapa-Sapa, Sibutu' (Sibutu), Simunul, Sitangkai, Tandubas. Sibutu intelligibility of Sama Central [sml] 77%, of the Simunul dialect 89%. Simunul intelligibility of Sama Central [sml] 77%, of the Sibutu dialect 80%. *Lg Use:* Vigorous. Home, neighborhood, local level official functions, religious services, commerce, and labor relations. Positive attitudes. Also use Central Sama [sml], English [eng], Filipino [fil], Malay [zlm], Mapun [sjm], Pangutaran Sama [slm], Tausug [tsg]. *Lg Dev:* Literacy rate in L1: 65%–70%. Literacy rate in L2: 40% in Tausug [tsg], 40% in Filipino [fil], 30% in Malay [zlm], 10% in English [eng]. 130,000 can read, 100,000 can write. Literature may not be acceptable to other dialect speakers due to marginal intelligibility and strong regional loyalties. Taught in primary schools, as language of instruction. Radio programs. Bible portions: 1979–2009. *Writing:* Latin script. *Other:* Simunul is central, prestige dialect. Bongao dialect from political, economic center of Southern Sama. Muslim. *Map:* 405:131.

Sambal [xsb] (Sambali, "Tina" *pej.*, "Tina Sambal" *pej.*). 70,000 (2000 SIL), decreasing. 0 monolinguals. Ethnic population: 70,000. Luzon, north Zambales Province, 5 towns; Pangasinan Province, 2 villages; Palawan Island, Quezon, Panitian village. *Status:* 4 (Educational). De facto language of provincial identity in Zambales province. *Class:* Austronesian, Malayo-Polynesian, Philippine, Central Luzon, Sambalic. *Dialects:* Iba, Masinloc, Santa Cruz. 70% intelligibility with Botolan [sbl]. *Lg Use:* Youth start using it at work if they do not go on to higher education; little use among children. Not used around outsiders, but they like it when outsiders learn Sambal. All domains among adults. Oral use in local commerce, occasional use in religion and political campaigning. Some letter-writing. Adults. 100% also use Filipino [fil]. 30% also use Ilocano [ilo]. *Lg Dev:* Literacy rate in L1: 98%. Literacy rate in L2: 98%. Orthography similar to Filipino. English and Filipino taught in school. Taught in primary schools, in Zambales. Poetry. Newspapers. Radio programs. Videos. Dictionary. Grammar. NT: 1999–2000. *Writing:* Latin script. *Other:* Christian (Protestant). *Map:* 403:39.

Sambal, Botolan [sbl] (Aeta Negrito, Ayta Hambali, Botolan Zambal). 32,900 (2000 SIL), increasing. Luzon, Zambales Province, Botolan and Cabangan municipalities. Affected by Mount Pinatubo eruption. *Status:* 5 (Developing). *Class:* Austronesian, Malayo-Polynesian, Philippine, Central Luzon, Sambalic. *Dialects:* Ayta Hambali (Hambali Botolan), Sambali Botolan. Among themselves, Ayta Hambali reportedly use some words that are similar to Ayta Mag-anchi [sgb]. *Lg Use:* Vigorous. All domains. Local administration, commerce, religion, letters. All ages. Also use Abellen Ayta [abp]. Used as L2 by Abellen Ayta [abp]. *Lg Dev:* Literacy rate in L1: 100%. Literacy rate in L2: 100%. All can read and write. Radio programs. Dictionary. NT: 1982. *Writing:* Latin script. *Map:* 403:41.

Sangil [snl] (Sanggil, Sangiré). 15,000 (1996 SIL). Mindanao, Balut and Sarangani islands. *Status:* 5 (Developing). *Class:* Austronesian, Malayo-Polynesian, Philippine, Sangiric, Northern. *Dialects:* Mindanao, Sarangani. Lexical similarity: 90% with Sangir [sxn]. *Type:* VSO; prepositions; genitives after noun heads; articles, adjectives, numerals all before noun heads; adjectives and numerals tend to follow noun heads; relatives are implied, so have no position in the clause; 4 prefixes, 4 suffixes; aspect; passives; nontonal; 18 consonants, 6 vowels. *Lg Use:* All ages. Proficiency in Cebuano [ceb]. Used as L2 by Sarangani Blaan [bps]. *Lg Dev:* Literacy rate in L1: 50%. Literacy rate in L2: 50%. Bible portions: 1981–2007. *Writing:* Latin script. *Other:* Muslim. *Map:* 405:153.

Sangir [sxn] (Sangihé, Sangirese). 55,000 in Philippines (1981 SIL). Mindanao, Balut and Sarangani islands. *Status:* 5 (Developing). *Lg Use:* Used as L2 by Sarangani Blaan [bps]. See main entry on page 188. *Map:* 405:154.

Sorsoganon, Northern [bks] (Northern Sorsogon, Sorsogon Bicolano, Sorsogon, Masbate). 85,000 (1975 census). Luzon, Sorsogon Province, Sorsogon city, Casiguran and Juban. *Status:* 6a (Vigorous). *Class:* Austronesian, Malayo-Polynesian, Philippine, Greater Central Philippine, Central Philippine, Bisayan, Central, Warayan. *Lg Use:* Also use Central Bikol [bcl], Filipino [fil]. *Map:* 404:83.

Sorsoganon, Southern [srv] (Bikol Sorsogon, Gubat, Sorsogon, Waray, Southern Sorsogon). 185,000 (1975 census). Luzon, south Sorsogon Province. *Status:* 6a (Vigorous). *Class:* Austronesian, Malayo-Polynesian, Philippine, Greater Central Philippine, Central Philippine, Bisayan, Central, Warayan, Gubat. *Dialects:* None known. Comprehension of Masbatenyo [msb] 63%–91%; of Central Bikol [bcl] (Naga) 71%–82%; of Filipino [fil] 85%–91%. Reportedly similar to Waray-Waray [war]. *Lg Use:* Also use Central Bikol [bcl], Filipino [fil], Masbatenyo [msb]. *Map:* 404:84.

Spanish [spa]. 2,660 in Philippines (1990 census). Mainly in Manila; Chavacano-speaking areas. *Status:* 5 (Dispersed). *Lg Use:* Formerly the official language. Used by a few families as L1. Used as L2 by Moyadan Itneg [ity]. *Other:* Christian. See main entry on page 322.

Subanen, Central [syb] (Sindangan Subanun). 140,000 (2000), increasing. Mindanao, east Zamboanga Peninsula; Sulu Archipelago. *Status:* 5 (Developing). *Class:* Austronesian, Malayo-Polynesian, Philippine, Greater Central Philippine, Subanon, Eastern. *Dialect:* Eastern Kolibugan (Eastern Kalibugan). Intelligibility of Southern Subanen [laa] 71%. Lexical similarity: 79% with Western Subanen [suc]. *Lg Use:* Community, home, church, informal education. All ages. Positive attitudes. Also use Cebuano [ceb], Hiligaynon [hil]. *Lg Dev:* Literacy rate in L1: 50%. Literacy rate in L2: 50%. Poetry. Dictionary. NT: 1992. *Writing:* Latin script, used since 1980s. *Other:* Value their language. Traditional religion. *Map:* 405:140.

Subanen, Eastern [sfe] (Guinselugnen). 7,000 (2011 SIL). Mindanao, eastern Zamboanga, Don Victoriano Chiongban, western slopes of Mount Malindang. *Status:* 6b (Threatened). *Class:* Austronesian, Malayo-Polynesian, Philippine, Greater Central Philippine, Subanon, Eastern. *Map:* 405:142.

Subanen, Northern [stb] (Tuboy Subanon). 85,400 (2010 SIL), increasing. 0 monolinguals. Ethnic population: 85,400. Mindanao, Zamboanga del Norte Province, Sergio Osmeña and Mutia municipalities; inland from Dipolog and Dapitan cities; Misamis Occidental Province, Northern Subanen: Jose Dalman (Linasan), Katipunan, La Libertad, Manukan (Linay and Pangandaw), Pinan, Polanco, President Manuel Roxas, Rizal (Disoy) Siayan (Dumugok), and Sibutad. *Status:* 5 (Developing). *Class:* Austronesian, Malayo-Polynesian, Philippine, Greater Central Philippine, Subanon, Eastern. *Dialects:* Dapitan, Dikayu, Miatan, Piyau, Salog (Salug). 63% intelligibility of Central Subanen [syb], 40% of Southern Subanen [laa]. Lexical similarity: 87% with Central Subanen [syb]. *Lg Use:* Home, church, community, group discussion. All ages. Positive attitudes. 86% also use Cebuano [ceb]. Acquired through community, school, travel, and some homes and churches. Used by Cebuanos who are married to Subanens. *Lg Dev:* Literacy rate in L1: 86%. Literacy rate in L2: 86%. Few local grade schools. Poetry. Grammar. NT: 2011. *Writing:* Latin script, used since 1991. *Other:* Christian, traditional religion. *Map:* 405:141.

Subanen, Southern [laa] (Lapuyen, Margosatubig, Subanen, Subanun, Lapuyan). 25,000 (1978 SIL). Mindanao, east Zamboanga del Sur, subpeninsulas. *Status:* 5 (Developing). *Class:* Austronesian, Malayo-Polynesian, Philippine, Greater Central Philippine, Subanon, Eastern. *Dialects:* None known. Southern Subanen speakers understand Central Subanen [syb] (85%), but not vice versa. *Lg Use:* Low comprehension of Cebuano [ceb]. *Lg Dev:* NT: 1982. *Writing:* Latin script. *Map:* 405:139.

Subanon, Kolibugan [skn] (Calibugan, Kalibugan, Kolibugan). 20,000 (1998 SIL). L2 users: Non-Kolibugan Subanon spouses. Mindanao, Zamboanga Peninsula, south Zamboanga del Norte and Zamboanga del Sur provinces. *Status:* 6a (Vigorous). *Class:* Austronesian, Malayo-Polynesian, Philippine, Greater Central Philippine, Subanon, Eastern. *Dialects:* None known. Reportedly similar to Western Subanon [suc], but limitations on inherent intelligibility between them. Lexical and grammatical differences. *Type:* VSO; prepositions; genitives after noun heads; articles, adjectives, and numerals before noun heads; relatives after noun heads; question word in sentence-initial position; 2 maximum prefixes, 3 maximum suffixes; word order distinguishes given and new information, topic and comment; affixes do not indicate case of noun phrases; verb affixes mark number; ergativity; passives; causatives; comparatives; nontonal. *Lg Use:* All domains. All ages. Positive attitudes. L2 acquired through public school, media and travel; L2 used in those domains. *Lg Dev:* Literacy rate in L1: 65%. Literacy rate in L2: 65%. *Writing:* Latin script, used since 2005. *Other:* Culture and attitudes separate Kolibugan from Western Subanon [suc]. Muslim, traditional religion. *Map:* 405:137.

Subanon, Western [suc] (Siocon). 125,000 (2011 SIL). Mindanao, Zamboanga Peninsula. *Status:* 5 (Developing). *Class:* Austronesian, Malayo-Polynesian, Philippine, Greater Central Philippine, Subanon. *Dialects:* Siocon, Western Kolibugan (Western Kalibugan). Lexical similarity: 89% between Siocon and Western Kolibugan dialects. *Type:* VSO; prepositions; genitives after noun heads; articles, adjectives, and numerals before noun heads; relatives before noun heads, and relatives without noun heads; question word in sentence-initial position; 2 maximum prefixes, 3 maximum suffixes; word order distinguishes subjects, objects and indirect objects, given and new information, topic and comment; affixes do not indicate case of noun phrases; verb affixes mark number; ergativity; passives; causatives; comparatives; CV, CVC, CVV, CCV, CCVV, CVVC; nontonal. *Lg Use:* All ages. *Lg Dev:* Literacy rate in L1: 39%. Literacy rate in L2: 39%. Multilingual education pilot program. Poetry. NT: 1996. *Writing:* Latin script. *Other:* Christian. *Map:* 405:138.

Sulod [srg] (Bukidnon, Mondo). 14,000 (1980 SIL). Capiz Province, Tapaz; Iloilo Province, Lambunao; Antique Province, Valderrama, Panay. *Status:* 6a (Vigorous). *Class:* Austronesian, Malayo-Polynesian, Philippine, Greater Central Philippine, Central Philippine. *Map:* 404:101.

Surigaonon [sgd] (Jaun-Jaun, Waya-Waya). 400,000 (2009 W. Hall). Mindanao, Surigao del Norte, north Agusan del Norte, north Surigao del Sur provinces. *Status:* 4 (Educational). *Class:* Austronesian, Malayo-Polynesian, Philippine, Greater Central Philippine, Central Philippine, Bisayan, South. *Dialects:* None known. Reportedly similar to Tandaganon [tgn]. Lexical similarity: 82% with Dibabawon Manobo [mbd], 81% with Agusan Manobo [msm], 69% with Butuanon [btw]. *Lg Use:* Speakers are rapidly shifting to Cebuano [ceb], especially in Surigao City and surrounding parts of Surigao del Norte. Language is much stronger in eastern Surigao del Norte and northern Surigao del Sur. *Lg Dev:* Taught in primary schools, in the Surigao provinces and Dinagat. *Map:* 404:93.

Tadyawan [tdy] (Balaban, Pula, Tadianan). 4,150 (2000). East central Mindoro. *Status:* 6a (Vigorous). *Class:* Austronesian, Malayo-Polynesian, Philippine, North Mangyan. *Lg Use:* Most Tadyawan understand Tawbuid [twb]. Much intermarriage with the Tawbuid. *Map:* 404:110.

Tagabawa [bgs] (Tagabawa Bagobo, Tagabawa Manobo).

43,000 (1998 SIL). Mindanao, Davao city, Mount Apo slopes. *Status:* 4 (Educational). *Class:* Austronesian, Malayo-Polynesian, Philippine, Greater Central Philippine, Manobo, South. *Dialects:* None known. Comprehension of Tigwa Manobo [mbt] 45%; low comprehension of Cebuano [ceb]. Lexical similarity: 62% with Sarangani Manobo [mbs]; 34% with Giangan [bgi]. *Lg Use:* Used as L2 by Obo Manobo [obo]. *Lg Dev:* Literacy rate in L2: 90%. Radio programs. NT: 2004. *Writing:* Latin script. *Other:* The official name is Tagabawa. *Map:* 405:146.

Tagakaulo [klg] (Kalagan, Tagakaulu, Tagakaolo). 83,000 (2000 census). 40,000 monolinguals. Ethnic population: 100,000. South Mindanao, Sarangani Province, Davao Del Sur. Many migrating to Davao City and other areas to find work (2007 SIL). *Status:* 4 (Educational). *Class:* Austronesian, Malayo-Polynesian, Philippine, Greater Central Philippine, Central Philippine, Mansakan, Western. *Dialects:* None known. About 85% intelligibility with Mansaka [msk]. *Type:* VOS, VSO; prepositions; genitives before noun heads; articles before adjectives, before and after numerals, before noun heads; relatives after noun heads; question word in sentence-initial position; 3 maximum prefixes, 2 maximum suffixes; word order distinguishes subjects, objects and indirect objects when case does not, word order distinguishes given and new information, topic and comment; affixes do not indicate case of noun phrases; verb affixes mark number; ergativity; passives; causatives; comparatives; CV, CVC, CVV; nontonal. *Lg Use:* Vigorous. All domains except church, trade. All ages. Positive attitudes. 60,000 also use Cebuano [ceb]. 60,000 also use Hiligaynon [hil]. *Lg Dev:* Literacy rate in L1: 20%–30%. Literacy rate in L2: 20%–30%. Literacy instruction continues for out-of-school youth and adults in non-public school and some church settings. Taught in primary schools in several tribal schools. Public schools taught in English (2007 SIL). Poetry. Radio programs. Videos. Bible portions: 1964–2009. *Writing:* Latin script. *Other:* Christian, traditional religion. *Map:* 405:156.

Tagalog [tgl]. 21,500,000 in Philippines (2000 census). Population total all countries: 24,245,200. Manila, most of Luzon, and Mindoro. Also in Canada, Guam, New Zealand, Saudi Arabia, United Arab Emirates, United Kingdom, United States. *Status:* 3 (Wider communication). De facto national working language. *Class:* Austronesian, Malayo-Polynesian, Philippine, Greater Central Philippine, Central Philippine, Tagalog. *Dialects:* Bataan, Batangas, Bulacan, Lubang, Manila, Marinduque, Puray, Tanay-Paete, Tayabas. *Lg Use:* Also use Bolinao [smk]. Used as L2 by Alabat Island Agta [dul], Calamian Tagbanwa [tbk], Caluyanun [clu], Central Bikol [bcl], Central Bontok [lbk], Central Sama [sml], Kalagan [kqe], Kamayo [kyk], Kayapa Kallahan [kak], Limos Kalinga [kmk], Lubuagan Kalinga [knb], Majukayang Kalinga [kmd], Manide [abd], Northern Bontok [rbk], Rinconada Bikol [bto]. *Lg Dev:* Fully developed. Bible: 1905. *Writing:* Braille script. Latin script, primary usage. Tagalog script, no longer in use. *Other:* Used as basis for the development of Filipino [fil]. Christian. *Maps:* 403:52, 404:52.

Tagbanwa [tbw] (Aborlan Tagbanwa, Apurawnon, Tagbanua). 10,000 (2002 SIL). 500 monolinguals. Palawan, scattered communities from about 120 km south to 60 km north on both sides of Puerto Princesa island. *Status:* 5 (Developing). *Class:* Austronesian, Malayo-Polynesian, Philippine, Greater Central Philippine, Palawanic. *Dialects:* None known. Intelligibility of Central Palawano [plc] 66%, of Cuyonon [cyo] 77%. Lexical similarity: 65% with Central Palawano [plc], 71% with Batak [bya], 54% with Cuyonon [cyo]. *Lg Use:* Used exclusively with other Tagbanwa in all situations. All ages. Negative attitudes. With non-Tagbanwa Filipinos, Tagbanwas are somewhat ashamed of being Tagbanwa, and speak Filipino [fil] as they can. Proficiency in Filipino [fil] varies; more proficiency on the East coast than the West. *Lg Dev:* Literacy rate in L1: 36%. Literacy rate in L2: 36%. NT: 1992. *Writing:* Latin script, primary usage. Tagbanwa script. *Other:* Traditional religion, Christian. *Maps:* 404:124, 405:124.

Tagbanwa, Calamian [tbk] ("Unggoy" *pej.*). 10,000 (2007 SIL), increasing. Ethnic population: 10,000. North Palawan Province, Coron, Busuanga, Culion, and Linapacan municipalities (Calamian and Linapacan Groups), Palawan Island, northeast coast, 3 Tagbanwa communities. *Status:* 5 (Developing). *Class:* Austronesian, Malayo-Polynesian, Philippine, Kalamian. *Dialects:* Baras, Binatuanen, Binuswanganen, Inawanwaanen, Kinalamiananen (Kinaramiananen), Lininipaknen, Tinalaanen. Baras dialect on Palawan Island 94% intelligibility with Calamian Tagbanwa. Lexical similarity: 80% with Calamian and Baras dialects; typologically unusual phenomenon with regard to pronoun ordering and marking. *Type:* VSO; 3 tense-aspects: past, future, and timeless. 16 consonants, 4 vowels; unusual pronoun ordering and marking (Ruch and Quakenbush 2006). *Lg Use:* Vigorous, except with inter-marriage with non-Tagbanwas. Home, church, neighborhood, work sites. All ages. Positive attitudes among themselves; negative attitudes around others. Also use Tagalog [tgl]. Used as L2 by Cuyonon [cyo]. *Lg Dev:* Literacy rate in L1: 40%–50%. Literacy rate in L2: 40% in Tagalog [tgl]. Fluency training much needed (2007 SIL). NT: 2009. *Writing:* Latin script. *Other:* Christian. *Map:* 404:118.

Tagbanwa, Central [tgt]. 2,000 (1985 SIL). North Palawan. *Status:* 8b (Nearly extinct). *Class:* Austronesian, Malayo-Polynesian, Philippine, Greater Central Philippine, Palawanic. *Dialects:* None known. Intelligibility of Tagbanwa [tbw] (Lamane) 29%, of Calamian Tagbanwa 56%, of Cuyonon [cyo] 61%. Lexical similarity: 56% with Tagbanwa [tbw] (Lamane), 57% with Calamian Tagbanwa [tbk], 48% with Cuyonon [cyo], 40% with Filipino [fil]. *Lg Use:* Low comprehension of Filipino [fil]. Also use Cuyonon [cyo]. *Map:* 404:121.

Tandaganon [tgn] (Naturalis, Tagon-on). 100,000 (2009 B. Hall). Mindanao, central Surigao del Sur, Tandag, Tago, Bayabas, and Cagwait towns. *Status:* 6a (Vigorous). *Class:* Austronesian, Malayo-Polynesian, Philippine, Greater Central Philippine, Central Philippine, Bisayan, South. *Dialects:* None known. Reportedly similar to Surigaonon [sgd]. *Lg Use:* Also use Cebuano [ceb]. *Lg Dev:* Radio programs. *Map:* 404:94.

Tausug [tsg] (Bahasa Sug, Moro Joloano, Sinug, Sulu, Suluk, Tausog, Taw Sug). 900,000 in Philippines (2000 SIL), increasing. Population total all countries: 1,062,000. 250,000 monolinguals. Jolo, Sulu Archipelago; Palawan island; Basilan island, Zamboanga city and environs. Also in Indonesia, Malaysia. *Status:* 3 (Wider communication). De facto language of provincial identity in Sulu and Tawi-Tawi provinces. *Class:* Austronesian, Malayo-Polynesian, Philippine, Greater Central Philippine, Central Philippine, Bisayan, South, Butuan-Tausug. *Lg Use:* Vigorous. All domains. All ages. Positive attitudes. Also use Kalagan [kqe]. Used as L2 by Balangingih Sama [sse], Central Sama [sml], Chavacano [cbk], Mapun [sjm], Pangutaran Sama [slm], Southern Sama [ssb], Yakan [yka]. *Lg Dev:* Literacy rate in L1: 50%. Literacy rate in L2: 50%. Taught in primary schools, in Sulu and Tawi-Tawi. Radio programs. Dictionary. NT: 1985–2002. *Writing:* Arabic script. Latin script. *Other:* Muslim. *Map:* 405:133.

Tawbuid, Eastern [bnj] (Bangon, Barangan, Batangan, Binatangan, Fanawbuid, Suri, Tabuid, Taubuid, Tiron). 7,190 (2000). Central Mindoro. *Status:* 5 (Developing). *Class:* Austronesian, Malayo-Polynesian, Philippine, Greater Central Philippine, South Mangyan, Buhid-Taubuid. *Dialects:* None known. Western Tawbuid [twb] is distinct. *Lg Dev:* NT: 1996. *Writing:* Latin script. *Map:* 404:111.

Tawbuid, Western [twb] (Batangan Taubuid, Fanawbuid, Western Taubuid). 6,810 (2000). Central Mindoro; Occidental Mindor, mainly Sablayan and Calintaan municipalities; Oriental Mindoro, Bongabon municipality. *Status:* 5 (Developing). *Class:* Austronesian, Malayo-Polynesian, Philippine, Greater Central Philippine, South Mangyan, Buhid-Taubuid. *Dialects:* None known. Eastern Tawbuid [bnj] is distinct. Reportedly most similar to Buhid [bku]. *Lg Use:* All ages. Also use Filipino [fil]. Used as L2 by Tadyawan [tdy]. *Lg Dev:* NT: 2001. *Writing:* Latin script. *Other:* Traditional religion, Christian. *Map:* 404:114.

Tboli [tbl] ("Tagabili" *pej.*, T'boli, Tiboli). 95,300 (2000). 10,000 monolinguals. Ethnic population: 100,000. Southwest Mindanao, South Cotabato Province. *Status:* 4 (Educational). *Class:* Austronesian, Malayo-Polynesian, Philippine, Bilic, Tboli. *Dialects:* Central Tboli, Southern Tboli, Western Tboli. *Type:* VSO; articles, adjectives, numerals all before and after noun heads; question word in sentence-initial position; maximum number of affixes: 1 prefix, 1 suffix; word order distinguishes subject, object and direct objects, given and new information, topic and comment; affixes indicate case of noun phrase; passives; causatives; comparatives; CV, CVC, CCV, CCVC; nontonal. *Lg Use:* Speak Tboli to each other freely in buses, surrounding towns, etc. All ages. Positive attitudes. Also use Ilongot [ilk]. Used as L2 by Koronadal Blaan [bpr], Sarangani Blaan [bps]. *Lg Dev:* Literacy rate in L1: Perhaps 50%–60%. Literacy rate in L2: Perhaps 50%–60%. Literacy program in previously unreached coastal mountain range. They operate their own government school. Poetry. Dictionary. Grammar. Bible: 2007. *Writing:* Latin script. *Other:* Christian, traditional religion. *Map:* 405:150.

Tiruray [tiy] (Teduray, Tirurai). 50,000 (2002 SIL). Ethnic population: 50,000. Mindanao, Upi and Cotabato. *Status:* 5 (Developing). *Class:* Austronesian, Malayo-Polynesian, Philippine, Bilic. *Lg Use:* Also use Cotabato Manobo [mta]. *Lg Dev:* Literacy rate in L1: 49%. Literacy rate in L2: 49%. NT: 1983. *Writing:* Latin script. *Map:* 405:148.

Waray-Waray [war] (Binisaya, Samaran, Samareño, Samarenyo, Samar-Leyte, Waray). 2,560,000 (2000 census). North and east Samar-Leyte. *Status:* 3 (Wider communication). Statutory language of provincial identity in Samar, Leyte islands (1991, ACFLC Section 3(f)). *Class:* Austronesian, Malayo-Polynesian, Philippine, Greater Central Philippine, Central Philippine, Bisayan, Central, Warayan, Samar-Waray. *Dialects:* Northern Samar, Samar-Leyte, Waray. *Lg Dev:* Bible: 1937–1984. *Writing:* Braille script. Latin script, primary usage. *Map:* 404:87.

Yakan [yka] (Yacan). 106,000 (1990 census), increasing. 86,900 in Basilan Province. 35,000 monolinguals. L2 users: Few outsiders learn Yakan. Some traders for commerce purposes. Sulu Archipelago, Basilan, and small surrounding islands; Sakol island; west Mindanao, Zamboanga east coast. Concentrated away from the coast. *Status:* 4 (Educational). De facto language of provincial identity in Basilan province. *Class:* Austronesian, Malayo-Polynesian, Greater Barito, Sama-Bajaw. *Type:* VOS, VSO; prepositions; genitives after noun heads; articles before noun heads, adjectives after noun heads, numerals before and after noun heads; question word in sentence-initial position; 2 prefixes, 1 suffix; word order distinguishes subjects, objects and indirect objects, given and new information, topic and comment; affixes do not indicate case of noun phrase; non-obligatory verb affixes indicate number; passives; causatives; comparatives; ergativity; CV, CCV, CVC; nontonal. *Lg Use:* Vigorous. All domains. Local administration, commerce, religion, oral traditional literature. Positive attitudes. Also use Chavacano [cbk], English [eng], Filipino [fil], Tausug [tsg]. *Lg Dev:* Literacy rate in L1: 35%. Literacy rate in L2: 25%. Taught in primary schools, in Basilan. Dictionary. Grammar. NT: 1984. *Writing:* Arabic script. Latin script. *Other:* Land division in families and increasing population pushes young people to seek employment in cities or other countries. Muslim. *Map:* 405:135.

Yogad [yog]. 16,000 (1990 census). Luzon, Isabela Province, Echague and nearby towns. *Status:* 6a (Vigorous). *Class:* Austronesian, Malayo-Polynesian, Philippine, Northern Luzon, Northern Cordilleran, Cagayan Valley, Ibanagic. *Dialects:* None known. Lexical similarity: 52% with Ilocano [ilo], 66% with Itawit [itv], 63% with Ibanag [ibg]. *Type:* VSO. *Lg Use:* Also use Ilocano [ilo]. *Lg Dev:* 77% literacy in Isabela in 1955. Dictionary. Grammar. *Map:* 403:28.

Qatar

State of Qatar. 1,700,000 (2010 census). Principal languages: Gulf Spoken Arabic, Standard Arabic. Literacy rate: 95% (2010 UNESCO). Immigrant languages: Malayalam (6,500), Tamil (2,200), Urdu (20,000). Deaf population: 31,100.

The number of individual languages listed for Qatar is 3. All are living languages. Of these, 2 are institutional and 1 is developing.

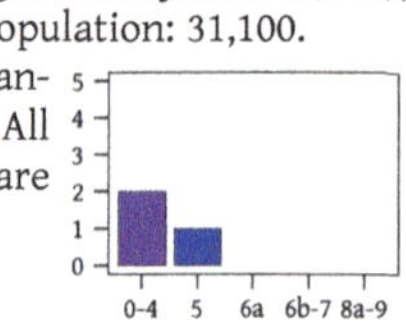

Arabic, Gulf Spoken [afb] (Gulf Arabic, Khaliji, Qatari). 104,000 in Qatar (1986). *Status:* 3 (Wider communication). De facto national working language, absent from formal education. *Dialects:* North Qatari Arabic, South Qatari Arabic. *Other:* Muslim. See main entry on page 213.

Arabic, Standard [arb]. Widespread. *Status:* 1 (National). Statutory national language (2003, Constitution, Article 1). *Lg Use:* Education, official purposes, formal speeches. See main entry on page 293.

Persian, Iranian [pes] (Persian). 73,000 in Qatar (1993). *Status:* 5 (Dispersed). *Other:* Muslim. See main entry on page 204.

Saudi Arabia

Kingdom of Saudi Arabia. 27,137,000 (2010 census). Principal languages: Najdi Spoken Arabic, Standard Arabic. Literacy rate: 81% (2010 UNESCO). Immigrant languages: Bengali (15,000), Chinese (58,000), Egyptian Spoken Arabic (300,000), English (60,000), French (22,000), Indonesian (37,000), Iranian Persian (102,000), Italian (22,000), Korean (66,000), Rohingya (400,000), Somali (42,700), Sudanese Spoken Arabic (86,000), Tagalog (700,000), Urdu (382,000), Uyghur (5,920), Western Cham (100). General references: Bateson 1967; Comrie 1987; Holes 1990; Ingham 1994; Johnstone 1967; Kaye 1987. Deaf population: 100,000.

The number of individual languages listed for Saudi Arabia is 5. All are living languages. Of these, 2 are institutional and 3 are vigorous.

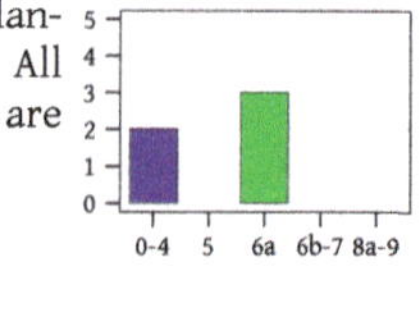

Arabic [ara]. A macrolanguage (see page 9). *Other:* Includes: Algerian Saharan Spoken Arabic [aao] (Algeria), Algerian Spoken Arabic [arq] (Algeria), Babalia Creole Arabic [bbz] (Chad), Baharna Spoken Arabic [abv] (Bahrain), Chadian Spoken Arabic [shu] (Chad), Cypriot Spoken Arabic [acy] (Cyprus), Dhofari Spoken Arabic [adf] (Oman), Eastern Egyptian Bedawi Spoken Arabic [avl] (Egypt), Egyptian Spoken Arabic [arz] (Egypt), Gulf Spoken Arabic [afb] (Kuwait), Hadrami Spoken Arabic [ayh] (Yemen), Hijazi Spoken Arabic [acw], Libyan Spoken Arabic [ayl] (Libya), Mesopotamian Spoken Arabic [acm] (Iraq), Moroccan Spoken Arabic [ary] (Morocco), Najdi Spoken Arabic [ars], North Levantine Spoken Arabic [apc] (Syria), North Mesopotamian Spoken Arabic [ayp] (Iraq), Omani Spoken Arabic [acx] (Oman), Sa'idi Spoken Arabic [aec] (Egypt), Sanaani Spoken Arabic [ayn] (Yemen), Shihhi Spoken Arabic [ssh] (United Arab Emirates), South Levantine Spoken Arabic [ajp] (Jordan), Standard Arabic [arb], Sudanese Creole Arabic [pga] (South Sudan), Sudanese Spoken Arabic [apd] (Sudan), Ta'izzi-Adeni Spoken Arabic [acq] (Yemen), Tajiki Spoken Arabic [abh] (Tajikistan), Tunisian Spoken Arabic [aeb] (Tunisia), Uzbeki Spoken Arabic [auz] (Uzbekistan).

Arabic, Gulf Spoken [afb] (Gulf Spoken). 200,000 in Saudi Arabia. North and south Eastern Province. *Status:* 6a (Vigorous). *Dialect:* Al-Hasaa. See main entry on page 213.

Arabic, Hijazi Spoken [acw] (Hijazi, West Arabian Colloquial Arabic). 6,000,000 in Saudi Arabia (1996). Population total all countries: 6,023,900. Red Sea coast and adjacent highlands. Also in Eritrea. *Status:* 6a (Vigorous). *Class:* Afro-Asiatic, Semitic, Central, South, Arabic. A member of macrolanguage Arabic [ara]. *Dialects:* Coastal Tihaamah, North Hijazi, South Hijazi, Valley Tihaamah. North Hijazi has 4 subvarieties, South Hijazi has 16.

Arabic, Najdi Spoken [ars]. 8,000,000 in Saudi Arabia. Population total all countries: 9,670,000. Also in Canada, Iraq, Jordan, Kuwait, Syria. *Status:* 3 (Wider communication). De facto national working language. *Class:* Afro-Asiatic, Semitic, Central, South, Arabic. A member of macrolanguage Arabic [ara]. *Dialects:* Central Najdi ('Ajmaan, Al-Qasiim, 'Awaazim, Biishah, Haayil, Hofuf, Mutair, Najraan, Rashaayda, Riyadh, Rwala, Sudair, 'Utaiba, Wild 'Ali), North Najdi (Bani Khaalid, Dafiir, Shammari), South Anjdi (Aal Murrah, Najran). Some dialects spoken by Bedouins. *Type:* SVO. *Lg Dev:* Bible portions: 2013. *Other:* Muslim.

Arabic, Standard [arb] (Al-'Arabiyya, Al-Fusha, Literary Arabic). 206,000,000 L1 speakers of all Arabic varieties (Wiesenfeld 1999). L2 users: 246,000,000 L2 speakers of all Arabic varieties (Wiesenfeld 1999). Widespread. Also in Algeria, Bahrain, Chad, Comoros, Denmark, Djibouti, Egypt, Eritrea, Iraq, Israel, Jordan, Kuwait, Lebanon, Libya, Mauritania, Morocco, Oman, Palestine, Philippines (Arabic), Qatar, Somalia, Sudan, Syria, Tanzania, Tunisia, United Arab Emirates, Western Sahara, Yemen. *Status:* 1 (National). Statutory national language (1992, Basic Law, Article 1). *Class:* Afro-Asiatic, Semitic, Central, South, Arabic. A member of macrolanguage Arabic [ara]. *Dialects:* Classical Arabic (Koranic Arabic, Quranic Arabic), Modern Standard Arabic (Modern Literary Arabic). Preserves the ancient grammar. *Type:* VSO. *Lg Use:* Not an L1. In most Arab countries only the well-educated have adequate proficiency in Standard Arabic, while over 100,500,000 do not. Education, official purposes, written materials, and formal speeches. Classical Arabic, with archaic vocabulary, is used for religion and ceremonial purposes. *Lg Dev:* Fully developed. Bible: 1865–2008. *Writing:* Arabic script, primary usage. Braille script. *Other:* Modern Standard Arabic is modernized Classical Arabic.

Saudi Arabian Sign Language [sdl]. *Status:* 6a (Vigorous). *Class:* Deaf sign language.

Singapore

Republic of Singapore, Republik Singapura. 5,080,000 (2010 census). Principal languages: English, Malay. Literacy rate: 94% (2010 UNESCO). Immigrant languages: Japanese (4,940), Korean (5,200), Sylheti, Thai (5,650), Urdu (3,000). Deaf institutions: 3.

The number of individual languages listed for Singapore is 24. All are living languages. Of these, 5 are institutional, 7 are developing, 1 is vigorous, 10 are in trouble, and 1 is dying.

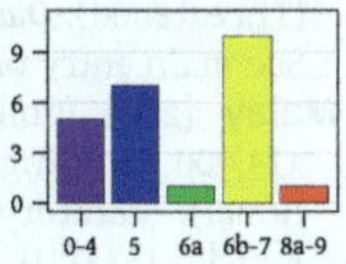

Bengali [ben]. 600 in Singapore (1985). Ethnic population: 80,000 (2006 People's Daily). *Status:* 6b (Threatened). *Other:* Hindu, Muslim. See main entry on page 54.

Chinese, Hakka [hak] (Hokka, Ke, Kechia, Kehia, Kek, Khek). 69,000 in Singapore (1980). Ethnic population: 233,000 (2010 census). *Status:* 6b (Threatened). See main entry on page 67.

Chinese, Mandarin [cmn] (Guoyu, Huayu). 1,210,000 in Singapore (2010 census). L2 users: 880,000 in Singapore. *Status:* 4 (Educational). Recognized language (1963, Constitution (amended), Article 153A(1)). *Lg Use:* Use is increasing. Some also use other Chinese varieties, minority languages, or English [eng]. Used as L2 by Baba Malay [mbf], Min Nan Chinese [nan]. *Lg Dev:* Literacy rate in L1: 65% (2001 census). Taught in primary and secondary schools. *Other:* 2,505,209 ethnic Chinese (2000 census). See main entry on page 67.

Chinese, Min Bei [mnp] (Min Pei). 4,000 in Singapore (1985). Ethnic population: 11,000. *Status:* 6b (Threatened). *Dialect:* Hokchia (Hockchew). See main entry on page 68.

Chinese, Min Dong [cdo]. 34,200 in Singapore (2000). Ethnic population: 54,200 (2010 census). *Status:* 5 (Developing). *Dialect:* Fuzhou (Foochow, Fuchow, Guxhou). See main entry on page 68.

Chinese, Min Nan [nan] (Min Nam, Southern Min). 333,000 in Singapore (2010 census). Ethnic population: 1,860,000 (2010 census). Includes 1,120,000 Hokkien, 562,000 Teochew, 178,0000 Hainanese. *Status:* 3 (Wider communication). *Dialects:* Hainanese, Hokkien (Amoy, Fujian, Fukienese, Xiamen), Teochew (Chaochow, Chaozhou, Taechew). *Lg Use:* Hokkien is most widely understood variety in Singapore (1979 E. Kuo). Home, food centres, army, friends. Also use Mandarin [cmn] or other Chinese varieties. Also use English [eng]. Used as L2 by Baba Malay [mbf]. See main entry on page 68.

Chinese, Pu-Xian [cpx]. 14,100 in Singapore (2000). Ethnic population: 25,600 (2010 census). *Status:* 5 (Developing). *Dialect:* Henghua (Hinghua, Xinghua). See main entry on page 68.

Chinese, Yue [yue] (Cantonese, Guangfu, Yue, Yueh). 121,000 in Singapore (2010 census). Ethnic population: 409,000 (2010 census). *Status:* 5 (Developing). *Lg Use:* Home, church, friends. Used as L2 by Baba Malay [mbf]. See main entry on page 69.

English [eng]. 1,100,000 in Singapore (2010 census). L2 users: 2,000,000 in Singapore (Crystal 2003). *Status:* 1 (National). Statutory national working language (1963, Constitution (amended), Article 153A(1)). *Lg Use:* Home, office, church, public institutions. *Lg Dev:* Taught in primary and secondary schools. See main entry on page 319.

Gujarati [guj] (Gujerathi, Gujerati). 4,120 in Singapore (2010 census). *Status:* 5 (Developing). *Other:* Hindu. See main entry on page 113.

Hindi [hin]. 13,100 in Singapore (2010 census). *Status:* 5 (Dispersed). See main entry on page 114.

Javanese [jav] (Djawa, Jawa). 800 in Singapore (1985). Ethnic population: 88,600 (2010 census). *Status:* 6b (Threatened). *Other:* Muslim. See main entry on page 164.

Madura [mad] (Madhura, Madurese). 900 in Singapore (1985). Ethnic population: 14,300 (1985). *Status:* 6b (Threatened). *Dialect:* Bawean (Boyanese). *Other:* Muslim. See main entry on page 175.

Malay [zlm] (Colloquial Malay, Local Malay, Malayu). 414,000 in Singapore (2010 census). *Status:* 1 (National). Statutory national language (1963, Constitution, Article 153A(2)), not dominant despite status. *Dialect:* Jugra-Muar-Melaka-Johor. *Lg Use:* Ethnic Malay speaking groups: Malay 339,000, 85%; Javanese 21,000, 5%; Indians 14,000, 4%; Bawean Madurese 14,000, 4%; Arabs 2,500, Below 1%; Bugis 500, Below 1%. English used at home by 7%. Also use English [eng], Standard Malay [zsm]. *Other:* Local Malay [zlm] in Singapore is distinguished from court-Malay-derived Standard Malay [zsm] by its sociolinguistic status as a vernacular, as well as by various linguistic features. Muslim (Sunni). See main entry on page 223.

Malay, Baba [mbf] (Baba, Chinese Malay, Straits Malay). 10,000 in Singapore (Pakir 1986). Population total all countries: 12,000. Ethnic population: 250,000 (1986). Mainly Katong District, east coast and surrounding Geylang and Jao Chiat districts. Also in Malaysia. *Status:* 7 (Shifting). *Class:* Creole, Malay based. *Dialects:* None known. It developed after 15th century from Low Malay with many Min Nan Chinese [nan] borrowings. Regional variants between Malacca and Singapore. Partially intelligible with Standard Malay [zsm]. It is generally believed that Baba of Malaysia is more, refined, and that of Singapore more, rough. Most learn Standard Malay and English in school. Distinct from Peranakan Indonesian [pea]. Baba in Melaka, Malaysia speak a Hokkien-influenced Malay creole; those in Penang, Malaysia speak a localized version of Hokkien [hnh] (2006, Tan Chee Beng). *Lg Use:* Mainly in the home. Mainly older adults. Also use Mandarin Chinese [cmn], Min Nan Chinese [nan], Standard Malay [zsm], Yue Chinese [yue]. Children now learn Mandarin [cmn] in school rather than Standard Malay [zsm]. Some who grew up with Chinese neighbors know Min Nan Chinese [nan], the Teochew dialect of Min Nan Chinese, or Yue Chinese [yue]. *Lg Dev:* NT: 1913. *Writing:* Latin script.

Malay, Standard [zsm] (Formal Malay, Malay, Malayu, Melayu, Melayu Baku). Few L1 speakers. L2 speakers include ethnic Malays and some others, particularly the older generation. *Status:* 6b (Threatened). *Lg Use:* Used as L2 by Baba Malay [mbf], Malay [zlm]. *Lg Dev:* Medium of instruction in some schools. *Other:* In Singapore, Standard Malay [zsm] exists in a diglossic relationship with Local Malay [zlm]. See main entry on page 224.

Malayalam [mal] (Alealum, Malayal, Malayalani, Malean, Maliyad, Mallealle, Mopla). 26,300 in Singapore (2010 census). *Status:* 6b (Threatened). *Other:* Christian. See main entry on page 128.

Orang Seletar [ors]. 880 in Singapore (2000). North coast; opposite the coast of Malaysia. *Status:* 8a (Moribund). See main entry on page 225.

Panjabi, Eastern [pan]. 5,670 in Singapore (2010 census). Ethnic population: 14,000 (1993). *Status:* 6b (Threatened). *Other:* Sikh. See main entry on page 138.

Sindhi [snd]. 3,970 in Singapore (2010 census). *Status:* 5 (Developing). See main entry on page 272.

Singapore Sign Language [sls]. 3,000 (2007 SIL). Very few monolinguals. Ethnic population: 4,000 (2007 SIL). *Status:* 6a (Vigorous). *Class:* Deaf sign language. *Dialects:* Contact Signing (Pidgin Signed English), Natural Sign Language. *Lg Use:* Home, church, commerce. Positive attitudes. 3,000 also use English [eng]. *Lg Dev:* Literacy rate in L1: 0%. Literacy rate in L2: 70% estimated in English and (or) Chinese. It is difficult for the deaf to learn to read and maintain their reading skills. Dictionary.

Sinhala [sin] (Chingalese, Singhalese, Sinhalese). 3,140 in Singapore (2010 census). Ethnic population: 12,000 (1993). *Status:* 6b (Threatened). *Other:* Great difference between the literary and colloquial language. Buddhist. See main entry on page 295.

Tamil [tam]. 111,000 in Singapore (2010 census). Ethnic population: 189,000 (2010 census). *Status:* 4 (Educational). Recognized language (1963, Constitution (amended), Article 153A(1)). *Lg Use:* Also use English [eng]. *Lg Dev:* Taught in primary and secondary schools. *Other:* Hindu. See main entry on page 145.

Telugu [tel]. 600 in Singapore (2000). *Status:* 5 (Developing). See main entry on page 145.

Korea, South

Republic of Korea, Taehan Min'guk. 48,580,000 (2010 census). Principal language: Korean. Literacy rate: 98% (2010 USDS). Immigrant languages: English (63,600), Mandarin Chinese (181,000). General references: Comrie 1987. Deaf institutions: 28.

The number of individual languages listed for Korea, South is 2. All are living languages. Of these, 2 are institutional.

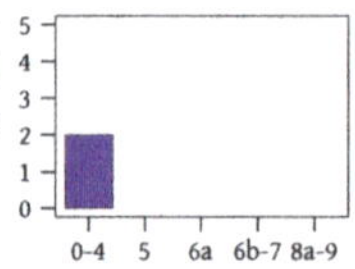

Korean [kor] (Hanguk Mal, Hanguk Uh). 48,400,000 in Korea, South (2010). Population total all countries: 77,166,230. Also in American Samoa, Australia, Azerbaijan, Bahrain, Belarus, Belize, Brazil, Brunei, Canada, China, Germany, Guam, Japan, Kazakhstan, North Korea, Kyrgyzstan, Libya, Mauritania, Mongolia, Mozambique, New Zealand, Northern Mariana Islands, Panama, Paraguay, Philippines, Russian Federation, Saudi Arabia, Singapore, Suriname, Tajikistan, Turkmenistan, Ukraine, United States, Uzbekistan. *Status:* 1 (National). De facto national language. *Class:* Language isolate. *Dialects:* Cheju Island, Chollado (North Chollado, South Chollado), Ch'ungch'ongdo (North Ch'ungch'ong, South Ch'ungch'ong), Kyongsangdo (North Kyongsangdo, South Kyongsangdo), Seoul (Kangwondo, Kyonggido). Scholars differ as to whether or not Korean is related to Japanese [jpn]. Some suggest that both languages are possibly distantly related to the Altaic group. Dialect boundaries generally correspond to provincial boundaries. Some dialects are not easily intelligible with others (Voegelin and Voegelin 1977). The suffix, -do, on dialect names means Province. Comprehension of standard Korean may be lower on Cheju Island. *Type:* SOV. *Lg Dev:* Literacy rate in L1: 98% (1995). Higher adult illiteracy is reported on Cheju Island. Fully developed. Bible: 1911–1993. *Writing:*

Braille script. Hangul and Han scripts, primary usage. Latin script, used for maps and signs. *Other:* Jeju (Cheju) has been identified as a language separate from Cheju Island dialect of Korean, but not yet assigned an ISO code (Moseley 2010). Buddhist, Christian.

Korean Sign Language [kvk]. *Status:* 4 (Educational). *Class:* Deaf sign language. *Dialects:* None known. Related to Japanese [jsl] and Taiwanese [tss] sign languages. *Type:* Finger-spelling system. *Lg Use:* Used since 1889. Signed interpretation required in court, used at important public events, and social services programs. Instruction for parents of deaf children. Many sign language classes for hearing people. *Lg Dev:* Primary schools for deaf children using sign language since 1908. TV. Dictionary.

Sri Lanka

Democratic Socialist Republic of Sri Lanka. 20,264,000 (2012 census). Principal languages: English, Sinhala, Tamil. Literacy rate: 90% (2010 UNESCO). General references: Gair 1998; Voegelin and Voegelin 1977. Deaf population: 73,340. Deaf institutions: 14.

The number of individual languages listed for Sri Lanka is 6. All are living languages. Of these, 3 are institutional, 1 is developing, 1 is vigorous, and 1 is in trouble. See map on page 399.

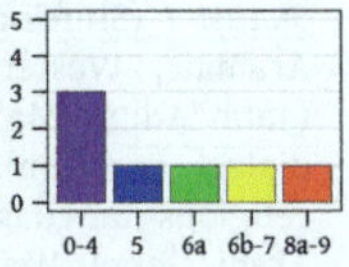

English [eng]. 10,000 in Sri Lanka (Crystal 2003). L2 users: 1,900,000 in Sri Lanka. *Status:* 3 (Wider communication). De facto national working language, used in government. *Lg Use:* Government. Used as L2 by Indo-Portuguese [idb], Sri Lankan Creole Malay [sci]. See main entry on page 319.

Indo-Portuguese [idb]. 30 in Sri Lanka (1992 P. Baker). 0 monolinguals. Ethnic population: 3,410. Trincomalee, Batticaloa. *Status:* 6b (Threatened). *Lg Use:* Many in the ethnic group may not know the creole well. Virtually no contact with Goa or Portugal since 1656. Home only. Most Burgher caste speak it at home. 100% also use Tamil [tam]. Also use English [eng], Sinhala [sin]. See main entry on page 116. *Map:* 399.

Sinhala [sin] (Cingalese, Singhala, Singhalese, Sinhalese). 15,500,000 in Sri Lanka (2007). Population total all countries: 15,579,980. L2 users: 2,000,000 in Sri Lanka (1997). Widespread except some districts north, east, and center. Also in Canada, Libya, Malaysia, Singapore, Thailand, United Arab Emirates, United States. *Status:* 1 (National). Statutory national language (1987, Constitution (amended), Article 18). *Class:* Indo-European, Indo-Iranian, Indo-Aryan, Sinhalese-Maldivian. *Dialect:* Rodiya. Great differences exist between literary and colloquial language. Rodiya dialect is spoken by low caste Rodiya people. *Type:* SOV; 7 long vowels, 7 short vowels, 24 consonants, including 4 which are prenasalized; gender, number, and case agreement between subject and verb in literary Sinhala. *Lg Dev:* Fully developed. Bible: 1823–1982. *Writing:* Braille script. Sinhala script, primary usage. *Other:* Buddhist. *Map:* 399.

Sri Lankan Creole Malay [sci] (Java Jati, Melayu Bahasa, Sri Lankan Malay). 46,000 (Ansaldo and Lim 2006), decreasing. Especially Colombo, Kandy, Badulla, Hambantota, and Kirinda cities. *Status:* 5 (Developing). *Class:* Creole, Malay based. *Dialects:* None known. Not intelligible of Standard Malay [zsm] due to phonological and syntactic differences, and strong influence from Tamil [tam]. May be similar to Malaccan Creole Malay [ccm] (Lim 1981). *Type:* SOV; postpositions; case; adjectives and genitives precede noun heads. *Lg Use:* Language shift taking place. Malay communities using either English [eng], Sinhala [sin], or Tamil [tam] favor Sri Lankan Creole Malay. Clear shift to English among youth in Colombo. Kirinda is the only vital community of Sri Lanka Malays who have youth who speak it as L1. There is also a desire to acquire Standard Malay [zsm] as a useful economic tool but still preserve Malay identity. Beginning to shift to Standard Malay even in Kirinda. Home, community. All ages only in Kirinda; being lost by youth in every other community. Also use English [eng], Sinhala [sin], Standard Malay [zsm], Tamil [tam]. *Lg Dev:* Newspapers. Radio programs. *Writing:* Latin script. *Other:* Malay vocabulary with grammatical structure based on Sri Lankan Moor Tamil. Muslim, traditional religion. *Map:* 399.

Sri Lankan Sign Language [sqs]. 12,800 deaf persons (Van Cleve 1986). *Status:* 6a (Vigorous). *Class:* Deaf sign language. *Type:* Two-handed finger-spelling derived from British Sign Language [bfi]. *Lg Use:* 14 deaf schools. Several sign languages used by different schools.

Tamil [tam]. 3,770,000 in Sri Lanka (2007). North and northeast coasts, a few pockets in the south. *Status:* 1 (National). Statutory national language (1987, Constitution (amended), Articles 22(1),24(1)), concentrated in North and East provinces; also in local administration and courts elsewhere. *Other:* Hindu, Muslim. See main entry on page 145. *Map:* 399.

Veddah [ved] (Beda, Bedda, Vaedda, Veda, Veddha, Weda, Weddo). Ethnic population: 2,500 (2002). Eastern mountains, Badulla and Polonnaruwa districts. *Status:* 8b (Nearly extinct). *Class:* Indo-European, Indo-Iranian, Indo-Aryan, Sinhalese-Maldivian. *Lg Use:* Shifting to Sinhala [sin]. Veddah reportedly no longer used (Breton 1997). *Other:* They live in small rural settlements and are more of a caste than a separate ethnic group. Generally accepted as equal in rank to the Sinhalese Goyigama caste. *Map:* 399.

Syria

Syrian Arab Republic. 17,921,000 (2004 census). Principal languages: North Levantine Spoken Arabic, Standard Arabic. Literacy rate: 77% (2010 UNESCO). Immigrant languages: Chaldean Neo-Aramaic (5,000), Egyptian Spoken Arabic (75,000), Iranian Persian (53,000), Turkmen (126,000). General references: Fischer and Jastrow 1980; Ingham 1982; Sebeok 1963. Deaf population: 902,600. Deaf institutions: 1.

The number of individual languages listed for Syria is 17. Of these, 16 are living and 1 is extinct. Of the living languages, 2 are institutional, 4 are developing, 4 are vigorous, 5 are in trouble, and 1 is dying. See map on page 379.

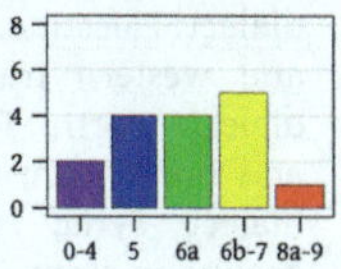

Adyghe [ady] (Adygey, West Circassian). 25,000 in Syria. *Status:* 5 (Developing). *Other:* Muslim (Sunni). See main entry on page 319. *Map:* 379.

Arabic, Levantine Bedawi Spoken [avl] (Bedawi). 70,000 in Syria. Southwest corner, Hawran region, from the border to within 35 km of Damascus. *Status:* 6a (Vigorous). *Other:* Muslim (Sunni), Christian. See main entry on page 319 (as Arabic, Eastern Egyptian Bedawi Spoken). *Map:* 379.

Arabic, Mesopotamian Spoken [acm] (Furati,

Mesopotamian Gelet Arabic, North Syrian Arabic). 1,800,000 in Syria. East. *Status:* 6a (Vigorous). *Dialect:* Euphrates Cluster. *Other:* Muslim, Christian, Jewish. See main entry on page 206. *Map:* 379.

Arabic, Najdi Spoken [ars] (Bedawi). 500,000 in Syria. Syrian desert. *Status:* 6a (Vigorous). *Lg Use:* Spoken by Bedouins. See main entry on page 293. *Map:* 379.

Arabic, North Levantine Spoken [apc] (Lebanese-Syrian Arabic, Levantine Arabic, North Levantine Arabic, Syro-Lebanese Arabic). 8,800,000 in Syria (1991). Population total all countries: 14,426,540. Also in Antigua and Barbuda, Argentina, Belize, Brazil, Cyprus, Dominican Republic, Egypt, French Guiana, Israel, Jamaica, Lebanon, Mali, Puerto Rico, Suriname, Trinidad and Tobago, Turkey. *Status:* 3 (Wider communication). De facto national working language. *Class:* Afro-Asiatic, Semitic, Central, South, Arabic. A member of macrolanguage Arabic [ara] (Saudi Arabia). *Dialects:* There is an urban standard dialect based on Damascus speech. Beiruti dialect well accepted. Aleppo dialect shows Mesopotamian (North Syrian) influence. *Lg Use:* Drama. Used as L2 by Northern Kurdish [kmr], Western Neo-Aramaic [amw]. *Lg Dev:* Radio programs. TV. Bible portions: 1973. *Writing:* Arabic script. *Other:* Druze, Christian, Jewish, Muslim. *Map:* 379.

Arabic, North Mesopotamian Spoken [ayp] (Mesopotamian Qeltu Arabic, Moslawi, Syro-Mesopotamian Arabic). 300,000 in Syria (1992). Far east. *Status:* 6a (Vigorous). *Other:* Muslim, Christian. See main entry on page 206. *Map:* 379.

Arabic, Standard [arb]. Widespread. *Status:* 1 (National). Statutory national language (1973, Constitution, Article 4). *Lg Use:* Education, print publications, official purposes, formal speeches. See main entry on page 293.

Armenian [hye] (Armjanski, Ermenice, Haieren, Somkhuri). 320,000 in Syria (1993). *Status:* 5 (Dispersed). *Dialect:* Western Armenian. *Other:* Christian. See main entry on page 51. *Map:* 379.

Assyrian Neo-Aramaic [aii] (Aisorski, Assyrian, Assyriski, Lishana Aturaya, Neo-Syriac, Suret, Sureth, Suryaya Swadaya). 30,000 in Syria (1995). Ethnic population: 700,000. North, Khabur river banks. Over 30 villages. *Status:* 6b (Threatened). See main entry on page 206. *Map:* 379.

Azerbaijani, South [azb]. 30,000 in Syria (1961 census). Homs and Hama. *Status:* 5 (Developing). *Lg Use:* Also use Arabic [ara]. *Other:* Ethnonym: Turkmen or Turkomen in Syria and Iraq. Not written in Syria. Muslim. See main entry on page 201. *Map:* 379.

Domari [rmt] (Barake, Gypsy, Kurbat, Middle Eastern Romani, Nawar, Tsigene). 37,000 in Syria (2005). Nawar dialect: Palestine, Syria, and Egypt; Kurbat dialect: Syria and western Iran; Helebi: Egypt and Libya; Karachi dialect: north Turkey, Russian Federation Caucasus, and north Iran; Domaki and Wogri-Boli: India; Barake dialect: Syria; Luli and Maznoug: Uzbekistan; other groups in Iran; Churi-Wali dialect: Afghanistan. *Status:* 8a (Moribund). *Dialects:* Barake, Beirut, Kurbati, Nablos, Nawar. *Other:* Arabic influence. Muslim. See main entry on page 202.

Kabardian [kbd]. 39,000 in Syria (2005 Circassian Association). Damascus; Aleppo. *Status:* 6b (Threatened). *Other:* Muslim (Sunni). See main entry on page 321.

Kurdish, Northern [kmr] (Kurdi, Kurmancî, Kurmanji). 938,000 in Syria (1993). North: Northern Cizire (Qamishlok), Kurd-Dagh (Ciyayê Kurdî, Afrin), Ain-Arab, Allepo, Damascus. *Status:* 5 (Developing). *Lg Use:* Also use North Levantine Spoken Arabic [apc]. *Other:* Muslim (Sunni), Yezidi. See main entry on page 305. *Map:* 379.

Lomavren [rmi] (Armenian Bosha, Arnebuab Bisa, Bosa, Bosha). *Status:* 6b (Threatened). See main entry on page 52.

Mlahsö [lhs]. No known L1 speakers. The last speaker died in 1998. Qamishli town; Diyarbakir Province, Turkey. *Status:* 10 (Extinct). *Class:* Afro-Asiatic, Semitic, Central, Aramaic, Eastern, Central, Northwestern. *Dialects:* None known. Reportedly similar to Turoyo [tru]. *Lg Use:* Mlahsö was still spoken by a handful of people in 1970s. One nearly deaf woman still knew Mlahsö well, but had no one to speak it to (1999). *Other:* A different language from Turoyo [tru], also called Suryoyo.

Turoyo [tru] (Surayt, Suryoyo, Syryoyo, Turani). 7,000 in Syria (1994). Ethnic population: 20,000 (1994). *Status:* 7 (Shifting). *Lg Use:* Home. Western Syriac [syc] used in church, Arabic in schools and trade. *Other:* Religious capital is Damascus; formerly at Tur 'Abdin, Turkey. Christian (Jacobite). See main entry on page 306. *Map:* 379.

Western Neo-Aramaic [amw] (Loghtha Siryanoytha, Maalula, Neo-Western Aramaic, Siryon). 15,000 (1996). 8,000 in Maaloula. Qalamoun mountains, 50 km north of Damascus, Ma'lula, Bakh'a, and Jubb 'Adin villages. *Status:* 7 (Shifting). *Class:* Afro-Asiatic, Semitic, Central, Aramaic, Western. *Dialects:* Bakh'a (Bax'a), Jub-'adin (Jubb 'Adi:n), Ma'lula (Maaloula, Maalula, Ma'lu:la). Little dialect variation. *Lg Use:* Home, and as literary and religious language. Also use North Levantine Spoken Arabic [apc]. *Writing:* Unwritten, efforts to introduce a writing system with old Aramaic characters and with Hebrew were not successful. *Other:* Christian. *Map:* 379.

Taiwan

Taiwan, Province of China. Also referred to as Republic of China, Chung-hua Min-kuo. 23,120,000 (2009 census). Principal languages: Mandarin Chinese, Min Nan Chinese. Literacy rate: 98% (2008 USDS). Immigrant languages: Halh Mongolian (6,000), Tibetan (2,000). General references: Li 1990; Sebeok 1971; Tryon 1995; Tsuchida 1976; Wurm 2000, 2007; Wurm and Hattori 1981. Deaf population: 104,000 (2004). Deaf institutions: 8.

The number of individual languages listed for Taiwan is 25. Of these, 21 are living and 4 are extinct. Of the living languages, 4 are institutional, 6 are developing, 1 is vigorous, 3 are in trouble, and 7 are dying. See map on page 347.

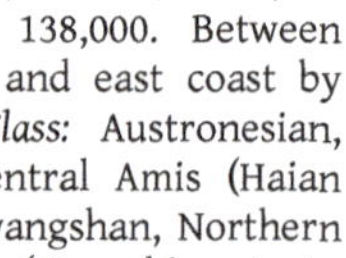

Amis [ami] (Ami, Amia, Bakurut, Lam-Si-Hoan, Maran, Pagcah, Pangcah, Pangtsah, Sabari, Tanah). 138,000 (CIP-EY 2002). Ethnic population: 138,000. Between Hualien and Taitung, valley plains and east coast by the sea. *Status:* 5 (Developing). *Class:* Austronesian, East Formosan, Central. *Dialects:* Central Amis (Haian Ami, Hsiukulan Ami), Chengkung-Kwangshan, Northern Amis (Nanshi Amis), Southern Amis (Hengch'un Amis, Peinan, Taitung), Tavalong-Vataan (Kuangfu, Kwangfu). Chengkung-Kwangshan dialect is most similar to Central Amis dialect. *Lg Use:* Also use Japanese [jpn], Mandarin Chinese [cmn]. Used as L2 by Kavalan [ckv]. *Lg Dev:* Dictionary. Grammar. Bible: 1997. *Writing:* Latin script. *Other:* Ethnic autonym: Amis. Ethnonym: Ami in Chinese. Traditionally matrilineal. Many migrating to cities and industrial areas. *Map:* 347.

Amis, Nataoran [ais] (Nataoran, Natawran, Tauran). 5 (Wurm 2000). Hualien area and north of Fenglin. *Status:*

8b (Nearly extinct). *Class:* Austronesian, East Formosan, Central. *Dialects:* Cikosowan, Kaliyawan (Kaliyuawan), Nataoran, Natawran, Pokpok, Ridaw, Sakizaya (Sakiray, Sakiraya). Not generally understood by other Amis. Sakizaya dialect is even more divergent from Central Amis [ami]. In recent years dialects converged. Lexical similarity: 50% with Central Amis. *Lg Use:* Moribund (2000 S. Wurm). Older adults. *Map:* 347.

Atayal [tay] (Ataiyal, Attayal, Bonotsek, Shabogala, Taijyal, Taiyal, Takonan, Tangao, Tayal, Tyal, Yukan). 84,300 (CIP-EY 2002). Northeast mountains, south of Ketagalan [kae] language area. *Status:* 5 (Developing). *Class:* Austronesian, Atayalic. *Dialects:* Sqoleq (Squliq), Ts'ole' (Ci'uli'). Mayrinax is a Ci'uli' subdialect. *Lg Use:* In active use in some areas. Used as L2 by Saisiyat [xsy]. *Lg Dev:* Dictionary. Grammar. Bible: 2002. *Writing:* Han script, Simplified variant. Han script, Traditional variant. Latin script. *Map:* 347.

Babuza [bzg] (Babusa, Favorlang, Favorlangsch, Jaborlang, Poavosa). No known L1 speakers. Ethnic population: 35. West central coast and inland, Tatu and Choshui rivers and beyond. *Status:* 9 (Dormant). *Class:* Austronesian, Western Plains, Central Western Plains. *Dialects:* Poavosa, Taokas. *Lg Dev:* Bible portions. *Other:* Sinicized.

Basay [byq] (Basai, Kawanuwan). No known L1 speakers. North, Tam Shui to Kungliao area, Fengtzulin, Taipei, Sangchung, and northeast Suao and east of Ilan area. *Status:* 10 (Extinct). *Class:* Austronesian, East Formosan, Northern. *Dialects:* Linaw-Qauqaul, Trobiawan. *Lg Dev:* Grammar. *Other:* Sinicized. Older people remember a few words.

Bunun [bnn] (Bubukun, Bunan, Bunti, Bunum, Vonun, Vunum, Vunun, Vunung). 38,000 (CIP-EY 2002). Ethnic population: 38,000. East central plain, south of the Sediq (Taroko) [trv] language area. *Status:* 5 (Developing). *Class:* Austronesian, Bunun. *Dialects:* Central Bunun (Takbanuao, Takevatan, Takivatan), North Bunun (Takebakha, Taketodo, Takibakha, Takitudu), Randai, Shibukun (Sibucoon, Sibukaun, Sibukun, Sivukun), South Bunun (Ishbukun), Takopulan, Tondai. *Lg Use:* Also spoken by Kanakanabu [xnb] and Saaroa [sxr]. *Lg Dev:* Dictionary. Grammar. Bible: 2000. *Writing:* Latin script. *Map:* 347.

Chinese, Hakka [hak]. 2,370,000 in Taiwan (1993). Taoyuan, Hsinchu, Miaoli, Pingtung counties. Shi Xien in north and south; Hi-Lu in central, north central. *Status:* 5 (Developing). *Dialects:* Hailu (Hi-Lu, Hoilluk, Hoiluk), Sanhsien (Shi Xien, Shigen, Shixien). *Lg Use:* Used as L2 by Saisiyat [xsy]. *Other:* Settled in Taiwan for 200 years. Sanhsien closely resembles Yuetai of Mainland China. Hailu closely resembles Yong-Ting or Yuqui of Mainland China. See main entry on page 67. *Map:* 347.

Chinese, Mandarin [cmn] (Guoyu, Kuoyu, Mandarin, Putonghua). 4,320,000 in Taiwan (1993). L2 users: 15,000,000 in Taiwan. Mainly Taipei and 5 provincial cities. *Status:* 1 (National). De facto national language. *Dialect:* Taibei Mandarin. *Lg Use:* Many 30–50-year-olds also use Taiwan Min Nan [nan]. *Lg Dev:* Kuoyu taught in all schools. *Other:* Traditional religion, Buddhist, Christian. See main entry on page 67. *Map:* 347.

Chinese, Min Nan [nan] (Min Nan, Minnan). 15,000,000 in Taiwan (1997 A. Chang). Tainan, Penghu Archipelago, east coast cities, western plain. *Status:* 3 (Wider communication). De facto language of national identity. *Dialect:* Taiwanese (Amoy, Chaenzo, Hokkien, Sanso). *Lg Use:* Adults over 60 also use Japanese [jpn]. 83% also use Mandarin Chinese [cmn]. Used as L2 by Kavalan [ckv], Mandarin Chinese [cmn], Rukai [dru]. *Other:* Taiwanese people are called Hoklo or Holo. Traditional religion, Buddhist, Christian. See main entry on page 68. *Map:* 347.

Japanese [jpn]. L2 users: 10,000 in Taiwan (1993). *Status:* 8b (Nearly extinct). *Lg Use:* A few older adult aboriginals. Used as L2 by Amis [ami], Min Nan Chinese [nan], Rukai [dru], Taroko [trv]. See main entry on page 210.

Kanakanabu [xnb] (Kanabu, Kanakanavu). 4 (2012 P. Jen-Kuei). A few other semi-speakers who have passive knowledge of the language (2012 P. Jen-Kuei). Ethnic population: 250 (UNESCO). Central, Sanmin Township, Kaohsiung County, Minchuan village area. *Status:* 8b (Nearly extinct). *Class:* Austronesian, Tsouic. *Lg Use:* Moribund (2000 S. Wurm). Shifted to Bunun [bnn], Taiwanese [nan], or Mandarin [cmn]. Also use Mandarin Chinese [cmn]. *Lg Dev:* Literacy rate in L2: 8%. Grammar. *Map:* 347.

Kavalan [ckv] (Cabaran, Kabalan, Kabaran, Kamalan, Kavanan, Kavarauan, Kbalan, Kibalan, Kiwaraw, Kiwarawa, Kuvalan, Kuvarawan, Kuwarawan, Kvalan, Shekwan). 24 (2000 P. Li). Ethnic population: 1,000 (Tsukida 2007). Northeast coast, above Toucheng to Ilan, nearly to Suao, and inland to Atayal [tay] language area. No longer spoken in the original area; a few migrants to the east coast, Hsishe village, Fengpin Township, Hualien County. *Status:* 8b (Nearly extinct). *Class:* Austronesian, East Formosan, Northern. *Dialect:* Kareovan (Kareowan). *Lg Use:* Moribund (2000 S. Wurm). Most shifted to Min Nan Chinese [nan] (Tsukida and Tsuchida 2007). Home. A few elderly speakers (Tsukida and Tsuchida 2007). Neutral attitudes. Also use Amis [ami], Min Nan Chinese [nan]. *Lg Dev:* Dictionary. Grammar. *Writing:* Latin script. *Other:* Sinicized.

Ketangalan [kae] (Ketagalan, Tangalan). No known L1 speakers. North central, Panchiao area and northwest, west, and southeast. *Status:* 10 (Extinct). *Class:* Austronesian, Unclassified. *Other:* Sinicized.

Kulon-Pazeh [uun] (Kulun). No known L1 speakers. West coast area, east of Tayal, Cholan area, Houli, Fengyuan, Tantzu, Taichung, Tungshih. *Status:* 10 (Extinct). *Class:* Austronesian, Northwest Formosan. *Lg Dev:* Dictionary. Grammar. *Writing:* Latin script. *Other:* Sinicized.

Paiwan [pwn] (Butanglu, Kadas, Kale-Whan, Kapiangan, Katausan, Li-Li-Sha, Paiuan, Payowan, Samobi, Samohai, Saprek, Stimul, Tamari). 66,100 (CIP-EY 2002). Ethnic population: 66,100. South, mountains southeast. *Status:* 5 (Developing). *Class:* Austronesian, Paiwan. *Lg Dev:* Dictionary. Grammar. NT: 1973–1993. *Writing:* Latin script. *Map:* 347.

Papora-Hoanya [ppu] (Bupuran, Hinapavosa, Papola, Vupuran). No known L1 speakers. North central coast around Lishui, Chingshui, Shalu, and inland to Taichung. *Status:* 10 (Extinct). *Class:* Austronesian, Western Plains, Central Western Plains. *Dialects:* Hoanya, Papora. *Other:* Sinicized.

Puyuma [pyu] (Kadas, Panapanayan, Pelam, Pilam, Piyuma, Pyuma, Tipun). 8,490 (CIP-EY 2002). Ethnic population: 8,490. East coast area south of Taitung and inland. *Status:* 7 (Shifting). *Class:* Austronesian, Puyuma. *Dialects:* Nanwang, Pinan. *Lg Use:* All domains. Mostly older adults. Used as L2 by Rukai [dru]. *Lg Dev:* Dictionary. Grammar. Bible portions: 1990. *Map:* 347.

Rukai [dru] (Banga, Bantalang, Bantaurang, Drukai, Drukay, Dukai, Dyokay, Kadas, Rutkai, Sarisen, Taloma, Tsalisen, Tsarisen). 10,500 (CIP-EY 2002). Some monolingual older adults. Ethnic population: 10,500. South central mountains, Ping Tung area, 11 villages; Taitung area, 2 or 3 villages; west of the Puyuma [pyu]. *Status:* 5 (Developing). *Class:* Austronesian, Rukai. *Dialects:* Budai, Labuan, Maga, Mantauran, Tanan, Tona. Mantauran, Tona, and Maga dialects are divergent. *Type:* VSO. *Lg Use:* All domains. Some older adults also use Japanese [jpn].

Budai people speak Taiwanese [nan]. Also use Puyuma [pyu]. *Lg Dev:* Dictionary. Grammar. NT: 2001. *Writing:* Latin script. *Other:* Some linguists classify it as Paiwanic. Paiwanic influence. *Map:* 347.

Saaroa [sxr] (Hla'alua, La'alua, La'arua, Lha'alua, Pachien, Paichien, Rarua, Saarua, Saroa, Shishaban, Sisyaban). 10 (2012 C. Pan). Ethnic population: 300 (2000 UNESCO). West central mountains, south and southeast of Minchuan, along Laonung River. *Status:* 8b (Nearly extinct). *Class:* Austronesian, Tsouic. *Dialects:* None known. Reportedly similar to Kanakanabu [xnb]. *Lg Use:* Moribund (2000 S. Wurm). Few remaining speakers in 1990. Shifting to Bunun [bnn]. Home. Mainly older adults. Neutral attitudes. *Lg Dev:* Grammar. *Map:* 347.

Saisiyat [xsy] (Amutoura, Bouiok, Saiset, Saisett, Saisiat, Saisiett, Saisirat, Saisyet, Saisyett, Seisirat). 4,750 (CIP-EY 2002). Tungho: more active use. Taai: a few speakers; nearly assimilated into Atayal [tay]. Ethnic population: 7,900. Western mountains, west of the Atayal [tay] language area, Nanchuang Township, Miaoli County and Wufong Township, Hsinchu County. *Status:* 6b (Threatened). *Class:* Austronesian, Northwest Formosan. *Dialects:* Taai (North Saiset), Tungho (South Saiset). Dialect differences are mainly phonological and lexical (1978 P. Li). *Lg Use:* Endangered (2000 S. Wurm). Many young speakers of the southern dialect are shifting to Hakka Chinese [hak]. Northern dialect already nearly assimilated to Atayal [tay] (Wurm 2007). All ages. Mildly positive attitudes. Also use Atayal [tay], Hakka Chinese [hak]. *Lg Dev:* Grammar. *Writing:* Latin script. *Map:* 347.

Siraya [fos] (Baksa, Formosan, "Pepohoan" *pej.*, "Pepo-Hwan" *pej.*, Sideia, Sideis, Sideisch, Siraia, Siraiya). No known L1 speakers. Southwest, Tainan area, Peimen to Hengchun to Tapu. *Status:* 9 (Dormant). *Class:* Austronesian, East Formosan, Southwest. *Dialects:* Lamai, Makatao (Makattao, Takaraya, Tta'o), Pangsoia-Dolatok, Siraya, Taivoan (Tevorang). *Lg Use:* Revitalization efforts since 1990s through Tainan Ping-pu Siraya Culture Association. *Lg Dev:* Dictionary. Bible portions: 1661. *Writing:* Latin script. *Other:* Still spoken in 1908 and some current semi-speakers. Sinicized.

Taiwan Sign Language [tss] (Taiwan Ziran Shouyu). 20,000 (2004), decreasing. *Status:* 4 (Educational). *Class:* Deaf sign language. *Dialects:* Kaohsiung, Tainan, Taipei. 2 major dialects. Sources from which the sign language developed were indigenous sign systems before 1895, Japanese occupation and education 1895–1946, Mainland Chinese Sign Language brought by refugees in 1949 and some from Hong Kong since. Lexical similarity: 50% with Japanese Sign Language [jsl]. *Lg Use:* Decreasing, but not likely to die out, as many deaf are not candidates for cochlear implants or hearing aids. Schools, sporting events, some homes, churches for the deaf. 5 to old age. Neutral attitudes. Most interaction with hearing people uses gestures or written Mandarin [cmn], unless the Deaf person has hearing aids or cochlear implants. *Lg Dev:* Literacy rate in L1: 0%. Literacy rate in L2: 60%–70%. 4 elementary, 3 high schools. Taught in primary and secondary schools. *Other:* Quite different from (Mainland) Chinese Sign Language [csl]; only a few signs the same or similar. Not related to Taiwanese languages. Some signs borrowed from Chinese characters, e.g. by drawing on the palm with a finger. There is also a Signed Mandarin (Wenfa Shouyu). 1,540 special education schools in Taiwan in 2002, which includes schools for the deaf.

Taroko [trv] (Bu-Hwan, Che-Hwan, Daiya-Ataiyal, Hogo, Iboho, Paran, Saediq, Sazek, Sedek, Sedeq, Sediakk, Sedik, Seedek, Seedeq, Seedik, Seediq, Sejiq, Shedekka, Taruku, Toda, Toroko, Truku). 20,000 (2008 R. Covell). Central, east, and coast; mountains north, Puli area; coast south of Hualien, south of the Atayal [tay]. *Status:* 4 (Educational). *Class:* Austronesian, Atayalic. *Dialects:* Tekedaya (Paran, Tkdaya), Teruku (Truku), Te'uda (Tuuda). Dialects differ mainly in phonology and lexicon, some in grammar. *Lg Use:* Elderly also use Japanese [jpn]. *Lg Dev:* Used as requested in special classes in schools. Dictionary. Grammar. Bible: 2005. *Writing:* Latin script. *Other:* 'Taroko', person, used by the coastals; 'Sediq', person, used by those in the mountains. *Map:* 347.

Thao [ssf] (Chui-Huan, Chuihwan, Sao, Sau, Shao, Suihwan, Vulung). 5 (Wurm 2000). Ethnic population: 300 (Tsukida 2007). Central, Sun Moon Lake southeast shore, Te-hua village, and Ta-p'ing-lin 14 km away. *Status:* 8b (Nearly extinct). *Class:* Austronesian, Western Plains, Thao. *Dialects:* Brawbaw, Shtafari. *Lg Use:* Most have shifted to Min Nan Chinese [nan] (Wurm 2007). Home. Elderly. Negative attitudes. *Lg Dev:* Dictionary. Grammar. *Writing:* Latin script. *Other:* Cooperation with the Bunun [bnn], intermarriage with Bunun women, loanwords from Bunun. *Map:* 347.

Tsou [tsu] (Namakaban, Niitaka, Tibola, Tibolah, Tibolak, Tibolal, Tso, Tsoo, Tsuou, Tsu-U, Tsu-Wo, Tzo). 2,130 (CIP-EY 2002). Ethnic population: 2,130. West central mountains southeast of Chiayi, Alishan (Mt. Ali) area. *Status:* 6a (Vigorous). *Class:* Austronesian, Tsouic. *Dialects:* Duhtu, Iimutsu, Luhtu, Tapangu, Tfuea. *Lg Use:* Iimutsu has no remaining speakers (Wurm and Hattori 1981). Many speak Tsou in daily life. Youth speak Mandarin. *Lg Dev:* Grammar. *Writing:* Latin script. *Other:* Some linguistic work done. *Map:* 347.

Yami [tao] (Botel Tabago, Botel Tobago, Lanyu, Tao, Tawu). 3,380 (CIP-EY 2002). Ethnic population: 3,380. Orchid Island, Botel Tobago (Lanyu) Island, southeast coast. *Status:* 6b (Threatened). *Class:* Austronesian, Malayo-Polynesian, Philippine, Bashiic, Yami. *Dialects:* None known. Reportedly similar to northern Philippines Ivatan [ivv]. *Lg Use:* Some young people, all adults. Also use Mandarin Chinese [cmn]. *Lg Dev:* Dictionary. Grammar. NT: 1994. *Writing:* Latin script. *Other:* Preferred ethnic autonym: Tao. Traditional religion. *Map:* 347.

Tajikistan

Republic of Tajikistan. 7,617,000 (2010 census). Principal languages: Russian, Tajiki. Literacy rate: 100% (2010 UNESCO). Immigrant languages: Armenian (6,000), Bashkort (5,410), Georgian (810), Kazakh (9,610), Korean (2,000), Lak (860), Lithuanian (470), Ossetic (8,000), Romanian (580), Tatar (80,000), Turkmen (14,000), Ukrainian (41,000), Uyghur (3,580), Western Balochi (4,840). General references: Akiner 1983; Comrie 1987; Kibrik 1991; Sebeok 1963.

The number of individual languages listed for Tajikistan is 13. All are living languages. Of these, 2 are institutional, 4 are developing, 3 are vigorous, and 4 are in trouble. See map on page 381.

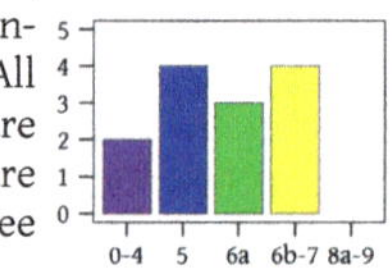

Arabic, Tajiki Spoken [abh] (Arabic, Bukhara Arabic, Buxara Arabic, Central Asian, Jugari, Tajiji Arabic). 1,000 in Tajikistan. Population total all countries: 6,000. Khatlon Province, Vakhsh Valley villages; Kuliab and Leninabad cities. Mainly small villages. Also in Afghanistan, Uzbekistan. *Status:* 6b (Threatened). *Class:* Afro-Asiatic, Semitic, Central, South, Arabic. A member of macrolanguage Arabic [ara] (Saudi Arabia). *Lg Use:* Only a few speak Arabic. Shifting to Tajiki [tgk]. No diglossia with Modern Standard Arabic [arb]. Also use Tajiki [tgk]. *Writing:* Arabic script. *Other:* Endogamous, do not mix with speakers of other languages. Muslim (Hanafi Sunni). *Map:* 381.

Ishkashimi [isk] (Ishkashim). 500 in Tajikistan (1990 A. Kibrik). Sumjin and Ryn villages, near Ishkashim. *Status:* 6a (Vigorous). *Lg Use:* Ishkashimi is very vital. This is because the fathers very much insist on their children acquiring Ishkashimi as their first language when they grow up. Home, village. All ages. Positive attitudes. *Other:* Muslim (Ismaili). See main entry on page 48. *Map:* 381.

Kyrgyz [kir]. 64,000 in Tajikistan. *Status:* 5 (Dispersed). See main entry on page 213. *Map:* 381.

Parya [paq] (Afghana-Yi Nasfurush, Afghana-Yi Siyarui, Laghmani, Pbharya). 3,000 in Tajikistan (2008). Population total all countries: 4,000. Hissar valley. Also in Afghanistan, Uzbekistan. *Status:* 6a (Vigorous). *Class:* Indo-European, Indo-Iranian, Indo-Aryan, Central zone, Unclassified. *Dialects:* May be Marwari [rwr] dialect, related to Panjabi [pan], or Laghman dialect of Southeast Pashayi [psi] of Afghanistan. Subgroups: Kalu, Jitain, Juni, Maggar, Bisiyan, Mussali, Shuiya. *Lg Use:* Despite small population, it is spoken more vigorously amongst themselves than larger language groups. Uzbek and Tajiki men who marry Parya women learn Parya and become assimilated into the community. Home. Also use Tajiki [tgk]. *Writing:* Unwritten. *Other:* Came in 1880 to Tajikistan from Laghman, Afghanistan. Ethnic autonym: Changgars. Subgroup names similar to Changgars of Lahore, and to names used for groups mistakenly called Gypsies. Muslim (Sunni). *Map:* 381.

Pashto, Southern [pbt]. 4,000 in Tajikistan (1970). *Status:* 5 (Dispersed). See main entry on page 50. *Map:* 381.

Persian, Iranian [pes] (Persian). 50,000 in Tajikistan (Johnstone and Mandryk 2001). *Status:* 5 (Dispersed). *Other:* Not a literary language in Tajikistan. Muslim (Shi'a). See main entry on page 204.

Russian [rus]. 237,000 in Tajikistan. *Status:* 3 (Wider communication). De facto national working language, no longer language of record in higher levels of government. *Lg Use:* Used as L2 by Tajiki [tgk], Yagnobi [yai]. See main entry on page 322.

Shughni [sgh] (Shugnan-Rushan). 40,000 in Tajikistan (1975 SIL). 20,000 Shugan, 1,500–2,000 Oroshor, 15,000 Rushan. Population total all countries: 80,000. Ethnic population: 73,800 (1990 A. Kibrik). Includes 50,000 Shugni, 2,000 Oroshor, 18,000 Rushan, 800 Khufi, 3,000 Bartang. Gorno-Bagakhshan, Pamir mountains. Also in Afghanistan. *Status:* 6a (Vigorous). *Class:* Indo-European, Indo-Iranian, Iranian, Eastern, Southeastern, Pamir, Shugni-Yazgulami. *Dialects:* Bartangi (Bartang), Khufi (Chuf, Khuf), Oroshor (Roshorvi), Rushani (Oroshani, Roshani, Rushan), Shughni (Khugni, Shighni, Shugan, Shugnan). Khufi and Bartangi dialects may be separate languages. Oroshani may be separate from Rushani. Not intelligible of Sarikoli [srh] (called, Tajiki, in China). *Lg Use:* Home. All ages. Positive attitudes. Tajiki [tgk] used as literary language. *Lg Dev:* Poetry. Dictionary. Bible portions: 2001. *Writing:* Arabic script, used in Afghanistan. Cyrillic script, used in Tajikistan. Latin script, used in Tajikistan. *Other:* Traditional territory and way of life. Muslim (Ismaili). *Map:* 381.

Tajiki [tgk] (Galcha, Tadzhik, Tajik, Tajiki Persian, Tojiki). 3,340,000 in Tajikistan (1991). Population total all countries: 4,479,650. Also in Iran, Kazakhstan, Kyrgyzstan, Russian Federation, Turkmenistan, Ukraine, United States, Uzbekistan. *Status:* 1 (National). Statutory national language (1994, Constitution, Article 2). *Class:* Indo-European, Indo-Iranian, Iranian, Western, Southwestern, Persian. *Dialects:* 4 groups of small dialects; no distinct boundaries. Dialect blending into Dari Persian [prs] in Afghanistan. *Lg Use:* Also use Northern Uzbek [uzn], Russian [rus]. *Lg Dev:* Radio programs. Bible: 1992. *Writing:* Arabic script, used until 1928. Cyrillic script, used since 1940, primary usage. Hebrew script, used by Bukharan Jews. Latin script, used from 1928–1940. *Other:* Russian sources refer to Persian dialects in Afghanistan as Tajiki. So-called Tajiki in China is actually Shugni [sgh] or Wakhi [wbl]. Some Tajiki-speaking Gypsy communities in Russian central Asia. Muslim (Sunni). *Map:* 381.

Uzbek, Northern [uzn]. 873,000 in Tajikistan. *Status:* 5 (Dispersed). *Lg Use:* Used as L2 by Tajiki [tgk]. See main entry on page 308. *Map:* 381.

Wakhi [wbl] (Guhjali, Khik, Vakhan, Wakhani, Wakhigi). 15,000 in Tajikistan (2012 M. Merritt). Ethnic population: 20,000 (1990 A. Kibrik). Gorno-Badakhshan, Pamir mountains. *Status:* 6b (Threatened). *Dialects:* Central Wakhi, Eastern Wakhi, Western Wakhi. *Lg Use:* Some domains. All ages. Positive attitudes. Also use Tajiki [tgk] as literary language. *Other:* Muslim (Ismaili). See main entry on page 51. *Map:* 381.

Yagnobi [yai] (Yaghnabi, Yaghnobi, Yaghnubi, Yagnabi, Yagnob, Yagnubi). 12,000 (2004 SIL). Zafarabad; north of Dushanbe; Yagnob river (the homeland), high mountain valley. *Status:* 6b (Threatened). *Class:* Indo-European, Indo-Iranian, Iranian, Eastern, Northeastern. *Dialects:* Eastern Yagnobi, Western Yagnobi. *Lg Use:* Also use Russian [rus] as literary language. Also use Tajiki [tgk] as literary language. *Lg Dev:* Grammar. *Writing:* Cyrillic script. *Other:* Were resettled in 1970s to Zafarabad in north Tajikistan on the border with Uzbekistan; changed from cool mountain valleys with water to irrigated desert plains. Muslim (Sunni). *Map:* 381.

Yazgulyam [yah] (Iazgulem, Yazghulomi, Yazgulam, Yazgulyami). 9,000 (2010). Gorno-Badakhshan Autonomous Province, Yazgulyam river valley, Motravn, Shavud, Budun, Vishkharv, Andarbag, Zhamag, Zaich, and Ubaghn; Kuybishev area; Dushanbe area. *Status:* 6b (Threatened). *Class:* Indo-European, Indo-Iranian, Iranian, Eastern, Southeastern, Pamir, Shugni-Yazgulami. *Dialects:* Lower Yazgulyam, Upper Yazgulyam. Little dialect difference. *Lg Use:* Home. All ages. Positive attitudes. Also use Tajiki [tgk]. *Lg Dev:* Bible portions: 2001. *Writing:* Cyrillic script. Latin script. *Other:* Muslim (Sunni), Muslim (Shi'a). *Map:* 381.

Thailand

Kingdom of Thailand. 65,479,000 (2010 census). Principal language: Thai. Literacy rate: 94% (2005 World Bank). Immigrant languages: Kayan (180), Rohingya (100,000). General references: Bradley 2007; Lebar, Hickey, and Musgrave 1964; Matisoff 1991; Matisoff, Baron, and Lowe 1996; Prachakij-karacak 1995; Purnell 1970; Smalley 1976; Wurm and Hattori 1981. Deaf population: 90,000–300,000. Deaf institutions: 22.

The number of individual languages listed for Thailand is 71. All are living languages. Of these, 2 are institutional, 27 are developing, 18 are vigorous, 17 are in trouble, and 7 are dying. See maps beginning on page 406.

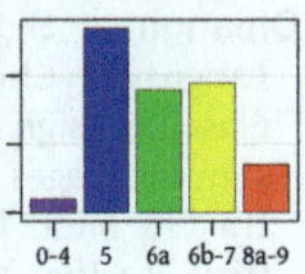

Aheu [thm] (Phon Soung, So, Sotawueng). 450 in Thailand (Bradley 2007). Population total all countries: 700. Ethnic population: 1,500 (Bradley 2007). Sakon Nakhon

Province, Song Daw district, Thavung, 3 villages. Also in Laos. *Status:* 6b (Threatened). *Class:* Austro-Asiatic, Mon-Khmer, Viet-Muong, Thavung. *Other:* Glossonym: So in Thailand. *Map:* 407:1.

Akeu [aeu] (Aki, Akui). 400 in Thailand (2006). Chiang Rai Province, Mae Suay and Wiang Papao districts. *Status:* 7 (Shifting). See main entry on page 62.

Akha [ahk] (Ahka, Aini, Aka, Ak'a, Ekaw, Ikaw, Ikor, Kaw, Kha Ko, Khako, Khao Kha Ko, Ko, Yani). 56,600 in Thailand (Bradley 2007). Chiang Mai, Chiang Rai, and Mae Hong Son provinces. 250 villages. *Status:* 5 (Developing). *Lg Use:* Also use Thai [tha]. *Lg Dev:* Literacy rate in L1: 1%–5%. Literacy rate in L2: 1%–50%. *Other:* Traditional religion, Christian. See main entry on page 230. *Map:* 406:2.

Ban Khor Sign Language [bfk]. East central, Maha Sarakham Province; a few villages. *Status:* 6a (Vigorous). *Class:* Deaf sign language. *Dialects:* None known. Not related to original sign languages of Thailand, but reportedly some similarities.

Bisu [bzi] (Lawa, Lua, Mbisu, Mibisu). Ethnic population: 700 (Bradley 2007). Chiang Rai Province, Doi Chomphu and Pui Kham villages. *Status:* 6b (Threatened). *Lg Use:* Not all young people speak Bisu (Bradley 2007). Also use Thai [tha]. *Lg Dev:* Literacy rate in L1: Below 1%. Literacy rate in L2: Below 5%. Literacy classes held at weekend in Doi Chompu. Oral and written materials developed. *Other:* The terms 'Lawa' and 'Lua' generally refer to Waic language varieties in Thailand: sometimes outsiders have classified unrelated languages such as Bisu in this category. Traditional religion, Christian. See main entry on page 64. *Map:* 406:3.

Blang [blr] (Bulang, Hkawa, K'ala, Kawa, Khon Doi, Kontoi, K'wa, Plang, Pula, Pulang, Sen Chun, Wa). 1,200 in Thailand (1998 SIL). Chiang Rai Province, north border area, Mae Sai; Mae Chan area; some west of Bangkok. *Status:* 6a (Vigorous). *Lg Use:* Also use Thai [tha]. *Lg Dev:* Literacy rate in L1: Below 1%. Literacy rate in L2: Below 10%. *Other:* Buddhist (Hinayana), Christian. See main entry on page 64. *Map:* 406:4.

Bru, Western [brv] (Baru, B'ru, Bruu). 20,000 in Thailand (1991). Ubon Ratchathani, Mukdahan, Nakhon Phanom, and Sakon Nakhon provinces. Also in United States. *Status:* 6a (Vigorous). *Class:* Austro-Asiatic, Mon-Khmer, Eastern Mon-Khmer, Katuic, West Katuic, Brou-So. *Dialects:* None known. Partially intelligible with Eastern Bru [bru]. *Lg Use:* Also use Thai [tha]. *Lg Dev:* Literacy rate in L1: 1%–5%. Literacy rate in L2: 80%. Bible portions: 2007. *Writing:* Lao script. Latin script. *Other:* Buddhist, Christian, traditional religion. *Map:* 407:56.

Cham, Western [cja] (Cambodian Cham, Cham, New Cham, Tjam). 4,000 in Thailand. Ban Khrue, Bangkok. *Status:* 6b (Threatened). *Lg Use:* Conflicting reports about whether those in Thailand still speak Cham or have shifted to Central Thai [tha]. *Other:* Austro-Asiatic influences. Thought to be remnants of Cham who fought in the Thai army about 200 years ago. Muslim. See main entry on page 60.

Chiangmai Sign Language [csd] (Chiengmai Sign Language). Chiang Mai Province. *Status:* 7 (Shifting). *Class:* Deaf sign language. *Dialects:* None known. Related to sign languages in Laos and Viet Nam (Haiphong, Hanoi, Ho Chi Minh City). Distinct from Thai Sign Language [tsq]. *Lg Use:* Younger signers use Thai Sign Language [tsq]. *Map:* 406:6.

Chinese, Hakka [hak] (Hakka). 58,800 in Thailand (1984). Cities. *Status:* 5 (Developing). See main entry on page 67.

Chinese, Mandarin [cmn]. 5,880 in Thailand (1984). Bangkok, provincial towns, and south in Kra peninsula. *Status:* 5 (Dispersed). *Dialect:* Ho (Cin Haw, Haw, Hui, Hui-Tze, Hwei, Panghse, Pantha, Panthe, Pathee, Western Mandarin, Yunnanese). *Other:* Traditional religion, Muslim (Hui). See main entry on page 67.

Chinese, Min Dong [cdo] (Eastern Min). *Status:* 5 (Developing). *Dialect:* Fuzhou (Foochow, Fuchow). See main entry on page 68.

Chinese, Min Nan [nan] (Min Nan, Minnan). 1,080,000 in Thailand (1984). 1,060,000 Chaochow (18%), 17,600 Fujian (less than 1%), 5,880 Hainanese (less than 1%) (1984). Cities. *Status:* 5 (Developing). *Dialects:* Hainan, Hokkien (Fujian, Fukien), Shantou (Swatow), Teochew (Chaochow, Chaozhou, Techu, Teochow, Tiuchiu). *Other:* Buddhist, traditional religion. See main entry on page 68.

Chinese, Yue [yue] (Cantonese, Yue, Yueh). 29,400 in Thailand (1984). *Status:* 5 (Developing). See main entry on page 69.

Chong [cog] (Chawng, Shong, Xong). 500. Chanthaburi Province, northwest of Par, 4 villages. *Status:* 8a (Moribund). *Class:* Austro-Asiatic, Mon-Khmer, Eastern Mon-Khmer, Pearic, Western, Chong. *Dialects:* None known. Related to Somray [smu] in Cambodia. *Writing:* Thai script. *Map:* 408:7.

Hmong Daw [mww] (Bai Miao, Chuan Miao, Hmong Der, Hmoob Dawb, Meo Kao, Pe Miao, Peh Miao, White Hmong, White Lum, White Meo, White Miao). 32,400 in Thailand (2000). Phetchabun, Tak, Mae Hong Son, Chiang Mai, Nan, Chiang Rai, Phitsanulok, Loei, Sukhothai, Kamphaeng Phet, Phrae, Phayao, Uttaradit, and Lampang provinces. *Status:* 5 (Developing). *Dialects:* Hmong Gu Mba (Hmong Qua Mba, Miao Lai, Striped Hmong), Petchabun Miao. *Lg Use:* Used as L2 by Mlabri [mra]. *Other:* Traditional religion, Christian. See main entry on page 72. *Map:* 406:9.

Hmong Njua [hnj] (Blue Meo, Ching Miao, Green Hmong, Green Meo, Hmong Leng, Hmong Nzhua, Hmoob Leeg, Lu Miao, Meo Dam, Meo Lai, Mong Leng, Mong Ntsua, Qing Miao, Tak Miao). 60,000 in Thailand (Hattaway 2000). Chiangrai, Chiangmai, Mae Hong Son, Tak, Phayao, Nan, Phrae, Loei, Sukhothai, Kamphaengphet, Uthai Thani, Uttaradit, and Phetchabun provinces. *Status:* 6a (Vigorous). See main entry on page 214. *Map:* 406:10.

Iu Mien [ium] (Highland Yao, Mian, Mien, Myen, Pan Yao, Yao, Yiu Mien, Youmian). 40,000 in Thailand (1999). Chiang Rai, Phayao, Lampang, Kamphaeng Phet, and Nan provinces; possibly in Chiang Mai and Sukhothai provinces. 159 villages. *Status:* 5 (Developing). *Dialect:* Chiangrai. *Lg Use:* Also use Northern Thai [nod]. *Other:* All Yao and Mien in Thailand are Iu Mien. Daoist, traditional religion. See main entry on page 73. *Maps:* 406:11, 407:11.

Jehai [jhi]. Ethnic population: 150 (Bradley 2007). Southern, Southwest Narathiwat Province. *Status:* 7 (Shifting). See main entry on page 221.

Karen, Phrae Pwo [kjt] (Northeastern Pwo Karen, Phrae, Prae, Pwo Phrae). 6,000 (Dawkins and Phillips 2009). Northeastern area; Phrae, Lampang, and Chiang Rai provinces. *Status:* 6a (Vigorous). *Class:* Sino-Tibetan, Tibeto-Burman, Karenic, Peripheral. *Dialects:* None known. Not intelligible with other Pwo Karen languages. Lexical similarity: 87% with Northern Pwo Karen [pww] of Thailand, 67%–71% with other Pwo Karen varieties. *Lg Use:* Also use Northern Thai [nod], S'gaw Karen [ksw]. *Lg Dev:* Literacy rate in L1: Below 1%. Literacy rate in L2: 50%–75%. *Writing:* Thai script. *Map:* 406:37.

Karen, Pwo Northern [pww] (Phlong). 60,000 (1983 SIL). Northwest; Chiang Mai, Mae Hong Son, Lamphun, and Tak provinces; Mae Sarieng town, Mae Ngaw along Salween river, 15–25 villages, Hot to Mae Sarieng. *Status:* 5 (Developing). *Class:* Sino-Tibetan, Tibeto-Burman, Karenic, Peripheral. *Dialects:* Mae Ping, Mae Sarieng,

Omkoi (Hod). Dialects mutually intelligible. Pwo Karen of Phrae [kjt], Kanchanaburi, and Hua Hin are not intelligible with these. Lexical similarity: 87% with Phrae Province Pwo Karen [kjt] of Thailand, 68%–73% with other Pwo Karen. *Type:* SVO. *Lg Use:* Little knowledge of Thai [tha] in Hot to Mae Sarieng area. *Lg Dev:* Literacy rate in L1: Below 1%. Literacy rate in L2: 25%–50%. NT: 2002. *Writing:* Thai script. *Other:* Traditional religion, Christian. *Map:* 406:43.

Karen, Pwo West-Central Thailand [kjp] (Phlou, Southern Pwo Karen). 50,000 in Thailand (1998). Phetchaburi, Kanchanaburi, Ratchaburi, and Uthai Thani provinces; Kanchanaburi dialect is north, Ratchaburi-Phetchaburi dialect is south. *Status:* 5 (Developing). *Dialects:* Kanchanaburi Pwo Karen, Ratchaburi Pwo Karen (Phetchaburi Pwo Karen). *Lg Use:* Also use Thai [tha]. *Lg Dev:* Literacy rate in L1: Below 1%. Literacy rate in L2: 15%–50%. See main entry on page 235 (as Karen, Pwo Eastern). *Maps:* 406:44 (as Karen, Pwo Western Thailand), 408:44 (as Karen, Pwo Western Thailand).

Karen, S'gaw [ksw] (Burmese Karen, Kanyaw, Karen, Paganyaw, Pwakanyaw, S'gau, S'gaw, S'gaw Kayin, White, Yang Khao). 200,000 in Thailand (2006 Mahidol University). Tak, Mae Hong Son, Chiang Mai, Kanchanaburi, and Kamphaeng Phet provinces, near Myanmar border. *Status:* 5 (Developing). *Dialects:* Palakhi (Palachi), Panapu. *Lg Use:* Also use Thai [tha]. Used as L2 by Phrae Pwo Karen [kjt], Western Lawa [lcp]. *Lg Dev:* Literacy rate in L1: 10%–30%. Literacy rate in L2: 25%–50%. *Other:* Traditional religion, Christian. See main entry on page 235. *Map:* 406:46.

Kayah, Eastern [eky] (Karennyi, Kayah, Kayay, Red Karen, "Yang Daeng" *pej.*). 18,000 in Thailand (2000). 2 camps of 15,000 refugees from Myanmar. Mae Hong Son Province, east of Salween river. *Status:* 6a (Vigorous). *Lg Use:* Home, religion, village. Also use Thai [tha]. *Lg Dev:* Literacy rate in L1: 1%–5%. Literacy rate in L2: 60% in Thai. *Other:* Strong feeling that all Kayah are the same ethnic group. Upper Eastern Kayah is north of Mae Hong Son provincial capital; Lower Eastern Kayah is south. Karieng Daeng means Red Karen in Central Thai. "Yang Daeng", Red Karen in Northern Thai, is pejorative. See main entry on page 236. *Map:* 406:8.

Kensiu [kns] (Belubn, Kense, Kenseu, Kensieu, Kensiw, Maniq, Mawas, Mengo, Meni, Menik, Moni, Monik, Moniq, Mos, Ngok Pa, Orang Bukit, Orang Liar, Sakai, Tiong). 300 in Thailand. South Yala, Phattaloong, Satun, and Narathiwat provinces, Thai-Malay border. *Status:* 7 (Shifting). *Lg Use:* Also use Southern Thai [sou]. *Lg Dev:* Literacy rate in L1: Below 1%. Literacy rate in L2: 5%–15%. *Other:* Negrito pygmies, nomads, small bands. Traditional religion. See main entry on page 222. *Map:* 408:12.

Khmer, Northern [kxm] (Khmer Lue, Thailand Khmer). 1,400,000 (2006 Mahidol University), decreasing. Very few monolingual. East, mainly Surin, Buriram, Sisaket, and Ubon Ratchathani provinces; also in Chanthaburi Province southeast of Bangkok. *Status:* 5 (Developing). *Class:* Austro-Asiatic, Mon-Khmer, Eastern Mon-Khmer, Khmer. *Dialects:* Buriram, Sisaket, Surin. Different from Central Khmer [khm]. Dialects mutually intelligible. Many local varieties. *Type:* SVO; prepositions; genitives, modifiers, relatives after noun heads; 1 prefix; CV, CVC, CCV; nontonal. *Lg Use:* Vigorous in towns; replaced by Isan [tts] and Thai in cities. A few Chinese shopkeepers speak it. Education, media, religious services, commerce. Positive attitudes. Also use Isan (a dialect of Northeastern Thai [tts]). Also use Central Khmer [khm], Thai [tha]. Used as L2 by Kuy [kdt]. *Lg Dev:* Literacy rate in L1: Below 1%. 1,000 can read Northern Khmer, 100 can write it. Literacy rate in L2: 50%–75%. 1,000 can read Northern Khmer, 100 can write it. Bible: 2003. *Writing:* Thai script. *Other:* Buddhist, Christian. *Maps:* 407:29, 408:29.

Khmu [kjg] (Kamhmu, Kammu, Kamu, Kha Khmu, Khamu, Khamuk, Khmu', Kmhmu, Luu, Mou, Pouteng, Tmooy). 31,400 in Thailand (2000). Chiangrai, Nan, Phayao, and scattered throughout Thailand. *Status:* 5 (Developing). *Other:* Traditional religion, Christian. See main entry on page 215. *Map:* 406:13.

Khün [kkh] (Gon Shan, Hkun, Khuen, Khun Shan, Tai Khun). 6,280 in Thailand (2000). Chiang Mai and Chiang Rai provinces. *Status:* 5 (Developing). *Other:* Different from Khuen [khf], a Mon-Khmer language of Laos. Buddhist. See main entry on page 236. *Map:* 406:14.

Kintaq [knq] (Kenta, Kintaq Bong, Kintk). 1 in Thailand (2007 SIL). Southern Yala Province. *Status:* 8b (Nearly extinct). *Other:* Negrito pygmies, nomadic. Traditional religion. See main entry on page 222.

Kuy [kdt] (Cuoi, Khamen-Boran, Kui, Kui Souei, Kuoy, Kuuy, Soai, Suai, Suay, Suei, Sui, Suoi). 400,000 in Thailand (2006 Mahidol University). Population total all countries: 452,800. Few monolinguals. Buriram, Surin, Sisaket, and Ubon Ratchathani provinces. Also in Cambodia, Laos. *Status:* 6b (Threatened). *Class:* Austro-Asiatic, Mon-Khmer, Eastern Mon-Khmer, Katuic, West Katuic, Kuay-Nheu. *Dialects:* Chang (Suai Chang), Kuay, Nheu. *Lg Use:* Positive attitudes. Have affection for Kuy and want to keep it. 99% also use Lao [lao]. 99% also use Northeastern Thai [tts]. 40% also use Northern Khmer [kxm]. Mainly older adults. 80% also use Thai [tha]. *Lg Dev:* Literacy rate in L1: Below 1%. Literacy rate in L2: 50%. Dictionary. NT: 1978. *Writing:* Khmer script, used in Cambodia. Lao script, used in Laos. Thai script. *Other:* Kuy villages often intermingled with those of Northern Khmer [kxm], Lao [lao]. Traditional religion, Buddhist, Christian. *Map:* 407:15.

Lahu [lhu] (Lohei, Muhso, Muhsur, Musser, Musso, Mussuh). 32,000 in Thailand (Johnstone and Mandryk 2001). Chiang Mai, Chiang Rai, Mae Hong Son, and Kamphaeng Phet provinces; 119 known villages. *Status:* 4 (Educational). *Dialects:* Na (Black Lahu, Loheirn, Musser Dam, Northern Lahu), Nyi (Luhishi, Luhushi, Musseh Daeng, Red Lahu, Southern Lahu), Shehleh. *Lg Use:* Also use Thai [tha]. *Lg Dev:* Literacy rate in L1: 30%–60%. Literacy rate in L2: 5%–15%. *Other:* Traditional religion, Christian. See main entry on page 76. *Map:* 406:16.

Lahu Shi [lhi]. 15,000 in Thailand (2007). Chiang Rai, Lampang, and Chiang Mai provinces; near Pua and Nan; separate enclaves in Tak and Phayao provinces. *Status:* 6a (Vigorous). *Lg Use:* Also use Thai [tha]. *Lg Dev:* Literacy rate in L1: Below 1%. Literacy rate in L2: 5%–15%. *Other:* Distinct from Kuy [kdt], which is Mon-Khmer. See main entry on page 76. *Map:* 406:17.

Lamet [lbn] (Kamet, Kha Lamet, Khamet, Lemet). 100 in Thailand. Language of Laos, no attested speakers in Thailand; perhaps in Chiang Rai. *Status:* 6a (Vigorous). *Dialects:* Lower Lamet, Upper Lamet. *Other:* Glossonym: Khamet in Thailand, Lamet in Laos. Traditional religion. See main entry on page 215.

Lawa, Eastern [lwl] (Bo Luang Lawa, "Lua" *pej.*). 7,000 (Nahhas 2007). Ethnic population: 8,000. L2 users: Some who marry into the community learn to speak it. North, Chiang Mai Province, Hot district, Bo Luang and Bo Sali subdistricts; 16 villages. *Status:* 6a (Vigorous). *Class:* Austro-Asiatic, Mon-Khmer, Northern Mon-Khmer, Palaungic, Eastern Palaungic, Waic, Lawa. *Dialects:* Bo Luang, Bo Sangae. Not intelligible with most Mae Hong Son Lawa dialects [lcp]. *Lg Use:* Very high language vitality. All domains except government and education (which are in Central Thai). All ages. Positive attitudes.

Interested in language maintenance. Proud of Lawa history and culture. 100% also use Northern Thai [nod]. Northern Thai [nod] is used for government and school. 100% also use Thai [tha]. Central Thai [tha] used with outsiders. *Lg Dev:* Literacy in Central Thai is common. *Writing:* Thai script. *Map:* 406:5.

Lawa, Western [lcp] (Lava, Lavüa, "Lua" *pej.*, Luwa, L'wa, Mae Hong Son Lawa, Mountain Lawa, Omphai Lawa). 8,000 (Nahhas 2007). Ethnic population: 8,500. L2 users: Some who marry into the community learn to speak it. Chiang Mai and Mae Hong Son provinces. *Status:* 5 (Developing). *Class:* Austro-Asiatic, Mon-Khmer, Northern Mon-Khmer, Palaungic, Eastern Palaungic, Waic, Lawa. *Dialects:* La-up, Northern Western Lawa, Omphai. Each village has a distinct accent. Ban Kok Luang, a village of the Northern group, has the most distinct dialect. *Lg Use:* Vigorous. All domains except government and education, which are in Central Thai [tha]. All ages. Some older adults also use Sgaw Karen [ksw]. Also use Northern Thai [nod], Thai [tha]. *Lg Dev:* Literacy in Mae Hong Son Lawa more common among Christians. Literacy in Central Thai has become more common as education becomes more available. Poetry. Dictionary. Grammar. Bible: 2001. *Writing:* Thai script. *Other:* Orthography and literature based on Ban La-up dialect. Traditional religion, Buddhist, Christian. *Map:* 406:57.

Lisu [lis] (Li-Hsaw, Lisaw, Li-Shaw, Liso, Lu-Tzu, Southern Lisu, Yao Yen, Yaw Yin, Yaw-Yen, Yeh-Jen). 40,000 in Thailand (Bradley 2007). Chiang Mai, Chiang Rai, Mae Hong Son, Tak, Phayao, and Kamphaeng Phet provinces. *Status:* 5 (Developing). *Dialect:* Lu Shi Lisu. *Lg Use:* Also use Thai [tha]. *Lg Dev:* Literacy rate in L1: 5%–10%. Literacy rate in L2: 50%–75%. *Other:* Traditional religion, Christian. See main entry on page 77. *Map:* 406:18.

Lü [khb] (Lu, Lue, Pai-I, Pai-Yi, Shui-Pai-I, Tai Lu, Tai Lue, Thai Lu). 83,000 in Thailand (Johnstone and Mandryk 2001). Phayao and Nan provinces; scattered in north. *Status:* 5 (Developing). *Dialect:* Yong. *Lg Use:* All domains. All ages. Positive attitudes. Also use Northern Thai [nod], Thai [tha]. *Lg Dev:* Literacy rate in L1: 1%–5%. Literacy rate in L2: 50%–75%. *Other:* Traditional religion, Buddhist. See main entry on page 78. *Map:* 406:19.

Lua' [prb] (East Pua Pray, Pray 2). 6,280 (2000). Nan Province, east of Pua district; Laos-Thailand border. *Status:* 7 (Shifting). *Class:* Austro-Asiatic, Mon-Khmer, Northern Mon-Khmer, Khmuic, Mal-Khmu', Mal-Phrai. *Lg Dev:* Bible portions: 1984. *Other:* Distinct from Mal [mlf], Prai [prt], and Pray 3 [pry]. Christian. *Map:* 406:20.

Mal [mlf] (Ht'in, Khatin, Thin, Tin, T'in). 3,000 in Thailand (1982 SIL). Nan Province, east of Pua district and Chiang Kam, valley near northern Laos border. *Status:* 5 (Developing). *Lg Use:* Also use Thai [tha]. Used as L2 by Pray 3 [pry]. *Lg Dev:* Literacy rate in L1: Below 1% literate. Literacy rate in L2: 1%–15%. *Other:* Ethnic autonym: T'in in Thailand. See main entry on page 216. *Map:* 406:21.

Malay, Pattani [mfa] (Baso Jawi). 1,000,000 (2006 Mahidol University). North, Songkhla Province, Chana region, south through Pattani, Narathiwat, Yala, Saiburi, and Tak Bai. *Status:* 5 (Developing). *Class:* Austronesian, Malayo-Polynesian, Malayo-Chamic, Malayic, Malay. A member of macrolanguage Malay [msa] (Malaysia). *Dialects:* None known. Different from Kedah Malay [meo] and Standard Malay [zsm]. *Lg Use:* Also use Thai [tha]. *Lg Dev:* NT: 1981. *Writing:* Arabic script. Thai script. *Other:* Preferable ethnonym: Jawi or Jawi-Malay. Ethnic authonym: oré Jawi. Muslim. *Map:* 408:36.

Malay, Satun [meo] (Kedah Malay). A few villages near Satun. Isolated. *Status:* 6a (Vigorous). *Lg Use:* Also use Thai [tha]. *Other:* More people in the area speak Thai than Pattani [mfa]. Most outside contacts in Thai centers of Songkhla, Phattalung, and Haad Yai; with west coast Malay states of Perlis and Kedah. Culturally Malay. Muslim. See main entry on page 224 (as Malay, Kedah). *Map:* 408:47.

Mlabri [mra] (Luang, Ma Ku, Mabri, Mla, Mla Bri, Mrabri, Phi Thong, Yellow Leaf, Yumbri). 130 in Thailand (Bradley 2007). Population total all countries: 154. Phayao, Nan, Phrae, Utaradit, Phitsanuloke, Loey, and perhaps other provinces. Laos border area. Also in Laos. *Status:* 8a (Moribund). *Class:* Austro-Asiatic, Mon-Khmer, Northern Mon-Khmer, Khmuic, Mlabri. *Lg Use:* Also use Hmong Daw [mww], Northern Thai [nod]. *Lg Dev:* Literacy rate in L1: Below 1%. Literacy rate in L2: 0%–1%. *Writing:* Thai script. *Other:* Mlabri are different from the Kha Tong Luang (Phi Tong Luang, Yellow Leaf) in Laos, who are Western Viet-Muong (Wurm and Hattori 1981). Sometimes employed by the Hmong. Some nomadic. Traditional religion. *Map:* 406:22.

Mok [mqt] (Amok, Hsen-Hsum, Muak, Muak Sa-aak). 7 (Wurm and Hattori 1981). Lampang Province; east northeast of Chiang Mai, on Wang river. *Status:* 8b (Nearly extinct). *Class:* Austro-Asiatic, Mon-Khmer, Northern Mon-Khmer, Palaungic, Eastern Palaungic, Angkuic. *Map:* 406:23.

Moken [mwt] (Basing, Chau Ko', Mawken, Salon, Salong, Selong, Selung). 2,000 in Thailand (Bradley 2007). South, west coast, Phuket, Phangnga, Krabi, and Ranong. *Status:* 7 (Shifting). *Dialects:* Jadiak, Moklen. *Lg Use:* Not spoken by youth in one Jadiak village (Bradley 2007). Also use Burmese [mya], Thai [tha]. *Lg Dev:* Various literacy materials in Karen, Burmese, Roman and Thai scripts (Bradley 2007). *Other:* Primarily live on boats, but occasionally settle on area islands. Traditional religion, Muslim. See main entry on page 237. *Map:* 408:24.

Moklen [mkm] (Chau Pok). 1,500 (1984 D. Hogan). Ethnic population: 4,000 (2000 D. Bradley). South, west coast, Phuket and Phangnga. *Status:* 6b (Threatened). *Class:* Austronesian, Malayo-Polynesian, Moklen. *Writing:* Thai script. *Other:* Heavy Thai and Mon-Khmer influence. Traditional religion, Muslim. *Map:* 408:25.

Mon [mnw] (Aleng, Mun, Peguan, Takanoon, Talaing, Taleng). 108,000 in Thailand (2000). 70,000–120,000, total population (Bauer 1984). 1983 census estimated 100,000; about 50,000 L1 speakers (Foster 1972; Smalley 1994). Kanchanaburi, Pathum Thani, Ratchaburi, Samut Sakhon, Nakhon Pathom, and Kanchanaburi provinces. *Status:* 6b (Threatened). *Lg Use:* Low or no usage among long-established groups. Widespread bilingualism; some language shift. Also use Thai [tha]. *Other:* Many seemingly integrated with the Thai; in other areas they are separate. Traditional religion, Buddhist. See main entry on page 237. *Maps:* 406:26, 408:26.

Mpi [mpz] (Kaw). 900 (Nahhas 2007), decreasing. Ethnic population: 1,500 (Nahhas 2007). North, Phrae Province, Ban Dong east of provincial capital; Nan Province, Ban Sakoen, east of Phayao Province border. 2 villages. *Status:* 7 (Shifting). *Class:* Sino-Tibetan, Tibeto-Burman, Ngwi-Burmese, Ngwi, Southern. *Dialects:* Ban Dong, Ban Sakoen. Ban Dong and Ban Sakoen Mpi are mutually intelligible (based on self-report of Ban Dong and Ban Sakoen residents). Lexical similarity: 86% between Ban Dong and Ban Sakoen dialects. *Type:* SOV. *Lg Use:* Children not speaking the language much. In one village only very old people spoke the language and in the other it was reported that only people over 40 spoke the language. Also use Northern Thai [nod], Thai [tha]. *Lg Dev:* Dictionary. Grammar. *Writing:* Thai script. *Other:* Kaw is used in Ban Sakoen. Possibly some in China who refer to their language as Pu Kaw. Buddhist. *Map:* 406:27.

Nyahkur [cbn] (Chao Dong, "Chaobon" *pej.*, "Chaobun" *pej.*, Chaodon, "Chaubun" *pej.*, Lawa, Niakuol, Niakuoll, Nyakur). 1,500 (2006 C. Shimmin), decreasing. 0 monolinguals. Ethnic population: 3,000 (Thongkum 1984). Central, northeast side, foot of Phetchabun mountains; mainly in Chaiyaphum Province; also in Bueng Kan, Sakon Nakhon, and Kalasin provinces; possibly in Phitsanulok and Phetchabun. *Status:* 7 (Shifting). *Class:* Austro-Asiatic, Mon-Khmer, Southern Monic. *Dialects:* Chaiyaphum users say they understand Petchabun only with difficulty, if at all. At least 91% lexical similarity among all dialects (Diffloth 1984). *Type:* SVO. *Lg Use:* Few children can speak Nyah Kur. Nearly extinct in Petchabun and Nakhon Ratchasima provinces (2007 SIL). Home. Mainly older adults. Mixed attitudes. Some have strong identity links to their language, others prefer to identify themselves as Thai (2002 P. Suwilai, 2007 SIL). 1,500 also use Thai [tha]. *Lg Dev:* Literacy rate in L1: 1%. Literacy rate in L2: 75%. Most men and the younger generation are literate in Thai. Literacy in Thai transfers easily to Nyah Kur. Dictionary. *Writing:* Thai script. *Other:* Buddhist, Christian, traditional religion. *Maps:* 406:31, 407:31.

Nyaw [nyw] (Jo, Nyo, Nyoh, Yo). 50,000 (Diller 1990). Sakon Nakhon, Nakhon Phanom, Udon Thani, Bueng Kan, Maha Sarakham provinces; isolated area on Cambodia border, Sa Kaeo Province. *Status:* 6a (Vigorous). *Class:* Tai-Kadai, Kam-Tai, Tai, Southwestern. *Dialects:* Reportedly similar to Northeastern Thai [tts] and the Luang Prabang dialect of Lao [lao]. *Lg Use:* Also use Northeastern Thai [tts]. *Other:* Maw may be an alternate name. Buddhist. *Maps:* 407:32, 408:32.

Nyeu [nyl] (Yeu, Yoe). 200. Sisaket. *Status:* 6b (Threatened). *Class:* Austro-Asiatic, Mon-Khmer, Eastern Mon-Khmer, Katuic, West Katuic, Kuay-Yoe. *Lg Use:* Also use Thai [tha]. *Lg Dev:* Literacy rate in L1: Below 1%. Literacy rate in L2: 25%–50%. *Map:* 407:33.

Palaung, Pale [pce] (Di-Ang, Ngwe Palaung, Palay, Pale, Silver Palaung, Southern Palaung, Ta-Ang). 5,000 in Thailand (1989). Chiang Mai Province. *Status:* 8a (Moribund). *Lg Use:* Also use Thai [tha]. *Lg Dev:* Literacy rate in L1: Below 1%. Literacy rate in L2: Below 5%. *Other:* Distinct from Shwe Palaung [pll] and Rumai Palaung [rbb]. See main entry on page 239 (as Palaung, Ruching). *Map:* 406:34.

Pa'o [blk] (Black Karen, Pa Oh, Pa'O, Pa'o Karen, Pa-U, Taungtu). 740 in Thailand (2000). Mae Hong Son Province. *Status:* 5 (Developing). *Dialect:* Southern Pa'o. See main entry on page 240. *Map:* 406:35.

Phu Thai [pht] (Phutai, Phuu Thai, Putai, Puthai). 470,000 in Thailand (2006 Mahidol University). Population total all countries: 866,000. Northeast; Sakon Nakhon, Kalasin, Mukdahan, Nakhon Phanom, Udon Thani, Yasothon, Amnat Charoen, and Roi Et provinces; possibly also in China. Also in Laos, United States, Viet Nam. *Status:* 6a (Vigorous). *Class:* Tai-Kadai, Kam-Tai, Tai, Southwestern. *Dialects:* Little dialect differentiation. Reportedly similar to Tai Dam [blt] and Tai Don [twh]. *Lg Use:* Also use Isan (a dialect of Northeastern Thai [tts]). *Lg Dev:* Literacy rate in L1: Below 1%. Literacy rate in L2: 75%–100%. *Other:* Buddhist. *Map:* 407:38.

Phuan [phu] (Lao Phuan, Phu Un). 200,000 in Thailand (2006 Mahidol University). Population total all countries: 307,000. Phetchabun, Phichit, Chaiyaphum, Lop Buri, Prachin Buri, Chachoengsao, Nakhon Nayok, and Sara Buri provinces; isolated area, Bueng Kan Province; 1 village south of Bangkok. Also in Cambodia (Lao Phuon), Laos. *Status:* 6a (Vigorous). *Class:* Tai-Kadai, Kam-Tai, Tai, Southwestern. *Dialects:* None known. Reportedly similar to Northern Tai [nod], Tai Dam [blt], Thai Song [soa], and Lao [lao]. *Lg Use:* Vigorous. *Other:* Strong sense of identity. Socially prominent group. Relocated to Thailand 1827–1890. The name is also used for Lao speakers in Thailand. Buddhist. *Maps:* 406:39, 407:39, 408:39.

Prai [prt] (Thin). 20,000 in Thailand (2001). Possibly 3,000 Ban Wen dialect speakers. Population total all countries: 41,900. North, Nan Province, Thung Chang, Chalerm Prakiat, Chiang Klang, Bo Klua, and Pua districts. Also in Laos. *Status:* 6a (Vigorous). *Class:* Austro-Asiatic, Mon-Khmer, Northern Mon-Khmer, Khmuic, Mal-Khmu', Mal-Phrai. *Dialects:* Ban Wen, Prai, Southern Prai. The main dialect of Prai has 2 subvarieties referred to as, R and Y, which are reportedly minimally different. Ban Wen dialect shares cognates with both Mal [mlf] and Prai, but is unintelligible to Mal speakers. *Lg Use:* Most Prai also speak Northern Thai [nod] (Kammüang). *Lg Dev:* Literacy materials include a set of primers and lessons. Dictionary. *Writing:* Thai script. *Other:* Distinct from Mal [mlf]. Lua is a self-reported language name for many Prai and Mal. The Southern dialect is called Longhouse (Jordan-Diller and Diller 2004). About 12 villages, mostly in Bo Klua District, with a few villages in Pua District. Ban Wen dialect speakers live in 10–15 villages, primarily in Bo Klua District, with some in Chalerm Prakiat District. *Map:* 406:41.

Pray 3 [pry]. 38,800 (2000). Nan Province; interspersed in Thung Chang and Pua districts among the Mal [mlf]. *Status:* 6a (Vigorous). *Class:* Austro-Asiatic, Mon-Khmer, Northern Mon-Khmer, Khmuic, Mal-Khmu', Mal-Phrai. *Dialects:* None known. Separate from Phai [prt] and Lua [prb]. *Lg Use:* Also use Mal [mlf]. *Lg Dev:* Literacy rate in L1: Below 1%. Literacy rate in L2: 25%–50%. *Map:* 406:42.

Saek [skb] (Sek, Tai Sek). 11,000 in Thailand (Johnstone 1993). Northeast; Nakhon Phanom Province; 5 villages. *Status:* 7 (Shifting). *Lg Use:* Also use Lao [lao]. *Other:* Buddhist. See main entry on page 217. *Map:* 407:45.

Shan [shn] (Great Thai, "Ngeo" *pej.*, "Ngiao" *pej.*, "Ngiaw" *pej.*, "Ngio" *pej.*, "Ngiow" *pej.*, Sam, Sha, Tai Luang, Tai Shan, Tai Yay, Thai Yay). 95,000 in Thailand (2006 Mahidol University). North, Mae Hong Son, Maehongson, Myuang Haeng, Chiangrai, Chiangmai, Maesai, and Tak provinces, on northwest border. *Status:* 5 (Developing). *Dialect:* Mae Hong Son. *Other:* Buddhist, Christian, traditional religion. See main entry on page 241. *Map:* 406:48.

Sô [sss] (Kha So, Thro). 70,000 in Thailand (2006 Mahidol University). Northeast, both sides of Mekong river; Nakhon Phanom and Sakon Nakhon provinces; Nong Kai and Kalasin. 53 villages. *Status:* 6a (Vigorous). *Dialects:* So Makon, So Phong, So Slouy, So Trong. *Lg Use:* Home. All ages. Also use Lao [lao], Thai [tha]. *Lg Dev:* Literacy rate in L1: Below 1%. Literacy rate in L2: 25%–50%. *Other:* Came from Laos, where the same dialect is spoken. Buddhist, Christian, traditional religion. See main entry on page 217. *Map:* 407:49.

Tai Dam [blt] (Black Tai, Jinping Dai, Tai Noir, Thai Den). 700 in Thailand (2004). Loei Province, Ban Na Pa Nat village. *Status:* 5 (Developing). *Other:* Arrived in Thailand in 1885. See main entry on page 315.

Tai Ya [cuu] (Huayaodai, Ya). 400 in Thailand (Dawkins and Kirkland 2008), decreasing. Ethnic population: 1,000. Chiang Rai Province. *Status:* 7 (Shifting). *Lg Use:* Weak. Home; mostly older people; occasionally with spouses and children. Neutral attitudes. Also use Northern Thai [nod], Thai [tha]. *Lg Dev:* Literacy rate in L2: High in Central Thai. *Other:* Some desire to preserve Tai Ya language. Christian. See main entry on page 90. *Map:* 406:51.

Thai [tha] (Central Tai, Siamese, Standard Thai, Thaiklang). 20,200,000 in Thailand (2000). 400,000 Khorat. 4,700,000 mother-tongue Thai are ethnic Chinese, or 80% of the Chinese (1984). Population total all countries: 20,396,930. L2 users: 40,000,000 in Thailand (2001 A. Diller). Central, centered in Bangkok. Khorat dialect: Ratchasima. Also in Cambodia, Canada, Denmark, Singapore, Sweden, United Arab Emirates, United States. *Status:* 1 (National). De facto national language. *Class:* Tai-Kadai, Kam-Tai, Tai, Southwestern. *Dialect:* Khorat Thai (Korat, Thaikorat). *Type:* SVO. *Lg Dev:* Fully developed. Bible: 1883–2011. *Writing:* Braille script. Thai script, primary usage. *Other:* Ethnonym: Siamese. Buddhist, Christian. *Maps:* 406:52, 407:52, 408:52.

Thai Sign Language [tsq]. 51,000 profoundly, prelingually deaf people in Thailand (1997 C. Reilly). 20% of deaf children go to school to learn it. Major regional centers and Bangkok. *Status:* 5 (Developing). *Class:* Deaf sign language. *Dialects:* None known. Signs used at the deaf school at Tak are reportedly very different. *Type:* Finger-spelling system. *Lg Use:* Total communication used in school: speaking and signing. Reported high mobility among most deaf people today. Sign language used in school and that used by deaf adults outside is different. Used by all deaf born since 1951; some older ones. Also use Thai [tha]. *Lg Dev:* Literacy rate in L2: Less than 10%. The 1st deaf school began in 1951, with help from Gallaudet University. Uses a combination of indigenous signs and American Sign Language [ase]. Educated deaf people have limited Thai literacy skills. Taught in primary schools. TV. Dictionary. *Other:* Buddhist.

Thai Song [soa] (Lao Song, Lao Song Dam, Song). 32,300 (2000). Kanchanaburi, Nakhon Pathom, and Phetchaburi provinces; Pitsanulok, Nakorn Sawaan; possibly in Suphan Buri Province. *Status:* 5 (Developing). *Class:* Tai-Kadai, Kam-Tai, Tai, Southwestern. *Dialects:* Slight dialect differences. Reportedly similar to Tai Dam [blt]. *Lg Dev:* Bible portions. *Writing:* Tai Viet script. Thai script. *Other:* Traditional religion. *Maps:* 406:53, 408:53.

Thai, Northeastern [tts] (Esarn, Isaan, Isan, Issan, Thai Isaan). 15,000,000 (1983 SIL). At least 1,000,000 in Bangkok. Kalerng has a few thousand speakers (1990 A. Diller). Northeast; 33 provinces. Kalerng subdialect: Sakon Nakhon and Nakhon Phanom. *Status:* 6a (Vigorous). De facto language of provincial identity in east, northeast provinces. *Class:* Tai-Kadai, Kam-Tai, Tai, Southwestern. *Dialects:* Central Isan (Kalerng, Kaleung, Kaloeng), Korat, Northern Isan, Southern Isan. Korat dialect is quite different, and may be a separate language. *Type:* SVO. *Lg Use:* 88% use Isan dialect in the home, 1% use Central Thai, 11% use both. Used as L2 by Kuy [kdt], Northern Khmer [kxm], Nyaw [nyw], Phu Thai [pht], Yoy [yoy]. *Writing:* Thai script. *Other:* Buddhist. *Maps:* 406:28, 407:28, 408:28.

Thai, Northern [nod] (Kam Mu'ang, Kammüang, Kammyang, Khon, Khon Meang, Khon Myang, La Nya, Lan Na, Lanatai, Lanna, Mu'ang, Mung, Myang, Northern Thai, Payap, Phayap, Phyap, Tai Nya, Tai Yon, Tai Yuan, Western Laotian, "Yuan" *pej.*). 6,000,000 in Thailand (1983 SIL). Population total all countries: 6,029,500. Chiang Mai, Chiang Rai, Lamphun, Lampang, Mae Hong Son, Sukhothai, Nan, Phayao, Phrae, Uttaradit, Tak, and Kamphaeng Phet provinces. Also in Laos. *Status:* 5 (Developing). De facto language of provincial identity in northern provinces. *Class:* Tai-Kadai, Kam-Tai, Tai, Southwestern. *Dialects:* Bandu, Nan, Tai Wang. Nan dialect is more distinct. *Lg Use:* 88% use Northern Thai in the home, 3% use Central Thai [tha], 10% use both. Also use Thai [tha]. Used as L2 by Eastern Lawa [lwl], Iu Mien [ium], Lü [khb], Mlabri [mra], Mpi [mpz], Phrae Pwo Karen [kjt], Prai [prt], Tai Ya [cuu], Western Lawa [lcp], Yong [yno]. *Lg Dev:* Newspapers. NT: 1914. *Writing:* Tai Tham (Lanna) script, limited usage. Thai script. *Other:* Yuan is their term for Vietnamese. The name 'Phyap' (Phayap) is Sanskrit, north. Buddhist. *Map:* 406:30.

Thai, Southern [sou] (Dambro, Pak Tai, Pak Thai, Paktay). 4,500,000 (2006 Mahidol University). Surat Thani, Chumphon, Nakhon Si Thammarat, Songkhla, Phatthalung, Ranong, Phangnga, Phuket, Krabi, Trang, Prachuap Khiri Khan, Pattani, Yala, and Satun provinces; Muslim Thai dialect. *Status:* 5 (Developing). De facto language of provincial identity in southeasternmost 15 provinces. *Class:* Tai-Kadai, Kam-Tai, Tai, Southwestern. *Dialects:* Tak Bai (Tai Tak Bai), Thai Malay (Tai Islam). A group of dialects more distantly related to other Tai languages. Border dialects are quite distinct from others. *Lg Use:* 81% use Southern Thai in the home, Muslim Tai (Thai Malay) speak only Southern Thai. Also use Thai [tha]. Used as L2 by Kensiu [kns]. *Lg Dev:* Read Central Thai. Bible portions: 2000. *Writing:* Thai script. *Other:* Buddhist, Christian, Muslim. *Map:* 408:50.

Tonga [tnz] (Mos). 180 in Thailand (2007). Population total all countries: 195. Ethnic population: 300 (2000 D. Bradley). South; Trang, Satun, and Phatthalung, and Songkhla provinces. Also in Malaysia. *Status:* 6b (Threatened). *Class:* Austro-Asiatic, Mon-Khmer, Aslian, North Aslian, Tonga. *Dialect:* Satun. Probably similar to Kensiu [kns]. *Map:* 408:54.

Ugong [ugo] (Gong, Lawa, Ugawng, 'Ugong). 80 (2000 D. Bradley). Ethnic population: 500. Suphan Buri Province, Kok Chiang village; Uthai Thani Province, Khok Khwai village. *Status:* 8a (Moribund). *Class:* Sino-Tibetan, Tibeto-Burman, Ngwi-Burmese, Ngwi, Unclassified. *Dialects:* Kok Chiang, Suphanburi. Not closely related to other languages. *Lg Use:* Extinct in traditional territory in western Kanchanaburi Province, moribund (youngest fluent speakers over 40, but revival activities underway) in Kok Chiang village in Suphanburi Province, endangered in Khok Khwai village in Uthai Thani Province, where they have recently lost their land and dispersed into the surrounding forests (Bradley 2007). Home. Mainly older adults. Also use Thai [tha]. *Other:* Distinct from Lawa [cbn] in the Palaung-Wa branch of Mon-Khmer. Relocated due to dam construction.

Urak Lawoi' [urk] (Chaw Talay, Chawnam, Lawoi, Lawta, Orak Lawoi'). 5,000 (2012 S. Pattemore). Krabi and Satun provinces; west coast, Phuket and Langta islands. *Status:* 6b (Threatened). *Class:* Austronesian, Malayo-Polynesian, Malayo-Chamic, Malayic. A member of macrolanguage Malay [msa] (Malaysia). *Dialects:* Adang, Phuket Old Peoples, Phuket Young Peoples. Aboriginal Malays with a unique Malay language. *Lg Use:* Often replaced by Thai [tha] or Malay or both when members of the group settle down (Bradley 2007). Most also use Thai [tha] and Malay (Bradley 2007). *Lg Dev:* Various Thai script and romanized literacy materials (Bradley 2007). Dictionary. Grammar. NT: 1998. *Writing:* Thai script. *Other:* Traditional religion, Christian. *Map:* 408:55.

Wa, Parauk [prk]. 6,700 in Thailand (2008 P. Hopple). Scattered; probably north, northwest. *Status:* 5 (Developing). See main entry on page 242.

Yong [yno] (Nyong). 12,600 (2000). Chiang Mai and Lamphun provinces. *Status:* 8a (Moribund). *Class:* Tai-Kadai, Kam-Tai, Tai, Southwestern. *Dialects:* None known. Phonology reportedly similar to Lü [khb]. *Lg Use:* Also use Northern Thai [nod]. *Other:* Buddhist. *Map:* 406:58.

Yoy [yoy] (Dioi, Jui, Yoi, Yooi, Yooy). 5,000 in Thailand (Diller 1990). Population total all countries: 6,000. Sakon Nakhon Province; small border enclave, Nakhon Phanom Province. Also in Laos. *Status:* 6a (Vigorous). *Class:* Tai-Kadai, Kam-Tai, Tai, Northern. *Lg Use:* Also use Northeastern Thai [tts]. *Map:* 407:59.

Turkey

Republic of Turkey, Türkiye Cumhuriyeti. 71,517,000 (2008 census). Principal language: Turkish. Literacy rate: 85% (2009 UNESCO). Immigrant languages: Chechen (8,000), Iranian Persian (500,000), Lak (300), Lezgi (1,200), North Levantine Spoken Arabic (500,000). General references: Andrews 1989; Comrie 1987; Izadi 1992; Sebeok 1963, 1970. Deaf population: 316,840. Deaf institutions: 12.

The number of individual languages listed for Turkey is 36. Of these, 35 are living and 1 is extinct. Of the living languages, 3 are institutional, 14 are developing, 7 are vigorous, 10 are in trouble, and 1 is dying.

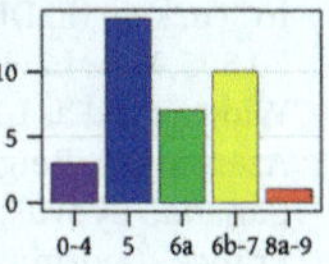

Abaza [abq] (Abazin, Abazintsy, Ahuwa, Tapanta). 10,000 in Turkey (1995). *Status:* 5 (Developing). *Dialects:* Ashkaraua (Ashkar), Bezshagh, Tapanta. *Lg Use:* Also use Turkish [tur]. *Other:* Muslim. See main entry on page 319.

Abkhaz [abk] (Abxazo). 4,000 in Turkey (1980). Ethnic population: 39,000 (Johnstone 2001). Northeast, Coruh; northwest; mainly Bolu and Sakarya provinces. *Status:* 6b (Threatened). *Dialects:* Abzhui, Bzyb, Samurzakan. *Lg Use:* Also use Turkish [tur]. *Other:* Muslim (Sunni). See main entry on page 99.

Adyghe [ady] (Adygey, Cherkes, Circassian). 278,000 in Turkey (2000). 6,410 monolinguals (1965 census). Central and western Anatolia, Kayseri, Tokat, Karaman Maras, and many other provinces. *Status:* 5 (Developing). *Lg Use:* Also use Turkish [tur]. *Other:* Muslim (Sunni). See main entry on page 319.

Albanian, Tosk [als] (Shqip). 15,000 in Turkey (1980). 1,100 monolinguals (1965 census). Ethnic population: 65,000. Western Turkey, scattered. *Status:* 6b (Threatened). *Lg Use:* Also use Turkish [tur]. *Other:* Muslim (Sunni). See main entry on page 319.

Arabic, Mesopotamian Spoken [acm]. 100,000 in Turkey. Diarbakir, Mardin, and Siirt provinces. *Status:* 6a (Vigorous). *Dialect:* Anatolian Cluster. *Other:* Christian, Jewish. See main entry on page 206.

Arabic, North Mesopotamian Spoken [ayp] (Syro-Mesopotamian Vernacular Arabic). 400,000 in Turkey (1992). Mardin and Siirt provinces. *Status:* 6a (Vigorous). *Lg Use:* Also use Turkish [tur]. *Other:* Do not read Arabic. Muslim, Christian. See main entry on page 206.

Armenian [hye] (Armjanski, Ermenice, Haieren, Somkhuri). 40,000 in Turkey (1980). 1,000 monolinguals (1965 census). Ethnic population: 70,000 (1980). Many in Istanbul; and scattered in east Turkey. Hemshin are Armenian Muslims, living near the Laz [lzz] language area. *Status:* 6b (Threatened). *Dialect:* Western Armenian. *Lg Use:* Also use Turkish [tur]. *Other:* Christian, Muslim. See main entry on page 51.

Azerbaijani, South [azb] (Azeri). 530,000 in Turkey. Kars Province. *Status:* 5 (Developing). *Dialect:* Kars. *Lg Use:* Also use Turkish [tur] as literary language. *Other:* Muslim. See main entry on page 201.

Balkan Gagauz Turkish [bgx] (Balkan Turkic). 327,000 in Turkey (Johnstone 1993). 7,000 Surguch (1965) and 320,000 Yuruk. Population total all countries: 331,000. Surguch dialect in Edirne region. Also in Bulgaria, Greece, Macedonia. *Status:* 7 (Shifting). *Class:* Altaic, Turkic, Southern, Turkish. *Dialects:* Gajol, Gerlovo Turks, Karamanli, Kyzylbash, Surguch, Tozluk Turks, Yuruk (Konyar, Yoruk). *Lg Use:* Probably no children. *Writing:* Latin script. *Other:* Distinct from Gagauz [gag] of Moldova, Bulgaria, and Romania. Christian.

Bulgarian [bul] (Pomak). 300,000 in Turkey (Johnstone and Mandryk 2001). Refugees from Bulgaria. Scattered in Edirne and other western provinces. *Status:* 5 (Dispersed). *Dialect:* Pomak. *Lg Use:* Spoken by Muslim Pomaks. Also use Turkish [tur]. *Other:* Muslim (Sunni). See main entry on page 319.

Crimean Tatar [crh] (Crimean Turkish). 2,000 in Turkey. Ankara Province, Polatli district, Karakuyu, several villages. *Status:* 5 (Developing). *Dialects:* Central Crimean, Northern Crimean (Crimean Nogai, Steppe Crimean), Southern Crimean. *Other:* Muslim. See main entry on page 319.

Domari [rmt] (Gypsy, Middle Eastern Romani, Tsigene). 28,500 in Turkey (Gunnemark and Kenrick 1985). Mainly west; some east. *Status:* 6a (Vigorous). *Dialects:* Beludji, Karachi, Marashi. *Other:* 500,000 Gypsies in Turkey speak Domari or varieties of Romani (Gunnemark and Kenrick 1985). Muslim. See main entry on page 202.

Georgian [kat] (Gruzin, Kartuli). 40,000 in Turkey (1980). 4,000 monolinguals (1965 census). Ethnic population: 91,000. North and northwest Anatolia, Artvin, Ordu, Sakarya, and other provinces. *Status:* 6b (Threatened). *Dialect:* Imerxev. *Lg Use:* Also use Turkish [tur]. *Other:* Muslim (Sunni). See main entry on page 99.

Greek [ell]. 4,000 in Turkey (1993). Istanbul, some in Izmir. *Status:* 5 (Dispersed). *Other:* Nearly all Greeks emigrated from Turkey. There were 1,500,000 in Turkey in 1900. See main entry on page 320.

Hértevin [hrt]. 1,000 (1999 H. Mutzafi). *Status:* 6a (Vigorous). *Class:* Afro-Asiatic, Semitic, Central, Aramaic, Eastern, Central, Northeastern. *Dialects:* Hértevin Proper (Arton), Jinet, Umraya. Considerable differences from other Northeastern Aramaic varieties, and not intelligible with any or most of them. *Lg Use:* Also use Northern Kurdish [kmr]. *Writing:* Syriac script. *Other:* Christian (Chaldean).

Kabardian [kbd]. 1,000,000 in Turkey (2005 Circassian Association). Uzun Yayla plateau east of Kayseri; Samsun area; Amasya; Çorum. *Status:* 5 (Developing). *Other:* Muslim (Sunni). See main entry on page 321.

Kazakh [kaz] (Kaisak, Kazakhi, Kazax, Kosach, Qazaqi). 600 in Turkey (1982). Manisa Province, Salihli; Istanbul; Kayseri Province. *Status:* 5 (Dispersed). *Other:* Muslim. See main entry on page 212.

Kumyk [kum] (Kumuk, Kumuklar, Kumyki). A few villages. *Status:* 6b (Threatened). *Dialects:* Buinak, Khaidak, Khasav-Yurt. *Other:* Different from the Kumux dialect of Lak [lbe]. Muslim. See main entry on page 321.

Kurdish, Northern [kmr] (Kermancî, Kirmancî, Kurdi, Kurdî, Kurmancî, Kurmanji). 15,000,000 in Turkey (McCarus 2009), decreasing. Very provisional figures for Northern Kurdish speaker population. Population total all countries: 20,210,890. 3,000,000 monolinguals. Especially in Hakkari and Shirnak provinces. Adiyaman, Agri, Batman, Bingol, Bitlis, Diyarbakir (Amed), Hakkari (Colemerg), Kars, Mardin, Shirnak, Siirt, Shanliurfa, and Van; also Ganziantep, Elazig, Erzincan, Erzurum, Kahramanmarash, Kayseri, Malatya, Sivas, Tunceli (Dersim), and other provinces; central Turkey, Konya, Cankiri and Cihanbeyli; many in Istanbul, Adana, Ankara, Izmir. Also in Armenia, Australia, Austria, Azerbaijan, Bahrain, Belgium, Canada, Denmark, Finland, France, Georgia, Germany, Greece, Iran, Iraq, Italy, Jordan, Kazakhstan, Kuwait, Kyrgyzstan, Lebanon, Netherlands, Norway, Russian Federation, Sweden, Switzerland, Syria, Turkmenistan, United Kingdom, United States. *Status:* 3 (Wider communication). *Class:* Indo-European, Indo-Iranian, Iranian, Western, Northwestern, Kurdish. A member of macrolanguage Kurdish [kur] (Iraq). *Dialects:* Ashiti, Bayezidi, Boti (Botani), Hekari, Marashi, Mihemedî, Shemdinani, Shikakî, Silivî. Dialect differences but all use the same written form. *Lg Use:* Home, market, political situations. Many are adults above age 30. Positive attitudes. 80% also use Turkish [tur]. Also use Northern Zazaki [kiu], Southern Zazaki [diq]. Used as L2 by Hértevin [hrt], Southern Zazaki [diq]. *Lg Dev:* Literacy rate in L1: Overall about 83%, but not differentiated by L1 or L2 usage. While overall speakers are decreasing, literates are increasing. Many literary works from 16th and 17th centuries onward. Poetry. Magazines. Newspapers. New media. Radio programs. Films. TV. Videos. Dictionary. Grammar. Bible: 2008. *Writing:* Arabic script, used in Iran, Iraq, Syria, and Lebanon. Cyrillic script, used in Russia and Armenia. Latin script, developed in 1932, used in Turkey. *Other:* Muslim (Sunni), Muslim (Alevi), Yezidi.

Kyrgyz [kir]. 1,140 in Turkey (1982). Van and Kars provinces. *Status:* 5 (Dispersed). *Other:* Refugees from Afghanistan; now Turkish citizens. Muslim (Sunni). See main entry on page 213.

Ladino [lad] (Dzhudezmo, Haketia, Hakitia, Judeo Spanish, Judezmo, Sefardi, Spanyol). 10,000 in Turkey (Salminen 2007). Ethnic population: 15,000. Mainly Istanbul; some in Izmir. *Status:* 7 (Shifting). *Lg Use:* Chief language of Sephardic Jews. The Donme are a Ladino-speaking group in Turkey, adherents of Shabbetai Zevi (Zvi). Most speakers are over 50 years old (Salminen 2007). Also use Turkish [tur]. *Other:* Jewish. See main entry on page 209.

Laz [lzz] (Chan, Chanuri, Chanzan, Laze, Zan). 20,000 in Turkey (Salminen 2007). Population total all countries: 22,000. Ethnic population: 92,000 (1980). Northeast, Rize, Kemer, Atin, Artasen, Vitse, Arkab, Hopa, and Sarp; Artvin, Sakarya, Kocaeli, and Bolu provinces. Also in Belgium, France, Georgia, Germany, United States. *Status:* 6b (Threatened). *Class:* Kartvelian, Zan. *Dialects:* None known. Officially considered a single language with Mingrelian [xmf], called, Zan, although not mutually inherently intelligible. *Lg Use:* Rapid language shift to Turkish [tur] (Salminen 2007). Also use Turkish [tur]. *Writing:* Georgian (Mkhedruli) script, used in Georgia. Latin script. *Other:* Muslim.

Pontic [pnt]. 300,000 in Turkey (2009 Z. Diakonikolaou). Northeast; easternmost area of European Turkey. *Status:* 6a (Vigorous). *Other:* Muslim. See main entry on page 321.

Romani, Balkan [rmn]. 25,000 in Turkey. West. *Status:* 6a (Vigorous). *Dialect:* Arlija (Erli). *Other:* Muslim. See main entry on page 322.

Serbian [srp] (Bosnian). 20,000 in Turkey (1980). 2,350 monolinguals (1965 census). Ethnic population: 61,000. Scattered in the west. *Status:* 6b (Threatened). *Lg Use:* Also use Turkish [tur]. *Other:* Muslim. See main entry on page 322.

Syriac [syc] (Ancient Syriac, Classical Syriac, Lishana Atiga, Suryaya, Suryoyo). No known L1 speakers. *Status:* 9 (Dormant). *Class:* Afro-Asiatic, Semitic, Central, Aramaic, Eastern. *Dialects:* Eastern Syriac, Western Syriac. Syrian churches: Eastern (Nestorian), Syrian Orthodox (Jacobite), and Syrian Catholic (Melkite, Maronite) developed a vast literature based on the Edessa (currently Sanliurfa, southeastern Turkey) variety of the Syrian dialect. Assyrian group (see Assyrian Neo-Aramaic in Iraq and elsewhere) separated denominationally from Chaldean (see Chaldean Neo-Aramaic in Iraq) and Jacobite (see Turoyo in Turkey and Syria) in the Middle Ages. Neo-Eastern Aramaic languages spoken by Christians are often dubbed Neo-Syriac although not directly descended from Syriac. *Lg Use:* Was used in Turkey, Iraq, and Syria. Became extinct in the 10th to 12th centuries. Still used, but rarely, as a secular literary language among followers of the churches listed. *Lg Dev:* Bible: 1645–1891. *Writing:* Syriac script. *Other:* Christian.

Tatar [tat]. Istanbul, perhaps elsewhere. *Status:* 5 (Developing). *Other:* Muslim. See main entry on page 322.

Turkish [tur] (Anatolian, Türkçe, Türkisch). 66,500,000 in Turkey (ELDIA 2006). Population total all countries: 70,805,930. L2 users: 350,000 in Turkey (ELDIA 2006). Widespread as L1 or L2. Also in Albania, Australia, Austria, Azerbaijan, Belgium, Bosnia and Herzegovina, Bulgaria, Canada, Cyprus, Denmark, Egypt, El Salvador, Finland, France, Georgia, Germany, Greece, Honduras, Iran, Iraq, Israel, Kazakhstan, Kyrgyzstan, Macedonia, Netherlands, Romania, Russian Federation, Serbia, Sweden, Switzerland, Tajikistan, Ukraine, United Arab Emirates, United Kingdom, United States, Uzbekistan. *Status:* 1 (National). Statutory national language (1982, Constitution, Article 3). *Class:* Altaic, Turkic, Southern, Turkish. *Dialects:* Danubian, Dinler, Edirne, Eskisehir, Gaziantep, Karamanli, Razgrad, Rumelian, Urfa. Danubian is west; other dialects east. *Type:* SOV. *Lg Use:* Karamanli are Turkish-speaking Greeks. 11,300,000 also use English [eng]. 2,660,000 also use Standard German [deu]. *Lg Dev:* Fully developed. Bible: 1827–2006. *Writing:* Arabic script, no longer in use. Braille script. Greek script, no longer in use. Latin script, used since 1928 or 1929, primary usage. *Other:* Muslim.

Turkish Sign Language [tsm] (Türk Isaret Dili). *Status:* 6a (Vigorous). *Class:* Deaf sign language.

Turkmen [tuk] (Trukhmen). 920 in Turkey (1982). Tokat Province. *Status:* 5 (Dispersed). *Other:* Refugees from Afghanistan; now Turkish citizens. Muslim (Sunni). See main entry on page 307.

Turoyo [tru] (Surayt, Süryani, Suryoyo, Syryoyo, Turani). 3,000 in Turkey (1994 H. Mutzafi). Population total all countries: 62,000. Ethnic population: 50,000 (1994). Southeast, Mardin Province. Also in Argentina, Belgium, Brazil, Canada, Germany, Iraq, Lebanon, Netherlands, Syria, United States. *Status:* 6b (Threatened). *Class:* Afro-Asiatic, Semitic, Central, Aramaic, Eastern, Central, Northwestern. *Dialects:* Anhil, 'Iwardo, Kfarze, Midin, Midyat, Raite. Turoyo subdialects divided between Town Turoyo (Midyat Turoyo), Village Turoyo, and Mixed (Village-Town) Turoyo. *Lg Use:* Mixed Turoyo, outside Tur 'Abdin, the language's original location, is increasingly used mainly by youth throughout the Jacobite diaspora. All also use their national languages or local lingua francas, and some are multilingual. *Lg Dev:* NT: 1992. *Writing:* Latin script, primary usage. Syriac script. *Other:* Glossonym: Tûrôyo, known among scholars almost exclusively; Suryoyo, is popular. Western Syriac, refers to the Classical Western Syriac [syc] liturgy and orthography used by Turoyo speakers. Christian (Jacobite).

Ubykh [uby] (Oubykh, Pekhi, Ubyx). No known L1 speakers. Last speaker died in 1992. Istanbul area, near the Sea of Marmara, Haci Osman village. *Status:* 10 (Extinct). *Class:* North Caucasian, West Caucasian, Ubyx. *Lg Use:* A century ago, there were 50,000 speakers in the Caucasus valleys east of the Black Sea. Shifted to a distinct dialect of Adyghe [ady]. *Writing:* Unwritten. *Other:* Most migrated to Turkey in 1894.

Uyghur [uig] (Uighur, Uigur, Uygur). 500 in Turkey (1981). Kayseri, Istanbul. Possibly in Iran. *Status:* 5 (Developing). *Other:* Muslim (Sunni). See main entry on page 92.

Uzbek, Southern [uzs]. 1,980 in Turkey (1982). Hatay, Gaziantep, and Urfa provinces. Possibly in Germany. *Status:* 5 (Developing). *Other:* Refugees from Afghanistan; now Turkish citizens. Distinct from Northern Uzbek [uzn] of Uzbekistan and China. Muslim (Sunni). See main entry on page 51.

Zaza [zza]. A macrolanguage (see page 9). *Other:* Includes: Northern Zazaki [kiu], Southern Zazaki [diq].

Zazaki, Northern [kiu] (Alevica, Dersimki, Dimilki, Kirmanjki, Northern Zaza, So-Bê, Zaza, Zonê Ma). 140,000 in Turkey. Tunceli Province, Tunceli merkez, Hozat, Nazmiye, Pülümür, and Ovacik subprovinces; Erzincan Province, Erzincan and Cayirli subprovinces; Elazig Province, Elazig merkez and Karakoqan subprovinces, 8 or more villages; Bingöl Province, Kigi and Karkiova subprovinces, 3 villages; Mush Province, Varto subprovince, 46 villages; Sivas Province, Zara, Imranli, Kangal, and Divrigi subprovinces, 15 or more villages; Erzerum Province, Hinis and Tekman subprovinces, 11 or more villages. Also in Austria, France, Germany, Netherlands, Switzerland, United Kingdom. *Status:* 4 (Educational). *Class:* Indo-European, Indo-Iranian, Iranian, Western, Northwestern, Zaza-Gorani. A member of macrolanguage Zaza [zza]. *Dialects:* Tunceli, Varto. Lexical similarity: 70% with Southern Zazaki [diq]. *Type:* SOV; prepositions and postpositions; genitives, articles, adjectives relatives after noun heads; numerals before noun heads; question word replaces content word in content questions; 2 prefixes, 2 suffixes, word order distinguishes subject, object, indirect object; noun affixes indicate case; verb affixes indicate person, number, gender; ergativity; passives; causatives; comparatives; V, VC, VCC, CV, CVC, CVCC; nontonal. *Lg Use:* Abroad, they use Northern Zazaki for close relationships. Home, community. All ages. Also use Turkish [tur]. Used as L2 by Northern Kurdish [kmr]. *Lg Dev:* Literacy rate in L2: School-age children to 40 years old, are literate in Turkish. Poetry. Magazines. Newspapers. New media. Radio programs. Films. TV. Videos. Dictionary. Grammar. Bible portions. *Writing:* Latin script. *Other:* Ethnonym for Alevi-Zaza: Kirmanj (Kirmanc), Kizilbash-Zaza. Muslim (Alevi).

Zazaki, Southern [diq] (Dimili, Dimli, Southern Zaza, Zaza, Zazaca). 1,500,000 (Paul 1998), decreasing. A few elderly monolinguals. Ethnic population: 3,000,000 (Paul 1998). East-central, Diyarbakir, Elazig and Bingö provinces. Mainly Cermik, Gerger, Egil, Siverek, Dicle, Palu, Bingöl, and Hani cities. *Status:* 5 (Developing). *Class:* Indo-European, Indo-Iranian, Iranian, Western, Northwestern, Zaza-Gorani. A member of macrolanguage Zaza [zza]. *Dialects:* Dersimki, Dumbuli (Dumbeli), Eastern Zazaki (Central Zazaki), Hazzu (Hazo), Kori, Motki (Moti), Sivereki. Dialects differ slightly, but mutually intelligible. *Type:* SOV; noun head initial; numerals, demonstratives, and quantifiers precede head; 2 genders; 3 cases: nominative, oblique, vocative; content-question word position in situ; split ergative system. *Lg Use:* In urban areas children still learn only L1 at home. Home, neighborhood, friends. All ages. Increasingly positive attitudes. 20% also use Northern Kurdish [kmr]. 80% also use Turkish [tur]. Used as L2 by Northern Kurdish [kmr]. *Lg Dev:* Poetry. Magazines. Newspapers. New media. Radio programs. Films. TV. Videos. Dictionary. Grammar. Bible portions. *Writing:* Latin script. *Other:* Muslim (Sunni).

Turkmenistan

Republic of Turkmenistan. 5,110,000 (2008 UNSD). Principal language: Turkmen. Literacy rate: 100% (2010 UNESCO). Immigrant languages: Armenian (32,000), Bashkort (2,610), Belarusan (5,290), Dargwa (1,600), Erzya (3,490), Georgian (1,050), Iranian Persian (8,000), Karakalpak (2,540), Kazakh (88,000), Korean (1,000), Lak (1,590), Lezgi (10,400), Lithuanian (220), North Azerbaijani (33,000), Ossetic (1,890), Romanian (1,560), Russian (349,000), Tabassaran (180), Tajiki (1,280), Tatar (40,400), Ukrainian (37,100). General references: Sebeok 1963.

The number of individual languages listed for Turkmenistan is 5. Of these, 4 are living and 1 is extinct. Of the living languages, 1 is institutional, 1 is developing, and 2 are vigorous. See map on page 409.

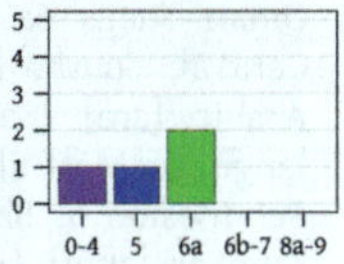

Balochi, Western [bgn] (Baloci, Baluchi, Baluci). 28,000 in Turkmenistan (1993). *Status:* 6a (Vigorous). *Lg Use:* Turkmen [tuk] is the literary language in Turkmenistan. *Other:* Distinct from Eastern [bgp] and Southern Balochi [bcc]. Muslim. See main entry on page 266. *Map:* 409.

Chagatai [chg] (Chaghatay, Jagatai). No known L1 speakers. *Status:* 10 (Extinct). *Class:* Altaic, Turkic, Eastern.

Kurdish, Northern [kmr] (Khorasani, Khorasani Kurmanji, Kurmancî, Kurmanji). 20,000 in Turkmenistan (Bakaev 1962). Ashkhabad area. *Status:* 6a (Vigorous). *Other:* Muslim (Shi'a). See main entry on page 305. *Map:* 409.

Turkmen [tuk] (Trukhmen, Trukhmeny, Turkmani, Turkmanian, Turkmenler, Turkomans). 3,430,000 in Turkmenistan (1995). Population total all countries: 7,560,560. Ethnic population: 3,470,000 (1995). Also in Afghanistan, Germany, Iran, Iraq, Kazakhstan, Kyrgyzstan, Pakistan, Russian Federation, Syria, Tajikistan, Turkey, United States, Uzbekistan. *Status:* 1 (National). Statutory national language (1992, Constitution, Article 13). *Class:* Altaic, Turkic, Southern, Turkmenian. *Dialects:* Anauli, Cawdur, Esari, Goklen, Khasarli, Nerezim, Nokhurli, Salyr, Saryq, Teke (Tekke), Yomud. *Lg Use:* Also use Russian [rus]. *Lg Dev:* Poetry. Magazines. Radio programs. TV. Dictionary. Grammar. NT: 1880–2005. *Writing:* Arabic script, used in Afghanistan and Iran. Cyrillic script, used in Turkmenistan, not used in Afghanistan. Latin script, official usage in Turkmenistan since 1991. *Other:* Turkmen in Syria, and possibly Iraq and Jordan, actually speak an ancient form of Turkmen; so-called Turkmen in Tibet may speak a different Turkic language. Muslim (Sunni). *Map:* 409.

Uzbek, Northern [uzn]. 317,000 in Turkmenistan. *Status:* 5 (Dispersed). See main entry on page 308. *Map:* 409.

United Arab Emirates

Ittihad al-Imarat al-Arabiyah, United Arab Emirates. 7,200,000 (2010 census). Principal languages: English, Standard Arabic. Literacy rate: 92% (2005 UNESCO). Immigrant languages: Bengali (70,000), Danish (160), Egyptian Spoken Arabic (100,000), French (250), Greek (100), Italian (400), Japanese (1,300), Malayalam (300,000), Omani Spoken Arabic (80,000), Polish (100), Serbian (100), Sinhala (25,000), Somali (46,400), Soqotri (7,000), Southern Pashto (26,100), Standard German (1,300), Swahili (2,500), Tagalog (80,000), Thai (3,000), Turkish (750). General references: Sebeok 1970. Deaf population: 109,200.

The number of individual languages listed for United Arab Emirates is 7. All are living languages. Of these, 3 are institutional, 3 are developing, and 1 is vigorous.

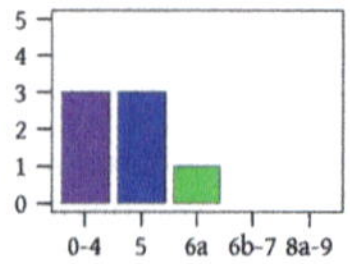

Arabic, Gulf Spoken [afb] (Gulf Arabic, Khaliji). 744,000 in United Arab Emirates. Gulf Bedu or village peoples. *Status:* 3 (Wider communication). *Other:* Muslim. See main entry on page 213.

Arabic, Shihhi Spoken [ssh] (Al-Shihuh, Shihhi, Shihu, Shihuh). 5,000 in United Arab Emirates (1995). Population total all countries: 27,000. Musandam peninsula. Also in Oman. *Status:* 6a (Vigorous). *Class:* Afro-Asiatic, Semitic, Central, South, Arabic. A member of macrolanguage Arabic [ara] (Saudi Arabia). *Lg Use:* Not a written language. Most Shihuh speak Shihhi, but the Kumazirah Subdivision of Shihuh, eg. the Dhahuriyin tribe, speak Kumzari [zum]. *Lg Dev:* Some may be literate in Standard Arabic [arb]. *Writing:* Unwritten. *Other:* Influenced by Farsi [pes]. Ethnonym: Shihuh. Muslim.

Arabic, Standard [arb]. Widespread. *Status:* 1 (National). Statutory national language (1996, Constitution, Article 7). *Lg Use:* Education, official purposes, formal speeches. See main entry on page 293.

Balochi, Southern [bcc] (Baloci, Baluchi, Baluci). 100,000 in United Arab Emirates. *Status:* 5 (Developing). *Dialect:* Makrani (Lotuni). *Other:* Come from Oman, Iran, and Pakistan. Muslim (Sunni). See main entry on page 266.

English [eng]. 100 in United Arab Emirates. L2 users: Used as L2 for communication among non-Arabic speakers. *Status:* 3 (Wider communication). De facto national working language. See main entry on page 319.

Pashto, Northern [pbu] (Pakhtoo, Pashtu, Passtoo, Pushto, Pusto). 100,000 in United Arab Emirates (1986). *Status:* 5 (Developing). *Other:* Came from Pakistan. Muslim. See main entry on page 271.

Persian, Iranian [pes] (Persian). 80,000 in United Arab Emirates (1986). *Status:* 5 (Dispersed). *Other:* Muslim. See main entry on page 204.

Uzbekistan

Republic of Uzbekistan. 28,661,000 (2013 World Factbook). Principal languages: Northern Uzbek, Russian. Literacy rate: 99% (2010 UNESCO). Immigrant languages: Armenian (50,000), Bashkort (35,000), Belarusan (29,000), Chuvash (8,870), Dargwa (1,340), Dungan (1,400), Erzya (14,200), Georgian (4,090), Iranian Persian (31,100), Karachay-Balkar (610), Korean (174,000), Kyrgyz (176,000), Lak (1,760), Lezgi (1,590), Lithuanian (1,040), Nogai (150), North Azerbaijani (44,000), Ossetic (6,000), Parya (1,000), Romanian (3,150), Standard German (40,000), Tabassaran (220), Tatar (468,000), Turkmen (228,000), Ukrainian (153,000), Uyghur (36,000). General references: Akiner 1983; Paper 1978; Sebeok 1963. Deaf population: 22,060.

The number of individual languages listed for Uzbekistan is 9. All are living languages. Of these, 2 are institutional, 5 are developing, 1 is vigorous, and 1 is dying. See map on page 409.

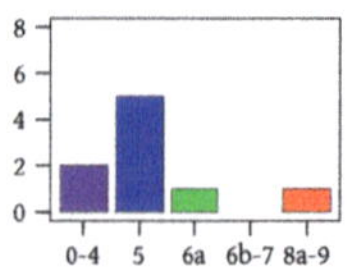

Arabic, Uzbeki Spoken [auz] (Central Asian Arabic, Jugari, Kashkadarya Arabic, Uzbeki Arabic). 700. Buxoro Region; Samarkand Region, middle and lower Zerafshan valley, a few in Katta-Kurgan town; small villages. *Status:* 8a (Moribund). *Class:* Afro-Asiatic, Semitic, Central, South, Arabic. A member of macrolanguage Arabic [ara] (Saudi Arabia). *Dialects:* Reportedly similar to North Mesopotamian Spoken Arabic [ayp]. Sharp dialect differences between Bukhara and Kashkadarya regions. Bukhara is strongly influenced by Tajiki [tgk], Kashkadarya by Uzbek [uzn] and other Turkic languages. May be a mixed language. *Lg Use:* Few ethnic group members speak Arabic. No diglossia with Modern Standard Arabic [arb]. Northern Uzbek [uzn] used to communicate and as literary language. *Other:* Endogamous and do not mix with speakers of other languages. Muslim (Hanafi Sunni). *Map:* 409:7.

Bukharic [bhh] (Bokharian, Bokharic, Bukharan, Bukharin, Judeo-Tajik). 10,000 in Uzbekistan (1995). Various areas. Buxoro is cultural center. *Status:* 6a (Vigorous). *Other:* Jewish. See main entry on page 208. *Map:* 409:1.

Crimean Tatar [crh] (Crimean Turkish). 150,000 in Uzbekistan (2006 A. Goriainov). *Status:* 5 (Developing). *Dialects:* Central Crimean, Northern Crimean (Crimean Nogai, Steppe Crimean), Southern Crimean. *Other:* In census counted with the Tatar [tat], but the languages are distinct. Muslim. See main entry on page 319. *Maps:* 409, 409:2.

Karakalpak [kaa] (Karaklobuk, Klobouki, Tchorny). 407,000 in Uzbekistan (1993 UBS). Population total all countries: 410,410. Ethnic population: 424,000. Along lower Amu Darya; south Aral Sea area. Also in Kazakhstan, Kyrgyzstan, Russian Federation, Turkmenistan. *Status:* 5 (Developing). Statutory language of provincial identity in Karakalpakstan (1995, Official Language Law (amended), 3561-XI, Article 3). *Class:* Altaic, Turkic, Western, Aralo-Caspian. *Dialects:* Northeastern Karakalpak, Southeastern Karakalpak. *Lg Use:* Also use Northern Uzbek [uzn], Russian [rus]. *Lg Dev:* NT: 2004. *Writing:* Cyrillic script. Latin script. *Other:* Some literature. Muslim (Sunni). *Maps:* 409, 409:3.

Kazakh [kaz]. 808,000 in Uzbekistan. *Status:* 5 (Dispersed). See main entry on page 212. *Maps:* 409, 409:4.

Russian [rus]. 1,660,000 in Uzbekistan. *Status:* 3 (Wider communication). De facto national working language. *Lg Use:* Used as L2 by Karakalpak [kaa], Northern Uzbek [uzn]. See main entry on page 322.

Tajiki [tgk]. 934,000 in Uzbekistan. *Status:* 5 (Dispersed). See main entry on page 299. *Maps:* 409, 409:6.

Turkish [tur] (Osmanli). 197,000 in Uzbekistan, Tajikistan, Kazakhstan, and Kyrgyzstan (based on 1979 census, not counting 56,000 Turks of Fergana, who speak an Uzbek dialect). *Status:* 5 (Dispersed). *Dialects:* Danubian, Dinler, Edirne, Eskisehir, Gaziantep, Karamanli, Razgrad, Rumelian, Urfa. *Lg Use:* Meskhetian Georgians, Khemshel Armenians, and Kurds in Uzbekistan speak Turkish [tur]. Also use North Azerbaijani [azj]. *Other:* Muslim (Sunni). See main entry on page 306.

Uzbek [uzb]. A macrolanguage (see page 9). *Other:* Includes: Northern Uzbek [uzn], Southern Uzbek [uzs] (Afghanistan).

Uzbek, Northern [uzn] (Özbek). 16,500,000 in Uzbekistan (1995 UN). Population total all countries: 18,968,250. East of the Amu Darya; south Aral Sea area. Possibly in Munich, Germany. Also in Australia, China, Israel, Kazakhstan, Kyrgyzstan, Russian Federation, Tajikistan, Turkey, Turkmenistan, Ukraine, United States. *Status:* 1 (National). Statutory national language (1995, Official Language Law (amended), 3561-XI, Article 1). *Class:* Altaic, Turkic, Eastern. A member of macrolanguage Uzbek [uzb]. *Dialects:* Karluk (Qarlug), Kipchak (Kypchak), Oghuz. Distinct from Southern Uzbek [uzs] of Afghanistan,

Pakistan, and Turkey. Russian [rus] influences in grammar, use of loanwords, and script. Oghuz may be a dialect of Khorasani Turkish [kmz] in Turkey rather than Uzbek. *Type:* SOV; has lost its historical vowel harmony and its vowel system now resembles that of Tajiki. *Lg Use:* Vigorous. Turks of Fergana and Samarkand speak Uzbek. Uzbek-speaking Gypsy communities in Russian central Asia. All ages. Positive attitudes. Also use Russian [rus]. *Lg Dev:* Literacy rate in L2: High. Taught in primary and secondary schools. Radio programs. TV. Dictionary. Grammar. NT: 1992–2010. *Writing:* Arabic script, officially abandoned in 1927, used in China. Braille script. Cyrillic script, officially adopted in 1940. Latin script, officially adopted in 1927 and abandoned in 1940, used in China. Sogdian script, used in China. *Other:* About a third urbanized. Much Persian influence in language and culture. Patrilineal. Sart is an obsolete name for sedentary Uzbek, possibly those who are ethnically Tajik. Muslim (Hanafi Sunni). *Maps:* 409, 409:5.

Viet Nam

Socialist Republic of Viet Nam. 85,847,000 (2009 census). Principal language: Vietnamese. 54 official ethnic communities. Literacy rate: 91% (2010 UNESCO). General references: Bradley 2007; Diller 2008; Edmondson and Solnit 1997; Ferlus 1996; Lebar, Hickey, and Musgrave 1964; Ostapirat 2000; Smith 1968, 1972, 1973; Thomas 1969, 1976, 1980; Thomas and Headley 1970; Wurm and Hattori 1981. Deaf institutions: 1.

The number of individual languages listed for Viet Nam is 109. Of these, 108 are living and 1 is extinct. Of the living languages, 1 is institutional, 15 are developing, 50 are vigorous, 37 are in trouble, and 5 are dying. See maps beginning on page 410.

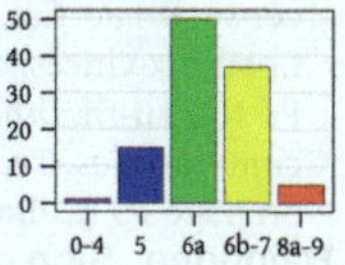

Akha [ahk] (Ahka, Aini, Aka, Ak'a, Ekaw, Ikaw, Kaw, Kha Ko, Khako, Khao Ikor, Ko, Yani). 1,260 in Viet Nam (1995 Institute for Southeast Asian Studies). Ethnic population: Hà Nhì ethnic group 21,725 (2009 census). Lao Cai, Lai Chau, and Dien Bien provinces, both sides of Viet Nam-Laos border. *Status:* 6b (Threatened). *Other:* Part of Hà Nhì official ethnic group. Traditional religion, Christian. See main entry on page 230. *Map:* 411:1.

Arem [aem] (A-Rem, Chombrau, Chomrau, Umo). 20 in Viet Nam (Ferlus 1996). Population total all countries: 40. Ethnic population: 100 (Ferlus 1996). Quang Binh Province, Bo Trach district, Tan Trach, 1 or 2 families of Thuong Trach. Also in Laos. *Status:* 8b (Nearly extinct). *Class:* Austro-Asiatic, Mon-Khmer, Viet-Muong, Chut. *Dialects:* Other dialects or ethnic names: Tu-vang, Pa-leng, Xo-lang, To-hung, Chà-cu, Tac-cui, Nhà Chút. *Lg Use:* Also use Vietnamese [vie]. *Other:* Part of Chút official ethnic community, including Sách, Mày Ruc, and Arem. *Map:* 414:2.

Bahnar [bdq] (Bana). 158,000 in Viet Nam (1999 census). Gai Lai, Kon Tum, and Binh Dinh provinces, central highlands. Also in United States. *Status:* 5 (Developing). *Class:* Austro-Asiatic, Mon-Khmer, Eastern Mon-Khmer, Bahnaric, Central Bahnaric. *Dialects:* Alakong (A-La Cong), Bahnar Bonom (Bomam), Golar, Jolong (Gio-Lang, Y-Lang), Kontum, Krem, Tolo. Other dialects or ethnic names: Roh, Kpang Cong. Reportedly most similar to Alak [alk], Tampuan [tpu], and Romam [rmx]. *Lg Use:* Also use Vietnamese [vie]. *Lg Dev:* Literacy rate in L1: 10%–30%. Literacy rate in L2: 50%–75%. Radio programs. Dictionary. NT: 1977–2008. *Writing:* Latin script. *Other:* Ba Na is an official ethnic community 227,715 (2009 census) that also includes Rengao [ren]. Traditional religion, Christian. *Map:* 414:3.

Brao [brb] (Braou, Brau, Brou, Lave, Laveh, Love, Proue, Rawe). 310 in Viet Nam (1999 census). Ethnic population: 400 (2009 census). Kon Tum Province, Cambodia-Laos border area. *Status:* 6a (Vigorous). *Dialect:* Palau. *Other:* Brâu is an official ethnic community. Traditional religion, Christian. See main entry on page 215 (as Lave). *Map:* 414:4.

Bru, Eastern [bru] (Brou, Bru, Quang Tri Bru, Van Kieu). 55,600 in Viet Nam (1999 census). Quang Binh, Quang Tri, and Dac Lac provinces. *Status:* 5 (Developing). *Dialects:* Mangkong, Tri. *Lg Use:* Also use Vietnamese [vie]. *Lg Dev:* Literacy rate in L1: 1%–5%. Literacy rate in L2: 15%–25%. *Other:* Bru Vân Kiêu is an official ethnic community of 74,506 (2009 census) that also includes Khua [xhv]. 'Bru', mountain people. Ethnic autonym: 'Bru' by the So people in Laos. Traditional religion, Christian. See main entry on page 214. *Map:* 414:16.

Cao Lan [mlc] (Cao, Caolan, Lan-Sán Chi, "Mán" *pej.*, "Man Cao-Lan" *pej.*, San Chay, San Chi, Sán-Chi). 169,000 (2009 census). San Chay mainly in Tuyen Quang, Lang Son, Bac Kan, and Thai Nguyen provinces; scattered in Yen Bai, Vinh Phuc, Phu Tho, Bac Giang, and Quang Ninh provinces. *Status:* 6a (Vigorous). *Class:* Tai-Kadai, Kam-Tai, Tai, Central. *Dialects:* None known. Maintain some features from Northern Tai [nod]. *Type:* Tonal. *Other:* Sán Chay is an official ethnic community. Possibly came from China in the 19th century. May speak a form of Yue Chinese [yue]. Traditional religion. *Map:* 412:8.

Cham, Eastern [cjm] (Bhamam, Chiem, Chiem Thành, Tjam). 72,900 in Viet Nam (2002). All Cham: 250,000 (Bradley 2007). Population total all countries: 73,790. Binh Thuan, Ninh Thuan, and Dong Nai provinces; Ho Chi Minh City. Also in United States. *Status:* 6b (Threatened). *Class:* Austronesian, Malayo-Polynesian, Malayo-Chamic, Chamic, Coastal, Cham. *Lg Use:* Being replaced by Vietnamese [vie] (Bradley 2007). Also use Vietnamese [vie]. *Lg Dev:* Literacy rate in L1: 5%–10%. Literacy rate in L2: 60%. Radio programs. Bible portions: 1973. *Writing:* Arabic script. Cham script, primary usage. Latin script. *Other:* Part of official Cham 161,729 (2009 census) ethnic community which includes Western Cham [cja] and Haroi [hro]. Remnants of a once-powerful kingdom. Austro-Asiatic influences. Traditional religion, Christian, Hindu. *Map:* 414:17.

Cham, Western [cja] (Cambodian Cham, Cham, Chiem, New Cham, Tjam). 25,000 in Viet Nam. All Cham: 250,000 (Bradley 2007). An Giang and Tay Ninh provinces; Ho Chi Minh City. *Status:* 6b (Threatened). *Lg Use:* Being replaced by Vietnamese [vie] (Bradley 2007). *Other:* Part of the official Cham 161,729 (2009 census) ethnic community which includes Eastern Cham [cjm] and Haroi [hro]. Differs a bit from Eastern Cham [cjm] of central Viet Nam. Muslim. See main entry on page 60. *Map:* 414:98.

Chinese, Yue [yue] (Chinese Nung, Ha Xa Phang, Hai Nam, Han, Hoa, Kiến, Liem Chau, Lowland Nung, Minh Huong, Nung, Phúc, Quang Dong, Samg Phang, Suồng Phóng, Triều Chau). 862,000 in Viet Nam (1999 census). Soc Trang, Can Tho, Vinh Long, Tra Vinh, Dong Nai, and Kieng Giang provinces; Ho Chi Minh, Hanoi, and Haiphong cities; north Viet Nam-China border regions. *Status:* 6b (Threatened). *Other:* Part of the official Hoa 823,071 (2009 census) ethnic community. Renowned fighters. Came from Canton, China as railroad workers and soldiers several decades ago. Distinct from Nung in the Tai family or Tibeto-Burman Nung (Nu) of China and

Myanmar. Daoist, Christian. See main entry on page 69.

Chrau [crw] (Chauro, Choro, Ro, Tamun). 7,000 (1995 census), decreasing. Few monolinguals. Ethnic population: 26,900 (2009 census). Dong Nai, Ba Ria-Vung Tau, and Binh Thuan provinces. *Status:* 6b (Threatened). *Class:* Austro-Asiatic, Mon-Khmer, Eastern Mon-Khmer, Bahnaric, South Bahnaric, Stieng-Chrau. *Dialects:* Chalah, Chalun, Dor (Doro), Jro, Mro, Prang, Tamun, Vajieng, Voqtwaq. *Lg Use:* Some parents pass it on to children. Informally used in education, oral and written use in religious services, oral literature. Positive attitudes. Also use Vietnamese [vie]. *Lg Dev:* Literacy rate in L1: 30%. Literacy rate in L2: 50%–75%. 5,000 can read Chrau, 500 can write it. Radio programs. Dictionary. Grammar. NT: 1982. *Writing:* Latin script. *Other:* Cho Ro is an official ethnic community. 'Chrau', mountain dweller. Traditional religion, Christian. *Map:* 414:11.

Chru [cje] (Cadoe Loang, Choru, Chrau Hma, Chu, Chu Ru, Churu, Cru, Kru, Seyu). 19,300 in Viet Nam (2009 census). Lam Dong, Ninh Thuan, and Binh Thuan provinces, inland from Malam area. Also in France, United States. *Status:* 6b (Threatened). *Class:* Austronesian, Malayo-Polynesian, Malayo-Chamic, Chamic, Highlands, Chru-Northern. *Dialects:* Noang (La-Dang), Rai. *Lg Use:* Being replaced by Vietnamese [vie] in many domains (Bradley 2007). Also use Vietnamese [vie]. *Lg Dev:* Literacy rate in L1: 5%–10%. Literacy rate in L2: 25%–50%. Radio programs. Dictionary. Bible portions: 1955. *Writing:* Latin script. *Other:* Chu Ru is an official ethnic community. *Map:* 414:12.

Chut [scb] (May, Ruc, Sach, Salang). 1,050 in Viet Nam (Bradley 2007). 450 May, 95 Ruc, 500 Sach (Bradley 2007). Population total all countries: 1,250. Ethnic population: 6,020 (2009 census). Quang Binh Province, Thuong Hoa, Hoa Son, Dan Hoa communes, near Laos border at the same latitude as Mu Gia Pass. Also in Laos. *Status:* 7 (Shifting). *Class:* Austro-Asiatic, Mon-Khmer, Viet-Muong, Chut. *Dialects:* May, Ruc (Kha Mu Gia, Tac Cui), Sach. *Writing:* Unwritten. *Other:* Chút is an official ethnic community which includes Arem, Mày, Sách, and Ruc. Traditional religion. *Map:* 414:13.

Côông [cnc] (Khoong, "Xa Coong" *pej.*, "Xa Xam" *pej.*, "Xa Xeng" *pej.*). 2,030 (2009 census). Lai Chau Province, Muong Te district, east of Sila, south of Mang. Ban Nam Luong, 4 villages; Kan Ho commune, Bo Lech; Nam Khao commune; Muong Toong commune, Ban Bo village; Dien Bien Province, Muong Nhé district, Nam Ke and Pa Thom communes, near the Lao border. *Status:* 6a (Vigorous). *Class:* Sino-Tibetan, Tibeto-Burman, Ngwi-Burmese, Ngwi, Southern. *Dialects:* None known. Quite different from Akha [ahk], Lahu [lhu], and Sila [slt] of this location. North and south varieties in Viet Nam are different, but mutually intelligible. Bisu [bzi], Pyen [pyy], and Mpi [mpz] are closely related. *Type:* No final consonants. *Lg Use:* Few domains. All ages. Mildly positive attitudes. *Other:* Cong is an official ethnic community. *Map:* 411:14.

Cua [cua] (Bòng Mieu, Bong Miew). 12,000 (Bradley 2007). Quang Ngai, Kon Tum, and Quang Nam provinces. *Status:* 6b (Threatened). *Class:* Austro-Asiatic, Mon-Khmer, Eastern Mon-Khmer, Bahnaric, North Bahnaric, East, Cua-Kayong. *Dialects:* Kol (Co, Col, Cor, Dot, Kor, Yot), Traw (Dong, Tràu). *Lg Dev:* Bible portions: 1973. *Writing:* Latin script. *Other:* Part of the Co official ethnic community. Traditional religion, Christian. *Map:* 414:15.

En [enc] (Nung Ven). 200 (1998 J. Edmondson). Cao Bang Province, Ho Quang district, Noi Thon village, 20 km east of Ho Quang city. *Status:* 6b (Threatened). *Class:* Tai-Kadai, Kra, Eastern Kra. *Dialects:* None known. Lexical similarity: less than 50% with Laha [lha], Qabiao [laq] (Laqua), Lachi [lbt], Gelao [giq], Hlai [lic]. *Type:* No uvular consonants; has its own number system. *Map:* 412:20.

Gelao, Green [giq] (Cape Draping Gelao, Hakhi, Hoki Gelao, Klau, Qau). 300 in Viet Nam (2002 J. Edmondson). Ha Giang Province, Yen Minh district, Dong Van district, Pho La and Dong Van communes. Also in China (Hagei). *Status:* 8b (Nearly extinct). *Class:* Tai-Kadai, Kra, Western Kra. *Lg Use:* Also use Hmong [hmn], Mandarin Chinese [cmn], Tày [tyz]. *Other:* Part of the Co Lao 2,636 (2009 census) official ethnic community. Not mutually intelligible with Red Gelao (2002 J. Edmondson). Traditional religion. *Map:* 412:22.

Gelao, Red [gir] (Vandu Gelao, Voa Dê). 20 in Viet Nam. Ha Giang Province, Yen Minh district. Also in China. *Status:* 8b (Nearly extinct). *Class:* Tai-Kadai, Kra, Western Kra. *Lg Use:* Shifting to Mandarin [cmn]. *Other:* Part of the Co Lao 2,636 (2009 census) official ethnic community. Not mutually intelligible with White Gelao [giw] (2002 J. Edmondson). Traditional religion. *Map:* 412:72.

Gelao, White [giw] (Southwestern Gelao, Telue, Tú Du). 20 in Viet Nam (2002 J. Edmondson). Ha Giang Province, Yen Minh district, Pho La and Dong Van. *Status:* 8b (Nearly extinct). *Other:* Part of the Co Lao 2,636 (2009 census). Not mutually intelligible with Red Gelao [gir] (2002 J. Edmondson). Traditional religion. See main entry on page 70 (as Duoluo). *Map:* 412:99.

Giáy [pcc] (Bo-I, Bouyei, Bo-Y, Buyi, Chang Chá, Chung Cha, Cùi Chu, Dang, Dioi, Giai, Giang, Nhaang, Niang, Nyang, Pau Thin, Pú Nà, Pui, Pu-I, Pu-Nam, Puyi, Sa, Trong Ggia, Tu-Dìn, Xa Chung Chá, Yai, Yay). 49,100 in Viet Nam (1999 census). Ethnic population: 58,600 (2009 census). Lao Cai, Yen Bai, Cao Bang, Ha Giang, and Lai Chau provinces. *Status:* 6b (Threatened). *Dialects:* Nhang, Pú Nà, Tu-Dí. *Other:* Giáy and Bo Y are both official ethnic communities. Traditional religion, Daoist. See main entry on page 65 (as Bouyei). *Maps:* 411:21, 412:21.

Haiphong Sign Language [haf]. Hai Phong. *Status:* 6a (Vigorous). *Class:* Deaf sign language. *Dialects:* None known. Related to sign languages in Hanoi, Ho Chi Minh City, Laos, and earlier sign languages in Thailand. *Map:* 412:23.

Halang [hal] (Koyong, Salang). 13,500 in Viet Nam (2000). Population total all countries: 17,500. Kon Tum Province. Also in Laos (Salang). *Status:* 6b (Threatened). *Class:* Austro-Asiatic, Mon-Khmer, Eastern Mon-Khmer, Bahnaric, North Bahnaric, West, Jeh-Halang. *Dialects:* None known. Reportedly similar to Jeh [jeh]. *Lg Use:* Also use Vietnamese [vie]. *Lg Dev:* Literacy rate in L1: 5%–10%. Literacy rate in L2: 25%–50%. Radio programs. Bible portions: 1970–1972. *Writing:* Latin script. *Other:* Part of the Xo Dang 165,501 (2009 census) official ethnic community. Traditional religion. *Map:* 414:24.

Halang Doan [hld] (Doan, Duan, Halang Duan). 2,000 in Viet Nam (Wurm and Hattori 1981). Population total all countries: 4,350. Kon Tum Province, between Sedang [sed] and Cua [cua] language areas. Also in Laos. *Status:* 6b (Threatened). *Class:* Austro-Asiatic, Mon-Khmer, Eastern Mon-Khmer, Bahnaric, North Bahnaric, West, Duan. *Dialects:* None known. May be intelligible of Takua [tkz], Kayong [kxy], Halang Daksut [hal], and Rengao [ren]. *Other:* Part of the Xo Dang 165,501 (2009 census) official ethnic community. *Map:* 414:25.

Hani [hni] (Ha Nhi, Hànhì, Haw, U Ní, Uni, Xá U Ní, Xauni). 17,500 in Viet Nam (1999 census). Ethnic population: 21,700 (2009 census). North, Lai Chau and Lao Cai provinces. 1 variety is east, 1 west of Muong Te city. *Status:* 6b (Threatened). *Other:* Hà Nhì is an official ethnic community in Viet Nam and China. 2 similar varieties in Viet Nam differ only in phonology and lexicon.

Traditional religion. See main entry on page 72. *Map:* 411:26.

Hanoi Sign Language [hab]. Ha Noi. *Status:* 6a (Vigorous). *Class:* Deaf sign language. *Dialects:* None known. Related to sign languages in Haiphong, Ho Chi Minh City, Laos, and earlier sign languages in Thailand. *Map:* 412:27.

Haroi [hro] (Aroi, Bahnar Cham, Hoi, Hroi, Hroy, Hrway). 35,000 (1998). Gai Lai and Phu Yen provinces. *Status:* 6a (Vigorous). *Class:* Austronesian, Malayo-Polynesian, Malayo-Chamic, Chamic, Coastal. *Writing:* Latin script. *Other:* Part of the Cham official ethnic community. *Map:* 414:28.

Hmong Daw [mww] (Bai Miao, Mán Tráng, Meo Kao, White Lum, White Meo). 1,068,000 in Viet Nam (2009 census). North, Son La, Dien Bien, Lao Cai, and Lai Chau provinces; others resettled in south. *Status:* 5 (Developing). *Dialect:* Hmong Xi (Meo Do). *Other:* Part of the H'mông official ethnic community. Largely intelligible with Hmong Njua [hnj]. No significant difference between White and Striped (Thailand) Hmong. Traditional religion, Christian. See main entry on page 72. *Map:* 411:29.

Hmong Dô [hmv]. Ha Giang Province, Dong Van and Meo Vae districts; Lao Cai Province, Bac Ha district. *Status:* 6a (Vigorous). *Class:* Hmong-Mien, Hmongic, Chuanqiandian. *Dialects:* None known. Lexical similarity: 80% with Hmong Daw [mww]. *Type:* Tonal, 8 tones. *Other:* Traditional religion, Christian. *Maps:* 411:30, 412:30.

Hmong Don [hmf]. Hoa Binh, Yen Bai, and Son La provinces. *Status:* 6a (Vigorous). *Class:* Hmong-Mien, Hmongic, Chuanqiandian. *Type:* Tonal, 7 tones. *Other:* Part of the H'mông official ethnic community. Traditional religion, Christian. *Maps:* 411:31, 412:31, 413:31.

Hmong Njua [hnj] (Mong Leng). Son La, Nghe An, Dien Bien, Lao Cai, Thanh Hoa, Lai Chau, and Hoa Binh provinces; scattered areas. *Status:* 6a (Vigorous). See main entry on page 214. *Maps:* 411:32, 412:32, 413:32.

Ho Chi Minh City Sign Language [hos]. Ho Chi Minh City. *Status:* 6a (Vigorous). *Class:* Deaf sign language. *Dialects:* None known. Related to sign languages in Hanoi, Hai Phong, Laos, and earlier sign languages in Thailand. *Map:* 414:33.

Hre [hre] (Cham-Re, Chom, Davach, Davak, Moi, Moi Da Vach, Moi Luy, Tachom). 94,000 (Bradley 2007). Ethnic population: 127,000 (2009 census). Quang Ngai, Binh Dinh, Gia Lai, and Kon Tum provinces. *Status:* 5 (Developing). *Class:* Austro-Asiatic, Mon-Khmer, Eastern Mon-Khmer, Bahnaric, North Bahnaric, West, Sedang-Todrah, Sedang. *Dialects:* Creq (Kare, Kre), Hre, Rabah (Tava). Reportedly most similar to Sedang [sed]. *Lg Use:* Also use Vietnamese [vie]. *Lg Dev:* Literacy rate in L1: 1%–5%. Literacy rate in L2: 15%–25%. Radio programs. Bible portions: 1967–1975. *Writing:* Latin script. *Other:* Hrê is an official ethnic community. Traditional religion, Christian. *Map:* 414:34.

Hung [hnu] (Cuói, K'katiam-Pong-Houk). 700 in Viet Nam (Ferlus 1996). Nghe An Province, Tuong Duong district, Tam Thai commune, Pong; Con Cuong district, Mon Son and Luc Da communes, Dan Lai and Ly Ha. *Status:* 7 (Shifting). *Dialects:* Dan Lai, Ly Ha, Pong (Khong Kheng, Phong, Pong 1, Pong 2, Poong, Tay Pong, Toum Phong, Xa La Vang). *Other:* Part of the Tho official ethnic community. See main entry on page 214. *Map:* 413:35.

Iu Mien [ium] (Dao Do, Dao Thanh Phan, Dìu, "Dong" *pej.*, Highland Yao, Kim Mien, "Mán" *pej.*, Mien, Myen, Red Dao, "Trai" *pej.*, "Xá" *pej.*, Yao, Yao Kimmien, Yao Ogang, Yu Mien). 350,000 in Viet Nam (1999 H. Purnell). Bac Giang, Bac Kan, Cao Bang, Ha Giang, Hoa Binh, Lai Chau, Lang Son, Lao Cai, Phu Tho, Quang Ninh, Son La, Thai Nguyen, Thanh Hoa, Tuyen Quang, Vinh Phuc, and Yen Bai provinces, scattered settlements in northern regions; Dac Lak Province south. *Status:* 5 (Developing). *Dialects:* Cham, Dao Do, Dao Lan Tien, Dao Lo Gang, Deo Tien, Quan Chet, Quan Trang. *Lg Use:* Same language as in Thailand and Laos. Not all ethnic Yao speak Mien; many speak Chinese. Part of the Viet Nam population figure may be for Kim Mun [mji]. *Other:* Part of the Dao 751,067 (2009 census) official ethnic community along with Kim Mun. Daoist, traditional religion. See main entry on page 73. *Maps:* 411:36, 412:36, 413:36.

Jarai [jra] (Chor, Cho-Rai, Chrai, Djarai, Gia-Rai, Gio-Rai, Jorai, Mthur). 242,000 in Viet Nam (Bradley 2007). Population total all countries: 262,800. Ethnic population: 411,000 (2009 census). Gai Lai, Binh Dinh, and Kon Tum provinces; some in Dac Lac Province. Also in Cambodia, United States. *Status:* 5 (Developing). *Class:* Austronesian, Malayo-Polynesian, Malayo-Chamic, Chamic, Highlands. *Dialects:* Aráp, Chuty, Golar, Habau (Ho-Bau), Hodrung (Hdrung), Jhue, Pleikly, Puan, Sesan, To-Buan. Cambodian dialects are all very similar, all displaying some significant differences with dialects in Vietnam. *Lg Use:* Also use Vietnamese [vie]. *Lg Dev:* Literacy rate in L1: 10%–30%. Literacy rate in L2: 50%–75%. Radio programs. NT: 1974. *Writing:* Latin script, used in Viet Nam and United States. *Other:* Gia Rai is an official ethnic community. Traditional religion, Christian. *Map:* 414:37.

Jeh [jeh] (Die, Gie, Yeh). 15,200 in Viet Nam (2002 SIL). Population total all countries: 25,800. Kon Tum and Quang Nam provinces. Also in Laos. *Status:* 5 (Developing). *Class:* Austro-Asiatic, Mon-Khmer, Eastern Mon-Khmer, Bahnaric, North Bahnaric, West, Jeh-Halang. *Dialects:* Jeh Bri La (Bri-La), Jeh Mang Ram. Related to Halang [hal]. *Lg Use:* Also use Vietnamese [vie]. *Lg Dev:* Literacy rate in L1: 1%–5%. Literacy rate in L2: 15%–25%. Radio programs. Dictionary. NT: 2012. *Writing:* Lao script. Latin script. *Other:* Part of the Gié Triêng offical ethnic community (50,962, 2009 census) which includes Triêng [stg]. *Map:* 414:38.

Katu, Eastern [ktv] (High Katu). 50,500 (1999 census). Quang Nam, Thua Thien-Hue, and Da Nang provinces. *Status:* 6a (Vigorous). *Class:* Austro-Asiatic, Mon-Khmer, Eastern Mon-Khmer, Katuic, East Katuic, Katu-Pacoh. *Dialects:* None known. Western Katu [kuf] is a different language with a different orthography in Laos. *Lg Use:* Also use Vietnamese [vie]. *Lg Dev:* Literacy rate in L1: Below 1%. Literacy rate in L2: 5%–15%. Radio programs. Dictionary. NT: 1978–2007. *Writing:* Latin script. *Other:* Part of the Co Tu official ethnic community (61,588, 2009 census) which includes Phuong [phg]. Traditional religion, Christian. *Map:* 414:18.

Katua [kta] (Ca Tua). 4,000 (Bradley 2007). Kon Tum Province, Mang Buk area, west of Kayong [kxy] language area. *Status:* 6a (Vigorous). *Class:* Austro-Asiatic, Mon-Khmer, Eastern Mon-Khmer, Bahnaric, North Bahnaric. *Other:* Part of the Xo Dang official ethnic community (165,501, 2009 census). *Map:* 414:39.

Kayong [kxy] (Ca Giong, Kagiuong, Katang). 25,000 (Bradley 2007). Kon Tum Province, remote mountains; also Quang Ngai Province. *Status:* 6a (Vigorous). *Class:* Austro-Asiatic, Mon-Khmer, Eastern Mon-Khmer, Bahnaric, North Bahnaric, East, Cua-Kayong. *Dialects:* None known. Reportedly similar to Takua [tkz] and Cua [cua]. *Other:* Part of the Xo Dang official ethnic community (165,501, 2009 census). *Map:* 414:40.

Kháng [kjm] (Bren, Hang, Khaang, Ksakautenh, Pouteng, Putenh, Quang Lam, Tay Hay, Tayhay, Teng, Theng, Xa, Xa Ai, Xa Bung, Xa Dang, Xa Don, Xa Hoc, Xá Khao, Xa Xua). 13,800 (2009 census). North, Son La, Dien Bien, Lai Chau, and Lao Cai provinces. *Status:* 8a (Moribund). *Class:* Austro-Asiatic, Mon-Khmer, Northern

Mon-Khmer, Khmuic, Xinh Mul. *Dialects:* Kháng Ai (Sakau, Xa Cau, Xa Khao), Kháng Clau. Related to Puoc [puo] and Phong-Kniang [pnx] in Laos. *Other:* Kháng is an official ethnic community. Traditional religion. *Map:* 411:41.

Khao [xao]. 10,000 (Wurm and Hattori 1981). Northwest; Son La and Dien Bien provinces, near ra River, north of Pa Ma. *Status:* 6a (Vigorous). *Class:* Austro-Asiatic, Mon-Khmer, Northern Mon-Khmer, Khmuic, Khao. *Dialects:* None known. Related to Bit [bgk] in Laos and China. *Other:* Part of the Xinh Mun official ethnic community (23,278, 2009 census). *Map:* 411:42.

Khmer, Central [khm] (Cambodian, Cu Tho, Cur Cul, Khmer Nam Bo, Kho Me, Khome, Krom, "Viet Goc Mien" *pej.*). 1,060,000 in Viet Nam (1999 census). Ethnic population: 1,260,000 (2009 survey). Hau Giang, Tra Vinh, Vinh Long, Kien Giang, An Giang, Bac Lieu, Ca Mau, Bin Duong, Can Tho, Dong Thap, Long An, Soc Trang, Bin Phuoc, and Tay Ninh provinces; Ho Chi Minh City. *Status:* 5 (Dispersed). *Dialects:* Central Khmer, Southern Khmer. *Other:* Kho Me is an official ethnic community. Buddhist, Christian. See main entry on page 61. *Map:* 414:9.

Khmu [kjg] (Cam Mu, Kha Cau, Khamu, Kho Mu, Khomu, Kmhmu, Mun Xen, Xa Cau). 56,500 in Viet Nam (1999 census). Ethnic population: 72,900 (2009 census). Dien Bien, Son La, Lai Chau, Thanh Hoa, Nghe An, and Yen Bai provinces. *Status:* 6b (Threatened). *Other:* Kho Mú is an official ethnic community. Traditional religion, Christian. See main entry on page 215. *Maps:* 411:43, 412:43, 413:43.

Khua [xhv]. 3,000 in Viet Nam (Wurm and Hattori 1981). Population total all countries: 5,000. West central; Quang Binh Province, southeast of Giap Tam. Also in Laos. *Status:* 6a (Vigorous). *Class:* Austro-Asiatic, Mon-Khmer, Eastern Mon-Khmer, Katuic, West Katuic, Brou-So. *Other:* Part of the Bru Vân Kieu official ethnic community (74,506, 2009 census). Distinct from Cua [cua]. *Map:* 414:44.

Kim Mun [mji] (Coc Mun, Dao Ao Dai, Dao Lam Dinh, Dao Quan Trang, Dao Thanh Y, Great Tunic Yao, Jinmen, Lan Ten, Lanten, Lantin, Lowland Yao, "Man Lan-Tien" *pej.*, Mun, Red Trouser Yao). 170,000 in Viet Nam (1999 J. Edmondson). Northeast region, Tuyen Quang, Bac Giang, Ha Giang, Lao Cai, Quang Ninh, Yen Bai provinces. *Status:* 6a (Vigorous). *Other:* Part of Dao official ethnic community (751,067, 2009 census). Lao Cai variety northwest of Lao City and Ha Giang at Na Khe village are very different phonetically. See main entry on page 75. *Maps:* 411:45, 412:45.

Koho [kpm] (Caho, Co Ho, Coho, Kohor). 166,000 in Viet Nam (2009 census). Lam Dong, Binh Thuan, Ninh Thuan, Dac Nong, and Dong Nai provinces. Also in United States. *Status:* 5 (Developing). *Class:* Austro-Asiatic, Mon-Khmer, Eastern Mon-Khmer, Bahnaric, South Bahnaric, Sre-Mnong, Sre. *Dialects:* Chil (Kil), Kalop, Kodu (Co-Don), Lac (Lach, Lat), Laya, Nop (Tu-Lop, Xre Nop), Pru, Rion, Sop, Sre, Tala (To La), Tring (Trinh). *Lg Use:* Also use Vietnamese [vie]. *Lg Dev:* Literacy rate in L1: 10%–30%. Literacy rate in L2: 50%–75%. Radio programs. Bible: 2010. *Writing:* Latin script. *Other:* Co Ho is an official ethnic community. Christian, traditional religion. *Map:* 414:46.

Kucong [lkc] (Cosung, Lahlu). 6,870 in Viet Nam (2007). Population total all countries: 46,870. Lai Chau Province, Muang Te district. Also in China. *Status:* 7 (Shifting). *Class:* Sino-Tibetan, Tibeto-Burman, Ngwi-Burmese, Ngwi, Central. *Dialects:* None known. Reportedly most similar to Lahu [lhu]. *Other:* Part of the La Hu official ethnic community (9,651, 2009 census). *Map:* 411:47.

Lachi [lbt] (Cù Te, Cu-Tê, La Chi, Lachí, Laji, Lati, Lipulio, Mia, Tai Lati, Y, Y Pí, Y Póng, Y To). 5,000 in Viet Nam (Bradley 2007). 3,990 women, in 1,450 households (Liang Min 1990), including Black Lachi 2,500 in 550 households, Long-Haired Lachi 4,500 in 900 households. 10,800 for all La Chi in Viet Nam (1999 census). Population total all countries: 5,200. Ethnic population: 7,860 (Bradley 2007). Ha Giang Province, west of Ha Giang in upper Clear River Valley (Riviere Claire) on China border. Black Lachi in Manyou, Long-Haired Lachi in Manpeng. Also in China. *Status:* 6b (Threatened). *Class:* Tai-Kadai, Kra, Western Kra. *Dialects:* Lipupi (Long-Haired Lachi), Liputiõ (Black Lachi). Related to Gelao. Lexical similarity: Long-Haired Lachi of Viet Nam: 80% with Flowery Lachi [lbt] of China, White Lachi [lwh] of Viet Nam: 30%–40% with the others, and should be considered a separate language, 36% with Gelao, 33% with Qabiao [laq], 22% with Dong [doc], 23% with Laka, 25% with Hlai [lic]. *Lg Use:* Continue to use the language. Also use Zhuang, Miao, Chinese varieties. *Other:* Part of the La Chí official ethnic community (13,158, 2009 census) which includes White Lachi [lwh]. 'Red', 'Flowery', refer to clothing color or other features of physical appearance. Traditional religion. *Map:* 412:48.

Lachi, White [lwh] (Lipupõ, White Lachi). 1,600 (Liang Min 1990). 300 households. North, south of Maguan in China, Ha Giang Province, Manbang and Manmei. *Status:* 7 (Shifting). *Class:* Tai-Kadai, Kra, Western Kra. *Dialects:* None known. Lexical similarity: 30%–40% with other Lachi. *Type:* Tonal. *Other:* Part of the La Chí official ethnic community (13,158, 2009 census) which includes White Lachi [lwh]. *Map:* 412:100.

Laghuu [lgh] (Laopa, Xá Phó). 300 (2002 J. Edmondson). Northwest; Lao Cai Province, Sa Pa district, Nam Sa village; 15 km south and east of Sa Pa City, in the valley below the highest mountain in Viet Nam, Phan Si Pan (3,198 m); small enclave in Son La Province. *Status:* 6b (Threatened). *Class:* Sino-Tibetan, Tibeto-Burman, Ngwi-Burmese, Ngwi, Southeastern. *Dialects:* None known. Unknown relationship to Laopang [lbg] (Laopa) of Myanmar, also in the Lolo group. *Maps:* 411:49, 412:49.

Laha [lha] (Khlá, Khlá Don, Khlá Dung, Khlá Phlao, Klá Dong, La Ha, La Ha Ung, Liik, Xá Chien, Xá Khao, Xá Lay). 5,690 (1999 census). Ethnic population: 8,180 (2009 census). Lai Chau and Son La provinces, along Red and Black rivers. *Status:* 6b (Threatened). *Class:* Tai-Kadai, Kra, Eastern Kra. *Dialects:* None known. Reportedly similar to Qabiao [laq]. *Lg Use:* In one village in Son La Province it is moribund, spoken only by those over 50; while in several villages in Lao Cai it is still spoken but potentially endangered (Bradley 2007). Mainly older adults. Those under 50 speak Thai [tha] and dress like the Tai Dam. *Other:* La Ha is an official community who live together with the Thai and Kháng. Traditional religion. *Maps:* 411:50, 412:50.

Lahu [lhu] (Kaixien, Lahuna, Laku, Launa, Lohei, Mooso, Muhso, Mussar, Musso, Mussuh, Namen). 9,650 in Viet Nam (2009 census). Northwest border with Laos, Lai Chau Province; Black Lahu north of Muong Te City near China border, at Ban Kiem Tra, Phu Nam Ma, Phu Nam Cau, and Phu Nam Ha; White Lahu in Muong Te, east of Nha Ca, 1 village. *Status:* 6b (Threatened). *Dialects:* Lahu Phung (White Lahu), Na (Black Lahu, Khucong, Musser Dam), Nyi (Musseh Daeng, Red Lahu), Shehleh. *Other:* La Hu is an official ethnic community. Distinct from Lahu Shi (Yellow Lahu) [lhi]. One source called them White Lahu. It is not clear if these are the same as Red Lahu, Black Lahu. Traditional religion. See main entry on page 76. *Map:* 411:51.

Lao [lao]. 10,000 in Viet Nam (Bradley 2007). Ethnic population: 14,900 (2009 census). *Status:* 5 (Dispersed). See main entry on page 215.

Lü [khb] (Duon, Lue, Nhuon, Pai-I, Shui-Pai-I, Tai Lu).

4,960 in Viet Nam (1999 census). Ethnic population: 5,600 (2009 census). North, Lai Chau Province, Tam Duong district, Ban Hon and Binh Lu communes. *Status:* 6b (Threatened). *Other:* Lu is an official ethnic community. Traditional religion, Buddhist. See main entry on page 78. *Map:* 411:52.

Maa [cma] (Chauma, Che Ma, Ma, Ma Krung, Ma Ngan, Ma To, Ma Xop, Maaq). 33,300 (1999 census). Ethnic population: 41,400 (2009 census). Lam Dong, Dong Nai, and Bin Phuoc provinces, widely scattered; possibly some in Dac Nong Province. *Status:* 6a (Vigorous). *Class:* Austro-Asiatic, Mon-Khmer, Eastern Mon-Khmer, Bahnaric, South Bahnaric, Sre-Mnong, Sre. *Dialects:* Sometimes considered a Koho [kpm] dialect. *Lg Use:* Also use Vietnamese [vie]. *Lg Dev:* Literacy rate in L1: 10%–30%. Literacy rate in L2: 50%–75%. *Other:* An official ethnic community. Traditional religion, Christian. *Map:* 414:53.

Maleng [pkt] (Malang, Malieng). 200 in Viet Nam (Ferlus 1996). Ha Tinh Province, Huong Khe district, Huong Lien commune; 2 or 3 villages bordering Laos, another southeast. Malieng dialect: Tuyen Hoa district, Thanh Hoa and Lam Hoa communes; Dan Hoa dialect: north Quang Binh Province, Minh Hoa district. *Status:* 6b (Threatened). *Dialects:* Dan Hoa, Kha Phong (Kha Nam Om, Maleng Bro, Maleng Kari), Malieng (Pa Leng). See main entry on page 216. *Map:* 414:54.

Mang [zng] (Ba'e, Chaman, Lá Vàng, Manbu, Mang U, Nieng Ó, Xá, Xá Mang, Xá Ó). 2,660 in Viet Nam (1999 census). Population total all countries: 3,165. Ethnic population: 3,700 (2009 census). Lai Chau Province, Muong Te and Sin Ho districts, triangle-shaped area between Song Da (Black River) and the Nam Na: Nam Nghe, Nam Xung, Nam Ban, Ban Nam Voi, and others. Also in China, Thailand. *Status:* 6b (Threatened). *Class:* Austro-Asiatic, Mon-Khmer, Northern Mon-Khmer, Mang. *Other:* M ang is an official ethnic community. Traditional religion. *Map:* 411:55.

Mantsi [nty] (Black Lolo, Flowery Lolo, Lolo, Red Mantsi). 1,100 (2002 J. Edmondson). Ha Giang Province, Meo Vac and Dong Van districts; also Cao Bang Province. *Status:* 6a (Vigorous). *Class:* Sino-Tibetan, Tibeto-Burman, Ngwi-Burmese, Ngwi, Southeastern. *Dialects:* None known. Called Southeast Vernacular, type of Yi. May be related to what is called Southeastern Yi or Guizhou Yi [yig] in China. Not intelligible with Sichuan Yi [iii] (Nosu). *Type:* Many uvular consonants, tense-lax voice quality; tonal, 5 tones. *Writing:* Yi script. *Other:* Part of the Lô Lô official ethnic community (4,541, 2009 census). *Map:* 412:56.

Mnong, Central [cmo] (Budang, Budong, Bunong, Phanong, Pnong). 32,500 in Viet Nam (2002 SIL). Population total all countries: 70,000. Mainly Dac Nong, west Dac Lak, and Bin Phuoc provinces, southwest of the Rade. Also in Cambodia. *Status:* 5 (Developing). *Class:* Austro-Asiatic, Mon-Khmer, Eastern Mon-Khmer, Bahnaric, South Bahnaric, Sre-Mnong, Mnong, Southern-Central Mnong. *Dialects:* Biat (Bhiét), Bu Dang, Bu Nar, Bu Rung, Dih Bri (Di-Pri), Préh (Pre). Biat dialect may be a separate language related to Eastern Mnong [mng]. *Lg Dev:* Radio programs. Bible: 2005. *Writing:* Khmer script. Latin script. *Other:* Part of the Mnông official ethnic community (102,741, 2009 census) which includes Eastern Mnong [mng] and Southern Mnong [mnn]. Traditional religion, Christian. *Map:* 414:10.

Mnong, Eastern [mng]. 30,000 in Viet Nam (2002 SIL). Dac Lak, Dac Nong, and Lam Dong provinces, southeast of the Rade. Also in United States. *Status:* 6a (Vigorous). *Class:* Austro-Asiatic, Mon-Khmer, Eastern Mon-Khmer, Bahnaric, South Bahnaric, Sre-Mnong, Mnong, Eastern Mnong. *Dialects:* Chil, Mnong Gar (Gar), Mnong Kwanh, Mnong Rolom (Ralam, Rlam, Rolam, Rolom). Biat dialect of Central Mnong [cmo] may be more similar to Eastern Mnong. *Lg Dev:* Bible portions: 1977. *Writing:* Latin script. *Other:* Part of the Mnông official ethnic community (102,741, 2009 census) which includes Central Mnong [cmo] and Southern Mnong [mnn]. *Map:* 414:19.

Mnong, Southern [mnn]. 30,000 (2002). Mostly Dac Nong and Bin Phuoc provinces, south of Central Mnong [cmo], north of Stieng [stt] language areas; some in Lam Dong Province. *Status:* 6a (Vigorous). *Class:* Austro-Asiatic, Mon-Khmer, Eastern Mon-Khmer, Bahnaric, South Bahnaric, Sre-Mnong, Mnong, Southern-Central Mnong. *Writing:* Khmer script. *Other:* Part of the Mnông official ethnic community (102,741, 2009 census). Ra-Ong, Bu Sre, Bu Dip, and Kuenh are possibly subgroups. *Map:* 414:78.

Monom [moo] (Bonom, Menam, Monam). 6,000 (Bradley 2007). East Gia Lai and Kon Tum provinces. *Status:* 6a (Vigorous). *Class:* Austro-Asiatic, Mon-Khmer, Eastern Mon-Khmer, Bahnaric, North Bahnaric, West, Sedang-Todrah, Todrah-Monom. *Other:* Part of the Xo Dang official ethnic community (165,501, 2009 census). *Map:* 414:57.

Muong [mtq]. 1,140,000 (1999 census). Ethnic population: 1,270,000 (2009 census). Mostly north central mountains, Hoa Binh, Thanh Hoa, Phu Tho, Ha Noi, Yen Bai, Son La, and Ninh Binh provinces. *Status:* 6a (Vigorous). *Class:* Austro-Asiatic, Mon-Khmer, Viet-Muong, Muong. *Dialects:* Ao Tá (Au Tá), Boi Bi (Moi Bi), Moi 1, Mol, Mual, Thang, Wang. Related to Chut [scb], May [scb], Ruc [scb], Arem [aem], and Aheu [thm]. *Lg Use:* Also use Vietnamese [vie]. *Lg Dev:* Literacy rate in L1: 1%–5%. Literacy rate in L2: 50%–70%. Radio programs. Dictionary. Bible portions: 1963. *Writing:* Latin script. *Other:* Muong is an official ethnic community. Traditional religion, Christian. *Maps:* 412:58, 413:58.

Ná-Meo [neo]. 1,200 (2002). Northwest Lang Son Province, Trang Dinh district, Cao Minh and Khuoi Phu Dao villages, Khanh Long hamlet; Cao Bang Province, Thach An district, Ca Liec village. *Status:* 6a (Vigorous). *Class:* Unclassified. *Other:* Possible immigrants from Guangxi Province in China. *Map:* 412:59.

Nguôn [nuo] (Ngouan). 1,000 (1995 census). Ethnic population: 2,000 (Bradley 2007). Western Quang Binh Province, 11 villages: Kwi-dat, An Duk, Ba nuong, Than long, Tan kieu; Ko liem, Bok tho (An tho), Kim bang, Tan li, and An lak. *Status:* 6b (Threatened). *Class:* Austro-Asiatic, Mon-Khmer, Viet-Muong, Muong. *Dialects:* None known. Diffloth (1992) groups Nguôn as a separate language similar to Vietnamese [vie], but Tran (1996) and Ferlus (1996) group it with Muong [mtq]. *Map:* 414:60.

Nung [nut] (Bu-Nong, Highland Nung, Nong, Tai Nung, Tay, Tày Nùng). 969,000 in Viet Nam (2009 census). Ethnic population: 969,000 (2009 census). North, mainly Cao Bang, Lang Son, Bac Kan, Tuyen Quang, Ha Giang, Lao Cai and Thai Nguyen provinces; possibly in Ho Chi Minh City and other sothern locations. Also in Canada, Laos, United States. *Status:* 5 (Developing). *Class:* Tai-Kadai, Kam-Tai, Tai, Central. *Dialects:* Giang, Khen Lài, Nùng An, Nùng Cháo, Nùng Inh, Nùng Lòi, Nùng Phan Slình (Nùng Fan Slihng), Nùng Qúy Rin (Guiren), Xuòng. Reportedly similar to Tày [tyz]. *Lg Use:* Ethnic group members preserved the language and culture more than the Tày. Also use Vietnamese [vie]. *Lg Dev:* Literacy rate in L1: 1%–5%. Literacy rate in L2: 50%–75%. Radio programs. Dictionary. Bible portions: 1971–1975. *Writing:* Latin script. *Other:* Different from Chinese Nung [yue] (Cantonese). Nùng is an official ethnic community. *Maps:* 411:62, 412:62.

O'du [tyh] (Haat, Hat, 'Iduh, O Du, "Tay Hat" *pej.*). 300 in

Viet Nam (1999 census). Population total all countries: 950. Ethnic population: 380 (2009 census). Nghe An Province, Tuong Duong district, Nga My commune. Also in Laos. *Status:* 7 (Shifting). *Class:* Austro-Asiatic, Mon-Khmer, Northern Mon-Khmer, Khmuic, Mal-Khmu', Khmu'. *Lg Use:* Middle-aged and older. *Other:* Official ethnic community. Call themselves O Du. Traditional religion. *Map:* 413:63.

Pa Di [pdi] (Padi). 300 in Viet Nam. Lao Cai Province, Muong Khuong district. *Status:* 6b (Threatened). See main entry on page 85. *Maps:* 411:64, 412:64.

Pacoh [pac] (Bo River Van Kieu, Paco, Pokoh). 16,000 in Viet Nam (2002). Population total all countries: 32,500. Quang Tri and Thua Thien-Hue provinces. Also in Laos. *Status:* 6b (Threatened). *Class:* Austro-Asiatic, Mon-Khmer, Eastern Mon-Khmer, Katuic, East Katuic, Katu-Pacoh. *Dialects:* Ka'do, Kanah, Pahi (Ba-Hi). *Lg Use:* Also use Vietnamese [vie]. *Lg Dev:* Literacy rate in L1: Below 1%. Literacy rate in L2: Less than 15%. Dictionary. Grammar. Bible portions: 1965–1969. *Writing:* Lao script. Latin script. *Other:* Part of the Tà Ôi official ethnic community (43,886, 2009 census). 'Koh' in Pacoh, mountain. *Map:* 414:66.

Pa-Hng [pha] (Baheng, Bahengmai, Pa Hng, Pà Hung, Pà Then, Paheng). 6,810 in Viet Nam (2009 census). Tuyen Quang and Ha Giang provinces. *Status:* 6b (Threatened). *Other:* Pà Then is an official ethnic community. Traditional religion. See main entry on page 85. *Map:* 412:65.

Phu Thai [pht] (Phutai, Putai, Puthai, Puthay). 209,000 in Viet Nam (2002). North central, Ha Tinh and Nghe An provinces; also in Laos. *Status:* 6a (Vigorous). *Other:* Part of Thái official ethnic community. See main entry on page 303. *Map:* 413:67.

Phula [phh] (Fu Khla, Phu Kha, Phu Khla, Phu La). 5,000 in Viet Nam (Pelkey 2008). Population total all countries: 10,000. Ethnic population: 11,000 (2009 census). Lao Cai Province, near Lao Cai City; Hà Giang Province, Xin Mun district, 1 village; Lai Chau and Son La provinces. Also in China (Phukha). *Status:* 6b (Threatened). *Class:* Sino-Tibetan, Tibeto-Burman, Ngwi-Burmese, Ngwi, Southeastern. *Type:* Tonal. *Lg Use:* Official minority nationality. Shifting to Vietnamese [vie]. *Other:* Phù Lá is an official ethnic community. *Maps:* 411:68, 412:68.

Phuong [phg] (Phuang, Phuong Catang). 15,100 (2000). Thua Thien-Hue Province, southeast of Pacoh [pac] language area; possibly some in areas further southeast. *Status:* 6a (Vigorous). *Class:* Austro-Asiatic, Mon-Khmer, Eastern Mon-Khmer, Katuic, East Katuic, Katu-Pacoh. *Other:* Part of Katu official ethnic community. *Map:* 414:69.

Puoc [puo] (Kha Puhoc, Ksing Mul, Mun, Pua, Puhoc, Puok, Sing, Xin Mul, Xinh Mul, Xinh-Mun). 18,000 in Viet Nam (1999 census). Population total all countries: 26,570. North, Lai Chau and Son La provinces, Laos border area. Also in Laos. *Status:* 6a (Vigorous). *Class:* Austro-Asiatic, Mon-Khmer, Northern Mon-Khmer, Khmuic, Xinh Mul. *Dialects:* None known. Related to Kháng [kjm] and Phong-Kniang [pnx]. *Other:* Part of the Xinh Mun official ethnic community (23,278, 2009 census).

Qabiao [laq] (Bendi Lolo, Ka Bao, Ka Biao, Laqua, Lolo, Pen Ti, Pu Péo, Pubiao, Pupeo). 690 in Viet Nam (2009 census). Population total all countries: 708. Ethnic population: Most of the ethnic group use the language (Bradley 2007). Ha Giang Province, Viet Nam-Yunnan-Kwangsi border, upper Clear river valley, Dunshi, Pugao, Pula, Pubang, and Manong; Yên Minh and Mèo Vac districts; Dông Van district, Phô Là and Sung Chang villages. Also in China. *Status:* 6b (Threatened). *Class:* Tai-Kadai, Kra, Eastern Kra. *Dialects:* None known. Lexical similarity: 38% with Gelao, 33% with Lachi [lbt], 30% with Northern Zhuang, 29% with Dong, 26% with Hlai [lic], 10% with Hmong, 7% with Iu Mien [ium]. *Other:* Pu Péo is an official ethnic community. Traditional religion. *Map:* 412:70.

Rade [rad] (De, E-De, Edeh, Raday, Rde, Rhade). 177,000 in Viet Nam (Bradley 2007). Ethnic population: 331,000 (2009 census). Dac Lak, Dac Nong, Phu Yen and Khanh Hoa provinces, Banmethuot area. Also in United States. *Status:* 5 (Developing). *Class:* Austronesian, Malayo-Polynesian, Malayo-Chamic, Chamic, Highlands. *Dialects:* Adham (A-Dham), Bih, Blo, Kodrao (Kdrao), Krung 1, Ndhur (Mdhur), Rde Kpa (Kpa). Bih (L1 pop. 1,000) may be a separate language. Krung 1 dialect is different from the Bahnaric language Kru'ng 2 [krr], in Cambodia. Other dialect or ethnic group names are: Ktul, Dlie, Rue, E-pan, Dong Kay, Arul, Kah. *Lg Use:* Also use Vietnamese [vie]. *Lg Dev:* Literacy rate in L1: 10%–30%. Literacy rate in L2: 50%–75%. Radio programs. Dictionary. NT: 1964. *Writing:* Latin script. *Other:* Ê Dê is an official ethnic community. Christian, traditional religion. *Map:* 414:71.

Rengao [ren] (Ro-Ngao). 18,000 (Bradley 2007). Kon Tum Province, northwest of Dak to southeast of Kontum city between Sedang and Bahnar. *Status:* 6b (Threatened). *Class:* Austro-Asiatic, Mon-Khmer, Eastern Mon-Khmer, Bahnaric, North Bahnaric, West, Rengao. *Dialects:* Bahnar-Rengao, Sedang-Rengao, Western Rengao. *Lg Use:* Also use Vietnamese [vie]. *Lg Dev:* Literacy rate in L1: 5%–10%. Literacy rate in L2: 25%–50%. Dictionary. Grammar. Bible portions: 1977. *Writing:* Latin script. *Other:* Part of the Ba Na official ethnic community (227,716, 2009 census). *Map:* 414:73.

Roglai, Cacgia [roc] (Ra-Glai). 3,000 (2002). Ninh Thuan Province, northeast of Phan Rang on the coast. *Status:* 6a (Vigorous). *Class:* Austronesian, Malayo-Polynesian, Malayo-Chamic, Chamic, Highlands, Chru-Northern, Northern Cham. *Dialects:* None known. Considerably different from other Roglai varieties. *Map:* 414:7.

Roglai, Northern [rog] (Adlai, La-Oang, Noang, Radlai, Ra-Glai, Rang Glai, Rayglay). 52,900 (2002). Ninh Thuan, Dac Lak, Binh Thuan, Khanh Hoa, and Lam Dong provinces, in the mountains west and south of Nhatrang; some near Dalat. *Status:* 5 (Developing). *Class:* Austronesian, Malayo-Polynesian, Malayo-Chamic, Chamic, Highlands, Chru-Northern, Northern Cham. *Lg Use:* Potentially shifting to Vietnamese [vie] (Bradley 2007). Also use Vietnamese [vie]. *Lg Dev:* Literacy rate in L1: 5%–10%. Literacy rate in L2: 25%–50%. Radio programs. Dictionary. Bible portions: 1966–1973. *Writing:* Latin script. *Other:* Part of the Ra Glai official ethnic community (122,245, 2009 census). Traditional religion, Christian. *Map:* 414:61.

Roglai, Southern [rgs] (Rai). 41,000 (1999 census). South, Binh Thuan, Khanh Hoa, and Ninh Thuan provinces. *Status:* 6a (Vigorous). *Class:* Austronesian, Malayo-Polynesian, Malayo-Chamic, Chamic, Highlands, Chru-Northern, Northern Cham. *Dialect:* Rai. Reportedly similar to Chru [cje] and Northern Roglai [rog]. *Lg Use:* Potentially endangered by Vietnamese [vie] (Bradley 2007). *Other:* Part of the Ra Glai official ethnic community (122,245, 2009 census). Traditional religion. *Map:* 414:79.

Romam [rmx] (Ro Mam). 200 (2013 SIL). Ethnic population: 440 (2009 census). Kon Tum Province, Mo Rai commune, Le village. Near Viet Nam-Cambodia border. *Status:* 6a (Vigorous). *Class:* Austro-Asiatic, Mon-Khmer, Eastern Mon-Khmer, Bahnaric, Central Bahnaric. *Other:* Kaco' [xkk] is possibly the same or a closely related language in Cambodia. Ro Mam is an official ethnic community. Traditional religion. *Map:* 414:74.

Sedang [sed] (Cadong, Dang, Hadang, Hdang, Hotea, Hoteang, Kmrang, Rotea, Roteang, Tang, Xa, Xodang).

97,000 in Viet Nam (Bradley 2007). Population total all countries: 97,520. Kon Tum, Quang Nam, and Quang Ngai provinces. Also in Laos. *Status:* 6a (Vigorous). *Class:* Austro-Asiatic, Mon-Khmer, Eastern Mon-Khmer, Bahnaric, North Bahnaric, West, Sedang-Todrah, Sedang. *Dialects:* Central Sedang, Dak Sut Sedang, Greater Sedang, Kon Hring Sedang, Kotua Sedang. Reportedly most similar to Hre [hre]. *Lg Use:* Also use Vietnamese [vie]. *Lg Dev:* Literacy rate in L1: 5%–10%. Literacy rate in L2: 25%–50%. Radio programs. Dictionary. *Writing:* Latin script. *Other:* Part of the Xo Dang official ethnic community (169,501, 2009 census). Sakau or Xa Cau may be an alternate name. Traditional religion, Christian. *Map:* 414:75.

Sila [slt] (Sida). 710 in Viet Nam (2009 census). Most members of the ethnic group speak the language (Bradley 2007). Lai Chau Province, Muong Tè district, Kan Ho commune, Ban Xeo Hai village; Dien Bien Province, Muong Nhé district, Chung Chai commune. *Status:* 6b (Threatened). *Lg Use:* Negative attitudes. *Other:* Si La is an official ethnic community who say they came from Laos. Traditional religion. See main entry on page 217. *Map:* 411:76.

Sinicized Miao [hmz] (Hmong Shua). 2,000 in Viet Nam (Hattaway 2000). Ha Giang Province. 3 villages. *Status:* 6a (Vigorous). *Other:* Traditional religion. See main entry on page 88. *Map:* 412:77.

Stieng, Budeh [stt] (Lower Stieng, Southern Stieng). 40,000 (2009 census). Part of the Xtiêng 85,436 (2009 census) official ethnic community which includes Bulo Stieng [sti]. Bin Phuoc Province, south Stieng area. *Status:* 6a (Vigorous). *Class:* Austro-Asiatic, Mon-Khmer, Eastern Mon-Khmer, Bahnaric, South Bahnaric. *Dialects:* None known. Different enough from Bulo Stieng [sti] that intelligibility is not functional. *Writing:* Latin script. *Other:* Part of the Xtiêng official ethnic community (85,436, 2009 census) which includes Bulo Stieng [sti]. *Map:* 414:5.

Stieng, Bulo [sti] (Budíp, Northern Stieng, Rangah, Upper Stieng, Xa-Dieng, Xtieng). 45,000 in Viet Nam (2009 census). Part of the Xtiêng 85,436 (2009 census) official ethnic community which includes Budeh Stieng [stt]. Population total all countries: 51,540. Bin Phuoc and Dac Nong provinces. Also in Cambodia. *Status:* 6a (Vigorous). *Class:* Austro-Asiatic, Mon-Khmer, Eastern Mon-Khmer, Bahnaric, South Bahnaric, Stieng-Chrau. *Lg Use:* Also use Vietnamese [vie]. *Lg Dev:* Literacy rate in L1: Below 1%. Literacy rate in L2: 15%–25%. Radio programs. Dictionary. Bible portions: 1971. *Writing:* Latin script. *Other:* Part of the Xtiêng official ethnic community (85,436, 2009 census) which includes Budeh Stieng [stt]. Christian, traditional religion. *Map:* 414:6.

Sui [swi]. 120 in Viet Nam (2002 J. Edmondson). Tuyen Quang Provimce, Chiem Hoa district. *Status:* 6a (Vigorous). *Other:* Lived in Viet Nam more than 150 years. See main entry on page 89. *Map:* 412:80.

Tai Daeng [tyr] (Daeng, Môc-Châu, Red Tai, Tai Deng, Tai Rouge, Táy-Môc-Châu, Thai Dang, Thai Do). 80,000 in Viet Nam (1995 census). Population total all countries: 105,000. Ethnic population: 100,000 (Bradley 2007). North central, Son La and Hoa Binh provinces; also in Thanh Hoa Province, south of Sam Nuea; small area in Yen Bai province. Also in Laos, Thailand, United States. *Status:* 6a (Vigorous). *Class:* Tai-Kadai, Kam-Tai, Tai, Southwestern. *Writing:* Tai Viet script. *Other:* Part of the Thái official ethnic community (1,550,423, 2009 census). Speakers in Viet Nam tend to identify with Tai Dam [blt] and deny they are Red Tai. *Maps:* 411:81, 412:81, 413:81.

Tai Dam [blt] (Black Tai, Tai Do, Tai Noir, Táy-Dam, Thái Den). 699,000 in Viet Nam (2002 SIL). Population total all countries: 763,754. North, along Red and Black rivers, Son La, Dien Bien, Yen Bai, Lai Chau, Lao Cai, and Phu Tho provinces; south, Lam Dong Province, Tung Nghia; Dac Lak Province, Tho Thanh; Gia Lai Province, Pleiku; elsewhere. Also in Australia, China, France, Laos, Thailand, United States. *Status:* 5 (Developing). *Class:* Tai-Kadai, Kam-Tai, Tai, Southwestern. *Dialect:* Táy Mu'ò'i (Meuay, Tai Mueai). Reportedly similar to Thai Song [soa] and Tai Dón [twh], but not inherently intelligible of Tai Dón. *Lg Use:* Also use Vietnamese [vie]. Used as L2 by Tai Dón [twh]. *Lg Dev:* Literacy rate in L1: 1%–5%. Literacy rate in L2: 50%–75%. Radio programs. Dictionary. NT: 2013. *Writing:* Lao script. Latin script. Tai Viet script. *Other:* Part of Thái official ethnic community (1,550,423, 2009 census), which also includes Tai Dón [twh] and Tai Daeng [tyr]. Officially included under Dai in China. Traditional religion. *Maps:* 411:82, 412:82.

Tai Do [tyj] (Tay Muoi, Tay Quy Chau, Tay Yo, Tay-Jo). 300 (2002). North, Nghe An Province. *Status:* 6a (Vigorous). *Class:* Tai-Kadai, Kam-Tai, Tai. *Writing:* Latin script. Tai Yo script, no longer in use. *Map:* 413:83.

Tai Dón [twh] (Tai Blanc, Tai Kao, Tai Lai, Táy Khao, Thái Tráng, White Tai). 280,000 in Viet Nam (2002). Population total all countries: 495,000. North, mainly along Red and Black rivers, Lai Chau, Dien Bien, Lao Cai, and Son La provinces; some in the south, Lam Dòng Province, Tung Nghia. Also in China, France, Laos. *Status:* 6a (Vigorous). *Class:* Tai-Kadai, Kam-Tai, Tai, Southwestern. *Dialects:* None known. Not intelligible of Tai Dam [blt]. Lao [lao] influenced the speech of some Tai Dón. *Lg Use:* Positive attitudes. Those with prolonged contact with Tai Dam [blt] have become bilingual in it. Many have not had that contact. *Lg Dev:* Dictionary. Bible portions: 1969–1992. *Writing:* Latin script. Tai Viet script. *Other:* Part of the Thái official ethnic community (1,550,423, 2009 census). Traditional religion, Buddhist. *Maps:* 411:84, 412:84.

Tai Hang Tong [thc] (Hàng Tong, Tày Muòng). 10,000 (2002). North, Nghe An Province. *Status:* 6a (Vigorous). *Class:* Tai-Kadai, Kam-Tai, Tai, Southwestern. *Other:* Part of Thái official ethnic community. *Map:* 413:85.

Tai Nüa [tdd]. 70,000 in Viet Nam (Bradley 2007). Ethnic population: 95,000 (Bradley 2007). Northwest, Son La Province, Laos border area. *Status:* 6b (Threatened). See main entry on page 89.

Tai Thanh [tmm] (Tai Man Thanh, Táy Thanh, Thanh). 20,000 (2002). North, Thanh Hoa and Nghe An provinces. *Status:* 6a (Vigorous). *Class:* Tai-Kadai, Kam-Tai, Tai, Southwestern. *Other:* Part of Thái official ethnic community. *Map:* 413:86.

Takua [tkz] (Langya, Quang Tin Katu). 6,000 (Bradley 2007). Quang Nam and Quang Ngai provinces. *Status:* 6a (Vigorous). *Class:* Austro-Asiatic, Mon-Khmer, Eastern Mon-Khmer, Bahnaric, North Bahnaric, East, Takua. *Dialects:* None known. Reportedly most similar to Cua [cua] and Kayong [kxy]. *Other:* Other Part of the Co official ethnic community (33,817, 2009 census) which includes Cua [cua]. *Map:* 414:87.

Ta'oih, Upper [tth] (Kantua, Ta Hoi, Tà-Oi, Tau Oi, Toi-Oi, T-Oy). 19,000 in Viet Nam (2002). 13,300 monolinguals. Thua Thien-Hue and Quang Tri provinces. *Status:* 6a (Vigorous). *Dialects:* Ha'aang (Sa'ang), Kamuan', Leem, Palee'n, Pasoom. *Lg Use:* Also use Vietnamese [vie]. *Lg Dev:* Literacy rate in L1: Below 1%. Literacy rate in L2: 5%–15%. *Other:* Tà Ôi is an official ethnic community (43,886, 2009 census). Traditional religion, Christian. See main entry on page 217. *Map:* 414:96.

Tày [tyz] (Ngan, Phen, Tai Tho, "Thô" *pej.*, Thu Lao, T'o). 1,630,000 in Viet Nam (2009 census). Central and northeast, near China border, Cao Bang, Lang Son, Bac Giang, Bac Kan, Thai Nguyen, Ha Giang, Tuyen Quang,

Yen Bai, and Hai Duong provinces, Bac Thai, Quang Ninh, Ha Bac; south in Lam Dong Province,Tung Nghia and Song Mao. Possibly in Laos. Also in France, United States. *Status:* 6b (Threatened). *Class:* Tai-Kadai, Kam-Tai, Tai, Central. *Dialects:* Central Tày, Eastern Tày, Northern Tày, Southern Tày, Tày Bao Lac, Tày Trung Khanh, Thu Lao. Reportedly similar to Nung [nut]. *Lg Use:* Also use Vietnamese [vie]. Used as L2 by Green Gelao [giq]. *Lg Dev:* Literacy rate in L1: 1%–5%. Literacy rate in L2: 50%–75%. Radio programs. Dictionary. Bible portions: 1938–1963. *Writing:* Latin script. *Other:* Tày is an official ethnic community. Traditional religion, Christian. *Maps:* 411:88, 412:88.

Tay Boi [tas] (Annamite French, Tay Boy, Vietnamese Pidgin French). No known L1 speakers. *Status:* 10 (Extinct). *Class:* Pidgin, French based. *Lg Use:* Developed about 1862. Influences from Vietnamese [vie], French [fra], English [eng], Javanese [jav], and Portuguese [por]. Used between French and Vietnamese until 1954, and lower levels of administration, the military, and police. No longer spoken (Wurm and Hattori 1981).

Tày Sa Pa [tys] (Tai Sa Pa). 300 (2002 J. Edmondson). Lao Cai Province, Muong Khuong district. *Status:* 6a (Vigorous). *Class:* Tai-Kadai, Kam-Tai, Tai, Southwestern. *Type:* Tonal. *Map:* 411:89.

Tày Tac [tyt]. Northwest, east Son La Province, Muong Tâc district. *Status:* 6a (Vigorous). *Class:* Tai-Kadai, Kam-Tai, Tai, Southwestern. *Type:* CN(C) in which N=V + tone, 22 consonants, 13 vowels, tonal, 6 tones on open syllables and those ending with a continuant, 3 tones on syllables ending with a stop. *Writing:* Latin script. Tai Viet script. *Other:* Part of the Thái official ethnic community. Women's blouses similar to that worn by White Tai women of Lai Châu, but without silver buttons. *Maps:* 411:90, 412:90.

Tho [tou] (Cuoi, Cuoi Cham, Ho Muong Meridional, Keo). 68,400 (1999 census). Ethnic population: 75,000 (2009 census). North Nghe An Province, highland areas, Cuoi Cham dialect in Tan Ky district, Tan Hop commune; also in Thanh Hoa Province. *Status:* 6a (Vigorous). *Class:* Austro-Asiatic, Mon-Khmer, Viet-Muong, Cuoi. *Dialects:* Cuoi Cham (Uy Lo), Mon. *Lg Dev:* Dictionary. *Writing:* Unwritten. *Other:* Tho is an official ethnic community. Associated culturally with other principal local ethnonyms Keo, Mon, Cuoi, Ho, Dan, Lai-Ly Ha, and Tay Poong. *Map:* 413:91.

Thu Lao [tyl]. 200 (2002 J. Edmondson). Near China border, Lao Cai Province; possibly in Laos. *Status:* 6b (Threatened). *Class:* Tai-Kadai, Kam-Tai, Tai, Southwestern. *Other:* Traditional religion, Christian. *Maps:* 411:92, 412:92.

Todrah [tdr] (Didra, Didrah, Kodra, Modra, Podra, Todrá). 6,000 (Bradley 2007). Kon Tum Province, northeast of Kon Tum city, Kon Hring to Kon Braih. *Status:* 6a (Vigorous). *Class:* Austro-Asiatic, Mon-Khmer, Eastern Mon-Khmer, Bahnaric, North Bahnaric, West, Sedang-Todrah, Todrah-Monom. *Other:* Part of the Xo Dang official ethnic community. Didra may be a separate language. *Map:* 414:93.

Trieng [stg] (Dgiéh, Giang Ray, Gie-Trieng, Pin, Strieng, Talieng, Tareh, Ta-Rieng, Treng). 15,000 (2002). Mainly Kon Tum and Quang Nam provinces. *Status:* 6a (Vigorous). *Class:* Austro-Asiatic, Mon-Khmer, Eastern Mon-Khmer, Bahnaric, North Bahnaric, West. *Dialects:* None known. May be related to Jeh [jeh] or Talieng [tdf] in Laos. May be the same language as Talieng. *Lg Dev:* Radio programs. *Other:* Part of the Gié Triêng official ethnic community (50,962, 2009 census). Traditional religion, Christian. *Map:* 414:94.

Ts'ün-Lao [tsl] (Lao). 10,000 (1993 D. Van). Northwest, scattered, Lai Chau, Dien Bien, and Son La provinces. *Status:* 6a (Vigorous). *Class:* Tai-Kadai, Kam-Tai, Tai, Central. *Other:* Lao is an official ethnic community (14,928, 2009 census), with associated names Lào Bóc and Lào Noi. Traditional religion. *Maps:* 411:95, 412:95.

Vietnamese [vie] (Annamese, Ching, Gin, Jing, Kinh, Viet). 65,800,000 in Viet Nam (1999 census). Population total all countries: 67,778,030. Ethnic population: 73,600,000 (2009 census). Widespread. Also in Australia, Cambodia, Canada, China, Taiwan, Côte d'Ivoire, Czech Republic, Denmark, Finland, France, Germany, Hungary, Laos, Martinique, Netherlands, New Caledonia, Norway, Philippines, Russian Federation, Senegal, Thailand, United Kingdom, United States, Vanuatu. *Status:* 1 (National). De facto national language. *Class:* Austro-Asiatic, Mon-Khmer, Viet-Muong, Vietnamese. *Dialects:* Central Vietnamese (Hue), Northern Vietnamese (Hanoi, Tonkinese), Southern Vietnamese. Numerous dialects. *Type:* SVO; prepositions; classifiers and numerals precede noun heads; possessor noun phrases and adjectives follow noun heads. *Lg Use:* Also use Vietnamese [vie]. *Lg Dev:* Literacy rate in L1: 94%. Literacy rate in L2: 80%. Fully developed. Bible: 1916–1994. *Writing:* Braille script. Han (Hanzi, Kanji, Hanja) script. Latin script, primary usage. *Other:* Kinh is an official ethnic community. Buddhist, Christian. *Maps:* 411:97, 412:97, 413:97, 414:97.

Zhuang, Dai [zhd] (Thu Lao, Tu, Tuliao, Tuzu, Wen-Ma Southern Zhuang). 200 in Viet Nam (2007). Very few monolinguals. Lao Cai Province, possibly Muong Khuong district. *Status:* 6b (Threatened). *Other:* Traditional religion, Buddhist (Mahayana), Daoist. See main entry on page 95.

Zhuang, Yang [zyg] (Thu Lao, Tu, Tuliao, Tuzu, Wen-Ma Southern Zhuang). North, Cao Bang Province, Ha Quang district. *Status:* 6a (Vigorous). *Lg Use:* Vigorous. All domains. All ages. *Other:* Officially classified within Nung nationality. Traditional religion, Buddhist (Mahayana), Daoist. See main entry on page 96.

Zhuang, Yongnan [zyn] (Long An, Long'an, Southern Zhuang, Yongnan Vernacular of the Southern Dialect of the Zhuang Language, Zhuangyu nanbu fangyan Yongnan tuyu). 10,000 in Viet Nam (2000 J. Edmondson). Cao Bang Province, Quang Ha district, Phuc Sen village; Doan Khon, Quoc Phong, Quoc Dan, Chi Thao, and Tu Do communes 37 km from Cao Bang city; Ha Quang district, Noi Thon commune; Ba Be district, Cao Che commune. *Status:* 6a (Vigorous). *Lg Use:* Vigorous. All domains. All ages. *Other:* Part of the Nùng official ethnic community (968,800, 2009 census). Traditional religion, Buddhist (Mahayana), Daoist. See main entry on page 96.

Zhuang, Zuojiang [zzj] (Nung Chao). 340,000 in Viet Nam (2000 census). 170,000 monolinguals. Ethnic population: Over 850,000 Nung nationality people in Viet Nam in 2000. Lang Son Province. *Status:* 6a (Vigorous). *Lg Use:* Vigorous. All domains. All ages. *Other:* Part of the Nùng official ethnic community (968,800, 2009 census). Traditional religion, Buddhist (Mahayana), Daoist. See main entry on page 97.

Yemen

Republic of Yemen. 23,852,000 (2011 World Factbook). Principal language: Standard Arabic. Literacy rate: 36% (2004 UNESCO). Immigrant languages: Egyptian Spoken Arabic (10,000), Hindi (233,000), Somali (679,000). General references: Johnstone 1967; Nyrop 1986; Sebeok 1970. Deaf population: 3,000.

The number of individual languages listed for Yemen is 10. All are living languages. Of these, 1 is institutional, 5 are vigorous, 1 is in trouble, and 3 are dying. See map on page 415.

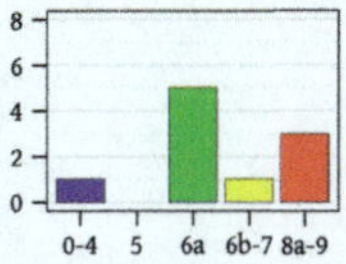

Arabic, Gulf Spoken [afb]. 10,000 in Yemen. *Status:* 6a (Vigorous). See main entry on page 213.

Arabic, Hadrami Spoken [ayh] (Hadrami, Hadromi). 300,000 in Yemen (1995). Population total all countries: 410,000. Hadramaut. Also in Eritrea, Kenya. *Status:* 6a (Vigorous). *Class:* Afro-Asiatic, Semitic, Central, South, Arabic. A member of macrolanguage Arabic [ara] (Saudi Arabia). *Lg Use:* Also use Standard Arabic [arb]. *Lg Dev:* Literacy rate in L2: 10%. *Other:* Distinct from Ta'izzi-Adeni Spoken Arabic [acq] and Sanaani Spoken Arabic [ayn]. Muslim. *Map:* 415.

Arabic, Judeo-Yemeni [jye] (Judeo-Yemeni, Yemenite Judeo-Arabic). 1,000 in Yemen (1995 H. Mutzafi). *Status:* 6a (Vigorous). *Dialects:* 'Aden, Be:da, Habban, San'a. *Other:* Jewish. See main entry on page 208.

Arabic, Sanaani Spoken [ayn] (Northern Yemeni Arabic). 7,600,000 (1996). Extends as far south as Dhamar. *Status:* 6a (Vigorous). De facto language of provincial identity in North Yemen. *Class:* Afro-Asiatic, Semitic, Central, South, Arabic. A member of macrolanguage Arabic [ara] (Saudi Arabia). *Lg Use:* Also use Standard Arabic [arb]. *Lg Dev:* Literacy rate in L2: 10%. *Other:* Distinct from Hadrami [ayh] and Ta'izzi-Adeni Arabic [acq]. Muslim (Zaydi). *Map:* 415.

Arabic, Standard [arb]. *Status:* 1 (National). Statutory national language (1991, Constitution, Article 2). *Lg Use:* Education, official purposes, formal speeches. See main entry on page 293.

Arabic, Ta'izzi-Adeni Spoken [acq] (Southern Yemeni Spoken Arabic). 6,760,000 in Yemen (1996). Population total all countries: 7,078,500. All provinces except the 2 east and the northeast ones. Probably a few in United Arab Emirates and Saudi Arabia. Also in Djibouti, Egypt, Eritrea, Kenya, Libya, Somalia, United Kingdom. *Status:* 6a (Vigorous). De facto language of provincial identity in South Yemen. *Class:* Afro-Asiatic, Semitic, Central, South, Arabic. A member of macrolanguage Arabic [ara] (Saudi Arabia). *Dialects:* Adeni, Ta'izzi. Ta'izzi dialect best accepted in Yemen. *Lg Use:* Also use Standard Arabic [arb]. *Lg Dev:* Literacy rate in L2: 10%. *Other:* Different from Hadrami [ayh] and Sanaani Arabic [ayn]. Muslim (Zaydi). *Map:* 415.

Bathari [bhm] (Bathara, Bautahari, Botahari). *Status:* 8b (Nearly extinct). *Other:* Muslim. See main entry on page 265.

Hobyót [hoh]. Near Oman border. *Status:* 8a (Moribund). See main entry on page 265. *Map:* 415.

Mehri [gdq] (Mahri). 50,000 in Yemen (2011). Population total all countries: 115,200. Mahrah Governorate. Also in Kuwait, Oman. *Status:* 7 (Shifting). *Class:* Afro-Asiatic, Semitic, South, South Arabian. *Dialects:* Eastern Mehri (Mehriyot), Western Mehri (Mehriyet). Within main dialects there are also differences between Bedouin and city varieties. *Lg Dev:* Dictionary. Bible portions: 1902. *Other:* Spoken by the Mahra. Many ethnic Mehri in Yemen are Arabic L1 speakers. Muslim. *Map:* 415.

Soqotri [sqt] (Saqatri, Socotri, Sokotri, Suqutri). 57,000 in Yemen (1990 census). Population total all countries: 64,000. Mainly Soqotra island; 'Abd al-Kuri island, Samha island in the Gulf of Aden. Also in United Arab Emirates. *Status:* 8a (Moribund). *Class:* Afro-Asiatic, Semitic, South, South Arabian. *Dialects:* 'Abd Al-Kuri, Central Soqotri, Northern Soqotri, Southern Soqotri, Western Soqotri. *Lg Dev:* Bible portions: 1902. *Writing:* Arabic script. Latin script. *Other:* North Soqotri includes North Central and Northwest Central (highland) Soqotri. Mostly monolingual in Soqotri. Muslim. *Map:* 415.

Other Languages

Abaza [abq] A language of Russian Federation. Population total all countries: 47,880. Also in: Germany, Turkey*Status:* 5 (Developing). *Class:* North Caucasian, West Caucasian, Abkhaz-AbazinSome dialects partially intelligible of Abkhaz [abk]. *Type:* SOV; ergative-absolutive agreement on the verb. *Lg Dev:* Newspapers. Radio programs. TV. Dictionary. Grammar. *Writing:* Cyrillic script. Latin script, used in Turkey.

Adyghe [ady] A language of Russian Federation. Population total all countries: 491,800. Also in: Egypt, France, Germany, Iraq, Israel, Jordan, Macedonia, Netherlands, Syria, Turkey, United States*Status:* 2 (Provincial). *Class:* North Caucasian, West Caucasian, CircassianReportedly similar to Kabardian [kbd]. *Type:* SOV. *Lg Dev:* Literacy rate in L1: 99% (Ministry of Education, Adygea Republic). Literacy rate in L2: 100% (Ministry of Education, Adygea Republic). Taught in primary schools. Newspapers. New media. Radio programs. TV. Dictionary. Grammar. NT: 1992. *Writing:* Arabic script, no longer in use. Cyrillic script. Latin script, used in Turkey.

Akhvakh [akv] A language of Russian Federation. Also in: Azerbaijan*Status:* 6b (Threatened). *Class:* North Caucasian, East Caucasian, Avar-Andic, AndicDiverse dialects. *Lg Dev:* Russian [rus] is a language of education. Dictionary. Grammar. *Writing:* Unwritten.

Albanian, Tosk [als] A language of Albania. Population total all countries: 1,778,200. Also in: Belgium, Croatia, Egypt, Germany, Greece, Sweden, Turkey, Ukraine, United States*Status:* 1 (National). *Class:* Indo-European, Albanian, ToskA member of macrolanguage Albanian [sqi]. Not intelligible with Arbëreshë [aae] of Italy. The basis of official standard Albanian since 1952. There is a transitional dialect zone which is neither Gheg [aln] nor Tosk. It is spoken in a few towns and villages around the Shkumbin river such as Shpat and Sulovë. *Type:* SVO. *Lg Dev:* Taught in primary schools. Fully developed. Bible: 1993. *Writing:* Elbasan script, no longer in use. Greek script, no longer in use. Latin script.

Amharic [amh] A language of Ethiopia. Population total all countries: 21,811,600. Also in: Canada, Djibouti, Egypt, Israel, United States*Status:* 1 (National). *Class:* Afro-Asiatic, Semitic, South, Ethiopian, South, Transversal, Amharic-Argobba*Type:* SOV; prepositions, postpositions, genitives, articles, and relatives precede noun heads; question word initial; case affixes; verb suffixes show person, number, gender of subject and (optionally) object; passives including deponents, causatives, CV, CVC, V, CVCC. *Lg Dev:* Literacy rate in L1: 28%. Literacy rate in L2: 28%. Taught in primary schools. Fully developed. Bible: 1840–1988. *Writing:* Braille script. Ethiopic script, primary usage.

Arabic, Eastern Egyptian Bedawi Spoken [avl] A language of Egypt. Population total all countries: 1,690,000. Also in: Israel (Levantine Bedawi Spoken Arabic), Jordan (Levantine Bedawi Spoken Arabic), Palestine (Levantine Bedawi Spoken Arabic), Syria (Levantine Bedawi Spoken Arabic)*Status:* 6a (Vigorous). *Class:* Afro-Asiatic, Semitic, Central, South, ArabicA member of macrolanguage Arabic [ara] (Saudi Arabia). Similar to some Hijazi dialects in northwestern Saudi Arabia. *Lg Dev:* TV. *Writing:* Arabic script.

Avar [ava] A language of Russian Federation. Population total all countries: 761,960. Also in: Azerbaijan, Georgia, Kazakhstan, Turkey*Status:* 4 (Educational). *Class:* North Caucasian, East Caucasian, Avar-Andic, Avar*Lg Dev:* Taught in primary and secondary schools. Newspapers. Radio programs. Dictionary. Grammar. NT: 2008. *Writing:* Cyrillic script.

Bezhta [kap] A language of Russian Federation. Population total all countries: 6,800. Also in: Georgia*Status:* 5 (Developing). *Class:* North Caucasian, East Caucasian, Tsezic, East Tsezic*Lg Dev:* Russian used for education. Dictionary. Bible portions: 1999–2007. *Writing:* Cyrillic script.

Bulgarian [bul] A language of Bulgaria. Population total all countries: 8,157,770. Also in: Canada, Croatia, Czech Republic, Greece, Hungary, Israel, Libya, Moldova, Romania, Russian Federation, Serbia, Slovakia, Turkey, Ukraine, United States*Status:* 1 (National). *Class:* Indo-European, Slavic, South, EasternPalityan dialect is functionally intelligible with standard Bulgarian. The Pomak dialect spoken in Greece is reportedly similar to Serbian [srp] and Bulgarian; geographical dialect variation toward each. *Type:* SVO. *Lg Dev:* Fully developed. Bible: 1864–1923. *Writing:* Braille script. Cyrillic script, primary usage.

Chechen [che] A language of Russian Federation. Population total all countries: 1,361,000. Also in: Georgia, Germany, Jordan, Kazakhstan, Kyrgyzstan, Syria, Turkey, Uzbekistan*Status:* 2 (Provincial). *Class:* North Caucasian, East Caucasian, Nakh, Chechen-IngushChechen partially intelligible with Ingush [inh]. Melkhi transitional dialect to Ingush. *Type:* Ergative case system; many consonants and vowels; extensive inflectional morphology, many nominal cases, several gender classes; complex sentences by chaining participial clauses; verbs have gender agreement with the direct object or intransitive subject, but no person agreement (Nichols 1995). *Lg Dev:* Taught in primary schools. Newspapers. New media. Radio programs. Dictionary. Grammar. Bible: 2012. *Writing:* Cyrillic script.

Crimean Tatar [crh] A language of Ukraine. Population total all countries: 475,540. Also in: Bulgaria, Kyrgyzstan, Moldova, Romania, Russian Federation, Turkey, United States, Uzbekistan*Status:* 5 (Developing). *Class:* Altaic, Turkic, Southern*Lg Dev:* Taught in a few schools. Two local universities have faculties of Crimean Tatar. Poetry. Newspapers. TV. NT: 1666–2011. *Writing:* Cyrillic script. Latin script, official use since 1997.

Dido [ddo] A language of Russian Federation. Also in: Georgia*Status:* 6b (Threatened). *Class:* North Caucasian, East Caucasian, Tsezic, West TsezicSahada most distinct. May be a separate language. *Lg Dev:* Taught in primary schools. *Writing:* Cyrillic script.

English [eng] A language of United Kingdom. Population total all countries: 335,148,868. L2 users worldwide: 505,000,000. Also in: American Samoa, Andorra, Anguilla, Antigua and Barbuda, Aruba, Australia, Bahamas, Bahrain, Bangladesh, Barbados, Belize, Bermuda, Bhutan, Botswana, British Indian Ocean Territory, British Virgin Islands, Brunei, Cambodia, Cameroon, Canada, Caribbean Netherlands, Cayman Islands, Chile, Hong Kong, Macao,

Cook Islands, Curacao, Czech Republic, Denmark, Dominica, Dominican Republic, Ecuador, Equatorial Guinea, Eritrea, Estonia, Ethiopia, Fiji, Finland, Gambia, Germany, Ghana, Gibraltar, Greece, Grenada, Guam, Guyana, Honduras, India, Indonesia, Ireland, Isle of Man, Israel, Italy, Jamaica, Japan, Kenya, Kiribati, South Korea, Lebanon, Lesotho, Liberia, Libya, Madagascar, Malawi, Malaysia, Maldives, Malta, Marshall Islands, Mauritius, Mexico, Micronesia, Montserrat, Mozambique, Namibia, Nauru, Nepal, New Zealand, Nigeria, Niue, Norfolk Island, Northern Mariana Islands, Norway, Oman, Pakistan, Palau, Papua New Guinea, Philippines, Pitcairn, Puerto Rico, Rwanda, Saint Barthélemy, Saint Kitts and Nevis, Saint Lucia, Saint Martin, Saint Pierre and Miquelon, Saint Vincent and the Grenadines, Samoa, Saudi Arabia, Seychelles, Sierra Leone, Singapore, Sint Maarten, Solomon Islands, Somalia, South Africa, South Sudan, Sri Lanka, Sudan, Suriname, Swaziland, Sweden, Switzerland, Tanzania, Tokelau, Tonga, Trinidad and Tobago, Turks and Caicos Islands, Tuvalu, Uganda, United Arab Emirates, United States, U.S. Virgin Islands, Vanuatu, Venezuela, Zambia, Zimbabwe*Status:* 0 (International). *Class:* Indo-European, Germanic, West, EnglishMany local English varieties around the world. Lexical similarity: 60% with German, 27% with French, 24% with Russian. *Type:* SVO; prepositions; genitives after noun heads; articles, adjectives, numerals before noun heads; question word initial; word order distinguishes subject, object, indirect objects, given and new information, topic and comment; active and passive; causative; comparative; consonant and vowel clusters; nontonal. *Lg Dev:* Fully developed. Bible: 1382–2002. *Writing:* Braille script. Deseret Alphabet, developed in 1854 with limited usage until 1877. Latin script, primary usage. Shavian (Shaw) script, no longer in use.

Erzya [myv] A language of Russian Federation. Population total all countries: 119,330. Also in: Armenia, Azerbaijan, Belarus, Estonia, Kazakhstan, Kyrgyzstan, Latvia, Lithuania, Turkmenistan, Ukraine, Uzbekistan*Status:* 5 (Developing). *Class:* Uralic, MordvinQuite different from Moksha [mdf]. *Lg Dev:* NT: 1827–2006. *Writing:* Cyrillic script.

French [fra] A language of France. Population total all countries: 74,980,460. Also in: Algeria, Andorra, Austria, Belgium, Benin, Burkina Faso, Burundi, Cambodia, Cameroon, Canada, Central African Republic, Chad, Comoros, Congo, Côte d'Ivoire, Czech Republic, Democratic Republic of the Congo, Djibouti, Equatorial Guinea, French Guiana, French Polynesia, Gabon, Guadeloupe, Guinea, Haiti, India, Israel, Italy, Lebanon, Libya, Luxembourg, Madagascar, Mali, Martinique, Mauritania, Mauritius, Mayotte, Monaco, Morocco, Mozambique, New Caledonia, New Zealand, Niger, Philippines, Puerto Rico, Réunion, Rwanda, Saint Barthélemy, Saint Martin, Saint Pierre and Miquelon, Saudi Arabia, Senegal, Seychelles, South Africa, Switzerland, Togo, Tunisia, United Arab Emirates, United Kingdom, United States, U.S. Virgin Islands, Vanuatu, Wallis and Futuna*Status:* 0 (International). *Class:* Indo-European, Italic, Romance, Italo-Western, Western, Gallo-Iberian, Gallo-Romance, Gallo-Rhaetian, Oïl, FrenchLexical similarity: 89% with Italian [ita], 80% with Logudorese Sardinian [src], 78% with Romansch [roh], 75% with Portuguese [por], Romanian [ron], and Spanish[spa], 29% with German [deu], 27% with English [eng]. *Type:* SVO. *Lg Dev:* Fully developed. Bible: 1530–2000. *Writing:* Braille script. Latin script, primary usage.

German, Standard [deu] A language of Germany. Population total all countries: 78,245,280. Also in: Argentina, Australia, Austria, Belgium, Bolivia, Bosnia and Herzegovina, Brazil, Canada, Chile, Croatia, Czech Republic, Denmark, Ecuador, Estonia, Finland, France, Hungary, Israel, Italy, Kazakhstan, Kyrgyzstan, Liechtenstein, Luxembourg, Moldova, Mozambique, Namibia, New Zealand, Paraguay, Philippines, Poland, Puerto Rico, Romania, Russian Federation, Slovakia, Slovenia, South Africa, Sweden, Switzerland, Tajikistan, Ukraine, United Arab Emirates, United States, Uruguay, Uzbekistan*Status:* 1 (National). *Class:* Indo-European, Germanic, West, High German, German, Middle German, East Middle German-Major related varieties are Bavarian [bar], Schwäbian [swg], Alemannisch [gsw], Mainfränkisch [vmf], Hessisch, Palatinian, Rheinfränkisch, Westfälisch [wep], Saxonian, Thuringian, Brandenburgisch, and Low Saxon [nds]. Many varieties are not mutually intelligible. Our present treatment is incomplete. Standard German is one High German variety, developed from the chancery of Saxony, gaining acceptance as the written standard in the 16th and 17th centuries. High German refers to dialects and languages in the upper Rhine region. Lexical similarity: 60% with English [eng], 29% with French [fra]. *Lg Dev:* Taught in primary and secondary schools. Fully developed. Bible: 1466–2004. *Writing:* Braille script. Latin script, primary usage. Latin script, Fraktur variant, used until 1940. Runic script, no longer in use.

Greek [ell] A language of Greece. Population total all countries: 13,432,940. Also in: Albania, Armenia, Australia, Austria, Bahamas, Bulgaria, Canada, Cyprus, Czech Republic, Democratic Republic of the Congo, Djibouti, Egypt, France, Georgia, Germany, Hungary, Italy, Jordan, Kazakhstan, Libya, Macedonia, Malawi, Mozambique, Paraguay, Poland, Romania, Russian Federation, Sierra Leone, South Africa, Sweden, Tunisia, Turkey, Ukraine, United Arab Emirates, United Kingdom, United States*Status:* 1 (National). *Class:* Indo-European, Greek, AtticKatharevousa is an archaic literary dialect, Dimotiki is the spoken literary and now official dialect. The Saracatsan are nomadic shepherds of northern Greece. The Greek of Italy and that of Corsica are probably distinct languages (1992 R. Zamponi). In Cyprus, the dialect is reportedly more similar to Classical Greek [grc] in some vocabulary and grammar than that spoken in Greece, and to have Latin [lat] and Turkish [tur] loanwords. Lexical similarity: 84%–93% with Greek [ell] in Cyprus. *Type:* SVO. *Lg Dev:* Fully developed. Bible: 1840–1994. *Writing:* Braille script. Cyrillic script, used in Ukraine. Greek script, primary usage.

Hungarian [hun] A language of Hungary. Population total all countries: 12,606,130. Also in: Australia, Austria, Canada, Croatia, Czech Republic, Israel, Moldova, Romania, Russian Federation, Serbia, Slovakia, Slovenia, Sweden, Ukraine, United States*Status:* 1 (National). *Class:* UralicReportedly most similar to the Uralic language Vogul (Mansi [mns]) in Siberia. Speakers of standard Hungarian have difficulty understanding the Oberwart dialect spoken in Austria, and considerable difficulty understanding the Moldavian Csángó dialect spoken in Rumania. *Type:* SVO. *Lg Dev:* Taught in primary and secondary schools. Fully developed. Bible: 1590–1991. *Writing:* Braille script. Latin script, primary usage.

Hunzib [huz] A language of Russian Federation. Population total all countries: 1,420. Also in: Georgia*Status:* 6b (Threatened). *Class:* North Caucasian, East Caucasian, Tsezic, East TsezicSeparate from Bezhta [kap] (1989 B. Comrie) but reportedly very similar to it. *Type:* 27 consonants, 16 vowels, word stress generally linked to prefinal vowel; 5 noun classes; agreement between nouns and coreferent adjectives, pronouns, verbs, and adverbs marked by prefixes; nominative-ergative system; demonstratives. *Lg Dev:* No literacy in Hunzib. Avar [ava] is literary language. Dictionary. Grammar. *Writing:* Unwritten.

Ingush [inh] A language of Russian Federation. Population total all countries: 322,900. Also in: Kazakhstan, Uzbekistan*Status:* 4 (Educational). *Class:* North Caucasian, East Caucasian, Nakh, Chechen-IngushSomewhat intelligible with Chechen [che], more so with contact. *Lg Dev:* Radio programs. Grammar. Bible portions: 2005. *Writing:* Arabic script. Cyrillic script. Latin script.

Judeo-Tat [jdt] A language of Russian Federation. Population total all countries: 96,010. Also in: Azerbaijan, Israel*Status:* 5 (Developing). *Class:* Indo-European, Indo-Iranian, Iranian, Western, Southwestern, Tat*Lg Dev:* Radio programs. Bible portions: 2000. *Writing:* Cyrillic script, primary usage. Hebrew script. Latin script, used in Azerbaijan.

Kabardian [kbd] A language of Russian Federation. Population total all countries: 1,628,500. Also in: Germany, Jordan, Syria, Turkey, United States*Status:* 5 (Developing). *Class:* North Caucasian, West Caucasian, CircassianReportedly similar to Adygey [ady]. *Lg Dev:* Taught in primary and secondary schools. Dictionary. Grammar. NT: 1993–2007. *Writing:* Cyrillic script.

Kalmyk-Oirat [xal] A language of Russian Federation. Population total all countries: 360,500. Also in: China, Taiwan, Germany, Kyrgyzstan, Mongolia (Oirat), United States*Status:* 6b (Threatened). *Class:* Altaic, Mongolic, Eastern, Oirat-Khalkha, Oirat-Kalmyk-DarkhatDiverged from other Mongolian languages. Called Kalmyk in the Russian Federation; Oirat in China and Mongolia; in the United States, Kalmyk not heavily influenced by Russian [rus]. Different from other varieties in China called Oirat [xal], which are sometimes called Asiatic Oirat. In Mongolia, some scholars consider Oirat to be a dialect of Halh Mongolian [khk]. *Lg Dev:* NT: 1827–2009. *Writing:* Cyrillic script, adopted in 1924, used in Russia and Mongolia. Mongolian script, Todo style, used in China.

Khakas [kjh] A language of Russian Federation. Population total all countries: 42,610. Also in: China*Status:* 5 (Developing). *Class:* Altaic, Turkic, NorthernKamass dialect is extinct (Salminen 2007). *Lg Dev:* Literacy rate in L1: 50% (2007 SIL). Literacy rate in L2: 95% in Russian. Khakas books often self-published and difficult to obtain. Taught in primary schools as medium in a few schools, as subject in about 100 schools. Taught in secondary schools as a subject in selected schools. Newspapers. Radio programs. TV. Dictionary. Grammar. Bible portions: 1995–2008. *Writing:* Cyrillic script.

Kumyk [kum] A language of Russian Federation. Population total all countries: 426,550. Also in: Kazakhstan, Turkey*Status:* 5 (Developing). *Class:* Altaic, Turkic, Western, Ponto-CaspianDialects quite divergent. *Lg Dev:* Literacy rate in L1: Higher where majority speak Kumyk. Literacy rate in L2: High in Russian. Taught in primary schools. Newspapers. Radio programs. Dictionary. Grammar. NT: 2007. *Writing:* Cyrillic script.

Lezgi [lez] A language of Russian Federation. Population total all countries: 788,720. Also in: Azerbaijan, Georgia, Kazakhstan, Kyrgyzstan, Turkey, Turkmenistan, Ukraine, Uzbekistan*Status:* 4 (Educational). *Class:* North Caucasian, East Caucasian, Lezgic, Nuclear Lezgic, East Lezgic*Lg Dev:* Newspapers. Radio programs. Dictionary. Grammar. Bible portions: 1990–2010. *Writing:* Cyrillic script.

Manem [jet] A language of Papua New Guinea. Population total all countries: 900. Also in: Indonesia*Status:* 6a (Vigorous). *Class:* Border, WarisLexical similarity: 50% with Waris [wrs]. *Lg Dev:* Significant literacy in Tok Pisin [tpi] and Bahasa Indonesia [ind].

Nanai [gld] A language of Russian Federation. Population total all countries: 1,390. Also in: China*Status:* 7 (Shifting). *Class:* Altaic, Tungusic, Southern, Southeast, NanajQuite distinct dialects. *Lg Dev:* Dictionary. Bible portions: 1884–2002. *Writing:* Cyrillic script.

Ninggerum [nxr] A language of Papua New Guinea. Population total all countries: 6,150. Also in: Indonesia*Status:* 5 (Developing). *Class:* Trans-New Guinea, Ok-Awyu, Ok, Lowland*Lg Dev:* Literacy rate in L1: 5%. Literacy rate in L2: 5%–15%. Taught in primary schools. *Writing:* Latin script.

Ossetic [oss] A language of Russian Federation. Population total all countries: 577,450. Also in: Azerbaijan, Georgia, Kazakhstan, Tajikistan, Turkey, Turkmenistan, Ukraine, Uzbekistan*Status:* 5 (Developing). *Class:* Indo-European, Indo-Iranian, Iranian, Eastern, Northeastern*Lg Dev:* Bible: 2010. *Writing:* Cyrillic script, used in Russia since 1844 and in Georgia since 1954. Georgian (Mkhedruli) script, used in Georgia until 1954. Latin script, used in Russia during the 1920s–1930s.

Plautdietsch [pdt] A language of Canada. Population total all countries: 394,900. Also in: Argentina, Belize, Bolivia, Brazil, Costa Rica, Germany, Kazakhstan, Mexico, Paraguay, Russian Federation, United States, Uruguay*Status:* 5 (Developing). *Class:* Indo-European, Germanic, West, Low Saxon-Low Franconian, Low Saxon50% intelligible of other Low German languages, Standard German [deu], Pennsylvania German [pdc], and Hutterite German [geh]. Plautdietsch has major differences from European Low German dialects still spoken along the North Sea and Baltic Ocean due to the various places where Mennonites lived during the past 150 years (Epp 1993). *Type:* SVO; prepositions; genitives after noun heads; question word initial; 5 prefixes; 2 suffixes; nontonal. *Lg Dev:* Literacy rate in L2: 95%. Bible: 2003. *Writing:* Latin script.

Polish [pol] A language of Poland. Population total all countries: 38,663,780. Also in: Australia, Austria, Azerbaijan, Belarus, Canada, Croatia, Czech Republic, Denmark, Estonia, Finland, Germany, Hungary, Israel, Kazakhstan, Latvia, Lithuania, Romania, Russian Federation, Serbia, Slovakia, Sweden, Ukraine, United Arab Emirates, United States*Status:* 1 (National). *Class:* Indo-European, Slavic, West, Lechitic*Type:* SVO. *Lg Dev:* Fully developed. Bible: 1561–1965. *Writing:* Braille script. Latin script, primary usage.

Pontic [pnt] A language of Greece. Population total all countries: 1,178,000. Also in: Azerbaijan, Canada, Georgia, Kazakhstan, Russian Federation, Turkey, United States*Status:* 6a (Vigorous). *Class:* Indo-European, Greek, AtticStandard Greek [ell] speakers cannot understand Pontic, and Pontic speakers reportedly do not understand or speak standard Greek [ell]. Pontic clubs and centers exist in the Athens-Peiraeus suburbs. *Lg Dev:* Grammar. *Writing:* Cyrillic script, rarely used. Greek script, primary usage. Latin script.

Portuguese [por] A language of Portugal. Population total all countries: 203,349,200. Also in: Andorra, Angola, Antigua and Barbuda, Belgium, Bermuda, Brazil, Canada, Cape Verde Islands, Macao, Congo, Curacao, East Timor, France, Germany, Guinea-Bissau, Guyana, India, Jamaica, Luxembourg, Malawi, Mozambique, Paraguay, Saint Vincent and the Grenadines, São Tomé e Príncipe, Senegal, South Africa, Spain, Suriname, Switzerland, United Kingdom, United States, Uruguay, Venezuela, Zambia*Status:* 1 (National). *Class:* Indo-European, Italic, Romance, Italo-Western, Western, Gallo-Iberian, Ibero-Romance, West Iberian, Portuguese-GalicianStandard Portuguese of Portugal based on Estremenho dialect (Lisbon and

Coimbra). *Type:* SVO. *Lg Dev:* Literacy rate in L2: 83%–84%. Fully developed. Bible: 1751–1995. *Writing:* Braille script. Latin script, primary usage.

Romani, Balkan [rmn] A language of Serbia. Population total all countries: 589,800. Also in: Bulgaria, France, Germany, Greece, Hungary, Iran, Italy, Macedonia, Moldova, Romania, Turkey, Ukraine*Status:* 5 (Developing). *Class:* Indo-European, Indo-Iranian, Indo-Aryan, Central zone, Romani, BalkanA member of macrolanguage Romany [rom] (Romania). Arlija dialect (252,000–367,000 total) understood by Greek Romani and Dzambazi. *Lg Dev:* Dictionary. Grammar. NT: 2008.

Romani, Sinte [rmo] A language of Serbia. Population total all countries: 318,920. Also in: Austria, Croatia, Czech Republic, France, Germany, Italy, Kazakhstan, Montenegro, Netherlands, Poland, Slovenia, Switzerland*Status:* 2 (Provincial). *Class:* Indo-European, Indo-Iranian, Indo-Aryan, Central zone, Romani, NorthernA member of macrolanguage Romany [rom] (Romania). Mutual intelligibility between Croatian Romani, Slovenian Romani, and Serbian Romani. Possibly quite distinct from German [deu] varieties. Sinte is characterized by German influence. Not intelligible of Vlax Romani [rmy]. *Lg Dev:* Grammar. NT: 2010. *Writing:* Latin script.

Romanian [ron] A language of Romania. Population total all countries: 23,782,990. Also in: Australia, Azerbaijan, Bulgaria, Canada, Croatia, Czech Republic, Finland, Hungary, Israel, Kazakhstan, Kyrgyzstan, Moldova (Moldovan), Mozambique, Russian Federation, Serbia, Sweden, Tajikistan, Turkmenistan, Ukraine, United States, Uzbekistan*Status:* 1 (National). *Class:* Indo-European, Italic, Romance, EasternLittle dialect variation. Bayash are Gypsies whose dialect is based on Banat, but influenced by Balkan Romani [rmn] and Hungarian [hun]. Lexical similarity: 77% with Italian [ita], 75% with French [fra], 74% with Sardinian [sdn], 73% with Catalan [cat], 72% with Portuguese [por] and Rheto-Romance [roh], 71% with Spanish [spa]. *Type:* SVO. *Lg Dev:* Fully developed. Bible: 1688–1989. *Writing:* Braille script. Cyrillic script, official usage in Moldova until 1991. Latin script, primary usage.

Russian [rus] A language of Russian Federation. Population total all countries: 167,332,230. Also in: Armenia, Azerbaijan, Belarus, Bulgaria, Canada, China, Croatia, Czech Republic, Estonia, Finland, Georgia, Germany, Greece, Hungary, Israel, Kazakhstan, Kyrgyzstan, Latvia, Lithuania, Moldova, Mongolia, Mozambique, Norway, Paraguay, Poland, Romania, Serbia, Slovakia, Sweden, Tajikistan, Turkmenistan, Ukraine, United States, Uruguay, Uzbekistan*Status:* 0 (International). *Class:* Indo-European, Slavic, East*Type:* SVO; prepositions; genitives after noun heads; adjectives, numerals before noun heads; question word initial; 1 prefix on a word; recursive addition of suffixes allowed; nontonal. *Lg Dev:* Fully developed. Bible: 1680–2011. *Writing:* Braille script. Cyrillic script, primary usage.

Rutul [rut] A language of Russian Federation. Population total all countries: 47,400. Also in: Azerbaijan*Status:* 4 (Educational). *Class:* North Caucasian, East Caucasian, Lezgic, Nuclear Lezgic, West LezgicDialects not sharply defined. *Lg Dev:* Not a literary language. Taught in primary schools. Grammar. Bible portions: 2004. *Writing:* Cyrillic script.

Serbian [srp] A language of Serbia. Population total all countries: 8,957,906. Also in: Albania, Australia, Bosnia and Herzegovina, Bulgaria, Canada, Croatia, Czech Republic, Denmark, Greece, Hungary, Libya, Macedonia, Montenegro (Montenegrin), Romania, Russian Federation, Switzerland, Turkey, Ukraine, United Arab Emirates, United States, Zambia*Status:* 1 (National). *Class:* Indo-European, Slavic, South, WesternA member of macrolanguage Serbo-Croatian [hbs]. *Type:* SVO; postpositions; genitives, articles, adjectives, numerals, relatives after noun heads; question word initial; 1 suffix; case determines subject, object; obligatory verb affixes mark person, number, gender of subject, object, other noun phrase; passive for each tense, not commonly used today; causatives marked by separate words; comparatives marked by prefix; CCVCVC; nontonal. *Lg Dev:* Fully developed. Bible: 1804–1868. *Writing:* Braille script. Cyrillic script, primary usage. Latin script.

Sowanda [sow] A language of Papua New Guinea. Population total all countries: 1,180. Also in: Indonesia*Status:* 6a (Vigorous). *Class:* Border, WarisMay be 2 languages.

Spanish [spa] A language of Spain. Population total all countries: 414,170,030. Also in: Andorra, Anguilla, Argentina, Aruba, Australia, Belgium, Belize, Bolivia, Canada, Caribbean Netherlands, Cayman Islands, Chile, Colombia, Costa Rica, Cuba, Curacao, Czech Republic, Dominican Republic, Ecuador, El Salvador, Equatorial Guinea, Finland, France, Germany, Gibraltar, Guatemala, Honduras, Israel, Jamaica, Mexico, Morocco, New Zealand, Nicaragua, Norway, Panama, Paraguay, Peru, Philippines, Puerto Rico, Sint Maarten, Sweden, Switzerland, Trinidad and Tobago, United States, U.S. Virgin Islands, Uruguay, Venezuela*Status:* 0 (International). *Class:* Indo-European, Italic, Romance, Italo-Western, Western, Gallo-Iberian, Ibero-Romance, West Iberian, CastilianLexical similarity: 89% with Portuguese [por], 85% with Catalan [cat], 82% with Italian [ita], 76% with Sardinian [src], 75% with French [fra], 74% with Ladin [lld], 71% with Romanian [ron]. *Type:* SVO; prepositions; genitives, relatives after noun heads; articles, numerals before noun heads; adjectives before or after noun heads depending on whether it is evaluative or descriptive; question word initial; (C(C))V(C); nontonal. Silbo Gomero whistled variety of Spanish used in Canary Islands. *Lg Dev:* Fully developed. Bible: 1553–2000. *Writing:* Braille script. Latin script, primary usage.

Swahili [swh] A language of Tanzania. Population total all countries: 15,457,390. Also in: Burundi, Canada, Kenya (Kiswahili), Libya, Mozambique, Oman, Rwanda, Somalia, South Africa, Uganda, United Arab Emirates, United States*Status:* 1 (National). *Class:* Niger-Congo, Atlantic-Congo, Volta-Congo, Benue-Congo, Bantoid, Southern, Narrow Bantu, Central, G, Swahili (G.42)A member of macrolanguage Swahili [swa]. Lexical similarity: Bajun dialect 85% with the Amu dialect, 78% with the Mvita dialect, 72% with the Mrima dialect; Mvita dialect 86% with Amu, 79% with Mrima; Mrima dialect 79% with Amu. *Type:* SVO. *Lg Dev:* Language of instruction in primary school. In secondary school taught as a subject. Taught in primary and secondary schools. Fully developed. Bible: 1891–2009. *Writing:* Braille script. Latin script.

Tatar [tat] A language of Russian Federation. Population total all countries: 5,406,110. Also in: Azerbaijan, Belarus, China, Estonia, Finland, Georgia, Kazakhstan, Kyrgyzstan, Latvia, Lithuania, Moldova, Tajikistan, Turkey, Turkmenistan, Ukraine, United States, Uzbekistan*Status:* 2 (Provincial). *Class:* Altaic, Turkic, Western, UralianEastern Tatar is divided into 3: Tobol-Irtysh, Baraba, and Tom. Tobol-Irtysh is divided into 5: Tyumen, Tobol, Zabolotny, Tevriz, and Tara (Tumasheva). Mixed dialects are: Astrakhan, Kasimov, Tepter, and Ural (Poppe). 43,000 Astrakhan (L1 speakers) have shifted to the Middle dialect. Kasim (5,000 L1 speakers) is between Middle and Western Tatar. Tepter (300,000 L1 speakers) is reportedly between the Tatar and Bashkort [bak] languages. *Type:* SOV. *Lg Dev:* Literacy rate in L2: High. Taught in primary schools. Taught in secondary schools and university. Magazines. Newspapers. New media. Radio programs. TV. Dictionary. Grammar. NT: 1820–2005. *Writing:* Cyrillic script. Latin script.

Tigrigna [tir] A language of Ethiopia. Population total all countries: 6,915,000. Also in: Canada, Djibouti, Eritrea, Germany, Israel, Sweden*Status:* 1 (National). *Class:* Afro-Asiatic, Semitic, South, Ethiopian, North*Lg Dev:* Literacy rate in L1: 1%–10%. Literacy rate in L2: 27%. Fully developed. Bible: 1956. *Writing:* Ethiopic script, used since 13th or 14th century.

Tuva [tyv] A language of Russian Federation. Population total all countries: 283,400. Also in: China, Mongolia*Status:* 4 (Educational). *Class:* Altaic, Turkic, NorthernSharp dialect differences. *Lg Dev:* Literacy rate in L2: 85% in Russian (2007 SIL). Taught in primary and secondary schools. Bible: 2011. *Writing:* Cyrillic script.

Ukrainian [ukr] A language of Ukraine. Population total all countries: 36,048,890. Also in: Argentina, Armenia, Azerbaijan, Belarus, Brazil, Bulgaria, Canada, Croatia, Czech Republic, Estonia, Georgia, Hungary, Kazakhstan, Kyrgyzstan, Latvia, Lithuania, Moldova, Poland, Romania, Russian Federation, Serbia, Slovakia, Tajikistan, Turkmenistan, United States, Uzbekistan*Status:* 1 (National). *Class:* Indo-European, Slavic, EastDialect differences slight. *Lg Dev:* Fully developed. Bible: 1903–2011. *Writing:* Cyrillic script.

Waris [wrs] A language of Papua New Guinea. Population total all countries: 4,000. Also in: Indonesia*Status:* 4 (Educational). *Class:* Border, WarisIntelligible at Imonda but not Amanab. Similar to Imonda [imn] and Amanab [amn]. *Type:* SOV. *Lg Dev:* Literacy rate in L1: 15%–20%. Literacy rate in L2: 50%. Taught in primary schools, in many villages. Poetry. Dictionary. NT: 2003. *Writing:* Latin script.

Bibliography

Abbi, A. 2006. *Endangered languages of the Andaman Islands*. LINCOM Studies in Asian Linguistics 64. Munich: LINCOM Europa.

Addleton, J. S. 1986. The importance of regional languages in Pakistan. *Al-Mushir* 28(2):55–80.

Adelaar, K. A. 1995. Borneo as a cross-roads for comparative Austronesian linguistics. In P. Bellwood, J. J. Fox, and D. Tryon (eds.), *The Austronesians: Historical and comparative perspectives*, pp. 75–95. Canberra: Department of Anthropology, Research School of Pacific and Asian Studies, Australian National University.

Akiner, S. 1983. *Islamic peoples of the Soviet Union*. London: Kegan Paul International.

Al-Tajir, M. A. 1982. *Language and linguistic origins in Bahrain: The Baharnah dialect of Arabic*. Library of Arabic Linguistics 5. London: Kegan Paul International.

Anderbeck, K. R. 2008. *Malay dialects of the Batanghari River Basin (Jambi, Sumatra)*, SIL e-Books 6. Dallas: SIL International.

Andrews, P. A. (ed.). 1989. *Ethnic groups in the Republic of Turkey*. Wiesbaden: Dr. Ludwig Reichert Verlag.

Anonby, E. and P. Yousefian. 2011. *A survey of language on Larak Islands*. Studia Iranica Uppsaliensia. Uppsala: Uppsala University.

Ansaldo, U. and L. Lim. 2006. Globalisation, empowerment and the periphery: The Malays of Sri Lanka. In R. Elangaiyan, R. M. Brown, N. D. M. Ostler, and M. K. Verma (eds.), *Vital voices: Endangered languages and multilingualism: Proceedings of the tenth Foundation for Endangered Languages conference*, pp. 39–46. Mysore, India: Central Institute of Indian Languages and Foundation for Endangered Languages.

Appell, G. N. 1965. *The nature of social groupings among the Rungus Dusun of Sabah, Malaysia*. Ph.D. dissertation, Australian National University.

Baart, L. G. and M. Z. Sagar. 2004. *Kalam Kohistani texts*. Islamabad: National Institute of Pakistan Studies and Summer Institute of Linguistics.

Bakaev, C. X. 1962. *Language of the Kurds of Turkmenistan (Govor Kurdov Turkmenii)*. Moscow: Nauk.

Bandhu, C. M. 1971. *Sinjali: Studies in linguistic behavior*. Kathmandu: Royal Nepal Academy.

Barr, D. F., S. G. Barr, and C. Salombe. 1979. *Languages of Central Sulawesi: Checklist, preliminary classification, language maps, wordlists*. Jayapura: Cenderawasih University.

Bashir, E. 2003. Dardic. In G. Cardona and D. Jain (eds.), *The Indo-Aryan languages*, pp. 818–894. Routledge Language Family Series. London and New York: Routledge.

Bateson, M. C. 1967. *Arabic language handbook*. Washington D. C.: Center for Applied Linguistics.

Bauer, C. 1984. Mon books in the National Library of Australia. *South East Asian Research Materials Group [SEARMG] Newsletter*, 27 [August].

Bauer, C. 1990. Language and Ethnicity: The Mon in Burma and Thailand. In G. Wijeyewardene (ed.), *Ethnic groups across national boundaries in mainland Southeast Asia*, pp. 17-23. Singapore: Institute of Southeast Asian Studies.

Benjamin, G. and C. Chou (eds.). 2003. *Tribal communities in the Malay world: Historical, cultural and social perspectives. 2nd ed.* Singapore: Institute of Southeast Asian Studies.

Bhaskararao, P. 2006. *The Dravidian languages*. London: Routledge.

Bickel, B. 1996. *Aspect, mood, and time in Belhare*. Zurich: Arbeiten des Seminars für Allgemeine Sprachwissenschaft (ASAS).

Bista, D. B. 1967. *People of Nepal*. 1st edition. Kathmandu: His Majesty's Government, Department of Publicity.

Bista, D. B. 1973. *Nepal in perspective*. Kathmandu: Center for Economic Development Agencies (CEDA).

Bista, D. B. 1996. *People of Nepal*. 6th edition. Kathmandu: Ratna Pustak Bhandar.

Blau, J. 1989. Gurani et Zaza. In R. Schmitt (ed.), *Compendium linguarum iranicarum*, pp. 336–340. Wiesbaden: Dr. Ludwig Reichert Verlag.

Blust, R. 2003. *The Austronesian languages*. Pacific Linguistics 501. Canberra: Australian National University.

Blust, R. A. 1974. *The Proto-North Sarawak vowel deletion hypothesis*. Ph.D. dissertation, University of Hawai'i.

Borg, A. 1985. *Cypriot Arabic*. Stuttgart: Deutsch Morgenländische Gesellschaft.

Boutin, M. E. 1986. *Indigenous groups of Sabah: An annotated bibliography of linguistic and anthropological sources: Supplement 1*. Sabah Museum Monographs 1, Part 2. Kota Kinabalu: Sabah Museum.

Boutin, M. E. and A. Y. Boutin. 1985. Report on the languages of Banggi and Balambangan. *Sabah Society Journal* 8(1):89–92.

Bradley, D. 1996. Bantawa Rai. In S. A. Wurm, P. Mühlhäusler, and D. T. Tryon (eds.), *Atlas of languages of intercultural communication in the Pacific, Asia, and the Americas, Vol. II: Texts*, pp. 773–774. Berlin: Mouton de Gruyter.

Bradley, D. 1997. Tibeto-Burman languages and classification. In D. Bradley (ed.), *Tibeto-Burman languages of the Himalayas: Papers in Southeast Asian linguistics, Vol. 14*, pp. 1–72. Pacific Linguistics A-86. Canberra: Australian National University.

Bradley, D. 2002. The subgrouping of Tibeto-Burman. In C. I. Beckwith (ed.), *Medieval Tibeto-Burman Languages, PLATS 2000: Tibetan Studies: Proceedings of the Ninth Seminar of the International Association for Tibetan Studies, Leiden, 2000*. Leiden: Brill.

Bradley, D. 2005. Sanie and language loss in China. *International Journal of the Sociology of Language* 173:159–176.

Bradley, D. 2007. East and Southeast Asia. In C. Moseley (ed.), *Encyclopedia of the world's endangered languages*, pp. 349–424. London: Routledge.

Bradley, D. 2007. Languages of Mainland South-East Asia. In O. Miyaoka, O. Sakiyama, and M. E. Krauss (eds.), *The vanishing languages of the Pacific Rim*, pp. 301–336. Oxford Linguistics. Oxford: Oxford University Press.

Brassett, P. R. and C. Brassett. 2005. Diachronic and synchronic overview of the Tujia language of Central South China. *International Journal of the Sociology of Language* 176:75–97.

Brauns, C. D. and L. G. Loffler. 1990. *Mru: Hill people on the border of Bangladesh*. Basel and Boston: Birkäauser Verlag.

Breton, R. J. L. 1997. *Atlas of the languages and ethnic communities of South Asia*. New Delhi: Sage Publications India.

Bright, W. (ed.). 1992. *Oxford international encyclopedia of linguistics, Vol. 1-4.* Oxford: Oxford University Press.

Bril, I. (ed.). 2010. *Clause linking and clause hierarchy: syntax and pragmatics.* Studies in languages companion series. Amsterdam: John Benjamins.

Burenhult, N. and C. Wegener. 2009. Preliminary notes on the phonology, orthography and vocabulary of Semnam (Austroasiatic, Malay Peninsula). . *Journal of the Southeast Asian Linguistics Society* 1:283–312.

Burling, R. 2003. The Tibeto-Burman languages of Northeast India. In G. Thurgood and R. J. LaPolla (eds.), *The Sino-Tibetan languages*, pp. 167–192. London and New York: Routledge.

Busenitz, R. L. 1991. Lexicostatistic and sociolinguistic survey of Balantak and Andio. In T. Friberg (ed.), *More Sulawesi sociolinguistic surveys, 1987-1991*, pp. 1–22. Workpapers in Indonesian Linguistics and Cultures 11. Ujung Pandang, Indonesia: Summer Institute of Linguistics.

CIP-EY. 2002. *National indigenous peoples population statistics.* Taipei, Taiwan: Council of Indigenous Peoples, Executive Yuan.

Cacopardo, A. M. and A. S. Cacopardo. 2001. *Gates of Peristan: History, religion, and society in the Hindu Kush.* Rome: Instituto Italiano per l'Africa e l'Oriente.

Cardoso, H. C. 2006. Challenges to Indo-Portuguese across India. In R. Elangaiyan, R. McKenna Brown, N. D. M. Ostler, and M. K. Verma (eds.), *Proceedings of the Tenth Annual Meeting of the Foundation for Endangered Languages*, pp. 23–30. Mysore, India Central Institute of Indian Languages and Foundation for Endangered Languages.

Castro, A. 2011. Southern Sui: a fourth Sui dialect. *Journal of the Southeast Asian Linguistics Society* 4(2):1-31.

Chauhan, A. 2002. *First-hand linguistic information on Kanash.* Shimla: Himachal Academy of Languages, Culture and Arts.

Chowdhury, J. N. 1996. *Arunachal Panorama.* Directorate of Research, Arunachal Pradesh. Itanagar, New Delhi: M/s. Himalayan Publishers.

Clouse, D., F. Ma, and M. Donohue. 2002. *Survey report of the north coast of Irian Jaya.* SIL Electronic Survey Reports 2002-078. Dallas: SIL International. http://www.sil.org/silesr/abstract.asp?ref=2002-078. Accessed 15 October 2012.

Cohen, D. 1985. Judeo-Arabic of North Africa. In J. A. Fishman (ed.), *Readings in the sociology of Jewish languages*, pp. 246–260. Leiden: E. J. Brill.

Collins, J. T. 1980. *Ambonese Malay and creolization theory.* Kuala Lumpur: Dewan Bahasa dan Pustaka.

Collins, J. T. 1983. *The historical relationships of the languages of Central Maluku, Indonesia.* Pacific Linguistics D-47. Canberra: Australian National University.

Collins, J. T. 2001. *Borneo and Malay dialectology*, Borneo Homeland Data Paper 5. Bangi: Institut Alam dan Tamadun Melayu.

Collins, J. T. 2003. *Malay and Malayic: The classification of the Menterap language.* Paper presented at Pertemuan Linguistik Lembaga Bahasa Atma Jaya. Jakarta.

Comrie, B. (ed.). 1987. *The world's major languages.* London: Routledge.

Cooper, R. L. 1989. *Language planning and social change.* Cambridge: Cambridge University Press.

Crevels, M. 2007. South America. In C. Moseley (ed.), *Encyclopedia of the world's endangered languages*, pp. 103–196. London: Routledge.

Crystal, D. 2003. *English as a global language.* 2nd edition. Cambridge and New York: Cambridge University Press.

Dai Qingxia and Duan Kuangle. 1995. *Haniy Gailun.* Kunming: Yunnan Minzu Chubanshe (Ethnic Affairs Commission of Simao Administrative Bureau of Yunnan Province).

Dawkins, E. and A. Phillips. 2009. *A sociolinguistic survey of Pwo Karen in northern Thailand.* Chiang Mai: Payap University.

Dawkins, E. and C. Kirkland. 2008. *A sociolinguistic survey of Tai Ya in Thailand.* SIL Electronic Survey Reports 2008-015. Dallas: SIL International. http://www/sil.org/silesr/abstract.asp?ref=2008-015. Accessed 15 October 2012.

Decker, K. D. and S. J. Decker. 1992. *Languages of Chitral.* Sociolinguistic Survey of Northern Pakistan 5. Islamabad: National Institute of Pakistan Studies, Quaid-i-Azam University and Summer Institute of Linguistics.

Decker, S. J., D. G. Hallberg, and C. R. Rensch. 1992. *Languages of Kohistan.* Sociolinguistic Survey of Northern Pakistan 1. Islamabad: National Institute of Pakistan Studies, Quaid-i-Azam University and Summer Institute of Linguistics.

Diffloth, G. 1984. *The Dvaravati Old Mon Language and Nyah Kur*, Monic language studies 1. Bangkok, Thailand: Chulalongkorn University Print. House.

Diffloth, G. and N. Zide. 1992. Austro-Asiatic languages. In W. Bright (ed.), *Oxford International Encyclopedia of Linguistics, Vol. 1*, pp. 137–158. New York: Oxford University Press.

Diller, A. 2008. *The Tai-Kadai languages.* London: Routledge Curzon.

Diller, A. and P. Juntanamalaga. 1990. "Full hearts" and empty pronominals in Thai. *Australian Journal of Linguistics* 10(2):231–255.

Dimmendaal, G. J. and F. K. E. Voeltz. 2007. Africa. In C. Moseley (ed.), *Encyclopedia of the world's endangered languages*, pp. 579–634. London: Routledge.

Doerfer, G., W. Hesche, H. Scheinhardt, and S. Tezcan. 1971. *Khalaj materials*, Uralic and Altaic Series 115. Bloomington: Indiana University Publications.

Donohue, M. 1998. Transitivity in Tukang Besi. *Studies in Language* 22(1):83–111.

Dreyer, J. T. 1976. *China's forty millions: Minority nationalities and national integration in the People's Republic of China.* Harvard East Asia Series 87. Cambridge, MA: Harvard University Press.

Drower, E. S. 1937. *The Mandaeans of Iraq and Iran.* Oxford: Clarendon Press.

Dupree, L. 1980. *Afghanistan.* Princeton: Princeton University Press.

ELDIA. 2006. *Europeans and their languages.* Eurobarometer 243. Brussels: Directorate-General Communication (European Commission).

ELDIA. 2012. *Europeans and their languages.* Special Eurobarometer 386. Brussels: Directorate-General Communication (European Commission). http://ec.europa.eu/public_opinion/archives/ebs/ebs_386_en.pdf.

Ebert, K. 1994. *The structure of Kiranti languages, comparative grammar and texts: Kiranti subordination in the South Asian areal context.* Zürich: Arbeiten des Seminars für Allgemeine Sprachwissenschaft (ASAS).

Edmondson, J. A. 1992. Eastern Cham as a tone language. *Mon Khmer Studies* 20:31–43.

Edmondson, J. A. and D. Solnit (eds.). 1997. *Comparative Kadai: The Tai branch.* Publications in Linguistics 124. Dallas: Summer Institute of Linguistics and the University of Texas at Arlington.

Epp, R. 1993. *The story of Low German and Plautdietsch.* Hillsboro, Kansas: The Reader's Press.

Farhadi, A. and G. Raven. 1967. *Languages.* Kabul: Kabul Times Publishing Agency.

Fattah, I. K. 2000. *Les dialectes Kurdes méridionaux.* Acta Iranica Étude linguistique et dialectologique. Louvain: Peters.

Ferguson, C. A. 1968. Language development. In J. A. Fishman, C. A. Ferguson, and J. Das Gupta (eds.), *Language problems of developing nations*, pp. 27–36. New York: Wiley and Sons.

Ferlus, M. 1996. Langues et peuples viet-muong. *Mon-Khmer Studies* 16:7–28.

Fischer, W. and O. Jastrow (eds.). 1980. *Handbuch der arabischen Dialekte.* Wiesbaden: Harrassowitz.

Fishman, J. A. (ed.). 1985. *Readings in the sociology of Jewish languages.* Leiden: E. J. Brill.

Fishman, J. A. 1991. *Reversing language shift.* Clevedon: Multilingual Matters.

Fleisch, H. 1974. *Études d'Arabe dialectal.* Beirut: Dar el-Machreq.

Florey, M. 2005. Language shift and endangerment. In A. Adelaar and N. P. Himmelman (eds.), *The Austronesian languages of Asia and Madagascar*, pp. 43–64. London: Routledge.

Forth, G. L. 1993. Ritual and ideology in Nage mortuary culture. *Asian Journal of Social Science* 21(2):37–61.

Foster, B. L. 1972. *Ethnicity and economy: The case of the Mons in the Thailand.* Ph.D. dissertation, University of Michigan.

Fox, J. J. 1991. The flow of life in Nusa Tenggara. In D. Pickell (ed.), *East of Bali: from Lombok to Timor*, pp. 30–35. Berkeley and Singapore: Periplus.

Friberg, T. and T. V. Laskowske. 1989. South Sulawesi languages. In J. N. Sneddon (ed.), *Studies in Sulawesi languages*, pp. 1–17. Linguistic Studies of Indonesian and Other Languages in Indonesia 31. Jakarta: Universitas Katolik Indonesia Atma Jaya.

GXLOUS. 2005. *Guangxi language and orthography use survey.* Guangxi Zhuang Autonomous Region Language Commission. Nanning, China: Guangxi Education Press.

Gair, J. W. 1998. *Sinhala and other South East Asian languages.* New York: Oxford University Press.

Gengxia Wengmu and Hu Shujin. 2008. Analysis of the linguistic island phenomenon in the multilingual environment of Daofu county. *Journal of the Southwest University of Nationalities: Humanities and Social Sciences* 29(5):86–90.

Gil, D. 2001. Creoles, complexity and Riau Indonesian. *Linguistic Typology* 5:325–371.

Go, K. Z. 1996. *A critical historical study of Bible translations among the Zo people.* Churachandpur, Manipur, India: Chin Baptist Literature Board.

Gold, D. L. 1974. Jewish intralinguistics. *Sociological Abstracts.* Supplement 47(1):344.

Gong, Q. 2007. *Zhabayu yanjiu [A study of the Zhaba language].* Beijing: Minzu Chuban She.

Gowda, K. K. 1976. Phonology of Sanket dialect. In R. C. Hiremath and J. S. Kulli (eds.), *Proceedings of the third all India conference of Dravidian linguists.* Dharwar: Extension Service and Publications, Karnatak University.

Gray, R. D., A. J. Drummond, and S. J. Greenhill. 2009. Language phylogenies reveal expansion pulses and pauses in Pacific settlement. *Science* 323(5913):479–483.

Grimes, B. D. 1991. Exploring the sociolinguistics of Ambonese Malay. In R. Harlow (ed.), *VICAL 2: Western Austronesian and contact languages, parts I and II: Papers from the fifth International Conference on Austronesian Linguistics, Auckland, New Zealand*, pp. 131–168. Auckland: Linguistic Society of New Zealand.

Grimes, B. D. 1991. The development and use of Ambonese Malay. In H. Steinhauer (ed.), *Papers in Austronesian Linguistics 1*, pp. 83-123. Pacific Linguistics A-81. Canberra: Australian National University.

Grimes, B. D. 1994. Cloves and nutmeg, traders and wars: Language contact in the Spice Islands. In T. E. Dutton and D. T. Tryon (eds.), *Language contact and change in the Austronesian world*, pp. 251–274. Trends in Linguistics: Studies and Monographs 77. Berlin: Mouton de Gruyter.

Grimes, C. E. 1982. *Report on a preliminary survey of the languages of North Maluku.* Jakarta: SIL International.

Grimes, C. E. and B. D. Grimes. 1987. *Languages of South Sulawesi.* Pacific Linguistics D-78. Canberra: Australian National University.

Grimes, C. E., T. Therik, B. D. Grimes, and M. Jacob. 1997. *A guide to the people and languages of Nusa Tenggara.* Center for Regional Studies, Paradigma, series B, no. 1. Kupang: Artha Wacana Press.

Grimes, J. E. 1974. *Word lists and languages.* Technical Report 2. Ithaca, NY: Cornell University, Department of Modern Languages and Linguistics.

Grimes, J. E. 1986. Area norms of language size. In B. F. Elson (ed.), *Language in global perspective: Papers in honor of the fiftieth anniversary of the Summer Institute of Linguistics*, pp. 5–20. Dallas: Summer Institute of Linguistics.

Grimes, J. E. 1995. Language endangerment in the Pacific. *Oceanic Linguistics* 34(1):1–12.

Grjunberg, A. L. 1968. *Languages of the Eastern Hindu Kush.* Moscow: Nauka Publishing House, Central Department of Oriental Literature.

Guillon, E. 1999. *The Mons, a civilization of Southeast Asia.* Bangkok: The Siam Society.

Gunnemark, E. and D. Kenrick. 1985. *A geolinguistic handbook.* Sweden: Gunnemark.

Gurung, H. 1997. *Faces of Nepal.* Kathmandu: Himal Books.

Gusain, L. 2002. *Endangered language: A case study of Sansiboli.* Language in India 2. http://www.languageinindia.com/dec2002/sansi.html. Accessed 15 October 2012.

Hajek, J. 2006. On the edge of the Pacific: Indonesia and East Timor. In D. Cunningham, D. E. Ingram, and K. Sumbuk (eds.), *Language diversity in the Pacific: endangerment and survival*, pp. 122–131. Clevedon, UK: Multilingual Matters.

Hajo, Z. 1994. *Die kurdische Sprache und ihre Dialekte. Ein Beitrag zur Standardisierung des Kurdischen.* Kurdologie Studien zu Sprache, Geschichte, Gesellschaft und Politik Kurdistans und der Kurden und Kurdinnen 73–82. Berlin: Allgemeiner Studierendenausschuss der Frei Univesität Berlin.

Hale, A. 1982. *Research on Tibeto-Burman languages.* Trends in Linguistics: State-of-the-Art Report 14. Berlin: Mouton.

Hansson, G. 1991. *The Rai of eastern Nepal: Ethnic and linguistic grouping. Findings of the Linguistic Survey of Nepal.* Kirtipur, Nepal: Centre for Nepal and Asian Studies, Tribhuvan University.

Hattaway, P. 2000. *Operation China.* Pasadena: William Carey Library.

Headland, T. H. 1989. Population decline in a Philippine Negrito hunter-gatherer society. *American Journal of Human Biology* 1:59–72.

Heegård Petersen, J. 2006. *Local case-marking in Kalasha.* Ph.D. dissertation, Department of Nordic Studies and Linguistics, University of Copenhagen.

Himmelmann, N. P. 2001. *Sourcebook on Tomini-Tolitoli languages: General information and word lists.* Pacific Linguistics 511. Canberra: Australian National University.

Himmelmann, N. P. and J. U. Wolff. 1999. *Toratán (Ratahan).* Languages of the World/Materials 130. Munich: LINCOM Europa.

Hinton, B. 2000. The languages of Wetar: Recent survey results and word lists with notes on Tugun grammar. In

C. E. Grimes (ed.), *Spices from the east: Papers in languages of eastern Indonesia*, pp. 105–139. Pacific Linguistics 503. Canberra: Australian National University.

Holes, C. 1988. The typology of Omani Arabic dialects, *Proceedings of the BRISMES International Conference on Middle Eastern Studies*, pp. 12–21. Leeds: University of Leeds.

Holes, C. 1990. *Gulf Arabic*. New York: Routledge.

Holm, J. A. 1989. *Pidgins and Creoles*. Cambridge: Cambridge University Press.

Huang, L. M. 2000. Focus system of Mayrinax Atayal: a syntactic, semantic and pragmatic perspective. *Oceanic Linguistics* 39:364–390.

Hudson, A. B. 1978. Linguistic relations among Bornean peoples with special reference to Sarawak, an interim report. *Studies in Third World Societies* 3:1–44.

Huffman, F. E. 1976. The register problem in fifteen Mon-Khmer languages. In P. N. Jenner, L. C. Thompson, and S. Starosta (eds.), *Austroasiatic studies, Vol. I*. Oceanic Linguistics Special Publications 13, pp. 567–589. Honolulu: The University of Hawai'i Press.

Hugoniot, R. D. (ed.). 1970. *A bibliographical index of the lesser known languages and dialects of India and Nepal*. Kathmandu: Summer Institute of Linguistics.

IMA. 1997. *Peoples of India*. Chennai, India: India Missions Association.

ISO. 2007. *ISO 639-3:2007: Codes for the representation of names of languages—Part 3: Alpha-3 code for comprehensive coverage of languages*. Geneva: International Organization for Standardization.

Ingham, B. 1982. *Northeast Arabian dialects*. London: Kegan Paul International.

Ingham, B. 1994. *Najdi Arabic: Central Arabian*. Amsterdam: John Benjamins.

Izadi, M. 1992. *The Kurds: A concise handbook*. Cambridge: Harvard University Press.

Janhunen, J. (ed.). 2003. *The Mongolic languages*. London: Routledge.

Janhunen, J. 1989. A Sino-Finnish joint expedition to the minority nationalities of northern China. *Suomalais-Ugrilaisen Seuran Aikakauskiria* 82:277–279.

Jastrow, O. 1978. *Die Mesopotamisch-Arabischen qeltu-Dialekte*. Wiesbaden: Franz Steiner GmbH.

Jiafa Ji. 1994. *Yi language dialect study: Project of the National Social Sciences*. Beijing: Minzu Press.

Jie, D. 2007. *Bumang language research*. Research into newly discovered languages of China, series D. Bejing: People's Publishing House.

Johnstone, P. 1993. *Operation world*. Grand Rapids: Zondervan Publishing House.

Johnstone, P. and J. Mandryk. 2001. *Operation world*. Waynesboro: Paternoster Lifestyle.

Johnstone, T. M. 1967. *Eastern Arabian dialect studies*. London: Oxford University Press.

Jones, R. B. 1988. Proto-Burmese as a test of reconstruction. In C. Duncan-Rose and T. Vennemann (eds.), *On Language+ Rhetorica, phonologica, syntactica: A festschrift for Robert P Stockwell*, pp. 203–211. London and New York: Routledge.

Jordan-Diller, K. and J. Diller. 2004. The Prai of Northern Thailand: A sociolinguistic survey of a Mon-Khmer language. *Mon-Khmer Studies* 34:19–45.

Kara, G. 1990. Ural-Altaische Jahrbücher. *Internationale Zeitschrift für Nord-Eurasien* 62:167–168.

Kawi, D., M. R. M. T. Lauder, B. Aritonang, N. Martis, Ayatrohaedi, F. A. Datang, H. Astar, and W. Kurniawati. 2002. *Penelitian Kekerabatan dan Pemetaan Bahasa-bahasa daerah di Indonesia: Provinsi Kalimantan Timur*. Jakarta: Pusat Bahasa.

Kaye, A. S. 1987. Arabic. In B. Comrie (ed.), *The world's major languages*, pp. 664–685. London: Croom Helm.

Kibrik, A. E. 1991. The problem of endangered languages in the USSR. In R. H. Robins and E. M. Uhlenbeck (eds.), *Endangered languages*, pp. 257–273. Oxford: Berg Publishers.

Kiefer, C. M. 2009. Parachi. In G. Windfuhr (ed.), *The Iranian languages*, pp. 693–720. London: Routledge.

King, J. K. and J. W. King (eds.). 1984. *Languages of Sabah: A survey report*. Pacific Linguistics C-78. Canberra: Australian National University.

King, J. T. 1994. Picking up where Hodgson left off: Further notes on Dhimal. *Journal of the Tibeto-Burman Area* 17(2):121–132.

Klamer, M. and M. A. F. Klamer. 2010. *A grammar of Tewa*. Berlin and New York: Mouton de Gruyter.

Kloss, H. and G. D. McConnell (eds.). 1974. *Linguistic composition of the nations of the world. Central and Western South Asia, Vol. 1*. Sainte-Foy: Les Presses de l'Université Laval.

Koentjaraninggrat (ed.). 1971. *Manusia dan kebudayaan di Indonesia*. Jakarta: Djambatan.

Koryakov, Y. B. 2006. . Moscow: Institute of Linguistics, Russian Academy of Sciences.

Koul, O. and R. Schmidt. 1983. *Kashmiri: A sociolinguistic survey*. Delhi: Madaan Publishers.

Krauss, M. E. 1992. The world's languages in crisis. *Language* 68:4–10.

Kroeger, P. R. 1985. Linguistic relations among the Dusunic groups in the Kota Marudu District. *Borneo Research Bulletin* 17(1):31–46.

Kroeger, P. R. 1986. Intelligibility patterns in Sabah and the problem of prediction. In P. A. Geraghty, L. Carrington, and S. A. Wurm (eds.), *FOCAL I: Papers from the Fourth International Congress on Austronesian Linguistics*, pp. 309–339. Pacific Linguistics C-93. Canberra: Australian National University.

Kruspe, N. 2009. Loanwords in Ceq Wong, an Austroasiatic language of Peninsular Malaysia. In M. Haspelmath and U. Tadmor (eds.), *Loanwords in the world's languages*, pp. 659–685. Berlin: De Gruyter Mouton.

Lal, M. (ed.). 1991. *Navaratri to Sarvasena*. New Delhi: Sahitya.

Laskowske, T. V. and K. B. Laskowske. 1987. Seko area (Kabupaten Luwu). In T. Friberg (ed.), *Universitas Hasanuddin-SIL South Sulawesi sociolinguistic surveys, 1983-1987*, pp. 41–57. Workpapers in Indonesian Languages and Cultures 5. Ujung Pandang: Summer Institute of Linguistics.

Lauder, M. R. M. T., F. Ayatrohaedi, H. Datang, B. Lapoliwa, F. Aritonang, S. Feirizal, N. Martis, W. Kurniawati, and H. Astar. 2000. *Penelitian kekerabatan dan pemetaan bahasa-bahasa daerah di Indonesia: Propinsi Sulawesi Tengah*. Jakarta: Pusat Pembinaan dan Pengembangan Bahasa, Departemen Pendidikan Nasional.

Lebar, F. M., G. C. Hickey, and J. K. Musgrave. 1964. *Ethnic groups of mainland Southeast Asia*. New Haven: Human Relations Area Files Press (HRAF).

Lee, M., B. Rai, B. K. Rai, and C. Boone. 2005. *Bayung Rai: A sociolinguistic survey*. Kirtipur, Nepal: Centre for Nepal and Asian Studies, Tribhuvan University.

Lewis, E. D. and C. E. Grimes. 1995. Sika: An introduction and wordlist. In D. T. Tryon (ed.), *Comparative Austronesian dictionary, part 1*, pp. 601–609. Berlin: Mouton de Gruyter.

Lewis, M. P. 1999. Language (development) as particle, wave, and field. *Notes on Sociolinguistics* 4(1):3–19.

Lewis, M. P. and G. F. Simons. 2010. Assessing endangerment: Expanding Fishman's GIDS. *Revue Roumaine de Linguistique* 55(2):103–120. http://www.lingv.ro/RRL 2 2010 art01Lewis.pdf. Accessed 11 January 2011.

Li Fang-gui. 1973. Languages and dialects of China. *Journal of Chinese Linguistics* 1:1–13.

Li Fengxiang and L. J. Whaley. 2009. Oroqen vocabulary. In M. Haspelmath and T. Uri (eds.), *Loanwords in the world's languages, a comparative handbook*, pp. 525–574. Berlin: De Gruyter.

Li Jinfang. 1997. *Buyang language research.* Beijing: Central Nationalities University Press.

Li Jinfang. 2006. *A survey of endangered languages of the Southwest Region.* Beijing: Central Nationalities University Press.

Li, P. J. K. 1990. Classification of Formosan languages: Lexical evidence. *The Bulletin of the Institute of History and Philology, Academia Sinica* 61(4):809–844.

Liang Min and Zhang Junru. 2002. *Study of the Biao language.* Beijing: Central Nationalities University Press.

Liang Min. 1990. The Buyang language. In J. A. Edmondson (ed.), *Kadai: Discussion in Kadai and Southeast Asian linguistics, Vol. 2*, pp. 13–55. Arlington, TX: University of Texas at Arlington.

Lieberson, S. 1981. *Language diversity and language contact.* Palo Alto: Stanford University Press.

Liljegren, H. 2008. *Towards a grammatical description of Palula: An Indo-Aryan language of the Hindu Kush.* Stockholm: Department of Linguistics, Stockholm University.

Lim, S. 1981. *Baba Malay, the language of the "Straits-born" Chinese.* M.A. thesis, Monash University, Australia.

Lin Xiangrong. 1993. *Jiarongyu yanjiu.* Chengdu: Sichuan Nationality Press.

Lobel, J. W. 2004. Old Bikol -um- vs- mag- and the loss of a morphological paradigm. *Oceanic Linguistics* 43(2):469–497.

Lobel, J. W. 2005. The angry register of the Bikol languages of the Philippines. In Hsiu-chuan Liao and C. R. Galvez Rubino (eds.), *Current issues in Philippine linguistics and anthropology: Parangal kay Lawrence A Reid*, pp. 149–166. Manila: Linguistic Society of the Philippines and SIL Philippines.

Lobel, J. W. 2010. Manide: An undescribed Philippine language. *Oceanic Linguistics* 29(2):478–510.

Lobel, J. W. 2012. *Issues in Philippine and Philippine-type languages.* Ph.D. dissertation, University of Hawaii.

Loski, R. A. and G. M. Loski. 1989. The languages indigenous to Eastern Seram and adjacent islands. *Workpapers in Indonesian Languages and Cultures* 6:103–142.

Lothers, L. and M. D. Lothers. 2007. *Pahari and Pothwari: A sociolinguistic survey.* Frontier Language Institute Language and Culture Series 2. Peshawar, Pakistan: Frontier Language Institute.

Lunsford, W. A. 2001. *An overview of linguistic structures in Torwali, a language of Northern Pakistan.* M.A. thesis, University of Texas at Arlington.

Maddieson, I. U. 1991. *Utset: A Chamic tone language of Hainan.* Paper presented at Sixth International Conference of Austronesian Linguistics. Honolulu.

Makoni, S. and A. Pennycook (eds.). 2006. *Disinventing and reconstituting languages.* Bilingual education and bilingualism. Bristol, UK: Multilingual Matters.

Manson, K. 2010. *A Grammar of Kayan, a Tibeto-Burman language.* Ph.D. dissertation, LaTrobe University.

Manson, K. 2011. The subgrouping of Karen. *Journal of the South East Asian Linguistics Society* 21:11–13.

Marrison, G. E. 1967. *The classification of the Naga languages of north east India.* Ph.D. dissertation, University of London.

Marshall, C. 2000. A phonological description of Fordata. In C. E. Grimes (ed.), *Spices from the east: Papers in languages of eastern Indonesia*, pp. 181–235. Pacific Linguistics 503. Canberra: Australian National University.

Martens, M. 1989. The Badaic languages of Central Sulawesi. In J. N. Sneddon (ed.), *Studies in Sulawesi linguistics, part 1*, pp. 19–53. NUSA: Linguistic Studies of Indonesian and Other Languages in Indonesia 31. Jakarta: Badan Penyelenggara Seri Nusa, Universitas Atma Jaya.

Martin, P. W. 1995. Whither the indigenous languages of Brunei Darussalem? *Oceanic Linguistics* 34(1):27–43.

Martin, P. W., C. Oxog, and G. Poedjosoedarmo (eds.). 1996. *Language use and language change in Brunei Darussalam.* Athens: Ohio University Center for International Studies.

Maryott, K. R. 1993. The Sangir language project: A status report (Penyelidikan bahasa dan perkembangan wawasannya), *Vol. 1*, pp. 320–358. Jakarta: Masyarakat Linguistik Indonesia.

Masica, C. P. 1991. *The Indo-Aryan languages.* Cambridge: Cambridge University Press.

Masinambow, E. K. M. and P. Haenen. 2002. *Bahasa Indonesia dan Bahasa Daerah.* Jakarta: Yayasan Obor.

Matisoff, J. A. 1991. Endangered languages of Mainland Southeast Asia. In R. H. Robins and E. M. Uhlenbeck (eds.), *Endangered languages*, pp. 189–228. Oxford: Berg Publishers.

Matisoff, J. A., S. P. Baron, and J. B. Lowe. 1996. *Languages and dialects of Tibeto-Burman.* Sino-Tibetan Etymological Dictionary and Thesaurus Monograph Series 1 and 2. Berkeley: University of California Press.

Matthias, W. 2011. Domaaki. In T. I. Oranskaia, Y. V. Mazurova, A. A. Kibrik, L. I. Kulikov, and A. Y. Rusakov (eds.), *Iazyki mira: novye indoariiskie iazyki (Languages of the world: New Indo-Aryan languages)*, pp. 165–194. Moscow: Academia.

McCarus, E. N. 2009. Kurdish. In G. Windfuhr (ed.), *The Iranian languages*, pp. 587–633. Routledge Language Family Series. London and New York: Routledge.

McConnell, G. D. (ed.). 1995. *The written languages of the world: A survey of the degree and modes of use.* Quebec City: Laval University Press.

Mead, D. E. 1999. *The Bungku-Tolaki languages of South-Eastern Sulawesi, Indonesia.* Pacific Linguistics D-91. Canberra: Australian National University.

Mead, D. E. 2001. A preliminary sketch of the Bobongko language. In W. D. Laidig (ed.), *Studies in Sulawesi linguistics*, pp. 61–94. NUSA Linguistic Studies of Indonesian and Other Languages in Indonesia 49. Jakarta: Badan Penyelenggara Seri Nusa, Universitas Katolik Indonesia Atma Jaya.

Mead, D. E. and M. Mead. 1991. *Survey of Pamona dialects of Kecamatan Bungku Tengah.* Workpapers in Indonesian Languages and Cultures. Ujung Pandaar: SIL and Universitas Hasanuddin.

Mead, D. E., M.-Y. Lee, and C. Neveux. 2007. *Mapping Indonesian Bajau communities in Sulawesi.* SIL Electronic Survey Reports 2007-019. Dallas: SIL International. http://www.sil.org/silesr/abstract.asp?ref=2007-019. Accessed 15 October 2012.

Meho, L. I. 2002. The Kurds in Lebanon. *The International Journal of Kurdish Studies* 16 (January 2002):59–82. http://www.accessmylibrary.com/article-1G1-132797081/kurds-lebanon-social-and.html. Accessed 18 October 2012.

Menon, M. T. (ed.). 1996. *Encyclopedia of Dravidian tribes, Vol. 1–2.* Thiruvananthapura: The DLA Publications.

Mohammed, N. 2009. *Bahasa Melayu kreol Chetti Melaka: deskripsi leksiko-fonologi.* Penang: Penerbit Universiti Sains Malaysia.

Moody, D. C. and J. R. Walton. 1984. The east coast Bajau

languages. In J. K. King and J. W. King (eds.), *Languages of Sabah: A survey report*, pp. 113–123. Pacific Linguistics C-78. Canberra: Australia National University.

Morey, S. 2006. Small languages in a polylingual situation—the case of Turung. In R. Elangaiyan, R. McKenna Brown, N. D. M. Ostler, and M. K. Verma (eds.), *Vital voices: Endangered languages and multilingualism: Proceedings of the Tenth Foundation for Endangered Languages Conference*, pp. 173–177. Mysore, India: Central Institute of Indian Languages and Foundation for Endangered Languages.

Morgenstierne, G. 1974. Languages of Nuristan and surrounding regions. In K. Jettmas (ed.), *Cultures of the Hindu Kush: Selected papers from the Hindu-Kush Cultural Conference held in Moesgard 1970*, pp. 1–10. Wiesbaden: Franz Steiner GmbH.

Morse, S. A. 1989. Five Rawang dialects compared plus more. In D. Bradley, E. J. A. Henderson, and M. Mazaudon (eds.), *Prosodic analysis and Asian linguistics: To honour R K Sprigg*, pp. 237–250. Pacific Linguistics C-104. Canberra: Australia National University.

Moseley, C. (ed.). 2010. *Atlas of the World's Languages in Danger. 3rd ed.* Paris: UNESCO Publishing.

Musa, M. 2011. The socioeconomic history of the Orang Kanaq of Johor. *Kajian Malaysia* 29(1):47–74.

Naby, E. 1975. Les Assyriens d'Union Sovietique. *Cahiers du Monde Russe et Sovietique* 16 (3–4):445–457. http://www.persee.fr/web/revues/home/prescript/article/cmr_0008-0160_1975_num_16_3_1249.

Nahhas, R. W. 2007. *Sociolinguistic survey of Mpi in Thailand.* SIL Electronic Survey Reports 2007-016. Dallas: SIL International. http://www.sil.org/silesr/abstract.asp?ref=2007-016. Accessed 15 October 2012.

Natarajan, G. V. 1985. *Abujmaria grammar.* Mysore: Central Institute of Indian languages.

Nikolić, H. 2008. *Relasi historis Bahasa Benuaq dalam silsilah kekerabatan Bahasa-bahasa Barito.* M.A. thesis, Universitas Sebelas Maret.

Noonan, M. 1996. The fall and rise and fall of the Chantyal language. *Southwest Journal of Linguistics* 15(1–2):121–136.

Noorduyn, J. 1991. *A critical survey of studies on the languages of Sulawesi.* Leiden: KITLV Press.

Nyrop, R. F. (ed.). 1986. *The Yemens: Country studies.* Washington, D. C.: American University.

Oberling, P. 1974. *The Qashqa'i nomads of Fars.* The Hague: Mouton.

Okamura, T. 2010. Dying language of the island: The direction the Tokunoshima dialect (Shimakuchi) is heading. *Kokubungaku Kaishaku-to Kansho* 75(1):164–167.

Omar, A. H. 1983. *The Malay peoples of Malaysia and their languages.* Kuala Lumpur: Dewan Bahasa Dan Pustaka, Kementerian Pelajaran Malaysia.

Opgenort, J. R. 2004. *A grammar of Wambule: Grammar, lexicon. texts and cultural survey of Rai-Kiranti tribe of eastern Nepal.* Brill's Tibetan Studies Library, Languages of the Greater Himalayan Region 2. Leiden: Koninklijke Brill.

Opgenort, J. R. 2005. *A grammar of Jero, with a historical comparative study of the Kiranti languages.* Brill's Tibetan Studies Library Languages of the Greater Himalayan Region 5/3. Leiden and Boston: Brill.

Ostapirat, W. 2000. Proto-Kra. *Linguistics of the Tibeto-Burman Area* 23(1):1–251.

Pakir, A. G. 1986. *A linguistic investigation of Baba Malay.* Ph.D. dissertation, University of Hawai'i.

Paldan, T. 2002. *Languages change: From preclassical Tibetan to modern spoken Ladakhi.* Paper presented at 8th Himalayan Languages Symposium, September 19–22, 2002. Berne, Switzerland.

Pallesen, A. K. 1985. *Culture contact and language convergence.* Berkeley: University of California Press.

Paper, H. H. (ed.). 1978. *Jewish languages: Theme and variation. 1st ed.* Cambridge, New York: Association for Jewish Studies.

Parkin, R. 1991. *A guide to Austro-Asiatic speakers and their languages.* Oceanic Linguistics Special Publication 23. Honolulu: University of Hawai"i.

Paul, L. 1998. *Zazi [Zazaki]: Grammatik und Versuch einer dialektologie.* Wiesbaden: Dr. Ludwig Reichert Verlag.

Paul, L. 2007. Zur Lage der Gōrānī-Dialekte im Iran und ihrer Erforschung. In M. Macuch, M. Maggi, and W. Sundermann (eds.), *Iranian languages and texts from Iran and Turan*, pp. 285–286. Wiesbaden: Harrassowitz Verlag.

Pawley, E. and M. Pawley. 2010. *Sociolinguistic survey of Jarai in Ratanakiri, Cambodia.* Phnom Phen: International Cooperation Cambodia.

Payne, J. R. 1987. Iranian languages. In B. Comrie (ed.), *The world's major languages, Vol. 13*, pp. 514–522. New York: Oxford University Press.

Pelkey, J. R. 2008. *The Phula languages in synchronic and diachronic perspective.* Ph.D. dissertation, La Trobe University.

Pelkey, J. R. 2011. *Dialectology as dialectic: Interpreting Phula variation.* Trends in Linguistics: Studies and Monographs 229. Berlin: Mouton de Gruyter.

Pike, K. L. 1959. Language as particle, wave, and field. *The Texas Quarterly* 2(2):37–54.

Poppe, N. 1955. *Introduction to Mongolian comparative studies.* Helsinki: Suomalais-Ugrilainen Seura.

Prachakij-karacak, P. 1995. *Some languages of Siam.* Mahidol: Institute of Language and Culture for Rural Development, Mahidol University.

Prentice, D. J. 1971. *The Murut languages of Sabah.* Canberra: Linguistic Circle of Canberra.

Prentice, D. J. 1987. Malay (Indonesian and Malaysian). In B. Comrie (ed.), *The world's major languages*, pp. 913–935. New York: Oxford University Press.

Price, D. S. and M. Donohue. 2009. *Report on the Ansus survey, West Yapen Island, Papua, Indonesia.* SIL Electronic Survey Reports 2009-001. Dallas: SIL International. http://www.sil.org/resources/publications/entry/9126.

Pstrusinska, J. and C. Gray (eds.). 1990. *Afghanistan 1989 in sociolinguistic perspective.* Central Asian Survey Incidental Papers. London: Society for Central Asian Studies.

Purnama, K. 1991. *The sociolinguistic pattern of use of Standard Malay in Brunei Darussalam.* Paper presented at Sixth International Conference of Austronesian Linguistics. Honolulu.

Purnell, H. C. 1970. *Toward a reconstruction of Proto-Miao-Yao.* Ithaca, NY: Cornell University Press.

Quick, P. 2007. *A grammar of the Pendau language of central Sulawesi, Indonesia.* Pacific Linguistics 590. Canberra: Australian National University.

Quilis, A. 1996. La lengua española en Filipinas. In M. Alvar (ed.), *Manual de dialectología hispánica: el español de América, Vol. 2.* Ariel Linguistica. Barcelona: Editorial Ariel.

Rajyashree, K. S. 2001. *Kodava speech community: An ethnolinguistic study.* Language in India 1. http://www.languageinindia.com/oct2001/kodavarajyashree.html. Accessed 15 October 2012.

Ramsey, R. 1987. *The languages of China.* Princeton: Princeton University Press.

Regmi, D. R. 2007. *The Bhujel language.* Ph.D. dissertation, Tribhuvan University.

Rehman, K. A. and J. L. G. Baart. 2005. *A first look at the language of Kundal Shahi in Azad Kashmir.* SIL Electronic Working Papers 2005-008. Dallas: SIL International. http://www.sil.org/silewp/abstract.asp?ref=2005-008. Accessed 15 October 2012.

Reid, L. A. 1971. *Philippine minor languages: Word lists and phonologies.* Oceanic Linguistics Special Publication 8. Honolulu: University of Hawaii Press.

Remijsen, A. C. L. 2001. *Word-prosodic systems of Raja Ampat languages.* Utrecht, The Netherlands: LOT (Netherlands Graduate School of Linguistics).

Rensch, C. R. 2006. Studies in the early Bidayuh language: Proto Bidayuh and its relatives. In C. R. Rensch, C. M. Rensch, J. Noeb, and R. S. Ridu (eds.), *The Bidayuh language: Yesterday, today and tomorrow*, pp. 135–442. Kuching, Sarawak, Malaysia: Dayak Bidayuh National Association.

Rensch, C. R., C. M. Rensch, J. Noeb, and R. S. Ridu (eds.). 2006. *The Bidayuh language: Yesterday, today and tomorrow.* Kuching, Sarawak, Malaysia: Dayak Bidayuh National Association.

Robinne, F. 2000. *Fils et maîtres du lac: relations interethniques dans l' État Shan de Birmanie.* Paris: Centre National de la Recherche Scientifique (CNRS).

Roesler, C. 1972. *The phonology of the Ajam dialect of Asmat.* M.A. thesis, Hartford Seminary Foundation.

Ross, M. D. 2005. Pronouns as a preliminary diagnostic for grouping Papuan languages. In A. Pawley, R. Attenborough, J. Golson, and R. Hide (eds.), *Papuan pasts: Cultural, linguistics and biological histories of Papuan-speaking peoples*, pp. 17–65. Pacific linguistics 572. Canberra: Australian National University.

Rubino, C. 2008. Zamboangueño Chavacano and the potentive mode. In S. Michaelis (ed.), *Roots of creole structures: Weighing the contribution of substrates and superstrates*, pp. 279–299. Creole Language Library 33. Amsterdam and Philadelphia: John Benjamins.

Ruch, E. and S. Quakenbush. 2006. *Pronoun ordering and marking in Kalamiani.* Paper presented at Tenth International Conference on Austronesian Linguistics, January 17-20, 2006. Puerto Princesa City, Palawan, Philippines. http://www-01.sil.org/asia/philippines/ical/papers/Quakenbush-Pronoun%20Ordering%20and%20Marking%20in%20Kalamianic.pdf.

Ruhlen, M. 1987. *A guide to the world's languages, Vol. 1, Classification.* Palo Alto: Stanford University Press.

Salleh, H. (ed.). 2006. *Peoples and traditions.* Encyclopedia of Malaysia 12. Kuala Lumpur: Archipelago Press.

Salman, A. and N. S. Kharusi. 2012. The sound system of Lawatiyya. *Journal of Academic and Applied Studies* 2(5):36-44. http://www.academians.org/articles/may3.pdf.

Salminen, T. 2007. Europe and North Asia. In C. Moseley (ed.), *Encyclopedia of the world's endangered languages*, pp. 211–282. London: Routledge.

Sandler, W., I. Meir, C. Padden, and M. Aronoff. 2005. The emergence of grammar in a new Sign Language. *Proceedings of the National Academy of Sciences* 102(7):2661–2665.

Schliessinger, J. 2003. *Ethnic groups of Laos.* Profile of Austro-Thai speaking peoples 3. Bangkok: White Lotus.

Sebeok, T. A. (ed.). 1963. *Soviet and East European linguistics.* Current Trends in Linguistics 1. The Hague: Mouton.

Sebeok, T. A. (ed.). 1967. *Linguistics in East Asia and Southeast Asia.* Current Trends in Linguistics 2. The Hague: Mouton.

Sebeok, T. A. (ed.). 1970. *Linguistics in Southwest Asia and North Africa.* Current Trends in Linguistics 6. The Hague: Mouton.

Sebeok, T. A. (ed.). 1971. *Linguistics in sub-Saharan Africa.* Current Trends in Linguistics 7. The Hague: Mouton.

Shackle, C. 1979. Problems of classification in Pakistan Panjab. *Transactions of the Philological Society* 77(1):191–210.

Shackle, C. 1980. Hindko in Kohat and Peshawar. *Bulletin of the School of Oriental and African Studies* 43(3):482–510.

Sharma, D. D. 1989. *Tibeto-Himalayan languages of Uttarkhand, Part 1.* Studies in Tibeto-Himalayan languages. New Delhi: Mittal Publications.

Sharma, D. D. 1994. *A comparative grammar of Tibeto Himalayan languages of Himachal Pradesh & Uttarakhand.* Studies in Tibeto-Himalayan Languages. New Delhi: Mittal Publications.

Sharma, H. B. and R. P. Gautam. 1999. *Record on Nepalese development: Nepal district profile. A distinctive socio-techno-economic profile along with a comprehensive national profile.* 4th edition. Kathmandu: Samudayik Printers.

Sharma, S. R. 2001. A sketch of Byangsi grammar. In Y. Nagano and R. LaPolla (eds.), *New research on Zhangzhung and related Himalayan languages.* Osaka: National Museum of Ethnology.

Shashi, P. and S. S. Shri. 1994. *Encyclopedia of Indian tribes.* New Delhi: Anmol Publications.

Shearer, W. and Sun Hong Kai. 2002. *Speakers of the Non-Han languages and dialects in China.* Lewiston, NY: Edwin Mellen Press.

Shibatani, M. 1990. *The languages of Japan.* Cambridge: Cambridge University Press.

Singh, K. S. (ed.). 1994. *Andaman and Nicobar Islands.* People of India 12. Oxford and Calcutta: Anthropolgocal Survey of India with Oxford University Press.

Singh, K. S. (ed.). 1994. *The scheduled tribes.* People of India 3. Calcutta and Delhi: Anthropological Survey of India with Oxford University Press.

Singh, K. S. (ed.). 1995. *Arunachal Pradesh.* People of India 14. Calcutta and Oxford: Anthropological Survey of Indian with Oxford University Press.

Singh, K. S. (ed.). 1995. *The scheduled castes. rev., Vol. 2.* People of India. Delhi: Anthropological Survey of India with Oxford University Press.

Singh, K. S. (ed.). 1998. *India's communities.* People of India 4, 5, 6. Delhi: Anthropological Survey of India with Oxford University Press.

Singh, K. S. (ed.). 1998. *Manipur.* People of India 31. Calcutta and Oxford: Anthropological Survey of India with Oxford University Press.

Singh, K. S. and S. Manoharan (eds.). 1993. *Languages and scripts.* People of India 9. Delhi: Anthropological Survey of India with Oxford University Press.

Singh, K. S., B. K. Bardoloi, and R. K. Athaparia (eds.). 2003. *Assam.* People of India 15. Calcutta: Seagull Books.

Singh, N. 1972. *Bhutan: A kingdom in the Himalayas.* New Delhi: Thomson.

Smalley, W. A. 1976. *Phonemes and orthography: Language planning in ten minority languages of Thailand.* Pacific Linguistics C-43. Canberra: Australian National University.

Smalley, W. A. 1994. *Linguistic diversity and national unity: Language ecology in Thailand.* Chicago: University of Chicago Press.

Smith, K. D. 1968. *Sedan dialects.* M.A. thesis, University of North Dakota.

Smith, K. D. 1972. *A phonological reconstruction of Proto-North-Bahnaric.* Language Data-Asia Pacific Studies 3. Santa Ana: Summer Institute of Linguistics.

Smith, K. D. 1973. Eastern north Bahnaric: Cua and Kotua. *Mon-Khmer Studies* 4:113–118.

Sneddon, J. 2003. *The Indonesian language: its history and role in modern society*. Sydney: University of New South Wales Press.

Sneddon, J. N. and H. T. Usup. 1986. Shared sound changes in the Gorontalic language group: Implications for subgrouping. *Bijdragen tot de Taal-Landen Volkenkunde* 142:407–426.

Soravia, G. 2002. *The Alas language (northern Sumatra)*. Bologna: Bologna University.

Soriente, A. 2003. *A classification of Kenyah variants in Sarawak and Kalimantan*. Ph.D., Universiti Kebangsaan Malaysia.

Soriente, A. 2005. *Linguistic classifications and local epistemology in Borneo: The case of Kenyah languages*. Paper presented at International ATMA-IKON Conference: The Languages and Literatures of Western Borneo: 144 years of research, 30 January–1 February 2005. Univesiti Kebangsaan Malaysia.

Soriente, A. 2006. *Mencaleny and Usung Bayung Marang: A collection of Kenyah stories in the Oma Longh and Lebu' Kulit language*. Jakarta: Atma Jaya University Press.

Stanzer, W. 1988. *Kordi: Leben, Knuepfen, Weben der Kurden Khorasans*. Vienna: Kollektion Adil Besim.

Statistical Bureau of Yunnan Province. 2004. *Yunnan Statistical Yearbook, Vol. 20*. Yunnan: China Statistics Press.

Stevens, A. M. 1968. *Madurese phonology and morphology*. New Haven: American Oriental Society.

Stewart, W. A. 1968. A sociolinguistic typology for describing national multilingualism. In J. A. Fishman (ed.), *Readings in the sociology of language*, pp. 530–553. The Hague: Mouton.

Strand, R. F. 1973. Notes on the Nuristani and Dardic languages. *Journal of the American Oriental Society* 93(3):297–305.

Strand, R. F. 2001. The tongues of Peristân. In A. M. Cacopardo and A. S. Cacopardo (eds.), *Gates of Peristân: History, religion and society in the Hindu Kush*, pp. 251–259. Rome: Instituto Italiano per l'Africa e l'Oriente.

Strecker, D. 1987. The Hmong-Mien languages. *Linguistics of the Tibeto-Burman Area* 10(2):1–11.

Strecker, D. 1989. *Hmongic noun prefixes*. Paper presented at Linguistic Society of America Annual Meeting, December 1989. Washington, D. C.

Strømme, K. J. 1987. Kabupaten Polewali Mamasa, west-central section. In T. Friberg (ed.), *Universitas Hasanuddin-SIL South Sulawesi sociolinguistic surveys, 1983–1987*, pp. 17–40. Workpapers in Indonesian Languages and Cultures 5. Ujung Pandang: Summer Institute of Linguistics.

Sun Hong Kai and Liu Guangkun. 2009. *A grammar of Anong: Language death under intense contact*. Brill's Tibetan Studies Library 9. Leiden: Brill.

Sáenz-Badillos, A. 1993. *A history of the Hebrew language*. Cambridge: Cambridge University Press.

Thomas, D. D. 1969. Mon-Khmer subgroupings in Vietnam. *Mon-Khmer Studies* 3:74–75.

Thomas, D. D. 1976. South Bahnaric and other Mon-Khmer numeral systems. *Linguistics* 174:65–80.

Thomas, D. D. 1980. The place of Alak, Tampuan, and West Bahnaric. *Mon-Khmer Studies* 8:171–186.

Thomas, D. D. and R. K. Headley, Jr. 1970. More on Mon-Khmer subgroupings. *Lingua* 25:398–418.

Thongkum, T. L. 1984. *Rhythmic groups and stress groups in Thai*. Paper presented at International Conference on Thai Studies Chulalongkorn University, Bangkok.

Thurgood, G. and R. LaPolla (eds.). 2003. *The Sino-Tibetan languages*. London: Routledge.

Thurston, E. and K. Rangachari. 1909. *Castes and tribes of Southern India, Vol. 5*. Madras: Madras Government Press.

Tjia, J. 2007. *A Grammar of Mualang: An Ibanic language of Western Kalimantan, Indonesia*. Leiden, Netherlands: Netherlands Graduate School of Linguistics.

Toba, S. 1976. National language and ethnic minority languages in Nepal. *Symposium Nepal Japan Nepal Society* 4:30–36.

Toba, S. 1983. *A phonological reconstruction of Proto-Northern Rai*. M.A. thesis, University of Texas at Arlington.

Toba, S. 1991. *A bibliography of Nepalese languages and linguistics*. Kathmandu: Linguistic Society of Nepal.

Toba, S., I. Toba, and N. K. Rai. 2002. *UNESCO Language survey report Nepal*. Kathmandu: UNESCO.

Toba, S., I. Toba, and N. K. Rai. 2005. *Diversity and endangerment of languages of Nepal*. UNESCO Kathmandu Series of Monographs and Working Papers 7. Kathmandu: United Nations Educational, Scientific and Cultural Organization.

Tryon, D. T. (ed.). 1995. *Comparative Austronesian dictionary: An introduction to Austronesian studies. Parts 1-4*. Berlin: Mouton de Gruyter.

Tsuchida, S. 1976. *Reconstruction of Proto-Tsouic phonology*. Tokyo: Institute of Asian and African Languages and Cultures, University of Foreign Language.

Tsukida, N. and S. Tsuchida. 2007. Indigenous languages of Formosa. In O. Miyaoka, Osamu Sakiyama, and Michael E. Krauss (ed.), *The vanishing languages of the Pacific Rim*, pp. 285-300. Oxford linguistics. Oxford: Oxford University Press.

Turin, M. 1999. Whence Thangmi? Historical ethnography and comparative morphology. In Y. P. Yadava and W. G. Glover (eds.), *Topics in Nepalese Linguistics*, pp. 451–477. Kathmandu: Royal Nepal Academy.

Turin, M. 2007. *Linguistic diversity and the preservation of endangered languages: A case study from Nepal*. Kathmandu: International Centre for Integrated Mountain Development (ICIMOD).

Utsumi, A. 2001. An overview of the syntactic structure of the Bantik language. *Tokyo daigaku gengogaku ronshū (Tokyo University Linguistics Papers)* 20:221–236.

Vail, I. W. 1991. Sociolinguistic survey report, Kabupaten Luwu: Report on the Rongkong-Luwu languages. In T. Friberg (ed.), *Universitas Hasanuddin-SIL: More Sulawesi sociolinguistic surveys, 1987-1991*, pp. 55–105. Workpapers in Indonesian Languages and Cultures 11. Ujung Pandang: Summer Institute of Linguistics

Valkama, K. 1987. Universitas Hasanuddin-SIL sociolinguistic survey: Kabupaten Majuju, Kabupatens Pinrang, Enrekang, Tana Toraja, Luwu and eastern part of Polewali Mamasa. In T. Friberg (ed.), *South Sulawesi sociolinguistic surveys*, pp. 99–136. Workpapers in Indonesian Languages and Cultures 5. Ujung Pandang: SIL.

Van Bik, K. 2006. *Proto-Kuki-Chin*. Ph.D. dissertation, University of California.

Van Cleve, J. V. (ed.). 1986. *Encyclopedia of Deaf people and deafness*. Washington, D. C.: Gallaudet University.

Van Driem, G. (ed.). 1997. *Current trends in linguistics: Himalayan linguistics*. Berlin: Mouton de Gruyter.

Van Driem, G. 1993. *The grammar of Dzongkha*. Bhutan: Dzongkha Development Commission, Royal Government of Bhutan.

Van Driem, G. 2001. *Languages of the Himalayas: An ethnolinguistic handbook of the greater Himalayan region containing an introduction to the symbiotic theory of language*. Leiden: Brill.

Van Driem, G. 2007. South Asia and the Middle East. In C. Moseley (ed.), *Encyclopedia of the world's endangered languages*, pp. 283–348. London: Routledge.

Varenkamp, B. K. 1996. *Tamang Tam: A sociolinguistic study of Eastern Tamang dialects (in Nepal)*. Kirtipur: Centre for Nepal and Asian Studies.

Verheijen, J. A. J. 1986. *The Sama/Bajau language in the lesser Sunda Islands*. Pacific Linguistics D-70. Canberra: Australian National University.

Voegelin, C. F. and F. M. Voegelin. 1977. *Classification and index of the world's languages*. New York: Elsevier.

Von Fürer-Haimendorf, C. 1975. *Himalayan traders*. London: John Murray Publishers.

Voorhoeve, C. L. and J. T. Collins. 1981. Moluccas (Maluku). In S. A. Wurm and S. Hattori (eds.), *Language atlas of the Pacific Area, part II: Japan area, Taiwan (Formosa), Philippines, mainland and insular south-east Asia* , pp. 45–46. Pacific Linguistics. Canberra: The Australian Academy of the Humanities in collaboration with the Japan Academy.

Voorhoeve, C. L. and L. E. Visser. 1987. *Sahu-Indonesian-English dictionary and Sahu grammar sketch*. Dordrecht: Foris Publications.

Wang Fushi and Mao Zongwu. 1995. *A phonological reconstruction of the ancient Miao-Yao/Hmong-Mien language*. Beijing: Chinese Academy of Social Sciences Press.

Wang Mingfu and E. Johnson. 2008. *Zhuang cultural and linguistic heritage (Yunnan sheng wenshan Zhuang zu miao zu zizhi zhou zhuang zu wenhua yichan ji Zhuang yu yanjiu)*. Kunming, China: Yunnan Nationalities Publishing House.

Watters, D. E. 2002. *A grammar of Kham*. Cambridge: Cambridge University Press.

Wei, J. and J. A. Edmondson. 2008. Sui. In A. Diller, V. Nostrand, J. A. Edmondson, and Y. Luo (eds.), *The Tai-Kadai languages*. Abingdon: Routledge.

Weinreich, U., W. Labov, and M. I. Herzog. 1968. Empirical foundations for a theory of language change. In W. P. Lehmann and Y. Malkiel (eds.), *Directions for historical linguistics*, pp. 95–188. Austin, Texas and London: University of Texas Press.

Whalen, D. and G. Simons. 2012. Endangered language families. *Language* 88(1):155–173.

Whinnom, K. 1956. *Spanish contact vernaculars in the Philippine Islands*. Hong Kong: Hong Kong University Press.

White, J. C. 1971. *Sikhim and Bhutan: Twenty-one years on the north-east frontier (1887–1908)*. Delhi: Vivek.

Wiesenfeld, L. P. 1999. *World almanac and book of facts*. Mahwah, NJ: World Almanac Books.

Wilde, C. P. 2001. *Preliminary phonological analysis of the Limi dialect of Humla Bhotia*. M.A., University of Helsinki.

Winter, W. and G. Hansson. 1991. *Linguistic survey of Nepal*. Kathmandu: Centre for Nepal and Asian Studies.

Wolff, J. U. 1988. The contribution of Banjar Masin Malay to the reconstruction of Proto-Malay (Monografi Sejarah Bahasa). In M. Zain, T. Ahmad, and M. Zaini (eds.), *Rekonstruksi dan cabang-cabang bahasa Melayu induk*, pp. 85–98. Kuala Lumpur: Dewan Bahasa dan Pustaka.

Wumbu, I. B., A. Kadir, N. Baso, and S. Maranua. 1986. *Inventarisasi bahasa daerah di propinsi Sulawesi Tengah*. Jakarta: Pusat Pembinaan dan Pengembangan Bahasa, Departemen Pendidikan dan Kebudayaan.

Wurm, S. A. 2000. *Ways and methods for maintaining and re-invigorating endangered languages* . Paper presented at Conference on Endangered Languages of the Pacific Rim, Nov 24–25, 2000. Kyoto Conference Hall, Kyoto, Japan.

Wurm, S. A. 2007. Australasia and the Pacific. In C. Moseley (ed.), *Encyclopedia of the world's endangered languages*, pp. 425–578. London: Routledge.

Wurm, S. A. and S. Hattori (eds.). 1981. *Language atlas of the Pacific area*. Canberra: The Australian Academy of the Humanities in collaboration with the Japan Academy.

Wurm, S. A., B. T'sou, D. Bradley, L. Rong, X. Zhenghui, Z. Zehnxing, F. Maoji, W. Jun, and Dob (eds.). 1987. *Language atlas of China, Parts 1, 2*. Pacific Linguistics C-102. Hong Kong: Longman Group.

Xiong, X. and X. Yang (eds.). 1991. *Encyclopedic dictionary of Chinese linguistics*. Nanchang, China: Jiangxi Educational Publishing House.

Xu Shixuan. 2005. Survey of the current situation of Laomian and Laopin in China. *International Journal of the Sociology of Language* 173:99–115.

Yamaguchi, M. and H. Nakashima. 2001. An interim report on the investigation of the Topoiyo language and the languages around it conducted in 2000. In T. Ikeda (ed.), *Preliminary reports on minority languages in East and Southeast Asia, Vol. A3-001*, pp. 79–88. Osaka, Japan: Endangered Languages of the Pacific Rim.

Yunbin, L. 2005. *Bugeng language research*. Beijing: Ethnic Publishing House.

Zhou Yaowen and Luo Meizhen. 2001. *Dai dialect research (Dai yu fangyan yanjiu)*. Beijing: The People's Publishing House.

Zhou Zhizhi, Qixiang Yan, and Guoqing Chen. 2004. *Wa language dialect research (Wayu fangyan yanjiu)*. Beijing: Min zu chu ban she.

Zorc, R. D. 1977. *The Bisayan dialects of the Philippines: Subgrouping and reconstruction*. Pacific Linguistics C-44. Canberra: Australian National University.

Zvelebil, K. 1970. *Comparative Dravidian phonology*. The Hague: Mouton.

Zvelebil, K. 1998. *A selection of papers on Tamil and Dravidian linguistics*. Prague: Charles University.

Part III
Language Maps

ASIA
Each dot represents the geographic center of the primary area where a language is spoken.
North Pacific Ocean
Indian Ocean
20°N
40°N
0°
20°S
20°E
40°E
60°E
80°E
100°E
120°E
140°E
160°E
Japan
North Korea
South Korea
Taiwan
Hong Kong (China)
Macao (China)
China
Mongolia
Philippines
Viet Nam
Laos
Cambodia
Thailand
Myanmar
Bhutan
Bangladesh
Nepal
India
Sri Lanka
Brunei
Malaysia
Singapore
Indonesia
East Timor
Kazakhstan
Kyrgyzstan
Tajikistan
Uzbekistan
Turkmenistan
Afghanistan
Pakistan
Maldives
British Indian Ocean Territory
Iran
Azerbaijan
Armenia
Georgia
Turkey
Cyprus
Lebanon
Israel
Palestine
Jordan
Syria
Iraq
Kuwait
Bahrain
Qatar
United Arab Emirates
Oman
Saudi Arabia
Yemen
Boundary in dispute
0 500 1,000 km
© 2014 SIL International

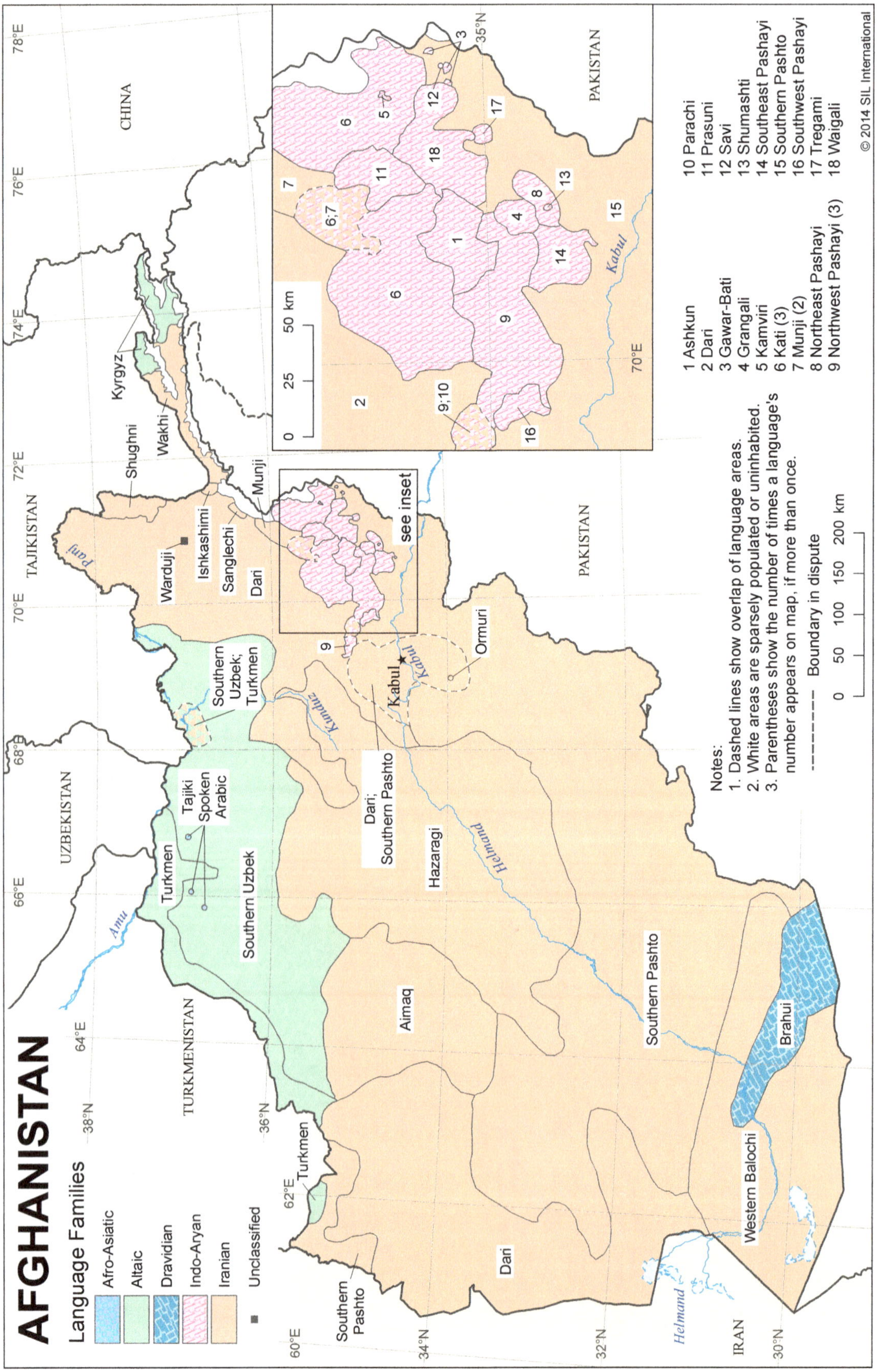
AFGHANISTAN
Language Families
Afro-Asiatic
Altaic
Dravidian
Indo-Aryan
Iranian
Unclassified
CHINA
TAJIKISTAN
UZBEKISTAN
TURKMENISTAN
PAKISTAN
IRAN
Amu
Panj
Kunduz
Kabul
Helmand
Kabul
Kyrgyz
Wakhi
Shughni
Munji
Ishkashimi
Sanglechi
Warduji
Dari
see inset
Southern Uzbek; Turkmen
Tajiki Spoken Arabic
Turkmen
Southern Uzbek
Dari; Southern Pashto
Hazaragi
Ormuri
Aimaq
Southern Pashto
Brahui
Western Balochi
Dari
Southern Pashto
Turkmen
9
0 25 50 km
1 Ashkun
2 Dari
3 Gawar-Bati
4 Grangali
5 Kamviri
6 Kati (3)
7 Munji (2)
8 Northeast Pashayi
9 Northwest Pashayi (3)
10 Parachi
11 Prasuni
12 Savi
13 Shumashti
14 Southeast Pashayi
15 Southern Pashto
16 Southwest Pashayi
17 Tregami
18 Waigali
Notes:
1. Dashed lines show overlap of language areas.
2. White areas are sparsely populated or uninhabited.
3. Parentheses show the number of times a language's number appears on map, if more than once.
Boundary in dispute
0 50 100 150 200 km
© 2014 SIL International

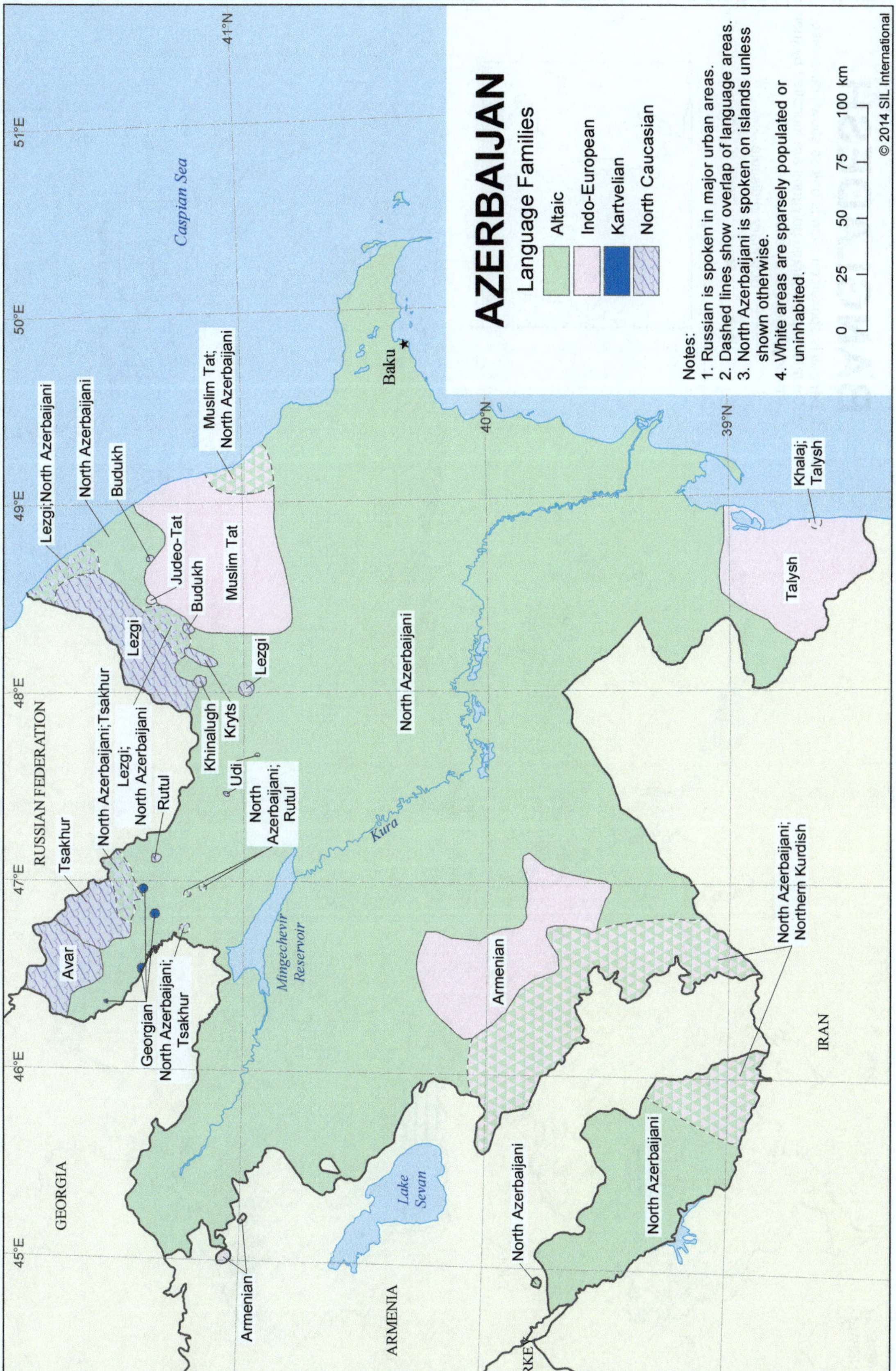
AZERBAIJAN
Language Families
Altaic
Indo-European
Kartvelian
North Caucasian
Notes:
1. Russian is spoken in major urban areas.
2. Dashed lines show overlap of language areas.
3. North Azerbaijani is spoken on islands unless shown otherwise.
4. White areas are sparsely populated or uninhabited.
0 25 50 75 100 km
© 2014 SIL International
Caspian Sea
RUSSIAN FEDERATION
GEORGIA
ARMENIA
IRAN
TURKEY
Lake Sevan
Mingechevir Reservoir
Kura
Baku
45°E
46°E
47°E
48°E
49°E
50°E
51°E
39°N
40°N
41°N
Avar
Tsakhur
North Azerbaijani;Tsakhur
Lezgi; North Azerbaijani
Rutul
Lezgi
Lezgi;North Azerbaijani
North Azerbaijani
Budukh
Judeo-Tat
Budukh
Muslim Tat
Muslim Tat; North Azerbaijani
Khinalugh
Kryts
Lezgi
Udi
North Azerbaijani; Rutul
Georgian
North Azerbaijani; Tsakhur
North Azerbaijani
Armenian
Armenian
North Azerbaijani; Northern Kurdish
North Azerbaijani
North Azerbaijani
Talysh
Khalaj; Talysh

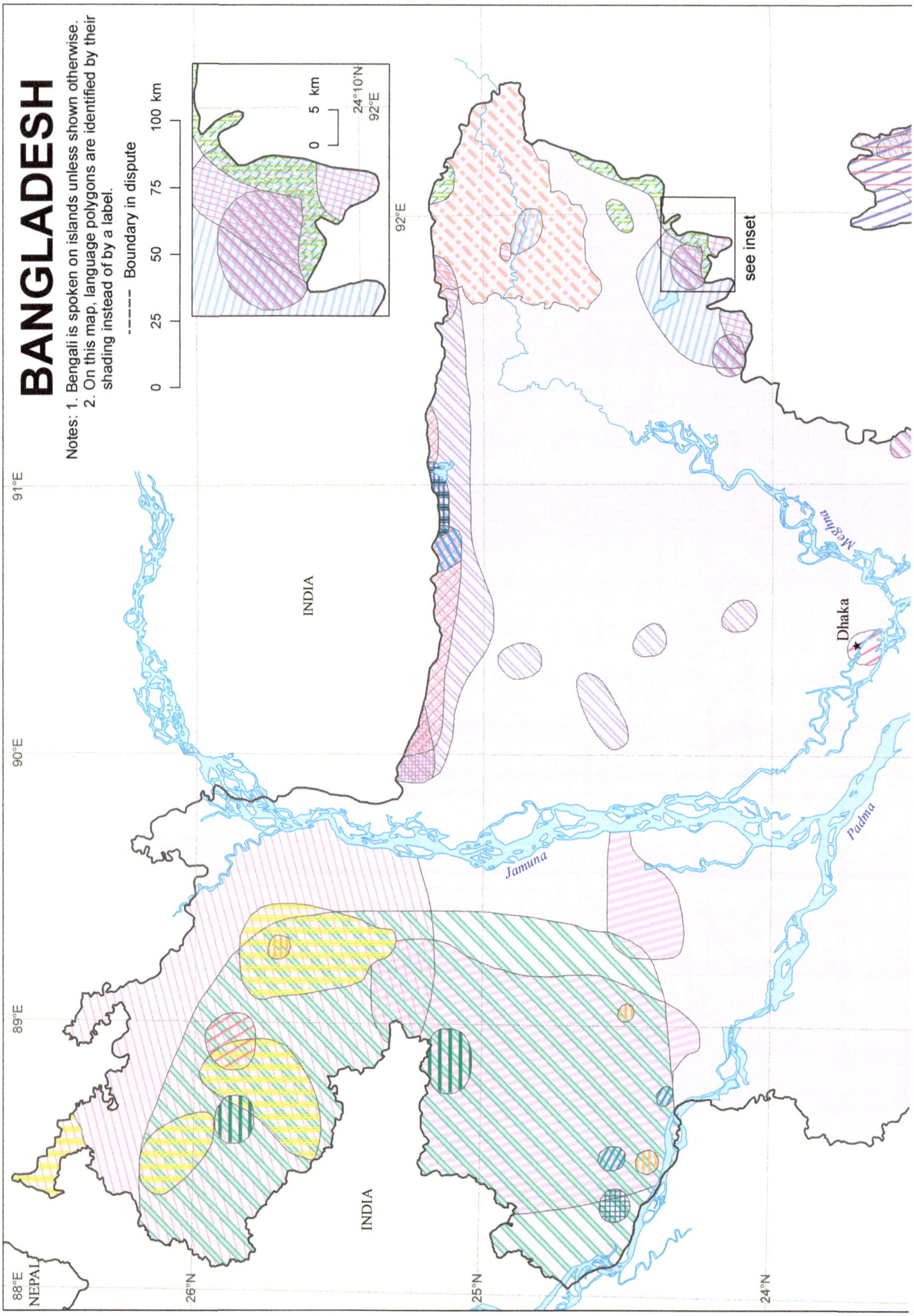
BANGLADESH
Notes: 1. Bengali is spoken on islands unless shown otherwise.
2. On this map, language polygons are identified by their shading instead of by a label.
Boundary in dispute
0 25 50 75 100 km
0 5 km
24°10'N
92°E
see inset
INDIA
NEPAL
Jamuna
Padma
Meghna
Dhaka
88°E
89°E
90°E
91°E
92°E
26°N
25°N
24°N

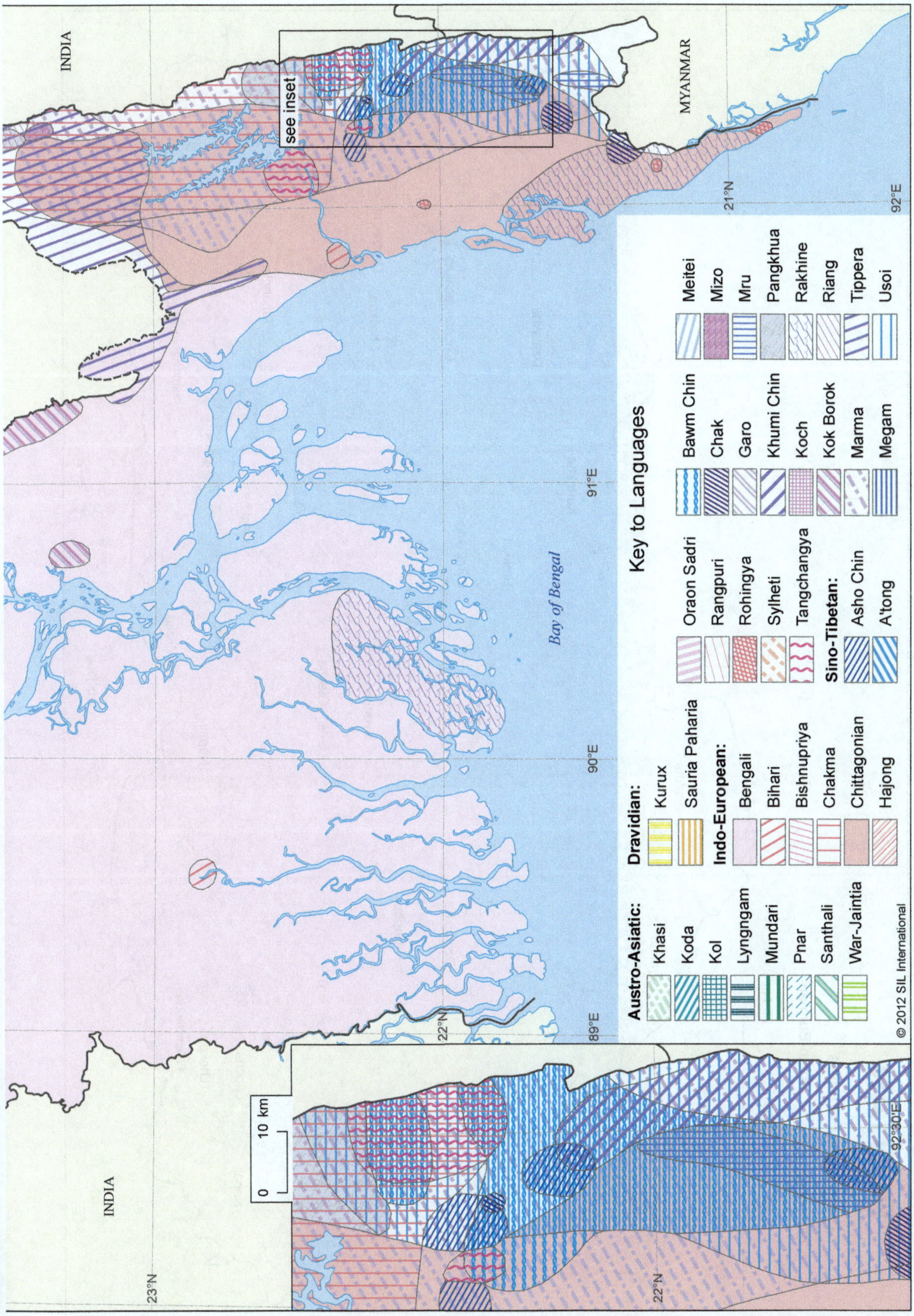
INDIA
MYANMAR
see inset
Bay of Bengal
23°N
22°N
21°N
89°E
90°E
91°E
92°E
92°30'E
0 10 km
Key to Languages
Austro-Asiatic:
Khasi
Koda
Kol
Lyngngam
Mundari
Pnar
Santhali
War-Jaintia
Dravidian:
Kurux
Sauria Paharia
Indo-European:
Bengali
Bihari
Bishnupriya
Chakma
Chittagonian
Hajong
Oraon Sadri
Rangpuri
Rohingya
Sylheti
Tangchangya
Sino-Tibetan:
Asho Chin
A'tong
Bawm Chin
Chak
Garo
Khumi Chin
Koch
Kok Borok
Marma
Megam
Meitei
Mizo
Mru
Pangkhua
Rakhine
Riang
Tippera
Usoi
© 2012 SIL International

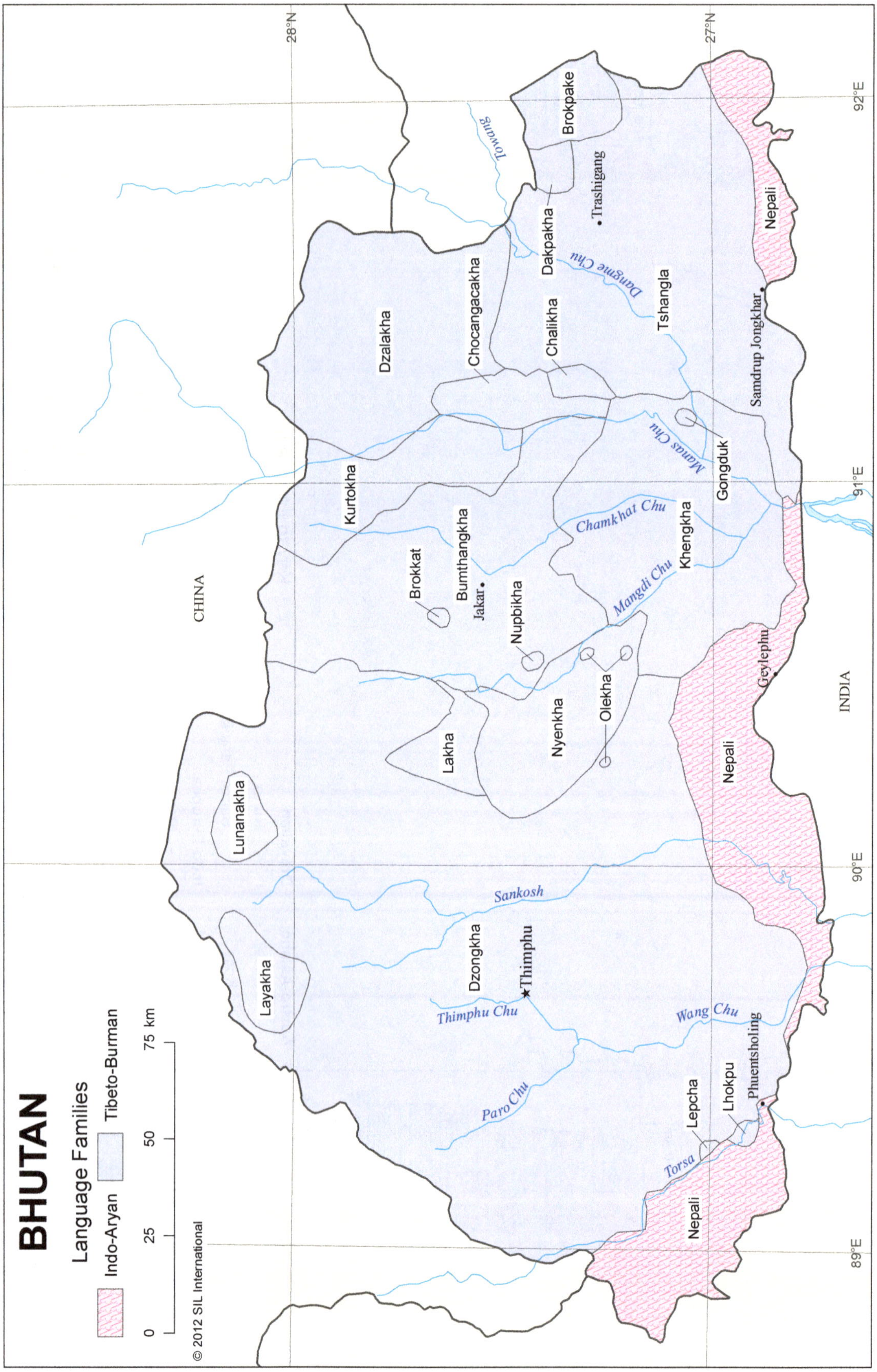
BHUTAN
Language Families
Indo-Aryan
Tibeto-Burman
0
25
50
75 km
© 2012 SIL International
28°N
27°N
89°E
90°E
91°E
92°E
CHINA
INDIA
Brokpake
Dakpakha
Trashigang
Towang
Dangme Chu
Nepali
Chocangacakha
Dzalakha
Chalikha
Tshangla
Samdrup Jongkhar
Gongduk
Manas Chu
Kurtokha
Bumthangkha
Chamkhat Chu
Khengkha
Brokkat
Jakar
Mangdi Chu
Nupbikha
Olekha
Nyenkha
Lakha
Geylephu
Nepali
Lunanakha
Sankosh
Dzongkha
Thimphu
Layakha
Thimphu Chu
Wang Chu
Paro Chu
Lepcha
Lhokpu
Phuentsholing
Torsa
Nepali

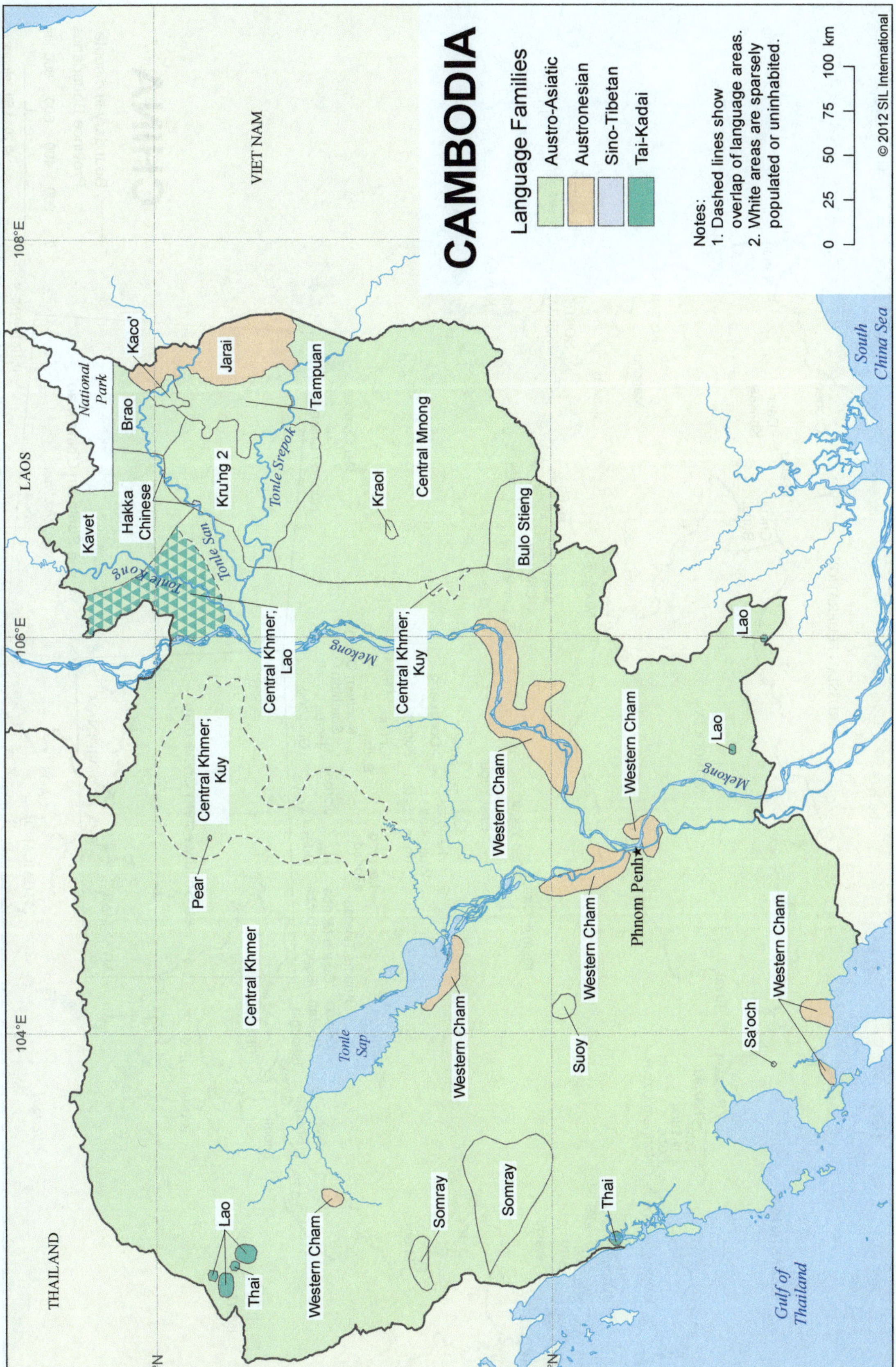
CAMBODIA
Language Families
Austro-Asiatic
Austronesian
Sino-Tibetan
Tai-Kadai
Notes:
1. Dashed lines show overlap of language areas.
2. White areas are sparsely populated or uninhabited.
0 25 50 75 100 km
© 2012 SIL International
THAILAND
LAOS
VIET NAM
South China Sea
Gulf of Thailand
14°N
12°N
104°E
106°E
108°E
Kavet
Hakka Chinese
Kru'ng 2
Brao
National Park
Kaco'
Jarai
Tampuan
Tonle Srepok
Tonle San
Tonle Kong
Central Mnong
Kraol
Bulo Stieng
Central Khmer; Lao
Central Khmer; Kuy
Central Khmer; Kuy
Mekong
Pear
Central Khmer
Western Cham
Western Cham
Western Cham
Western Cham
Western Cham
Western Cham
Phnom Penh
Lao
Lao
Lao
Thai
Thai
Tonle Sap
Suoy
Sa'och
Somray
Somray

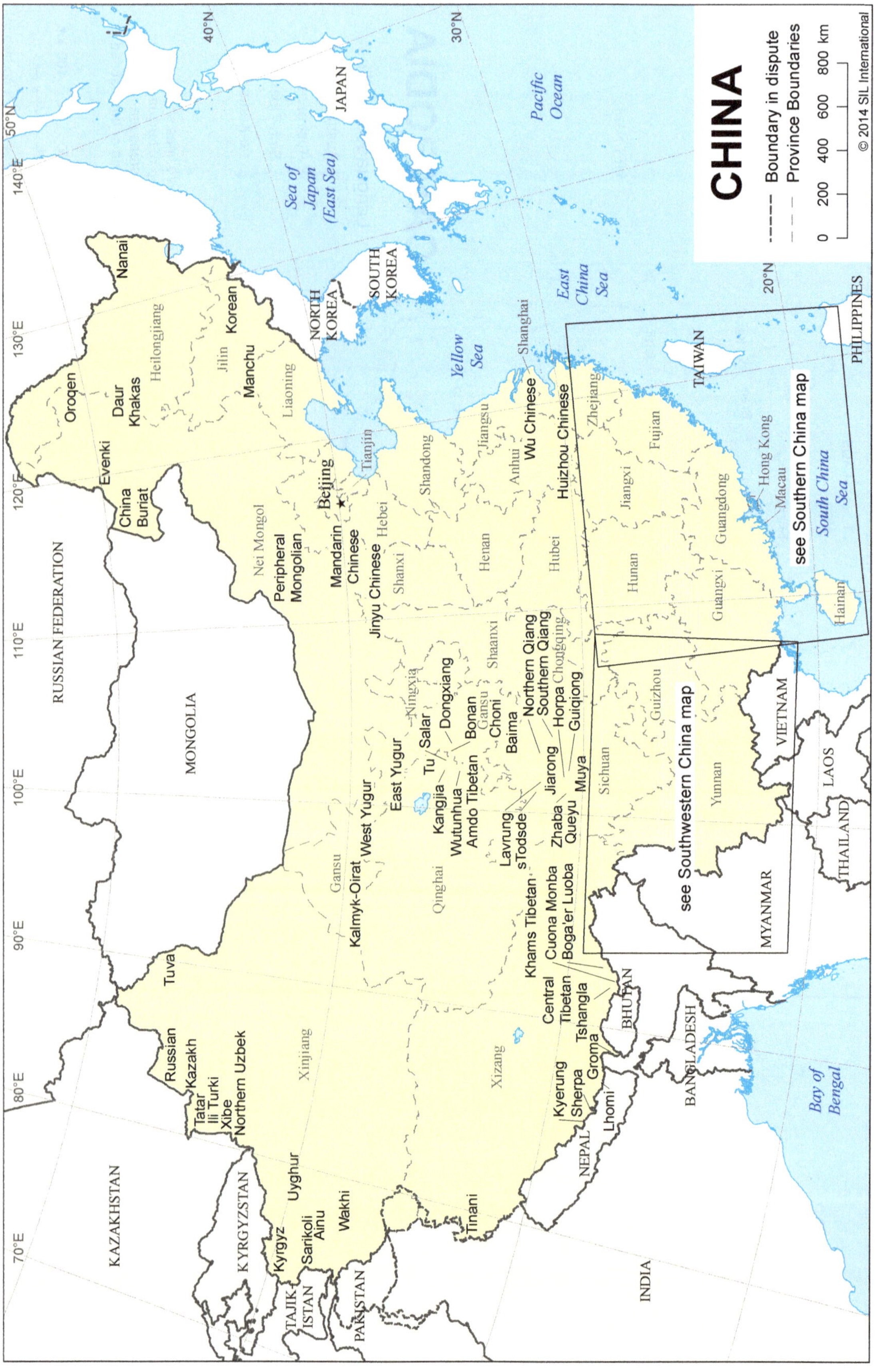
CHINA
Boundary in dispute
Province Boundaries
0 200 400 600 800 km
© 2014 SIL International
see Southern China map
see Southwestern China map
RUSSIAN FEDERATION
MONGOLIA
KAZAKHSTAN
KYRGYZSTAN
TAJIKISTAN
PAKISTAN
INDIA
NEPAL
BHUTAN
BANGLADESH
MYANMAR
THAILAND
LAOS
VIETNAM
PHILIPPINES
TAIWAN
JAPAN
NORTH KOREA
SOUTH KOREA
Sea of Japan (East Sea)
Pacific Ocean
Yellow Sea
East China Sea
South China Sea
Bay of Bengal
Heilongjiang
Jilin
Liaoning
Nei Mongol
Beijing
Tianjin
Hebei
Shandong
Jiangsu
Shanghai
Anhui
Zhejiang
Fujian
Jiangxi
Henan
Shanxi
Shaanxi
Hubei
Hunan
Guangdong
Hong Kong
Macau
Guangxi
Hainan
Guizhou
Chongqing
Sichuan
Yunnan
Ningxia
Gansu
Qinghai
Xizang
Xinjiang
Nanai
Oroqen
Daur
Khakas
Evenki
China Buriat
Korean
Manchu
Peripheral Mongolian
Mandarin Chinese
Jinyu Chinese
Wu Chinese
Huizhou Chinese
Northern Qiang
Southern Qiang
Dongxiang
Salar
Tu
Bonan
Choni
Baima
Horpa
Guiqiong
East Yugur
Kangjia
Wutunhua
Amdo Tibetan
Jiarong
Muya
Lavrung
sTodsde
Zhaba
Queyu
West Yugur
Kalmyk-Oirat
Khams Tibetan
Cuona Monba
Boga'er Luoba
Central Tibetan
Tshangla
Groma
Kyerung
Sherpa
Lhomi
Tuva
Russian
Kazakh
Tatar
Ili Turki
Xibe
Northern Uzbek
Uyghur
Kyrgyz
Sarikoli
Ainu
Wakhi
Tinani
70°E
80°E
90°E
100°E
110°E
120°E
130°E
140°E
50°N
40°N
30°N
20°N

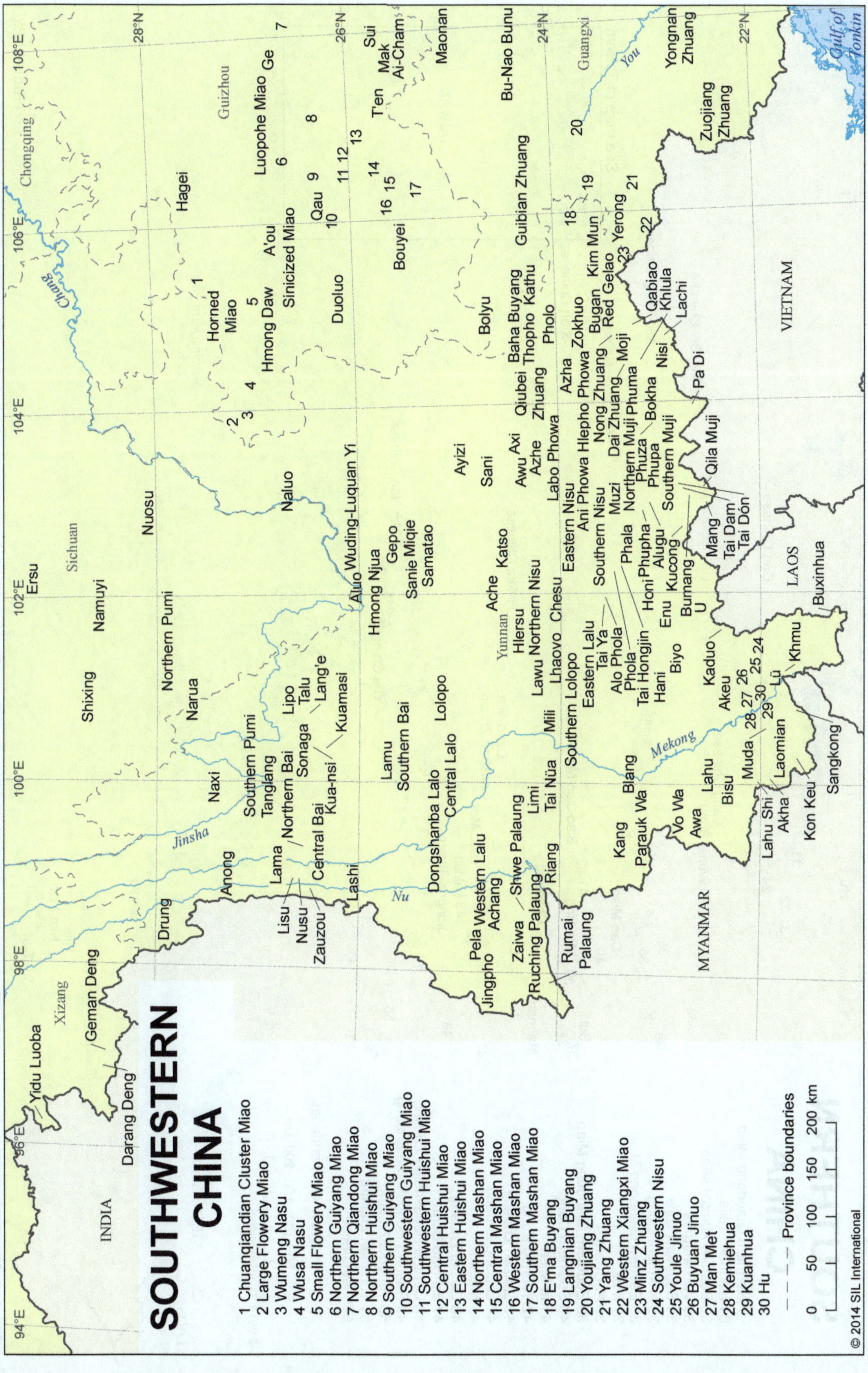

SOUTHWESTERN CHINA
1 Chuanqiandian Cluster Miao
2 Large Flowery Miao
3 Wumeng Nasu
4 Wusa Nasu
5 Small Flowery Miao
6 Northern Guiyang Miao
7 Northern Qiandong Miao
8 Northern Huishui Miao
9 Southern Guiyang Miao
10 Southwestern Guiyang Miao
11 Southwestern Huishui Miao
12 Central Huishui Miao
13 Eastern Huishui Miao
14 Northern Mashan Miao
15 Central Mashan Miao
16 Western Mashan Miao
17 Southern Mashan Miao
18 E'ma Buyang
19 Langnian Buyang
20 Youjiang Zhuang
21 Yang Zhuang
22 Western Xiangxi Miao
23 Minz Zhuang
24 Southwestern Nisu
25 Youle Jinuo
26 Buyuan Jinuo
27 Man Met
28 Kemiehua
29 Kuanhua
30 Hu
Province boundaries
0 50 100 150 200 km
© 2014 SIL International
INDIA
Xizang
Sichuan
Chongqing
Guizhou
Yunnan
Guangxi
MYANMAR
LAOS
VIETNAM
Gulf of Tonkin
Jinsha
Nu
Mekong
Chang
You
Yidu Luoba
Darang Deng
Geman Deng
Drung
Anong
Lisu
Nusu
Zauzou
Lama
Northern Bai
Central Bai
Southern Pumi
Tanglang
Naxi
Narua
Northern Pumi
Shixing
Namuyi
Ersu
Nuosu
Hagei
Horned Miao
Hmong Daw
A'ou
Sinicized Miao
Luopohe Miao
Ge
Qau
Duoluo
Naluo
Wuding-Luquan Yi
Aluo
Hmong Njua
Gepo
Sanie
Miqie
Samatao
Lipo
Talu
Lang'e
Sonaga
Kuamasi
Kua-nsi
Lashi
Lamu
Southern Bai
Lolopo
Dongshanba Lalo
Central Lalo
Pela
Western Lalu
Achang
Jingpho
Zaiwa
Shwe Palaung
Ruching Palaung
Riang
Rumai Palaung
Limi
Tai Nüa
Mili
Lhaovo
Chesu
Lawu
Northern Nisu
Hlersu
Ache
Katso
Ayizi
Sani
Awu
Axi
Azhe
Labo Phowa
Qiubei Zhuang
Baha Buyang
Thopho
Kathu
Bolyu
Pholo
Bouyei
Guibian Zhuang
T'en
Mak
Ai-Cham
Sui
Maonan
Bu-Nao Bunu
Southern Lolopo
Eastern Lalu
Eastern Nisu
Ani Phowa
Hlepho Phowa
Azha
Zokhuo
Southern Nisu
Nong Zhuang
Bugan
Red Gelao
Kim Mun
Yerong
Qabiao
Khlula
Lachi
Dai Zhuang
Moji
Muzi
Northern Muji
Phuma
Phuza
Phupa
Bokha
Nisi
Southern Muji
Pa Di
Qila Muji
Tai Ya
Alo Phola
Phola
Phala
Honi
Phupha
Alugu
Kucong
Tai Hongjin
Hani
Enu
Bumang
U
Mang
Tai Dam
Tai Dón
Biyo
Kaduo
Akeu
Buxinhua
Khmu
Lü
Kang
Parauk Wa
Blang
Vo Wa
Awa
Lahu
Bisu
Muda
Laomian
Lahu Shi
Akha
Kon Keu
Sangkong
Zuojiang Zhuang
Yongnan Zhuang
94°E
96°E
98°E
100°E
102°E
104°E
106°E
108°E
28°N
26°N
24°N
22°N

SOUTHERN CHINA
7 Northern Qiandong Miao
31 Northern Tujia
32 Eastern Xiangxi Miao
33 Waxianghua
34 Southern Tujia
35 Northern Dong
36 Eastern Qiandong Miao
37 Mak
38 Ai-Cham
39 Southern Qiandong Miao
40 Southern Dong
41 Iu Mien
42 Younuo Bunu
43 Liuqian Zhuang
44 Liujiang Zhuang
45 Mulam
46 Guibei Zhuang
47 Bu-Nao Bunu
48 Central Hongshuihe Zhuang
49 Eastern Hongshuihe Zhuang
50 Yongbei Zhuang
51 Yongnan Zhuang
52 Vietnamese
Province boundaries
0 50 100 150 200 km
© 2014 SIL International
See map of Taiwan
TAIWAN
PHILIPPINES
South China Sea
Gulf of Tonkin
VIETNAM
LAOS
Zhejiang
Fujian
Jiangxi
Hubei
Hunan
Guangdong
Guangxi
Guizhou
Chongqing
Hainan
Hong Kong
Macao
Min Dong Chinese
Min Bei Chinese
Min Zhong Chinese
Pu-Xian Chinese
Min Nan Chinese
Gan Chinese
Hakka Chinese
She
Yue Chinese
Xiang Chinese
Wunai Bunu
Biao-Jiao Mien
Dzao Min
Lianshan Zhuang
Biao
Biao Mon
Lakkia
Jiongnai Bunu
Cao Miao
Pa-Hng
Chadong
Ge
Sui
Maonan
E
Lingao
Hlai
Kim Mun
Jiamao
Tsat
Cun
Gan
Xiang
Yuan
Dong
Bei
Xi
You
120°E
115°E
110°E
105°E
25°N
20°N

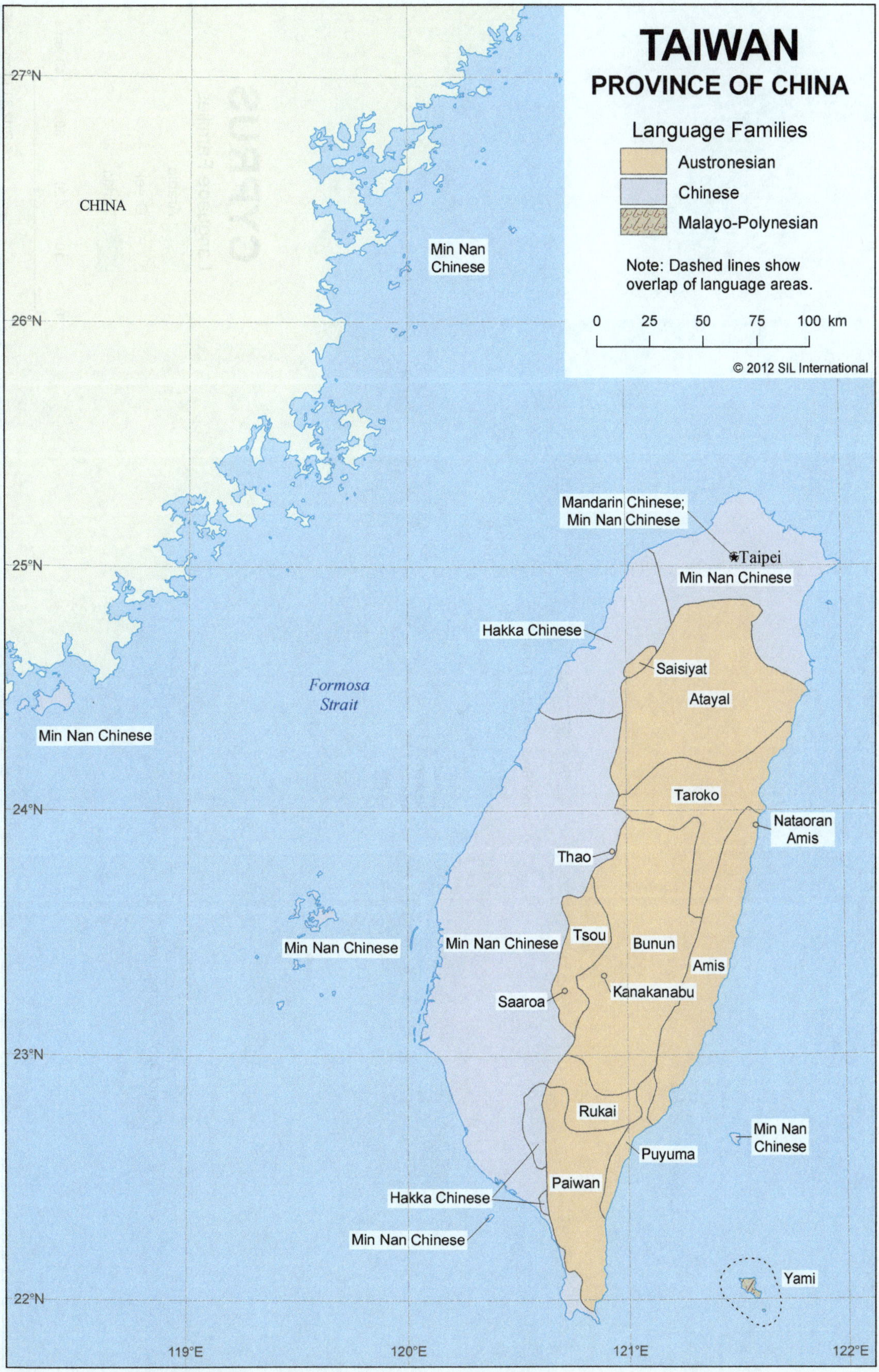
TAIWAN
PROVINCE OF CHINA
Language Families
Austronesian
Chinese
Malayo-Polynesian
Note: Dashed lines show overlap of language areas.
0 25 50 75 100 km
© 2012 SIL International
CHINA
Min Nan Chinese
Formosa Strait
Min Nan Chinese
Mandarin Chinese; Min Nan Chinese
Taipei
Min Nan Chinese
Hakka Chinese
Saisiyat
Atayal
Taroko
Nataoran Amis
Thao
Min Nan Chinese
Min Nan Chinese
Tsou
Bunun
Amis
Kanakanabu
Saaroa
Rukai
Min Nan Chinese
Puyuma
Paiwan
Hakka Chinese
Min Nan Chinese
Yami
27°N
26°N
25°N
24°N
23°N
22°N
119°E
120°E
121°E
122°E

CYPRUS
Language Families
Arabic
Greek
Turkic
0 10 20 30 40 km
© 2012 SIL International
35°N
34°E
33°E
Turkish
Cypriot Spoken Arabic;Turkish
Nicosia
Cypriot Spoken Arabic; Greek
Greek
Cypriot Spoken Arabic;Greek
Mediterranean Sea

Language data from Centre for Regional Studies, Universitas Kristen Artha Wacana (1997)

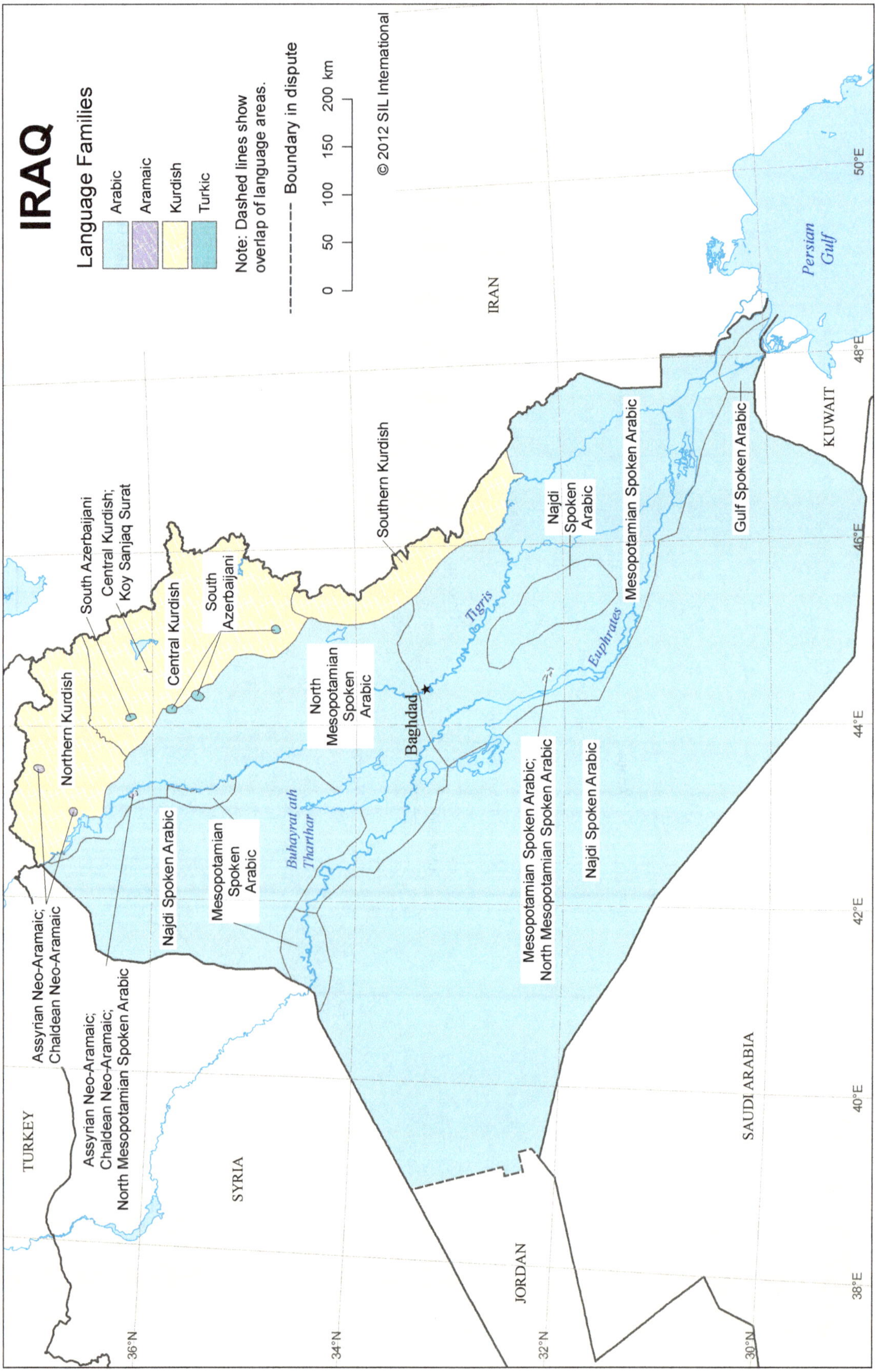
IRAQ
Language Families
Arabic
Aramaic
Kurdish
Turkic
Note: Dashed lines show overlap of language areas.
Boundary in dispute
0 50 100 150 200 km
© 2012 SIL International
TURKEY
SYRIA
JORDAN
SAUDI ARABIA
KUWAIT
IRAN
Persian Gulf
Assyrian Neo-Aramaic; Chaldean Neo-Aramaic
Assyrian Neo-Aramaic; Chaldean Neo-Aramaic; North Mesopotamian Spoken Arabic
Northern Kurdish
South Azerbaijani
Central Kurdish; Koy Sanjaq Surat
Central Kurdish
South Azerbaijani
Southern Kurdish
Najdi Spoken Arabic
Mesopotamian Spoken Arabic
Buhayrat ath Tharthar
North Mesopotamian Spoken Arabic
Baghdad
Tigris
Euphrates
Mesopotamian Spoken Arabic; North Mesopotamian Spoken Arabic
Najdi Spoken Arabic
Najdi Spoken Arabic
Mesopotamian Spoken Arabic
Gulf Spoken Arabic
36°N
34°N
32°N
30°N
38°E
40°E
42°E
44°E
46°E
48°E
50°E

INDIA
Scheduled Languages
Language Families
Austro-Asiatic
Indo-Aryan
Dravidian
Tibeto-Burman
Note:This map and the Non-Scheduled Languages maps should be used together. See those maps for details of the languages spoken in the white areas on this map.
0 250 500 750 km
© 2012 SIL International
Boundary in dispute
State boundaries
Index to Maps of Non-Scheduled Languages
1
2
3
4
5
6
7
8
9
see inset on map 9
AFGHANISTAN
PAKISTAN
CHINA
NEPAL
BHUTAN
BANGLADESH
MYANMAR
SRI LANKA
MALDIVES
Kashmiri
Urdu
Dogri
Eastern Panjabi
New Delhi
Hindi
Sanskrit
Maithili
Nepali
Assamese
Hindi
Bodo
Meitei
Santhali
Bengali
Bengali
Sindhi
Gujarati
Oriya
Konkani
Marathi
Telugu
Kannada
Tamil
Malayalam
Arabian Sea
Bay of Bengal
Andaman Sea
Indian Ocean
35°N
30°N
25°N
20°N
15°N
10°N
70°E
75°E
80°E
85°E
90°E
95°E

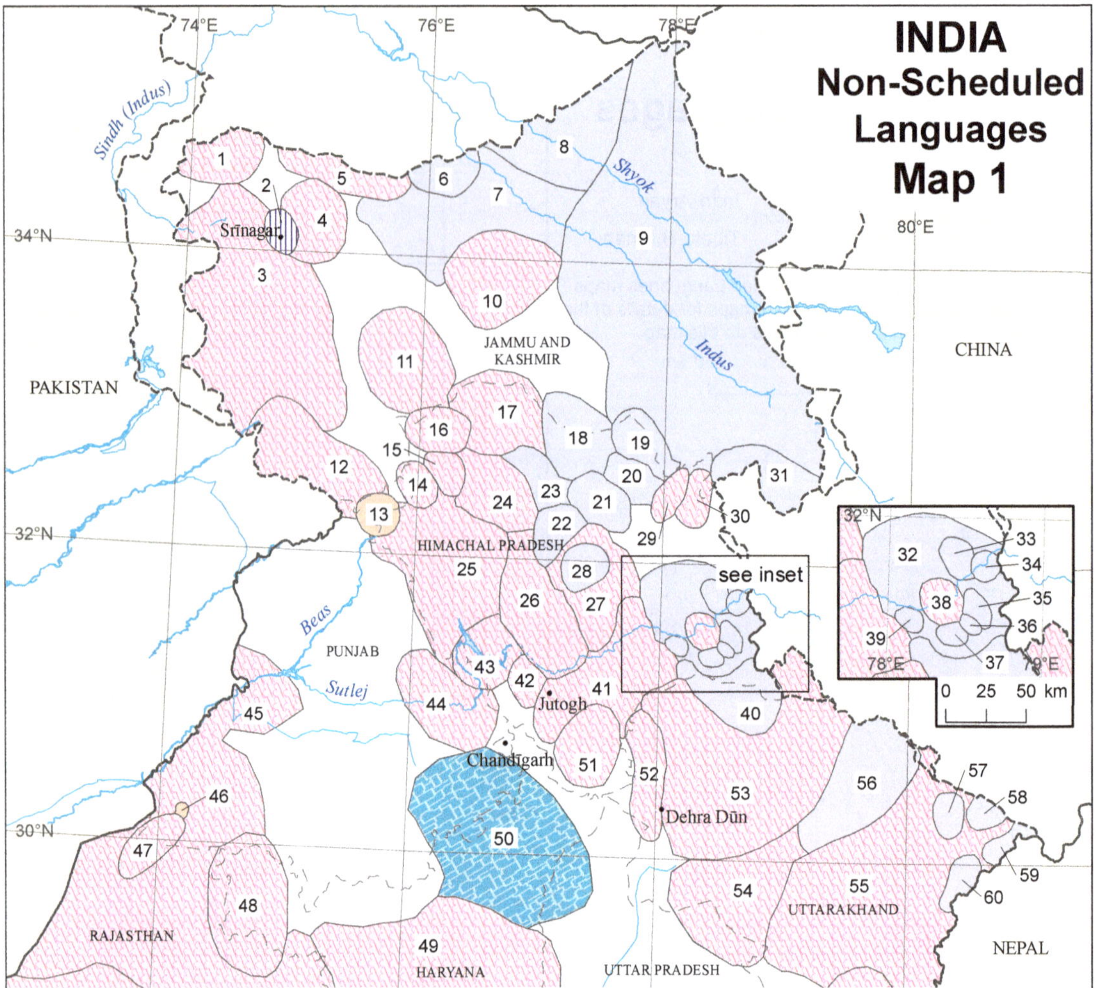

1 Mirpur Panjabi
2 Burushaski
3 Gujari
4 Bateri
5 Shina
6 Zangskari
7 Purik
8 Balti
9 Ladakhi
10 Brokskat
11 Bhadrawahi
12 Western Panjabi
13 Northern Pashto
14 Bhattiyali
15 Chambeali
16 Churahi
17 Pangwali
18 Pattani
19 Spiti Bhoti
20 Stod Bhoti
21 Tinani
22 Kanashi
23 Gahri
24 Gaddi
25 Kangri
26 Mandeali
27 Kullu Pahari
28 Mugom
29 Chinali
30 Lahul Lohar
31 Changthang
32 Kinnauri
33 Shumcho
34 Sunam
35 Bhoti Kinnauri
36 Jangshung
37 Chitkuli Kinnauri
38 Pahari Kinnauri
39 Tukpa
40 Jad
41 Mahasu Pahari
42 Hinduri
43 Bilaspuri
44 Bauria
45 Bagri
46 Eastern Balochi
47 Seraiki
48 Sansi
49 Haryanvi
50 Bazigar
51 Sirmauri
52 Jaunsari
53 Garhwali
54 Buksa
55 Kumaoni
56 Rongpo
57 Darmiya
58 Byangsi
59 Rawat
60 Chaudangsi

Language Families
Dravidian
Indo-Aryan
Iranian
Language isolate
Tibeto-Burman

Boundary in dispute
State boundaries

Note: See the Scheduled Languages map for details of the languages that are spoken in the white areas.

0 50 100 150 200 km

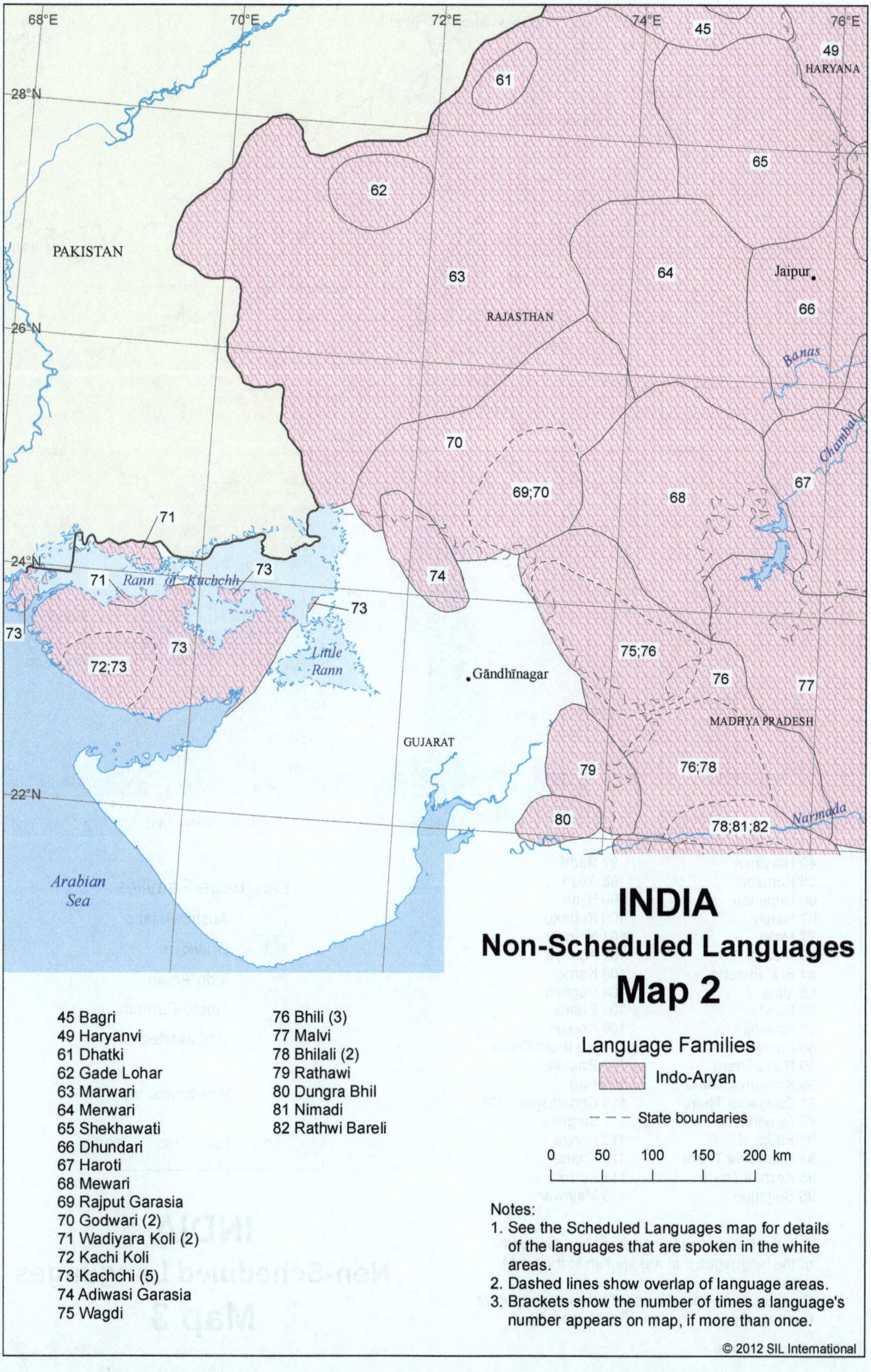
68°E
70°E
72°E
74°E
76°E
28°N
26°N
24°N
22°N
PAKISTAN
RAJASTHAN
HARYANA
GUJARAT
MADHYA PRADESH
Jaipur
Gāndhīnagar
Banas
Chambal
Narmada
Rann of Kachchh
Little Rann
Arabian Sea
45
49
61
62
63
64
65
66
67
68
69;70
70
71
72;73
73
74
75;76
76
77
76;78
78;81;82
79
80
INDIA
Non-Scheduled Languages
Map 2
Language Families
Indo-Aryan
State boundaries
0 50 100 150 200 km
45 Bagri
49 Haryanvi
61 Dhatki
62 Gade Lohar
63 Marwari
64 Merwari
65 Shekhawati
66 Dhundari
67 Haroti
68 Mewari
69 Rajput Garasia
70 Godwari (2)
71 Wadiyara Koli (2)
72 Kachi Koli
73 Kachchi (5)
74 Adiwasi Garasia
75 Wagdi
76 Bhili (3)
77 Malvi
78 Bhilali (2)
79 Rathawi
80 Dungra Bhil
81 Nimadi
82 Rathwi Bareli
Notes:
1. See the Scheduled Languages map for details of the languages that are spoken in the white areas.
2. Dashed lines show overlap of language areas.
3. Brackets show the number of times a language's number appears on map, if more than once.
© 2012 SIL International

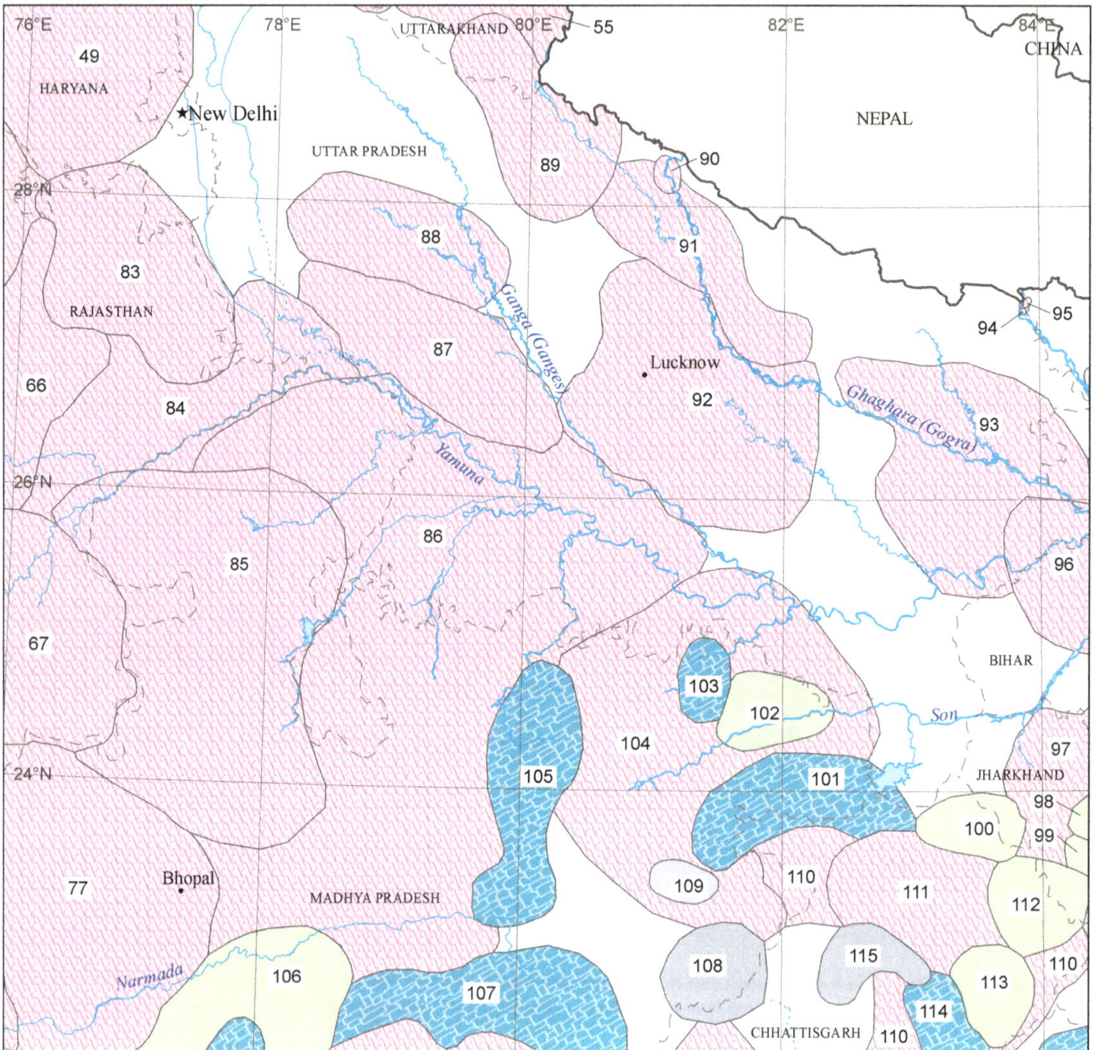

49 Haryanvi
55 Kumaoni
66 Dhundari
67 Haroti
77 Malvi
83 Mewati
84 Braj Bhasha
85 Mina
86 Bundeli
87 Kanauji
88 Kanjari
89 Rana Tharu
90 Kathariya Tharu
91 Dangaura Tharu
92 Awadhi
93 Bhojpuri
94 Chitwania Tharu
95 Kochila Tharu
96 Surjapuri
97 Sadri
98 Asuri
99 Bijori
100 Kodaku
101 Khirwar
102 Agariya
103 Kamar
104 Bagheli
105 Bharia
106 Korku
107 Northern Gondi
108 Bhatola
109 Pao
110 Chhattisgarhi (3)
111 Surgujia
112 Korwa
113 Kharia
114 Kurux
115 Majhwar

Language Families

- Austro-Asiatic
- Dravidian
- Indo-Aryan
- Tibeto-Burman
- Unclassified

State boundaries

0 50 100 150 200 km

Notes:

1. See the Scheduled Languages map for details of the languages that are spoken in the white areas.
2. Brackets show the number of times a language's number appears on map, if more than once.

INDIA
Non-Scheduled Languages
Map 3

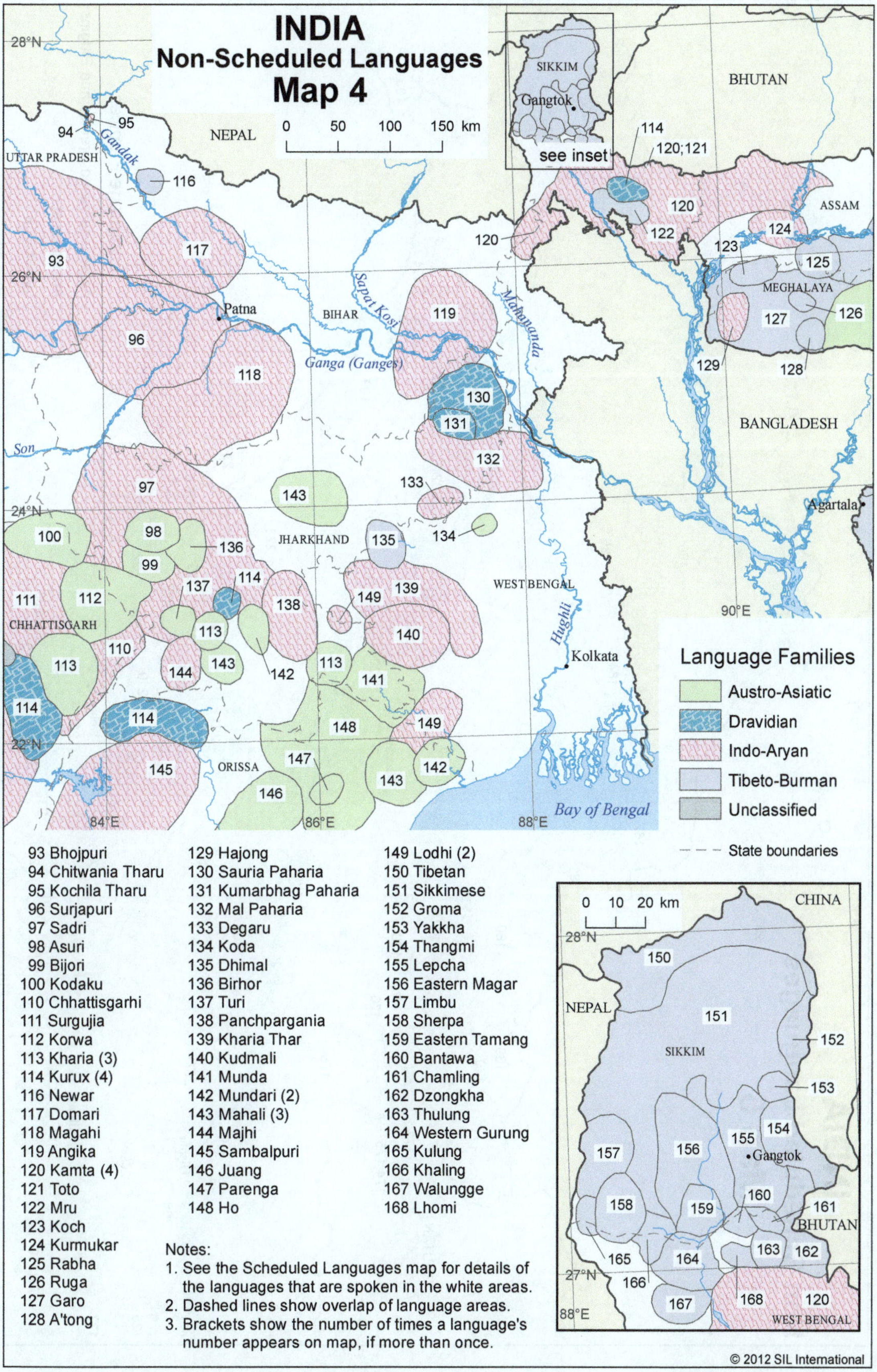
INDIA
Non-Scheduled Languages
Map 4
0 50 100 150 km
NEPAL
UTTAR PRADESH
BIHAR
JHARKHAND
CHHATTISGARH
ORISSA
WEST BENGAL
BHUTAN
ASSAM
MEGHALAYA
BANGLADESH
SIKKIM
Gangtok
see inset
Patna
Kolkata
Agartala
Gandak
Son
Sapat Kosi
Mahananda
Ganga (Ganges)
Hughli
Bay of Bengal
28°N
26°N
24°N
22°N
84°E
86°E
88°E
90°E
Language Families
Austro-Asiatic
Dravidian
Indo-Aryan
Tibeto-Burman
Unclassified
State boundaries
93 Bhojpuri
94 Chitwania Tharu
95 Kochila Tharu
96 Surjapuri
97 Sadri
98 Asuri
99 Bijori
100 Kodaku
110 Chhattisgarhi
111 Surgujia
112 Korwa
113 Kharia (3)
114 Kurux (4)
116 Newar
117 Domari
118 Magahi
119 Angika
120 Kamta (4)
121 Toto
122 Mru
123 Koch
124 Kurmukar
125 Rabha
126 Ruga
127 Garo
128 A'tong
129 Hajong
130 Sauria Paharia
131 Kumarbhag Paharia
132 Mal Paharia
133 Degaru
134 Koda
135 Dhimal
136 Birhor
137 Turi
138 Panchpargania
139 Kharia Thar
140 Kudmali
141 Munda
142 Mundari (2)
143 Mahali (3)
144 Majhi
145 Sambalpuri
146 Juang
147 Parenga
148 Ho
149 Lodhi (2)
150 Tibetan
151 Sikkimese
152 Groma
153 Yakkha
154 Thangmi
155 Lepcha
156 Eastern Magar
157 Limbu
158 Sherpa
159 Eastern Tamang
160 Bantawa
161 Chamling
162 Dzongkha
163 Thulung
164 Western Gurung
165 Kulung
166 Khaling
167 Walungge
168 Lhomi
Notes:
1. See the Scheduled Languages map for details of the languages that are spoken in the white areas.
2. Dashed lines show overlap of language areas.
3. Brackets show the number of times a language's number appears on map, if more than once.
0 10 20 km
CHINA
NEPAL
SIKKIM
BHUTAN
WEST BENGAL
28°N
27°N
88°E
© 2012 SIL International

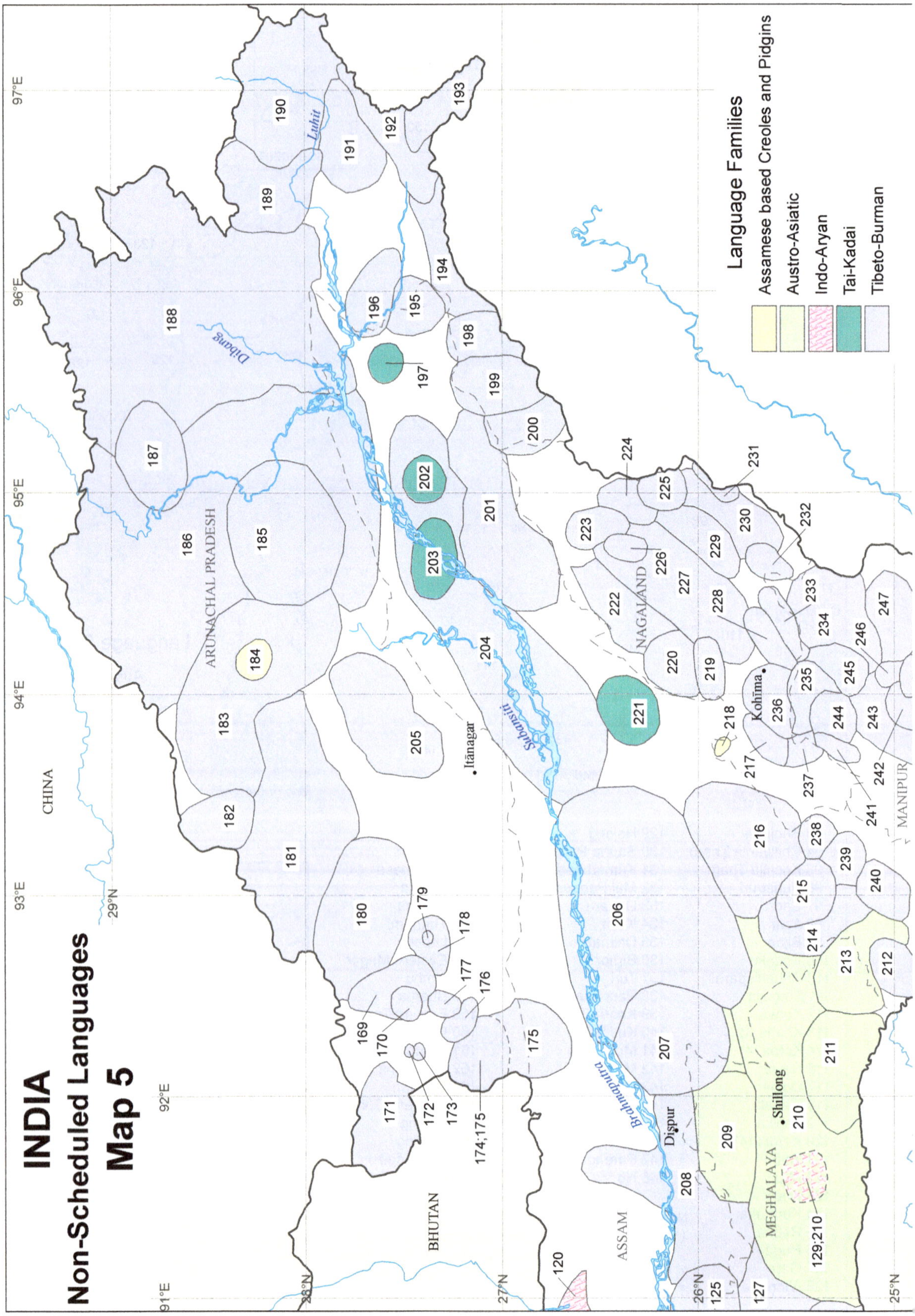
INDIA
Non-Scheduled Languages
Map 5
Language Families
Assamese based Creoles and Pidgins
Austro-Asiatic
Indo-Aryan
Tai-Kadai
Tibeto-Burman
CHINA
BHUTAN
ARUNACHAL PRADESH
ASSAM
NAGALAND
MEGHALAYA
MANIPUR
Itānagar
Dispur
Shillong
Kohīma
Dibang
Luhit
Subansiri
Brahmaputra
91°E
92°E
93°E
94°E
95°E
96°E
97°E
29°N
28°N
27°N
26°N
25°N
120
125
127
129;210
169
170
171
172
173
174;175
175
176
177
178
179
180
181
182
183
184
185
186
187
188
189
190
191
192
193
194
195
196
197
198
199
200
201
202
203
204
205
206
207
208
209
210
211
212
213
214
215
216
217
218
219
220
221
222
223
224
225
226
227
228
229
230
231
232
233
234
235
236
237
238
239
240
241
242
243
244
245
246
247

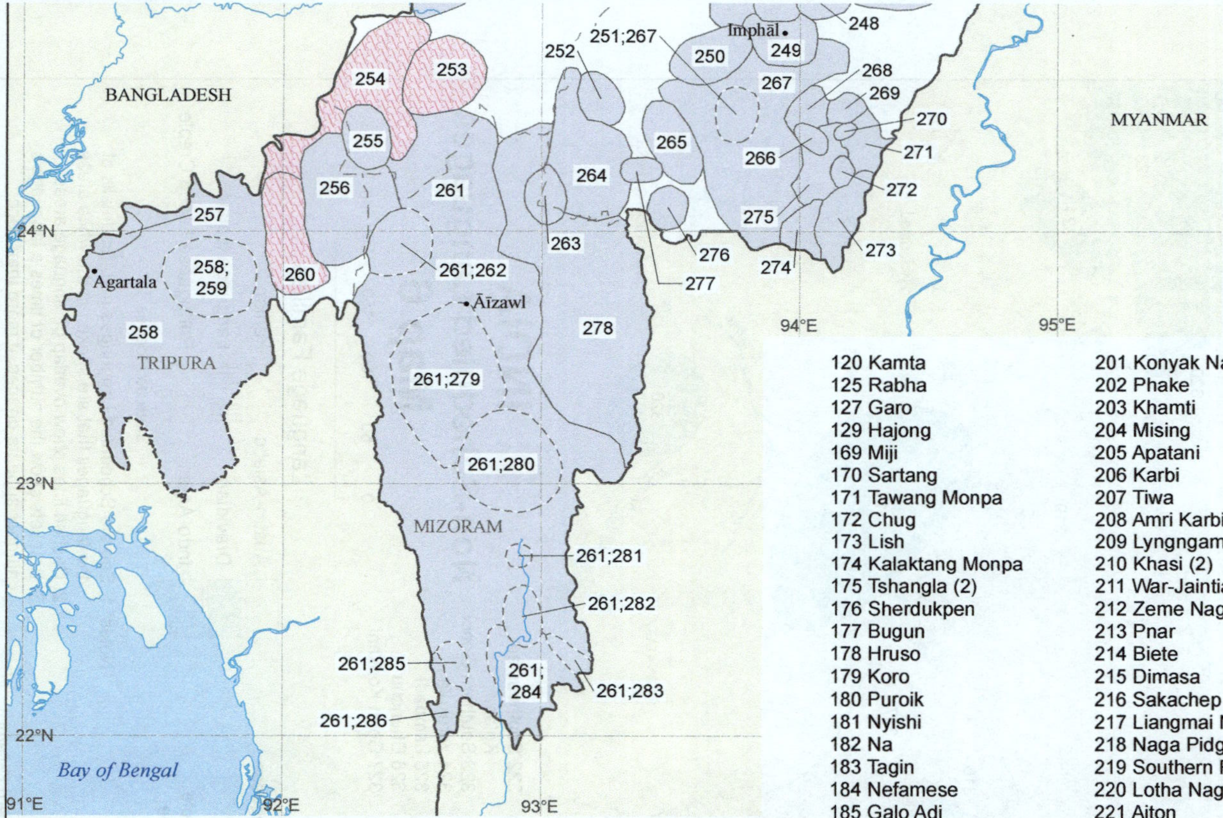

Boundary in dispute
State boundaries

Notes:
1. See the Scheduled Languages map for details of the languages that are spoken in the white areas.
2. Dashed lines show overlap of language areas.
3. Parentheses show the number of times a language's number appears on map, if more than once.

0 25 50 75 100 km

120 Kamta
125 Rabha
127 Garo
129 Hajong
169 Miji
170 Sartang
171 Tawang Monpa
172 Chug
173 Lish
174 Kalaktang Monpa
175 Tshangla (2)
176 Sherdukpen
177 Bugun
178 Hruso
179 Koro
180 Puroik
181 Nyishi
182 Na
183 Tagin
184 Nefamese
185 Galo Adi
186 Adi
187 Khamba
188 Idu-Mishmi
189 Digaro-Mishmi
190 Miju-Mishmi
191 Zakhring
192 Rawang
193 Lisu
194 Tase Naga
195 Singpho
196 Deori
197 Khamyang
198 Tutsa Naga
199 Nocte Naga
200 Wancho Naga
201 Konyak Naga
202 Phake
203 Khamti
204 Mising
205 Apatani
206 Karbi
207 Tiwa
208 Amri Karbi
209 Lyngngam
210 Khasi (2)
211 War-Jaintia
212 Zeme Naga
213 Pnar
214 Biete
215 Dimasa
216 Sakachep
217 Liangmai Naga
218 Naga Pidgin
219 Southern Rengma Naga
220 Lotha Naga
221 Aiton
222 Ao Naga
223 Phom Naga
224 Chang Naga
225 Khiamniungan Naga
226 Northern Rengma Naga
227 Sumi Naga
228 Khezha Naga
229 Sangtam Naga
230 Yimchungru Naga
231 Makuri Naga
232 Pochuri Naga
233 Chokri Naga
234 Poumei Naga
235 Mao Naga
236 Angami Naga
237 Mzieme Naga
238 Kachari
239 Hrangkhol
240 Hmar
241 Puimei Naga
242 Koireng
243 Thangal Naga
244 Rongmei Naga
245 Maram Naga
246 Kharam Naga
247 Tangkhul Naga
248 Purum Naga
249 Inpui Naga
250 Chiru
251 Kom
252 Simte
253 Bishnupriya
254 Sylheti
255 Falam Chin
256 Riang
257 Darlong
258 Kok Borok (2)
259 Ranglong
260 Chakma
261 Mizo (10)
262 Marma
263 Ralte
264 Paite Chin
265 Vaiphei
266 Moyon Naga
267 Thado Chin (2)
268 Aimol
269 Monsang Naga
270 Tarao Naga
271 Chothe Naga
272 Khoibu Naga
273 Anal
274 Lamkang
275 Maring Naga
276 Zou
277 Gangte
278 Tedim Chin
279 Matu Chin
280 Pankhu
281 Zyphe Chin
282 Haka Chin
283 Bawm Chin
284 Mara Chin
285 Khumi Chin
286 Shendu

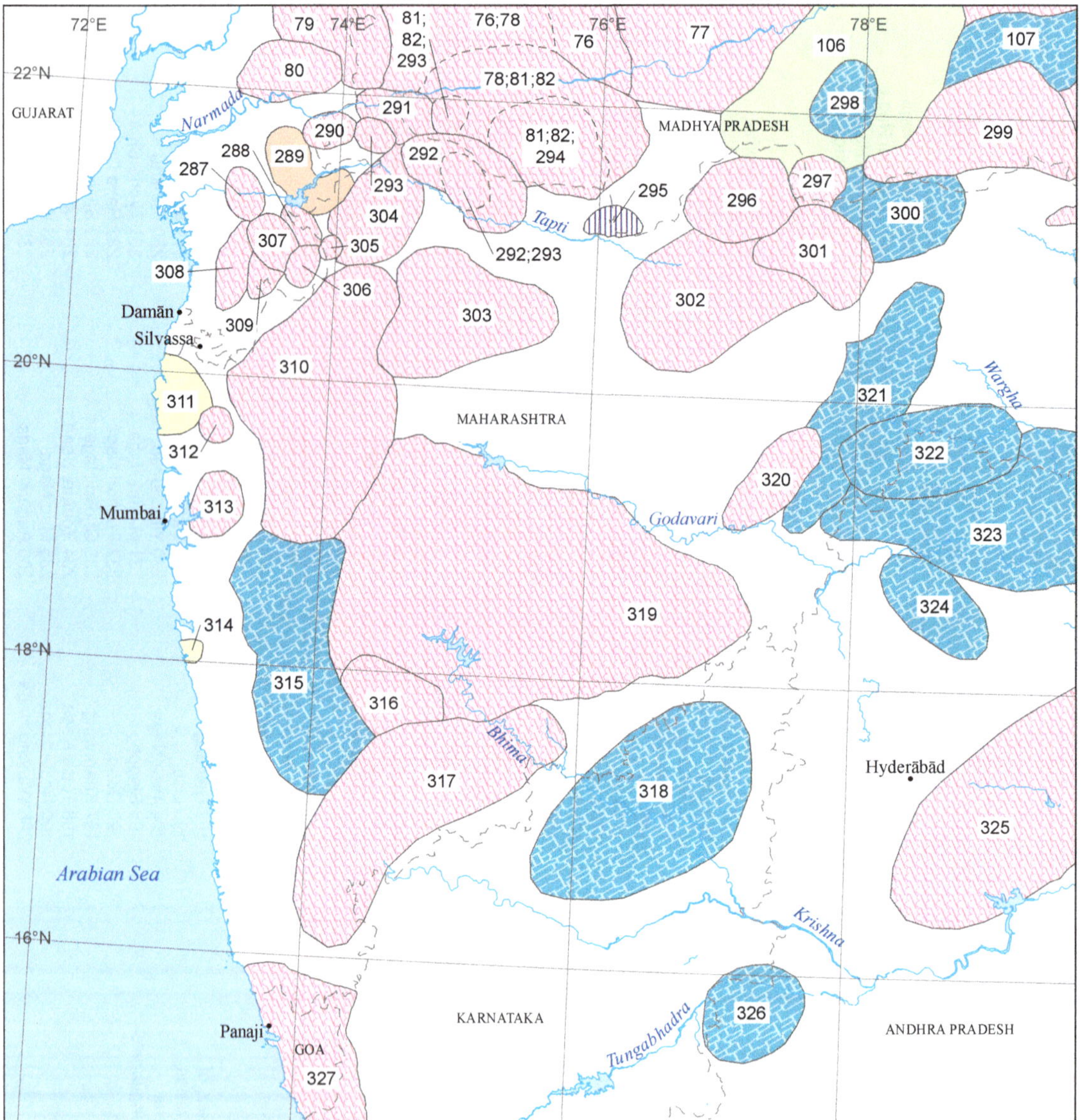

76 Bhili (2)
77 Malvi
78 Bhilali (2)
79 Rathawi
80 Dungra Bhil
81 Nimadi (3)
82 Rathwi Bareli (3)
106 Korku
107 Northern Gondi
287 Dubli
288 Gamit
289 Parsi
290 Vasavi
291 Pauri Bareli
292 Nahali (2)
293 Noiri (3)
294 Palya Bareli
295 Nihali
296 Gowlan
297 Bhalay
298 Pardhan
299 Powari
300 Kaikadi
301 Gowli
302 Varhadi-Nagpuri
303 Ahirani
304 Khandesi
305 Mawchi
306 Dhanki
307 Chodri
308 Dhodia
309 Kukna
310 Varli
311 Indo-Portuguese
312 Phudagi
313 Katkari
314 Korlai Creole Portuguese
315 Waddar
316 Samvedi
317 Pardhi
318 Holiya
319 Deccan
320 Andh
321 Northwestern Kolami
322 Southeastern Kolami
323 Southern Gondi
324 Yerukula
325 Lambadi
326 Chenchu
327 Goan Konkani

INDIA
Non-Scheduled Languages
Map 6

0 50 100 150 200 km

Language Families

Austro-Asiatic
Iranian
Dravidian
Language isolate
Indo-Aryan
Portuguese based Creole

State boundaries

Notes: 1. See the Scheduled Languages map for details of the languages that are spoken in the white areas.
2. Dashed lines show overlap of language areas.
3. Brackets show the number of times a language's number appears on map, if more than once.

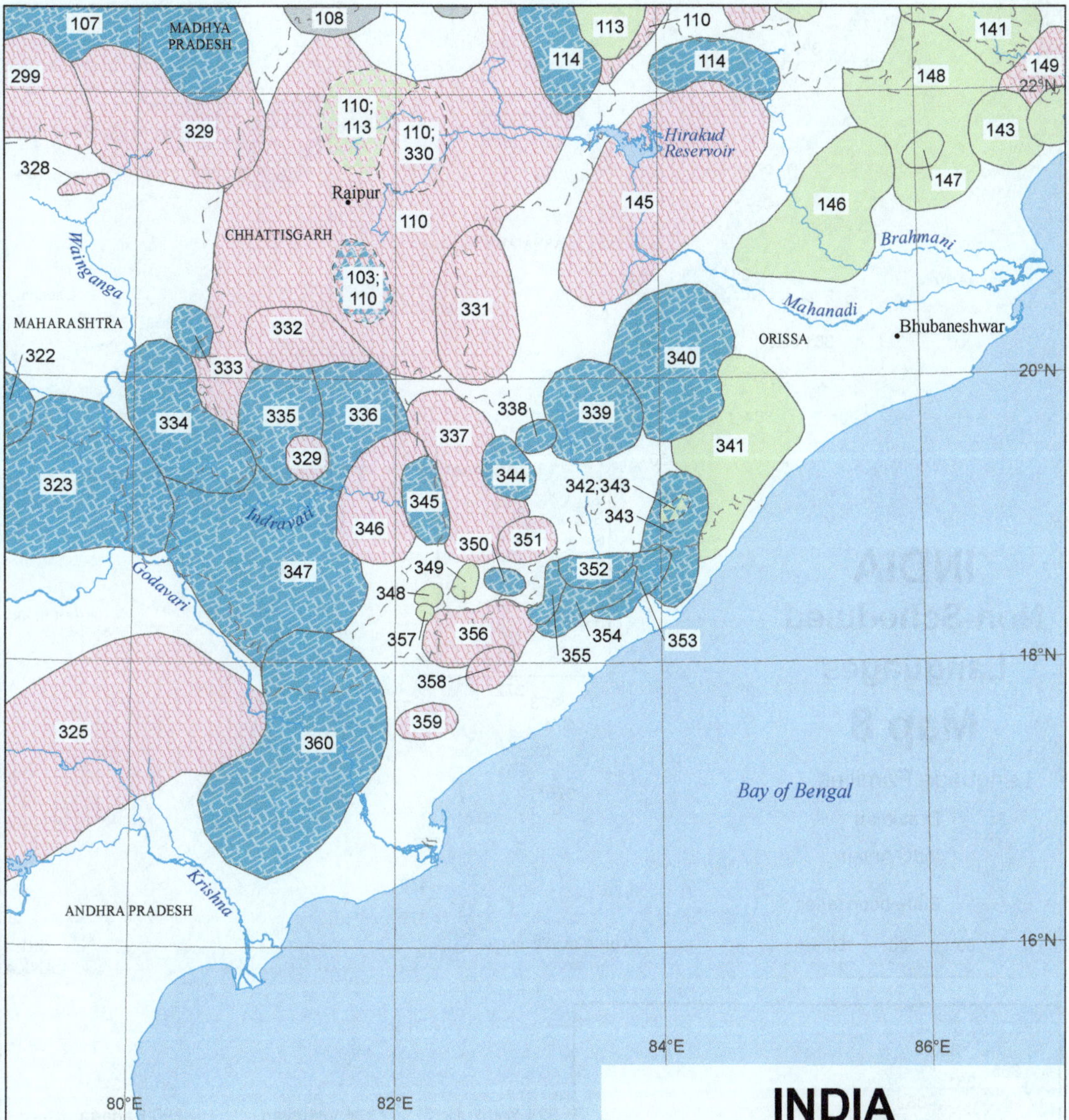

103 Kamar
107 Northern Gondi
108 Bhatola
110 Chhattisgarhi (5)
113 Kharia (2)
114 Kurux (2)
141 Munda
143 Mahali (2)
145 Sambalpuri
146 Juang
147 Parenga
148 Ho
149 Lodhi
299 Powari
322 Southeastern Kolami
323 Southern Gondi
325 Lambadi
328 Chamari
329 Halbi (2)
330 Nahari
331 Bhunjia
332 Mirgan
333 Far Western Muria
334 Maria
335 Western Muria
336 Eastern Muria
337 Desiya
338 Manda
339 Kuvi
340 Kui
341 Sora
342 Juray
343 Savara (2)
344 Pengo
345 Duruwa
346 Bhatri
347 Dandami Maria
348 Bondo
349 Bodo Gadaba
350 Pottangi Ollar Gadaba
351 Bodo Parja
352 Konda-Dora
353 Mukha-Dora
354 Manna-Dora
355 Mudhili Gadaba
356 Adivasi Oriya
357 Gata'
358 Reli
359 Kupia
360 Koya

INDIA
Non-Scheduled Languages
Map 7

Language Families

Austro-Asiatic — Indo-Aryan
Dravidian — Unclassified

— — — State boundaries

0 50 100 150 200 km

Notes: 1. See the Scheduled Languages map for details of the languages that are spoken in the white areas.
2. Dashed lines show overlap of language areas.
3. Brackets show the number of times a language's number appears on map, if more than once.

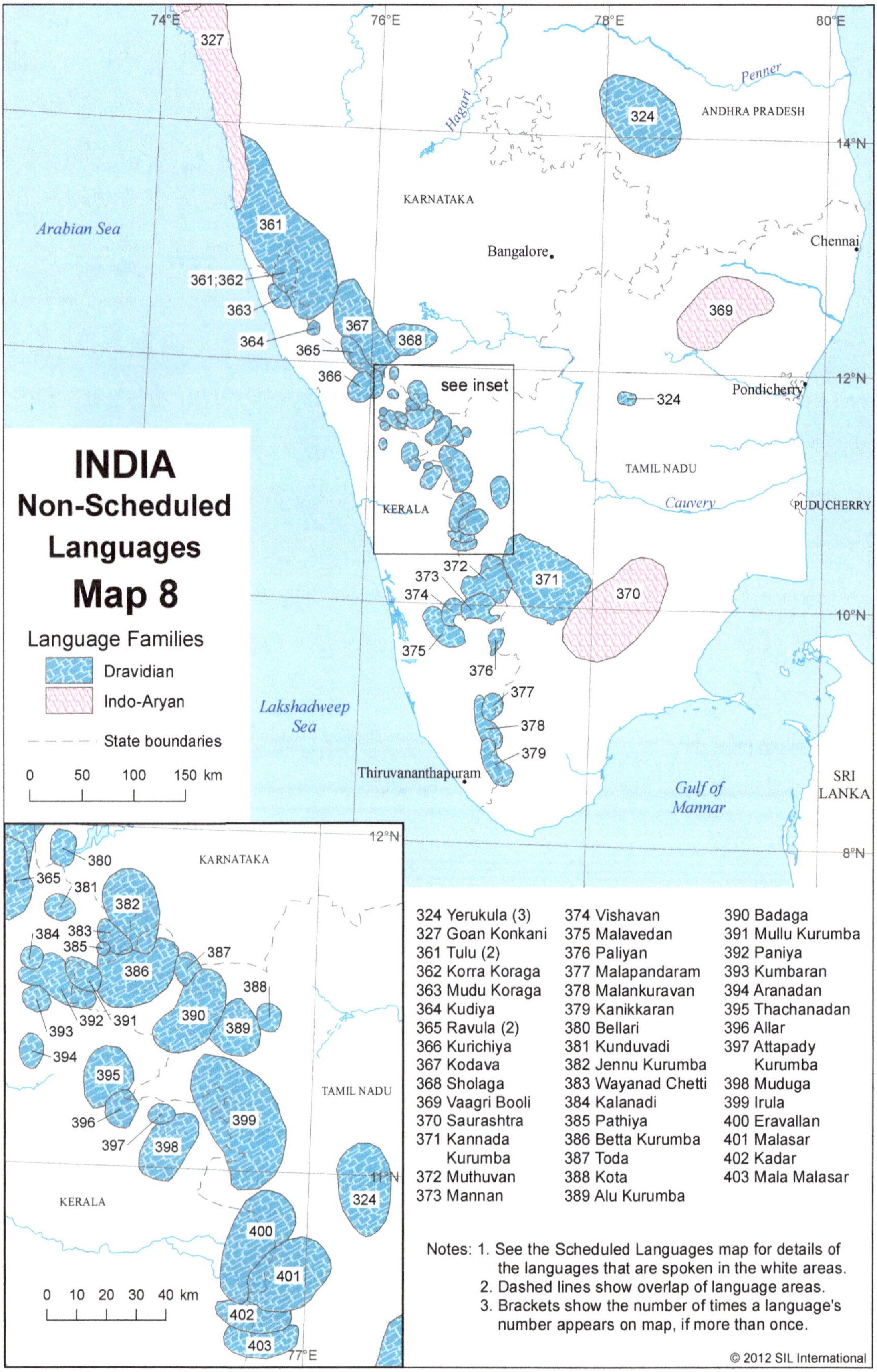
INDIA
Non-Scheduled
Languages
Map 8
Language Families
Dravidian
Indo-Aryan
State boundaries
0 50 100 150 km
Arabian Sea
Lakshadweep Sea
Gulf of Mannar
KARNATAKA
ANDHRA PRADESH
TAMIL NADU
KERALA
PUDUCHERRY
SRI LANKA
Bangalore
Chennai
Pondicherry
Thiruvananthapuram
Penner
Hagari
Cauvery
74°E
76°E
78°E
80°E
14°N
12°N
10°N
8°N
11°N
77°E
see inset
0 10 20 30 40 km
324 Yerukula (3)
327 Goan Konkani
361 Tulu (2)
362 Korra Koraga
363 Mudu Koraga
364 Kudiya
365 Ravula (2)
366 Kurichiya
367 Kodava
368 Sholaga
369 Vaagri Booli
370 Saurashtra
371 Kannada Kurumba
372 Muthuvan
373 Mannan
374 Vishavan
375 Malavedan
376 Paliyan
377 Malapandaram
378 Malankuravan
379 Kanikkaran
380 Bellari
381 Kunduvadi
382 Jennu Kurumba
383 Wayanad Chetti
384 Kalanadi
385 Pathiya
386 Betta Kurumba
387 Toda
388 Kota
389 Alu Kurumba
390 Badaga
391 Mullu Kurumba
392 Paniya
393 Kumbaran
394 Aranadan
395 Thachanadan
396 Allar
397 Attapady Kurumba
398 Muduga
399 Irula
400 Eravallan
401 Malasar
402 Kadar
403 Mala Malasar
Notes: 1. See the Scheduled Languages map for details of the languages that are spoken in the white areas.
2. Dashed lines show overlap of language areas.
3. Brackets show the number of times a language's number appears on map, if more than once.

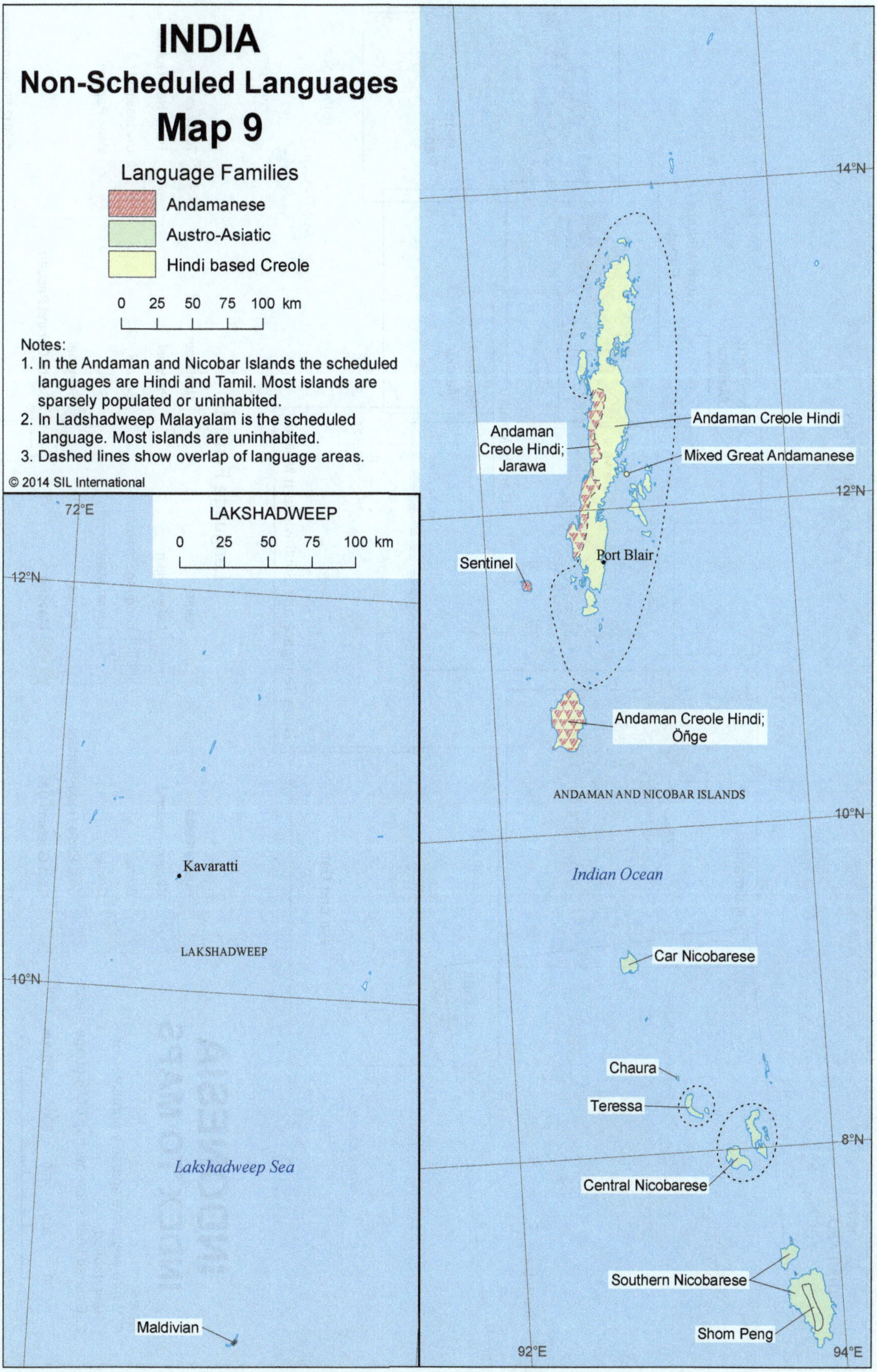
INDIA
Non-Scheduled Languages
Map 9
Language Families
Andamanese
Austro-Asiatic
Hindi based Creole
0 25 50 75 100 km
Notes:
1. In the Andaman and Nicobar Islands the scheduled languages are Hindi and Tamil. Most islands are sparsely populated or uninhabited.
2. In Ladshadweep Malayalam is the scheduled language. Most islands are uninhabited.
3. Dashed lines show overlap of language areas.
© 2014 SIL International
LAKSHADWEEP
0 25 50 75 100 km
72°E
12°N
10°N
Kavaratti
LAKSHADWEEP
Lakshadweep Sea
Maldivian
14°N
12°N
10°N
8°N
92°E
94°E
Andaman Creole Hindi
Andaman Creole Hindi; Jarawa
Mixed Great Andamanese
Port Blair
Sentinel
Andaman Creole Hindi; Öñge
ANDAMAN AND NICOBAR ISLANDS
Indian Ocean
Car Nicobarese
Chaura
Teressa
Central Nicobarese
Southern Nicobarese
Shom Peng

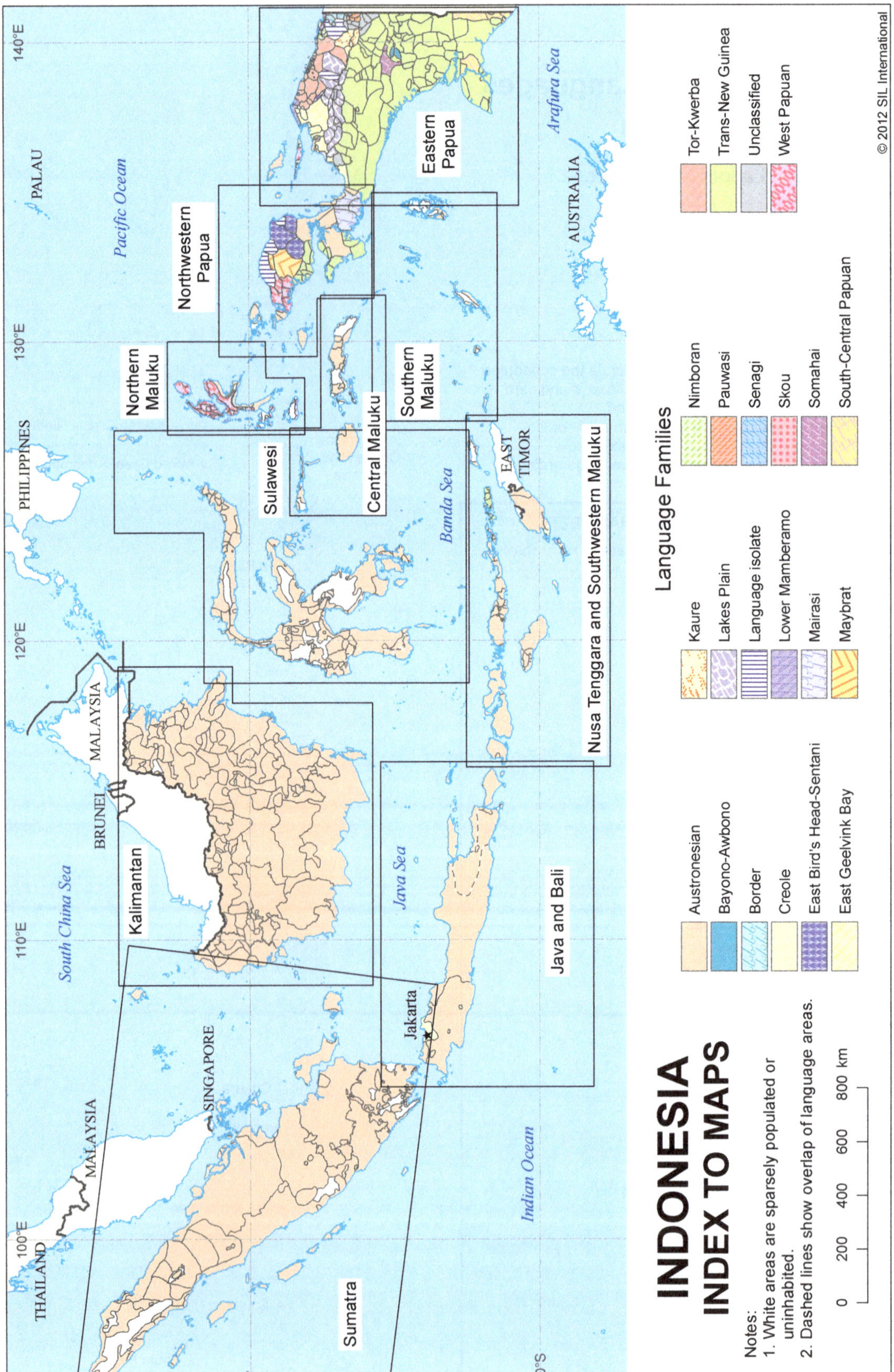
INDONESIA
INDEX TO MAPS
Notes:
1. White areas are sparsely populated or uninhabited.
2. Dashed lines show overlap of language areas.
0 200 400 600 800 km
Language Families
Austronesian
Bayono-Awbono
Border
Creole
East Bird's Head-Sentani
East Geelvink Bay
Kaure
Lakes Plain
Language isolate
Lower Mamberamo
Mairasi
Maybrat
Nimboran
Pauwasi
Senagi
Skou
Somahai
South-Central Papuan
Tor-Kwerba
Trans-New Guinea
Unclassified
West Papuan
© 2012 SIL International
Sumatra
Kalimantan
Java and Bali
Sulawesi
Nusa Tenggara and Southwestern Maluku
Central Maluku
Northern Maluku
Southern Maluku
Northwestern Papua
Eastern Papua
THAILAND
MALAYSIA
SINGAPORE
BRUNEI
PHILIPPINES
PALAU
EAST TIMOR
AUSTRALIA
Jakarta
South China Sea
Java Sea
Indian Ocean
Pacific Ocean
Banda Sea
Arafura Sea
100°E
110°E
120°E
130°E
140°E
0°
10°S

INDONESIA
JAVA AND BALI
Language Families
Creole
Deaf sign language
Javanese
Malayic
other Malayo-Polynesian
Notes:
1. White areas are sparsely populated or uninhabited.
2. Dashed lines show overlap of language areas.
0 50 100 150 km
© 2012 SIL International
SUMATRA
Java Sea
Indian Ocean
106°E
108°E
110°E
112°E
114°E
6°S
8°S
10°S
Malay
Madura
Kangean; Madura
Bali; Balinese Malay; Bengkala Sign Language
Bali; Balinese Malay
Osing
Badui
Tengger
Javanese; Madura
Javanese
Betawi
Jakarta
Petjo
Sunda

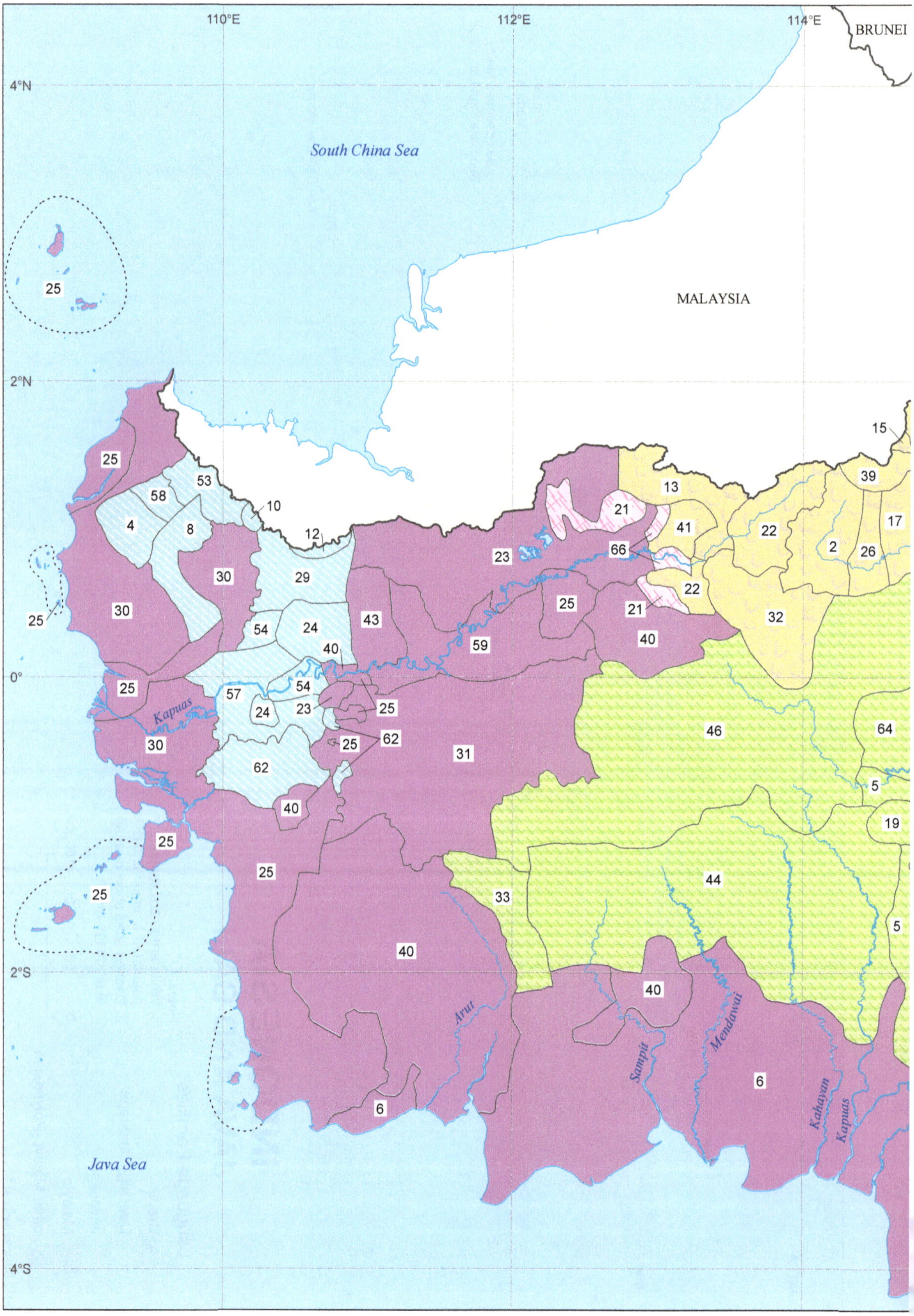
110°E
112°E
114°E
BRUNEI
4°N
South China Sea
MALAYSIA
2°N
0°
2°S
4°S
Kapuas
Arut
Sampit
Mendawai
Kahayan
Kapuas
Java Sea
25
53
58
4
8
10
12
29
30
30
25
54
24
40
43
23
66
21
13
41
22
39
17
2
26
22
21
25
59
40
32
15
25
57
54
24
23
25
62
25
31
46
64
30
62
40
5
19
25
25
25
33
44
5
40
40
6
6

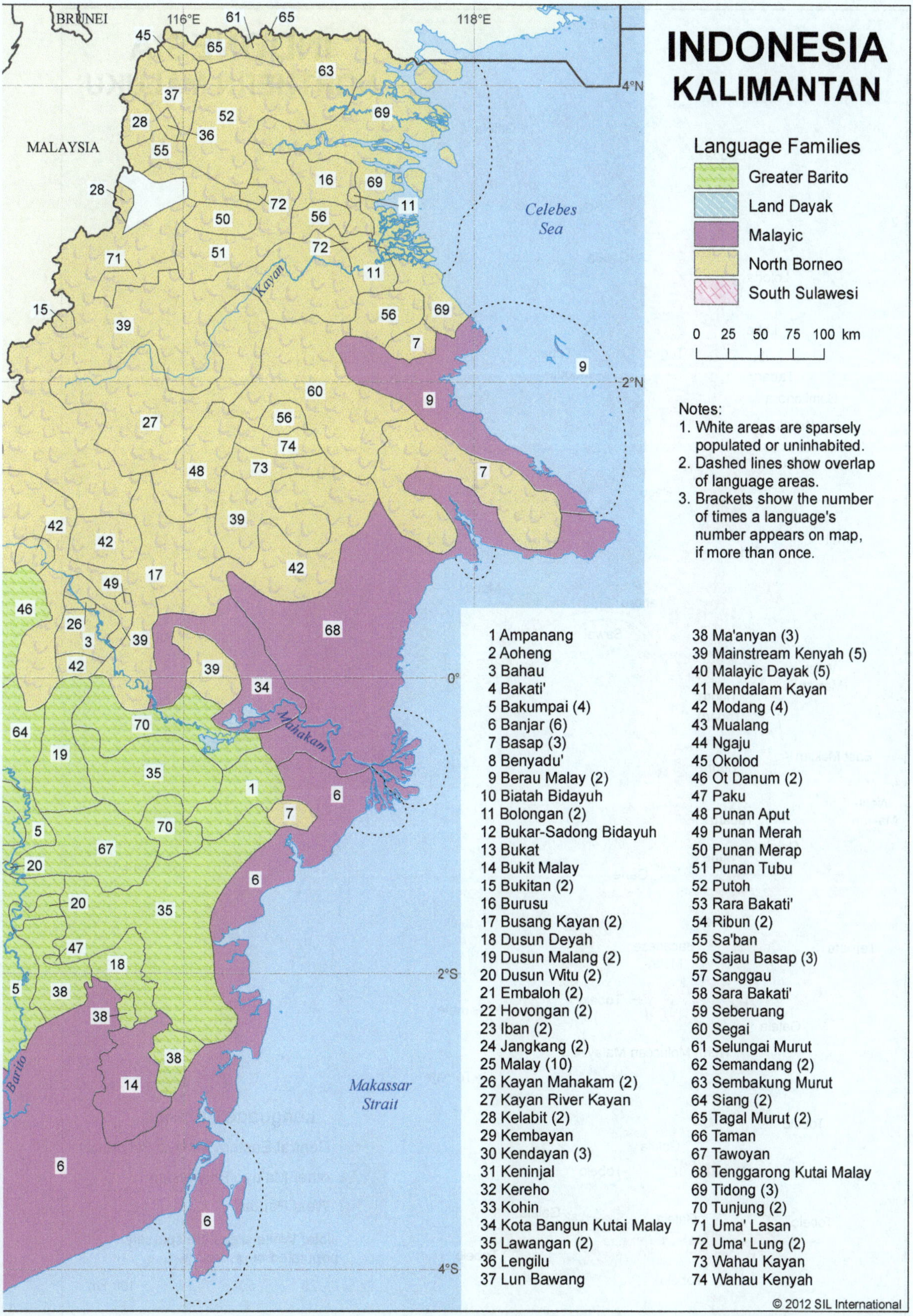
INDONESIA
KALIMANTAN
Language Families
Greater Barito
Land Dayak
Malayic
North Borneo
South Sulawesi
0 25 50 75 100 km
Notes:
1. White areas are sparsely populated or uninhabited.
2. Dashed lines show overlap of language areas.
3. Brackets show the number of times a language's number appears on map, if more than once.
BRUNEI
MALAYSIA
116°E
118°E
4°N
2°N
0°
2°S
4°S
Celebes Sea
Makassar Strait
Kayan
Mahakam
Barito
1 Ampanang
2 Aoheng
3 Bahau
4 Bakati'
5 Bakumpai (4)
6 Banjar (6)
7 Basap (3)
8 Benyadu'
9 Berau Malay (2)
10 Biatah Bidayuh
11 Bolongan (2)
12 Bukar-Sadong Bidayuh
13 Bukat
14 Bukit Malay
15 Bukitan (2)
16 Burusu
17 Busang Kayan (2)
18 Dusun Deyah
19 Dusun Malang (2)
20 Dusun Witu (2)
21 Embaloh (2)
22 Hovongan (2)
23 Iban (2)
24 Jangkang (2)
25 Malay (10)
26 Kayan Mahakam (2)
27 Kayan River Kayan
28 Kelabit (2)
29 Kembayan
30 Kendayan (3)
31 Keninjal
32 Kereho
33 Kohin
34 Kota Bangun Kutai Malay
35 Lawangan (2)
36 Lengilu
37 Lun Bawang
38 Ma'anyan (3)
39 Mainstream Kenyah (5)
40 Malayic Dayak (5)
41 Mendalam Kayan
42 Modang (4)
43 Mualang
44 Ngaju
45 Okolod
46 Ot Danum (2)
47 Paku
48 Punan Aput
49 Punan Merah
50 Punan Merap
51 Punan Tubu
52 Putoh
53 Rara Bakati'
54 Ribun (2)
55 Sa'ban
56 Sajau Basap (3)
57 Sanggau
58 Sara Bakati'
59 Seberuang
60 Segai
61 Selungai Murut
62 Semandang (2)
63 Sembakung Murut
64 Siang (2)
65 Tagal Murut (2)
66 Taman
67 Tawoyan
68 Tenggarong Kutai Malay
69 Tidong (3)
70 Tunjung (2)
71 Uma' Lasan
72 Uma' Lung (2)
73 Wahau Kayan
74 Wahau Kenyah
© 2012 SIL International

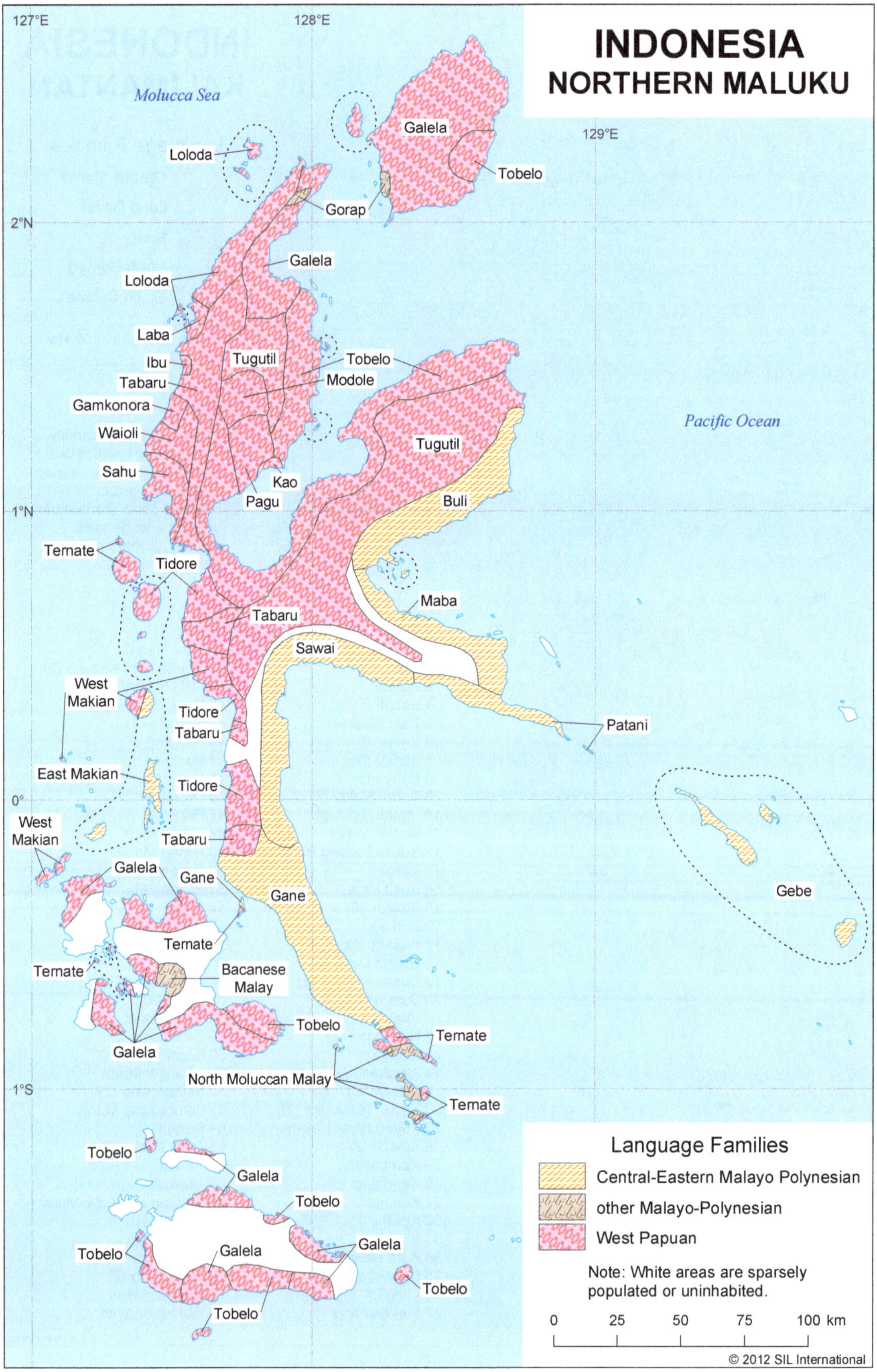
INDONESIA
NORTHERN MALUKU
127°E
128°E
129°E
2°N
1°N
0°
1°S
Molucca Sea
Pacific Ocean
Galela
Tobelo
Loloda
Gorap
Galela
Loloda
Laba
Ibu
Tugutil
Tobelo
Tabaru
Modole
Gamkonora
Waioli
Tugutil
Sahu
Kao
Pagu
Buli
Ternate
Tidore
Maba
Tabaru
Sawai
West Makian
Tidore
Tabaru
Patani
East Makian
Tidore
West Makian
Tabaru
Gebe
Galela
Gane
Gane
Ternate
Ternate
Bacanese Malay
Tobelo
Galela
Ternate
North Moluccan Malay
Ternate
Tobelo
Galela
Tobelo
Tobelo
Galela
Galela
Tobelo
Tobelo
Language Families
Central-Eastern Malayo Polynesian
other Malayo-Polynesian
West Papuan
Note: White areas are sparsely populated or uninhabited.
0 25 50 75 100 km
© 2012 SIL International

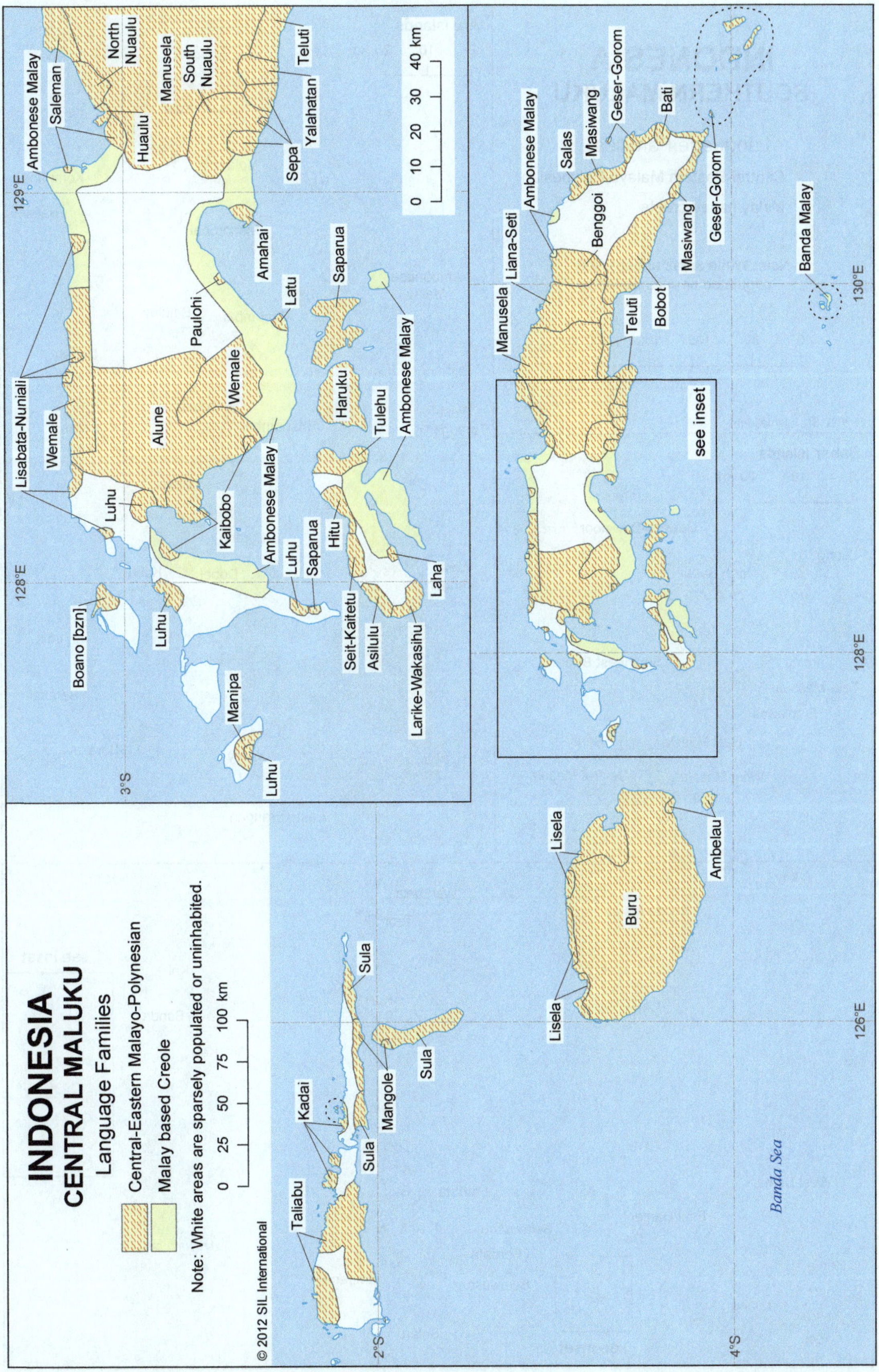
INDONESIA
CENTRAL MALUKU
Language Families
Central-Eastern Malayo-Polynesian
Malay based Creole
Note: White areas are sparsely populated or uninhabited.
0 25 50 75 100 km
© 2012 SIL International
Taliabu
Kadai
Sula
Mangole
Lisela
Buru
Ambelau
Banda Sea
see inset
Manusela
Liana-Seti
Ambonese Malay
Salas
Masiwang
Geser-Gorom
Bati
Benggoi
Bobot
Teluti
Banda Malay
2°S
4°S
3°S
126°E
128°E
129°E
130°E
0 10 20 30 40 km
Saleman
North Nuaulu
South Nuaulu
Huaulu
Yalahatan
Sepa
Amahai
Lisabata-Nuniali
Wemale
Alune
Paulohi
Latu
Saparua
Haruku
Tulehu
Luhu
Kaibobo
Hitu
Laha
Seit-Kaitetu
Asilulu
Larike-Wakasihu
Boano [bzn]
Manipa

INDONESIA
SOUTHERN MALUKU
Language Families
Central-Eastern Malayo-Polynesian
Malay based creole
Note: White areas are sparsely populated or uninhabited.
0 50 100 150 200 km
© 2012 SIL International
Aru Islands
0 10 20 km
Kola
Kola
Kola
Kompane
Ujir
Batuley
Manombai
Ambonese Malay
Manombai
Batuley
Dobel
6°S
Dobel
West Tarangan
Manombai
Mariri
Dobel
Lola
Lorang
West Tarangan
Dobel
Koba
Lola
Barakai
Karey
Barakai
East Tarangan
134°E
Babar Islands
0 10 20 km
Dawera-Daweloor
Luang
North Babar
Imroing
Southeast Babar
8°S
Tela-Masbuar
Emplawas
East Masela
Serili
West Masela
Central Masela
130°E
128°E
130°E
132°E
134°E
Watubela
Banda Malay
Teor
see inset
Kei
Kur
Banda
Banda Sea
Kei
Kei
6°S
West Damar
Fordata
East Damar
Seluwasan
Dai
Arafura Sea
Roma
Fordata
Yamdena
Seluwasan
8°S
Luang
Leti
Selaru
see inset

INDONESIA
NUSA TENGGARA AND
SOUTHWESTERN MALUKU
Flores Sea
SULAWESI
Timor Sea
EAST TIMOR
EAST TIMOR
see enlargement
see enlargement
see inset
Bali
Sasak
Sumbawa
Bima
Komodo
Bima
Manggarai
Laura
Mamboru
Wejewa
Kodi
Lamboya
Wanukaka
Anakalangu
Kambera
Hawu
Hawu
Sika
Helong;Kupang Malay
Bilba;Kupang Malay
Kupang Malay;Uab Meto
Amarasi;Kupang Malay
Amarasi
Uab Meto
Tetun
Bunak
Kemak
Ili'uun
Aputai
Perai
Tugun
Galolen
Kisar
Oirata
Roma
Leti
0 10 20 km
Rikou
Bilba
Termanu
Lole
Tii
Dengka
Dhao
Dela-Oenale
123°E
11°S
6°S
8°S
10°S
12°S
116°E
118°E
120°E
122°E
124°E
126°E
Language Families
Central-Eastern Malayo-Polynesian
Malay based Creole
other Malayo-Polynesian
Trans-New Guinea
Notes:
1. White areas are sparsely populated or uninhabited.
2. Dashed lines show overlap of language areas.
0 50 100 150 200 km
© 2012 SIL International
Language data from Centre for Regional Studies, Universitas Kristen Artha Wacana (1997)

Language data from Centre for Regional Studies, Universitas Kristen Artha Wacana (1997)

INDONESIA
NORTHWESTERN PAPUA

1 Kawe
2 Legenyem
3 Waigeo (2)
4 Biak (4)
5 Wauyai
6 As
7 Moi (2)
8 Ma'ya (2)
9 Maden
10 Duriankere
11 Matbat
12 Biga
13 Seget
14 Kalabra
15 Tehit
16 Moraid
17 Abun
18 Karon Dori
19 Mpur
20 Meyah
21 Hatam
22 Manikion
23 Moskona
24 Mai Brat
25 Kais
26 Konda
27 Yahadian
28 Suabo
29 Puragi
30 Kokoda
31 Kaburi
32 Arandai
33 Kemberano (2)
34 Wandamen (2)
35 Tanahmerah
36 Irarutu
37 Mor [moq]
38 Erokwanas
39 Bedoanas
40 Arguni
41 Sekar
42 Onin (2)
43 Iha
44 Baham (2)
45 Uruangnirin
46 Karas
47 Buruwai
48 Kamberau
49 Kowiai (3)
50 Mairasi
51 Semimi
52 Mer
53 Yeretuar
54 Kuri
55 Meoswar
56 Roon
57 Yaur
58 Yeresiam
59 Ekari
60 Kamoro

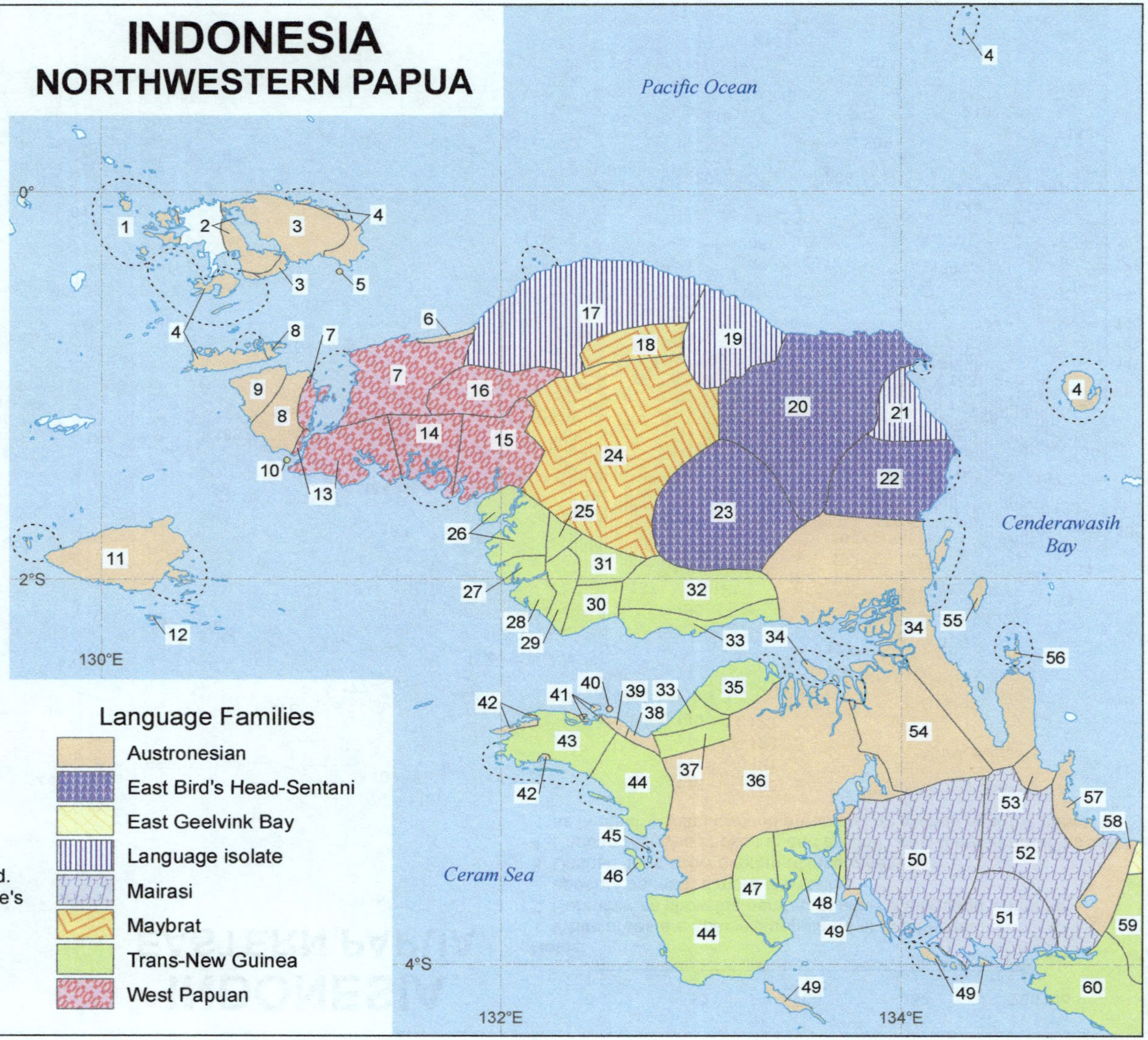

0 50 100 150 200 km

Notes:
1. White areas are sparsely populated or uninhabited.
2. Parentheses show the number of times a language's number appears on map, if more than once.
3. Papuan Malay is spoken in and around coastal urban areas as well as in other coastal lowland areas and on islands near the coast.

INDONESIA
EASTERN PAPUA
0 50 100 150 200 km
Notes:
1. White areas are sparsely populated or uninhabited.
2. Parentheses show the number of times a language's number appears on map, if more than once.
3. Dashed lines show overlap of language areas.
4. Papuan Malay is spoken in and around coastal urban areas as well as in other coastal lowland areas and on islands near the coast.
136°E
138°E
140°E
2°S
4°S
South Pacific Ocean
Cenderawasih Bay
Mamberamo
Rouffaer
Idenburg
Vriendschaps
4 Biak (3)
51 Semimi
52 Mer
53 Yeretuar
57 Yaur
58 Yeresiam
59 Ekari
60 Kamoro
109 Yoke
110 Massep
111 Samarokena
112 Liki
113 Sobei
114 Mo
166 Jofotek-Bromnya
167 Itik
168 Berik (2)

61 Moni (2)
62 Damal
63 Sempan
64 Central Asmat (5)
65 North Asmat
66 Nduga (2)
67 Silimo
68 Hupla
69 Lower Grand Valley Dani
70 Mid Grand Valley Dani
71 Upper Grand Valley Dani
72 Walak
73 Nggem
74 Western Dani
75 Wano
76 Dem
77 Wolani
78 Dao
79 Auye
80 Tunggare
81 Burate (2)
82 Waropen (3)
83 Kehu
84 Tause (3)
85 Mor [mhz]
86 Awera
87 Woria (2)
88 Rasawa
89 Demisa
90 Tefaro
91 Kofei
92 Barapasi
93 Sauri
94 Ambai
95 Saweru
96 Serui-Laut
97 Papuma
98 Ansus (2)
99 Woi
100 Pom
101 Marau
102 Munggui
103 Busami
104 Yawa
105 Wabo
106 Kurudu
107 Anasi
108 Warembori
115 Keijar
116 Dabe
117 Masimasi
118 Vitou
119 Sunum
120 Betaf
121 Kwinsu (2)
122 Mawes (2)
123 Fedan
124 Yarsun
125 Anus
126 Bonggo
127 Dineor
128 Mekwei
129 Sowari
130 Sentani
131 Tabla
132 Ormu
133 Tobati (2)
134 Kayupulau
135 Skou
136 Nafri
137 Taikat
138 Manem
139 Waris
140 Sowanda
141 Zorop
142 Dera
143 Tebi
144 Emem
145 Towei
146 Yetfa
147 Murkim
148 Kimki
149 Lepki
150 Kembra
151 Tofanma
152 Usku
153 Namla
154 Molof
155 Viid
156 Elseng
157 Awyi
158 Kemtuik
159 Gresi
160 Orya
161 Mlap
162 Nimboran
163 Tarpia
164 Kaptiau
165 Wares
169 Beneraf
170 Kwesten
171 Isirawa
172 Kwerba
173 Mander
174 Kwerba Mamberamo
175 Kauwera
176 Airoran
177 Bagusa
178 Nisa
179 Trimuris
180 Bauzi
181 Burmeso
182 Eritai
183 Sikaritai
184 Obokuitai
185 Biritai
186 Kirikiri
187 Fayu
188 Edopi
189 Iau
190 Duvle
191 Doutai
192 Kwerisa
193 Waritai
194 Diebroud
195 Kaiy
196 Papasena
197 Abinomn
198 Foau
199 Sause
200 Kapauri
201 Kaure
202 Kosare
203 Narau
204 Nipsan
205 Angguruk Yali
206 Pass Valley Yali
207 Kosarek Yale
208 Nalca
209 Eipomek
210 Ketengban
211 Una
212 Korupun-Sela
213 Ninia Yali
214 Momuna (2)
215 Momina
216 Kopkaka
217 Awbono
218 Diuwe (2)
219 Bayono (2)
220 Korowai (2)
221 Komyandaret (2)
222 Kwer
223 Burumakok
224 Tangko
225 Nakai
226 Ngalum
227 Morop
228 North Muyu (2)
229 Ninggerum
230 Wambon
231 Ketum (2)
232 Tsaukambo
233 Wanggom
234 Kombai
235 Citak
236 Tamnim Citak
237 Yaosakor Asmat
238 Warkay-Bipim
239 Sawi
240 Casuarina Coast Asmat
241 Atohwaim
242 Asue Awyu
243 Tamagario (2)
244 Kayagar
245 Yaqay (2)
246 Central Awyu
247 Aghu
248 North Awyu
249 Mandobo Atas
250 South Muyu
251 Mandobo Bawah
252 Jair Awyu
253 Edera Awyu
254 South Awyu (2)
255 Yelmek
256 Riantana
257 Kimaghima (3)
258 Koneraw
259 Mombum (2)
260 Ndom (2)
261 Marind (3)
262 Maklew
263 Bian Marind
264 Yei
265 Sota Kanum
266 Ngkâlmpw Kanum
267 Morori
268 Bädi Kanum
269 Smärky Kanum

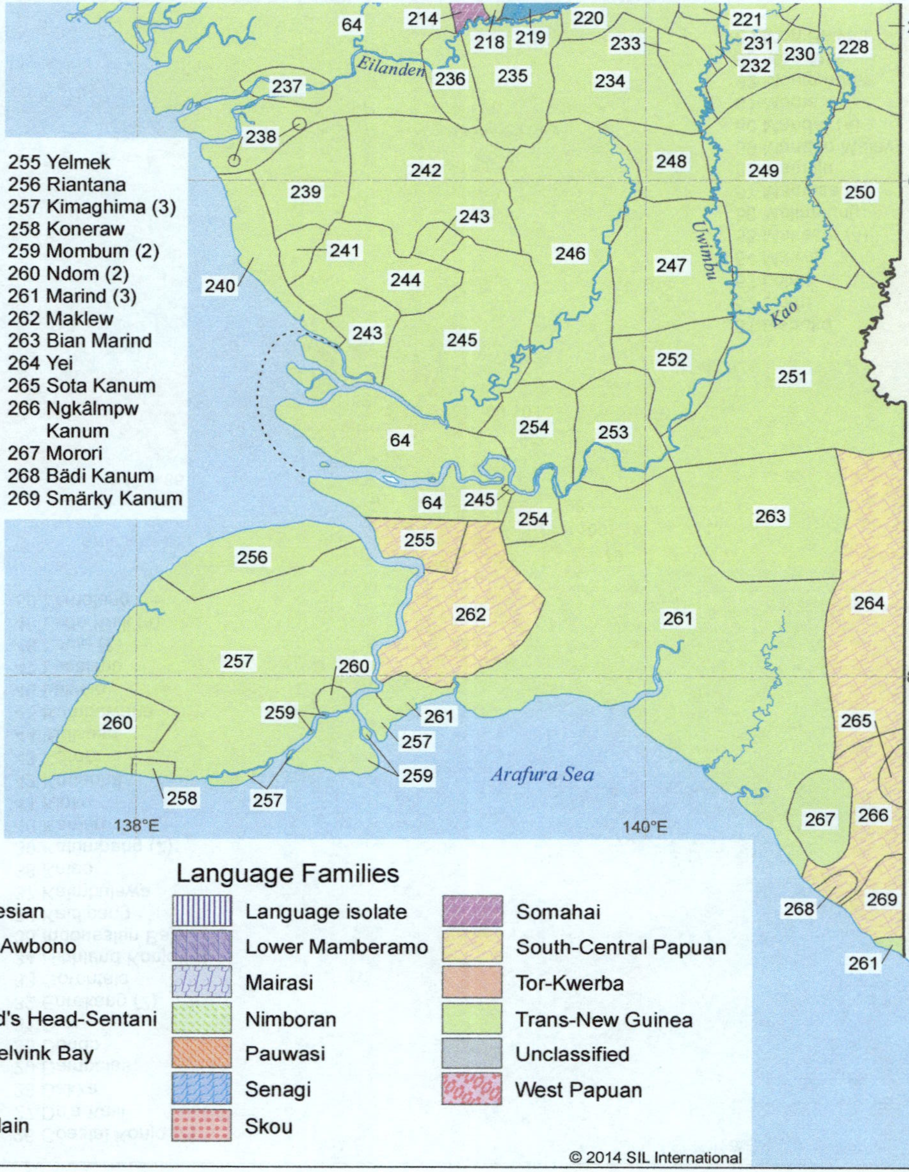

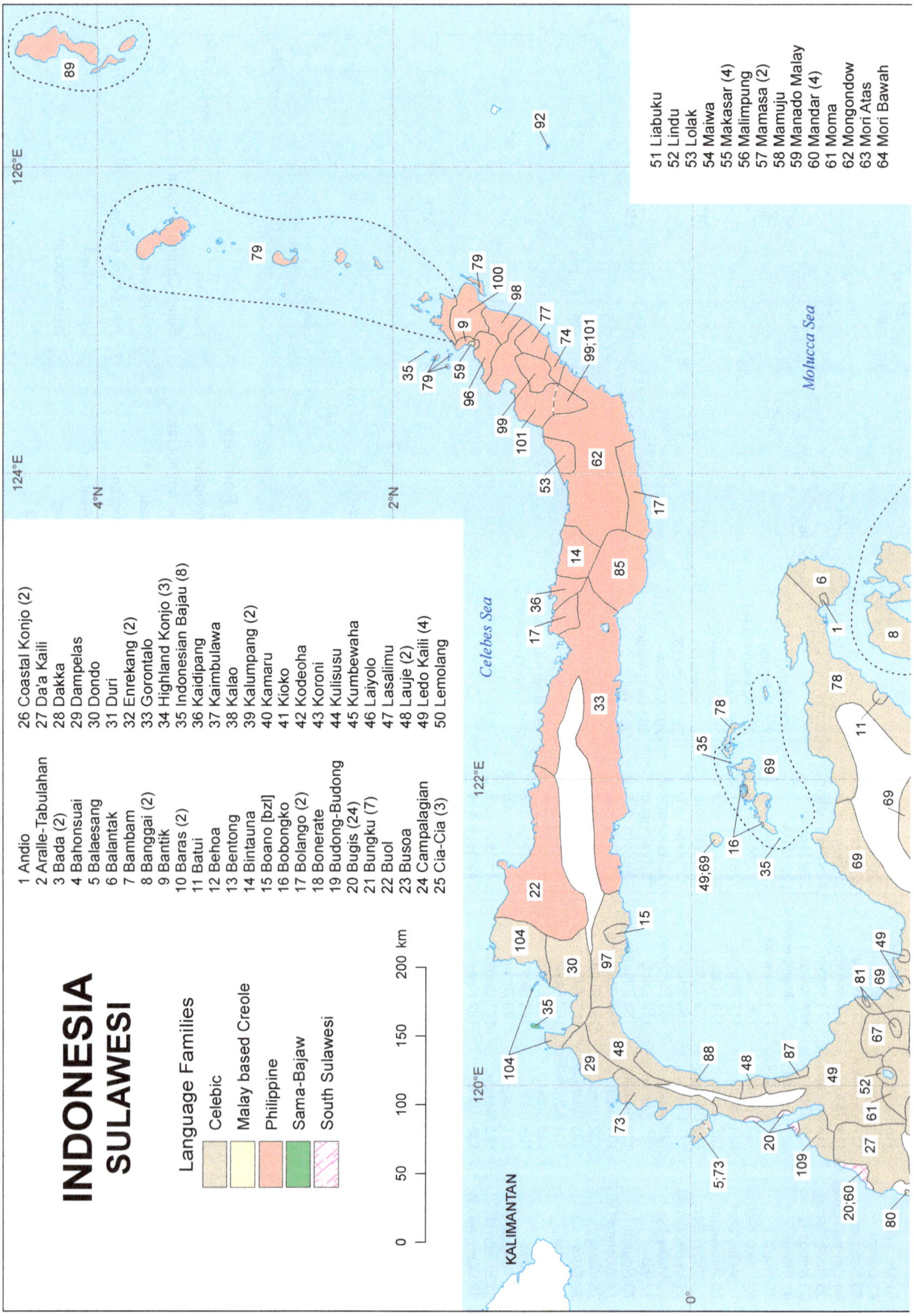
INDONESIA
SULAWESI
Language Families
Celebic
Malay based Creole
Philippine
Sama-Bajaw
South Sulawesi
0 50 100 150 200 km
1 Andio
2 Aralle-Tabulahan
3 Bada (2)
4 Bahonsuai
5 Balaesang
6 Balantak
7 Bambam
8 Banggai (2)
9 Bantik
10 Baras (2)
11 Batui
12 Behoa
13 Bentong
14 Bintauna
15 Boano [bzl]
16 Bobongko
17 Bolango (2)
18 Bonerate
19 Budong-Budong
20 Bugis (24)
21 Bungku (7)
22 Buol
23 Busoa
24 Campalagian
25 Cia-Cia (3)
26 Coastal Konjo (2)
27 Da'a Kaili
28 Dakka
29 Dampelas
30 Dondo
31 Duri
32 Enrekang (2)
33 Gorontalo
34 Highland Konjo (3)
35 Indonesian Bajau (8)
36 Kaidipang
37 Kaimbulawa
38 Kalao
39 Kalumpang (2)
40 Kamaru
41 Kioko
42 Kodeoha
43 Koroni
44 Kulisusu
45 Kumbewaha
46 Laiyolo
47 Lasalimu
48 Lauje (2)
49 Ledo Kaili (4)
50 Lemolang
51 Liabuku
52 Lindu
53 Lolak
54 Maiwa
55 Makasar (4)
56 Malimpung
57 Mamasa (2)
58 Mamuju
59 Manado Malay
60 Mandar (4)
61 Moma
62 Mongondow
63 Mori Atas
64 Mori Bawah
KALIMANTAN
Celebes Sea
Molucca Sea
120°E
122°E
124°E
126°E
4°N
2°N
0°

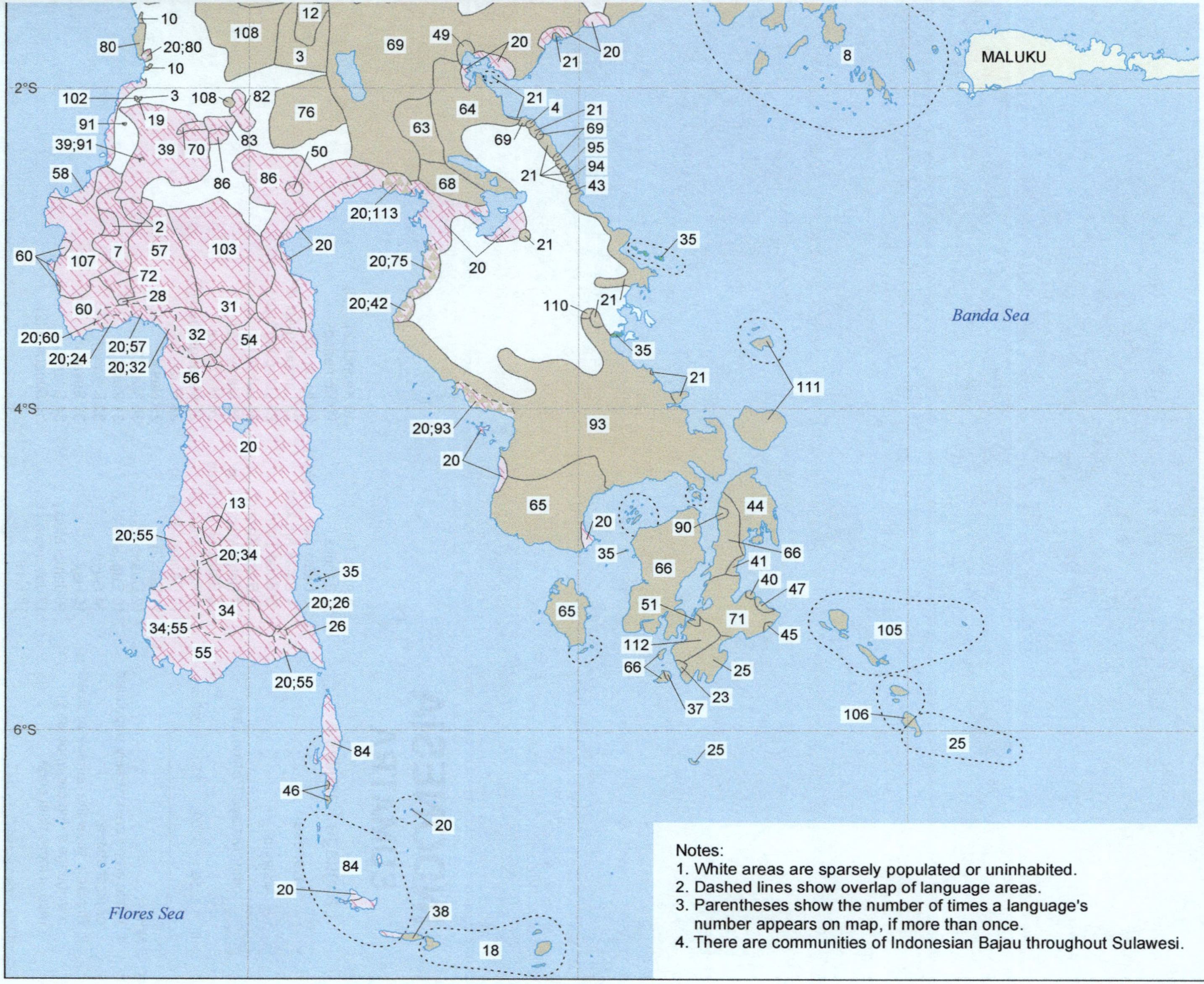

65 Moronene (2)
66 Muna (3)
67 Napu
68 Padoe
69 Pamona (8)
70 Panasuan
71 Pancana
72 Pannei
73 Pendau (2)
74 Ponosakan
75 Rahambuu
76 Rampi
77 Ratahan
78 Saluan (2)
79 Sangir (3)
80 Sarudu (3)
81 Sedoa
82 Seko Padang
83 Seko Tengah
84 Selayar (2)
85 Suwawa
86 Tae' (2)
87 Taje
88 Tajio
89 Talaud
90 Taloki
91 Talondo' (2)
92 Tidore
93 Tolaki (2)
94 Tomadino
95 Tombelala
96 Tombulu
97 Tomini
98 Tondano
99 Tonsawang (2)
100 Tonsea
101 Tontemboan (2)
102 Topoiyo
103 Toraja-Sa'dan
104 Totoli (2)
105 Tukang Besi North
106 Tukang Besi South
107 Ulumanda'
108 Uma (2)
109 Unde Kaili
110 Waru
111 Wawonii
112 Wolio
113 Wotu

Notes:
1. White areas are sparsely populated or uninhabited.
2. Dashed lines show overlap of language areas.
3. Parentheses show the number of times a language's number appears on map, if more than once.
4. There are communities of Indonesian Bajau throughout Sulawesi.

INDONESIA
SUMATRA
Language Families
Javanese
Malayic
other Malayo-Polynesian
0 50 100 150 200 km
Notes:
1. White areas are sparsely populated or uninhabited.
2. Brackets show the number of times a language's number appears on map, if more than once.
1 Aceh (4)
2 Bangka
3 Batak Alas-Kluet (2)
4 Batak Angkola
5 Batak Dairi
6 Batak Karo (2)
7 Batak Mandailing
8 Batak Simalungun
9 Batak Toba (2)
10 Central Malay (3)
11 Col (2)
12 Duano (2)
13 Enggano
14 Gayo
15 Haji
16 Jambi Malay
17 Javanese (13)
18 Kaur
19 Kerinci (2)
20 Komering
21 Kubu (2)
22 Lampung Api (5)
23 Lampung Nyo
24 Lubu
25 Malay (12)
26 Mentawai
27 Minangkabau (6)
28 Musi
29 Nasal
30 Nias (2)
31 Pekal
32 Rejang
33 Sekak (5)
34 Sikule
35 Simeulue (2)
Malacca Strait
Indian Ocean
Toba
Rokan
6°N
4°N
2°N
0°
2°S
4°S
96°E
98°E
100°E
102°E
© 2012 SIL International

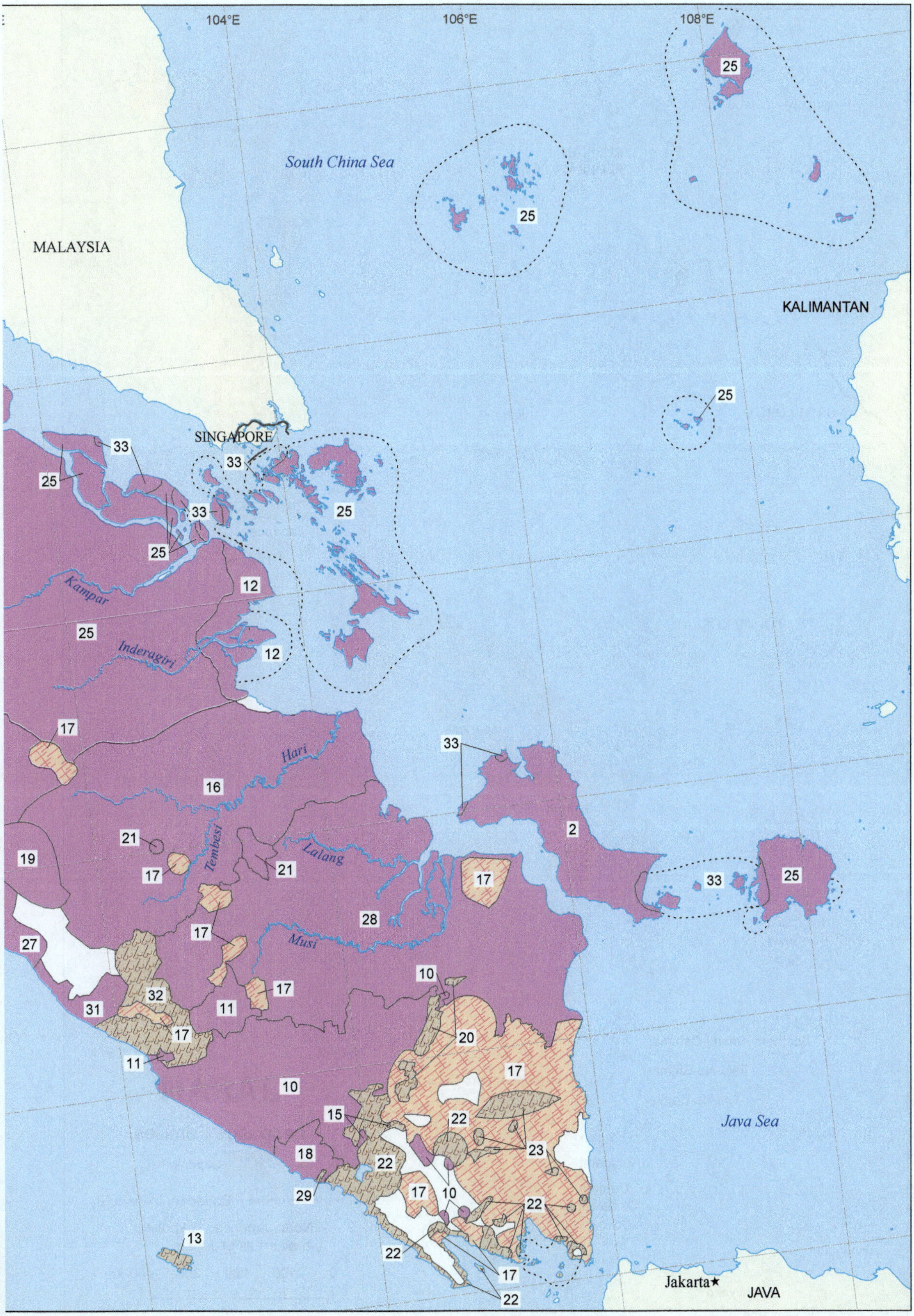
104°E
106°E
108°E
South China Sea
MALAYSIA
KALIMANTAN
SINGAPORE
Kampar
Inderagiri
Hari
Tembesi
Lalang
Musi
Java Sea
Jakarta★
JAVA
25
33
12
17
16
21
19
27
28
2
31
32
11
10
20
15
22
23
18
29
13

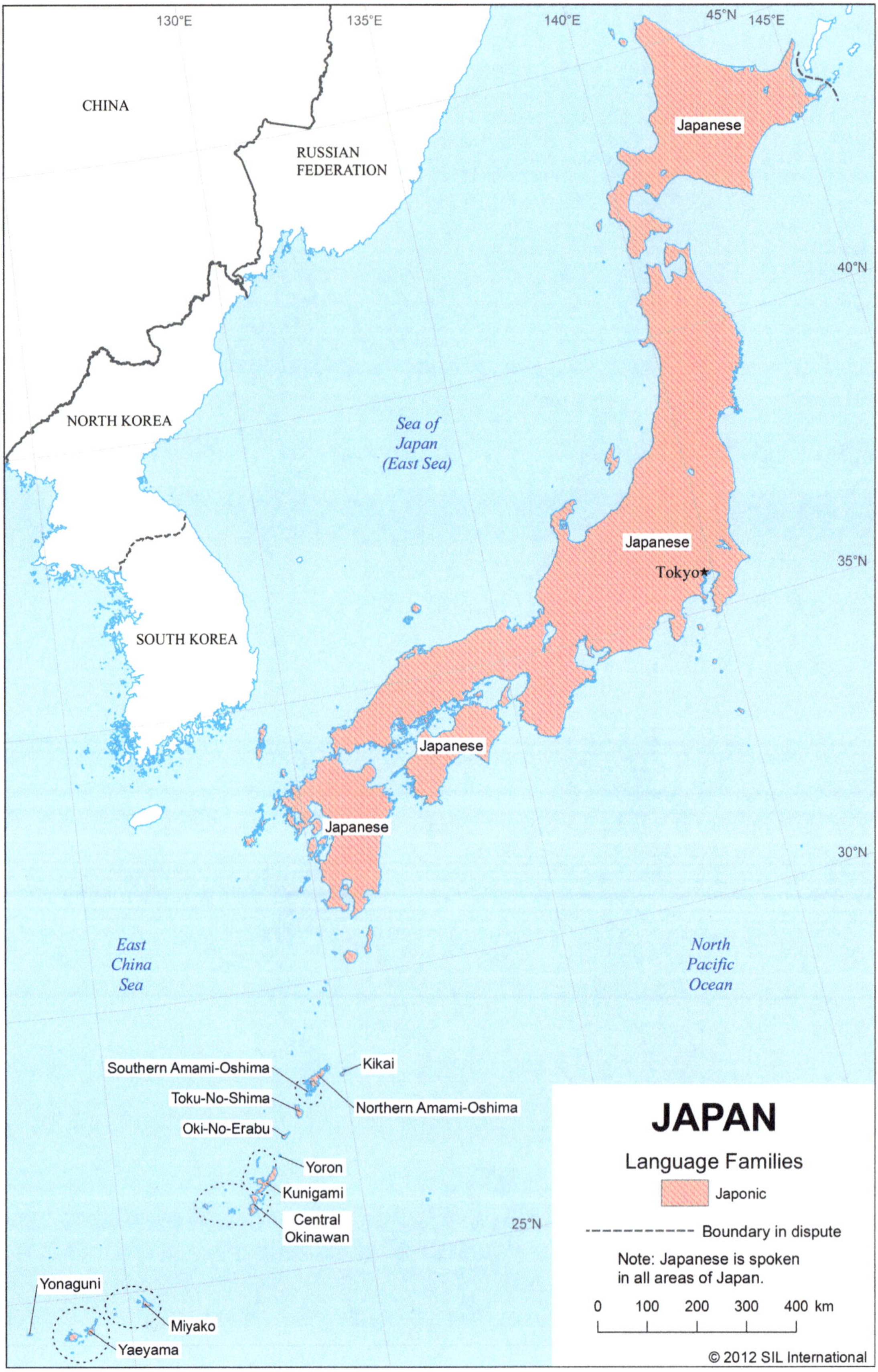
130°E
135°E
140°E
45°N
145°E
CHINA
RUSSIAN FEDERATION
Japanese
40°N
NORTH KOREA
Sea of Japan (East Sea)
Japanese
35°N
Tokyo
SOUTH KOREA
Japanese
Japanese
30°N
East China Sea
North Pacific Ocean
Southern Amami-Oshima
Kikai
Toku-No-Shima
Northern Amami-Oshima
Oki-No-Erabu
Yoron
Kunigami
Central Okinawan
25°N
Yonaguni
Miyako
Yaeyama
JAPAN
Language Families
Japonic
Boundary in dispute
Note: Japanese is spoken in all areas of Japan.
0 100 200 300 400 km
© 2012 SIL International

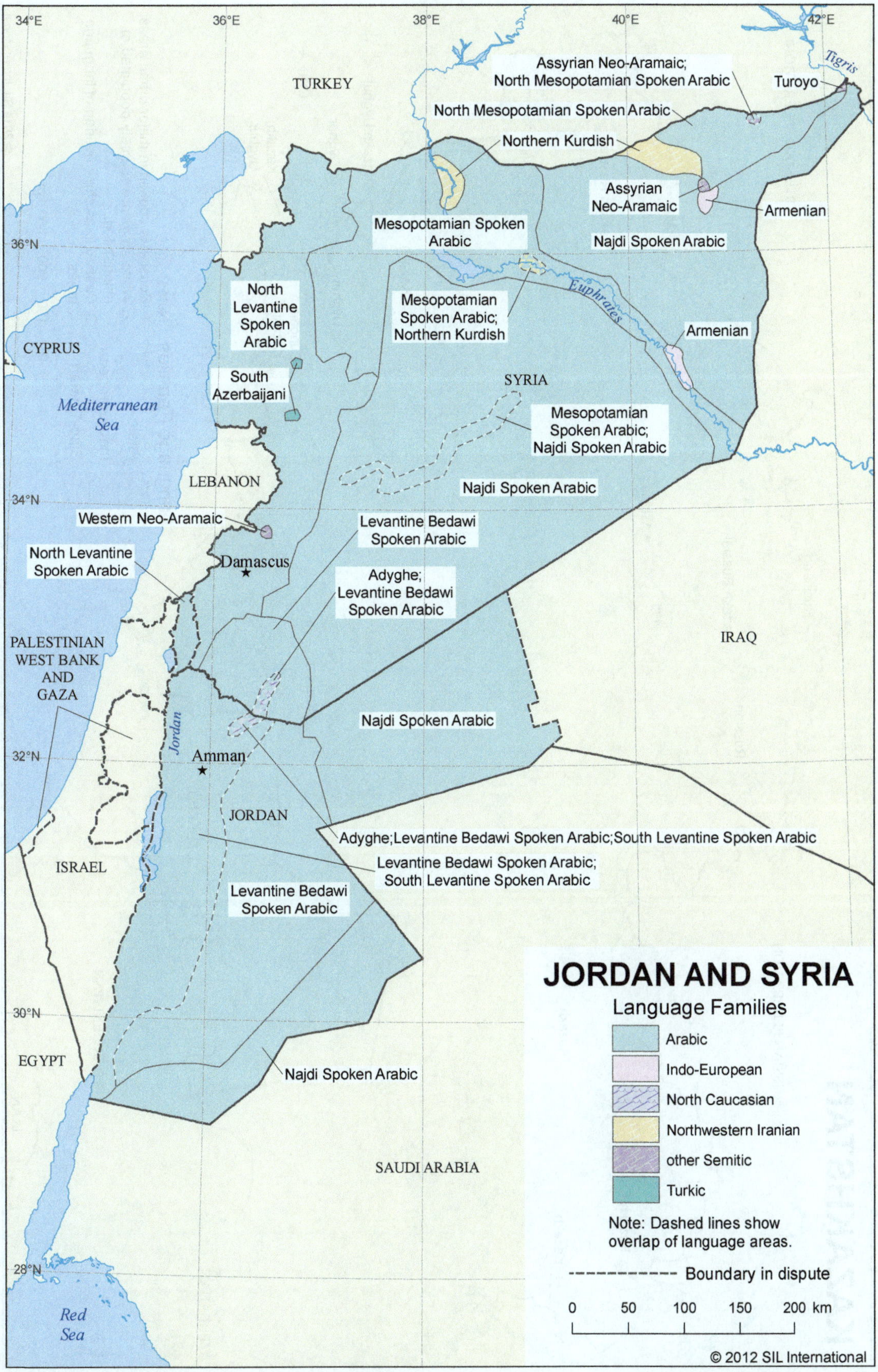
34°E
36°E
38°E
40°E
42°E
36°N
34°N
32°N
30°N
28°N
TURKEY
CYPRUS
Mediterranean Sea
LEBANON
SYRIA
IRAQ
JORDAN
ISRAEL
PALESTINIAN WEST BANK AND GAZA
EGYPT
SAUDI ARABIA
Red Sea
Tigris
Euphrates
Jordan
Damascus
Amman
Assyrian Neo-Aramaic; North Mesopotamian Spoken Arabic
Turoyo
North Mesopotamian Spoken Arabic
Northern Kurdish
Assyrian Neo-Aramaic
Armenian
Mesopotamian Spoken Arabic
Najdi Spoken Arabic
North Levantine Spoken Arabic
Mesopotamian Spoken Arabic; Northern Kurdish
Armenian
South Azerbaijani
Mesopotamian Spoken Arabic; Najdi Spoken Arabic
Najdi Spoken Arabic
Western Neo-Aramaic
Levantine Bedawi Spoken Arabic
North Levantine Spoken Arabic
Adyghe; Levantine Bedawi Spoken Arabic
Najdi Spoken Arabic
Adyghe;Levantine Bedawi Spoken Arabic;South Levantine Spoken Arabic
Levantine Bedawi Spoken Arabic; South Levantine Spoken Arabic
Levantine Bedawi Spoken Arabic
Najdi Spoken Arabic
JORDAN AND SYRIA
Language Families
Arabic
Indo-European
North Caucasian
Northwestern Iranian
other Semitic
Turkic
Note: Dashed lines show overlap of language areas.
Boundary in dispute
0 50 100 150 200 km
© 2012 SIL International

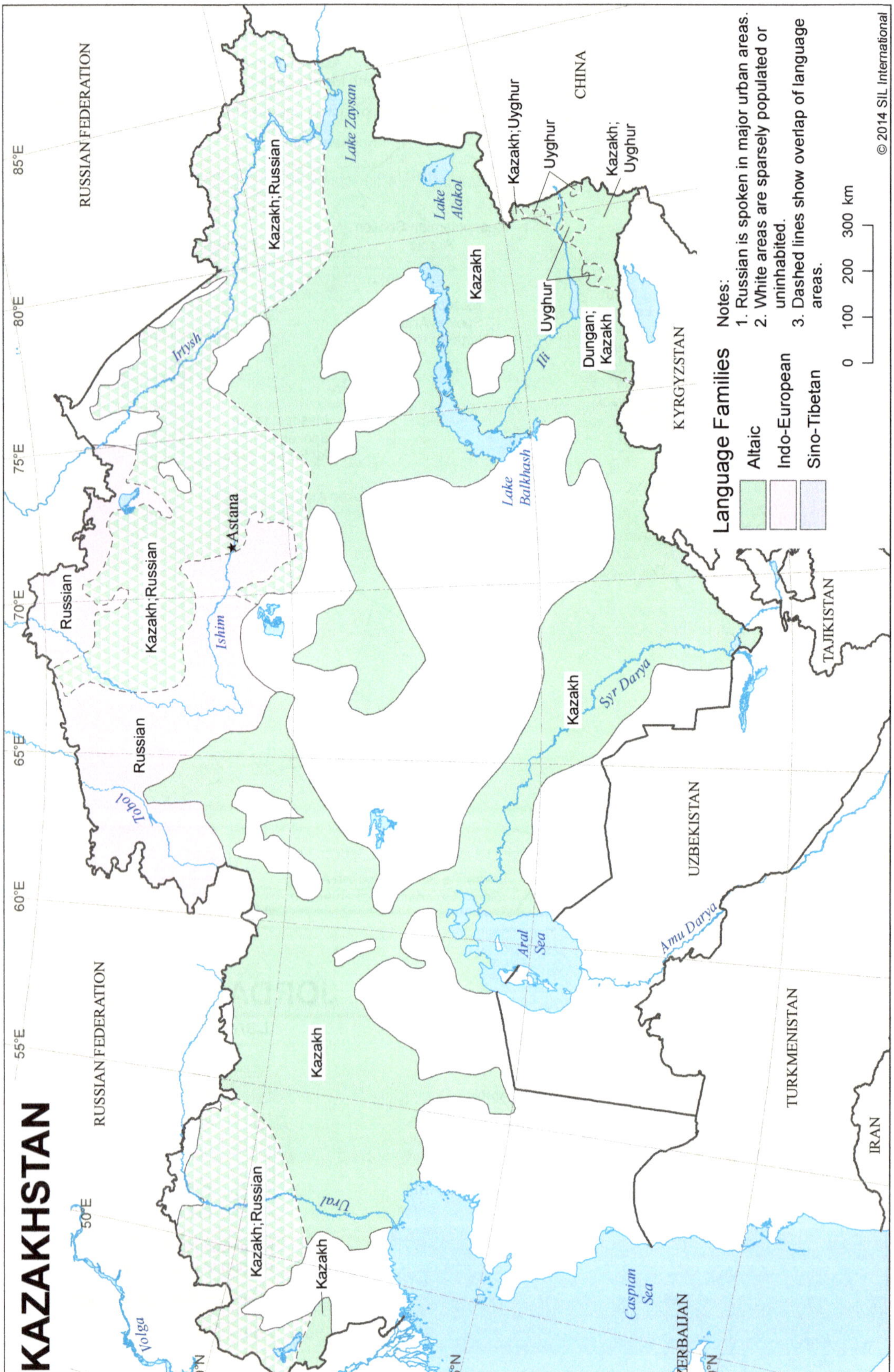
KAZAKHSTAN
RUSSIAN FEDERATION
RUSSIAN FEDERATION
CHINA
KYRGYZSTAN
TAJIKISTAN
UZBEKISTAN
TURKMENISTAN
IRAN
AZERBAIJAN
Kazakh;Russian
Kazakh;Russian
Kazakh;Russian
Russian
Russian
Kazakh
Kazakh
Kazakh
Kazakh
Kazakh;Uyghur
Uyghur
Kazakh; Uyghur
Uyghur
Dungan; Kazakh
Astana
Irtysh
Ishim
Tobol
Ural
Volga
Ili
Syr Darya
Amu Darya
Lake Zaysan
Lake Alakol
Lake Balkhash
Aral Sea
Caspian Sea
85°E
80°E
75°E
70°E
65°E
60°E
55°E
50°E
50°N
45°N
40°N
Language Families
Altaic
Indo-European
Sino-Tibetan
Notes:
1. Russian is spoken in major urban areas.
2. White areas are sparsely populated or uninhabited.
3. Dashed lines show overlap of language areas.
0 100 200 300 km
© 2014 SIL International

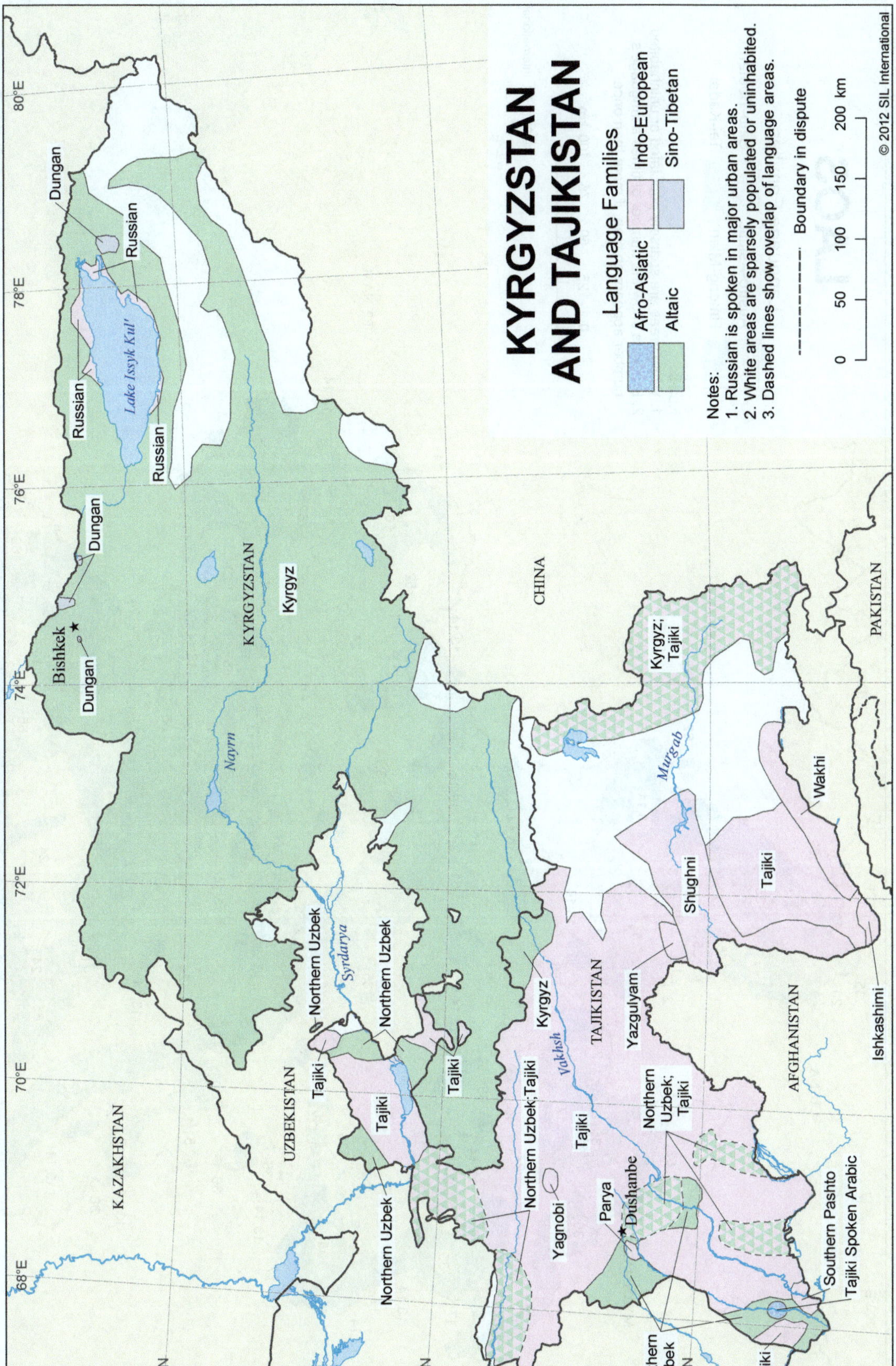
KYRGYZSTAN AND TAJIKISTAN
Language Families
Afro-Asiatic
Altaic
Indo-European
Sino-Tibetan
Notes:
1. Russian is spoken in major urban areas.
2. White areas are sparsely populated or uninhabited.
3. Dashed lines show overlap of language areas.
Boundary in dispute
0 50 100 150 200 km
© 2012 SIL International
KAZAKHSTAN
UZBEKISTAN
KYRGYZSTAN
TAJIKISTAN
CHINA
AFGHANISTAN
PAKISTAN
Bishkek
Dushanbe
Lake Issyk Kul'
Nayrn
Syrdarya
Vakhsh
Murgab
Dungan
Russian
Kyrgyz
Northern Uzbek
Tajiki
Kyrgyz; Tajiki
Wakhi
Shughni
Yazgulyam
Ishkashimi
Northern Uzbek; Tajiki
Yagnobi
Parya
Southern Pashto
Tajiki Spoken Arabic
Northern Uzbek
80°E
78°E
76°E
74°E
72°E
70°E
68°E
42°N
40°N
38°N

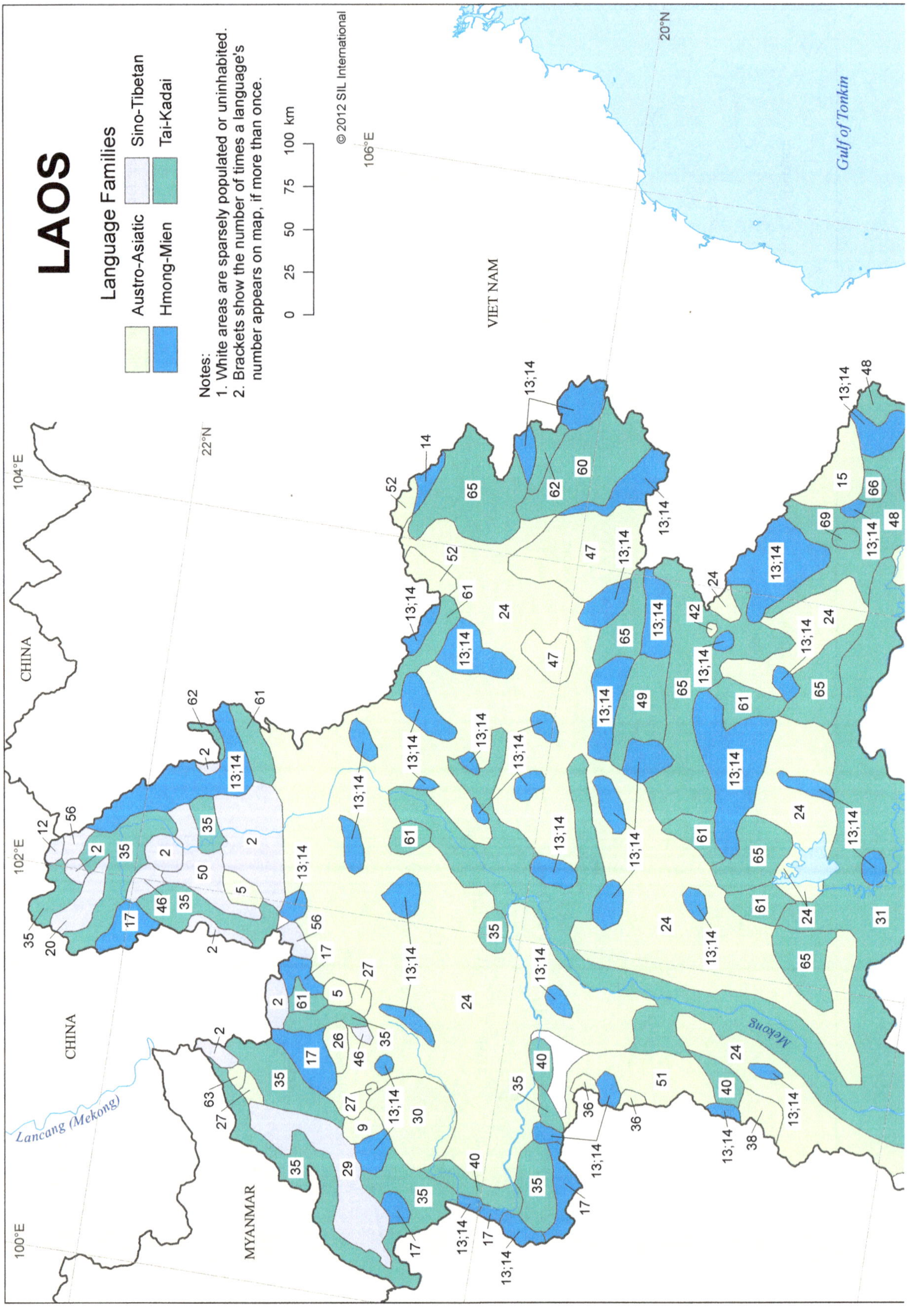
LAOS
Language Families
Austro-Asiatic
Sino-Tibetan
Hmong-Mien
Tai-Kadai
Notes:
1. White areas are sparsely populated or uninhabited.
2. Brackets show the number of times a language's number appears on map, if more than once.
0 25 50 75 100 km
© 2012 SIL International
CHINA
VIET NAM
MYANMAR
Gulf of Tonkin
Lancang (Mekong)
Mekong
22°N
20°N
100°E
102°E
104°E
106°E

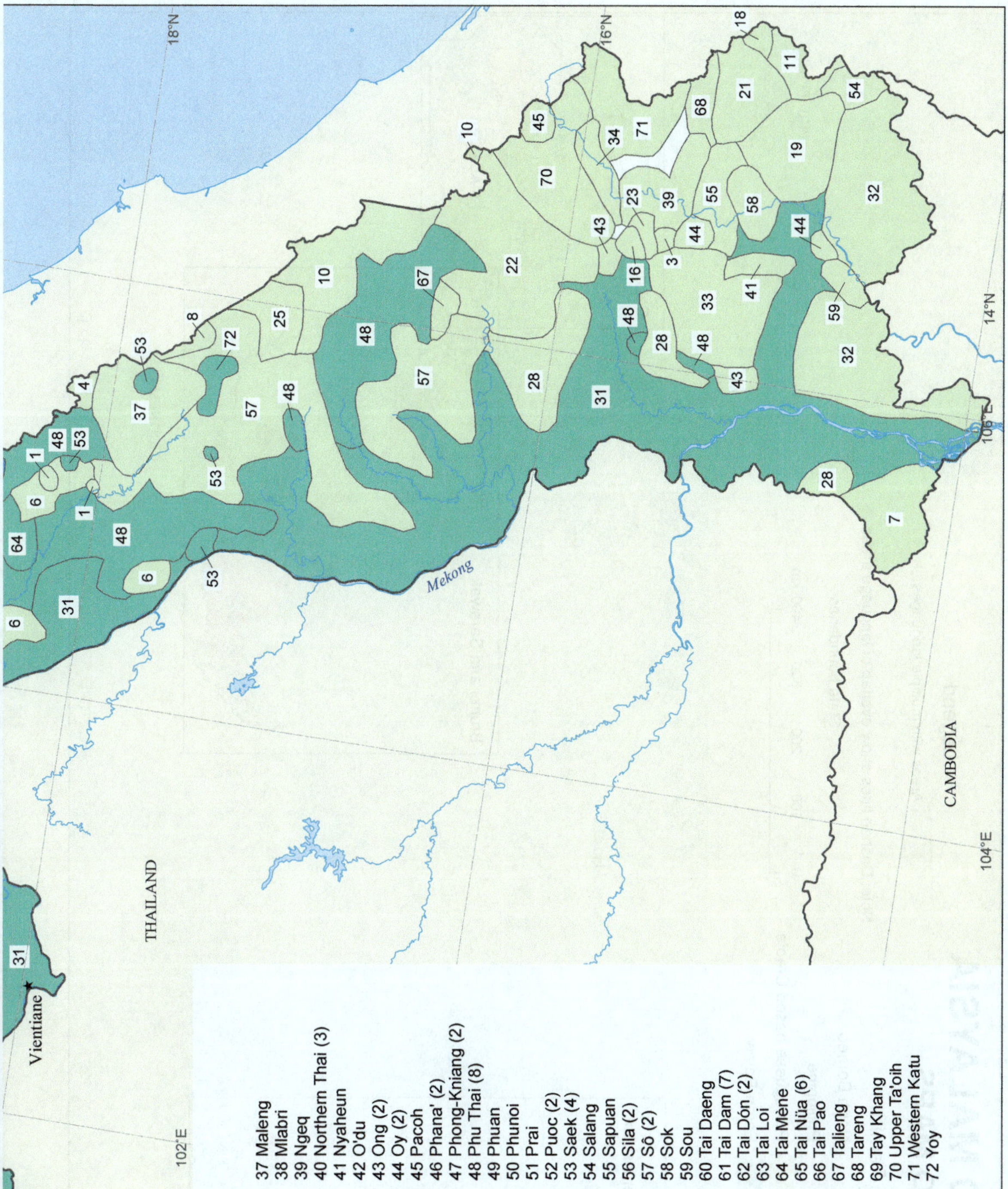

THAILAND
CAMBODIA
Vientiane
Mekong
18°N
16°N
14°N
102°E
104°E
106°E
1 Aheu (2)
2 Akha (7)
3 Alak
4 Arem
5 Bit (2)
6 Bo (3)
7 Central Khmer
8 Chut
9 Con
10 Eastern Bru (2)
11 Halang Doan
12 Hani
13 Hmong Daw (31)
14 Hmong Njua (32)
15 Hung
16 Ir
17 Iu Mien (6)
18 Jeh
19 Jeng
20 Kaduo
21 Kasseng
22 Kataang
23 Khlor
24 Khmu (8)
25 Khua
26 Khuen
27 Kiorr (3)
28 Kuy (3)
29 Lahu
30 Lamet
31 Lao (5)
32 Lave (2)
33 Laven
34 Lower Ta'oih
35 Lü (11)
36 Mal (2)
37 Maleng
38 Mlabri
39 Ngeq
40 Northern Thai (3)
41 Nyaheun
42 O'du
43 Ong (2)
44 Oy (2)
45 Pacoh
46 Phana' (2)
47 Phong-Kniang (2)
48 Phu Thai (8)
49 Phuan
50 Phunoi
51 Prai
52 Puoc (2)
53 Saek (4)
54 Salang
55 Sapuan
56 Sila (2)
57 Sô (2)
58 Sok
59 Sou
60 Tai Daeng
61 Tai Dam (7)
62 Tai Dón (2)
63 Tai Loi
64 Tai Mène
65 Tai Nüa (6)
66 Tai Pao
67 Talieng
68 Tareng
69 Tay Khang
70 Upper Ta'oih
71 Western Katu
72 Yoy

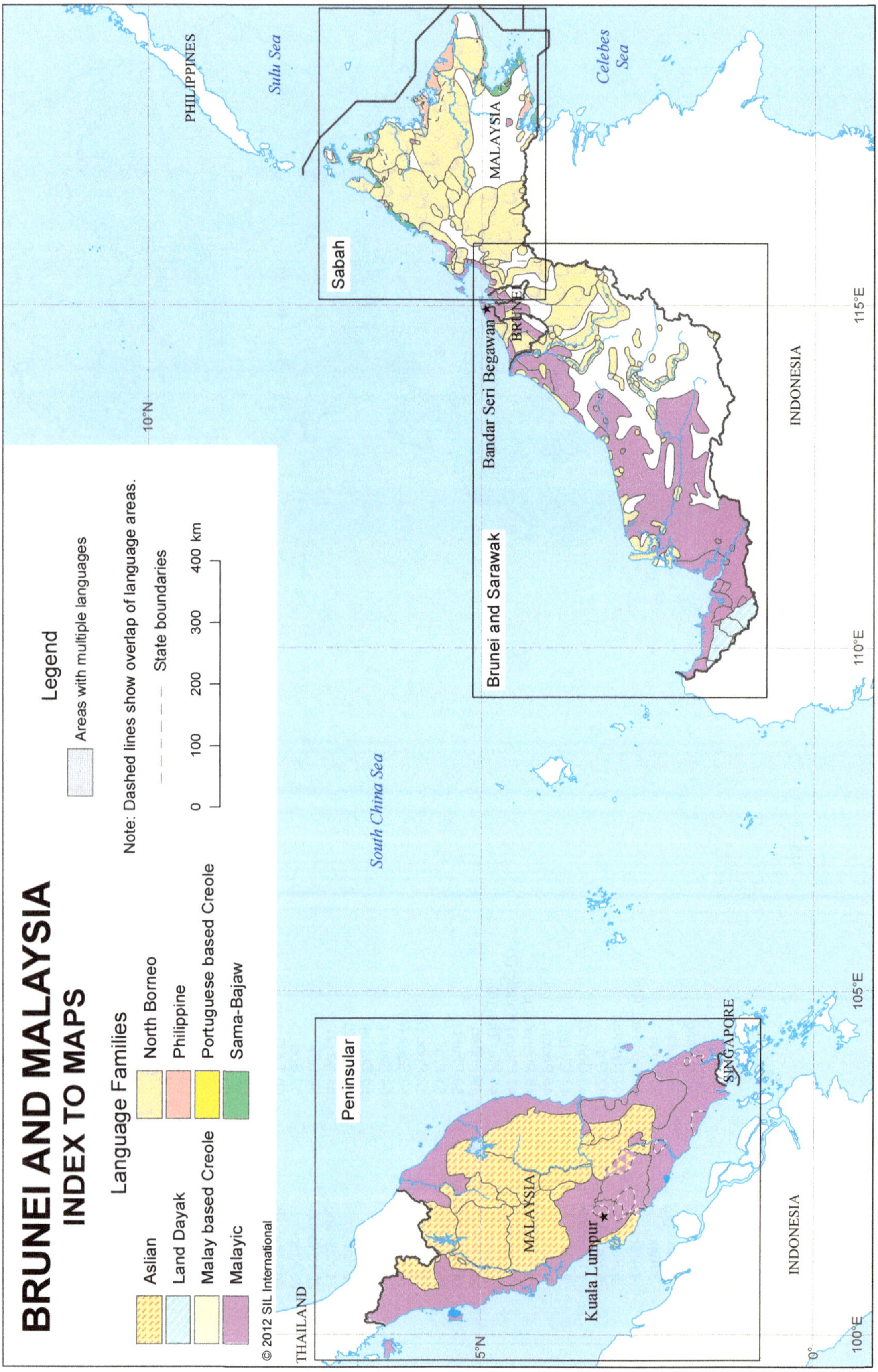

BRUNEI AND MALAYSIA
INDEX TO MAPS
Language Families
Aslian
Land Dayak
Malay based Creole
Malayic
North Borneo
Philippine
Portuguese based Creole
Sama-Bajaw
Legend
Areas with multiple languages
Note: Dashed lines show overlap of language areas.
State boundaries
0
100
200
300
400 km
© 2012 SIL International
Peninsular
Brunei and Sarawak
Sabah
PHILIPPINES
Sulu Sea
Celebes Sea
MALAYSIA
BRUNEI
Bandar Seri Begawan
INDONESIA
South China Sea
THAILAND
Kuala Lumpur
SINGAPORE
10°N
5°N
0°
100°E
105°E
110°E
115°E

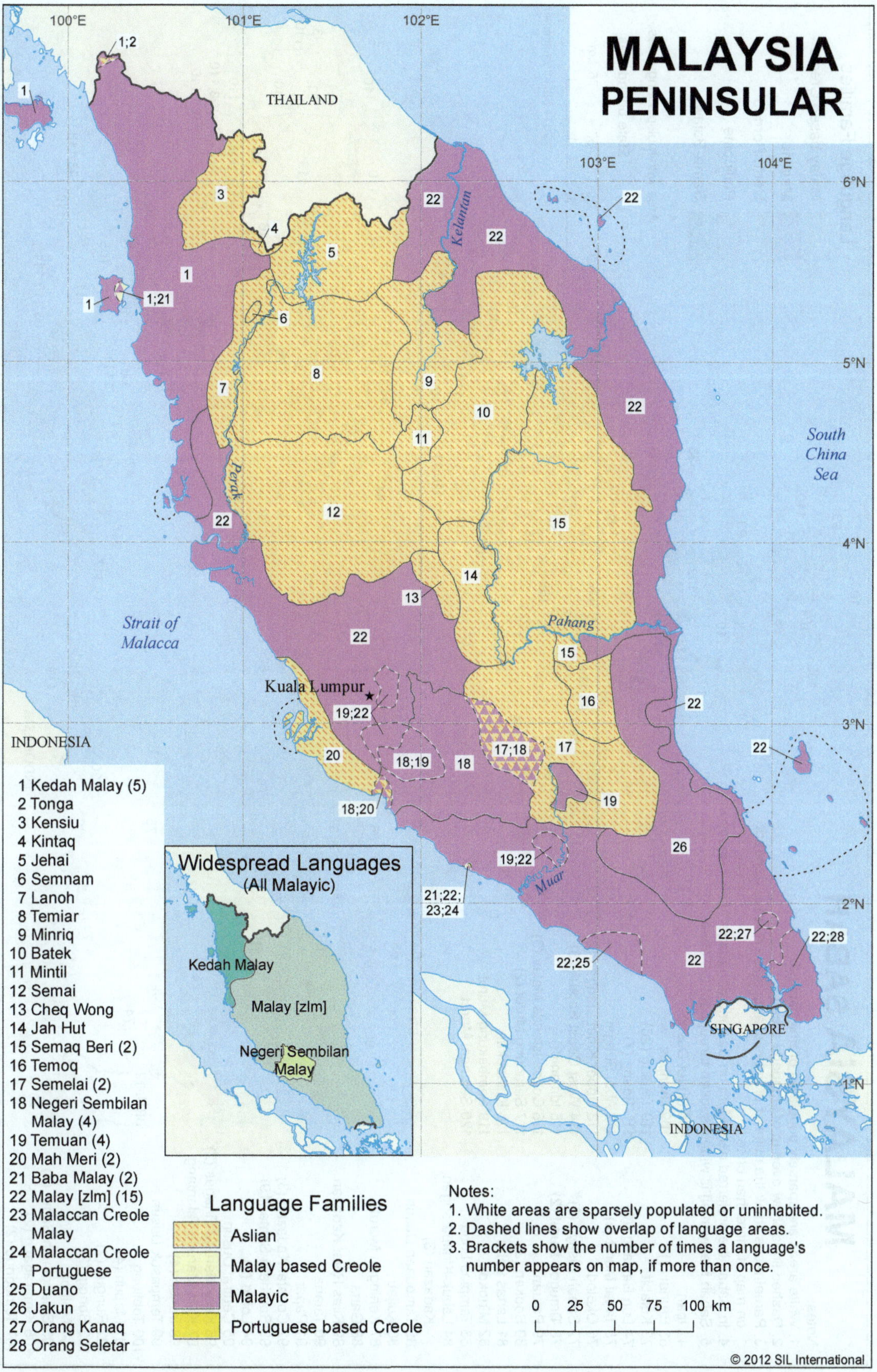
MALAYSIA
PENINSULAR
100°E
101°E
102°E
103°E
104°E
6°N
5°N
4°N
3°N
2°N
1°N
THAILAND
INDONESIA
SINGAPORE
Strait of Malacca
South China Sea
Kelantan
Perak
Pahang
Muar
Kuala Lumpur
1;2
1;21
19;22
18;19
18;20
17;18
21;22; 23;24
22;25
22;27
22;28
Widespread Languages
(All Malayic)
Kedah Malay
Malay [zlm]
Negeri Sembilan Malay
1 Kedah Malay (5)
2 Tonga
3 Kensiu
4 Kintaq
5 Jehai
6 Semnam
7 Lanoh
8 Temiar
9 Minriq
10 Batek
11 Mintil
12 Semai
13 Cheq Wong
14 Jah Hut
15 Semaq Beri (2)
16 Temoq
17 Semelai (2)
18 Negeri Sembilan Malay (4)
19 Temuan (4)
20 Mah Meri (2)
21 Baba Malay (2)
22 Malay [zlm] (15)
23 Malaccan Creole Malay
24 Malaccan Creole Portuguese
25 Duano
26 Jakun
27 Orang Kanaq
28 Orang Seletar
Language Families
Aslian
Malay based Creole
Malayic
Portuguese based Creole
Notes:
1. White areas are sparsely populated or uninhabited.
2. Dashed lines show overlap of language areas.
3. Brackets show the number of times a language's number appears on map, if more than once.
0 25 50 75 100 km
© 2012 SIL International

MALAYSIA SABAH

Notes:

1. White areas are sparsely populated or uninhabited.
2. Dashed lines show overlap of language areas
3. Parentheses show the number of times a language's number appears on map, if more than once.
4. In Sabah the preferred name for Lun Bawang (language 74) is Lundayeh.
5. Sabah Malay [msi] is widely spoken throughout the state.

42 Iban
63 Brunei (7)
73 Kelabit
74 Lun Bawang[3] (3)
75 Tagal Murut (2)
76 Okolod
77 Sabah Bisaya (2)
78 Timugon Murut (2)
79 Paluan
80 Bookan (2)
81 Lanas Lobu
82 Minokok
83 Tampias Lobu
84 Labuk-Kinabatangan Kadazan (3)
85 Tambunan Dusun
86 Kuijau
87 Keningau Murut
88 Gana
89 Klias River Kadazan
90 Tatana
91 Papar
92 Coastal Kadazan (3)
93 Southern Sama (19)
94 Lotud (2)
95 Central Dusun
96 Kota Marudu Tinagas (2)
97 Kota Marudu Talantang
98 Iranun (4)
99 Tempasuk Dusun
100 Tobilung
101 Mapun (4)
102 Rungus (2)
103 Bonggi (2)
104 Molbog
105 Balangingih Sama (4)
106 Kimaragang (2)
107 Tombonuo (2)
108 Sugut Dusun
109 Dumpas
110 Tausug (26)
111 Tidong (7)
112 Abai Sungai
113 Upper Kinabatangan (2)
114 West Coast Bajau (13)
115 Ida'an (3)
116 Cocos Islands Malay (3)
117 Serudung Murut (2)
118 Kalabakan
119 Sembakung Murut
120 Selungai Murut

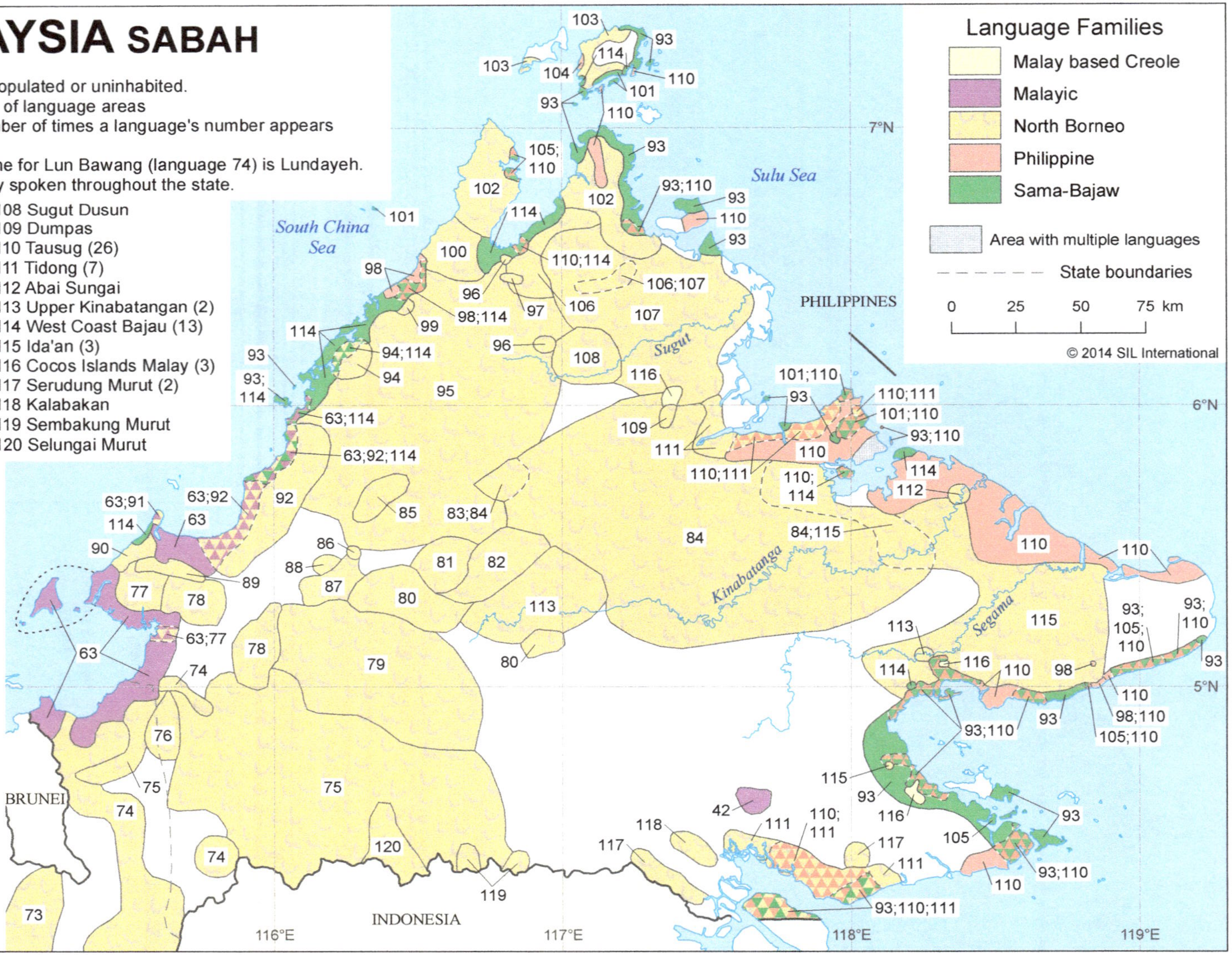

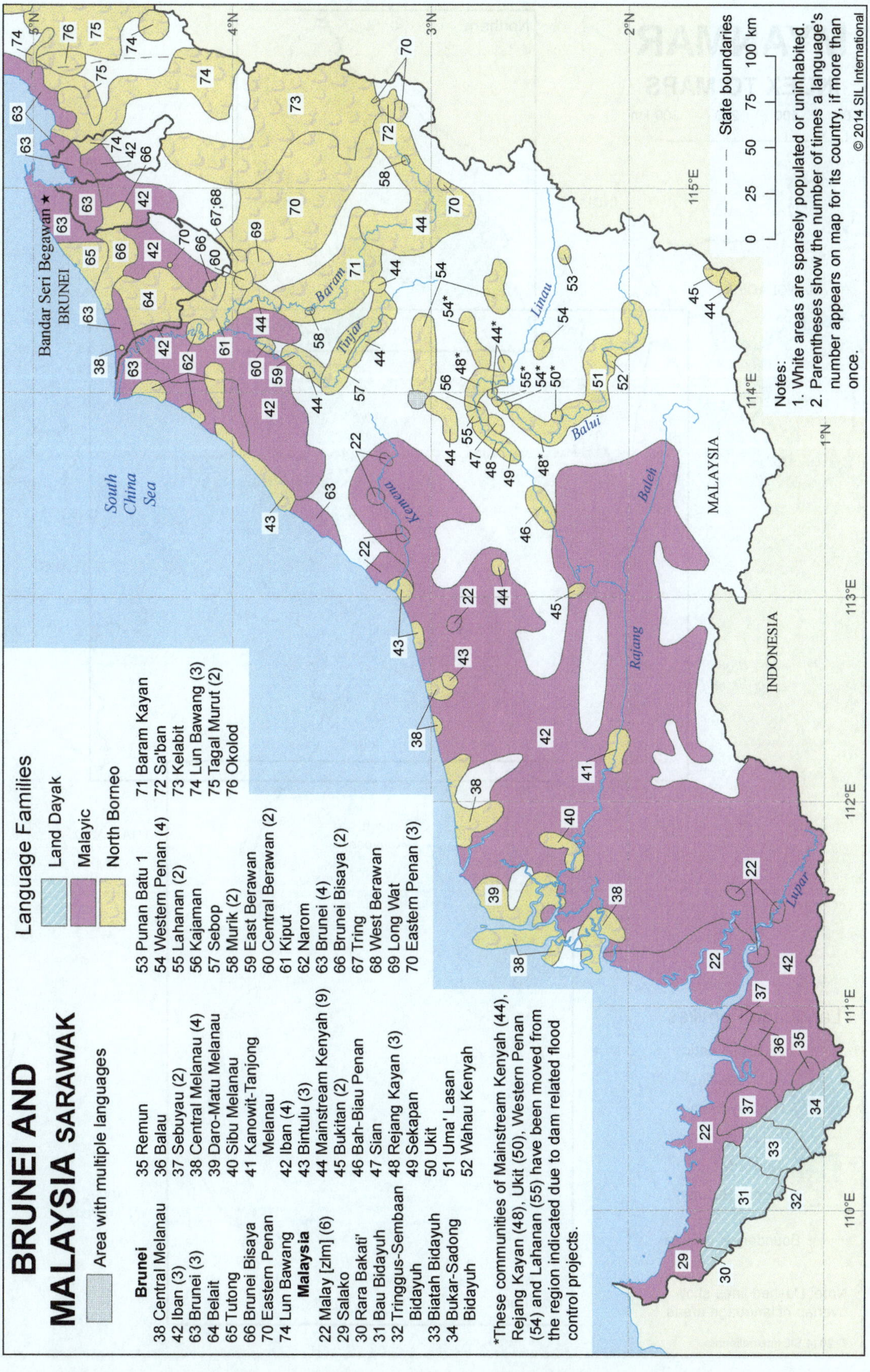
BRUNEI AND
MALAYSIA SARAWAK
Area with multiple languages
Language Families
Land Dayak
Malayic
North Borneo
Brunei
38 Central Melanau
42 Iban (3)
63 Brunei (3)
64 Belait
65 Tutong
66 Brunei Bisaya
70 Eastern Penan
74 Lun Bawang
Malaysia
22 Malay [zlm] (6)
29 Salako
30 Rara Bakati'
31 Bau Bidayuh
32 Tringgus-Sembaan Bidayuh
33 Biatah Bidayuh
34 Bukar-Sadong Bidayuh
35 Remun
36 Balau
37 Sebuyau (2)
38 Central Melanau (4)
39 Daro-Matu Melanau
40 Sibu Melanau
41 Kanowit-Tanjong Melanau
42 Iban (4)
43 Bintulu (3)
44 Mainstream Kenyah (9)
45 Bukitan (2)
46 Bah-Biau Penan
47 Sian
48 Rejang Kayan (3)
49 Sekapan
50 Ukit
51 Uma' Lasan
52 Wahau Kenyah
53 Punan Batu 1
54 Western Penan (4)
55 Lahanan (2)
56 Kajaman
57 Sebop
58 Murik (2)
59 East Berawan
60 Central Berawan (2)
61 Kiput
62 Narom
63 Brunei (4)
66 Brunei Bisaya (2)
67 Tring
68 West Berawan
69 Long Wat
70 Eastern Penan (3)
71 Baram Kayan
72 Sa'ban
73 Kelabit
74 Lun Bawang (3)
75 Tagal Murut (2)
76 Okolod
*These communities of Mainstream Kenyah (44), Rejang Kayan (48), Ukit (50), Western Penan (54) and Lahanan (55) have been moved from the region indicated due to dam related flood control projects.
South China Sea
Bandar Seri Begawan
BRUNEI
MALAYSIA
INDONESIA
Baram
Tinjar
Linau
Balui
Baleh
Rajang
Kemena
Lupar
5°N
4°N
3°N
2°N
1°N
110°E
111°E
112°E
113°E
114°E
115°E
State boundaries
0 25 50 75 100 km
Notes:
1. White areas are sparsely populated or uninhabited.
2. Parentheses show the number of times a language's number appears on map for its country, if more than once.
© 2014 SIL International

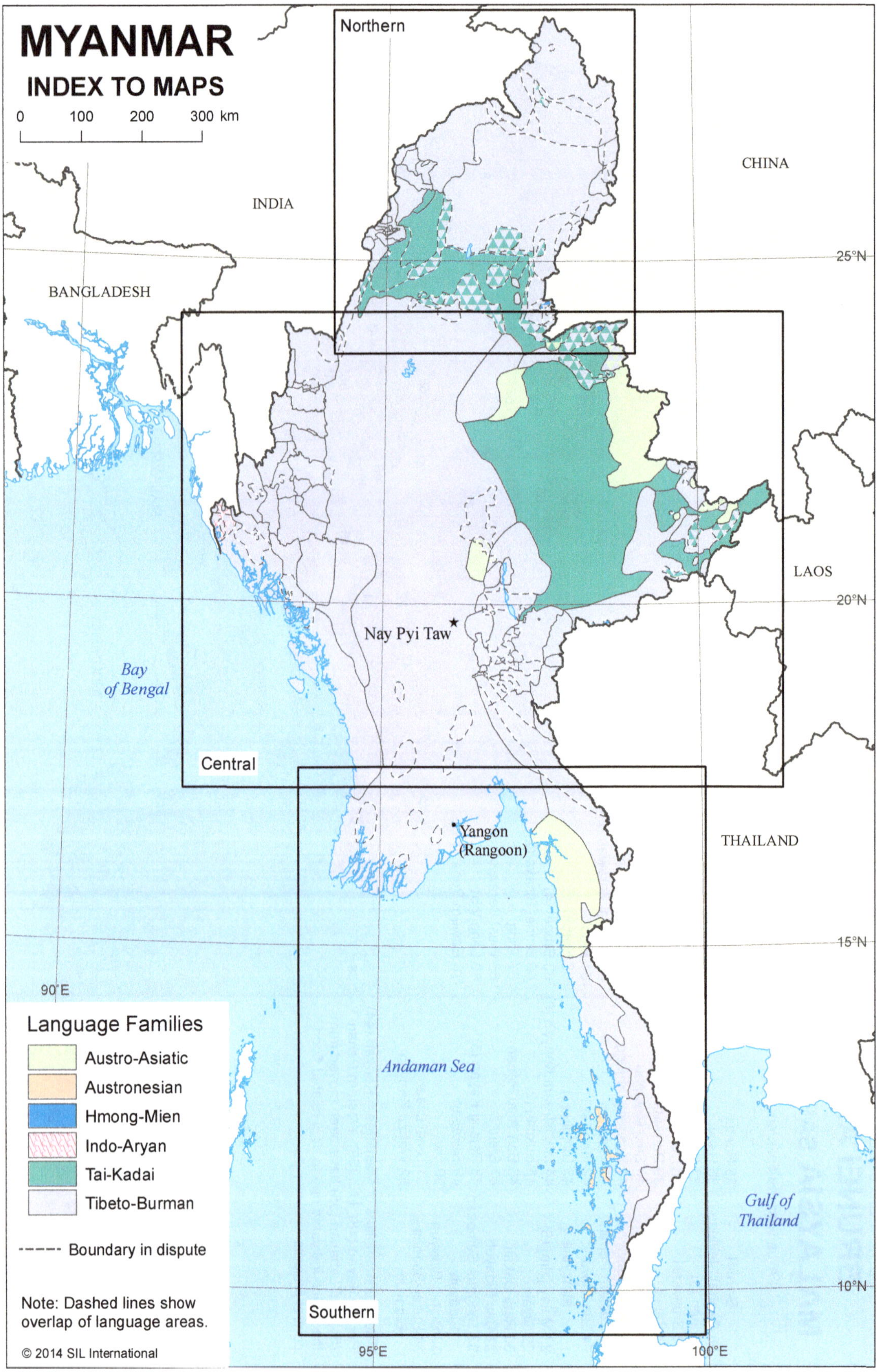
MYANMAR
INDEX TO MAPS
0 100 200 300 km
Northern
Central
Southern
INDIA
CHINA
BANGLADESH
LAOS
THAILAND
Nay Pyi Taw
Yangon (Rangoon)
Bay of Bengal
Andaman Sea
Gulf of Thailand
25°N
20°N
15°N
10°N
90°E
95°E
100°E
Language Families
Austro-Asiatic
Austronesian
Hmong-Mien
Indo-Aryan
Tai-Kadai
Tibeto-Burman
Boundary in dispute
Note: Dashed lines show overlap of language areas.
© 2014 SIL International

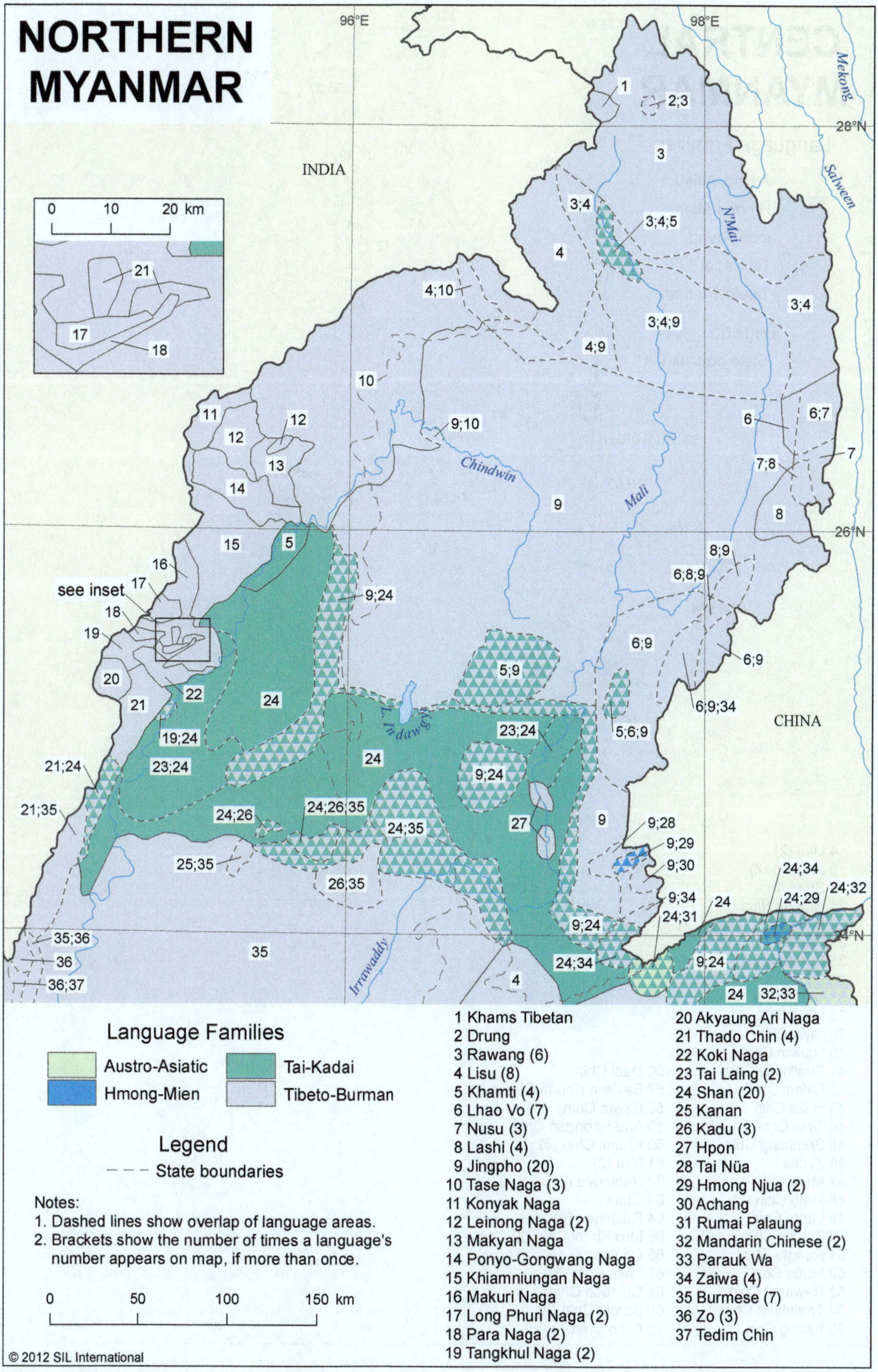
NORTHERN
MYANMAR
96°E
98°E
28°N
26°N
24°N
INDIA
CHINA
Mekong
Salween
N'Mai
Mali
Chindwin
L. Indawgyi
Irrawaddy
see inset
0 10 20 km
Language Families
Austro-Asiatic
Hmong-Mien
Tai-Kadai
Tibeto-Burman
Legend
State boundaries
Notes:
1. Dashed lines show overlap of language areas.
2. Brackets show the number of times a language's number appears on map, if more than once.
0 50 100 150 km
1 Khams Tibetan
2 Drung
3 Rawang (6)
4 Lisu (8)
5 Khamti (4)
6 Lhao Vo (7)
7 Nusu (3)
8 Lashi (4)
9 Jingpho (20)
10 Tase Naga (3)
11 Konyak Naga
12 Leinong Naga (2)
13 Makyan Naga
14 Ponyo-Gongwang Naga
15 Khiamniungan Naga
16 Makuri Naga
17 Long Phuri Naga (2)
18 Para Naga (2)
19 Tangkhul Naga (2)
20 Akyaung Ari Naga
21 Thado Chin (4)
22 Koki Naga
23 Tai Laing (2)
24 Shan (20)
25 Kanan
26 Kadu (3)
27 Hpon
28 Tai Nüa
29 Hmong Njua (2)
30 Achang
31 Rumai Palaung
32 Mandarin Chinese (2)
33 Parauk Wa
34 Zaiwa (4)
35 Burmese (7)
36 Zo (3)
37 Tedim Chin
© 2012 SIL International

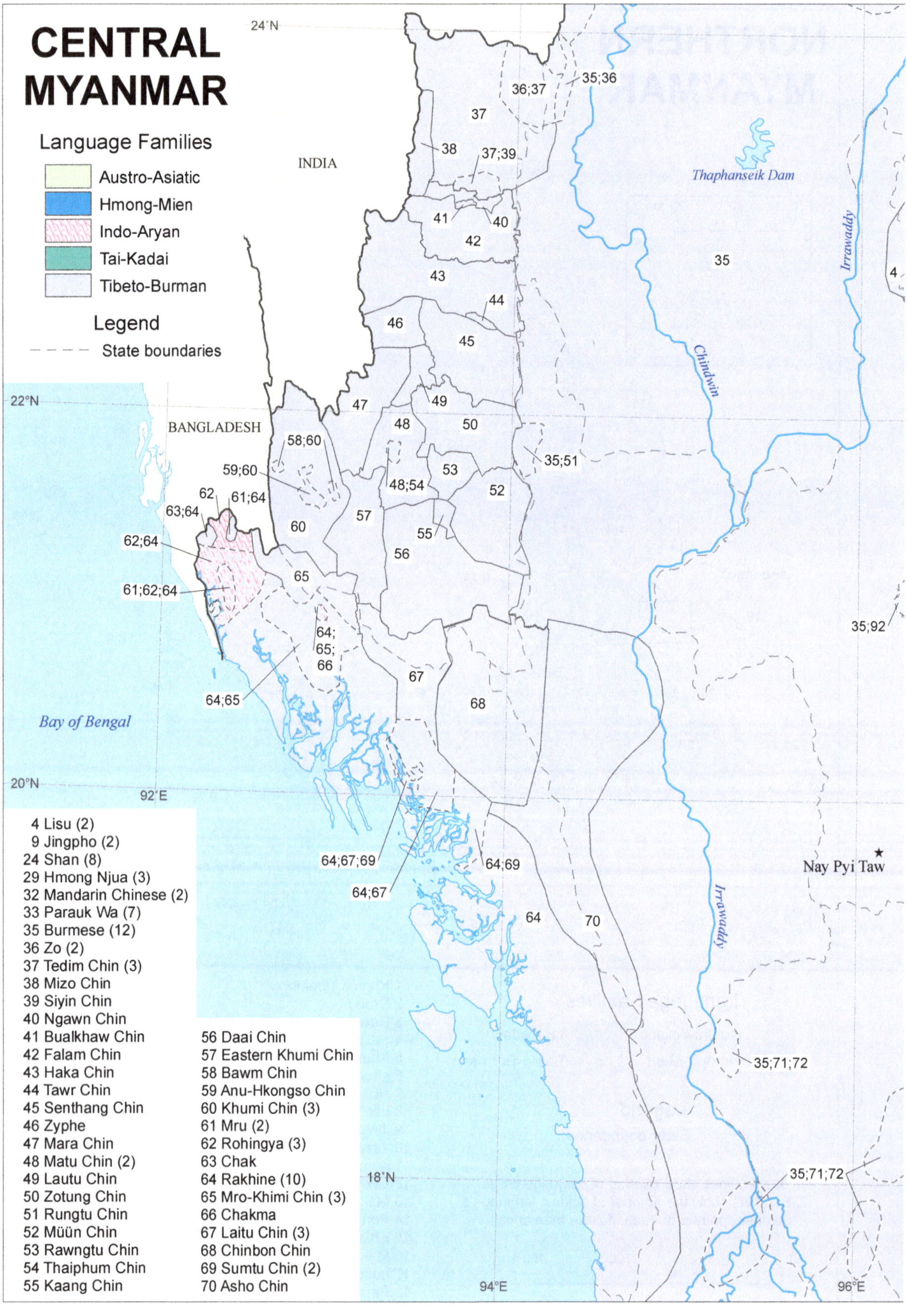
CENTRAL MYANMAR
Language Families
Austro-Asiatic
Hmong-Mien
Indo-Aryan
Tai-Kadai
Tibeto-Burman
Legend
State boundaries
INDIA
BANGLADESH
NORTHERN MYANMAR
Thaphanseik Dam
Chindwin
Irrawaddy
Bay of Bengal
Nay Pyi Taw
24°N
22°N
20°N
18°N
92°E
94°E
96°E
4 Lisu (2)
9 Jingpho (2)
24 Shan (8)
29 Hmong Njua (3)
32 Mandarin Chinese (2)
33 Parauk Wa (7)
35 Burmese (12)
36 Zo (2)
37 Tedim Chin (3)
38 Mizo Chin
39 Siyin Chin
40 Ngawn Chin
41 Bualkhaw Chin
42 Falam Chin
43 Haka Chin
44 Tawr Chin
45 Senthang Chin
46 Zyphe
47 Mara Chin
48 Matu Chin (2)
49 Lautu Chin
50 Zotung Chin
51 Rungtu Chin
52 Müün Chin
53 Rawngtu Chin
54 Thaiphum Chin
55 Kaang Chin
56 Daai Chin
57 Eastern Khumi Chin
58 Bawm Chin
59 Anu-Hkongso Chin
60 Khumi Chin (3)
61 Mru (2)
62 Rohingya (3)
63 Chak
64 Rakhine (10)
65 Mro-Khimi Chin (3)
66 Chakma
67 Laitu Chin (3)
68 Chinbon Chin
69 Sumtu Chin (2)
70 Asho Chin

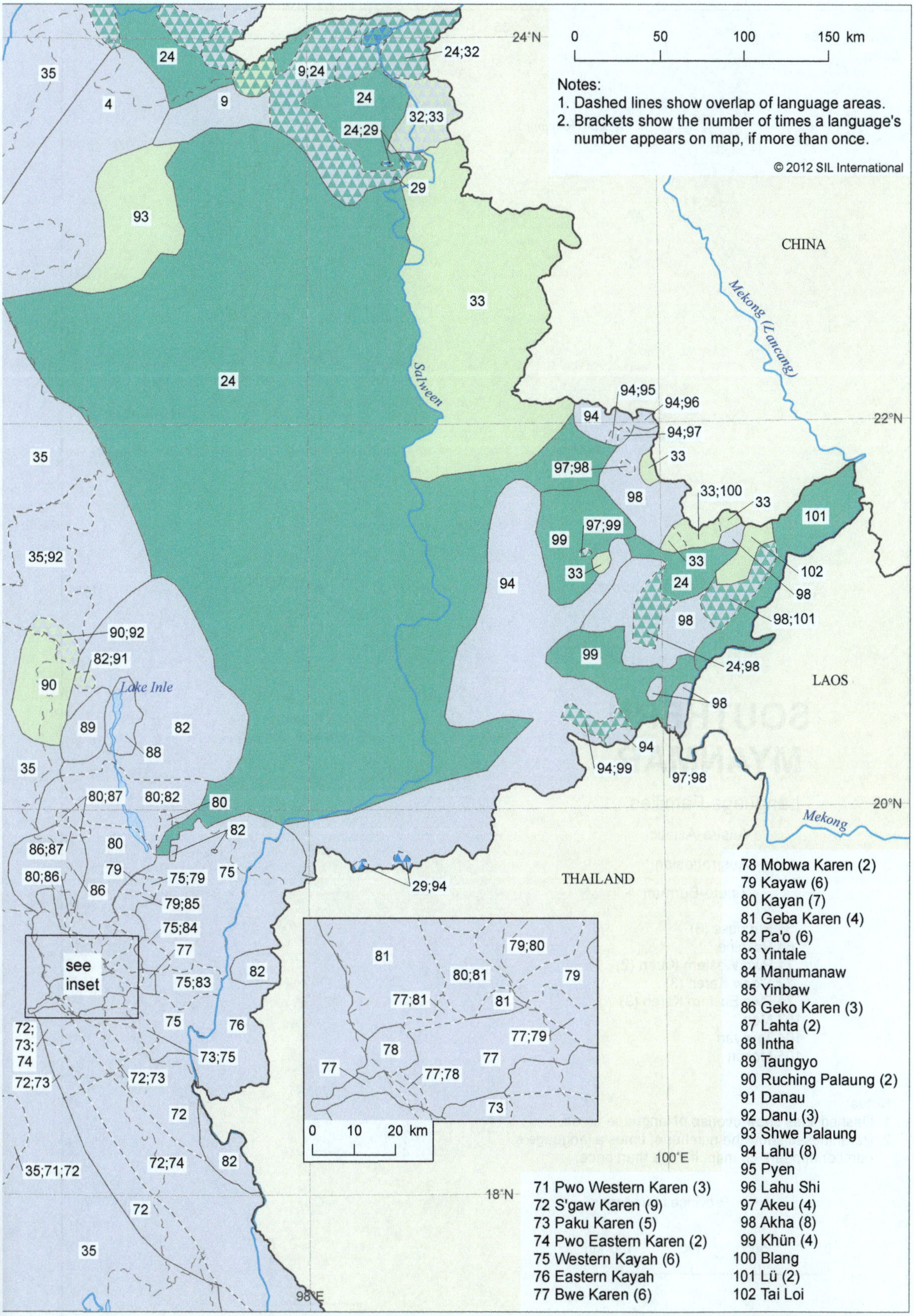
0 50 100 150 km
Notes:
1. Dashed lines show overlap of language areas.
2. Brackets show the number of times a language's number appears on map, if more than once.
© 2012 SIL International
24°N
22°N
20°N
18°N
98°E
100°E
CHINA
LAOS
THAILAND
Salween
Mekong (Lancang)
Mekong
Lake Inle
see inset
0 10 20 km
71 Pwo Western Karen (3)
72 S'gaw Karen (9)
73 Paku Karen (5)
74 Pwo Eastern Karen (2)
75 Western Kayah (6)
76 Eastern Kayah
77 Bwe Karen (6)
78 Mobwa Karen (2)
79 Kayaw (6)
80 Kayan (7)
81 Geba Karen (4)
82 Pa'o (6)
83 Yintale
84 Manumanaw
85 Yinbaw
86 Geko Karen (3)
87 Lahta (2)
88 Intha
89 Taungyo
90 Ruching Palaung (2)
91 Danau
92 Danu (3)
93 Shwe Palaung
94 Lahu (8)
95 Pyen
96 Lahu Shi
97 Akeu (4)
98 Akha (8)
99 Khün (4)
100 Blang
101 Lü (2)
102 Tai Loi

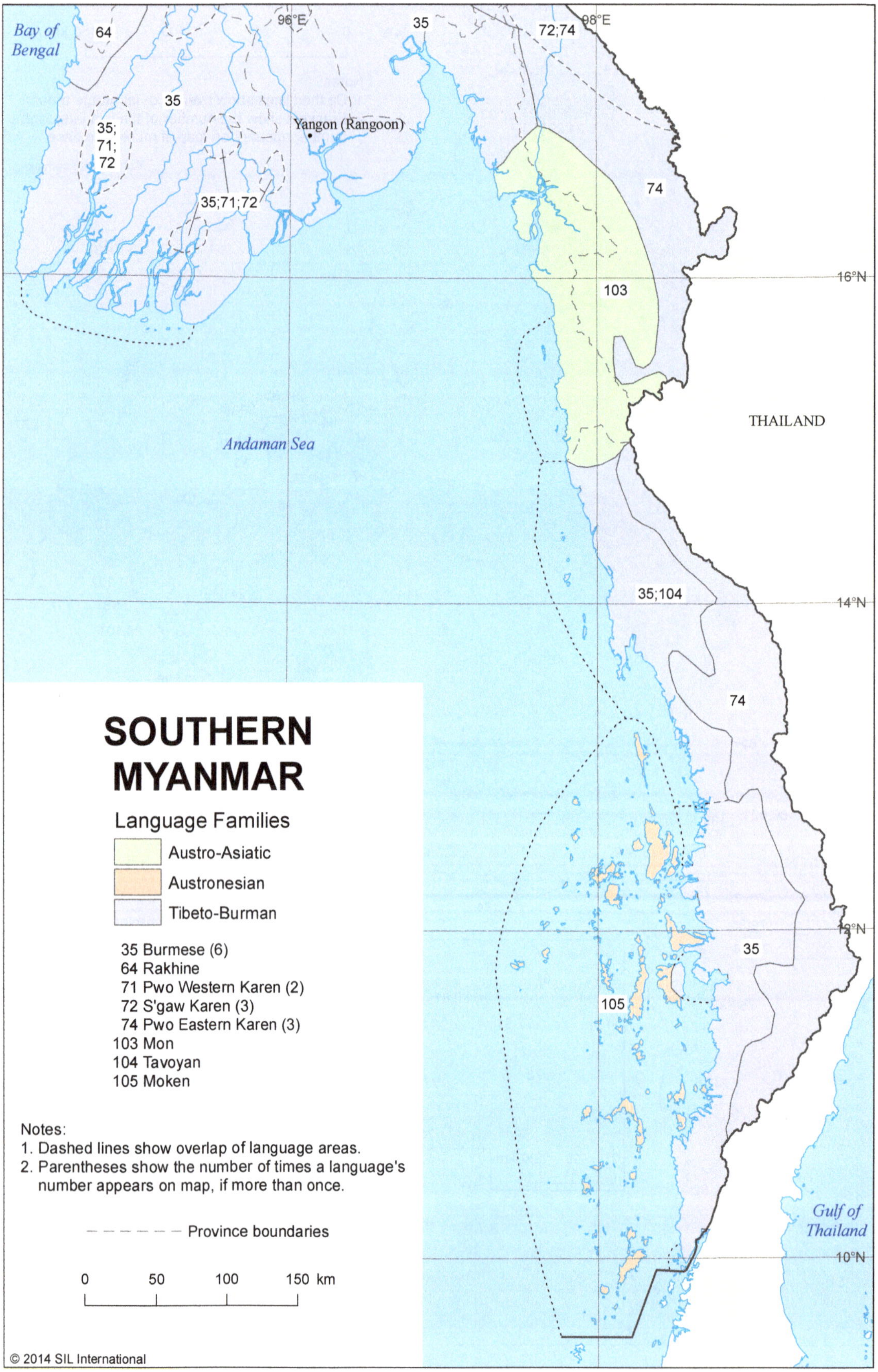
Bay of Bengal
64
96°E
35
72;74
98°E
35
35; 71; 72
Yangon (Rangoon)
35;71;72
74
16°N
103
THAILAND
Andaman Sea
35;104
14°N
74
SOUTHERN MYANMAR
Language Families
Austro-Asiatic
Austronesian
Tibeto-Burman
35 Burmese (6)
64 Rakhine
71 Pwo Western Karen (2)
72 S'gaw Karen (3)
74 Pwo Eastern Karen (3)
103 Mon
104 Tavoyan
105 Moken
12°N
35
105
Notes:
1. Dashed lines show overlap of language areas.
2. Parentheses show the number of times a language's number appears on map, if more than once.
Province boundaries
0 50 100 150 km
Gulf of Thailand
10°N
© 2014 SIL International

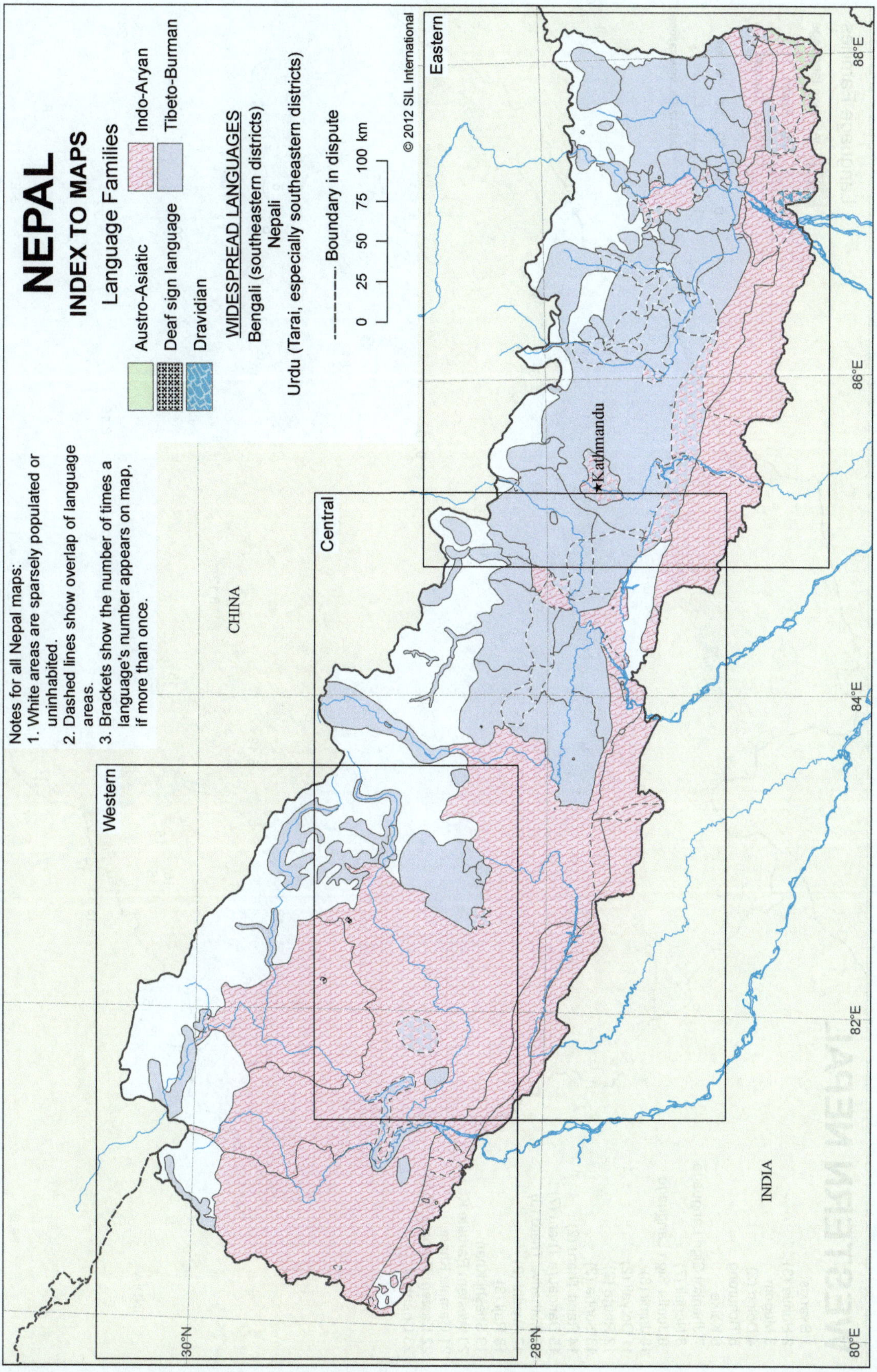
NEPAL
INDEX TO MAPS
Language Families
Austro-Asiatic
Deaf sign language
Dravidian
Indo-Aryan
Tibeto-Burman
WIDESPREAD LANGUAGES
Bengali (southeastern districts)
Nepali
Urdu (Tarai, especially southeastern districts)
Boundary in dispute
0 25 50 75 100 km
© 2012 SIL International
Notes for all Nepal maps:
1. White areas are sparsely populated or uninhabited.
2. Dashed lines show overlap of language areas.
3. Brackets show the number of times a language's number appears on map, if more than once.
Western
Central
Eastern
CHINA
INDIA
Kathmandu
30°N
28°N
80°E
82°E
84°E
86°E
88°E

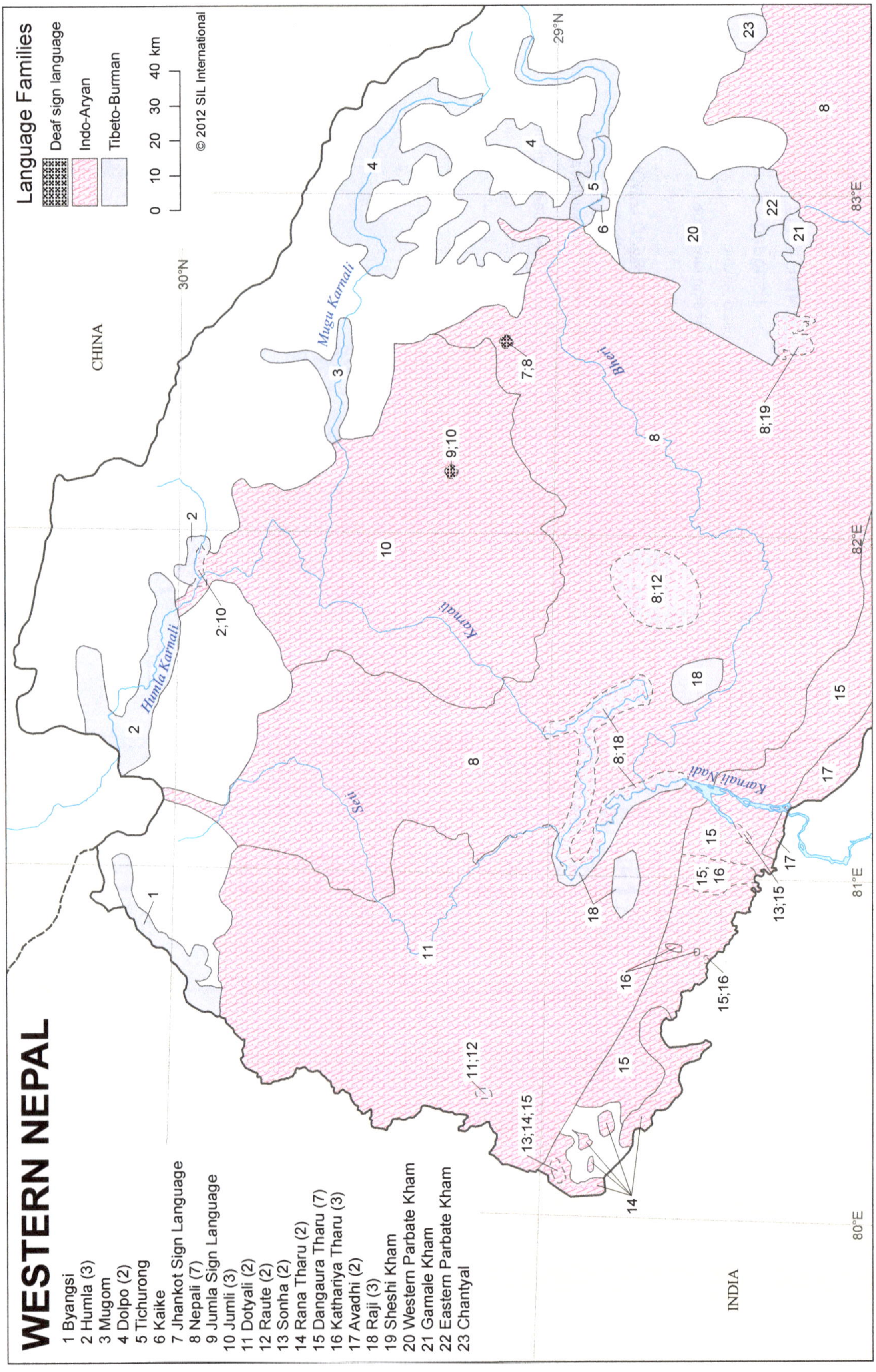

WESTERN NEPAL
1 Byangsi
2 Humla (3)
3 Mugom
4 Dolpo (2)
5 Tichurong
6 Kaike
7 Jhankot Sign Language
8 Nepali (7)
9 Jumla Sign Language
10 Jumli (3)
11 Dotyali (2)
12 Raute (2)
13 Sonha (2)
14 Rana Tharu (2)
15 Dangaura Tharu (7)
16 Kathariya Tharu (3)
17 Avadhi (2)
18 Raji (3)
19 Sheshi Kham
20 Western Parbate Kham
21 Gamale Kham
22 Eastern Parbate Kham
23 Chantyal
Language Families
Deaf sign language
Indo-Aryan
Tibeto-Burman
0 10 20 30 40 km
© 2012 SIL International
CHINA
INDIA
30°N
29°N
80°E
81°E
82°E
83°E
Humla Karnali
Mugu Karnali
Karnali
Seti
Bheri
Karnali Nadi

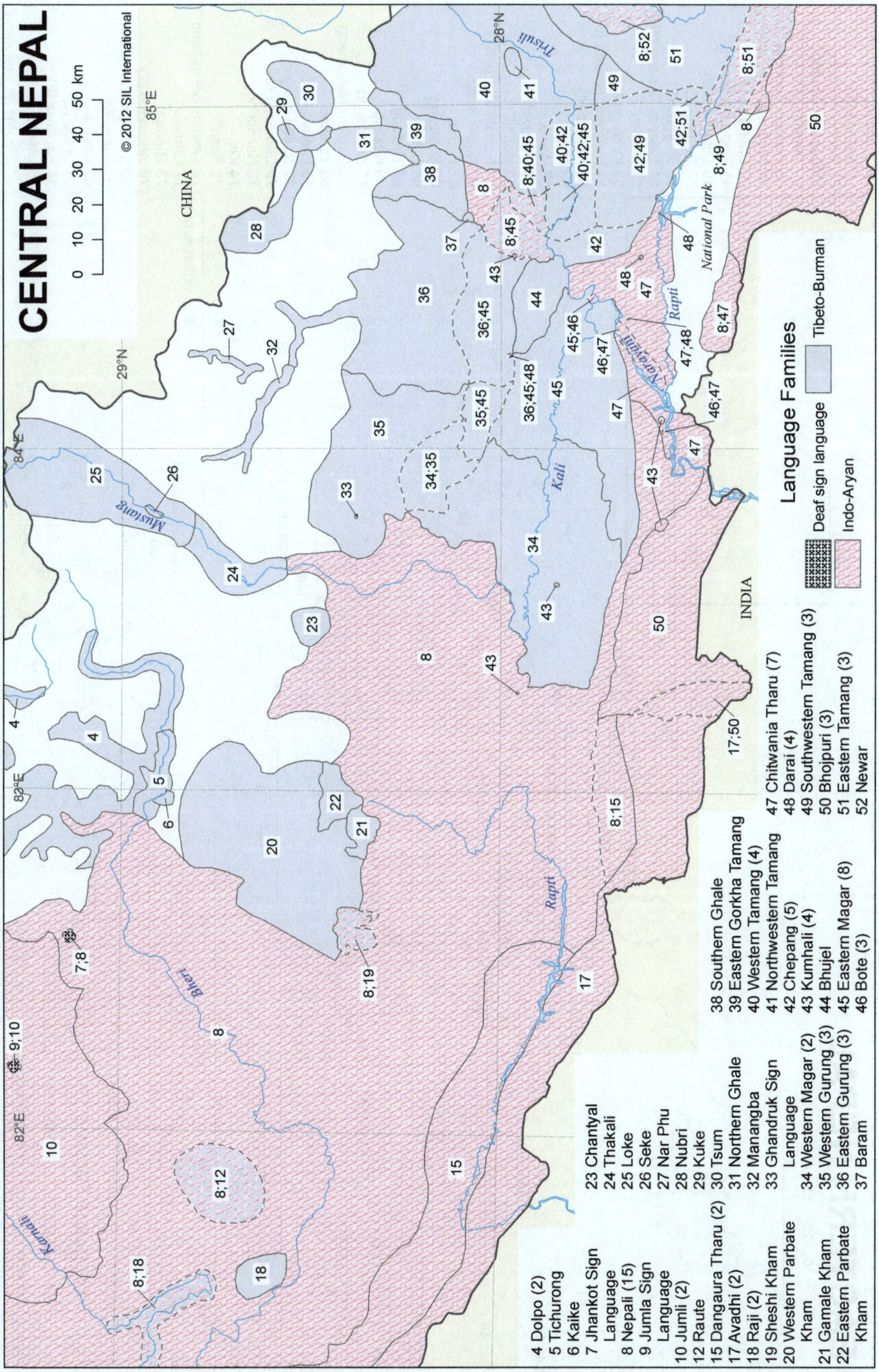
CENTRAL NEPAL
0 10 20 30 40 50 km
© 2012 SIL International
CHINA
INDIA
Karnali
Bheri
Rapti
Kali
Mustang
Trisuli
Narayani
National Park
82°E
83°E
84°E
85°E
28°N
29°N
Language Families
Deaf sign language
Indo-Aryan
Tibeto-Burman
4 Dolpo (2)
5 Tichurong
6 Kaike
7 Jhankot Sign Language
8 Nepali (15)
9 Jumla Sign Language
10 Jumli (2)
12 Raute
15 Dangaura Tharu (2)
17 Avadhi (2)
18 Raji (2)
19 Sheshi Kham
20 Western Parbate Kham
21 Gamale Kham
22 Eastern Parbate Kham
23 Chantyal
24 Thakali
25 Loke
26 Seke
27 Nar Phu
28 Nubri
29 Kuke
30 Tsum
31 Northern Ghale
32 Manangba
33 Ghandruk Sign Language
34 Western Magar (2)
35 Western Gurung (3)
36 Eastern Gurung (3)
37 Baram
38 Southern Ghale
39 Eastern Gorkha Tamang
40 Western Tamang (4)
41 Northwestern Tamang
42 Chepang (5)
43 Kumhali (4)
44 Bhujel
45 Eastern Magar (8)
46 Bote (3)
47 Chitwania Tharu (7)
48 Darai (4)
49 Southwestern Tamang (3)
50 Bhojpuri (3)
51 Eastern Tamang (3)
52 Newar

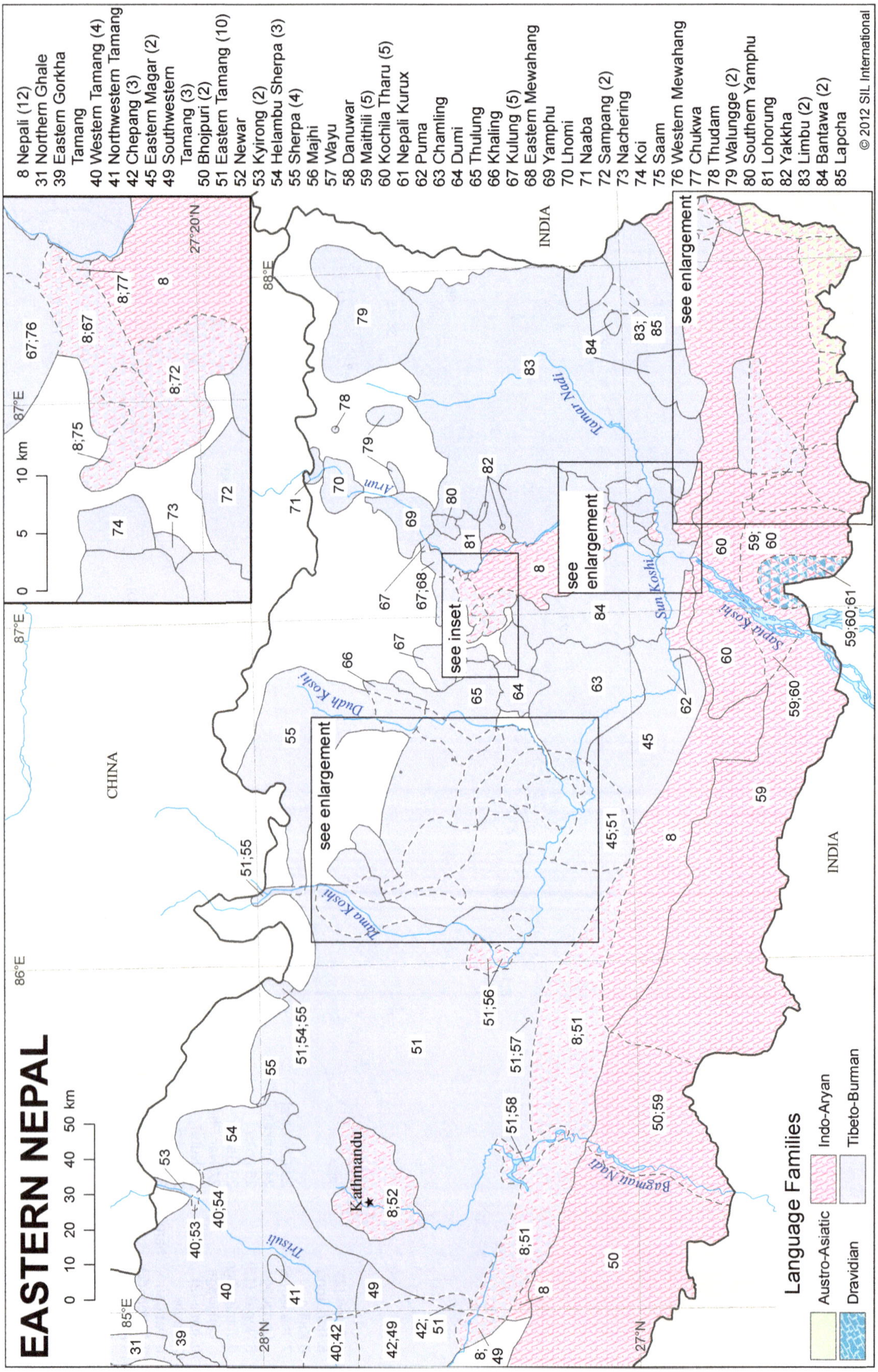
EASTERN NEPAL
0 10 20 30 40 50 km
CHINA
INDIA
Kathmandu
Trisuli
Bagmati Nadi
Tama Koshi
Dudh Koshi
Sun Koshi
Sapta Koshi
Arun
Tamar Nadi
see enlargement
see inset
85°E
86°E
87°E
88°E
28°N
27°N
27°20'N
0 5 10 km
Language Families
Austro-Asiatic
Dravidian
Indo-Aryan
Tibeto-Burman
8 Nepali (12)
31 Northern Ghale
39 Eastern Gorkha Tamang
40 Western Tamang (4)
41 Northwestern Tamang
42 Chepang (3)
45 Eastern Magar (2)
49 Southwestern Tamang (3)
50 Bhojpuri (2)
51 Eastern Tamang (10)
52 Newar
53 Kyirong (2)
54 Helambu Sherpa (3)
55 Sherpa (4)
56 Majhi
57 Wayu
58 Danuwar
59 Maithili (5)
60 Kochila Tharu (5)
61 Nepali Kurux
62 Puma
63 Chamling
64 Dumi
65 Thulung
66 Khaling
67 Kulung (5)
68 Eastern Mewahang
69 Yamphu
70 Lhomi
71 Naaba
72 Sampang (2)
73 Nachering
74 Koi
75 Saam
76 Western Mewahang
77 Chukwa
78 Thudam
79 Walungge (2)
80 Southern Yamphu
81 Lohorung
82 Yakkha
83 Limbu (2)
84 Bantawa (2)
85 Lapcha
© 2012 SIL International

NEPAL ENLARGEMENTS

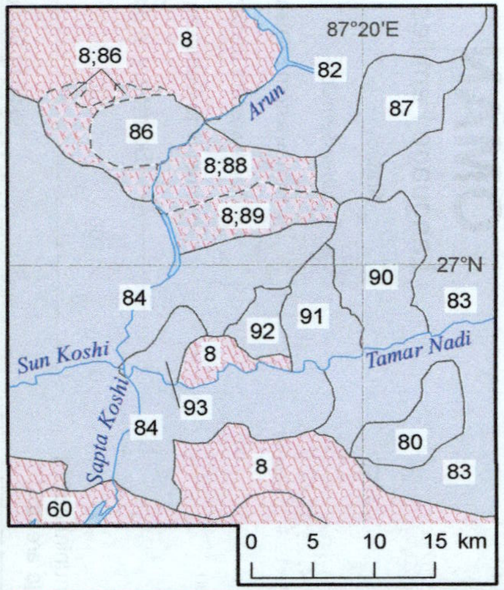

8 Nepali (8)
45 Eastern Magar (2)
51 Eastern Tamang (11)
55 Sherpa (8)
57 Wayu
59 Maithili (3)
60 Kochila Tharu (4)
63 Chamling (3)
65 Thulung (2)
66 Khaling
80 Southern Yamphu
82 Yakkha
83 Limbu (3)
84 Bantawa (3)
86 Dungmali (2)
87 Lumba-Yakkha
88 Phangduwali
89 Mugali
90 Athpariya
91 Belhariya
92 Chhulung
93 Chhintang
94 Rajbanshi (10)
95 Dhimal (4)
96 Angika (2)
97 Kharia
98 Santhali
99 Mundari
100 Kisan (3)
101 Meche (2)
102 Thangmi (2)
103 Jirel (2)
104 Tibetan (2)
105 Sunwar (5)
106 Kagate
107 Bahing (4)
108 Jerung
109 Wambule
110 Tilung

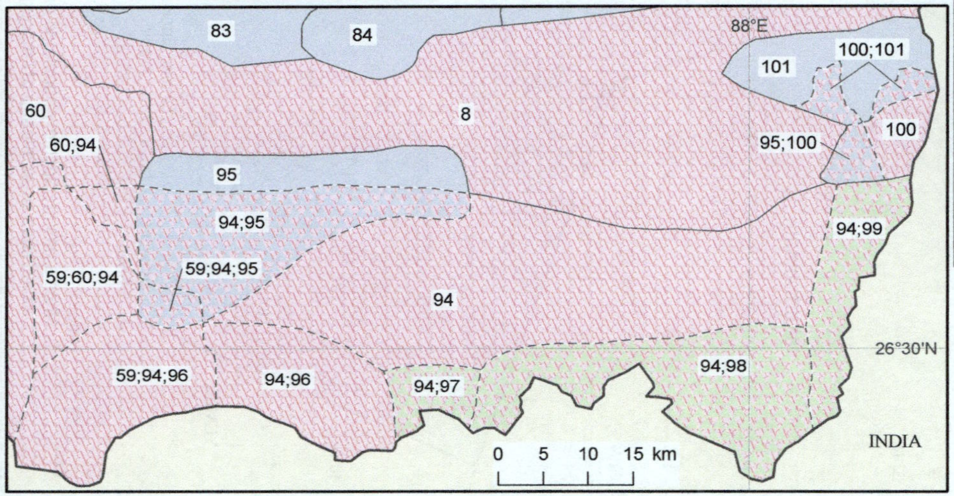

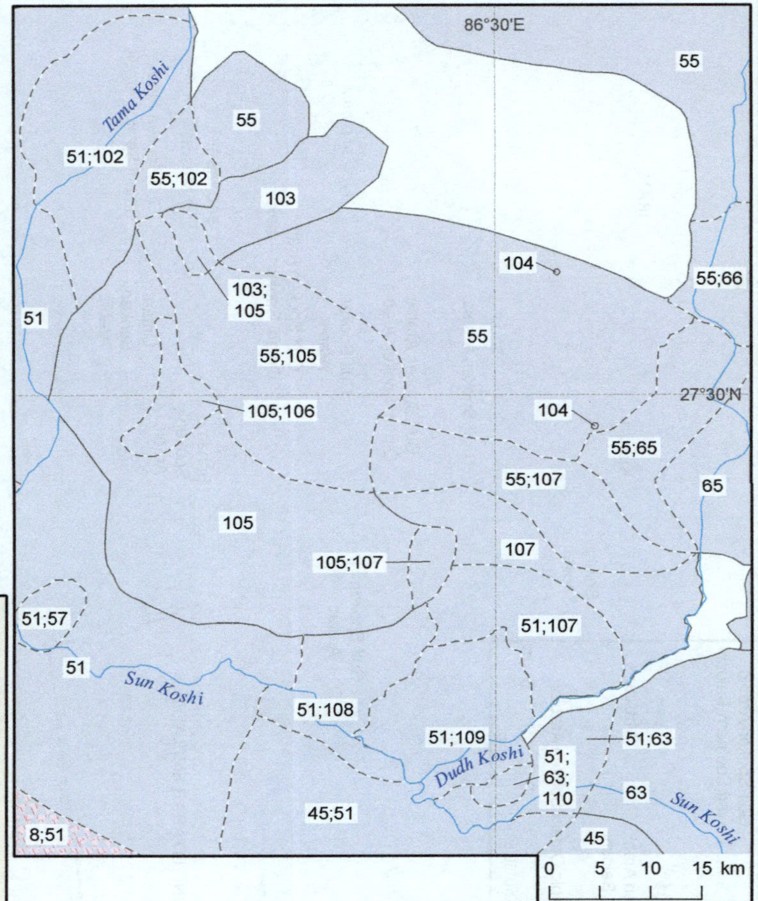

Language Families

Austro-Asiatic
Tibeto-Burman
Indo-Aryan

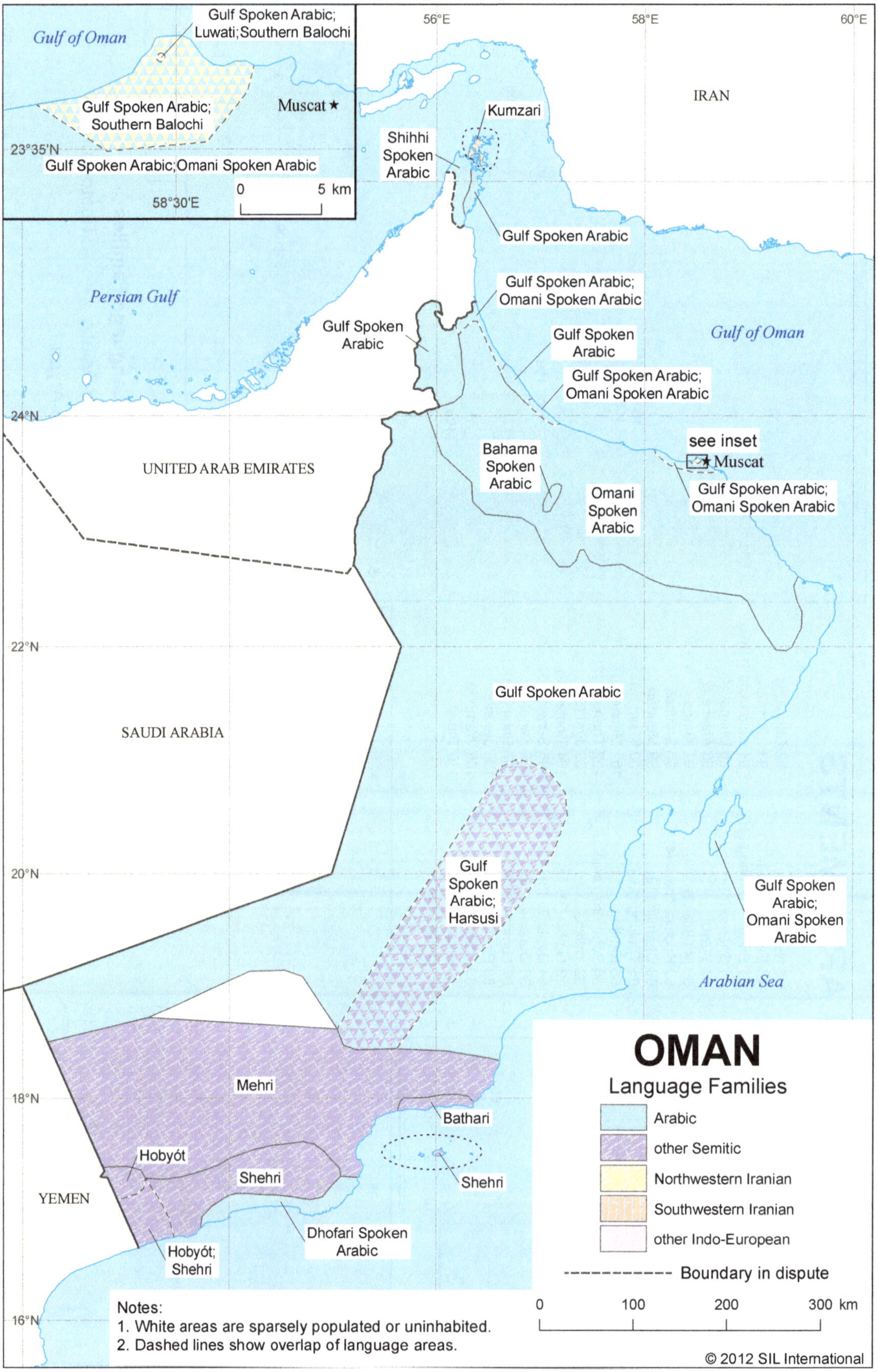
Gulf of Oman
Gulf Spoken Arabic; Luwati; Southern Balochi
Gulf Spoken Arabic; Southern Balochi
Muscat
23°35'N
Gulf Spoken Arabic; Omani Spoken Arabic
0 5 km
58°30'E
56°E
58°E
60°E
IRAN
Kumzari
Shihhi Spoken Arabic
Gulf Spoken Arabic
Gulf Spoken Arabic; Omani Spoken Arabic
Persian Gulf
Gulf Spoken Arabic
Gulf Spoken Arabic
Gulf of Oman
Gulf Spoken Arabic; Omani Spoken Arabic
24°N
see inset
Muscat
UNITED ARAB EMIRATES
Baharna Spoken Arabic
Omani Spoken Arabic
Gulf Spoken Arabic; Omani Spoken Arabic
22°N
Gulf Spoken Arabic
SAUDI ARABIA
20°N
Gulf Spoken Arabic; Harsusi
Gulf Spoken Arabic; Omani Spoken Arabic
Arabian Sea
OMAN
Language Families
Arabic
other Semitic
Northwestern Iranian
Southwestern Iranian
other Indo-European
Boundary in dispute
18°N
Mehri
Bathari
Hobyót
Shehri
Shehri
YEMEN
Dhofari Spoken Arabic
Hobyót; Shehri
16°N
Notes:
1. White areas are sparsely populated or uninhabited.
2. Dashed lines show overlap of language areas.
0 100 200 300 km
© 2012 SIL International

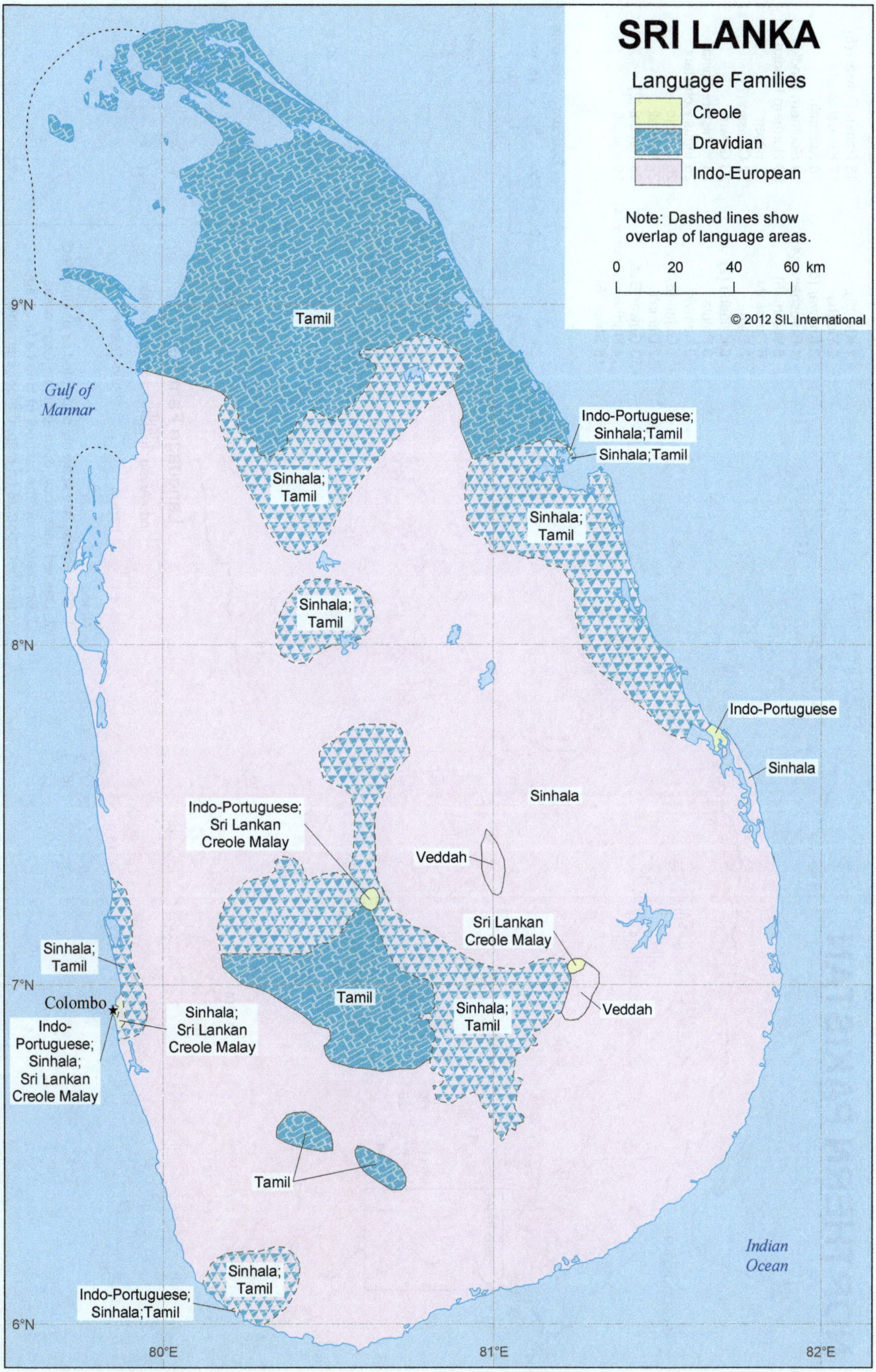
SRI LANKA
Language Families
Creole
Dravidian
Indo-European
Note: Dashed lines show overlap of language areas.
0 20 40 60 km
© 2012 SIL International
9°N
8°N
7°N
6°N
80°E
81°E
82°E
Gulf of Mannar
Indian Ocean
Tamil
Sinhala; Tamil
Indo-Portuguese; Sinhala;Tamil
Sinhala;Tamil
Sinhala; Tamil
Sinhala; Tamil
Indo-Portuguese
Sinhala
Sinhala
Indo-Portuguese; Sri Lankan Creole Malay
Veddah
Sri Lankan Creole Malay
Sinhala; Tamil
Colombo
Indo-Portuguese; Sinhala; Sri Lankan Creole Malay
Sinhala; Sri Lankan Creole Malay
Tamil
Sinhala; Tamil
Veddah
Tamil
Sinhala; Tamil
Indo-Portuguese; Sinhala;Tamil

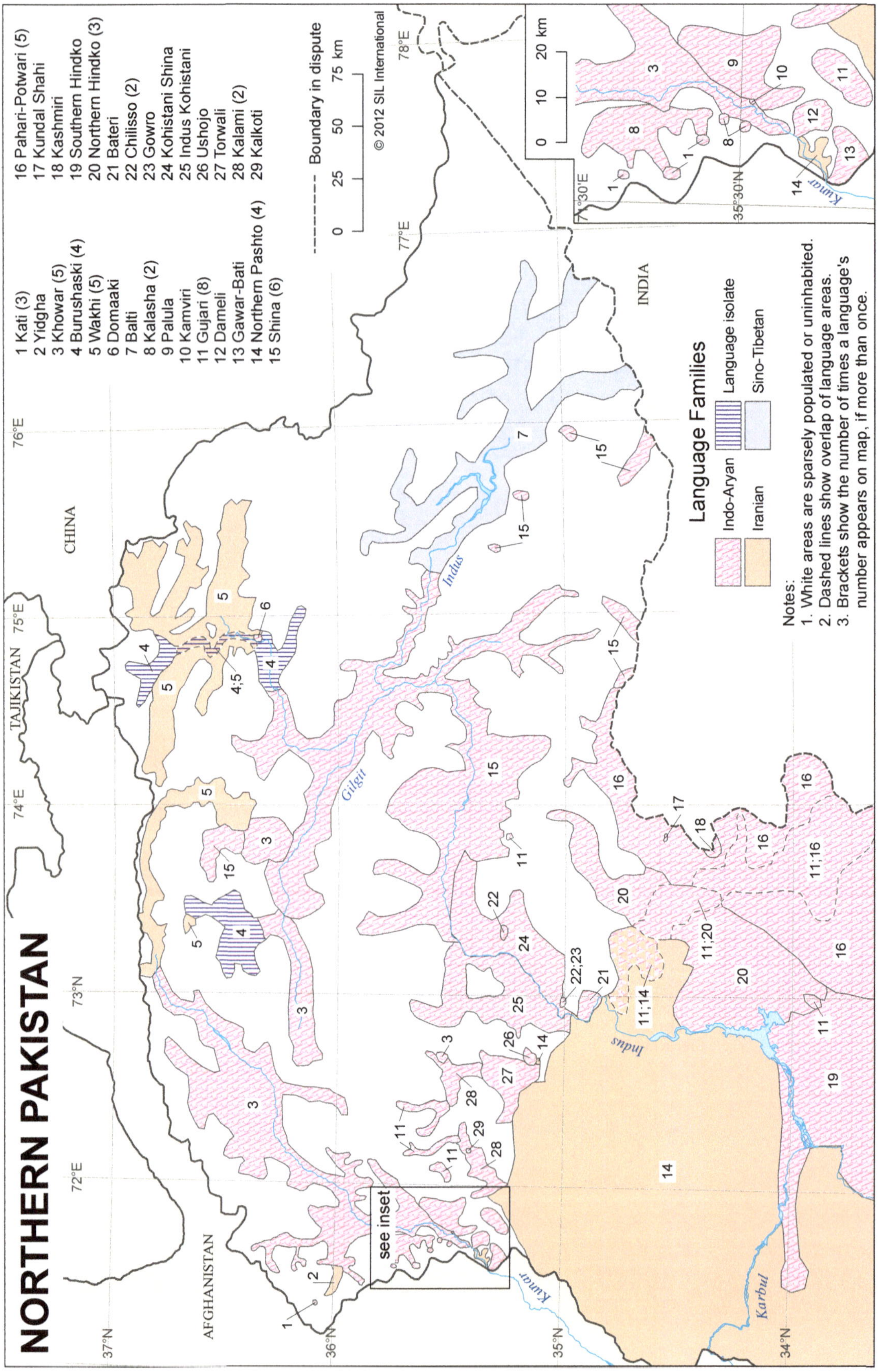
NORTHERN PAKISTAN
1 Kati (3)
2 Yidgha
3 Khowar (5)
4 Burushaski (4)
5 Wakhi (5)
6 Domaaki
7 Balti
8 Kalasha (2)
9 Palula
10 Kamviri
11 Gujari (8)
12 Dameli
13 Gawar-Bati
14 Northern Pashto (4)
15 Shina (6)
16 Pahari-Potwari (5)
17 Kundal Shahi
18 Kashmiri
19 Southern Hindko
20 Northern Hindko (3)
21 Bateri
22 Chilisso (2)
23 Gowro
24 Kohistani Shina
25 Indus Kohistani
26 Ushojo
27 Torwali
28 Kalami (2)
29 Kalkoti
Boundary in dispute
0 25 50 75 km
© 2012 SIL International
0 10 20 km
Language Families
Indo-Aryan
Iranian
Language isolate
Sino-Tibetan
Notes:
1. White areas are sparsely populated or uninhabited.
2. Dashed lines show overlap of language areas.
3. Brackets show the number of times a language's number appears on map, if more than once.
CHINA
TAJIKISTAN
AFGHANISTAN
INDIA
Gilgit
Indus
Kunar
Karbul
see inset
72°E
73°N
74°E
75°E
76°E
77°E
78°E
37°N
36°N
35°N
34°N
71°30'E
35°30'N

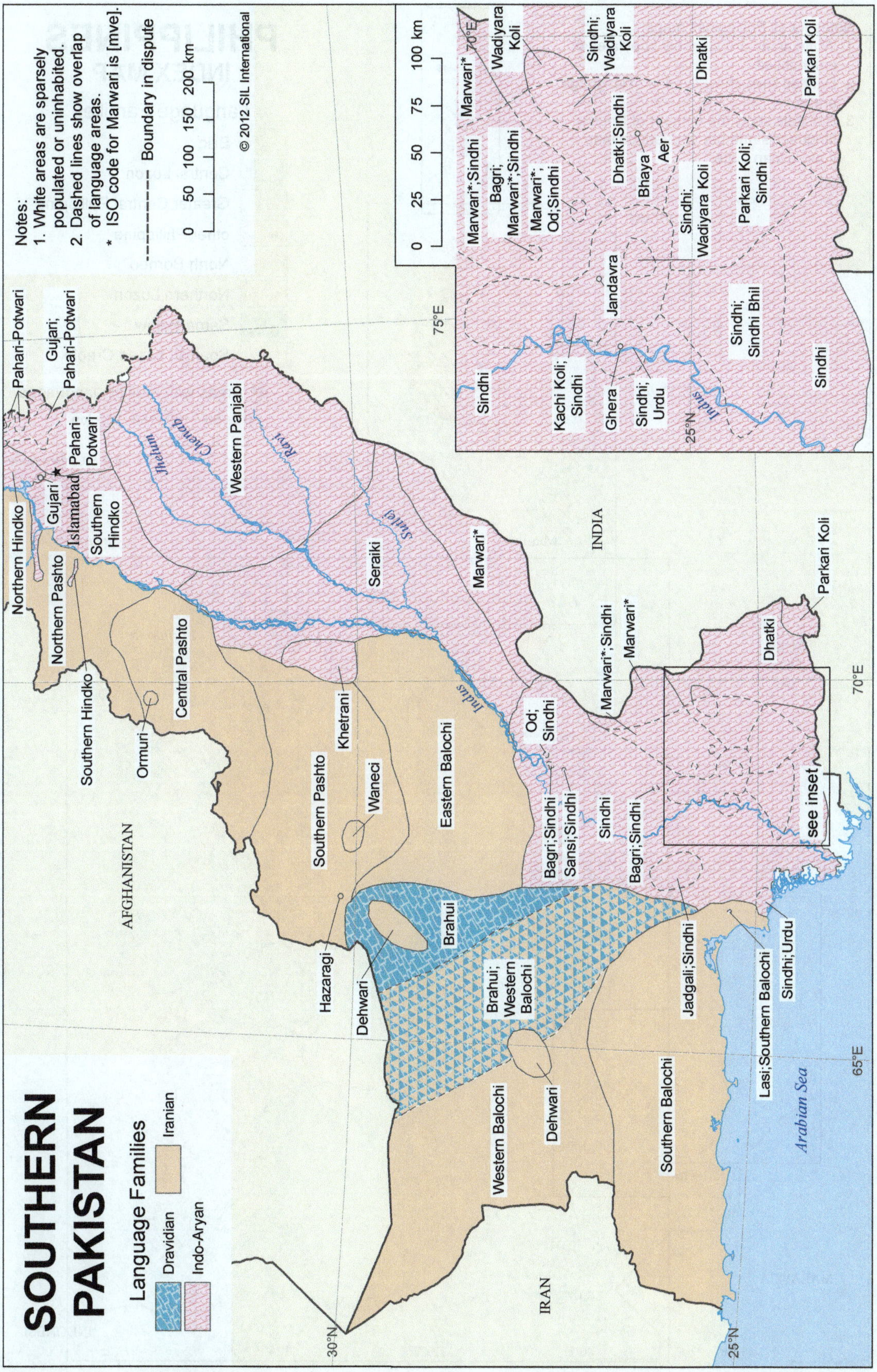
SOUTHERN PAKISTAN
Language Families
Dravidian
Indo-Aryan
Iranian
Notes:
1. White areas are sparsely populated or uninhabited.
2. Dashed lines show overlap of language areas.
* ISO code for Marwari is [mve].
Boundary in dispute
0 50 100 150 200 km
0 25 50 75 100 km
© 2012 SIL International
AFGHANISTAN
IRAN
INDIA
Arabian Sea
Indus
Jhelum
Chenab
Ravi
Sutlej
30°N
25°N
65°E
70°E
75°E
Northern Hindko
Northern Pashto
Pahari-Potwari
Gujari; Pahari-Potwari
Gujari
Islamabad
Pahari-Potwari
Southern Hindko
Western Panjabi
Central Pashto
Ormuri
Southern Pashto
Khetrani
Waneci
Seraiki
Marwari*
Eastern Balochi
Hazaragi
Dehwari
Brahui
Brahui; Western Balochi
Western Balochi
Southern Balochi
Jadgali;Sindhi
Lasi;Southern Balochi
Sindhi;Urdu
Od; Sindhi
Bagri;Sindhi
Sansi;Sindhi
Sindhi
Marwari*;Sindhi
Marwari*
Dhatki
Parkari Koli
see inset
Wadiyara Koli
Sindhi; Wadiyara Koli
Marwari*;Sindhi
Bagri; Marwari*;Sindhi
Marwari*; Od;Sindhi
Dhatki;Sindhi
Bhaya
Aer
Jandavra
Kachi Koli; Sindhi
Ghera
Sindhi; Urdu
Sindhi; Wadiyara Koli
Parkari Koli; Sindhi
Sindhi; Sindhi Bhil

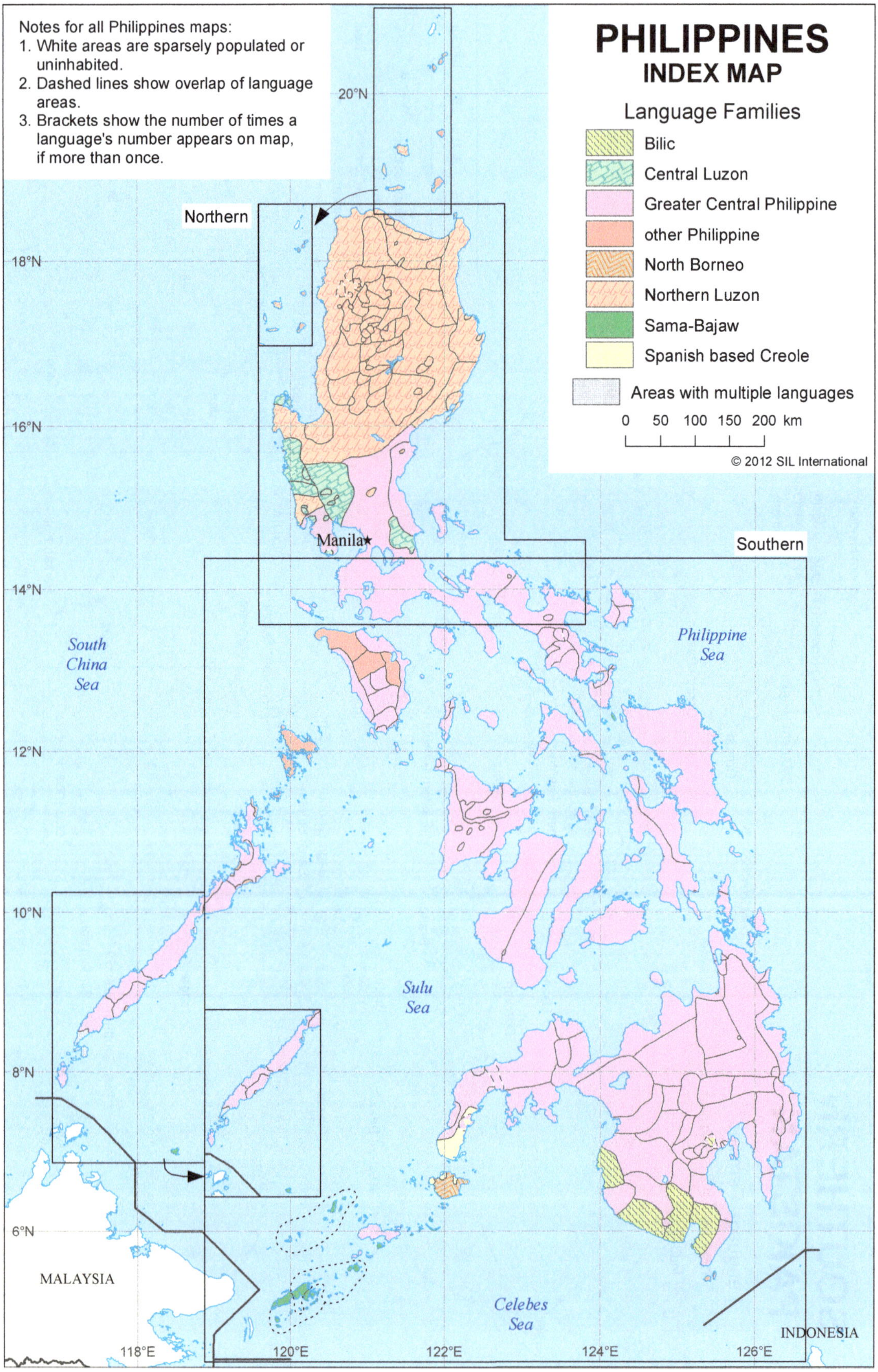
Notes for all Philippines maps:
1. White areas are sparsely populated or uninhabited.
2. Dashed lines show overlap of language areas.
3. Brackets show the number of times a language's number appears on map, if more than once.
PHILIPPINES
INDEX MAP
Language Families
Bilic
Central Luzon
Greater Central Philippine
other Philippine
North Borneo
Northern Luzon
Sama-Bajaw
Spanish based Creole
Areas with multiple languages
0 50 100 150 200 km
© 2012 SIL International
Northern
Southern
Manila
South China Sea
Philippine Sea
Sulu Sea
Celebes Sea
MALAYSIA
INDONESIA
20°N
18°N
16°N
14°N
12°N
10°N
8°N
6°N
118°E
120°E
122°E
124°E
126°E

NORTHERN PHILIPPINES
Language Families
Central Luzon
Greater Central Philippine
other Philippine
Northern Luzon
0 25 50 75 km
1 Ivatan
2 Ilocano (9)
3 Ibatan
4 Inlaod Itneg
5 Adasen
6 Mabaka Valley Kalinga
7 Isnag
8 Pamplona Atta
9 Pudtol Atta
10 Faire Atta
11 Central Cagayan Agta
12 Dupaninan Agta
13 Paranan
14 Pahanan Agta
15 Ibanag (3)
16 Itawit
17 Limos Kalinga
18 Ga'dang
19 Mayoyao Ifugao
20 Batad Ifugao
21 Tinoc Kallahan
22 Amganad Ifugao
23 Kankanaey
24 Keley-i Kallahan
25 Karao
26 Gaddang (2)
27 Tuwali Ifugao
28 Yogad
29 Casiguran Dumagat Agta (2)
30 Kasiguranin
31 Arta
32 Ilongot
33 Isinai
34 Kayapa Kallahan
35 Ibaloi
36 I-wak
37 Pangasinan
38 Bolinao
39 Sambal
40 Abellen Ayta
41 Botolan Sambal
42 Pampangan
43 Mag-antsi Ayta (2)
44 Mag-Indi Ayta (2)
45 Ambala Ayta
46 Magbukun Ayta
47 Southern Alta
48 Northern Alta
49 Umiray Dumaget Agta
50 Remontado Dumagat
51 Alabat Island Agta
52 Tagalog (5)
53 Northern Kankanay
54 Moyadan Itneg
55 Masadiit Itneg
56 Maeng Itneg
57 Binongan Itneg
58 Banao Itneg
59 Tanudan Kalinga
60 Lubuagan Kalinga
61 Southern Kalinga
62 Butbut Kalinga
63 Northern Bontok
64 Majukayang Kalinga
65 Balangao
66 Eastern Bontok
67 Central Bontok
68 Southern Bontok
69 Southwestern Bontok
70 Manide
71 Central Bikol
72 Isarog Agta
Northern Islands
0 25 50 km
Cagayan
see inset
Philippine Sea
South China Sea
Manila
18°N
20°N
16°N
14°N
122°E
120°E
121°E
17°N
0 25 km
© 2014 SIL International

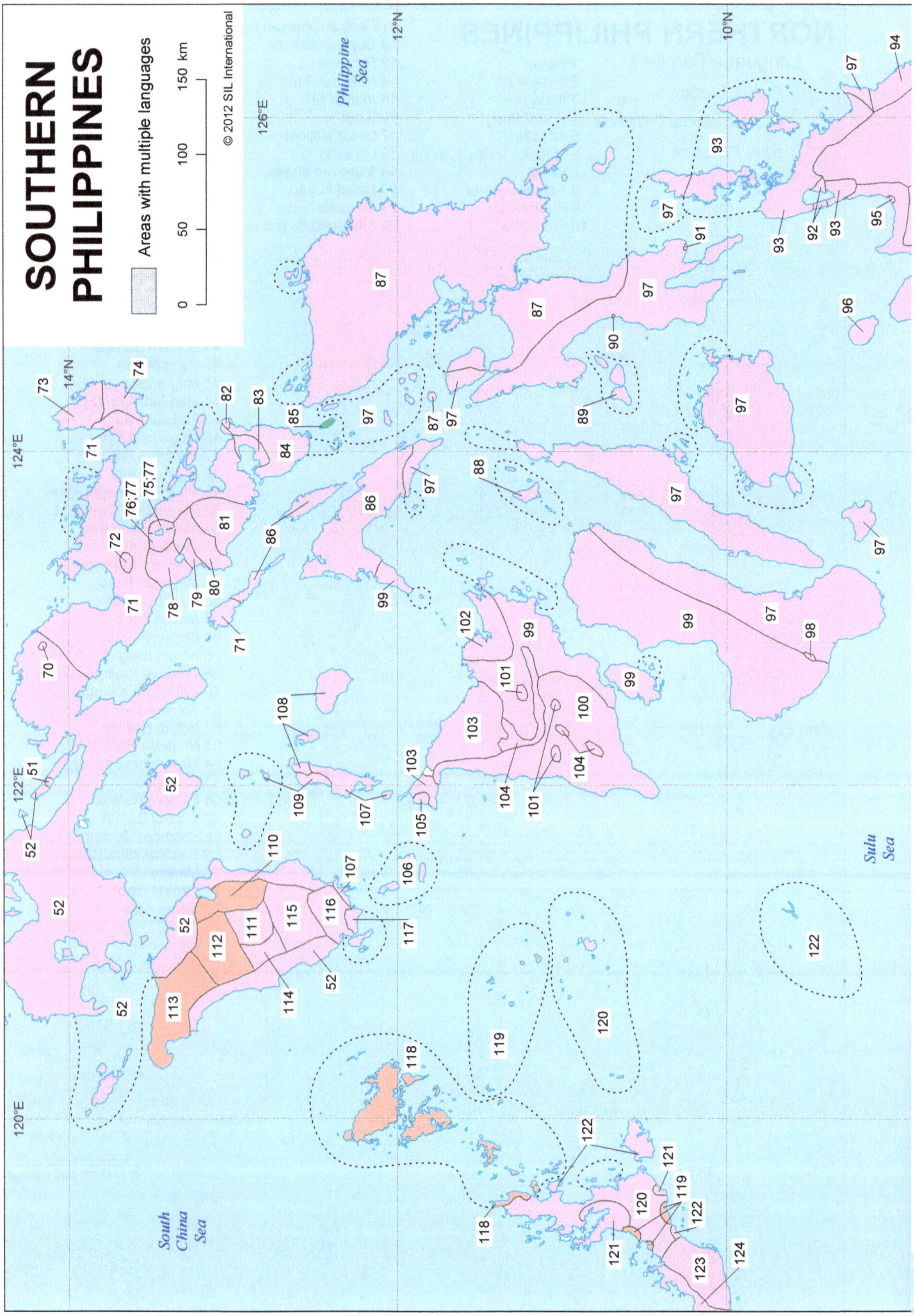
SOUTHERN PHILIPPINES
Areas with multiple languages
0 50 100 150 km
© 2012 SIL International
Philippine Sea
South China Sea
Sulu Sea
14°N
12°N
10°N
120°E
122°E
124°E
126°E

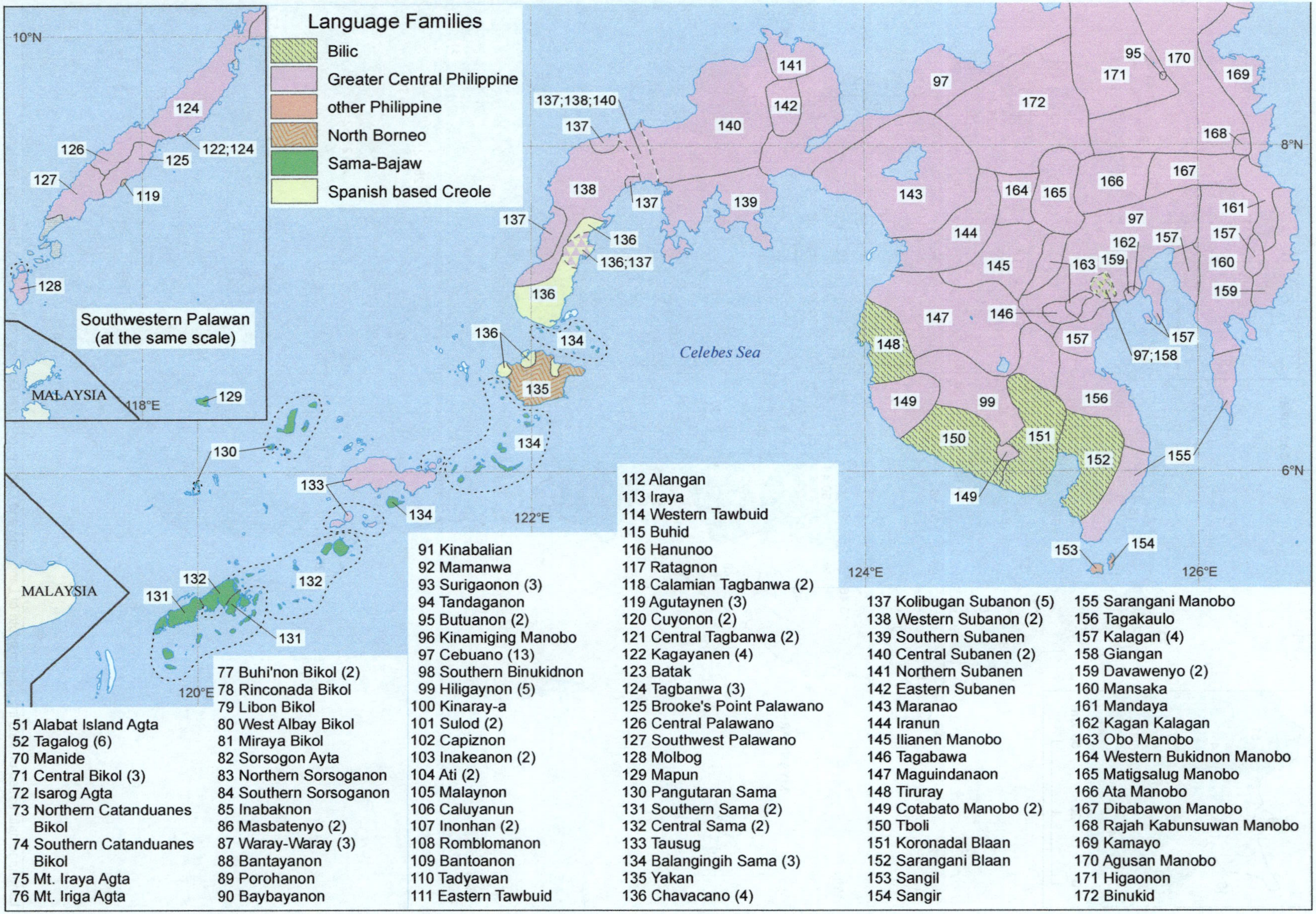
Language Families
Bilic
Greater Central Philippine
other Philippine
North Borneo
Sama-Bajaw
Spanish based Creole
Southwestern Palawan
(at the same scale)
MALAYSIA
Celebes Sea
10°N
8°N
6°N
118°E
120°E
122°E
124°E
126°E
51 Alabat Island Agta
52 Tagalog (6)
70 Manide
71 Central Bikol (3)
72 Isarog Agta
73 Northern Catanduanes Bikol
74 Southern Catanduanes Bikol
75 Mt. Iraya Agta
76 Mt. Iriga Agta
77 Buhi'non Bikol (2)
78 Rinconada Bikol
79 Libon Bikol
80 West Albay Bikol
81 Miraya Bikol
82 Sorsogon Ayta
83 Northern Sorsoganon
84 Southern Sorsoganon
85 Inabaknon
86 Masbatenyo (2)
87 Waray-Waray (3)
88 Bantayanon
89 Porohanon
90 Baybayanon
91 Kinabalian
92 Mamanwa
93 Surigaonon (3)
94 Tandaganon
95 Butuanon (2)
96 Kinamiging Manobo
97 Cebuano (13)
98 Southern Binukidnon
99 Hiligaynon (5)
100 Kinaray-a
101 Sulod (2)
102 Capiznon
103 Inakeanon (2)
104 Ati (2)
105 Malaynon
106 Caluyanun
107 Inonhan (2)
108 Romblomanon
109 Bantoanon
110 Tadyawan
111 Eastern Tawbuid
112 Alangan
113 Iraya
114 Western Tawbuid
115 Buhid
116 Hanunoo
117 Ratagnon
118 Calamian Tagbanwa (2)
119 Agutaynen (3)
120 Cuyonon (2)
121 Central Tagbanwa (2)
122 Kagayanen (4)
123 Batak
124 Tagbanwa (3)
125 Brooke's Point Palawano
126 Central Palawano
127 Southwest Palawano
128 Molbog
129 Mapun
130 Pangutaran Sama
131 Southern Sama (2)
132 Central Sama (2)
133 Tausug
134 Balangingih Sama (3)
135 Yakan
136 Chavacano (4)
137 Kolibugan Subanon (5)
138 Western Subanon (2)
139 Southern Subanen
140 Central Subanen (2)
141 Northern Subanen
142 Eastern Subanen
143 Maranao
144 Iranun
145 Ilianen Manobo
146 Tagabawa
147 Maguindanaon
148 Tiruray
149 Cotabato Manobo (2)
150 Tboli
151 Koronadal Blaan
152 Sarangani Blaan
153 Sangil
154 Sangir
155 Sarangani Manobo
156 Tagakaulo
157 Kalagan (4)
158 Giangan
159 Davawenyo (2)
160 Mansaka
161 Mandaya
162 Kagan Kalagan
163 Obo Manobo
164 Western Bukidnon Manobo
165 Matigsalug Manobo
166 Ata Manobo
167 Dibabawon Manobo
168 Rajah Kabunsuwan Manobo
169 Kamayo
170 Agusan Manobo
171 Higaonon
172 Binukid

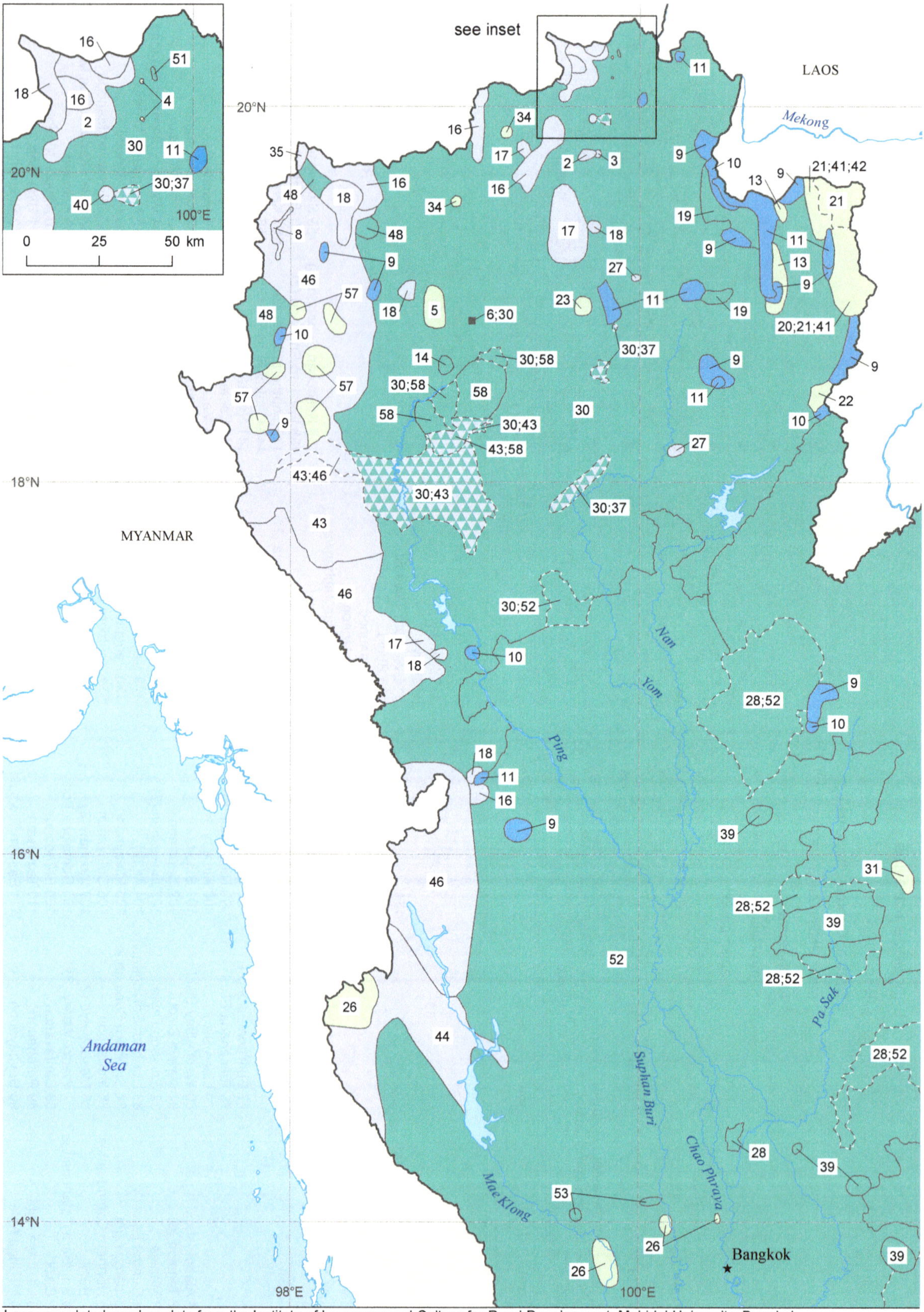

Language data based on data from the Institute of Language and Culture for Rural Development, Mahidol University, Bangkok

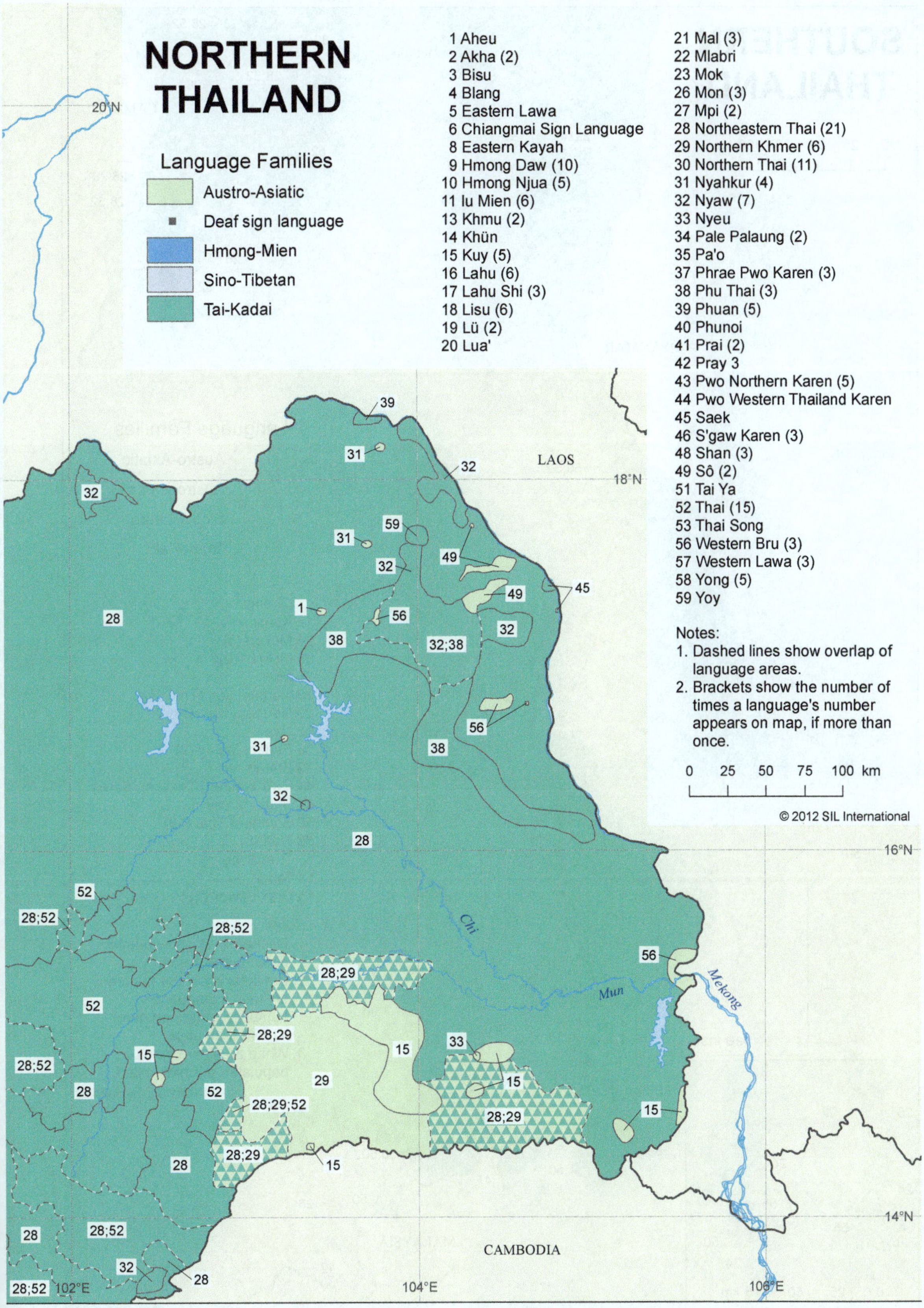
NORTHERN THAILAND
Language Families
Austro-Asiatic
Deaf sign language
Hmong-Mien
Sino-Tibetan
Tai-Kadai
1 Aheu
2 Akha (2)
3 Bisu
4 Blang
5 Eastern Lawa
6 Chiangmai Sign Language
8 Eastern Kayah
9 Hmong Daw (10)
10 Hmong Njua (5)
11 Iu Mien (6)
13 Khmu (2)
14 Khün
15 Kuy (5)
16 Lahu (6)
17 Lahu Shi (3)
18 Lisu (6)
19 Lü (2)
20 Lua'
21 Mal (3)
22 Mlabri
23 Mok
26 Mon (3)
27 Mpi (2)
28 Northeastern Thai (21)
29 Northern Khmer (6)
30 Northern Thai (11)
31 Nyahkur (4)
32 Nyaw (7)
33 Nyeu
34 Pale Palaung (2)
35 Pa'o
37 Phrae Pwo Karen (3)
38 Phu Thai (3)
39 Phuan (5)
40 Phunoi
41 Prai (2)
42 Pray 3
43 Pwo Northern Karen (5)
44 Pwo Western Thailand Karen
45 Saek
46 S'gaw Karen (3)
48 Shan (3)
49 Sô (2)
51 Tai Ya
52 Thai (15)
53 Thai Song
56 Western Bru (3)
57 Western Lawa (3)
58 Yong (5)
59 Yoy
Notes:
1. Dashed lines show overlap of language areas.
2. Brackets show the number of times a language's number appears on map, if more than once.
0 25 50 75 100 km
© 2012 SIL International
20°N
18°N
16°N
14°N
102°E
104°E
106°E
LAOS
CAMBODIA
Chi
Mun
Mekong

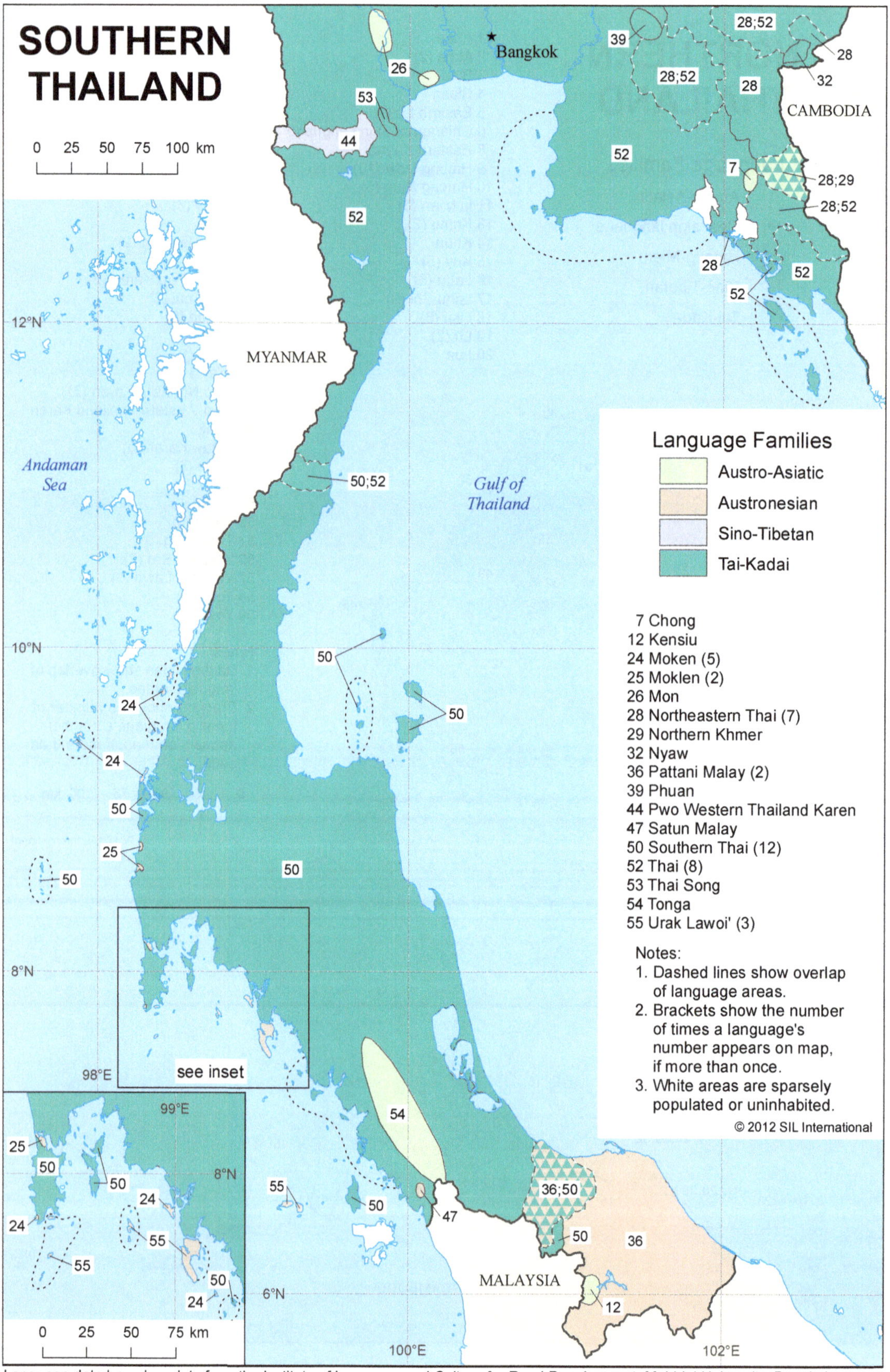

Language data based on data from the Institute of Language and Culture for Rural Development, Mahidol University, Bangkok

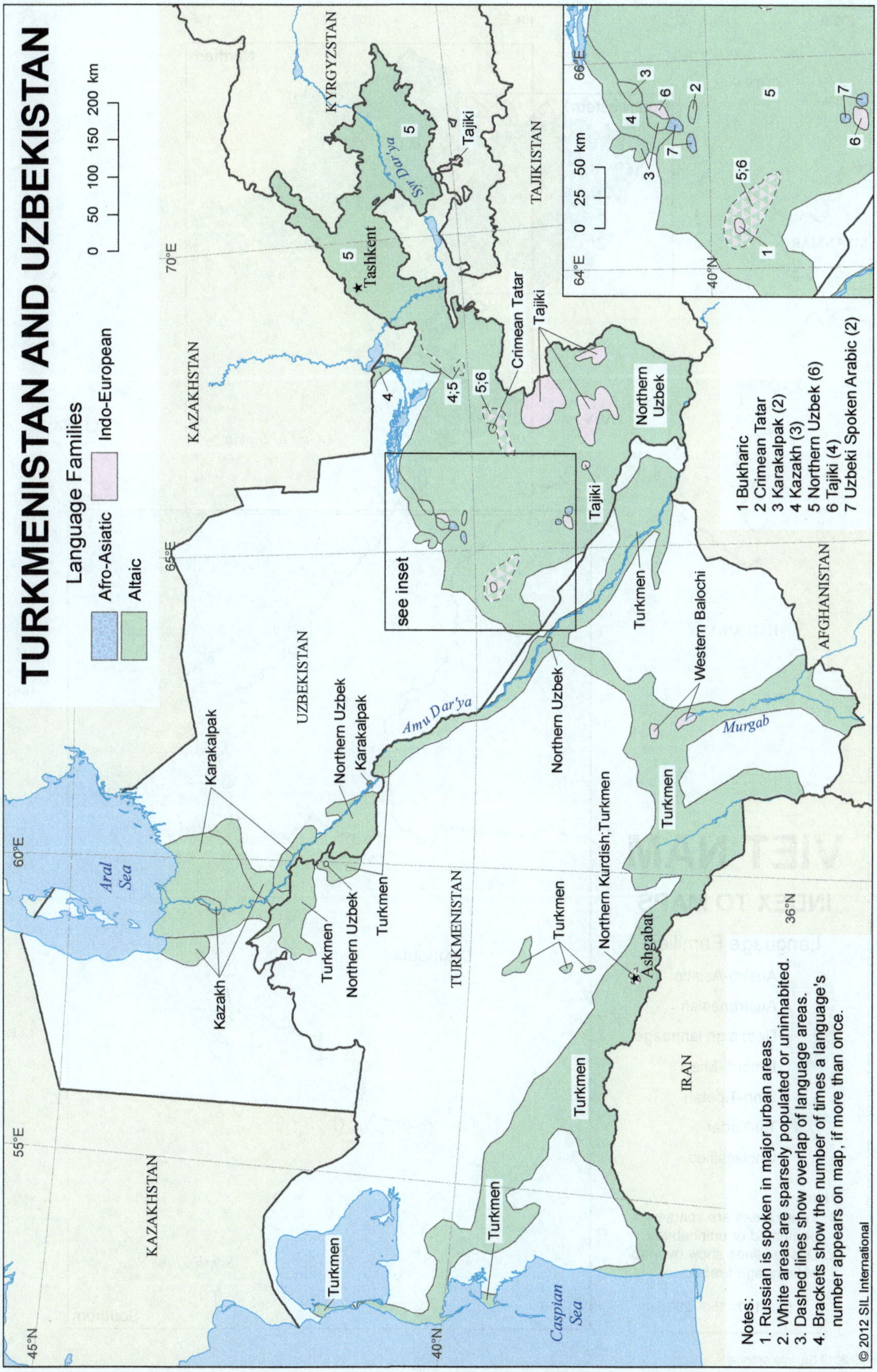
TURKMENISTAN AND UZBEKISTAN
Language Families
Afro-Asiatic
Altaic
Indo-European
0 50 100 150 200 km
KAZAKHSTAN
KYRGYZSTAN
TAJIKISTAN
UZBEKISTAN
TURKMENISTAN
AFGHANISTAN
IRAN
Aral Sea
Caspian Sea
Amu Dar'ya
Syr Dar'ya
Murgab
Tashkent
Ashgabat
Karakalpak
Kazakh
Turkmen
Northern Uzbek
Northern Kurdish; Turkmen
Western Balochi
Tajiki
Crimean Tatar
see inset
1 Bukharic
2 Crimean Tatar
3 Karakalpak (2)
4 Kazakh (3)
5 Northern Uzbek (6)
6 Tajiki (4)
7 Uzbeki Spoken Arabic (2)
Notes:
1. Russian is spoken in major urban areas.
2. White areas are sparsely populated or uninhabited.
3. Dashed lines show overlap of language areas.
4. Brackets show the number of times a language's number appears on map, if more than once.
© 2012 SIL International

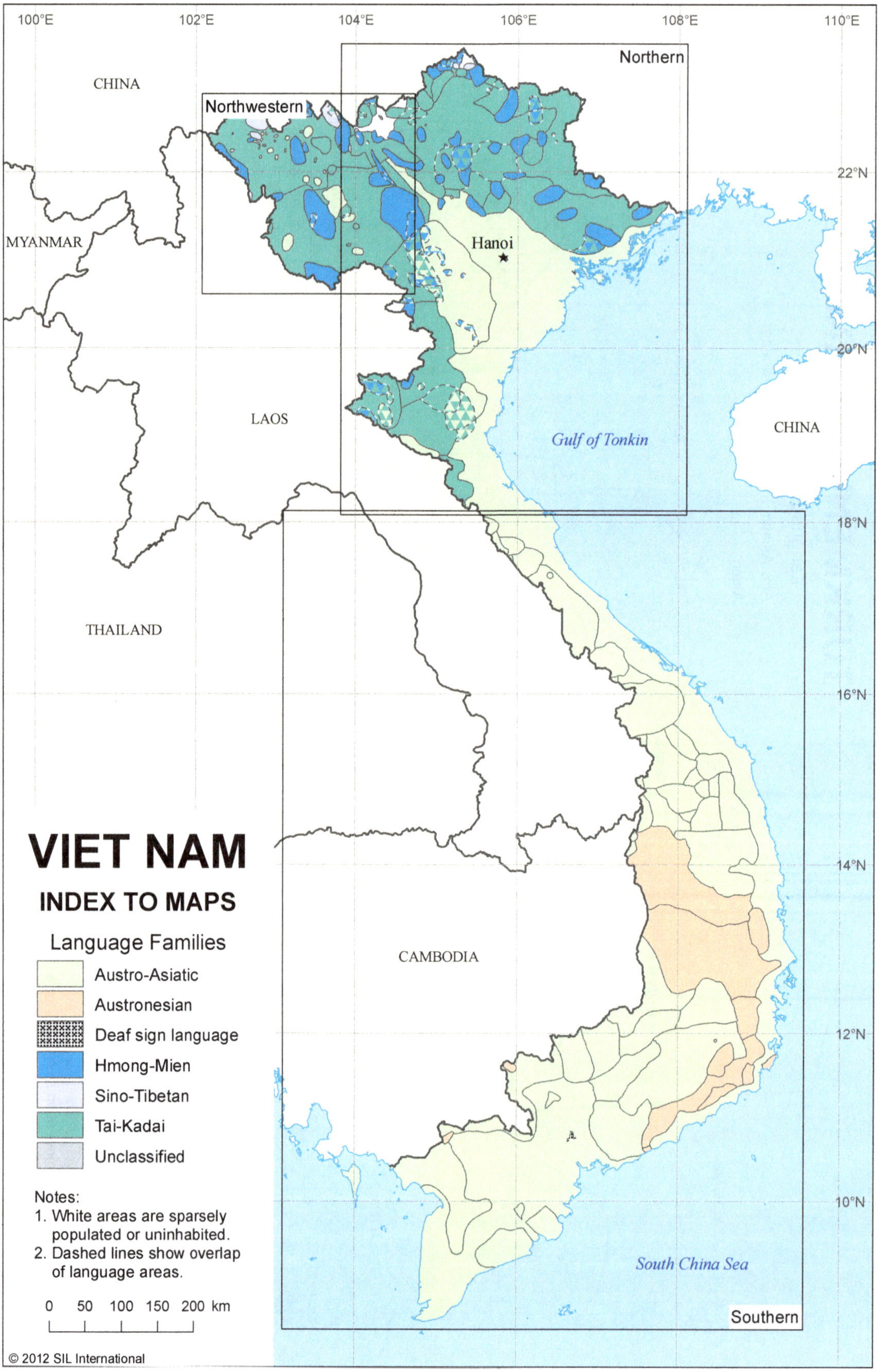

100°E
102°E
104°E
106°E
108°E
110°E
22°N
20°N
18°N
16°N
14°N
12°N
10°N
Northern
Northwestern
Southern
CHINA
MYANMAR
LAOS
THAILAND
CAMBODIA
Hanoi
Gulf of Tonkin
South China Sea
VIET NAM
INDEX TO MAPS
Language Families
Austro-Asiatic
Austronesian
Deaf sign language
Hmong-Mien
Sino-Tibetan
Tai-Kadai
Unclassified
Notes:
1. White areas are sparsely populated or uninhabited.
2. Dashed lines show overlap of language areas.
0 50 100 150 200 km
© 2012 SIL International

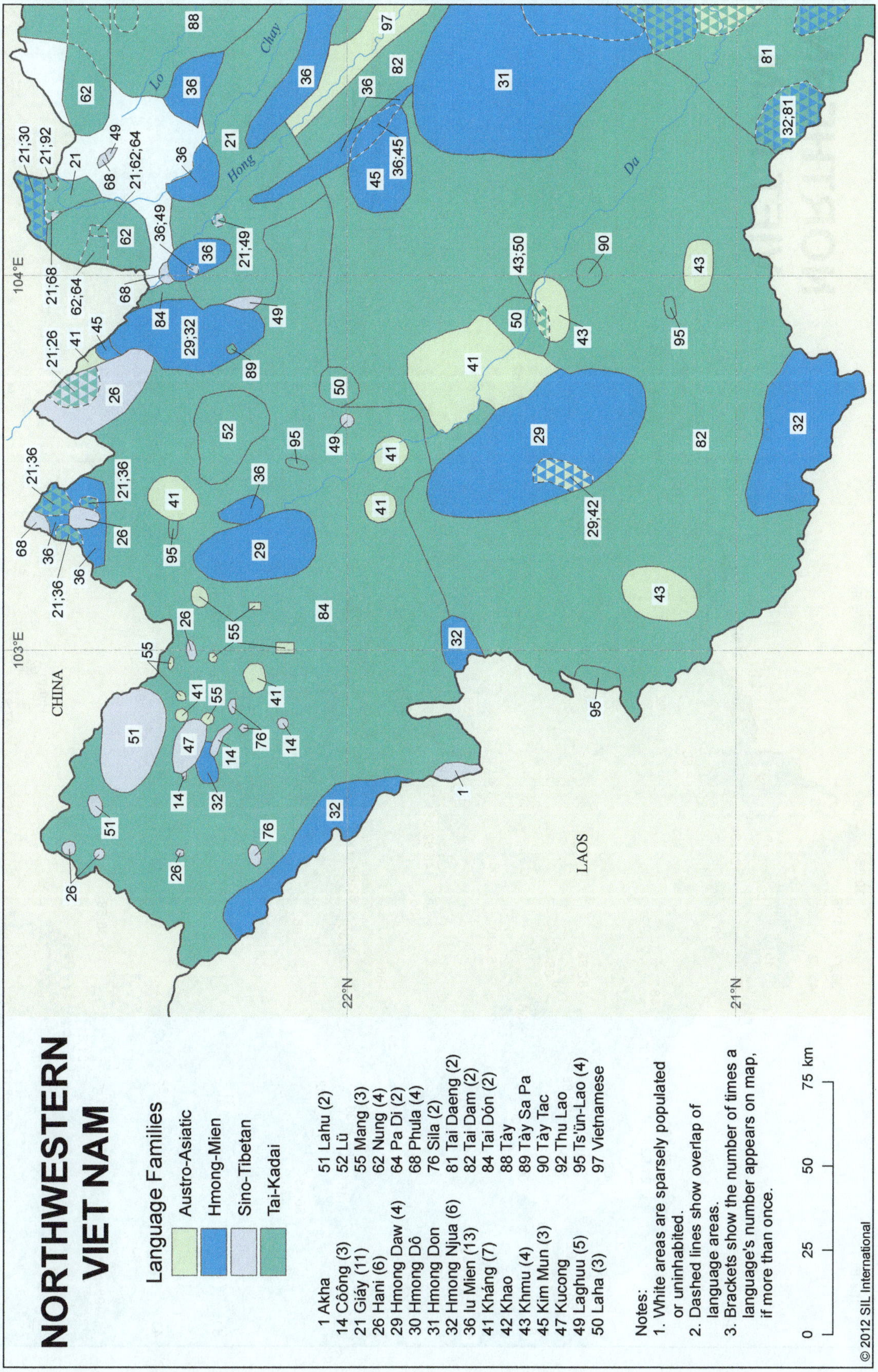
NORTHWESTERN VIET NAM
Language Families
Austro-Asiatic
Hmong-Mien
Sino-Tibetan
Tai-Kadai
1 Akha
14 Côông (3)
21 Giáy (11)
26 Hani (6)
29 Hmong Daw (4)
30 Hmong Dô
31 Hmong Don
32 Hmong Njua (6)
36 Iu Mien (13)
41 Kháng (7)
42 Khao
43 Khmu (4)
45 Kim Mun (3)
47 Kucong
49 Laghuu (5)
50 Laha (3)
51 Lahu (2)
52 Lü
55 Mang (3)
62 Nung (4)
64 Pa Di (2)
68 Phula (4)
76 Sila (2)
81 Tai Daeng (2)
82 Tai Dam (2)
84 Tai Dón (2)
88 Tày
89 Tày Sa Pa
90 Tày Tac
92 Thu Lao
95 Ts'ün-Lao (4)
97 Vietnamese
Notes:
1. White areas are sparsely populated or uninhabited.
2. Dashed lines show overlap of language areas.
3. Brackets show the number of times a language's number appears on map, if more than once.
0 25 50 75 km
© 2012 SIL International
CHINA
LAOS
Lo
Chay
Hong
Da
103°E
104°E
22°N
21°N

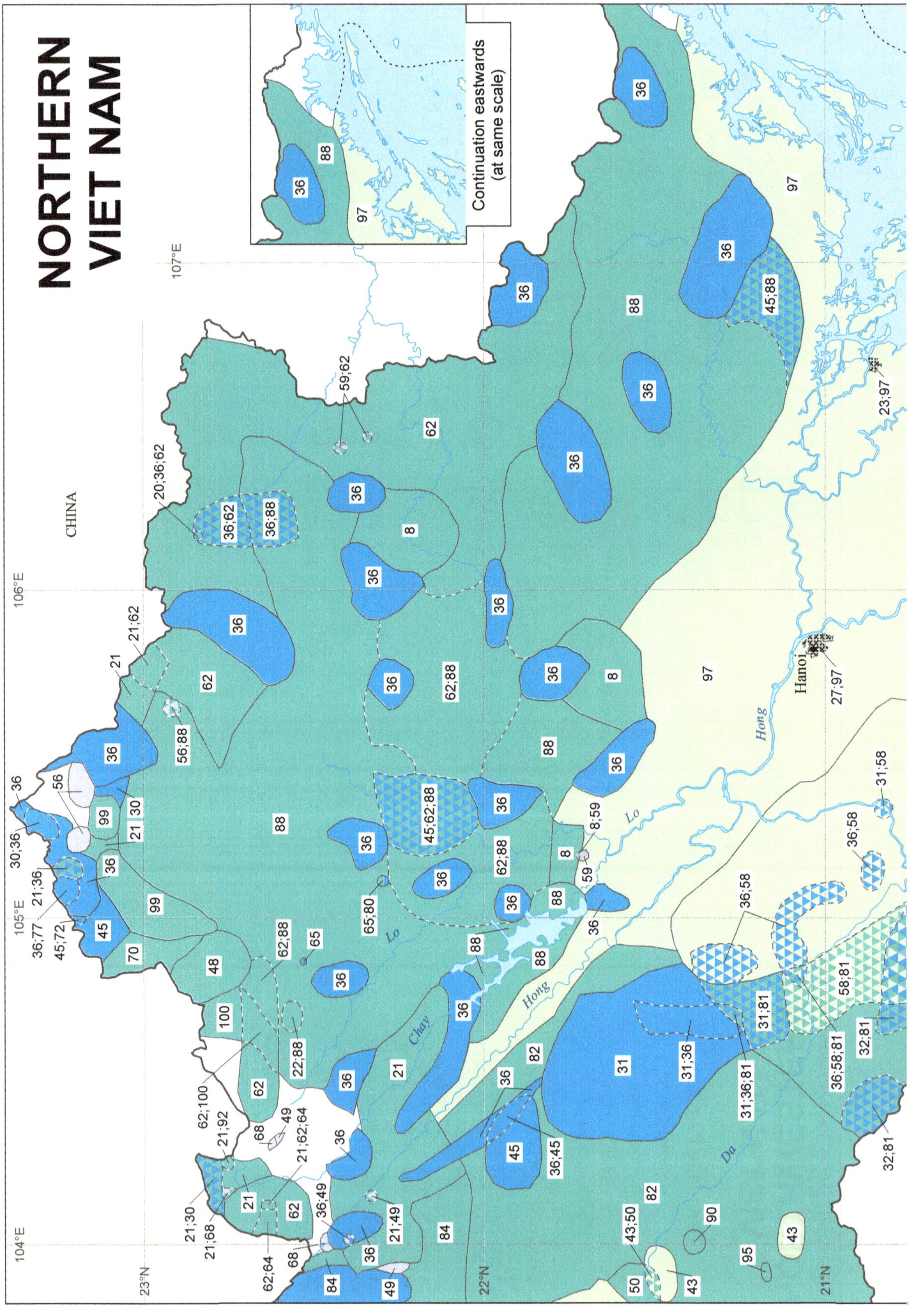
NORTHERN VIET NAM
Continuation eastwards (at same scale)
CHINA
Hanoi
Hong
Lo
Chay
Da
104°E
105°E
106°E
107°E
23°N
22°N
21°N

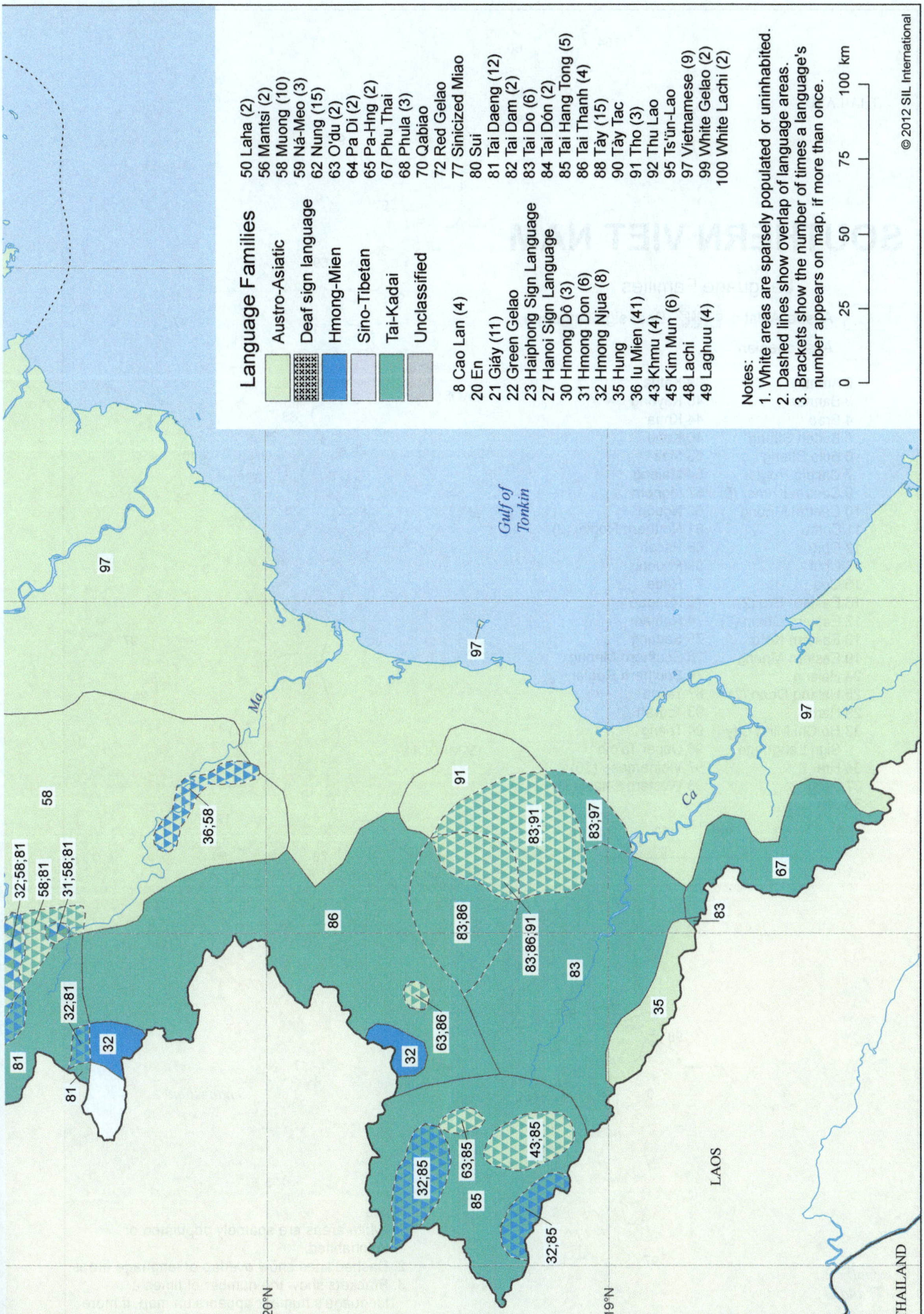
Language Families
Austro-Asiatic
Deaf sign language
Hmong-Mien
Sino-Tibetan
Tai-Kadai
Unclassified
8 Cao Lan (4)
20 En
21 Giáy (11)
22 Green Gelao
23 Haiphong Sign Language
27 Hanoi Sign Language
30 Hmong Dô (3)
31 Hmong Don (6)
32 Hmong Njua (8)
35 Hung
36 Iu Mien (41)
43 Khmu (4)
45 Kim Mun (6)
48 Lachi
49 Laghuu (4)
50 Laha (2)
56 Mantsi (2)
58 Muong (10)
59 Ná-Meo (3)
62 Nung (15)
63 O'du (2)
64 Pa Di (2)
65 Pa-Hng (2)
67 Phu Thai
68 Phula (3)
70 Qabiao
72 Red Gelao
77 Sinicized Miao
80 Sui
81 Tai Daeng (12)
82 Tai Dam (2)
83 Tai Do (6)
84 Tai Dón (2)
85 Tai Hang Tong (5)
86 Tai Thanh (4)
88 Tày (15)
90 Tày Tac
91 Tho (3)
92 Thu Lao
95 Ts'ün-Lao
97 Vietnamese (9)
99 White Gelao (2)
100 White Lachi (2)
Notes:
1. White areas are sparsely populated or uninhabited.
2. Dashed lines show overlap of language areas.
3. Brackets show the number of times a language's number appears on map, if more than once.
0 25 50 75 100 km
© 2012 SIL International
Gulf of Tonkin
Ma
Ca
LAOS
THAILAND
20°N
19°N

SOUTHERN VIET NAM
Language Families
Austro-Asiatic
Deaf sign language
Austronesian
2 Arem
3 Bahnar
4 Brao
5 Budeh Stieng
6 Bulo Stieng
7 Cacgia Roglai
9 Central Khmer (8)
10 Central Mnong
11 Chrau
12 Chru
13 Chut
15 Cua
16 Eastern Bru (2)
17 Eastern Cham (3)
18 Eastern Katu
19 Eastern Mnong
24 Halang
25 Halang Doan (2)
28 Haroi
33 Ho Chi Minh City Sign Language
34 Hre
37 Jarai
38 Jeh
39 Katua
40 Kayong
44 Khua
46 Koho
53 Maa
54 Maleng
57 Monom
60 Nguôn
61 Northern Roglai (2)
66 Pacoh
69 Phuong
71 Rade
73 Rengao
74 Romam
75 Sedang
78 Southern Mnong
79 Southern Roglai
87 Takua
93 Todrah
94 Trieng
96 Upper Ta'oih
97 Vietnamese (10)
98 Western Cham (2)
0 50 100 150 200 km
THAILAND
LAOS
CAMBODIA
Gulf of Tonkin
South China Sea
Gulf of Thailand
Mekong
18°N
16°N
14°N
12°N
10°N
104°E
106°E
108°E
Notes:
1. White areas are sparsely populated or uninhabited.
2. Dashed lines show overlap of language areas.
3. Brackets show the number of times a language's number appears on map, if more than once.
© 2012 SIL International

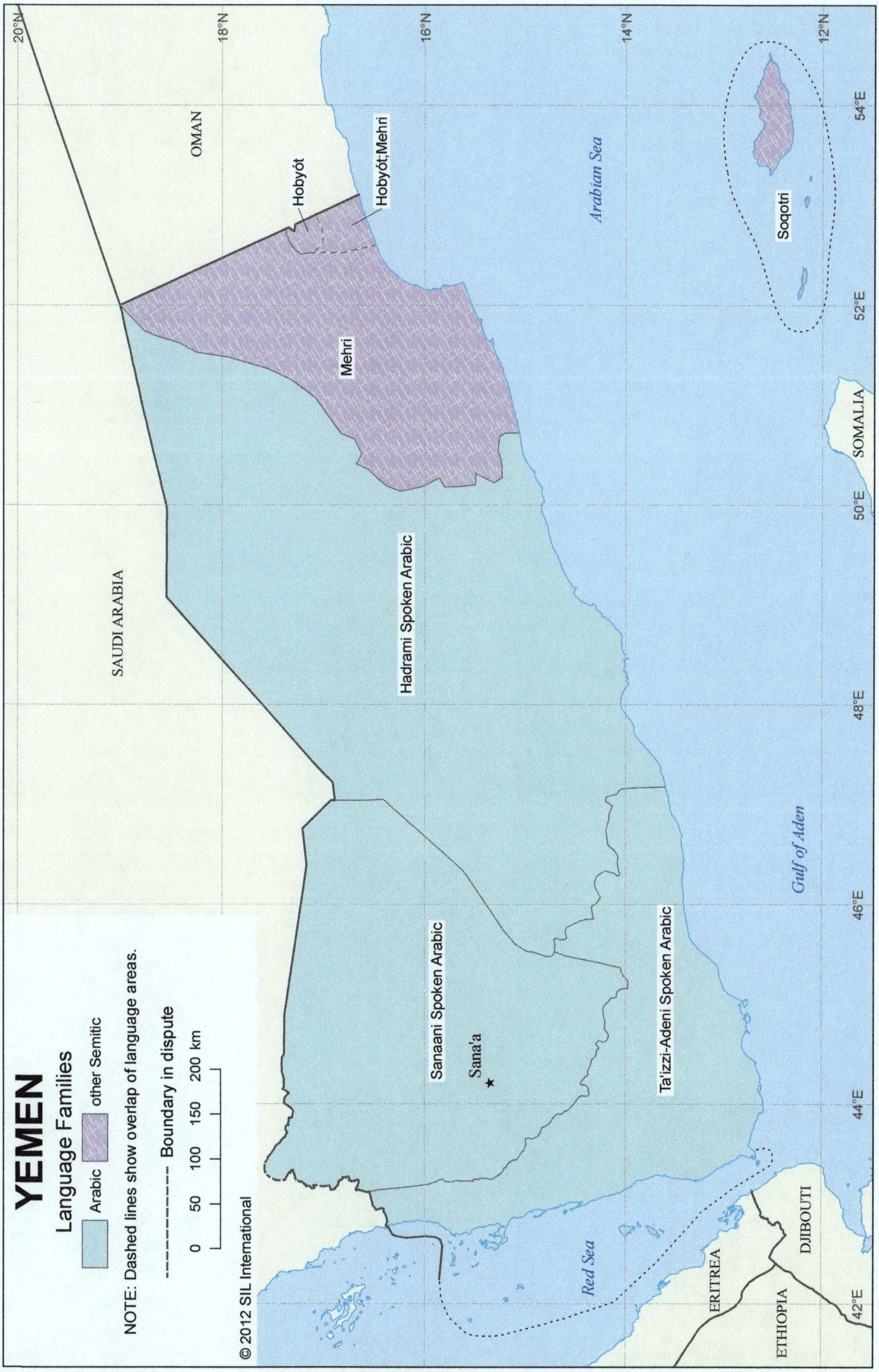
YEMEN
Language Families
Arabic
other Semitic
NOTE: Dashed lines show overlap of language areas.
Boundary in dispute
0 50 100 150 200 km
© 2012 SIL International
OMAN
SAUDI ARABIA
Hobyót
Hobyót;Mehri
Mehri
Hadrami Spoken Arabic
Sanaani Spoken Arabic
Sana'a
Ta'izzi-Adeni Spoken Arabic
Soqotri
Arabian Sea
Gulf of Aden
Red Sea
SOMALIA
DJIBOUTI
ERITREA
ETHIOPIA
20°N
18°N
16°N
14°N
12°N
42°E
44°E
46°E
48°E
50°E
52°E
54°E

Part IV
Indexes

Language Name Index

This index lists every name that appears in the language listings as a primary or alternate name of a language or dialect. The following abbreviations are used in the index entries: *alt.* 'alternate name for'; *alt. dial.* 'alternate dialect name for'; *dial.* 'primary dialect name for'; *pej. alt.* 'pejorative alternate name for'; and *pej. alt. dial.* 'pejorative alternate dialect name for'. The index entry gives the primary name for the language with which the given name is associated, followed by the unique three-letter ISO 639 language code in square brackets. The numbers identify the pages on which the language entries using the indexed name may be found. If the list of page references includes the entry in the primary country, it is listed first. The entry for a primary name also lists page numbers for the maps on which the language occurs.

Language Code Index

This index gives an alphabetical listing of all 2,429 three-letter codes that are used in this work to uniquely identify languages. The referenced page contains the main entry that describes the language. All codes listed are part of the ISO 639-3 standard; see http://www.sil.org/iso639-3/.

Country Index

CPSIA information can be obtained at www.ICGtesting.com
Printed in the USA
BVOW11*1403090315

390175BV00004B/14/P

9 781556 713705